# LEARNING EMPIRE

The First World War marked the end point of a process of German globalization that began in the 1870s, well before Germany acquired a colonial empire or extensive overseas commercial interests. Structured around the figures of five influential economists who shaped the German political landscape, *Learning Empire* explores how their overseas experiences shaped public perceptions of the world and Germany's place in it. These men helped to define a German liberal imperialism that came to influence the "World Policy" (*Weltpolitik*) of Kaiser Wilhelm, Chancellor Bülow, and Admiral Tirpitz. They devised naval propaganda, reshaped Reichstag politics, were involved in colonial and financial reforms, and helped define the debate over war aims in the First World War. Looking closely at German worldwide entanglements, *Learning Empire* recasts how we interpret German imperialism, the origins of the First World War, and the rise of Nazism, inviting reflection on the challenges of globalization in the current century.

ERIK GRIMMER-SOLEM is Professor in the Departments of History and German Studies at Wesleyan University. He is the author of numerous works including *The Rise of Historical Economics and Social Reform in Germany* (2003). He was a University of Chicago Harper Fellow and has received awards from the Fritz Thyssen Foundation and the Leverhulme Trust as well as two distinguished teaching prizes from Wesleyan University. His research on the Wehrmacht's involvement in the Holocaust was discussed in the newsweekly *Der Spiegel* and debated in German parliament in 2014.

# LEARNING EMPIRE

Globalization and the German Quest for
World Status, 1875–1919

ERIK GRIMMER-SOLEM
*Wesleyan University*

# CAMBRIDGE
## UNIVERSITY PRESS

University Printing House, Cambridge CB2 8BS, United Kingdom

One Liberty Plaza, 20th Floor, New York, NY 10006, USA

477 Williamstown Road, Port Melbourne, VIC 3207, Australia

314–21, 3rd Floor, Plot 3, Splendor Forum, Jasola District Centre, New Delhi – 110025, India

79 Anson Road, #06–04/06, Singapore 079906

Cambridge University Press is part of the University of Cambridge.

It furthers the University's mission by disseminating knowledge in the pursuit of education, learning, and research at the highest international levels of excellence.

www.cambridge.org
Information on this title: www.cambridge.org/9781108483827
DOI: 10.1017/9781108593908

© Erik Grimmer-Solem 2019

This publication is in copyright. Subject to statutory exception and to the provisions of relevant collective licensing agreements, no reproduction of any part may take place without the written permission of Cambridge University Press.

First published 2019

Printed in the United Kingdom by TJ International Ltd. Padstow Cornwall

*A catalogue record for this publication is available from the British Library.*

*Library of Congress Cataloging-in-Publication Data*
Names: Grimmer-Solem, Erik, author.
Title: Learning empire : globalization and the German quest for world status, 1875–1919 / Erik Grimmer-Solem.
Description: Cambridge, United Kingdom ; New York, NY : Cambridge University Press, 2019. | Includes bibliographical references and index.
Identifiers: LCCN 2019011889 | ISBN 9781108483827 (hardback : alk. paper) | ISBN 9781108705158 (pbk. : alk. paper)
Subjects: LCSH: Germany–Foreign relations–1871–1918. | Germany–Politics and government–1871–1918. | Germany–Colonies–History. | Imperialism–History–19th century. | Imperialism–History–20th century.
Classification: LCC DD221.5 .G73 2019 | DDC 327.43009/034–dc23
LC record available at https://lccn.loc.gov/2019011889

ISBN 978-1-108-48382-7 Hardback

Cambridge University Press has no responsibility for the persistence or accuracy of URLs for external or third-party internet websites referred to in this publication and does not guarantee that any content on such websites is, or will remain, accurate or appropriate.

# CONTENTS

*List of Illustrations*     viii
*Acknowledgments*     x
*List of Abbreviations*     xiii

**Introduction**     1

> PART I   **Absent-Minded Empire, 1875–1897**     27

1  **Frontier Empire: The United States**     29
   Gustav Schmoller and the University Germanosphere     29
   Labor Frontiers – Henry Farnam and American Trade Unionism     38
   From Strasbourg to Minnesota – Max Sering in North America     43
   Contiguous Colonies     56
   Hermann Schumacher and Ernst von Halle in Chicago     60
   The American Challenge     66

2  **Island Empire: Japan**     79
   Prussians in Edo     79
   The Meiji Six Society and "German Studies"     82
   From Strasbourg to Tokyo – Karl Rathgen in Japan     87
   Political Economy at Tokyo University     90
   The Association School and the Reform of Japanese Law     98
   "Yellow Peril"     107

3  **World Economy: China and Venezuela**     119
   Naval Arms, Neutrality, and the Erosion of Security     119
   From Berlin to Peking – Hermann Schumacher in China     128
   Karl Rathgen, Imperial Preference, and the Threat of "Panamerica"     141
   The Venezuela and Transvaal Crises     146
   From Hamburg to Caracas – Ernst von Halle in Venezuela     151
   Germany at the Crossroads     159

PART II  Empire Imagined, 1897–1907   163

4  **World Policy**   165
   Naval Dreams   165
   From *Weltwirtschaft* to *Weltpolitik*   169
   Alfred Tirpitz   177
   Bernhard von Bülow   185
   Bülow's *Weltpolitik*   192
   The Fleet Professors   197

5  **The High Seas Fleet and Power Politics**   213
   The Spanish-American War and the Samoa Question   213
   The Second Navy Bill and the Free Union for Naval Lectures   220
   Gustav Schmoller: Germany's Economic Future   223
   Max Sering: The Trade Policy of the Great States   227
   Ernst von Halle: The German Shipping Industry   233
   Hermann Schumacher: Germany's Interests in China   236
   Germany as Hammer or Anvil   242

6  **National Efficiency and the New Mercantilism**   250
   The "Yangtze Accord" and Anglo-German Estrangement   250
   National Efficiency   258
   Blue Riband   262
   The Bülow Tariff and the New Mercantilism   266
   The Politics of Anglo-German Trade   280
   The New Fleet Politics   285

7  **Formal and Informal Empire**   290
   *Weltpolitik* and the German Colonies – Karl Helfferich   290
   The Baghdad Railway   298
   The Retreat of "Germandom" in Japan   302
   The Second Venezuela Crisis   310
   Inventing the "German Menace"   316
   The Russo-Japanese War   319
   Full Steam to Bankruptcy   329

8  **Empire in Crisis**   340
   The Colonial Crisis   340
   The "Hottentot Elections"   344
   The Colonial-Political Action Committee   349
   The *Colonial-Political Guide* and *The Railways of Africa*   355

CONTENTS

The Baghdad Railway and the Young Turks – Karl Helfferich in Constantinople     361
The Kaiser's Professor – Hermann Schumacher in New York     368
The American Empire     374

PART III   **Empire Lost, 1908–1919**     389

9   **Colonial Dreams**     391
    Bernhard Dernburg's Colonial Reforms     391
    Karl Rathgen and the Hamburg Colonial Institute     397
    Tropical Fever – Hermann Schumacher in Southeast Asia     407
    Morocco and Espirito Santo     416
    King Leopold's Ghost in Dixie – Karl Rathgen in the American South     420
    Inner Colonization     426
    Max Sering and Hermann Schumacher in Russia     431
    Karl Helfferich and the Balkan Shatterbelt     438

10  **World Policy Contained**     446
    Fleet Enthusiasm     446
    Deterrent Illusions     451
    Financial Reform and the Limits of Professorial Politics     464
    The Baghdad Railway and Mesopotamian Oil     482
    "World Policy and No War!"     489

11  **From World Policy to World War**     494
    The Last Roosevelt Professor     494
    July Crisis     496
    The End of *Weltwirtschaft*     509
    The U-Boat Professors     519

12  **War Aims, Peace Resolutions, and Defeat**     541
    *Weltpolitik* by Other Means     541
    "New Germany"     558
    The Jewish Question     568
    The Friends of the Fatherland     578
    Elusive Peace     591

*Epilogue*     600
*Selected Bibliography*     604
*Index*     624

# ILLUSTRATIONS

## Figures

1.1 Gustav Schmoller ca. 1872. Bildarchiv des Mathematischen Forschungsinstituts Oberwolfach, CC BY-SA 2.0 DE. 34
1.2 Henry Walcott Farnam ca. 1900. Courtesy of Henry Walcott Farnam III. 42
1.3 Max Sering in 1890. Photograph by Bildagentur-online / UIG via Getty Images. 58
2.1 Karl Rathgen, Kudanzaka, Japan, May 1890. Fotosammlung des Geographischen Institutes der Humboldt-Universität zu Berlin. 88
3.1 Hermann Schumacher ca. 1900. Edwin R. A. Seligman, "Dr. Schumacher and the Kaiser Wilhelm Lectureship," *American Monthly Review of Reviews* XXXIV, no. 5 (1906): 548. 131
3.2 Ernst von Halle ca. 1905. © Universitätsbibliothek der Humboldt-Universität zu Berlin, Porträtsammlung: Ernst von Halle. 157
4.1 Alfred Tirpitz ca. 1895. Bettmann / Getty Images. 179
4.2 Bernhard von Bülow ca. 1895. Bundesarchiv Bildarchiv. 189
5.1 "The New World Order: A View into the Twentieth Century, by Bellamy-Jingo," *Kladderdatsch*, August 14, 1898 (Zweites Beiblatt). Digitale Bibliothek der Universität Heidelberg, CC-BY-SA-3.0. 219
7.1 Karl Helfferich in 1898. Source: Karl Lumm, *Karl Helfferich als Währungspolitiker und Gelehrter* (Leipzig: C. L. Hirschfeld, 1926), frontispiece. 292
7.2 "The German Fleet Dragon," *Der wahre Jacob*, June 26, 1906. Digitale Bibliothek der Universität Heidelberg, CC-BY-SA-3.0. 332
8.1 Bernhard Dernburg ca. 1915. Photograph by Paul Thompson / FPG / Getty Images. 347
10.1 "Fleet Increases," *Der wahre Jacob*, April 28, 1908, 5788. Digitale Bibliothek der Universität Heidelberg, CC-BY-SA-3.0. 474
11.1 Henry Walcott Farnam ca. 1910. Yale University, Harvey Cushing/John Hay Whitney Medical Library 496
11.2 Max Sering in 1910. Bildarchiv preußischer Kulturbesitz/Wilhelm Fechner, Art Resource, NY. 521
11.3 Karl Helfferich in 1915. Photograph by Ernst Sandau / Ullstein Bild via Getty Images. 526

ILLUSTRATIONS

12.1 Karl Rathgen ca. 1920. Bildarchiv preußischer Kulturbesitz, Art Resource, NY.   543
12.2 Hermann Schumacher ca. 1910. Photograph by Nicola Perscheid / Ullstein Bild via Getty Images.   557
12.3 Gustav Schmoller ca. 1915. Photograph by Nicola Perscheid / Ullstein Bild via Getty Images.   576

## Maps

1.1 Max Sering's journey through the United States and Canada, Feb. 23–Sept. 26, 1883.   48
1.2 Ernst von Halle's travels through the United States, ca. March 1893–ca. March 1894.   73
1.3 Ernst von Halle's journey through the American South, Sept. 3–Dec. 23, 1894.   77
2.1 Karl Rathgen's journey to Korea, China, and southern Japan, July 3–Sept. 9, 1886.   95
2.2 Karl Rathgen's journey to Formosa and China, May 25–Aug. 25, 1890.   112
2.3 Karl Rathgen's journey from Yokohama to Hamburg via the United States, Sept. 3–Oct. 23, 1890.   114
3.1 Hermann Schumacher's journey to China, Korea, and Japan, Jan.–Aug. 1897.   133
3.2 Ernst von Halle's journey to the United States, Caribbean, and Venezuela, Jan. 8–March 14, 1896.   156
8.1 Hermann Schumacher's journey through the United States and to Cuba, Jan.–April 1907.   377
9.1 Hermann Schumacher's journey to Malaya, Java, and Sumatra, Jan.–ca. May 1911.   410
9.2 Karl Rathgen's journey to the American South, Caribbean, Panama, and Honduras, Feb. 5–April 28, 1914.   425
9.3 Hermann Schumacher and Max Sering's journey to the Russian Empire, May–June 1912.   433

# ACKNOWLEDGMENTS

This book has been more than a decade in the making, and I have accumulated debts to many people and institutions along the way.

Wesleyan University offered numerous project grants and generous sabbaticals that allowed extended research in archives and libraries. I also received travel grants to attend conferences at which drafts of some of the chapters were presented. I am much indebted for this invaluable institutional support.

Many archivists and librarians assisted me in gaining access to many of the sources that are the foundation of this book. I am especially grateful to Frau Schleicher and Herr Baumgarten at the Bundesarchiv Koblenz for their accommodation in allowing me to use the uncatalogued and normally inaccessible Nachlass Helfferich and for their help in making duplicates from the Nachlass Sering. I am also deeply grateful to the Heisenberg family for their permission to use Hermann Schumacher's unpublished memoir. Frau Kohl in the Historical Archives of the Germanisches Nationalmuseum in Nuremberg was most helpful in allowing unencumbered access to this manuscript in the Nachlass Schumacher. I am especially grateful to Nils Goldschmidt for facilitating full access to this material. The staff of the Politisches Archiv der Ausärtigen Amts and Geheimes Staatsarchiv preußischer Kulturbesitz in Berlin as well as the Bundesarchiv Freiburg and Lichterfelde offered much valued assistance and expertise over numerous visits that span many years and always did so with consummate professionalism. Many other librarians and curators have been helpful in locating and making available materials to me. These include Kimberly Reynolds, Curator of Manuscripts at the Boston Public Library, and the archivists at the Hessisches Staatsarchiv in Wiesbaden and Warburg Institute in London. I also thank Henry W. Farnam III for his kindness in making available a photograph of his grandfather for use in this book.

A special expression of gratitude is due Dr. Barthold Witte of Bad Godesberg, who through his kindness and generosity allowed access to the private correspondence of his great grandfather Karl Rathgen. I also benefited enormously from his wealth of knowledge of Rathgen's liberal milieu in Germany as well as his work in founding the Hamburg Colonial Institute, now the University of Hamburg. I am very grateful to Professor Emeritus Dr. Christian Scheer of the University of Hamburg for introducing me to Dr. Witte.

Robert Nelson and Greg Zieren offered many valuable tips on archival and other research as well as stimulating conversations that helped this project along. I am also much indebted to Bärbel Holtz and Rainer Paetau through whose initiative I was able to participate in a Berlin-Brandenburg Academy of Sciences project in 2008–9 on the Prussian cultural state that offered the opportunity to present my initial findings on Japan and who gave much useful critical and stimulating feedback. An invitation to a conference organized by Sophus Reinert and Robert Fredona at Harvard Business School in 2013 gave me another venue to present my findings that proved enormously fruitful in helping to synthesize my ideas about the relationship between economic thought, empire, and policy. My thanks go out to them for that very valuable experience.

Many other colleagues in North America, Japan, and Europe have been incredibly helpful over the years. A special thank-you especially to Courtney Fullilove, Hoi-eun Kim, Alfred Reckendrees, Christian Spang, Ying Jia Tan, and Kazuhiro Tekii for the valuable feedback on earlier drafts of various chapters of the book. Jim Retallack gave very helpful advice on the book proposal, while Geoff Eley and Hartmut Pogge von Strandmann were kind enough to read through the completed manuscript, making helpful suggestions for revision before publication. All have my deepest gratitude. Any remaining omissions or errors are mine alone. I thank my commissioning editor at Cambridge University Press, Liz Friend-Smith, for her faith in this project and advocacy for the book.

It has been a privilege to work with so many gifted students of history at Wesleyan whose thesis projects touched on aspects of this book and who have often been an important direct and indirect source of inspiration, especially Ari Edmundson, Jared Fineberg, Elena Green, Jack Guenther, Stephen Lazer, Carolyn Lipp, Gillian Mahoney, Anna Mageras, John McNeil, Max Shafer-Landau, Mihai Olteanu, Anneliese Rapp, Maddy Smith-Huemer, and Heather Stanton. Colin T. Casey was a fastidious research assistant when this book project first took vague form in academic year 2004–5. Lucie Benz was a very helpful intern in the fall of 2012, while Jack Guenther assisted me splendidly as a research assistant during the final stage of this project in academic year 2017–18. For their assistance in making maps using geospatial software, my thanks go out to Azher Jaweed, Elizaveta Kravchenko, Melissa Mischell, and Sam Raby.

While researching in Berlin, Boston, Freiburg, Hamburg, Koblenz, and London over the years, many friends have offered their kind hospitality for which I am very grateful. These include Friederike Becker, Roman and Dagmar Benz, Christoph Burkhard and Stefanie Ostendorf, Kishwer and

Robert Falkner, Jana Ferguson, Fouad Hashem, Michaela Hinnenthal, Robert Nitsch and Frauke Zipp, Nicolas Weidtman, and Joachim Zweynert.

My wife Miwa and daughter Emma have suffered a spouse and father frequently away researching, busy reading and writing, or distracted with thought while this book was coming together. For the enduring patience and love you have shown me, I dedicate this book to you.

# ABBREVIATIONS

| | |
|---|---|
| BArch K | Bundesarchiv Koblenz |
| BArch L | Bundesarchiv Lichterfelde |
| BArch M | Bundesarchiv Militärarchiv, Freiburg |
| BdI | Bund der Industriellen |
| BPL | Boston Public Library |
| CDI | Centralverband deutscher Industrieller |
| GNN HA | Historisches Archiv, Germanisches Nationalmuseum, Nuremberg |
| *GPEK* | *Große Politik der Europäischen Kabinette* |
| GStA PK | Geheimes Staatsarchiv preußischer Kulturbesitz, Berlin |
| HAPAG | Hamburg-Amerikanische Paketfahrt-Aktien-Gesellschaft |
| HHStA | Hessisches Hauptstaatsarchiv, Wiesbaden |
| HUB UA | Humboldt-Universität zu Berlin, Universitätsarchiv |
| *JbbfNS* | *Jahrbücher für Nationalökonomie und Statistik* |
| *JbfGVV* | *Jahrbuch für Gesetzgebung, Verwaltung und Volkswirtschaft im Deutschen Reich* (after 1913 *SJ*) |
| *MOAG* | *Mitteilungen der Ostasiatischen Gesellschaft* |
| NDL | Norddeutscher Lloyd |
| Nl. | Nachlass (papers) |
| OAG | Ostasiatische Gesellschaft (Deutsche Gesellschaft für Natur- und Völkerkunde Ostasiens) |
| OHL | Oberste Heeresleitung (Supreme Army Command) |
| PA AA | Politisches Archiv des Auswärtigen Amts, Berlin |
| PNFBW | Privatnachlass Familie Barthold C. Witte, Bonn-Bad Godesberg |
| RMA | Reichsmarineamt (Imperial Navy Office) |
| SBB | Staatsbibliothek Berlin |
| SdVfS | Schriften des Vereins für Socialpolitik |
| *SJ* | *Schmollers Jahrbuch* (before 1913 *JbfGVV*) |
| SPD | Sozialdemokratische Partei Deutschlands (Social Democratic Party) |
| SUB | Staats- und Universitätsbibliothek Hamburg |

| | |
|---|---|
| StaHH | Staatsarchiv Hamburg |
| *StenBerVR* | *Stenographische Berichte über die Verhandlungen des Deutschen Reichstages* |
| WIA | Warburg Institute Archives, London |
| YUL MA | Yale University Library, Manuscripts and Archives |

# Introduction

In Erskine Childers' spy novel *The Riddle of the Sands,* the English college chums Davies and Carruthers go on a duck hunting holiday by sail to the Schleswig fiords. En route Davies diverts his yacht to the German East Frisian islands. Worried about England's weak North Sea coast defenses and chased off by the aptly-named German gunboat *Blitz,* the two begin to suspect something sinister afoot. Under cover of thick fog, the pair navigate the treacherous sandbanks to discover a nefarious plot: hidden away on the island of Memmert they spy hundreds of German barges readied for the invasion of England and overhear invasion-scheming German officers. Davies, it turned out, had visited the East Frisian islands previously and had fallen in love with a beautiful German girl, Clara. It was then that he had started to suspect that her father, Dollmann, might be an English double agent and that something suspicious was brewing on the island. Discovered, Davies, Carruthers, Clara, and Dollmann escape, the disgraced Dollmann sacrificing himself to the rough seas on the way back to England where the plot is revealed to the Admiralty.

Published in 1903, *Riddle of the Sands* was enormously popular in its time and remains a fascinating document of Edwardian Britain's love-hate relationship with Imperial Germany: admired for its efficiency and industrial progress yet also feared as an economic and imperial rival. It also tapped into real invasion fears. Indeed, it was itself only barely a novel, based as it was on Childers' own suspicions about Germany awakened by the Transvaal Crisis and then deepened while serving as an artillery driver during the Boer War. As a yachting enthusiast Childers had cruised along the Frisian coast to Cuxhaven and through the Kiel Canal all the way to Schleswig in 1897. There, as an amateur spy of sorts, he had taken note of canal and railway work along the German coast. Indeed, reviewers of the book had a hard time reading it as fiction.[1]

---

[1] Erskine Childers, *The Riddle of the Sands: A Record of Secret Service Recently Achieved,* with an introduction by Eric J. Grove (1903; Annapolis: Naval Institute Press, 1991), ix–xvi; see also Richard Scully, *British Images of Germany: Admiration, Antagonism & Ambivalence, 1860-1914* (Basingstoke, Hampshire: Palgrave Macmillan, 2012).

As reflected in *Riddle of the Sands* and in many other British invasion novels from that era, Imperial Germany's naval and world power ambitions had anchored themselves into the British psyche as a menace years before the High Seas Fleet posed any kind of threat to Britain and long before the First World War. Yet it is almost impossible today to separate fictive images animating Edwardian paranoia from the real rivalry between Germany and Britain that contributed to the outbreak of the First World War. Indeed, nearly the entire history of the German Empire has come to be narrated as a prelude to war. Imperial Germany has effectively become synonymous with cataclysm, its history a pathology of dysfunctional illiberal and authoritarian politics, persistent Junker militarism, and the erratic, warmongering Kaiser Wilhelm II.

While this narrative of German menace was well formed before the First World War, it coalesced during wartime into the full image of "beastliness." This was informed by the German invasion of Belgium, the mistreatment of Belgian civilians, and the policy of unrestricted submarine warfare that led to the sinking of the *Lusitania* in 1915, events that offered endless material for Entente and US wartime propaganda. The postwar issues of German war guilt, reparations, and loss of the bulk of the German navy and colonies were of course much invested in that image. The longevity and persistence of the pathological image of Imperial Germany can clearly also be explained by its appeal as a prelude to the Third Reich, giving the Great War – a war that many Europeans and Americans had come to view as pointless by the late 1920s – some meaning. The rise of Hitler and then the outbreak of the Second World War merely confirmed what many British historians like Louis Namier and A. J. P. Taylor had known about the Germans all along.[2]

After the Second World War, the rehabilitation of West Germany, and its integration into a Western alliance bloc, German historians like Walther Hubatsch and Gerhard Ritter sought to salvage the imperial past in their reassessments of German history as a usable legacy for a German identity that was, unlike the Third Reich, part of a Western and Christian civilizational trajectory. While these narratives went too far in claiming a radical break with that path in 1933, they contributed to a reassessment of Imperial Germany less haunted by the Great War and began to resituate that history and war in a context of global entanglements and great power diplomacy putting Imperial Germany into a comparative imperial context.[3]

---

[2] L. B. Namier, *1848: The Revolution of the Intellectuals* (London: G. Cumberlege, 1944); A. J. P Taylor, *The Course of German History: A Survey of the Development German History Since 1815* (London: H. Hamilton, 1945).

[3] Walther Hubatsch, *Die Ära Tirpitz: Studien zur deutschen Marinepolitik* (Göttingen: Musterschmidt-Verlag, 1955); Gerhard Ritter, *Staatskunst und Kriegshandwerk: Das Problem des "Militarismus" in Deutschland*, 4 vols. (Munich: Oldenbourg, 1954–68).

That all changed with the publication of Fritz Fischer's book *Griff nach der Weltmacht* in 1961 (translated as *Germany's Aims in the First World War*).[4] He exposed the apologetic tendentiousness of Gerhard Ritter's interpretation of German policy in the First World War, but Fischer's intervention had the unintended effect of also shifting attention away from comparisons of Imperial Germany with other imperial powers. Fischer also reaffirmed the continuities of thinking and policy between the Kaiserreich and Third Reich, notably in the policies of conquest and annexation in eastern Europe.[5] This work and especially his follow-up book, *Krieg der Illusionen* (*War of Illusions*), likewise cast Imperial Germany's global entanglements before the war in uniquely sinister terms as a prelude to the First World War, a war German leaders allegedly actively planned and then precipitated.[6] While Germany's global wartime strategy was an important component of Fischer's *Griff nach der Weltmacht*, the focus on the domestic German origins of the war very much overshadowed it. Likewise overshadowed were the strong continuities of liberal imperialism in evidence in German *Weltpolitik* (World Policy) initiated after 1895.[7]

One interesting consequence of the success of Fischer's interpretation was that the difficult and contradictory legacy of liberal imperialism in Britain, France, and the United States escaped critical scrutiny, undoubtedly welcome in Britain and France, which had both expanded their colonial empires after 1918 and retained formal colonies well into the 1960s and beyond. Because of the clear continuities that Fritz Fischer also identified between German war aims in the First and Second World Wars, German peculiarity could be highlighted, and the many parallels that in fact existed between British, French, American, and German imperialism and their common links to Western liberalism were almost entirely obscured.[8] In contemporaneous treatments and thereafter German liberalism was narrated as an obvious failure and compared unflatteringly with British, French, and American liberalism, a

---

[4] Fritz Fischer, *Griff nach der Weltmacht: Die Kriegszielpolitik des Kaiserlichen Deutschland 1914/18*, 2d ed. (Düssledorf: Droste Verlag, 1962); Fischer, *Germany's Aims in the First World War*, with an introduction by Hajo Holborn and James Joll (New York: W. W. Norton, 1967). Due to problems with this translation, notably abridgements and inaccuracy, I will be using the German edition of this work throughout.

[5] See Fritz Fischer, *World Power or Decline: The Controversy over Germany's Aims in the First World War*, trans. Lancelot L. Farrar, Robert Kimber, and Rita Kimber (New York: W. W. Norton, 1974), 113–24.

[6] Fritz Fischer, *Krieg der Illusionen: Die deutsche Politik von 1911 bis 1914* (Düssledorf: Droste Verlag, 1969); Fischer, *War of Illusions: German Policies from 1911 to 1914*, trans. Marian Jackson (New York: W. W. Norton, 1975).

[7] See Jennifer Jenkins, "Fritz Fischer's 'Programme for Revolution': Implications for a Global History of Germany in the First World War," *Journal of Contemporary History* 48, no. 2, Special Issue: The Fischer Controversy after 50 years (April 2013): 397–417.

[8] See Fritz Fischer, *From Kaiserreich to Third Reich: Elements of Continuity in German History, 1871–1945*, trans. Roger Fletcher (London: Allen & Unwin, 1979).

perspective that conveniently overlooked the realities of British and French violent colonial tutelage and Algerian, American, Australian, Canadian, and South African settler colonialism, genocide, racial segregation, and non-white disenfranchisement.[9] According to that narrative, the stagnation and fragmentation of the German liberal movement in the 1890s made the German Protestant middle strata susceptible to the siren song of *Weltpolitik*, drawing them out of liberal party politics into the mushrooming nationalist associations where they could be mobilized against their traditional Catholic and Socialist enemies to defend the authoritarian political status quo.[10]

This interpretation of German imperialism with its narrative of liberal failure became a pillar of critical German historiography in West Germany in the early 1970s in what we might call the Kehr-Fischer-Wehler synthesis, an argument that drew on the earlier work of Eckart Kehr on German naval policy and then Hans-Ulrich Wehler's works on Bismarck and German imperialism that stressed the domestic political purposes of German overseas imperialism and pointed to Germany's uniquely illiberal, authoritarian, and militaristic historical trajectory since the nineteenth century.[11] More recently, the influence of this argument has shaped the development of a parallel interpretation among scholars seeking to establish a link between Germany's allegedly peculiarly violent colonial history and German atrocities in the First World War and under National Socialism.[12]

In light of the power of these narratives of Imperial German prewar aggression and menace, it may come as a surprise to some readers that Imperial Germany waged no wars of conquest between its founding and the

---

[9] Leonard Krieger, *The German Idea of Freedom: History of a Political Tradition* (Boston: Beacon Press, 1957); Ralf Dahrendorf, *Society and Democracy in Germany* (Garden City, NY: Doubleday, 1967); Fritz Stern, *The Failure of Illiberalism: Essays on the Political Culture of Modern Germany* (New York: Knopf, 1972); James J. Sheehan, *German Liberalism in the Nineteenth Century* (Chicago: University of Chicago Press, 1978). Cf. Ben Kiernan, *Blood and Soil: A World History Genocide and Extermination from Sparta to Darfur* (New Haven and London: Yale University Press, 2007), 213–390.

[10] Sheehan, *German Liberalism*, 276–78.

[11] Eckart Kehr, *Schlachtflottenbau und Partei-Politik 1894–1901: Ein Versuch eines Querschnitts durch die innenpolitischen, sozialen und ideologischen Voraussetzungen des deutschen Imperialismus* (Berlin: Emil Ebering, 1930); Kehr, *Der Primat der Innenpolitik: Gesammelte Aufsätze zur preussisch-deutschen Sozialgeschichte im 19. und 20. Jahrhundert* (Berlin: Walter de Gruyter & Co, 1965); Hans-Ulrich Wehler, *Bismarck und der Imperialismus*, 3rd ed. (Cologne: Kiepenheuer & Witsch, 1972).

[12] See Jürgen Zimmerer and Joachim Zeller, eds., *Völkermord in Deutsch-Südwest Afrika: Der Kolonialkrieg (1904–1908) in Namibia und seine Folgen* (Berlin: Ch. Links, 2003), 45–63; Jürgen Zimmerer, "The Birth of the 'Ostland' out of the Spirit of Colonialism: A Post-Colonial Perspective on Nazi Policy of Conquest and Extermination," *Patterns of Prejudice* 39, no. 2 (June 2005): 197–219; Isabel V. Hull, *Absolute Destruction: Military Culture and the Practices of War in Imperial Germany* (Ithaca and London: Cornell University Press, 2005).

outbreak of the First World War. Between 1895 and 1914 Germany was also one of the only major world powers that did not wage war to acquire new colonial territory, and what it did acquire by negotiation, purchase, or lease was extremely modest by international comparison: parts of French Congo abutting Cameroon, half of Samoa, the tiny Caroline, Palau, and Mariana Islands in the Pacific, and the isolated Chinese leasehold of Kiaochow (Jiaozhou). Just for perspective, in those same years the British gained control of the Sudan, Nyasaland, Rhodesia, the Transvaal, Swaziland, Amantongaland (Maputaland), the Chinese leasehold Weihaiwei (Weihai), and Tonga. The French seized control of Mauritania, Morocco, Upper Volta, Madagascar, Laos, and the Chinese leasehold Kwangchow Wan (Guangzhouwan), while the Japanese gained Port Arthur (Lüshunkou) and Talien (Dalian), colonized Formosa and Korea, and expanded their position in southern Manchuria. The Americans, for their part, gained control of the Philippines, half of Samoa, Guam, Hawaii, Puerto Rico, and the Panama Canal Zone, and they intervened militarily in Cuba, Nicaragua, Honduras, and Mexico. Even a relatively weak power like Italy gained Cyrenaica and Tripolitania (Libya).

The other major objectives of German *Weltpolitik* fared no better. The Berlin-Baghdad railroad was not completed by 1914, still some 800 kilometers of track short. Germany also "lost" the dreadnought arms race with Britain by 1912, and the political purposes of the fleet as a diplomatic lever to force Britain into a neutrality agreement or colonial concessions achieved nothing. The reality is that Germany's navy never acquired the strength to threaten the British Isles, much less Britain's trade or its colonies, and it obviously also ultimately failed to deter war. Perhaps not surprisingly, German foreign policy in the decade before the First World War was roundly denounced as weak, adrift, and feckless by the German public. Indeed, the prevailing perception by 1914 was that in most arenas that mattered, *Weltpolitik* had failed. Thus Imperial Germany's actual provocations and actions before 1914 stand in remarkable contrast to the perceptions of those actions, especially in Britain and the United States.

The bifocal vision adopted in interpreting the German Empire from the perspective of 1918 and 1945 and the inordinate attention given its brief formal colonial gambit in Africa have also almost completely buried Germany's many other overseas entanglements that long predated the founding of the German Empire and that continued to be a very important part of its presence overseas after unification. There is, indeed, little if any wider awareness of the length and depth of those connections. We are accustomed to viewing the Age of Discovery and Europe's overseas expansion as Portuguese, Spanish, Dutch, and later French and English affairs, ones in which German-speakers did not much participate. Though less conspicuous, Germans were nevertheless aboard Portuguese caravels, Spanish galleons, and Dutch fluyts in the sixteenth and seventeenth centuries as crewmembers, missionaries, cartographers, scientists, physicians, merchants, bank agents, planters, and mercenaries. In the eighteenth and early nineteenth centuries Germans were aboard Dutch and British ships in similar capacities and often important agents of description, translation, and mediation between Europe and the rest of the world. For example, two German physicians in Dutch service in Japan, Engelbert Kaempfer (1651–1716) and Philipp Franz von Siebold (1796–1866), would play key roles both in the transmission of European medical knowledge to the Tokugawa shogunate and in shaping Europe's perceptions of Japan.[13]

The ranks of such German traveler-scientists would swell in the nineteenth century, led by such legendary figures as Alexander von Humboldt (1769–1859), whose extraordinary journeys gave names to many plants, animals, rivers, mountain ranges, and other places in the Americas. He would be followed by a whole host of German geographers, geologists, naturalists, and ethnographers, such as the brothers Adolf, Hermann, and Robert Schlagintweit (1829–57, 1826–82, 1833–85, respectively), whose extraordinary investigative journeys from the Himalayas down the Deccan plateau to Ceylon produced a monumental survey of India in 1861 commissioned by the British India Office. Only a few years later in the late 1860s Ferdinand von Richthofen (1833–1905) would undertake extensive geological expeditions in China and come to play a major role in Western perceptions of opportunity in the Middle Kingdom. He was followed by Johannes Justus Rein (1835–1918), whose multivolume work on the flora, fauna, and people of Japan based on his extensive excursions deep into the archipelago in the early 1870s was considered definitive at the time and immediately translated into multiple languages.[14]

Beyond the familiar story of German emigration to North America, Germans had also developed isolated settler communities, missions, and merchant diasporas not only in many parts of the British Empire but also in such places as Mexico, Venezuela, Brazil, West Africa, the Ottoman Empire, the Dutch East Indies, Samoa, and China by the 1860s. Meanwhile, between 1816 and 1860 the tonnage of shipping entering Hamburg increased fivefold,

---

[13] Josef Kreiner, ed., *Deutschland-Japan: Historische Kontakte* (Bonn: Bouvier Verlag Herbert Gundermann, 1984); Edgar Franz, "Deutsche Mediziner in Japan – ein Beitrag zum Wissenstransfer in der Edo-Zeit," *Japanstudien – Jahrbuch des Deutschen Instituts für Japanstudien* 17 (2005): 31–56.

[14] See Andrea Wulf, *The Invention of Nature: Alexander von Humboldt's New World* (New York: Alfred Knopf, 2015); Ulrike Kirchberger, *Aspekte deutsch-britischer Expansion: Die Überseeinteressen der deutschen Migranten in Großbritannien in der Mitte des 19. Jahrhunderts* (Stuttgart: Franz Steiner, 1999); Kris Manjapra, *Age of Entanglement: German and Indian Intellectuals across Empire* (Cambridge, MA and London: Harvard University Press, 2014), 27; Shellen Xiao Wu, *Empires of Coal: Fueling China's Entry Into the Modern World Order, 1860-1920* (Stanford: Stanford University Press, 2015); Matthias Koch and Sebastian Conrad, eds., *Johannes Justus Rein: Briefe eines deutschen Geographen aus Japan 1873-1875* (Munich: Iudicium, 2006).

INTRODUCTION 7

driven in large part by rapidly-growing trade with North and South America. By 1860 nearly one million tons of goods was entering its harbor.[15]

As already alluded to, the prominence of university-educated people – geographers, scientists, physicians, and clerics – in this German exploration and discovery is a striking feature, and it may not come as a surprise that university scholarship was a cornerstone of Germany's worldwide influence long before Germany was unified. Indeed German research universities had by 1870 gained a truly global reputation, attracting students from all over the world and serving as a nexus for scholarly connections that entangled Germany with the outside world decades before Germany ever acquired formal colonies, a navy, or significant industrial export markets and overseas investments. German universities would remain one of the most powerful institutions of German global connection and play a key role both in the dissemination of imperial information and in imperial politics up to and during the First World War. It is thus odd that while valuable contributions have been made to our understanding of the global and transnational entanglements and the global economic context of Imperial Germany's history, the key role of universities in that globalization is missing almost entirely.[16] Even in histories of the nineteenth century that aspire to be global, such as Jürgen Osterhammel's impressive *Transformation of the World,* the German university is treated as a European export to the rest of the world rather than as a node of global connection that brought the world to Germany and then facilitated many active personal links to such places as Japan, China, Latin America, and the United States.[17]

This is a book about Germany's global scholarly connections after it was founded as a modern state in 1871 and how these fatefully intersected with the later quest for formal colonies and the national ambition to become a world power. It is about how this "empire of learning" became entangled with the task of learning about the world and devising an imperial strategy, hence the double

---

[15] Niall Ferguson, *Paper and Iron: Hamburg Business and German Politics in the Era of Inflation, 1897–1927* (Cambridge: Cambridge University Press, 1995), 33.

[16] See Sebastian Conrad, *Globalisation and the Nation in Imperial Germany,* trans. Sorcha O'Hagan (Cambridge: Cambridge University Press, 2010); Niels P. Petersson, "Das Kaiserreich in Prozessen ökonomischer Globalisierung," in *Das Kaiserreich transnational: Deutschland in der Welt 1871–1914,* ed. Sebastian Conrad and Jürgen Osterhammel (Göttingen: Vandenhoeck & Ruprecht, 2004), 49–67; Cornelius Torp, *The Challenges of Globalization: Economy and Politics in Germany, 1860–1914,* trans. Alex Skinner (New York: Berghahn Books, 2014). Two notable recent exceptions are Ho-eun Kim, *Doctors of Empire: Medical and Cultural Encounters between Imperial Germany and Meiji Japan* (Toronto: University of Toronto Press, 2014); Manjapra, *Age of Entanglement.*

[17] Jürgen Osterhammel, *The Transformation of the Word: A Global History of the Nineteenth Century,* trans. Patrick Camiller (Princeton: Princeton University Press, 2014), 798–808.

meaning of the book's title *Learning Empire*. It is a story about the German Empire told from the globe inward toward Germany. While this may seem an odd strategy, the intention is to highlight how misleading it is to treat Imperial Germany purely endogenously and its later imperial gambits as emanating from the metropole outward. In reality the transportation and communications revolution unfolding in the decade before German unification – exemplified by transcontinental railways such as the Union Pacific, transoceanic steamships, undersea telegraph cables, and the completion of the Suez Canal – rapidly accelerated the transfer of people and ideas that were already part of the fabric of German life at the empire's founding. Those experiences entered German consciousness and parlance by the burgeoning newspaper, journal, and book print media, where the term *Weltwirtschaft* (world economy, i.e., globalization) was increasingly common by the 1880s.[18] Detailed scholarly and journalistic treatments of the process of agricultural and industrial development, urbanization, and colonization from overseas thus accompanied Germany's own modern development and became important metrics of its progress. The rapid traffic of university-educated people and the dissemination of their ideas through journalistic and scholarly description, comparison, and analysis was at the very heart of the formation of mental maps of the world that later came to justify *Weltpolitik* as a response to the challenges of globalization. That is, Imperial Germany's history was inescapably global from the very beginning, not as the result of policies of outward colonial expansion or the forces of industrialization and urbanization in the 1880s and 1890s.[19]

Another important ambition of this book is to recover the strands of liberal imperialism that made up the cloth of German *Weltpolitik*. This is important for a number of reasons. The heavy investment in narratives of "liberal failure" and imperialism as an authoritarian ruse has largely written liberalism out of German *Weltpolitik*. This has wider implications. As Adam Tooze has argued, the hold of Mark Mazower's "Dark Continent" thesis to explain the tragedy of interwar history that culminated in fascism and National Socialism gives excessive weight to the resurgence of the supposedly illiberal and atavistic imperialistic impulses of the "old world" against the forces of progress.[20] This thesis overlooks the genuine novelty of the new global imperialism that took form around 1900 and that ultimately contributed to the outbreak of world

---

[18] Jürgen Osterhammel and Niels P. Petersson, eds., *Geschichte der Globalisierung: Dimensionen, Prozesse, Epochen* (Munich: C. H. Beck, 2003), 63–70; Quinn Slobodian, "How to See the World Economy: Statistics, Maps, and Schumpeter's Camera in the First Age of Globalization," *Journal of Global History* 10 (2015): 307–22.

[19] See Conrad, *Globalisation and the Nation*, 15–20.

[20] Adam Tooze, *The Deluge: The Great War, America and the Remaking of the Global Order, 1916–1931* (New York: Viking, 2014), 17–20, 22; cf. Mark Mazower, *Dark Continent: Europe's Twentieth Century* (New York: Vintage Books, 1998), x–xv, 3–40; Arno J. Mayer, *The Persistence of the Old Regime: Europe to the Great War* (New York: Pantheon, 1981).

war in 1914, which in war and after would morph into interwar militarism and fascism. This was an imperialism that before 1914 had grown out of liberal nationalism, was often self-consciously progressive, and that managed to mobilize the democratized masses not just in Britain and France, but also in Germany, Japan, Italy, and the United States.[21] Indeed, the mutated DNA of liberalism can be found in the interwar right and in the metastasis of fascism.

We are familiar with narratives of interwar instability that treat the prewar liberal *Pax Britannica* as a force for peace, stability, and international order only to be ultimately shattered by world war.[22] That reading tends to overlook the fact many of the destabilizing forces of the period before 1914 can be traced back to Britain's violent outward expansion in the Victorian era, the battleship arms race it started with its imperial rivals France and Russia in the late 1880s, and the strategic realignments that were necessary due to its imperial overextension undertaken in the Edwardian era. Globalization required the acceptance of certain international rules largely defined by Britain, but the very legitimacy of those rules was being undermined by the tensions that emerged between Britain's imperial claims and its actual power, and along with that, its self-serving abuse of those very rules as it found itself increasingly overstretched.[23]

Clear definitions of German liberalism and liberal imperialism are in order before continuing any further. For the purposes of this study, "liberalism" is understood not as a party designation but rather as a broader political ideology linked intimately to German nationalism and associated closely with the Protestant and Jewish urban middle classes of Imperial Germany. Like its close cousins in Britain and France, this liberalism placed the emancipated individual (not class, church, or king) at its core, was committed to representative government (if not necessarily parliamentarism or democracy), and saw scientific, social, economic, and cultural progress as desirable and the result of individual freedom, initiative, and upward mobility. It was an ideology that gave priority to civil society (*bürgerliche Gesellschaft*) and market forces in creating social order and in that march of progress, yet one that was

---

[21] Eric Hobsbawm, *Age of Empire 1875–1914* (London: Weidenfeld & Nicolson, 1987), 56–83.

[22] See, for example, John Darwin, *Unfinished Empire: The Global Expansion of Britain* (London: Allen Lane, 2012); Niall Ferguson, *Empire: The Rise and Demise of the British World Order and the Lessons for Global Power* (New York: Basic Books, 2002); Robert Gilpin, *The Political Economy of International Relations* (Princeton: Princeton University Press, 1987); Charles P. Kindleberger, *The World in Depression, 1929–1939*, rev. ed. (Berkeley, Los Angeles, and London: University of California Press, 1986).

[23] See Antoinette Burton, *The Trouble with Empire: Challenges to Modern British Imperialism* (Oxford: Oxford University Press, 2015); Harold James, *The Roman Predicament: How the Rules of International Order Create the Politics of Empire* (Princeton: Princeton University Press, 2006).

also committed to older German ideals of a classless civil society (*Mittelstandsgesellschaft*), the rule of law (*Rechtsstaatlichkeit*), and the state as a patron and guarantor of religious, educational, scientific, and artistic freedoms (*Kulturstaatlichkeit*).

German liberal imperialism was the projection abroad of those liberal values and ideals to become the equal of other great world powers. In practice that involved gaining both formal colonies and informal spheres of influence. While committed to colonization and the spread of *Deutschtum* (Germandom), liberal imperialists came to criticize colonial bureaucratic tutelage (*Kolonial-Assessorismus*) and the abusive practices of colonial concession companies. Instead, they sought greater colonial self-administration and to incentivize colonial subject people into becoming rational (firmly-settled and docile, yet acquisitive) producers and consumers, aiming at their integration into a German and worldwide division of labor through investments in colonial railways and more scientific forms of colonial policy. They hoped to turn the colonies into sources of key imported raw materials, a market for German manufactured goods, and where feasible, a destination for Germany's emigrant population otherwise lost to the United States and British Empire.

In the Wilhelmine period, German liberal imperialists fully embraced Germany's industrial future and the challenges of *Weltwirtschaft*, prioritizing free trade and private overseas investments to expand German export markets and spheres of interest well beyond formal colonies into such places as Latin America, China, and the Ottoman Empire. This reflected the waning popularity of settler colonialism within their ranks due to the disappointing record of Germany's African colonies as settler destinations. Even so, a significant coterie of liberal imperialists continued to place much stock in the liberating potential of settler colonies and never quite gave up hope for securing them somewhere. They saw them as valuable laboratories of self-reliance, self-government, and social mobility on the model of American and British experience in North America, and they believed they would heal deficiencies in the German national character inherited from centuries of princely tutelage and status snobbery. Finally and most importantly, German liberal imperialists were deeply invested in the German navy as a symbol of national unity and guarantor of Germany's maritime destiny as a major trading and aspiring world power.

Some readers may find the prominence given in this book to liberalism surprising given the still prevalent notion of German "liberal failure." Much research since the 1980s on German bourgeois society, liberalism, and German political culture has come to question this thesis and its supporting trope of the supposedly apolitical German bourgeoisie.[24] While it is true that the

---

[24] See David Blackbourn and Geoff Eley, *The Peculiarities of German History: Bourgeois Society and Politics in Nineteenth-Century Germany* (Oxford: Oxford University Press, 1984); Dieter Langewiesche, *Liberalism in Germany,* trans. Christiane Banerji (Princeton:

democratization of the German polity before its parliamentarization marginalized the liberal parties at the Reich level, they dominated at the state and municipal levels, where restricted franchises prevailed and the educated and propertied urban *Bürgertum* became exceptionally active in social reform policy, philanthropy, and the women's movement.[25] Bourgeois political energies did witness a shift out of liberal party politics into radical nationalist associations in the 1890s, though it cannot be claimed that this was due to manipulation from above to preserve the authoritarian features of the Reich – indeed, if anything this activity made the authoritarian system less stable and more difficult to govern.[26] The closer one looks at this activity, the more untenable the claims about the apolitical bourgeoisie and "liberal failure" seem to become.

Following the colonial turn in German history in the 1990s, a sizable body of scholarship has come to reveal that the German bourgeoisie was exceptionally active in colonial and naval politics and that German imperialism retained a deep strain of liberalism well into the twentieth century.[27] In those areas where the *Bildungsbürgertum* (university-educated bourgeoisie) retained the upper hand, Birthe Kundrus has shown that German colonialism had unmistakably modern and liberal features, with progress, science, and technology assuming very prominent roles in the articulation of German colonial aims.[28] Indeed and as will be argued throughout this book, the promise of scientific,

---

Princeton University Press, 2000); Margaret Lavinia Anderson, *Practicing Democracy: Elections and Political Culture in Imperial Germany* (Princeton: Princeton University Press, 2000).

[25] Kevin Repp, *Reformers, Critics and the Paths of German Modernity: Anti-Politics and the Search for Alternatives, 1890–1914* (Cambridge, MA and London: Harvard University Press, 2000); Thomas Adam, *Philanthropy, Civil Society, and the State in German History* (Rochester, NY: Camden House, 2016).

[26] Geoff Eley, *Reshaping the German Right: Radical Nationalism and Political Change after Bismarck* (New Haven: Yale University Press, 1980; repr., Ann Arbor: Michigan University Press, 1991); Roger Chickering, *We Men Who Feel Most German: A Cultural Study of the Pan-German League 1886–1914* (Boston: Allen and Unwin, 1984).

[27] Susanne Zantop, *Colonial Fantasies: Conquest, Family, and Nation in Precolonial Germany, 1770–1870* (Durham, NC: Duke University Press, 1997); Matthew Jeffries, *Contesting the German Empire 1871–1918* (Malden, MA: Blackwell, 2008); Bradley Naranch and Geoff Eley, eds., *German Colonialism in a Global Age* (Durham, NC and London: Duke University Press, 2014).

[28] Birthe Kundrus, *Moderne Imperialisten: Das Kaiserreich im Spiegel seiner Kolonien* (Cologne, Weimar, & Vienna: Böhlau Verlag, 2003), 286–87. See also Dirk van Laak, *Imperiale Infrastruktur: Deutsche Planungen für eine Erschließung Afrikas 1880 bis 1960* (Paderborn: Ferdinand Schöningh, 2004), 132–33; Erik Grimmer-Solem, "Die preußische Bildungspolitik im Spannungsfeld des internationalen Kulturwettbewerbs: der Fall Japan (1869–1914)," in *Kulturstaat und Bürgergesellschaft: Preußen, Deutschland und Europa im 19. und frühen 20. Jahrhundert*, ed. Bärbel Holtz and Wolfgang Neugebauer (Berlin: Akademie Verlag, 2010), 203–21.

technological, and material progress, and greater individual freedom and opportunity, along with the worldwide spread of a supposedly superior German *bürgerliche Gesellschaft* and *Kultur* were core ambitions of German liberal imperialism as embodied in *Weltpolitik*. Much like their British counterparts on which they modeled themselves, many German liberal imperialists came to view unfamiliar cultures and peoples as provisional, incomplete, and backward as well as in need of guidance to attain higher levels of organization, freedom, and stability. Where native people were seen in the way of that march of progress, the thinking went, they had to be dealt with severely.[29]

Here it is important to clarify that liberalism and radical nationalism were not necessarily antagonistic worldviews in Wilhelmine Germany. For example, Lora Wildenthal has analyzed the thought and activity of radical nationalists as they were shaped by the colonial encounter, revealing that left liberal feminist aspirations and radical nationalist colonial ambitions could coexist and how colonial hierarchies based on race could be used by women as tools of democratic mobilization.[30] Others have underscored this point, demonstrating that members of the left liberal milieu – those who could be counted among the most progressive, modern, and forward-looking in Germany – became uncompromising imperialists because of the way their imperialism was fused with a liberal civilizing mission.[31] These contributions and more recent work on the German Navy League and the continuities of liberal nationalism in southwestern Germany into the 1930s support the conclusion that radical nationalism and liberalism, far from having gone separate ways, remained closely tied, and that the German overseas empire and navy acted to reinforce that tie.[32]

---

[29] Matthew P. Fitzpatrick, *Liberal Imperialism in Germany: Expansionism and Nationalism, 1848-1884* (Oxford and New York: Berghahn Books, 2008), 205-11; cf. Uday Singh Mehta, *Liberalism and Empire: A Study in Nineteenth-Century British Liberal Thought* (Chicago and London: University of Chicago Press, 1999), 191.

[30] See Lora Wildenthal, *German Women for Empire, 1884-1945* (Durham, NC and London: Duke University Press, 2001); Wildenthal, "'She is the Victor': Bourgeois Women, Nationalist Identities, and the Ideal of the Independent Woman Farmer in German Southwest Africa," in *Society, Culture, and the State in Germany, 1870-1930*, ed. Geoff Eley (Ann Arbor: University of Michigan Press, 1996), 371-95.

[31] Helmut Walser Smith, "The Talk of Genocide, the Rhetoric of Miscegenation: Notes on Debates in the German Reichstag Concerning Southwest Africa, 1904-14," in *The Imperialist Imagination: German Colonialism and Its Legacy*, ed. Sara Friedrichsmeyer, Sara Lennox, and Susanne Zantop (Ann Arbor: University of Michigan Press, 1998), 107-23; Smith, "The Logic of Colonial Violence: Germany in Southwest Africa (1904-1907): The United States in the Philippines (1899-1902)," in *German and American Nationalism: A Comparative Perspective*, ed. Hartmut Lehmann and Hermann Wellenreuther (Oxford and New York: Berg, 1999), 205-31.

[32] Sebastian Diziol, *"Deutsche, werdet Mitglieder des Vaterlandes!": Der Deutsche Flottenverein 1898-1934*, 2 vols. (Kiel: Solivagus Praeteritum, 2015); Oded Heilbronner, *From*

There is today an extensive literature on French and British liberal imperialism that has served to reinforce this interpretation. Alice Conklin, Uday Mehta, and Jeanne Morefield have highlighted the liberal and modernizing content of aggressive strains of British and French imperialism noting the close links between British liberal and French republican thought and the emergence of an orientalizing anthropology unable to consider the claims and culture of the colonized "other."[33] Likewise, Jennifer Pitts has shown that such paragons of the British and French liberal traditions as John Stuart Mill (1806–73) and Alexis de Tocqueville (1805–59) came to fully embrace and justify the colonial projects in India and Algeria in the 1840s by internalizing more restrictive, hierarchical, and biologistic definitions of national character and new heroic notions of national progress that emerged in the wake of suffrage reform, the abolition of slavery, industrialization, and the spread of Christian missionary activity in the colonies.[34] Interestingly and in some contrast, German anthropology in the nineteenth century was a self-consciously cosmopolitan, pluralist, and humanistic discipline oriented toward *Bildung*.[35] It was not until Germany gained a colonial project, and as importantly, a democratized visual culture with a predilection for imperialistic show that the turn toward race and nation was made within the discipline.[36] It is now much more fully appreciated how this affected the self-understandings and perceptions not only of the German middle-class public and bourgeois political parties but also the working classes and Social Democratic Party. All gradually internalized new colonial and racial tropes after the turn of the twentieth century through popular culture and the important place the colonies gained in German public life, especially during and after the elections of 1907.[37]

---

*Popular Liberalism to National Socialism: Religion, Culture and Politics in South-Western Germany, 1860s–1930s* (London and New York: Routledge, 2016).

[33] Alice L. Conklin, *A Mission to Civilize: The Republican Idea of Empire in France and West Africa, 1895–1930* (Stanford, CA: Stanford University Press, 1997); Mehta, *Liberalism and Empire*; Jeanne Morefield, *Covenants without Swords: Idealist Liberalism and the Spirit of Empire* (Princeton: Princeton University Press, 2004).

[34] Jennifer Pitts, *A Turn to Empire: The Rise of Imperial Liberalism in Britain and France* (Princeton and Oxford: Princeton University Press, 2005).

[35] H. Glenn Penny and Matti Bunzl, eds., *Worldly Provincialism: German Anthropology in the Age of Empire* (Ann Arbor: University of Michigan Press, 2003), 2, 9–11.

[36] H. Glenn Penny, "Bastian's Museum: On the Limits of Empiricism and the Transformation of German Ethnology," in *Worldly Provincialism*, ed. Penny and Bunzl, 86–126.

[37] Oliver Sobich, *"Schwarze Bestien, rote Gefahr": Rassismus und Antisozialismus im deutschen Kaiserreich* (Frankfurt am Main: Campus, 2006); Erik Grimmer-Solem, "The Professors' Africa: Economists, the Elections of 1907, and the Legitimation of German Imperialism," *German History* 25, no. 3 (2007): 313–47; John Phillip Short, *Magic Lantern Empire: Colonialism and Society in Germany* (Ithaca and London: Cornell University Press, 2012).

These and other studies suggest that German imperialism was neither uniquely violent nor uniformly malevolent and, indeed, in important respects unexceptional, falling in line with broader patterns already seen in Britain and France after Germany gained a colonial foothold.[38] Comparative studies have only served to reinforce this interpretation, revealing the many common themes that united the liberal bourgeois milieux of Britain, France, and Germany in encounters with non-European peoples.[39] Germany's encounter with the United States explains the most about the expectations and formal contours of German liberal imperialism in the late nineteenth and early twentieth centuries. As Jens-Uwe Guettel and Glenn Penny have shown, the interactions between Americans and Germans, and particularly the long and deep experience of Germans living and traveling in the United States, was quite possibly the most important single reference point in the development of German liberal imperialism, just as it was in the development of perceptions of racial otherness.[40] Sven Beckert and Andrew Zimmerman have also revealed that the American "New South" was likewise a significant laboratory for new regimes of German colonial exploitation and domination.[41] Similarly, Dirk Bönker has shown that the development of naval militarism in the United States and Germany shows many striking parallels that reveal close reciprocal observation and common lines of development.[42] What is still missing is integrating these insights into a new, wider narrative about German expansionism and its relationship to prewar diplomacy, the July Crisis, and the war aims debate during the First World War as well as their relationship to the longer-term trajectory of German history in the twentieth century.[43]

---

[38] Georg Steinmetz, *The Devil's Handwriting: Precoloniality and the German Colonial State in Qingdao, Samoa, and Southwest Africa* (Chicago and London: University of Chicago Press, 2007); Susanne Kuss, *German Colonial Wars and the Context of Military Violence*, trans. Andrew Smith (Cambridge, MA and London: Harvard University Press, 2017).

[39] See, for example, Frederick Cooper and Ann Laura Stoler, eds., *Tensions of Empire: Colonial Cultures in a Bourgeois World* (Berkeley: University of California Press, 1997); Ulrich van der Heyden and Holger Stoecker, eds., *Mission und Macht im Wandel politischer Orientierungen: Europäische Missionsgesellschaften in politischen Spannungsfeldern in Afrika und Asien zwischen 1800 und 1945* (Stuttgart: Franz Steiner, 2005).

[40] Jens-Uwe Guettel, *German Expansionism, Imperial Liberalism, and the United States, 1776–1945* (Cambridge and New York: Cambridge University Press, 2012); H. Glenn Penny, *Kindred By Choice: Germans and American Indians Since 1800* (Chapel Hill: University of North Carolina Press, 2013).

[41] Sven Beckert, "From Tuskegee to Togo: The Problem of Freedom in the Empire of Cotton," *Journal of American History* 92, no. 2 (Sept. 2005): 498–526; Andrew Zimmerman, *Alabama in Africa: Booker T. Washington, the German Empire, & the Globalization of the New South* (Princeton: Princeton University Press, 2010).

[42] Dirk Bönker, *Militarism in a Global Age: Naval Ambitions in Germany and the United States before World War I* (Ithaca: Cornell University Press, 2012).

[43] Geoff Eley, "Empire by Land and Sea? Germany's Imperial Imaginary, 1840–1945," in Naranch and Eley, *German Colonialism in a Global Age*, 19–45, here 24–29, 37.

A second important interpretive line of *Learning Empire* draws on insights from diplomatic history. The tradition of German diplomatic history represented by Gerhard Ritter focusing on Imperial Germany's precarious geographical position as the key constraint and determinant of its international politics continued to have adherents after the Fischer controversy. It was reaffirmed by Klaus Hildebrand, Andreas Hillgruber, and Michael Stürmer in the 1970s and 1980s and contributed to heated debates that culminated in the *Historikerstreit* of 1986–89.[44] While the strongest versions of this argument are untenable without serious qualifications and were to varying degrees colored by conservative politics at the time, a growing body of research on German and British foreign policy over the last several years has come to the conclusion that the ultimate failure of the German *Weltpolitik* and the outbreak of war in 1914 cannot be explained adequately by focusing only on German leaders and domestic politics. Metropolitan German imperial politics were internationally mediated through the press and in a constant dialogue with those same processes going on in the United States and Great Britain. All great powers were reacting to tectonic shifts occurring in the global balance of power. For example, Germany's ambitions in China and Latin America strained formerly very close relations with Japan and the United States, and the noisy and internationally mediated domestic German politics of naval, colonial, and trade policy in turn distorted British and American public perceptions of Germany. These processes made it possible for an overextended Britain to abandon the Western Hemisphere to the United States, negotiate an alliance with Japan, and reconcile with its traditional imperial rivals France and Russia. The domestic German politics of *Weltpolitik* were thus tied in complex ways to an Edwardian strategy of German containment. This interpretation draws on a now large body of work by Magnus Brechtken, Konrad Canis, Ragnhild Fiebig-von Hase, Dominik Geppert, Ute Mehnert, Nancy Mitchell, Thomas Otte, Andreas Rose, and Gregor Schöllgen, who have all given British imperial politics, the global balance of power, the media, and public opinion a much more prominent place in the ultimate fate of German *Weltpolitik*.[45]

---

[44] See esp. Klaus Hildebrand and Reiner Pommerin, eds. *Deutsche Frage und europäisches Gleichgewicht: Festschrift für Andreas Hillgruber zum 60. Geburtstag* (Cologne: Böhlau Verlag, 1985); Andreas Hillgruber, *Zweierlei Untergang: Die Zerschlagung des Deutschen Reiches und das Ende des europäischen Judentums* (Berlin: Seidler, 1986); Michael Stürmer, *Das ruhelose Reich: Deutschland 1866–1918* (Berlin: Severin und Seidler, 1983).

[45] Magnus Brechtken, *Scharnierzeit 1895–1907: Persönlichkeitsnetze und internationale Politik in den deutsch-britisch-amerikanischen Beziehungen vor dem Esten Weltkrieg* (Mainz: Philipp von Zabern, 2006); Konrad Canis, *Von Bismarck zur Weltpolitik: Deutsche Aussenpolitik 1890 bis 1902* (Berlin: Akademie Verlag, 1997); Ragnhild Fiebig-von Hase, *Lateinamerika als Konfliktherd der deutsch-amerikanischen Beziehungen 1890–1903: Vom Beginn der Panamerikapolitik bis zur Venezuelakrise von 1902/03*, 2 parts

German *Weltpolitik* still poses a number of questions that have yet to be adequately resolved. The policy's strikingly modest achievements recounted earlier were hardly worth the huge risks the country ran and the enormous costs it bore by building the second largest navy in the world by 1907. Various strategies have been devised by historians to deal with this apparent contradiction. As already touched on, some have come to view *Weltpolitik* as little more than a sham, a cynical social-imperialist ploy by Germany's political elite to legitimate the authoritarian nation state and distract the middle- and working-class masses and thus prevent political reform. As Hans-Ulrich Wehler has argued, the volatile character of *Weltpolitik* hid what was in fact a "coolly-calculated instrumentalization of expansionist politics for domestic political purposes."[46] John Röhl, taking this interpretative line a step further, attributes *Weltpolitik* to the peculiar obsessions and character flaws of Kaiser Wilhelm, who was at the time bent on establishing much more direct personal rule over Germany by appointing Bernhard von Bülow foreign secretary and chancellor and Alfred Tirpitz head of the Navy Office, a duo that implemented *Weltpolitik* largely according to his preferences.[47] The volatility and failings of the policy can thus largely be chalked up to the personal failings of a monarch in a system without adequate checks and balances.

Other historians of Germany such as Christopher M. Clark have taken a different line, seeing Bülow as a new kind of chancellor who channeled popular opinion to bolster his position against the Kaiser.[48] Yet other than in its brash new style and tone, he sees little deviation in *Weltpolitik* from prevailing German foreign policy precepts. It was, he writes, "the old policy of the free hand with a larger navy and more menacing mood music."[49] A more strictly functionalist interpretation of *Weltpolitik* offered by Woodruff Smith

(Göttingen: Vandenhoeck & Ruprecht, 1986); Dominik Geppert, *Pressekriege: Öffentlichkeit und Diplomatie in den deutsch-britischen Beziehungen (1896–1912)* (Munich: Oldenbourg, 2007); Ute Mehnert, *Deutschland, Amerika und die „Gelbe Gefahr": Zur Karriere eines Schlagworts in der großen Politik, 1905–1917* (Stuttgart: Franz Steiner, 1995); Nancy Mitchell, *The Danger of Dreams: German and American Imperialism in Latin America* (Chapel Hill and London: University of North Carolina Press, 1999); T. G. Otte, *The China Question: Great Power Rivalry and British Isolation, 1894–1905* (Oxford: Oxford University Press, 2007); Andreas Rose, *Zwischen Empire und Kontinent: Britische Aussenpolitik vor dem Ersten Weltkrieg* (Munich: R. Oldenbourg, 2011); Gregor Schöllgen, *Imperialismus und Gleichgewicht: Deutschland, England und die orientalische Frage* (Munich: R. Oldenbourg, 1984).

[46] Hans-Ulrich Wehler, *Deutsche Gesellschaftsgeschichte*, vol. 3 (Munich: C.H. Beck, 1995), 1139.
[47] John C. G. Röhl, *Wilhelm II: The Kaiser's Personal Monarchy*, trans. Sheila de Bellaigue (Cambridge: Cambridge University Press, 2004), 799–879, 924–65, 999–1039.
[48] Christopher Clark, *Kaiser Wilhelm II* (Harlow: Longman, 2000), 92–118, 123–54.
[49] Christopher Clark, *The Sleepwalkers: How Europe Went to War in 1914* (New York: Harper, 2013), 151.

sees *Weltpolitik* as an economic imperialism driven by the growing prominence of banking, industry, and economic interest groups in Wilhelmine politics, groups who sought the state's assistance to secure overseas export markets, access to raw materials, and investment opportunities in such places as China, the Near East, and South America. The inconsistencies and zig-zags observed in implementing this policy were due to its tensions and incompatibilities with other imperialist pressure groups and policy that sought settler colonies.[50]

While there are elements of truth in some of these interpretations of *Weltpolitik*, they tend to give excessive voice to highly visible political agents in the formulation of the aims of *Weltpolitik* and reflect the deficiency of attempting to reconstruct *Weltpolitik* largely from the official record. The traditional overreliance on diplomatic, military, naval, and colonial papers by political historians has led them to over-privilege visible political agents and the very selective, fragmentary, and often self-serving record they left behind. This has obscured the workings of informal foreign policy agents and networks and has played down or ignored the role of civil society and global structural forces in German political outcomes. This is especially true with regard to the complex multilateral processes and unspoken and unwritten assumptions that undergirded decision-making shaped strongly by a climate of public opinion in which these political agents were themselves inescapably immersed.[51] In any case, it has been difficult to square the Kaiser, Bülow, and Tirpitz-centered narratives of German prewar imperialism with the overwhelming evidence of strong middle-class initiative in creating that policy. Similarly, it is difficult to reconcile the spontaneous effusion of expansive war aims drafted by bourgeois scholars and publicists during the First World War with an allegedly coherent centralized plan for European and world hegemony advanced by the Kaiser, Chancellor Bethmann Hollweg, and the German military leadership. Indeed, often the same figures who had been active in formulating *Weltpolitik* in the decades prior were at the forefront of the war aims debate during the war.

There has long been an awareness that there was an elaborate revolving door between diplomacy, colonial policy, business, banking, and universities

---

[50] Woodruff D. Smith, *The Ideological Origins of Nazi Imperialism* (New York and Oxford: Oxford University Press, 1986), 52–140. See also, Smith, "'Weltpolitik' und 'Lebensraum,'" in *Das Kaiserreich transnational: Deutschland in der Welt 1871–1914*, ed. Sebastian Conrad and Jürgen Osterhammel (Göttingen: Vandenhoeck & Ruprecht, 2004), 29–48. Cf. Dennis Sweeney, "Pan-German Conceptions of Colonial Empire," in Naranch and Eley, *German Colonialism in a Global Age*, 265–82.

[51] See James Joll, *1914: The Unspoken Assumptions, An Inaugural Lecture Delivered 25 April 1968* (London: Weidenfeld & Nicolson, 1968).

that shaped foreign policy in the Wilhelmine period.[52] The German Foreign and Navy Offices, for example, were often short of resources and expertise and drew extensively on outside experts who were coopted to overcome or mask internal incapacity and incompetence. Indeed, as anyone who has critically scrutinized these and other official German sources knows, far more improvisation and chaos than meets the eye in official papers occurred in German colonial, naval, and foreign policymaking in this era. Likewise, there is much evidence that Kaiser Wilhelm was himself remarkably sensitive to the opinions of the educated German middle class and often simply parroted their views in his speeches and policy statements, raising the interesting question of how much he was actually leading German public opinion rather than following it.[53] Even Chancellor Bülow and Admiral Tirpitz had only a limited grasp of the opportunities and challenges that existed out there in the wider world, while the German Foreign Office itself was a hidebound and reactive institution still dominated by an often bumbling aristocratic elite hostile to the new informed assertiveness of the increasingly well-traveled and experienced educated middle classes in Wilhelmine Germany.

These and many other accumulated insights along with the points introduced earlier about German liberal imperialism raise anew the question of what forces were really at work in shaping the content of *Weltpolitik* and why Imperial Germany embarked on it given the risks that it entailed and the meager results that it produced by 1914?

What were the perceptions of Germany's place and status in the world, who gathered them, where and when, and how were they articulated and disseminated? How did a more active policy for asserting Germany's place in the world come together and then get on the political agenda?

What priorities were set and why, and what were the forces and agents that did so? Why did *Weltpolitik* gain such strong support among the German middle classes despite the huge risks and massive material costs attending Germany's naval ambitions? Why did the naval arms race persist even as the diplomatic and strategic rationale for such a navy disappeared and as the wharves building these ships often lost money?

What were the connections between the definition of Germany's place in the world and the development of a more populist imperialism in the late Wilhelmine era, and what accounts for its peculiar features and durability as an ideology that would evolve into an increasingly radical and populist imperialism by the eve of the First World War?

---

[52] John G. Williamson, *Karl Helfferich 1872–1924: Economist, Financier, Politician* (Princeton: Princeton University Press, 1971), 80.
[53] See especially Thomas A. Kohut, *Wilhelm II and the Germans: A Study in Leadership* (New York and Oxford: Oxford University Press, 1991), 118–23, 130–40.

Finally, how did *Weltpolitik* figure in the reasons that Germany went to war in 1914, in the content of Germany's war aims, and in the way the war was prosecuted? How was *Weltpolitik* shaped by the war and what legacy did it bequeath to the Weimar Republic and National Socialism?

This is admittedly a very tall order, but it highlights just how much is at stake in really coming to grips with German *Weltpolitik*. Indeed, tackling this problem afresh and informed by the latest scholarship offers an opportunity to thoughtfully link the development of German liberal imperialism to National Socialism and thus to a fundamental reinterpretation of the path of German history in the twentieth century, one in which the German bourgeoisie played a much more central role.

*Learning Empire* will argue that *Weltpolitik* was an improvised response to the opportunities and challenges of globalization that emerged in the 1870s and 1880s that was largely communicated to the German metropole by university-educated bourgeois scholars who had been living and working overseas. It was less an intended policy than the end result of an accretion of insights that were later adapted into scholarship and popularized in naval and colonial propaganda by these men. The most influential subset within this group of scholars was a small group of economists who saw Germany as a new industrial power with a now global reach in a world already defined by naval rivalry and competition over trade and spheres of influence, a world then being shaken up by the simultaneous rise of the United States and Japan as new industrial and increasingly imperial world powers. Germany was closely tied to these two countries by a common heritage of late industrialization, civil war, and national disunity. An awareness of that common heritage was enabled by the linkages between Germany, the United States, and Japan created by German universities. The German economists who are the subject of this book were active in these university links to both the United States and Japan as well as in the exploration of overseas opportunities in China, Venezuela, and the Caribbean, and they were later drawn into government advising because of their valued global expertise. Thus *Weltpolitik's* roots can be traced back to the discovery of *Weltwirtschaft* in the 1880s and 1890s in encounters in North America, the Caribbean, Venezuela, Japan, and China. How this perspective came together and shaped imperial policymaking has until now escaped attention because it was largely elided from the official record.

The book will approach the topic from the perspective of six economists: the American Henry Farnam and the Germans Ernst von Halle, Karl Helfferich, Karl Rathgen, Hermann Schumacher, and Max Sering. All were students of or connected to the influential professor and public intellectual Gustav Schmoller. All were middle class and Protestant, and after their educations in Germany, all traveled or worked extensively overseas, especially in the United States, Japan, China, and the Ottoman Empire. The Germans among them eventually became professors of political economy specializing in the new subfield of *Weltwirtschaft* and thus Wilhelmine Germany's leading authorities on globalization, defining much of the content of *Weltpolitik* well before it ever entered the political agenda. Through their training in the then dominant paradigm of German historical political economy, these men had an historical and statistical training that made them particularly attentive to the different stages and trajectories of economic development observed in the many places they traveled and studied. This empirical but also evolutionary perspective enabled them to connect relative economic status and trajectories of development with the imperial rivalries they witnessed overseas. It also enabled them to communicate effectively with policymakers and the public about Germany's past, its current place in the world, and the challenges to its ambitions as an emerging "world power." They thus wielded powerful investigative modalities of formal and informal empire shaping mental maps that would have a remarkable hold on the German political imagination in the Wilhelmine era and beyond.[54]

While the work of Ludwig Dehio, Wolfgang Marienfeld, Fritz Ringer, Gerhard Ritter, and Klaus Schwabe did highlight the influence of German professors on imperialist politics before and during the First World War, it was Rüdiger vom Bruch who opened up this field to contemporary research.[55] His first book offered a detailed overview of the various ways that German scholars in the humanities and social sciences in Wilhelmine Germany influenced public opinion, politics, and the government.[56] This and later works also offered a critical analysis of these scholars' self-perceptions as civil servants and exemplars of *Bildung*, men claiming to stand above the fray of politics and offering a privileged, objective voice. The extraordinary public influence enjoyed by German professors from that perch set them apart from their colleagues in Great Britain, France, and the United States.[57] Nevertheless like

---

[54] Cf. Bernard S. Cohn, *Colonialism and its Forms of Knowledge: The British in India* (Princeton: Princeton University Press, 1996); C. A. Bayly, *Empire and Information: Intelligence Gathering and Social Communication in India, 1780–1870* (Cambridge: Cambridge University Press, 1996).

[55] Ludwig Dehio, *Deutschland und die Weltpolitik im 20. Jahrhundert* (Vienna: Verlag für Geschichte und Politik, 1955); Wolfgang Marienfeld, *Wissenschaft und Schlachtflottenbau in Deutschland 1897–1906*, Beiheft 2 der *Marine Rundschau* (April 1957) (Berin: E. S. Mittler Verlag, 1957); Fritz Ringer, *The Decline of the German Mandarins: The German Academic Community, 1890–1933* (Hanover, NH and London: Wesleyan University Press/University Press of New England, 1990); Ritter, *Staatskunst*, vol. 2, 175; Klaus Schwabe, *Wissenschaft und Kriegsmoral: Die deutschen Hochschullehrer und die politischen Grundfragen des Ersten Weltkriegs* (Göttingen, Zurich and Frankfurt: Musterschmidt-Verlag, 1969).

[56] Rüdiger vom Bruch, *Wissenschaft, Politik und öffentliche Meinung: Gelehrtenpolitik im Wilhelminischen Deutschland (1890–1914)* (Husum: Matthiesen Verlag, 1980).

[57] Rüdiger vom Bruch, *Weltpolitik als Kulturmission: Auswärtige Kulturpolitik und Bildungsbürgertum in Deutschland am Vorabend des Ersten Weltkriegs* (Paderborn:

his predecessors, vom Bruch largely overlooked the context of global travel and university connections that informed professorial politics (*Gelehrtenpolitik*) in Imperial Germany.

With the exception of Helfferich, no biographies exist of Farnam, von Halle, Schmoller, Schumacher, Sering, or Rathgen, and apart from perhaps Schmoller and Helfferich, the rest are little known beyond a highly specialized historical subfield and thus rarely figure in more general narratives of German imperialism.[58] Where they have been discussed, they are usually mentioned as highly influential but treated only in passing or relegated to footnotes, and the overseas context of their ideas and writings is missing entirely, as for example in the treatments of Eckart Kehr and Fritz Fischer and the many other scholars who followed in their path.[59] Indeed, with the notable exception of the work of Robert L. Nelson, the context of this worldwide travel is even missing in the work of scholars of *Weltpolitik* who have treated the ideas of these men in greater detail.[60]

The narrative of this book is based on many unknown, unused, underused, or very obscure manuscript and published primary sources that include an unpublished memoir by Hermann Schumacher and the private correspondences, travelogues, and other personal papers of Schumacher, Henry Farnam, Karl Helfferich, Gustav Schmoller, Max Sering, and Karl Rathgen. In some instances gaining full access to this material required taking up direct contact with the families of the men covered in the book. Most of these sources and the other related personal papers and institutional documents were drawn from fifteen archives and library special collections in Germany, the United States, and the United Kingdom. The approach of this book is to link the individual biographies and prosopography of this group with the high politics of Alfred Tirpitz, Chancellor Bülow, Kaiser Wilhelm, and the Foreign Office. While these historical sources are fragmentary and have their own limits and biases, they do allow making that connection in a striking number of instances. Even where that is not always possible, they yield a contemporaneous global perspective on Weltpolitik too often missing or lost entirely in

---

F. Schöningh, 1982); vom Bruch, *Gelehrtenpolitik und akademische Diskurse in Deutschland im 19. und 20. Jahrhundert*, ed. Björn Hofmeister and Hans-Christoph Liess (Stuttgart: Franz Steiner, 2006).

[58] Williamson, *Karl Helfferich*.

[59] See, for example, Kehr, *Schlachtflottenbau*, 20n39, 64n130, 101, 103, 105, 177, 216, 246n67; 257; 262–63n49; 271n74; 277n2; 279n12; 289n47; 290n50, 290n51, 29n52, 306n3, 419, 423, 425, 427, 428, 432, 441–44; Fischer, *Griff nach der Weltmacht*, 18–19, 20, 30, 33.

[60] Robert L. Nelson, "From Manitoba to the Memel: Max Sering, Inner Colonization and the German East," *Social History* 35, no. 4 (Nov. 2010): 439–57. Cf. Söhnke Neitzel, *Weltmacht oder Untergang: Die Weltreichslehre im Zeitalter des Imperialismus* (Paderborn: F. Schöningh, 2000), 27, 27n31; Smith, *Ideological Origins*, 86, 89.

the usual treatment of this policy from the perspective of diplomacy, domestic German politics, public opinion, and German imperialist ideology.

To fill in the gaps left by the primary sources, the book will draw on a wide range of secondary sources. Much effort has been made to integrate the extraordinarily large historiography that surrounds the topic, which is all the more challenging because a good part of this book is set in the Americas, Japan, China, and the Ottoman Empire and thus required mastering these additional historical literatures. Because it ranges so widely and over five decades, the reconstruction of the context of great power diplomacy, trade policy, naval policy, the Baghdad railroad, aspects of colonial policy, and the outbreak of the First World War will necessarily draw heavily on the latest scholarship in those fields. It relies here on a wider historical literature that has revised Germany's role in the European diplomacy of imperialism and the outbreak of the First World War, and it is informed by much newer literature that has altered our understanding of prewar German navalism and the dreadnought arms race. This includes the work of John Charmley, Christopher M. Clark, Rolf Hobson, Patrick J. Kelly, Nicholas A. Lambert, Sean McMeekin, Thomas Otte, Jan Rüger, Stefan Schmidt, and Keith Wilson.[61]

The first part of the book (Absent-Minded Empire, 1875–1897) comprising the first three chapters explores the emergence of *Weltwirtschaft* and how informed comparisons gleaned from extensive travel and study overseas came to inform *Weltpolitik*. As these chapters show, it was not Africa but rather the United States, Japan, China, and Venezuela that were the most important initial arenas of German *Weltpolitik*. The United States, not Great Britain, emerged as the most important reference point for German ambitions from these overseas observations and comparisons. Similarly, the United States, and not Great Britain, came to be perceived as the greatest potential long-term threat to German globalization. Although often overlooked, the United States

---

[61] John Charmley, *Splendid Isolation? Britain, the Balance of Power and the Origins of the First World War* (London: Hodder & Stoughton, 1999); Rolf Hobson, *Imperialism at Sea: Naval Strategic Thought, the Ideology of Sea Power, and the Tirpitz Plan, 1875–1914* (Boston and Leiden: Brill, 2002); Patrick J. Kelly, *Tirpitz and the Imperial German Navy* (Bloomington and Indianapolis: Indiana University Press, 2011); Nicholas A. Lambert, *Planning Armageddon: British Economic Warfare and the First World War* (Cambridge, MA: Harvard University Press, 2012); Sean McMeekin, *July 1914: Countdown to War* (New York: Basic Books, 2013); T. G. Otte, *July Crisis: The World's Descent Into War, Summer 1914* (Cambridge: Cambridge University Press, 2014); Jan Rüger, *The Great Naval Game: Britain and Germany in the Age of Empire* (Cambridge: Cambridge University Press, 2007); Stefan Schmidt, *Frankreichs Außenpolitik in der Julikrise 1914: Ein Beitrag zur Geschichte des Ausbruchs des Ersten Weltkriegs* (Munich: Oldenbourg, 2009); Keith Wilson, *The Policy of the Entente: Essays on the Determinants of British Foreign Policy 1904–1914* (Cambridge: Cambridge University Press, 1985).

and the threat of "Panamerica" were also very prominent in the justifications later given for an expanded German battleship navy after 1897. By exploring the enmeshment of the subjects of the book in the agricultural and industrial expansion of the United States, the modernization of Japan, the scramble for China, and the demarcation of German spheres of influence in the Ottoman Empire, Caribbean, and South America, the global context of *Weltpolitik* is revealed for the first time.

What makes these men, their travel, and their scholarship worthy of sustained attention is not just their role defining *Weltwirtschaft* and *Weltpolitik* but also their remarkable influence on formal policy. Their influence was enabled by their connections to Alfred Tirpitz and Bernhard von Bülow, mediated in many instances by their teacher and colleague Gustav Schmoller. This occurred both through the formal channels of publication in Schmoller's *Jahrbuch* – one of the most widely read and respected public policy journals in Imperial Germany – and the personal lines of connection Schmoller had cultivated with these men well before they came to power in 1897. This led directly to these economists' involvement in the Imperial Navy Office's pro-fleet propaganda that eased passage of the landmark navy laws of 1898 and 1900. It also involved them in the debates over the Bülow tariff of 1902. The influence of these men on German policy was also felt as German naval policy made the dreadnought leap and during the colonial crisis of 1904–7, as well as in the so-called "Hottentott" elections of 1907. The elections forged the Bülow Bloc of liberal and conservative parties, and as a byproduct of that election, a potent new imperialist ideology that fused settler colonialism with navalism and increasingly saw Germany's worldwide mission in racialized terms. The economists covered in this book also participated actively in academic *Weltpolitik*, notably the professorial exchanges negotiated between the United States and Germany before 1914. The overseas travel and experiences this facilitated informed the movement for colonial reform and also led to a gradual rethinking of Germany's colonial ambitions and opportunities for overseas expansion. These and other related topics are covered in Chapters 4–8 that make up Part II of the book (Empire Imagined, 1897–1907).

The third and last part of the book (Empire Lost, 1908–1919), comprised of the final four chapters (Chapters 9–12), explores the constraints on *Weltpolitik* in the last years of peace, the outbreak and prosecution of the First World War, and the failure of the Paris Peace following Germany's defeat in 1918. Chapter 9 and 10 analyze the involvement of the economists covered in this book in Bülow and Colonial Secretary Bernhard Dernburg's colonial reforms, including the founding of the Hamburg Colonial Institute in 1908, their involvement in the politics of the dreadnought arms race, and their effort to get imperial financial reforms passed in order to continue *Weltpolitik*. Likewise, their involvement in the negotiations over the construction of the Baghdad Railway before 1914, as well as their participation in important exchanges between Russia and Germany shortly before the outbreak of First World War will be analyzed. These chapters thus also connect these agents with shifts in the European and global balances of power that would ultimately spell the end of "World Policy" and the beginning of an age of world wars.

The final two chapters deal with the First World War. Chapter 11 offers a nuanced picture of the July Crisis informed by recent scholarship and the previous chapters. It analyzes how the unfolding world war shattered the strong lines of scholarly connection with the United States and the global division of labor of the railway and steamship era. It also reveals how active the subjects of the book were in the German response to the British blockade, notably in the decisions to rationalize wartime food production and launch unrestricted submarine warfare in 1915. Chapter 12 discusses the role of the subjects of the book in the formulation of some of the most expansive annexationist war aims during the First World War, thus providing the essential prewar global context for German wartime policy that was largely missing in the work of Fritz Fischer and his students. Yet as will be argued, extreme and annexationist though these war aims were, they were firmly within the orbit of liberal imperialism. The bitter politics of the last two years of the war also featured these men prominently, whether in the controversy raised by the army's notorious "Jewish census" in 1916 or in the backlash to the Reichstag's July 1917 peace resolution and the development of the populist Fatherland Party. This was a radicalized liberal imperialist ideology that would survive to inform Weimar-era revisionism and the nationalist right. This final chapter thus also offers a nuanced reinterpretation of the failure of the Paris Peace and the influences that enabled the rise of National Socialism in the 1920s and 1930s.

Since it traces the thought and activities of six men from their student days in Strasbourg and Berlin to their extensive travel overseas, and from there to the development of their careers and involvement in imperial politics from 1875 until 1919, *Learning Empire* offers a novel retelling of the entire history of the German Empire from a simultaneously local prosopographical and global perspective. The broader ambition is not just to open up a hidden window to the making of *Weltpolitik* but to reshape our understanding of Germany's past and offer a reinterpretation of the full arc of its history, and thus a new perspective on the deeper origins of the First World War. *Learning Empire* makes it possible to view German history between 1875 and 1919 as concurrent with the rise and demise of the first era of globalization, which was linked directly to the profound changes in the global system brought on by the emergence of Germany, the United States, and Japan as new world powers. In doing that, it brings the world back into German *Weltpolitik* where it has long been missing due to the dominant historiographical preoccupation with the domestic origins of German imperialism and the still very Eurocentric frame of German history. At the same time, it connects the history of American westward expansion and industrialization and the modernization of Meiji-era Japan with Germany in ways that help to revise the exceptionalist master narratives still dominant in these two historiographies. Alternating fluidly between the perspectives of historical agents, their personal networks, and the wider national, imperial, and global contexts, this book is at its core a profound human drama in a broader unfolding tragedy that would come to define much of the twentieth century. The perspective it offers changes how we view the German question and thus the history of the twentieth century, inviting reflection on the problem of disorder and instability accompanying globalization in the twenty-first century.

# PART I

Absent-Minded Empire, 1875–1897

# 1

## Frontier Empire

### The United States

### Gustav Schmoller and the University Germanosphere

In early September 1878, Henry Walcott Farnam entered New York harbor on a steamer from Bremen. He had been away for three years of graduate study in Germany that had taken him to the Berlin, Göttingen, and Strasbourg Universities. With a doctorate in political economy in hand and a published dissertation, Farnam was looking forward to a teaching position that had been offered to him at his alma mater, Yale College.

Across New York harbor in a house on Grymes Hill on the northeastern side of Staten Island, ten-year-old Hermann Schumacher was regularly watching the clipper ships and steamers entering the harbor against New York's skyline. Himself the son of the German General Consul to New York, Schumacher's childhood impressions would strongly shape his later scholarly interests in the world economy. He would be sent back to Bremen in 1882 to complete his schooling and would enter university in 1887, encountering some of the same professors that had taught Farnam ten years earlier.

Some seven thousand miles away along Tokyo Bay, thirteen-year-old Kanai Noburu was also pondering the steam and clipper ships entering the harbor and the *gaijin* (foreigners) they brought to Japan. He would later be taught by a German professor of political economy who had studied with Farnam in Strasbourg in the 1870s and who was then employed by the Japanese government in the 1880s to teach at the new University of Tokyo. In turn, Kanai would be sent to extend his studies in Germany in 1886 and be taught by the same common professor, extending further the international threads of connection created by German universities in this first period of globalization.[1] Farnam, Schumacher, and Kanai were all part of a growing web of intellectual and personal links made possible by transoceanic steamships, undersea telegraph cables, the Suez Canal, and the Union Pacific Railroad.

---

[1] Erik Grimmer-Solem, "Bismarck von einem Kontinent zum anderen: Der Transfer sozialpolitischer Ideen nach Japan und in die Vereinigten Staaten," *Francia* 43 (2016): 417–24.

Farnam was one of an estimated 9,000 Americans who would travel to Germany for graduate education between 1820 and 1920.[2] The choice of German universities was driven by the unparalleled breadth of research they encompassed, the excellence of their professors, and their accessibility as public, nondenominational institutions, which also made them comparatively inexpensive.[3] The dearth of graduate programs in American higher education – which in the 1870s was still a collection of denominational colleges – meant that advanced study was only possible abroad. The German-speaking lands' historical fragmentation had resulted in more universities in the territory of the German and Austrian Empires than in the rest of Europe combined, and it was common practice to switch from one university to another until one found the right *Doktorvater*, a mentor for a dissertation. More broadly, Germany was much admired in the United States at the time as a leader in cultural and intellectual pursuits. There was an acute awareness among many educated Americans of the superficiality and dilettantism of Anglo-Saxon scholarly and scientific traditions and an acknowledgment of the puritanical crudeness and underachievement of Anglo-Saxon artistic and musical culture. The loyal support given the Union by the states of the German Confederation and the disproportionate role of German American soldiers and officers in the Union victory all also helped to cement strong German American ties in the 1870s that clearly also encouraged study in Germany.[4] By contrast, most British sympathies had been with the Confederacy, and a majority in Parliament and most leading statesmen from William Gladstone (1809–98) to Lord Salisbury (Robert Gascoyne-Cecil, 1830–1903) had sympathized with the Confederacy's bid for independence.[5] A Transatlantic "Anglosphere," later

---

[2] Jurgen Herbst, *The German Historical School in American Scholarship: A Study in the Transfer of Culture* (Ithaca, NY: Cornell University Press, 1965), 1, 8–9.

[3] Konrad H. Jarausch, "American Students in Germany, 1815–1914: The Structure of German and U.S. Matriculants at Göttingen University," in *German Influences on Education in the United States to 1917*, ed. Henry Geitz, Jürgen Heideking, and Jurgen Herbst (Washington, DC: German Historical Institute, 1995; Cambridge: Cambridge University Press, 1995), 195–211; Daniel T. Rodgers, *Atlantic Crossings: Social Politics in a Progressive Age* (Cambridge, MA: Harvard University Press, 1998), 85; Anja Werner, *The Transatlantic World of Higher Education: Americans at German Universities, 1776–1914* (New York: Berghahn Books, 2013).

[4] Jörg Nagler, "From Culture to *Kultur*: Changing American Perceptions of Imperial Germany, 1870–1914," in *Transatlantic Images and Perceptions: Germany and America Since 1776*, ed. David E. Barclay and Elisabeth Glaser-Schmidt (Washington, DC: German Historical Institute; Cambridge: Cambridge University Press, 1997), 131–54, here 131, 134.

[5] David Steele, *Lord Salisbury: A Political Biography* (London: University College London Press, 1999), 109; Sven Beckert, *Empire of Cotton: A Global History* (New York: Knopf, 2015), 258–63; Sheldon Vanauken, *The Glittering Illusion: English Sympathy for the Southern Confederacy* (Lanham, MD and Washington, DC: Regnery Gateway, 1989).

projected anachronistically back into the nineteenth century by British politicians and historians such as Winston Churchill, hardly existed at the time, and if it did, it united the British Empire with the Confederacy in a shared tradition of violent colonial exploitation and white planter supremacy.[6]

There were other important factors that drew American students to Germany. As Henry Farnam himself later reflected, Germany and the United States had both been through civil wars in the 1860s, and in the 1870s were facing many similar questions related to the role of federal government and the challenges posed by the rise of new social and economic questions: in the United States the emancipation of slaves had raised the "negro question" while in Germany the birth of trade unionism and social democracy in the 1860s had raised a new "worker question." The rapid growth of commerce and industry in both countries also raised important questions about tariffs and money as well as the regulation of banking, railways, and industrial corporations, and with it, the challenge of developing administrative capacities and coherent economic and social policies.[7] In short, both countries were in the throes of nation building under conditions of rapid social and economic change. Germany's research universities were places where new knowledge about these problems was being actively generated, and Germany's deep, practical administrative traditions, long part of German political economy (*Staatswissenschaften*), attracted Americans in the 1870s.[8] For many of the same reasons, Japanese students of political economy would be drawn to study in Germany beginning in the 1880s, as Japan – much like Germany and the United States – was struggling with many of the same challenges of nation building following its own civil war, legal and administrative reforms, and breakneck economic modernization, something that will be analyzed in depth in Chapter 2.

Farnam was part of an unusually large cohort of Americans who went to Germany in the 1870s to study political economy and/or history, many of whom would later become prominent in the development of American higher

---

[6] See Anthony Bundage and Richard Cosgrove, *British Historians and National Identity* (Abingdon, Oxon and New York: Taylor and Francis, 2014); Srdjan Vucetic, *The Anglosphere: A Geneology of Racialized Identity in International Relations* (Stanford, CA: Stanford University Press, 2011), 22–52.
[7] Henry Farnam, "Deutsch-Amerikanisch Beziehungen in der Volkswirtschaftslehre," in *Die Entwicklung der deutschen Volkswirtschaftslehre im neunzehnten Jahrhundert: Gustav Schmoller zum siebzigsten Wiederkehr seines Geburtstags, 24. Juni 1908*, ed. S. P. Altmann et al. (Leipzig: Duncker & Humblot, 1908), vol. 1, ch. XVII, 1–31, here 7–8; cf. Stig Förster and Jörg Nagler, eds., *On the Road to Total War: The American Civil War and the German Wars of Unification, 1861–1871* (Washington, DC: German Historical Institute; Cambridge and New York: Cambridge University Press, 1997).
[8] See esp. David Lindenfeld, *The Practical Imagination: The German Sciences of State in the Nineteenth Century* (Chicago and London: University of Chicago Press, 1997), 1–9.

education, the social sciences, and in the Progressive movement.[9] This group included Herbert B. Adams (1850–1901), John W. Burgess (1844–1931), John Bates Clark (1847–1938), Richard T. Ely (1854–1943), Arthur T. Hadley (1856–1930), Edmund J. James (1855–1925), Simon N. Patten (1852–1922), Edwin R. A. Seligman (1861–1939), Albion W. Small (1854–1926), William G. Sumner (1840–1910), and Frank W. Taussig (1859–1940).[10] For example, Burgess established the first department of political science at Columbia University in 1880, while Ely, James, and Seligman would go on to found the American Economic Association in 1885. In turn, Small and Sumner were the first to establish sociology as a discipline in the United States at the University of Chicago and Yale, respectively. These men would send a stream of graduate students back to Germany in the 1880s and 1890s, deepening the transatlantic intellectual connection between the United States and Germany that would later be supplemented by a series of professorial exchanges in the first decade of the twentieth century.[11] The German cultural and intellectual influences were so extensive by 1901 that the German ambassador to the United States, Theodor von Holleben (1838–1913), even spoke of the "intellectual annexation" of the United States.[12] As we shall see in Chapter 2, he had said much the same about Japan, where he had served as head of the German legation.

While the influences of the German university experience on American students have been explored,[13] largely overlooked is the fact that these Americans also facilitated a much greater familiarity with the United States by Germans in the period 1875–95 that would itself profoundly shape German perceptions of their place in the world and that would in turn shape Germany's *Weltpolitik* in the late 1890s. The ease of travel opened up by the completion of the American transcontinental railroad in 1869 and the faster,

---

[9] See Rodgers, *Atlantic Crossings* and Axel R. Schäfer, *American Progressives and German Social Reform, 1875–1920: Social Ethics, Moral Control, and the Regulatory State in a Transatlantic Context* (Stuttgart: Franz Steiner, 2000).

[10] See Albion W. Small, "Some Contributions to the History of Sociology. Section XIX. The Emergence of Sociology in the United States," *American Journal of Sociology*, 30, no. 3 (Nov. 1924): 310–36, here 312n2.

[11] Rodgers, *Atlantic Crossings*, 84–85, 86–111; Bernhard vom Brocke, "Der deutschamerikanische Professorenaustausch: Preußische Wissenschaftspolitik, internationale Wissenschaftsbeziehungen und die Anfänge einer deutschen Auswärtigen Kulturpolitik," *Zeitschrift für Kulturaustausch* 31 (1981): 128–82; Ragnhild Fiebig-von Hase, "Die politische Funktionalisierung der Kultur: Der sogenannte 'deutsch-amerikanische' Professorenaustausch von 1904–1914," in *Zwei Wege in die Moderne: Aspekte der deutschamerikanischen Beziehungen 1900-1918*, ed. Ragnhild Fiebig-von Hase and Jürgen Heideking, (Trier: Wissenschaftlicher Verlag Trier, 1998), 45–88.

[12] Nagler, "From Culture to *Kultur*," 153.

[13] Rodgers, *Atlantic Crossings*; Dorothy Ross, *The Origins of American Social Science* (Cambridge: Cambridge University Press, 1991), 55, 58, 60, 68, 104–12.

cheaper, and more reliable steamship connections between the two continents in the early 1880s driven by the expansion of trade and a new wave of European emigration allowed German scholars to visit, travel in, and study the United States to an unprecedented degree. The similar yet also profoundly different social conditions and economic life they encountered played an important role in understanding the rapid changes gripping their own country and the risks attending globalization as well as the destabilizing shifts in world power that were occurring in these years. Henry Farnam would himself play an important role as a bridge between Germany and the United States through the strong contacts he maintained with professors and students he had met during his studies in Germany.

Farnam's connections to Germany were much deeper than most of the rest of his American cohort. He was born in New Haven, Connecticut in 1853, the youngest of five children of Ann Sophia Whitman and the canal and railway tycoon Henry Farnam (1803–83), who made his fortune with the Chicago, Rock Island, and Pacific Railway. During the American Civil War in 1863, Farnam Sr. retired from the presidency of railway and moved his family to Europe. Henry Jr. thus attended schools in both France and Germany, attaining early fluency in both languages. Most of his higher school education was completed in Germany, where he was a pupil from 1865 to 1869, first in Heidelberg, and then in Weimar.[14] In Weimar the Farnam family became friendly with the family of Bernhard Hederich Rathgen (1802–80) and his wife Cornelia Niebuhr, with Henry drawing close to their children, especially their daughter Lucie and youngest son Karl, with whom Henry attended *Gymnasium*.[15] Bernhard Rathgen was president of the Grand Duchy of Sachse-Weimar's General Commission, and Cornelia Niebuhr was the daughter of the diplomat and pioneering historian Barthold Niebuhr (1776–1831). Their daughter Lucie would marry Gustav Schmoller (1838–1917) in 1869, who would himself become one of the most prominent economists and public intellectuals in Imperial Germany. Henry returned to the United States in 1869 and entered Yale College in 1870, completing his A.B. Phi Beta Kappa in 1874. One year later he completed an A.M. at Yale and then returned to Germany to embark on his graduate studies.

It was not entirely coincidental that Farnam would wind up in Strasbourg to research and write his dissertation. The Swabian economist Gustav Schmoller had been appointed to this newest of German universities in 1872 as part of a concerted effort to bring some of Germany's best and brightest to this colonial outpost of Germandom in the new *Reichsland* of Alsace-Lorraine, which was

---

[14] *Dictionary of American Biography,* vol. 21, Supplement 1 (New York: Charles Scribner's Sons, 1943), 293–95.
[15] YUL MA, Farnam Family Papers, Group 203, Series II, Box 89, Folder 933, Karl Rathgen to Henry Farnam, Tokyo, Jan. 9, 1884.

**Figure 1.1**  Gustav Schmoller ca. 1872.

administered directly from Berlin. The new university was a conscious effort at intellectual recolonization in which economic historians like Schmoller played an important part.[16] His research project on Strasbourg's medieval economic history focusing on the guilds was unquestionably an attempt to recover the German roots of this disputed region. But it was his ability as a captivating lecturer, his open and engaging manner, and the great individual care he gave when instructing his students in his seminar that helped to establish his growing reputation.[17] His scholarship on the workers' question, his cofounding of the Verein für Socialpolitik (Association for Social Policy) in 1873, and his open polemic with Heinrich von Treitschke (1834–96) in 1874 had by 1876 given him a national reputation. In that dispute Schmoller had argued forcefully for reforms that reduced class divisions and enhanced social mobility.[18] His work on the Strasbourg clothier and weaver guilds – which culminated in two famous rectorial addresses in 1874 and 1875 – was in fact bound up closely with his preoccupation with contemporary class tensions and social

---

[16] See Nelson, "From Manitoba to the Memel," 443. See also John E. Craig, *Scholarship and Nation Building: The Universities of Strasbourg and Alsatian Society, 1870–1939* (Chicago: University of Chicago Press, 1984), 78–83.

[17] Wilhelm Stieda, "Zur Erinnerung an Gustav Schmoller und seine Straßburger Zeit," *SJ* 45 (1921): 1155–93.

[18] Erik Grimmer-Solem, *The Rise of Historical Economic and Social Reform in Germany 1864–1894* (Oxford: Clarendon Press; New York: Oxford University Press, 2003), 127–98.

discord.[19] Schmoller argued that Strasbourg's guilds came into being during an economic revolution of the thirteenth century, which had created a prosperous class of artisans. Nevertheless, the wealthy patricians and aristocrats denied the guilds any representation in Strasbourg's city council, which along with growing disparities of wealth, led to social friction and eventually to revolution and bloodshed when militarized guilds seized control of the city in 1332. Schmoller concluded that timely municipal reforms and accommodation of the new artisan class might have prevented this upheaval and loss of life.[20] In Germany of the 1870s the challenge was integrating a growing urban working class into German civil society without revolution. To men like Schmoller this meant coming to terms with trade unionism and social democracy peacefully and constructively.

In 1875 Schmoller was joined in Strasbourg by the other figure indelibly associated with Strasbourg *Staatswissenschaften*, Georg Friedrich Knapp (1842–1926). Knapp, who was from Giessen, Hesse, and also a co-founder of the Association for Social Policy, was a specialist in agricultural history who focused on the problems of peasant emancipation and tenure reform. Knapp was a particularly sharp critic of the long-term negative legacy in Germany of *Gutswirtschaft*, the Junker-based manorial economy of East-Elbian Mecklenburg and Prussia. Indeed, he drew explicit parallels between the American and Caribbean plantation slave economy and *Gutswirtschaft* as forms of coercive capitalism, and he became an advocate of land reforms breaking up eastern German latifundia into medium-sized peasant holdings as existed in western Germany.[21]

We know that by summer semester of 1876 Henry Farnam had moved from Göttingen to Strasbourg University to be instructed by Schmoller for his doctoral dissertation in time to participate in the fifth anniversary *Stiftungsfest* of the university held May 1, 1876.[22] His childhood friend Lucie Rathgen was now Schmoller's spouse, and undoubtedly that connection played a role in this decision. In any case, Farnam flourished in Strasbourg and developed a strong personal friendship with Schmoller, with whom he would correspond for the rest of Schmoller's life. It did not take long for Karl Rathgen, who had started his own studies in Halle and then Leipzig in 1876, to follow Farnam to Strasbourg in 1878. However, by the end of the summer semester 1878 Farnam

---

[19] Gustav Schmoller, "Rede über Strassburgs Blüte und die volkswirtschaftliche Revolution im XIII. Jahrhundert," in *Der Rectoratswechsel an der Universität Strassburg am 31. October 1874* (Strasbourg: Karl J. Trübner, 1874), 17–53; Schmoller, *Strassburg zur Zeit der Zunftkämpfe und die Reformen seiner Verfasung und Verwaltung im XV. Jahrhundert: Rede Gehalten zur Feier des Stiftungsfestes der Universität Strassburg am 1. Mai 1975* (Strasbourg: Karl. J. Trübner, 1875).
[20] Grimmer-Solem, *Historical Economics*, 165–66.   [21] Ibid., 223–24, 229–32.
[22] YUL MA, Farnam Family Papers, Group 203, Series II, Box 300, Folder 3607, Fünftes Stiftungsfest der Universität Strassburg am 1. Mai 1876: Commerslieder.

had already completed his doctoral dissertation in Schmoller's seminar on "The Internal Commercial Policy of France from Colbert to Turgot," receiving his Dr. rer. pol. (*rerum politicarum*) magna cum laude.[23] While in Strasbourg Rathgen was himself undecided about pursuing a career either as a lawyer or economist, but on his father's wishes he completed his *Referendar* examinations (the equivalent of a bar examination) in Naumburg in 1880 in preparation for a career in the civil service. In the end Rathgen returned to Strasbourg to write a doctoral dissertation under Schmoller and Knapp on the origins of fairs and markets in Germany, receiving his own Dr. rer. pol. magna cum laude in 1881.[24] As will be discussed at length in Chapter 2, Rathgen would be offered a professorship at Tokyo University in 1882 and would in turn teach and mentor Kanai Noburu in the mid-1880s.

By odd circumstance, Farnam did not overlap in Strasbourg with another important student of Schmoller and Knapp who will figure in this book: Max Sering. Sering was born in Barby on the River Elbe in Prussian Provincial Saxony in 1857, the son the music teacher Friedrich Wilhelm Sering (1822–1901) and Elisabeth Friedländer, the daughter of the Jewish schoolteacher Abraham Salomo Friedländer.[25] After attending Gymnasium in Magdeburg and then completing his schooling at the Imperial Lyceum in Strasbourg in 1876, he studied law and *Staatswissenschaften* at Strasbourg and Leipzig Universities, completing his *Referendar* examination in 1879 while working in civil administration in Colmar. In 1879, the year after Farnam had returned to the United States, Sering rematriculated at Strasbourg University to complete a doctoral dissertation on the history of Prusso-German iron duties in *Staatswissenschaften* under Knapp and Schmoller, finishing the Dr. rer pol. magna cum laude in 1881.[26] As will be discussed, Sering would later embark on an extensive journey to North America to investigate its agricultural economy.

One of the many advantages of being a student of a rising star like Schmoller was easy publication of research. Schmoller had close personal connections to Carl Geibel Jr. (1842–1910), who owned the venerable

---

[23] Henry W. Farnam, *Die innere französische Gewerbepolitik von Colbert bis Turgot*, Staats- und socialwissenschaftliche Forschungen, vol. 1 (Leipzig: Duncker & Humblot, 1878). These were much shorter than dissertations today, equivalent to MA theses. See Grimmer-Solem, *Historical Economics*, 46–47.

[24] StaHH, 361–66 Hochschulwesen – Dozenten- und Personalakten, IV 815 Personalangelegenheiten betr. Professor Dr. Rathgen, n.d.; Karl Rathgen, *Die Entstehung der Märkte in Deutschland* (Darmstadt: Buchdruckerei von G. Otto, 1881).

[25] HUB, UA, UK Personalia, S 84, Max Sering, Bd. 1 und 2, Max Sering to Rector of the Friedrichs-Wilhelms University of Berlin, Berlin, March 2, 1936 with attached biographical questionnaire.

[26] Max Sering, *Geschichte der preussisch-deutschen Eisenzölle von 1818 bis zur Gegenwart*, Staats- und socialwissenschaftliche Forschungen, vol. 4 (Leipzig: Duncker und Humblot, 1882).

publishing house Duncker & Humblot in Leipzig, which published the works of Leopold von Ranke (1795–1886). Geibel, who had a strong interest in economic and social policy, had along with Schmoller and Knapp been a co-founder of the Association for Social Policy and served as that body's secretary for many years.[27] He became, not surprisingly, the publisher of the association's proceedings, the *Schriften des Vereins für Socialpolitik*, as well as the monograph series *Staats- und socialwissenschaftliche Forschungen* tied to Schmoller's seminar in Strasbourg. More significantly, Geibel also published the *Jahrbuch für Gesetzgebung, Verwaltung und Volkswirtschaft im Deutschen Reich* (Annual for Legislation, Administration and Economics in the German Empire), an economics and public policy journal with a large national and later international readership. In 1880 Schmoller would take over as editor of this journal, which would thereafter become known informally as Schmoller's *Jahrbuch*, giving him and his students an outlet for their research and a mouthpiece for policy advocacy. Many articles published in this journal were intended to influence public opinion, and as the journal was read by members of the German bureaucratic and governing elite, the social and economic policy issues raised in this journal often got on the political agenda.[28]

When promising students finished their studies at the university that was usually not the end of their association with Schmoller and his ongoing research program. Schmoller was driven by a deep, almost maniacal hunger for knowledge and was himself almost constantly working, frequently tapping his former students to head new research projects or to write articles in their areas of expertise. When Farnam returned to the United States in the autumn of 1878 he already had a commission organized by Schmoller from the Association for Social Policy to investigate American trade unions. At the time, interest in American industrial conditions had grown quite considerably following the impressive American industrial displays at the Centennial Exposition in Philadelphia in 1876 and the many reports in the German press about America's impressive industrial development little more than ten years after the Civil War.[29] By this point the United States had already pioneered and mastered precision manufacturing with identical interchangeable parts – American sewing machines, textile machinery, steam engines, agricultural machinery, and firearms had already astonished visitors at the 1867 Paris Exposition Universelle.[30] The contrast to the German goods on display in

---

[27] Grimmer-Solem, *Historical Economics*, 73–75, 186–89.   [28] Ibid., 80–82, 84, 202–7.
[29] See Bruno Giberti, *Designing the Centennial: A History of the 1876 International Exhibition in Philadelphia* (Lexington: University Press of Kentucky, 2002).
[30] Gregory Zieren, "Engineer Hermann Grothe (1839–1885): American Technology and the German Patent Law of 1877," in *Technologie und Kultur: Europas Blick auf Amerika vom 18. Bis zum 20. Jahrhundert*, ed. Michael Wala and Ursula Lehmkuhl (Cologne: Bölau Verlag, 2000), 55–75, here 60–63.

Philadelphia was glaring. Open letters published in German newspapers condemned the German goods as "cheap and nasty."[31] Indeed, it was abundantly clear that the United States was rapidly emerging as the most modern and dynamic industrial competitor of Germany. For that reason, too, American labor conditions offered a window into the European future, as it was axiomatic at the time that the country with the most modern economy would also have the most highly-developed working class movement and trade unions, just as had been the case with Britain in the decades prior.

## Labor Frontiers – Henry Farnam and American Trade Unionism

Soon after Farnam had settled in at home in New Haven he was receiving letters from Schmoller asking about the progress of his research on American trade unions. This was, as Farnam wrote back, a slow-going process: the dearth of literature on the topic as well as the demise of many trade unions since the crash of 1873 meant that there was only the shallowest documentary history to investigate.[32] Farnam's strategy around these problems was to write directly to trade union leaders to request material and answers to his queries as well as to interview trade union leaders. But even with some modest success, his expectations were low. As he wrote Schmoller: "Our trade unions have no prehistory like the European ones and we have never had a guild system. Furthermore there are very few unions that have a history of any length. They come into being easily and go under easily given the economic mobility of our life."[33] An added difficulty was the lack of congressional inquiries or surveys, laws, and regulations relating to them. While he was able to remedy this by traveling to Boston, Chicago, and other cities with sizable trade union movements, by January 1879 Farnam's own work as a Latin "tutor" at Yale College began absorbing his time and prevented additional travel.[34] Nevertheless by May 1879 Farnam had compiled enough material to complete the study and sent it to Germany, where it was published as volume 18 in the *Schriften des Vereins für Socialpoilitik,* the series published by the Association for Social Policy.[35]

---

[31] Ibid., 71.
[32] GStA PK, VI. HA Nl. Schmoller, Nr. 175, fols. 142–45, Henry Farnam to Gustav Schmoller, Sept. 13, 1878.
[33] GStA PK, VI. HA Nl. Schmoller, Nr. 175, fols. 136–37, Henry Farnam to Gustav Schmoller, Nov. 15, 1878.
[34] Ibid.; GStA PK, VI. HA Nl. Schmoller, Nr. 176, fols. 65–67, Henry Farnam to Gustav Schmoller, Feb. 9, 1879.
[35] GStA PK, VI. HA Nl. Schmoller, Nr. 176, fols. 68–69, Henry Farnam to Gustav Schmoller, May 23, 1879; Henry W. Farnam, *Die amerikanischen Gewerkvereine*, SdVfS, vol. 18 (Leipzig: Duncker & Humblot, 1879); cf. Philip S. Foner, *History of the Labor Movement in the United States* (New York: International Publishers, 1947), vol. 1, 454–524; vol. 2,

While other studies of American working conditions had been published that touched on trade unionism by the time Farnam's study went to print, Farnam's was the first to be based on a systematic, critical analysis of trade union documents and interviews, offering the first detailed and reliable survey of this movement.[36] It was also one of the first to offer a generally positive assessment of them. Appealing perhaps to existing German tropes about America, Farnam evoked the image of settling a wilderness with his project:

> In any period of European history it is easy to find sources, indeed, sometimes one is even overwhelmed by them, making the task of mentioning them disconcerting and exhausting. In the worst cases some predecessor has already shown or prepared a path for research. This is very different for those who seek to examine social developments in the New World. Here everything is still complete primordial forest. Not even the rawest preparatory work of chopping down the trees has been completed, much less removing the stumps and stones. One has to take up this task from the beginning and alone.[37]

A central conclusion that emerged from Farnam's study that would influence German perceptions of the American worker and American working conditions was what set American trade unions apart from their European counterparts: the unusually large size of American industrial firms, the lack of legal hurdles in incorporating unions in the states of the Union, and the existence of a western frontier. The lack of legal hurdles encouraged the formation of many trade unions. The already pronounced tendency toward large enterprises in the United States (in contrast to Europe) was a further boon to trade unions, as it brought large masses of workers face to face with one employer.[38]

While Farnam was critical of some of the abuses of a few American trade unions (such as wildcat strikes and embezzlement in the Brotherhood of Locomotive Engineers), his general conclusions about American trade unions were positive.[39] American unions focused on the practical work of securing high wages for their members by peaceful collective bargaining and control of apprenticeships. Indeed, Farnam was at pains to dispel the impression of American trade unions as engaging in widespread work stoppages and strikes or their alleged involvement in civil unrest. He noted that the Pennsylvania railway riots of February 1877, which gained international press attention and were blamed by many newspapers on trade union activity, could not be

---

11–74; Leon Fink, *Workingman's Democracy: The Knights of Labor and American Politics* (Urbana: University of Illinois Press, 1983).

[36] Albert Sidney Bolles, *Industrial History of the United States, from the Earliest Settlements to the Present Time* (Norwich, CT: H. Bill, 1878), 881–88, 891–903; Arthur von Studnitz, *Nordamerikanische Arbeiterverhältnisse* (Leipzig: Duncker & Humblot, 1879), 269–79; cf. Farnam, *Die amerikanischen Gewerkvereine*, 1.

[37] Farnam, *Die amerikanischen Gewerkvereine*, 1.   [38] Ibid., 2–3.   [39] Ibid., 15.

attributed to trade unions or to any plan at all. Rather, the riots were a result of spontaneous unrest sparked by wage reductions and a speedup on the Pennsylvania Railroad as well as the dereliction of duty of the mayor of Pittsburgh in controlling a growing mob, which led to the mobilization of the militia and much unnecessary bloodshed.[40]

A related conclusion was that most American trade unions had "nothing to do with socialism," which contrasted particularly starkly with trade unions in which the German element predominated, such as Union of Cigarmakers and Union of Furniture Workers of North America, which, as Farnam noted, even recognized the socialist newspapers *Vorbote* and *Arbeiterstimme* as their organs.[41] By contrast, "the other trade unions have no sense of utopias. They certainly want no upheaval of existing production methods, no changes in the relationship between capital and labor; they simply seek just negotiations and a wage reflective of their effort (*Leistungen*)."[42] The lack of radicalism in American trade unionism Farnam attributed not only to a greater pragmatism but to the existence of a western frontier:

> The stock of uninhabited land in the West enables anyone who is unhappy with his lot as a wage laborer to flee the tyranny of his employer [*Brodherrn*; lit. "bread lord"] and to live independently. He will, of course, not always improve the comfort of his life but at least he will be independent; he need never complain to himself that he was condemned to slavery through wage labor. He always has the prospect of beginning something for himself, and through the possibility of this escape, the trade union becomes more dispensable to him. Furthermore, the transfer from one trade to another is hardly something uncommon in the United States; the American is a quick learner and loves change if he sees a pecuniary advantage in it: thus he goes from one business to another with the greatest of ease. That has a twofold negative effect on the trade unions. First, no one joins a trade union with the intention of staying in it all his life; he can change his trade and domicile at any time; he must thus be able to sever ties to it [the union] easily. This is not reconcilable with the arrangements from which he can only take advantage after years, such as sickness insurance funds, old-age pension funds, accident insurance funds and such, all the things that are the main attractions of English unions. For that reason such funds, if they exit at all, are almost without exception separated from one another and from the general fund, and subscription to them is voluntary. Through this a useful bond and means for the perpetuation of the trade union is lost.[43]

In other words, the western frontier and the independence, personal initiative, and social mobility it offered American workers naturally reduced the discontent with wage labor that fueled socialism. Furthermore, the only workers in

---

[40] Ibid., 33–37.  [41] Ibid., 19, 24–25, 32.  [42] Ibid., 32–33.  [43] Ibid., 4.

America beholden to dreams of upheaval and socialist utopia were German American workers with ties to their homeland with its pinched horizons, limited social mobility, and social democracy peddling revolutionary panaceas. That said, Farnam was clearly aware that the western frontier and the social and vocational mobility it afforded had a negative effect on trade unions.[44]

By the time that Farnam published his study, trade unions and collective bargaining were generating great interest in Germany. Indeed, the Association for Social Policy had held numerous conferences dealing with trade unions and punishment of breach of contract in work stoppages since 1873, commissioning no fewer than three different studies on these topics by 1879.[45] Farnam's work was thus undoubtedly widely read, and not just by members of the Association for Social Policy and other economists, but a wider educated public that included journalists, trade union officials, employers, and members of the civil service that participated in the conferences of the association. Schmoller himself liked Farnam's study.[46] The vivid image of the American western frontier diffusing radicalism and encouraging independence, initiative, vocational flexibility, and social mobility would have been unmistakable and rendered credible to these German readers. They meshed with similar views of the American frontier then just being published by the German geographer Friedrich Ratzel (1844–1904), who had undertaken an extensive investigative journey to Cuba, Mexico, and the United States in the mid-1870s.[47] Farnam and Ratzel's reflections on the role of America's vast frontier tapped into an existing strand of thought developed by such earlier European travelers to North America as Alexis de Tocqueville, Alexander von Humboldt, Gottfried Duden (1785–1855), Friedrich List (1789–1846), and Friedrich Gerstäcker (1816–72), in which settlement of the North American

---

[44] Cf. Werner Sombart, *Warum Gibt es in den Vereinigten Staaten keinen Sozialismus* (Tübingen: J. C. B Mohr [Paul Siebeck], 1906); Sombart, *Why Is There No Socialism in the United States*, trans. Patricia M. Hocking and C. T. Husbands (London: Macmillan, 1976); Eric Foner, "Why Is There No Socialism in the United States?" *History Workshop* 17 (Spring 1984): 57–80; Friedrich Lenger, "'Warum gibt es in den Vereinigten Staaten keinen Sozialismus?' Werner Sombart, die deutsche Sozialwissenschaft und Amerika," in *Zwei Wege in die Moderne: Aspekte der deutsch-amerikanischen Beziehungen 1900–1918*, ed. Ragnhild Fiebig-von Hase and Jürgen Heideking (Trier: Wissenschaftlicher Verlag Trier, 1998), 105–15.

[45] Franz Boese, *Geschichte des Vereins für Sozialpolitik, 1872–1932*, SdVfS, vol. 188 (Berlin: Duncker & Humblot, 1939), 17–18, 22–23, 31, 32–33, 305–6; see also Grimmer-Solem, *Historical Economics*, 70–71, 178–81.

[46] GStA PK, VI. HA Nl. Schmoller, Nr. 176, fols. 186–87ab, Henry Farnam to Gustav Schmoller, July 29 1879.

[47] Friedrich Ratzel, *Die Vereinigten Staaten von Nord-Amerika*, 2 vols. (Munich: Oldenbourg, 1878–80).

Figure 1.2    Henry Walcott Farnam ca. 1900.

frontier was closely linked to the fulfillment of liberal-national ideals of independence, self-government, and national unity.[48]

Farnam's interpretations of American labor would be reinforced by additional research on US trade unions conducted in the early 1880s by Farnam's contemporary, the German economist August Sartorius von Waltershausen (1852–1938). Waltershausen traveled in the United States from 1880 to 1881 to investigate the American workers' movement. He then published a series of articles based on his travels in the *Jahrbücher für Nationalökonomie und Statistik* that were later expanded into an 1886 book, drawing on Farnam's work far more than he credited.[49] In any case, he did not question Farnam's basic premises about the western frontier defusing radicalism, even though he, unlike Farnam, was investigating unions at a time of rising wages, renewed growth in union membership, and labor activism. Waltershausen added a new

---

[48] See Guettel, *German Expansionism*, 43–78; Guettel, "From the Frontier to German South-West Africa: German Colonialism, Indians, and American Westward Expansion," *Modern Intellectual History* 7, no. 3 (2010): 523–52; Pitts, *A Turn to Empire*, 204–39.

[49] A. Sartorius Freih. v. Waltershausen, *Die nordamerikanischen Gewerkschaften unter dem Einfluss der fortschreitenden Produktionstechnik* (Berlin: Hermann Bahr, 1886).

dimension to the narrative of American labor exceptionalism by emphasizing the role of technology. While he believed that the remarkable sophistication of the American division of labor and the rapid pace of technical innovation that he witnessed were the central constraints on the American labor movement, he also recognized these as the sources of American workers' unusually high wages and prosperity.[50] Like Farnam, he believed that the high pay, mobility, and adaptability of American workers limited the appeal of compulsory insurance and hindered the development of both union-provided and factory-based benefit funds.[51]

## From Strasbourg to Minnesota – Max Sering in North America

By the early 1880s the US western frontier was being felt in Germany in other, more immediate ways: the strong price pressure that farmers were feeling from the vast expansion of arable land in Illinois, Iowa, Minnesota, and the Dakotas. The Mary's Fall Canal connecting the Great Lakes with the Erie Canal, the expansion of American railways to and from the grain and livestock hub of Chicago, and the improved efficiency of steamship travel had created a global grain market by the late 1870s. Just one metric of this globalization is the dramatic reduction in the cost of transporting bulk cargoes. For example, the cost of moving a ton of goods 1,000 miles fell from $173.82 in 1830 to $ 22.43 in 1910.[52] The North American Great Plains were now flooding Germany and the rest of Europe with inexpensive wheat. While in 1879 grain tariffs had passed the Reichstag, such and subsequent attempts at price support were completely overwhelmed by the continued fall in world grain prices, which also highlighted endemic problems in German agriculture itself. These included excessive debts accumulated in land speculation when grain prices were rising before 1873, technological backwardness, hidebound peasant traditionalism, excessive subdivision in south and southwest Germany, and unsustainable grain cultivation on large estates on the sandy soils of the Prussian east.[53] A closely related set of issues was migration from the land (*Landflucht*) accelerated by very rapid German population growth and the crisis gripping German farming. That led to more rapid urbanization, downward pressure on urban wages, overseas emigration, and concerns about the "Polonization" of

---

[50] August Sartorius von Waltershausen, *The Worker's Movement in the United States*, ed. David Montgomery and Marcel van der Linden (Cambridge and New York: Cambridge University Press, 1998), 77–83, 101.

[51] Ibid., 186–87, 197–229.

[52] William J. Bernstein, *A Splendid Exchange: How Trade Shaped the World* (New York: Atlantic Monthly Press, 2008), 330. Dollar prices are in 2007 values.

[53] Gustav Schmoller, "Die amerikanische Konkurrenz und die Lage der mitteleuropäischen, besonders der deutschen Landwirthschaft," *JbfGVV* 6 (1882): 247–84. See also Grimmer-Solem, *Historical Economics*, 224–29.

the rural German-Polish borderlands in Prussia's eastern "colonial" provinces of West Prussia and Posen.[54]

In the late spring of 1882 the chairman of the Royal Prussian Land Economy Collegium (Landesökonomiekollegium), Leopold von Schuhmann (1815–86), and a senior official in the Prussian Ministry of Agriculture, Hugo Thiel (1839–1918), contacted Max Sering about traveling to the United States and Canada to investigate the causes and likely future course of North American agricultural competition.[55] Schuhmann and Thiel had first approached Schmoller about a suitable candidate for such an adventure and he had recommended Sering.[56] By this point Sering had completed his doctorate in Strasbourg and had decided on an academic career, going to Bonn University to discuss beginning a *Habilitation* with Professor Erwin Nasse (1829–90). This second dissertation was needed for the *venia legendi* to begin a career as a lecturer (*Privatdozent*) in a German or Austrian university, a first step toward a professorship. Sering seems to have taken up Schuhmann and Thiel's offer eagerly and began gathering material in preparation for his trip to North America, using it to write his *Habilitation* thesis in the months before his departure in early 1883.[57] Henry Farnam provided valuable advice, sources, and contacts to Sering. In June 1882 Sering was in touch with him with questions about the reliability of US official statistics and with a request to send him US government documents and census materials that were missing in the Berlin libraries.[58] While putting the final touches on his *Habilitation* and making preparations for his passage to New York in December 1882, Sering was discussing the possibility of staying with Farnam in New Haven as a jumping off point for his North American journeys.[59] By January Farnam had written back that Sering would be very warmly welcome to stay with him.[60]

On February 11, 1883 Sering boarded the new Norddeutscher Lloyd (NDL) steamer *Werra* in Bremen, arrived in New York on February 23, and then continued on to New Haven to prepare for what would become an epic

---

[54] See Grimmer-Solem, *Historical Economics*, 90–94, 224–35.
[55] Max Sering, *Die landwirthschaftliche Konkurrenz Nordamerikas in Gegenwart und Zukunft: Landwirthschaft, Kolonisation und Verkehrswesen in den Vereinigten Staaten und Britisch-Nordamerika* (Leipzig: Duncker & Humblot, 1887), v; YUL MA, Farnam Family Papers, Group 203, Series II, Box 89, Folder 932, Max Sering to Henry Farnam, Berlin, June 10, 1882.
[56] Nelson, "From Manitoba to the Memel," 442.   [57] Ibid., 444.
[58] YUL MA, Farnam Family Papers, Group 203, Series II, Box 89, Folder 932, Max Sering to Henry Farnam, Berlin, June 10, 1882.
[59] GStA PK, VI. HA Nl. Schmoller, Nr. 141, fols. 119–20, Max Sering to Gustav Schmoller, Straßburg, Dec. 16, 1882.
[60] GStA PK, VI. HA Nl. Schmoller, Nr. 121, fols. 32–33, Henry Farnam to Gustav Schmoller, New Haven, Jan. 9, 1883.

journey through most of the grain-growing regions of North America.[61] In New Haven Farnam was very pleased to welcome Sering and to hear news about Schmoller and his family. Farnam subsequently introduced Sering to Professor William Brewer (1828–1910), a botanist and colleague of Farnam in the Sheffield Scientific School at Yale, and he advised Sering to go to Washington, DC. Undoubtedly Farnam helped open many doors in the capital. In any case Sering was very well received by the German Minister Plenipotentiary Karl von Eisendecher (1841–1934), who had just been reassigned to the United States from Japan the previous year and who was able to give Sering additional advice. In Washington he also met with the eminent German-trained historian and politician George Bancroft (1800–91), who was able to give Sering many valuable recommendations and introductions. Sering was later able to visit senior officials and statisticians in the US General Land Office, Department of Agriculture, and the Treasury, who answered his many queries.[62]

From Washington, Sering returned to New York via Baltimore, and on March 19 boarded a Pennsylvania Central train to travel to San Francisco via the Union Pacific Railroad.[63] It is worth noting that in 1883 such transcontinental railway travel was still a relative novelty, as it was only in May 1869 that the Union Pacific Railroad's transcontinental connection had been completed. The significance was not only that it was now possible to reach the Pacific coast in little more than a week's journey but also that travelers returning to Europe from East Asia could opt to take a steamer to San Francisco and return to Europe via New York (or, for that matter, to travel to East Asia via New York and San Francisco). As we shall see in the chapters to follow, many prominent German travelers to China and Japan would be exposed to the vast expanses of the North American continent in just this way, shaping their perceptions of the United States, the world, and Germany's place in it.

The first short stops Sering made on his journey to San Francisco were in Chicago and Omaha, then continuing on to Cheyenne and Denver (with an excursion to Colorado Springs and Manitou), and from Denver on to Salt Lake City.[64] From Salt Lake City he took the Central Pacific to Sacramento. Sering was overwhelmed by the dimensions of the country. Writing Gustav Schmoller from San Jose, CA, on April 15, he said it would be impossible to convey the abundance of impressions he had gathered traveling right across a massive continent. What had in the past been "fantasies based on books and maps" was in front of his eyes, or as he wrote, "rushed past me like a giant

---

[61] Sering, *Die landwirthschaftliche Konkurrenz*, xii.
[62] Ibid., ix; GStA PK, VI. HA Nl. Schmoller, Nr. 178, fols. 185–86, Henry Farnam to Gustav Schmoller, New Haven, March19, 1883; GStA PK, VI. HA Nl. Schmoller, Nr. 141, fols. 193–200, Max Sering to Gustav Schmoller, Auzerais House, San Jose, CA, April 15, 1883.
[63] Sering, *Die landwirthschaftliche Konkurrenz*, ix.   [64] Ibid., 457–61.

panorama."[65] His eye was particularly primed to observe the vast variety of farming and stock rearing that encompassed the United States, from the farm landscapes of Pennsylvania that reminded him of Westphalia to the corn fields of Illinois, from the forest to the prairie regions, and on eventually into the "dry steppes" where his train disturbed gigantic herds of cattle and horses. He described the monotony of the alkaline flats in the high plateaus of the West where hundreds of thousands of cattle grazed and the isolated but flourishing Mormon farm communities that had established themselves along the Weber and Humboldt Rivers in Utah and Nevada as well as the vast salt flats and deserts where not even sage brush survived. It was, he wrote, "like being in a dream retiring to ones sleeping quarters in the palace car while crossing through the region of Nevada to wake up in the morning to the sight of the indescribably lush vegetation covering the foothills of the Sierra Nevada and then the broad, deep green wheat fields covering the Sacramento Valley."[66] The railroad that Sering was traveling on, the Union Pacific – built at breakneck speed as a Union initiative during the Civil War with federal bond subsidies, vast land grants, and the manpower of the US Army – had itself become the spearhead of an American frontier empire, leading directly to the near extinction of the vast herds of bison that Sering would have seen had he traveled just twenty years earlier. The Union Pacific and other Pacific railway projects also annulled the land claims of the Plains Indians and enabled the mass movement of federal troops to the frontier, which in turn led directly to the military decimation and concentration of these people, opening the way to the vast European colonization project of the Homestead Act.[67]

---

[65] GStA PK, VI. HA Nl. Schmoller, Nr. 141, fols. 193–200, Max Sering to Gustav Schmoller, Auzerais House, San Jose, CA, April 15, 1883.

[66] Ibid.

[67] See John W. Starr, Jr., *Lincoln and the Railroads* (New York: Dodd, Mead & Company, 1927); Robert G. Athearn, *Union Pacific Country* (Chicago: Rand McNally, 1971); H. Craig Miner, *The Corporation and the Indian: Tribal Sovereignty and Industrial Civilization in Indian Territory, 1865–1907* (Columbia: University of Missouri Press, 1976); Lloyd J. Mercer, *Railroads and Land Grant Policy: A Study in Government Intervention* (New York: Academic Press, 1982); Maury Klein, *Birth of a Railroad: 1862–1893*, vol. 1, Union Pacific (Garden City, NY: Doubleday, 1987); David Haward Bain, *Empire Express: Building the First Transcontinental Railroad* (New York: Viking Penguin, 1999); Robert G. Angevine, *The Railroad and the State: War, Politics, and Technology in Nineteenth-Century America* (Stanford: Stanford University Press, 2004); Brian Balogh, *A Government Out of Sight: The Mystery of National Authority in Nineteenth-Century America* (Cambridge: Cambridge University Press, 2009); William G. Thomas, *The Iron Way: Railroads, the Civil War, and the Making of Modern America* (New Haven: Yale University Press, 2011); Richard White, *Railroaded: The Transcontinentals and the Making of Modern America* (New York: W. W. Norton & Company, 2011); Jared Fineberg, "Wayward Child of the State: The Union Pacific Railroad and the Challenge of Mixed Enterprise, 1862–1879" (BA thesis, Wesleyan University, 2017).

In California Sering stayed in San Francisco from April 3 through April 5 and then until April 18 was able to visit a number of significant farms in the Sacramento, San Joaquin, Salinas, and Santa Clara Valleys, passing through Sacramento, Berkeley, Merced, Salinas, Monterey, San Jose, Vina, and Chico along the way.[68] Sering was impressed by the exceptional hospitality he enjoyed on these farms and the "model family life" he imagined flourishing there. On the farm of John Bidwell (1819–1900) near Chico he began to see the agricultural future of California, writing that

> Here on one of the giant farms of California I also met people for the first time who were not robbing out the soil to amass money but who take joy in the gorgeous natural surroundings and run a sensible, diverse agriculture, protect forest stands, and have a heart for their workers. It was on the ranch of the elderly General Bidwell in Chico. He has 22,000 acres in pasture and forest – mostly in the foothills of the Sierra Nevada – , 4,000 acres in grain (wheat and barley), 1,000 for hay, about 2,000 in summer fallow, 1,000 for fruit and wine.[69]

Sering wrote that this division of cultivation was unusual on the old farms of California, which were mostly under wheat, but he very much doubted that wheat had a future in California. On average fruit, wine, hops, and other horticulture was much more profitable in the California climate and did not rob its soils of their nutrients like wheat with the endemic common practice of summer fallowing. He noted that the trend toward these "finer" forms of agriculture in California was already well underway, and the people would adapt quickly. They were, he wrote, "born speculators, energetic, pliable; an American farmer can never get into hardship, it was said to me in the east, in New England, and there is something true in that."[70] Clearly, Sering had a very penetrating eye, recognizing California's horticultural future after less than two weeks of on-the-ground observation. No doubt it was a heady prospect to imagine a vast vegetable, fruit, and wine growing region nearly the size of the entire German Empire. But it was not California that he had come to study. It was, rather, the vast new wheat growing region of the upper Midwest.

On April 18 Sering departed California by steamer for Portland, and from that base went on various excursions organized and accompanied by the German-born president of the Northern Pacific Railroad, Henry Villard (1835–1900), joined by a staff of railway officials and engineers. He traveled the California, Oregon, and other railroads, went up the Snake River by steamer to Lewiston, Idaho, and on to Walla Walla, the Willamette Valley,

---

[68] Sering, *Die landwirthschaftliche Konkurrenz*, x.
[69] GStA PK, VI. HA Nl. Schmoller, Nr. 141, fols. 193–200, Max Sering to Gustav Schmoller, Auzerais House, San Jose, CA, April 15, 1883.
[70] Ibid.

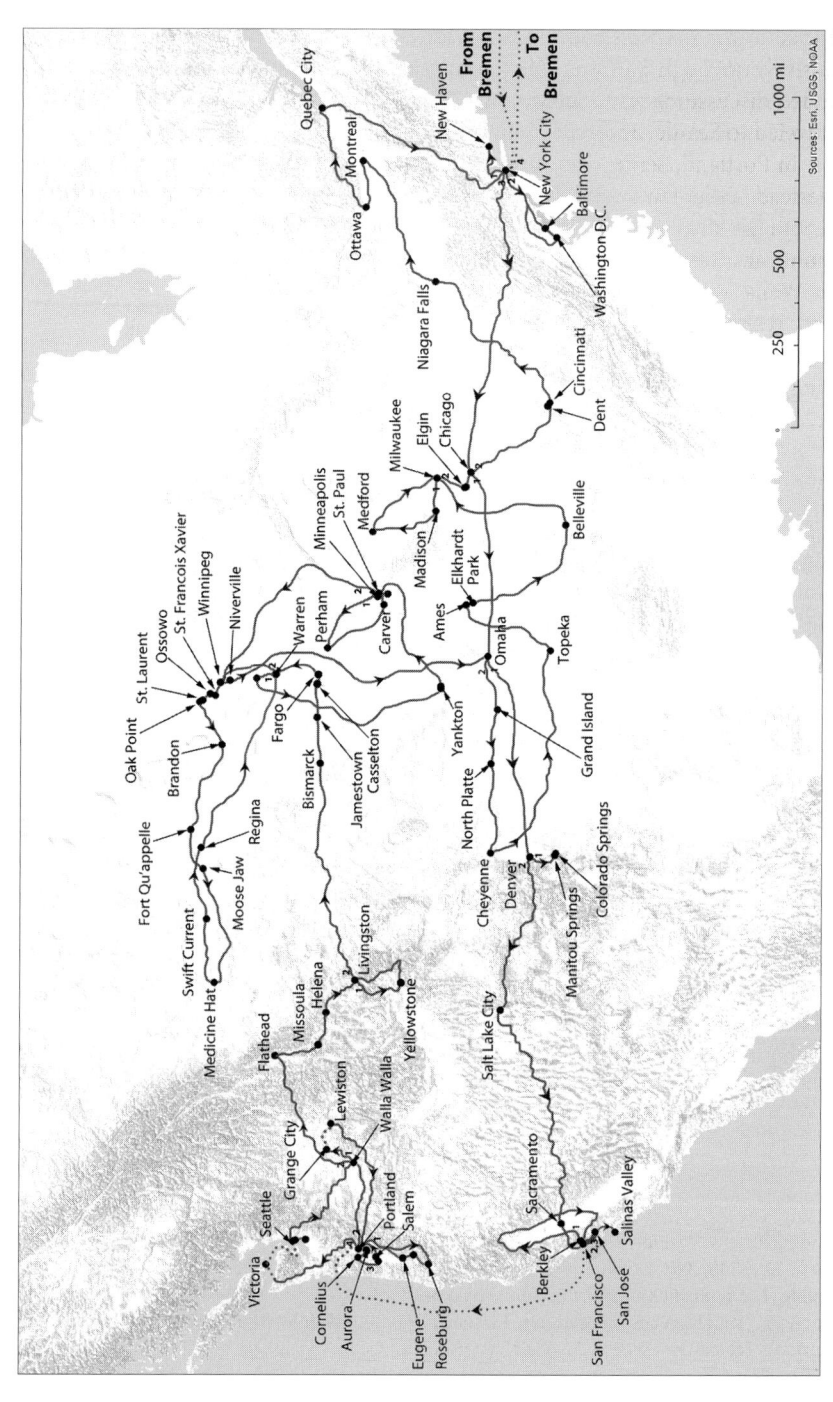

Map 1.1 Max Sering's journey through the United States and Canada, Feb. 23–Sept. 26, 1883.

and then to the German communist community in Aurora. Later he traveled extensively through western Washington and to Vancouver Island, which included discussions with the Minister of Agriculture in Victoria. From there he traveled to Seattle, and on through the Duwamish and White River Valleys. While in Portland, Sering was also able to undertake a detailed investigation of homestead settlements with the land agent of the Northern Pacific Railroad, Paul Schulze.[71]

From May 24 to June 6 Sering traveled through the Rocky Mountains, first from Walla Walla to the terminus of the Northern Pacific at the Flathead Indian reservation, and from there by wagon accompanied by the chief engineer of the Northern Pacific through the Mullan Tunnel in Montana, visiting various farms and the largest cattle breeding operation in the territory. As in all the other states and territories he visited, Sering had opportunity to meet with Montana territorial officials in Helena.[72] He was impressed with the farmers and ranchers of Montana whom he had a chance to interview, some telling him that they had entered the territory in the mid-1860s with a few hundred dollars and were now rich, having since abandoned their log cabins for comfortable stone homes.[73] After passing through the Yellowstone Valley by wagon, he traveled on the Northern Pacific from Livingston to Bismarck in the Dakota Territory, and from there, into the northwestern prairie regions, the heartland of North American wheat production, spending eleven days in Dakota, sixteen days in Minnesota, and twenty-six days in Manitoba, Saskatchewan and the Northwest Territories from a base in St. Paul between June 6 and July 29, 1883.[74]

It was in this region that he was able to witness larger-scale German immigrant settlements for the first time in both the US and Canadian parts of the northern Great Plains.[75] In the Park Region of Minnesota, northwest of St. Paul specifically, there were many German immigrant farms that he had the opportunity to visit. He later observed that these farms were among the most beautiful and prosperous in all of North America. He was impressed with the tidy wood-frame houses fitted with lightning rods, good stables with haylofts, and the well-filled machine sheds and storage houses. He observed the ubiquitous well-tended vegetable gardens and orchards. Their fields were in the best order he had seen of any farm region he visited while in North

---

[71] Sering, *Die landwirthschaftliche Konkurrenz*, x, 261–305.   [72] Ibid., x, 218–21.
[73] Ibid., 220.   [74] Ibid., xi, 403–49.
[75] Ibid., 311, 335, 370–73, 388; cf. Nelson, "From Manitoba to the Memel," 444; Courtney Fullilove, *The Profit of the Earth: The Global Seeds of American Agriculture* (Chicago and London: The University of Chicago Press, 2017), 83–118; John Warkentin, "Mennonite Agricultural Settlements of Southern Manitoba," *Geographical Review* 49, no. 3 (July 1959): 324–68.

America. He was charmed by the landscape, with its hilltop copses and many valley waterways separating alternating fields of grain and pasture, which contrasted starkly with the bleak uniformity of the Dakota prairie. The only things disturbing this picture of bucolic orderliness were the unfinished roads and numerous fresh forest clearings.[76] It was undoubtedly a familiar scene to Sering's central European eyes.

More substantively, he noticed that on German farms crop rotation and the manuring of fields were routine – even in newly-settled areas on the western edge with virgin soils, such as Perham, Minnesota, crop rotation was introduced by the German farmers after only five or six years of wheat cultivation, a scene that contrasted with other farmers in the region, who repeated wheat crops twelve, thirteen, or more years resulting in diminishing returns and soil exhaustion. The Germans were, he noticed, much more thorough farmers than the Americans, and with respect to commercial dexterity, were quick learners from their new compatriots. Unlike the Americans, they were also not afraid to start small and work their way up through frugality, avoiding big speculative ventures to achieve their prosperity. The Germans he spoke with in Perham and Carver, Minnesota had started off with little – eight to ten acres of land and a borrowed team of oxen – but then gradually expanded their holdings and were now all living in "secured abundance" [*gesichertem Wohlstand*] without larger debts.[77] The superiority of the German farmers, in Sering's estimation, was due also to the fact that they had large families where everyone helped out on the farm. It was a custom among the German farmers – but not the native-born farmers – that women took charge of the poultry yard and vegetable garden and prepared their own butter. While American farmer sons often sought their fortunes as businessmen in cities, Sering observed, the German families stuck together and gradually accumulated the surrounding lands of the Anglo-Americans. As Sering concluded: "if all of North America had been settled by Germans, we would feel the competition even more acutely because the Germans produce more cheaply and are less susceptible to changing economic conditions than the American farmers, [who are] more reliant on outside help with their one-sided operation."[78]

But would the German settlers in North America remain German? The assimilationist pressures were enormous, even on the frontier. The battlefield of identity was then being fought in the local primary schools over German language instruction. It was while pondering this problem in Minnesota in

---

[76] Sering, *Die landwirthschaftliche Konkurrenz*, 416; cf. Kathleen Neils Conzen, *Germans in Minnesota* (St. Paul, Minn.: Minnesota Historical Society Press, 2003); Conzen, *Immigrant Milwaukee, 1836–1860: Accommodation and Community in a Frontier City* (Cambridge, MA: Harvard University Press, 1976); Fullilove, *The Profit of the Earth*, 106–16.
[77] Sering, *Die landwirthschaftliche Konkurrenz*, 416.    [78] Ibid., 416–17.

mid-July 1883 after extensive travel through Manitoba that Sering had an epiphany. From Ramsey's farm near Warren, Minnesota – about 150 miles northwest of Perham – he wrote Gustav Schmoller:

> The week that I spent in St. Paul and Minneapolis is among my most pleasant travel memories. The Germans here are still aware of the advantages of their nationality and eager to preserve it. The main topic of discussion is German instruction in primary school which the Americans sought to displace. I am convinced that German nationality cannot be maintained in this land for many generations, and as a result I have become, mainly for this reason, an enthusiastic supporter of the idea of German colonies. It is my most fervent desire to later visit South America, to study the sources about this land and to eventually bring German emigrants to these territories where a dying European population resides who are of no threat to the unique qualities of our compatriots. I am ever more convinced that we do have many advantages over the Yankee and that it is a shame if our compatriots, forced by the external circumstances of making a living, are compelled to assimilate and subordinate themselves to him. All of the great economic and psychological processes which a wide and untapped territory offers a nation would become ours through colonies, [and] much damage to our national life would be healed.[79]

This is a very intriguing and revealing passage. It shows that Sering must have been entertaining the idea that the massive flow of German immigrants to the United States offered the prospect of a permanent German presence in North America, a German colony of some kind. But what he saw and heard on the spot was that assimilation was swift, that the German language and identity had no future in North America. One had to look elsewhere to fulfill the dream of a permanent German settler colony.[80]

Although he does not say, undoubtedly Sering was thinking of Brazil and Venezuela, where there were sizable German settlements by the 1880s.[81] Sering was of course writing one year before Germany became a formal overseas colonial power in Africa in 1884, but as we shall see, these German protectorates would ultimately not offer much of an outlet for German settler farmers. Migrationist colonial enthusiasts like the Protestant mission director Friedrich Fabri (1824–91) and others then began to press the Bismarck

---

[79] GStA PK, VI. HA Nl. Schmoller, Nr. 141, fols. 185–92, Max Sering to Gustav Schmoller, Ramsey's Farm near Warren, MN, July 16, 1883.
[80] Cf. Horst Gründer, *Geschichte der deutschen Kolonien*, 5th ed. (Paderborn: Ferdinand Schöningh, 2004), 17.
[81] Ibid., 19. See also Conrad, *Globalisation and the Nation*, 275–333; Fiebig-von Hase, *Lateinamerika also Konfliktherd*, 68–88, 193–247; Holger Herwig, *Germany's Vision of Empire in Venezuela 1871–1914* (Princeton: Princeton University Press, 1986).

government to seize lands somewhere in the temperate zone.[82] South America would thus continue to animate many Germans, yet there is evidence that by the time Sering published his lengthy study of North American agricultural competition in 1887 he had already shifted his colonial thinking elsewhere. In any case, he never made it to South America, nor did he engage in any sustained study of its colonization, much less of Germany's colonization of Africa.

Another fascinating aspect of this passage in Sering's letter is the reference to the "great economic and psychological processes which a wide and untapped territory offers a nation" and the prospect of healing "damage to our national life" through such colonization. To be sure, these included the classic liberal nationalist aspirations for what the settler colonies would do for national life, but there is an interesting German twist here of a "damaged" national life in need of repair.

Sering remained in the United States until late September 1883 and continued his pattern of study into Nebraska, Kansas, Iowa, Illinois, and Missouri, followed by Wisconsin, Ohio, Ontario, and Quebec. Most of his substantive conclusions about American agricultural competition had nevertheless already been formed while in the upper Midwest.[83] By the time he reached Montreal in mid- September, Sering estimated that he had traveled 20,000 miles. He had collected a vast volume of impressions and materials that he intended to compile into an objective and critical study that offered the German legislator and farmer information from which to take a practical stand in response to the challenges posed by North American agriculture.[84]

On September 26 Sering boarded the *Elbe* in New York and was back in Germany on October 6 in time for the start of the winter semester at Bonn University.[85] In March 1884 he was hopeful to have his study completed by the end of the next semester (August), but as the study took form it expanded dramatically in scale and was not completed until August 1887 and finally between covers in November of that year.[86] At 759 pages it was quite a tome, but its conclusions as they relate to the questions previously raised are relatively easy to summarize. Sering referred to the settlement of the American frontier as a colonization project and called such measures as the Pre-emption

---

[82] Smith, *Ideological Origins*, 40. See especially Klaus J. Bade, *Friedrich Fabri und der Imperialismus der Bismarckzeit: Revolution, Depression, Expansion* (Freiburg i. Br. and Zurich: Atlantis, 1975).
[83] Sering, *Die landwirthschaftliche Konkurrenz*, xi–xii, 316–26, 400–403, 406–407, 451–91.
[84] GStA PK, VI. HA Nl. Schmoller, Nr. 141, fols. 181–84, Max Sering to Gustav Schmoller, Montreal, Quebec, Sept. 14, 1883.
[85] Sering, *Die landwirthschaftliche Konkurrenz*, xii.
[86] GStA PK, VI. HA Nl. Schmoller, Nr. 141, fols. 176–80, Max Sering to Gustav Schmoller, Strassburg, March 26, 1884; fols. 145–48, Max Sering to Gustav Schmoller, Bonn, Aug. 19, 1887; fols. 141–44, Max Sering to Gustav Schmoller, Bonn, Nov. 10, 1887.

and Homestead Acts "colonization policy."[87] Indeed, he noticed the many similarities that existed between the laws of American territorial government and the laws of British crown colonies.[88] While he was definitely critical of many aspects of American "colonization," he recognized the advantage of the American practice of surveying and homesteading 80 or 160 acre parcels in the speed with which it could be brought under cultivation without any of the complications of scattered strips that German farmers had to contend with.[89] But American homestead settlement also had a valuable psychological effect, as to his mind it encouraged greater intellectual alertness and the courage to welcome novelty in farming. The "laming traditions and prejudices" of the old country were largely swept aside by the complete freedom to dispose of property and the lack of village bonds, which inspired an "energetic feeling of independence" and "strong individuality" among North American settler farmers.[90] Indeed, the Pre-emption and Homestead Acts represented important chapters in land reform that empowered the small free farmers of the North to create a bulwark against the expansion of slavery-based agriculture [91] At the same time, by offering the land free or at low cost, agricultural production in the West had effectively been publicly subsidized, heightening the competitive pressures on Europe.[92]

To be sure, Sering was critical of many aspects of the Homestead Act, such as the failure to repeal the Pre-emption Act with passage of the homestead laws and the lack of competent and honest officials, which led to much land speculation. The lack of sufficient working capital in the hands of the homesteaders had moreover led to unsustainable, predatory agriculture.[93] Still, Sering acknowledged that within the United States small and middling landownership now predominated and that therefore it had been a success.[94] There was no widespread indebtedness and there were few tenant farmers in the wheat growing areas east of the Rockies. They comprised a healthy, independent, self-reliant, confident middle class that now determined the future of the country. The "American farmer" differentiated himself from the European peasant by his "frank, confident presence" shaped by "an awareness of a vast continent open to him and his children which give him a feeling of calm

---

[87] Sering, *Die landwirthschaftliche Konkurrenz*, 104–73.
[88] Ibid., 105. Cf. Christopher Clark, "The Agrarian Context of American Capitalist Development," in *Capitalism Takes Command: The Social Transformation of Nineteenth-Century America*, ed. Michael Zakim and Gary John Kornblith (Chicago and London: University of Chicago Press, 2012), 13–37; Paul W. Gates, *Landlords and Tenants on the Prairie Frontier: Studies in American Land Policy* (Ithaca, NY: Cornell University Press, 1973); Eric Foner, *Free Soil, Free Labor, Free Men: The Ideology of the Republican Party before the Civil War* (New York: Oxford University Press, 1970); Johnathan A. Glickstein, *Concepts of Free Labor in Antebellum America* (New Haven: Yale University press, 1991).
[89] Sering, *Die landwirthschaftliche Konkurrenz*, 108.   [90] Ibid., 109.   [91] Ibid., 118.
[92] Ibid., 119–20.   [93] Ibid., 120, 124–25.   [94] Ibid., 140, 151.

security and keen entrepreneurial courage, [while] the novelty of all conditions stimulates contemplation and inventiveness."[95]

Here Sering was beginning to get at the "damage" that had been done to German national life on account of the lack of a frontier: the old caste prejudices in Germany "that persuade city dwellers that they are better than country folk, that a noble estate owner was more than the peasant, [that] the scholar, official or soldier stood higher in status than those engaged in commerce." Of all occupations in Germany, Sering observed, farming suffered more than any other from such arrogance. "Such caste spirit," he wrote, "was a sad inheritance of earlier centuries."[96] In the equal regard given to all work, in the respect accorded farmers, in the reduced class divides and the increased social mobility he witnessed in North America, Germany had much to learn, and it would be this, Sering believed, that would ultimately increase Germany's productivity and allow them to effectively meet the American competition.[97] The challenge was a psychological one as much as it was a physical matter of getting a hold of land for German settlers.

In short, a class of prosperous, robust, independent, inventive, and entrepreneurial middle-class settler farmers was what Germany needed, confident and with broad horizons not plagued by class and caste prejudice and those perennial German faults of self-doubt, quibbling, and impractical, otherworldly dreaming. This would help to shake off the German Michel's lethargy, his provincial and sectarian attachments, his hidebound customs and outdated traditions, and in turn sharpen his commercial and administrative acumen, boost his initiative, and unleash his inventive and entrepreneurial potential. But where on earth would that happen? That was the big unanswered question.

While that question remained open, Sering believed that in the meantime much could be done within Germany to remedy some of the endemic problems in the way of a healthier farm sector. And perhaps some of those sturdy and industrious German emigrants could be persuaded to stay in Germany so they were not lost to the nation only to strengthen the American rival. One of the insights that emerged from Sering's analysis of the patterns of emigration from Germany was that it was strongest in the places you would least expect it to be: in those areas with the lowest population densities such as Mecklenburg-Schwerin, Pomerania, Posen, and West Prussia. He concluded that it was the social conditions and property relations in these places that were the root of the problem, notably the historical legacy of *Gutswirtschaft* and the continued predominance of large estates, and with it, the hurdles in the way of farm laborers to secure their own land. It was this problem that led people to leave the country, as they saw no other way to a better future. Elsewhere in Germany where primogeniture predominated and large, closed peasant lands

---

[95] Ibid., 152–53.    [96] Ibid., 153.    [97] Ibid., 154.

were common, large numbers of rural people also became landless every year and so also emigrated, as in northwestern Germany.[98] The key was therefore land reforms that broke up large estates and royal and state domain lands, changed land inheritance laws (such as entail), and allowed parceling of land to peasant "homesteaders." These developments would reduce the amount of emigration, he believed. Indeed, in his 1887 book Sering was already freely using the term "inner colonization" for such a process.[99]

Still, land reforms in Germany were not enough to stem the crisis in German agriculture. Sering recognized that German immigrant settlers enhanced American agricultural competitiveness and that this was driving further waves of German emigration, as it lowered grain prices and made extensive grain farming less and less viable in Germany over time. The process would continue so long as new lands were available to colonize in North America.[100] Rather than emulating North American methods, Sering proposed taking advantage of Germany's smaller farm units, dense population, and more abundant capital by encouraging more intensive forms of farming, specifically industrial crops such as oil seeds, fine legumes, fiber plants, hops, seed production, wine, sugar beets, and potatoes, niches where North America presented no competition. Sugar beets in particular were a promising crop on account of the potential of North America as a promising export market for German sugar.[101] Even more important than these crops was the improvement and expansion of stock rearing and dairying in Germany, which Sering noted was very backward and could be much improved by making better use of pasture, cultivating winter forage crops, and systematically improving the quality of German dairy products, meat livestock, and poultry. In terms of grain agriculture, Sering recommended switching from wheat to fine brewing barley and rye. Where wheat was still cultivated, finer strains would have to be developed and more attention given to systematic fertilization and soil preparation, where Germany had advantages over North America.[102]

Sering also recommended continuing in the promising trend of organizing agricultural cooperatives to eliminate middlemen and thus gain access to the sales market directly to improve sale prices. Where American farmers had the most to teach German peasants was in their "cast of mind, economic proficiency, elasticity and alertness" as well as their "self-esteem, energy, willingness to learn, and commercial skill."[103] Sering closed by noting that the "American competition" was not, as was commonly believed, a conjunction of favorable agricultural conditions but rather "a struggle of intelligences." The economic superiority of the American farmer ultimately rested on the high social status afforded him. The challenge for Germany was breaking with the old feudal

---

[98] Ibid., 98.  [99] Ibid., 100.  [100] Ibid., 100, 103.  [101] Ibid., 710–11.
[102] Ibid., 711–14.  [103] Ibid., 715.

hierarchies that hindered the kind of productive cooperation and exchange of ideas needed for a renewal of German farming to master the American challenge.[104]

## Contiguous Colonies

In 1886, one year before Sering published his book on North American agricultural competition, the Prussian government created the Prussian Settlement Commission for the Provinces of West Prussia and Posen with a 100 million mark fund to purchase German or Polish gentry estate lands and to resettle them with German peasants.[105] While the policy was definitely inspired by colonial notions, it was influenced by older Prussian Germanization measures dating back to the 1830s and ultimately came about in a deal between Bismarck and the National Liberals in the Prussian Landtag.[106] Its primary motivation was stemming the tide of Russian Polish migrant workers entering Germany and countering the surging Polish and shrinking German population in these borderlands. The aims were thus explicitly political and linguistic-cultural: to turn areas with a German-speaking minority into a majority. It was preceded by the expulsion of some 40,000 foreign migrant workers (mostly Russian Poles and Jews) in 1885 and accompanied by later legislation that restricted the disposal of Polish-owned land (quasi-entail), imposed restrictions on Polish building and settlement permits, offered debt-relief to German peasant farms via credit subsidies (annuity properties), and in 1908, empowered the Settlement Commission to forcibly purchase up to 70,000 hectares of land for settlement.[107]

While Sering found aspects of the Settlement Commission's project appealing, he was himself sharply critical of the use of coercive measures and of efforts to restrict property rights and bind people to the land through entailment, which he compared explicitly to antebellum Southern slavery and

---

[104] Ibid., 716.
[105] William W. Hagen, *Germans, Poles, and Jews: The Nationality Conflict in the Prussian East, 1872–1914* (Chicago and London: University of Chicago Press, 1980), 134–35, 156–57.
[106] See Robert Lewis Koehl, "Colonialism inside Germany, 1886–1918," *Journal of Modern History* 25, no. 3 (Sept. 1953): 255–72, here 261. See also Conrad, *Globalisation and the Nation*, 146–47; Hagen, *Germans, Poles, and Jews*, 87–91; Philipp Ther, "Deutsche Geschichte als imperial Geschichte: Polen, slawophone Minderheiten und das Kaiserreich als kontinentales Empire," in Conrad and Osterhammel, *Das Kaiserreich transnational*, 129–48.
[107] Scott M. Eddie, "The Prussian Settlement Commission and Its Activities in the Land Market, 1886–1918," in *Germans, Poland, and Colonial Expansion to the East: 1850 Through the Present*, ed. Robert L. Nelson (New York: Palgrave Macmillan, 2009), 39–63, here 41–51.

indentured servitude.[108] In any case, the extensive surveys and research that Sering initiated in the Association for Social Policy in the early 1890s led to very different proposals.[109] In a report at the annual meeting of the Association for Social Policy in March 1893 summarizing the findings of this research project, Sering was sharply critical of large East-Elbian estates regardless of the nationality of their owners. Instead, he proposed creating a broad peasant middle class and propertied class of agricultural workers, making unfavorable comparisons between, on the one hand, East-Elbian, and on the other, North American and western German farmsteads.[110] He likewise criticized tenant farming and debt servitude, advocating for the protection of agricultural wage laborers from capitalist exploitation.[111] At the same time, he was hostile to proposals to bureaucratically regulate farm credit and mortgages or to impose entail or homestead regulations on new peasant lands created by parceling large estates.[112] Thus while the nationality issue always figured in Sering's proposals, far greater weight was given the task of overcoming class and status divisions produced by the unequal distribution of land in all of East Elbia (not just Polish areas). Sering's ultimate goal of creating an independent, productive, and entrepreneurial rural middle class showed the unmistakable imprint of his experiences in North America.[113]

In July 1893, just four months after Sering had given his paper to the Association for Social Policy, Frederick Jackson Turner gave his famous address on the historical significance of the American frontier to a meeting of the American Historical Association held in conjunction with the World's Columbian Exposition in Chicago. Turner, who had himself grown up on the Wisconsin frontier, observed that in 1890 the Superintendent of the US Census had declared that there was no longer an American frontier line, and with that, an era of history that had long defined American development was over. The frontier had offered Americans a return to primitive conditions, and with it, a continual rebirth, he argued.[114] The frontier kept alive the "stalwart rugged

---

[108] Robert L. Nelson, "*The Archive for Inner Colonization*, the German East, and World War I," in Nelson, *Germans, Poland, and Colonial Expansion to the East*, 65–93, here 77.

[109] Max Sering, *Die innere Kolonisation im östlichen Deutschland*, SdVfS, vol. 56 (Leipzig: Duncker & Humblot, 1893); Grimmer-Solem, *Historical Economics*, 229–32.

[110] Max Sering, "Die Bodenbesitzverteilung und die Sicherung des Kleingrundbesitzes" [Referat], in *Verhandlungen des am 20. und 21. März in Berlin abgehaltenen Generalversammlung des Vereins für Socialpolitik über die ländliche Arbeiterfrage und über die Bodenbesitzverteilung und die Sicherung des Kleingrundbesitzes*, ed. Ständiger Ausschuß des Vereins für Socialpolitik, SdVfS, vol. 58 (Leipzig: Duncker & Humblot, 1893), 135–50, here 137, 139, 140–41.

[111] Ibid., 142–43, 146, 147, 148. [112] Ibid., 144–46, 147

[113] Cf. Zimmerman, *Alabama in Africa*, 16, 80, 107, 195, 238.

[114] Frederick Jackson Turner, "The Significance of the Frontier in American History" [1893], in *The Frontier in American History* (New York: Henry Holt, 1920), 1–38, here 1–2.

Figure 1.3   Max Sering in 1890.

qualities of the frontiersman," it had "Americanized" a composite nation, decreased economic dependence on England, encouraged the development of national government in such things as the disposal of public lands and incorporating new states.[115] It created a democratic, tolerant, national society not bound by region or sect. The frontier had extended the franchise and reinvigorated republican virtues of self-government and self-reliance.[116]

While Turner was aware of the dark side of "democracy born of free land" (selfishness, individualism, populist intolerance, the spoils system, land speculation, poor business ethics, wildcat banking, and inflated paper currency, to name a few),[117] he extolled the frontier's lasting imprint on the American mind: "That coarseness and strength combined with acuteness and inquisitiveness; that practical, inventive turn of mind, quick to find expedients; that masterful grasp of material things, lacking in the artistic but powerful to affect great ends; that restless, nervous energy, that dominant individualism, working for good and for evil, and withal that buoyancy and exuberance which comes with freedom."[118] The frontier had offered "escape from the bondage of the past; and freshness, and confidence, and scorn of older society."[119] Intriguingly, Turner seemed to have already anticipated the overseas imperial turn with the closing of the frontier: "American energy will continually demand a wider field for its exercise."[120]

The strong parallels between Turner's vision of the frontier and Sering's own conclusions are striking, which itself opens the intriguing question of their possible connection. That this is not as far-fetched as it might seem is supported by the links between Turner and Friedrich Ratzel. Ratzel's positive assessments of westward expansion in his work on the cultural, political, and economic geography of the United States, *Die Vereinigten Staaten von Amerika,* was very well received in the United States, and Turner was one of Ratzel's

---

[115] Ibid., 15, 22–26.   [116] Ibid., 28–30.   [117] Ibid., 32.   [118] Ibid., 37.
[119] Ibid., 38.   [120] Ibid., 37.

most influential American admirers.[121] Ratzel, perhaps best known (and later notorious) for his development of the concept *Lebensraum*, was nevertheless unquestionably a political liberal who, as noted previously, had himself traveled extensively in the United States. He admired the *laissez-faire* process of westward expansion, which he linked to political stability and the stimulation of economic and cultural development in the United States.[122] As it turned out, Sering's own work found its way into the later and much expanded and revised second edition of Ratzel's American political geography published in 1893. This edition was completed in June 1893 and made admiring use of Seringss's 1887 book. Ratzel noted that he very much subscribed to Sering's conclusion about the potential of the American wheat growing regions to double their production in the next twenty years, and not just by the expansion of arable land, but by increasing the productivity of the land and of the special importance in that process of *"der Geist und die Thatkraft"* [the spirit and the active energy] of the American farmer.[123] Referring to Sering's work and its spatial focus, and then quoting the Comte de Paris' history of the Civil War, Ratzel also noted the essentially expansive nature of the American people, "like a liquid that nothing holds back" and thus the inability to keep them confined to the borders of 1848. American economic and political expansion went hand in hand.[124]

While Turner could not have yet read the revised and expanded edition of Ratzel's work, it is quite likely that he was familiar with Sering's work on account of its sheer importance to the field and Ratzel's clear admiration of it. Certainly Sering was himself primed for a liberal imperialist view of the frontier by his own reading of Ratzel's political geography, but much more important to the argument of this chapter is that the *Weltpolitik* with which Sering would later be closely associated had a fundamentally American reference point. Indeed it almost certainly had its origins in his experiences in Minnesota in 1883. What Ratzel, Turner, and Sering shared, then, was a common experience of the North American frontier that had reinforced and amplified a preexisting ideological belief in the liberating and emancipating force of frontier lands for national development.[125]

---

[121] Guettel, *German Expansionism*, 97–100; Guettel, "From the Frontier," 535–39. See also Richard Hofstadter and Seymour Martin Lipset, eds., *Turner and the Sociology of the Frontier* (New York: Basic Books, 1968); Richard Slotkin, *The Fatal Environment: The Myth of the Frontier in the Age of Industrialization, 1800–1890* (Norman: University of Oklahoma Press, 1998).

[122] Guettel, *German Expansionism*, 98.

[123] Fredrich Ratzel, *Die Vereinigten Staaten von Amerika*, 2nd ed., vol. 2, Politische und Wirtschafts-Geographie (Munich: Oldenbourg, 1893), 382.

[124] Ibid., 97.   [125] Cf. Smith, *Ideological Origins*, 89.

## Hermann Schumacher and Ernst von Halle in Chicago

Sering's book on North American agriculture established his reputation as the leading authority on the subject in Germany, and his knowledge was perhaps unrivaled anywhere else in Europe at the time. In 1889 he left Bonn for a professorship at the Landwirtschaftliche Hochschule (Higher School of Land Economy) in Berlin and thereafter also began lecturing at the University of Berlin. He was made a member of the Prussian Land Economy Collegium in 1891, and in 1893 was appointed to an extraordinary professorship at the University of Berlin. Sering's former teacher and mentor, Gustav Schmoller, had himself been called from Strasbourg to take a professorship at the University of Berlin in 1882. Together with his colleague Adolph Wagner (1835–1917), Schmoller had helped turn Berlin into the most important center for the study of *Staatswissenschaften* in the German Empire, which in the late 1880s and early 1890s drew a very talented cohort of German and international students to the University, including the likes of Emily Greene Balch (1867–1961), W. E. B. Du Bois (1868–1963), Max Weber (1864–1919), and Werner Sombart (1863–1941). Less well known in that cohort but of importance to the development of German *Weltpolitik* in the late 1890s were Hermann Schumacher and Wilhelm Ernst von Halle.

Hermann Albert Schumacher was born in Bremen in 1868, but as already noted earlier, spent much of his childhood in Bogota and New York. The son of a successful lawyer and *Syndikus* (legal representative) of the Bremen Chamber of Commerce, H. A. Schumacher (1839–90), and Therese Grote, scion of an old Bremen merchant family, Hermann and his family moved to Bogota, Columbia, in 1872 when he was only four years old after his father was named German Minister-Resident to Columbia. From there his family moved to New York City three years later in 1875, when his father was appointed to the post of German Consul General.[126] Hermann Schumacher had very fond memories of his youth in New York, highlights of which included witnessing the first electric lights in Madison Square, a demonstration of Edison's phonograph, seeing the arm and torch of the still incomplete Statue of Liberty, and visiting the Philadelphia Centennial Exposition and Independence Hall with his parents in 1876. Other powerful memories of his youth in New York included the massive growth of the city on account of immigration, close contacts to the family of the great German American statesman Carl Schurz (1829–1906), summers spent on the Hudson north of the city, many diplomatic visitors with stories from all corners of the earth, and witnessing the arrival of the first NDL express steamer *Elbe* in New York harbor in 1881. Many hours or his youth were spent watching the busy ship traffic in and out

---

[126] Schumacher-Vereinigung, ed., *Hermann Schumacher* (Wiesbaden and Berlin: B. Behr's Verlag, 1958), 5; GNN HA, Nl. Schumacher, I, B-6a, fols. 1–29.

of New York harbor, which left a powerful impression of a world connected by threads of communication and commerce.[127] Likewise, booming German immigration to the United States and the expansion of American grain exports to Germany were phenomena that the young Schumacher took note of and connected with the improvements in shipping and the opening of the Midwest to farming in those years. Schumacher recalled that this had turned his father's work as consul into one approximating a "colonial director."[128]

In 1882, one year before Sering traveled to the United States, Schumacher's father was named Minister-Resident in Lima, now a position of great importance since a significant part of the trade in Peruvian guano and Chile saltpeter had been in the hands of Bremen merchants but was now threatened by the War of the Pacific between Peru and Chile.[129] Schumacher and his younger brother Fritz did not join their father in Peru but were sent back to Bremen instead to complete their schooling. After completing *Gymnasium* in 1887 Schumacher began his studies at the University of Freiburg, where he was exposed to economics for the first time in the economic policy lectures of Eugen von Philippovich (1858–1917). Philippovich awakened in Schumacher an interest in contemporary practical economic questions that connected easily to his existing interest in international trade and commerce awakened by his youth in New York and Bremen.[130]

Schumacher deepened his study of *Staatswissenschaften* in Munich and Vienna, but the death of his father in 1890 and the financial difficulties that it brought to the Schumacher family forced him to accelerate and focus his studies. He thus began to prepare for the *Referendar* examination in law with an eye to serving Bremen as a lawyer as his father had, switching his studies to complete his degree in law and moving to the University of Berlin in the autumn of 1890. While attending the necessary lectures and preparing for the law examinations, Schumacher continued to pursue his interest in *Staatswissenschaften*, joining the seminar led by Gustav Schmoller and his colleague Adolph Wagner. In 1891 Schumacher passed the *Referendar* examination in Berlin, moving from there to the University of Jena to complete his doctoral degree in law (Dr. iur.) summa cum laude that same year.[131]

Starting in September 1891 Schumacher served as a superior court clerk in Alt-Landsberg, switching to a superior court in Berlin in 1892. While working as *Referendar* in Berlin in 1892 Schumacher was able to once again continue

---

[127] GNN HA, Nl. Schumacher, I, B-6b, fols. 30–53.   [128] Ibid., fols. 53–54.
[129] Ibid., fols. 56/57–58. See Ekkehard Böhm, *Überseehandel und Flottenbau: Hanseatische Kaufmannschaft und deutsche Seerüstung 1879–1914* (Düsseldorf: Bertelsmann Universitätsverlag, 1972), 35–37.
[130] GNN HA, Nl. Schumacher, I, B-6d, fols. 94–95; Schumacher-Vereinigung, *Hermann Schumacher*, 6.
[131] Schumacher-Vereinigung, *Hermann Schumacher*, 8.

his studies in economics in Gustav Schmoller's, Adolph Wagner's, and Max Sering's respective seminars, also joining the Association for Social Policy that year.[132] As he himself recollected, Schumacher was particularly interested in getting to know "the actual economy that had expanded to a *Weltwirtschaft* (world economy) in the age of steamship travel, railways, and telegraphs."[133] Thus Sering became an important teacher and mentor to Schumacher because unlike the other professors of *Staatswissenschaften*, he was not a *"Binnenländer"* (landlubber) – he had spent considerable time abroad and knew the country of Schumacher's childhood and youth from direct experience. At the time, Sering's seminar was dealing with the question of a central European customs union (*"Mitteleuropa"*), an idea that had been reawakened by the Austro-German industrialist and politician Alexander von Peez (1829–1912) and the German historian and journalist Constantin Rößler (1820–96).[134]

In Berlin Schumacher developed contacts to many later very significant economists and sociologists who were there to complete their studies or begin their academic careers. In Schmoller's seminar, for example, Schumacher befriended the American students Emily Greene Balch and W. E. B. Du Bois, and through his membership in the Association for Social Policy, Staatswissenschaftliche Gesellschaft (Political Economy Society), and the Staatswissenschaftliche Vereinigung (Political Economy Union), he met Max Weber. Weber, a man with expansive intellectual and physical appetites – Schumacher recalled that in post-seminar soirees in Berlin beer halls Weber would start by ordering himself two beefsteaks and two mugs of beer! – was then completing his *Habilitation* in two different faculties at the University of Berlin.[135] Through Weber he also met his brother Alfred Weber (1868–1958) and the later prominent historians Erich Marcks (1861–1938) and Otto Hintze (1861–1940).[136] Max Weber had then just completed a large study on German agricultural laborers in East Elbia that Sering had initiated in the Association for Social Policy in 1890.[137] In Berlin Schumacher also developed contacts to the geologist and geographer Ferdinand von Richthofen who was by then

---

[132] GNN HA, Nl. Schumacher, I, B-6d, fols. 90–121; GNN HA, Nl. Schumacher, I, B-6e, fols. 122–45; GNN HA, Nl. Schumacher, I, B-6f, fols. 146–70; B-6g, fol 171–92; Schumacher-Vereinigung, *Hermann Schumacher*, 7–8; David Levering Lewis, *W. E. B. DuBois: Biography of a Race, 1868–1919* (New York: H. Holt, 1993), 137, 142–46; Lewis, *W. E. B. Du Bois: A Biography* (New York: Henry Holt, 2009), 98–106.

[133] GNN HA, Nl. Schumacher, I, B-6g, fol. 173.   [134] Ibid., fol. 174.

[135] Ibid., fol. 177.

[136] GNN HA, Nl. Schumacher, I, B-6g, fols. 176–78; B-6o, fol. 436; B-6p, fol. 459.

[137] Max Weber, *Die Verhältnisse der Landarbeiter in Deutschland*, vol. 3: *Die Verhältnisse der Landarbeiter im ostelbischen Deutschland*, SdVfS, vol. 55 (Leipzig: Duncker & Humblot, 1892); Grimmer-Solem, *Historical Economics*, 232.

world famous for his work on China,[138] and through Richthofen, to many others who had traveled extensively in Africa, Asia, and the Americas. It was Richthofen who reinforced in Schumacher a desire "to grasp the economy of the entire earth," and it was at this time that Schumacher began to see a career as an economist as personally more fulfilling given that much was in motion and yet to be discovered in this field as opposed to the established and dogmatic field of law.[139]

It was thus not surprising that in 1893 Schumacher applied for one of the scholarships that had been funded by Henry Villard (as discussed, the German-born founder of the Northern Pacific Railroad) to enable young German engineers to attend the Columbian Exposition in Chicago.[140] The scholarships were administered by the German Chancellor's Office. While not himself an engineer, Schumacher proposed to undertake a study of the organization of American grain exchanges, which was then relevant to the drafting of a new German commodity and stock exchange law and about which practically nothing was known in Germany. By 1890 the internal German debate about American agricultural competition had been jolted by the sudden and massive entry of Argentina into the global grain market. It was becoming clear by this point that German agriculture would only survive this additional onslaught by initiating the reforms Sering had proposed and improving the efficiency of the internal German grain market. Here, once again, it was thought that the United States offered models, as it had one of the most efficient internal grain markets in the world. Knowledge about how exactly it was organized was nevertheless sketchy in Germany. It was Schumacher's aim to fill this gap. The Chancellor's Office agreed that his proposal merited funding, giving Schumacher a stipend of 2,000 marks.[141] Schumacher would subsequently spend the autumn of 1893 in the United States, initially in New York but then for the bulk of his stay in Chicago as a guest of the Board of Trade.

Joining Schumacher in the United States in 1893 was Ernst Levy von Halle. He was born Wilhelm Ernst Hermann Levy in Hamburg in 1868 to observant Jewish parents, the prominent attorney and longstanding member of the Hamburg Assembly (Bürgerschaft) Dr. Heymann Baruch Levy (1834–1904) and Louise Meyersberg, herself from a prominent Jewish merchant family with roots in Hamburg and Paderborn. Ernst Levy, who began to adopt the name von Halle from his maternal grandmother's side of the family in 1892 due to his conversion to Protestantism in 1888, attended the prestigious Johanneum

---

[138] Ferdinand von Richthofen, *China: Ergebnisse eigener Reisen und darauf gegründeter Studien*, 3 vols. (Berlin: Dietrich Reimer, 1876–1883).
[139] GNN HA, Nl. Schumacher, I, B-6g, fols. 180–82.
[140] On this scholarship, Henry Villard, *Memoirs of Henry Villard, Journalist and Financier*, vol. 2 (Boston and New York: Houghton, Mifflin and Company, 1902), 375–76.
[141] GNN HA, Nl. Schumacher, I, B-6g, fol. 183.

Gymnasium in Hamburg, completing his *Abitur* in 1887.[142] The Johanneum was unusual in that it was the first in Germany that required English in its curriculum, aiding the international engagement of its graduates. Among the other students in von Halle's class in the Johanneum was the future diplomat, writer, and bon vivant Count Harry Kessler (1868–1937). From an early age von Halle developed a deep appreciation for Hamburg's dependence upon overseas trade, particularly the importance of its trade with the Americas.[143]

Von Halle began studying law and *Staatswissenschaften* in 1887 at the University of Munich, switching to the University of Bonn in 1888, where he was taught by Max Sering, who helped redirect his studies from law toward political economy. There is no question that Sering made a very positive impression on the young von Halle, but as previously discussed, Sering left the University of Bonn for an appointment at the Berlin Landwirtschaftliche Hochschule in 1889 and seemed to have advised von Halle to switch from Bonn to the University of Leipzig to attend the research seminar of Lujo Brentano (1844–1931), one of the other co-founders of the Association for Social Policy who was an expert on British economic conditions.[144] Von Halle completed his doctoral dissertation in political economy in Leipzig in 1891 summa cum laude with a thesis on the history of the Hamburg Girobank, a topic Sering had suggested and which when it was published in book form von Halle dedicated to Max Sering as a sign of his appreciation.[145]

---

[142] Gregory Zieren, "Ernst von Halle and the U.S. Navy in German Naval Propaganda, 1897–1907," paper delivered at the Fifth International and Interdisciplinary Conference, Alexander von Humboldt, 2009: Travels Between Europe and the Americas, Free University of Berlin (July 27–31, 2009), 1–2; Guenther Roth, "Der politische Kontext von Max Webers Beitrag über die deutsche Wirtschaft in der *Encyclopedia Americana*," *Zeitschrift für Soziologie* 36, no. 1 (Feb. 2007): 65–77, here 69n16; Jürgen Sielemann, *Quellen zur jüdischen Familiengeschichtsforschung im Staatsarchiv Hamburg: Ein Wegweiser für die Spurensuche* (Hamburg: Hamburg University Press/Verlag der Staats- und Universitätsbibliothek Hamburg, 2015), 72–77; Lars U. Scholl, "Ernst von Halle und die wissenschaftliche Propaganda für den 'Tirpitz-Plan,'" in Tjard Schwarz and Ernst von Halle, *Die Schiffbauindustrie in Deutschland und im Ausland*, ed. Lars U. Scholl (Düsseldorf: VDI-Verlag, 1987), v–xxxi, here viii; BPL, Hugo Münsterberg Collection, Ser. 1, Box 7, Folder 1768, Ernst von Halle to Hugo Münsterberg, Grunewald, Oct. 9, 1907 and Ernst von Halle to Hugo Münsterberg, Grunewald, Jan. 3, 1908; GStA PK, VI. HA Nl. Schmoller, Nr. 126, fols. 20–21, Ernst von Halle to Gustav Schmoller, Boston, May 5, 1894.

[143] See Ernst von Halle, ed. *Amerika: Seine Bedeutung für die Weltwirtschaft und seine wirtschaftliche Beziehungen zu Deutschland insbesondere zu Hamburg* (Hamburg: Verlag der Hamburger Börsenhalle, 1905).

[144] Ernst Levy von Halle, *Die Hamburger Giro-Bank und ihr Ausgang* (Berlin: Puttkammer & Mühlbrecht, 1891), vii. On Brentano, see James J. Sheehan, *The Career of Lujo Brentano: A Study of Liberalism and Social Reform in Imperial Germany* (Chicago and London: University of Chicago Press, 1966).

[145] von Halle, *Giro-Bank*, dedication page.

Like Schumacher, von Halle was frustrated by the fact that the subject of overseas trade was still a "stepchild" of German economic research. He attributed this to deep-seated, provincial prejudices that saw merchants as second-class citizens compared to farmers, industrialists, and civil servants.[146] In any case, like Schumacher, von Halle's Hanseatic background made him aware of the global web of exchange in which the German economy was entangled and eager to witness this overseas. In 1892 von Halle moved to the University of Berlin with the intention of beginning his *Habilitation* to embark on an academic career in *Staatswissenschaften*, becoming part of the exciting intellectual milieu in and around Gustav Schmoller's and Max Sering's seminars.[147] One year later he would be on his way to the United States.

As none of von Halle's papers have survived, the exact circumstances of how he found his way to North America in 1893 cannot be established. It is likely that through the mediation of either Schmoller or Sering and on account of his superb command of English that von Halle was asked to be part of the sizable German delegation attached to the German educational exhibits at the Chicago World's Fair, which formed one of the centerpieces of the very extensive German exhibition.[148] As is also known and will be discussed in depth later, von Halle received a commission from the Association for Social Policy in the spring of 1893 to investigate American industrial trusts. He was asked to write a monograph for the association's series in advance of the association's annual meeting in the autumn of 1894.[149] It is thus possible that he received some kind of stipend from the association for this research. In any case, von Halle disposed of considerable private means from his family that would have covered his passage and that then allowed him to stay in the United States for more than two years from the early spring of 1893 to mid-1895.

Von Halle was based initially in Chicago but then later in New York and Boston, where he was much assisted by both the German American psychologist Hugo Münsterberg (1863–1916) and the English economic historian William James Ashley (1860–1927), both of whom then held positions at Harvard University and with whom von Halle developed close friendships.[150]

---

[146] Ibid., vii.    [147] Zieren, "Ernst von Halle," 4.    [148] Ibid., 5.
[149] Gustav Schmoller, "Vorrede," in *Über wirtschaftliche Kartelle in Deutschland und im Auslande: Fünfzehn Schilderungen nebst einer Anzahl Statuten und Beilagen*, ed. Ständiger Ausschuß des Vereins für Socialpoltik, SdVfS, vol. 60 (Leipzig: Duncker & Humblot, 1894), v.
[150] GStA PK, VI. HA Nl.. Schmoller, Nr. 201a, fols. 123–24, William Ashley to Gustav Schmoller, June 30, 1909. On Ashley, A. P. Usher, "William J. Ashley: A Pioneer in the Higher Education," *Canadian Journal of Economics and Political Science* 4, no. 2 (May 1938): 151–63.

## The American Challenge

By the time Schumacher and von Halle arrived in the United States in 1893, a perceptible change in mood had occurred toward Germany and German immigrants compared to the 1870s. This was a result of the rise of populism and labor unrest in the late 1880s that had been brought to national attention by the Haymarket Riot of May 4, 1886 and its aftermath. In the subsequent investigation and trials it was discovered that five of the six rioters who were given the death sentence were German Americans. Thereafter fear grew within the American public that Germans were bringing a radical and dangerous European political ideology to the United States.[151] It also affected public perceptions of labor activism for such things as the eight-hour day, which were now seen as potentially subversive.[152] As Dorothy Ross has noted, this event "sent shock waves through the upper and middle classes" and began a nativist reaction to the socialist and social reforming ideas that many German-trained American economists and other social scientists had absorbed and then disseminated in American universities in the 1870s.[153]

Heightened American nationalism was also to be seen in an increasingly skeptical and critical attitude toward the German educational system and scholarship that had accompanied a generational change in the 1880s and early 1890s. American institutions of higher learning were improving in quality and developing graduate programs so that it was no longer necessary to study overseas. Rather than the reverential attitudes about German culture of the generation of the 1870s, the generation of American scholars coming of age in the early 1890s were much more self-assertive and critical of German culture and Germany's authoritarian political system.[154] The movements for prohibition, Sabbatarianism, compulsory English-language schooling, and regulating parochial schools that arose in these years also had implicitly anti-German valences.[155] Parallel and closely related to this was the failure of Reconstruction, the rise of white supremacy under Jim Crow laws, and the

---

[151] Foner, *History of the Labor Movement*, vol. 2, 105–31; cf. Hartmut Keil, "The German Immigrant Working Class of Chicago, 1875–90: Workers, Labor Leaders, and the Labor Movement," in *American Labor and Immigration History, 1877–1920s: Recent European Research*, ed. Dirk Hoerder (Urbana, Chicago, and London: University of Illinois, 1983), 156–76.

[152] Nagler, "From Culture to *Kultur*," 148; Hartmut Keil and John B. Jentz, eds., *German Workers in Industrial Chicago 1850–1910: A Comparative Perspective* (DeKalb: Northern Illinois University Press, 1983); Michaela Bank, *Women of Two Countries: German-American Women, Women's Rights and Navivism, 1848–1890* (New York: Berghahn Books, 2012).

[153] Ross, *The Origins of American Social Science*, 115.

[154] Nagler, "From Culture to *Kultur*," 138–44.

[155] Frederick C. Luebke, *Bonds of Loyalty: German-Americans in World War I* (DeKalb: Northern Illinois University, 1974), 60–62.

growing backlash to the Catholic and Jewish "new immigration" from eastern and southern Europe, which led American nativists and populists to begin constructing the American nation in ever more racialized and exclusively "Anglo-Saxon" Protestant terms.[156]

American nativist backlash was also evident in the passage of the Tariff Act of 1890 sponsored by Representative (and future president) William McKinley (1843–1901), which raised duties on many imports to the United States to nearly 50 percent. While tariffs on raw sugar were lowered, bountied sugar (effectively all German sugar, a major export good to the United States) was subject to new surtaxes. Additionally, a vast range of American industrial goods enjoyed tariff protection, including iron goods, steel, tools, medical equipment, and cotton fabrics, which hit German exporters hard.[157] When Hermann Schumacher visited his old family friend Carl Schurz while staying in New York in September 1893 before continuing to Chicago, Schurz himself denounced the McKinley tariff as "setting a course of imperialism for the American ship of state."[158] The fact was that the United States was now not just an agricultural but also a major industrial power competing with the Germans both for the large American domestic market as well as markets overseas. The United States was by far the world's largest producer of cotton. Railroad, oil, steel, tobacco, and shipping trusts now also dominated the American economy and seemed to be setting their sights on markets overseas. It was at this time, too, that voices were first raised to restrict the immigration of contract laborers to protect the wages of domestic American workers.

Some of these developments were reflected in Chicago and the Columbian Exposition itself. Chicago – this most American city – had grown at a breathtaking pace from a town of just over 4,000 in 1837 to a metropolis exceeding one million by 1890, becoming the single largest railway hub in the New World.[159] The White City built for the exposition on Chicago's South Side was an ebullient expression of American artistic creativity and symbolized American self-confidence and independence from Europe. Yet not far from

---

[156] C. Vann Woodward, *The Strange Career of Jim Crow* (Oxford and New York: Oxford University Press, 1955), 49–95; John Higham, *Strangers in the Land: Patterns of American Nativism, 1860–1925* (New Brunswick and London: Rutgers University Press, 1983), 35–105; Jörg Nagler, *Nationale Minoritäten im Krieg: "Feindliche Ausländer"und die amerikanische Heimtafront während des Ersten Weltkriegs* (Hamburg: Hamburger Edition, 2000), 88–89.

[157] Mitchell, *The Danger of Dreams*, 15; Pommerin, *Der Kaiser und Amerika*, 27–49; Tom E. Terrill, *The Tariff, Politics and American Foreign Policy: 1874–1901* (Westport, CT: Greenwood Press, 1973), 159–83.

[158] GNN HA, Nl. Schumacher, I, B-6g, fol. 185.

[159] Ibid., fols. 196/97–198; cf. John F. McDonald, *Chicago: An Economic History* (London and New York: Routledge, 2016), 27, 32.

the gleaming exposition and the skyscrapers of the Loop, visitors could see the stockyards, the ramshackle immigrant tenements, and the soot and filth of a seething metropolis challenged by crime and corruption.[160] On October 28, 1893, five days before the closing of the Columbian Exposition, the mayor of Chicago was murdered in his home. This jarring image of contrasts – this picture of a restless, dynamic, and potentially menacing republic with powerful nativist forces and industrial trusts that would not be contained by the closing of the frontier – would increasingly shape German and other European perceptions of the United States over the next two decades. Competition and rivalry would increasingly define the German-American relationship, and these images of America would themselves increasingly inform German auto- and heterostereotypes that shaped Wilhelmine German identity and Germany's place in the world. The new American images of German immigrants and Germans would do the same in the United States during the Progressive era.[161]

Schumacher began his journey to the United States on September 2, 1893 boarding an NDL steamer in Bremen for New York. On arriving in the city in mid-September, Schumacher briefly reconnected with family friends on Staten Island and Manhattan, including Carl Schurz, and paid a visit to his benefactor, Henry Villard, who invited Schumacher to his country home in Dobbs Ferry to meet his family. Villard had gained control of the Oregon and Northern Pacific Railways with the assistance of the Deutsche Bank, and with other German interests including Siemens & Halske and Allgemeine Electrizitäts Gesellschaft (AEG), he had organized, financed, and directed the Edison General Electric Company in 1889. At the time of Schumacher's visit, Villard had been forced to relinquish control of both and was active as owner of the *New York Evening Post*, which employed Carl Schurz as a regular contributor on behalf of the cause of political reform, sound money, and free trade.[162]

Schumacher got to work investigating the American commodity markets soon after these courtesy stops, visiting New York's gigantic Produce Exchange on Broadway, much impressed by the strong trend toward concentration of New York commercial life that it embodied. Yet the actual significance of this commodity exchange was disappointing to Schumacher: at the time it had already been eclipsed by Chicago. Oddly, New York – despite its secondary status as a grain exchange – remained the largest grain exporting hub in the United States and as such was then the largest single grain exporting port in the world. This was puzzling to Schumacher and in contrast to major German

---

[160] See Arnold Lewis, *An Early Encounter with Tomorrow: Europeans, Chicago's Loop and the World's Columbian* Exposition (Urbana: University of Illinois Press, 1997); William Cronon, *Nature's Metropolis: Chicago and the Great West* (New York and London: W. W. Norton, 1991), 341–70.
[161] Nagler, "From Culture to *Kultur*," 146.
[162] GNN HA, Nl. Schumacher, I, B-6g, fols. 185–86; cf. Villard, *Memoirs*, vol. 2, 272–374.

grain exchanges and ports. As Schumacher would later discover, the reason for the relative decline of the New York grain exchange had to do with the fact that American grain – on account of the massive quantities involved and the vast distances it moved as part of a worldwide grain market – was graded, priced, and exchanged well before it ever reached American export hubs. Unlike German grain, American wheat was continuously transported and stored not in sacks but loosely as a dry fluid. Thus it was not only that American grain exchanges were organized differently but that the American grain market had been shaped by very different rules and institutions. Understanding the differences fully, he realized, meant traveling to Chicago to investigate its Board of Trade.[163]

Chicago was entirely new to Schumacher, though not without German contacts from his time at university. He visited the constitutional historian Hermann von Holst (1841–1904) at the University of Chicago, whose lectures he had heard at Freiburg University and who had been lured to the new University of Chicago to head the History Department.[164] Nevertheless it seemed to Schumacher that von Holst had failed to establish much of a rapport with his colleagues or students. He found Holst very homesick and unwell when he called on him. While staying with a student friend from Freiburg – a German physician who had immigrated after completing his medical studies – Schumacher also gained an indelible impression of the crime problems in the city. When he was needed at night, his friend traveled with a loaded revolver and was the victim of a holdup while Schumacher was staying with him in Chicago. Schumacher even became part of the private posse of medical students that his friend organized and that managed to gain access to the many criminal dives of Chicago to apprehend the bandit. In their quest they made their way to one of the "hotels" of organized crime trading in immigrant girls as well as cocaine and opium dens, where Schumacher even witnessed what appeared to be upper-class women indulging in drugs.[165]

Schumacher saw more than Chicago's seedy underbelly. Indeed, visiting the Columbian Exposition and seeing the White City was one of the high points of Schumacher's visit to the United States.[166] In Chicago he also visited Hull

---

[163] GNN HA, Nl. Schumacher, I, B-6h, fols. 193–99.
[164] Jörg Nagler, "Mediator between Two Historical Worlds: Hermann von Holst and the University of Chicago," in *German Influences on Education in the United States,* ed. Henry Geitz, Jürgen Heideking and Jurgen Herbst (Washington, DC: German Historical Institute; New York: Cambridge University Press, 1995), 257–74; Peter Novick, *That Noble Dream: The "Objectivity Question" and the American Historical Profession* (Cambridge and New York: Cambridge University Press, 1988), 25–26.
[165] GNN HA, Nl. Schumacher, I, B-6h, fols. 199–99a; cf. David T. Courtwright, *Dark Paradise: Opiate Addiction in America before 1940* (Cambridge, MA: Harvard University Press, 1982).
[166] GNN HA, Nl. Schumacher, I, B-6g, fols. 188–92.

House, modeled on the settlement house Toynbee Hall in England, and he got to know its head, the social reformer and suffragette Jane Addams (1860–1935).[167] And quite in contrast to the cool reception he had been given at New York's Produce Exchange, Schumacher was warmly received by officials at the Chicago Board of Trade, who were eager to answer his queries and offer their assistance.

Schumacher was given use of an office on the seventeenth floor of a neighboring "*Turmhaus*" (skyscraper) to go through the material that Board officials freely supplied him with for his investigation. These materials included the annual reports of the Board of Trade and Commissioners of Railroads and Warehouses as well as records of legal cases involving the exchange and many trade periodicals. Gradually Schumacher gained insight into the system of country and terminal grain elevators and the interconnected railway and shipping networks that graded, moved, and stored the loose grain between producers and consumers with astonishing speed. He also began to grasp how the powerful elevator corporations had formed and why individual farmers felt helpless against their buying power, in turn spawning "anti-elevator," "anti-grading," "anti-exchange," and "anti-option" movements. Moreover, he gained insights into the problem with commodity speculation, such as deliberate cornering of the market for grain on the options and futures exchange as well as the profusion of many unregulated secondary exchanges that greatly increased price volatility.[168]

Schumacher later traveled to Minneapolis to study the extraordinarily concentrated American grain milling industry, meeting both Charles Pillsbury (1842–99) and W. D. Washburn (1831–1912), who as heads of two giant milling operations (Pillsbury and what later became General Mills) had themselves been active in the anti-option movement and who discussed the need to reform American commodity exchanges. To Schumacher's surprise these proposals were in striking accord with the findings of the German Exchange Survey Commission (Börsen- Enquênte-Kommission) to, among many other things, better regulate the options and futures exchanges and restrict the scope of secondary trading.[169]

Schumacher returned to Germany in late December 1893 pleased with the "harvest" of his three-month investigative journey. By then the debate over the reform of German commodity exchanges was reaching a high pitch. Before he had time to write and publish his study, Schumacher was asked by Gustav Schmoller to present his preliminary findings to branches of the Prussian

---

[167] GNN HA, Nl. Schumacher, I, B-6o, fols. 438–39.
[168] GNN HA, Nl. Schumacher, I, B-6h, fols. 199b-205; cf. Cronon, *Nature's Metropolis*, 97–147; Guy A. Lee, "The Historical Significance of the Chicago Grain Elevator System," *Agricultural History* 11, no. 1 (Jan. 1937): 16–32.
[169] GNN HA, Nl. Schumacher, I, B-6h, fols. 206–208.

government and scholarly societies in Berlin. Together with the long, serialized article he published on the topic in the *Jahrbücher für Nationalökonomie und Statistik* in 1895 and 1896, this established his credentials as an economist.[170]

Two important overarching observations emerged from that study that deserve to be highlighted. One was that the vast scale of American wheat growing and the mechanization of its transportation and storage under conditions of *laissez faire* had encouraged consolidation, concentration, and monopolization of the intermediaries in the American grain trade (elevator and warehouse companies). Anti-trust legislation and other ad hoc interventions of the relatively weak American state had been largely ineffective against this trend.[171] At the same time, certain qualities of that trade – notably the fungibility of the grain, the system of elevator grading of grain, and the institution of warehouse receipts – translated into advantages of quality control, transparency, simplicity, cost, and speed in the grain futures market, which ultimately made for a much more efficient market in the United States than in Germany.[172] American agricultural capitalism's advantages were thus not only geographical but also organizational and institutional.

By the time Schumacher returned to Germany in December 1893, Ernst von Halle had been living in Chicago for nearly a year and was well on his way to completing a major study on American industrial trusts. In that time he had developed contacts to Professor Laurence Laughlin (1850–1933) at the University of Chicago, who was interested in publishing translations of Schmoller's essays in the *Journal of Political Economy* and for which he solicited von Halle's assistance.[173] In May 1893 a member of the Standing Committee of the Association for Social Policy had written von Halle from Germany with a request to compile a report on American industrial combinations in advance of the association's annual meeting in the autumn of 1894 that was to be devoted to the subject of cartels and trusts.[174] For the remainder of 1893 as he traveled the length of the country to the west coast and back to Chicago and

---

[170] Ibid., fols. 212–14; Hermann Schumacher, "Die Organisation des Getreidehandels in den Vereinigten Staaten von Amerika," *JbbfNS* III. Folge, 10 (1895): 361–92, 801–22; 11 (1896): 35–73, 161–236. Reprinted in Hermann Schumacher, *Weltwirtschaftliche Studien: Vorträge und Aufsätze* (Leipzig: Veit & Comp., 1911), 209–400.

[171] Schumacher, "Die Organisation des Getreidehandels," in *Weltwirtschaftliche Studien*, 210–33.

[172] Ibid., 318–25.

[173] GStA PK, VI. HA Nl. Schmoller, Nr. 126, fols. 24–25, Ernst Levy von Halle to Gustav Schmoller, Chicago, May 17, 1893. See Gustav Schmoller, "The Idea of Justice in Political Economy," *Annals of the American Academy of Political and Social Science* 4 (March 1894): 1–41; Ernst von Halle, "Münchener Volkswirtschaftliche Studien: Lujo Brentano, Walther Lotz," *Journal of Political Economy* 2, no. 3 (June 1894): 464–68.

[174] Ernst von Halle, *Trusts or Industrial Combinations and Coalitions in the United States* (New York and London: Macmillan & Co., 1896), xiii; GStA PK, VI. HA Nl. Schmoller, Nr. 126, fols. 22–23, Ernst Levy von Halle to Gustav Schmoller, Boston, April 6, 1894.

then to New York and Boston, this study absorbed most of von Halle's energies. In the process he was able not only to collect and synthesize an immense volume of literature but also interview many managing officials and legal representatives of various companies, bankers, stock exchange and trade union officials, politicians, and academics on the topic.[175]

An awareness of a marked trend toward concentration in many branches of American industry, such as Schumacher had observed in the grain trade, had already been awakened in the late 1870s. An official survey undertaken by the State of New York on abuses in the railway industry had revealed that the oil industry was concentrated in the hands of a small but powerful interest group, the Standard Oil Trust. By the late 1880s public concern had grown as a consequence of press reports that had revealed that such collusive behavior had spread to many other branches of the American economy beside railways and oil into agricultural commodities and raw materials. This included the sugar, salt, meat, milk, grain, livestock, iron, copper, lead, wood, and coal trades. This had in turn sparked a lively public debate about the threat posed by such "exploitative capitalists" to the freedom of the individual, the community, and American democratic government itself.[176]

While collusion, pools, and corners had existed in the past, the new concerns centered on trusts, which had the capacity to control the production of entire industries to an unprecedented degree through the New York stock exchange. That had led to additional investigations conducted by the State of New York and the US House of Representatives and the passage of the Interstate Commerce Act in 1887 and the first federal anti-trust legislation in 1890 as countermeasures.[177] Von Halle saw the trust issue bound up fundamentally with the creation of a comprehensive North American railway network, marked by the completion of the Canadian Pacific Railway in 1881, which had created a large coherent North American market. This had encouraged speculative investment and led to breakneck expansion, ruinous competition, spectacular bankruptcies, and in turn to ever-greater concentration and collusion. Trusts had emerged under these conditions as an improvement on pools by forging a permanent common interest through the legal instrument of trusteeship. The weak American regulatory-administrative state, rampant political corruption, the existence of multiple competing federal states with different legal statutes, and political controversy over the legality of such

---

[175] Ernst Levy von Halle, "Industrielle Unternehmer- und Unternehmungsverbände in den Vereinigten Staaten von Nordamerika," in *Über wirtschaftliche Kartelle in Deutschland und im Auslande: Fünfzehn Schilderungen nebst einer Anzahl Statuten und Beilagen*, ed. Ständiger Ausschuß des Vereins für Socialpoltik, SdVfS, vol. 60 (Leipzig: Duncker & Humblot, 1894), zweiter Teil [part two], 93–322, here 97–98.

[176] Ibid., 93–94.     [177] Ibid., 95–97, 108.

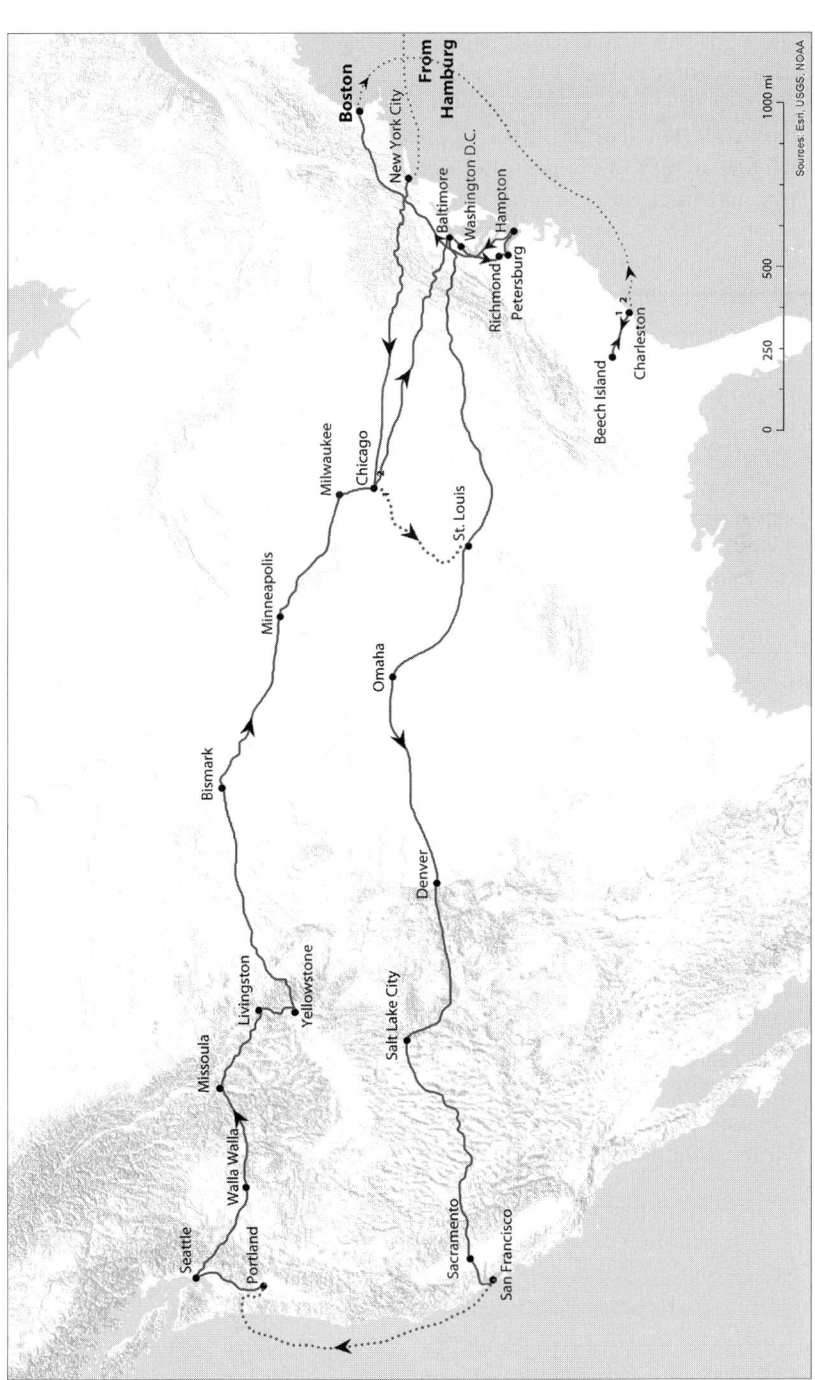

Map 1.2  Ernst von Halle's journey through the United States, ca. March 1893–ca. March 1894. This is not an exact route but a reconstruction based on known stops made and then existing railway and steamship lines.

combinations had enabled trusts to flourish and spread into many areas of the American economy.[178]

Von Halle believed that the anti-trust legislation prohibiting a wide range of business collusion drafted by some twenty states, five territories, and the federal government was largely an outgrowth of populist agitation and demagoguery and had created a legal mess that was difficult to enforce.[179] Some forms of collusive behavior that were subsequently deemed beneficial to prevent ruinous competition, such as railway pools, were re-legalized, while other forms of collusion, combination, and concentration in railways, rolling stock, insurance, docks, shipping, telegraphy, anthracite coal, coke, mining, and cotton seed oil prevailed successfully despite prohibitions. The McKinley tariff's protection and America's recurring panics and economic downturns had only served to further reinforce such collusion and concentration. That said, von Halle was well aware that concentration was also being driven by the technical and economic rationalization of production to achieve lower costs through scale economies.[180] Whether organized into formal trusts or not, the trend toward concentration and centralization in American business was a fact, had not been stopped by anti-trust measures, and had yet to reach its zenith.[181]

Von Halle was nevertheless optimistic that the American people would come to terms with this development and the social strife it entailed peacefully given their faith in progress and the advantageous circumstances of facing no external threats. As von Halle concluded, an observation of American conditions had persuaded him that Germany would only meet similar challenges peacefully by "purposeful corporative organization."[182] While he did not elaborate on it in his study, it was implicit that highly rationalized and concentrated American industrial enterprises shielded by the McKinley tariff might ultimately pose a major threat to much smaller German firms and more fragmented German industrial sectors.

Along with the concentration of industry in the United States, a recurring pattern of financial crises seemed to also plague the country. In 1893 both Schumacher and von Halle witnessed one of the most severe of such panics, one that resulted in a major stock market crash, widespread bankruptcy of railroad companies, and bank runs.[183] In 1894 von Halle would also observe the Pullman Railway Strike and Coxey's Army of unemployed men marching on Washington, part of a much wider series of strikes and episodes of labor

---

[178] Ibid., 107–30    [179] Ibid., 131–33, 181–82.
[180] Ibid., 139–47, 148–52, 153–54, 159–61, 163.    [181] Ibid., 197–98.
[182] Ibid., 199–200.
[183] See Douglas Steeples and David O. Whitten, *Democracy in Desperation: The Depression of 1893* (Westport, CT and London: Greenwood Press, 1998).

unrest that unfolded in 1894 in wake of the panic.[184] Von Halle would subject the Panic of 1893 to closer scrutiny and write an article about it for Schmoller's *Jahrbuch* published in the summer of 1894.[185] As von Halle observed, in recent years panics had broken out repeatedly – most recently in 1890 – following speculative booms. The severity of the depression that followed the 1893 panic left the unmistakable impression that the American colossus was prone to speculative excesses and regular financial crises that now had worldwide repercussions.

The panic was due to an unsavory mix of unsound US Treasury policies (attempting a bimetallic standard through silver purchases) arising from populist pressure, the lack of adequate regulation or uniform legislation, arbitrary economic policy driven by partisan interest and corrupt business elites, and the absence of either a professional civil service or a central bank with a uniform discounting policy.[186] American protectionism had meanwhile plunged many of the South American economies into turmoil.[187] Von Halle also openly worried about the more muscular assertions of the Monroe Doctrine and plans for a Panamerican union being discussed in the United States at the time, which he saw along with the McKinley tariff as deliberately anti-European measures.[188] On account of the United States' growing economic and financial weight, these developments were beginning to negatively affect the world economy. American financial instability and rising protectionism were thus seen as real emerging risks attending Germany's globalization.

After completing his study on trusts and the American economic crisis in the spring of 1894, von Halle shifted his attention to American cotton in the hopes of using the resulting study as a *Habilitation* thesis when he returned to Germany.[189] By the early 1890s the German cotton industry had grown into one of Europe's largest and would by 1900 be the third largest in the world after that of Great Britain and the United States, employing no fewer than one in eight industrial workers by 1913.[190] All of Germany's raw cotton came from abroad, making it far and away the costliest raw material to import and the German cotton industry the most susceptible to overseas disruptions in supply, as the cotton famine during the American Civil War had shown most painfully. This highlighted another fact: the lion's share of the world's raw cotton was produced in the United States. While the acquisition of a German overseas colonial empire had been stimulated in part by the desire to

---

[184] See Foner, *The Labor Movement*, vol. 2, 235–26.
[185] Ernst von Halle, "Die Wirtschaftliche Krisis des Jahres 1893 in den Vereinigten Staaten von Nordamerika," *JbfGVV* 18 (1894): 1181–249.
[186] Ibid., 1197, 1206–7, 1209, 1240–49.     [187] Ibid., 1185–86.     [188] Ibid., 1183–84.
[189] GStA PK, VI. HA Nl. Schmoller, Nr. 126, fols. 18–19, Ernst von Halle to Gustav Schmoller, Boston, June 12, 1894.
[190] Beckert, *Empire of Cotton*, 355.

gain some cotton "autonomy" – and though high hopes had been invested in colonial cotton cultivation, notably in German East Africa – these had by 1893 proven very disappointing.[191] Fears were also growing that the United States lacked the cheap labor needed to cultivate and process this incredibly labor-intensive commodity. Indeed, the world price of cotton was rising in the 1890s and would in fact no less than double between 1898 and 1904, further stoking these fears. A *Baumwollkulturkampf* (the struggle to cultivate cotton) had thus emerged which prompted German manufacturers to create and fund the Kolonial-Wirtschaftliches Komitee (Colonial Economic Committee) in 1896.[192]

Von Halle's interest in cotton must be set in this context. While his intention was originally to write an economic history of the southern states – a much neglected topic, he noted – von Halle soon realized that cotton was the ideal lens through which to take an historical view of the South's economic development.[193] In January and February 1894 von Halle began the preparatory work in libraries and government agencies in Baltimore and Washington, DC for an extensive direct investigation of the economy of the South. At the end of February he started the first leg of his investigative journey, passing through the tobacco cultivating areas of Virginia via Richmond and Petersburg – and then after a return to Boston – continued his investigations to Charleston, South Carolina in late April 1894. He spent the rest of the spring and summer of 1894 in Boston and New York libraries, deepening his study of the literature on the subject and attending William Ashley's lectures on economic history at Harvard.[194] In September he returned to the South to continue his investigations embarking on an extensive three-month journey into the cotton belt, passing through North and South Carolina, Georgia, Alabama, Mississippi, Louisiana, Texas, Arkansas, Tennessee, and Missouri, completing his journey shortly before Christmas 1894.[195]

On the basis of these travels and his exhaustive analysis of the literature and available statistics, von Halle came to better understand the dramatic expansion of cotton cultivation into the new, open lands of the Deep South, with

---

[191] Ibid.
[192] Ibid., 356. See also Beckert, "From Tuskegee to Togo," 498–526; George A. Schmidt, *Das Kolonial-Wirtschaftliche Komitee: Ein Rückblick auf seine Entstehung und seine Arbeiten aus Anlass des Gedenkjahres 50-Jähriger deutscher Kolonialarbeit* (Berlin: Kolonial-Wirtschaftliches Komitee, 1934).
[193] Ernst von Halle, *Baumwollproduktion und Pflanzungswirtschaft in den Nordamerikanischen Südstaaten*, vol. 1: Die Sklavenzeit (Leipzig: Duncker & Humblot, 1897), xviii, ix.
[194] Ibid., ix, xiv–xv; GStA PK, VI. HA Nl. Schmoller, Nr. 126, fols. 22–23, Ernst Levy von Halle to Gustav Schmoller, Boston, April 6, 1894; fols. 18–19, Ernst von Halle to Gustav Schmoller, Boston, June 12, 1894.
[195] von Halle, *Baumwollproduktion*, vol. 1, ix; GStA PK, VI. HA Nl. Schmoller, Nr. 126, fols. 15–17, Ernst von Halle to Gustav Schmoller, Savannah, GA, Oct. 22, 1894.

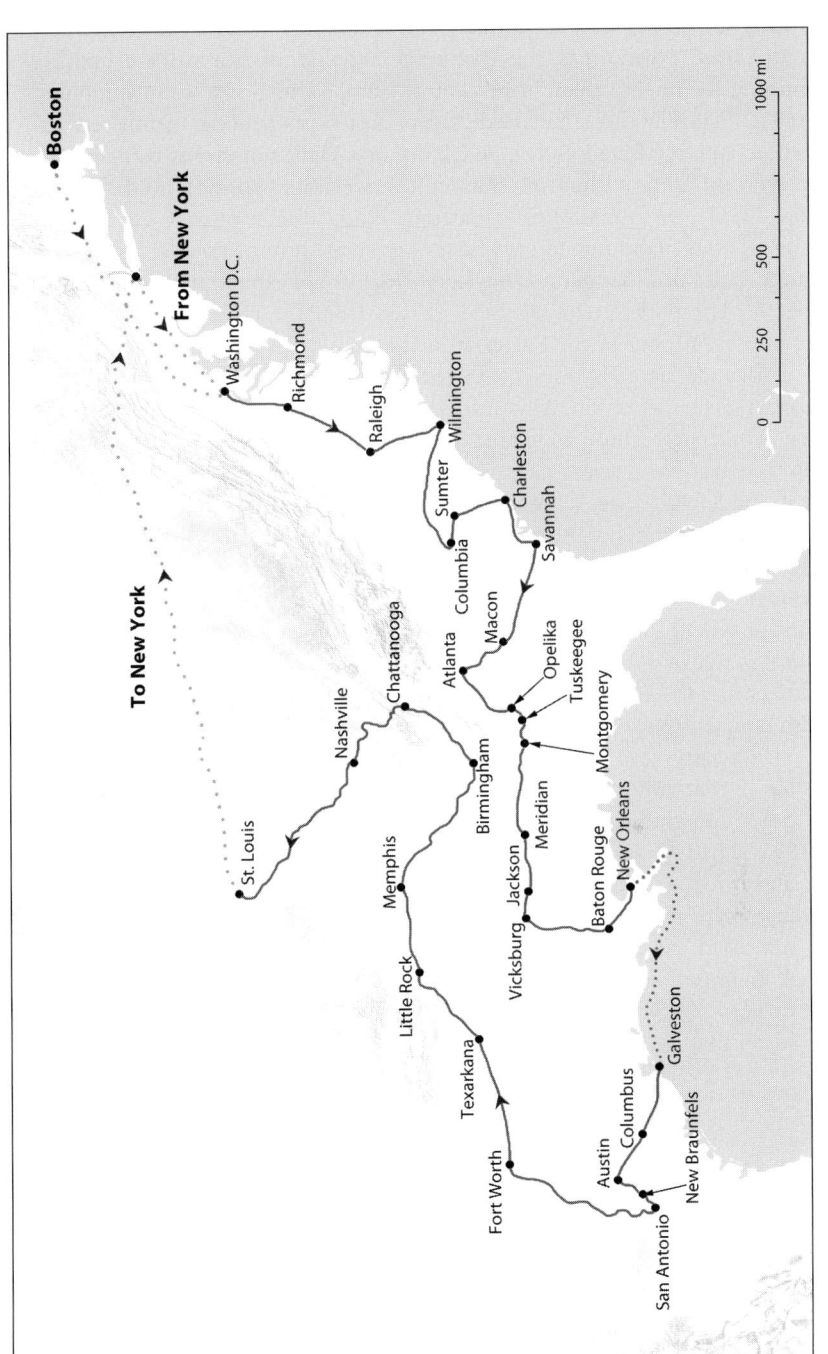

**Map 1.3** Ernst von Halle's journey through the American South, Sept. 3, 1894–Dec. 23, 1894. This is not an exact route but a reconstruction based on known stops made and then existing railway and steamship lines.

their ideal soil and climate for cotton growing and how that had cemented the United States' position as the dominant supplier of the world's cotton, accounting for no less than 74 percent of Europe's total raw cotton imports by 1891.[196] While there had been some success expanding cotton output elsewhere, notably Brazil, Egypt, and India, von Halle noted that these places offered no challenge to the United States' overwhelming position in worldwide cotton supply on account of competing crops like sugarcane or limited additional arable land due to population pressures. It remained yet to be seen whether Africa or other parts of South America could expand their raw cotton output.[197] The parallel emergence of cotton from the most insignificant to most important fiber in the European textile industry and the almost unlimited worldwide demand for cotton textiles had thus created a dangerous industrial dependence on American cotton.[198] What is more, the United States, while increasing production quite robustly since the collapse of the 1860s, was using a growing proportion of its own crop domestically, particularly in the South, where a cotton industry was developing.[199] In light of von Halle's earlier analysis of the processes of rationalization and concentration in many other areas of the American economy, it was not hard to draw the conclusion that it might only be a matter of time before Germany and the rest of Europe would be at the mercy of an American cotton trust. Indeed, just a few years later in 1903 William Perry Brown and his financial backers managed to corner the US cotton market, causing great hardship for the American, British, and European cotton industry.[200]

Over a twenty-year period, the entanglement with the United States made possible by Farnam, and deepened by Sering, Schumacher, and von Halle, had forged and gradually transformed the German image of the United States. By 1895 it had become both an important reference point and a potential rival and threat in a still emerging German *Weltpolitik*. The other important reference point in this proto-*Weltpolitik* was Japan. Indeed, the perception of an "American peril" (*amerikanische Gefahr*) in the Western Hemisphere served in important respects as a template for the later construction of a "yellow peril" (*gelbe Gefahr*) centered on China and Japan in East Asia.[201] It is to Japan that we now turn.

---

[196] von Halle, *Baumwollproduktion*, vol. 1, 182.   [197] Ibid., 173–80, 183.
[198] Ibid., 183.
[199] Ibid., Produktion und Konsumption von Baumwolle in Ballen [chart 1790–1895], 156–57, 182.
[200] See Bruce E. Baker and Barbara Hahn, *The Cotton Kings: Capitalism and Corruption in Turn-of-the-Century New York and New Orleans* (New York: Oxford University Press, 2016), 55–60.
[201] Mehnert, "Gelbe Gefahr," 42.

# 2

# Island Empire

## Japan

### Prussians in Edo

Germans played an extraordinary role in the modernization of Japan, and their connections to that country would shape German perceptions of East Asia and the basic contours of *Weltpolitik* in lasting ways. Nevertheless German-Japanese contacts since the opening of Japan in the early 1850s gave few signs of the "special relationship" that would develop between the two nations in the 1880s and the extraordinary influence that Germany would come to enjoy in the archipelago. After the end of the Tokugawa shogun's policy of managed foreign relations (*sakoku*) through the expeditions of Commodore Perry from 1853 to 1854, there was growing interest among a number of states of the German Confederation in a treaty to regulate diplomatic and trade relations with Japan, China, and other East Asian countries. This culminated in the Prussian naval expedition of Friedrich zu Eulenburg (1815–81) on behalf of Prussia, the German Customs Union, and the Hanseatic states to Japan, China, and Siam in 1860–62.[1]

Beyond trade relations, Prussia's ambitions were much in the pattern of the gunboat diplomacy of the time and included hopes for acquiring naval bases, treaty ports, and overseas colonies.[2] Initially Prussian eyes fell on Formosa, the Tokara chain, the Gōtō and Ryuku Islands, and then later Hokkaido. A small fleet of four Prussian warships (a corvette, a frigate, a schooner, and a transport ship) were sent off in March 1860 and finally reached Japan in September after a rendezvous in Singapore in August, losing the schooner *Frauenlob* with all hands in a ferocious typhoon along the way.[3] Once in Edo, difficult negotiations with the shogun stretched out for months, eventually

---

[1] See Bradley Naranch, "Made in China: Austro-Prussian Overseas Rivalry and the Global Unification of the German Nation," *Australian Journal of Politics and History* 56, no. 3 (2010): 366–80.

[2] Kreiner, *Deutschland-Japan*, 42.

[3] Anon., *Die preussische Expedition nach Ost-Asien nach amtlichen Quellen*, vol. 1 (Berlin: Verlag der Königlichen Geheimen Ober-Hofbuchdruckerei [R. v. Decker], 1864), vii–xvii, 190–256. On the loss of the *Frauenlob*, vol. 1, xvi–xvii, 191, 242, 253; vol. 2 (1866), 102; vol. 4 (1873), 93, 97.

resulting in a commercial treaty going into effect in 1861, but only with Prussia – their Japanese counterparts had a difficult time making much sense of the tangled politics of the other German states.[4]

As a result of the treaty with Prussia, the military attaché of the Eulenburg expedition, Max von Brandt (1835–1920), became Prussian consul in Yokohama. During the chaos of the Boshin War in 1868 between the Tokugawa shogun and the forces of the Meiji emperor, von Brandt became an energetic advocate of seizing Hokkaido, but these and other colonial dreams were dashed when the Meiji emperor's forces prevailed in 1869.[5] Thereafter a much more promising and practical avenue appeared in exploiting Japan's economic potential, not only to secure an export market for German goods, but also to discover the manufacturing secrets of the much-valued Japanese luxury exports in order to aid Prussian and other German firms.

In 1872 von Brandt, now Prussian and German resident minister in Japan, recommended that Prussian Minister of Trade Heinrich Achenbach (1829–99) send an expert to Japan to discover the advantages of Japanese craftsmanship and industry and then make these techniques available to Germans.[6] Thereupon the much-traveled Hessian geographer and naturalist Johannes Justus Rein was brought into service by the Prussian Ministries of Trade and Culture and sent to Japan, where he spent the years 1873–75. With the aid of von Brandt, Rein managed to travel into the deepest reaches of Japan's interior, into areas that had never before been visited by Europeans, exploring and studying not only Japanese craft and industry, but also the land, people, flora, and fauna of these regions in encyclopedic detail. During his time in Japan, Rein was an active member of the Deutsche Gesellschaft für Natur- und Völkerkunde Ostasiens (German Society for the Study of the Nature and Peoples of East Asia, commonly known as the East Asiatic Society) founded on von Brandt's initiative by German scholars and merchants in 1873, and Rein published his first essays on Japan in its bulletin.[7]

These activities heightened existing Japanese interest in German scholarship that had begun in Tokugawa times due to the translation of German medical texts and contact with German physicians and naturalists in Dutch service in Deshima near Nagasaki, particularly Engelbert Kaempfer and Philipp Franz

---

[4] See Holmer Stahncke, *Die diplomatischen Beziehungen zwischen Deutschland und Japan 1854–1868* (Stuttgart: Franz Steiner, 1987), chs. 6 & 7.

[5] Kreiner, *Deutschland-Japan*, 46.   [6] Koch and Conrad, *Johannes Justus Rein*, 28–29.

[7] Ibid., 58. Dr. J. J. Rein, "Naturwissenschaftliche Reisestudien in Japan – Nikko," *MOAG* 1 (1873–1876), Heft 6: 60–61 and *MOAG* I (1873–1876), Heft 7: 21–26; Rein, "Naturwissenschaftliche Reisestudien in Japan – Die Kueste von Sendai und Nambu," *MOAG* 1 (1873–1876), Heft 7: 26–29. See also Christian W. Spang, "Anmerkungen zur frühen OAG-Geschichte bis zur Eintragung als 'japanischer Verein' (1904)" *MOAG* 179–80 (2006): 67–91.

von Siebold.[8] The two-volume work that Rein later published on Japan after his return to Germany, *Japan nach Reisen und Studien* (1881–86), was quickly recognized as one of the most important works on Japan in existence and translated into English before the publication of the second volume in 1884.[9] Rein's work was particularly influential in establishing an ethnographic register for German encounters with the Japanese in the 1880s, which while still burdened with the conventions of European Sinophobia, also presented the Japanese in flattering terms as a clean, frugal, modest, stoic, and disciplined people of steady habits and high cultivation, who loved flowers and gardens.[10] This was an image with which Germans, and Prussians in particular, could more easily identify and with which they were primed through Rein's work in their first encounters with the Japanese.

Beyond the scientific and ethnographic significance of Rein's work, Rein's activity in Japan should not be overlooked as an act of economic reconnaissance for access to Japan with distinctly mercantilist and imperial overtones. The many samples of raw materials and products made of bronze, iron, enamel, ceramic, copper, lacquer, leather, paper, and silk which Rein collected in Japanese workshops and sent to Berlin along with his extensive accompanying reports were received with much enthusiasm by the Prussian Ministry of Trade and later put on official display. In a direct petition by Minister Achenbach to Kaiser Wilhelm I to bestow the Order of the Red Eagle on Rein for his services to Germany, he noted that Rein's journey had led to "recognition by members of foreign nations that the German government had done more for the scientific and industrial exploration of the country than any other."[11]

Given what turned out to be very constrained opportunities for German colonial expansion in Asia and the Pacific in the 1870s and 1880s, Imperial Germany made a considerable investment to attain intellectual prominence in Japan and thus to keep the door open for German influence in East Asia. It would do so by building on foundations grounded in *Wissenschaft*, for

---

[8] Franz, "Deutsche Mediziner in Japan," 31–56.
[9] Johannes Justus Rein, *Japan nach Reisen und Studien im Auftrage der königlich preussischen Regierung dargestellt*, vol. 1: *Natur und Volk des Mikadoreiches* (Leipzig: Wilhelm Engelmann, 1881); Rein, *Travels and Researches Undertaken at the cost of the Prussian Government* (New York: A. C. Armstrong and Son, 1884). See also Koch and Conrad, *Johannes Justus Rein*, 40.
[10] See Rein, *Japan nach Reisen und Studien*, vol. 1, 483, 485, 486, 494, 498, 501, 508–11, 529–35; cf. Steinmetz, *The Devil's Handwriting*, 384–416.
[11] GStA PK, I. HA Rep. 89 Geheimes Zivilkabinett, jüngere Periode, Nr. 13369, fols. 30–32, Achenbach to his Imperial and Royal Majesty, Berlin, March 21, 1876; Johannes Justus Rein, *Japan nach Reisen und Studien im Auftrage der königlich preussischen Regierung dargestellt*, vol. 2: *Land- und Forstwirtschaft, Industrie und Handel* (Leipzig: Wilhelm Engelmann, 1886).

which the OAG was an important Japanese beachhead.[12] Indeed, it is no exaggeration to see this as the very beginning of German *Weltpolitik*. Karl Rathgen would be part of a large cohort of German scholars and advisors who made their way to Japan in the early 1880s and who would help turn this into Meiji Japan's "German decade." The Japanese government had by that point identified Germany as offering the highest degree of worldwide expertise in a whole range of arts and sciences including astronomy, botany, chemistry, geology, medicine, pharmacology, physics, political science, and economics.[13] According to one estimate, no fewer than 70 of these German *oyatoi-gaikokujin* (foreign advisors and teachers) were working in Japan by 1888.[14]

### The Meiji Six Society and "German Studies"

Many processes conspired to give the Germans, who were among the most unlikely candidates for influence in Japan, unusual opportunities in the late 1870s. In the minds of the samurai oligarchy that had restored imperial rule in 1868, the violation of Japanese sovereignty imposed by the unequal treaties negotiated with the Western powers and the ongoing threat of colonization made a Western-style defensive modernization urgent. The vehicle for the spread of Western thought throughout Japan in these years were scholars, societies, and journals associated with the *bunmei-kaika* (civilization and enlightenment) movement, which in its early guise meant systematically eradicating Japanese institutions and the wholesale embrace of British, French, or American educational, legal, administrative, political, social, and economic models.[15] The outstanding proponents of such a pattern of Westernization were samurai associated with the *meirokusha* (the Meiji Six Society, named after the year it was founded, year six of the Meiji era [1874]) and its journal, the *Meiroku Zasshi*. Among them were Fukuzawa Yukichi (1835–1901), Mori Arinori (1847–89), Nakamura Masanao (1832–91), and Nishi Amane (1829–97). Younger proponents of *bunmei-kaika* included the liberal economist Taguchi Ukichi (1857–1905, founder of the *Tokyo Keizei Zasshi* modeled on the London *Economist*) and Tokutomi Sohō (1863–1957).

---

[12] For example, Albrecht Wernich, "Ueber einige Formen nervoeser Stoerungen bei den Japanern," *MOAG* 1 (1873–76), Heft 10: 16–19.

[13] Scott L. Montgomery, *Science in Translation: Movements of Knowledge through Cultures and Time* (Chicago: University of Chicago Press, 2000), 220–21.

[14] Bernd Martin, *Japan and Germany in the Modern World* (Providence and Oxford: Berghahn Books, 1995), 44.

[15] Hirakawa Sukehiro, "Japan's Turn to the West," in *The Cambridge History of Japan*, vol. 5, ed. Marius B. Jansen, 432–98; D. Eleanor Westney, *Imitation and Innovation: The Transfer of Western Organizational Patterns to Meiji Japan* (Cambridge, MA: Harvard University Press, 1987).

While hardly a uniform group of thinkers, the *meirokusha* identified with English liberal thought, drawing particularly radical implications from it and advocating extreme forms of individualism, materialism, utilitarian ethics, *laissez-faire*, and hostility to government. As the pages of the *Meiroku Zasshi* reveal, a number of those associated with this movement went so far as to advocate radical reform or abandonment of such things as Japanese familial patterns, religion, and language.[16] More often, this mid-century British liberal thought was rendered into familiar Confucian terms and modified to suit Japanese perceptions and conditions (Henry Buckle's *History of Civilization* [1857–61], Samuel Smiles' *Self Help* [1859] Herbert Spencer's *Social Statics* [1851] and John Stuart Mill's *On Liberty* were particularly popular in translation).[17]

By the late 1870s, however, there were growing signs of a backlash to this radical program of Westernization among the Meiji oligarchy and even by prominent members of the *meirokusha* itself, such as Nishi Amane.[18] American teachers and advisors working in Japan at the time, such as Ernest Fenollosa (1853–1908) and David Murray (1830–1905), were encouraging a more critical stance to things Western in general, particularly to English and American models in education. Murray, who was retained by the Meiji government as superintendent of education to advise on school reform, was a persistent proponent of a German-style compulsory education system with centralized, national administration and equality of educational opportunity.[19] Indeed, around this very time German pedagogical models were ascending in the United States.[20] As was discussed in Chapter 1, this was especially the case

---

[16] William Reynolds Braisted, ed., *Meiroku Zasshi: Journal of the Japanese Enlightenment* (Cambridge, MA: Harvard University Press, 1976); Chuhei Sugiyama, *Origins of Economic Thought in Modern Japan* (London: Routledge, 1994), 1–11, 40–63, 85–97; Nagai Michio, *Higher Education in Japan: Its Take-off and Crash*, trans. Jerry Dusenbury (Tokyo: University of Tokyo Press, 1971), 166–96.

[17] Earl H. Kinmonth, *The Self-Made Man in Meiji Japanese Thought: From Samurai to Salary Man* (Berkeley: University of California Press, 1981), 9–43; Douglas R. Howland, *Translating the West: Language and Political Reason in Nineteenth-Century Japan* (Honolulu: University of Hawaii Press, 2002), 31–60.

[18] See Kenneth B. Pyle, *The New Generation in Meiji Japan: Problems of Cultural Identity, 1885–1895* (Stanford: Stanford University Press, 1969), 23–98; Pyle, "Meiji Conservatism," in Jansen, *The Cambridge History of Japan*, vol. 5, 674–720, 676–720.

[19] Kaneko Tadashi, "Contributions of David Murray to the Modernization of School Administration in Japan," in Burks, *The Modernizers*, 301–21, here 313–18; Makoto Asō and Ikuo Amano, *Education and Japan's Modernization* (n.p. [Tokyo]: Ministry of Foreign Affairs, 1972), 19–41.

[20] See esp. Karl-Heinz Günther, "Interdependence between Democratic Pedagogy in Germany and the Development of Education in the United States in the Nineteenth Century," in *German Influences on Education in the United States to 1917*, ed. Henry Geitz, Jürgen Heideking, and Jurgen Herbst (Washington, DC: German Historical Institute; Cambridge: Cambridge University Press, 1995), 43–56.

in higher education, as revealed by the large number of Americans in German universities. In medicine, for example, the Dutch-American Guido Verbeck (1830–98), one of the earliest advisors to the Meiji government, recommended following German models given the worldwide prestige of German medical research at the time. The work of two German military doctors who entered Japanese service in 1872 through Max von Brandt's mediation, Leopold Müller (1822–93) and Theodor Eduard Hoffmann (1837–94), then assured the dominance of German medical training and medical terminology in Japan by the late 1870s.[21] This was later reinforced by the German Naval Hospital (Deutsches Marinehospital) in Yokohama, which while mainly treating foreign patients, was in operation between 1877 and 1911 and served as an important conduit for the spread of German medical expertise in Japan.[22]

Thus from early on, command of the German language became an indispensable prerequisite for the study of medicine in the medical school in Tokyo, and language instructors were brought from Germany to staff its attached language school. Among these was the Berlin linguist Rudolf Lange (1850–1933) who began teaching German and Latin at the medical school in 1874. Lange mastered spoken and written Japanese and later returned to Germany publishing Japanese language textbooks and becoming one of the founders of Japanology at the Berlin Seminar for Oriental Languages.[23] The medical school and its attached language school formed the core of what would develop into Tokyo University in 1877.

There were also political reasons that drew Japan closer to German models. Over the course of the 1870s, a "Freedom and People's Rights" movement (*jiyū minken undō*) grew out of *bunmei-kaika*. This national political movement, through the new Liberal Party (*jiyūtō*, formed in 1880), put pressure on the imperial ministries and court to create representative political institutions. This, along with inflation, a squeeze on government finances, and scandal over plans to sell government assets pressed finance minister Ōkuma Shigenobu (1838–1922), a partisan of Anglo-American liberal thought, to propose a constitution modeled on Britain. Under the sway of his secretary, Inoue Kowashi (1844–95), Itō Hirobumi (1841–1909), and others from the Satsuma-Chōshu samurai clans, who advocated a form of modernization

---

[21] See Hermann Heinrich Vianden, *Die Einführung der deutschen Medizin in Japan in der Meiji-Zeit* (Düssledorf: Triltsch, 1985); Yoshio Mishima, "The Dawn of Surgery in Japan, with Special Reference to the German Society for Surgery,"*Surgery Today* 36 (2006): 395–402.

[22] Berthold J. Sander-Nagashima, "Naval Relations Between Japan and Germany from the Late Nineteenth Century until the end of World War II," in *Japanese German Relations, 1895–1945: War Diplomacy and Public Opinion*, ed. Christian W. Spang and Rolf-Harald Wippich (London and New York: Routledge, 2006), 40–41.

[23] BArch L, R 901/39187, excerpted transcription to UI. 2614 of a memorandum by W. Dönitz on the University of Tokyo, n.d.

which was less expressly "Western" and more Japanese, the emperor was pressed to force Ōkuma out of office in 1881 and give an imperial rescript that promised a constitution and the opening of a national parliament in 1890. Inoue and Itō were drawn to German constitutional models and to the German system of education, and it is notable that the fifth item of a new policy declared in November 1881 encouraged the study of German to overcome the dominance of French and English thought and thereby to create more "conservative-minded men."[24]

By the early 1880s a marked turn away from the French model in military training and organization toward Germany was also underway. French advisors, French military drill and organization, and an officer school modeled on the École spéciale militaire in Saint-Cyr had given Japan's military a strongly French orientation, but with France's defeat by Prussia and the smaller German states and as more and more young Japanese officers went to Germany for their studies or served as military attachés and aids in the Japanese diplomatic mission in Germany, a German orientation began to compete in the army, reinforced by negative impressions of French military instructors, who compared unfavorably with their German counterparts in terms of discipline and professionalism.[25] This reorientation toward the German military was due in no small measure to the strong influence of War Minister Yamagata Aritomo (1838–1922) and Katsura Taro (1848–1913), the latter himself also later war minister in successive Meiji cabinets and then prime minister.[26] That Katsura ended up in Germany was itself pure happenstance. He had originally learned French and was slated to receive his military education in France, but when he arrived in London in 1870, Paris was under siege by the Prussians. He thus opted to go to Berlin and received his military education there instead from 1870 to 1873, later deepening his knowledge of the German military while serving as Japanese military attaché in Berlin from 1875 to 1878, even attending political economy and law lectures at the University of Berlin in those years.[27]

Despite entrenched opposition from his French-oriented colleagues, on his return to Japan in 1878 Katsura made the case for major military reforms along Prussian lines following the poor performance of the army during its expedition to Formosa and in samurai revolts. With the support of Yamagata,

---

[24] Hirakawa Sukehiro, "Japan's Turn to the West," in Jansen, *The Cambridge History of Japan*, vol. 5, 494.

[25] See Sven Saaler, "The Imperial German Army and Germany," in *Japanese-German Relations, 1895–1945: War Diplomacy and Public Opinion*, ed. Christian W. Spang and Rolf-Harald Wippich (London and New York: Routledge, 2006), 21–39, here 23–24.

[26] On Yamgata Aritomo, see Roger F. Hackett, *Yamagata Aritomo and the Rise of Modern Japan, 1838–1922* (Cambridge, MA: Harvard University Press, 1971).

[27] Stewart Lone, *Army, Empire and Politics in Meiji Japan: The Three Careers of Katsura Tarō* (Basingstoke, Hamps. and London: Macmillan, 2000), 9–14.

he successfully pushed through the formation of a Prussian-inspired general staff with full control over military operations and under the direct command of the emperor in 1878.[28] Katsura proposed and then served as aid on the one-year Japanese military mission led by General Ōyama Iwao (1842-1916) to Europe in 1884 and 1885, which spent most of its time in Germany. In the 1880s and early 1890s Katsura would then lead major military reforms that gave the Japanese army an unmistakably German shape, such as the founding of the Army War College (*rikugun daigakkō*) on the model of the Prussian *Kriegsakademie* (War Academy) in 1882, the hiring of the first German military instructor in 1884 (Major Klemens Meckel [1842-1905]), the reorganization of the standing army along divisional lines in 1888, and new drill regulations in 1891, all closely following German blueprints.[29] In 1886 Hermann von Blankenburg was sent to Japan as a military advisor, followed by Erich von Wildenbruch in 1888, and then Alexander von Grutschreiber in 1891.[30]

In the early 1880s Katsura was part of an entire cohort of influential Japanese men who knew German or had studied in Germany and were trying to foster the study of the German language and spread knowledge of German scholarship in Japan. This group was led by Katsura and Yamagata, but also included Aoki Shūzō (1844-1914), Katō Hiroyuki (1836-1916), Nishi Amane (previously mentioned), and Yajirō Shinagawa (1843-1900), who together founded the *doitsugaku kyōkai* (Verein für deutsche Wissenschaft; Association for German Scholarship) for that purpose in 1881.[31] A prodigious effort was made by the association to translate German economic and legal texts, among them the existing volumes of Wilhelm Roscher's (1817-94) *System der Volkswirtschaft* (5 vols. [1854-94]) and Friedrich List's *Das nationale System der politischen Ökonomie* (1841). The acute financial and monetary problems of the Meiji government at the time also led to the translation and publication of numerous German and Austrian texts on public finance, among them those of Adolph Wagner, Lorenz von Stein (1815-90), and Rudolf von Gneist.[32] The German orientation of the government was then underscored

---

[28] Ibid., 10-16.
[29] Saaler, "The Imperial German Army," 24; Lone, *Army Empire and Politics*, 18-19.
[30] Sven Saaler, "Das Deutschlandbild in Japans Politik und Gesellschaft 1890-1914," in *Das Deutsche Kaiserreich 1890-1914*, ed. Bernd Heidenreich and Söhnke Neitzel (Paderborn, Munich, Vienna, and Zurich: Ferdinand Schöningh, 2011), 285-302, here 291.
[31] Yanagisawa Osamu, "Das Übersetzen von deutscher wirtschaftswissenschaftlicher Literatur vor dem Zweiten Weltkrieg in Japan," in *Übersetzen, verstehen, Brücken bauen. Geisteswissenschaftliches und literarisches Übersetzen im internationalen Kulturaustausch*, ed. Paul Armin Frank et al., (Berlin: Erich Schmidt, 1993), 393-404, here 395; William G. Beasley, *Japan Encounters the Barbarian: Japanese Travelers in America and Europe* (New Haven: Yale University Press, 1995).
[32] Yanagisawa ,"Das Übersetzen," 396.

by Itō Hirobumi's visit to Germany and Austria from 1882 to 1883, during which time he engaged in discussions with Rudolf von Gneist in Berlin and Lorenz von Stein in Vienna on constitutional matters.[33] It was in fact on Gneist and Schmoller's recommendation to Aoki Shūzō, then Japanese envoy in Berlin, that Karl Rathgen was chosen for a professorship of law and political economy at Tokyo University.[34]

### From Strasbourg to Tokyo – Karl Rathgen in Japan

Shortly after signing his contract with Aoki Shūzō in Berlin in early February 1882, Rathgen began the long journey from Strasbourg to Tokyo via Munich, Bologna, and Brindisi, and from there aboard the P & O steamer *Tanjore* to Alexandria, arriving in Egypt on February 16th.[35] He then continued the next day by rail to Cairo, where he stayed until February 26th, undertaking numerous excursions with local German consular contacts to various points of interest in and outside the city, including the Citadelle, Bulaq, the pyramids and sphinx of Giza, Memphis, Bedrashan, and the necropolis of Saqqara.[36] He continued on to Suez where he boarded the French steamer *Shagalien* on February 28th for the journey through the Red Sea, Gulf of Aden, and Indian Ocean.[37]

The journey passed Mocha to Aden, where coal was taken on for the journey through the Gulf of Aden to the Indian Ocean, then passed the Somali coast on to Ceylon, whose distant mountains were visible on March 12th.[38] Since the ship was delayed, only a short excursion was possible in Colombo, whose exotic heat and humidity as well as lush tropical vegetation Rathgen was

---

[33] On Itō's study of constitutions in Berlin and Vienna, see the now definitive study by Junko Ando, *Die Entstehung der Meiji-Verfassung: Zur Rolle des deutschen Konstitutionalismus im modernen japanischen Staatswesen* (Munich: Iudicium, 2000), 59–75; Takii Kazuhiro, *The Meiji Constitution: The Japanese Experience of the West and the Shaping of the Modern State*, trans. David Noble (Tokyo: International House of Japan, 2007). Also very useful but based only on German sources is Paul Christian Schenck, *Der deutsche Anteil an der Gestaltung des modernen japanischen Rechts- und Verwaltungswesens: Deutsche Rechtsberater im Japan der Meiji-Zeit* (Stuttgart: Franz Steiner, 1997), 143–64.

[34] Toshiro Nozaki, "Karl Rathgen in Japan (1882–1890)," in *Karl Rathgen (1856–1921) Nationalökonom und Gründungsrektor der Universität Hamburg: Reden, gehalten beim akademischen Festakt zum 150. Geburtstag, 24. Januar 2007* (Hamburg: Universität Hamburg, Fakultät Wirtschafts- und Sozialwissenschaften, 2009), 19–31, here 21–22.

[35] PNFBW, Karl Rathgen to Bernhard Rathgen et al., on board the Tanjore, Feb. 13, 1882; Karl Rathgen to Bernhard Rathgen et al., on board the Tanjore, Feb. 15, 1882.

[36] PNFBW, Karl Rathgen to Bernhard Rathgen et al., Cairo, Feb. 17, 1882; Karl Rathgen to Bernhard Rathgen et al., Cairo, Feb. 20, 1882 [with insertions from Feb. 21–26, 1882].

[37] PNFBW, Karl Rathgen to Bernhard Rathgen et al., on board the Shagalien between 16° and 17° N latitude, March 3, 1882 [with insertions from March 4, 1882].

[38] Ibid.

**Figure 2.1** Karl Rathgen, May 1890.

at a loss to describe.[39] Coal was loaded at Point de Galle for the journey past Sumatra on to Singapore. Singapore was reached on March 20th where many passengers of the ship departed for other ships destined for Sumatra, Java, and the Philippines.[40] The next day the journey continued aboard the *Shagalien* to French Indochina and north along the Mekong delta on to Saigon, arriving in the city early on March 23rd.[41] In Saigon Rathgen noted how pleased he was to see a German steam ship on his journey for the first time. He also observed that beside many soldiers there were very few French in the city. Until 1870 Saigon's rice trade had been in German hands exclusively. Even after being driven out by the French after the war of 1870–71 it was still mainly in German hands, though he noted now subject to increased competition from the Chinese. The next day Rathgen made excursions to the zoo and the garden

---

[39] PNFBW, Karl Rathgen to Bernhard Rathgen et al., on board the Shagalien in the Straits of Malacca, March 19, 1882.
[40] PNFBW, Karl Rathgen to Bernhard Rathgen et al., on board the Shagalien on the coast of Cambodia, March 21, 1882.
[41] PNFBW, Karl Rathgen to Bernhard Rathgen et al., on board the Shagalien in Nashan, March 27, 1882.

of the governor's palace, noting in letters to his siblings how acclimatized he looked in his white linen suit, white shoes, and pith helmet.[42]

The journey continued early the next morning on to Hong Kong, which was reached after a passage through high wind and seas on March 27th. Here the *Shagalien* had to take on repairs in dock.[43] Rathgen was thus forced to change ships in order to continue on to Yokohama in reasonable time. In Hong Kong Rathgen took a room in the Hong Kong Hotel and visited the Bremen merchants of Melchers & Co., where he was warmly received by Herr Reiners, the local director. With Reiners' introduction Rathgen and his German travel companion, Hirth, were welcomed into the German Club. Rathgen's main impression was of the endless drinking of cocktails – "hellish brew, American invention" – and the Anglicized habits and language of the German merchants in Hong Kong, who worked in an "office" rather than in a *Geschäft*.[44]

While in Hong Kong, Rathgen and Hirth visited the German vice-consul and linguist Paul von Möllendorff (1847–1901), with whom they lunched and then toured the city in sedan chairs, returning for dinner in the German Club, where Rathgen met many men of "colonial significance."[45] Groggy from the many toasts that evening in the club, Rathgen's journey continued the next morning, March 29th, on the *Menzalek*. This smaller ship had fewer passengers – Rathgen, the Japanese passengers from the *Shagalien*, and a French captain of a cannon boat anchored in Yokohama.[46] The journey passed through very heavy seas along the southern coast of China past northern Formosa and then on into the open ocean with its massive waves, which Rathgen watched crashing on the ship and which induced terrible seasickness among the passengers.[47] The first Japanese islands came into view April 2nd despite heavy rain, finally clearing up April 4th as Rathgen entered Tokyo Bay toward Yokohama. Glad to be back on land after a rough passage, Rathgen spent the first night in the Grand Hotel in Yokohama, proceeding the next day to present himself to the president of the Tokyo University, Katō Hiroyuki, and the German consul, Carl Eduard Zappe (d. 1888).[48] Katō, one of the first in Japan to learn German, originally mastered the language in order to be able

---

[42] Ibid.
[43] PNFBW, Karl Rathgen to Bernhard Rathgen et al., on board the Menzalek, April 4, 1882.
[44] Ibid.
[45] See Walter Leifer, *Paul Georg von Möllendorff: Ein deutscher Staatsmann in Korea* (Saarbrücken: Homo et Religio, 1988); Yur-Bok Lee, *West goes East: Paul Georg von Möllendorff and Great Power Imperialism in late Yi Korea* (Honolulu: University of Hawaii Press, 1988).
[46] PNFBW, Karl Rathgen to Bernhard Rathgen et al., on board the Menzalek, April 4, 1882.
[47] Ibid.
[48] PNFBW, Karl Rathgen to Bernhard Rathgen et al., Tokyo, April 6, 1882 [with insertions from April 21, 1882 and May 12, 1882].

to operate a steam engine and Siemens telegraph given as gifts of the Prussian mission to the last Tokugawa shogun.[49]

The following day Rathgen collected his luggage at the customs house and was accompanied from Yokohama via rail to Tokyo to the *seyoken*, a guest house for foreigners in Tokyo. He continued in rickshaw to the university, where he was greeted by President Katō and then on to the nearby house intended for Rathgen, No. 8 Kaga Yashiki, not yet ready for its new denizen but where he would live the next eight years of his life. He then made his way to Ueno where two professors of the university greeted him, the Swiss physiologist Ernst Tiegel and the German anatomist Joseph Disse (1852–1912), who were both extremely surprised by the arrival of a new foreign professor for the "Literature Department."[50]

## Political Economy at Tokyo University

When Rathgen arrived at Tokyo University, founded just five years earlier, his department was housed in what was then called the *san gakkubu* (the Three-School Section), which included the Law, Science, and Literature Departments. In addition to Rathgen, one Englishman and one American (along with a number of Japanese) taught in the Literature Department. According to Rathgen, the Science Department had three Germans and three "Anglo-Americans," while the Law Department had a single foreigner, an American.[51] There were many other Germans and German-speakers at the university, notably in the medical school (in addition to Tiegel and Disse, Erwin Baelz [1849–1913] and Julius Scriba [1848–1905]) as well as in the agricultural and veterinary school, but not in the *san gakkubu*. And unlike in the medical school where the German language predominated, the language of instruction in the *san gakkubu* was English. Outside the university there were then two German economic advisors employed by the Japanese government, the *Staatswissenschaftler* Hermann Roesler (1834–94) and Paul Mayet (1846–1920), the former then advising on the draft of the Japanese commercial code in the Foreign Ministry and the latter on the development of savings banks in the Finance Ministry.[52]

---

[49] BArch L, R 901/39188, Attachment to Report B 266 [AA IIIb 16445], Oct. 30, 1903, Die deutsche Sprache in Japan; Takenaka Tōru, "Business Activities of Siemens in Japan: A Case Study of German-Japanese Economic Relationships before the First World War," in *Japan and Germany: Two Latecomers to the World Stage, 1890–1945*, vol. 1, ed. Kudō Akira, Tajima Nobuo, and Erich Pauer (Folkstone, Kent: Global Oriental, 2009), 120.

[50] PNFBW, Karl Rathgen to Bernhard Rathgen et al., Tokyo, April 6, 1882 [with insertions from April 21, 1882 and May 12, 1882].

[51] Ibid.

[52] Ibid. On Hermann Roesler's work, see Anna Bartels-Ishikawa, ed., *Hermann Roesler: Dokumente zu seinem Leben und Werk* (Berlin: Duncker & Humblot, 2007). On Mayet,

Beyond adjusting to a strange new country, new foreign colleagues, and teaching in English, Rathgen also had to be initiated into the very different university system in Tokyo, and rather quickly, as the new term started April 8, 1882.[53] Apart from the three-term academic calendar modeled on Anglo-American colleges, there were also final exams at the end of each term and a long summer break running from early July to early September. And unlike in German universities, the course of study was prescribed and ran four years. Moreover, while Rathgen had been hired to teach political economy to students in their last two years of study, in his first term he was asked to lecture on public administration and "political science," the latter a six-hour weekly course combining both the junior and senior classes, which as both a qualified lawyer and *Staatswissenschaftler,* he was nevertheless well equipped to do.[54] By "political science" his superiors had in mind general constitutional law, particularly Johann Caspar Bluntschli's (1808–81) *Allgemeines Staatsrecht* (2 vols., 1863), which had just been translated into Japanese in 1880 by none other than Katō Hiroyuki himself. Unlike some of his predecessors, Rathgen was given considerable freedom to determine the curriculum and the content of his lecturing, so he opted to teach his new class as a course in comparative constitutional law.[55] On April 24th Rathgen began his lectures in front of fourteen young men in "blue dressing gowns and straw sandals" whose identities he had a hard time differentiating initially, but gradually he grew accustomed to his new routine.[56]

Even as Rathgen was settling in, President Katō was eager to draw on Rathgen's expertise to improve the curriculum, asking him for a memo of suggestions.[57] One thing that Rathgen made note of early was that his students lacked foundational knowledge and thought in far too superficial, speculative, and theoretical terms – "always vague ideas of people's rights, separation of powers, chunks of Herbert Spencer about evolution etc." – with too little grasp of the historical background, for which he blamed American and Japanese dilettantes.[58] Worse than the ignorance itself was the "confident semi-education" this encouraged.[59] Moreover, the students seemed to know more about conditions in Europe than in Japan[60]; indeed, until recently, Rathgen noted, it had even been forbidden to ask exam questions about conditions in Japan. Above all, the institution needed to be improved so that students could learn

---

see Paul Mayet, "Deutsches wirken im Japan der Meiji Zeit," *Nippon: Zeitschrift für Japanologie* (1935): 217–24.
[53] PNFBW, Karl Rathgen to Bernhard Rathgen et al., Tokyo, April 6, 1882 [with insertions from April 21, 1882 and May 12, 1882].
[54] Ibid.   [55] Ibid.   [56] Ibid.
[57] PNFBW, Karl Rathgen to Bernhard Rathgen et al., Tokyo, June 2, 1882.
[58] PNFBW, Karl Rathgen to Bernhard Rathgen et al., Tokyo, June 12, 1882.   [59] Ibid.
[60] Nozaki, "Karl Rathgen in Japan," 23.

how to do their own scientific work. To that end, Rathgen proposed allowing his students into a seminar to do common readings and for the students to produce their own small research papers, an idea at first greeted with friendly laughter by President Katō.[61]

Rathgen's fist examination results confirmed many of these fears, revealing that his students were very good at rote learning but had only a vague grasp of the material and showed no evidence of original thinking.[62] At a long meeting that followed with President Katō, Vice-president Hattori, and the deans of the Literature and Law Departments, Tayama and Hozumi on June 29, 1882, Rathgen persuaded these men that a knowledge of the law was very valuable in political economy. He also argued that it was sensible to allow students of law to attend courses in "political science" covering such subjects as administration and comparative constitutional law – previously, students could only attend courses in their respective departments. Moreover, given the lack of knowledge of existing conditions, he succeeded in persuading the men of the value of lectures on statistics, offering to teach such a course so long as he was not also burdened with teaching political economy and finance. The meeting also resulted in promises to give Rathgen access to material on Japanese administrative institutions. Finally, despite Katō's initial rejection, Rathgen also persuaded them to allow him to create a seminar. As he wrote to his brother in a tone of modest triumph rounded with irony:

> I bear the possibly pointless hope that I will find a few people who will conduct investigations of Japanese conditions, which the foreigner cannot undertake because of the language. It is a real shame that the few foreigners who know the written Japanese language and Chinese are only interested in antiquaria. Even my colleague in political economy here (who is, by the way, not a language scholar) responded to various questions of mine about the organization of trade, banking etc. that he is only interested in the "high problems of sociology."[63]

In that same letter written to Bernhard but addressing all of his siblings, including his brother-in-law Gustav Schmoller – the letters were shared for reasons of distance – Rathgen asked Schmoller to pay special heed to the fact that seven Japanese students were currently at the University of Berlin studying *Staatswissenschaften*. If one of them should "lose his way" into Schmollers' seminar, Schmoller would do that student a great service by having him study guilds. This was a topic, he wrote, "of incredible importance to Japan," as much of the economic life in Japanese cities, even in wholly new trades,

---

[61] PNFBW, Karl Rathgen to Bernhard Rathgen et al., Tokyo, June 12, 1882.
[62] PNFBW, Karl Rathgen to Bernhard Rathgen et al., Tokyo, July 5, 1882.
[63] Ibid. This is very likely a conversation that Rathgen had with Ernest Fenollosa.

continued to operate through guilds and other trade associations whose heads negotiated the prices that outsiders paid. As Rathgen wrote, "the lovely theory that supply and demand regulate prices is absolutely untrue here. In all the internal commerce in Japan prices are determined by custom and negotiation."[64] In general Rathgen was surprised by how little information there was about the Japanese economy – even economic specialists advising the government for years like Paul Mayet did not know where to find this material.[65]

In short, Rathgen believed that it was necessary to understand law, institutions, and administration, to have a grasp of statistics and history, and to engage in original empirical research cultivated and presented in seminars if one had any hope of understanding Japan's economy. Political economy in Japan could not afford to remain a system of abstract dogmas to be memorized if its students had any hope of addressing the practical problems Japan faced. This was especially urgent because most of his Japanese graduates usually entered influential civil service positions.

The students were themselves very enthusiastic about these changes when the new term started in autumn of 1882, with the lectures on statistics and the seminar both fully enrolled.[66] Notably popular was the seminar, where some of Rathgen's best students volunteered to tackle specific subjects like Japanese banking, taxation, and vital statistics.[67] The students were pleasantly surprised to learn about the specific workings of foreign constitutions rather than the usual general judgments and theories and also welcomed their new ability to come to Rathgen directly with their own personal wishes and questions.[68] Appropriately, one of Rathgen's Japanese colleagues, a physicist trained in Germany, described the new scientific methods Rathgen was introducing as "the medical method" due to its detailed, hands-on, and empirical orientation.[69] The curricular steps to reform and reorganize the "*staatswissenschaftliches Studium*" at Tokyo were given final approval at a university conference in June 1884.[70] By that point Rathgen was already quite pleased with the papers and dissertations submitted by his students, which he said he enjoyed reading and a number of which, he noted, were really quite good.[71] Starting that year he was assisted in these efforts by Wadagaki Kenzō (1860–1919), who had just returned to Japan from his graduate studies at the University of Berlin and was immediately appointed to replace Ernest Fenollosa as professor

---

[64] PNFBW, Karl Rathgen to Bernhard Rathgen et al., Tokyo, July 5, 1882.
[65] PNFBW, Karl Rathgen to Bernhard Rathgen et al., Tokyo, Oct. 25, 1882.   [66] Ibid.
[67] PNFBW, Karl Rathgen to Bernhard Rathgen et al., Tokyo, Oct. 16, 1882.
[68] PNFBW, Karl Rathgen to Bernhard Rathgen et al., Tokyo, Nov. 18, 1882.   [69] Ibid.
[70] PNFBW, Karl Rathgen to Bernhard Rathgen et al., Tokyo, June 24, 1884. On these curricular changes to political economy and their impact, see also Nozaki, "Karl Rathgen in Japan," 23–24.
[71] PNFBW, Karl Rathgen to Bernhard Rathgen et al., Tokyo, July 10, 1884.

of political economy at the university.[72] Less than a year later, the Japanese government requested that Rathgen's contract be renewed for an additional three years.[73]

Taken together, the changes at Tokyo University would shape the Japanese discipline of political economy in ways that were distinctively German and much indebted to the "younger" German Historical School led by Rathgen's teacher and brother-in-law, Gustav Schmoller.[74] German in flavor, too, was the elimination of the examinations at the end of each term and their replacement with an exam at the end of the academic year, an arrangement that Rathgen thought was sensible despite the fact that it ate into the summer break.[75] Distinctly in the tradition of German *Staatswissenschaften* was Rathgen's involvement in moving the disciplines political science and political economy from the Literature Department to the Law Department in 1885 and the creation of a unified institute with both subjects and law in 1886.[76] One year later in 1887, the first scholarly society in political and economic science, the *kokka gakkai* (Association of Political and Social Sciences) and its scholarly journal, the *Kokka Gakkai Zasshi*, were founded.[77] It was in the *Kokka Gakkai Zasshi* that translations of the works of the leading German economists, including the works of Gustav Schmoller, would be published.[78] What all of this amounted to was nothing short of transforming political economy from a system of general axioms and dogmas into a critical scholarly discipline capable of generating new knowledge.

Given his scholarly inclinations, it should not surprise that Rathgen was a very interested observer of Japan's industrial development during his lengthy summer travels throughout Japan over his eight years in the country. He noted with interest, for example, the sudden extensive use of water wheels in silk spinning on the Tenryu River, the expansion of the cotton industry in Hamamatsu, and the production of large-caliber canons in Osaka as well as the ubiquitous construction of railways throughout Japan.[79] He was also a keen observer of the extraordinary role of the samurai class as Japanese industrial

---

[72] On Wadagaki's career, see Yanagisawa, "Das Übersetzen," 395.
[73] PNFBW, Karl Rathgen to Bernhard Rathgen et al., Tokyo, March 2, 1885.
[74] Kenneth B. Pyle, "Advantages of Followership: German Economics and Japanese Bureaucrats," *The Journal of Japanese Studies* 1 (1974): 127–64; Martin, *Japan and Germany*, 48–49; cf. Erik Grimmer-Solem, "German Social Science, Meiji Conservatism, and the Peculiarities of Japanese History," *Journal of World History* 16 (2005): 187–222.
[75] PNFBW, Karl Rathgen to Bernhard Rathgen et al., Tokyo, July 5, 1882.
[76] Nozaki, "Karl Rathgen in Japan," 25.
[77] Yanagisawa ,"Das Übersetzen," 394; see also PNFBW, Karl Rathgen to Bernhard Rathgen et al., Tokyo, March 18, 1887. In this letter Rathgen calls it the "Staatswissenschaftliche Gesellschaft."
[78] Yanagisawa, "Das Übersetzen," 396.
[79] PNFBW, Karl Rathgen to Bernhard Rathgen et al., Tokyo, [n.d.] July 1887.

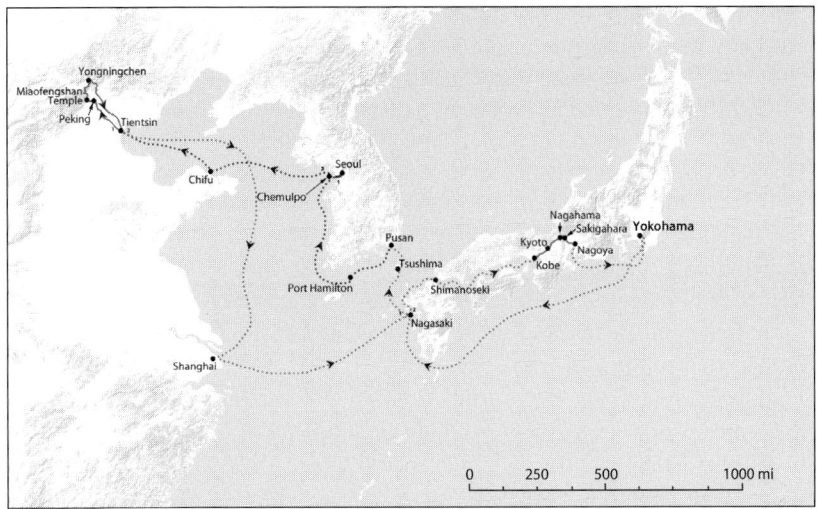

Map 2.1  Karl Rathgen's journey to Korea, China, and southern Japan, July 3–Sept. 9, 1886.

entrepreneurs.[80] In his last year in Japan in 1889 he noted how much places he had visited earlier in his time in Japan had undergone remarkable change.[81] He was also astonished by the rapid process of economic concentration he observed in Japan, which showed distinct signs of monopoly.[82] One unmistakable insight, which would later figure prominently in Rathgen's scholarly work published on Japan after his return to Germany, was the central role that steamships and railways had played in creating a Japanese division of labor for the first time as a foundation for Japan's industrial development.[83] As in the United States and in Germany, this had occurred with considerable state investments and subsidies. Here Japan stood in glaring contrast to its Asian neighbors China and Korea, which Rathgen visited over extensive journeys in the summers of 1886 and 1890.

Of the many advanced Japanese students that Rathgen taught and mentored in his seminar, there were some who learned German and who would then

---

[80] PNFBW, Karl Rathgen to Bernhard Rathgen et al., Tokyo, Nov. 5, 1883; Karl Rathgen to Bernhard Rathgen et al., Tokyo, Jan. 9, 1884.
[81] PNFBW, Karl Rathgen to Bernhard Rathgen et al., Tokyo, Jan. 7, 1889.
[82] PNFBW, Karl Rathgen to Bernhard Rathgen et al., Tokyo, Dec. 7, 1888.
[83] See Karl Rathgen, *Japans Volkswirtschaft und Staatshaushalt*, vol. 10, Staats- und socialwissenschaftliche Forschungen (Leipzig: Duncker & Humblot, 1891), 259–61; and especially Rathgen, *Die Japaner und ihre wirtschaftliche Entwicklung* (Leipzig: Teubner, 1905), 4, 29–33.

work as his research assistants for a very lengthy work on the Japanese economy that Rathgen later published as his *Habilitation* after his return to Germany.[84] Among these was Kanai Noburu (1865-1933), who stood out for his abilities and served as Rathgen's assistant translating Japanese statistics in 1885-86.[85] With the aid of Kanai, Rathgen was able to give a public lecture on Japanese population statistics to the German East Asiatic Society in late March 1887.[86] On Rathgen's recommendation, Kanai was urged to go to Germany to continue his studies of political economy, which he did in the years 1886-90 studying with the leading lights of German *Staatswissenschaften*, including Karl Knies (1821-98) in Heidelberg, Johannes Conrad (1839-1915) in Halle, Carl Menger in Vienna, and above all, with Gustav Schmoller, who had by that time moved to the University of Berlin.[87]

In Berlin Kanai was very warmly received and mentored by Schmoller, and it was through this contact in Schmoller's seminar and as a guest in his home in Berlin-Charlottenburg that Kanai developed a deep and abiding interest in social questions.[88] Indeed, Kanai would himself take up direct study of the "social question" in England in 1889, living in London to investigate the "homes" for destitute children of Thomas Barnardo, Toynbee Hall, and studying the London dockworkers' strike.[89] Clearly Rathgen's insistence on the importance of empirical work was reinforced by Kanai's studies in Germany and directed by Schmoller toward an interest in the "social question." In all, Kanai would spend a year in England doing field research of various kinds and attending Alfred Marshall's (1842-1924) lectures in Cambridge.[90] Writing to Schmoller from Saigon on his way back to Japan after his year in England in

---

[84] Rathgen, *Japans Volkswirtschaft*.
[85] Nozaki, "Karl Rathgen in Japan," 25-26; see also Byron K. Marshall, *Academic Freedom and the Japanese Imperial University, 1868-1939* (Berkeley, Los Angeles, and Oxford: University of California Press, 1992), 36-37.
[86] See PNFBW, Karl Rathgen to Bernhard Rathgen et al., Tokyo, April 14, 1887; Dr. K. Rathgen, "Ergebnisse der amtlichen Bevölkerungsstatistik in Japan" (mit einer Karte), *MOAG* 4 (1884-88), Heft 37: 322-40.
[87] Wolfgang Schwentker, "Fremde Gelehrte: Japanische Nationalökonomen und Sozialreformer im Kaiserreich," in *Intellektuelle im Deutschen Kaiserreich*, ed. Gangolf Hübinger and Wolfgang Mommsen (Frankfurt a.M.: Fischer, 1993), 177-81; Hannah Kreis and Bertram Schefold, "Die Einführung des Gedankenguts der Deutschen Historischen Schule in Japan: Karl Rathgen und Noburu Kanai – eine weitreichende Lehrer-Schüler-Beziehung und die Gründung des Japanischen Vereins für Sozialpolitik," in *Der Einfluss deutschsprachigen wirtschaftswissenschaftlichen Denkens in Japan*, ed. Heinz D. Kurz (Berlin: Duncker & Humblot, 2012), 29-46, here 37-38.
[88] Schwentker, "Fremde Gelehrte," 180.
[89] GStA PK, VI. HA Nl. Schmoller, Nr. 182, Kanai Noburu to Gustav Schmoller, London, Oct. 3, 1889.
[90] Schwentker, "Fremde Gelehrte," 181; Kreis and Schefold, "Die Einführung des Gedankenguts," 38.

October 1890, Kanai mentioned that he had completed his study of the "social question" in England and had now left "the land of classical political economy," intending to pursue an academic career on his return to Japan.[91] He thanked Schmoller again for the kindness he had shown him during his studies in Berlin and especially regretted that he would miss his old teacher Rathgen when he arrived in Tokyo, who had by that time returned to Germany. As it turned out, Rathgen was just then himself on a steamer between New York and Hamburg, having left Yokohama on September 3rd for San Francisco.[92]

On returning to Japan in November 1890 Kanai was immediately appointed to a professorship in political economy at his alma mater, renamed the Imperial University in 1886.[93] In some of his first lectures Kanai criticized the Japanese adherents of orthodox economic liberalism, who did not grasp the specific historical and social context of economic developments in Japan. He was particularly harsh toward Taguchi, the editor of the *Tokyo Keizei Zasshi* and prominent figure in the *meirokusha*. The policy of *laissez-faire*, Kanai argued, had not prevented grave social problems and the emergence of a radical labor movement in Europe, and even in England, the doctrine's homeland, increasing state intervention had become necessary in dealing with these challenges, just as it had in Germany through the passage of social insurance laws.[94] Above all, it was necessary to develop a Japanese model of economic development that took into account Japan's peculiarities and could guide social reforms that might prevent these social problems, ones that were sure to emerge as Japan industrialized – there was no point repeating the mistakes that had been made in Europe.[95] As such, Kanai was one of the first to introduce the term "social question" (*shakai mondai*) into Japanese economic discourse.[96]

In 1896 Kanai along with another professor of political economy at the Imperial University, Kuwata Kumazō (1868–1932), who had himself only recently returned to Japan from higher studies in economics in Germany, together with their students founded the *nihon shakai seisaku gakkai* (Japanese Scholars for Social Policy). It was consciously modeled on the German

---

[91] GStA PK, VI. HA Nl. Schmoller, Nr. 183, Kanai Noboru to Gustav Schmoller, Saigon, Oct. 30, 1890.
[92] PNFBW, Karl Rathgen to Bernhard Rathgen et al., on board the Gaelic between Yokohama and San Francisco, Sept. 17, 1890; Karl Rathgen to Bernhard Rathgen et al., New York, Oct. 3, 1890; Karl Rathgen to Bernhard Rathgen et al., New York, Oct. 20, 1890.
[93] Kreis and Schefold, "Die Einführung des Gedankenguts," 29–46; Schwentker, "Fremde Gelehrte," 182.
[94] Kreis and Schefold, "Die Einführung des Gedankenguts," 39.    [95] Ibid., 39–40.
[96] Ibid., 40.

Association for Social Policy (as discussed in Chapter 1, founded by Gustav Schmoller and other economists in 1873) to turn social reform ideas into policy.[97] In 1907 the first annual conference was held, and by 1909 it counted no fewer than 122 members and was by that point the official association of Japanese social scientists.[98] The ideas of the *shakai seisaku gakkai* began to have an influence on senior Meiji officials shortly after its founding and would ultimately aid the passage of the first Japanese factory law in 1911. In 1898 Kanai served as a delegate to the Third Higher Council on Agriculture, Commerce and Industry, where he expressed his views to senior bureaucrats.[99] At the council meetings the discussion turned to the hazards of dangerous working conditions and the role of the state in remedying these through factory legislation. Similar initiatives were also underway in the Japanese Home Ministry, where the physician Gotō Shimpei (1857–1929), who had studied the German social insurance system in Germany, was appointed chief of the Bureau of Health and Sanitation in 1892, which began drafting the first proposals for a sickness insurance law in 1898.[100] In 1900 a Factory Survey Office was established by the Ministry of Agriculture, which recruited Kuwata Kumazō as an investigator and produced its first labor survey in 1903, documenting the many social problems accompanying Japan's rapid industrial development, notably child labor. Other surveys by the Home Ministry highlighted the deteriorating health and fitness of factory workers and its potential impact on Japan's military strength. Together these pressures produced the Factory Law of 1911, introducing minimum health and safety standards, restrictions on child and women's labor, factory liability for job-related injuries, and a state factory inspectorate for the first time.[101]

### The Association School and the Reform of Japanese Law

The German "fashion" had, of course, never been confined to political economy and was especially marked in the field of law. Japanese interest in foreign law began with Japan's coerced opening to the West and was born of a desire to find a "civilized" legal basis for revising the hated unequal treaties. These

---

[97] Sumiya Etsuji, *Nihon keizaigakushi* (Kyoto: Minerva, 1958), 151–98, 250–90; Pyle, "Advantages of Followership," 139–48; Iida Kanae, "Nihon shakai seisaku gakkai to keizaigaku kenkyū," in *Nihon no keizaigaku: Nihonjin no keizaiteki shisui no kiseki*, ed. Takaynagi Hiroshi (Tokyo: Tōyō keizai shimpo-sha, 1984), 51–92; Sheldon Garon, *The State and Labor in Modern Japan* (Berkeley, Los Angeles, and London: University of California Press, 1987), 25–33; Schwentker, "Fremde Gelehrte," 184–85; Sugiyama, *Origins of Economic Thought*, 11–19; Tessa Morris-Suzuki, *A History of Japanese Economic Thought* (London: Routledge, 1989), 62–70.
[98] Kreis and Schefold, "Die Einführung des Gedankenguts," 41–42.
[99] Garon, *The State and Labor*, 26.   [100] Ibid., 26–27.   [101] Ibid., 27–28.

treaties were imposed under massive outside pressure and resulted in the opening of select Japanese ports to foreigners, loss of Japanese sovereignty over tariffs, and the right of foreigners to, live, conduct business, and travel in the country under consular jurisdiction. Creating a modern constitutional state with the rule of law was thus indispensable to revising the treaties and regaining Japanese sovereignty.

Some of the first steps undertaken by the Japanese Ministry of Justice were establishing a school to study and test foreign law in 1871, followed by the creation of a law school in 1874 to study Anglo-American law, to which was added a section on French civil law in 1875. While the British and Americans had applied their case law method in drafting and enforcing their treaties with Japan, this turned out to be irreconcilable with Japanese legal tradition and thus not adopted, despite strong Japanese orientation to these countries at the time. This fact and the Meiji oligarchy's desire to centralize power resulted in greater interest in the civil law tradition of continental Europe, and in particular the Code Napoléon of France.[102] As the process of translating and adopting civil law advanced, tensions between the natural law concepts of the Code and Japanese legal traditions grew and came to a head over the abolition of samurai privileges, bringing the process of codifying a civil law along French lines to a standstill in 1878.[103]

Around the same time, awareness developed that German legal and constitutional models afforded greater scope for the integration of Confucian and Japanese norms, institutions, and notions of legitimate power, most notably a sovereign emperor.[104] These models were also broadly attractive as a legal foundation for positive state action directly relevant to the process of Japanese state building, which was more circumscribed in Western legal codes and constitutions informed by natural law concepts and Enlightenment social contract theory. France's tumultuous political history (no fewer than three revolutions between 1830 and 1871) and the US Civil War had certainly also made these legal-constitutional models less attractive to Japanese legal reformers like Inoue and Itō.

Reflecting these changes in Japanese legal thinking, in 1878 the Bavarian *Staatswissenschaftler* Hermann Roesler was brought to Japan, initially to help draft a Japanese commercial code but later also to draft a constitution. A conservative Catholic and a harsh critic of Bismarck, Roesler drew heavily on the work of Lorenz von Stein.[105] Roesler argued that economic laws were

---

[102] Schenck, *Der deutsche Anteil*, 89–97, 254–55.   [103] Ibid., 97–98.
[104] Ibid., 130–42; Ando, *Die Entstehung der Meiji-Verfassung*, 47–57.
[105] On von Stein, see Pasquale Pasquino, "Introduction to Lorenz von Stein," *Economy and Society* 10 (Feb. 1981): 1–6 ; Karl-Hermann Kästner, "From the Social Question to the Social State," *Economy and Society* 10 (Feb. 1981): 7–26; Giles Pope, "The Political Ideas of Lorenz von Stein and their Influence on Rudolf Gneist and Gustav Schmoller" (DPhil

not universal but instead depended on social institutions and the legal structure of a given society.[106] Crucially, this meant that a modern society was something more than the sum of commercial interests and that positive state action was needed to prevent the capture and use of state institutions by a predominant social class to further its own interests. Roesler's relevance for Japan was that his legal thought provided justifications for state policy that went beyond the defense of the negative liberties of individuals, and his ideas would prove influential later in Itō's drafting of the Meiji constitution.[107] In that process the organicist theories of state developed by the Swiss legal scholar Bluntschli would prove particularly influential. His relevance to Japanese constitutional law was assured by the emperor's tutor and later rector of Tokyo University, Katō Hiroyuki, who as mentioned earlier, had translated Bluntschli's *Allgemeines Staatsrecht* in 1881.[108]

While drafting a constitution and commercial code were themselves challenging enough, equally daunting was training lawyers, judges, and civil servants who would apply the law and administer justice. And with the new orientation toward German legal models, an additional hurdle was gaining a command of German, as English was by far the most predominant foreign language taught and in use in Japan at the time. As it had with German political economy, the *doitsugaku kyōkai* played a very important role in this process. Not only did it translate German legal texts and publish these in its own monthly, it also created its own school in 1883, the *doitsugaku kyōkai gakko* (School of the Association for German Scholarship, commonly known as the "Association School" ["Vereinschule" in German]). Its purpose was to train Japanese students both in the German language and German law and political economy.[109] The school was intended as a counterweight to the dominance of Anglo-American and French law at Tokyo University at the time.[110] Karl Rathgen was made an honorary member of the *doitsugaku kyōkai* at a meeting on April 22, 1883, attended by members of the imperial

---

diss., University of Oxford, 1985). On von Stein's influence in Japan, see Ernst Grünfeld, "Lorenz von Stein und Japan," *Jahrbücher für Nationalökonomie und Statistik* 45 (Neue Folge 100) (1913): 345–61.

[106] See esp. Ando, *Die Entstehung der Meiji-Verfassung*, 77–145; Joseph Pittau, *Political Thought in Early Meiji Japan 1867–1889* (Cambridge, MA: Harvard University Press, 1967), 131–57; Schenck, *Der deutsche Anteil*, 102–7, 132–35; Johannes Siemes, *Hermann Roesler and the Making of the Meiji State* (Tokyo: Sophia University Press, 1966), 3–7.

[107] Schenck, *Der deutsche Anteil*, 15–16.    [108] Ibid., 196–97.

[109] See Dokument B, Report of Ambassador von Holleben to Chancellor von Bismarck of Nov. 24, 1886 with memorandum on the school statutes of the Doitsugaku Kyōkai Gakko, in Bert Becker, ed., *Georg Michaelis: Ein preußischer Jurist im Japan der Meiji-Zeit; Briefe, Tagebuchnotizen, Dokumente, 1885–1889* (Munich: Iudicium, 2001), 584–97; Schenck, *Der deutsche Anteil*, 240.

[110] Schenck, *Der deutsche Anteil*, 240.

family and many prominent Japanese statesmen, including Prince Kitashirakawa Yoshihisa (1847–95), who was its president.[111] The pressure of the impending constitutional and administrative reforms along German lines required ever more trained Japanese civil servants able to read, interpret, and translate German books and laws.

In 1884 the the *doitsugaku kyōkai gakko* opened its doors led by Nishi Amane, the first director of the school. By March of 1885 the association also planned to begin offering Japanese officials with a command of German courses in "*Rechts- und Staatswissenschaft*," which Rathgen volunteered to teach.[112] In these years the Association School received considerable subsidies from the Japanese Ministry of Justice, the Ministry of Education, and from the Imperial court, which enabled it to acquire property and a building in Kanda-Tokyo as well as a library and to hire teaching staff from Germany. Among them was the qualified judge and later German imperial chancellor Georg Michaelis (1857–1936), who served as the school's first full-time director of education beginning in the fall of 1885.[113] It thus took on a much more permanent form as a semi-official institution whose primary goal became producing a new generation of Japanese civil servants able to administer the new Japanese laws.[114] For these purposes, a six-year general course at the level of German *Gymnasium* was implemented, supplemented by a three-year special course at the university level. The "general" *Gymnasium*-level course included instruction in Chinese, German, geography, history, Japanese, and gymnastics and was taught by ten Japanese instructors and the Swiss-German pastor Wilfried Spinner (1854–1918) of the Allgemeiner Evangelisch-Protestantischer Kirchenverein (a.k.a "Weimar Mission"), founder of the Evangelical Lutheran Congregation in Yokohama in 1885. The foreign instructor teaching the "general" course was the German *Gymnasium* teacher Otto Hering (b. 1858).[115] As can be seen here, the school showed a degree of cultural syncretism that anticipated by many years the policy of rapprochement and cultural exchange implemented in the German leasehold of

---

[111] PNFBW, Karl Rathgen to Bernhard Rathgen et al., Tokyo, May 13, 1883; Karl Rathgen to Bernhard Rathgen et al., Tokyo, March 20, 1884; Karl Rathgen to Bernhard Rathgen et al., Tokyo, Nov. 5, 1884.

[112] PNFBW, Karl Rathgen to Bernhard Rathgen et al., Tokyo, March 11, 1885.

[113] See Georg Michaelis, *Für Staat und Volk: Eine Lebensgeschichte* (Berlin: Furche Verlag, 1922), 98–101, 127–30; PNFBW, Karl Rathgen to Bernhard Rathgen et al., Tokyo, Oct. 3, 1885.

[114] Schenck, *Der deutsche Anteil*, 241, 244.

[115] BArch L, R 901/39186, Report of Holleben, Imperial Embassy Tokyo, to Bismarck, Foreign Office, Tokyo, Nov. 24, 1886 with transcript of a memorandum on and the statutes of the Doits-Gaku Kiokai Gakko; see also duplicate in GStA PK, I. HA Rep 76 Kultusministerium, V c Sekt. 1, Tit. 11, Teil VII, Nr. 22, Bd. 1, fols. 86–98; Becker, *Georg Michaelis*, 584–97.

Kiaochow after 1905, notably the creation of the German-Chinese Seminar (Deutsch-Chinesisches Seminar) in Tsingtao (Qingdao), a *Gymnasium* for adolescent boys founded in 1905 by the same Weimar Mission.[116] A similar model was followed in the Deutsch-Chinesische Hochschule (German-Chinese Higher School [college]), founded in 1909, which had attached to it a six-year preparatory school with a very similar curriculum synthesizing German and Chinese subjects.[117]

The Association School's "special" course was in the subjects of *Staatswissenschaften* and law, with supplemental instruction in Latin and history, and structured in such a way that its students, on completing the course, could be admitted to the state examinations for entry into the Japanese higher civil service.[118] Michaelis was specifically employed by the Japanese government to teach constitutional and administrative law and political economy in the "special course" at the school.[119] But mirroring changes that had occurred in the curriculum of political economy at Tokyo University, Michaelis tried new methods of teaching that conveyed a scientific conception of law and legal rights and emphasized active learning in his students. One way this was done was by comparative analysis of legal praxis using Rudolf von Jhering's (1818–92) *Jurisprudence of Everyday Life* to discuss the daily life of the students as these entailed legal relations, such as for example in their interactions with landlords, bookstores, and railway companies.[120] By revealing through such examples that similar notions of law and justice existed in Japan and Germany, and that these were based in turn on Roman law concepts, he was able to hone his student's analytical thinking. Michaelis then worked with his students to apply their understandings of law and legal practice to Japanese customary law, with the students themselves providing the comparative material to reveal how these had inherent notions of legality and order not unlike those found in Roman law.[121]

Like Rathgen, Michaelis also implemented the seminar method of instruction.[122] The Prussian training of legal clerks (*Referendarsausbildung*) with its emphasis on legal praxis served as a model, which Michaelis integrated into the curriculum of the school.[123] Once again, this anticipated by many years policy in the later German leashold Kiaochow, where on initiative of the Imperial Navy Office the Deutsch-Chinesische Hochschule was founded. This

---

[116] See Steinmetz, *The Devil's Handwriting*, 479–80.   [117] Ibid., 486.
[118] BArch L, R 901/39186, Report of Holleben, Imperial Embassy Tokyo, to Bismarck, Foreign Office, Tokyo, Nov. 24, 1886 with transcript of a memorandum on and the statutes of the Doits-Gaku Kiokai Gakko.
[119] Dokument A, Employment contract for Georg Michaelis of May 8, 1885, in Becker, *Georg Michaelis*, 581.
[120] Michaelis, *Für Volk und Staat*, 128.   [121] Ibid.   [122] Ibid., 129.
[123] Schenck, *Der deutsche Anteil*, 242–43.

combined a six-year preparatory school with an upper school that included a section for law and *Staatswissenschaften*. As in the Association School, religion was absent from the curriculum and courses were taught by both German and native instructors.[124]

The experiments with new forms of teaching at the Association School were highly successful as measured by the growing numbers of students enrolled. At the start of the year in 1885, Michaelis only had 12 students in the special course; by 1887 there were already some 50, with the school enrolling 561 students in all, taught by 5 German and 12 Japanese teachers.[125] By that point the German teachers at the school included the future president of the German Imperial Statistical Office, Ernst Delbrück (1858–1933), and his cousin, Felix Delbrück (1859–1924), later state court president in Göttingen and future director of the Imperial Patent Office.[126] It is no exaggeration to describe the school in these years as an elite civil service academy of a rapidly expanding Japanese bureaucratic apparatus. Since the school had the status of a higher school, many of the graduates who did not enter the civil service matriculated in Tokyo University. Of the students trained at the Association School in the 1880s, many went on to pursue successful careers as judges, councilors of state, governors, professors of law, and influential parliamentarians. Of these, a number of them continued their studies or spent time in Germany, including Arimatsu Hideyoshi (1863–1927).[127] Arimatsu entered the Association School in February 1884 and completed his studies in 1888, successfully passing his exams for entry into the higher civil service.[128] After working in numerous courts, Arimatsu became an influential senior figure in the Japanese Ministry of Interior and then chief of the Imperial Police Bureau who spearheaded the development and expansion of a modern Japanese police force and passage of the Public Safety Law in 1900.[129]

In addition to those Germans teaching in the Association School, the Japanese government retained a large number of German *Staatswissenschaftler*

---

[124] Steinmetz, *The Devil's Handwriting*, 486.
[125] Michaelis, *Für Volk und Staat*, 128; Dokument C, Report of Ambassador von Holleben to Chancellor von Bismarck of Aug. 12, 1887 with text of a speech given by Georg Michaelis on June 7, 1887, in Becker, *Georg Michaelis*, 598–605, here 599.
[126] Michaelis, *Für Volk und Staat*, 129–30; PNFBW, Karl Rathgen to Bernhard Rathgen et al., Tokyo, April 14, 1887; Anna Bartels-Ishikawa, Hansgerd Delbrück, and Itō Yushi, eds., *Die schönste Zeit meines Lebens: Ernst und Felix Delbrücks Briefe aus Japan aus den Jahren 1887 bis 1889* (Dunedin: University of Otago Department of Languages and Cultures, German Section, 2014).
[127] Michaelis, *Für Volk und Staat*, 130.
[128] Maik Hendrik Sprotte, *Konfliktaustragung in autoritären Herrschaftssystemen: Eine historische Fallstudie zur frühsozialistischen Bewegung im Japan der Meiji-Zeit* (Marburg: Tectum Verlag, 2001), 146.
[129] Ibid., 147–56.

and lawyers in the 1880s to teach law at Tokyo University or to advise the process of codifying Japanese law and reforming Japanese public administration. In 1884 an American lawyer was dismissed from Tokyo University and replaced by the Hannover *Landrichter* (privincial judge) Otto Rudorff (1845–1922), who assumed a professorship of law specializing in Roman law.[130] In 1885 the Law School of the Japanese Ministry of Justice was moved to Kaga Yashiki and slowly integrated into the Law Department of Tokyo University.[131] In 1886 another German lawyer, Heinrich Weipert (1856–1905), replaced Rudorff as professor of Roman law at Tokyo University.[132] In 1889 yet another German, Ludwig Lönholm (b. 1854), was appointed to a chair of law at the university. What is more, German was introduced to the university as a language of instruction outside of medicine from 1888 on.[133] By 1895 there was even an independent section for German law in the Law Department at the university. The impact of these developments was a rapid increase in the numbers of students enrolled in the German section of the Law Department in the late 1890s and an almost reciprocal decline in the numbers enrolled in the English section: in 1898 there were 81 enrolled in the German section and 340 in the English section; by 1903 there were 364 enrolled in the German and 197 in the English section.[134]

Many more German lawyers and *Staatswissenschaftler* worked as legal and administrative advisors. As early as 1883 Rathgen had been asked to give private lectures in German on administrative science (*Verwaltungslehre*) to members of the Japanese State Council and various ministries, which were translated by interpreter and then printed in Japanese in outline form.[135] These lectures began in January 1884 and included administrative organization, administrative science, and constitutional law.[136] In 1883 Privy Counselor Carl Rudolph (1841–1915), an administrative jurist and *Regierungsrat* in Oppeln, Prussia, was given leave and entered Japanese service to reform Japanese public administration.[137] In 1886, the Berlin *Landrichter* Albert

---

[130] GStA PK, I. HA Rep. 89 Geheimes Zivilkabinett, Jüngere Periode, Nr. 13370, fols. 6–7, Otto Rudorff to Wilmowsky, Lauenstein, Aug. 23, 1887; PNFBW, Karl Rathgen to Bernhard Rathgen et al., Tokyo, Feb. 2, 1884; Karl Rathgen to Bernhard Rathgen et al., Tokyo, April 9, 1884.

[131] PNFBW, Karl Rathgen to Bernhard Rathgen et al., Tokyo, Sept. 16, 1885.

[132] PNFBW, Karl Rathgen to Bernhard Rathgen et al., Tokyo, Dec. 26, 1886; Bartels-Ishikawa, Delbrück and Itō, *Die schönste Zeit meines Lebens*, 259n201.

[133] PNFBW, Karl Rathgen to Bernhard Rathgen et al., April 26, 1884 [with insertions from May 15, 1884].

[134] BArch L, R 901/39189, Attachment to AA IIIb 4948, April 4, 1904, Report B51 of the Imperial German Embassy in Tokyo, transcript of a memo by Professor Dr. Lönholm, Tokyo, Jan. 16, 1904.

[135] PNFBW, Karl Rathgen to Bernhard Rathgen et al., Tokyo, Dec. 23, 1883.

[136] PNFBW, Karl Rathgen to Bernhard Rathgen et al., Tokyo, Jan. 9, 1884.

[137] PNFBW, Karl Rathgen to Bernhard Rathgen et al., Tokyo, Feb. 27, 1884.

Mosse (1846–1925), one of Rudolf von Gneist's brightest students, was retained by the Japanese government as a legal advisor to the Japanese Ministry of State to aid in revising the foreign treaties and in drafting a new constitution.[138] Early in 1887 yet another Prussian judge, Johannes Ernst Bergmann (1845–1935) *Landrichter* in Magdeburg, was employed to aid in the codification of Japanese law.[139]

Beyond his private lectures on administration to senior Japanese civil servants, Rathgen was also put to work by the Japanese government to advise on a new stock exchange law in 1886, visiting the rice and securities exchanges to gain a detailed understanding of their operations and participating in lengthy discussions with Japanese officials drafting the legislation.[140] He was retained again in 1887 to produce a memo to the Chinese government on the value for Sino-Japanese trade of establishing an orderly silver currency in China, as well as to advise on managing the Japanese national debt.[141] In 1888 Rathgen and Mosse began lecturing in the Selbstverwaltungsverein (Association for Self-Governance) to Japanese officials and nobles intended for the future Japanese House of Lords on the impending laws on administrative reform and local governance, with Mosse covering the legal and Rathgen the economic side of these reforms. These lectures were translated by interpreter and transcripts were published, with excerpts appearing in Japanese newspapers.[142]

When the constitution was finally promulgated in early 1889 Rathgen approved of the draft, which he saw as a carefully worked out law, that while informed by German constitutional literature, was drafted by the Japanese very much on their own terms.[143] Indeed, it was hardly the slavish imitation of the Prussian constitution or as authoritarian as has often been claimed.[144]

---

[138] GStA PK, I. HA Rep. 89 Geheimes Zivilkabinett, Jüngere Periode, Nr. 13370, fol. 9, Friedburg, Ministry of Justice, to his Majesty the Kaiser und King, Bad Ems, Aug. 4, 1886; Historische Kommission bei der Bayerischen Akademie der Wissenschaften, ed., *Neue Deutsche Biographie*, vol. 18 (Berlin: Duncker & Humblot, 1997), 216–18. On Mosse's years in Japan, Albert Mosse and Lina Mosse, *Fast wie mein eigen Vaterland: Briefe aus Japan, 1886–1889*, ed. Shirō Ishii, Ernst Lokowandt, and Yūkichi Sakai (Munich: Iudicium, 1995); Ando, *Die Entstehung der Meiji-Verfassung*, 146–80, 218–19.

[139] GStA PK, I. HA Rep. 89 Geheimes Zivilkabinett, Jüngere Periode, Nr. 13370, fol. 11, Bismarck and Friedburg, Ministry of Justice to his Majesty the Kaiser und King, Berlin, Dec. 15, 1886.

[140] PNFBW, Karl Rathgen to Bernhard Rathgen et al., Tokyo, Nov. 11, 1886; Karl Rathgen to Bernhard Rathgen et al., Tokyo, Dec. 26, 1886.

[141] PNFBW, Karl Rathgen to Bernhard Rathgen et al., Tokyo, Nov. 29, 1887.

[142] PNFBW, Karl Rathgen to Bernhard Rathgen et al., Tokyo, Nov. 16, 1888; Karl Rathgen to Bernhard Rathgen et al., Tokyo, May 27, 1889.

[143] PNFBW, Karl Rathgen to Bernhard Rathgen et al., Tokyo, Feb. 15, 1889.

[144] Cf. Martin, *Japan and Germany*, 45–46.

Significant departures from German and Western legal thinking can be seen in the persistent influence of Confucian and Japanese legal traditions and genuine Japanese innovations: a unitary family-state with a deified emperor at its head had no precedent in modern German or Western law, and the Japanese Diet was elected with a more restricted franchise and granted even fewer powers than its counterpart under the Prussian constitution. Yet despite the conservative inclination of its drafters, the Meiji constitution was in practice quite flexible and gradually evolved into a parliamentary form of rule by the time of the Meiji *tennō's* death in 1912.[145] And with its checks on imperial power, an independent judiciary, formal legal equality, guaranteed basic rights of free speech, assembly, and association, and considerable scope for local self-government, many features of it were unquestionably modern, indeed even liberal.[146] It was, in fact, highly praised and defended by most contemporary American and western European constitutional experts at the time.[147]

Giving so many highly-trained men extensive leaves of absence to work for the Meiji government was a considerable investment by the Prussian and Imperial German governments that only makes fuller sense when placed in the context of the fierce competition between rival Western powers for trade, spheres of influence, and bases of operation in East Asia in the 1880s. Indeed, it is useful to see this heavy involvement of Germans in Meiji-era state building as a continuation by other means of what had begun with the Eulenburg expedition in the early 1860s and von Brandt in the late 1860s and early 1870s: *Weltpolitik*. In lieu of a large bluewater navy, spheres of influence, or formal colonies in Asia, German influence overseas could spread by means of *Geist* much as it had in the United States in the 1870s. In a report from Ambassador von Holleben to Chancellor Bismarck in 1886, Holleben was confident enough to write: "Germany will only be delighted if it gradually manages to acquire its intellectual dominion [*geistige Herrschaft*] over Japan without having to make material sacrifices."[148]

---

[145] Ando, *Die Entstehung der Meiji-Verfassung*, 211–15; Ann Hastings, *Neighborhood and Nation in Tokyo, 1905–1937* (Pittsburgh: University of Pittsburgh Press, 1995); Jeffrey E. Hanes, *The City as Subject: Seki Hajime and the Reinvention of Modern Osaka* (Berkeley: University of California Press, 2002).

[146] Schenck, *Der deutsche Anteil*, 192–93, 200, 211–14, 225–26; Ando, *Die Entstehung der Meiji-Verfassung*, 218–19.

[147] Schenck, *Der deutsche Anteil*, 225–39.

[148] BArch L, R 901/39186, Report of Holleben, Imperial Embassy Tokyo, to Bismarck, Foreign Office, Tokyo, Nov. 24, 1886 with transcript of a memorandum on and the statutes of the Doits-Gaku Kiokai Gakko; Becker, *Georg Michaelis*, 595.

## "Yellow Peril"

Early in his stay in Japan, Rathgen was well aware of the role he played in helping to secure *Deutschtum* ("Germandom") in East Asia. In 1883 he had complained about how little the German embassy supported the German cause, remarking that the embassy had nothing at all to do with the current fashion for things German in Japan and how little it did to foster German trade.[149] Indeed, Otto von Döhnhoff (1835–1904), who was ambassador between 1883 and 1885, was unusually passive and unengaged, and unlike his predecessors and successors, did not serve as chairman of the OAG.[150] Another ongoing early cause of concern was the negative press the Germans were receiving from some English newspapers in Yokohama as well as in the Anglophile Japanese press, including the newspaper of the influential Fukuzawa Yukichi, the *Jiji Shinpo*. As Rathgen noted, the Germans were being caricatured unfairly as "*Dunkelmänner* [unenlightened men] and Absolutists."[151] By the spring of 1884 there were very extensive discussions in the Japanese press about the value of German versus English scholarship, in which the pro-English Japanese voices were heard spreading what were to Rathgen's mind "childishly ignorant" stories of the dangers of German authoritarianism.[152] The fact that the Japanese government was taking German institutions as models also meant that the study of German books in Japan grew very rapidly, which generated additional outrage among the English and those Japanese who had learned English.[153] That anger led to a dismissal of the standing of all German scholarly fields in Japan as purely a creature of political favoritism. As Yokohama's *Japan Weekly Mail* noted in March of 1884:

> That Germans now have the preference in Japan, as teachers, in almost all branches of science and literature, is probably due to the fact that the more conservative members of the Government feel that the country has progressed rather too rapidly toward free thought and free institutions, and believe the political system of Germany to be more in accord with that desirable for Japan, than those of England and America. The students

---

[149] PNFBW, Karl Rathgen to Bernhard Rathgen et al., Tokyo, May 13, 1883.
[150] Spang, "Anmerkungen zur frühen OAG-Geschichte," 74.
[151] PNFBW, Karl Rathgen to Bernhard Rathgen et al., Tokyo, Oct. 25, 1882.
[152] PNFBW, Karl Rathgen to Bernhard Rathgen et al., April 26, 1884 [with insertions from May 15, 1884]. For example, the *Hochi Shimbun* asserted that Germany was backward in politics, economy, and law. See "The Growing Taste for German Literature" (translated from the *Nichi Nichi Shimbun*), *The Japan Weekly Mail* (Yokohama), May 17, 1884; cf. "The Recent Newspaper Controversy in Tokiyo [sic]," *The Japan Weekly Mail* (Yokohama), May 24, 1884.
[153] PNFBW, Karl Rathgen to Bernhard Rathgen et al., May 29, 1884.

themselves, however, much prefer the English language and English and American books, even as regards medicine, and it is chiefly from these sources that the present literature is derived.[154]

In part this was a reflection of the disproportionate number of Germans now teaching at Tokyo University. As Rathgen noted in a letter to his old friend and university companion Henry Farnam, by January 1884 no fewer than 9 Germans as opposed to only 2 Americans, 2 Englishmen, 1 Scot, 1 Canadian, 1 Swiss, and 1 Dutchman taught at the university.[155]

When Theodor von Holleben returned to Tokyo in 1885, now as German ambassador, it marked the beginning of much more active German diplomatic engagemen in Japan that would draw on Rathgen's knowledge. Rathgen's seminar at Tokyo University as well as the work of Rathgen's many advanced student assistants in finding and translating Japanese sources for Rathgen, put him in a position with unrivaled knowledge of Japan's economic history, institutions, statistics, administration, and state finances.[156] So valuable was Rathgen to "Germandom" in Japan that as of February 1887 he was formally employed as a paid Foreign Office assistant and advisor to von Holleben.[157] As Rathgen's Foreign Office personnel file and private correspondences with his family reveal, this additional activity was focused on conveying information about the budgetary rights in the draft Japanese constitution to the German government and on improving the Japanese public's understanding of Germany by countering bad press in the local English and Japanese newspapers.[158] On the latter, he worked with the American editor F. W. Eastlake of the *Tokyo Independent* to place positive stories on Germany and the Germans working in Japan.[159] To that end he also developed contact to Fukuzawa Yukichi and the *keiō gijuku* (Keiō Public School), the latter then in the process of establishing a Department of Economics, Law, and Literary Study and becoming a university.[160] Further, he was active assisting German merchants and shipping companies in gaining a competitive footing in Japan. His contacts seem to have been particularly active with M. Raspe & Co. and Carl

---

[154] "The Present State of Medicine in Japan," *The Japan Weekly Mail*, March 15, 1884.
[155] YUL MA, Farnam Family Papers, Box 89, Folder 93, Karl Rathgen to Henry Farnam, Tokyo, Jan. 9, 1884.
[156] Nozaki, "Karl Rathgen in Japan," 26.
[157] PA AA, P 11799, zu AA I 4965 von Holleben, Imperial German Embassy Tokyo, to Prince von Bismarck, Tokyo, Feb. 14, 1887.
[158] PA AA, P 11799, Attachment to report C. No. 72 A. of July 30, 1890, "Das Budgetrecht nach der japanischen Verfassung."
[159] PNFBW, Karl Rathgen to Bernhard Rathgen et al., Tokyo, June 11, 1886; Karl Rathgen to Bernhard Rathgen et al., Tokyo, June 11, 1886; May 4, 1887; Georg Michaelis was apparently also involved in this effort. See Bartels-Ishikawa, Delbrück, and Itō, *Die schönste Zeit meines Lebens*, 122.
[160] PNFBW, Karl Rathgen to Bernhard Rathgen et al., Tokyo, Nov. 29, 1887.

Rohde & Co., the latter an agent for both Siemens and Krupp in Japan.[161] Krupp was at the time in fierce completion with Armstrong for coastal defenses and other military contracts in Japan, which was the most important industrial export market for German firms in East Asia in these years.[162] Likewise, German shipyards were at that time active selling torpedo boats and other ships to the Japanese navy.[163] Rathgen noted the tremendous progress of German steamer lines, which by 1888 were faster than the English, French, and American competition, and German steel exports to Asia, and Japan in particular, were likewise to his mind superior to those from Britain and the United States and in increasing demand.[164] Indeed, in these years Rathgen was seriously contemplating entering the German consular service to work in such a capacity on returning to Germany. Von Holleben formally recommended him to the Foreign Office, and officials in Berlin were positively disposed to the idea.[165]

Beyond immediate concerns about Germany's place and standing in Japan, Rathgen was also a very well-informed observer of the great power frictions and conflicts in Asia in the 1880s marked by the rapid growth of the Chinese Northern Fleet, Sino-French War (1884–85), and various efforts by China, Japan, Russia, and Britain to jockey for harbors and influence in Korea, about which he was well informed by Paul von Möllendorff, who was then in service of the powerful Chinese Viceroy Li Hongzhang (1823–1901) as an advisor to the Korean king.[166] The tensions in Korea in particular convinced Rathgen that Germany needed more warships to assert its own interests in the region.[167] He was also an interested observer of the fierce competition for

---

[161] PNFBW, Karl Rathgen to Bernhard Rathgen et al., Tokyo, June 11, 1886; Sept. 22, 1886; April 16, 1889; Takenaka, "Business Activities of Siemens in Japan," 120–21.

[162] Kudō Akira, Tajima Nobuo, and Erich Pauer, "Changing Japanese-German Economic Relations: Competition and Cooperation," in Akira, et al., *Japan and Germany*, vol. 1: 47–50; Saaler, "The Imperial Japanese Army and Germany," 23–27.

[163] "Japan's Purchases Abroad," *The Japan Weekly Mail* (Yokohama), Oct. 12, 1889.

[164] PNFBW, Karl Rathgen to Bernhard Rathgen et al., Tokyo, March 29, 1888. He was particularly impressed with the steamers of Norddeutscher Lloyd, PNFBW, Karl Rathgen to Bernhard Rathgen et al., Tokyo, Dec. 10, 1886; July 8, 1889. See also Kudō, et al., "Changing Japanese-German Economic Relations," 47–48.

[165] PA AA, P 11799, I 17084 von Holleben to Chancellor von Caprivi, Tokyo, Aug. 27, 1890; adI. 17084, memorandum on Rathgen, Berlin, Oct. 5, 1890; PNFBW, Karl Rathgen to Bernhard Rathgen et al., Tokyo, June 11, 1886 and Feb. 22, 1887.

[166] PNFBW, Karl Rathgen to Bernhard Rathgen et al., Nikko, Aug. 26, 1884; Tokyo, Dec. 22, 1884; Jan. 19, 1885; Jan. 26, 1885; April 2, 1885; April 16, 1885; May 11, 1885; May 25, 1885; May 27, 1885; June 13, 1885; Sept. 16, 1885; Oct. 3, 1885; Nov. 23, 1885; Dec. 4, 1885; Dec. 18, 1885; Jan. 23, 1886; June 23, 1888; Sept. 27, 1888. On naval tensions between the English and Russians, PNFBW, Karl Rathgen to Bernhard Rathgen et al., Nikko, April 16, 1885; May 27, 1885; Jan. 19, 1887.

[167] PNFBW, Karl Rathgen to Bernhard Rathgen et al., Tokyo, April 16, 1885.

railway construction and military contracts between the Americans, British, French, and Germans in China.[168] It was at this time that Germany became a Pacific colonial power with new protectorates in New Guinea and New Britain (Bismarck Archipelago) (1884) and the Marshall Islands (1885) and a growing German merchant presence in Samoa. As a board member and librarian of the OAG and chairman of the German Colonial Society in Japan, Rathgen was both well informed and deeply-interested in these developments, following them very closely.[169] But he was also a frequent critic of the pettiness of the Reichstag and German public, which to his mind did not give the German navy, German shipping companies, the colonial endeavor, and German activities in China and Korea sufficient material support.[170]

At this time, Japan began to serve as a stopping off point for many German scientific expeditions to and from these new colonies, and the OAG frequently hosted lectures by German ethnographers and scientists which Rathgen attended.[171] With its new Pacific colonial presence, the German Cruiser Squadron made more frequent port calls to Yokohama in the 1880s, which resulted in various receptions and festivities involving the German embassy and the local German colony, to which Rathgen was a frequent guest.[172] These visits also served a clear commercial purpose, as von Holleben and Chancellor Caprivi were eager to impress upon the Japanese the quality of German ships and Krupp artillery for purchase.[173] Two institutions which served as meeting points for these formal and informal connections were – beyond the German embassy and OAG – the German Club "Germania" (founded in Yokohama 1863) and the German Evangelical Lutheran Congregation (founded in 1885 in Yokohama and Tokyo) by the Weimar Mission under the leadership of Pastor Wilfried Spinner. Rathgen thought very highly of Spinner and was quite close to him, and he considered the Evangelical Lutheran Congregation an "expansion of the German colony" in Japan.[174] As already mentioned, Rathgen's contacts to German merchants and shipping firms in Yokohama were quite extensive; he even served as a legal advisor to some of these in the absence of German lawyers and law firms in Yokohama.[175]

---

[168] PNFBW, Karl Rathgen to Bernhard Rathgen et al., Tokyo, Sept. 16, 1885; May 24, 1886.
[169] PNFBW, Karl Rathgen to Bernhard Rathgen et al., n.d. [Sept. 1885]; Tokyo, Oct. 28, 1887; Nov. 15, 1889.
[170] PNFBW, Karl Rathgen to Bernhard Rathgen et al., Tokyo, March 11, 1885; May 11, 1885; Oct. 3, 1885; Dec. 4, 1885; March 31, 1886; May 5, 1886.
[171] PNFBW, Karl Rathgen to Bernhard Rathgen et al., Tokyo, April 12, 1888.
[172] PNFBW, Karl Rathgen to Bernhard Rathgen et al., Tokyo, May 10, 1888.
[173] Böhm, *Überseehandel und Flottenbau*, 41.
[174] PNFBW, Karl Rathgen to Bernhard Rathgen et al., Tokyo, Oct. 23, 1885; Heyo E. Hamer, *Mission und Politik* (Aachen: Verlag an der Lottbeck, 2002).
[175] PNFBW, Karl Rathgen to Bernhard Rathgen et al., March 20, 1884.

Beyond these points of contact to German interests in Japan, Asia, and the Pacific, Rathgen traveled nearly all corners of the Japanese archipelago as both a tourist and an astute observer of Japan's rapid economic development. As mentioned earlier, Rathgen also traveled extensively in Korea, Formosa, and China in 1886 and 1890, enabled by his close ties to von Holleben and good contacts to German ambassadors, consular officials, and advisors to the Chinese and Korean governments, such as Max von Brandt and Paul von Möllendorff.[176] The conditions he observed and his impressions of their significance to Germany were conveyed to Gustav Schmoller via many lengthy and very detailed letters Rathgen wrote to his brother Bernhard and his sisters. Among other things, he observed German military advisors and engineers active in Formosa rebuilding fortifications and coastal batteries for the Chinese governor Lui Mingchuang (1836–96).[177] Rathgen was also a regular correspondent on Japanese and Asian affairs for the liberal *National-Zeitung* in Berlin, helping to disseminate his views to a wider audience at home.[178]

The unambiguous picture that Rathgen painted was of a very fragile German presence in Asia, under attack within Japan by the English and those in Japan who sympathized with them and without any firm foothold elsewhere. Within Japan, Rathgen realized that Japanese sympathies for Germany were pragmatic, geared toward legal and constitutional reform with an eye to national unity, industrialization, a modernized military, and a revision of the unequal treaties. Once those goals were achieved, he had no illusions that the Germans in Japan would continue to enjoy any special advantage over the other tolerated foreigners. Indeed, the Japanese were adept at playing the various nationalities off against each other for their own ends.[179] Outside of Japan, German merchants and missionaries were at the mercy of English, French, and Chinese goodwill, since Germany lacked the naval muscle or an East Asian base of operation to secure a more advantageous and permanent position in Korea or China.

After his lengthy journey to Shanghai, up the Yangtze to Hankou and back, and through Formosa and southern China between late May and late August 1890, Rathgen returned to Tokyo one last time for a reunion with his old childhood and university friend Henry Farnam, who was on a journey to Japan with his wife and then staying Yokohama. Despite a very warm reunion with Henry, Rathgen could not help but note to his family how he had almost

---

[176] PNFBW, Karl Rathgen to Bernhard Rathgen et al., Aboard the P & O steamer Thibet, July 3, 1886; Tientsin (Tianjin), July 29, 1886 (with insertions from July 16–Aug. 28, 1886); Shanghai, June 6, 1890.
[177] PNFBW, Karl Rathgen to Bernhard Rathgen et al., on board the *Namoa* between Foochow (Fuzhou) and Amoy (Xiamen), July 30, 1890.
[178] PNFBW, Karl Rathgen to Bernhard Rathgen et al., Tokyo, March 1, 1889.
[179] PNFBW, Karl Rathgen to Bernhard Rathgen et al., Tokyo, Dec. 27, 1887; May 28, 1888.

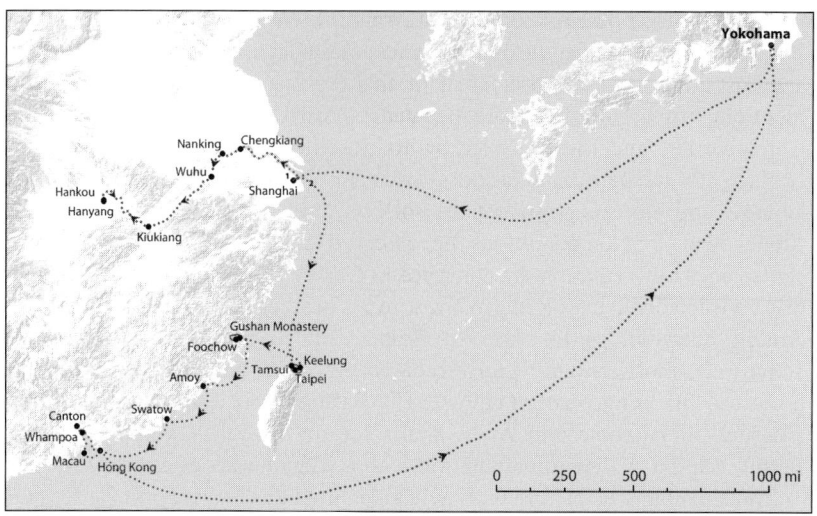

Map 2.2  Karl Rathgen's journey to Formosa and China, May 25–Aug. 25, 1890.

barely recognized Henry with his new beard, who to his mind "had taken on the external appearance of the typical Yankee." He was also surprised by his "pure American" speech, as he had only ever heard him speaking German in the past.[180] The years in Japan seem to have made Rathgen more, not less, sensitive to national differences and frictions. That said, Rathgen's return to Germany in early September 1890 went via San Francisco and New York, and he would spend a very pleasant week with Farnam in New Haven in early October before his passage to Hamburg.[181]

As it would turn out, Ambassador von Holleben's hopes for a permanent German intellectual dominance over Japan were wildly optimistic. When Rathgen left Japan in September 1890, there had already been a significant exodus of German teachers and advisors from Japan, marking an end to the so-called "German decade."[182] One year later, von Holleben was named ambassador to the United States and left Japan, replaced in 1892 by the far less capable Felix von Gutschmidt (1843–1905). The Japanese leadership was in any case by this point eager to reduce its reliance on foreign advisors and teachers and to begin to replace them by suitably-trained Japanese, emblematic of which was Kanai Noburu's appointment to a professorship of political economy at the Imperial University in 1890. The enactment of the Meiji

---

[180] PNFBW, Karl Rathgen to Bernhard Rathgen et al., on board the *Gaelic* between Yokohama and San Francisco, Sept. 17, 1890.
[181] PNFBW, Karl Rathgen to Bernhard Rathgen et al., Washington, DC, Oct. 16, 1890.
[182] PNFBW, Karl Rathgen to Bernhard Rathgen et al., Tokyo, March 19, 1890.

constitution that same year and the renegotiation of foreign treaties this enabled, as well as the many steady advances in Japanese industry and the modernization of its military, meant that Japan was now also legally and militarily much more self-reliant. Arguably, it had been Germans more than any other foreigners who had helped to bring this about so swiftly.

The drift in German-Japanese relations was bound up closely with Germany's growing commercial interests in China and the hold that China had on the imagination as both a promising market and possible field of German colonial activity. In 1885 a first commission of German bankers and industrialists visited China to explore investment and export opportunities in the Middle Kingdom, and direct steamship traffic subsidized by the Reichstag began between Germany and China in the year following. In 1890 the Deutsch-Asiatische Bank and the Consortium for Asian Business were founded, and soon thereafter China replaced Japan to become the most important Asian export market for German arms manufacturers. Likewise German military men were very active as advisors to the Qing government and in the reform of its armed forces in the 1880s and 1890s.[183] The German Cruiser Squadron was then also being used increasingly in both "shows of force" and "shows for sale" in Asia, the Chinese being especially good customers for German naval ships from such wharves as Bremer Vulkan and Howaldtwerft.[184] Indeed Krupp enjoyed a near monopoly in China as an arms supplier, and German merchants were by the early 1890s the second most active foreign commercial presence in China after the British.[185]

The upshot was that German policy in Asia was being pulled in two different directions: on the one hand, Germany had invested heavily in the spread of German influences in Japan, a process that had been dominated by

---

[183] PNFB, Karl Rathgen to Bernhard Rathgen et al., Tokyo, Jan. 19, 1885; Wippich, *Japan und die deutsche Fernostpolitik,* 94; Richard S. Horowitz, "Beyond the Marble Boat: The Transformation of the Chinese Military, 1850–1911," in *A Military History of China,* ed. David A. Graff and Robin Higham (Lexington: University of Kentucky Press, 2012), 153–74, here 158; William C. Kirby, *Germany and Republican China* (Stanford: Stanford University Press, 1984), 8–10.

[184] Heiko Herold, *Reichsgewalt bedeutet Seegewalt: Die Kreuzergeschwader der Kaiserlichen Marine als Instrument der deutschen Kolonial- und Weltpolitik 1885 bis 1901* (Munich: Oldenbourg, 2013), 102–4; Canis, *Von Bismarck zur Weltpolitik,* 238.

[185] Harold James, *Krupp: A History of the Legendary German Firm* (Princeton and Woodstock: Princeton University Press, 2012), 51; Kelly, *Tirpitz,* 117–18. See also Georg Baur, *China um 1900: Aufzeichnung eines Krupp-Direktors,* ed. Elisabeth Kaske (Cologne, Weimar, Vienna: Böhlau Verlag, 2005); Chunxiao Jing, *Mit Barbaren gegen Barbaren: Die chinesische Selbststärkungsbewegung und das deutsche Rüstungsgeschäft im späten 19. Jahrhundert* (Münster, Hamburg, London: LIT Verlag, 2002), 70–152; Sun Lie, "The Tactics and Channels of Ordnance Procurement of the Northern Navy as Revealed by a Letter from Li Hongzhang to Alfred Krupp," *Studies in Dialectics of Nature* 27, no. 6 (2011): 93–97.

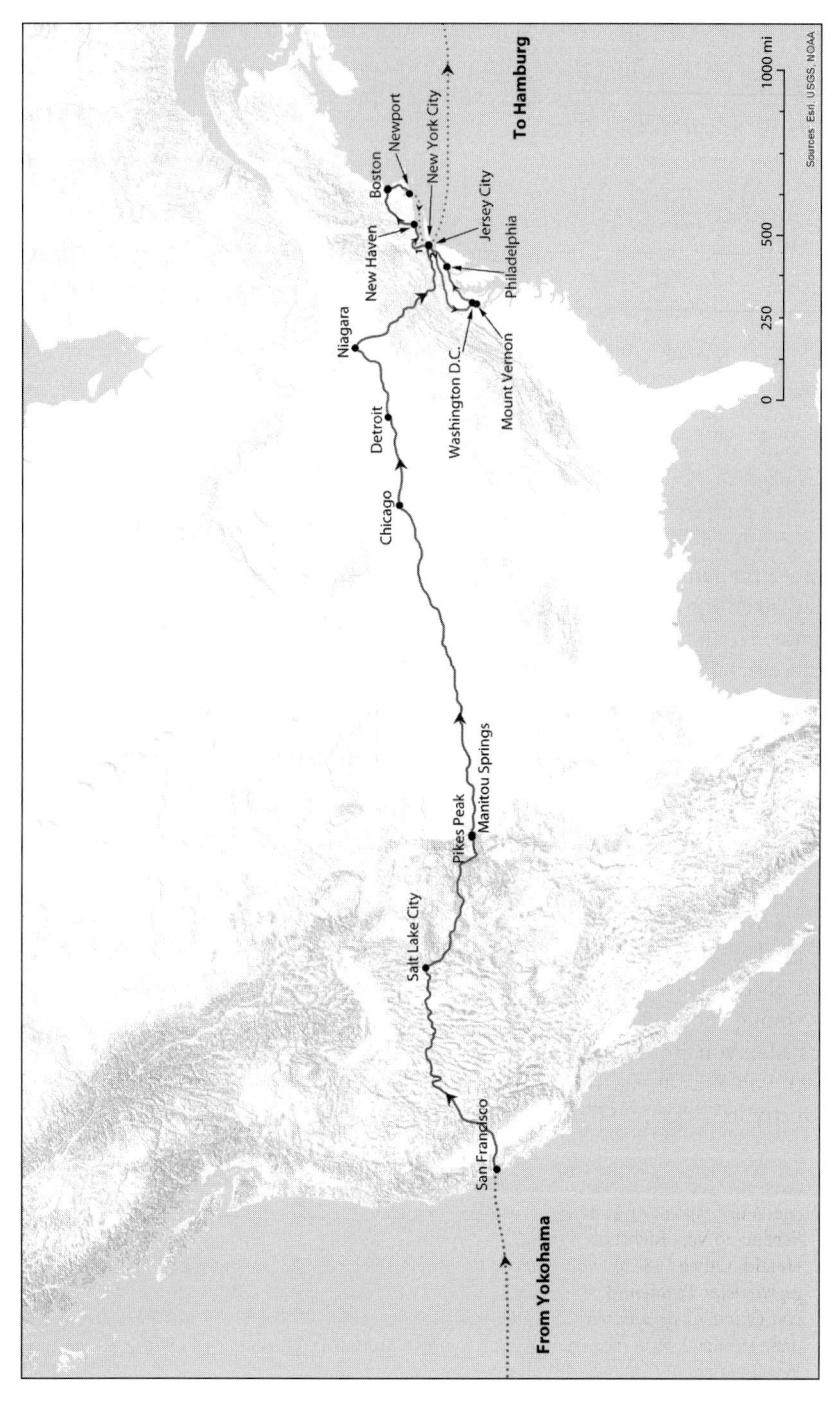

Map 2.3 Karl Rathgen's journey from Yokohama to Hamburg via the United States, Sept. 3–Oct. 23, 1890.

the *Bildungsbürgertum* and supported by the Foreign Office so long as German opportunities elsewhere in Asia were constrained. The logic of this policy was reinforced by Germany's very feeble cruiser force and its reliance on the ports of Hong Kong and Nagasaki for coal and repairs and the German Naval Hospital in Yokohama for the care of its sailors. Soon however, the Foreign Office began to pursue a more China-centered policy strongly supported by Max von Brandt. As was previously discussed, von Brandt had been part of the Eulenburg expedition to East Asia in the early 1860s that had established diplomatic and commercial relations with Japan, China, and Siam. The geologist Ferdinand von Richthofen had served as legation secretary to Eulenburg on that expedition, and Richthofen would subsequently play a very similar role in making China accessible to the Germans that Johannes Justus Rein had played for Japan.[186]

Richthofen had spent six years working as a field geologist in California and Nevada gold fields after his initial travels to East Asia from 1860 to 1862, which he followed up with a more extensive series of expeditions in China between 1868 and 1872 funded by the Bank of California, which was interested in information about China's mineral bounty.[187] These geological expeditions resulted in the publication of a series of letters to the Shanghai Chamber of Commerce focusing on the mineral wealth of China and then a groundbreaking work on China after Richthofen's return to Germany, the latter partially subsidized by the Prussian government and published in three volumes from 1877 to 1883 and in two folios of geological maps of China in 1885.[188] The significance of von Richthofen's work was his conviction of the vast mineral wealth that China possessed, notably coal and iron ore deposits, and his belief that the construction of railways would allow the rapid industrial development of China and its integration into the world economy. Shansi (Shanxi) province and the Shantung Peninsula appeared as particularly coal-rich and promising. His subsequent status as eminent geographer and geologist of international reputation and his public lecturing and contacts in Berlin to German high officials did much to spread these views throughout Germany.[189]

Among those very much persuaded by Richthofen's work and arguments was Max von Brandt. While German Imperial envoy to China from 1875 to 1893, von Brandt was quite aggressive in promoting the interests of German industry in China and in gaining influence among the powerful Qing viceroys

---

[186] See Wu, *Empires of Coal*, 33–65.   [187] Ibid., 41–45.
[188] Ferdinand von Richthofen, *Baron Richthofen's Letters, 1870–72* (Shanghai: North-China Herald Office, 1872); von Richthofen, *China: Ergebnisse eigener Reisen und darauf gegründeter Studien*, 3 vols. (Berlin: Dietrich Reimer, 1876–83); von Richthofen, *Atlas von China: Orographische und geologische Karten, zu des Verfassers Werk: China, Ergebnisse eigener Reisen und darauf gegründeter Studien* (Berlin: Dietrich Reimer, 1885).
[189] Wu, *Empires of Coal*, 46–48, 61–64.

by placing German engineers in their service as advisors in the hopes of securing railway and mining concessions for German firms.[190] He also worked to increase the influence of Gustav Detring (1842–1913), a German serving as commissioner of Chinese Customs in Tientsin, with Li Hongzhang.[191] Brandt, despite his stint as resident minister in Japan between 1872 and 1875, was nevertheless known for his dismissive and hostile attitude toward the Japanese, which had grown during his long tenure in China. After his retirement and return to Germany in 1893, von Brandt spread his views in Germany in many publications, and his status as a leading expert on China assured him much influence advising both the Kaiser and the Foreign Office through a number of memoranda.[192]

Brandt successfully pushed for a policy focused on gaining a formal sphere of influence in China and increasingly hostile to Japan, which he saw as a threat to the European powers in China and East Asia more broadly. Indeed, more than any other single person in Germany, von Brandt was active in spreading the fear of a Japanese "yellow peril" in Germany, gaining a particularly receptive ear in the young Kaiser, who made the crusade against this *fata morgana* a personal cause.[193] This coincided with efforts in the Foreign Office and by the Kaiser to try to curry favor with the Russians in order to break the Franco-Russian alliance since the lapse of the Reinsurance Treaty in 1890.[194] As a major arms supplier to China, Germany also sought to gain favor with the Chinese with an eye also toward ultimately securing an exclusive base of operation and a formal sphere of influence in China.[195] Thus German foreign policy drifted in a direction at odds with maintaining good relations with Japan, coming to a head in 1895 over Japan's claims to the Liaotung Peninsula in the Treaty of Shimonoseki ending the Sino-Japanese War.

Liaotung and Port Arthur were considered within the Russian sphere of interest, which was at that time building the Trans-Siberian Railway to connect Russia with its Far Eastern territories and Manchuria. Moreover,

[190] Ibid., 103–4.
[191] Hans van de Ven, "Robert Hart and Gustav Detring during the Boxer Rebellion," *Modern Asia Studies* 40, no. 3 (2006): 631–62, here 650–56.
[192] Wippich, *Japan und die deutsche Fernostpolitik*, 90–94; Mehnert, "Gelbe Gefahr," 113.
[193] Mehnert, "Gelbe Gefahr," 156–60; Röhl, *The Kaiser's Personal Monarchy*, 745–60. On the Japanese "Yellow Peril," Heinz Gollwitzer, *Die gelbe Gefahr: Geschichte eines Schlagworts: Studien zum imperialistischen Denken* (Göttingen: Vandenhoeck & Ruprecht, 1962); Mehnert, "Gelbe Gefahr," 28–29, 35–59, 112–19; Iikura Akira, "The 'Yellow Peril' and Its Influence on Japanese-German Relations," in *Japanese-German Relations, 1895–1945: War Diplomacy and Public Opinion*, ed. Christian W. Spang and Rolf-Harald Wippich (London and New York: Routledge, 2006), 80–97.
[194] Canis, *Von Bismarck zur Weltpolitik*, 149–64; Röhl, *The Kaiser's Personal Monarchy*, 749–60.
[195] Wippich, *Japan und die deutsche Fernostpolitik*, 146–47; Canis, *Von Bismarck zur Weltpolitik*, 155.

Liaotung would have put Japan in the driver's seat in determining the future status of Korea. While German public opinion, reflecting the strong German cultural and scientific engagement in Japan since the 1870s, was firmly supportive of the Japan in its war with China, the German government – reflecting the Sinophile positions of the Foreign Office establishment and the Kaiser influenced by von Brandt and von Richthofen and the Chinese interests of German exporters – was by this point squarely focused on gaining advantages in China.[196] Despite its very good relations with Japan and the formal declarations of neutrality by the German government, German illegal merchant trade in "war contraband" to China flourished during the hostilities, which led to uncharacteristic tensions with the Japanese.[197] Then, in a shocking about-face marked by entirely gratuitous diplomatic insults to the Japanese from the German ambassador to Japan, the German government agreed to intervene with France and Russia against Japan in April 1895, effectively threatening Japan with war if it did not cede its claims in Liaotung.[198]

Faced with the prospect of naval conflict with three European powers simultaneously and the risk of being cut off from its troops in China, the Japanese relinquished their claims ignominiously, while retaining Formosa and the nearby Pescadores Islands (Penghu). The Japanese would never forget this betrayal by the Germans. The British had themselves played the role of defender of the Chinese status quo throughout the conflict and been very much opposed to Japan gaining a foothold in Formosa, which threatened British interests in coastal China from the Yangtze Valley all the way to Hong Kong, but British statesmen preferred a policy of appeasement over confrontation with Japan and so in the end acquiesced to Japan's seizure of the islands as a prize of war.[199] Similar timidity in the face of a potentially powerful foe informed British policy vis-à-vis Russia in northern China when in early April the Russians began to hint of their displeasure over Japan's acquisition of the Liaotung Peninsula.[200]

The damage to Japanese-German relations caused by the Intervention of Shimonoseki was as lasting as the diplomatic advantage Germany thought it had secured with St. Petersburg and Peking was fleeting: no wedge came between the Franco-Russian alliance, and the Qing government was aloof to German overtures for a naval base or treaty port in China as a gift of gratitude for its intervention. Likewise, no railway concessions were offered the

---

[196] See Rolf-Harald Wippich, "Japan Enthusiasm in Wilhelmine Germany: The Case of the Sino-Japanese War, 1894–95," in *Japanese-German Relations, 1895–1945: War Diplomacy and Public Opinion*, ed. Christian W. Spang and Rolf-Harald Wippich (London and New York: Routledge, 2006), 61–79. Canis, *Von Bismarck zur Weltpolitik*, 154–55.
[197] Herold, *Reichsgewalt bedeutet Seegewalt*, 221–22.
[198] See Wippich, *Japan und die deutsche Fernostpolitik*, 129–43, 145.
[199] Otte, *The China Question*, 54, 56, 61–63, 72.     [200] Ibid., 57, 64–65, 72–73.

Germans, and since Chinese state coffers were emptied by the war and the indemnities paid to Japan, there was little prospect for export of German-made weaponry and ships to China.[201] Simultaneously, a wave of anti-German sentiment swept Japan. If Japan's betrayal by its former teacher was particularly hard to swallow, its diplomatic and military isolation following its conflict with China was nevertheless a crash course in the brutal politics of imperialism. Japan was, as ever, a quick study and gradually moved closer to Britain, later culminating in the 1902 Anglo-Japanese Alliance.[202] The German Foreign Office's unsuccessful foray into a more active China policy thus threatened to squander more than twenty years of German *Kulturarbeit* in Japan and investment in good relations with the Japanese with next to nothing to show for it in return – for all their efforts, the Chinese were only willing to offer the Germans minor trading concessions in Hankou and Tientsin.[203] This was not a promising start for a new round of German *Weltpolitik*.

While Bismarck's intention had been to use German colonial expansion in the 1880s to push European conflicts to the periphery, the growing German commercial, financial, and trade ties to Asia, the South Pacific, South America, and Ottoman Turkey increasingly divorced German foreign policy from European diplomatic considerations and created abundant new avenues for entanglements and conflicts that would ultimately reverberate back to Europe, affecting an already precarious balance of power. Indeed, these areas and China in particular would emerge in the 1890s as a realm of tension and potential conflict of the first order. Due to Britain's position as indirect arbiter of the balance of power in Europe, growing Anglo-German tensions were very likely to result.[204] But these entanglements also brought Germany into conflict with non-European powers. As will be discussed in the next chapters, the seizure of Kiaochow in 1897, the Spanish-American War in 1898, the partitioning of Samoa in 1899, the suppression of the Boxer Rebellion from 1899 to 1901, and the Second Venezuela Crisis of 1902–3 brought Germany into a series of diplomatic conflicts with China and the United States for the first time, events keenly observed by Schmoller and his students shaping the political economy of *Weltwirtschaft* and in turn informing their perspectives on German naval arms and colonial policy in the making of *Weltpolitik*.

---

[201] Niels P. Petersson, *Imperialismus und Modernisierung: Siam, China und die europäischen Mächte 1895–1914* (Munich: Oldenbourg, 2000), 47–48; Wippich, *Japan und die deutsche Fernostpolitik*, 285–97.
[202] Wippich, *Japan und die deutsche Fernostpolitik*, 160–70.
[203] Canis, *Von Bismarck zur Weltpolitik*, 164.
[204] Schöllgen, *Imperialismus und Gleichgewicht*, 4.

# 3

# World Economy

## China and Venezuela

### Naval Arms, Neutrality, and the Erosion of Security

Two unmistakable themes that emerged from the wide-ranging travel of Sering, Rathgen, Schumacher, and von Halle in the United States and Japan in the 1880s and early 1890s were that the world was now much smaller and that there was much greater worldwide competition – for markets, spheres of influence, and colonies – than there had been only a few years earlier. Quite clearly, it was also perceived by Schmoller's students and many other observers as a more dangerous world, and that perception was, if anything, heightened in the years between 1895 and 1897. While this more competitive international dynamic was driven to a large degree by economic imperatives and the reality of the rise of two powerful industrial competitors to Britain – the United States and Germany – British colonial and naval policy of the previous forty years bears a great degree of responsibility for creating that more menacing climate. Any hope of understanding the origins and driving forces of German *Weltpolitik* must start here, and this requires unpacking the changes in British naval and strategic thinking and policy that took place in these decades.

Steamships, railways, and telegraphs – the very technologies that had enabled the wide-ranging travel recounted in the previous two chapters – had once been celebrated by British liberals at the time of the Crystal Palace Exhibit in 1851 as promising to usher in a more peaceful and secure world.[1] What many British observers of the exhibit breezily overlooked was that these same technologies were ushering in an unprecedented and violent expansion of the British Empire. There was no centralized or coherent plan for the remarkable outward expansion of Britain in the Victorian era. It was driven instead by old networks and multiple lobbies of investors, merchants, speculators, emigrants, scientists, adventurers, humanitarians, and missionaries able to influence British public opinion and make their cases to the "official mind" in Whitehall.[2] While not planned per se, it was not a natural, inevitable, or

---

[1] "The Exhibition – The Crystal Palace," *The Economist*, Jan. 4, 1851.
[2] John Darwin, *The Empire Project: The Rise and Fall of the British World-System, 1830–1970* (Cambridge: Cambridge University Press, 2009), 24.

much less a peaceful process. From 1855 to 1895, during which the size of the British Empire roughly doubled, the British fought wars in the Crimea (1854–56), Persia (1856–57), India (1857–59), China (1856–60), New Zealand (1860–66), Ethiopia (1867–68), West Africa (1873–84), Afghanistan (1878–80), Zululand (1879), South Africa (1880–81), Egypt (1882), the Sudan (1884–85), Burma (1885–86), and Chitral in northwestern India (1895).[3] Gladstone himself described the foreign policy of this era as having been "Imbued with the spirit of territorial grab."[4]

The first of these British wars, the Crimean War, humiliated Russia and shattered the European balance of power, enabling Italian and German unification and catalyzing in the decades following great power rivalries, imperial scrambles, and naval arms races. After Russia's stunning victories in the Russo-Turkish War of 1877–78, Britain (along with Austria) threatened Russia with war and pressed it to relinquish most of its territorial claims at the Congress of Berlin, gaining British control over Cyprus. As mediator in the dispute, Berlin neither sought nor gained territory but harvested St. Petersburg's lasting enmity (much of the rest was reserved for Vienna, which gained control over Bosnia-Herzegovina). This led to the signing of the Austro-German Dual Alliance in 1879 and would over time lead Russia to withdraw from the Holy Alliance in 1887 and into a military entente with France in 1892. There is a line from these developments to the two Balkan wars in 1912–13 and ultimately to the outbreak of the First World War.[5] It can thus be argued that Great Britain's sprawling colonial interests and sweeping claims in the Mediterranean became key catalysts for instability and conflict in Europe before 1914.

While Britain had been last successfully invaded by the Dutch in 1688 and enjoyed unquestioned naval superiority after 1815, British national identity had been shaped strongly by recurring invasion and naval scares and sensationalist invasion stories since the Napoleonic era.[6] The British liberal politician Richard Cobden was himself an astute observer and critic of these recurring "panics" fed by absurd or improbable rumors of French invasion that had riled the British public repeatedly in 1848, 1851–53, and again in 1859–61, and led to needless increases in naval spending.[7] Indeed, as Cobden noted, there was even something of an American invasion panic in Britain during the US Civil War, as outlandish as that was.[8]

---

[3] Darwin, *Unfinished Empire*, 117.   [4] Quoted in Wilson, *The Policy of the Entente*, 4.
[5] See Dominic Lieven, *The End of Tsarist Russia: The March to World War I and Revolution* (New York: Viking, 2015), 77–83.
[6] Linda Colley, *Britons: Forging the Nation, 1707–1837* (New Haven and London: Yale University Press, 2009), 289–325.
[7] Richard Cobden, *The Three Panics: An Historical Episode*, 5th ed. (London: Ward & Co. 1862).
[8] Ibid., 139–43.

German invasion of Britain made its debut in George Tomkyns Chesney's anonymously published yarn "The Battle of Dorking" in 1871, before a German navy even existed. Published in the Tory political journal *Blackwood's Magazine*, it managed to cause such a public stir that Gladstone was pressed by the Foreign Office to warn of the dangers of alarmism.[9] Forts were nevertheless erected at Box Hill and Ranmore in the "Dorking gap" in the chalk hills of the North Downs shortly thereafter.[10] This is all the more striking given that British naval supremacy between 1865 and 1890 was so complete that the Royal Navy could successfully fend off "any combination of naval rivals."[11] Such invasion fear continued to operate as a major factor in British defense policy well through the nineteenth century and would witness a renewed upsurge after 1900.[12] The point to be made here is that invasion fear was a peculiar fixture of British domestic politics long before Germany ever posed a credible naval or military threat to Britain, and it retained a life of its own in British public opinion not bound to objective assessments by Admiralty and other defense specialists of the actual naval threats posed to the British Isles.

Before 1880, British national defense had focused on coastal fortifications, fortified dockyards, and ironclad defensive steamships whose range was restricted by the need for close access to coastal coaling stations and repair docks.[13] A few years prior to the Dorking panic in the immediate aftermath of the US Civil War, Captain J. C. R. Colomb (1838–1909) of the Royal Marines raised the question of British defense in a new way that vastly inflated the definition of national security to include not only the defense of Great Britain and Ireland, but also all of British maritime commerce and India, arguing that the British Empire's welfare depended on the security of its commerce and safe communications in the event of a sudden war.[14] The British people, he later argued, were but dimly aware of their dependence on maritime trade for food and raw materials. Dismissing the effectiveness of defensive convoys out of hand on false assumptions, he and his followers argued that Britain needed to extend its defensive frontier to the enemy's coastline to impose a close blockade of enemy ports in order to secure command of the sea. Only by putting an overwhelming bluewater navy at the center of British defense, they argued, could the security of the Empire be assured.[15]

---

[9] Gertjan Dijink, *National Identity and Geopolitical Visions: Maps of Pride and Pain* (London: Routledge, 1996), 38; Scully, *British Images*, 93–103.
[10] Kathryn Atherton, *Dorking in the Great War* (Barnsley, South Yorkshire: Pen and Sword, 2014), 21.
[11] Hobson, *Imperialism at Sea*, 25.
[12] See Rose, *Zwischen Empire und Kontinent*, 189–237.
[13] Hobson, *Imperialism at Sea*, 29–30.   [14] Ibid., 87.
[15] Ibid., 88–93; Avner Offer, *The First World War: An Agrarian Interpretation* (Oxford: Oxford University Press 1989), 221.

To be sure, these Bluewater School ideas, which began to dominate British Admiralty thinking by the early 1880s, were informed by changes in ship and weapons technology that extended the range, accuracy, and lethality of naval ships.[16] But they were also legitimated by arguments that drew from a very selective reading of naval history and were premised on a very expansive definition of contraband in war to the point of violating neutral rights.[17] Indeed, there was no clear line by the 1870s between a military and economic blockade involving entire industrial societies in wars of attrition, as the US Civil War had shown. In any case, it is hard to miss the pedigree of hysteria from a long history of invasion scares in the inflationary logic of imperial defense of the Bluewater School, and not surprisingly, it ultimately prevailed in altering British naval strategy in the late 1880s following yet another naval panic.

Significant increases in the size and capability of French navy, tensions with the French and Russians, and massive popular agitation aroused by a new naval scare in 1884 put pressure on the British government to expand the Royal Navy. In 1888 the Admiralty, now beholden to bluewater strategic thinking, evaluated maneuvers that had tested the feasibility of imposing a blockade with existing naval technology and came to the conclusion that Britain should proceed immediately to create an overwhelming naval force centered on battleships with the aim of coastal blockade and command of the sea.[18] A "Two Power Standard" was then formalized for the Royal Navy through the Naval Defence Act in March 1889. This sought to expand the number of first-class battleships to at least the size of the next two largest navies combined – at the time, those of France and Russia, respectively.[19]

As France, Germany, and other European countries had industrialized by 1889 and were more reliant than ever on overseas trade, command of the sea as formalized under the Two Power Standard was an offensive weapon to which they were now much more vulnerable.[20] The defence act's intention was, of course, to *deter* the naval ambitions of France and Russia, as well as to secure parliamentary funding for the navy for a timeframe of five years to allow a continuity of construction uninterrupted by yearly budgetary politics.[21] While 10 new British battleships were built for a total of 22 first-class battleships (ships of the line), by 1893 the deterrent had failed: France and Russia more than matched that together with a total of 25.[22] In 1892, moreover, the Russians and French forged a military entente that became a formal

---

[16] Hobson, *Imperialism at Sea*, 30–33, 91–92.   [17] Ibid., 92–95.   [18] Ibid., 95.
[19] Arthur J. Marder, *The Anatomy of British Sea Power: A History of British Naval Policy in the Pre-Dreadnought Era, 1880–1905* (New York: Knopf, 1940), 65–74, 105–43, esp. 119–43.
[20] Hobson, *Imperialism at Sea*, 37–38.   [21] Marder, *British Sea Power*, 143, 143n48.
[22] Ibid., 175; Offer, *The First World War*, 325; Wilson, *The Policy of the Entente*, 10.

alliance in 1894. Ongoing tensions with France over Siam and Egypt, fears that Russia and France might attack India, and Franco-Russian naval cooperation in the Mediterranean then prompted yet another British navy scare that swept the country in the autumn of 1893 with much press agitation to increase the size of the Royal Navy immediately.[23] Despite the spuriousness of the arguments of the British navalists – as Admiralty experts pointed out, Britain's fleet was qualitatively superior to the combined Franco-Russian battleship fleets – the agitation resulted in large supplemental naval appropriations (the Spencer Programme) in March 1894 for seven new first-class battleships and significant increases in permanent naval personnel from 83,400 in 1894 to 106,390 by 1898.[24]

Just as this naval arms race was underway, the status of neutral shipping in war was also in some flux. The Crimean War had led to an agreement exchanging a commitment from France to cease privateering in exchange for Britain granting greater protections to neutral goods and vessels in war. This was formalized legally at the peace ending the Crimean War in the Declaration of Paris of 1856 and ratified by all of the European great powers. Accordingly, neutral ships carrying enemy goods could not be seized unless carrying contraband, and neutral goods on enemy ships (unless contraband goods) could not be seized in war. Previously Britain had made wide and indiscriminate use of what it termed the Rule of War (1756) that prohibited neutrals from carrying out any trade with Britain's enemies in war, and it often seized all enemy goods on neutral vessels.[25] The Paris Declaration also asserted that blockades in war, in order to be legally binding, had to be effective, that is, maintained by a sufficient force to be able to prevent maritime access to an enemy coast. Simple declarations of a blockade (i.e., "paper" blockades) used by Britain to scare off trade with belligerents thus also became illegal.[26] This was a significant restriction of the belligerent prerogatives of de facto British naval hegemony, though one loophole existed in that contraband was never defined in the declaration.

While the protests of powerful neutrals like the United States helped assure enforcement of the Declaration of Paris after 1856, Britain nevertheless clung tenaciously to the doctrine of "continuous voyage" and never abandoned it. This doctrine claimed the right in war to search any ships and cargos for contraband goods on the high seas – even if the destination was a neutral port – if there was any suspicion that the cargo's ultimate destination was

---

[23] Marder, *British Sea Power*, 179–80.   [24] Ibid., 204–5.
[25] Lance Davis and Stanley Engerman, *Naval Blockades in Peace and War: An Economic History Since 1750* (Cambridge: Cambridge University Press, 2006), 7.
[26] Wolff Heintschel von Heinegg, "Naval Blockade and International Law," in *Naval Blockades and Seapower: Strategies and Counter-Strategies*, ed. Bruce A. Ellerman and S. C. M Paine (London and New York, 2006), 12–13.

enemy hands. It also opposed clearer definitions of effective blockade.[27] The experience of the Union blockade in the US Civil War, the spread of bluewater strategic thinking, and a larger American navy by the late 1890s likewise led the United States to gradually embrace "continuous voyage," prefer looser rules of proof in determining contraband, and to oppose additional restrictions on blockade.[28] The gradual drift of the United States into these positions – once one of the most powerful traditional defenders of neutral rights – thus represented a de facto erosion of neutral rights, though its full impact on international law would not be felt until after 1900.

Britain's insecurity, its tensions with Russia and France, and the escalating costs of imperial defense were all tied up to varying degrees with the massive territorial expansion of the British Empire between 1855 and 1895 discussed earlier. As the Naval Defense Act of 1889 and Spencer Programme of 1894 make plain, the strains on Britain's resources were growing by the mid-1890s due to these various commitments and tensions. By 1897–98 both Lord Salisbury and Joseph Chamberlain (1836–1914) voiced open concern that any additional expansion of the empire was financially burdensome and that Britain faced grave challenges protecting it all given that Britain's interests conflicted with nearly everyone else's.[29] The gradual strategic pivot that would occur in British foreign policy between 1895 and 1907 resulting from these pressures drew Britain out of its "splendid isolation" back to Europe. This was justified to the British public by the Foreign Office and various British governments as Britain playing its supposedly "traditional role" in maintaining the balance of power in Europe. In reality, it was a major departure from the long-prevailing Palmerstonian doctrine of the Victorian era which had sought to maintain flexibility by avoiding both permanent alliances and permanent rifts with other great European powers. It was thus an admission of vulnerability, weakness, and a strategic retreat into the arms of European allies on which the fate of the British overseas empire would now increasingly hinge.[30] As will be discussed in detail in the chapters to follow, rather than balancing power in its European geopolitical center, the Triple Entente that was the end result of this British diplomacy upset that balance profoundly and became a major contributing factor in the outbreak of the First World War.[31]

In 1895 it remained to be seen how Britain would align itself on the European continent, but it was already doubtful by then that it would be with

---

[27] See John W. Coogan, *The End of Neutrality: The United States, Britain and Maritime Rights 1899–1915* (Ithaca and London: Cornell University Press, 1981).

[28] Ibid., 22–24, 56–69, 114–16, 122.

[29] Wilson, *The Policy of the Entente*, 4–5, 6, 11, 15–16.

[30] Ibid., 59–84; Rose, *Zwischen Empire und Kontinent*, 353–62.

[31] Charmley, *Splendid Isolation*, 6–7, 313–95; Wilson, *The Policy of the Entente*, 1–16, 59–99.

Imperial Germany. Britain had rejected an alliance proposal from Germany in 1890, and Germany's own geography and alliance with Austria-Hungary and Italy posed unattractive additional defensive liabilities to the British government after 1895, which by that point wanted to *reduce* not increase those liabilities and their attending costs. At the same time, Germany's naval impotence and small colonial presence offered little in return to cover Britain's sprawling imperial commitments. Thus, when Salisbury headed a new government in 1895 his priority was to improve relations with France and Russia, which was at odds with the new Colonial Secretary Joseph Chamberlain's inclination to seek an alliance with Germany. In the Wilhelmstrasse, Britain's increasing isolation and strategic overextension as well the cues coming from Chamberlain were misread as offering Germany leverage with Britain.[32]

This basic bargaining asymmetry between Great Britain and Germany meant that Britain was the dominant partner and largely determined the direction of the Anglo-German relationship in these years.[33] This was seen clearly in the series of English rebuffs and affronts reflecting indifference or casual disregard of German interests overseas between 1892 and 1895, which had cooled Anglo-German relations even before the Kruger Telegram. The British tolerated or encouraged colonial subimperialism in Portuguese Africa, the Transvaal, and Samoa and refused a German protectorate in Samoa (despite a longstanding German merchant presence in the islands). The British also allowed incursions into the hinterlands of German Cameroon, signed a treaty with Belgium violating Germany's rights in eastern Congo, prohibited Singaporean coolies from working in German New Guinea, and opposed a German railway concession in Anatolia.[34] Salt was rubbed into these wounds by the fact that news reportage from the colonies and elsewhere overseas was in the hands of British correspondents working for Reuters using a nearly exclusive British network of undersea telegraph cables, which tended to slant reporting in a pro-British direction. This enabled London to shape European and world public opinion in disputes with Berlin in ways that were useful to Whitehall.[35] In 1894, for example, the Wilhelmstrasse complained that Reuters paid insufficient heed to German interests in Samoa.[36] Then, as now, information was power.

---

[32] See Canis, *Von Bismarck zur Weltpolitik*, 291–94, 372–75, 400; Charmley, *Splendid Isolation*, 227–43, 246, 254–60, 264; Rose, *Zwischen Empire und Kontinent*, 145–55; Bernhard Fürst von Bülow, *Denkwürdigkeiten*, vol. 1 (Berlin: Ullstein, 1930), 310–32. Cf. Friedrich Meinecke, *Geschichte des deutsch-englischen Bündnisproblems* (Munich and Vienna: Oldenbourg, 1927).
[33] Canis, *Von Bismarck zur Weltpolitik*, 396.
[34] Canis, *Von Bismarck zur Weltpolitik*, 130–37; Paul M. Kennedy, *The Rise of Anglo-German Antagonism, 1860–1914* (London and Boston: Allen & Unwin, 1980), 210, 214.
[35] Geppert, *Pressekriege*, 80–89.   [36] Ibid., 80.

While these rebuffs to German initiatives were more irritations than hostile actions, Britain was increasingly seen as a hindrance to German overseas ambitions in Berlin, where the realization dawned that German foreign policy had no effective pressure points for more accommodating British diplomacy and nothing to offer in return for British colonial "favors." For its part, the British government was prone to see the Germans as pushy, rude, and demanding given their weak position. Clumsy German diplomacy and the impolitic interventions of the Kaiser in German foreign policy heightened those impressions, as did German public opinion reflected in the press. In a summary of a conversation with Prime Minister Salisbury, the new British ambassador to Germany Frank Lascelles (1841–1920) observed in early December 1895 that

> In commercial and colonial matters Germany was most disagreeable. . . . The rudeness of German communications, much increased since Bismarck's time, was perhaps due to the wish of smaller men to keep up the traditions of the great Chancellor. . . . In the Far East, the Germans are up to every sort of intrigue, asking for concessions & privileges of all sorts, with a view to cutting us out. The only way of meeting them is by countermining, & we are in a position to do so.[37]

The basic dilemma of the Anglo-German relationship was later captured in its essence in a remarkable conversation between C. F. Moberly Bell (1847–1911), director of the London *Times*, and the acting German ambassador in London, Paul Wolff Metternich zur Gracht (1853–1934) in 1901, the latter of whom was trying to make the case for the identity of interests between Britain and Germany in Europe and thus show the logic of an alliance. Bell responded:

> Precisely because they are identical therefore there is no need of it. We should be wiser to choose that ally which can singly do us harm. That is not Germany. In the event of war, what can Germany do? She recalls you. What next? She declares war. What next? How can you touch us? We can blockade Hamburg, take Samoa, drive you out of South Africa, or try to do all three. But what can you do? Absolutely nothing.[38]

It is important to reiterate that these basic features of the Anglo-German relationship were in place *before* Germany ever embarked on a concerted program to expand its navy in 1897. Even after 1900, British foreign policy was driven less by any actual German threat (naval or otherwise) than by questions of imperial defense, domestic politics, and British public opinion.[39] With its expanding presence in Persia, Central Asia, and the Far East, Russia was the single greatest threat to British imperial security, and for that reason

---

[37] Quoted in Kennedy, *Anglo-German Antagonism*, 220.
[38] Quoted in Rose, *Zwischen Empire und Kontinent*, 154.
[39] Wilson, *The Policy of the Entente*, 100–120; Rose, *Zwischen Empire und Kontinent*, 573–90.

British foreign secretaries from Rosebery to Grey were continually seeking a policy of rapprochement with Russia – the Anglo-Russian convention of 1907 thus cannot be reduced to growing Anglo-German enmity between 1895 and 1907 as it often is.[40] This is even more true of the Anglo-French Entente Cordiale of 1904: France was not only a major imperial rival to Britain in West Africa, Egypt, the Sudan, Siam, and southern China, but as we have seen, was also Britain's chief naval rival. Simply put, rapprochement with these powers offered Britain far more than closer ties to Germany or entry into the Triple Alliance.

As will be discussed in this chapter and in the chapters to follow, by far the most important forces at work in Europe's diplomatic realignment after 1895 were not actually in Europe but rather in Asia: the emergence of Japan as a great power, the Sino-Japanese War of 1894–95, and the scramble for Chinese concessions among the great powers as the Qing Empire slowly disintegrated between 1895 and 1901. This led to an Anglo-Russian crisis over Manchuria in 1901, an Anglo-Japanese alliance in 1902, and an Anglo-French Entente in 1904. The Russo-Japanese War, the culmination of these processes in East Asia, would in turn profoundly alter the European power balance in ways ultimately unfavorable to Germany. While little of that had much to do with Germany, the China question did serve to highlight how difficult Anglo-German cooperation was and how irreconcilable British imperial defense and German continental security ultimately were.[41] The greatest irony in this unfolding story was that few countries had contributed more to Japan's emergence as a great power by 1895 than Germany.

The upshot of the shift in British naval strategy to coastal blockade, the growing tenuousness of maritime neutrality, Britain's strategic overstretch, the naval arms race between Britain and the Franco-Russian Dual Alliance, and the cooling of Anglo-German relations was that by late 1895 Germany's maritime trade and overseas interests appeared more vulnerable than ever. This was a conclusion reinforced by Hanseatic merchants and traders who had complained about inadequate German naval protection since the late 1860s and voiced those concerns more vociferously during the interruptions to the saltpeter trade caused by the Chilean Civil War in 1891, when they were left to begging for protection from the Royal Navy. During the Brazilian Naval Revolts of 1893–94 the German navy intervened with two cruisers, but this only served to highlight just how strapped it was for ships. The Hamburg Chamber of Commerce ultimately petitioned the Hamburg Senate in August 1894 to press the Reich into increasing its naval armaments on the grounds

---

[40] Keith Neilson, *Britain and the Last Tsar: British Policy and Russia 1894–1917* (Oxford: Clarendon Press; New York: Oxford University Press, 1995), 370.
[41] See Otte, *The China Question*.

that Germany's image as a first-rate commercial power was now at stake.[42] In light of these pressures, it is a striking fact that by 1895 the size of Germany's navy had been in decline since the mid-1880s.[43] To be sure, increasing the size of the German navy was in the air in 1895, but what shape that would take was far from certain. Kaiser Wilhelm II's own naval enthusiasm and attempt to chart a new "world" foreign policy course ultimately played a role in this new direction, but the Reichstag was hostile to the fleet expansion proposals coming from the Kaiser and the Imperial Navy Office before 1897, which seemed to lack any coherent plan or strategy.[44] Two very important catalysts for a change of course in German naval thinking were the China and Venezuela questions. As important was wider engagement of the German middle class public with these questions. Karl Rathgen, Hermann Schumacher, and Ernst von Halle would play no small role in giving these questions systematic thought, drawing on their own travels in East Asia and South America, and in turn giving these questions a much larger public profile through various publications.

## From Berlin to Peking – Hermann Schumacher in China

Since all German diplomatic efforts to secure a treaty port or naval base in China had fallen flat by early 1896, consensus between the Admiralty, the Kaiser, and the Foreign Office began to coalesce around seizing such a Chinese port by force at the next available opportunity.[45] An important factor in this decision was disappointment over prospects for German involvement in the modernization of China's military and infrastructure following the Sino-Japanese War and Triple Intervention. Thinking thus shifted to exerting more direct pressure on China as the French had done in southern China in order to gain a preferential position in mining and railway concessions and facilitate the Reich's economic penetration of the Chinese market.[46] The most

---

[42] Böhm, *Überseehandel und Flottenbau*, 38–65; Wilhelm Deist, *Flottenpolitik und Flottenpropaganda: Das Nachrichtenbureau des Reichmarineamts 1897–1914* (Stuttgart: Deutsche Verlags-Anstalt, 1976), 27; Herwig, *Vision of Empire*, 145–47; Bradley Naranch, "Between Cosmopolitanism and German Colonialism: Nineteenth-Century Hanseatic Networks in Emerging Tropical Markets," in *Cosmopolitan Networks in Commerce and Society 1660–1914*, ed. Andreas Gestrich and Margit Schulte Beerbühl (London: German Historical Institute, 2011), 99–132, here 127–28. See also Jack Guenther,"'Gateway to the World': Hamburg and the Global German Empire, 1881–1914" (BA thesis, Wesleyan University, 2018).

[43] Peter Winzen, "Zur Genesis von Weltmachtkonzept und Weltpolitik," in *Der Ort Kaiser Wilhelms II. in der deutschen Geschichte*, ed. John C. G. Röhl (Munich: Oldenbourg, 1991), 189–222, here 192–93.

[44] Ibid., 195; Clark, *Kaiser Wilhelm II*, 130–35; Röhl, *The Kaiser's Personal Monarchy*, 732–41, 745–60, 924–38, 999–1016.

[45] Canis, *Von Bismarck zur Weltpolitik*, 162–63, 237–38, 256–76; Herold, *Reichsgewalt bedeutet Seegewalt*, 245–47; Wippich, *Japan und die deutsche Fernostpolitik*, 271–85.

[46] Petersson, *Imperialismus und Modernisierung*, 49–50.

promising sites for a German treaty port were deemed to be Amoy (Xiamen), Samsa Bay, the Chusan Islands, or Kiaochow (Jiaozhou) Bay.[47] In June 1896, Alfred Tirpitz (1849-1930) arrived in Shanghai from Hamburg via San Francisco and Yokohama to assume command of the German East Asian Cruiser Squadron (formed in 1894) and proceeded to investigate these possibilities with an eye to their economic potential and suitability as well as strategic value as naval bases.[48] After directly inspecting Kiaochow Bay and Tsingtao (Qingdao) in mid-August 1896, he concluded that this was by far the most promising site and urged the Admiralty to focus on seizing it from the Chinese.[49] This was then formalized into German policy by Kaiser Wilhelm himself, based on reconnaissance by a German naval engineer earlier that summer, who also approved seizing Kiaochow Bay.[50] The German gambit was part of a wider scramble among the great powers for concessions and spheres of influence in China following the Sino-Japanese War, which had revealed how weak the Qing state was and made it appear that the dismemberment of China was a real possibility.

Early in November of 1896, while working in the Prussian Ministry of Public Works, Hermann Schumacher received word from Wilhelm Hirsch (1861-1918) of the Central Association of German Industrialists (CDI) that the Reich was planning a trade commission to China, which was being financed in large part by German heavy industry and to a lesser degree by the Reich, Prussia, and Saxony. Ten representatives of industries with interests in East Asia along with an economic expert were to comprise the expedition, with Schumacher tapped to serve as that expert.[51] In some ways the commission was similar in purpose to the expedition to Japan of Johannes Justus Rein from 1873 to 1875 that had been commissioned and funded by the Prussian Ministries of Trade and Culture discussed in Chapter 2. Nevertheless, the timing of this mission to China likely had something to do with what seemed, by November 1896 at least, to be dimming prospects for German involvement in railway projects in China as a consequence of the British winning out over the Germans for a lucrative contract to build the Shanghai-Woosung-Nanking Railway. Earlier that year Friedrich Alfred Krupp (1854-1902) had also refused an offer to take over management of China's

---

[47] Alfred von Tirpitz, *My Memoirs*, vol. 1 (London: Hurst & Blackett, 1919), 70.
[48] Ibid., 70-75; Herold, *Reichsgewalt bedeutet Seegewalt*, 247; Kelly, *Tirpitz*, 120.
[49] Kelly, *Tirpitz*, 121.
[50] Herold, *Reichsgewalt bedeutet Seegewalt*, 248-49, 253-56, 265; Wippich, *Japan und die deutsche Fernostpolitik*, 285-97.
[51] GNN HA, Nl. Schumacher, I, B-6j, fol. 245; Gollwitzer, *Die gelbe Gefahr*, 29; Hartmut Kaelble, *Industrielle Interessenspolitik in der Wilhelminischen Gesellschaft: Centralverband Deutsche Industrieller* (Berlin: Walter de Gruyter, 1967), 159-60. Cf. Henry Axel Bueck, *Der Centralverband deutscher Industrieller 1876-1901*, 3 vols. (Berlin: Deutscher Verlag/J. Guttentag, 1902-5).

only modern iron foundry, the Hanyang Iron Works in Hubei province, which had been developed with much expense by the Viceroy of Hu-Guang, Zhang Zhidong (1837–1909), and had involved German engineers as senior advisors and many German suppliers of equipment.[52] The trade commission was thus intended to gather detailed information about Chinese market opportunities and other potential railway investments in order to draw German industrial exporters and investors to China in a climate of growing international competition. The broader context in which this must be seen was that German industrial production was expanding robustly in these years while domestic consumption was growing much more slowly, putting a premium on export markets. Alas, in the last half of 1896 the German steel and iron industry reported declines in exports, particularly to some of those markets seen as most promising for the future, namely in South America, Ottoman Turkey, and China.[53]

While Schumacher was initially unsure he was qualified to serve as an economic expert on the expedition owing to his lack of knowledge and inexperience in East Asia, he agreed to join, serving as its official secretary.[54] There was a great sense of urgency about the expedition, which Schumacher did not quite understand at the time and which precluded much in the way of preparation. Nor was he given any specific instructions about his duties on the expedition, which made Schumacher suspect that this trade commission had political goals.[55] The commission left Genoa for Hong Kong on an NDL steamer in late January 1897 traveling via Port Said, the Suez Canal, and Aden, and then on to Colombo, Singapore, and finally Hong Kong. While on the journey, the commission held regular meetings working out questionnaires for those branches of German industry with interests in East Asia. When they arrived in Hong Kong the German Consul Wilhelm Knappe (1855–1910) took over leadership of the commission, proposing that two members of it make visits to every German merchant house in the colony.

Schumacher was very impressed with Hong Kong harbor, which reminded him much of the scenes of New York harbor he had taken in from Staten Island during his youth. Docked in the harbor was the German cruiser *Prinzess Wilhelm*, and Schumacher recalled that it was "possibly characteristic" of the German trade commission to China that their first dining invitation would be aboard this German cruiser as guests of Korvettenkapitän (Lieutenant Commander) Thiele.[56] Later at a dinner as guest of the president of the Chinese Chamber of Commerce, Ho Amei, Schumacher had opportunity to discuss the further development of economic access to China's hinterland and learn of

---

[52] Wu, *Empires of Coal*, 106–14, 121–22.
[53] See Canis, *Von Bismarck zur Weltpolitik*, 234–35.
[54] GNN HA, Nl. Schumacher, I, B-6j, fol. 246.  [55] Ibid., fols. 246–47.
[56] Ibid., fols. 249–50.

Figure 3.1   Hermann Schumacher ca. 1900.

the importance of Chinese contacts in that endeavor. On investigating further, Schumacher, like Rathgen before him, was surprised by the outsized commercial role that German merchants played in the colony: no fewer than 21 major German trading companies, 5 brokerage firms, and 8 retail stores were present in Hong Kong, which compared favorably to the 28 major English trading companies and an equal number of smaller Indian firms. No fewer than 4 of the 11 board members of the Hong Kong and Shanghai Bank were German, as were 3 of the 7 board members of the Whampoa Dock Company. This discovery filled Schumacher with much pride.[57] But in attempting to make statistical inquiries into the nature of Hong Kong's German trade, Schumacher was surprised to discover that the colony maintained only shipping statistics but no statistics on transported goods, making it impossible to determine the source and destiny of those goods and thus to get a clearer picture of the extent of German trade with China. This made it necessary to investigate the Chinese hinterland. Soon after arriving in Hong Kong the commission thus began a journey by river steamer to Canton.[58] From Canton Schumacher journeyed to Macau via Hong Kong (where he received an overdue inoculation for smallpox – someone had died of the disease in the inn he was staying in) – and then

---

[57] Ibid., fol. 256.   [58] Ibid., fol. 257.

up the Xunjiang River to the open ports of Samshui (Sanshui) and Wuchow (Wuzhou). The primary interest of the expedition was central China, which was seen as the region most promising to Germany's economic future, so after four weeks in southern China the expedition journeyed to Shanghai and the Yangtze River delta.[59]

Along the way to Shanghai, Schumacher was surprised to observe that piracy was still a significant problem along the Chinese coast, and that unlike English, American, and French merchants, Germans could not rely on effective protection of naval forces under German flag. The Chinese exploited that political weakness turning it into a commercial disadvantage for the German traders and merchants operating in these waters. It was on observing these conditions directly that Schumacher began to realize the interdependence of naval and commercial power for the first time: "It is no coincidence that England is simultaneously leading in world trade and ruler of the seas. Whoever, like England, depends upon international trade to feed and employ its people must sooner or later take similar paths."[60] This conclusion was then confirmed on visiting the coastal treaty ports of Swatow (Shantou), Amoy (Xiamen), and Foochow (Fuzhou): "I even gained the impression that those who do not take into account power relations cannot gain a fully valid judgement of world trade. This knowledge made the presence of the German cruiser in Hong Kong understandable to me after the fact."[61]

In Shanghai the dominance of English trade was even more pronounced than it had been in Hong Kong, with imports of cotton goods accounting for 130 million taels and Indian opium 19 million taels. The rest of Shanghai's imports amounted to 46 million taels, including "German knick-knack" as they were described locally. Schumacher's impression of Shanghai's economy and that of the Yangtze delta were nevertheless more positive than what he had witnessed in southern China; it appeared wealthier and more dynamic, and industrial cotton textile production was, if still in its infancy, showing promise.[62]

From Shanghai Schumacher and the German trade commission traveled to Soochow (Suzhou) and Hangchow (Hangzhou), which had been opened up recently to foreign trade by the Treaty of Shimonoseki. A concession for the construction of a railway between Shanghai, Soochow, and Nanking had also been given, making this particularly attractive to the German visitors. As Schumacher had made his mark in the Ministry of Public Works through his research on internal waterways, his eyes fell immediately on the very elaborate canal and river system connecting this region with Peking to the north and far into the western interior of China nearly to Central Asia, and he

---

[59] Ibid., fols. 257–64.   [60] Ibid., fol. 265.
[61] Ibid. Parts of this passage were crossed out in the manuscript.   [62] Ibid., fol. 270a.

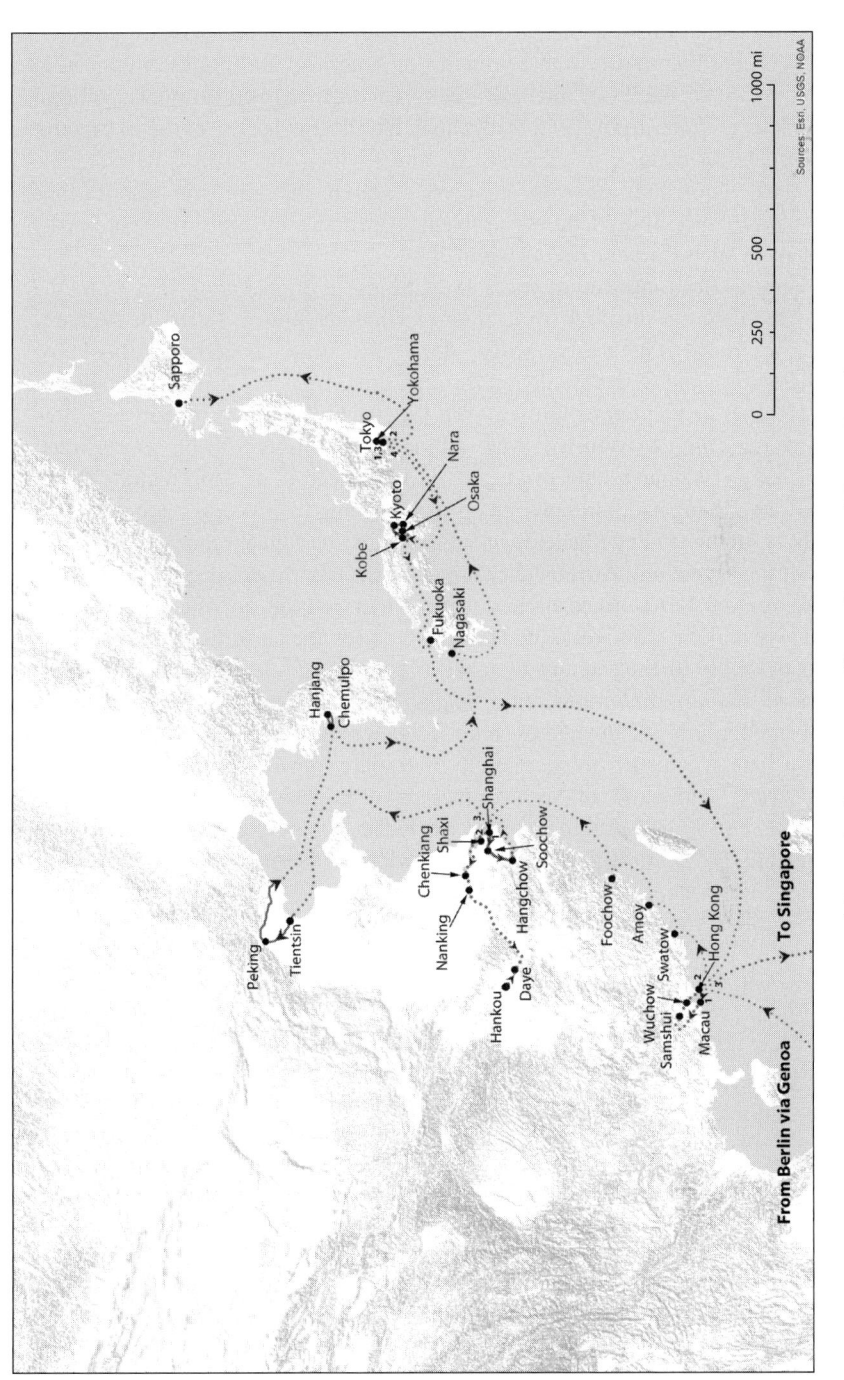

Map 3.1   Hermann Schumacher's journey to China, Korea, and Japan, Jan.–Aug. 1897.

concluded that this was the basis of the region's wealth and political power.[63] He was sensitive to the sizable presence of American and English missions in this region, especially of medical missions with their own hospitals, some of which were quite sizable as in Hangchow. He also made note of the impressive French Jesuit mission in Zikawei (Xujiahui) which was making considerable scholarly contributions with its own research institute and publications devoted to specifically Chinese problems. Germans, by contrast, were largely absent in such Chinese *Kulturarbeit*.[64]

Schumacher's journey to study the Chinese economy took him from the Yangtze delta up the river by steamer to Hankou (now a district in Wuhan), visiting numerous treaty ports along the way, including Chenkiang (Zhenjiang), and then partially up through the Gorges in Chinese river vessels. In Hankou he had opportunity to visit the neighboring city of Hanyang (now Hanyang District, Wuhan) with China's only modern iron works, and Wuchang (Wuhan), the residence of the viceroy of Hu-Huang, Zhang Zhidong. Zhang had been advised on the Hanyang Iron Works by the German railway engineers Peter Scheidtweiler and Heinrich Hildebrand, who sought – albeit unsuccessfully, Schumacher noted – to get German firms involved in its development.[65] As noted earlier, Krupp had refused an offer to purchase the loss-making iron works in 1896 on grounds that insufficient coking coal was available in the vicinity to make it profitable.[66] It had been purchased instead, Schumacher noted, by a Belgian firm – he regretted this as a clear lost opportunity for greater German influence in China.[67] Scheidtweiler had nevertheless managed to successfully ingratiate himself with Zhang through his strong command of both Chinese and English and intrigued against Belgian and English engineers who were also competing for contracts from Hanyang. He ultimately secured sizable orders for German pumps, drills, coke ovens, dynamite, locomotives, cement, and tools in the early 1890s.[68] However, under Heinrich Hildebrand, who became Scheidtweiler's successor at Hanyang in 1894, the works had to be idled for lack of coal, precipitating the losses which resulted in the sale of the ironworks.[69]

While in Hankou, Schumacher also made an excursion to the nearby Daye iron ore mines in Jinshandiazhen (now Daye, Huangshi), which were under the supervision of the German mining engineer Gustav Leinung, learning that the outlook for future steel production in this area was promising given the ample available iron ore.[70] The main problem for industry in the Hankou region at that time was that – despite large coal deposits and very extensive

---

[63] Ibid., fol. 271.   [64] Ibid., fols. 273–74.   [65] Ibid., fols. 276–79.
[66] Wu, *Empires of Coal*, 121.
[67] GNN HA, Nl. Schumacher, I, B-6j, fol. 279; cf. Wu, *Empires of Coal*, 114.
[68] Wu, *Empires of Coal*, 108–10.   [69] Ibid., 111.
[70] Ibid., 111, 117. GNN HA, Nl. Schumacher, I, B-6j, fol. 280.

investment in coal mining by Zhang at Moganshan some 60 miles southeast – the coal was of an inferior grade for iron smelting, and the closest known Chinese sources of coking coal were in Chihli (Zhili) province, hundreds of miles to the north and ruinously expensive to transport given the lack of Chinese railway infrastructure.[71]

On the way down the Yangtze back to Shanghai, Schumacher stopped in Nanking and Shaxi (now Shaxizhen District, Suzhou, Jiangsu). Nanking was site of the headquarters of the German military mission in China, which was then training a modern Chinese army under General Erich von Falkenhayn (1861-1922), later chief of the German General Staff during the first years of First World War. It was in Nanking as a guest of Falkenhayn's that Schumacher would enjoy the most impressive spectacle he would experience in East Asia: a Chinese military parade. The German-trained Chinese troops he observed were surprisingly impressive, filling Schumacher with much pride. He thought that if this was the lesson learned from the defeat by the Japanese in 1895, there was hope yet for the country.[72]

Back in Shanghai, the German expedition then headed north up the coast to the Yellow Sea passing the Shantung and Liaotung Peninsulas into the Bohai Sea and then on to the city of Tientsin (Tianjin). It was notable to Schumacher that there were no treaty ports from Shanghai to the northern tip of the Shantung Peninsula and only one coaling station along the way to Tientsin at Chih-fu (Zhifu), making it a strategically important ice-free harbor that had been much used by various foreign navies during the recent Sino-Japanese War.[73] As the gateway to Peking, Tientsin was itself a key port city ahead of Canton and Hankou in terms of trade volume, and as Schumacher noted, the extension of the Trans-Siberian Railway would bring this part of China into direct connection with Europe.[74] As importantly, Tientsin was the seat of the most powerful Qing official, Li Hongzhang, viceroy of Chihli who had retained a number of German advisors, notably the director of Chinese Maritime Customs Gustav Detring, the port engineer Constantin von Hanneken (1854-1925), and director of Chinese Maritime Customs for Korea, Paul von Möllendorff, the latter also serving in Rathgen's time in Japan as advisor to the Korean king.[75] The connections between foreigners and foreign interests and the Qing political leadership were of course far more direct and intense in Tientsin and Peking than they were in Shanghai, much less Hong Kong. As discussed in the previous chapter, the German ambassador to the Qing court, Max von Brandt and his successors Gustav Schenck zu

---

[71] Wu, *Empires of Coal*, 112–13. Indeed, Wu notes that Taiwanese coal was cheaper to deliver to Shanghai at the time than coal from Kaiping.
[72] GNN HA, Nl. Schumacher, I, B-6j, fol. 282. [73] Ibid., fols. 284–85.
[74] Ibid, fols. 285–85a. [75] Ibid., fol. 286.

Schweinsberg (1843–1909) and Edmund von Heyking (1850–1915), had done much to cultivate those contacts between German advisors and Li Hongzhang.

On arriving in Tientsin, Schumacher and the rest of the commission met Vice-Consul Arthur Zimmermann (1864–1940) of later Zimmermann Telegram notoriety before heading to Peking on horseback.[76] In Peking Schumacher met with Sir Robert Hart (1835–1911), inspector general of Chinese Maritime Customs and perhaps the most knowledgeable person on the Chinese economy in China at the time, and utilized the economic records of the German embassy made available to him by Ambassador von Heyking. He was struck with how interlinked power/political and economic matters were in Peking after attending a dinner hosted by the newly-appointed British ambassador Claude Macdonald (1852–1915) at which Li Hongzhang was preset and very much the center of attention. The great powers that had protested the terms of the Peace of Shimonoseki were at this time eager to find (or force) solutions to the coaling station question in northern China.[77] The war with Japan had revealed China's weakness to the world, and all countries with sizable interests in China were aware that they had to provide for their own protection in the future. Indeed, the German acquisition of Kiaochow Bay and Tsingtao was then only a few months in the future.[78] Anticipating this and very likely in direct response to a request from the German trade commission and CDI, in 1897 Gustav Detring put in a request to the Qing court on behalf of a syndicate of German manufacturers for a concession to build railways and open mines.[79]

While the rest of the commission traveled from Peking directly to Yokohama via Tientsin, Schumacher and Knappe sought to visit Manchuria and Korea (the latter, in Schumacher's words "the most unknown land in Asia beside Tibet"[80]) before joining their colleagues in Japan and so traveled from Tientsin to Chemulpo (Incheon). Manchuria was of great interest because of its fertile soils, soybean production, natural resources (especially coal), and because one year earlier, in 1896, the Russians had secured a concession from the Chinese to extend the Siberian Railway through Manchuria as a shortcut between Chita and Vladivostok. The planned railway construction, as Schumacher put it, "integrated this fertile and resource rich territory into the world economy [*Weltwirtschaft*], and since it was the first big railway contract signed by China, it had a significance beyond Manchuria."[81] Russia's Manchurian railway interests were, as Schumacher noted, bound up with gaining access to an ice-free port in southern Manchuria. Unfortunately, time did not allow Schumacher to travel there.

---

[76] Ibid.  [77] Ibid., fols. 288–93.  [78] Ibid., fol. 294.
[79] Wu, *Empires of Coal*, 124; Petersson, *Imperialismus und Modernisierung*, 55–61.
[80] GNN HA, Nl. Schumacher, I, B-6k, fol. 295.  [81] Ibid.

Once in Hanjang (Seoul), Schumacher and Knappe witnessed the powerful rivalry between the Japanese and Russians for predominance in Korea as guests of the Korean king. King Gojong (formally Emperor Gwangmu, 1852–1919) was then under the protection of the very competent Russian ambassador Karl von Waeber (1841–1910) following the assassination of his wife, Queen Min (formally Empress Myeongseong, 1851–95), by Japanese agents in 1895.[82] Since Karl Rathgen's visit in 1886, Korea had ceased being a tributary state of Qing China following the Treaty of Shimonoseki and was now formally independent, though increasingly part of a Japanese sphere of influence. Already during Rathgen's time in Japan, Korea had emerged as an object of intense rivalry between Russia and Japan that extended to Manchuria, a rivalry that was clearly intensifying in 1897 and promising to sideline Germany even more now that Li Hongzhang and Möllendorff were out of the picture on the Korean Peninsula. Indeed, later on his journey while in Japan Schumacher would be surprised to learn from the pioneering Japanese banker, industrialist, and president of the Tokyo Chamber of Commerce, Shibusawa Eiichi (1840–1931), just how strong Japan's ambitions were in Korea, which according to Shibusawa was to be turned into a Japanese model colony.[83]

In Japan itself, Schumacher was astonished by the fast pace of railway construction and modernization more generally, which contrasted starkly with conditions he had seen in China and Korea, but also by the deep public consternation of the Japanese over Germany's participation in the Triple Intervention in 1895 – and its diplomatic tactlessness in that process, not least the Kaiser's "yellow peril" bugbear – which had forced Japan to relinquish claims to Port Arthur and the Liaotung Peninsula. At the same time, Schumacher observed that the English had switched their diplomatic sympathies from the Chinese to the Japanese, which English newspapers in Japan, such as the *Japan Weekly Mail*, were exploiting to agitate against Germany with a vehemence that Schumacher noted he "had not previously experienced."[84] In light of the unusually prominent role that Germans had played in Japan's modernization, this was particularly disappointing for Schumacher.[85]

Schumacher traveled Japan widely as part of the commission in order to discover future opportunities for German merchants and industrialists, traveling from Nagasaki on to Yokohama and Tokyo, and then later to Hokkaido, Kobe, Osaka, Nara, Kyoto, and Fukuoka. Throughout these travels he observed factories, railways, wharves, ports, coaling stations, and merchant vessels. He also came into contact with a number of important Japanese scholars, bureaucrats, and industrialists. These included the Japanese economist Wadagaki

---

[82] Ibid., fols. 298–99.   [83] Ibid., fol. 310b.   [84] Ibid., fols. 302–4.
[85] Ibid., fols. 303, 308a–9.

Kenzō, who as discussed in the previous chapter, had studied in Berlin and taught political economy with Karl Rathgen at Tokyo University, the previously mentioned banker and industrialist Shibusawa of the Dai Ichi Kokuritsu Ginkō (First National Bank), and the bureaucrat and industrialist Hayakawa Senkichirō (1863–1922) of the Mitsui Trading Company.[86] Schumacher's conversations with the former Tokyo University professor of law and then secretary of the German legation in Japan, Heinrich Weipert, and the German shipbuilding engineer, teacher, and long-serving board member of the OAG, Rudolph Lehmann (1842–1914), offered additional insights from a German perspective.[87] Lehmann himself was at the time representing the Hamburg trading company Raspe & Co., which specialized in the export of German machinery to Japan.[88] These observations and conversations left no doubt that Japan was well on its way to becoming the leading industrial and trading power in East Asia, that the Japanese state was actively assisting these efforts where it could, and that German merchants and industrialists were facing stiff Japanese competition for markets in Japan and the rest of East Asia now and into the future.[89]

The breakneck developments Schumacher had observed in Japan stood in stark contrast to China, whose development, Schumacher surmised, would in any case be much slower owing to its proud, ancient culture and vast geographic expanse. Nevertheless, once on that path, he believed development would be more sustainable in China than in Japan.[90] Certainly, there were more opportunities for German industry.

During a meeting of the German trade commission in early August 1897 before their planned return to Europe later that year, Wilhelm Knappe reported in confidence that a decision would soon be made about the acquisition of a German coaling station in China, and that it was desirable that the commission form judgments about the economic significance of that place and its hinterland based on their own observations. The commission greeted this news enthusiastically.[91] As previously discussed, by that point the German navy and Foreign Office had settled upon seizing Kiaochow Bay on the southern Shantung Peninsula at the first available opportunity, and in late July 1897 an Anglo-German agreement had effectively sanctioned this, granting Germany economic predominance over Shantung in return for recognizing the same for the British in the Yangtze Valley. When Knappe wrote the German embassy in Peking about the desire of the commission to undertake these investigations, however, the ambassador responded that it was presently too

---

[86] Ibid., fols. 310a–310b, 311, 316, 322–23, 324–28.　[87] Ibid., fols. 309a–310.
[88] Gerd Hoffmann, "Rudolph Lehmann (1842–1914) – Ein Lebensbild," *OAG-Notizen* (Sept. 2006): 17–39, here 30–31.
[89] GNN HA, Nl. Schumacher, I, B-6k, fols. 305a, 307–8, 312–13, 329–30.
[90] Ibid., fol. 330a.　[91] Ibid.

dangerous for such travel to the area – there had been unrest in Shantung recently.[92] Nevertheless, the CDI and supporting federal state governments in Germany proposed extending the journey of the commission beyond the planned year, with Schumacher given the offer to extend his investigations to Siam and the Philippines, in particular Manila.[93] At the time there was growing concern that France's aggressive territorial ambitions in former Siamese Cambodian provinces and Siam from its colonial base in Indochina would ultimately edge out any German participation in Siam's modernization.[94]

Schumacher was by that point already so overwhelmed trying to get a grasp of the material he had gathered on China that he declined this offer, as much as he would have enjoyed getting to know these new areas.[95] He thus made his way back to Hong Kong intending to return to Germany, but given that sufficient leave was offered by the Ministry of Public Works to visit the Philippines and Siam, he decided to take his time on his return in order to get to know Ceylon and Egypt along the way.[96] News of unusually cold weather in Germany received in Aden later reinforced that decision.[97] In Egypt he became witness to the swift advance of a British camel regiment up along the Nile shortly after he had toured the temple complex of Karnak, part of the British effort to reconquer the Sudan which would later participate in the Battle of Omdurman on September 2, 1898. There the English under Herbert Kitchener (1850–1916) decisively defeated the much larger army of Abdallahi ibn Muhammad (1846–99) but where Britain's military reputation would be tarnished by Kichener's desecration of Muhammad Ahmad's (1844–85) tomb and the deliberate slaughter of wounded Mahdists.[98]

Before Schumacher returned home, events unfolded that ultimately led Germany to seize a presence for itself in Shantung. Using the pretext of retaliation for attacks on two German Catholic missionaries in western Shantung, and after gaining vague assurances from the Russian tsar that no Russian opposition to a retaliatory action was to be feared, three German cruisers with a 700-man landing corps commanded by Admiral Otto von Diederichs (1843–1918) were sent to Kiaochow, which was seized without Chinese resistance on November 14, 1897.[99] On March 6, 1898, the Germans negotiated a 99-year lease with the Chinese for Kiaochow Bay, the town of Tsingtao, and a 50 km wide surrounding neutral zone on the Shantung Peninsula. That very day Hermann Schumacher had finally arrived back in Berlin by train from Genoa. It was his thirtieth birthday.[100]

---

[92] Ibid.   [93] Ibid., fol. 331.
[94] Petersson, *Imperialismus und Modernisierung*, 91–100, 109–13.
[95] GNN HA, Nl. Schumacher, I, B-6k fol. 331.
[96] GNN HA, Nl. Schumacher, I, B-6l, fol. 332.   [97] Ibid., fol. 335.   [98] Ibid., fol. 337.
[99] See Herold, *Reichsgewalt bedeutet Seegewalt*, 270–90.
[100] GNN HA, Nl. Schumacher, I, B-6l, fol. 337.

Once back and settled in, Schumacher was instructed by the head of the trade commission to get to work immediately on the commission's East Asian exhibit to be held in the Reichstag. This involved organizing the 5,000 samples collected by the commission in East Asia, which included European and American export goods in demand in East Asia (mainly black satins, velvets, plushes, and English cotton goods), as well as Chinese pongees and Japanese habutais, the latter two of which there were some 2,000 silk and cotton samples alone.[101] A large collection of ribbons and trimmings, raw silk, ramie, jute, banana fiber, and wools from camel, sheep, and goats rounded out the exhibition of textiles.[102] Samples of locks, knives, scissors, razors, buttons, gold and silver wire articles, opium pipes, and tanned hides were also on display – "the wellspring" as Schumacher put it, of the German knick-knack trade.[103] One is reminded of the similarity both in content and purpose between this exhibit and the one of Japanese goods collected by Johannes Justus Rein from 1873 to 1875 and put on display by the Prussian Ministry of Trade in 1876 discussed in Chapter 2.

Schumacher needed time both to organize the exhibit and work through the materials he had collected on the Chinese economy and transportation system and so sought permission from the Ministry of Public Works for leave from his regular duties until October 1, 1898, which was granted.[104] The preoccupation with the "superficial" matter of the exhibit in light of the wealth of information he needed to work through on the Chinese economy initially puzzled Schumacher, but this began to make more sense once he got news of the recent German lease of Kiaochow.[105] The exhibit that Schumacher organized for the commission was opened on April 19 and was restricted to politicians, officials, members of chambers of commerce, and others with permission from the CDI, but measured by the number of visitors and the positive newspaper reports about it, it was widely attended and quite a success.[106] One of Schumacher's additional tasks was to lead senior officials and politicians through the exhibit, and it was in this capacity that he got to know nearly every prominent figure in German politics at the time. Interestingly, one of the few with a deeper interest in East Asian industrial competition was the leader of the German Social Democratic Party (SPD), August Bebel (1840–1913), who held forth about it at length to Schumacher.[107]

---

[101] Ibid., fol. 339; "Exhibit of Samples Collected by the German Commercial Mission to the Far East," *Board of Trade Journal* XXIV (Jan.–June 1898): 578–80, here 579; Gollwitzer, *Die gelbe Gefahr*, 29.

[102] "Exhibit of Samples Collected by the German Commercial Mission," 579–80.

[103] Ibid., 580; GNN HA, Nl. Schumacher, I, B-6l, fol. 339.   [104] Ibid.

[105] Ibid., fol. 338.

[106] Ibid., fol. 340; "Exhibit of Samples Collected by the German Commercial Mission," 578–79; cf. *Norddeutsche Zeitung*, April 20, 1898.

[107] GNN HA, Nl. Schumacher, I, B-6l, fol. 340.

The exhibit in the Reichstag finished April 28, and Schumacher was very pleased when he had packed it up and sent it off to Krefeld (a major German textile production center) so that he could finally get started with his written work on China before returning to his regular duties in the ministry in October.[108] For Schumacher the lease of Kiaochow less than two months earlier had settled any lingering doubts that it would be China, and not Japan, that would now be the focus of any future German commercial expansion into Asia, with the Chinese treaty ports already open to foreign trade serving as the starting point of his general analysis of the economic opportunities offered to Germany by China.[109] In those areas of China not yet open to foreign trade, the transport question predominated, as he knew all too well from the difficulties he had himself encountered firsthand while traveling in China's interior. Here the railway question took center stage. Over the course of the spring, summer, and early autumn of 1898, Schumacher devoted himself to detailed analyses of the Chinese treaty ports and railways, which culminated in two longer studies: the first a two-part article appearing in 1898 and early 1899 in the *Jahrbücher für Nationalökonomie* on the economic position and significance of Chinese treaty ports[110]; the second a long report on railway construction and railway plans in China synthesizing recent English, French, and other official sources, which was then published under the auspices of the Prussian Ministry of Public Works in its journal *Archiv für Eisenbahnwesen* in 1899 and 1900.[111]

## Karl Rathgen, Imperial Preference, and the Threat of "Panamerica"

Just as new opportunities opened up for German trade and investment in China, they appeared to be closing elsewhere. Among those concerned about these developments and making public statements about the attending dangers was Karl Rathgen. Rathgen had ultimately declined going into the German diplomatic corps after his return from Japan in 1890, embarking instead on an academic career in Germany by completing his *Habilitation* at the University of Berlin under Gustav Schmoller in 1892 with a monograph on the economy and state finances of Japan, which synthesized the vast material he had collected while in Japan with the aid of Kanai Noburu and many other of his students there.[112] It quickly became the standard work on the subject in

---

[108] Ibid., fol. 341. [109] Ibid.
[110] Hermann Schumacher, "Die chinesischen Vertragshäfen, ihre wirtschaftliche Stellung und Bedeutung," *JbbfNS* III. Folge, 16 (1898): 577–97, 721–93; III. Folge 17 (1899): 55–70, 289–331.
[111] Hermann Schumacher, "Eisenbahnbau und Eisenbahnpläne in China," *Archiv für Eisenbahnwesen* 22 (1899): 901–78, 1194–226; 23 (1900): 1–115.
[112] Rathgen, *Japans Volkswirtschaft*.

Germany. After serving as a *Privatdozent* (lecturer) at the University of Berlin for two years, he was called to a position as *ausserordentlicher Professor* (associate professor) representing Professor Hermann Paasche (1851–1925) at the University of Marburg in 1893. In March 1895 he became full professor (*ordentlicher Professor*) at Marburg.[113]

In 1896 Rathgen pointed to what he saw as definite tendencies toward imperial protectionism in Britain after the appointment of Joseph Chamberlain as British secretary of state for the colonies in June 1895 and analyzed the plan for the proposed imperial customs union in an article in the *Preußische Jahrbücher*.[114] Chamberlain's was not an isolated voice. In August 1895 an article in the *Saturday Review* had complained about German trade competition, openly invoking the long English tradition of destroying its chief trade rivals by war.[115] Then in the spring of 1896 the Welsh journalist Ernest Edwin Williams (1866–1935) published a series of exaggerated and alarmist articles in the *New Review* with the title "Made in Germany." His articles attracted much public attention and were then published as a book that caused a national sensation in Britain, running through four editions by the end of 1896.[116] Motivated by the steady increase in the share of German imports to Britain and the British Empire and the perceived displacement of British merchants and manufacturers – and trafficking in familiar "invasion" tropes sure to prick ears in Britain – he warned of the omnipresence of German goods on the British market, how steadily Britain's industrial supremacy had been eroded in every branch of industry, and how the dogma of free trade had blinded the public to the danger.[117] Williams also recounted the various ways he believed the Germans had given the British "a handsome beating" by borrowing or purloining British technology, protective tariffs and export bounties, subsidized shipping and preferential railway rates, better technical education and consular support, and better adaptation to local markets.[118] It concluded with a list of countermeasures that included retaliatory tariffs and penalties.[119] The stir Williams's book caused pressed the British government to ask the Board of Trade to investigate the matter, which affirmed some of Williams's findings in an 1898 report.[120]

---

[113] StaHH, 361–66 Hochschulwesen – Dozenten- und Personalakten, IV 815 Personalangelegenheiten betr. Professor Dr. Rathgen, n.d.

[114] Karl Rathgen, "Über den Plan eines britischen Reichszollvereins," *Preußische Jahrbücher* 86 (1896): 481–523.

[115] "Our True Foreign Policy," *Saturday Review*, Aug. 24, 1895.

[116] Ernest Edwin Williams, *"Made in Germany,"* 5th ed. (London: William Heinemann, 1897).

[117] Ibid., 1–22, 23–129.    [118] Ibid., 17, 130–63.    [119] Ibid., 164–75.

[120] Walter E. Minchinton, "E. E. Williams: 'Made in Germany' and After," *Vierteljahrschrift für Sozial- und Wirtschaftsgeschichte* 62, no. 2 (1975): 229–42, here 236–37.

Without warning in July 1897, the British government announced the termination in July 1898 of the Anglo-German trade treaty of 1865 that had granted the Zollverein and its successor, the German Empire, most favored nation status and had prevented Britain from imposing differential tariffs around its colonies. The treaty had also granted the German states the same trade access in the colonies as in the British Isles. In August 1897 Karl Rathgen wrote an article published in Schmoller's *Jahrbuch* that was discussed extensively by other newspapers and journals and so gained national attention analyzing the potential economic threat this posed to Germany.[121] Rathgen argued in this essay that the termination of the trade treaty was undoubtedly the first step in creating preferential tariffs and an imperial federation between Britain and her colonies as had been proposed by Chamberlain in 1895 and as had been at the top of the agenda of the June–July 1897 Colonial Conference on the occasion of Queen Victoria's Diamond Jubilee.[122] What was surprising was that this measure, long demanded by Britain's protectionist Dominions, now had the hearty applause of the British public and even the support of the formerly free-trading Cobden Club.[123]

Rathgen, who had become something of a specialist on English emigration through a large study done for the Verein für Sozialpolitik in 1896, also made note of some other facts that framed this initiative, such as the various efforts put in place by the United Kingdom over the previous twenty years to channel British emigration to the Dominions, notably to Canada.[124] Likewise, he mentioned that the British book trade was flush with tracts on "Greater Britain."[125] Nevertheless, the immediate practical purpose of Chamberlain's idea of an imperial federation was imperial defense and trade, two issues closely interlinked. The intent, Rathgen wrote, was to reduce the burdens of imperial defense, and the initiatives for greater imperial cohesion were coming from the Dominions, particularly Canada, which had been particularly hard hit by the extreme protectionism of the United States. It had been Canada that proposed the imperial preference to Britain as a countermeasure to additional American protectionism promised by President McKinley in 1896 that then ultimately passed in the form of the Dingley Act in July 1897.[126] The Canadian tariff bill that was approved by its parliament in April 1897 offered successive

---

[121] Karl Rathgen, "Die Kündigung des englischen Handelsvertrags und ihre Gefahr für Deutschlands Zukunft," *JbfGVV* 21 (1897): 1369–86; "Handelsvertrag und die Flottenfrage," *Die Grenzboten* 56, no. 45 (Nov. 11, 1897): 263–71.

[122] Rathgen, "Die Kündigung," 1369, 1374.    [123] Ibid., 1370.

[124] Karl Rathgen *Englische Auswanderung und Auswanderungspolitik im 19. Jahrhundert*, SdVfS, vol. 72 (Leipzig: Duncker & Humblot, 1896), 3–212.

[125] Rathgen, "Die Kündigung," 1375–76; cf. Duncan Bell, *The Idea of Greater Britain: Empire and the Future of World Order, 1860–1900* (Princeton and Oxford: Princeton University Press, 2007).

[126] Rathgen, "Die Kündigung," 1377–78.

reductions in tariffs on goods from countries that allowed Canadian goods in duty free. As it turned out, Rathgen observed, the only places that did so were Great Britain and New South Wales. The Canadian tariff law, Rathgen showed, was in fact a creature of long discussions with Chamberlain over the winter of 1896–97.[127] The only way that Britain could reciprocate with its own preferences for Canada was by abrogating the longstanding trade treaties it had with Belgium and Germany because these contained most favored nation clauses that would have obliged Britain to extend to them any reduction in duties negotiated with Canada or any other part of the British Empire.[128]

It remained to be seen, Rathgen wrote, if the United States would retaliate, but for Germany, whose trade with Canada was rather modest by comparison, the impact would be small. Rathgen believed it would become a problem if other parts of the British Empire followed suit because Germany's trade with these colonies was substantial. It was true that the great bulk of all industrial goods imported to the British colonies still originated from Britain, so a system of imperial preferences was less about Britain expanding its current exports than "securing a market for the future."[129] Rathgen believed the grossly exaggerated claims made by Williams in "Made in Germany" about the increased industrial competition Britain faced from Germany in its own colonies were preparing the ground for measures preferential to British industry.[130] The most immediate practical question for Germany was thus whether or not to revise the most favored nation clauses in its own trade treaties. Rathgen observed that the United States only granted most favored nation status in exchange for trade concessions, not as a matter of course. With that in mind and with the moves now occurring in the British Empire, Rathgen wondered whether it might not be wise for Germany to extend most favored nation status only as a treaty right between a small group of economically integrated central European states.[131]

As should be clear from Rathgen's discussion of British imperial trade preferences, the 800-pound protectionist gorilla at the time was the United States. It was now also an outwardly expanding power. Ever since its leading role in the opening of Japan in the 1850s, the United States had been an important player in East Asia and the South Pacific with commercial interests not only in Japan but also China, the Philippines, and Samoa. After the overthrow of the Hawaiian monarchy in 1893 was followed by the islands' formal annexation by the United States in 1898, the US had gained a coveted exclusive foothold in the South Pacific. British diplomats had in fact encouraged such bold American unilateralism.[132] On the other hand, when

---

[127] Ibid., 1379.  [128] Ibid., 1380–81.  [129] Ibid., 1381–82.  [130] Ibid., 1383.
[131] Ibid., 1384.
[132] Pommerin, *Der Kaiser und Amerika*, 82; Mehnert, "Gelbe Gefahr," 62–63.

Germany – taking note of the Hawaiian annexation treaty in July 1897 – sought compensation by opening up the question of Samoa (where German merchants had a longstanding and sizable presence) the British Foreign Office brushed them off easily.[133]

It was not only in Asia and the South Pacific that America's presence was felt by Germans but especially in the Caribbean and South America. Trade disputes with the United States had, of course, been running themes in German and US relations since the 1870s. The United States had imposed duties on German sugar in 1875, and the Germans placed tariffs on American grain in 1879 and bans on American pork in the 1880s.[134] In 1889 the first Panamerican Congress was held in Washington, DC, with the aim of tying the Latin American economies more closely to the United States. After passage of the protectionist McKinley Tariff in 1890 (which raised average American import duties to nearly 50 percent), the Union sought to reach that goal by negotiating reciprocity treaties with Brazil, Santo Domingo, El Salvador, and Honduras as well as with the Spanish and British West Indies, which made access to the American market for such important Latin American export commodities as sugar and coffee conditional on the preferential treatment of American exporters. These reciprocity treaties effectively discriminated against German and other European trade with Latin America and the Caribbean and hit such German export sectors as textiles, iron and steel, and sugar as well German shipping companies particularly hard.[135] Under Chancellor Caprivi, trade treaties were signed that lowered tariffs in 1892 and extended most favored nation trade status to the United States. While American tariffs were in turn lowered in 1894, they were reinstated and raised to 52 percent on average with William McKinley's election in 1896 and the passage of the previously mentioned Dingley Act.[136] Indeed, the ad valorem equivalent tariff on manufactured imports to the United States imposed by this legislation was 44 percent, which along with the extraordinarily high import tariffs on manufactured goods in Mexico, Brazil, and Argentina at the time, were far and away among the highest tariffs in the world and contributed to very large American trade surpluses with the European states.[137] Fears were thus growing in the 1890s that it was only a matter of time before the United States would close off the Western Hemisphere to German trade, in turn animating

---

[133] Canis, *von Bismarck zur Weltpolitik*, 244–45.
[134] See Pommerin, *Der Kaiser und Amerika*, 21–49.
[135] Fiebig-von Hase, *Lateinamerika als Konfliktherd*, 272–73; Herwig, *Vision of Empire*, 196.
[136] See Mitchell, *The Danger of Dreams*, 12–17; Pommerin, *Der Kaiser und Amerika*, 41–49.
[137] Findlay and O'Rourke, *Power and Plenty*, 403, table 7.3; Torp, *The Challenges of Globalization*, 228–41.

the idea of a central European customs union as a countermeasure to the *amerikanische Gefahr* (American peril).[138] It is notable that Karl Rathgen had himself warned of the dangers emerging from such American trade policy in the pages of the *Preußische Jahrbücher* as early as 1892.[139]

## The Venezuela and Transvaal Crises

American and Panamerican protectionism was being combined at the time with aggressive US diplomacy. In July 1895, in response to a rising tide of American public hostility stoked by a British military intervention in Nicaragua in 1894 and an anti-British pamphlet on a long-festering border dispute between British Guiana and Venezuela, the US Secretary of State Richard Olney (1835–1917) invoked the Monroe Doctrine in a note to the British Foreign Office.[140] Among other things, the note warned of the unnatural and dangerous European political influences in the Americas and asserted that the "United States is practically sovereign on this [American] continent, and its fiat is law upon the subjects to which it confines its interposition."[141] It also demanded that the British submit to immediate US arbitration to settle the entire Venezuelan boundary matter.[142] The note had little immediate impact in the Foreign or Colonial Offices – indeed, Joseph Chamberlain was ready to press the matter with the Americans, thinking that the border region was another gold-filled Transvaal.[143] The condescending response of Lord Salisbury which arrived late in 1895 argued that the Monroe Doctrine was incompatible with international law and that the United States was not entitled to assume that it had an interest in matters between sovereign American states simply because these states were situated in the Western Hemisphere.[144]

In a tone of deep disappointment, President Grover Cleveland (1837–1908) responded on December 17, 1895 by reaffirming the Monroe Doctrine unequivocally and effectively threatening Great Britain with war if it did not submit unconditionally to American arbitration and the findings of a presidential border commission:

---

[138] Fiebig-von Hase, *Lateinamerika als Konfliktherd*, 287–92. See also Pommerin, *Der Kaiser und Amerika*, 23–43.
[139] Karl Rathgen, "Moderne Handelspolitik," *Preußische Jahrbücher* 69 (1892): 84–97. See also Fiebig-von Hase, *Lateinamerika als Konfliktherd*, 288–89.
[140] R. A. Humphries, "Presidential Address: Anglo-American Rivalries and the Venezuela Crisis of 1895," *Transactions of the Royal Historical Society*, 5th Series, 17 (1967): 131–64, here 143–50.
[141] Quoted in Humphries, "Presidential Address," 150. [142] Ibid. [143] Ibid., 151.
[144] Ibid., 153.

When such a report is made and accepted, it will, in my opinion, be the duty of the United States to resist by every means in its power, as a willful aggression upon its rights and interests, the appropriation by Great Britain of any lands or the exercise of governmental jurisdiction over any territory which after investigation we have determined of right belongs to Venezuela.

In making these recommendations I am fully alive to the responsibility incurred and keenly realize all the consequences that may follow.

I am, nevertheless, firm in my conviction that while it is a grievous thing to contemplate the two great English-speaking peoples of the world as being otherwise than friendly competitors in the onward march of civilization and strenuous and worthy rivals in all the arts of peace, there is no calamity which a great nation can invite which equals that which follows a supine submission to wrong and injustice and the consequent loss of self-respect and honor, beneath which are shielded and defended a people's safety and greatness.[145]

It was, at bottom, a question of honor, and the United States was prepared to go to war to preserve it.

The message was shocking and bewildering to the British government and public alike.[146] While there were a few belligerent responses in the British press, the overall British reaction was remarkably subdued.[147] The British government backed down quickly and submitted to US demands, in effect accepting the Monroe Doctrine and ceding Britain's formerly preeminent position in the Caribbean and Latin America to the Americans without a fight.[148] This astonishing result can only be explained by the fact that the Dominion of Canada was catastrophically vulnerable to US invasion – at the time Sir John Ardagh (1840–1907), then head of military intelligence in the War Office, assessed a defense of Canada as "the most hazardous military enterprise that we could possibly be driven to engage in."[149] And despite its vast naval superiority, the Royal Navy had no ships to spare in late 1895 and early 1896 to bolster the West Indian and North American squadrons in case of war because the margin of superiority over the Dual Alliance was still deemed too slim.[150] As pointed out earlier, however, this was as much a consequence of the vastly inflated definition of British national defense that

---

[145] Special Message on the Venezuela Boundary Dispute, Washington, DC, December 17, 1895, in Grover Cleveland, *Addresses, State Papers and Letters*, ed. Albert Ellery Bergh (New York: Sun Dial Classics, 1909), 380–81.
[146] Humphries, "Anglo-American Rivalries," 156; Marder, *British Sea Power*, 254.
[147] Marder, *British Sea Power*, 254–55.
[148] Humphries, "Anglo-American Rivalries," 163.
[149] Quoted in Richard Preston, *Defense of the Undefended Border: Planning for War in North America* (Montreal & London: McGill-Queen's University Press, 1977), 130.
[150] Marder, *British Sea Power*, 255.

had come about through the triumph of the Bluewater School in the 1880s, which had turned enemy coastlines into Britain's frontier and had shifted naval strategy from coastal defenses to blockade of enemy ports and command of the sea as embodied in the Naval Defense Act of 1889.

British anger over its humiliating capitulation in the Venezuelan matter was quickly and easily vented toward Germany following the Kaiser's January 3, 1896 Kruger Telegram, which followed almost immediately after the Venezuela Crisis.[151] In it, the Kaiser congratulated President Paul Kruger of the Transvaal South African Republic for defeating Dr. Jameson's British irregulars without the aid of "friendly Powers" (*befreundeter Mächte*) and thus securing the independence of his country from "outside aggression" *(Angriffe von außen)*.[152] As is now known, the Kruger Telegram was not an impulsive gaffe by Kaiser Wilhelm but an official German response initiated by Foreign Secretary Marschall von Bieberstein (1842–1912) jointly formulated by the Kaiser, the foreign secretary, Chancellor Hohenlohe-Schillingsfürst (1819–1901), and German naval officials in response to British aggression in the Transvaal. It was also calculated to impress upon the British the dangers of their increasing isolation in hopes of nudging Britain toward the Triple Alliance.[153] The telegram was widely applauded in Germany's press, even in the normally reserved and moderate *Vossische Zeitung* and very critical Social Democratic *Vorwärts*.[154] Moreover, it was factually correct: the Jameson Raid was organized and funded by Cecil Rhodes (1853–1902), governor of the Cape Colony, had the support of the Cape Colony's high commissioner, and was intended to topple Paul Kruger's South African Republic and seize the Transvaal.[155]

Nevertheless, the Germans had overplayed their hand. The violence of the British public's reaction to the mildly-worded telegram was astonishing and far out of proportion to the provocation – *The National Review* admitted frankly that Cleveland's speech was a far greater affront and injury to Britain than the telegram.[156] Within days a new Royal Navy "flying squadron" of two

---

[151] William L. Langer, *The Diplomacy of Imperialism 1890–1902*, 2nd ed. (New York: Knopf, 1960), 243.

[152] "Das Krüger-Telegramm (1896), in *Deutsche Geschichte in Quellen und Darstellungen* ed. Rüdiger vom Bruch and Björn Hofmesiter, vol. 8 (Stuttgart: Reclam, 2000), 271–73, here 273; see also Röhl, *The Kaiser's Personal Monarchy*, 783–88.

[153] Willem-Alexander van't Padje, "The 'Malet Incident,' October 1895: A prelude to the Kaiser's 'Krüger Telegram' in the Context of the Anglo-German Imperialist Rivalry," in *Wilhelminism and Its Legacies: German Modernities, Imperialism, and the Meanings of Reform, 1890–1930*, ed. Geoff Eley and James Retallack (New York and Oxford: Berghahn Books, 2003), 138–53, here 142; Charmley, *Splendid Isolation*, 239–40; Clark, *Kaiser Wilhelm II*, 132.

[154] Geppert, *Pressekriege*, 95–96.   [155] Darwin, *The Empire Project*, 232.

[156] Langer, *The Diplomacy of Imprialism*, 243; Rose, *Zwischen Empire und Kontinent*, 64. This was also observed in Germany, Geppert, *Pressekriege*, 100.

battleships and four cruisers was on its way to the Mediterranean.[157] Later that month British navalist writers such as Herbert Wrigley Wilson (1866–1940) and Arnold White (1848–1925) began expressing alarm about German naval ambitions, despite the fact that Germany's navy was tiny, the plans for it still vague, and nowhere remotely directed at the Royal Navy. In fact, Admiral Alfred Tirpitz's appointment to head the German Navy Office was more than a year in the future.[158]

The Kruger Telegram was not the first or only example of British overreaction. German settlers were a sizable demographic in the Boer republics, and Germans owned about one-fifth of all invested capital in the South African Republic in 1895, at the time an independent state recognized by Britain.[159] In 1894 a railway line from Pretoria to Laurenço Marques on Delagoa Bay in Portuguese Mozambique was nearing completion, a project financed in large part by German investors. The railway line would give the landlocked country access to an ocean port not controlled by Britain. Both the Deutsche and Dresdner Bank had offices in the republic, and Krupp and Siemens & Halske were major suppliers to the railways and gold mining industry, where German investors were likewise very active.[160] Fearing the loss of economic control over South Africa by the new railway line, Britain began reasserting phony sovereign claims over the republic in the fall of 1894.[161] When on November 20, 1894, the German ambassador to Britain, Paul von Hatzfeldt (1831–1901), presented the German government's position insisting that the territorial status quo in South Africa be preserved, Britain's Foreign Secretary Lord Kimberley (John Wodehouse, 1826–1902) was unpleasantly surprised and perturbed, responding that Britain was, after all, the greatest naval power and would "not recoil from the spectre of war" to assert its interests in South Africa.[162] During the Drifts Crisis in October 1895 Sir Edward Malet (1837–1908), the departing British ambassador in Berlin, told Chancellor Hohenlohe and Foreign Secretary Marschall that South Africa was a "black spot" on Anglo-German relations and Germany risked "serious complications" with Britain if it did not cease encouraging the Boers.[163] Marschall later reported that Malet had in fact used the term "war" but Marschall omitted it in his memo of the conversation because "it looked so bad on paper!"[164]

---

[157] Röhl, *The Kaiser's Personal Monarchy*, 788.
[158] Geppert, *Pressekriege*, 101–8; Kennedy, *Anglo-German Antagonism*, 248; Langer, *The Diplomacy of Imperialism*, 237–46.
[159] Clark, *Kaiser Wilhelm II*, 131–32; Darwin, *The Empire Project*, 226.
[160] Canis, *von Bismarck zur Weltpolitik*, 142.    [161] Ibid., 143.
[162] Quoted in Kennedy, *Anglo-German Antagonism*, 217.
[163] van't Padje, "The 'Malet Incident,'" 145, 147; Canis, *Von Bismarck zur Weltpolitik*, 177.
[164] Quoted in van't Padje, "The 'Malet Incident,'" 148.

After the Kruger Telegram British diplomats became even more blunt. In March 1897 Sir Francis Bertie, assistant under-secretary of the British Foreign Office, told the acting German ambassador in London that the United Kingdom would use every measure including war against Germany if it intervened in the slightest way in the Transvaal. If it were to come to war, Bertie said, "the entire English nation would be behind it, and a blockade of Hamburg and Bremen and the annihilation of German commerce on the high seas would be child's play for the English fleet."[165] On April 22, 1897 British warships entered Delagoa Bay (a neutral port), and there was nothing the German government could do about it, leaving it with no choice but to withdraw from any further confrontation. It was later compensated for relinquishing any involvement in the future of the Transvaal in exchange for trifling British concessions.[166] Indeed, one is tempted to see in what might be called the "Malet Doctrine" a British version of the Monroe Doctrine for the Boer republics of South Africa.

These British overreactions to what were rather minor German provocations grew out of a complex of imperial entitlement, strategic anxiety, and irritation over successful German economic competition, not a nonexistent larger German navy. Imperiousness and overreaction were luxuries the British afforded themselves because Germany was weak, a *quantité négligeable* that could offer Britain little diplomatically. A number of historians have argued that appeasement and opposition, respectively, became patterns in British responses to American and German provocation after 1895, bound up closely with the perceived relative strength of these powers vis-à-vis Britain.[167] The disproportionate British reactions to American and German provocations from 1895 to 1897 were not lost on German observers at the time, not least Kaiser Wilhelm, who began to press for an aggressive expansion of the German navy to gain diplomatic leverage with Britain, albeit without much success against a recalcitrant Reichstag. This will be treated in detail in the next chapter.

---

[165] Quoted in Clark, *Sleepwalkers*, 149. See also Harald Rosenbach, *Das Deutsche Reich, Großbritannien und der Transvaal: Anfänge Deutsch-Britischer Entfremdung* (Göttingen: Vandenhoeck & Ruprecht, 1994), 70.
[166] Canis, *Von Bismarck zur Weltpolitik*, 244.
[167] Niall Ferguson, *The Pity of War* (New York: Basic Books, 1999), 52–55; Clark, *Sleepwalkers*, 151–52. See also Mitchell, *Danger of Dreams*, 64–107; Rose, *Zwischen Empire und Kontinent*, 279–300; Joachim Remak, *The Origins of World War I: 1871–1914* (New York: Holt, Rinehart and Winston, 1967), 30–46, 71–82; Wilson, *The Policy of the Entente*, 100–120.

## From Hamburg to Caracas – Ernst von Halle in Venezuela

The dual prospect of American expansion into the South Pacific and the closing off of German trade to the Western Hemisphere by more muscular invocations of the Monroe Doctrine began to worry many Germans, including Ernst von Halle, whose family was closely connected to Hamburg's merchant and trading elite. As discussed in Chapter 1, over his time in the United States, which extended from 1893 to 1895, von Halle had become an expert not only on American industrial enterprises and trusts, but also on American cotton cultivation, which he had opportunity to study directly by traveling through the American South in the late summer and autumn of 1894, at which point he had opportunity to visit Booker T. Washington's Tuskegee Institute.[168] These materials were used to write a major study on the history of cotton production in the American South, the first part of which was published in 1897, which together with his work on American trusts and syndicates discussed in Chapter 1, firmly established von Halle, alongside Max Sering and Hermann Schumacher, as one of the leading specialists on the American and world economy in Wilhelmine Germany.

Beyond the United States, von Halle had a very deep interest in Latin America and the Caribbean, not only as a potential site of German cotton cultivation but also as a destination for German investment and possible German colonization. As was discussed in Chapter 1, Max Sering had already come to the realization that North America was hopeless territory for German colonization because of tremendous Yankee assimilationist pressure on German settlers. He had become – on the Minnesota prairie in 1883, no less – an ardent advocate instead of German colonization of South America. Von Halle's own observations of North America in the early 1890s would have only confirmed this view.

There had been organized private efforts in Germany since the late 1840s to redirect German emigration from North America to Brazil, albeit with only very modest success. These plans were revived in the 1880s by German colonial enthusiasts who sought to purchase tracts of land in Brazil, Chile, Paraguay, and Uruguay for German colonists, though again without much success.[169] Nevertheless, this dream of a "German India" never quite died and gained renewed energy after 1890 with initiatives of the German Colonial Society and Pan-German League to direct investment and colonization to South America.[170] This was, in must be emphasized, not an official German policy – the German Foreign Office was skeptically aloof and often hostile to these projects because of their diplomatic implications for relations with the United States, especially after the First Venezuela Crisis, and it was not until

---

[168] GStA PK VI HA, Nl. Schmoller, Nr. 126, fols. 15–26, von Halle to Schmoller, Savannah, Georgia, Oct. 22, 1894.
[169] Herwig, *Vision of Empire*, 181–84.
[170] Ibid., 185; Fiebig-von Hase, *Lateinamerika als Krisenherd*, 193–248.

1898 that a 1859 Prussian rescript prohibiting emigration to Brazil was revoked. This ban, the Heydt Rescript, had stopped all emigration to Brazil due to fear of loss of agricultural laborers and the abuses of emigration brokers bringing Germans to Brazil under conditions akin to indentured servitude.[171]

With the rapid expansion of German trade with the United States after 1850, Hanseatic merchants had meanwhile expanded their activity into the Caribbean and Central and South American markets very robustly, notably in Venezuela.[172] Hanseatic trade with "Little Venice" centered on exports of coffee, cacao, and tobacco, and through state subsidies to the steamer lines HAPAG and Norddeutscher Lloyd, Germany had established direct steamer service to Venezuela via the Caribbean in the 1880s.[173] By the turn of the century the Hanseatic merchant colony included 38 merchant houses that dominated the Venezuelan economy, controlling about one-third of all commerce and fully two-thirds of its foreign trade in manufactured goods.[174] Hanseatic coffee planters such as H. G. & L. F. Blohm, Breuer, Möller & Co., and Van Dissel, Rhode & Co. were particularly influential, effectively monopolizing the coffee trade and serving as important money lenders. What gave these Hanseatic merchants an edge over the competition was their ability to assimilate themselves to local conditions: learning Spanish, adopting local customs, and paying close attention to the needs of the local market.[175]

Large-scale German industrial investments had also been drawn to Venezuela in the 1880s. In 1887 Friedrich Krupp signed a contract with President Antonio Guzmán Blanco (1829–99) to build a small-spur, single track railway line between Caracas and Valencia, part of an effort for deeper German commercial penetration of South America at a time of economic depression and growing worldwide protectionism. In 1888 the Große Venezuelabahn (Great Venezuela Railway; Gran Ferrocarril de Venezuela) was founded in Hamburg and financed jointly by the Disconto-Gesellschaft and Norddeutsche Bank and became the single largest German overseas investment at the time.[176] Royal Prussian railway engineers were employed to survey and oversee the construction of the railway project, which commenced in late 1888 and drew exclusively from German contractors for its supplies: steel rails, wheels, and axels from Krupp in Essen; passenger and freight cars from Zypen & Charlier in Cologne; steel railway ties from Dortmunder Union; and locomotives from Sächsische Maschinenfabrik in Chemnitz.[177]

---

[171] Herwig, *Vision of Empire*, 178, 185.
[172] Fiebig-von Hase, *Lateinamerka als Konfliktherd*, 68–88.
[173] Herwig, *Vision of Empire*, 17, 21.   [174] Ibid., 22.   [175] Ibid., 22–27.
[176] Ernst von Halle, *Reisebriefe aus Westindien und Venezuela: Skizzen während einer 10 wöchentlichen Tour mit dem Schnelldampfer "Columbia" der Hamburg-Amerika Linie* (Hamburg: A.G. "Neue Börsen-Halle," 1896), 75–76; cf. Fiebig-von Hase, *Lateinamerika als Krisenherd*, 88–193.
[177] Herwig, *Vision of Empire*, 37–39.

In all, between 1888 and 1894 some 50,000 tons of German material valued at 8 million marks was transported to Venezuela.[178] Krupp also became the supplier of some 212 steel viaducts and bridges for the line, which covered very challenging, mountainous terrain between Caracas and Las Tejerias. It was completed in February 1894, despite Venezuelan political unrest in 1892 and severe flooding, which damaged the railway line.[179] Due to the mountainous terrain and mudslides, the construction costs of the railway more than doubled, putting great pressure on Norddeutsche Bank to come up with additional capital. Likewise, the Venezuelan government had difficulty paying the 7 percent per kilometer guarantee it had signed with its German creditors and Krupp.[180] The gala grand opening of the railway on February 1, 1894 was a star-crossed affair, marred by the sudden cancellation of President Joaquín Crespo (1841–98), the absence of German Resident Minister Friedrich von Kleist (1851–1936), who was taken ill, and a mudslide on the tracks preventing a ceremonial meeting of trains at La Victoria. Relations between the German merchant community and German mission were also frayed over their exclusion from celebrations marking the event.[181]

In early January 1896 Ernst von Halle embarked on a second journey to the Americas, this time aboard the HAPAG steamer *Columbia,* taking him to the West Indies and Venezuela. Typical of the melding of pleasure and purpose, of private and public, this journey involved a sizable German group (some 80 men and women) on what appeared, on the surface at least, a pleasure cruise to the Caribbean and Venezuela aboard one of HAPAG's newest and fastest steamers. In reality, it was – also – a carefully-planned and organized inspection tour of the Great Venezuela Railway. All evidence suggests this tour of the railway had a dual purpose: to celebrate the opening of the line and thus put the mess of the 1894 gala behind the railway and to attract German investor interest in it, given the cost overruns of the project. Since Albert Ballin's (1857–1918) HAPAG was involved and Ballin's known close ties to the Kaiser, it is also likely that this tour of the railway was intended to offer publicity for German investment and engagement abroad of a status equal to other European great powers. Indeed, the German Foreign Office included photographs and other exhibits of the Great Venezuela Railway at the Industrial Exhibition in Berlin that opened in May 1896.[182] It must thus also count as one of the first public displays of Germany's new *Weltpolitik*, which will be discussed in detail in the next chapter.

Von Halle's journey started in Genoa January 8, 1896, taking him via Naples to Algiers, and from there via Gibraltar and Madeira to New York. After a two-day stop in New York for resupply, the journey continued to the

---

[178] Ibid., 39.  [179] von Halle, *Reisebriefe*, 76–78, 84.  [180] Herwig, *Vision of Empire*, 40.
[181] Ibid., 41.  [182] Ibid., 44.

Caribbean. As von Halle noted in his travelogue, German merchants and traders, notably Hanseatic traders, predominated in large parts of the West Indies and Central and South America, though Germany – unlike Spain, England, France, Denmark, and the Netherlands – lacked any formal presence in the West Indies or a coaling station for large ships of the sort Great Britain had at Castries on St. Lucia.[183] In the Caribbean von Halle and his group made numerous stops, embarking on tours in Haiti and Santo Domingo, St. Thomas, and Barbados, with a longer stop made in Trinidad. From there many of the Lesser Antilles were visited, including St. Kitts and St. Lucia, finally arriving in La Guaira, Venezuela February 11.[184] One of the running themes in von Halle's account of this journey was Spanish colonial mismanagement, exploitation, and decay, notably in Cuba and Puerto Rico and in the former Spanish possessions he visited.[185]

With the *Columbia* anchored at La Guaira, President Joaquín Crespo's entourage lunched with the German group on their arrival, which was followed by a tour by the German consul Cesar Müller (1854–1918) and the German director of the Great Venezuela Railway, Gustav Knoop (1850–1925).[186] At the time tense negotiations were occurring between the German ambassador Arthur von Rex (1856–1926) and Crespo's government about repayment of debts incurred during construction of the railway, and von Halle and the other Germans were witness to a bit of German gunboat diplomacy with the arrival at La Guaira of the navy cruisers *Hardenberg, Stosch*, and *Stein* to strengthen Rex's hand.[187] Von Halle observed that Venezuela's foreign trade was at the time almost exclusively in German merchant hands, to the point where common Venezuelans referred to any strangers as "*Allemenos.*"[188] Indeed, German-Venezuelan trade had risen sharply since 1889, which in 1894 was valued at 26.6 million marks, was beginning to rival Venezuela's trade with the United States (30.6 million marks), and was more than one-third larger than Venezuela's trade with Britain (16.6 million marks).[189]

After traveling by rail on the poorly-built English La Guaira Railway from La Guaira to Caracas, von Halle was introduced to many of the prominent Germans in the city, notably the botanist and polymath Adolf Ernst (1832–99) of the Central University of Venezuela, an extraordinarily knowledgeable interlocutor on the land, people, and economy of Venezuela.[190] The German Club in Caracas served as a meeting point for many of these contacts.[191] Von Halle noted that Germans were highly regarded in Venezuela for their entrepreneurial activity, even with the heightened diplomatic tensions over

---

[183] von Halle, *Reisebriefe*, 13, 26.   [184] Ibid., 17–48.
[185] Ibid., 12, 18, 49, 56, 59, 107–18.   [186] Ibid., 52.   [187] Ibid., 55.   [188] Ibid., 52.
[189] ibid., 82; cf. Rose, *Zwischen Empire und Kontinent*, 284.
[190] von Halle, *Reisebriefe*, 60, 68–69.   [191] Ibid., 62, 65.

Venezuelan loans. This was in some contrast to the Americans who, though arrogating to themselves the role of protector in the recent Venezuela Crisis, continued to be disliked in the country, von Halle noted.[192]

In the days that followed a *treno especial* (special train; *Sonderzug*) of the Great Venezuela Railway was prepared for von Halle's group, and on February 14th the train departed Caracas for the 250 kilometer journey to Valencia.[193] Along on the ride and indicating the semi-official status of the journey was Baurat Wilhelm Böckmann (1832–1902), who had been active as an architect to the Meiji government and the technical attaché of the German embassy in Washington, DC, and Bauinspektor Höch.[194] Von Halle was a close observer of the potential economic impact of the railway in connecting Venezuelan urban and overseas consumer markets with those areas along the line producing coffee, cacao, sugar, maize, and cattle.[195] To his mind there had been far too little of this sort of large-scale German industrial investment abroad financed with German capital, employing German engineers, and supplied by German industrial firms, much to the detriment of Germany's standing in its competition with other nations.[196] Venezuela with some 200 million marks of invested German capital was thus a notable exception.[197] As he observed, the Gran Ferrocarril – in contrast to the primitive colonial railways usually built by the Americans and English, as exemplified by the ramshackle, narrow-gauge La Guaira Line – "has from the beginning been carried out absolutely complete technically" so that even the bureaucrats of the Prussian State Railways would not be able to find fault with it.[198]

Indeed, von Halle was very impressed with the technical mastery of the challenging terrain the railway covered, rising from 911 meters above sea level in Caracas to 1,227 meters after 30 kilometers and then descending uninterrupted for 44 kilometers at a 2 percent grade with "mighty curves and countless bridges and tunnels" back down to 500 meters above sea level at Las Tejerias.[199] As he remarked later in his travelogue, "no railway known to me in Europe or America can be compared with this section of the Great Venezuela Railway in terms of the wild grandeur of its scenery."[200] Further along on the journey, von Halle was also sensitive to the potential of some regions covered by the railway as a destination for German colonists and of the new railway in assisting that endeavor, notably as craftsmen and coffee planters in and around Valencia and San Esteban near Puerto Cabello, which both already had German colonies of planters and merchants.[201]

From Puerto Cabello, von Halle and his group bid Venezuela farewell and re-boarded the *Columbia* to return to the United States via Jamaica, Cuba,

---

[192] Ibid., 64–65, 92–93.   [193] Ibid., 75, 89.   [194] Ibid., 75.   [195] Ibid., 80.
[196] Ibid., 81.   [197] Ibid., 83.   [198] Ibid.   [199] Ibid., 84.   [200] Ibid., 88.
[201] Ibid., 85, 87, 90, 91; cf. Herwig, *Visions of Empire*, 54, 63.

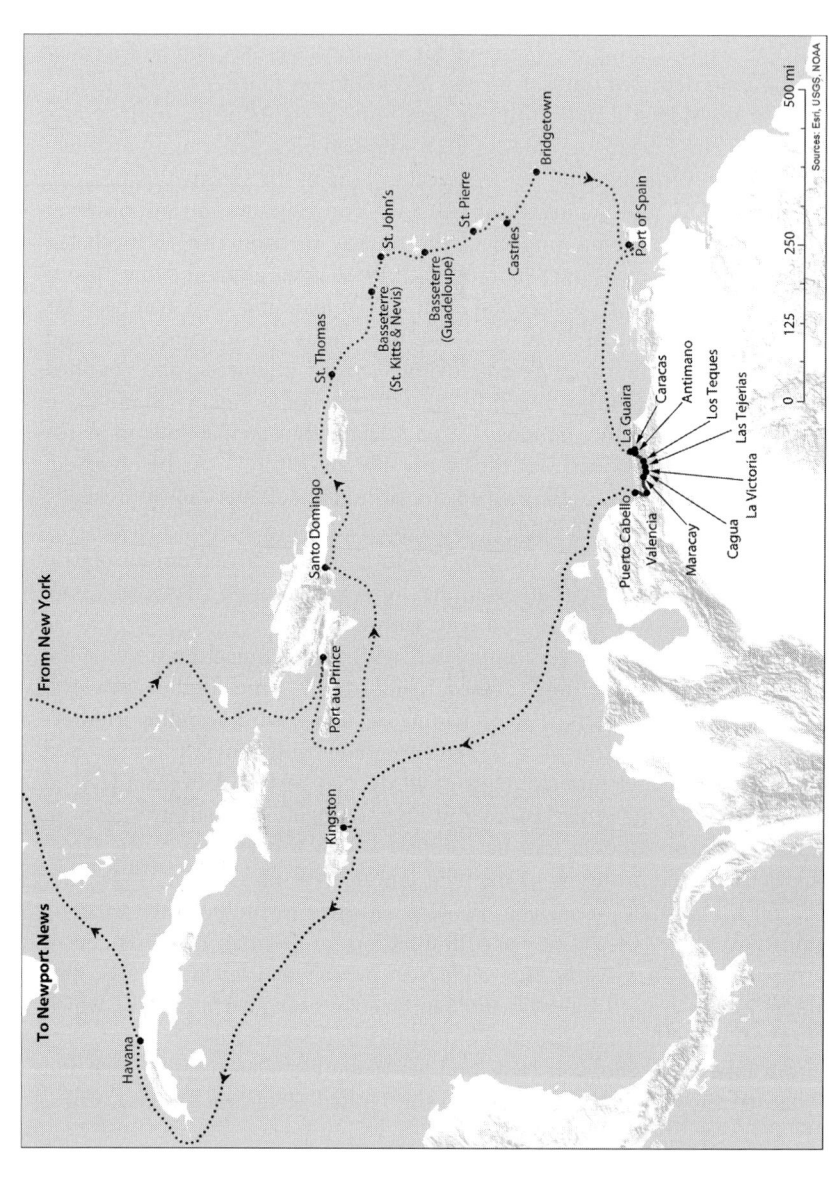

Map 3.2 Ernst von Halle's journey to the United States, Caribbean, and Venezuela, Jan. 8–March 14, 1896.

**Figure 3.2** Ernst von Halle ca. 1905.

and New York. Kingston was reached February 17th.[202] The arrival in Havana of von Halle's party four days later was clouded by the ongoing Mambi rebellion, and so the Spanish authorities subjected those disembarking to tedious searches for contraband, highlighting to von Halle the administrative incompetence of Spanish rule.[203] The rebellion itself was to von Halle indicative of native hatred of Spanish misrule. The inferior Spanish troops sent to quell the insurrection, Cuba's currency mess, and the appalling sanitary conditions he witnessed there rounded out a picture of Spanish misrule on the verge of collapse in the Caribbean.[204]

Von Halle's journey continued from Havana to Old Point Comfort and Newport News, from where von Halle disembarked to continue on to Washington, New York, and Boston by river boat and rail. At the opening of Chesapeake Bay at Old Point Comfort between Hampton and the Norfolk Naval Yards, von Halle could see some fifteen "mostly extremely impressive looking" American warships, among them the *New York,* the *San Francisco,* and the *Minneapolis.*[205] He was also very impressed with the expansion of the

---

[202] von Halle, *Reisebriefe,* 99.   [203] Ibid., 110.   [204] Ibid., 114–16.   [205] Ibid., 119.

harbor and port facilities at Old Point Comfort and Hampton, which coincided with the expansion of the US Navy.[206] With respect to the Venezuela Crisis, von Halle was himself convinced that most of Britain's claims in South America were valid, which made the recent British retreat all the more out of character.[207] Seeing these impressive warships and expanded American harbors would only have reinforced his conviction that American naval muscle had been the decisive factor in Britain's uncharacteristic about-face.

Shortly after his return to Germany in March of 1896, von Halle published an article in Schmoller's *Jahrbuch* that distilled his recent impressions of Venezuela, the Caribbean, and the United States.[208] He was deeply concerned in this article about the growth of jingoistic and belligerent public opinion in the United States that he himself had witnessed from 1893 to 1895. He was also worried that the new more muscular Monroe Doctrine invoked in Venezuela, together with America's very high protective tariffs and powerful trusts, would eventually exclude German merchants and exporters from the Western Hemisphere, a dire prospect given the leading role Germans played in the trade of many South American countries, notably Venezuela.[209] He urged the German government to purchase the Danish Caribbean island of Saint Thomas before it fell into American hands to assure German traders a tariff-free port to Central and South American markets.[210] He also proposed coordinating retaliatory tariffs between Germany and the countries of continental Europe in a customs union in order to force the American market open to European trade.[211] Finally von Halle proposed shifting German immigration away from the United States toward South America and developing alternative sources of cotton in German colonies with the aid of Texas German planters as additional leverage over the Americans.[212]

It is certain that von Halle had by this time steeped himself in the writings of the American naval officer Captain Alfred Thayer Mahan (1840–1914), whose *Influence of Sea Power upon History, 1660–1783* (1890) and *Influence of Sea Power upon the French Revolution and Empire, 1783–1812* (1892) had been published shortly before von Halle's first journey to the United States and quickly became influential in both the United States and Germany.[213] Von

---

[206] Ibid., 120.   [207] Ibid., 92–93.
[208] Ernst von Halle, "Das Interesse Deutschlands an der amerikanischen Präsidentenwahl des Jahres 1896," *JbfGVV* 20 (1896): 1353–86; cf. Humphries, "Anglo-American Rivalries," 131–64.
[209] von Halle, "Das Interesse Deutschlands," 1359–61, 1371–73.
[210] Ibid., 1373–1374; cf. Fiebig-von Hase, *Lateinamerika als Konfliktherd*, 431–46.
[211] von Halle, "Das Interesse Deutschlands," 1380–81.
[212] Ibid., 1382–83; cf. von Halle, *Baumwollproduktion*, vol. 1, 200.
[213] See James R. Holmes, "Mahan, a 'Place in the Sun' and Germany's Quest for Sea Power," *Comparative Strategy* 23 (2004): 27–61.

Halle's writings on the history of American cotton production as well as his subsequent writings on the role of the Union blockade in the defeat of the Confederacy demonstrate that he drew parallel conclusions from this more recent episode of history. As he was to write, "Nearly half of the German people is directly or indirectly dependent upon industries reliant on the import of raw materials and semi-manufactured goods and export of semi-manufactured and manufactured goods. If these suffered restrictions limiting the possibilities of work and commerce, a terrible crisis would doubtless ensue."[214]

## Germany at the Crossroads

On March 31, 1897, Joseph Chamberlain gave a remarkable speech to the Royal Colonial Institute in which he argued that forces were at work that were gradually bringing about greater cohesion in the British Empire and concentrating all power in the hands of similar greater empires. Smaller kingdoms that did not move forward with the times would be relegated to subordinate status:

> We want to promote a closer and firmer union between all members of the great British race, and in this respect we have in recent years made great progress.... Let us, gentlemen, keep our ideal always before us. For my own part I believe in the practical possibility of a federation of a British race – (loud cheers).
> ... That such a result would be desirable, would be in the interests of all our colonies as well as ourselves, I do not believe any sensible man will doubt. It seems to me that the tendency of the time is to throw all power into the hands of the greater Empires, and the minor kingdoms – those which are non-progressive – seem to be destined to fall into a secondary and subordinate place. But if Greater Britain remains united, no empire in the world can ever surpass it in area, in population, in wealth, or in the diversity of its resources.[215]

The speech, while couched in the language of progress and confidence, was nevertheless unmistakably defensive in tone, reflecting the growing strategic anxiety of British statesmen about Britain's sprawling imperial commitments, escalating defense costs, and the centrifugal forces pulling at the Dominions.

---

[214] Ernst von Halle, *Die Blockade der nordamerikanischen Südstaaten* (Berlin: Mittler und Sohn, 1900), 34; cf. von Halle, *Baumwollproduktion und Pflanzungswirtschaft in den Nordamerikanischen Südstaaten*, vol. 2, Sezessionskrieg und Rekonstruktion: Grundzüge einer Wirtschaftsgeschichte der Baumwollstaaten von 1861–80, Staats- und sozialwissenschaftliche Forschungen, vol. 26, no. 2 (Leipzig: Duncker & Humblot, 1906), 146–64.

[215] Joseph Chamberlain, "The True Conception of Empire," *Foreign and Colonial Speeches* (London: Routledge, 1897), 241–48, here 246–47.

Chamberlain's speech drew immediate attention in Germany, as it seemed to throw the Germans an existential challenge, as the German Empire was neither a greater empire nor a minor kingdom.

Karl Rathgen, himself an Anglophile and an informed observer of British colonialism since his return from Japan, commented that while Chamberlain's ideas of a "Greater Britain" might make Germans uncomfortable and could ultimately pose a danger to Germany, it would be foolish for Germans to condemn British politicians for ruthlessly pursuing Britain's own interests.[216] Chamberlain was simply giving expression to a certain indifference to the damage caused others by the English pursuit of progress and freedom. Chamberlain thus embodied "the apparent contradiction of the defense of freedom and peaceful progress driven to the point of suppressing foreign freedom by a striving to rule which characterizes the English people as a whole and has made it what it is."[217] This insouciance would, however, invariably lead to tensions:

> As painful as it may be for anyone filled with admiration for what the English people have accomplished for themselves and for humanity, and much as we admire England for what she has accomplished and what we may still learn from our English cousins, the final consequence is nevertheless: the struggle over world power leads us necessarily to a conflict of interest with England as we have to fear from no other European power.[218]

The struggle, Rathgen continued, was one over which markets remained open. It was true, he admitted, that Germany's own colonial possessions could absorb but little of Germany's exports for the foreseeable future, and the rest of the world had been divvied up. Still, he noted, "we should not forget that around 1600 the world had been divvied up too between the Spanish and the Portuguese until the Netherlands, France and above all England became sea powers and divided overseas colonial lands anew. What had once occurred could occur again."[219] Clearly, Rathgen, too, had been reading Alfred Thayer Mahan.

Beyond Germany's colonial empire, a few promising markets remained open to German exporters and offered attractive prospects, particularly China and Turkey – Rathgen did not believe in an "awakening of China" along lines analogous to Japan.[220] The Chinese were a race not a nation and were hardworking and pliable subjects if one did not interfere too much with their customs and habits, Rathgen argued. They had been habituated to foreign rule over many centuries, and their rulers [the Qing] were rotten to the core, much as the Moghuls of India had been in the eighteenth century. Like Moghul

---

[216] Rathgen, "Die Kündigung," 1383–84. [217] Ibid., 1384. [218] Ibid., 1384–85.
[219] Ibid., 1385. [220] Ibid.

India, Chinese rule was now decaying, drawing in foreign conquerors from overseas. As then, the struggle over China's future would be determined by those states that put the greatest and most decisive effort to command the sea. England came to rule over India for precisely this reason, and England's status in the world and welfare rested most significantly on its rule of India.[221]

As in India in the past, foreign merchants were the starting point for entrepreneurial activity in China. But there was one difference: there were no German merchants in the counting houses of India while there was a profusion of them in the harbors of East Asia who had established their place proficiently and calmly, as Rathgen himself had had ample opportunity to witness over his many years in East Asia. Yet, on the borders of China today, Rathgen warned, Russia, Japan, England, and France were waiting to pounce with treachery and violence and seize Chinese lands for themselves.[222] The eighteenth century had been decided by the struggle for India and North America, while the nineteenth century witnessed the dissolution of much of the Spanish colonial empire and the division of Africa. The dawning twentieth century, Rathgen believed, would be determined by the struggle for China. Would that massive market be divided up alone by Germany's "economic opponents"?[223] He closed his essay returning to Chamberlain's speech and posing a final question:

> All power is being concentrated in the hands of the great world empires, as Jos. Chamberlain said. Will we Germans be satisfied to belong to the "secondary" countries, "that do not progress" or will we be as proud as the English thinking of the significance of our nationality [*Volkstums*] for humanity, of our national strength, our national mission, our national honor? Then we must be clear that only sea power can become world power. Then we too must have the will to make the sacrifice without which we cannot assert ourselves among the great nations.[224]

---

[221] Ibid.  [222] Ibid., 1385–86.  [223] Ibid., 1386.  [224] Ibid.

# PART II

## Empire Imagined, 1897–1907

# 4

# World Policy

## Naval Dreams

Germany's growing economic engagement in East Asia and the Americas witnessed and analyzed directly by Rathgen, Schumacher, Sering, and von Halle offered a picture of vulnerability and opportunity much heightened by the international phenomenon of "navalism." As discussed in Chapter 3, by 1897 an international naval arms race in heavily armed and armored battleships was well underway between Great Britain and the Dual Alliance, by which point it also began sweeping in the up-and-coming powers of the United States, Germany, and Japan.[1] Very much at the center of this process was the growing influence of the American naval strategist Alfred Thayer Mahan, who connected colonial expansion, shipping, and overseas commerce with larger bluewater navies. This was tied closely to the gradual doctrinal eclipse of the French *jeune école* emphasizing small, fast warships (light cruisers, torpedo boats) for *guerre de course* (commerce raiding) in favor of destroyers and heavy cruisers with powerful cannons for decisive battle at sea.[2] In part this was a lesson from the Japanese naval victory over the Chinese at the Yalu River estuary in August 1894, but it was also as much a creature of the Social Darwinian and neomercantilist zeitgeist of the of the "new imperialism" epitomized by Joseph Chamberlain's March 1897 speech discussed at the end of the previous chapter.[3] New naval technology, particularly in steel armor plate, heavy long-range cannons, and tube boilers were also important in ushering this age of the battleship.[4] Not to be overlooked, either, was the professional zeal and hunger for power and prestige of senior naval officers, organized naval agitation spearheaded by navy leagues (e.g., the British Navy League, founded in 1894), and lobbying by defense contractors.[5] Finally, there was the growing naval enthusiasm of the public, notably the

---

[1] Marder, *British Sea Power*, 166–68; Offer, *The First World War*, 325; Hobson, *Imperialism at Sea*, 154–77.
[2] Hobson, *Imperialism at Sea*, 84–109.   [3] See Hobsbawm, *Age of Empire*, 56–83.
[4] William McNeill, *The Pursuit of Power: Technology, Armed Force and Society since A.D. 1000* (Chicago: University of Chicago Press, 1982), 262–306.
[5] Bönker, *Militarism in a Global Age*.

middle classes, who marveled at the technology and saw battleships as symbols of great power status and national prestige.[6] All of these developments were reflected in the naval preoccupations of prominent national leaders in the United States, Germany, and Japan, notably Theodore Roosevelt (1858–1919), Kaiser Wilhelm II, and Yamamoto Gonnohyōe (1852–1933).[7]

Alfred Thayer Mahan's work, which as already discussed was exercising great influence in Germany, was itself hardly unbiased historical scholarship but rather navalist and imperialist propaganda, as it was directed in the first instance toward the American public to gain support for a larger bluewater navy and an expansionist overseas program.[8] For these reasons Mahan's ideas had particular resonance not only in the United States but also in other newer naval and colonial powers such as Germany and Japan.[9] Appealing in these contexts was Mahan's blurring of the distinction between sea power in war and peace, particularly the notion that economic growth and the expansion of peaceful overseas commerce and shipping created a need for naval stations and colonies, which in turn all necessitated a larger navy for their protection. In this way the size of a navy was easily (and erroneously) equated with the size of a country's overseas commercial and colonial interests, and when combined with then-current Social Darwinism and neomercantilism, made such overseas expansion seem both necessary and inevitable.[10] In Britain – where the Bluewater School had originated, command of the sea in wartime was the Royal Navy's strategic doctrine, and a vast navy, expansive overseas empire, and a network of naval and coaling stations and transoceanic telegraph cables were not aspiration but reality – Mahan's ideas were not taken

---

[6] Rüger, *The Great Naval Game*; J. Charles Schencking, "The Politics of Pragmatism and Pageantry: Selling a National Navy at the Elite and Local Level in Japan, 1890–1913," in *Nation and Nationalism in Japan,* ed. Sandra Wilson (London: RoutledgeCurzon, 2002), 21–37.

[7] See Clark, *Kaiser Wilhelm II*, 130–34; Holger H. Herwig, *"Luxury" Fleet: The Imperial German Navy 1888–1918* (London and Atlantic Highlands, NJ: Ashfield, 1987), 17–32; Peter Karsten, "The Nature of 'Influence': Roosevelt, Mahan and the Concept of Sea Power," *American Quarterly* 23, no. 4 (Oct. 1971): 585–600; Edmund Morris, *The Rise of Theodore Roosevelt* (1979; New York: Modern Library, 2001), 137–38, 182, 433–34, 560–61, 581, 592–616; Morris, *Theodore Rex* (New York: Random House, 2001), 180, 186, 455–56; David C. Evans and Mark R. Peattie, *Kaigun: Strategy, Tactics, and Technology in the Imperial Japanese Navy, 1887–1941* (Annapolis, MD: Naval Institute Press, 1997), 20–22, 57–65; Röhl, *The Kaiser's Personal Monarchy*, 999–1039; J. Charles Schencking, *Making Waves: Politics Propaganda, and the Emergence of the Imperial Japanese Navy, 1868–1922* (Stanford: Stanford University Press, 2005), 78–200.

[8] Walter LaFeber, "A Note on the 'Mercantilist Imperialism' of Alfred Thayer Mahan," *The Mississippi Valley Historical Review* 48, no. 4 (March 1962): 674–85; Hobson, *Imperialism at Sea*, 154–70.

[9] Rose, *Zwischen Empire und Kontinent*, 185.

[10] Hobson, *Imperialism at Sea*, 163–64, 167.

very seriously.[11] As will be discussed in Chapter 7, the British counterpart to Mahan, the influential naval historian and strategist Julian Corbett (1854–1922), doubted the importance of decisive battle and advocated instead the use of Royal Navy sea power to blockade enemy ports as the ultimate naval weapon.

While international in scope, navalism in Germany had some German features that need to be highlighted in order to fully understand the later active pro-fleet activity of von Halle Rathgen, Schmoller, Schumacher, and Sering beginning in 1897. First of all, the navy (unlike the Prusso-German army) was one of the only German national institutions defined by the 1871 constitution of the very fragmented and decentralized Reich, and an institution that had been associated with national unity by the German liberal bourgeoisie since the 1848 Revolution.[12] As such, it was perceived by the German middle classes as a liberal nationalist counterforce to the powerful centrifugal tendencies pulling at Germany. It was also associated with Britain's status as a wealthy, unrivaled great power and free constitutional nation-state, and thus German bourgeois ambitions for similar status.[13] Beyond that – and this is a very important point for understanding the psychology of German middle-class naval enthusiasm – the navy was seen as a manifestation of the strength and validity of German values, a German way of life, and German institutions. As a floating agent of such on the open waters, it was hoped that it would unite "Germandom" (*Deutschtum*) both at home and overseas.[14] This view of the Imperial Navy can be traced back to the Revolution of 1848 and even earlier and had become the stock in trade of German liberal nationalism during the 1870s and 1880s. Overseas imperial expansion and liberalism were thus very closely linked ideologies in German political culture. As already explored in Chapter 1, the links between the North American settler colonization and German visions of overseas settler colonies were strong and likewise informed liberal nationalist hopes to achieve a more unified, independent, entrepreneurial, and self-governing Germany.

Not surprisingly, the German navy drew overwhelmingly from children of the educated bourgeoisie, notably the professions, merchants, and manufacturers, for its officer cadets and as such was associated with education and

---

[11] Rose, *Zwischen Empire und Kontinent*, 185–89.
[12] Jonathan Steinberg, *Yesterday's Deterrent: Tirpitz and the Birth of the German Battle Fleet* (New York: Macmillan, 1965), 32, 36–37. The sections of the 1871 constitution dealing with the Navy were Par. II, Art. 4, Sec. 14; Par. II, Art. 5; and especially Par. IX, Art. 53, 54 & 55.
[13] Steinberg, *Yesterday's Deterrent*, 38; Fitzpatrick, *Liberal Imperialism in Germany*, 27–43.
[14] Steinberg, *Yesterday's Deterrent*, 38; cf. Paul Rohrbach, *Deutschland unter den Weltvölkern: Materialien zur auswärtigen Politik* (Berlin-Schöneberg: Buchverlag der "Hilfe," 1903); Friedrich Naumann, *Demokratie und Kaisertum: Ein Handbuch für innere Politik* (Berlin-Schöneberg: Buchverlag der "Hilfe," 1905), 212–20.

meritocracy to an unusual degree.[15] Unlike the army, the German navy had no exclusively noble units, and its highly technical apparatus – at the forefront of developments in machine building, metallurgy, ballistics, optics, hydraulics, electro-mechanics, cartography, and civil engineering – required a specialist engineer-officer corps and extensive contacts between the navy and civilian contractors, making it a quintessentially modern and bourgeois service where *Bildung*, technical mastery, and ambition counted for far more than in the army.[16] As Jonathan Steinberg observes, "[b]y 1890 the new Navy had absorbed the entire standard of values of German bourgeois liberalism."[17] Research on the German military-industrial complex has also cautioned against the Marxist thesis that German battleship construction and navalism were largely a creature of bourgeois material interests. Firms like Krupp did not actively create the demand for German naval arms and were in fact rather more passive players in the processes that led to a much larger German navy after 1897.[18] Politicians and military figures retained the upper hand in naval objectives, procurement, and propaganda, and arms suppliers like Krupp supported a larger navy not only because it was profitable but because they too supported the navy as an institution of national cohesion and a tool of *Weltpolitik*.[19]

Of ultimately much greater importance for the construction of a larger German fleet was the naval enthusiasm of Kaiser Wilhelm II. Wilhelm had taken a deep personal interest in the navy from an early age, encouraged by his English mother, Empress Consort Victoria (1840–1901), the oldest daughter of Queen Victoria and a free-thinking anti-militarist. He had an unusually bourgeois education attending a mixed Gymnasium in Kassel and later preferred the company of navy men, even appointing a naval officer as a personal adjutant, quite out of the ordinary for a Hohenzollern monarch whose dynasty was practically synonymous with the Prussian army. By the mid-1890s he had also steeped himself in the navalist writings of Mahan and contemporary German naval literature.[20] It would thus be misleading to see Wilhelm's interest in the navy as an outgrowth of "militarism"; closer to the mark is that

---

[15] Steinberg, *Yesterday's Deterrent*, 39–40; Holger H. Herwig, *The German Naval Officer Corps: A Social and Political History, 1890–1918* (Oxford: Clarendon Press, 1973), 40–43.
[16] Steinberg, *Yesterday's Deterrent*, 40–41; Herwig, *German Naval Officer Corps*, 42, 103–33.
[17] Steinberg, *Yesterday's Deterrent*, 43.
[18] Michael Epkenhans, "Krupp and the Imperial German Navy, 1898–1914," *Journal of Military History* 64, no. 2 (April 2000): 335–69. Cf. Volker Berghahn, *Der Tirpitz Plan; Genesis und Verfall einer innenpolitischen Krisenstrategie unter Wilhelm II* (Düsseldorf: Droste Verlag, 1971), 129–57.
[19] Epkenhans, "Krupp and the Imperial German Navy," 341–46; 365–67; James, *Krupp*, 108–16.
[20] Clark, *Kaiser Wilhelm II*, 130–31; Kohut, *Wilhelm II*, 114–16; John C. G. Röhl, *Young Wilhelm: The Kaiser's Early Life, 1859–1888*, trans. Jeremy Gaines and Rebecca Wallach

his navalism was a creature of his youthful Anglophilia, revealing how much his own ideas had been shaped by English and especially German educated bourgeois opinion, reflected also in the unusually wide range of his other interests in the arts, sciences, education, social policy, and industry.[21] Indeed, it was often noted what a modern monarch he was by the standards of the time, a point made by many contemporary observers who knew him, such as the US historian and diplomat Andrew Dickson White (1832–1918), who spent a decade in Berlin over two assignments as ambassador between 1879 and 1903 and who was struck both by Wilhelm's unusual range of interests and his depth of knowledge on maritime and naval matters.[22]

As discussed in the previous chapter, the ferocious British backlash to the Kruger Telegram and the multiple threats of war and destructive naval blockades of German ports uttered by British foreign secretaries and diplomats before, during, and after the Transvaal Crisis had made a profound impression on the Kaiser that Germany was effectively at Britain's mercy in the absence of a navy that Britain respected.[23] Even so, the Kaiser's naval enthusiasm and British naval threats were not enough on their own to secure an expansive naval program, as all efforts to induce the Reichstag to significantly increase naval appropriations after the humiliations of the Transvaal Crisis had come to naught by 1897. As we shall see, it was ultimately other agents who would prove decisive in nudging the Reichstag into a more accommodating course regarding the navy, and at that, not in the strategic direction that Wilhelm wished.[24]

## From *Weltwirtschaft* to *Weltpolitik*

As was discussed at length in the previous chapters, *Weltpolitik* was in important respects a political response to the realities of *Weltwirtschaft* driven forward by the concurrence of economic interests, ideological forces, great power rivalries and domestic German politics. Otto Hammann (1852–1928), who served as chief of the press division in the German Foreign Office from 1893 to 1917, later argued that German *Weltpolitik* was not driven in the first instance by political power or military interests as the imperialism of Russia, France, Spain, and Britain had been but rather more by the pressure of population growth, the expansion of German industry, and with it, the growth of German overseas commerce and trade, as well as by the desire to keep the

---

(Cambridge: Cambridge University Press, 1998), 82–92, 201–28, 396–402; Röhl, *The Kaiser's Personal Monarchy*, 153–58, 355–60, 999–1039.
[21] See Ritter, *Staatskunst und Kriegshandwerk*, 2nd rev. ed., vol. 2, 171.
[22] Andrew D. White, *Autobiography*, vol. 2 (London: Macmillan and Co., 1905), 224–44.
[23] Kohut, *Wilhelm II*, 178–81.     [24] Cf. Röhl, *The Kaiser's Personal Monarchy*, 1025.

door open to overseas investments, raw materials, and export markets.[25] That is as accurate a description of *Weltpolitik* as one can find anywhere in the literature on German imperialism. That said, it was not "capitalism" or the economic system per se that were driving German *Weltpolitik*; the bourgeois thinkers and politicians behind *Weltpolitik* were imagining the future development and standing of Germany's political and economic power and its national prestige bound up with German achievements, talents, and institutions as well as the desire to secure that power and prestige into the future. It was quite consciously a liberal imperialism modeled on Britain and the British Empire and similar to American overseas imperialism of these years, even if in practice it was often defined in terms of opposition to Britain and the United States.[26]

It is important to underscore once again that with *Weltpolitik* we are dealing not simply with an ideological epiphenomenon. As the previous three chapters have sought to show, *Weltwirtschaft* and *Weltpolitik* were a new problem field and a policy response based on real experiences and observations *in the world*. Historians who have focused on the development of imperialist ideology have produced much valuable knowledge about the ideas shaping an imperialist zeitgeist, but they have usually not engaged in the historical spadework to uncover the context that catalyzed the perceptions behind these ideas. For example, Söhnke Neitzel's excellent comparative study of the doctrine of "world empires" in Germany, Britain, and the United States concluded that little could be said about the specific motivations of Gustav Schmoller or Max Sering in disseminating this idea in Imperial Germany, claiming that their personal papers offered no useful material to come to conclusions about these motivations.[27] As has also been pointed out by critics of the history of ideas and ideology, the concrete situational context that gave rise to the perceptions that informed these ideas and the forms of their dissemination through the media require investigation before one can attempt to gauge their historical significance.[28]

While not just an ideological construct, the specific aims of *Weltpolitik* are much harder to pin down. German public discussion about Germany's place in the wider world and the role in that of its economy and colonial empire had been simmering for close to a decade by 1897; but since the British reaction

---

[25] Otto Hammann, *The World Policy of Germany, 1890–1912*, trans. Maude A. Huttman (New York: Knopf, 1927), 53–54.
[26] See Smith, *Ideological Origins*, 69, 71, 74–75; Brechtken, *Scharnierzeit*, 28.
[27] Neitzel, *Weltmacht oder Untergang*, 27, 27n31. A similar approach to *Weltpolitik* focused on ideas and concepts is taken by van Laak, *Imperiale Infrastruktur*, 67–99.
[28] Ute Daniel, "Einkreisung und Kaiserdämmerung: Ein Versuch der Kulturgeschichte der Politik vor dem Ersten Weltkrieg auf die Spur zu kommen," in *Was heißt Kulturgeschichte des Politischen?* ed. Barbara Stollberg-Rilinger, Zeitschrift für Historische Forschung, Beiheft 35 (Berlin: Duncker & Humblot, 2005), 279–328, here 282–83.

to the Kruger Telegram, the discussion had been brought to a boil. Settler colonial enthusiasts were bitter that no suitable land had been seized in the temperate zone under Bismarck.[29] The Heligoland-Zanzibar Treaty of June 1890 signed between Great Britain and Germany had resulted in another major backlash in German colonial circles that the government had conceded far too much to Britain. Britain's aggressive imperialism, the disappointing resume of thwarted German colonial initiatives between 1892 and 1896, and the repercussions of the Kruger Telegram had further served to increasingly discredit the government and the Kaiser.[30] This fueled the formation of a number of populist nationalist societies criticizing the government and pushing for a much more aggressive policy abroad, notably the Pan-German League, founded on the initiative of the colonial hero Carl Peters (1856–1918) and others in 1894.[31]

Such nationalist movements had the blessing of the *fronde* centered around the retired Chancellor Otto von Bismarck, who had been critical of the Heligoland-Zanzibar Treaty and "New Course" charted by the Caprivi government since his dismissal in 1890. Caprivi had also allowed the Reinsurance Treaty with Russia to lapse, had liberalized trade and domestic policy, and sought better relations with Britain with an eye to alliance, all with very little to show by 1897.[32] Despite approvals from a bitter Bismarck in Friedrichsruh for populist nationalism, *Weltpolitik* and the navalism with which it became closely associated remained a quintessential creature of the German bourgeoisie, particularly prominent members of the *Bildungsbürgertum* who defined its ambitions and content.[33]

What did Germany's educated bourgeoisie imagine *Weltpolitik* to be? Before his death in 1896, Heinrich von Treitschke's, the *spiritus rector* of the Pan-German movement, had argued in his immensely popular lectures and writings that Wilhelm II had been too pro-British and that Germany needed to build a powerful navy to challenge England's maritime hegemony in order to preserve German and European *Kultur*.[34] Reflecting similar views, Max Weber

---

[29] Smith, *Ideological Origins*, 40.
[30] Canis, *Von Bismarck zur Weltpolitik*, 241; Wolfgang J. Mommsen, *Bürgerstolz und Weltmachtstreben: Deutschland unter Wilhelm II. 1890 bis 1918* (Berlin: Propyläen, 1995), 281, 289–95.
[31] Chickering, *We Men*, 48–55.
[32] Ibid., 46–47, 51; Kennedy, *Anglo-German Antagonism*, 208–209, 21, 215. On the Bismarck fronde, see Chickering, *We Men*, 46–47, 51; Daniel, "Einkreisung und Kaiserdämmerung," in Stollberg-Rilinger, *Was heißt Kulturgeschichte*, 298–304; Otto Pflanze, *Bismarck and the Development of Germany*, vol. 3 (Princeton: Princeton University Press, 1990), 381–95; Jonathan Steinberg, *Bismarck: A Life* (Oxford and New York: Oxford University Press, 2011), 452–64.
[33] Canis, *Von Bismarck zur Weltpolitik*, 333–34.
[34] See Peter Winzen, *Bülow's Weltmachtkonzept: Untersuchungen zur Frühphase seiner Außenpolitik 1897–1901* (Boppard am Rhein: Harald Boldt Verlag, 1977), 32–33; see also

argued in 1895 that a *Weltmachtspolitik* [world power policy] was the next obvious step after German unification to establish Germany as a world power.[35] Hans Delbrück (1848-1929) agreed and believed it was time for Germany to break out of the stagnation of its narrowly European constraints and to broaden its horizons in order to take its place as an equal alongside established European world empires like those of Russia, France, and Great Britain.[36] Yet oddly, *Weltpolitik* as voiced by these scholars and publicists was not directed at any specific territorial goals in the world. To be sure, as it had evolved and been shaped by *Weltwirtschaft*, it became a policy focused less on formal colonies and more on foreign trade, investment, and spheres of interest, not in Africa (which by the mid-1890s nearly everyone agreed had been a disappointment), but in China, Brazil, Venezuela, and Ottoman Turkey.[37] Indeed, this was widely seen by many industrialists as one of the only ways to effectively stimulate the German industrial economy in the wake of the long deflation that had spanned from 1873 to 1896.[38] Still, *Weltpolitik* did not exclude the possibility of new formal colonies, and many of its supporters eyed Belgian, Portuguese, and Spanish African, Caribbean, and Pacific colonies as potential candidates. One such idea later popularized by Wilhelm Solf (1862-1936) and Paul Rohrbach (1869-1956) was forging a *"Mittelafrika"* ("Central Africa") out of a belt of African colonial territory that included German Cameroon, the Belgian Congo, and German East Africa.[39]

*Weltpolitik* would lend Germany world "validity" (*Geltung*) and "standing" (*Stellung*) – the equal respect and status of other world powers, especially Britain – yet there was no specific goal that could confirm having achieved that status.[40] England was in the way, nearly all observers agreed, yet apart from within the Pan-German fringe, it was not England's status as a universal power and naval hegemon that bourgeois *Weltpolitik* sought to gain for Germany.[41] Rather, it would assure, as Paul Rohrbach and others argued, that smaller nations of the world would not be devoured under an expansive Greater Britain, Panamericanism, or Panslavism – smaller nations, it was imagined,

---

Winzen, "Zur Genesis von Weltmachtkonzept," 198-99; Kennedy, *Anglo-German Antagonism*, 209; Mommsen, *Bürgerstolz und Weltmachtstreben*, 297.

[35] Max Weber, *Gesammelte politische Schriften* (Munich: Drei Masken Verlag, 1921), 7-30, here 29; cf Roth, "Der politische Kontext," 69-72; Mommsen, *Bürgerstolz und Weltmachtstreben*, 307.

[36] Hans Delbrück, "Stagnation in der inneren und äußeren Politik,"*Preußische Jahrbücher* 81 (1895): 383-91, esp. 388-91.

[37] See Smith, *Ideological Origins*, 70-71.

[38] Canis, *Von Bismarck zur Weltpolitik*, 233-40.

[39] Smith, *Ideological Origins*, 68-69, 129-40.

[40] Thomas Nipperdey, *Deutsche Geschichte 1866-1918*, vol. 2, 2nd ed. (Munich: C. H. Beck, 1993), 630; Mommsen, *Bürgerstolz und Weltmachtstreben*, 303.

[41] Dehio, *Germany and World Politics*, 80.

would coexist with Germany as their protector.[42] This connected quite easily to the older idea of *"Mitteleuropa"* ("Central Europe"), a German-dominated continental trading system that included the Netherlands, Switzerland, Austria-Hungary, and Italy (and sometimes also Scandinavia and western Russia), first proffered by Friedrich List and then taken up again in the 1880s and early 1890s by Alexander von Peez, Constantin Rößler, Gustav Schmoller, and others mentioned in Chapter 1.[43]

Others argued that *Weltpolitik* would strengthen Germany's "free hand" in foreign policy, but it would also draw partners into alliance. It would slowly unite a scattered global *Deutschtum*, but it would also serve to unite a fissiparous Germany. It would help reconcile, as Friedrich Naumann (1860–1919) later believed, *Demokratie* and *Kaisertum* by ushering in an internal liberalization program and social reforms.[44] It would spread German *Wissenschaft*, *Bildung*, and *Kultur* peacefully for the benefit of the world, yet it would also be prepared to confront – with *Gewalt* (force), if need be – any encroachment on Germany's rightful claims and standing. The aims of *Weltpolitik* were nebulous yet demanded action, something described by the left liberal Reichstag deputy Eugen Richter (1838–1906) sardonically if fittingly as an *"Überall-dabei-sein-Wollens"* – an urge to be involved everywhere.[45] This lack of clear-cut goals made *Weltpolitik* appear impossible to satisfy and allowed it to be inflated abroad into an all-pervasive menace, especially in Britain, where hysterical invasion scares and navy panics had been rooted in the political culture since the Napoleonic era.[46]

While the Kaiser sought to deploy *Weltpolitik* to gain favor with the educated middle classes and thus burnish the tarnished prestige of the crown with the aspiration of creating a "personal regime," he was reacting to criticisms leveled at himself and the German government that German foreign policy was weak, adrift, and had been far too accommodating to Britain, as much as acting on his own long-standing interest in the navy. Indeed,

---

[42] Ibid., 86–87; Rohrbach, *Deutschland unter den Weltvölkern*.
[43] Schmoller, "Die amerikanische Konkurrenz" [1882], 283; Schmoller, "Neuere Litteratur über unsere handelspolitische Zukunft," *JbfGVV* 15 (1891): 275–82, esp. 281; Alexander von Peez, *Zur neuesten Handelspolitik: Sieben Abhandlungen* (Vienna: Commissions-Verlag von Georg Szelinski, 1895). Cf. Jörg Brechtfeld, *Mitteleuropa and German Politics* (New York: St. Martin's, 1996), 35–38; Henry Cord Meyer, *Mitteleuropa in German Thought and Action 1815–1945* (The Hague: Martinus Nijhoff, 1955), 11–16, 60, 63–64, 82–115; Dirk Stegman, *Die Erben Bismarcks: Parteien und Verbände in der Spätphase des wilhelminischen Deutschland, Sammlungspolitik 1897–1918* (Cologne: Kiepenheuer & Witsch, 1970), 55–56; Smith, *Ideological Origins*, 78–80.
[44] Naumann, *Demokratie und Kaisertum*, 221–29.
[45] Quoted in Mommsen, *Bürgerstolz und Weltmachtstreben*, 309.
[46] See James Joll, *The Origins of the First World War*, 2nd ed. (London and New York: Longman, 1992), 181–83.

bourgeois opinion on the matter was far ahead of both the Kaiser and Foreign Office.[47] Not surprisingly, the Kaiser's understanding of *Weltpolitik* was largely derivative of the ideas of the German educated bourgeoisie and similarly vague.[48] Just how vague and unoriginal his notions were is revealed by a famous dinner speech the Kaiser gave in the royal palace in Berlin to a group of prominent merchants and industrialists on January 18, 1896, on the twenty-fifth anniversary of German unification, normally taken as his first public utterance on the topic of *Weltpolitik*:

> The German Empire has become a world empire. Everywhere in the distant parts of the earth thousands of our compatriots reside. German goods, German knowledge, German industriousness travel over the ocean. In thousands of millions is estimated the value of goods Germany has going by sea. To you, dear gentlemen, is given the serious duty to help me integrate this greater German Reich firmly to the homeland.[49]

Tellingly, the Kaiser's speech was greeted by bourgeois publicists and writers as reflective of hopes and aspirations they had long been pressing for.[50]

There is a diplomatic and strategic side to the emergence of *Weltpolitik* that too often gets short shrift: it must also be seen as a response to a disintegrating Bismarckian system. Reflecting Germany's inherently vulnerable geostrategic position and the difficulties this posed to defending the Reich, Bismarck's alliance system had already fallen apart by the mid-1880s and become a fragile policy of expedients by the time of his departure as chancellor in 1890. This involved a tangle of treaties and alliances that were contradictory (the Reinsurance Treaty with Russia [1887] was at odds with the Austro-German Dual Alliance [1879]), offered no longer-term solution to the security dilemmas, and in fact created new problems by encouraging Russian expansion into the Ottoman Empire. Increases in agricultural tariffs in 1885 and 1887 and restrictions on Russian access to the German credit market (*Lombardverbot*) pushed through by Bismarck had in turn contributed to rapidly deteriorating relations with Russia, shifting Russian borrowing to France, and in turn opening a path to closer Franco-Russian relations.[51] And while it is tempting

---

[47] Mommsen, *Bürgerstolz und Weltmachtstreben*, 298, 303; Winzen, *Bülows Weltmachtkonzept*, 69–72.

[48] Röhl, *The Kaiser's Personal Monarchy*, 926–27, 936–38, 1018–23; cf. Kohut, *Wilhelm II*, 190–93.

[49] Quoted in Winzen, *Bülows Weltmachtkonzept*, 69.

[50] Ibid., 69–70; Böhm, *Überseehandel und Flottenbau*, 38–65.

[51] Barbara Vogel, *Deutsche Rußlandpolitik: Das Scheitern der deutschen Weltpolitik unter Bülow* (Düsseldorf: Bertelsmann Universitätsverlag, 1973), 13–16; Mommsen, *Bürgerstolz und Weltmachtstreben*, 275–79; Andreas Rose, "International Relations," *The Ashgate Research Companion to Imperial Germany*, ed. Matthew Jeffries (Farnham, Surrey: Ashgate, 2015), 347–66, here 352–53.

to see in *Weltpolitik* a major departure from Bismarckian tenets, it was in many ways the unintended outcome of policies pursued under the Iron Chancellor since the late 1870s of rapid industrial development, the expansion of overseas trade, greater commercial engagement in East Asia, the Caribbean, and South America, the acquisition of protectorates in Africa and the South Pacific, and closer ties to Austria, which in turn drew Germany into the Balkans and especially to Turkey.

Finally, *Weltpolitik* was also the result of Chancellor Caprivi's failure to achieve rapprochement with Great Britain on account of the fundamental irreconcilability of German and British security interests, the failure of a German entente with Russia following the intervention of Shimonoseki, an escalating international naval arms race sparked by British naval policy in 1889, and Germany's growing maritime vulnerability on account of its expanding international trade and investment. German foreign policy was, as we have seen, sometimes clumsy and contradictory, but it was usually not wantonly provocative, and as will be discussed, certainly much less aggressive and violent than other rising powers of the time, notably the United States. When asked by the English journalist Sindney Whitman in 1898 by what means deteriorating Anglo-German relations might be remedied, Bismarck responded that he knew of only one and it was not applicable: restricting Germany's commercial industry.[52]

There is no doubt that the inconsistencies observed in Germany's *Weltpolitik* after 1896 were reflections of the many different (and sometimes conflicting) views of how Germany would achieve its "world standing" between the Foreign Office, the navy, and the Kaiser, complicated by the lack of accountability of German governments to the Reichstag, the lack of civilian control over the military, and the lack of strategic coordination between the services. The erratic tendencies of Kaiser Wilhelm II and his frequent meddling in foreign policy did not help matters. But as will be argued later, *any* political system would have been challenged by the geopolitics of *Weltpolitik*. And as the violent outward expansion of Great Britain after 1832 and the United States following the Civil War make clear, a more accountable, democratic polity would likely have made German *Weltpolitik* more aggressive, expansive, and uncompromising, not less.[53]

By announcing *Weltpolitik* in 1896 with its unclear complex of soaring end goals, domestic expectations were awakened that were bound to be disappointed given that much of the earth had by that point already been divvied up. Such a forceful outward stance given Germany's weight in Europe was also

---

[52] Count Rantzau to Sidney Whitman, Friedrichsruh, April 1898 in Sidney Whitman, *Personal Reminiscences of Prince Bismarck* (New York: D. Appleton & Co., 1903), 288.

[53] See Dominic Lieven, *Aristocracy in Europe 1815-1914* (New York: Columbia University Press, 1993), 243-53.

by its very nature likely to generate frictions with neighbors that would serve to highlight Germany's latent continental European hegemony and thus accelerate a process of European counterbalancing.[54] In this sense *Weltpolitik* was over time more likely to constrain the political room for maneuver than enhance it given Germany's unfavorable geostrategic position and ultimately unleash forces that would lead to greater German diplomatic isolation regardless of who was at the helm of German foreign policy.[55] Gregor Schöllgen is thus on the mark in seeing a certain tragedy in the "belated" nation embarking on *Weltpolitik*, and by doing so, undermining its very basis, a process he called *Selbstentmachtung* (self-disempowerment).[56]

There is another side to this process that has so far often been overlooked because it took place outside of Europe: Germany's *Selbstentmachtung* was accelerated by the rise of the United States and Japan as world powers, a process in which Germans, as we have seen, were deeply entangled. As discussed in the previous chapters, there is also a tendency to blithely overlook the destabilizing role that Great Britain played in these processes on account of its sprawling colonial interests, notably its direct responsibility for undermining the European balance of power by its multiple humiliations of Russia that encouraged the formation of European alliance blocs, led to a British naval arms race with France and Russia, and pushed Russia to focus its expansionist ambitions into Asia and the Pacific, where it would – rather ironically – in turn generate tensions with Britain over Persia, Afghanistan, and Tibet and with Japan (and Britain) over northern China, Manchuria, and Korea. While far from blameless in Germany's eventual diplomatic isolation, there has been a tendency in German historiography – with its Eurocentric frame of reference – to overburden individual political agents and elites with responsibility for policy ideas and outcomes that were often reactions to decisions and forces set in motion far beyond Germany. This found its apogee in Hans-Ulrich Wehler's judgment that *Weltpolitik* was a "coolly calculated instrumentalization of expansionist politics for domestic political purposes."[57]

The other interpretive extreme is to dismiss *Weltpolitik* as nothing more than old wine in new bottles. Was *Weltpolitik* just "the old policy of the free hand with a larger navy and more menacing mood music," as Christopher

---

[54] Klaus Hildebrand, "Zwischen Allianz und Antagonismus: Das Problem bilateraler Normalität in den britisch-deutschen Beziehungen des 19. Jahrbunderts (1870–1914)," in *Weltpolitik, Europagedanke, Regionalismus: Festschrift für Heinz Grollwitzer zum 65. Geburtstag am 30. Januar 1982*, ed. Heinz Dollinger, Horst Gründer and Alwin Hanschmidt (Münster: Aschedorff, 1982), 305–31, here 325; Schöllgen, *Imperialismus und Gleichgewicht*, 435–36.

[55] See Imanuel Geiss, *Der lange Weg in die Katastrophe: Die Vorgeschichte des Ersten Weltkriegs, 1815–1914* (Munich: Piper, 1990), 116–41, 204–27.

[56] Schöllgen, *Imperialismus und Gleichgewicht*, 441.

[57] Wehler, *Gesellschaftsgeschichte*, vol. 3, 1139.

Clark has pithily put it?[58] Perhaps from the hindsight of its extremely modest achievements by 1909, but like Wehler's perspective this risks downplaying or overlooking the novel involvement of the educated bourgeoisie in identifying and analyzing *Weltwirtschaft* and in defining the aims of *Weltpolitik*. In 1897 the mood was ebullient, the horizons appeared wide, and confidence in Germany's capacities ran high, even if fears always nagged that Germany might have started too late, that jealous competitors were bent on hindering it, and that Germany might come up short again. That overconfidence was shared by the generation of government men coming into positions of power and influence in these years, such as Alfred Tirpitz and Bernhard von Bülow, part of a generation that had experienced the unification of Germany in their early adulthoods and then the breathtaking industrial development of the country. Having experienced these developments, they believed in progress and were prone to see a future full of opportunity and to overlook the always lurking danger of German isolation.[59] Such *Weltpolitiker* tended to also over-inflate the economic significance of export markets and colonies, and they had unclear notions about how a larger German navy would work to secure them.[60] That is, a strong strain of liberal nationalist idealism clouded their vision and would continue to be a major factor in *Weltpolitik* until its ultimate demise in the First World War.

## Alfred Tirpitz

The man indelibly associated with *Weltpolitik* was of course Alfred Tirpitz, who would assume the position of secretary of state of the Imperial Navy Office in the summer of 1897. A misleading picture of Tirpitz emerges if one peruses only his activities in the wartime Fatherland Party and his postwar apologetic writings, where he does appear, as Gerhard Ritter once observed, as "typical 'Pan-German' and 'militarist.'"[61] As the more recent masterful biography by Patrick J. Kelly makes plain, however, before the war Tirpitz was more moderate and liberal, and the naval component of *Weltpolitik* which he embodied was very much in the mold of Anglo-Saxon liberal imperialism.[62]

Born in Küstrin in the Prussian Neumark in 1849 to a bourgeois judge, Tirpitz entered the Prussian navy as a cadet in 1865 and rose swiftly through the ranks as a gunnery officer and then commander of cruisers and torpedo boats. He gained the attention of Kaiser Wilhelm as a junior captain in the torpedo boat section in 1891, who appointed him chief of staff to the navy's Executive Command in 1892 with a commission to develop new tactics for the

---

[58] Clark, *The Sleepwalkers*, 151.
[59] Canis, *Von Bismarck zur Weltpolitik*, 308–9; Smith, *Ideological Origins*, 56–60.
[60] Hobson, *Imperialism at Sea*, 299–300.   [61] Ritter, *Staatskunst*, vol. 2, 174–75.
[62] See Kelly, *Tirpitz*.

German navy.[63] In that capacity, Tirpitz developed new squadron tactics and began to steep himself in the writings of Alfred Thayer Mahan, which led to his abandonment of cruiser warfare and embrace open-seas warfare with battleships.[64] The culmination of his thinking was worked out in a tactical and strategic memo of June 1894 (*Dienstschrift IX*), which argued that the fleet's natural purpose was not defensive but rather to pursue the strategic offensive to achieve mastery of the seas. The navy's specific missions were thus blockading an enemy's coast, restricting its commerce with neutrals, hindering its transatlantic maritime traffic, and bombarding its coastal cities.[65] According to Tirpitz, the lessons of history showed that maritime interests were equivalent to world interests and required a maritime show of force beyond territorial waters to support investments and business interests abroad. Here the business-oriented United States was, he believed, leading the way, building an offensive navy in order to expand its maritime trade and overseas interests.[66] A similar offensive force in German hands, he argued, would act as a deterrent and thus enhance Germany's diplomatic position and value as an ally.[67] In practical terms, this new strategy meant rationalizing the number of ship types in the German navy to ships of the line (heavily armed and armored battleships), fast heavy and light cruisers, and torpedo boats, as well as maintaining a one-third superiority over the larger of the two rival navies of France and Russia.[68]

Beyond these tactical innovations, Tirpitz was also at the forefront of developing new tools for actively shaping public opinion in advance of naval legislation. While the first initiatives to publicize the navy this way came from the Kaiser, Tirpitz went well beyond that to solicit articles sympathetic to the navy from outside journalists and then have them planted in a broad range of newspapers.[69] He developed contacts to wire services and newspaper editors to disseminate a regular stream of pro-fleet reportage very widely and revamped naval publications to appeal to a more popular audience by covering such subjects as fisheries, maritime trade, the colonies, and yachting.[70] Newspapers hostile to the navy were brought into line by starving them of naval press releases or by working directly with their editors and journalists.[71] In short, many of the tools of modern propaganda campaigns had been worked out by Tirpitz and his colleagues by 1896.

While in the Executive Command, Tirpitz repeatedly clashed with Friedrich von Hollmann (1842–1913), state secretary of the Imperial Navy Office (RMA) and a proponent of cruiser warfare. Tirpitz would fight a vicious

---

[63] Tirpitz, *Memoirs*, vol. 1, 46–48; Steinberg, *Yesterday's Deterrent*, 69; Kelly, *Tirpitz*, 85, 89, 93–94, 111–12.
[64] Tirpitz, *Memoirs*, vol. 1, 55, 58; James Holmes, "Mahan, a 'Place in the Sun' and Germany's Quest for Sea Power," *Comparative Strategy* 23, no. 1 (2004): 27–61.
[65] Kelly, *Tirpitz*, 92.   [66] Ibid., 92–95.   [67] Ibid., 95.   [68] Ibid.
[69] Deist, *Flottenpolitik*, 32–35.   [70] Ibid., 35–38.   [71] Ibid., 41.

Figure 4.1    Alfred Tirpitz ca. 1895.

campaign against Hollmann aided by his allies Admiral Eduard Knorr (1840–1920) and Admiral Gustav von Senden-Bibran (1847–1909), the latter chief of the Kaiser's Navy Cabinet and the single most important naval advisor to the Kaiser.[72] In his memoranda Tirpitz continually argued for the tactical and political necessity of a battleship fleet for both German sea power and protecting German maritime interests – otherwise, he later wrote, "Germany's position in the world resembled a mollusc without a shell."[73] Aware of Germany's growing population and heavy reliance on industrial exports, he took to heart the dictum that "commerce either engenders a navy which is strong enough to protect it, or else it passes into the hand of foreign merchants, who already enjoy such protection."[74] What the other great powers, particularly the United States, had in land Germany needed to secure by overseas trade and investment:

> The "Open Door," which could easily be closed, was to us what their broad plains and inexhaustible natural wealth were to the other Powers. This, combined with our hemmed-in and dangerous continental position,

---

[72] Steinberg, *Yesterday's Deterrent*, 70–71; Kelly, *Tirpitz*, 98–101.
[73] Tirpitz, *Memoirs*, vol. 1, 58.
[74] Ibid., 59. This was apparently a quotation from *The Fortnightly Review* of 1893.

strengthened me in my conviction that no time was to be lost in beginning the attempt to constitute ourselves as a sea-power. For only a fleet which represented alliance-value to other great Powers, in other words a competent battle fleet, could put into the hands of our diplomats the tool which, if used to good purpose, could supplement our power on land. The object in view had to be the institution of a constellation of Powers at sea, which would remove the possibility of any injury to or attacks upon our economic prosperity, and would transform the treacherous brilliance of our world-policy into a really independent position in the world.[75]

What is striking about this passage is how much it seemed to accord with the conclusions that von Halle, Sering, Rathgen, and Schumacher had drawn from their own experiences abroad observing *Weltwirtschaft*. That a major reference point for the evolution of Tirpitz's thinking in these years was not just England but the United States has already been suggested and is confirmed by what is known of his experiences in 1896 and 1897 in the United States and Far East before he was appointed as state secretary of the Imperial Navy Office. In all, he would spend that year in East Asia traveling through the United States twice along the way, strongly shaping his perspective of the world.

Quite gloomy about the future of his naval plans, Tirpitz stepped down as chief of staff in September 1895 due to ongoing conflicts with the Admiralty.[76] While awaiting his new commission in early January 1896, he completed yet another memo and had an audience with the Kaiser arranged by Admiral Senden-Bibran at which he argued for a naval spending program that kept more battleships and heavy cruisers in reserve for the home fleet on the grounds that the risk it posed would result in greater conciliation from England and make Germany more attractive as an alliance partner, an early version of his "risk theory."[77] He wrote Admiral Albrecht von Stosch (1818–96) in February 1896 about the uproar in the British press in response to the Kruger Telegram, which he saw as symptomatic of Germany's naval impotence: "England puts up with a slight from America because the latter is a source of anxiety to her, and more than anything else because America is an unpleasant opponent, and Germany pays the bill because at the moment she has no sea power of any weight."[78] This was a reference to Britain's appeasement of provocation by the United States in the First Venezuela Crisis.

In April of 1896 Tirpitz was ordered to depart for Shanghai to take over command of the East Asian Cruiser Squadron, steaming from Hamburg to New York on May 2, 1896.[79] From New York he took the overland express to Chicago, a city whose rapid growth from nothing in so short a time was astonishing to him. Heavy German immigration had by that point made

---

[75] Tirpitz, *Memoirs*, vol. 1, 60.   [76] Kelly, *Tirpitz*, 107.
[77] Steinberg, *Yesterday's Deterrent*, 83–84; Röhl, *The Kaiser's Personal Monarchy*, 1021.
[78] Tirpitz, *Memoirs*, vol. 1, 63–64, 66.   [79] Ibid., 69; Kelly, *Tirpitz*, 119.

Chicago the "third largest German city in the World."[80] In his memoirs Tirpitz would later observe that "Many millions of Germans who emigrated were lost to us both morally and actually, and enriched those countries which were afterwards our worst enemies."[81] He also regretted how quickly Germans assimilated into American culture, attributing it to a "lack of national pride, sentiment and obligation."[82] From Chicago he traveled on to Salt Lake City aboard the Union Pacific, where he visited the Mormon Tabernacle and heard the Swabian dialect and of fruitful missionary efforts in Germany, contributing to the "10,000,000 North Americans of German origin."[83] From Salt Lake City he traveled on to San Francisco, observing its prosperous farms and busy commerce, regretting he could not stay in California longer. He then took passage to Tokyo aboard the American steamer *China* on May 21, stopping in Hawaii along the way and noting the improvements that had been made recently to Pearl Harbor by the US Navy. On June 9th he arrived in Japan, and four days later was in Shanghai to take command of the East Asian Cruiser Squadron.[84]

As already recounted in Chapter 3, one of Tirpitz's tasks in the summer of 1896 was to inspect prospective sites for a German naval base in China.[85] This experience in East Asia heightened his sense of the beleaguered nature of "Germandom abroad" that had already been sparked by observations on his travels through the United States. By contrast, the English seemed strikingly cohesive and loyal overseas and "became almost as a matter of course an agent of the 'Foreign Office' as soon as English interests were at stake."[86] The Germans that had gone abroad had the disadvantage that they were scattered all over the globe making it difficult to keep German interests alive, he thought.[87] He saw the Imperial Navy as an important agent of connection, a "pioneer of '*Germanism*'" which worked to strengthen links between Germans overseas and would be easier to achieve in East Asia than elsewhere, Tirpitz noted.[88] As discussed in Chapter 2, this was something that Rathgen had himself experienced and had commented on at length in his letters home while living in Japan and participating in the celebrations attending visits of the German Cruiser Squadron to Tokyo and Yokohama in the late 1880s.

Over his time in East Asia, Tirpitz visited Japan for an extended stay, which included an audience with Emperor Meiji in Tokyo and a tour of the royal palace in early October 1896.[89] Japan much impressed him, and later in his memoirs he would write that he very much regretted the pall that had fallen over German-Japanese relations following the Triple Intervention, writing that "we should have done everything in our power to correct the mistake of Shimonoseki." He wrote that he "constantly worked for good understanding

---

[80] Kelly, *Tirpitz*, 119.   [81] Tirpitz, *Memoirs*, vol. 1, 81.   [82] Ibid., 82.
[83] Ibid., 82–83.   [84] Kelly, *Tirpitz*, 119.   [85] Tirpitz, *Memoirs*, vol. 1, 69.
[86] Ibid., 83.   [87] Ibid.   [88] Ibid., 83–84, 85.   [89] Kelly, *Tirpitz*, 120–21.

with Tokyo" but the matter of better relations with Japan was, he argued, never a priority in the German government.[90] Clearly, Tirpitz had become more sensitive to the fragility of the German presence in East Asia much along the lines articulated by Rathgen while in Japan and Schumacher while in China. That awareness was made acute by his command of the largely obsolete and repair-prone East Asian Squadron, which as he recalled, "could be rendered useless on the slightest provocation."[91] While Tirpitz was in East Asia, events were conspiring in Berlin that would ultimately catapult him to the head of the Navy Office. The Kaiser, though still very much attached to the cruiser war strategy, was increasingly eager to expand the navy in light of the Transvaal Crisis and lost patience with Hollmann when in early March 1897 the Reichstag's Budget Commission cut the Navy Office's budget proposals.[92] By that point Senden-Bibran had been priming the emperor to appoint Tirpitz as Hollmann's replacement for some time.[93] Shortly thereafter Hollmann was put on leave and Tirpitz was ordered to Berlin to become the new state secretary of the Navy Office.[94]

Tirpitz debarked at Bremerhaven in early June 1897 sick with a lung infection but was soon thereafter summoned to see the Kaiser.[95] On June 15, 1897, he met the Kaiser to Potsdam, where he presented a new memo much along the lines of the one from January 1896: he proposed abandoning cruiser warfare as impractical given the lack of German overseas bases and instead to focus Germany's naval strength in home waters against England, their most dangerous naval foe.[96] He proposed spending a total of 408 million marks over 7 years to build 19 battleships, 8 armored coastal battleships, and 16 heavy and 30 light cruisers, all to be completed by 1905.[97] He further requested full cooperation from Chancellor Hohenlohe and permission to take the lead in presenting the legislation to the Reichstag and to be able to speak openly about the tactical and strategic aims of the proposal. He also insisted on a free hand in selecting those who would assist him, complete control over the content of naval propaganda, a new division within the Navy Office dedicated specifically to pro-fleet propaganda, and that the Kaiser avoid any confrontations with the Reichstag while the legislation was pending. Much to Tirpitz's surprise, the Kaiser agreed to every point.[98] Tirpitz was well aware of the Kaiser's inept confrontational tactics with the Reichstag, so removing him from the campaign for the navy bill was essential for it to have any hope of success.[99]

[90] Tirpitz, *Memoirs*, vol. 1, 88–89.   [91] Ibid., 93.
[92] Kelly, *Tirpitz*, 126–27. See also Steinberg, *Yesterday's Deterrent*, 112–16.
[93] Röhl, *The Kaiser's Personal Monarchy*, 1018–19.   [94] Kelly, *Tirpitz*, 127–28.
[95] Steinberg, *Yesterday's Deterrent*, 125; Kelly, *Tirpitz*, 129.
[96] Tirpitz, *Memoirs*, vol. 1, 92–93; Steinberg, *Yesterday's Deterrent*, 126–27.
[97] Steinberg, *Yesterday's Deterrent*, 128.   [98] Kelly, *Tirpitz*, 132–33.
[99] Röhl, *The Kaiser's Personal Monarchy*, 1021, 1024–1025, 1027.

Much has been made of Tirpitz's June 1897 memorandum identifying England as Germany's "most dangerous naval enemy at the present time" in the voluminous scholarship on the German fleet and Tirpitz, with many scholars viewing it as a dangerous decision bound to antagonize Britain and thus as a step that set forces in motion culminating in the First World War.[100] However, that reads too much into the memo and ignores its international context. France and Russia also figured in the memo as they had in *Dienstschrift IX*, and as already mentioned with reference to the 1889 British Naval Defence Act, it was common practice to measure naval strength against the most formidable potential foes – indeed, up until the 1904 Entente Cordiale, French naval strategy was directed against Britain, aiming to starve it into submission.[101] The June 1897 memo must also be set in the context of the Malet incident, the Jameson Raid, and the vicious anti-German backlash to the Kruger Telegram. The British had formed a new Royal Navy "flying squadron" during the Transvaal Crisis in January 1896 to prepare for a possible war with Germany, in effect making Britain a possible naval opponent for the first time. As a result, operational plans for war with Britain had been worked out for the first time within the Admiralty in March 1896 and were later sanctioned by the Kaiser.[102]

As has already been shown, the United States loomed at least as large and as a much greater long-term challenge to Germany's world interests in Tirpitz's *Weltbild* than Britain. Indeed, in his view Britain was in gradual decline and its empire was in a slow process of liquidation – the ultimate struggle down the road was not with Britain as much as with the United States.[103] The importance of Latin America to Germany's trade and investment and as a destination for German settlement and a possible site of a future settler colony, as well as the threat posed to Germany by Panamerican trade policy and more assertive interpretations of the Monroe Doctrine, all figured centrally in Tirpitz's naval ambitions and were shared and articulated by many like-minded German observers.[104] Due to Britain's obstructing physical presence in Germany's maritime geography and the lack of German overseas naval bases, any leverage against the United States would have to operate from a British fulcrum as a geographical fact. Although Tirpitz's grand strategy was still being worked out before 1900, he believed such naval pressure would force Britain to take Germany seriously, make concessions to it, as well as draw France or Russia

---

[100] Reprinted in Steinberg, *Yesterday's Deterrent*, 208–23, here 209, para. 2 and 3; see also Steinberg, *Yesterday's Deterrent*, 126; Berghahn, *Der Tirpitz Plan*, 173–201; Mommsen, *Bürgerstolz und Weltmachtstreben*, 305–306.
[101] Reprinted in Steinberg, *Yesterday's Deterent*, 209, para. 5.
[102] Winzen, "Zur Genesis von Weltmachtkonzept," 197.
[103] Herwig, *Vision of Empire*, 156–57, 161–63; Mehnert, "Gelbe Gefahr," 105–6.
[104] See especially Fiebig-von Hase, *Lateinamerika als Krisenherd*, 367–85.

into alliance with Germany.[105] British appeasement of American provocations after 1895 only served to reinforce the logic of a policy of strength brought to bear against Britain. All of that said, the 1897 memo saw the larger German navy explicitly as "political power factor" to *deter* England and enhance Germany's alliance value, not to provoke or wage a war with it.[106] It was, as Hans Delbrück termed it, a strategy of "dry war," or as Ludwig Dehio later observed in more familiar contemporary language, a strategy of "cold war": an offensive strategy meant to achieve those political aims peacefully.[107]

This notion of the *political* utility of a battle fleet concentrated in home waters proportionate to Germany's overseas commercial interests was *the* defining characteristic of German naval policy under Tirpitz.[108] As should be clear by now and as has been argued by Rolf Hobson, Michael Salewski, and others, Tirpitz's plans for expanding the German navy in 1897, 1899, and beyond were motivated by the long-standing liberal nationalist ambitions for the navy as an emblem of national unity and equal standing in the world, by the liberal imperialist ideology of sea power popularized by Mahan, by the vogue of Bluewater strategic thinking in the 1890s, and by Germany's rise as an international economic power.[109] There is in fact little convincing evidence for the argument first posed by Eckart Kehr and then taken up by Volker Berghahn and Hans-Ulrich Wehler that Tirpitz's plans were ever conceived as a social imperialist initiative – that is, as a palliative against the rise of social democracy to stabilize the monarchical regime by rallying the bourgeoisie, peasants, and aristocratic landowners with various payoffs to defend the existing order.[110] This claim rests only on a single passage made in passing in a letter that Tirpitz wrote Admiral von Stosch in December 1895.[111] Even Wilhelm Deist, who built on Berghahn's interpretation in his exhaustive study of pro-fleet propaganda, was forced to qualify Berghahn's claim by arguing that any "system stabilizing" aims were secondary to getting the naval

---

[105] Kelly, *Tirpitz*, 114–15, 133.
[106] Reprinted in Steinberg, *Yesterday's Deterrent*, 209, para. 2; Tirpitz, *Memoirs*, vol. 1, 67.
[107] Dehio, *Germany and World Politics*, 76; cf. Fürst von Bülow, *Deutsche Politik* (Berlin: Reimar Hobbing, 1916), 43.
[108] Hobson, *Imperialism at Sea*, 297.
[109] Ibid., 324; Rödel, *Krieger, Denker, Amateure*, 52–64; Michael Salewski, *Tirpitz: Aufstieg-Macht-Scheitern* (Göttingen: Musterschmidt, 1979), 63–66.
[110] Eckart Kehr, *Battleship Building and Party Politics: A Cross-Section of the Political, Social and Ideological Preconditions of German Imperialism*, ed. and trans. and with an introduction by Pauline R. Anderson (Chicago: University of Chicago Press, 1975), 217; Berghahn, *Der Tirpitz-Plan*, 226–48, esp. 236; Wehler, *Gesellschaftsgeschichte*, vol. 3, 1134–35, 1138–41; Wehler, *Bismarck und der Imperialismus*, 486–502.
[111] Letter by Tirpitz to Stosch, Kiel, Dec. 21, 1895, in Corrado Pirzio-Biroli, *My Great-Grandfather Grand-Admiral von Tirpitz* (Bloomington, IN: Archway, 2016), Appendix 4, 317–19.

legislation passed.[112] More recently Patrick Kelly has gone further, arguing that if there was any "Tirpitz Plan" it was one directed not only at securing long-term funding against Reichstag opposition but also against the meddling of the Kaiser and the navy – the "system" Tirpitz was trying to uphold with the navy laws was not the Prusso-German monarchical system but rather his own control over the direction of strategy in the navy.[113]

### Bernhard von Bülow

On June 28, 1897, a little over a week after Tirpitz's audience with the Kaiser, Berhnard von Bülow was named acting foreign state secretary (Kommissarischer Staatssekretär), and later that year, on October 20, 1897, was formally appointed the successor of Adolf Marschall von Bieberstein, who had opposed a change of course in foreign policy in the direction of *Weltpoltiik*.[114] Bülow was a career diplomat who had advanced rapidly through the ranks not only due to his ability and charm but also his excellent personal contacts, ambition, and scheming. The scion of the Holstein line of landless Mecklenburg lesser nobility and one of Hamburg's wealthiest burgher merchant families, Bülow was born in 1849 in Klein Flottbeck near Hamburg and grew up in privileged and worldly surroundings as the son of Bernhard Ernst von Bülow (1815–79), a diplomat in Danish service, minister of state of Mecklenburg-Strelitz, and ultimately, state secretary of the German Foreign Office (1873–79) as well as one of Bismarck's closest and most loyal colleagues. The younger Bülow thus had early and deep connections to the Bismarck family and enjoyed the patronage of both Otto von Bismarck and his son Herbert (1849–1904), the latter also state secretary of the Foreign Office (1885–90) during Bülow's swift career to the top as a diplomatic attaché in Rome, St. Petersburg, Vienna, and Paris, and then as German ambassador in Bucharest and Rome.[115]

As important for his advancement and of critical importance to his appointment as foreign secretary by the Kaiser was his relationship to two powerful figures in the German Foreign Office, Friedrich August von Holstein (1837–1909) and Philipp zu Eulenburg (1847–1921), the latter in particular, who was very close to Kaiser Wilhelm II. It was through Eulenburg that Bülow

---

[112] Deist, *Flottenpolitik*, 13–14; cf. Herwig, *"Luxury" Fleet*, 35–36, 39, 41–42; Mommsen, *Bürgerstolz und Weltmachtstreben*, 306.
[113] Kelly, *Tirpitz*, 11–12.
[114] Bülow, *Deutsche Politik*, 20–21; Winzen, *Bülows Weltmachtkonzept*, 63, 70.
[115] See Katherine Anne Lerman, *The Chancellor as Courtier: Bernhard von Bülow and the Governance of Germany, 1900–1909* (Cambridge: Cambridge University Press, 1990), 10–18.

managed to ingratiate himself with the Kaiser by much calculated flattery and sycophancy.[116] The scheming, sycophantic side of Bülow was criticized by his colleagues and Otto and Herbert von Bismarck, and along with his association with *Weltpolitik* and Germany's diplomatic isolation during his tenure as chancellor (1900–1909), they have made Bülow a controversial figure in German historiography, with many taking a very critical view of his legacy for Germany.[117] That negative assessment, while undoubtedly true in many particulars, has nevertheless gone too far and been shaped strongly by an interpretation of the Wilhelmine period that places excessive weight on the role of *Weltpolitik* and the German fleet in British and European prewar diplomacy as well as later German diplomatic isolation, a perspective that tends to underappreciate Germany's geostrategic vulnerability, exaggerate Germany's diplomatic room for maneuver, and reify a "German menace" largely invented by the British press and influential members of the British Foreign Office after 1900.[118]

The newer historiography, which undergirds the interpretive framework offered in the opening section of Chapter 3 and earlier in this chapter, shifts more agency in the Anglo-German relationship to Britain and greater weight to changes in the global balance of power in these developments and thus invites a reassessment of Bülow. This is all the more necessary because what historians have chosen to highlight as both the key influences in Bülow's foreign and domestic policy and the ultimate aims of *Weltpolitik* are bound up closely with that negative post hoc assessment of Bülow's legacy. For example, Peter Winzen's otherwise excellent studies of Bülow have chosen to focus on the influence of Heinrich von Treitschke on Bülow's alleged Anglophobia to assert that his foreign policy aimed at conflict with England and German world hegemony, even though there is no evidence that Bülow knew Treitschke or was ever a serious student of his writings.[119] Winzen's short biography of Bülow carries the tendentious subtitle "World Power Strategist without Fortune – Forerunner of the Great Catastrophe" and begins with a

---

[116] Ibid., 22–25.
[117] See, for example, Willy Becker, *Fürst Bülow und England 1897–1909* (Greifswald: L. Bamberg, 1929); Brechtken, *Scharnierzeit*, 322–30; Lerman, *The Chancellor as Courtier*, 250–58; Peter Winzen, *Reichskanzler Bernhard Fürst von Bülow: Weltmachtstratege ohne Fortune – Wegbereiter der großen Katastrophe* (Göttingen: Muster-Schmidt Verlag, 2003); Winzen, *Bülows Weltmachtkonzept*, 432–34; and most recently, John C. G. Röhl, *Wilhelm II: Into the Abyss of War and Exile, 1900–1941*, trans. Sheila de Bellaigue and Roy Bridge (Cambridge: Cambridge University Press, 2014), 96–126.
[118] See especially Canis, *Von Bismarck zur Weltpolitik*, 285–87, 294, 308, 325, 330; Clark, *The Sleepwalkers*, 159–67; Rose, *Zwischen Empire und Kontinent*, 121–27, 362–427.
[119] See Peter Winzen, "Prince Bülow's Weltmachtpolitik," *Australian Journal of Politics & History* 22, no. 2 (1976): 227–42; Winzen, *Bülows Weltmachtkonzept*, 27–35, 48, 80, 120; Winzen, "Zur Genesis von Weltmachtkonzept," 189, 212, 218–20. Cf. Lerman, *The Chancellor as Courtier*, 20; Canis, *Von Bismarck zur Weltpolitik*, 336n192.

gossipy introduction focused almost exclusively on Bülow's possible homosexuality.[120] Other aspects of his background have been overlooked or ignored, particularly Bülow's strong ties to Hamburg, his admiration of England, deep respect for British political traditions, and avowed sympathy for parliamentary government as well as his close intellectual and personal connection to Gustav Schmoller. While Bülow's self-serving memoirs must be read critically and cautiously, when set in context and supplemented by private correspondences and other sources that have not been used before, many valuable new insights emerge that allow a more balanced and accurate assessment of Bülow and the influences that shaped him and his policies.

Bülow was related to Hamburg's merchant elite through his mother's family, the Rückers, and his maternal grandmother was the daughter of the Hamburg Senator Martin Johann Jenisch (1793–1857) whose fortune had been made through shipping and banking as a partner in the prominent bank house Jenisch & Godeffroy.[121] As already noted, Bülow was himself born in the Rücker country house in Klein Flottbeck on the outskirts of Hamburg between Altona and Blankenese overlooking the Elbe River, and though he grew up in Frankfurt, Bülow always considered Flottbeck his actual home.[122] Like Schumacher's youth in Manhattan and Staten Island overlooking New York harbor, Bülow had many memories from his youth of watching the shipping traffic on the Elbe and of Hamburg harbor.[123] There is no question that these ties to Hamburg shaped his worldview and his appreciation of the importance of Germany's trade, as did the very cosmopolitan features of his family – the Rückers were very pro-Danish and the Bülow family, as was the custom in many Hanseatic burgher families, spoke English and French at home.[124] Bülow would later inherit the Rücker estate in Klein Flottbeck and make it his permanent home.[125]

Though Bülow spent very little time in Britain (London was conspicuously missing in his diplomatic resume), he was completely fluent in English, and much in keeping with his Hanseatic background, he wrote very highly of England and had a deep respect for British statesmen and British parliamentary political traditions, which he often compared favorably with Germany's own politics and political culture.[126] The Anglophobia imputed to Bülow arises from a conflation of Bülow's (and much of the rest of Germany's foreign policy establishment's) disappointment with Britain's refusal to give firm commitments to Germany and the Triple Alliance, Britain's "countermining" of German overseas aims throughout the 1890s, and its menacing and breezily

---

[120] Winzen, *Reichskanzler*, 7–14.
[121] Bernhard Fürst von Bülow, *Denkwürdigkeiten*, vol. 4 (Berlin: Ullstein, 1931), 30, 33–34.
[122] Ibid., 37, 247.   [123] Ibid., 30, 40.   [124] Ibid., 51–53.
[125] Bernhard Fürst von Bülow, *Denkwürdigkeiten*, vol. 3 (Berlin: Ullstein, 1931), 7, 24–25.
[126] Ibid., vol. 1, 187–88, 292, 315, 332–34.

arrogant treatment of Germany as a *quantité négligeable* during the Transvaal Crisis, with some kind of deeply-seated emotional animosity for England.[127] Indeed, *Weltpolitik* was in many ways the outgrowth of a great many Germans whose Anglophilia had been mugged by reality in the decade of the 1890s, as we saw very vividly in the case of Karl Rathgen.

While Bülow was completing the last two years of *Gymnasium* as a boarding student in the Royal Prussian Pädagogium in Halle an der Saale from 1865 to 1867, he heard Gustav Schmoller lecture as a young professor for the first time, which made a strong and lasting impression on him.[128] Bülow later studied at the University of Leipzig where he was particularly drawn to the political economy lectures of Wilhelm Roscher.[129] Roscher's textbook *System der Volkswirtschaft* (multiple editions between 1854 and 1901) became a very important intellectual foundation, one that helped Bülow recognize that social democracy and communism were not unprecedented developments but rather "illnesses" that emerged in highly cultivated nations at specific points in their development and had both the noblest and lowest intellectual supporters.[130] Thus to Bülow it was not surprising that with Germany's rapid industrial development and rising inequality there were many hard-working and honorable workers that were drawn to socialism. He wrote that he saw it as the prime task of government to overcome conflicts of interest and find just accommodations through social reforms.[131]

Particularly influential to this insight, Bülow recalled, was Gustav Schmoller's programmatic essay on taking over the editorship of the *Jahrbuch für Gesetzgebung* published in 1881, which he had opportunity to read while serving as a young diplomatic attaché in Paris.[132] This article reinforced Bülow's commitment to promoting social reforms, stronger centralized imperial institutions, and shaping the economy on the basis of law and social justice.[133] Bülow wrote that ever since he had become an "eager reader" of Schmoller's *Jahrbuch*, which he "read through the years with interest and to advantage," just as he had become a supporter of "a generous and continuous

---

[127] This older interpretation has been put forward by Volker Berghahn, Paul Kennedy, and Peter Winzen. See, for example, Winzen, *Bülows Weltmachtkonzept*, 78, 78n74, which draws heavily from Paul Kennedy's and Volker Berghahn's perspectives. In his biography Winzen alleges Bülow took on his Halle school teacher's Anglophobia wholesale and that this had fateful consequences for German and European history, Winzen, *Reichskanzler*, 28. Cf. Canis, *von Bsimarck zur Weltpolitik*, 285–87, 290, 308, 317, 325, 330, 336, 351, 371.

[128] Bülow, *Denkwürdigkeiten*, vol. 2, 285; vol. 4, 72–73. Cf. Winzen, *Reichskanzler*, 19–20.

[129] Bülow, *Denkwürdigkeiten*, vol. 4, 118–19.  [130] Ibid., 119.  [131] Ibid.

[132] Ibid., 120; Gustav Schmoller, "Ueber Zweck und Ziele des Jahrbuchs," *JbfGVV* 5 (1881): 1–18.

[133] Bülow, *Denkwürdigkeiten*, vol. 4, 120; cf. Schmoller, "Ueber Zweck und Ziele," 15–16.

Figure 4.2   Bernhard von Bülow ca. 1895.

social policy."[134] Bülow would himself get to know Schmoller personally after 1897 because Schmoller was both a member of the Prussian Council of State (since 1884) and representative of the University of Berlin in the Prussian Upper House of the Diet (since 1899), and in these capacities was involved in much preparatory work on legislative commissions as well as in legislation. Bülow later described Schmoller as a "venerable friend" whose advice and personal company be valued very highly, one who stood by Bülow's side with "benevolence and loyal friendship" throughout his time in office and after.[135] As will be seen, this intellectual and personal connection was significant during Bülow's tenure as foreign secretary and especially chancellor, giving Schmoller and his former students direct access to the very top of German government, where they would exercise a significant influence on the contours of *Weltpolitik*. As a self-professed avid reader of Schmoller's *Jahrbuch*, Bülow's exposure to the essays of von Halle, Schumacher, Sering, and Rathgen during the 1890s almost certainly played a role in shaping his perceptions of

---

[134] Bülow, *Denkwürdigkeiten*, vol. 2, 285; vol. 4, 120; GStA PK, VI. HA, Nl. Schmoller, Nr. 205b, fols. 102–4, Berhard von Bülow to Gustav Schmoller, Dec. 20, 1913.
[135] Bülow, *Denkwürdigkeiten*, vol. 2, 285–86, 454; vol. 3, 22, 220, 225, 349.

Germany's political economy and its place in the world. This would be reinforced by the fact that, as will be discussed, Schmoller knew Tirpitz personally, and von Halle, Schumacher, and Sering would later work closely and directly on the pro-fleet research and propaganda of the Navy Office's Communications Bureau after 1897. Particularly, the importance given to the East Asian and South American markets, the rising global protectionism, and the threats posed to German economic interests by "world empires" analyzed at length by these men would resonate very strongly with both Tirpitz and Bülow.

One of Bülow's preoccupations both as foreign secretary in 1897 and then chancellor after 1900 was national unity, namely bringing together the liberal, Catholic, and conservative political forces in Germany so that Germany could be freed from domestic problems to enter the world of great power politics.[136] He was critical of the *Kulturkampf* which had alienated German Catholics and had contributed much to Germany's domestic divisions.[137] He also opposed legal repression of the Social Democrats, another deviation from Bismarck, whom he otherwise held in very high esteem. Likewise he opposed any extreme solutions to domestic political impasses of the sort that had sometimes been threatened by Bismarck and were entertained by the young Kaiser in his fits of anger, such as a royal *Staatsstreich* (coup) and constitutional revision. He also believed that Bismarck's hostility to the "New Course" of his successor Caprivi had been a mistake.[138] By strengthening the "Reich idea" and by bringing together conservatives, most of the liberals, and the Catholic Center Party, he believed a broader coalition could be forged that would even draw in the Social Democratic masses.[139] Bülow also believed that after the dismissal of Bismarck – which he thought was handled terribly and left a negative political legacy[140] – Germany should have evolved into a more parliamentary system:

> Above all Bismarck should only have been allowed to be sent off if the Kaiser was determined to take a more liberal direction, that is even if not immediately introducing a parliamentary system in the Western European sense, nevertheless to move closer to one. A dictatorship of Bismarck should not have been allowed to be followed by a dictatorship of William II, as Bismarck was a genius, William II was not.[141]

While this reflection on the 1890s was written after the First World War, there is nevertheless no reason to believe that this was not Bülow's view before and

---

[136] Winzen, *Bülows Weltmachtkonzept*, 41.
[137] Clark, *Kaiser Wilhelm II*, 96; Lerman, *The Chancellor as Courtier*, 20, 24–25.
[138] Lerman, *The Chancellor as Courtier*, 22–23.   [139] Ibid., 24.
[140] Bülow, *Denkwürdigkeiten*, vol. 1, 225.
[141] Ibid., vol. 4, 638; see also ibid., vol. 3, 327–28.

during his time as foreign secretary and chancellor, as that is reflected in how he actually governed. Indeed, a major aim of his while in power was to recover the powers of the chancellor that had been eroded under his predecessors Caprivi and Hohnelohe.[142] That he would not divulge such views to Eulenburg through whom Bülow sought to curry favor with the Kaiser is obvious; these letters – on which many claims about Bülow's political outlook and aims have been based – cannot be read literally, as the bold flattery of the Kaiser, devotion to the Kaiser's political authority, and support for the Kaiser's desire to rule more directly were calculated to gain the Kaiser's favor.[143]

To be sure, Bülow affected a highly compliant and conciliatory manner with the Kaiser that played on his personal connection with the monarch, and he did not shy away from extraordinary displays of obsequiousness. Nevertheless, there is no doubt that Bülow had a dim view of Wilhelm, his character, and his suitability as a monarch that predated his appointment, and while in office he effectively manipulated the Kaiser by concealing his own agenda and largely succeeded in imposing his own preferences by getting Wilhelm to believe that these were his.[144] This was most effective before 1902 and became more difficult thereafter, revealing that there were always limits to Bülow's power and that the Kaiser remained a powerful and volatile fixture of German politics. But even in those instances where the Kaiser succeeded in imposing his own wishes, it is remarkable how often Bülow managed to reverse these and gain the Kaiser's compliance in most areas of policy after 1902, especially in foreign policy. In the later years of his tenure as chancellor, keeping the upper hand relied ever more on deception and increasingly brutal methods with the Kaiser (the Harden-Eulenburg and *Daily Telegraph* affairs, come to mind) that ultimately undermined Bülow's own position, reliant as it always was on the Kaiser's good graces. Still, it also involved open disagreement with the Kaiser, threats to resign, and direct appeals to the Reichstag that showed an unmistakably parliamentary style unlike any imperial chancellor before or after Bülow.[145] That does not mean that Bülow aspired for constitutional revisions in that direction while in office – numerous statements of his and his later handling of the *Daily Telegraph* Affair make it abundantly clear that he did not – but a liberal nationalist and conciliatory social reforming theme runs through his correspondences, speeches, writings, and policies that was shaped to an unusual degree by educated bourgeois opinion and resonated very strongly in that quarter.

---

[142] Canis, *Von Bismarck zur Weltpolitik*, 350–51.
[143] Lerman, *The Chancellor as Courtier*, 23, 24.
[144] Clark, *Kaiser Wilhelm II*, 93–98; Lerman, *The Chancellor as Courtier*, 27–31; Winzen, *Bülows Weltmachtkonzept*, 166–68.
[145] Canis, *Von Bismarck zur Weltpolitik*, 350; Clark, *Kaiser Wilhelm II*, 97, 99, 108.

## Bülow's *Weltpolitik*

As already touched on, Bülow's desire for national unity – his notion of *Sammlungspolitik* – was not focused on domestic stability for its own sake but rather as a means to support an effective foreign policy. Domestic politics had a decidedly secondary status and had to serve Germany's European position as a great power. In Bülow's view, foreign policy always had a higher priority than domestic politics, as he saw foreign policy mistakes as far more dangerous and harder to reverse than those made domestically.[146] Before his appointment in 1897, Bülow's foreign policy views were vaguely – and sometimes too breezily and superficially – "Bismarckian," in that he valued friendly relations with Russia but wanted to retain a free hand for Germany and was averse to formal alliances. To be sure, like Bismarck, he was very skeptical of British European policy and was wary of Germany being used by Britain for European cover in its imperial rivalry with Russia.[147] He drew lessons from the Triple Intervention of Shimonoseki of 1895 as offering the prospect of shifting attention to the non-European periphery to reduce the danger of a war in Europe. While the successful seizure of Kiaochow that followed soon after his appointment as foreign secretary seemed to vindicate a policy of retaining a free hand, like Tirpitz (and unlike the Kaiser) he advocated for better relations with Japan as a growing regional power to check French and especially Russian expansionism in China.[148]

Bülow saw the Franco-Russian alliance as fundamentally shaky. The basic premise of his position was, however, that Anglo-Russian antagonism – over the Ottoman Empire, Persia, India, and China – made a future conflict between Britain and Russia very likely. In the meantime, Germany could exploit that antagonism by sitting aside patiently and avoiding alliance entanglements with either power. While at the same time avoiding any permanent rifts with either Russia or Britain, Bülow believed tensions between the two powers could be encouraged subtly to Germany's advantage.[149] This view was hardly Bülow's alone but was shared widely within the German Foreign Office at the time, even though it tended to overlook the fact that both Russia and Britain were aware that a conflict between them would serve to strengthen Germany and so they themselves sought to avoid one.[150] It also underestimated the degree to which British diplomats were continually

---

[146] Winzen, *Bülows Weltmachtkonzept*, 41; cf. Bülow, *Deutsche Politik*, 54.
[147] Bülow, *Deutsche Politik*, 34–35; Canis, *Von Bismarck zur Weltpolitik*, 291–94.
[148] Canis, *Von Bismarck zur Weltpolitik*, 288; Wippich, *Japan und die deutsche Fernostpolitik*, 366–67.
[149] Winzen, *Bülows Weltmachtkonzept*, 43–59.
[150] Canis, *Von Bismarck zur Weltpolitik*, 241–43; Mommsen, *Bürgerstoltz und Weltmachtstreben*, 280. On the German dogma of the impossibility of an Anglo-Russian entente, see Vogel, *Deutsche Rußlandpolitik*, 118–23.

seeking accommodation with Russia because of the direct threat it posed to their overseas empire.[151]

On June 23 and 24, 1897, shortly before he was named acting foreign secretary, Bülow had a set of discussions with Eulenburg, Holstein, Marschall, and Hohenlohe, where he learned that his appointment was mainly motivated by the Kaiser's desire to have Tirpitz's naval program shepherded through the Reichstag. Subsequent discussions with the Kaiser in Kiel then made it clear that the primary foreign policy tasks put to Bülow were the development of German trade, the transition to *Weltpolitik*, and the creation of the larger fleet without precipitating conflict with England.[152] In a letter Bülow wrote Gustav Schmoller after his retirement, he described the task of transitioning to *Weltpolitik* by defining it in illuminating detail:

> Our transition to *Weltpolitik* (trade, shipping, overseas interests, the consequences of the enormous development of our industry, our growing prosperity, the growth in population) and above all to enable the construction of the German fleet without conflict with England, whom we were at the time in no way a match, but with the preservation of our dignity [*Würde*] and standing [*Stellung*] on the Continent.[153]

As this passage shows, *Weltpoltiik* was linked in Bülow's mind directly with Germany's growing population, industry, trade, shipping, overseas interests, and prosperity, a description in striking accord with that of Otto Hammann recounted earlier. The role of "dignity" and "standing" in this description should also be highlighted here, as they continued to figure centrally in German aspirations for *Weltpolitik* well after Bülow's resignation in 1909 and as a justification for Germany's naval program long after its strategic rationale had expired.

On August 3, 1897 Bülow met with Kaiser Wilhelm in Kiel to accompany him on a state visit to St. Petersburg. In the ensuing discussions with the monarch, Bülow mentioned that he had long thought an expansion of the German navy was justified.[154] Later that month Bülow was summoned to Schloss Wilhelmshöhe in Kassel for extensive discussions with Alfred Tirpitz and the Kaiser that took place between August 18 and 21. The main point of these discussions was working out a strategy for passage of the new navy bill proposed by Tirpitz and coordinating German foreign policy in a way that would enable undisturbed fleet construction. Tirpitz and Bülow agreed that the

---

[151] Neilson, *Britain and the Last Tsar*, 370.
[152] Winzen, *Bülow's Weltmachtkonzept*, 61–64, 64n11. Cf. Bülow, *Deutsche Politik*, 11–12, 19–21.
[153] GStA PK, VI. HA Nl. Schmoller, Nr. 204a, fols. 4–13, Bernhard von Bülow to Gustav Schmoller, Feb. 9, 1912.
[154] Bülow, *Denkwürdigkeiten*, vol. 1, 56, 104; Winzen, *Bülow's Weltmachtkonzept*, 74.

Reichstag and allied governments in the Bundesrat should be presented with a clear, coherent, and limited bill that would resonate with the great majority of the German people and thus find acceptance in the Reichstag.[155] Bülow was himself initially skeptical of focusing primarily on a battleship fleet stationed in home waters rather than cruisers in protecting Germany's overseas interests. Tirpitz, now supported by the Kaiser, countered that the ship-of-the-line strategy was justified because Germany lacked overseas bases and coaling stations; only a fleet concentrated in home waters, Tirpitz argued, could provide the pressure that Germany's diplomatic representatives lacked in their negotiations with England. Bülow was brought around to Tirpitz's view by the opportunities that he saw a battle fleet offering German diplomacy once it had grown to become a real power factor with Britain, especially as Germany became a more attractive alliance partner among powers feared by Britain. Bülow agreed that Germany should not become dependent upon Britain, as this would not allow Germany's continued economic development and expansion overseas. Once in a stronger bargaining position, Bülow believed Germany would be able to enter negotiations with Britain over colonial matters firmly and confidently.[156] Bülow claimed that the longer-term goal was that Germany would ultimately enter into an advantageous military alliance with either Britain, France, or Russia and become through such an alliance the guarantor of perpetual peace on the European continent.[157]

In essence the larger fleet offered by Tirpitz's plan was complimentary to Bülow's strategy of the free hand and "alliance abstinence" with view to a rapprochement and eventual alliance with Russia without arousing undue tensions between Germany and Britain. Tirpitz and Bülow both agreed that Germany would only be able to participate as an equal partner in the partitioning and economic development of the remaining unclaimed parts of the world by reducing Germany's diplomatic dependence on Britain and by eroding Britain's naval hegemony, as it was this that had afforded the British the luxury to do deals with Germany as they pleased and always on their own terms. Tirpitz and Bülow also agreed that the only way this goal could be achieved was not alone, but with other alliance partners.[158] The primary difference between the two was that Tirpitz's rather inflexible, binary thinking led him to believe a war between Russia and Britain was rigidly inevitable. He was also more hostile toward Britain than Bülow. Tirpitz's animus toward Britain was influenced by Heinrich von Treitschke, whose books he had read

---

[155] Bülow, *Denkwürdigkeiten*, vol. 1, 107–8, 115.
[156] Ibid., 115–16; cf. Winzen, *Bülow's Weltmachtkonzept*, 75–78; Kelly, *Tirpitz*, esp. 195–202, 446–66.
[157] Winzen, *Bülows Weltmachtkonzept*, 80–81; Canis, *Von Bismarck zur Weltpolitik*, 288, 307–9, 323–24, 340–41, 369.
[158] Bülow, *Denkwürdigiten*, vol. 1, 116–17; Winzen, *Bülow's Weltmachtkonzept*, 79–81.

and lectures he had audited at the University of Berlin as a young officer in 1876. It was apparently also given impulse by witnessing British competition for influence in China while commanding the German East Asian Squadron in 1896. This led him to believe that at some point conflict between Germany and England was unavoidable and that Britain was capable of a preventive strike against Germany's fleet-in-being (the so-called "Copenhagen complex"), all views that neither Bülow nor the Kaiser shared.[159]

With hindsight of the Anglo-Russian Convention of 1907, the dangers of such an independent foreign policy from a position of naval strength are all too apparent, yet viewed in context no viable alternatives to this policy really existed in 1897. No offers of alliance had been extended to Germany, and foreseeing the dangers would have required superhuman foresight and a voluntary step into the ranks of a second-rate power, a decision that would not have been politically viable in Germany, or for that matter, in any other European great power given the then prevailing zeitgeist.[160] Again, it is worth being reminded that Germany was hardly alone in deciding to build a battleship navy in these years.

Immediately after the Wihelmshöhe talks, Tirpitz set off to Friedrichsruh to seek the blessing of Bismarck for his fleet plans, while Bülow began working to change the views of the Foreign Office and other government quarters about *Weltpolitik*, making quite surprising inroads with senior ministers. Bülow even took the extraordinary step of having an audience with the Pope and senior missionaries in Rome to try to convince them of the need to expand the German fleet and thus to preempt any negative interventions of the Holy See that might influence the Center Party. Similar discussions were held between Bülow and Prince-Bishop of Breslau Georg von Kopp (1837–1914).[161] Tirpitz, meanwhile, cultivated members of the Hamburg and Bremen Senate, the Hanseatic cities' merchant and shipping elite, as well as key figures in German industry and banking.[162]

Bülow's Reichstag debut as new foreign secretary on December 6, 1897 was the occasion of his famous "Place in the Sun" speech which is indelibly associated with the aims and aspirations of *Weltpolitik* held during the thick

---

[159] Bülow, *Denkwürdigiten*, vol. 1, 110, 116, 283; Tirpitz, *Memoirs*, vol. 1, 144; Kelly, *Tirpitz*, 56, 72; Rafael Scheck, *Alfred von Tirpitz and German Right Wing Politics, 1914–1930* (Atlantic Highlands, NJ: Humanities Press, 1998), 12–14; Jonathan Steinberg, "The Copenhagen Complex," *Journal of Contemporary History* 1, no. 3 (July 1966): 23–46. Canis, *Von Bismarck zur Weltpolitik*, 288, 302, 307–9, 323–24, 337–38, 340–41, 368–69, 383; Kohut, *Wilhelm II*, 199–223; Clark, *Kaiser Wilhelm II*, 131–38, 197–214. Cf. Winzen, *Reichskanzler*, 67.
[160] Canis, *Von Bismarck zur Weltpolitik*, 287, 302, 306, 308, 325, 328–30, 331, 375; Offer, *The First World War*, 325.
[161] Winzen, *Bülows Weltmachtkonzept*, 81–84.
[162] Böhm, *Überseehandel und Flottenbau*, 91–102.

of the budget debate over the new navy bill.[163] It was an impromptu response to questions posed to the government by a Social Democratic deputy about Germany's recent occupation of Kiaochow. The speech reflected to an uncanny degree the priorities that had been given in *Weltpolitik* to China and the West Indies, so-called lands with a rich and promising future:

> In East Asia Deputy Dr. Schoenlank[164] seemed to fear that we wish to plunge into a risky adventure. Do not fear anything, Gentlemen! Mr. Reichschancellor is not the man and his staff are not the people to pursue useless undertakings. We also definitely do not feel the need to have a finger in every pie. But we are also of the opinion that it is unwise, from the outset, to exclude Germany from competition with other nations in lands with a rich and promising future. (Bravo!) The days when Germans granted one of its neighbors the earth, the other the sea, and reserved for themselves the sky, where pure doctrine reigns (laughter – Bravo!) – those times are past. We see it as our foremost task to foster and cultivate the interests of our shipping, our trade, and our industry, particularly in the East. . . . We are happy to respect the interests of other great powers in China, secure in the knowledge that our own interests will also receive the recognition they deserve. (Bravo!) In a word: we do not want to put anyone in our shadow, but we also demand our place in the sun. (Bravo!) In East Asia as in the West Indies we will be anxious to protect our rights and our interests without harshness, but also without weakness, true to the traditions of German politics.[165]

As this passage reveals yet again and as the earlier sections of this and prior chapters have shown, *Weltpolitik* was a complex of ideas originally defined by the German educated bourgeoisie that were then profoundly shaped by the encounter with *Weltwirtschaft* in the Americas and East Asia. *Weltpolitik* was never focused on Britain, much less bent on attaining Britain's naval hegemony or seizing its colonial empire. It was focused on establishing Germany alongside the Americans, Japanese, Russians, French and British as one of a number of newer and established world powers with interests in China and elsewhere in the world that deserved to be respected. From that perspective, Britain would have to cede its naval monopoly to a more polycratic order and be prodded to revise the colonial status quo in favor of Germany as it had done with other newer world powers, notably Japan in Formosa and the United States in Hawaii and Venezuela. Germany would cease being a "junior partner" and supplicant.

---

[163] Bülow, *Denkwürdigkeiten*, vol. 1, 192.
[164] Bruno Schoenlank (1859–1901), writer, Social Democratic politician, and Reichstag deputy from 1893 to 1901.
[165] *StenBerVR, IX. Legislaturperiode, 4. Sitzung, 1897/98*, vol. 1 (Dec. 6, 1897), 60A–D, here 60B.

As will become much more apparent later in this chapter and in those to follow, there was a very strong consensus between Bülow, Tirpitz, Schmoller, and Schmoller's students on these issues that grew out of the important role that von Halle, Rathgen, Schumacher, and Sering had played in their travels and observations in East Asia and the Americas in defining new objectives and in identifying the challenges to German foreign policy at a time of unprecedented international expansion of German ideas, capital, ships, and goods. As has been shown in abundant detail in the previous chapters, many of these ideas had long been in incubation and were articulated well before Tirpitz became state secretary of the Navy Office and Bülow took charge as acting foreign secretary. Bülow usually deferred to Tirpitz for the ideas animating *Weltpolitik*, and Tirpitz in turn turned to scholars such as Schmoller and his students for their theoretical and historical underpinnings.[166] While the common experiences abroad had brought men like Rathgen, Sering, Schumacher, von Halle, and Tirpitz together in their *Weltbild* and commitment to a larger navy, it was Schmoller who offered the personal lines of connection between Tirpitz, Bülow, and his students and the public mouthpiece of his *Jahrbuch*.[167]

## The Fleet Professors

Given Tirpitz's commitment to working with the Reichstag in gaining support for *Weltpolitik* and the fact that its centerpiece, his naval program, sought to bind the Reichstag to a fixed program of increased spending, a sustained political effort was needed over many years spearheaded by a massive propaganda campaign to bring about changes in public opinion. For that purpose a new propaganda department within the Navy Office had been created just two days after Tirpitz's meeting with the Kaiser on June 17, 1897: the Section for Communications and General Parliamentary Affairs MII (Communications Bureau). It was headed by one of Tirpitz's most trusted colleagues from the torpedo service, August von Heeringen (1855–1927).[168] There was broad unanimity within the Navy Office that it was essential to persuade Germany's educated classes of the necessity of developing the Reich's maritime power to bring about these changes in public opinion, and Heeringen had given this point special emphasis in his supplements to Titpitz's famous January 1896 memorandum. This included proposals to establish professorial posts devoted to German maritime interests at various universities.[169] Thus Heeringen and

---

[166] See Herwig, *"Luxury" Fleet*, 40; Lerman, *The Chancellor as Courtier*, 33.
[167] vom Bruch, *Wissenschaft*, 100–101, 238–39.
[168] Deist, *Flottenpolitik*, 71–72; Marienfeld, *Wissenschaft und Schlachtflottenbau*, 79.
[169] Deist, *Flottenpolitik*, 102.

Tirpitz were particularly keen to get university professors involved, as their influence on educated opinion in Germany was enormous.[170]

Heeringen set out almost immediately to visit leading German professors for their assistance, and in the list that Heeringen compiled of those to be visited, Tirpitz added Gustav Schmoller's name. Tirpitz later recalled that it was the economists who were most willing to give their enthusiastic support, naming in particular Lujo Brentano, Schmoller, Sering, Schumacher, and Adolph Wagner.[171] Schmoller and his former students did not need to be pressed, much less "goaded" by von Heeringen to lend their voice to support German naval construction.[172] As was discussed in the previous chapters, Schmoller had been in close contact with his former students over the previous years and agreed with their position on the need for Germany to build a larger naval force in order to be taken seriously by rival powers. To be sure, that view was reinforced by Tirpitz himself, whom Schmoller had known personally for many years.[173] In any case, von Heeringen paid a visit to Schmoller in mid-July 1897. A letter from Schmoller to his colleague Lujo Brentano in Munich reveals Tirpitz and Heeringen's broader, long-term strategy to change public opinion in order to sustain naval construction over an entire generation in remarkable candor:

> Through his deceased father-in-law the deputy Liepke [sic][174] I have known Secretary of State Tirpitz since old times. He recently sent Lieutenant Commander von Heeringen to me to discuss how one could, and better than hitherto, awaken in broader circles an understanding not so much for fleet plans as for the German colonies, exports, the significance of international power struggles with England, etc. Since on the whole I am on the same standpoint as he is and also have found in previous conversations with Tirpitz that he has clear and sensible views about our trade policy, etc., I therefore gladly declared my willingness to be helpful, yet I did not conceal that under the current government all efforts to quickly gain something for the fleet would be futile. Com. v. H [eeringen] agreed completely and repeated his intention with precision: voting in the next budget years is less the aim than constantly producing a change in views about the significance of our external trade, German exports, the colonies, the power questions. Only a permanent change in the whole of

---

[170] Ibid.  [171] Ibid.; Tirpitz, *Memoirs*, vol. 1, 111.
[172] Cf. Eley, *Reshaping the German Right*, 85.
[173] See BArch M, N253 Nl. Tirpitz, Nr. 263, fol. 180, Ludwig von Schmoller to Alfred von Tirpitz, Tübingen, Aug. 1922.
[174] Gustav Lipke (1820–89) was a lawyer as well as the National Liberal deputy in the Prussian Chamber of Deputies for Waldenburg-Reichenbach from 1874 to 1879 and National Liberal and then Liberal Union (Liberale Vereinigung) deputy in the Reichstag for Schwarzburg-Sonderhausen from 1880 to 1889.

> public opinion can guarantee us the sort of fleet building [that] is needed and so spread itself over a generation.
>
> He wishes to establish contacts with literary and economic experts in south Germany and mentioned your name. I declared my wiliness to write you and ask that you respond in such a way that I might show him your response. He was also willing to visit you on occasion in Munich.
>
> What is wished is one cleverly-written article in the Allg. Zeitung[175] or in the Neueste Münchener Nachrichten (even better in all Ultramontane papers) which enlightens Bavaria about the fact that while south Germany happens to be distant from the coast, it is nevertheless involved in these questions.[176]

As this letter also makes clear, from the very beginning, and at least as far back as Schmoller's first discussions with Tirpitz, the matter of the fleet was linked very closely to colonial policy, German exports, and international power struggles. Indeed, these appear very much the ends of any expansion of the fleet and therefore also seem to be the basis for consensus with Schmoller. Heeringen was also remarkably candid about the long-term goal of sustaining investments in a larger navy over an entire generation and therefore the need to bring about a permanent change in public opinion.

Lujo Brentano was an Anglophile and a left liberal free trader, yet this did not stop him from lending his strong support to Heeringen's initiative, notably because of the dependence of Germany on industrial exports and the danger of British imperial and American protectionism. As he wrote in response to Schmoller:

> Every policy that effectively works toward raising our exports is assured my support. For – whether one may view it as a fortune or misfortune – it is nevertheless a fact that Germany is now an industrial state. Since this is how things are, the most important concern is to find sales markets for its products, and particularly the export of its industrial products. On this the sales will now depend, namely, even the domestic sales market of our agricultural products. For our domestic sales market is dependent upon whether we have a solvent working population. The solvency of the industrial working population has replaced the old [saying]: "if the farmer has money, so does everybody." The future of agriculture lies in the purchasing power of our industrial working population, the development of its necessities, the increase of its efficiency, and the adjustment of agricultural production to its needs. Yet the solvency of our working population has as a precondition the development of our exports.
>
> The future of our export is, however, currently very threatened. The development of the relationship between England and its colonies could

---

[175] *Allgemeine Zeitung,* Munich.
[176] BArch K, N 1001, Nl. Brentano, Nr. 57, fols. 107–8, Gustav Schmoller to Lujo Brentano, July 23, 1897.

> become very detrimental to us. Similarly, our senseless bounty policy has given us the American Dingley Bill,[177] whose horrors will likely be felt even sooner. Decades of work of our businesspeople could be endangered by it. Under such conditions it is natural that one looks about for alternatives. To expect this from our colonies would be childish. But in Asia and South America there may still be very much to be had. From this viewpoint, an increase in the German fleet appears justified.[178]

Much like Schumacher and von Halle, Brentano recognized opportunities for expanded trade were not in the colonies but in Asia and South America – a larger fleet would assure that these markets remained open to German trade. The focus in these letters is squarely on Germany in the international arena, jostling for export markets and spheres of influence vis-à-vis the other powers in a climate of rising protectionism. One also finds an explicit understanding that Germany, as a major industrial power and exporter, would need a larger fleet to protect its interests by standing on a more equal maritime footing with Britain and challenging the ambitions of the United States. That is, a larger fleet was seen clearly as a deterrent to imperialist aggression and protectionism and as starting point for bolstered credibility in negotiations over trade treaties and alliances. Indeed, the unanimity with Tirpitz on these matters is quite remarkable.

While on sick leave in Bad Ems in late July 1897, Tirpitz himself wrote Schmoller that with his appointment as state secretary his ideas for the navy had finally prevailed to turn it into a *defensive* tool against the encroachments on German maritime and economic interests overseas, but that the path ahead was going to be rocky:

> Since the [18]80s I have been fighting for our fleet to be understood as a function of our maritime interests and to be constructed accordingly. This opinion has finally prevailed. Over the last year in Asia I have once again been able to convince myself of what influence this "agency" of the German Empire is in the preservation of Germandom abroad and in the assertion of our economic interests, once it is sufficiently powerful and properly handled. I could give you countless reports about this. I have been able to observe the ruthless advance of Pan-Americanism, the tremendous successes of Russia, and the entirely astonishing growth in strength of the British Empire idea from close proximity with alarm. How depressing and alienating by comparison is the effect made by our political situation in general, and the position of our Reichstag majorities on the question of the fleet in particular. Daily detailed reports by

---

[177] A reference to the Dingley Act passed in July 1897, the highest and longest-lived American protective tariff which amounted to 52 percent ad valorem on average.

[178] GStA PK, VI. HA Nl. Schmoller, Nr. 114, fols. 275–76, Lujo Brentano to Gustav Schmoller, July 27, 1897; cf. Sheehan, *Lujo Brentano*, 180.

telegraph come to Hong Kong on the position of the Reichstag regarding the development of the fleet; such interest and such understanding is compelled for this question by the English in Asia. I may have the pleasure to discuss these things and the economic prospects in Asia over the course of the winter. Since I am known everywhere and have first-rate contacts, a post as admiral is incomparably favorable for gaining a certain overview of these things.[179]

It is noteworthy that here once again the United States is given such prominence as a threat to Germany, but this should not come as any surprise given the earlier elaboration of the importance of the United States both in Tirpitz's navalist worldview and as a danger to Germany's maritime interests and industrial exports in some of the most promising international markets. The response from Schmoller reveals that there was already broad agreement between the two men by that point about these threats facing Germany and the connection between an expanded fleet, export markets, and bilateral trade treaties:

I am very pleased if those conducting German trade policy grasp the enormous dangers of Panamericanism, the English agitation for Greater Britain, and Russian plans for world power.... And naturally all our plans for the fleet are tied in the closest possible way to future German trade policy. I only fear the penetration of agrarian interests will hinder a keen policy oriented toward the future. If a system of high tariffs in the Bismarck-Kardorffian[180] sense were to be introduced then one cannot pursue export and naval policy.

Naturally I still have hopes for Hohenlohe,[181] who as an old free trader will not be had easily for excessive protective tariffs. But we must also not neglect our trade treaties if we do not want to destroy our industry and exports.[182]

Clearly the fleet was seen as offering leverage in difficult upcoming bilateral trade treaties with the expiration of the Caprivi trade laws in 1902. There can be no doubt that the most difficult and important negotiations were going to be with the Americans, who were perceived not only as an important export market in their own right but as the lynchpin for access to the entire Caribbean and South American market now so important to German trade and investment.

---

[179] GStA PK, VI. HA Nl. Schmoller, Nr. 189a, fols. 83–84, Alfred Tirpitz to Gustav Schmoller, July 28, 1897.
[180] Wilhelm von Kardorff (1828–1907), confidant of Bismarck, trade protectionist, and cofounder of the Free Conservative Party (Deutsche Reichspartei).
[181] Prince Chlodwig von Hohenlohe-Schillingsfürst, German Chancellor 1894–1900.
[182] BArch M, N 253 Nl. Tirpitz, Nr. 40, fols. 154–55, Gustav Schmoller to Alfred Tirpitz, Berlin, July 29, 1897.

As it came into being in the summer of 1897, Heeringen's Communications Bureau was staffed by two younger officers as department heads and assisted on an ad hoc basis by a number of other senior naval officers. In addition to this naval staff, there were many important non-navy collaborators and assistants who worked very closely with the bureau to produce its economic and statistical research and compile memoranda that accompanied draft legislation. The most important of these was unquestionably Ernst von Halle, who began working with von Heeringen in early August 1897 on Schmoller's recommendation and who subsequently became editor of all memoranda and publications produced by the RMA that illuminated the economic aspects of navy construction intended for both the Reichstag and the public.[183] The memoranda von Halle compiled for the Reichstag on Germany's maritime interests drew heavily on sources supplied by Hamburg and Bremen merchants and shipping companies on request of the Navy Office and von Halle.[184] It was also through von Halle (and very likely Schmoller) that Sering, Schumacher, and later Karl Helfferich came to work as collaborators with the Navy Office, including as anonymous contributors to the Navy Office's propaganda publications. The first of these publications was edited by von Halle and published under the pseudonym *Nauticus* in February and March 1898 during the third reading of the navy bill.[185] In 1899 a journal, *Jahrbuch für Deutschlands Seeinteressen*, was founded and edited under the same pseudonym.[186] The tone of these publications was sober and nonpolemical, intended to convey arguments for the navy by weight of reasoned argument and scholarship. While acknowledging the RMA's financial support of *Nauticus*, Tirpitz tried to maintain secrecy about the identity of the editor and the degree of cooperation that in fact existed between *Nauticus* and the RMA's Communications Bureau. In reality *Nauticus* was none other than Ernst von Halle.[187] Von Halle's offices, which he maintained privately away from the Navy Office, were themselves a veritable hive of activity, as Schumacher later recalled. Von Halle, who had inherited a large fortune, had an exceptional private library and used all of the newest technology in his work, including typewriters and stenotype machines, and he employed a secretary and assistants. As Schumacher recalled, von Halle was "one of the first in Germany to fit out

---

[183] Deist, *Flottenpolitik*, 113; Marienfeld, *Wissenschaft und Schlachtflottenbau*, 79; Scholl, "Ernst von Halle," viii, xi.
[184] Böhm, *Überseehandel und Flottenbau*, 102–6.
[185] Nauticus, *Altes und neues zur Flottenfrage: Erläuterungen zum Flottengesetz* (Berlin: Mittler und Sohn, 1898).
[186] Marienfeld, *Wissenschaft und Schlachtflottenbau*, 79–80; Deist, *Flottenpolitik*, 80n33, 107, 107n125, 113, 221.
[187] Scholl, "Ernst von Halle," xi.

his work into a scholarly giant enterprise [*Grossbetrieb*]." He was amazed by what von Halle was able to produce in a short period of time.[188]

There were many other and more subtle connections between the Communications Bureau and the group of scholars around Schmoller. Heeringen himself worked through many intermediaries to secure duplicates of articles that had a pro-fleet tendency to avoid the appearance of too close a connection between the Navy Office and pro-fleet publicity. For example, Tirpitz and von Heeringen had been much taken by Karl Rathgen's essay discussing the cancellation of the Anglo-German trade treaty in which he had taken up Joseph Chamberlain's challenge and made a strong plea for German naval expansion, which they had been given by Schmoller in manuscript form in August 1897 as it was about to go to press in Schmoller's *Jahrbuch*. Von Heeringen subsequently contacted Schmoller to request and pay for offprints of Rathgen's article for wider distribution through the intermediary Adolph von Wenckstern (1862–1914), one of Schmoller's former students and *Privatdozent* at Berlin University, who had himself only returned from three years of teaching at the Imperial University in Tokyo the year prior.[189] Wenckstern notified Schmoller that Rathgen had agreed to have his article distributed as an offprint and that Heeringen's office would cover the costs but wanted to avoid taking up contact with the publisher Duncker & Humblot "for fear that it would appear that he has a hand in the game of distributing the article." He thus requested that Schmoller take up the matter with publisher and that "beyond the circle that knows, no one else learn of it."[190]

While spearheading the scholarly side of the propaganda effort in the Communications Bureau from 1897 to 1898, von Halle gave speeches on behalf of the fleet that were often organized with the assistance of the Communications Bureau. In December of 1897, in the very thick of the campaign for the first navy bill, von Halle gave a lecture to the International Union for Comparative Jurisprudence and Political Economy, which was then published in Schmoller's *Jahrbuch* in early 1898.[191] This speech connected the emerging *Weltwirtschaft* and expanded German naval interests even more explicitly in light of his recent experiences abroad and study of Mahan's writings, drawing heavily from a June 1897 memorandum that had accompanied the draft navy law Tirpitz had presented to the Kaiser.[192]

---

[188] GNN HA, Nl. Schumacher, I, B-6l, fols. 351–52. This passage was crossed out in the manuscript.
[189] GStA PK, VI. HA, Nl. Schmoller, Nr. 189c, fols. 254–55, Adolph von Wenckstern to Gustav Schmoller, Berlin, Aug. 25, 1897.
[190] Ibid.
[191] Ernst von Halle, "Die Seeinteressen Deutschlands," *JbfGVV* 22 (1898): 221–45; reprinted in Halle, *Volks- und Seewirthschaft: Reden und Aufsätze*, vol. 1 (Berlin: Mittler und Sohn, 1902), 136–71. Cf. Kelly, *Tirpitz*, 146.
[192] Kelly, *Tirpitz*, 146.

Von Halle began his speech by pointing out how much the world economy and foreign trade had been neglected by German statisticians, economists, and the German public, preoccupied as they had been by domestic policy since the founding of the Reich.[193] The result was a distinct lack of knowledge, even among specialists, and the susceptibility of German maritime and foreign trading interests to unwarranted attacks from agrarian interests and the Social Democrats.[194] Narrowly domestic and protectionist interests of this sort were hardly confined to Germany, he noted, but were particularly influential in the United States, which was restricting imports and turning itself into a closed market; in England similar initiatives were being hatched in the guise of an imperial customs union to create a "greater" Britain. Russia was pursuing similar aims by expanded cotton cultivation in the Transcaspian region, as was France through its absorption of Algiers into its customs zone and recent expansion of colonial territory.[195] He drew particular attention to the United States, which he reported was well on its way to integrating Cuba and other West Indian Islands into its own economy for the supply of tropical agricultural products like tobacco, sugar, coffee, and spices. As he concluded: "All four peoples have submitted to what nowadays is understood as imperialism, the ambition to bring giant expanses of the earth under the rule of a uniform, national political and economic system; territories which guarantee their people all elements of independence even while further increasing their power to expand and extend their spheres of power."[196] Electrical light and power, mechanical refrigeration, and other technologies had improved the conditions of life of Europeans in the tropics and offered the prospect of the spread of industry to these climactic zones and the elimination of the advantages enjoyed by the countries of the temperate zones.[197] With that in mind, Germany stood at a distinct territorial disadvantage vis-à-vis the other four states; nevertheless, through its rapidly-growing population, Germany had a demographic advantage over France, and its organizational abilities in statecraft and industry were superior to those of Russia. Indeed, von Halle argued that Germany's *capacities* for expansion were the equal of England, but in terms of the *need* for new opportunities for expansion stood well ahead of all four rival powers.[198]

The fact that England enjoyed such unrivaled opportunities and that Germany lacked them was an accident of history, von Halle argued. Making references to Alfred Thayer Mahan and the English historian John Robert Seeley (1834–95), von Halle argued that it had been decided in a struggle for mastery of the seas that had played out in European and colonial wars between 1650 and 1815 in which Britain ultimately prevailed through it synergetic

---

[193] von Halle, "Die Seeinteressen Deutschlands," 136–38.　[194] Ibid., 138–39.
[195] Ibid., 139–41.　[196] Ibid., 141.　[197] Ibid., 142–43.　[198] Ibid., 144–45.

cultivation of its merchant marine and navy.[199] Germans, he said, were largely ignorant of this process and its significance due to their parochial concerns and unworldly, German-centered school education.[200] The Hanseatic city states were subsequently excluded from many ports, reduced to the mercy of the great trading powers, and only left a small secondary trade, surviving through their utility as neutrals in wartime and their own agile diplomacy.[201] Well into the nineteenth century foreign trading powers, above all the English, prevailed in terms of traded tonnage in Hamburg. Even the most powerful German state, Prussia, could do little to mitigate the dangers of the Barbary pirates and so was excluded from Mediterranean and South American trade and had to seek protection from the Swedes.[202]

These trends were only slowly reversed by the expansion of German trade with the United States, Latin America, and Danish, Dutch and French colonies, the repeal of the English Navigation Acts, and the elimination of discriminatory tariffs. The Prussian East Asian expedition of 1859 to 1861 and the pooling of trade negotiation power under the North German Confederation and Reich then also opened many other ports to German trade.[203] Today, von Halle said, over two-thirds of Germany's foreign trade was overseas trade, it having grown in terms of value by no less than three-fifths since 1872 – this was a disproportionate increase, as in that same period the value of all world trade had risen by less than one quarter, putting Germany second only to England.[204] At the same time, Germany's neighboring states France, Russia, Switzerland, Belgium, and Austria had all increased protective tariffs, and Britain moved to purchase foreign goods formerly acquired in German ports in their place of origin.[205] Increasingly, von Halle pointed out, more and more of Germany's foreign trade was intercontinental, as German firms had grown or acquired their necessary raw materials or sold their finished goods on overseas markets.[206] Indeed this overseas export market was over time a more promising field than Germany's neighboring states.[207] Thus he predicted that those areas that had seen the most rapid upswing in German overseas trade in recent decades, above all Central and South America, but also the independent states of Africa and Asia, the Balkans, and those empires that did not close themselves off to foreign trade would grow in importance to Germany.[208] As he observed:

> Germany controls more than half of the shipping commerce in its harbors. Its flag dominates in its overseas commerce. And its sphere of economic interest abroad has expanded substantially. Billions in German capital works abroad, partially in enterprises, partially as loan capital

---

[199] Ibid., 148.  [200] Ibid., 148–49.  [201] Ibid., 150–51.  [202] Ibid., 152–53.
[203] Ibid., 154–55.  [204] Ibid., 156–57.  [205] Ibid., 158–59.  [206] Ibid., 159.
[207] Ibid., 160.  [208] Ibid., 161–62.

> extended to foreign borrowers. 500–600 million flow back into the country through channels of German ownership of foreign stocks and bonds, [and] the income from overseas commercial operations of German trade and industry can be estimated to be no less. Abroad one has trading posts and plantations, factories and mines, warehouses, merchant houses, and banks. The yields of our maritime fisheries, once minimal, have possibly increased to 20 million [marks]. We have begun to develop colonies. We have started to establish a navy. The elements for further progress in this direction are given.[209]

It would be foolish, von Halle argued, to throttle these developments due to the complaints of German agriculture about foreign competition in grain production. Foreign trade benefited German industry and guaranteed ongoing employment for German workers without wages falling along with other prices and leading to emigration. Above all, German industry was reliant on the importation of raw materials and had to export in order to be able to pay for these. Allowing German capital to work abroad where its yields were higher allowed the country to be in a position to support domestic agriculture and to improve the lot of domestic workers.[210]

For these reasons it was necessary to prevent Germany from being damaged abroad. It remained an open question whether Germany would be able to maintain its advantageous trade relations given the growing world competition on all markets "in view of the political aspirations of overseas powers, the United States, Japan, possibly this or that South American state and British imperialism."[211] Nothing would be more foolish than for Germany to withdraw itself from these developments:

> Situated in the middle of Europe, crossroads to important and significant commercial arteries, it must go along or go under. It has the population and the productive organization. It has a part of the military machinery, which despite the hoped-for substantial continued development of international law, has been in the end and in all ages decisive in questions of world power. It must provide for a growing population, and in view of the consolidation of the four great world-political [*weltpolitischen*] and world-economic [*weltwirtschaftlichen*] entities, must be anxious to secure the existential conditions that assure it is equal to these future competitive challenges.[212]

Von Halle concluded that freedom of international commerce and world trade could only be maintained by being sufficiently armed to deter any power seeking to restrict Germany. In the current age of a shrinking world through modern transportation technology, growing competition for limited raw materials, increasing global supply of industrial products, population pressures,

---

[209] Ibid., 164–65.    [210] Ibid., 165–66.    [211] Ibid., 166.    [212] Ibid., 167.

and of the law of diminishing returns to agriculture and increasing returns to industry, frictions were beginning to emerge.[213] The only conclusion one could draw, von Halle argued, was that Germany had to pursue "world power politics" and put itself in a position where it is was on the same footing as the other nations in the coming era.[214] "The treaties of the future will only be agreed and held between equals, [but] will be dictated and interpreted to the weak."[215] As in the past, the future would be decided by access to the seas.[216]

One of the interesting features of von Halle's speech on Germany's maritime interests is how often the United States appears as a threat to Germany's overseas commerce and trade alongside the looming menace of Chamberlain's "Greater Britain." One area of potential conflict with the Americans was the uncertain status of Spain's moribund colonial empire, which von Halle had observed firsthand in Cuba in 1896. Years before the start of the Spanish-American War, Berlin had an eye to gaining Spanish colonial territory in the Philippines and South Pacific in order to supplement Germany's possessions in New Guinea, the Bismarck Archipelago, and German merchant interests in Samoa with coaling stations and naval bases, aware that Germany's rival in any such initiative would likely be the United States.[217]

The first navy bill was accepted by a vote of 272 to 139 in the Reichstag on April 10, 1898, approving a navy budget of over 408 million marks to construct 19 battleships, 8 armored cruisers, and 12 heavy and 30 light cruisers by April 1904.[218] Passage of the law by such a wide margin was unquestionably the product both of the Imperial Navy Office's effective propaganda effort, which prepared the ground, and Tirpitz's clear plans and winning manner in intense negotiations with the parties of the Reichstag, notably with the Center Party.[219] The tactics he employed included pressure, the element of surprise, and concealment of the true extent of his plans.[220] There is nevertheless little evidence that *Sammlungspolitik* played much of a role in these negotiations or that Tirpitz was after anything more than an expansion of the fleet.[221]

Schumacher himself began working with Tirpitz and Heeringen shortly after his return from East Asia in March 1898 when he was back in the Prussian Ministry for Public Works. In fact he received a request from Tirpitz to present his views on Kiaochow to him in person.[222] Arriving at the state

---

[213] Ibid., 168.  [214] Ibid., 169.  [215] Ibid., 170.  [216] Ibid.
[217] See Herold, *Reichsgewalt bedeutet Seegewalt*, 302–3.
[218] Herwig, *"Luxury" Fleet*, 42; Röhl, *The Kaiser's Personal Monarchy*, 1029.
[219] Röhl, *The Kaiser's Personal Monarchy*, 1028; Berghahn, *Der Tirpitz-Plan*, 112–57; Kelly, *Tirpitz*, 140–55.
[220] Berghahn, *Der Tirpitz Plan*, 123–24.  [221] Kelly, *Tirpitz*, 153; Deist, *Flottenpolitik*, 14.
[222] GNN HA, Nl. Schumacher, I, B-6l, fol. 344.

secretary's office on the appointed day for the discussion, Schumacher was astounded to encounter, along with Tirpitz, a "stately circle of uniformed men" who had arrived for Schumacher's "report."[223] While at first somewhat uncomfortable, Schumacher was put at ease by "the winning naturalness and almost astonishing openheartedness" of Tirpitz and the keen interest that Tirpitz showed in his ideas. This stood in marked contrast to the much more guarded and stiff interaction he was used to in the army. The powerful personality of von Heeringen particularly impressed Schumacher.[224] Tirpitz raised many questions at that session, quite a number of which Schumacher had himself not thought of or was unable to answer, which Tirpitz asked him to consider and submit to him as a memorandum the next day, which he did.[225] Thereafter Tirpitz drew on Schumacher's expertise on China on a regular basis, which included a surprising invitation to dinner at Tirpitz's home. Soon thereafter Schumacher became a collaborator on the series and journal edited by *Nauticus* and was flooded with requests to give lectures, which Schumacher was sure the Navy Office had had a hand in encouraging. As Schumacher recalled, "Thus I became part of the movement for the new [second] navy bill almost without noticing."[226] By early December 1899 Schumacher was on friendly terms and working closely with Heeringen in the Communications Bureau on the pro-fleet propaganda for the second navy bill.[227]

When a large meeting was organized by the Social Democrat Karl Liebknecht (1871–1919) opposed to the second navy bill in late 1899, Schumacher attended and requested to speak immediately after Liebknecht.[228] As Schumacher recalled, he was not distracted or intimidated by the crowd's distracting hisses and catcalls and soon had their attention. Discussing the piracy he had recently witnessed firsthand on the Chinese coast, he explained that just as many of the main thoroughfares of Berlin required police monitoring, the streets of world commerce on which they were all dependent required a degree of naval protection.[229] He continued by arguing that while this was an extreme example, in general one's security was threatened if one had the reputation of not being able to protect oneself. Since involvement in world markets was now an existential question for Germany much as it was for the English, one could not evade the resulting consequences. When Liebknecht launched into a vehement rebuttal of Schumacher's remarks, he was happy to take up each one of his points and concerns with additional responses. Slowly the mood at the meeting shifted to become one increasingly

---

[223] Ibid.  [224] Ibid., fols. 344–44a.  [225] Ibid., fol. 345.  [226] Ibid.
[227] GNN HA, Nl. Schumacher, I C-104, August von Heeringen to Hermann Schumacher, Berlin, Dec. 5, 1899.
[228] Cf. Deist, *Flottenpolitik*, 127.  [229] GNN HA, Nl. Schumacher, I, B-6l, fol. 345a.

favorable to Schumacher, which then led the chairman to end the discussion prematurely and close the meeting.[230]

One of the public lectures supporting the fleet that Schumacher gave while working with von Halle for the Communications Bureau was on the organization of foreign trade in China, presented to the International Union for Comparative Jurisprudence and Political Economy in the winter of 1898–99, before the campaign for the second navy bill was started. The lecture was then published in Schmoller's *Jahrbuch* in 1899.[231] Together with his contemporary work on Chinese treaty ports and railways mentioned earlier, this and other publications reveal the development of Schumacher's thinking about the German presence in the Chinese economy in light of his year in East Asia and how that justified a larger navy.

As was discussed in the previous chapter, Schumacher had been pleasantly surprised by the prominence of German merchants and trading firms in Chinese treaty ports, but he recognized missed opportunities for German industrial investment in the Chinese interior. With Tientsin emerging second only to Shanghai in terms of its trade volume, he also saw China's economic center of gravity shifting northward and so the utility of an enhanced German naval presence for protecting German trade from coastal piracy and improving the negotiating position of German merchants and firms in China.[232] Schumacher argued that the Shantung Peninsula, an area three times the size of Rhineland-Westphalia with a population of some 25 million, would thus be sure to grow in economic significance.[233] With an excellent harbor at Kiaochow, a healthy climate, high-quality silk production, pongee exports, cotton cultivation, and rich deposits of coal, he believed it was only a matter of overcoming the transportation problems on the peninsula for this region to flourish.[234] Reestablishing the canal connection between Tsinan (Jinan) and Kiaochow would make most of Shantung's mines accessible, and by further connecting the harbor to the mouth of the Yellow River, it would be possible to connect the populous and iron ore and coal-rich province of Shansi (Shanxi) to ocean-going shipping.[235] Schumacher believed railways would play a central role in making China's interior accessible in the future, not just to merchant interests, but especially to those of industry and mining.[236] North American continental railway development, he observed, was the inspiration for many of these Chinese railway plans, not least those of the Russians.[237] The Trans-Siberian Railway's astonishingly rapid construction and expansion into

---

[230] Ibid., fols. 345–46.
[231] Hermann Schumacher, "Die Organisation des Fremdhandels in China," *JbfGVV* 23 (1899): 657–91; reprinted in Schumacher, *Weltwirtschaftliche Studien*, 430–62.
[232] Schumacher, "Die chinesischen Vertragshäfen," 303.   [233] Ibid., 307.
[234] Ibid., 317, 319–21.   [235] Ibid., 309–10.
[236] Schumacher, "Eisenbahnbau und Eisenbahnpläne," 903.   [237] Ibid., 913–14.

Manchuria with the 1896 Chinese concession as well as the 1898 Russian lease of ports on the Liaodong Peninsula now offered the promise of a direct rail link between China and Europe.[238] While Schumacher acknowledged the powerful rivalry between Russia and Japan for Manchuria and Korea, he thought that it was now only a matter of time before Manchuria would be absorbed by Russia.[239] Schumacher was nevertheless aware that Japan was emerging as a powerful rising competitor of German firms in the Chinese market. Indeed, the Japanese were already flooding China with cheap imitations of European and American wares.[240]

With fast steamers, intercontinental telegraph lines, Chinese railways, and many more competitors for a share of the Chinese market, Schumacher was convinced that the age of the sort of Chinese trading houses exemplified by Jardine, Matheson & Co. had passed. Firms in that mold suffered from a short-term, speculative perspective, lacked capital, and thus did not reinvest capital in a sustained way.[241] Moreover, their dismissal of all things Chinese and isolation from Chinese society, lack of command of the language, limited knowledge of the Chinese consumer market, and thus overreliance on compradors had weakened their position.[242] German merchants were, to Schumacher's mind, easily the equal of the English and superior to all other foreign competitors in China, and now that the interior and north of China were opening to foreign merchants, they could strengthen their position by exploiting their often better command of local languages and customs.[243] In short, a *Weltwirtschaft* was emerging in the great power contest for China that involved large, sustained investments in railway infrastructure, industry, and mining, as well as deeper and more informed penetration of the Chinese consumer market that needed the support of a more muscular German naval presence.

While von Halle and Schumacher's writings and speeches would have a direct impact on German public opinion during the campaign for the second navy bill in 1900, they were also highly valued as a foundation for institutional initiatives supported by the Imperial Navy to establish "world economy," "world trade," and "oceanography" as new disciplines in German universities, an initiative that had been outlined in Tirpitz's 1896 memorandum and that Heeringen was now actively promoting.[244] Von Halle drafted an 1898 memorandum for the Prussian Ministry of Culture arguing for the creation of a new oceanographic institute at the University of Kiel to specifically serve the interests of the navy.[245] Schumacher and von Halle were widely considered the two preeminent specialists on these subjects in Germany at the time.

---

[238] Ibid., 907–8, 915–20.   [239] Ibid., 908.
[240] Schumacher, "Die Organisation des Fremdhandels," 444.   [241] Ibid., 437–39.
[242] Ibid., 448–49   [243] Ibid., 458–62.   [244] Deist, *Flottenpolitik*, 102.
[245] Scholl, "Ernst von Halle," xiii.

In June 1898 Friedrich Althoff (1839–1908), director of the university section in the Prussian Ministry of Culture, offered Schumacher an extraordinary professorship at Kiel University, where a new oceanographic institute (Institut für Meereskunde) was established with an economics section, which later evolved into the Königliches Institut für Seeverkehr und Weltwirtschaft (Royal Institute for Ocean Traffic and World Economy).[246] Schumacher accepted this position and held it from 1899 until 1901, though he was given a leave of absence to conduct his research and never actually lectured there.[247] Simultaneously, Ernst von Halle was called to an extraordinary professorship at Berlin University specializing in "world economy," where on the initiative of the RMA and the Kaiser an Institut für Meereskunde (Institute for Oceanography) was to be founded. In 1906 a Museum für Meereskunde followed.[248]

While on leave from teaching at Kiel, Schumacher was offered and accepted a professorship in *Handelswissenschaften* (commercial studies) and became director of studies of the newly founded Handelshochschule (Higher School of Commerce) in Cologne in 1901, one of the very first business schools in the world.[249] A large bequest from the industrialist Gustav Mevissen (1815–99) and the Bund der Industriellen (BdI) – a business association founded in 1895 by smaller and medium-sized German manufacturers who embraced free trade – funded the Cologne Handelshochschule, and the municipal organizers had apparently taken note of Schumacher's writings and speeches on the organization of trade with the United States and China.[250] Althoff, who had by that point anyway thought of appointing Schumacher to a more established position at the nearby University of Bonn, encouraged Schumacher to accept the Cologne offer, as in the meantime Schumacher had been specially selected – likely on Tirpitz's recommendation to the Kaiser himself and Schmoller's recommendation to Althoff – to serve as private lecturer in economics to the German Crown Prince Wilhelm (1882–1951) at Bonn. And so it came about that Schumacher was appointed to dual professorships at Cologne and Bonn, though Schumacher switched to Bonn permanently

---

[246] GNN HA, Nl. Schumacher, I, B-6l, fol. 354.
[247] Schumacher Vereinigung, ed., *Hermann Schumacher*, 10. Cf. Manjapra, *Age of Entanglement*, 145–55.
[248] Scholl, "Ernst von Halle," xiii–xiv; GNN HA, Nl. Schumacher, I, B-6l, fols. 349–52.
[249] See Hermann Schumacher, "Einleitung," in *Die städtische Handels-Hochschule in Köln, die erste selbständige Handels-Hochschule in Deutschland, eröffnet am 1. Mai 1901*, 3rd ed. (Berlin: Julius Springer, 1903), 5–8; Dieter Schneider, "The Creation of Business Economics as a Discipline," *Journal of Economic Studies* 20, no. 4/5 (1993): 262–74; Tribe, *Strategies of Economic Order*, 95–139.
[250] GNN HA, Nl. Schumacher, I, B-6l, fol. 356; Keith Tribe, *Strategies of Economic Order: German Economic Discourse, 1750–1950* (Cambridge: Cambridge University Press, 1995), 106–9.

in 1904 after he had seen through the founding years of the Cologne Handelshochschule.[251] Schumacher was in any case eager to connect his teaching to the practical problems of economic life and German industry, and the proximity to Rhenish-Westphalian heavy industry offered by that location was ideal. He would devote his career to connecting economic theory to economic reality, focused particularly on Germany's commercial connections to the rest of the world.[252]

As is clear from these developments, scholarship and politics became ever more closely enmeshed in this new era of *Weltpolitik*. Professors would play a major role not only in the naval politics of the second navy bill from 1899 to 1900, but also in the campaign for the Bülow tariff bill from 1901 to 1902, the colonial reforms initiated in 1904, the formation of the liberal-conservative Bülow Bloc in 1906 and 1907, and in the campaign for financial reform from 1908 to 1909.

---

[251] GNN HA, Nl. Schumacher, I, B-6l, fols. 357–59; GNN HA, Nl. Schumacher, I, B-6m, fols. 376–81, 387–90; GNN HA, Nl. Schumacher, I B-1, Lebenslauf.
[252] GNN HA, Nl. Schumacher, I, B-6m, fols. 363–66; B-6n, fol. 401.

# 5

# The High Seas Fleet and Power Politics

### The Spanish-American War and the Samoa Question

When war broke out between the United States and Spain in April 1898, it caught everyone in Germany by complete surprise, not least Tirpitz. On March 16, 1898, a month after the sinking of the *Maine*, Tirpitz reported to Bülow via Reinhold Klehmet (1859–1940) in the Foreign Office that the Spanish-American conflict came too early for him, as he would have preferred it to have arisen when Germany possessed the sort of naval power it would have as a result of the new navy law. Even so, he advocated sending several ships to the theaters of the conflict to show that Germany had something to say in the matter.[1] Tirpitz believed that, with the United States distracted by its conflict with Spain, a last chance was offered for Germany to purchase Curaçao from the Netherlands and St. Thomas from Denmark as had long been advocated by von Halle, and he believed the United States could not object to this as it would be compensated with Cuba. He also believed that England would welcome such a permanent German presence in the Americas. Tirpitz argued that if Germany failed to take advantage of the constellation of events, South America would be lost permanently as a German export market once the United States completed a Panama or Nicaragua canal.[2] With respect to China, Tirpitz advocated purchasing a German settlement on the Yangtze, ideally in Woosung (Wusong), as the time would come when heighted economic competition between the Germans and British in the Yangtze region would result in German firms being excluded from English settlements. It was also absolutely essential, Tirpitz argued, for German ships to show the German merchant flag far inland on the Yangtze, and German postal steamers would have to be impelled to do so by the Reich.[3]

It should be obvious from the previous chapters that these ideas were hardly formed in a vacuum but rather a product of Tirpitz's own experiences in East

---

[1] Reinhold Klehmet to Berhard von Bülow, Berlin, March 16, 1898, in Bülow, *Denkwürdigkeiten*, vol. 1, 188.
[2] Ibid.; cf. Fiebig-von Hase, *Lateinamerika als Krisenherd*, 428–72.
[3] Bülow, *Denkwürdigkeiten*, vol. 1, 188–89.

Asia and those of von Halle in the Americas in 1893–96, as well as von Halle's memoranda and writings, views that were confirmed by Schumacher's own experiences in China in 1897 and subsequent memoranda and publications, and not least his conversations with Tirpitz. Indeed, the evidence is overwhelming that von Halle and Schumacher were very important sources of Tirpitz's ideas. While Bülow was much more wary of antagonizing the United States, he would himself draft a list of desiderata for the German Empire later communicated to the German ambassador in London Paul von Hatzfeld in June 1898 of territories that he hoped could be purchased or negotiated: in Africa, the southern parts of Angola, Walvis Bay, the islands of Zanzibar and Pemba, and northern Mozambique to the Zambesi; and in Asia, Timor, the Sulu Archipelago, one of the main Philippine islands (preferably Mindanao), the Caroline Islands, and the Samoan Islands.[4]

During the Spanish-American War Germany contemplated seizing the Caroline Islands, the Sulu Archipelago, and the Philippine islands of Mindanao and Palwan. Originally Tirpitz had proposed seizing Manila, but holding such a naval base was only feasible after the expansion of the fleet.[5] Still, the American ambassador in Berlin, Andrew White, told the German Foreign Office that the United States had no objections to these German ambitions.[6] On May 18th the German East Asian Cruiser Squadron in Kiaochow was ordered to dispatch its flagship *Kaiser*, the cruiser *Cormoran*, and three other mostly obsolete cruisers (*Kaiserin Augusta*, *Prinzess Wilhelm*, and *Irene*) to Manila to make the German presence known and inspect various prospective Philippine islands.[7] The French, English, and Japanese also sent naval squadrons to observe the US naval blockade of the Philippines, to evacuate their nationals if necessary, and to gain advantage should opportunity arise, yet the US government became particularly alarmed by the German presence. While this American mistrust was due in part to the size of the German armada and its orders to learn from the conflict by close observation of Spanish-American naval engagement, the British government was eager to exploit these tensions in order to block any German initiatives in the Philippines.[8] Already in May 1898 the American ambassador in London, John Hay, had received a string of ominous letters from his friend in the British Embassy in Berlin, Cecil Spring-Rice (1859–1918), warning of Germany's dangerous "designs" in the Pacific.[9]

---

[4] Winzen, *Reichskanzler*, 88.
[5] Herwig, *"Luxury" Fleet*, 99–100; Canis, *Von Bismarck zur Weltpolitik*, 279.
[6] Mitchell, *The Danger of Dreams*, 27.
[7] Herwig, *"Luxury" Fleet*, 100; Herold, *Reichsgewalt bedeutet Seegewalt*, 302–13. Cf. Mitchell, *The Danger of Dreams*, 29–30.
[8] Bülow, *Denkwürdigkeiten*, vol. 1, 221; Canis, *Von Bismarck zur Weltpolitik*, 279.
[9] Mitchell, *The Danger of Dreams*, 27.

German public opinion showed definite sympathies for Spain, which may have added to these suspicions.[10]

That mistrust was shared by the American commanding admiral in the Philippines, George Dewey (1837–1917), who viewed every German action as a provocation and easily lost his temper.[11] The German admiral, Otto von Diederich, nevertheless observed strict neutrality and refused to accept Dewey's arbitrary (and illegal) demand to board neutral vessels as Diederich was scouting out islands in the archipelago – at the time there was no expectation that the United States intended to annex the islands.[12] Behind the scenes the British press fanned the flames of distrust between the two admirals, and as the British controlled the cable to the United States, sent disparaging reports on the Germans to the United States. Together with Dewey's later complaints when back in Washington, these press reports began to spread a distorted picture in the United States of Germany as an aggressive bully.[13]

The British, for their part, responded much as they had during the Venezuela Crisis of 1895 and annexation of Hawaii by bending over backward to appease this aggressive American expansionism in the Caribbean and Pacific, putting their own naval bases and cables at American disposal. Indeed, Colonial Secretary Chamberlain praised the American victory in the Philippines and hoped it would help forge an Anglo-Saxon alliance.[14] The British were at the time eager to draw in the Americans for help against Russian encroachment in China and Korea.[15] The German Foreign Office had thought that German claims to some parts of the Philippines were legitimate compensation for the effective US annexation of Hawaii in 1893 (formalized in 1898), but the move required both British and American agreement for which the British had effectively poisoned the well.[16] The president of the Dominican Republic, fearing US annexation, offered the Germans an island for lease, but Bülow had to decline for fear of antagonizing the United States even more.[17] For similar reasons nothing ever became of plans to purchase Curaçao and St. Thomas.

After the arrival of American naval reinforcements and the surrender of Manila by the Spanish in mid-August 1898, Germany de-escalated the tensions in the Philippines by withdrawing their cruisers and essentially giving up any hope of gaining territory in the Philippines. Instead they focused on the Spanish South Pacific. Following negotiations with the United States, Spain, and Britain, the Germans managed only to purchase the tiny and far-flung Caroline, Palau, and Mariana Islands (excepting Guam) from Spain in

---

[10] Bülow, *Deutsche Politik*, 47; Carroll, *Germany and the Great Powers*, 411–16.
[11] Mitchell, *The Danger of Dreams*, 29; Herwig, *"Luxury" Fleet*, 100–101.
[12] Mitchell, *The Danger of Dreams*, 29–30.   [13] Ibid., 30–31.   [14] Ibid., 31.
[15] Canis, *Von Bismarck zur Weltpolitik*, 278.   [16] Ibid., 279–80.   [17] Ibid., 280.

February 1899, a very modest prize indeed given earlier ambitions in the Philippines.[18] The jewels of the Spanish Empire – Guam, the Philippines, Puerto Rico, and other parts of the Spanish West Indies – along with Wake Island had, of course, been seized by the United States. It now had its springboard to China and controlled the deepwater passages to a future canal on the Central American isthmus – indeed, Tirpitz's nightmare of "Panamericanism" seemed to be looming on the horizon.

Henry Farnam wrote Gustav Schmoller in September 1898 of his pleasure with the successful completion of the Spanish-American War in light of the limited training of the soldiers. He also believed that Puerto Rico and Cuba ought to be linked to the United States, given the close economic ties, but he was opposed to the annexation of the Philippines, where over the next three years the United States would wage a savage war that would leave 20,000 Filipino fighters and an estimated 200,000 Filipino civilians dead.[19] Indeed, Farnam could not fail to express his concern with the widespread jingoistic sentiments then current in America:

> Apparently there is a large number, possibly a majority of my countrymen, who embrace the so-called imperialism. Various motivations are heard. There are some who believe that the conquest of distant islands is necessary for our trade; the others impose the duty to take them out of pure philanthropy in order to grace them with our free institutions. That others might have something to say about it does not enter the thought of our "jingos." There are already signs of a retreat of public opinion. The voice of the workers is very important, who see that Imperialism must as a consequence lead to the suspension of the current restrictions on immigration and who must feel threatened in their life circumstances.[20]

Not surprisingly, the Spanish-American War and the robust expansion of American exports that accompanied it heightened already existing concerns among German shipping companies, merchants, bankers, industrialists, and

---

[18] Herold, *Reichsgewalt bedeutet Seegewalt*, 321–22; Canis, *Von Bismarck zur Weltpolitik*, 280. See also Herwig, *"Luxury" Fleet*, 101–2; Mommsen, *Bürgerstolz und Weltmachtstreben*, 315.

[19] GStA PK, VI. HA Nl. Schmoller, Nr. 190b, fols. 184–85, Henry Farnam to Gustav Schmoller, Sept. 7, 1898; George C. Herring, *From Colony to Superpower: U.S. Foreign Relations since 1776* (Oxford and New York: Oxford University Press, 2009), 329; Glenn Anthony May, "Was the Philippine-American War a 'Total War,'" in *Anticipating Total War: The German and American Experiences, 1871–1914*, ed. Manfred Boemeke, Roger Chickering, and Stig Förster (Washington, DC: German Historical Institute; Cambridge: Cambridge University Press, 1999), 437–57; Smith, "The Logic of Colonial Violence," 205–31.

[20] GStA PK, VI. HA Nl. Schmoller, Nr. 190b, fols. 184–85, Henry Farnam to Gustav Schmoller, Sept. 7, 1898. See Stephen Kinzer, *The True Flag: Theodore Roosevelt, Mark Twain, and the Birth of American Empire* (New York: Henry Holt, 2017).

farmers about *die amerikanische Gefahr* (the American peril) and the country's Panamerican ambitions.[21] Apart from highlighting Germany's naval and diplomatic weakness – and thus reinforcing the logic of a larger bluewater navy – the Spanish-American War marked the United States' emergence as an overseas imperial power, one far more aggressive than Germany yet appeased by Britain at nearly every turn. Once again, despite alliance overtures from Chamberlain, the British had reacted aggressively to German weakness and accommodated American strength in a great reshuffling of European colonial territory.

Be that as it may, mixed signals were coming out of Whitehall in 1898, and definite shifts in British policy driven by perceptions of imperial vulnerability and diplomatic isolation were afoot that still appeared to offer opportunities for German *Welltpolitik*. In a speech given by Chamberlain in Birmingham on May 13, 1898, he openly advocated for an alliance with Germany and the United States, and on initiative of Chamberlain, a secret Anglo-German agreement to partition the Portuguese colonies in the event of a Portuguese default on British loans was signed in August 1998, giving credence to the idea that Britain's desire for an alliance could be used to extract colonial concessions. The near clash of France and Britain at Fashoda on the Upper Nile that autumn lent credibility to the related notion that differences between Britain and the Franco-Russian Alliance could also be exploited to Germany's advantage.[22]

Despite the modesty of Kiaochow and the Spanish territory purchased in the Pacific, by 1899 Germany had become an Asian and Pacific power, a *Weltmacht* in reach, if not yet in naval grasp. Of crucial importance was some kind of coaling station between Kiaochow and German East Africa and a base for a necessary submarine cable network connecting the Chinese leasehold with Berlin and the rest of the German overseas empire. For these purposes Tirpitz had his eye on the Siamese island of Langkawi in the Straits of Malacca. While that was still a longer-term ambition, in the meantime eyes fell on Samoa as an important naval base between Kiaochow and South America and a submarine cable point between South America, German New Guinea, and East Africa, offering also some prospect of control over the sea lanes that would open up by an isthmian canal in Central America.[23]

The Germans felt they had a strong entitlement to control the Samoan Islands as a German protectorate due to the long involvement of Hanseatic merchants in Samoa dating back to 1856. By the 1870s the Hamburg firm Johann Cesar Godeffroy & Sohn had managed to monopolize the Samoan

---

[21] See esp. Fiebig-von Hase, *Lateinamerika als Konfliktherd*, 320–60.
[22] See Hammann, *The World Policy of Germany*, 78–82; Charmley, *Splendid Isolation*, 262–69.
[23] Herwig, "Luxury Fleet," 101–2.

copra trade, expanding its operations to the Society, Fiji, Caroline, and Palau Islands and acquiring land in Samoa and elsewhere for coconut and cotton plantations.[24] These were operated by its Samoan company, Deutsche Handels- und Plantagen-Gesellschaft (DHPG) based in Apia, Samoa, which in 1879 employed no fewer than 1,879 people on over 4,000 acres of plantation land, along with a merchant fleet of some 100 vessels in its South Pacific trade. A German naval base also began operating in Apia in the 1880s, and the company's representative served as German consul.[25] By that point British missionaries and traders and the American navy also operated in the islands, if on a smaller scale than the Germans.[26] Elsewhere in the South Pacific, Britain had annexed the Fiji Islands in 1874, and one year later the United States signed a treaty with the Hawaiian king that secured exclusive trading rights in the archipelago. By 1883 DHPG's plantations were being raided with impunity by native Samoans while Germany's claims in Samoa were being openly challenged by New Zealanders demanding the annexation of the islands by Wellington. The Germans responded by pressing the Samoan king Malietoa Laupepa (1841–98) into a German-Samoan agreement in 1884, which granted the Germans de jure control over the islands' police force, judiciary, and treasury.[27]

When German consular officials tried to install the head of a pro-German native royal faction as Samoan king in 1887, the Americans responded by sending warships to the South Pacific leading Berlin to back down and broker a US-British-German condominium over the Samoan Islands in 1889.[28] Not satisfied with the Hawaiian Islands, whose monarchy they had toppled in 1893, American interests began to expand in the eastern Samoan Islands in the mid-1890s, notably on the Island of Tatuila, where they sought to establish a coaling station. When Malietoa Laupepa died in August 1898, Mata'afa Iosefo (1832–1912) returned from exile to claim the throne, sanctioned by the Samoan assemblies and supported by the Germans. The Americans and British feared a German takeover of the islands and came to support Malietoa Tanumafili (1879–1939) of a rival Samoan royal faction for leadership. In the

---

[24] Gründer, *Geschichte der deutschen Kolonien*, 90.
[25] Ibid., 90–91. On the dominance of German trade in Samoa by the 1880s, see Paul M. Kennedy, *The Samoan Tangle: A Study in Anglo-German Relations 1878–1900* (New York: Harper & Row, 1974), 6–25; Alfred Vagts, *Deutschland und die Vereinigten Staaten in der Weltpolitik*, vol. 1 (London: Lovat Dickinson & Thompson, 1935), 637; Hartmut Pogge von Strandmann, *Imperialismus vom grünen Tisch: deutsche Kolonialpolitik zwischen wirtschaftlicher Ausbeutung und „zivilisatorischen" Bemühungen* (Berlin: Links, 2009), 301.
[26] See Vagts, *Deutschland und die Vereinigten Staaten*, vol. 1, 636–47.
[27] Kennedy, *The Samoan Tangle*, 28, 32–38.
[28] Gründer, *Geschichte der deutschen Kolonien*, 95–96; see also Vagts, *Deutschland und die Vereinigten Staaten*, vol. 1, 637–95.

Figure 5.1   "The New World Order: A View into the Twentieth Century, by Bellamy-Jingo," *Kladderdatsch*, Aug. 14, 1898.

ensuing civil strife, the Americans sent warships to Samoa. In March 1899 Apia was bombarded by US and British ships and marines were landed, damaging German plantations and occupying the German consulate. Germany and the United States only narrowly avoided a naval clash sparked by these tensions.[29]

German public opinion, particularly Pan-German and pro-colonial voices within it, were convinced that Britain and the United States had violated the terms of the Samoan condominium and feared Germany's humiliation in the Philippines would be repeated, this time in an area of direct German interest.[30] While Bülow recognized the importance of Samoa to German public opinion and sought ways to secure the islands, he acknowledged that Germany's navy was too weak to assert claims in the islands vis-à-vis Britain or the United States. The only solution, he argued, was a negotiated settlement.[31] Bülow and

---

[29] *GPEK*, vol. 14, 567–68, 567n; Charmley, *Splendid Isolation*, 269–71; Hammann, *The World Policy of Germany*, 84–88. In greater detail, see Kennedy, *The Samoan Tangle*, 51–155; Vagts, *Deutschland und die Vereinigten Staaten*, vol. 1, 797–884.
[30] See for example "Bülow von Upulu," *Die Zukunft* 27 (Apr. 22, 1899): 145–49. See also Kennedy, *Anglo-German Antagonism*, 238.
[31] Pogge von Strandmann, *Imperialismus vom grünen Tisch*, 308–9.

the rest of the government were subsequently much criticized for following what was seen as too pro-British a line.[32] Both the Spanish-American War and the Samoan troubles offer a context for understanding the unfavorable official German position regarding the disarmament proposals of Tsar Nicholas II that culminated in the First Hague Conference held in May–July 1899.[33]

## The Second Navy Bill and the Free Union for Naval Lectures

The humiliations of the Spanish-American War and then the tensions in Samoa in 1899 were like fuel to the fires of naval enthusiasm in Germany. With growing public support for the navy and then the outbreak of the Boer War on October 11, 1899, the Kaiser gave an impetuous speech about the urgent need to increase the size of the fleet at a banquet of the Hamburg Senate on October 18th. Shortly thereafter, Tirpitz, Bülow, and Hohenlohe agreed to take advantage of the situation by introducing a new navy bill much earlier than originally planned.[34] The new bill was announced by the Kaiser to the federal princes on November 2, 1899, and a draft of the bill was promised for the winter. Tirpitz justified the new bill in the Federal Council on the grounds that the Spanish-American War had made the thinner-armored ships of the Germany navy obsolete.[35]

A draft bill gradually emerged from feverish activity within the Imperial Navy Office that autumn. Particular pressure was on von Halle, who was charged with gathering the statistics, compiling the tables, and drafting the memoranda to accompany the bill when it was to be presented to the Reichstag, materials that were deemed crucial for securing its passage.[36] As it took form the bill represented a quantum leap for Germany into the ranks of first-rate naval powers, calling for one additional squadron of 8 battleships, along with 2 heavy and 6 light cruisers. Additionally, 3 other heavy cruisers were proposed to protect shipping and show the flag overseas.[37] Among the reasons given to justify the bill, it was argued – in orthodox Mahanian terms – that the United States and Japan were expanding their navies in line with their expanding trade. Thus, the German navy needed to grow commensurate with Germany's own growing maritime commercial interests. Above all, it needed to be of sufficient strength to survive attack from the greatest of all sea powers – a barely-veiled reference to Great Britain.[38]

---

[32] Canis, *Von Bismarck zur Weltpolitik*, 312.
[33] Cf. Mommsen, *Bürgerstolz und Weltmachtstreben*, 318–20.
[34] Deist, *Flottenpolitik*, 156; Winzen, *Bülows Weltmachtkonzept*, 99–101.
[35] Kelly, *Tirpitz*, 180–81.
[36] On his role in this activity, see Deist, *Flottenpolitik*, 80, 80n33, 113–15.
[37] Kelly, *Tirpitz*, 181.    [38] Ibid., 182.

Unquestionably, the Navy Office intended to leverage the anti-British public sentiment whipped up by the Samoa tensions and Boer War in order to assure passage of the new bill. While Tirpitz began actively courting Reichstag allies in the Center Party for the campaign to come, the Navy Office's Communications Bureau scrambled to action to cultivate public opinion, drawing once again on the fleet professors who had been mobilized so effectively by Heeringen in 1897.[39] By this point Tirpitz and Heeringen were drawing on the findings of a lengthy memorandum commissioned by the RMA and written by the German naval attaché in London in November 1897 on the effective naval publicity methods deployed by the Royal Navy during the naval campaigns of 1887, 1888, and 1893, which had included planting news stories in the press via sympathetic journalists and newspaper editors, speeches by prominent naval officers, pamphlets, maritime novels, gala ship christenings, naval exhibits, and the founding of the Navy League in 1894. Key to the effective British campaign, the memo noted, was the careful cultivation of the press to affect a longer-term change in public opinion toward a national consensus supportive of the navy irrespective of party political affiliation.[40]

Like von Halle and Schumacher, Gustav Schmoller had been giving speeches and writing articles on the theme of German *Weltpolitik* and the role of the German fleet beginning in 1898, contributing to such newspapers and journals as *Die Jugend, Tägliche Rundschau,* and *Die Woche,* and he was solicited for many more.[41] Schmoller and the other fleet professors were invited to join the new German Navy League in June 1898, which had been founded in April of that year by representatives of German heavy industry and banking. However, they stipulated that they would join only on condition that the composition of its managing board be broadened to include opinions besides those of conservative industrialists.[42] These concerns were shared by Heeringen, who himself had a strained relationship with the Navy League's secretary, the Krupp-affiliated Victor Schweinburg, over coordination of the pro-fleet propaganda.[43] The refusal of the Navy League to meet these conditions led Schmoller and his colleagues – supported by the Communications Bureau of the RMA – to found their own body in November 1899, the Free Union for Naval Lectures (Freie Vereinigung für Flottenvorträge), to deliver

---

[39] Deist, *Flottenpolitik*, 156–57.   [40] Geppert, *Pressekriege*, 235–38.
[41] For example, "Was lehren uns die Vorgänge in Samoa?" *Die Woche* 1, no. 5 (1899). Schmoller was asked in January 1898 to write an article in the *Neuste Nachrichten* by the editor, Otto Friedrich Koch, under the heading "Was ist uns China?" GStA PK, VI. HA Nl. Schmoller, Nr. 190a, fols. 216–17, Otto Koch to Gustav Schmoller, Jan. 4, 1898.
[42] GStA PK, VI. HA Nl. Schmoller, Nr. 190c, fol. 171. Gustav Schmoller to Victor Schweinburg [draft], June 15, 1898. See also Deist, *Flottenpolitik*, 153; Eley, *Reshaping the German Right,* 85–86; Kehr, *Schlachtflottenbau,* 171.
[43] Deist, *Flottenpolitik*, 157–58.

popular lectures on behalf of the fleet throughout Germany.[44] A loose association inspired and co-founded by the nationalist writer Julius Lohmeyer (1835-1903), the Free Union was nevertheless quite a sophisticated and effective pressure group because of the broad range of expertise from which it drew, its apparent disinterestedness and independence, and the academic authority of many of its participants.[45] Its founding appeal of November 18, 1899, was signed by no fewer than sixty-seven prominent academics, writers, artists, and businessmen, including the painter Max Liebermann (1847-1935), the novelist Wilhelm Raabe (1831-1910), and the industrialist Wilhelm von Siemens (1855-1919) as well as by Schmoller and Sering.[46]

The appeal made much of the connections between the necessary expansion of the fleet and Germany's domestic cultural and material life, but it also made distinctly Pan-German (and Tirpitzian) claims by arguing that the larger fleet would help to preserve Germandom abroad by connecting German settlers dispersed in the world with the fatherland and its language, culture, and *Wissenschaft*.[47] But above all it argued that recent history had shown how essential naval power now was. It made the case that in wake of the Spanish-American War, an effective battle fleet was now a matter of life or death for any great power. It argued that France's capitulation at Fashoda and Maskat and Germany's humiliation in Samoa were due to insufficient naval arms. Germany's larger navy would help uphold world peace, and it would make Germany a sought-after friend and a feared enemy.[48] The undersigned hoped to awaken an appreciation for the "urgent political, economic, and moral necessity of maritime trade, maritime life, [and] sea power" in those circles still closed to the idea. The speakers would offer lectures in north and south Germany in a popular tone independent of any political party united in their common conviction that only a nation's standing at sea makes it rich and strong.[49] The appeal thus echoed most of the themes that were at the center of German navalism and *Weltpolitik* discussed at length in Chapter 4.

The success of the professors associated with the Free Union in influencing public opinion on behalf of the second navy bill meant that the Navy League was initially eclipsed as the organizational locus of fleet advocacy coordinated by the Navy Office.[50] What is more, Schmoller and his colleagues succeeded in imposing fundamental changes to the Navy League's managing board to include liberals and social reformers. Pressure was put on Victor Schweinburg,

---

[44] Marienfeld, *Wissenschaft und Schlachtflottenbau*, 86; Deist, *Flottenpolitik*, 158-59.
[45] GStA PK, VI. HA Nl. Schmoller, Nr. 192a, fols. 42-43, Julius Lohmeyer, Cenralstelle der "Freien Vereinigung für deutsche Flottenvorträge" to Gustav Schmoller, Berlin, March 3, 1900. See also Deist, *Flottenpolitik*, 113.
[46] Anhang, Anlage 1: Gründingsaufruf der Freien Vereinigung für Flottenvorträge, in Marienfeld, *Wissenschaft und Schlachtflottenbau*, 108-9.
[47] Ibid., 108.   [48] Ibid.   [49] Ibid., 108-9.   [50] Deist, *Flottenpolitik*, 103, 158-59.

to resign, and Schmoller played a key role in forcing the resignation of Octavio von Zedlitz-Neukirch (1840–1919).[51] This had to do with Schmoller's own personal hostility toward Zedlitz because the latter had subjected Schmoller and other "socialists of the chair" to withering criticism in the debates over university expenditures in the Prussian Diet in 1897. Zedlitz, along with the industrialist Carl Ferdinand Stumm (1836–1901), had not only attacked the commitment to social reform and supposed softness on socialism of Schmoller and other academics, but also had questioned their very competence as scholars.[52] With Zedlitz and Schweinburg gone, the basis for closer cooperation between the Navy League, the fleet professors, and the Navy Office's Communications Bureau was finally established, allowing the transformation of the Navy League into a mass organization less burdened by its associations with heavy industry.[53] It grew quite dramatically in the second half of 1899, nearly doubling its membership between June and December to almost 250,000.[54]

## Gustav Schmoller: Germany's Economic Future

The speeches given for the Free Union for Naval Lectures are revealing for how consistently they emphasized the importance of the battle fleet to Germany's international power struggles with Russia, the United States, and England, the struggle for export markets in a rising climate of protectionism, and the role of the fleet in sustaining and expanding German commercial and colonial interests worldwide. In his capacity as a member of the Free Union, Schmoller himself crisscrossed Germany in late 1899 and early 1900 on a lecture tour that generated extensive German and international press attention.[55] The speech Schmoller first gave in the Berlin Philharmonic November 28, 1899 and then in Strasbourg and Hanover in late January 1900 was later published in revised form as "The Economic Future of Germany and the Navy Bill" in a collected volume published by the Free Union under the appropriate

---

[51] GStA PK, VI. HA Nl. Schmoller, Nr. 191b, fols. 170–71, Secretariat of the German Navy League to Gustav Schmoller, Dec. 14, 1899; cf. Deist, *Flottenpolitik*, 159; Kelly, *Tirpitz*, 183.

[52] Prussian Landtag, Stenographische Berichte, Haus der Abgeordneten, vol. 3, 75th session (May 4, 1897), 2380–83; Prussian Landtag, Stenographische Berichte, Herrenhaus, vol. 1, 19th session (May 28, 1897), 382–88.

[53] Deist, *Flottenpolitik*, 159–63; Diziol, *Flottenverein*, vol. 1, 58–59, 64–65, 91–127.

[54] Kelly, *Tirpitz*, 168.

[55] "Professor Schmoller über die Flotte," *Hamburgerischer Correspondent*, Nov. 29, 1899; "Eine Flottenrede von Gustav Schmoller," *Breslauer Zeitung*, Morgen-Ausgabe, Nov. 30, 1899; "Die deutschen Universitäten und die Flottenbewegung," *Hamburgerischer Correspondent*, Morgen-Ausgabe, June 10, 1900; "Talk of German Future," *Chicago Tribune*, July 14, 1900.

title *Handels- und Machtpolitik* (Trade and Power Politics).[56] It is worth discussing in detail because it drew very heavily from the insights his students Sering, Rathgen, Schumacher, and von Halle had gained in North America, Japan, China, South America, and the Caribbean.

Schmoller began with a discussion of the disappointing economic upswing of 1894–1900 and the admonition that Germany had better accustom itself to a more difficult international economic climate or else broaden its economic horizons and secure a sufficient economic basis, particularly in light of its rapidly growing population. With growth of 1 percent yearly, Schmoller projected no fewer than 104 million Germans by 1965, and as many as 208 million by 2135, a demographic expansion that demanded an international outlet, given the European territorial strictures of the Reich. More fearsome than these figures were those he cited of the French publicist Henri Leroy-Beaulieu (1842–1912), who predicted no fewer than 200 million Germans by 1999. Interestingly, Schmoller was positively enthusiastic about this population surplus as it assured Germany's place in the international *"Wasserwanderung"* (water migration) for new settlements, a development that had yet to reach its climax and would ultimately determine the rank of nations.[57] In light of the vast size of the populations of the three great world empires, growth in the German population to 100–150 million was "neither a fantasy nor undesired. It should, it will, it must come, if we want to remain a great and powerful people. And it cannot be accommodated exclusively in the old homeland. We must have farmer colonies and territories of cultivation that can absorb this surplus. Let us see to it if and by how much we can increase our home population."[58] There is not much handwringing here about demographic time bombs and their social implications for Germany.

Equally interesting about this speech is that Schmoller was resigned to the fact that German agricultural productivity had strict limits and that therefore Germany would remain a country that imports a substantial portion of its food grains. Unlike agriculture, however, he noted that industry had no such strictures, encouragingly mentioning that the latest economic upswing was based much more on a boost in domestic consumption than on exports of industrial goods. Nevertheless, with rising population density, exports needed to expand to ensure the importation of foodstuffs, raw materials, and colonial goods. The fact was, he asserted, that no large nation could exist and move

---

[56] Gustav Schmoller, Max Sering, and Adolf Wagner, eds., *Handels- und Machtpolitik: Reden und Aufsätze im Auftrage der "Freien Vereinigung für Flottenvorträge,"* vol. 1, 2nd ed. (Stuttgart: J. G. Cotta, 1900), 1–38; reprinted in Gustav Schmoller, "Die wirtschaftliche Zukunft Deutschlands und die Flottenvorlage," in *Zwanzig Jahre Deutscher Politik (1897–1917): Aufsätze und Vorträge von Gustav Schmoller*, ed. Lucie Schmoller (Munich and Leipzig: Duncker & Humblot, 1920), 1–20.
[57] Schmoller, "Die wirtschaftliche Zukunft," in *Zwanzig Jahre*, 1–6.    [58] Ibid., 6.

forward without vast imports and exports, without being interwoven into the world economy, and the threats posed by this dependence on the world market receded to the degree that a state had colonies and naval power. Germany's "impotence on the seas" would therefore have to end. With the stagnation of exports over the last twenty-five years, only the highest degree of technical, intellectual, organizational, and social political progress would lead to an export expansion, but only on the basis of a far-sighted trade policy and good trade treaties, so that the production of food and colonial goods, as well as the importation of German industrial goods in the colonies, were secured. All of these things necessitated a larger fleet. Aided by the fleet, colonial development could also retain for Germany the twenty million emigrants projected for the twentieth century.[59]

Much of the remainder of Schmoller's speech was based on the insight that trade policy could no longer be pursued independently of the power politics of states. Only by following the most ruthless piracy, destruction of rival shipping, seizure of colonies, and fraudulent trade treaties, through harsh navigation laws, steep tariffs, and import-export prohibitions, he recalled, had England emerged following the Napoleonic wars with a consolidated economy and an unchallenged international position. This had facilitated the spread of the liberal economic doctrine that became the basis for the long era of peace from 1815 to 1870 that had so benefited Germany, providing the conditions for the humane commercial interaction of states in the modern world economy.[60] This, he reminded his audience, was possible as long as Cobden's ideas held sway and Gladstone led Britain. Had Britain abandoned its fleet and colonies as Cobden and Gladstone had proposed, Schmoller noted, Germany would not have any "*Flottensorgen*" (fleet worries).[61]

Schmoller believed that rising international competition and growing populations after 1870, combined with a new scramble for colonial possessions and protected spheres of influence, demonstrated that international competitive struggles remained power struggles. Britain under Disraeli helped to initiate an era in which prohibitions, tariffs, blockades, search and seizure of shipping, and prohibitions on the use of sea cables and coaling stations had become the order of the day. While announcing in 1876 that Britain was satiated and not an aggressive power, Disraeli had seized Natal, Cyprus, Egypt, and Burma. The territory of Great Britain between 1866 and 1899, Schmoller mentioned, had grown from 12.6 to 27.8 million square kilometers, thirty times that of the German Empire. The United States between 1800 and 1900 grew from over 2 to 9.3 million square kilometers and Russia between 1866 and 1899 from 12.9 to 22.4 million square kilometers. He believed that events over the last generation had created a wholly changed world and a

---

[59] Ibid., 6–9.  [60] Ibid., 9–12.  [61] Ibid., 12.

different foundation for international economic relations. In place of a community of equal and peaceful states, three conquering world empires emerged against which all other smaller states paled. Only France and Germany had a position in between these three "conquering and colonizing empires" and the smaller states.[62] Moreover, it was in the freest states, Britain and the United States, that tendencies to conquest, plans for imperialism, and hostility to up-and-coming economic competitors had emerged out of popular sentiment fanned by unscrupulous plutocratic leaders. The conquest by the United States of Cuba and the Philippines and its tendency to seek to exclude the Europeans from North and South American markets, as well as Britain's war against the Boers and its plans to dominate sub-Saharan Africa and bring the British Empire into a closer union to the exclusion of others, all necessarily led to greater conflicts with other states.[63]

In the final sections of his speech, Schmoller asserted that the dangers to Germany's trade and colonies by a "relapse to mercantilism" had long existed and were hardly created by plans for a larger fleet. But Germany, he claimed, did not aspire to a chauvinistic *Weltmachtspolitik*; it did not wish to become a naval and colonial power of the rank of Britain but only to expand its trade and industry, support a growing population, defend its colonies, and acquire a farmer colony somewhere. It was Germany's aim, he asserted, to oppose the exaggerated "robber mercantilism" and division of the earth by the three great world empires. To do so, a larger fleet was needed; the larger fleet would deter attack from these powers and at the same time win over the smaller and medium-sized states of Europe, who by joining into peaceful economic union with Germany could have their own colonies protected. In any case, according to Schmoller, Germany had become too large and powerful, and its competition too uncomfortable to the great world empires, to allow the competitive struggle to be conducted without proper naval armaments.[64]

Some of Schmoller's concluding proposals were not without Pan-German accents, such as his call to establish a large German settler colony in southern Brazil or Venezuela and to forge a customs union with Switzerland, Austria, Scandinavia, and Holland.[65] Closer customs, trade, and colonial ties to Holland were particularly enticing to Schmoller; Germany could gain access to colonial ports, coaling stations, and undersea telegraph cables in return for guaranteeing Holland's political independence and colonial possessions. More broadly, Schmoller asserted, it was only through a fleet and a leasehold such as Kiaochow in China that the East Asian and Central and South American markets, with such promise for the future, could be held open.[66] But as he noted in his conclusion, the matter at hand was not to put up a defensive

---

[62] Ibid., 13.    [63] Ibid., 14.    [64] Ibid., 14–19.
[65] Ibid., 19; cf. Fiebig-von Hase, *Lateinamerika als Krisenherd*, 216.
[66] Schmoller, "Die wirtschaftliche Zukunft Deutschlands," 20.

bulwark against encroachment and play second fiddle to rivals. Rather, Germany's many achievements demanded an outward expansion from which the rest of the world would benefit:

> [Germany] no longer wishes to be the nursery and schoolroom of the rest of the world, a land that sends out millions of its sons abroad so that they cease being Germans in the next generation. Its state, its energy, its scholarship and its technology, its trade and its reputation in the world are so great ... [and] its moral und intellectual qualities, its affective life, its fine arts, its diligence, its institutions stand so high that it can demand in the interest of the *Kultur* of humanity to assert, on the basis of its own law, own colonies, own stations, its own influence of power, its place in the world economy next to and following the great three world empires.[67]

Schmoller's speech is noteworthy for the degree to which it remained focused on international economic competition and tensions, particularly on the strategic threats of the new imperialism for Germany, which he saw increasingly squeezed by the United States, Russia, and, especially, Great Britain. He envisioned Germany as a player in this international premier league, and it was implicit, if not always explicit, that he sought to establish Germany as the fourth great world empire. Just as importantly, the justifications for *Weltpolitik* and the fleet were neither vague nor had they been quickly cooked up to serve a naval agenda; they were based upon scholarly convictions that had emerged out of the direct investigations of Germany's *Weltwirtschaft* by his students and conversations with Tirpitz that predated the first and second German navy bills of 1897 and 1899.

## Max Sering: The Trade Policy of the Great States

It should not be surprising that Max Sering, Ernst von Halle, and Hermann Schumacher would also play a direct role in the Free Union's activities. Max Sering gave a speech in the Berlin Philharmonic on February 14, 1900, entitled "The Trade Policy of the Great States and the Battle Fleet" that was published in the second volume of *Handels- und Machtpolitik*.[68] Likewise, both Ernst von Halle and Hermann Schumacher contributed essays to that volume for the Free Union.[69] Ernst von Halle's essay "The Development and Significance of

---

[67] Ibid.
[68] Max Sering, "Die Handelspolitik der Grossstaaten und die Kriegsflotte," in *Handels- und Machtpolitik: Reden und Aufsätze im Auftrage der "Freien Vereinigung für Flottenvorträge,"* ed. Gustav Schmoller, Max Sering, and Adolph Wagner, vol. 2, 2nd ed. (Stuttgart: J. G. Cotta, 1900), 1–44.
[69] Ernst von Halle, "Die Entwicklung und Bedeutung der deutschen Reederei," in *Handels- und Machtpolitik*, vol. 2, 127–74; Hermann Schumacher, "Deutschlands Interessen in China," in *Handels- und Machtpolitik*, vol. 2, 175–246.

German Shipping Industry" and Hermann Schumacher's essay "Germany's Interests in China" were added to fully round out the topics offering reasons for an expanded navy. Both the latter two's direct and close involvement with Tirpitz and the Communications Bureau and their junior status were likely among the reasons they were not part of the Free Union's lecture circuit. In any case, these essays are worth discussing in some detail because they reflect not only their respective experiences abroad and thus the transnational origins of Germany's *Weltpolitik* to an uncanny degree, but also because, in the case of von Halle and Schumacher, they represent positions closest to those held by Tirpitz.

Sering's speech was his first attempt to link his deep knowledge of the United States with German power politics and navalism. He took as his starting point Schmoller's position that the economy was inseparable from matters of state, and both were currently governed by forces of expansion, a process that had begun to accelerate in the 1870s. Today, Sering argued, Germany was heavily reliant on imported minerals and other raw materials and consumed ever larger quantities of imported foodstuffs and luxuries, currently amounting to imports worth 5.5 billion marks. All of this was driven primarily by the rapid growth of Germany's population, the growth of its needs, and new technology. Germany's world trade, he surmised, had turned it into an "ocean state" (*Seestaat*) in a true sense.[70] Hamburg was now the second largest port on the European continent, and Germany possessed the second largest merchant marine in the world, which was involved not only in meeting the needs of domestic commerce but also in coastal trade worldwide, from South America to East Asia. Germany was now the leading exporter to Austria-Hungary, Russia, and Scandinavia, and second only to Great Britain in its exports to Italy, the United States, nearly all South American countries and British India, and in third place next to Britain, France, and the United States, respectively, in its exports to France, England, Canada, Australia, and the Cape Colony.[71]

Britain's free trade, achieved through ruthless trade and colonial wars of conquest conducted over hundreds of years and culminating in the near complete destruction of rival naval and merchant ships during the Napoleonic era, was the foundation of Britain's undisputed hegemony in trade, a policy that was in the interests of Britain's great industries.[72] But this did not prevent Britain from expanding its possessions and protectorates in the tropics through bloody wars in East India, China, and many places along the route to India.[73] Reiterating points made in Schmoller's speech, Sering argued that so long as ideas of liberal free trade and equality of peoples predominated and Britain assured access to world markets, no one imagined Germany needed

---

[70] Sering, "Die Handelspolitik," 4–5.   [71] Ibid., 6.   [72] Ibid., 7–9.   [73] Ibid., 11.

much more than a small cruiser fleet to defend its overseas interests. All of that had been shattered, however, by the Spanish-American and Boer Wars. These were not wars fought to protect threatened vital interests or to fulfill great national ideals, nor were they fought to conquer and open up semi-civilized lands. Rather, these were wars waged against other Europeans to impose foreign rule, and they were bound up closely with gaining economic advantages and capitalist expansion. These were authentic trade wars of the sort that were once fought in the age of mercantilism, premised on might and the right of the "Anglo-Saxon race" and its supposed superior culture to rule the world.[74]

The wars of aggression that had ushered in a new phase of "*Weltwirtschaft* and *Weltpolitk*" were not the result of individual hotheaded ministers or admirals but the expression of powerful popular movements, the starting points of which were the United States and Russia.[75] New technologies in railways, steamships, and telegraphs allowed the economic integration of these vast continental territories within a few decades and their emergence as true world powers, ones which by the size of their population and compactness of their territory were already now superior to the British Empire.[76] Railways had brought their grain and livestock to world agricultural markets, which they now dominated. Their great mineral wealth had led to the rapid development of efficient heavy industry, and with it great changes in the social and political structures of these states. These great changes had begun in the 1860s with the US Civil War and the freeing of the Russian serfs. In the United States, the triumph of the Union over the Confederacy meant the triumph of farmers and the distribution of free public lands to them through the Homestead Act. The spoils of war for northern commerce was the protective tariff of 1864, which had been continued to the present day through the McKinley and Dingley Acts of 1890 and 1897 under the influence of powerful of investment rings and industrial trusts, "the actual rulers of the North American republic." These were pursuing a "formal violent policy against foreign competition."[77] Together with the aid of abundant natural resources in coal, iron, copper, precious metals, and cotton, their staple industries had monopolized the internal market and were beginning to expand outward now that western frontier settlement had slowed. Economic considerations thus played a major role in the seizure of Spanish territory. Drawing directly from his extensive travels through the United States, Sering noted that the country currently encompassed a vast uninterrupted territory that extended from the summer wheat areas of the north, through to maize, cotton, and tropical zones to the south, enabling it to produce nearly every food and luxury crop domestically, an unprecedented degree of self-sufficiency.[78]

[74] Ibid., 13–14.  [75] Ibid., 14.  [76] Ibid., 16.  [77] Ibid., 17.  [78] Ibid., 18–19.

Now, however, the United States sought to expand further southward. Quoting Friedrich Ratzel, Sering claimed that just as the American settlers occupied Texas, great American capitalists were at work expanding their railway networks through Mexico, the Panama Railway through the isthmus, and the Transandine Railway in South America. Sering argued that wherever the "North Americans" gained political control, it spelled the end of European imports. Britain and Germany, the main suppliers of industrial goods to Latin America, were bound to suffer. Now with the US presence secured in the Pacific with the seizure of Guam and the Philippines, the Americans were bound to expand their reach into Asia.[79] Likely with the recent memory of Samoa on his mind, Sering argued the ruthless dynamism of the American republic should never be underestimated:

> One should not fool oneself! As much as the simultaneously exclusive and expansive policy of the United States is bound up with great capitalists, it is also carried forward by the sentiment of the public ... the American people, this selection of the energetic elements from Ireland, Germany and Great Britain, has not only been lent intellectual agility and centrifugal force by the newness of the conditions and the wide expanse of their field of activity; their great and easily-achieved successes have accustomed them to look down dismissively at other peoples. No people is less inclined to view foreign rights and interests as equal.[80]

Echoing Frederick Jackson Turner's observations in Chicago in 1893, Sering argued the closure of the American frontier posed particular challenges since a sizable proletariat was now filling American cities, and it was now widely acknowledged in the United States "that it had not been the county's democratic institutions but rather the unoccupied public lands that had spared American society the evils of the old world."[81] Conquest and colonization were the only means the country knew for abating those evils, and the recent easy victory over Spain had only emboldened those sentiments. Germans had to be prepared for a continuation of "an American policy of conquest that would continue only until the country confronted equal opponents."[82] The new invocation of the Monroe Doctrine, he claimed, meant nothing less than the seizure of the entire Western Hempisphere and further expansion into the Pacific.[83]

In other parts of his speech, Sering switched his discussion to the challenges emanating from Russia. Just as American heavy industry was bound up with the idea of "Panamericanism" so it was with the giant enterprises and cartels of southern Russia and "Panslavism" in creating a vast and protected autarkic economic zone. The new period of Russian expansion since the 1880s was motivated by economic goals, such as access to cotton in Turkestan and access

---

[79] Ibid., 19–20.   [80] Ibid., 20.   [81] Ibid., 21.   [82] Ibid.   [83] Ibid.

to Chinese and Pacific markets via railway expansion into Manchuria, the ice-free ports of Talien Bay and Port Arthur on the Liaotung Peninsula, and expanding Russian influence in Korea.[84] While not as grave or direct a challenge as the United States or Russia, France too had vastly expanded its colonial territory in Africa after 1871, a territory that now extended from the Gulf of Tunis to Congo and from Senegal to the reaches of the upper Nile, one that included significant French settlement in North Africa. It, too, was becoming a closed, self-sufficient economic system with the high tariffs imposed in 1892.[85]

Britain had been put into the defensive as a consequence of the expansionist tendencies of the United States. The founding of the Dominion of Canada in 1867, the construction of the Canadian Pacific Railway, and expansion of the naval harbor in Halifax, and relocation of the British Pacific Fleet to Esquimalt (British Columbia) was a direct response to the victory of the Union over the Confederacy and the dangerous expansionist forces this unleased.[86] Sering then discussed the various efforts to consolidate the British Empire, which had itself expanded sizably under Disraeli and how British imperialism had since embedded itself as a popular idea in Britain. Nevertheless, Sering argued that it had been trade tensions with the United States in Canada, notably American protectionism, that were behind plans for greater British imperial commercial cohesion.[87] His conclusion was very similar to Schmoller's: the potential consequence for Germany was exclusion from British colonial trade and monopolization of the world's raw materials and agricultural commodities by the "world empires."[88] Only once Germany had the means to be taken seriously as an equal, Sering argued, would it be able to negotiate fair access to this world trade. Germany's lack of leverage with the United States in trade negotiations had, for instance, led to stagnation of German exports to the United States over the last decade while American exports to Germany had expanded robustly.[89]

Germany's fate was now tied to a small European territory in danger of being excluded and ultimately overwhelmed by the "world empires," a process analogous to the relationship of the Hanseatic cities to the new territorial states of the Middle Ages, which ended in the Hanseatic League's economic decline and loss of autonomy.[90] "The calling of 'Anglo-Saxons' to rule foreign lands," Sering argued, would result in "the desolate uniformity of the English language and customs." Quoting the Cornell University professor Harry Huntington Powers (1859–1936) as a partisan of this Anglo-Saxon dominance, he noted that his ilk saw the elimination of "Boer, Maori and Castilian" and other minor nations as akin to the extinction of the Pterodactyl and

---

[84] Ibid., 22–23.   [85] Ibid., 24–25.   [86] Ibid., 27.   [87] Ibid., 28–29.   [88] Ibid., 31.
[89] Ibid., 32.   [90] Ibid., 34.

Mastodon; it was easier and more economic to eliminate these people, Powers argued, rather than "to educate these races up to our level." To that mindset this was not a loss but progress.[91]

Sering countered that in his own travels to England and the United States he was not able to recognize any superiority: no northern European land had a more depraved *Lumpenproletariat* than England, and hardly any country had a more corrupt administration than the United States.[92] Germany was envied because of its vitality and the steady advances it had made in open competition, yet because it lacked naval arms it was subject to frivolous attacks from rivals. Under such circumstances, the old policy of free trade was an anachronism, and it was a blessing that Germany had not heeded that siren song in agriculture, as it would have destroyed its middle class peasantry, as it had in England.[93]

Given Germany's reliance on imported tropical goods, copper ores, lignite, petroleum, wood, fodder grains, and fertilizer for its industrial exports, access to world markets was now a matter of life and death for Germany.[94] Under the existing circumstances, these challenges could not be met with the tools of domestic economic policy, customs unions, or alliances. With an eye squarely on the United States and its conduct in the Spanish-American War and the British and Americans in Samoa, Sering concluded that this required naval power:

> If we seek to secure our development as an independent nation, we need to expand our territory, we need colonies. ... [T]here are still significant stretches of land which have not been seized by the great world empires; a fierce struggle has broken out over the commercial, capitalistic, and political domination of these areas. And our future, our prosperity, our cultural and political significance depend on whether we are able to gain our own foothold there or prevent these areas from becoming the spoils of the already overpowering empires. This desire does not mean a restless policy of conquest, but rather the demand that we be viewed as an equal power and not be pushed aside in the still pending great liquidations, in all great questions and changes of *Weltpolitik*.
>
> The irrefutable precondition for this is a significant strengthening of our battle fleet.[95]

All German classes, including the working classes, had a common interest in the preservation of German greatness, he said. The hopes of the German social democrats that Britain's democratization through the franchise reforms

---

[91] Ibid., 35; cf. H. H. Powers, "The Ethics of Expansion," *International Journal of Ethics* 10, no. 3 (Apr. 1900): 288–306, here 294.
[92] Sering, "Die Handelspolitik," 35–36.   [93] Ibid., 37–38.   [94] Ibid., 38–39.
[95] Ibid., 40–41.

of 1867 and 1885 would usher in a more peaceful foreign policy had been shattered:

> The force of imperialist ideas and goals of conquest lies precisely in the fact that they are supported by the mass of the English-American workers. Nowhere is one further from cosmopolitan tendencies than here. Nowhere do the workers have a more spirited understanding of the inner connection between wealth and political power, between the welfare of the individual, class, and the whole – thanks to the political education they have gained through long-lived freedoms of social mobility and participation in public life.[96]

Sering hoped that the broadening of national horizons that came from "overseas politics" would clear away the petty perspectives of narrowly domestic German public life. The shattering of Germany's place as a world power would affect German farmers no less gravely than industrialists. Here the lessons of history should be heeded, as it had happened before when the disunited German states of the Holy Roman Empire confronted the new Spanish, Dutch, French, and English nation states.[97]

As this speech makes plain, Sering's deep familiarity with conditions in North America markedly heightened his sense of Germany's vulnerability. It is striking, too, how he drew many parallels between the United States and Russia, not only as vast, self-sufficient railroad empires astride entire continents, but also as the two most aggressively expansionist, protectionist, and thus menacing world powers.

## Ernst von Halle: The German Shipping Industry

Ernst von Halle's contribution to the volume *Handels- und Machtpolitik* was originally an anonymous article in *Nauticus* and dealt with the growth of the German shipping industry as a justification for a larger battle fleet, a particularly Mahanian argument and one to which Tirpitz himself much subscribed.[98] This also tapped into an area of von Halle's expertise on which he later published widely.

Von Halle began his essay by discussing the precipitous decline of Germany's flourishing Baltic, North Sea, and oceanic shipping at the turn of the nineteenth century, beginning with the British blockade of the Elbe in 1804 and then the French embargo of British trade beginning in 1806.[99] After

---

[96] Ibid., 42.   [97] Ibid., 43–44.
[98] [Ernst von Halle], "Die Entwicklung und Bedeutung der deutschen Reederei," *Nauticus* 12 (1900): 339–77; cf. Marienfeld, *Wissenschaft und Schlachtflottenbau*, 80–81.
[99] von Halle, "Die Entwicklung und Bedeutung," in *Handels- und Machtpolitik*, vol. 2, 129–31.

the Napoleonic era, the German shipping industry recovered only very slowly, as many ships were no longer seaworthy, lacked naval protection from the Barbary pirates, and the British Navigation Acts severely restricted trade of German ships with Britain and its empire.[100] Before 1850 English dominance of Hanseatic shipping was thus pronounced, English ships accounting in 1830 for no fewer than 50 percent of all ships entering into Hamburg harbor. Most of the rest were US or Scandinavian ships.[101] Only after the repeal of the British Navigation Acts, greater freedom of navigation in France and the Netherlands, the suppression of the Barbary pirates, the conclusion of trade treaties with North and South America, and the opening up of East Asia to trade after 1850 did German shipping really recover.[102] It was particularly through trade with the United States and with former Spanish and Portuguese colonies that German shipping received its first big boost, beginning what von Halle termed a transition to "*Weltwirtschaft*" (world economy) and "*Weltverkehr*" (world commerce), from which the North Sea ports in particular benefited.[103] The construction of railways worldwide, Germany's industrial development, and the rapid growth of central European emigration in the 1840s all also contributed to a successive rapid expansion of German shipping tonnage and traffic, particularly under steam. While in 1850 Hamburg still had only 9 ships driven by steam with 2,800 tons of capacity, by 1898 it had no fewer than 377 steam ships with some 514,950 register tons capacity.[104]

Despite some severe setbacks caused by the US Civil War in the 1860s and the Depression of the 1870s, the German shipping industry had made steady progress. Important steps along the way were the establishment of postal steamer connections from Hamburg and Bremen in the 1860s, and then development of weekly passenger traffic to New York, Baltimore, New Orleans, and Havana. The flag of the North German Confederation and then German Empire gave German ships greater protection in war and peace, while rapid improvements in technology allowed the construction of larger and more efficient steam ships that increased the speed of passage and reduced coal consumption.[105] Moreover, German wharves developed the capacity not only to repair foreign steam ships, but also to build their own. Undersea cables had transformed the flow of information to ships worldwide, reducing the costs and increasing the efficiency of shipping traffic, while massive investments had been made in dredging shipping channels, reinforcing costal areas, and modernizing harbor and dock facilities to make Germany's coasts and rivers accessible and safer for oceanic shipping. Together with improvements in navigation, this had reduced insurance rates. As von Halle observed, "All of these developments worked together with other technological progress to

---

[100] Ibid., 131–32.   [101] Ibid., 133.   [102] Ibid., 134–35.   [103] Ibid., 132.
[104] Ibid., 136–37.   [105] Ibid., 138–40.

create the fitting transportation instrument for world economic development to satisfy the emerging and increasing needs for the regular supply of mass goods from all over the earth."[106]

Von Halle noted that the dramatic growth of the Hamburg-America Line (HAPAG) and Norddeutscher Lloyd (NDL) in Bremen – controlling three-fourths of Germany's steamer tonnage – and which had since "entered the first ranks of the great international ocean transport companies," had been much assisted by the imperial subsidies for postal steamer service to routes little or not served by regular steamer traffic.[107] The subsidies of 1885, 1888, and 1893 enabled NDL to develop regular steamer routes through the Mediterranean to Ceylon, the Dutch East Indies, and China, with branch connections to Japan, German New Guinea, and Australia. Subsidies passed in 1890 enabled the German East Africa Line, while many other companies, including HAPAG and NDL, developed new worldwide lines independent of subsidies. In 1899 Germany's merchant marine comprised no fewer that 3,541 ships with a tonnage of 1,639,652 register tons. In having 22 steamers with a cargo capacity of over 10,000 tons each, Germany led the rest of the world in that category.[108] Nevertheless, the most important route to the German shipping industry remained the American route for which there were multiple weekly crossings with fast steamers from NDL and HAPAG to New York.[109]

Taken together, von Halle argued, "It would be impossible to overstate the significance of the upswing of the German shipping industry for Germany's maritime interests and even for the country's general economic expansion."[110] A strong German shipping industry had enabled the development of modern German shipbuilding, which in turn stimulated the metal, machine, and wood industries. German shipping firms tended to have their ships repaired and supplied in home harbors, which in turn benefited domestic suppliers of grain, meat, canned goods, delicacies, beer, wine, textiles, furniture, and wallpaper. The ability to move traded goods on German ships also improved Germany's balance of payments, he argued. German shipping had worked very closely with German industry and the German railways to fix rates in order to ease movement of transit freight. Merchants were thus spared delays, and loading, storage, and reloading charges.[111]

For many centuries, von Halle argued, other nations had recognized the many advantages to the economy of an expanding shipping industry and structured their navigation and shipping policy accordingly. That expansion was in a symbiotic relationship with the expansion of a powerful and effective navy. Some 45,000 people worked on German ships and gained a valuable education for service in the Imperial Navy, making the merchant marine a

---

[106] Ibid., 141–42, here 142.   [107] Ibid., 147–48.   [108] Ibid., 148–51, 152–53.
[109] Ibid., 168.   [110] Ibid., 170.   [111] Ibid., 170–72.

necessary reservoir of reserve forces for the German navy. The navy, in turn, provided valuable skills to sailors who returned to the merchant marine after completing their military service. In case of war, von Halle argued, the great steamers would serve the navy as axillary cruisers, troop transports, as well as coaling, resupply, and repair ships.[112] As he concluded,

> Whether the ship follows the flag or the flag the ship are unfruitful academic questions that are resolved in practice as needed in varying ways. Our people need both in order to be able to send them out ahead should the situation arise, as even in the future these relations will not cease. Germany can neither dispense with a constantly strengthening shipping industry nor a powerful and growing war fleet [*Kriegsflotte*] for the procurement of its maritime transport services on the great highway [*Hochstrasse*] of the globe.[113]

Von Halle's essay clearly leveraged his intimate knowledge of his native Hamburg and its economy's increasing reliance on ocean-going trade and shipbuilding, cleverly turning what had long been Hanseatic maritime interests into German global economic interests that now demanded a much expanded imperial fleet.

### Hermann Schumacher: Germany's Interests in China

Hermann Schumacher's extensive essay on Germany's interests in China published in the second Free Union volume drew from his recent travels to China and the pieces on Chinese treaty ports, railways, and foreign trading operations in China that he had published shortly after his return to Germany in 1898. What was new in this essay was the emphasis he placed on naval arms in light of the interplay between East Asian power politics and German Chinese trade and investments during the then raging Boxer Rebellion. Like von Halle's contribution, it had originally been an anonymous *Nauticus* contribution.[114]

After discussing the historical process of Anglo-Russian and French encroachment on East Asia and China and the importance of the Sino-Japanese War in drawing the world's attention to northeastern China and Korea, Schumacher noted that China, while still largely territorially intact, was military impotent and unable to enforce its own policies and treaty obligations.[115] With the emerging transition from foreign merchant trading to large-scale foreign capital investments in industry, railways, and mining in China, fair treatment of foreigners and protection from agitated Chinese

---

[112] Ibid., 173.   [113] Ibid., 173–74.
[114] Marienfeld, *Wissenschaft und Schlachtflottenbau*, 81.
[115] Schumacher, "Deutschlands Interessen in China," 177–85.

mobs, destructive rebellions, and overreaching, arbitrary Mandarins were thus acute needs.[116] The fragile Chinese state was now heavily reliant upon foreign powers to maintain order, and if Germany intended to play a role in resolving these problems with the other great powers, it would need a major upgrade of its naval forces.[117]

Schumacher declared that the tiny, obsolete, and unreliable German East Asian cruiser fleet reliant on the docks of Hong Kong and Nagasaki for protection and repairs was an anachronism. He noted that in recent years every county with interests in China had increased their battle fleets to an extraordinary degree. Japan had amassed a wide-ranging naval force amounting to no less than 140,000 tons, while England and Russia had each increased their East Asian naval presence to between 80,000 and 90,000 tons, which amounted to no less than one-third of the entire German navy. The United States was close behind the British and Russians in East Asia, with 60,000 tons, followed by France with more than 40,000 tons.[118] Germany thus had no choice but to try to keep pace and in recent years had upgraded its East Asian squadron to 6 cruisers and 2 gunboats amounting to 36,000 tons. Despite the upgrades that were part of the first navy law of 1898, this increase in the East Asian squadron was only achieved at the cost of weakening the home fleet by two large reconnaissance vessels.[119] Germany's naval weakness stood in glaring contrast to its commercial interests in East Asia, which were second only to those of England.[120] Quoting the then pending navy bill, Schumacher argued that "for an effective representation of our interests, more ships would have had to be sent to East Asia if only they had been available."[121] He also made a point of the fact that until the recent occupation of Kiaochow, of all European powers in the Far East, only Germany had lacked a naval base of operation.[122] The independence afforded by Kiaochow was thus not only a strategic economic necessity but also a political one.[123]

Schumacher reflected on the prospects for an actual partitioning of China between the great powers along African lines and argued that Germany would have to participate in "seizing a share of the spoils for itself according to its European power position," yet he much doubted it would ever come to that.[124] The sheer size of the population, its ancient cultural cohesiveness, and hostility to foreigners would make the task of governing China far too difficult – it would be a repetition but on a much grander scale of the difficulties Japan was encountering with native rebellions in Formosa and the United States in the Philippines.[125] Rather, German aims in China were to secure an open door and to protect Germans and German enterprise from the encroachments of the Chinese and foreign competitors.

---

[116] Ibid., 186–87, 188–89. [117] Ibid., 191–92. [118] Ibid., 192. [119] Ibid.
[120] Ibid., 193. [121] Ibid. [122] Ibid. [123] Ibid., 193–94. [124] Ibid., 196.
[125] Ibid., 196–97.

That was the task of the German navy.[126] The open door and a German sphere of interest were only viable if China remained an independent state and its finances and administration were reformed. Britain sought to gain undue influence to pursue its own interests by leading such reforms, so Germany should not allow itself to be pushed aside in that work. After all, Germans had played important roles as advisors to the Chinese military in constructing fortifications and in the new Chinese Office of Railways and Mines.[127]

Schumacher argued that the policy of a sphere of interest, unlike the policy of the open door, was not bound up with trade but rather with investment, notably investments in railways and mines. Since securing railway and mining concessions from the Chinese government in March 1898, a German sphere of interest existed on the Shantung Peninsula. In June 1899 the Shantung Railway Company (Schantung-Eisenbahngesellschaft) was founded with capital of 54 million marks to build a railway line between Tsingtao und Tsinan (Jinan), and in September 1899 construction began on two sites of this line. The rails, rolling stock, and bridges would, Schumacher noted, be supplied by German firms, and German steamers would deliver the material from Germany, three of which were already loaded and on their way.[128] By early 1901 it was hoped that a 100 km stretch would be opened. The entire 450 km railway line was to be completed by 1905. At the same time, Germany was working with Britain to complete the 1,000 km-long North-South Railway from Tientsin to Chenkiang (Zhenjiang), and it was expected that in the future a transport artery would be constructed connecting Kiaochow Bay with Shansi (Shanxi) Province.[129] The completion of railways in Shantung would enable modern mining in the region for the first time. Schumacher pointed out that the German concession allowed the mining of coal and other minerals on a 15 km buffer zone along the length of the railway, where surveys had determined minable coal deposits were present.[130] The Shantung Mining Company (Schantung-Bergbaugesellschaft) with capital of 12 million marks had been founded recently to develop these deposits and transport inexpensive coal to Kiaochow harbor by the time of the opening of the Tsingtao-Tsinan railway line. Thus both de jure and de facto the Shantung Peninsula was a German sphere of interest to a degree no other foreign power had yet accomplished elsewhere in China.[131]

Shantung was a secured starting point for the economic development of the Chinese interior, Schumacher argued. Already there were signs of increased entrepreneurial activity and shipping traffic in Tsingtao. Once the harbor works were completed and the railways connected to mining and the hinterland, a marked upswing would commence. Indeed, what had been achieved in

---

[126] Ibid., 198–99.   [127] Ibid., 200–2.   [128] Ibid., 202–4.   [129] Ibid., 204–5.
[130] Ibid., 205.   [131] Ibid., 206.

Kiaochow in only 2 years was well beyond expectations, even with the recent Boxer unrest.[132] Nevertheless, Schumacher pointed out that the intention was not to create a German Hong Kong but rather to secure access to all of China with the aid of a naval base. The potential of China, even as the Qing state had decayed, remained unexhausted. By applying modern technology to its outstanding natural endowment of land in the temperate zone and its rich, largely untouched mineral wealth, these could be developed to their full potential. China's population was no less than one-fourth of the earth's population, and despite epidemics, urban overcrowding, filth, and rebellions, had not lost any of its original strength – nowhere on earth were a people more driven to earn and acquire as well as bound by a such a strong sense of familial ties.[133] Schumacher was sure industrial investment promised a bright future in China:

> What perspectives open up once the Chinese people arise from the narrow circle of this petty, all energy-absorbing struggle for existence, once it succeeds ... in applying its labor power [*Arbeitskraft*] more successfully with the aid of modern technology and effective organization than heretofore, and ... once it gathers up it's family-based sense of community and directs it into a lively national consciousness.[134]

A glimpse of that potential was offered by the fact that the Chinese had spread to many parts of the earth, driven as they were by severe privations caused by overpopulation and a surplus of entrepreneurial energy that could not find outlets at home. They made up important diasporas in Southeast Asia, in the Pacific, Canada, the United States, South America, Australia, and South Africa. The strong reactions against Chinese workers in such places, Schumacher observed, were indicative of their economic significance.[135]

At this point in Schumacher's essay he had to very diplomatically banish the specter of the "yellow peril," diplomatically because this was a pet obsession of the Kaiser. Making direct reference to the Kaiser's warnings, Schumacher wrote that no one would dare deny that a distant danger may lurk in the Asian people being brought together by nationalism and once again threatening European *Kultur* as had occurred during the Mongol invasions of the Middle Ages and as the active national energy of the "little Japanese people" [*japanisches Völkchen*] had suggested might once again be possible.[136] While no one could predict when such a danger might arise in the future, in a nod to the Kaiser he said a policy of prudent watchfulness even for distant possibilities was justified.[137] He then continued by changing the subject, noting that today what most people thought of as the "yellow peril" was not the national mobilization of the Chinese people but rather the economic competition they posed, both for work in North America and Australia, as

---

[132] Ibid., 208–11.   [133] Ibid., 211–15.   [134] Ibid., 215.   [135] Ibid., 216–17.
[136] Ibid., 217–18.   [137] Ibid., 218.

well as an industrial reserve army to challenge European and American industry.[138]

Drawing on his own direct observation of Japanese industrial conditions in 1897, Schumacher noted that the costs of Japan's headlong rush into industry had been steep: the new giant industries faced severe crises and had not met expectations; wages had risen sharply and deplorable working conditions had undermined the health and safety of Japanese workers. Thus the relationship between productivity and wages had become unfavorable to Japan.[139] Only in a few sectors, such as cotton and silk spinning that drew on the skills of the indigenous cottage industry and that were based on relatively simple technology, had industry successfully taken root. Wherever more complicated production processes and machinery were involved, such as in most branches of heavy industry, there could be no talk of massive competition from East Asia. Likewise, the likelihood that East Asian labor would take the same sharp, competitive form beyond North America and Australia was not very great. Thus nothing was to be feared from Germany opening up and developing the Chinese economy.[140] Moreover, experience in Japan had shown that industrial development did not interrupt but in fact stimulated imports from abroad – during Japan's industrial development over the last 15 years, Schumacher noted, its overall imports had quintupled, and its imports from Germany had grown nearly twentyfold. Similarly favorable trends for German exporters were to be expected with China's industrial development.[141]

So far, Schumacher observed, German capital investments in Chinese industry had been relatively modest. Nevertheless, along with the English, Germans had ventured into numerous larger enterprises, such as cotton spinning, silk throwing, dockworks, towing and barging, wharves, grain milling, and gasworks with investments valued at 10 million marks in Shanghai and 27 million silver dollars in Hong Kong. They were also well represented on the boards of the largest firms, even English ones such as the Whampoa Dock Company in Hong Kong, which repaired all English warships in Asian waters.[142] German industrial exports to China were bound to grow dramatically with China's development, and nothing would stimulate that more than the development of railways and mining. Since Germany was heavily reliant on food and raw material imports due to its rapidly growing population, the expansion of exports to pay for these was a necessity and nothing should be spared, Schumacher argued, in developing a full share of the promising Chinese export market. In light of the protectionism elsewhere, the more important places like China became to German industry[143]:

---

[138] Ibid., 218–19.   [139] Ibid., 219.   [140] Ibid., 220.   [141] Ibid., 221.
[142] Ibid., 221–23.   [143] Ibid., 223–24.

German entrepreneurial energy, German work and perseverance have already succeeded in conquering for Germandom [*Deutschtum*] in the Far East, and especially in China, a status that is still better known and appreciated abroad, above all in England, than in our own fatherland, whose inhabitants have only to a vanishingly-small part learned to take their eyes beyond the borders of their own homeland to broad oceans and distant parts of the earth.[144]

Official statistics, Schumacher noted, understated German exports to China since so much of Germany's trade went via non-German ports. In any case, the value of German exports to China between 1881 and 1885 had increased four and one-half times and had doubled in value in the years between 1889 and 1899.[145] The extent of German shipping in China and the numbers of Germans working in China reflected in the statistics of Chinese Maritime Customs also understated the German presence; when one looked beyond the major ports of China to the outer treaty ports, for example, Germans firms were present in numbers very near those of the English. In 1897 the Germans had 47 such firms operating in these outer ports compared to 54 English firms. Indeed, outside the Yangtze Valley there were no fewer than 36 German firms compared to 35 English firms working in China.[146]

In the concluding sections of his essay, Schumacher pointed to distinct advantages that German industry had in China over the British competition. As a late entrant into the Chinese market, German firms were not ashamed or too proud to export all kinds of articles to China, such as sewing needles, wire, and buttons – often derisively described by the English as "German articles, German Nicknack [*sic.*], or muck and truck trade."[147] The Germans exported anything for which there was demand and were very active and informed, taking great care in cultivating those markets. Indeed, such "sundries" made up the largest increase in Chinese imports and were almost exclusively in German hands.[148] Along with areas of heavy industry such as iron goods – where American firms had been particularly successful in China – these were far more promising branches of industrial export to China than English cotton goods, for which the Chinese market was already saturated. German industry, Schumacher believed, would be the pioneers in China in developing new markets in contrast to the English, who were focused on protecting the old and familiar. No country had more favorable prospects "in conquering this great export market of the future" than Germany.[149]

In order to assure Germany an equally respected and secured position overseas as on the European continent, Germany could not miss the opportunity to develop her naval force along lines other countries already possessed,

---

[144] Ibid., 224.  [145] Ibid., 225.  [146] Ibid., 226, 229, 233.  [147] Ibid., 236.
[148] Ibid., 236–37.  [149] Ibid., 240–42.

not only to impress upon the Chinese the German will with the same vigor that these other countries did, but also so that

> the fear of our home battle fleet [*Schlachtflotte*] by any one of our competitors, even the strongest, holds [them] back from arbitrary intervention into Germany's commercial development, from any injury to the German flag! Then it will be possible to fulfill a task unfortunately neglected for far too long. Then it will be possible to finally make useful for the national interest that rich surplus of peoples' power [*Volkskraft*] superior to all other nations which gives us natural candidature to remain in the ranks of the leading peoples of the earth, even in a future given evident shape by the rise of great empires as has not been known before in world history. Then it will not be so easy for the German abroad to become disloyal to his fatherland, no longer serving almost wholly as the fertilizer of nations [*Völkerdünger*] strengthening our rivals! Then we will finally be able to harvest for ourselves the fruits of German energy, German diligence and German education and cultivation [*Bildung*] that ripen beyond our German fatherland.[150]

While unquestionably vigorous in tone, imbued with much nationalist pathos, and intended to persuade the German public of the necessity of a much expanded German navy, these speeches and essays for the Free Union were not just jingoist propaganda. They were informed reflections on Germany's economic potential, its enmeshment in *Weltwirtschaft*, and its vulnerable position vis-à-vis the other great powers informed by lengthy direct observation and study in East Asia, North America, the Caribbean, and Venezuela. It is only with this context that the persuasive force of these arguments can be fully appreciated.[151]

## Germany as Hammer or Anvil

As the fleet professors were giving speeches for the second navy bill, the Samoa question was resolved by agreement between Germany and the United States. Following the violence in Samoa in the spring of 1899, Bülow and the Foreign Office learned that the Americans were prepared to agree to a partition of the islands. With the Americans on board and the Germans convinced that they were in the right both legally and morally – and supported by a massive outpouring of anti-English sentiment in the German press sparked by the Boer War – Bülow put pressure on Britain to agree to the German proposals, including a threat to break off diplomatic relations.[152] Britain, for its part,

---

[150] Ibid., 245–46.
[151] Cf. Fischer, *Krieg der Illusionen*, 71–72, 74; Berghahn, *Der Tirpitz-Plan*, 132–33, 143, 143n117.
[152] See Canis, *Von Bismarck zur Weltpolitik*, 313–14; Kennedy, *The Samoan Tangle*, 155–88.

was facing fierce opposition from Australia and New Zealand over relinquishing any of its claims in the archipelago. In November, Bülow traveled to England and successfully brokered an agreement with the Salisbury government, agreeing to all of Chamberlain's conditions and compensating Britain for relinquishing its Samoan claims with Tonga, Savage Island, Lord Howe Island, and the German North Solomon Islands. The resulting Tripartite Convention on Samoa formalizing the partition was signed jointly by Germany, Great Britain, and the United States in December 1899. It ceded the largest Samoan Islands Savaii and Upolu to Germany, while Tutuila and some smaller islands were given to the United States. Britain, which was at the time in an isolated and somewhat vulnerable position due to the Boer War, was thus ultimately forced into a more accommodating position regarding the German proposals.[153] While a diplomatic coup of sorts for Bülow – and presented by him as a success in the Reichstag – the partition of Samoa was nevertheless unfavorable to Germany from a material point of view.[154] Not surprisingly, many Germans were dissatisfied, convinced that legal treaties had been broken and that Germany had once again been bullied by Britain and the United States into less than it deserved.[155] The contrast to the successful American coup d'état against the Hawaiian queen in 1893 and President McKinley's formal annexation of the Hawaiian islands in July 1898 – or, for that matter, the massive annexations following the Spanish-American War – could not have been more glaring, not least since this American aggression had met with little opposition and, more often, with encouragement from London.[156]

The tenuousness and vulnerability of Germany's position was itself admitted by Bülow in his famous "Hammer or Anvil" speech given in the Reichstag on December 11, 1899, during the first reading of the 1900 navy bill, barely two weeks after Schmoller had given his speech on Germany's economic future in the Berlin Philharmonic. That speech is in uncanny accord with the public lectures and essays produced by the Free Union for Naval Lectures. As Bülow reflected with the recent scramble over Samoa in mind:

> In our nineteenth century, England has expanded its colonial empire, the largest the world has seen since the days of the Romans, ever further and

---

[153] Canis, *Von Bismarck zur Weltpolitik*, 315–16; Gründer, *Geschichte der deutschen Kolonien*, 96; Vagts, *Deutschland und die Vereinigten Staaten*, vol. 1, 884–938. See also Charmley, *Splendid Isolation*, 270–72; Hammann, *The World Policy of Germany*, 85–86; Mommsen, *Bürgerstolz und Weltmachtstreben*, 315. In greater detail, Kennedy, *The Samoan Tangle*, 189–239.

[154] Kennedy, *The Samoan Tangle*, 240; Kennedy, *Anglo-German Antagonism*, 238.

[155] For example "Maßgebliches und Unmaßgebliches: Was Lehrt Samoa?" *Die Grenzboten* 58 (1899): 161–66.

[156] See Vagts, *Deutschland und die Vereinigten Staaten*, vol. 1, 723–24, 791–94.

further; the French have put down firm roots in North Africa and East Africa and created for themselves a new empire in Southeast Asia; Russia has begun its mighty run of victory in Asia, leading it to the high plateau of the Pamir and to the coasts of the Pacific Ocean. Four years ago the Sino-Japanese War, barely one and a half years ago the Spanish-American War have thrown things further in motion, leading to great, momentous, far-reaching decisions, shaken old empires, and added new and serious ferment into development. ... The English prime minister said some time ago that the strong states were getting stronger and stronger and the weak ones weaker and weaker. ... We don't seek to step on the toes of any foreign power, but at the same time we don't want our own feet trampled by any foreign power (Bravo!) and we don't intend to be shoved aside by any foreign power, neither in political nor in economic terms. (Lively applause.) ... The rapid increase of our population, the unprecedented boom of our industries, the prowess of our merchants, in short the tremendous vitality of the German people have woven us into the world economy [*Weltwirtschaft*] and pulled us into world politics [*Weltpolitik*]. If the English speak of a Greater Britain, if the French speak of a Nouvelle France, if the Russians open up Asia, then we, too, are entitled to a greater Germany (*Bravo! from the right, laughter from the left*), not in the sense of conquest, but rather in the sense of peaceful extension of our trade and its bases of operation [*Stützpunkte*]. [...]But we'll only be able to keep ourselves at the heights when we realize that there is no well-being for us without power, without a strong army and a strong fleet. (Very true! from the right. Objections from the left) The means, gentlemen, for a people of soon 60 million – dwelling in the middle of Europe and, at the same time, stretching its economic antennae out in all directions – to successfully struggle for its existence in this world without strong armaments on land and sea have not yet been found. (Very true! from the right.) In the coming century the German people will be hammer or anvil.[157]

A first test over whether Germany would be hammer or anvil came a little over two weeks later as the Boer War began to get bogged down.

As already discussed in Chapter 3, the naval policy Britain began to pursue formally after 1889 was premised on using its maritime hegemony to search and seize shipping and impose blockades by defying the Paris Declaration of 1856. This included applying the dubious doctrine of "continuous voyage" to assert belligerent rights to search all neutral vessels. Surprised by the effective resistance put up by the Boers and their penetration deep into British territory, the British became convinced – wrongly, as it would later turn out – that the Boers were being supplied with contraband goods by neutral vessels calling at

[157] Michael Behnen, ed., *Quellen zur deutschen Aussenpolitik im Zeitalter des Imperialismus: 1890-1911* (Darmstadt: Wissenschaftliche Buchgesellschaft, 1977), 231–34.

the port of Lourenço Marques (Maputo) in Portuguese Mozambique. On October 21, 1900, Lord Salisbury, invoking the doctrine of "continuous voyage," authorized the search and seizure of any neutral ships suspected of carrying contraband. Especially controversial was that the list of contraband included not just arms and ammunition, but also food. As it turned out a formal report by the British Law Officers rejected the legal basis of Salisbury's authorization.[158]

In mid-December 1899, a series of severe British military setbacks in South Africa forced the British Army into full retreat. Conveniently, Salisbury blamed the debacle not on incompetence within the army but on the failure of the Royal Navy to intercept contraband goods, despite the fact that there was no evidence that such goods were being smuggled to the Boers from Lourenço Marques.[159] Soon thereafter the Royal Navy was pressed to begin seizing neutral merchant vessels on the flimsiest of pretexts (and in violation of its own manual on prize rules) with the explicit aim of illegally blockading Delagoa Bay, a neutral port.[160] In late December 1899 and early January 1900 the German postal and merchant steamers *Bundesrath*, *Herzog* and *Hans Wagner* were illegally seized by the Royal Navy in Delagoa Bay and taken to the Cape Colony on suspicion of carrying contraband.[161] Shortly thereafter the German postal steamer *General* was stopped and boarded at Aden for similar reasons. No contraband was ever found on any of these vessels, but the British took their time searching them, thereby putting great strain on relations with Germany.[162] Among the vessels seized, the *Herzog* was on a humanitarian mission carrying a Red Cross party personally sponsored by the German empress, but it was treated no differently than the *Bundesrath*, with Salisbury stubbornly refusing to release the ships. Bülow warned the British ambassador of the Kaiser's anger and of the severe strain on Anglo-German relations caused by Britain's illegal and arbitrary actions.[163] A common refrain heard at the time was "Britannia rules the waves because she waives the rules." On January 3, 1900, the *Allgemeine Zeitung*, a newspaper widely read by the German educated *Bürgertum*, came to just this conclusion:

> The organs of the British government are accustomed to the fact that they can act freely on the open sees. It is now obvious that the only states which can hope to deter such pretentions are those with the validity offered by possessing a fleet that England respects. All games with big words have no practical value and thus the only proper raison d'être to be

---

[158] Coogan, *The End of Neutrality*, 32–34.  [159] Ibid., 35–36, 42.  [160] Ibid., 36–37.
[161] See "Aufbringung eines deutschen Dampfers in Südafrika," *Münchener Neueste Nachrichten*, Dec. 30, 1899; "Die Affäre 'Bundesrath,'" *Berliner Tageblatt*, Jan. 3, 1900; "Die Beschlagnahme deutscher Schiffe durch Engländer," *Berliner Lokal-Anzeiger*, Jan. 3, 1900. See also Coogan, *The End of Neutrality*, 37–38.
[162] Coogan, *The End of Neutrality*, 40–42.  [163] Ibid., 40.

learned from this incident is strengthening the fleet in the form of legal commitments for a "giant step" which we feel compelled to take and carry out as quickly as possible.[164]

Eventually Salisbury was forced to relent, and the British Admiralty ordered the release of the *Herzog* on January 7th.[165] However, it was not the German anger but rather the vigorous protests of the United States about the illegal seizure of US property on the high seas that forced Salisbury's hand, conceding every major point to the Americans and revealing the bankruptcy of Britain's belligerent rights doctrine.[166] Yet again the British government proved to be remarkably accommodating to great powers such as the United States negotiating from a position of strength. Even so, the ability to detain and search neutral vessels and impose illegal blockades in violation of the Declaration of Paris remained the cornerstone of British naval strategy in war and thus prewar deterrence maintaining freedom of the seas.[167]

As it turned out, the second navy bill and its accompanying materials were delivered to the Kaiser while in the thick of the steamer incidents on January 15th. For the home fleet, the bill called for no fewer than 16 new battleships (in 2 squadrons) and 1 fleet flagship, along with 2 heavy and 8 light cruisers, as well as 2 battleships and 3 cruisers in reserve. For overseas service, 5 heavy cruisers or battleships were to be built.[168] The formal justification given to the Reichstag for a fleet of that size was deterring blockade by a more powerful sea power – attacking the German fleet would in future entail so much risk to such a power that its very status as a great power would be threatened.[169] The final objective of the legislation was the creation of a German naval deterrent of 2 German for every 3 British ships to be achieved by the 1920s.[170] It was believed by Tirpitz that Germany's rapidly growing economy would allow it to compete successfully with Britain in the construction of ships. Moreover, it was thought that compulsory military service gave Germany a leg up in naval personnel costs, while it was assumed that British imperial commitments would not allow concentrating the Royal Navy in home waters, thus making the numerically inferior German navy an effective deterrent to a British blockade.[171]

---

[164] "Deutsches Reich: Eine bittere Lehre," *Allgemeine Zeitung*, Jan. 3, 1900.
[165] Coogan, *The End of Neutrality*, 40–41.   [166] Ibid., 41–42.
[167] Offer, *The First World War*, 270–99; Davis und Engerman, *Naval Blockades*, 13.
[168] Kelly, *Tirpitz*, 185.   [169] Ibid., 185–86.   [170] Hobson, *Imperialism at Sea*, 252.
[171] Ibid., 253–55, 272–73; Kelly, *Tirpitz*, 200. Cf. Paul Kennedy, "Tirpitz, and the Second Navy Law of 1900: A Strategical Critique," *Militärgeschichtliche Mitteilungen* 2 (1970): 22–57.

The wave of anti-English emotion that swept Germany in a flood of newspaper articles and editorials in the aftermath of the *Bundesrath* and *Herzog* affairs contributed greatly to the Center Party and agrarian conservatives dropping their opposition to the navy bill and ultimately played an important role in its later passage. As Tirpitz would himself later tell Kaiser Wilhelm, "Your Majesty ought to confer an Order on the English commander as a reward for getting the Navy Bill through," a direct reference to the *Bundesrath* affair.[172] While the steamer incidents were exploited by the Kaiser, Bülow, and Tirpitz to generate propaganda for the navy bill, German Anglophobic public opinion followed its own unpredictable dynamic that the government had only a very limited capacity to influence and that could pose its own perils. That was no less true in Britain with the rising tide of anti-German opinion cultivated in the conservative British press after 1901, notably in *The Times*, *Spectator*, and *National Review*. Indeed, the press and public opinion on both sides of the North Sea worked to complicate foreign policy in both countries and lead it in new directions that markedly worsened Anglo-German relations.[173]

The second navy bill was approved by the Reichstag unchanged on June 14, 1900, by a two-to-one margin.[174] The new law approved a naval budget to double the size of the fleet to 38 battleships, 20 armored cruisers, and 38 light cruisers, setting no cost limits to achieving this strength and ultimately funding its construction by issuing imperial debt (*Reichsanleihen*).[175] By 1905 no fewer than 12 new battleships would be built making Germany the second largest naval power in the world in 1906.[176] The response in Britain to the new German navy law was surprisingly muted, with *The Times* even expressing some sympathy for Germany's naval ambitions – few could have predicted then that it would lead to an eventual Anglo-German naval arms race.[177] Indeed, in late 1900 of much greater concern in Whitehall was the much larger navy law passed in France – First Lord of the Admiralty William Selborne (William Palmer, 2nd Earl of Selborne, 1859–1942) was concerned also about France's alliance partner Russia as well as the danger posed by the United States and urged the foreign secretary to seek an alliance with Berlin for that very reason.[178] That is, Germany's larger fleet appeared to be making it a more attractive alliance partner within some quarters of the British Admiralty, seemingly confirming the political logic of Tirpitz's Risk Fleet. Ultimately, as we shall see, that was only very short-lived, as the political

---

[172] Tirpitz quoted in Röhl, *The Kaiser's Personal Monarchy*, 1036.
[173] See Daniel, "Einkreisung und Kaiserdämmerung," in Stollberg-Rilinger, *Was heißt Kulturgeschichte*, 304–15; Geppert, *Pressekriege*, 151–83; cf. Bülow, *Deutsche Politik*, 56–57.
[174] Kelly, *Tirpitz*, 189.   [175] Herwig, *"Luxury" Fleet*, 42.   [176] Ibid., 43.
[177] Kelly, *Tirpitz*, 190, 195; Geppert, *Pressekriege*, 248–49.
[178] Rose, *Zwischen Empire und Kontinent*, 191.

utility of accommodation with France given its existing naval strength and the size of its colonial empire was much greater than offered by any accommodation with Germany. The German decision did, however, shock the Russians into an accelerated improvement of their naval forces, which in turn led the Japanese to pass a supplemental naval bill in 1903 to counter the Russian threat, turning Japan into the fourth largest naval power in the world by 1904.[179] That would have much more profound implications for the future balance of world power and thus the course of *Weltpolitik* after 1905 than the larger German fleet, as will be discussed in the next two chapters.

The important role of the "fleet professors" in the passage of the 1900 navy law was acknowledged in both word and deed by Tirpitz, Bülow, and the Kaiser. Gustav Schmoller had already received the order *Pour le mérite* in 1899 for his scholarly achievements and his services mobilizing the professoriate for the matter of the navy. Tirpitz wrote Schmoller personally in early February 1900 thanking him for the "extraordinarily effective support" in "enlightening the German people about the necessity of strengthening our battle fleet" through Schmoller's public lectures for the Free Union.[180] Later that month Tirpitz also wrote Hermann Schumacher thanking him for his many valued efforts in "supporting and fostering the work of persuading the German people of the necessity of strengthening our power means at sea [*Verstärkung unserer Machtmittel zur See*]."[181] It is almost certain that Sering and von Halle would have been thanked similarly. In any case, von Halle's work was deemed so important that he was awarded the Order of the Crown (*Kronenorden*) by the Kaiser.[182] Even the Navy League's leadership acknowledged the extraordinary effectiveness of the speeches and publications of the Free Union for Naval Lectures in the ultimate passage of the 1900 law.[183]

On June 12, 1900 Tirpitz would himself be elevated to the German hereditary nobility by the Kaiser for this achievement.[184] Bernhard von Bülow was rewarded by appointment as German Chancellor in October 1900.[185] This would open the door to even more influence on German foreign and domestic policy by Schmoller and his students. Bülow would draw on Schmoller's

---

[179] Evans and Peattie, *Kaigun*, 64.
[180] GStA PK, VI. HA Nl. Schmoller, Nr. 192a, fol. 19, Alfred Tirpitz to Gustav Schmoller, Berlin, Feb. 8, 1900.
[181] GNN HA, Nl. Schumacher, I, B-26a, Alfred Tirpitz to Hermann Schumacher, Berlin, Feb. 28, 1900.
[182] Sielemann, *Familiengeschichtsforschung*, 77; cf. Bülow, *Deutsche Politik*, 231.
[183] GStA PK, VI. HA Nl. Schmoller, Nr. 193, fols. 128–29, Kanzleramt des deutschen Flottenvereins to Gustav Schmoller, Berlin, Sept. 3, 1901.
[184] BArch M, N 253 Nl. Tirpitz, Nr. 398, fols. 28–29, Gustav Schmoller to Marie Tirpitz, Berlin, June 15, 1900.
[185] See Röhl, *The Kaiser's Personal Monarchy*, 843–87; Röhl, *Into the Abyss of War and Exile*, 96–126.

friendship and advice during his time in office, Bülow acknowledging the remarkable lasting influence of Schmoller's scholarship on his views on matters of economic and social policy.[186] As will be seen in the chapters to follow, during the debate over tariffs and trade treaties in 1901–2, over colonial reform sparked by the colonial crises in 1904–6, and then during the struggle for financial reform in 1908–9, Bülow's would draw on the advice and political support of Schmoller and his students to an extraordinary degree.

---

[186] GStA PK, VI. HA Nl. Schmoller, Nr. 116, fols. 1–2, Bernhard von Bülow to Gustav Schmoller, Aug. 18, 1903.

# 6

# National Efficiency and the New Mercantilism

### The "Yangtze Accord" and Anglo-German Estrangement

As Germany made its naval leap in 1900, China reemerged as a center of great power tensions of the first order that would ultimately overshadow the Boer War. The events in China would also initiate a diplomatic and strategic realignment with profound longer-term repercussions for German *Weltpolitik*. The scramble for Chinese concessions among the great powers following the First Sino-Japanese War had greatly destabilized the Qing state. The German seizure of Kiaochow in 1897 – which initiated the concession grabbing that led to new Russian, British, and French leaseholds in 1898 – as well as the railway construction and missionary activity in Shantung and other foreign concessions angered many in northern China. Here massive flooding of the Huang-ho (Yellow) River in 1898 had destroyed thousands of villages, displaced millions of people, and produced famine. The scale of the flooding was itself symptomatic of the weakness of the Qing government, which had shifted its limited resources away from flood control in the 1890s.[1] This was compounded by a severe drought that affected the region in 1899. Under these dire circumstances, popular anger was directed at the foreign presence, whose Christian church towers, railways, and telegraph lines were blamed for creating geomantic imbalances that had led to these natural disasters. Anger was also festering against foreign Christian missionaries for subverting local law and political order through their conversion of the Chinese.[2] Railway construction – notably the German railway projects in Shantung – had, moreover, disrupted traditional property and social structures and displaced those working in river, canal, and road transport. Thus, as vivid symbols of foreign occupation, railways and Christian missions became objects of growing Chinese popular hostility.[3]

---

[1] Robert A. Bickers, *The Scramble for China: Foreign Devils in the Qing Empire, 1832–1914* (London: Allen Lane, 2011), 338–39.

[2] Ibid., 339–41.

[3] Canis, *Von Bismarck zur Weltpolitik*, 339; Klaus Mühlhahn, *Herrschaft und Widerstand in der „Musterkolonie" Kiautschou: Interaktionen zwischen China und Deutschland, 1897–1914* (Munich: Oldenbourg, 2000), 112–84; Mühlhahn, "A New Imperial Vision? The

All of these developments became fertile ground for the *yihequan*, the Righteous and Harmonious Fists (Boxers), a popular anti-foreigner movement that sought to purge China of foreign pollution and which began attacking missions, Christian villages, and the German railways on the Shantung Peninsula in 1899.[4] The Qing government was at the time on the defensive and wary of inflaming anti-foreigner sentiment by too hard a crackdown against the Boxers for fear of the movement turning anti-Qing. It was also eager to contain the Christian presence in China.[5] A *coup d'etat* in Peking in September 1898 had brought to power a reactionary Manchu faction led by the empress dowager Tz'u-Hsi (1835–1908), pushing aside reformers who were seen as too accommodating to foreigners.[6] With the British bogged down in their South African war and the United States preoccupied with the Philippine-American War (1899–1902), there was, moreover, less fear of foreigner backlash in the Qing court for not suppressing the Boxers more vigorously.[7] Thus the Boxer movement grew in 1899–1900, drawing on the ranks of young unemployed men and spreading from Shantung to Chihli province and then to the northern Chinese plain to Tientsin and Peking, attacking converts and burning churches along the way. When the Boxers entered Peking in June 1900 and the foreign legations responded by moving their coastal troops to Peking in a failed effort to protect their threatened diplomats, the Qing court sided with the Boxers, and Boxer and Chinese Imperial forces subsequently jointly laid siege to the Peking legation quarter.[8] In the ensuing chaos the German plenipotentiary in Peking, Clemens von Ketteler (1853–1900), was shot and killed on June 19, and on June 21, 1900, the Qing court effectively declared war on the foreigners.

While the British were eager to consolidate their dominant presence in the Yangtze region into a British sphere of influence, they were at the same time committed to an "open door" policy in China fearing that any foreign suppression of the Boxers would lead to a new wave of concession grabbing.[9] Especially worrisome were the Russians, who had been seeking concessions to link Peking with the northern railway network at Newchwang (Yingkou) in 1899 and had taken advantage of the Boxer unrest to raid Chinese cities along the Amur River in early July 1900. They also started moving some 200,000 troops into Manchuria on the pretext of protecting the China Eastern Railway (Trans-Manchurian Railway). This Chinese concession was critical to the Russians, as it allowed completion of the Trans-Siberian Railway between

---

Limits of German Colonialism in China," in *German Colonialism in a Global Age*, ed. Naranch and Eley, 129–46, here 137–39.
[4] Mühlhahn, *Herrschaft und Widerstand*, 378–96; Canis, *Von Bismarck zur Weltpolitik*, 339.
[5] Bickers, *The Scramble for China*, 342.  [6] Otte, *The China Question*, 178.
[7] Bickers, *The Scramble for China*, 343.  [8] Ibid., 343–44.
[9] See Otte, *The China Question*, 179–81.

Chita and Vladivostok. The Russians were also interested in linking Vladivostok with their Chinese leasehold in Port Arthur, thus seeking to control southern Manchuria and Korea, thereby putting the Russians on a collision course with the British and Japanese.[10] Indeed, in early July the Russians had seized the Taku-Tientsin section of the British-built and run China Northern Railway, as well as the section of from Tangku (Tanggu) to Shan-hai-kwan (Shanhaiguan), in open violation of the Anglo-Russian Scott-Muravev Agreement of 1899, which had demarcated British and Russian railway interests in China.[11]

The British were at that time in a remarkably isolated diplomatic position and rather pinched financially on account of the Boer War. At the same time, other parts of the British Empire appeared vulnerable. Russian troops were massing along the Afghan border and the French were entering the disputed region between Algeria and Morocco. There was even a French invasion scare that swept Britain in the spring and summer of 1900.[12] This had led Salisbury to delay action on the Boxer issue and forced the British to work with other great powers affected by the violence in China and committed to the open door, such as the United States, Japan, and especially, Germany, which the British Foreign Office hoped could be deployed as a bulwark against Russian encroachment in northern China.[13]

Meanwhile in Germany, the attacks on the German legation, the assasination of Ketteler, heavy damage to the German gunboat *Iltis* (by Chinese-bought Krupp cannons, no less), and news that Russia was dispatching four thousand men to Peking enraged the Kaiser and pressed him to take some kind of action against the Boxers. Without informing either Bülow or Tirpitz, he impetuously ordered Field Marshall Alfred von Waldersee (1832–1904) – his "*Weltmarschall*" – to lead an expeditionary corps of twenty thousand men to China, accompanied by a naval force that was to include some of Germany's newest battleships and cruisers.[14] However, the lack of sufficient German naval vessels and the delicate diplomatic situation in China between Russia and Britain forced the Kaiser to scale back his ambitions on Bülow's urging, who persuaded him to have Waldersee lead what became an eight-nation expeditionary force instead.[15]

Bülow recognized that the Anglo-Russian standoff in China offered Germany an opening to retake the diplomatic lead among the European great powers and opportunities to improve Germany's economic position in China,

---

[10] Ibid., 182–83; Bickers, *The Scramble for China*, 345–48; Wippich, *Japan und die deutsche Fernostpolitik*, 359–400, esp. 371–84.
[11] Otte, *The China Question*, 220–22.  [12] Kennedy, *Anglo-German Antagonism*, 242.
[13] Canis, *Von Bismarck zur Weltpolitik*, 341–42.  [14] Kelly, *Tirpitz*, 232.
[15] Canis, *Von Bismarck zur Weltpolitik*, 341–42. See also Petersson, *Imperialismus und Modernisierung*, 164.

particularly in the Yangtze Valley. The German Foreign Office, the Deutsch-Asiatische Bank, and the Shantung Syndicate were by this point disappointed by Shantung province and were keen to expand German railway activity into richer Chinese provinces to the south, fearing that the Yangtze Valley was becoming exclusively British.[16] Ultimately, Bülow also hoped to improve his own domestic political position by demonstrating to the German public through a Chinese intervention that the government was protecting German honor abroad and that *Weltpolitik* could yield tangible economic benefits.[17] The lack of German qualms in the summer of 1900 about violating prior agreements over Anglo-German spheres of influence in China needs to be set against Britain's secret abrogation the Anglo-German Angola Treaty of 1898 through the Windsor Treaty signed with Portugal in 1899 and the multiple violations of neutral rights by the Royal Navy during first phase of the Boer War in late 1899 and early 1900. Warm relations these were not.

While Salisbury and the rest of the British government were understandably wary of the German proposal, they were in no position on account of the Boer War and fear of Russian encroachment in Manchuria to do much on their own. They were also aware that their dithering in China had allowed the Boxer uprising to swell into the monster that it had become. Despite Salisbury's strong objections, the British thus agreed to give the Germans the lead on condition that all of the other powers place their forces under German command, to which the other powers including the Russians and Japanese agreed.[18] The multinational intervention that Germany would eventually lead would be the single largest German overseas military engagement in the era of *Weltpolitik*. As will be discussed more shortly, beyond punishing the Boxers and extracting an indemnity from the Qing court, German policy was directed to an unusual degree by perceptions of economic opportunity, which Hermann Schumacher, perhaps more than any other single person besides Richthofen, had helped get on the policy agenda.

As Waldersee was heading to China, an eigthteen-thousand man strong Allied force comprised of Russian, Japanese and British troops entered Peking from Tientsin on August 9 to relieve the besieged foreign legations, ending the siege shortly thereafter.[19] On August 26 the Russians precipitously withdrew their legation and troops to Tientsin, threatening to fracture the international coalition. They had the powerful Chinese Viceroy Li Hongzhang on their side for their ambitions in Manchuria and were thus eager to quickly reinstall the Qing government in Peking to restore the status quo. This created a potentially embarrassing situation for Waldersee, who would have no international force to command when he arrived in China.[20] Bülow and the German Foreign

---

[16] Mommsen, *Bürgerstolz und Weltmachtstreben*, 312.
[17] Canis, *Von Bismarck zur Weltpolitik*, 340–41, 346–47.
[18] Otte, *The China Question*, 192–95.   [19] Ibid., 195–96.   [20] Ibid., 196–97.

Office were forced to scramble to salvage the international coalition by proposing an Anglo-German agreement on the Yangtze region that they hoped the other powers would join. This was initially met with extreme mistrust by the British, but Salisbury had unwisely landed thirty thousand British marines in Shanghai in mid-August, a decision that emboldened the French, Japanese, and Germans to send their own naval vessels and land troops in the Yangtze basin in late August as fear of the Boxer movement spread.[21] On September 8, the British received a consular report that the Russians had taken over large stretches of the China Northern Railway, and by October 1 all of Manchuria was effectively under Russian military occupation.[22] These events made the British more amenable to working with the Germans, even if the British cabinet and Foreign Office had legitimate concerns about German aims in the Yangtze Valley.

The impression that German ambitions in China extended well beyond the Shantung Peninsula into the Huang-ho and Yangtze Valleys would have been obvious to anyone familiar with Schumacher's extensive writings and speeches on China between 1898 and 1900, which included significant pro-fleet propaganda that had gained a high degree of publicity. His piece published as part of the collection of speeches and essays for the Free Union for Naval Lectures, which, as discussed in the previous chapter, gained a wide circulation and German and international press coverage, made no secret of German ambitions to extend the German "sphere of interest" at Kiaochow Bay deep into the Chinese hinterland along the Huang-ho to Shansi province, as well as the goal of connecting Tientsin in the north to Chenkiang and the Yangtze Valley to the south. He reported on the steady gains that German merchants and industry were making on the English everywhere in China and of the special interest they had in continued German commercial penetration of the Yangtze Valley. Schumacher was considered one of the foremost German experts on the Chinese economy, and as discussed previously, had very close ties to Tirpitz and Heeringen in the RMA, as well the confidence of the Kaiser, whose son he was tutoring in Bonn. He also had ties to Chancellor Bülow and the army and was called to advise the German government as a China expert in 1900–1901, participating in a confidential conference on the military mobilization to suppress the Boxer Rebellion. He was even invited by the army to participate as an observer of the military expedition to China, but had to decline. Chancellor Bülow later asked him to complete a memorandum for the German Foreign Office on covering the costs of the German military expedition to China.[23] Indeed, Bülow's China policy in 1900–1901 was geared toward maintaining the open door only until Germany was sufficiently strong

---

[21] Ibid., 197–200.   [22] See ibid., 216–22.
[23] GNN HA, Nl. Schumacher, I, B-6l, fol. 348.

to assert itself as an equal in order to pursue these wider aims, with a significant shift of interest southward toward the Yangtze Valley.[24]

This was hardly lost on Lord Salisbury and influential figures in the British Foreign Office, such as Sir Francis Bertie, who had suspected all along that German ambitions extended well beyond the Shantung Peninsula and that they would exploit the Boxer unrest to gain concessions along the Hwang-ho and between there and the north bank of the Yangtze.[25] For that reason Bertie vehemently opposed the Anglo-German agreement signed on October 16, 1900, which while omitting specific reference to the Yangtze region had also excluded – as a consequence of a major cartographical blunder by Salisbury – all Chinese territory north of the 38th parallel north latitude, meaning northern China and Manchuria were exempted from an earlier draft of the agreement. While reference to the 38th parallel was removed from the final draft of the accord, it was replaced by language so vague that it allowed quite elastic geographic interpretations.[26]

The Anglo-German accord that was finally signed committed both powers to preventing the partition of China by (1) maintaining the open door, (2) renouncing additional territorial acquisitions, (3) preventing third powers from doing the same, and (4) seeking territorial compensation in case a third power gained Chinese territory.[27] The terms of the agreement were nevertheless interpreted in Berlin as assuring German access to the Yangtze, and it was telling – and indeed galling in London – that the agreement was commonly referred to as the "Yangtze Accord" in Germany and read to exclude Manchuria, of which the British press was quick to take note and claim that the British government had been duped by the Germans. By contrast, the German press was uniformly positive about the agreement and the assurances it gave German firms for access to the wider Chinese market.[28]

Throughout their intervention in China, the Germans pursued a very hard, uncompromising line with the Chinese bent on extracting maximum indemnities and advantage for German commercial interests; shipping companies like HAPAG, mining companies and railway suppliers, as well as the existing German railway and mining companies and banks in Kioachow were all eager to expand their operations in China through concessions to new ports and markets and so added pressure to pursue such a policy.[29] Waldersee's soldiers and the other Eight Nation forces he ostensibly "directed" (but did not directly command) also engaged in many bloody revenge actions, indiscriminate acts

---

[24] Canis, *Von Bismarck zur Welpolitik*, 344–45, 364–65.
[25] Otte, *The China Question*, 207–8.  [26] Ibid., 210.  [27] Ibid., 208–9.
[28] Canis, *Von Bismarck zur Weltpolitik*, 347–49; Carroll, *Germany and the Great Powers*, 458.
[29] Canis, *Von Bismarck zur Weltpolitik*, 344–45; Petersson, *Imperialismus und Modernisierung*, 168–70.

of violence, and much looting, which tarnished Germany's international image.[30] At the same time, the Germans pushed the British for a favorable indemnity, better treatment of German investors, and access to the Yangtze basin. Even after the punitive Boxer Protocol was signed between the Eight Nation Alliance and the Qing government in September 1901, German diplomats continued to press the Chinese, refusing to withdraw German troops from Shanghai until guarantees were given by the local Chinese viceroys that no one country would be favored in the Yangtze Valley. This generated much negative press in Britain.[31]

Bülow and Waldersee were in a tricky position navigating between London and St. Petersburg and had to be mindful not to antagonize either party unduly. They tended, however, to appease Russian provocations in Manchuria as leverage over the British in order to achieve German economic objectives, which took a toll on relations with London.[32] German public opinion, appalled like much of the rest of the world by the scorched-earth tactics used in the Boer War, would have in any case hardly been favorable to assisting the British in China. In January 1901 news leaked out that the Qing government had offered the Russians a protectorate over Manchuria, and by early March Russia and Britain were on the brink of war over Manchuria.[33] On March 15, 1901, Bülow announced in the Reichstag that the October 1900 Anglo-German Accord was a purely commercial agreement that did not concern Manchuria. He also noted that the Qing government could not enter into agreements on concessions with Russia or any other power until the terms of a peace treaty were fulfilled.[34] While Bülow was attempting to appease both the Russians and the British, any hopes London had of containing Russia with German assistance were now dead. Subsequently British China policy switched to accommodation with the Russians and to a mutual de-escalation of the crisis.[35]

On the face of it, Bülow's interpretation of the Anglo-German agreement was – in narrow legal terms – correct: Germany had not made a commitment to preserve China's territorial integrity.[36] And his China policy was right out of a British playbook that Lord Salisbury had perfected in his dealings with Germany and other weaker powers since the 1890s, but Germany was neither

---

[30] Bickers, *The Scramble for China*, 346–51; Canis, *Von Bismarck zur Weltpolitik*, 352–53; Otte, *The China Question*, 231–32.
[31] Carroll, *Germany and the Great Powers*, 473.
[32] See Bülow, *Denkwürdigkeiten*, vol. 1, 512–15.
[33] On the run-up to the "war-in-sight" crisis, see Otte, *The China Question*, 232–46.
[34] Ibid., 259–60; Canis, *Von Bismarck zur Weltpolitik*, 353–54.
[35] Otte, *The China Question*, 260–65. See also Charmley, *Splendid Isolation*, 283.
[36] Ibid., 266.

splendidly isolated nor yet anywhere close to as powerful as Britain. Even if Bülow had wanted to, he could not have checked Russian ambitions in China without endangering the Reich's security on the European continent. Bülow, with visions of Yangtzean bounty in his head, did manage to keep this region open to German trade and investment – indeed by 1902 there were clear signs of increased German commercial activity in the Yangtze Valley – but he had burned bridges to London in the process.[37] While it is untrue, as has often been claimed, that a military alliance between Britain and Germany was in the offing in 1900–1901 and that the Germans missed that opportunity on account of Bülow's China policy, the impression of German unreliability took a lasting toll on Anglo-German relations, just as it brought Britain and Japan closer together.[38] On account of their common interests in northern China, Manchuria, and Korea, only Japan had proven itself a reliable partner to the British. The negative impression of German unscrupulous opportunism and menace would harden into the official image of Germany in British cabinets and especially in the Foreign Office from this point on. In January 1902, *The Fortnightly Review* carried a piece that described that emerging image vividly:

> [T]he first article in the foreign policy of Germany ever since Bismarck shaped and moulded it is to keep on good terms with Russia, whatever may happen. … His policy still reigns in the German Foreign Office; a fact of which we had painful example in what Count von Bülow ostentatiously called "the Yangtze Agreement" – a public avowal, which was preceded by private intimations to Russia, that the Anglo-German agreement was intended to admit Germany into the British sphere of influence, but not to interfere with Russian policy in the Far East. The object of this was to persuade Russia that England was her enemy and Germany her friend. Count Waldersee pursued the same policy all through the international occupation of Pekin [sic]; doubtless in obedience to instructions from Berlin.
>
> The position is therefore perfectly plain. It is impossible to arrive at a working understanding with Germany. It is her interest to supplant us in the field of commerce and to destroy our supremacy at sea, and all nations – Germany most of all and least scrupulous of all – will pursue the policy which makes for their interest.[39]

---

[37] Ibid., 308.
[38] Becker, *Fürst Bülow und England*, 162–201, 269–93; Kennedy, *Anglo German Antagonism*, 244–46. Cf. Canis, *Von Bismarck zur Weltpolitik*, 372–75; Charmley, *Splendid Isolation*, 277–93; Otte, *The China Question*, 266–67, 297–99, 326–37; Rose, *Zwischen Empire und Kontinent*, 145–69.
[39] Canon Malcolm MacCall, "Russia, Germany and Britain: A Warning and a Moral," *The Fortnightly Review* CCCCXXI (Jan. 1, 1902): 21–38, here 24.

## National Efficiency

As the Boxer intervention made clear, this was an important turning point in British public opinion, when for the first time a "German threat" was perceived that had to be countered.[40] A very a similar turn in perceptions occurred in the United States at this time, reinforcing Anglo-American rapprochement around this supposed common German threat. Those perceptions – not the actual existence of a German threat – played a significant role in Germany's gradual diplomatic isolation in the years following. The British anxieties about Germany have often been ascribed rather too breezily to the growing German navy, but as the industrialist Walther Rathenau (1867–1922) observed rather trenchantly, these anxieties were at root economic and colonial. The former anxiety, he argued, was the sense of being left behind in newer industries like machine building, chemicals, and electrical equipment on account of defective technical knowledge and poor organization. The later anxiety was driven by the centrifugal forces in the British Empire, which England had nothing to counter other than with the Royal Navy.[41] As Rathenau reflected,

> It is highly remarkable that both anxieties, the industrial and the colonial, shift the English gaze toward Germany. Here sits the competitor and rival. From every conversation with educated English people it emerges, at times as a compliment at others as an accusation, at yet others as irony: you will surpass us, you have surpassed us. And a third weighty impulse is added of which we from our home vantage point are not always aware: the evaluation of Germany by those viewing her from a distance. One takes a look from the outside at the cauldron of peoples of the Continent and takes note of a people of restless activity and enormous physical expansion locked in by stagnating nations. Eight hundred thousand new Germans every year! Every five years [*Lustrum*] additional population nearly equal to Scandinavia or Switzerland! And one asks, how long can an evacuated France withstand the atmospheric pressure of this population. Thus every English dissatisfaction substantiates and localizes itself in the concept Germany. And what appears as motivated conviction among the educated expresses itself among the people, within the youth, in the provinces as prejudice, as hatred and fantasy to a degree that goes far beyond our journalistic apperceptions. It would be feeble and superficial were one to believe that small pleasantries, deputation visits, or press maneuvers could quell dissatisfaction that flows from such a deep source.[42]

While these observations were made in early 1909 after Anglo-German relations had deteriorated significantly, they capture a British public mood

---

[40] Kennedy, *The Rise of Anglo-German Antagonism*, 251.
[41] Bülow, *Denkwürdigkeiten*, vol. 2, 427.   [42] Walther Rathenau quoted in ibid., 428.

of decline well documented by 1904 and very much heightened by the Boer War and its aftermath. The war cost £ 200 million, dragged on for more than two years, and resulted in heavy British casualties of 45,000 men fighting a Boer force that numbered only 50,000–70,000. It revealed major deficiencies in the physical fitness of British soldiers and the quality of training, organization, command, equipment, and medical care in the British Army.[43] Farm burnings in reprisal for Boer guerilla activity and the detention in concentration camps of Boer civilians by the British Army, where an estimated 26,000 Boer women and children died of disease and malnutrition, also did lasting damage to Britain's image.[44] It was a severe blow to British national confidence and led to much soul-searching about Britain's national fitness, reinforcing public perceptions of Britain's relative economic decline vis-à-vis Germany and the United States that were already current.[45]

Public anxiety about British decay was underscored by the report of the Elgin Commission, a Royal commission investigating the failings of the South African War, which did not publish its findings until August 1903. In pointing to the deficiencies of the British war effort, it was striking how often the testimony given to the commission highlighted the superior organization and efficiency of the German military. The report pointed to, among other things, the superior planning of the German General Staff and the higher levels of health, education, and training of German soldiers as well as the German Army's superior command and control, more efficient procurement and supply, and superior weapons, military hospitals, medical care, sanitary measures, and cartography.[46] While humiliating in and of itself, the Elgin report served to heighten both admiration and fear of Germany in the British public, as extensive excerpts of the report were published in British newspapers.[47]

One effect of the Boer War fiasco was that it reinforced a movement for British national efficiency that predated the war and crossed partisan lines.

---

[43] See G. R. Searle, *The Quest for National Efficiency: A Study in British Politics and Political Thought, 1899–1914* (London and Atlantic Highlands: Ashfield Press, 1990), 34–53; Rhodri Williams, *Defending the Empire: The Conservative Party and British Defence Policy 1899–1915* (New Haven and London: Yale University Press, 1991), 6–22.

[44] David Brooks, *The Age of Upheaval: Edwardian Politics, 1899–1914* (Manchester and New York: Manchester University Press, 1995), 34–35.

[45] See David S. Landes, *The Unbound Prometheus: Technological Change and Industrial Development in Western Europe from 1750 to the Present*, 2nd ed. (Cambridge and New York: Cambridge University Press, 2003), 326–58; Barry Supple, "Fear of Failing: Economic History and the Decline of Britain," *Economic History Review* XLVII, 3 (1994): 441–58.

[46] Royal Commission on the War in South Africa, *Minutes of Evidence Taken Before the Royal Commission on the War in South Africa*, 2 vols. (London: Wyman and Sons, 1903), vol. 1, 16–17, 36, 182, 184, 199, 210, 218, 234, 237–38, 375, 436, 447–48, 474–75, 479–80, 482; vol. 2, 69, 125–26, 228, 139–40.

[47] "Report on the Royal Commission on the South African War," *The Times*, Aug. 29, 1903.

This was led to some extent by Archibald Primrose (5th Earl of Rosebery, 1847-1929) and included such disparate figures as William Ashley, Joseph Chamberlain, Richard Haldane (1856-1929), Willam A. S. Hewins (1865-1931), Sir Halford Mackinder (1861-1947), Leo Maxse (1864-1932), Alfred Milner (1st Viscount Milner, 1854-1925), Bertrand Russell (3rd Earl Russell, 1872-1970), George Bernard Shaw (1856-1950), Beatrice Webb (née Potter, 1858-1943), Sidney Webb (1859-47), and H. G. Wells (1866-1946).[48] Devotees of this movement saw the root causes of the South African debacle primarily in failed British institutions, notably incompetent, amateurish government, a failing education system at all levels, and the need for long-overdue social reforms.[49] Not surprisingly, many supporters of British national efficiency tended to look to Imperial Germany, and to a lesser degree Japan, for models, even though a number of them – notably Chamberlain – also saw Germany as a potential threat to vital British interests. The challenge, then, was to become more like Germany in order to more effectively compete with it.[50] In some cases, the new sense of national vulnerability could mutate into rabid hatred of all things German, as was the case with Leo Maxse, editor of the *National Review*.[51] For Maxse, a prominent figure in the British Navy League, this aversion to Germany was undoubtedly shaped by his envy of the superiority of the German Navy League over its British counterpart in terms of membership numbers, organization, and effective publicity.[52]

In a very lengthy letter to Gustav Schmoller of January 1901 as the Boer War was still raging, Henry Farnam recounted a longer stay in England the previous summer, during which he was able to chat with William Hewins, the first director of the London School of Economics (LSE). The very well-traveled Farnam, with a keen eye for all things economic and administrative, wrote that "what I especially noticed in England was the lack of progress since my last visit."[53] Clearly, even to Americans like Farnam, all was not well in England. Hewins would have certainly reinforced that impression, since as an important ally of Beatrice and Sidney Webb and a member of their Co-Efficient Club he was in agreement about the urgent need for wide-ranging British governmental, social, and educational reforms.[54] Sidney and Beatrice Webb were, as it turned out, admirers of Gustav Schmoller's scholarship and activity as a social reformer, as they were of the German education system and social insurance

---

[48] Searle, *National Efficiency*, 107-41.  [49] Ibid., 53-106.
[50] Ibid., 29-30, 31-32, 53-60, 67, 169-72, 249; Smith, *Ideological Origins*, 75.
[51] Rose, *Zwischen Empire und Kontinent*, 58-69, 75-81, 118-28; on the Co-Efficients, see also Searle, *National Efficiency*, 150-52.
[52] Geppert, *Pressekriege*, 240-41.
[53] GStA PK, VI. HA Nl. Schmoller, Nr. 193, fols. 16-19, Henry Farnam to Gustav Schmoller, New Haven, Jan. 2, 1901.
[54] Searle, *National Efficiency*, 4, 83, 85-86, 150; GStA PK, VI. HA Nl. Schmoller, No. 187, fols. 44-45, W. A. S. Hewins to Gustav Schmoller, Aug. 17, 1895.

schemes.[55] In 1895 Sidney Webb wrote Schmoller praising the service he had done to "economic science," noting "we are slowly beginning to realize in England how inadequate any merely insular conception of economic science must be, and how much we owe to the patient labours of yourself and others in Germany."[56] The founding of the LSE that year by the Webbs, Graham Wallas (1858-1932), and George Bernard Shaw gave these reform ambitions practical expression, explicitly intended as the LSE was to address Britain's endemic poverty and inequality, governmental amateurism, and administrative disorganization, which were known problems well before the Boer War.[57] William Hewins was himself later an ardent supporter of Joseph Chamberlain's campaign for tariff reform and imperial federation.[58] Indeed, social reform and imperialism were in no way contradictory forces at the time, as Joseph Chamberlain himself embodied like few others.

The economist William Ashley, a former student of Arnold Toynbee (1852-83) at Oxford, much respected Germany's system of education and administration and was one of Chamberlain's strongest intellectual supporters.[59] Ashley had long been an admirer of Gustav Schmoller's work going back nearly twenty years.[60] He had, In fact, become intimately familiar with Schmoller's oeuvre and was so impressed with Schmoller's work on the history of mercantilism that he actually took the trouble to translate and publish the piece in English in 1896.[61] As discussed in Chapter 1, Ashley had developed a friendship with Ernst von Halle while the latter was living in the United States in 1893-95, contacts that were mediated by Schmoller. Schmoller and Ashley corresponded regularly, and Schmoller wrote a letter of reference for Ashley

---

[55] GStA PK, VI. HA Nl. Schmoller, No. 198, fols. 29-30, Sidney Webb to Gustav Schmoller, Feb. 27, 1906.

[56] GStA PK, VI. HA Nl. Schmoller, No. 188a, fols. 10-11, Sidney Webb to Gustav Schmoller, London, Oct. 8, 1895.

[57] See Ralf Dahrendorf, *LSE: A History of the London School of Economics and Political Science 1895-1995* (Oxford: Oxford University Press, 1995), 10-67. Searle, *National Efficiency*, 4.

[58] Dahrendorf, *LSE*, 67-71.

[59] Alon Kadish, *The Oxford Economists in the Late Nineteenth Century* (Oxford: Clarendon Press; New York: Oxford University Press, 1982); Gerard M. Koot, *English Historical Economics, 1870-1926: The Rise of Economic History and Neomercantilism* (Cambridge and New York: Cambridge University Press, 1987).

[60] GStA PK, VI. HA Nl. Schmoller, Nr. 153, fols. 25-26, William Ashley to Gustav Schmoller, Nov. 24, 1887.

[61] Gustav Schmoller, *The Mercantile System and Its Historical Significance Illustrated Chiefly from Prussian History*, trans. William J. Ashley (New York: Macmillan, 1896). Cf. Schmoller, "Studien über die wirtschaftliche Politik Friedrichs des Großen und Preußens überhaupt von 1680-1786," *JbfGVV* 8 (1884): 1-61, 345-421, 999-1091; 10 (1886): 1-45, 327-73, 675-727; 11 (1887): 1-58, 789-883; Schmoller, "Das Merkantilsystem in seiner historischen Bedeutung," in *Umrisse und Untersuchungen zur Verfassungs-, Verwaltungs- und Wirtschaftsgeschichte* (Leipzig: Duncker & Humblot, 1898), 1-60.

that enabled him to secure a professorship at the new Faculty of Commerce at the University of Birmingham, whose charter had been secured by none other than Joseph Chamberlain, who also served as its first chancellor.[62] Like the LSE, the University of Birmingham was intended to remedy what were deemed by Chamberlain, Haldane, Rosebery, the Webbs, and many others to be deficiencies in British higher education, which was seen as wholly ill-prepared to meet the challenges of modern life that required practical scientists and technicians, professional administrators, and business managers.[63] German universities, technical universities, and business schools (*Handelshochschulen*) naturally became examples of this sort of reform. In particular, the Higher School of Commerce in Cologne, which Hermann Schumacher had helped to organize and then directed, served as the model for the effort that Ashley was spearheading in Birmingham, as Ashley himself acknowledged to Schumacher in private.[64] Indeed German economists were important facilitators of a North Atlantic milieu of reformers that included Fabian, Liberal, and Unionist reformers in Britain no less than American Progressives such as Farnam.[65] In the case of Liberal Unionists like Hewins, Ashley, and Chamberlain, admiration and fear of Germany were often opposite sides of the same coin.

## Blue Riband

One particularly sensitive area where admiration and fear of Germany were being expressed in Britain in these years was in the astonishing growth of the German shipbuilding industry and merchant marine, something von Halle had highlighted in his many pro-fleet essays and speeches. Between 1870 and 1900 the German shipbuilding industry had witnessed a breathtaking transformation. While in 1870 there were only 9 wharves with an estimated invested capital of 4.8 million marks, by 1900 there were no fewer than 30 with some 59 million marks of invested capital.[66] The number of workers employed in shipbuilding grew in that same period from 3,500 to no fewer than 42,000.[67] Likewise between 1873 and 1898 the tonnage of the German merchant marine grew nearly tenfold.[68] While in 1886 HAPAG ranked 22nd in the world well behind the British mammoths P&O, British-India, and J. A. Allan, by 1900 it

---

[62] GStA PK, VI. HA Nl. Schmoller, Nr. 193, fol. 109, William Ashley to Gustav Schmoller, July 31, 1901.
[63] Searle, *National Efficiency*, 76, 120–22.
[64] GNN HA, Nl. Schumacher, I, C-20, William Ashley to Hermann Schumacher, Birmingham, May 19, 1901; William Ashley to Hermann Schumacher, Birmingham, Nov. 15, 1901; Tribe, *Strategies of Economic Order*, 95–97, 98–99, 106–15.
[65] See esp. Rodgers, *Atlantic Crossings*.
[66] Epkenhans, *Die wilhelminische Flottenrüstung*, 213.    [67] Ibid.    [68] Ibid., 214.

possessed the single largest merchant marine in the world. NDL's fleet was third largest. By the time of the First World War, HAPAG and NDL were by far the world's two largest shipping companies, accounting for nearly half the tonnage of the German merchant marine.[69]

Henry Farnam's return journey from Britain to the United States in 1900 was aboard the new NDL express steamer *Kaiser Wilhem der Große*, which in 1898 held the record for the fastest westbound transatlantic crossing and was unrivaled by anything British in terms of speed, size, or luxury.[70] Indeed, between 1898 and 1906 German express steamers owned by NDL and HAPAG completely dominated the Blue Riband prizes for the fastest transatlantic crossings, records that had been held almost exclusively by British ships since the advent of steamships.[71] To be sure, firms like NDL and HAPAG had received some Reich subsidies to develop their global shipping routes and had benefited from large-scale public works expanding German harbors. And they were not above colluding in pools to secure their profits. But their underlying success was ultimately based on better organization and management, willingness to innovate, and superior service at lower prices.[72] Ships like *Kaiser Wilhem der Große* and HAPAG's *Deutschland* (which won the Blue Riband on its maiden voyage in 1900) thus became potent symbols of German technological, commercial, and maritime prowess, of which the wider world took note, not least the British.[73] Indeed, one can hardly imagine a more painful rebuke to a nation with such a long and proud maritime tradition.

The British Admiralty was not as insulated from such developments as has been imagined, and British naval policy was not always as rational and sensible as it has often been made out to be by the hindsight of the First World War.[74]

---

[69] Lamar Cecil, *Albert Ballin: Business and Politics in Imperial Germany, 1888–1918* (Princeton: Princeton University Press, 1967), 21; Gerhard A. Ritter, "The Kaiser and His Ship-Owner: Albert Ballin, the HAPAG Shipping Company, and the Relations between Industry and Politics in Imperial Germany and the Early Weimar Republic," in *Business in the Age of Extremes: Essays in Modern German and Austrian Economic History*, ed. Hartmut Berghoff, Jürgen Kocka, and Dieter Ziegler (Washington, DC and Cambridge: German Historical Institute and Cambridge University Press, 2013), 15–39, here 19.

[70] GStA PK, VI. HA Nl. Schmoller, Nr. 193, fols. 16–19, Henry Farnam to Gustav Schmoller, New Haven, Jan. 2, 1901; Arnold Kludas, *Record Breakers of the North Atlantic: Blue Riband Liners 1838–1952* (London: Chatham, 2000), 85–94.

[71] Kludas, *Record Breakers*, 147–50.

[72] See Cecil, *Ballin*, 22–26, 39–58; see also Ritter, "The Kaiser and His Ship-Owner," 20–23.

[73] Kludas, *Record Breakers*, 95. Matthew S. Seligmann, *The Royal Navy and the German Threat, 1901–1914: Admiralty Plans to Protect British Trade in a War against Germany* (New York: Oxford University Press, 2012), 11–12; Seligmann, "Germany's Ocean Greyhounds and the Royal Navy's First Battle Cruisers: An Historiographical Problem," *Diplomacy and Statecraft* 27, no. 1 (2016): 162–82, here 163–64.

[74] Kennedy, *Anglo-German Antagonism*, 420; cf. Rose, *Zwischen Empire und Kontinent*, 189–237.

British Admiralty papers are notoriously incomplete, with only some 2 percent surviving, and it is beyond doubt that many unflattering documents were deliberately removed and destroyed, while those that did survive were often subject to stringent censorship as it related to Anglo-German antagonism and the outbreak and prosecution of the First World War.[75] While the Royal Navy had largely been spared the relentless criticisms directed at the British Army during and after the Boer War, all was not well in this organization by 1900. Behind the façade of spit and polish was a lumbering, creaking organization with hidebound traditions and a bloated budget that, like much else in Victorian Britain, had not kept up with new organizational methods, new forms of education and training, and new technology.[76] Incompetence, inefficiency, and lack of preparedness were thus hardly problems confined to the British Army. Indeed, the Boer War affected an almost overnight mood shift in the Royal Navy from "jingo complacency" to "insecurity and defensiveness."[77]

It is interesting that around this very time the German navy was increasingly admired for its efficiency in other countries, particularly in the United States and Japan. The Americans had adopted the model of the German General Staff in their reorganization of the Navy Department in the mid-1890s, reforms that emphasized professionalism, the operational science of war, and long-term planning.[78] Indeed, after 1900 and well into the First World War senior American naval officers often made unfavorable organizational comparisons between the German and British navies. Rear Admiral Bradley Fiske (1854–1942), for example, argued that the German navy was the most efficient in the world and had eclipsed the Royal Navy in that respect.[79] British Admiralty papers from before 1904 that have survived reveal a degree of hostility toward Germany far out of proportion to the negligible military threat it then posed. This hostility goes well beyond periodic dismissive and bellicose utterances made by members of the Admiralty to imputing imaginary offensive capabilities to the German navy and merchant marine.[80] It might be argued that this can only be fully explained by the dual role Germany began to play in early Edwardian Britain as both model and menace. One vivid example should serve to drive this point home.

---

[75] Matthew S. Seligmann, "Naval History by Conspiracy Theory: The British Admiralty before the First World War and the Methodology of Revisionism," *Journal of Stratgic Studies* 38, no. 7 (2015): 966–84, here 969–70; Lambert, *Planning Armageddon*, 7–15.
[76] John Sumida, *In Defence of Naval Supremacy: Finance, Technology and British Naval Policy* (Boston: Unwin Hyman, 1989), 18–28; Williams, *Defending the Empire*, 25–32.
[77] Williams, *Defending the Empire*, 29.
[78] Bönker, *Militarism in a Global Age*, 193–99, 263–74.   [79] Ibid., 269.
[80] Matthew S. Seligmann, Frank Nägler, and Michael Epkenhans, eds., *The Naval Route to the Abyss: The Anglo-German Naval Race, 1895–1914* (Furnham, Surrey and Burlington, VT: Ashgate, 2015), 103–54.

In a sequence of events that might have furnished material for George Bernard Shaw's 1924 play *Saint Joan* – "no Englishman is ever fairly beaten" – a House of Commons committee was formed in 1901 to investigate the alleged unfair competition from subsidized foreign steamship companies, and not surprisingly German steamship lines which had made British headlines with their record-breaking Atlantic crossings became the primary focus of the committee, whose hearings gained much British press attention.[81] HAPAG's owner, Albert Ballin, took note of the accusations against German steamer lines, which prompted him to write an open letter to *The Times* refuting these assertions, arguing that government subsidies did not confer unfair advantages to his company and that the German steamship lines did not even receive the government subsidies given the British lines for their use as auxiliary ships of the Royal Navy in wartime. Similar services, he wrote, were promised to the German navy without payment of government subsidies.[82]

This last sentence got the attention of the director of Naval Intelligence, Sir Reginald Custance (1847–1935), who was sufficiently alarmed to alert the Admiralty, which subsequently launched an investigation.[83] By late January 1902 this supposed "dangerous situation" had been brought to the attention of First Lord of the Admiralty William Selborne by the Parliamentary and Financial Secretary Hugh Arnold-Forster (1855–1909), even though it was not until March 1902 that German Admiralty Staff ever even gave the use of merchantmen as auxiliary cruisers serious consideration or devised a plan for such, suggesting that the source was most likely German naval propaganda and Arnold-Forster's fertile imagination.[84] It may be recalled from Chapter 5 that Ernst von Halle had claimed that Germany's fast steamers would serve as auxiliary cruisers in war in his propaganda essays that appeared anonymously in the Communications Bureau's *Nauticus* series and then under his name for the Free Union for Naval Lectures, both published in 1900.[85] It is quite possible that this served as the hard evidence for what came to be seen as a threat to Britain's maritime security.

The initial response to this "dangerous situation" was very heavy British government subsidies for the construction of the large Cunard Line ships *Lusitania* and *Mauretania* in 1902, but these liners failed to meet Admiralty expectations after their launch.[86] The situation was deemed so inadequate that

---

[81] Seligmann, *The Royal Navy*, 25–26.   [82] Ibid., 26.   [83] Ibid., 27.
[84] Ibid., 28, 28n7. Cf. Graf v. Posadowski-Wehner, "Kaperei und Seekriegsrecht," *Marine-Rundschau* 13, no. 3 (1902): 255–64.
[85] See von Halle, "Die Entwicklung und Bedeutung der deutschen Reederei," in *Handels- und Machtpolitik*, vol. 2, 173; [von Halle], "Die Entwicklung und Bedeutung der deutschen Reederei," *Nauticus* 12 (1900): 339–77.
[86] Seligmann, "Germany's Ocean Greyhounds," 167–69; Seligmann, *The Royal Navy*, 46–88. Cf. Kludas, *Record Breakers*, 104, 147.

it ultimately prompted the Royal Navy to develop a new class of lightly-armored, fast heavy cruiser, the *Invincible*, in 1906. It is odd but telling that the original impetus for these ships can be traced back to a 1901 panic over fast German transoceanic steamers.[87]

## The Bülow Tariff and the New Mercantilism

One of the most important and consequential arenas of Anglo-German and US-German friction in the years 1901–4 was trade, but as with the perceptions of the German navy, the image of German protectionism often shaped American and British opinion more than its reality. The heated and sometimes bellicose rhetoric that accompanied the debates over trade in these years served to raise American and British mistrust and would have lasting negative consequences for German *Weltpolitik*.

Germany ran persistent trade deficits between 1899 and 1913.[88] Because these deficits in the current account could not be fully balanced by returns on German foreign investments (which while growing, still remained modest), Germany had to borrow much of the difference, often from British lenders. As Germany's population was growing extremely rapidly in these same years (from 49.4 million in 1890 to 64.9 million in 1910), Germany's longer-term prosperity was dependent upon increasing its exports more than its growing consumption of imported food and raw materials, especially as world food and commodity prices rose relative to industrial goods in the first decade of the twentieth century, worsening Germany's terms of trade.[89] More broadly, German overseas trade was growing more rapidly than its gross national product, and so its reliance on world markets was increasing relative to Britain. And while with hindsight Germany's demographic transition to lower fertility was just around the corner and began to manifest itself in the last years before the First World War, the Malthusian fears about Germany's ever-expanding population in the first decade of the twentieth century were real and understandable.[90] So was the desire driven in part by these fears to find a

---

[87] See Seligmann, *The Royal Navy*, 68–88, esp. 69, 77, 83–85. Cf. Admiral Sir R. H. Bacon, *The Life of Lord Fisher of Kilverstone: Admiral of the Fleet*, vol. 1 (Garden City, NY: Doubleday, Doran, 1929), 255–56.

[88] N. Molodowsky, "Germany's Foreign Trade Terms in 1899–1913," *Quarterly Journal of Economics* 41, no. 4 (Aug. 1927): 664–83, here 666.

[89] Ibid., 673–74; Volker Hentschel, *Wirtschaft und Wirtschaftspolitik im wilhleminischen Deutschland: Organisierter Kapitalismus und Interventionsstaat?* (Stuttgart: Klett-Cotta, 1978), 88, Tabelle 20; 238–59.

[90] Jean-Claude Chesnais, *The Demographic Transition: Stages Patterns, and Economic Implications: A Longitudinal Study of Sixty-Seven Countries Covering the Period 1720–1984* (Oxford: Clarendon Press; New York: Oxford University Press, 1992), 543, Table A2.1.

viable German settler colony, which unlike France (Algeria) or Britain (Canada, Australia, New Zealand) Germany did not have. The only German settler colony, German Southwest Africa, had a very limited carrying capacity on account of its extremely arid climate, and as will be discussed in the following chapters, the pressure of the limited number of white settlers there (only some 4,500 in 1904) would precipitate a major native uprising beginning in January 1904.[91] Without grasping these dynamics, it is difficult to understand the anxiety surrounding overseas trade that had so animated the debates over increases in the size of the German navy and that would come to the fore again in the debate over German tariff and trade policy in 1901–4.

As was discussed in previous chapters, a protectionist and now imperialist United States excluding Europe from North and South American markets as well as the prospect of Britain closing off its empire to German trade in an imperial federation were major themes in Schmoller's, Sering's, Schumacher's, Rathgen's, and von Halle's justifications for a larger fleet. As Schmoller believed – very much concurring with Sering, the specialist on American matters – the precedents for this turn had been set by the United States and Great Britain, where to his mind populism and jingoism fueled imperialist expansion and protectionism to an unusual degree:

> The turnaround of world conditions, the necessary liquidation of dying empires, the necessary division of the earth between *Kulturnationen* [cultural nations], which alone rule [and] can create advanced economic conditions and institutions, [and] the heightened competition in the world economy have created the new state of affairs from which today's tensions, envy of trade, and conflicts of all kinds came into being. We must not forget that it was precisely in the freest states, in England and North America, that popular and mass instinct fed conquering tendencies, imperialist plans, and hatred of up-and-coming economic competitors, where their leaders emerged from the ranks of great speculators with manners half those of pirates, half of stock brokers, possess billions and at the same time serve as party leaders and ministers.[92]

Undoubtedly the "party leaders" and "ministers" Schmoller had in mind were Joseph Chamberlain and William McKinley, the former taking moves to create a British imperial customs union and the latter ratcheting up tariffs to some of the highest in the world at the time, harming German exporters. Indeed, in 1901 Henry Farnam wrote Gustav Schmoller complaining of America's "bad example" with respect to protective tariffs and his belief that "the world is surely large enough for both peoples [Americans and Germans], and each can

---

[91] Gründer, *Geschichte der deutschen Kolonien*, 115–21.
[92] Schmoller, "Die wirtschaftliche Zukunft Deutschlands," 14.

advance without necessarily harming the other."[93] Zero-sum thinking about trade was encouraged by the growing economic crisis enveloping the German industrial economy and the heightened international competition for overseas consumers for its goods. Meanwhile in England a backlash to the massive rebalancing of Anglo-German bilateral trade that was occurring in these years was taking hold. In 1900 Germany had exported 7.9 million marks worth of iron goods to England, while importing 54.9 million marks of such goods from England. In just two years that had been almost completely reversed in Germany's favor, with German iron exports to England in 1902 worth 49.3 million while German imports of such goods from England were worth only 7.2 million marks.[94]

The origins and significance of the "new mercantilism," the heightened international economic tensions and the accompanying increase in naval armaments, remained a topic on which Schmoller, von Halle, Schumacher, and Sering spoke and wrote about after 1901, and in these pieces many of the themes in the Free Union speeches and essays were reiterated.[95] Schmoller described this new era as one in which a synthesis between mercantilism and free trade had been established. Indeed, he even wrote as if such a rebalance between national special interests and an international division of labor had been bound to develop and was therefore quite normal.[96] Schmoller here could speak from authority, as he had himself played a role in both free trade and protectionism, pressing for the free trade treaty between the Zollverein and France in the early 1860s (an act that had ended all prospects for a career in his native Württemberg), as well as participating in the passage of protective tariffs in the late 1870s.[97] Indeed, he had come to occupy a pragmatic middle ground between doctrinaire free trade and mercantilism, justifying moderate protective tariffs for agriculture on the grounds of preserving and modernizing German farming in the face of fierce international competition – thereby avoiding massive foreclosures and the sort of dire rural poverty he knew of in Britain – yet mindful that such tariffs could and should be used as a negotiating tool to secure beneficial trade treaties, as they had been in signing

---

[93] GStA PK, VI. HA Nl. Schmoller, Nr. 194a, fols. 3–6, Henry Farnam to Gustav Schmoller, Aug. 4, 1901.
[94] Canis, *Von Bismarck zur Weltpolitik*, 369.
[95] Gustav Schmoller, "Die Wandlungen in der europäischen Handelspolitik des 19. Jahrhunderts: Eine Säkularbetrachtung," *JbfGVV* 24 (1900): 373–82.
[96] Ibid., 378.
[97] [Gustav Schmoller], *Der französische Handelsvertrag und seine Gegner: Ein Wort der Verständigung von einem Süddeutschen* (Frankfurt a.M.: Sauerländers's Verlag, 1862); Gustav Schmoller, "Korreferat über die Zolltarifvorlage," in *Verhandlungen der sechsten Generalversammlung des Vereins für Socialpolitik über die Zolltarifvorlage am 21. Und 22. April 1879*, SdVfS, vol. 16 (Leipzig: Duncker & Humblot, 1879), 19–29.

the Caprivi treaties.[98] As far back as the early 1880s, Schmoller had also been advocating the strategic trade goal of creating a central European customs union.[99]

Bernhard von Bülow shared this pragmatic middle ground on trade with Schmoller to an uncanny degree. He viewed moderately higher agricultural tariffs as offering some legitimate protection to German farming and relief from too rapid a process of urbanization in light of Germany's dramatic demographic expansion, while also serving as a negotiating tool for securing new trade treaties with Russia, Austria, Italy, Romania, and Switzerland to benefit German industry.[100] As a self-confessed keen reader of Schmoller's *Jahrbuch* there is no reason to doubt that he had come to form his views from a perusal of its pages as well as conversations with Schmoller.

The issue of keeping markets open and negotiating better bilateral trade treaties had figured among the justifications for the larger battleship fleet discussed in the previous chapters and would come to the fore again in September 1901, when the Association for Social Policy made the impact of current and goals of future trade policy as it related specifically to social policy one of the topics of its annual meeting in Munich. The impulse was the debate over the Bülow's tariff bill, which had been introduced in 1900 with proposals to increase certain manufactured good and agricultural tariffs with the expiration of the Caprivi treaties in 1903 in preparation for new trade treaties.[101] Hermann Schumacher had been slated to submit a report in advance of the meeting on the "trade and competitive conditions on the East Asian market" but was hindered in doing so by his appointment to the Handelshochschule Cologne that year.[102] Nevertheless he did give a paper at the meeting that is worth discussing because of its focus on trade relations with the United States and because Sering, Schmoller, and Helfferich also participated in the debate about trade policy that followed.[103]

The ultimate aim of trade treaties, Schumacher argued, was to achieve valuable concessions from trading partners, and in that process tariff rates had to be seen as negotiating chips, which while high enough to be taken seriously by Germany's trading partners, were not so high that they harmed

---

[98] Schmoller, "Neuere Litteratur," 275–82.
[99] Schmoller, "Die amerikanische Konkurrenz," 283.
[100] Bülow, *Denkwürdigkeiten*, vol. 1, 282–83.
[101] Torp, *The Challenges of Globalization*, 139–202; Bülow, *Denkwürdigkeiten*, vol. 1, 531–33, 591–94.
[102] Gustav Schmoller, "Vorrede," in *Beiträge zur neuesten Handelspolitik Deutschlands*, SdVfS, vol. 93 (Leipzig: Duncker & Humblot, 1901), v; GNN HA, Nl. Schumacher, I, B-6m, fol. 382.
[103] Hermann Schumacher, "II. Referat," in *Verhandlungen des Vereins für Socialpolitik über die Wohnungsfrage und die Handelspolitik*, ed. Ständiger Ausschuss des Vereins für Socialpolitik, SdVfS, vol. 98 (Leipzig: Duncker & Humblot, 1902), 153–81.

certain domestic sectors.[104] He judged the proposed tariffs of 6 marks on rye and 6.5 marks on wheat per quintal not too high, and certainly not when compared to the high tariff rates abroad. Moreover, the bill was tailored to favor the export of finished goods and import of raw materials and semi-finished goods.[105] So long as most favored nation clauses could not be invoked, bilateral treaties were valuable, Schumacher said, because they created interested parties in their renewal and thus banished the specter of maximal tariff rates.[106]

In trade treaties it was important to negotiate with the strongest competitors first. The United States, which was both highly protectionist as well as one of the leading exporters in the world, posed special challenges, not least since trade relations between Germany and the United States of the last decade had left much to be desired and lacked legal clarity.[107] If the United States were to abandon the Dingley Act, which allowed only very little in the way of bilateral concessions, then the United States would have to accept the negative consequences of reciprocity. Even so, the prospects for American tariff reductions were low, he reported – these rates were on average 4–7 times higher than in Germany, and since they financed US federal expenditures which were rising rapidly, were unlikely to be reduced.[108] If no agreements could be reached with the Americans, then Schumacher argued Germany had a right to retaliate against American tariff rates that were raised drastically no less than twice over the last decade. If bilateral negotiation could not reduce the American rates, then retaliatory measures could be taken against certain American goods by imposing the same onerous customs regulation that the United States imposed on German goods. Other proposals made by Schumacher included restricting most favored nation trade provisions in any treaty with the United States.[109]

As much as it was desirable to improve trade relations between the United States and Germany given that Germany accounted for one-sixth of all American trade, Schumacher judged the prospects for a treaty as dim. Moreover, even modest German retaliation could spark a trade war that would harm both countries, Germany most especially given its dependence upon difficult to replace American raw materials such as raw cotton and copper.[110] If a trade war were to erupt – Germany's honor and status as a world power, he noted, would not accept every American provocation – Germany would have to confront "real American jingoism" with the only thing that impresses it: "fearless confidence, moved only by objective reasons."[111]

If some kind of trade treaty were negotiated with the United States, Schumacher argued, it would be much easier to negotiate treaties with European

[104] Ibid., 157, 164.  [105] Ibid., 165.  [106] Ibid., 166.  [107] Ibid., 168.
[108] Ibid., 168–69.  [109] Ibid., 169–71.  [110] Ibid., 172–73.  [111] Ibid., 173.

countries, notably central European states, especially treaties granting most favored nation status and reducing tariffs on agricultural goods. The countries of central Europe had a common interest in their trade policy with the United States, both to reduce tariff rates between one another and to protect themselves from American food and manufactured imports, and he hoped that a customs union could be negotiated and slowly realized in practice in the future.[112] He saw Russia not as a threat but as a potential trading ally to central Europe. He pointed out that its agricultural expansion into Siberia posed no real threat to Europe and that its Asian territories in the Assur and Amur regions and Central Asia would eventually be connected to Siberia and China by railway. These were all net food importing areas and "might offer more favorable markets than in the West."[113] Russia posed "no economic threat comparable to the United States" and had good reasons to come to a trade agreement with Germany on account of the content of it trade with Germany, which was more easily substitutable than America's.[114]

After discussing the growing tariff autonomy of many parts of the British Empire and the potential protectionist threats this posed, Schumacher concluded his presentation by arguing that the competition between nations meant that future trade negotiations would increasingly move away from general most favored nation clauses toward custom-tailored, bilateral trade agreements with special provisions on tariffs. This international struggle would forge an "international division of labor" in constant flux, offering both opportunities and posing dangers that required a proactive and flexible trade policy:

> [T]his division of labor will itself be in a constant flux of development. Processes in different parts of the earth influence it; and with the organization of communications and capital, changes can occur with the greatest suddenness, such as has been proved now in the United States on a large scale and recently in Japan on a small one. Because of this suddenness, these changes would demand great sacrifices. To slow this suddenness and to reduce the sacrifices of increasing economic development is one of the main tasks of today's trade policy. But even more important is to keep watch that the economic division of labor does not turn to our constant disadvantage.... This task directed toward slowing the international division of labor is one side [of trade policy] and is joined by another, which is to keep foreign markets open and to foster the international division of labor.[115]

That Schumacher's sights were squarely on the United States with regard to the dangers of division of labor shifting to Germany's disadvantage is underscored by a speech he gave shortly after the conference at the Oceanographic

---

[112] Ibid., 174–75.   [113] Ibid., 175–76.   [114] Ibid., 176.   [115] Ibid., 179–80.

Institute in Kiel in October 1901. This was entitled "German Shipping Interests in the Pacific," a treatise that drew heavily from his Association for Social Policy paper but which focused on the significance of the entire Pacific to German trade and the dangers posed to it by American plans to construct an exclusive Panama canal.[116]

Sering and Schmoller participated at the conference as discussants in the debate that followed Schumacher's paper with extensive prepared remarks. Sering, who was the first to speak in the debate, prefaced his comments by reminding his audience that the topic of the conference was trade policy as it related to social policy, and that his arguments were relevant only to agricultural tariffs.[117] He argued that the social constitution of a country is a unitary organism and that agriculture was its foundation. He claimed Germany was a "*Bauernland*" since three-quarters of its used acreage was devoted to middling and small peasant agriculture and that grain tariffs were only justified if they preserved this peasantry. Without tariff protection a large part of the peasantry would be endangered.[118] He then offered the counterexample of England's free trade policy and the dire consequences this had had for British agriculture. The latest British government surveys of 1893–95 had revealed, for example, that much of western Britain's farmland had been turned into pasture as a consequence of the competitive pressures of the world economy and its wet climate. In the drier grain-growing regions of eastern England the commission predicted that falling grain prices could end grain cultivation altogether, as had already occurred in the southeast.[119] Unlike more humid Britain, approximately one-half of Germany's land area was climatically suitable only for grain growing and had only very limited capacity to switch to stock rearing. No less that 56 percent of the grain-growing lands in cultivation in eastern Germany were farmed by peasants, not great landlords, and their soils were less fertile than England's. Price pressures on grain thus had the potential to do even more harm in Germany than in Britain.[120]

Sering made a special point of the fact that his conclusions about German farming were not anecdotal but based upon his own direct observation and careful study of farming in the east. The unusually low prices of 1893–97, exacerbated by accumulated debts resulting from inheritance obligations, would have bankrupted many farmers and led to desolation of these regions had there not been German grain tariffs. Industry would also have suffered due to the resulting reduced domestic sales. It was thus false to assume that grain producers and consumers were starkly opposed in their interests. The

---

[116] Hermann Schumacher, "Die deutschen Schiffahrtsinteressen im Stillen Ozean" [1901], in *Weltwirtschaftliche Studien: Vorträge und Aufsätze* (Leipzig: Veit & Comp., 1911), 463–97.
[117] Max Sering, in *Verhandlungen,* SdVfS, vol. 98, 238.   [118] Ibid.   [119] Ibid., 238–39.
[120] Ibid., 240.

German nation and industrial workers had an interest in preserving the independent farmers that made up a large part of the peasant middle class, which Sering argued comprised no less than three-fifths of Germany's middle class.[121] Quite obviously drawing from his experiences studying American frontier homesteading and his internalization of the classical republican virtues expressed in Turner's frontier hypothesis, Sering argued that an independent middle class peasantry had a profound influence upon the character of the whole nation:

> I cannot imagine our people without these independent, powerful, ready defenders. The entire character of our people would be a different one without them. Rural social conditions are reflected everywhere, even in our urban areas because the urban population continues to be complemented and renewed by the land. Where there is a powerful peasantry, handicrafts flourish in those still viable niches because they can draw on the necessary well-reared and prepared younger generation streaming from the land. And wherever landed property is in the hands of self-employed ... economically independent farmers, the urban working class stands tall and less starkly separated from the other classes. Compare the social development of industry in England, on the one hand, with that of central and western Germany, on the other. In England a massive *Lumpenproletariat*, descended from British, primarily Irish rural laborers and petty leaseholders. Only a small upper class of educated workers has worked itself up from this misery through fierce struggles over a century and a half with the aid of the trade unions. In the main centers of German industry, German workers could enjoy a higher standard of living from the beginning without fierce struggles because industry recruited its ranks from the sons of peasants and those of rural workers who participated in the ordered family life of peasants. We have a high-standing working class because we have a large peasant class. If you allow their proletarianization, you will destroy the foundation of our entire social constitution and thereby endanger the superstructure, the social standing and living standard of the workers.[122]

A farsighted social policy thus began with steps to preserve Germany's *Bauernstand*. Sering thus supported the modest minimal tariffs proposed by the government, such as 75 pfennigs per hundredweight on rye, equivalent to a one-quarter to one-third average reduction in interest obligations in Silesian villages.[123] In turn Sering sought some compensation for the consumers burdened by such tariffs by eliminating tariffs on coffee, petroleum, and other goods. He also proposed using state funds to purchase large East-Elbian estates and to parcel these out into peasant farms to be colonized by German peasants to stem the tide of proletarianized Slavic migrant laborers.[124] He bemoaned

---

[121] Ibid., 241–43.  [122] Ibid., 244–45.  [123] Ibid., 245.  [124] Ibid., 246.

the fact that little if anything had been done in this area beyond the remit of the Prussian Settlement Commission in Posen and West Prussia. Experience thus far had shown that "capitalist enterprise alone was incapable of solving this great national task to the necessary scope and degree."[125] He was thus a supporter of higher grain tariffs as long as they were part of a "great social program," otherwise he opposed them.[126] Sering's comments were followed by very long and and lively applause from the conference attendees, indicating that his ideas resonated with many of them.[127]

The debate over the Bülow tariff bill was one of the first appearances in the Association for Social Policy of the young Karl Helfferich, who will henceforth also figure in this book as a significant economist of *Weltwirtschaft* and *Weltpolitik*. Helfferich was born in the town of Neustadt an der Hardt in the Bavarian Rheinkreis (Rhenish Palatinate) in 1872, the son of the textile factory owner Friedrich Helfferich (1845–1917) and Auguste Knöckel, likewise the daughter of a factory owner. After studies in law and political economy (*Staatswissenschaften*) at the Universities of Munich and Berlin (where he attended the lectures of Lujo Brentano and Gustav Schmoller, respectively), Helfferich moved to the University of Strasbourg and wrote a dissertation on the Austro-German currency union of 1857 under Georg Friedrich Knapp, receiving his Dr. rer pol *summa cum laude* in 1894.[128]

In some contrast to both Schumacher and Sering, Helfferich took the position of a free trader in his comments, though not without some accommodation of Schumacher and Sering's position. He argued that while he was no less an advocate of the German worker and German economy, one had to assess the tariffs proposed by the Bülow government and endorsed by most of the speakers of the conference not as a means to and end but rather according to their overall effects. Agricultural tariffs would without question raise the cost of living of the working class – on that, he said, there seemed to be complete unanimity at the conference.[129] He argued further that what Sering proposed – a far sighted social reform of agriculture as part of any increase in grain tariffs – was not possible given the current constellation of political power and tendency of economic policy in the Reich.[130] The question was thus whether the planned increases in grain tariffs and the resulting higher food prices could be compensated. Higher industrial tariffs were no recompense, as they hurt the urban working class disproportionately who, unlike peasants, were significant consumers of industrial goods. It was therefore false, as was

---

[125] Ibid.  [126] Ibid., 256–47.  [127] Ibid., 247.
[128] Karl Helfferich, *Die Folgen des deutsch-österreichischen Münzvereins von 1857: Ein Beitrag zur Geld- und Währungs-Theorie* (Strasbourg: Karl J. Trübner, 1894).
[129] Karl Helfferich, in *Verhandlungen*, SdVfS, vol. 98, 254–55.  [130] Ibid., 255.

often claimed, that it was the peasants who bore the weight of industrial tariffs.[131]

Helfferich also dismissed the alleged benefits of greater self-sufficiency, arguing that he could not see how national welfare was in any way enhanced by the purchase of domestically produced goods that could have been bought more cheaply abroad. The end result would be lower national output. Even if a larger part of this smaller national output was gained by cartelized industry and landowners, he could not but see how this would lead to a lowering of the share of output of workers.[132] A more self-sufficient economy was not more stable; instead, Germany's interdependence with the world economy spread risk over broader areas and thus assured greater economic stability, as shown in the reduced volatility of world agricultural prices and capital markets. There were thus fewer swings in production. Indeed, German exports had acted as a "parachute" to German industry, which would have otherwise experienced a much harder landing following the recent contraction of German demand. While Helfferich agreed that German agriculture was an important sector and that some parts of it were in difficulty, he wondered if there were not better ways to help it than through tariffs.[133]

Helfferich concluded his response with a jab at the neo-Malthusian agricultural protectionists who feared an industrial state, notably Karl Oldenberg (1864–1936) and Ludwig Pohle (1869–1926), the latter of whom had given a paper at the conference advocating high agricultural tariffs following directly on Schumacher's paper on trade treaties. The reliance of a growing population upon agriculture that had limited capacity to increase its yields was not a newer but an ancient problem, Helfferich said. Yet despite this constraint, human beings had managed to master the problem by better technology and economic organization resulting not in a decline but in a significant improvement in living standards. This progress had been possible in the past, and he was optimistic it would continue into the future.[134] No country had ever had the luxury to decide whether it should make the step to becoming an industrial state. Powerful natural forces were at work in that transition against which legislation and other forms of intervention were largely ineffective.[135] The fact was Germany had already become an industrial state:

> Germany is an industrial state, whether you like it or not. We are reliant to a large extent upon exports, and if we decrease our competitiveness by raising the cost of living of workers [thus] increasing the production costs of industry, or even make the conclusion of trade treaties impossible and thereby squander large sales markets – then I fear the crises that Oldenberg prophesies for 1950 will be conjured up in the very near future.[136]

---

[131] Ibid., 255–56. [132] Ibid., 256. [133] Ibid., 257. [134] Ibid., 258.
[135] Ibid., 258–59. [136] Ibid., 259.

Helfferich's comments were here interrupted by lively applause in the chamber, but he continued:

> Since we are an industrial state, since farmers have already fallen behind the industrial population in numbers, tax payments etc. . . . we must adapt our economic policy rules accordingly. I see the greatest danger not in the industrial state as such but that we pursue an agrarian policy in the industrial state. . . . The future of our fatherland rests not only on agriculture but on the state of happiness of the broad mass of the people, the industrial workers. Therefore the great national economic task of our times lies not in fighting the industrial state and a policy of extreme tariffs, but rather that we find the means that support the one pillar without damaging the other, means that help pull up agriculture without depressing the workers in their standard of living and cultural status and [so] embitter and provoke them against the existing order.[137]

When he concluded with these words lively applause filled the chamber once again.

Schmoller's own remarks were given after those of Sering and Helfferich and seemed to seek a middle ground between the positions articulated by Schumacher and Sering, on the one hand, and Helfferich on the other. Much like Schumacher, Schmoller argued that trade policy was a tool of power in an international competitive struggle, which, when applied correctly and moderately, could foster a national economy. While trade often benefited both parties, the formation of prices and distribution of the share of gains could be determined by the relative power of the trading parties, and here the weaker party, particularly the "undeveloped nation," as he put it, had a right and duty to protect itself.[138] Schmoller continued by noting that while in 1879 he had supported a position in favor of moderate industrial and agrarian tariffs because of the "agrarian and industrial crisis," his primary motivation for supporting them was his hope that they would be used as a negotiating chip to arrive at favorable trade treaties. But echoing Helfferich to some extent, Schmoller noted that he had warned of the dangers posed by escalating protectionism driven by interested parties – tariffs were a cumbersome instrument to be used with great care and discretion. He recalled that he had become very skeptical when higher tariffs were negotiated than he had wanted, especially with subsequent increases in the rates, which he saw as an excessive burden on consumers and industry. As in the more democratic states, France and the United States, the tariffs had been exploited in Germany to forge parliamentary majorities. For this reason, the Caprivi trade treaties had had his hearty support.[139]

---

[137] Ibid.  [138] Gustav Schmoller, in *Verhandlungen*, SdVfS, vol. 98, 264–65.
[139] Ibid., 265–66.

While he could support moderate tariff increases as a preparation for a trade treaty, he viewed the current bill with increasing concern. The official organs of the Reich had for years now taken a narrowly protectionist position and privileged the opinions of iron industrialists and large estate owners; worse, the preparations for the bill had been shrouded in bureaucratic secrecy.[140] Following the bad French example, German tariffs had become so extensive and complex that they delayed and obstructed cross-border trade. Schmoller noted that he had tried to understand the logic of the current bill but had failed – it remained "a book with seven seals."[141] As such, he concluded, it was an attempt by the government to win "all voices outside and within the Reichstag."[142]

At this point Schmoller reiterated his interpretation of mercantilism and the origins of what he called "*Neomerkantilismus.*" While protectionism, deployed felicitously, could be beneficial, Russia, France, and the United States had regressed into a "*Hochschutzzollsystem,*" and indeed "to a trade policy of raw power and violence of the worst kind." Under such circumstances, Germany had to employ certain trade "countermeasures," which he hoped could then be used to secure better trade treaties. Neomercantilism, he emphasized, would have to be fought by means of trade treaties "to bring about a reasonable measure of equitable and just trade policy in the entire international commerce of the civilized world."[143] Schmoller concluded with the wish that the German federal governments pursue the general interest by resisting excessive influences of industrial magnates and large landowners alike.

One might be excused for seeing a double standard underlying Schumacher's, Sering's, and Schmoller's arguments: only the protectionism of the United States, France, and Russia was neomercantilism, not that of Germany. Still, the danger of a retaliatory cycle of tariffs and escalating trade wars had also been acknowledged. In their Free Union speeches Schmoller, Sering, and Schumacher had all claimed that one of the purposes of the High Seas Fleet was to help secure trade treaties on better terms for Germany, and the prevailing assumption of great power diplomacy of the time was that this was always done from a position of strength. The common thread here, if worn a little thin in places and not always shared by Helfferich, was an interpretation of the new imperialism and mercantilism that had grown out of experiences and observations of conditions abroad, particularly that states and state power were being used to secure and consolidate markets on terms more beneficial than would otherwise be possible under free trade – after all, the Spanish-American War and Samoan Crisis were in recent memory, Russia had just put Manchuria under military occupation, and the Boer War was still raging.

---

[140] Ibid., 267.  [141] Ibid., 268.  [142] Ibid., 269.  [143] Ibid., 271.

It is interesting that in the debate over the Bülow tariff bill in the Association for Social Policy neither Schmoller, Schumacher, Sering, nor Helfferich couched their arguments in any way suggestive that they viewed protectionism as a reward to agrarian interests in Germany for their approval of the Second navy law of 1900. Agricultural protectionism, where it was supported at all, was justified as a means to other ends (bilateral trade treaties and securing midsized peasant tenure reforms in East Elbia), not to pay off agrarian support for naval appropriations. Recent careful re-examination of both the decision-making processes in the German ministerial bureaucracy in drafting the tariff bill and the negotiations in the Reichstag before passage of the law in 1902 by Cornelius Torp has failed to find any evidence that the tariff increases were tied to passage of the second naval law as a political barter deal between German industrial and agricultural interests, as has been claimed by Eckart Kehr and as underpins Volker Berghahn's arguments about a "Tirpitz Plan."[144] Very tellingly, the CDI representing heavy industry supported the agricultural tariff increases as a bargaining chip for long-term bilateral trade treaties; even the BdI representing the export-oriented finished goods industry initially supported the tariffs to extract tariff concessions from the protectionist United States.[145] Still, the bill was one of the most contentious pieces of legislation that Bülow managed to get through the Reichstag, and once again, he had been given the support of most of Schmoller's students. It was ultimately accepted at five a.m. on December 14, 1902, after a 19-hour session, one of the longest in Reichstag history. It was a remarkable victory for Bülow, due in no small measure to his pragmatism and skill as a politician. That day, Kaiser Wilhelm rewarded Chancellor Bülow by elevating him to the status of prince.[146]

The new law doubled the tariffs for wheat, rye, oats, and malt to levels slightly higher than the tariff of 1887, and it raised duties on a wider range of industrial goods by 40–80 percent.[147] However, it did not come into force until

---

[144] Torp, *The Challenges of Globalization*, 201–2. Kehr, *Battleship Building*, 217; Berghahn, *Der Tirpitz-Plan*, 226–48, esp. 236; Deist, *Flottenpolitik*, 13–14; Herwig, "*Luxury*" *Fleet*, 35–36, 39, 41–42; Wehler, *Gesellschaftsgeschichte*, vol. 3, 1134–35, 1138–41. Cf. Geoff Eley, "Sammlungspolitik, Social Imperialism and the Navy Law of 1898," in *From Unification to Nazism: Reinterpreting the German Past* (Boston: Allen and Unwin, 1986), 110–53; Hentschel, *Wirtschaft und Wirtschaftspolitik*, 184, 190; Fiebig-von Hase, *Lateinamerika als Krisenherd*, 395.

[145] Torp, *The Challenges of Globalization*, 158–61; Hans-Peter Ullmann, *Der Bund der Industriellen: Organisation, Einfluß und Politik klein und mittelbetrieblicher Industrieller im deutschen Kaiserreich* (Göttingen: Vandenhoeck & Ruprecht, 1976), 168–70, 181–92.

[146] Kenneth D. Barkin, *The Controversy over German Industrialization, 1890–1902*, (Chicago: University of Chicago Press. 1970), 211–45; Bülow, *Denkwürdigkeiten*, vol. 1, 591–95, esp. 594–95.

[147] Paul Bairoch, "European Trade Policy, 1815–1914," in *The Cambridge Economic History of Europe*, vol. 8, ed. Peter Mathias and Sidney Pollard (Cambridge: Cambridge University Press, 1989), 1–196, here 74.

March 1906 and so allowed the negotiation of bilateral trade treaties. The Mitteleuropäischer Wirtschaftsverein (Central European Economic Association) was formed in Berlin in January 1904 by industrialists in the BdI and other bodies to encourage that process.[148] Ultimately, the German Empire successfully negotiated such treaties with ten countries in 1904-5, including Belgium, Russia, Romania, Italy, Switzerland, and Austria-Hungary, thus mitigating the effects of the tariff in much of continental Europe and moving central Europe toward something closer to a customs union.[149] It should be added here that after the law came into effect German import duties on all goods (with the exception of rye and oats) were not particularly high by either European or world standards at the time. Indeed, before 1913 France, Spain, Italy, and a few smaller European countries had higher duties on wheat, and Austria-Hungary, France, Italy, Spain, Denmark, and Sweden all had higher average tariffs on manufactured goods. Average tariffs on manufactured imports were also higher in Australia, Canada, New Zealand, and Japan and over three times higher in the United States than in Germany.[150]

The Bülow tariff and the bilateral trade treaties it initiated worked to stabilize the international trading system away from such extreme protectionism.[151] An exchange between Schmoller and Bülow after the last and one of the most important of the trade treaties was signed with Austria-Hungary in January 1905 underscores this point. Gustav Schmoller was very pleased with the outcome though still worried about the damage protectionism could do German industry. Bülow responded:

> Of the many friendly messages that have been sent to me lately, your letter is especially valued, not only because of the warm and trusting attitude expressed toward my person but also as much because of the critical observations which you give the matter [of trade]. I recognize therein the expression of basic views on economic policy which are in no way opposed to my own which lead you, dear professor, in the field of economics and me in the field of practical politics to a mediating position. A shared axiom of ours is that we cannot let our agriculture perish. The direction I took in my efforts to help agriculture was by way of tariff policy. One of my tasks therein was in fact to direct the stream influenced by high protectionist agitation in such a way that it did not go overboard. I believe that I've achieved that, and that despite higher agricultural tariffs,

---

[148] Ullmann, *Der Bund der Industriellen*, 205-7.
[149] Bairoch, "European Trade Policy," 74n95; Bülow, *Denkwürdigkeiten*, vol. 2, 45-49; Barkin, *The Controversy*, 245-52; Vogel, *Deutsche Rußlandpolitik*, 124-53, 174-200.
[150] Bairoch, "European Trade Policy," 76, Table 9; Ronald Findlay and Kevin H. O'Rourke, *Power and Plenty: Trade, War, and the World Economy in the Second Millenium* (Princeton, NJ: Princeton University Press, 2007), 397, Figure 7.4; 403, Table 7.3.
[151] Hentschel, *Wirtschaft und Wirtschaftspolitik*, 185-90; William Mulligan, *The Origins of the First World War* (Cambridge: Cambridge University Press, 2010), 195.

industry did not do poorly. I had to take into account protectionist efforts in foreign countries, and I do not know whether you possibly underestimate their role in similar aspirations as we had [trade treaties]. We gained experience in our negotiations that so far offer but little encouragement for the lovely idea of a central European economic union [*mitteleuropäischen Wirtschaftsunion*]. For now we must do what we can, and I am heartily pleased that the manner in which this occurred has earned me your exceedingly valuable acclamation.[152]

In the domestic German context, the regressive impact of the Bülow tariff has been routinely exaggerated by historians who see it as having benefited mainly the Junker squirearchy.[153] The truth of the matter is that the new agricultural tariffs benefited small and medium-sized peasant farms in western and southern Germany too and that for this reason the Center Party had been a supporter of higher agricultural tariffs in 1901–2. What is more, significant productivity increases in potato and dairy farming helped to offset higher prices for grain and meat so that the ultimate impact of the tariffs on worker incomes was modest.[154] This was enabled by technological innovation and a move to more intensive farming encouraged by improved agricultural education, research stations, trial plots, and scientific research, all areas where Germany led Europe at the time.[155]

### The Politics of Anglo-German Trade

German industry did not require any protection to be competitive. About that Helfferich had been quite right. Since its international embarrassment at the Centennial Exhibition in Philadephia in 1876, German industry had successfully made the investments in plant, skills, and technology to move up the value-added chain into such newer sectors as chemicals and pharmaceuticals, electrical equipment, machinery, and specialty steel goods. While in the early

---

[152] GStA PK, VI. HA Nl. Schmoller, Nr. 197a, fol. 39, Bernhard von Bülow to Gustav Schmoller, Feb. 25, 1905. Cf. Bülow, *Deutsche Politik*, 317–20.
[153] See, for example, Barkin, *The Controversy*, 253–70. Cf. Hentschel, *Wirtschaft und Wirtschaftspolitik*, 195–204.
[154] Hentschel, *Wirtschaft und Wirtschaftspolitik*, 195–204.
[155] Oliver Grant, *Migration and Inequality in Germany 1870–1913* (Oxford: Clarendon Press, 2004), 224–46; Niek Koning, *The Failure of Agrarian Capitalism: Agrarian Politics in the United Kingdom, Germany, The Netherlands and the USA* (London and New York: Routledge, 1994), 99–102; J. A. Perkins, "The Agricultural Revolution in Germany 1850–1914," *Journal of European Economic History* 10 (Spring 1981): 71–118; J. L. van Zanden, "The First Green Revolution: The Growth of Production and Productivity in European Agriculture, 1870–1914," *Economic History Review* 44, no. 2 (1991): 215–39; S. B. Webb, "Agricultural Protection in Wilhelmian Germany," *Journal of Economic History* 42, no. 2 (1982): 309–26.

1890s beet sugar and textiles were still Germany's most valuable exports, by 1913 they were chemicals and machinery.[156] By contrast British industry had not made many investments in these newer fields but had continued in sectors of traditional British strength, such as textiles, coal, and iron. Even in these fields, Britain was being pushed out of many industrial markets in Europe and North America by German, American, and western European competitors, retreating to export markets in the empire and non-industrialized countries, such as in Latin America. Britain's persistent trade deficits were balanced by much so-called invisible trade comprised of services and returns on investments overseas, where Britain had much expertise, namely in banking, insurance and shipping services, railroad investments, and in commodity trading.[157] In reality, the British and German economies were highly complimentary and deeply interdependent – as British and imperial markets had grown in significance to German industrial exporters, raw material and food imports from the British Empire to Germany rose continuously, and Germans relied heavily on British commercial services and lending.[158]

As was already discussed in Chapter 3, the superficial optic of the changing Anglo-German trade relationship lent itself easily to politicization. The context of the ongoing trade war between Germany and Canada that had started in 1897 as a consequence of the preferences Canada had extended to imports from the rest of the British Empire were particularly ripe for politics. Those preferences, it will be recalled, were themselves countermeasures to American protectionism. Germany's own countermeasures to Canada and then the threat made by the German Foreign Office in April 1903 that Germany would retaliate against other British self-governing colonies that followed Canada's example made it appear in Britain that Germany was seeking to prevent a federation of the British Empire by punishing Canada.[159]

On May 15, 1903, Joseph Chamberlain, having just returned from a long journey to South Africa, bursting with imperialist fervor, and now at the end of his tether on the matter of "unfair" trade with Germany, launched his surprise populist campaign for tariff reform and imperial federation before his constituents in Birmingham.[160] This would begin a chain of events that would ultimately bring down the Balfour government. Speaking of Canada's preference and the inability of Britain to reciprocate, Chamberlain observed the dilemmas he faced as colonial minister forced to toe the government's line on trade:

---

[156] Kennedy, *Anglo-German Antagonism*, 293; Beckert, *Empire of Cotton*, 355.
[157] Kennedy, *Anglo-German Antagonism*, 294, 301–2.   [158] Ibid., 294–95.
[159] Ibid., 262.
[160] Joseph Chamberlain, "A Demand for Inquiry," in *Imperial Union and Tariff Reform: Speeches Delivered from May 15 to Nov. 4, 1903* (London: Grant Richards, 1903), 1–18; Geppert, *Pressekriege*, 199–204.

That is a fair offer, that is a generous offer, from your point of view, and it is an offer which we might ask our people to accept. But, speaking for the Government as a whole, and not solely in the interests of the Colonies, I am obliged to say that it is contrary to the established fiscal policy of this country; that we hold ourselves bound to keep open market for all the world, even if they close their markets to us (laughter); and that, therefore, so long as that is the mandate of the British public, we are not in a position to offer any preference or favour whatever, even to our own children. We cannot make any difference between those who treat us well, and those who treat us badly ("Shame"). Yes, but that is the doctrine which, I am told, is the accepted doctrine of the Free Traders, and we are all Free Traders (cries of "No, no," and laughter).

... We may well, therefore, have supposed that an agreement of this kind by which Canada does a kindness to us, was a matter of family arrangement, concerning nobody else. But, unfortunately, Germany thinks otherwise.[161]

As was recounted previously, William Ashley became a strong supporter of this line of argument in 1903, yet as a letter to Schmoller from 1901 reveals, in his capacity as a professor at Birmingham, Ashley had earlier sought to defuse growing tensions between Britain and Germany. In it he wrote: "I do hope that in my new position I may do something to draw England & Germany more closely together. They are natural allies – if we look at the large tendencies of economic development and away from the pressing causes of friction." Yet in the very next line Ashley went on to observe: "I have learnt very much of late from your paper in *Macht und Handelspolitik* [sic]," a reference to Schmoller's speech for the Free Union for Naval Lectures.[162] How much he would have learned in this tract about peace and understanding between Germany and Britain is of course questionable. Nevertheless, Ashley seems to have been a very good student of both Schmoller's writings on mercantilism and Germany's new *Weltpolitik*: two years later Ashley would write that his own sympathies were now strongly with Chamberlain's plans for customs reform and imperial federation and that he expected Chamberlain to be elected with a mandate for his policies.[163]

Just how strongly was revealed in Ashley's 1903 book *The Tariff Problem*, which promoted an imperial system of preferential tariffs to draw the British Empire into closer economic union, just the thing Chamberlain was promoting and over which Schmoller and his students had fretted in their speeches for the Free Union in 1900 and in the debate over the Bülow tariff in the

---

[161] Ibid., 14–15.
[162] GStA PK, VI. HA Nl. Schmoller, Nr. 193, fol. 109, William Ashley to Gustav Schmoller, July 31, 1901.
[163] GStA PK, VI. HA Nl. Schmoller, Nr. 195b, fols. 58–59, William Ashley to Gustav Schmoller, Sept. 19, 1903.

Association for Social Policy in 1901.[164] The irony is capped by what Ashley wrote to Schmoller in April 1904, just as the Russo-Japanese War had started and the Entente Cordiale between Britain and France was being signed:

> You will find many indications of the way in which I have been affected by German methods of thought. Unlucky I do not find much *direct* assistance in dealing with our problems in current German writing. German literature deals mainly with the desirability of agricultural protection in Germany & in a lesser degree with the question of industrial protection in its relation to a given state. Our problem here – or so I conceive it – is that of binding together the very loosely connected members of a world empire by economic links.
>
> You will be glad to hear that there is now very little averse reference to Germany in the public discussion of fiscal policy.
>
> ... PS: You may, perhaps, have noticed that the well known sociological writer, Mr. Benjamin Kidd, has been referring to your essay on *Mercantilism*; & at Mr. Kidd's request I sent a copy of my translation to the Prime Minister. But I do not know whether he has read it.[165]

There are many interesting ironies here. One is that Schmoller's naval propaganda from 1899 to 1900 served to actually reinforce a movement for British imperial federation that had become a major cause for concern and an argument for a larger German fleet in 1897. Moreover, nothing had quite galvanized Joseph Chamberlain's campaign for an imperial preference and gradual imperial federation as the passage of the Bülow tariff in 1902, which had opened Germany up to the charge of dumping its goods abroad while sheltering behind a tariff wall.[166] Preference and tariff reform became so contentious within the Liberal Unionist Party and the British cabinet that Chamberlain ultimately resigned from the government in September 1903, precipitating a major split within the Conservative and Liberal Unionist government. This, in turn, led directly to the resignation of the Balfour government in December 1905, a general election, and then the landslide victory of the Liberal Party in February 1906, one of the greatest electoral reversals in British history. As we shall see in the next chapters, that new Liberal government would come to pursue a much more deliberate policy of containing German *Weltpolitik*.

The fact that the speeches and essays of the Free Union and the debate over the Bülow tariff were read and reported on widely not only in Germany but in

---

[164] William J. Ashley, *The Tariff Problem* (London: P. S. King & Son, 1903); cf. Gustav Schmoller, "Die künftige englische Handelspolitik, Chamberlain und der Imperialismus," *JbfGVV* 28 (1904): 829–52.
[165] GStA PK, VI. HA Nl. Schmoller, Nr. 196a, fols. 17–18, William Ashley to Gustav Schmoller, April 9, 1904.
[166] Kennedy, *Anglo-German Antagonism*, 260–61.

Britain and the United States points to one of the unanticipated hazards of *Weltpolitik* by published speech, journal essay, and memo. To be sure, Schmoller and his students could speak most authoritatively and convincingly, not only about Germany's industrial and commercial capacities and global interests – which many of them had observed directly – but also about the double standards and ruthlessness that they had witnessed accompanying a world being carved up between the United States, Great Britain, and Russia. Nevertheless, open and often boastful discussions of Germany's rapid demographic expansion, its dominance of higher education, its cultural and scientific creativity, its administrative and organizational superiority, its extraordinary success in the newest and most promising fields of industry, its flourishing entrepreneurship and industrial exports, the massive growth of its merchant marine, its record-breaking steamships, its expanding investments and interests in China, Venezuela, and Turkey, and its plans for Brazil and Venezuela and the remnants of Spain and Portugal's colonial empires as sites of future colonization were guaranteed to stir unease abroad.

With characteristically German directness they also pointed to the exorbitant luxury of the vast expanses of settler land enjoyed by the United States. They called out the sanctimonious cant of American manifest destiny and the Monroe Doctrine behind which a greedy, grasping, and violent republic corrupted by money and driven by demagoguery pursued its own ruthless imperial expansionism. They pointed to the sky-high tariffs behind which it pursued a global beggar-thy-neighbor policy and threatened to shut out any competitors in Latin America and the Caribbean. The only thing the Yankees paid heed to, they argued, was raw power and dogged determination, and that was exactly what they had coming from Germany in trade negotiations and in divvying up South America and the Caribbean.

With similar frankness they questioned British imperial entitlement to rule vast expanses of the globe in light of the complacency, growing industrial, technological and entrepreneurial stagnation, and administrative incompetence they saw. They took British hypocrisy to task and pointed to the dire poverty and jingoism at home, the wars of aggression abroad motivated by greedy politicians, the abuse of naval hegemony, and the toadying appeasement of strength whenever Britain was confronted by more powerful rivals like the United States. They outlined how they had eaten Britain's lunch in most export markets and were ready to put a fork in the Yangtze Valley. And, most importantly, they demanded that Germany build a battle fleet to confront both the United States and Britain directly to secure Germany's place in the sun alongside them, at the same time broadcasting – just as frankly – Germany's multiple current vulnerabilities and weaknesses.

Such pointed observations and aspirations, however valid and justified some of them might have been, were bound to raise hackles abroad, isolate Germany, and thus make German *Weltpolitik* even more difficult. It was especially unfortunate that these observations were publicized at a time when Britain's dirty laundry was being aired during and after the Boer War and when a crisis of confidence was rocking nearly every British institution. Karl Helfferich would later identify just such brusqueness as an important factor that served to isolate Germany diplomatically in the prewar period, namely "the loud and widely-heard words with which we loved to underscore our will to peace through a much too clear emphasis on our preparedness for war. ... In this manner we fostered the myth of our warlike intentions and helped forge an international atmosphere that provided the mass psychological foundation for the formation of a coalition directed against us."[167]

These negative perceptions of Germany extended to the United States, despite the strong ties established by German immigration and American university study in Germany, as Ernst von Halle observed.[168] Indeed, von Halle saw that improved Anglo-American relations since 1896 were tied directly to deteriorating US-German relations in those same years.[169] For the first time epithets such as "Hun" had started to appear in American newspapers.[170] By gist of Wilhelmine Germany's sheer weight as a great power and the "immense forces of elemental civilization at its command," the blunt rhetoric of *Weltpolitik* was bound to be viewed as threatening by rival powers.[171] The growing role of populism within German naval politics would serve only to amplify those concerns.

## The New Fleet Politics

After passage of the second navy law in 1900, pro-navy propaganda was developed into a sophisticated operation within the RMA's Communications Bureau, which thereafter relied less on professors and ad hoc campaigns than on careful coordination between the RMA and the swiftly growing Navy League in a program of sustained naval propaganda that could draw on the local initiatives of the German middle class.[172] As was revealed in Chapter 5, the personnel changes in the Navy League's leadership that Heeringen and von Halle in the Communications Bureau and Schmoller, Sering, and others in the Free Union for Naval Lectures had pushed through in 1899 had broadened its leadership and membership base and led most of the so-called fleet professors, including Schmoller, to eventually join the Navy League in 1900. Sering

---

[167] Helfferich, *Der Weltkrieg*, vol. 1, 37.
[168] Ernst von Halle, "Deutschland und die öffentliche Meinung in den Vereinigten Staaten," *Preussische Jahrbücher* 107, no. 2 (1902): 189–212; Fiebig-von Hase, *Lateinamerika als Krisenherd*, 329–30, 330n195, 786–87, 948–49.
[169] Fiebig-von Hase, *Lateinamerika als Krisenherd*, 948.
[170] Nagler, "From Culture to *Kultur*," 136. [171] Dehio, *Germany and World Politics*, 75.
[172] See Deist, *Flottenpolitik*, 163–71; Diziol, *Flottenverein*, vol. 1, 64–83.

himself entered the executive committee of the organization in December 1899, helping to push through those changes.[173] Additional reforms passed in 1902 strengthened regional and local branches of the organization and transformed the league into a true mass organization.[174] Lifted on a tide of middle-class naval enthusiasm, by 1906 the league counted no less than 315,000 members, making it by far the largest nationalist pressure group in the Reich.[175]

Apart from Sering, among the other new faces in the leadership of the organization after 1900 was August Keim (1845–1926), who was asked to join the executive committee in July 1900 and by 1901 had taken control of the league's propaganda efforts.[176] A bourgeois former major general whose military career was cut short by journalistic politicking, Keim was a radical nationalist who saw himself as a misunderstood outsider to the establishment and devoted himself to the league on a full-time basis. He took pride in flouting the normal courtesies afforded high state officials and did not flinch to take on the government or the Kaiser if he saw either betraying what he saw as the national interest.[177] Keim was very much an example of the new breed of bourgeois activists in Wilhelmine Germany who, as Geoff Eley observed, "entered national politics through the back door."[178] As will be seen, men like Keim and their grass roots supporters in the Navy League were not easily controlled by the RMA's Communications Bureau or by Tirpitz, giving *Flottenpolitik* a new unforeseen populist dynamic. Particularly problematic was that Navy League agitation pressed for huge increases in naval arms increasingly divorced from any fiscal, parliamentary, strategic, or foreign policy considerations.[179] Indeed, it might be said that the fleet professors and the RMA's Communications Bureau had perhaps been *too* successful in deepening popular German naval enthusiasm after 1897.

As regards the more formal affiliation between the fleet professors and the Communications Bureau, Ernst von Halle continued his work in this office, advancing to become admiralty councilor and reporting councilor in 1906 while also continuing as a professor at the University of Berlin and Technische Hochschule Berlin.[180] Along with Helfferich, Schumacher, and Sering, he also continued to edit and write pro-fleet and pro-*Weltwirtschaft* pieces for

---

[173] Eley, *Reshaping the German Right*, 93.
[174] Ibid., 104; Deist, *Flottenpolitik*, 164–67; Diziol, *Flottenverein*, vol. 1, 65, 91–127.
[175] Eley, *Reshaping the German Right*, 102.   [176] Ibid., 111.
[177] Ibid., 108–10. See also Chickering, *We Men Who Feel Most German*, 255.
[178] Eley, *Reshaping the German Right*, 111.
[179] Deist, *Flottenpolitik*, 174–78; Diziol, *Flottenverein*, vol. 1, 72–83.
[180] Peter-Christian Witt, *Die Finanzpolitik des Deutschen Reiches von 1903 bis 1913: Eine Studie zur Innenpolitik des Wilhelminischen Deutschlands* (Lübeck and Hamburg: Matthiesen, 1970), 217–18.

*Nauticus*, *Marine-Rundschau* and many other publications after 1900.[181] In 1906 he began editing a journal entitled *Die Weltwirtschaft*, which carried articles on these themes.[182] Still, what is quite conspicuous about his publications after 1900 is that explicit pro-fleet advocacy waned considerably, with focus shifting to *Weltwirtschaft*, particularly trade and shipping in the Americas.[183] This can be explained both by the fact that the Navy League had assumed this function and could do so with an unparalleled network of local activists and that within the RMA there was in these years little needed in the way of active pro-fleet propaganda, as no new legislation was anticipated until 1904 at the very earliest. Even then, what was foreseen was a relatively modest request for the six overseas cruisers that had been struck from 1900 law and an extension of the pace of building three new ships annually (which would end in 1906) to 1912-13.[184] While secret planning for larger navy bills was underway in these years, it is clear that Tirpitz's immediate objective was to pass through the "danger zone" without provoking a British attack and so assure fulfillment of the construction plan outlined in the 1900 law. He had in fact opposed Germany's foreign adventure in China and on just such grounds. The primary immediate tasks to assure those goals were to insulate the RMA from the Kaiser's interference, maintain control over the Navy League's propaganda, and to cultivate good relations with the Center Party in the Reichstag, as his yearly cost projections were quite optimistic and quickly outstripped by the rising price of naval construction.[185]

Rising naval costs were not a problem confined to Germany and must be set in the context of the British Two Power Standard and the naval arms race between Britain, France, and Russia that had started in the 1890s discussed in Chapter 3. The British Naval Defence Acts of 1889 and 1893 and the Naval Works Acts of 1895 and 1896 had led to growth in expenditure of no less than 65 percent from £ 15.88 in 1889-90 to nearly £ 24 million in 1896-97.[186]

---

[181] Deist, *Flottenpolitik*, 107. For a list of some of the publications contributed to *Nauticus* by Helfferich, Schumacher, and Sering, see ibid., 107n125.
[182] Witt, *Die Finanzpolitik*, 218.
[183] For example, Ernst von Halle, "Die wirthschaftliche Entfaltung Mexicos und der Weltmarkt," [1901] in *Volks- und Seewirthschaft*, vol. 2, 84-146; Tjard Schwarz and Ernst von Halle, ed., *Die Schiffbauindustrie in Deutschland und im Auslande* (Berlin: Mittler, 1902); von Halle, "Der Panamakanal und seine wirtschaftliche Bedeutung," *Die Woche* 5, no. 8 (Feb. 21, 1903): 321-26; von Halle, "Die neueste Phase der Chamberlainschen Handels- und Schiffahrtspolitik," *Marine-Rundschau* 15 (1904): 145-68; von Halle, "Die drei Hauptbewerber auf dem Weltmarkt," *Marine-Rundschau* 16 (1905): 537-52; 762-44; Ernst von Halle, ed., *Amerika: Seine Bedeutung für die Weltwirtschaft und seine wirtschaftlichen Beziehungen zu Deutschland, insbesondere zu Hamburg* (Hamburg: Hamburger Börsenhalle, 1905).
[184] Deist, *Flottenpolitik*, 167.
[185] See Kelly, *Tirpitz*, 240-47; Berghahn, *Der Tirpitz-Plan*, 305-30.
[186] Sumida, *In Defence of Naval Supremacy*, 18.

Competitive increases in expenditure itself accelerated changes in the design and size of battleships, making them much more expensive by 1904.[187] This was a classic arms race cost spiral, where larger naval defense expenditures led to rapid technological change, a more rapid rate of obsolescence, and thus to demands for ever larger naval expenditures. For example, unit costs for first-class cruisers were more than triple in 1904–5 than they had been in 1889.[188] Between fiscal year 1897–98 and fiscal year 1904–5 alone, Royal Navy personnel costs grew by some 42 percent and expenditure on new barracks, docks and port facilities shot up nearly fivefold.[189] By 1904–5 navy estimates were no less than 78 percent higher than they had been in 1897–98. Under the strain of the Boer War, this naval expense spiral had contributed to a significant increase in the British national debt.[190] By 1904 the Exchequer's Office warned the British cabinet that Britain's financial resources were at their limits and could not bear any more increases in naval spending, forcing the Admiralty to agree to large decreases in naval estimates for 1905–6.[191]

In Germany, naval expenditure had risen from 131.25 million marks in 1898 to 246.14 million marks in 1905, an 87 percent increase.[192] Rising ship construction costs and increased naval expenditure exposed a structural problem in Reich finances that hinged on the constitutional limits the Reich had in imposing direct taxes and a growing problem with Reich deficits by 1905, which would prove to be the Achilles heel of all future fleet planning and which needs to be understood in order to grasp the crisis of Bülow's *Weltpolitik* after 1905. The basic problem was that the Reich's revenues from indirect taxes were inelastic in economic upswings and elastic during downswings, making the revenue stream unpredictable and inadequate. This led to Reich deficits that had to be covered with rising matricular contributions from the imperial states or with borrowing. All attempts to increase Imperial indirect taxes on beer, brandy, or tobacco faced stiff opposition from the liberals, the Center Party, and states such as Bavaria, Württemberg, and Saxony, while attempts to introduce direct taxation was fiercely opposed by the states as an intrusion on their fiscal sovereignty.[193] The dilemmas this presented Tirpitz and the RMA are obvious when one considers how reliant they had been on the Center Party for passage of the navy law of 1900 and would likely be in any future amendments to cover higher naval estimates. The problem was exacerbated by the economic downswing after 1900. By 1903 a 119 million mark deficit was recorded that was mostly covered by borrowing, and by 1904 the red ink had swollen to 805 million marks.[194] Thus by 1904–5 budgetary pressures on both sides of the North Sea were actually auspicious

---

[187] Ibid., 18–19.   [188] Ibid., 20.   [189] Ibid., 21.   [190] Ibid., 22–23.
[191] Ibid., 24–25.   [192] Epkenhans, *Die wilhelminische Flottenrüstung*, 465, Tabelle Nr. 14.
[193] Hentschel, *Wirtschaft und Wirtschaftspolitik*, 164.   [194] Ibid., 165.

for slowing the pace of battleship construction in the future. Yet for various reasons, this did not happen.

With Germany's growing fiscal problem, a compromise tax reform package was introduced by the Prussian Ministry of State in March 1905 that aimed at introducing a general Imperial inheritance tax, stiff increases in tobacco and cigarette taxes, new brewery taxes, and stamp duties that were to bring in 230 million annually.[195] While a decent compromise, it was bound to offend just those Reichstag constituents on which the funding the fleet depended. Slowly but steadily, fleet politics and Reich financial reform became intermeshed issues that, as will be discussed in the next chapters, would seriously destabilize Bülow's chancellorship. While Tirpitz and the RMA were largely successful in mastering these challenges for the time being, events unfolding in Asia in 1904–5 would usher in circumstances that would undermine many of the assumptions of the "Risk Fleet," throw the RMA's carefully worked-out fleet plans into disarray, and put impossible strains on Reich finances.

---

[195] Ibid., 166.

# 7

# Formal and Informal Empire

## *Weltpolitik* and the German Colonies – Karl Helfferich

If Germany was making great headway by 1904 in its maritime trade, this could not be said about its overseas empire, both its formal protectorates in Africa and the Pacific and its informal empire in Ottoman Turkey, Japan, and Venezuela. While the economist Karl Helfferich was introduced in the previous chapter in the debate over the Bülow tariff in 1901, his own first direct involvement in *Weltpolitik* predated this and actually began with German colonial policy, and he would later become an important influence on the colonial reforms implemented under Bernhard Dernburg (1865–1937) as state secretary of a new Colonial Office in 1907. As will be revealed in this and subsequent chapters, Helfferich's activities and writings are very important for understanding the contours of German *Weltpolitik* after 1900, especially also through his direct involvement in the construction of the Berlin-Baghdad railroad after 1906.

Helfferich had moved from Strasbourg to Berlin after completing his doctorate under Georg Friedrich Knapp in 1894. He began his *Habilitation* at Berlin University on the currency reform and introduction of the gold standard in the German Empire, making extensive use of material at the Reichsbank in Berlin, where he also developed good contacts to Richard Koch (1834–1910), its president. He completed this study in 1898 and submitted it to the University of Berlin for the *venia legendi*. Helfferich then traveled to Egypt to recover from a recurring lung ailment in the winter and spring of 1898–99. While staying at the Shepheard's Hotel in Cairo, he chanced upon Oscar Wilhelm Stübel (1846–1921).[1] Stübel, who had been German consul in Samoa and Shanghai (the latter where Schumacher had been a frequent guest in 1897), had just been tapped to head the Colonial Section of the Foreign Office. Helfferich impressed Stübel with the clarity of his thought, and upon receiving the necessary recommendations, Stübel offered Helfferich an entry-level probationary position in the Colonial Section as an economic consultant

---

[1] Karl von Lumm, *Karl Helfferich als Währungspolitiker und Gelehrter* (Leipzig: C. L. Hirschfeld, 1926), 94.

(*wirtschaftlicher Referent*) in a new economic department, which Helfferich accepted, beginning work there in October 1, 1901.[2] Incidentally, Helfferich's fellow junior assistant in the Colonial Section at the time was Arthur Zimmermann, whom Hermann Schumacher had met during his journey to China in 1897.[3]

In the meantime, Helfferich's *Habilitation* had been accepted by the Berlin faculty, despite the vehement opposition of Professor Adolph Wagner, who objected to Helfferich's uncompromising criticism of bimetallism, the Junker landowners, and agricultural protectionism. This had come to light not so much in his *Habilitation* thesis as through a polemic Helfferich had waged in the press against the Free Conservative Reichstag deputy Otto Arendt (1854–1936), the most vocal supporter of bimetallism in Germany at the time.[4] As it turned out, Gustav Schmoller, who happened to be serving as rector of the University of Berlin at the time, was of a notably friendly disposition toward Helfferich and full of praise for his *Habilitation* thesis, turning into an important ally of his in the faculty deliberations and helping to assure his acceptance as *Privatdozent* by arguing strongly in his favor.[5]

In the winter of 1899–1900, while lecturing for the first time at the University of Berlin, Helfferich accepted a lecturing engagement organized by the General Lecture Agency of the Upper Schools Board in Hamburg (Allgemeines Vorlesungswesen der Oberschulbehörde, the predecessor of the Hamburg Colonial Institute), which allowed him to distill his thoughts on trade policy in a lecture series that was later published by Duncker & Humblot.[6] His lectures, while elaborating the history and theory of trade policy going back to the age of mercantilism, had a distinctly contemporary point of reference, stressing the significance of *Weltwirtschaft* and foreign trade in the German economy and the important decisions that would arise with the expiry of Germany's trade treaties with its most important trading partners in 1903.[7] These lectures also revealed the extent to which Helfferich had internalized the messages that Schmoller and his students had disseminated about the role that power politics were now playing in determining the terms of trade and access to markets, as well as the importance of a strong fleet to deter those who would

---

[2] Ibid.; Williamson, *Karl Helfferich*, 60; van Laak, *Imperiale Infrastruktur*, 134.
[3] Williamson, *Karl Helfferich*, 61.
[4] Ibid., 36–38. On Helfferich's involvement in the bimetallist controversy, a libel suit, and its complications for his *Habilitation*, see ibid., 22–36; von Lumm, *Karl Helfferich*, 20–30. Cf. Barkin, *The Controversy*. Helfferich's *Habilitation* was published as Karl Helfferich, *Die Reform des deutschen Geldwesens nach der Gründung des Reiches*, 2 vols. (Leipzig: Duncker & Humblot, 1898).
[5] von Lumm, *Karl Helfferich*, 82–83, 87; Williamson, *Karl Helfferich*, 36, 37.
[6] Karl Helfferich, *Handelspolitik: Vorträge, gehalten in Hamburg im Winter 1900/01 im Auftrag der Hamburgischen Oberschulbehörde* (Leipzig: Duncker & Humblot, 1901).
[7] Helfferich, *Handelspolitik*, 6.

Figure 7.1  Karl Helfferich in 1898.

encroach on Germany's peaceful worldwide commercial successes.[8] Indeed, he was quite explicit in pointing to the United States' defeat of Spain and seizure of its colonies, the two-year bloody war it was then waging against the "formerly free people of the Philippines," and Britain's war with the Transvaal for its gold mines. To Helfferich these were vivid examples of the menace of a new "imperialism," which, he noted, was in fact nothing more than trade wars to gain political control over valuable land and resources.[9] Indeed, as an advocate of German industry and *Weltwirtschaft* but also of a navally-armed and assertive *Weltpolitik*, his views were much like those of Rathgen, von Halle, and Schumacher except that he had not yet had a chance to spend much time abroad. These views made him an ideal candidate for lecturing on *Weltwirtschaft* at the Oceanographic Institute in Kiel, a position, as will be recalled, that was first offered to Hermann Schumacher in 1899 but that was then extended to Helfferich in October 1900 by the Prussian Ministry of Culture. He also agreed to give similar such lectures at the Seminar for Oriental Languages in Berlin.[10]

By the late 1890s neither private investors nor the Reichstag had shown much interest or given much support to Germany's overseas colonies. This meant that colonial development had been left largely in the hands of private

---

[8] Ibid., 83–84.   [9] Ibid., 82–83.   [10] Williamson, *Karl Helfferich*, 38–39.

concession companies that had been granted monopolistic rights. These companies had concentrated most colonial assets in their hands, which led over time to unsustainable exploitation of the land, natural resources, and especially the peoples of the colonies, notably in Africa. At the same time, underqualified and inexperienced colonial officials (often drawn to the colonies for lack of career prospects in Germany) exercised excessive bureaucratic control and discretion (decried at the time as *Kolonial-Assessorismus*) that often weighed like a dead hand on indigenous economic development. The wide latitudes given colonial justice and the military – and its frequent deployment at the behest of the concession companies – had led to high-handed treatment and violent abuse of the native peoples.[11]

When Helfferich entered the Colonial Section in 1901 the German colonial project was already under the pall of a number of colonial scandals. These had been uncovered most spectacularly in the case of Carl Peters, founder of German East Africa, who was recalled to Germany in 1892 for executing his concubine and manservant and later dishonorably discharged from imperial service.[12] Carl Peters' company, the German East Africa Company (DOAG), had conducted it affairs very cavalierly, generating frictions with Arab coastal traders and then leading to a major uprising in 1888–89 that the DOAG was in no position to suppress. Troops had to be dispatched from Germany, and by 1891 the territory had come under direct control of its first German colonial governor. Extensive military campaigns had to be waged between 1891 and 1897 just to pacify the territory, with much of the eastern parts of the country remaining under indirect rule or ungoverned. The region around Mount Kilimanjaro was particularly troublesome in this respect because of the influx of white settlers in the 1890s. The DOAG and the colonial government had sought to develop large-scale plantation cash crop production and to systematically exploit the human and natural resources of the colony to this end. Village cotton production was made compulsory by the administration and traditional hunting was prohibited or restricted. Lands were expropriated and native labor was recruited, often forcibly, to work the plantations.[13]

In German Cameroon, scandals, abusive practices, and uprisings of various kinds were running themes and had already made German headlines alongside the case of Peters in 1893 relating to the brutality of its governor Heinrich Leist (1859–1910).[14] As in German East Africa, large plantations dominated the economy, notably the West African Plantation Company Victoria, the

---

[11] Werner Schiefel, *Bernhard Dernburg 1865-1937: Kolonialpolitiker und Bankier im Wilhelminischen Deutschland* (Zurich: Atlantis Verlag, 1974), 31–35.
[12] See Arne Perras, *Carl Peters and German Imperialism 1856-1918. A Political Biography* (Oxford: Clarendon Press, 2004), 185–229; Guettel, "From the Frontier," 539–42.
[13] Gründer, *Geschichte der deutschen Kolonien*, 85–89, 154–69, esp. 157–62.
[14] Ibid., 139.

single most important planter company in the colony and a favorite of Leist's successor, Jesko von Puttkamer (1855–1917), who was a shareholder. With the connivance of the colonial government, the company systematically expropriated native lands in the Cameroon highlands, destroying village life and removing the natives to reservations or turning them into plantation laborers subject to much coercion and abuse. In August 1900 reports of such abuses appeared in the German press, and by March 1901 complaints about Puttkamer's abusive and corrupt regime even reached the floor of the Reichstag.[15]

Karl Rathgen was one of the first of Schmoller's students to articulate a more humane and rational program for German colonization that emphasized a civilizing mission. He did so at the annual conference of the Evangelical Social Congress in Karlsruhe in June 1900, and his views enjoyed much resonance with the audience, eventually forming the basis of the organization's colonial program.[16] Rathgen argued that the challenge to Evangelical-Lutheran morality and to the church posed by global trade and the new imperialism was to spread itself to lower cultures and thus enable their material and intellectual progress. That is, rather than a search for profits or the extension of political power, colonization was a civilizational duty. The subordination of less civilized peoples was only legitimate, he argued, if it made contributions to the improvement of those people. He saw this very much akin to the obligations that the upper classes had in morally justifying their privileges by looking after the welfare of the lower classes. As he argued,

> Conquest and subordination without subsequent work raising the culture is without value; conquest only with the aim of exploitation is reprehensible.... No reward at the cost of those ruled, no advantage without simultaneous elevation of the conquered. Just as the hierarchy of social classes and the better conditions of the higher orders will never disappear but must be morally justified by dedication to the whole and care for the lower-standing classes, so it is as well in the relationship between ruler and ruled peoples and races.[17]

Two years later at the first German Colonial Congress in Berlin in 1902 Gustav Schmoller expressed views similar to Rathgen's but with a more economic focus. Here Schmoller criticized colonial plantation farming because it reduced the natives to the status of proletarianized wage laborers, leading to

---

[15] Ibid., 146–49.
[16] Evangelisch-Sozialer Kongress, *Die Verhandlungen des Elften Evangelisch-sozialen Kongresses, abgehalten zu Karlsruhe am 7. und 8. Juni 1900: Nach den stenografischen Protokollen* (Göttingen: Vandenhoeck & Ruprecht, 1900).
[17] Ibid., 134.

short-term profits but in the long run to the economic ruin of the colonies.[18] Instead, he supported "native farming" (*Eingeborenenkulturen*) and fostering the technical improvement of "native small businesses" (*Eingeborenenkleinbetrieb*), which he saw as working toward the intellectual and "economic upbringing" (*wirtschaftliche Erziehung*) and for the future of the "subdued lower races" (*unterworfenen niedrigen Rassen*).[19] What is remarkable about these ideas is that they mesh almost seamlessly with the kinds of policies that Schmoller and his colleagues in the Association for Social Policy had been advocating in Germany since the late 1860s, notably securing, modernizing, and integrating the *Mittelstand* trades into an industrial economy and fostering land reform in Prussian East Elbia, in the case of the latter, to break up large estates into family farms and foster a move to modern intensive farming.[20] Despite the racial hierarchies evoked by references to "lower races," transferring German developmental strategies to the colonial subjects made the rather liberal assumption that the "natives" were receptive to incentives and could be integrated into an evolving modern capitalist economy without resort to compulsions (as some continued to advocate), and that technical improvements could pave the way to better material conditions for the native population and longer-term prosperity.[21]

Karl Helfferich would come around to similar views. In the Colonial Section Helfferich had gained considerable hands-on experience, where he had initiated the introduction of the mark as currency in most of the German colonies, been closely involved in a currency reform in German East Africa, and worked

---

[18] Deutscher Kolonialkongress, *Verhandlungen des Deutschen Kolonialkongresses 1902 zu Berlin am 10. und 11. Oktober 1902* (Berlin: D. Riemer, 1903), 515. See also Franz-Josef Schulte-Althoff, "Koloniale Krise und Reformprojekte: Zur Diskussion über eine Kurskorrektur in der deutschen Kolonialpolitik nach der Jahrhundertwende," in *Weltpolitik, Europagedanke, Regionalismus: Festschrift für Heinz Gollwitzer zum 65. Geburtstag am 30. Januar 1982*, ed. Heinz Dollinger, Horst Gründer, and Alwin Hanschmidt (Münster: Aschendorff, 1982), 407–25, here 412–13.

[19] Deutscher Kolonialkongress, *Verhandlungen*, 515.

[20] Grimmer-Solem, *Historical Economics*, 144–49, 223–45; cf. Gustav Schmoller, *Zur Geschichte der deutschen Kleingewerbe im 19. Jahrhundert: Statistische und Nationalökonomische Untersuchungen* (Halle: Verlag der Buchhandlung des Waisenhauses, 1870); Schmoller, *Korreferat über innere Kolonisation mit Rücksicht auf die Erhaltung und Vermehrung des mittleren und kleineren ländlichen Grundbesitzes*, SdVfS, vol. 33 (Leipzig: Duncker & Humblot, 1886), 90–101; Sebastian Conrad, "'Eingeborenenpolitik' in Kolonie und Metropole: 'Erziehung zur Arbeit' in Ostafrika und Ostwestfalen," in Conrad and Osterhammel, *Das Kaiserreich transnational*, 107–28; Zimmerman, *Alabama in Africa*.

[21] Kolonialkongress, *Verhandlungen*, 516; cf. G. K. Anton, "Über die neuere Agrarpolitik der Holländer in Java," *JbfGVV* 23 (1899): 1337–62.

to increase the pace of railroad investments in German colonial Africa.[22] He was an unusually industrious assistant and quickly rose through the ranks of the Foreign Office after his probationary period ended in 1902. He had by that time already gained the attention of Chancellor Bülow, to whom Helfferich had been recommend by Ludwig Bamberger (1823–99) and Georg von Siemens (1839–1901), the cofounder and director, respectively, of the Deutsche Bank, who both knew Helfferich's father from their common work in the left liberal Freisinnige Partei.[23]

By 1904 Helfferich had been elevated to *Legitionsrat* (legation councilor) and was participating as a government representative in deliberations of the Reichstag's Budget Commission. By that point he was on familiar terms with Bülow and involved in developing the chancellor's program for the reform of colonial administration, which among other things aimed at separating the civilian from military administration, fostering greater colonial self-government, and creating a new Reich Colonial Office with its own state secretary.[24] As an indication of his rising status, by 1905 Helfferich, only 33 years old at the time, had advanced to the rank of *Vortragender Rat* (reporting councilor), a position usually only granted much more experienced and senior men.[25] Meanwhile, he gained the title of "professor" from the Prussian government but declined professorships in political economy at both the Technische Hochschule Karlsruhe in 1902 and at the University of Bonn in 1904.[26]

To Helfferich's mind, railways were particularly important to colonial development because the climate and geography of German Africa put strict limits on river transport.[27] In order to unlock the potential of the African colonies and stimulate German investment and native enterprise, railways would have to be built to create a colonial division of labor and link the colonies to *Weltwirtschaft*. That would allow the systematic production of such important staples as cotton, thereby reducing Germany's dependence on foreign (e.g., American) sources of this fiber and thus also improving

---

[22] Williamson, *Karl Helfferich*, 60–68; von Lumm, *Karl Helfferich*, 39–45. See esp. Helfferich's East African coinage memorandum: BArch K, N 1123, Nl. Helfferich, Paket 7, Denkschrift über die Neuordnung des Münzwesens in Deutsch-Ostafrika, [signed Dr. Helfferich], (Für den Gebrauch der Kolonial-Abteilung. *Streng Vertraulich!*) (Berlin: Reichsdruckerei, 1902); "Neuordnung des deutsch-ostafrikanischen Münzwesens, I" *National-Zeitung*, May 3, 1904; "Neuordnung des deutsch-ostafrikanischen Münzwesens, II" *National-Zeitung*, May 4, 1904; "Banken in den deutschen Schutzgebieten," *National-Zeitung*, Oct. 14, 1904; "Die parlamentarische Behandlung der afrikanischen Eisenbahnen," *National-Zeitung*, May 3, 1904; "Die beiden Afrika-Bahnen," *National-Zeitung*, June 14, 1904.

[23] Bülow, *Denkwürdigkeiten*, vol. 1, 219. Cf. Smith, *Ideological Origins*, 81.

[24] Karl Helfferich, "Das Kolonialprogramm des Reichskanzlers," *National-Zeitung*, Dec. 11, 1904; Williamson, *Karl Helfferich*, 76; Helfferich, *Der Weltkrieg*, vol. 1, 35.

[25] Williamson, *Karl Helfferich*, 76.   [26] Ibid., 78; von Lumm, *Karl Helfferich*, 94.

[27] Williamson, *Karl Helfferich*, 67–68.

Germany's negotiating position with other trading partners such as the United States.[28] Yet Helfferich recognized Germany had only started colonial railway investments very late and that the record of state-directed construction and operation of such railways was poor.[29] New approaches were thus needed.

Helfferich elaborated on some of these ideas in a speech that he gave at the plenary session of the second Colonial Congress in Berlin in October 1905.[30] In it, Helfferich acknowledged that the German colonies were at the very beginning of their economic development and that Germany had both an obligation and an interest to assure their rapid growth into higher levels of productivity and consumption.[31] He highlighted Germany's disadvantageous position compared to Great Britain and the United States – the United States, he noted, could pursue its economic expansion, strengthen is maritime means of power [*maritime Machmittel*], and vastly expand its external colonial empire in parallel. Other nations possessed colonial empires whose significance was vastly greater than the metropole's external economic relations. That was quite the reverse of Germany, he noted, whose significance as an overseas trading and shipping power was second only to Great Britain yet which had a colonial empire of still only modest economic significance. To secure Germany's future position in the world [*Weltstellung*], its fate was tied to the question of whether it could make up lost time to give its global economic interests [*weltwirtschaftlichen Interessen*] the needed protection against foreign violations [*fremde Vergewaltigungen*] by expanding its naval deterrent and giving its colonial possessions the needed territorial basis for development. Germany needed productive colonies not to close them off to other nations, but rather as important means to secure favorable trading conditions worldwide, just as England's colonies had been to England in opening the world's doors to its trade.[32]

Modern technology allowed Germany to overcome the natural disadvantages of its colonies – notably poor natural harbors and the lack of navigable rivers into the hinterland – by building ports and railways, and it was in this area that state initiative and assistance had to become effective, as the sheer size of the necessary investments and the uncertainty over future profitability

---

[28] "Die Baumwollfrage: Ein weltwirtschaftliches Problem," *National-Zeitung*, June 5, 1904; "Die Baumwollfrage: Ein weltwirtschaftliches Problem," *Marine-Rundschau* 15 (June 1904): 641–67; "Deutsch-koloniale Baumwollkultur in amerikanischer Beleuchtung" *Nation und Welt*, July 20, 1904 in BArch K, N1123, Nl. Helfferich, Paket 8, [Rotes Lederband mit Zeitungsausschnitte vom Jahr 1904]. Cf. Beckert, *Empire of Cotton*, 362–75; Smith, *Ideological Origins*, 76–78; Zimmerman, *Alabama in Africa*, 112–65.

[29] Williamson, *Karl Helfferich*, 68.

[30] BArch K, N 1123, Nl. Helfferich, Paket 7, Karl Helfferich, "Die Bedeutung der Kolonien für die deutsche Volkswirtschaft," *Sonderabdruck aus den Verhandlungen des deutschen Kolonialkongresses 1905:* 571–84. [Plenarsitzung am 5. Oktober, Vormittag].

[31] Ibid., 571–72, 577.    [32] Ibid., 579–80.

made it difficult for private investors to play that role. Only through the extension of transportation though a methodical construction of railways and roads would it be possible to create the conditions under which private entrepreneurship could become an active participant in the economic development and utilization of the colonies.[33] But as will be discussed more in Chapter 8, Helfferich's view was that the best way for the state to foster the construction of railways and other such infrastructure in the colonies was not by direct involvement but rather by providing interest and loan guarantees and minimum operating expenses to enable construction by private firms, just as had been done in the construction of the Germany's railway network at home.[34] Indeed, as liberal Helfferich believed that Germans had a misplaced faith in the capacities of state administration and administrative reforms to achieve progress in the colonial endeavor. What an effective colonial administration could do "was mostly confined to clearing away obstacles and frictions... The actual forward driving force does not lie in the formal organization but in the living people, in the personalities that give our colonial policy direction, in the officials that embody our colonial organization, and not least in the people itself, without whose support and participation Prince Bismarck had already declared any colonial policy as hopeless."[35] It was Helfferich's belief, shared by Schmoller and the rest of his students, Bülow, and Dernburg, that the key to the elevation of both African *Kultur* and economic development was railways, just as it was hoped it would be on the Shantung Peninsula and elsewhere in China.

## The Baghdad Railway

Venezuela, German colonial Africa, and the Shantung Peninsula were not the only places where railways promised to serve as bridgeheads of German *Weltpolitik*. By 1900 the Turkish Empire had entered the picture in what would ultimately become the single largest German railway investment overseas, eclipsing even the Great Venezuela Railway: the Baghdad Railway, better known as the Berlin-Baghdad railroad. In 1906 Helfferich would himself be appointed as a managing director of the Anatolian Railway which controlled the Baghdad Railway and that will be elaborated in Chapter 9, but by way of background, a brief account of its development until 1905 is in order.

There had been plans to build a comprehensive railway system for the Ottoman Empire going back to the early 1870s. This had aimed at enhancing Constantinople's military and administrative reach and in developing thinly-populated Anatolia, but this had been delayed due to Turkey's national

---

[33] Ibid., 583.   [34] Williamson, *Karl Helfferich*, 68.
[35] BArch K, N 1123, Nl. Helfferich, Paket 7, Karl Helfferich, *Zur Reform der kolonialen Verwaltungs-Organisation* (Berlin: Mittler und Sohn, 1905), 47.

bankruptcy in 1875.[36] In these years a bridgehead for German influence was first formed by German military advisors sent to Turkey on request of Sultan Abdul Hamid II (1842–1918) following Turkey's defeat in war with Russia in 1878.[37] In the 1880s ideas for such a railroad were resurrected with plans to build a railway from Haydarpasha (near Constantinople on the Asian side of the Bosporus) to Ankara. At the time, the Ottoman government was heavily reliant on French lending and the Paris bourse, so it was eager to involve British or German banks to counterbalance this French influence. British banks showed little interest in financing such a railway, nor did German ones for that matter until the Württembergische Vereinsbank was offered a concession to build the railroad in 1888. As the project was too large for this provincial bank, it was passed to the Deutsche Bank, which accepted the project after the Turkish government offered to guarantee the interest on the capital and Bismarck assured some diplomatic backing.[38] The British approved the project because they, too, were keen to counterbalance French influence in Turkey and the Mediterranean at the time and wary of Russian designs on the Straits and expansion into Asian Turkey and Persia.[39] In early October 1888 the concession to build and run the railway was signed between a consortium of banks led by the Deutsche Bank and the Ottoman government. Soon thereafter the Ottoman Anatolian Railway Company (Société du Chemin de Fer Ottoman d'Anatolie) was founded in Constantinople. As was the case with the Great Venezuela Railway discussed in Chapter 4, all of the materials for the railroad were sourced from German firms, notably Philipp Holzmann & Co. for the construction work, Krupp for the rails, and a number of other German firms for the rolling stock that included Krauss & Co., J.A. Maffei, Hannoverischer Maschinenbau A.G., and Maschinenfabrik Esslingen.[40]

Although the stretch of railway to Ankara was completed in 1893, and that year the company received a concession to build a railway between Eskisehir and Konya, financing the railway project proved challenging, and extending the line beyond Ankara to Baghdad as Abdul Hamid II was keen to do would involve the costly business of crossing the Taurus and Amanus mountains and the political risks of entering the Russian sphere of influence.[41] Yet for precisely the latter reason the railway began to attract the attention of the German Foreign Office. After Marschall von Bieberstein was appointed German ambassador to the Sublime Porte in 1897, and then with Kaiser

---

[36] Gall et al., *The Deutsche Bank*, 67.
[37] See Schöllgen, *Imperialismus und Gleichgewicht*, 32–37.
[38] Ibid., 39–41; Lothar Gall et al., *The Deutsche Bank, 1870–1995* (London: Weidenfeld & Nicolson, 1995), 68–69; Helfferich, *Der Weltkrieg*, vol. 1, 123.
[39] Schöllgen, *Imperialismus und Gleichgewicht*, 41–46.
[40] Gall et al., *The Deutsche Bank*, 69–70.
[41] Ibid., 70–71. See also Schöllgen, *Imperialismus und Gleichgewicht*, 80–85.

Wilhelm, Bülow, and Siemens' visit to the Middle East in 1898, the railway grew in political significance. The sultan approved concessions to the railway to build harbor facilities at Haydarpasha and lay telegraph cables between Constanta and Constantinople.[42] Kurt Zander, the new director of the railway, and Marschall worked to gain the concession to extend the railway to Baghdad and keep the project in German hands.[43] When the sultan, aware of the Kaiser's enthusiasm for the project, offered the Germans a concession to extend the Eskisehir-Konya railway all the way to Baghdad, Siemens and the Deutsche Bank were pushed into this undertaking very reluctantly on account of the disappointing returns on the Anatolian Railway and a tight German capital market.[44] Nevertheless in November 1899 the pre-concessions to build the railway all the way to Basra were secured, and by Christmas the Baghdad Convention was signed.[45]

Meanwhile back in Germany, the idea of a German presence and civilizing mission in Anatolia and Mesopotamia began to animate educated middle class opinion as a new prong of *Weltpolitik* to acquire a "German India."[46] The strategic significance of such a project – one of which Siemens was well conscious – was that it could link central Europe directly to the Persian Gulf and Indian Ocean and thus by a much shorter and faster land route that avoided the British-controlled chokepoint at Suez. For example, while a journey between Vienna and Bombay required 16 ½ days via the Mediterranean and Suez Canal, the same journey was projected to require only 9 ½ days via railway through the Balkans, Asia Minor, and Mesopotamia and then by sea from the Persian Gulf.[47] In its potential to connect India and Europe, Karl

---

[42] See Manfred Pohl, *Von Stambul nach Bagdad: Die Geschichte einer berühmten Eisenbahn* (Munich and Zurich: Piper, 1999), 51–56; Bülow, *Denwürdigkeiten*, vol. 1, 242–60; Helfferich, *Der Weltkrieg*, vol. 1, 12; Schöllgen, *Imperialismus und Gleichgewicht*, 107–31.

[43] Mommsen, *Bürgerstolz und Weltmachtstreben*, 354–56.

[44] Pohl, *Von Stambul nach Bagdad*, 55–56.

[45] Ibid., 59–61; see also Canis, *Von Bismarck zur Weltpolitik*, 295–96, 299, 361–63; Gall, et al., *The Deutsche Bank*, 71; Sean McMeekin, *The Berlin-Baghdad Express: The Ottoman Empire and Germany's Bid for World Power* (Cambridge, MA: Harvard University Press, 2010), 38–43.

[46] Canis, *Von Bismarck zur Weltpolitik*, 300–301, 363–64; Dietrich Eichholtz, *Die Baghdadbahn, Mesopotamien und die deutsche Ölpolitik bis 1918: Aufhaltsamer Übergang ins Erdözeitalter* (Leipzig: Leipziger Universitätsverlag, 2007), 21; Malte Fuhrmann, *Der Traum vom deutschen Orient: Zwei deutsche Kolonien im Osmanischen Reich 1851-1918* (Frankfurt and New York: Campus Verlag, 2006), 47–82. Cf. Friedrich Naumann, *"Asia": Athen, Konstantinopel, Baalbek, Damaskus, Nazaret, Jerusalem, Kairo, Neapel*, 3rd ed. (Berlin-Schöneberg: Verlag der "Hilfe," 1900); Paul Rohrbach, *Die Bagdadbahn* (Berlin: Wiegandt & Grieben, 1902). See also Boris Barth, *Die deutsche Hochfinanz und die Imperialismen: Banken und Aussenpolitik vor 1914* (Stuttgart: Franz Steiner, 1995), 219–21; Pohl, *Von Stambul nach Bagdad*, 116–19.

[47] Pohl, *Von Stamabul nach Bagdad*, 122.

Helfferich called it nothing less than a *"Weltlinie ersten Ranges"* (world line of the first order).[48]

Since the Deutsche Bank could not manage to finance this massive undertaking on its own, Siemens had long sought the participation of the Ottoman Public Debt Administration (Caisse Dette Publique Ottoman) and British, American, and French banks, but the American and British banks were skeptical, and large-scale involvement of foreign investors was rejected by Marschall, who insisted on it remaining a purely German undertaking.[49] But even the Prussian state bank, the Seehandlung, and the Reichsbank rejected offering the project any state guarantees, despite the Kaiser's pleading.[50] It was thus not until April 1903 that Deutsche Bank actually managed to organize the financing, secure all the concessions, and found the Baghdad Railway Company (Société Imperial Ottoman du Chemin de Fer de Bagdad).[51] After Siemens' death in 1901, Deutsche Bank's Arthur Gwinner (1856–1931) took overall charge of Deutsche Bank's Turkish railway investments as president of the Anatolian Railway and again attempted to gain British investors for the project, which was supported by Lansdowne and Balfour, but as will be touched on later in this chapter, elicited howls of protest in the British parliament and press in the aftermath of the Second Venezuela Crisis in the spring of 1903 and so had to be abandoned.[52] In the end the enterprise was nevertheless successfully internationalized to some degree, with Deutsche Bank holding 40 percent of the shares, the Banque Impérial Ottomane (30 percent), the Anatolian Railway Company (10 percent), the Wiener Bankverein and Credit Suisse (7.5 percent each), as well as a number of Italian and Turkish banks holding 5 percent of the shares.[53] Despite official opposition from the Quai d'Orsay, the cooperation of French banks (with significant interests in Banque Impérial Ottomane) and access to the French capital market were secured and would prove fundamental to financing construction,[54] which only serves to highlight the irrational distrust of the undertaking by the British public.[55] Gwinner was chairman, while the statutes of the company stipulated two vice-chairman, one French and the other German.[56] Kurt Zander, General Director of the Anatolian Railway, was appointed director of the company. In 1906 Karl Helfferich was appointed Second Director of the Anatolian Railway

---

[48] Helfferich, *Der Weltkrieg*, vol. 1, 125.
[49] Barth, *Die deutsche Hochfinanz*, 221–22; Gall et al., *The Deutsche Bank*, 71–72; Pohl, *Von Stambul nach Bagdad*, 57, 64.
[50] Pohl, *Von Stambul nach Bagdad*, 63.    [51] Ibid., 64–72, 119.
[52] Helfferich, *Der Weltkrieg*, vol. 1, 128–31; Rose, *Zwischen Empire und Kontinent*, 300–312; Kennedy, *Anglo-German Antagonism*, 260–61; Mommsen, *Bürgerstolz und Weltmachtstreben*, 357.
[53] Gall et al., *The Deutsche Bank*, 73.    [54] Barth, *Die deutsche Hochfinanz*, 208–9, 212–13.
[55] Ibid., 228.    [56] Gall et al., *The Deutsche Bank*, 73–74.

by Gwinner, and in that capacity served as the German vice-chairman of the Bagdad Railway, its subsidiary.[57]

On March 5, 1903, a convention was signed by the Turkish government and Deutsche Bank giving the bank a ninety-nine-year concession to build the first stretch of the Baghdad Railway.[58] A coup of sorts for the Deutsche Bank was securing a forty-year preliminary concession in July 1904 to exploit the oil fields of Mesopotamia, with the Anatolian Railway given the right to explore the area between Mosul and Baghdad for oil.[59] Indeed, Gwinner was aware that the Bagdad Railway could be equipped to move that oil and that over the longer run this might make the German market independent of Standard Oil – the significance of oil was growing for the German economy, and at the time the Deutsche Bank was already a majority shareholder in the largest Romanian oil company, Steaua, and active in oil production in Austrian Galicia.[60] However, in order to make the enterprise profitable in the immediate term in light of the enormous outlays of capital, Gwinner sought to extend the railway beyond Baghdad to Basra near the Persian Gulf, but this met with vehement opposition from the British, as transport between Baghdad and the Gulf was in the hands of a British river transport company.[61] It also opened up the specter of a German presence in the British sphere of influence in Persia, Kuwait, and the Persian Gulf, with a possible faster route to India and the Far East. Likewise the Russians saw the growing German presence in Turkey as stabilizing the Ottoman state and viewed the railway with growing alarm as it drew closer to the Caucasus and its own sphere of interest in Persia. So while the Baghdad Railway was already under construction in 1905, it was increasingly the object of an intense diplomatic tug of war in Constantinople that opened up new fields of conflict with both Britain and Russia that over the longer term encouraged an Anglo-Russian entente.[62]

## The Retreat of "Germandom" in Japan

Of all the areas of German informal empire, the one that was most neglected in the first years of the twentieth century was Japan, despite the enormous investment of German human capital in that country in the 1880s and Japan's

---

[57] Helfferich, *Der Weltkrieg*, vol. 1, 131–32; Gall et al., *The Deutsche Bank*, 77; Williamson, *Karl Helfferich*, 78–80.
[58] Helfferich, *Der Weltkrieg*, vol. 1, 129, 131; Barth, *Die deutsche Hochfinanz*, 210.
[59] Eichholtz, *Die Bagdadbahn*, 22–24.  [60] Ibid., 25–26.
[61] Gall et al., *The Deutsche Bank*, 74.
[62] See Schöllgen, *Imperialismus und Gleichgewicht*, 132–76; Canis, *Von Bismarck zur Weltpolitik*, 303–5, 396; Konrad Canis, *Der Weg in den Abgrund: Deutsche Aussenpolitik 1902–1914* (Paderborn: F. Schöningh, 2011), 49–59; McMeekin, *Berlin-Baghdad Express*, 46–52.

central importance in German "precoloniality," as was explored at length in Chapter 2. That neglect was bound up directly with Germany's ambitions in China, which had put Germany at odds with Japan. Yet even as Japan declined as a German priority, Japan's regional strategic significance grew steadily. The British, worried about the Russian presence in Manchuria and northern China and German provocations in the Yangtze basin, were warming to the idea of a regional military alliance with Japan by 1901.[63] This ultimately enabled Japan to confront Russia militarily in 1904, and the military, diplomatic, and strategic consequences of that engagement would ultimately shatter Russia as an Asian power and have far-reaching consequences for Germany.

The starting point of the chill in German-Japanese official relations was of course the sudden German intervention with Russia and France against Japan in 1895 and Japan's humiliating surrender of conquered Chinese territory in the Peace of Shimonoseki. Ever since relinquishing Port Arthur and the Liaotung Peninsula in 1895, diplomatic relations between Japan and Germany were poor, and those with Russia very tense. With Russia then securing a leasehold over the Liaotung Peninsula and Port Arthur in 1897 – which then added to the diplomatic humiliation of Japan – the Japanese had grown increasingly worried about the Russian presence in East Asia and were nudging closer to Russia's great rival in China, Britain. In 1898 the Russians had started building a spur line between Harbin and Port Arthur while building fortifications in the port, further inflaming relations. Likewise, relations between Berlin and Tokyo deteriorated further as Germany gained a foothold in Shantung and tried to exploit Russo-Japanese and Anglo-Russian tensions to its own advantage in China.[64]

The aftermath of the Boxer Rebellion only served to greatly magnify Japanese fears about Russia's Manchurian ambitions. As was discussed in Chapter 6, on the pretext of protecting its Manchurian railway concession, Russia had moved nearly 200,000 troops into Manchuria in 1900 and refused to withdraw them even after the Boxer Protocol was signed in September 1901.[65] Throughout the anti-Boxer intervention, only Britain had shown itself a reliable partner to the Japanese, bound by the common necessity of containing Russian expansionism in East Asia. The British cabinet had itself come around to a similar view about Japan. By the autumn of 1901 there was also broad agreement within the British cabinet that Britain's position among the great powers had been greatly diminished by the dual Boer-Boxer crises, which had highlighted Britain's strategic overstretch, diplomatic isolation, and its

---

[63] See Otte, *The China Question*, 292–306.
[64] See Wippich, *Japan und die deutsche Fernostpolitik*, 359–400, esp. 371–84; Vogel, *Deutsche Rußlandpolitik*, 104–18.
[65] Otte, *The China Question*, 182–83.

inability to respond effectively to multiple emergencies overseas. The tremendous costs of the Boer War added to the appeal of burden-sharing via an alliance. Quite simply, Whitehall could no longer hold it together in the British Empire and its spheres of influence without alliance partners, and the only realistic option in early 1902 became a regional military alliance with Japan.[66]

It should not be overlooked that an alliance between Japan and Britain only became a viable option because Japan had decided – just like Germany – to greatly expanded its bluewater navy in 1896–97, turning it into the fourth largest naval force in the world by 1904.[67] In contrast to Tirpitz, Yamamoto Gonnohyōe had drawn the correct strategic conclusions from bluewater naval thinking: the Japanese Imperial Navy would pursue the offensive and deploy battleships and armored cruisers to gain command of the seas around Japan in case of war.[68] In other words, Japan had *not* opted for the strategic defensive of a battleship "Risk Fleet" as Germany had. Japan had also drawn the right conclusions from the Sino-Japanese War about the proper deployment of smaller flotilla units to support the main battle fleet. While it had *not* opted to build a raiding force as France had, it did integrate these smaller units as part of an effective naval force.[69] To be sure, Japan's geostrategic position was much akin to Britain's. Still, the clarity of Japanese thinking about the appropriate types and mix of naval weapons and tactics to pursue its strategic objectives – in a context of rapid changes in ship design and technology, swift evolution of naval doctrines, and widespread (and often misleading) Mahanist "sea power" ideology – betrayed a superior grasp of the purposes of a modern navy than was the case not only in Germany, but also in France and Russia.[70]

Japan, on account of these naval advantages to Britain – as well as the financial pressure of escalating naval defense costs due to changes in ship design, the acceleration of the French and Russian naval programs, and as importantly, the congruence of Japan's interests with Britain in containing Russia in East Asia – was, in short, truly "alliance worthy."[71] For their part, Japanese statesmen were worried about confronting the Russians on their own, which had the world's third largest navy at the time. As was mentioned in Chapter 5, in 1903 Japan had passed supplemental naval appropriations to significantly increase the size of its navy in response to accelerated Russian naval construction sparked by the German navy law of 1900.[72] The prospect of

---

[66] Ibid., 291–92. David Schimmelpennick van der Oye, "The Immediate Origins of the War," in *The Russo-Japanese War in Global Perspective: World War Zero*, ed. John W. Steinberg et al., vol. 1 (Leiden and Boston: Brill, 2005), 23–44. Ian Nish, "Stretching out to the Yalu: A Contested Frontier," in *Russo-Japanese War*, ed. Steinberg, vol. 1, 45–64; Charmley, *Splendid Isolation*, 295–311.
[67] Evans and Peattie, *Kaigun*, 64.   [68] Ibid.   [69] Ibid., 65.   [70] Ibid., 64–65.
[71] Otte, *The China Question*, 292.   [72] Evans and Peattie, *Kaigun*, 64.

another Tripartite intervention as in 1895 also haunted the Japanese, so a powerful ally in such a scenario was valued. The Anglo-Japanese Alliance that was agreed in early January 1902 and signed later that month did not commit either party to come to the aid of the other in case of war with a single third power; *casus foederis* was only invoked if war broke out with two or more enemies. It was also valid only in East Asia and for a period of five years. The alliance recognized Japan's special economic interests in Korea and its right to defend them if challenged by a third power in return for Japanese assurances to Britain that it had no aggressive intentions on the peninsula.[73] In addition to the formal terms of the alliance, the Japanese and British navies developed combined wartime naval operational plans, exchanged intelligence, and provided for mutual coaling stations and docking facilities.[74]

Oddly, when news of the alliance reached Berlin in February, neither the government nor the press saw any disadvantages in it for Germany; many saw it as strengthening Germany's mediating position and assuring the open door in China, from which Germany might profit. On similar grounds, Bülow refused an invitation to join a Russo-French declaration to preserve the status quo in China, devised as a Russian countermeasure to the Anglo-Japanese Alliance and offering Germany prospects for a continental alliance in the future.[75] By this point it was clear to both London and St. Petersburg that Germany was bent on pursuing its own expansion at the cost of others. This perception, and Germany's growing power potential, would gradually pave the way to eventual rapprochement between Britain and Russia.[76]

As explored at the end of Chapter 2, in the years preceding the Anglo-Japanese Alliance, German-Japanese relations had been on something of a two-way street of official disengagement. The Japanese government was eager to end its reliance on foreign advisors and to reassert its sovereignty with the aid of its German-inspired constitution, legal code, administrative apparatus, and military. This meant that the institutions through which German influence in Japan had flowed came to be neglected. For example, the Association School in Tokyo, which had played such an extraordinary role in training the Meiji judicial and bureaucratic elite, found itself increasingly short of the staff and resources needed to offer its "special course" on a regular basis. In

---

[73] Otte, *The China Question*, 305; Evans and Peattie, *Kaigun*, 65.
[74] Evans and Peattie, *Kaigun*, 65–66. See also Canis, *von Bismarck zur Weltpolitik*, 281–92, 303, 315–16, 319–23, 347–48, 369–75; Otte, *The China Question*, 271–91, 297–99, 303; Rose, *Zwischen Empire und Kontinent*, 300–311.
[75] Carroll, *Germany and the Great Powers*, 470–71; Röhl, *Into the Abyss*, 173. In greater depth, see Canis, *Von Bismarck zur Weltpolitik*, 295–307, 383–84, 393–94; Vogel, *Deutsche Rußlandpolitik*, 108–23.
[76] Canis, *Von Bismarck zur Weltpolitik*, 394.

1892 the Japanese Diet cut the subsidies the school had received from the Japanese Ministries of Justice and Education, and in 1895 the "special course" had to be suspended entirely.[77]

When in December 1901 the Association School along with its sizable German library of 13,000 volumes burned to the ground in a fire, the German ambassador, Count Emmerich von Arco-Valley (1852-1909), did not even bother to report the matter to Berlin, so low was it on the list of German diplomatic priorities at the time. Only after this disaster had been reported in the German press in February 1902 and the Kaiser himself began showing a personal interest in it through these reports did it become clear that there was an embarrassing lack of information about it in the Foreign Office, setting diplomatic wheels in motion.[78] Even so, the German ambassador telegrammed Berlin that a contribution toward rebuilding the school was not necessary as the school would be rebuilt on account of its significant student body. Count Acro suggested to the Foreign Office that the Kaiser might offer a 1,000 yen gift (then about 2,000 marks) if he felt it was necessary.[79]

In contrast to the lethargy and indifference of the ambassador and German Foreign Office, the destruction of the Association School and its library elicited much concern and sympathy in segments of the Japan-friendly German public. Indeed, rebuilding the school and restocking its library became an organized private cause spearheaded by many German "old Japan hands" including Rathgen, Michaelis, Mayet, Lange, and others who had worked and taught in Japan in the 1870s and 1880s. Ōmura Jintarō (1863-1907), a former director of the school, was at the time visiting Berlin and became engaged in mobilizing German participation in the rebuilding efforts through articles in the press, particularly in restocking the library, a matter that he himself described as "fostering Germandom abroad."[80] An appeal was signed by many German professors and teachers who had taught in Japan culminating in a "Tokyo Festival," organized by the German Japan Society "Wa-Doku-Kai" (founded in 1888 by Lange and his colleagues at the Berlin Seminar for Oriental Languages). This festival was intended as a fundraiser to restock the library and rebuild the school and was held in the Berlin Philharmonic on

---

[77] PNFBW, Karl Rathgen to Bernhard Rathgen et al., Tokyo, July 8, 1889; BArch L, R 901/39188, Report B 33 [AA IIIb, March 21, 1902] von Arco-Valley, Imperial German Legation in Tokyo, to Reich Chancellor Bülow, Tokyo. Feb. 20, 1902; Schenck, *Der deutsche Anteil*, 249.

[78] *Tägliche Rundschau*, Feb. 5, 1902; BArch L, R 901/39188, Telegram draft to IIIb 1784 of the Foreign Office to the Imperial German Legation in Tokyo, Feb. 11, 1902.

[79] BArch L, R 901/39188 [AA IIIb 2066], Telegram of the Imperial German Legation in Tokyo to the Foreign Office, Feb. 15, 1902.

[80] BArch L, R 901/39188 [AA IIIb 3305], Jintaro Omura, "Die deutsche Schule in Tokio," *Asien* 5 (Feb. 1902): 32-33.

April 3, 1902.[81] It raised 3,000 marks, while larger German booksellers made additional generous book and money contributions.[82] Some 6,000 marks were raised in total along with a very large number of books, whose shipment to Japan some officials in the Prussian Ministry of Culture, acting in a private capacity, later coordinated.[83]

On account of being overshadowed by the success of this private initiative, not a *Pfennig* was contributed to this effort by the Imperial Treasury or the Kaiser.[84] Thanks in part to the private generosity the school could be rebuilt quickly and reopen in late November 1902. Count Arco was unaware of these facts when he participated in the festive reopening of the school as official representative of the Reich on November 29, 1902, announcing pompously "that through the grace of His Majesty the Kaiser, a collection of teaching materials has been made available to the school."[85] Japanese newspapers later reported on the Kaiser's generosity sympathetically.[86] When Friedrich Althoff in the Prussian Ministry of Culture was later informed of Arco's speech, he could not resist notifying the Foreign Office that the German ambassador had been mistaken, laying out the rather embarrassing truth about the source of the books.[87] In any case, in the years following the Association School thrived, becoming Dokkyo Middle School, and in 1947, a private university, Dokkyo Daigaku, retaining many elements of its German orientation.

The German ambassador did gain an appreciation of the importance of German-language instruction to German *Weltpolitik* in Asia through this episode. As he reported to Bülow in September 1903:

> What comes to light for the field of sales of our industry is true of all other fields. There is naturally a constant interplay between German language instruction here in Japan and on the other hand the political situation, the higher or lower standing of our influence and our sympathies, and the manifold relations between both counties. But it is also certain that our share in the further development of the country, our

---

[81] BArch L, R 901/39188, [AA IIIb 3506] March 18, 1902 Invitation to the Tokyo-Festival of the German-Japanese Society Wa-Doku-Kai in Berlin on Thursday, April 3, 1902.
[82] BArch L, R 901/39188, [AA IIIb 49993] P. Brunn to Lentze, Foreign Office, Berlin, April 18, 1902; [AA IIIb 5730] Brunn to Lentze, Berlin, April 27, 1902; BArch L, R901/39188 [AA IIIb 7935], Report B 126 of the Imperial German Legation, Tokyo, May 16, 1902.
[83] BArch L, R 901/39188 [AA IIIb 4556, March 24, 1903] (UII. Nr. 270), Althoff, Prussian Ministry of Culture, to the Prussian Minister of Foreign Affairs, Berlin, March 18, 1903.
[84] BArch L, R 901/39188, Note on AA IIIb 15041, Berlin, Nov. 27, 1902.
[85] BArch L, R 901/39188, [AA IIIb 350], Report B 293 of the Imperial German Legation in Tokyo to Reich Chancellor von Bülow, Tokyo. Dec. 6, 1902.
[86] Ibid.
[87] BArch L, R 901/39188 [AA IIIb 4556 {UII. Nr. 270}], Althoff by commission of the Minister of Culture to the Minister of Foreign Affairs, Berlin, March 18, 1903.

influence and our sales and finally *our position in the competitive struggle with England and America* will be dependent to a high degree on how German language instruction is preserved and develops.[88]

According to Count Arco, Germany was indeed in a precarious position vis-à-vis the "Anglo-Saxons" considering the significant role that American and British mission schools were playing, which he described as "seedbeds" for English. There were according to him no fewer than 776 Anglophone compared to only six German-speaking missionaries in the country.[89] One year prior, in 1902, the German consul in Nagasaki had already written the Foreign Office about the strongly predominating and spreading "Anglo-American" influence in southern Japan, which he attributed to the activity of English and American missionaries.[90] This report noted that German-language instruction was only represented in a few state schools and that only three German teachers were working in southern Japan. The consul urged that German teachers be recruited though the relevant German school associations, particularly teachers who could be employed in technical and commercial schools.[91]

Alas, such pleas fell on deaf ears in the German Foreign Office, which viewed initiatives like these as aiming "not to preserve Germandom so much as artificially carrying it into a foreign people."[92] One later example illustrates this particularly vividly. When Prussian Catholics and German Jesuits led by Cardinal Kopp planned to establish a major new German-language university near imperial palaces and the Austrian embassy in Tokyo, it was initially met with considerable hostility from both the German legation in Tokyo and Foreign Office, despite the specially German character of the institution from its language of instruction to its intellectual traditions and the explicit exclusion of religious instruction in its curriculum.[93] The Jesuits nevertheless prevailed and founded Sophia University (Jōchi Daigaku) in 1913, which thereafter established itself as a leading Japanese university.[94] As usual, the German legation in Tokyo was later eager to claim some credit for it, going so

---

[88] BArch L, R901/39188 [AA IIIb 16445], Report B 266 of the Imperial German Legation in Tokyo to Reich Chancellor von Bülow, Tokyo, Sept. 28, 1903. Emphasis in the original.
[89] Ibid.
[90] PA AA, R 62407 [AA IIIb 2358], Imperial German Consulate to the Foreign Office, Nagasaki, Jan. 6, 1902.
[91] Ibid.  [92] PA AA, R 62407, Note to IIIb 2358, Feb. 24, 1902.
[93] PA, AA R 63159, Enclosure 8 to IIId 596, Pastoral Letter of Cardinal-Princebishop Kopp, Fulda, Aug. 23, 1910; PA, AA R 63159, Transcript to G II 31 U I 1, Cardinal Kopp to the Prussian Minister of Culture, Breslau, Jan. 4, 1913.
[94] See "Die Deutsche Jesuitenschule in Tokio," *Kölnische Zeitung*, Apr. 25, 1913; "Höhere Lehranstalt in deutscher Sprache," *Neue Preußische Zeitung* [*Kreuzzeitung*], May 9, 1913; "Die neugegründete Universität der deutschen Jesuiten in Tokio," *Reichspost*, June 25, 1913.

far as to assert that "the value it can bring for the spread of German culture cannot be overestimated."[95]

Perhaps nothing quite symbolized the intellectual withdrawal of Germany from Japan in these years as the 1911 closure of the German Naval Hospital in Yokohama, which had played such an important role as a conduit for the transmission of German medical knowledge and thus also the German language to Japan, it having been replaced by that point by newer facilities in the German leasehold in Kiaochow.[96] Indeed the contrast between the official neglect in Japan and focus on Kiaochow is quite startling: by 1907 more than 100 million marks had been invested in Germany's tiny Chinese leasehold, more than in any other individual German colony – Bülow later called Tsingtao "our nicest and most promising colony," which is itself a very telling statement.[97] This massive investment in infrastructure, capped by the official opening of the Tsingtao Wharf in May 1907, was accompanied by extensive cultural imperialism much in the mold of German efforts in Japan prior to that point. This included the opening of the German-Chinese School in 1898, the German-Chinese Seminar of the Weimar Mission in 1901, two state-funded elementary schools (*Volksschulen*) in 1905, and the opening of German-Chinese Higher School (college) in 1909.[98] Despite this massive investment, a determined and effective Chinese containment policy prevented the Germans from expanding their influence beyond central Shantung.[99] And very ironically, it was not German but rather Japanese trade that came to dominate the leasehold by 1914.[100]

It is nevertheless a remarkable testament to the durability of the German-oriented path set in Japanese education, law, administration, and the military in the 1870s and 80s – and the ongoing active engagement of German civil society and German educational institutions – that far and away the largest number of Japanese students going overseas for their studies continued to go to Germany. Indeed, the trend was even upward after 1895. In the year 1901,

---

[95] PA AA R 63159, Memorandum B 163 to the Decree IIId 4513/30082 No. 90 from the Imperial German Embassy to Reich Chancellor Bethmann Hollweg, Tokyo, May 10, 1913, fol. 3.
[96] Mühlhahn, *Herrschaft und Widerstand*, 255–62.
[97] Bülow, *Deutsche Politik*, 53; Gründer, *Geschichte der deutschen Kolonien*, 191. By 1913 the total sum invested in Kiaochow is estimated at nearly 200 million marks. See Herwig, *"Luxury" Fleet*, 103–6.
[98] See Mühlhahn, *Herrschaft und Widerstand*, 236–55; Chin-Shik Kim, *Deutscher Kulturimperialismus in China: Deutsches Kolonialschulwesen in Kiautschou (China) 1898–1914* (Stuttgart: Franz Steiner, 2004); Steinmetz, *The Devil's Handwriting*, 479–86; Petersson, *Imperialismus und Modernisierung*, 191–94, 211–13.
[99] John E. Schrecker, *Imperialism and Chinese Nationalism: Germany in Shantung* (Cambridge: Harvard University Press, 1971), 210–45; Mühlhahn, "A New Imperial Vision?" 129–46. See also Mühlhahn, *Heerschaft und Widerstand*, 268–81.
[100] Herwig, *"Luxury" Fleet*, 105.

for example, of the 28 Japanese with state-funded scholarships to study abroad, no fewer than 22 went to Germany.[101] This does not include the significant number of privately-funded students in such fields as medicine and law, for example, who went to Germany in these years to complete their studies, or the nearly uninterrupted flow of Japanese Education Ministry officials, parliamentarians, university rectors, and schoolmasters who went to Germany before 1914 to investigate German schools, universities, and other institutions of learning.[102] Even the Japanese Army General Staff sent by far the most Army Staff College students to study in Germany, with no fewer than 81 sent to Germany before 1914, compared with only 33 to France, 29 to Russia, and 24 to Great Britain.[103]

Another important informal link that was maintained between Germany and Japan was facilitated by the bold involvement of German Jewish bankers in underwriting Japanese loans during and after the Russo-Japanese War, notably Jacob Schiff (1847–1920) of Kuhn, Loeb & Co. in New York and Max Warburg (1867–1946) of the M.M. Warburg Bank in Hamburg.[104] Schiff, who was an Orthodox Jew originally from Frankfurt and whose daughter Frieda was married to Max Warburg's brother Felix (1871–1937), had made his name through the 1897 reorganization of the Union Pacific Railroad and served an illustrious list of clients that included Westinghouse, Western Union, U.S. Rubber, and American Smelting and Refining.[105] As we shall see in later chapters, Schiff was a fierce Germanophile and would later be involved in many important US-German transatlantic philanthropic initiatives.

## The Second Venezuela Crisis

As was discussed in Chapter 3, Venezuela had a sizable German presence, both in terms of merchants and invested capital. Venezuela's financial obligations to German creditors were also substantial, and it is no exaggeration to describe it as part of an informal German overseas empire by 1901. No less than $ 476 million (20 percent of Germany's overseas capital) had been invested by Germans in Central and South America by 1900, which was some three times greater than in Asia ($ 160 million) and nearly eight times greater than in

---

[101] Grimmer-Solem, "Die preußische Bildungspolitik," 212.
[102] See Kim, *Doctors of Empire*.
[103] Lone, *Army, Empire and Politics*, 17. See also Saaler, "Das Deutschlandbild in Japans Politik," 288–98.
[104] Cf. Edward Miller, "Japan's Other Victory: Overseas Financing of the Russo-Japanese War," in *Russo-Japanese War*, ed. Steinberg, vol. 1, 465–83, here 471–82; Max Warburg, *Aus meinen Aufzeichnungen* (New York: Eric M. Warburg, 1952), 19–22.
[105] Ron Chernow, *The Warburgs: The Twentieth Century Odyssey of a Remarkable Jewish Family* (New York: Random House, 1993), 46–52.

Ottoman Turkey ($ 60.69 million).[106] That year, Latin America was the destination of 5 percent of Germany's total exports and accounted for 9.4 percent of its total imports.[107]

In early 1901 Venezuelan President Cipriano Castro (1858-1924), who had seized power in 1899, unilaterally declared his country's obligations to foreign creditors from before his presidency null and void. At the same time, he began to take hold of the lands and assets European settlers and merchants and to seize and destroy ships under foreign flags.[108] In the winter of 1901-2 Germany began to contemplate an intervention. Wary of another invocation of the Monroe Doctrine as in 1895 and also consciously attempting to cultivate closer relations between Germany and the United States, German diplomats assured the United States that any intervention was for debt collection only and then cautiously sent three smaller cruisers to the Venezuelan coast to put pressure on Castro, ruling out any additional action unless approved by Washington and supported by London–Venezuela also had very large financial obligations to Britain.[109] By July 1902 Britain's own patience with Castro was at an end and London proposed an Anglo-German naval blockade of Venezuela under British leadership if Castro refused to heed its ultimatum.[110] There is some indication that the British were at that time trying to test the Monroe Doctrine and thus far less concerned about American sensibilities than the Germans.[111] On November 11, 1902, an Anglo-German agreement was signed for a joint operation to seize Venezuelan gunboats. Even at this early stage the British conservative press led by *The Spectator* and *National Review* was hostile to the agreement as soon as it got wind of Germany's participation.[112]

As is now known, President Roosevelt viewed German involvement in Venezuela in 1902 with suspicion, fearing that the Germans were interested in seizing land or a naval base. This was reinforced by a memorandum by Rear Admiral Henry Clay Taylor (1845-1904), who warned that the only thing Venezuela could offer to settle its debts and indemnify Germany was land.[113]

---

[106] Brechtken, *Scharnierzeit*, 6-7n29.
[107] Fiebig-von Hase, *Lateinamerika als Konfliktherd*, Anhang IIIa and IIIb.
[108] See Rose, *Zwischen Empire und Kontinent*, 279-84; Fiebig-von Hase, *Lateinamerika also Krisenherd*, 850-52.
[109] Pommerin, *Der Kaiser und Amerika*, 113-20; Fiebig-von Hase, *Lateinamerika als Krisenherd*, 852-75, 984-1003; Rose, *Zwischen Empire und Kontinent*, 284, 291; Morris, *Theodore Rex*, 177.
[110] Fiebig-von Hase, *Lateinamerika als Krisenherd*, 875-80, 966-84; Rose, *Zwischen Empire und Kontinent*, 285-90.
[111] Rose, *Zwischen Empire und Kontinent*, 291.
[112] Geppert, *Pressekriege*, 183-88; Mitchell, *The Danger of Dreams*, 73-74.
[113] Edmund Morris, "'A Matter of Extreme Urgency': Theodore Roosevelt, Wilhelm II, and the Venezuela Crisis of 1902," *Naval War College Review* 55, no. 2 (Spring 2002): 73-85, here 75.

Roosevelt, like Taylor, became convinced that the Germans were after land in Latin America in part by a passage in Germany's written commitment to Britain over Venezuela that stated they would consider the temporary occupation of Venezuelan harbors.[114] The German diplomat Hermann Speck von Sternburg (1852–1908) had already conveyed to Roosevelt that Bülow and Tirpitz did not take the Monroe Doctrine seriously and that Germany had ambitions in Brazil, which as was discussed in Chapter 3, had a large German settler presence.[115] Suspicions of German intentions in Brazil and Venezuela had also spread widely in the United States by the excerpts of speeches and essays on Germany's economic future and role in the world given for the Free Union for Naval Lectures, which had appeared in such US newspapers as the *Chicago Tribune* in July 1900.[116] It is also a fact that after 1900 American naval strategists recognized Germany as the primary maritime threat and proceeded to concentrate naval forces in the North Atlantic Fleet.[117] Likewise, operational planning for a naval engagement between the United States and Germany had started in the General Board of the Navy in 1900.[118]

While there is dispute about the degree of Roosevelt's alarm over the Anglo-German operations in Venezuela,[119] Roosevelt had long adopted a maximalist position on the Monroe Doctrine and had clear designs on Panama, and he began to take precautionary measures as the Venezuela Crisis came to a head. On November 21, 1902, four battleships of the US North Atlantic Squadron arrived at Culebra Island near Puerto Rico, where four warships of the Caribbean Squadron awaited, all under the command by Admiral George Dewey, the same admiral who nearly came to blows with the German navy in the Philippines in July 1898 and a notorious Germanophobe.[120]

On November 25, Britain and Germany notified the US State Department that they intended to begin their joint blockade of Venezuela.[121] Meanwhile, the US naval force at Culebra was joined by numerous support vessels, and further south near Trinidad – only 125 miles from the Venezuelan coast – 2 US battleships and 4 cruisers from the US European and South Atlantic squadrons rendezvoused. Together Admiral Dewey eventually had some 53 ships at his disposal to counter 29 British and German ships, the largest

---

[114] Ibid.  [115] Ibid., 76.
[116] "Talk of German Future," *Chicago Tribune*, July 14, 1900.
[117] Bönker, *Militarism in a Global Age*, 116–17.
[118] Mitchell, *The Danger of Dreams*, 55. In greater detail, Fiebig-von Hase, *Lateinamerika als Krisenherd*, 788–839. See also David Trask, "Naval Operations Plans Between Germany and the United States of America, 1898–1913: A Study of Strategic Planning in the Age of Imperialism," *Militärgeschichtliche Mitteilungen* 2 (1970): 5–32; Lambi, *The Navy*, 186, 226–31. Cf. Mitchell, *The Danger of Dreams*, 46–53.
[119] Mitchell, *Danger of Dreams*, 75–79; cf. Morris, "A Matter of Extreme Urgency," 75–76.
[120] Morris, "A Matter of Extreme Urgency," 76, 78.  [121] Ibid., 78.

naval armada that the United States had ever assembled.[122] On December 7, 1902, the Germans and British issued their ultimatum to Castro. According to a disputed later account by Roosevelt, the following day the German ambassador von Holleben was told by the president that the United States would go to war with Germany if Germany seized any territory in Venezuela or elsewhere in the Caribbean.[123] On December 9 the first violent actions of the blockade were taken by the Germans, with the new German gunboat *Panther* seizing three Venezuelan naval ships. Castro then took 200 English and German nationals hostage in Caracas, whereupon the *Panther* was ordered to sink the three unmanned ships and steam to La Guaira to prevent the German consul and his family from falling into Castro's hands.[124] Castro, in a panic, then appealed to the United States to arbitrate the matter, and shortly thereafter, the United States made an offer of arbitration to both Berlin and London.[125] The German ambassador von Holleben, flatly refused.[126] In the meantime, the US newspapers began to report on the crisis in terms very hostile to Germany.[127]

On December 13, the Royal Navy, assisted by a German warship, bombarded the Venezuelan coastal fortresses at Puerto Caballo and landed marines in retaliation for the boarding of British merchant vessel by the Venezuelans. Despite the lead the British took in this operation, Roosevelt was convinced that Germany was the more dangerous party in the alliance and that the British would back down immediately once the Monroe Doctrine were invoked.[128] In the meantime, the US Navy was being readied to move from Culebra to Trinidad to engage the Germans in Venezuela.[129] At that time a vitriolic anti-German press campaign was beginning in Britain that reached a crescendo when on December 15 the British Foreign Office finally released the White Paper on the terms of the agreement between Berlin and London over the Venezuelan matter. The British government was raked over the coals for joining Germany in the Venezuelan misadventure and for potentially offending the United States in both the press and in parliament.[130]

---

[122] Ibid., 79; Hendrix, *Naval Diplomacy*, 40–49.
[123] Morris, "A Matter of Extreme Urgency," 79–81; Henry J. Hendrix, *Theodore Roosevelt's Naval Diplomacy: The U.S. Navy and the Birth of the American Century* (Annapolis, MD: Naval Institute Press, 2009), 40–53. Cf. Herwig, *Vision of Empire*, 197–207, 225–35; Pommerin, *Der Kaiser und Amerika*, 124–26; Mitchell, *Danger of Dreams*, 87–88, 87n89.
[124] Rose, *Zwischen Empire und Kontinent*, 292.
[125] Morris, "A Matter of Extreme Urgency," 80–81; Fiebig-von Hase, *Lateinamerika als Krisenherd*, 1013–27.
[126] Morris, "A Matter of Extreme Urgency," 79–80.    [127] Ibid., 81.    [128] Ibid., 82.
[129] Ibid., 83.
[130] Mitchell, *The Danger of Dreams*, 89–97. See also Geppert, *Pressekriege*, 188–89.

On December 16th the US government once again forwarded Castro's proposal for American arbitration to the British and German embassies, this time giving it a strong endorsement. By this point much evidence suggests that the US Navy was on the brink of intervention. Dewey had established an emergency hospital ward in Puerto Rico, an unusual move that suggests the Americans were anticipating conflict and casualties. Sick men were also called back to ship from hospitals in order to fully man Dewey's armada, which was concentrated and loaded with coal and ammunition by December 17th.[131] With Britain falling into line, the growing diplomatic fallout for Anglo-German relations, and with the growing risk of offending the United States, Ambassador von Holleben cabled Berlin and the German government accepted the United States' offer. Two days later, on December 19th, both London and Berlin gave Roosevelt a formal invitation to arbitrate the Venezuelan conflict.[132] After an impressive diplomatic career in Japan, South America, and the United States, Theodor von Holleben was recalled as ambassador and left the United States hurriedly January 10, 1903.[133] Little can be seen here of the "fearless confidence, moved only by objective reasons" recommended by Schumacher in dealing with the Yankees.

Throughout the crisis, the American and British press focused almost exclusively on alleged German brutality and expansionism, with British papers claiming the Venezuelan blockade was a German ruse into which the Balfour government had been strong-armed to spark a conflict between Britain and the United States.[134] By mid-December the leading British papers were falling over themselves to emphasize the importance of good relations with the United States, and by late December 1902 the British government began watering down its Venezuelan demands.[135] At the opening of Parliament in 1903 a British government spokesman even had the audacity to claim that "the principle of the Monroe Doctrine has always received the unwavering support of successive Ministries in this country."[136] Earlier in November 1902 the Colonial Office had forwarded a secret memorandum on the defense of British possessions in the Caribbean and western Atlantic to the Admiralty and War Office for comment. The War Office concluded that in a conflict with the

---

[131] Hendrix, *Naval Diplomacy*, 43–47.
[132] Mitchell, *The Danger of Dreams*, 97–101; Fiebig-von Hase, *Lateinamerika als Krisenherde*, 1040–44. Cf. Morris, "A Matter of Extreme Urgency," 83–84; Hendrix, *Naval Diplomacy*, 40–41, 44, 48.
[133] Morris, "A Matter of Extreme Urgency," 84.
[134] Rose, *Zwischen Empire und Kontinent*, 293–96; Kennedy, *Anglo-German Antagonism*, 259. Cf. Bülow, *Denkwürdigkeiten*, vol. 1, 558; Herwig, *Vision of Empire*, 228–30.
[135] Rose, *Zwischen Empire und Kontinent*, 296–300.
[136] Humphries, "Anglo-American Rivalries," 163–64. See also "Brilliant Show in Parliament," *Chicago Tribune*, Feb. 18, 1903.

United States, Britain's colonies in the Western Hemisphere were effectively indefensible. Worse, the US Navy now had the capacity to intercept Britain's overseas grain supplies from Canada and Argentina. The memo acknowledged the necessity of maintaining good relations with the United States.[137]

As the Venezuela talks in Washington were underway in mid-January 1903, Germany and Britain maintained their blockade of Venezuela. When two German gunboats, *Panther* and *Falke*, entered the lagoon of Maracaibo on January 17th giving chase to a blockade-evading Venezuelan vessel, *Panther* was fired upon by the Venezuelan fort at San Carlos and damaged. In a retaliatory move, *Panther* flattened the fort with its cannons.[138] While arguably justified and no different to how American or British gunboats would have responded under similar circumstances, the German move generated very negative American press and became a public relations disaster, the British bombardment of Puerto Cabello and the landing of its marines in December 1903 now all but forgotten.[139] In February 1903 Roosevelt told Speck von Sternburg, now German ambassador, that the US Navy considered the German fleet its primary future target.[140]

On January 24, 1903, Britain signed the Hay-Herbert Convention with the United States to settle the Alaskan boundary dispute between the United States and Canada by a six-member tribunal. It was composed of three Americans, two Canadians, and the British Lord Chief Justice, Richard Alverstone (1842–1915). The three Americans were Secretary of War Elihu Root (1845–1937), Senator Henry Cabot Lodge (1850–1924), and the former senator George Turner (1850–1932), all Roosevelt loyalists and known partisans of a maximalist US position on the Alaskan boundary.[141] Unsurprisingly, the tribunal became locked in a bitter dispute between the Americans and Canadians, as both sides refused to compromise. In October the tribunal nevertheless made major territorial concessions to the United States as a result of Lord Alverstone siding with the Americans, despite Canadian outrage and warnings of seceding from the empire. As it turned out, Roosevelt had threatened the British government with military occupation of the disputed territory should the tribunal side with Canada.[142]

On January 22, 1903 – while the Anglo-German Venezuela blockade was still in effect – the United States signed the Hay-Herrán Treaty with Columbia

---

[137] Hendrix, *Naval Diplomacy*, 164.
[138] Mitchell, *The Danger of Dreams*, 101–2. See also Herwig, *Vision for Empire*, 230–31.
[139] Mitchell, *The Danger of Dreams*, 102–3; Pommerin, *Der Kaiser und Amerika*, 126–27; Fiebig-von Hase, *Lateinamerika als Krisenherd*, 1044–69.
[140] Röhl, *Into the Abyss*, 244.
[141] Howard Jones, *Crucible of Power: A History of U.S. Foreign Relations Since 1897* (Lanham, MD: SR Books, 2001), 43, 45; Morris, *Theodore Rex*, 254.
[142] Jones, *Crucible of Power*, 44–45; Morris, *Theodore Rex*, 281.

to lease a six-mile strip of land through the Isthmus of Panama to allow construction of the canal. It was never ratified by the Columbian Senate. Using the flimsy pretext of a rebellion in Panama, the United States launched a naval flotilla with a battalion of marines toward Panama in October 1903, supporting the rebellion and actively hindering the Columbian military. With the rebels victorious, the dubious Hay–Bunau-Varilla Treaty was signed on November 18, 1903, whereby the new Panamanian Republic leased the Canal Zone to the United States into perpetuity.[143] Britain had, of course, already ceded exclusive rights to the Canal Zone to the United States through the Hay-Pauncefote Treaty in 1901 in the aftermath of the First Venezuela Crisis.

## Inventing the "German Menace"

The Second Venezuela Crisis was a gift from heaven to the US Navy. The lurid press image of German warships in the Caribbean helped to end a 1901 moratorium on naval spending and led to significant congressional increases in the US Navy's budget that Roosevelt marshaled to build no fewer than ten battleships and four cruisers by the time he left office in 1909.[144] For the third time in less than five years, the United States had nearly provoked war with Germany while pursuing its own very aggressive *Weltpolitik*, each time appeased or sanctioned by Britain. The arc of Britain's silent strategic pivot toward the United States since the First Venezuela Crisis was shortening.[145] The speed by which England had come to be constructed as friend and Germany as a foe in the United States was nevertheless bewildering to many thoughtful Americans. In the immediate aftermath of the crisis, the journalist and historian Henry Adams (1838–1918), who had himself studied law at the University of Berlin in the late 1850s, observed that

> Nothing is more curious to me than the sudden change of our national susceptibilities. Down to 1898 our *bête noire* was England. Now we pay little or no attention to England; we seem to regard her as our property; but we are ridiculous about Germany. The idea of a wretched little power like Germany, with no coast, no colonies and no coal, attacking us, seems to me too absurd for a thought, but Cabot and Theodore and the Senate and Moody seem to have it on the brain.[146]

With the resolution of disputes between Washington and London over the Western Hemisphere, the myth of the "special relationship" between Britain

---

[143] On the US seizure of the Canal Zone, see Morris, *Theodore Rex*, 197, 216, 254, 276–80, 297–98.

[144] Pommerin, *Der Kaiser und Amerika*, 127.  [145] See Geppert, *Pressekriege*, 189.

[146] Henry Adams to Elizabeth Cameron, March 22, 1903, quoted in Brechtken, *Scharnierzeit*, 25. The name references are to Henry Cabot Lodge, Theodore Roosevelt, and Navy Secretary William Henry Moody (1853–1917).

and the United States was actively propagated in Britain by such politicians as Arthur Balfour, Joseph Chamberlain, Winston Churchill, and Edward Grey (1862–1933), senior members of the Admiralty like John "Jackie" Fisher (1841–1920), the influential *Times* editor and journalist Valentine Chirol (1852–1929), and the editor of *The Spectator*, John St. Loe Strachey (1860–1927).[147] The related notion of an "Anglosphere" was a new racialized Anglo-Saxon identity that had emerged in the 1890s in violent British colonial encounters and with the failure of Reconstruction and the revival of white supremacy and nativism in the Jim Crow United States. It also served liberal imperialist desires to counter the centrifugal tendencies in the British Dominions. A common German enemy was the glue that held it together.[148]

In the United States Roosevelt's successful great power politics in defense of his version of the Monroe Doctrine with expanded naval power resonated with many Americans, including those who had once been critical of imperialism. While still very skeptical about American overseas empire, in July 1904 Farnam would write Gustav Schmoller that he strongly supported Theodore Roosevelt in the upcoming presidential election.[149]

With uncanny similarity to the First Venezuela Crisis and the uproar over the Kruger Telegram, as the British were backing down over Venezuela and the Alaskan boundary, and as the Americans were preparing to seize the Canal Zone, Britain found itself in the throes of yet another invasion scare, this time directed against Germany. This scare had almost nothing to do with Germany's now larger navy. Instead it was whipped up by senior British army officers disturbed by Britain's poor military preparedness, morale, and performance in the Boer War, along with ambitious younger officers who used the specter of German invasion to try to secure funding for the British Army during a time defense reform and cost cutting.[150] There is nevertheless no doubt that it was driven by a deeper, pervasive sense of unease and vulnerability that the noisy German campaign for the second navy bill and Bülow tariff had deepened. The wide popularity of Erskine Childers' invasion novel *Riddle of the Sands* (published in 1903) speaks to that, as do the many British press articles and letters to the editor that accompanied the scare, which actually cited and discussed von Halle, Schmoller, Sering, and Schumacher's articles on behalf of the second navy bill, notably aggressive conservative papers like *The*

---

[147] Herwig, *Vision of Empire*, 233–34; Kennedy, *Anglo-German Antagonism*, 405.
[148] Vucetic, *The Anglosphere*, 22–52.
[149] GStA PK, VI. HA Nl. Schmoller, Nr. 196b, fols. 35–39, Henry Farnam to Gustav Schmoller, July 19, 1904. See also Gustav Schmoller, "Die Amerikaner," *JbfGVV* 28 (1904): 1477–94; William E. Leuchtenberg, "Progressivism and Imperialism: The Progressive Movement and American Foreign Policy 1898–1916," *The Mississippi Valley Historical Review* 39 (Dec. 1952): 483–504.
[150] Rose, *Zwischen Empire und Kontinent*, 203–6.

*Spectator.*[151] In any case, the army lobby aided by the press managed to turn it into national campaign, culminating in the Norfolk Commission, which held eighty-two official meetings and hearings between May and November 1903.[152]

The baseless arguments offered by the army and its supporters in these hearings and the press about the threat of German invasion and the need to have a "nation in arms" were repeatedly shown to be nonsense by the Committee of Imperial Defence and the most senior and informed British defense experts, such as the Second Sea Lord Jackie Fisher, the Director of Naval Intelligence Prince Louis of Battenberg (1854–1921), State Secretary of the Admiralty Hugh Arnold-Foster, and Prime Minister Balfour. British naval superiority, they argued, was both quantitatively and qualitatively overwhelming, precluding any invasion of the British Isles.[153] The Anti-German clamor of the British press in the spring of 1903 was nevertheless hardly isolated to the bogus threat of the German navy. Conservative magazines led by Leo Maxse's *National Review* and Strachey's *Spectator,* along with such papers as *The Times* and *Daily Mail* denounced with equal relish Anglo-German cooperation on the Baghdad Railway and the imbalance in Anglo-German trade.[154] This was symptomatic of a much more general unease about Germany that transcended any one issue like the German navy and reinforces the observations of Walther Rathenau, quoted in the previous chapter, that these British anxieties were at root economic and colonial.

In 1904 the British journalist and editor Austin Harrison (1873–1928) published a book on "Pan-Germanism" pitched to both an English and American audience receptive to the related idea of "Anglo-Saxonism."[155] The book was not devoted to the Pan-German movement in Germany per se but rather sought to illuminating the ideas animating the movement to unite Germandom as propagated by a wide range of German authors, with particular attention paid to the voice of "the professors – political, economic, naval and philological."[156] This remarkably thorough and largely dispassionate tract drew from an impressive body of German literature that included many works by von Halle on shipping and ocean commerce, his travelogue through the Caribbean and Venezuela, and the two volumes of essays

---

[151] See Kennedy, *Anglo-German Antagonism,* 251–52; cf. "Correspondence. German Expectations and Aspirations," *The Spectator,* Feb. 21, 1903; "Correspondence. Germany, Russia and the East," *The Spectator,* Mar. 28, 1903; "Germany and Britain Once More," *The Spectator,* Apr. 11, 1903.

[152] Rose, *Zwischen Empire und Kontinent,* 210–11.   [153] Ibid., 206–9, 212–18.

[154] Kennedy, *Anglo-German Antagonism,* 260–64. See also Barth, *Die deutsche Hochfinanz,* 211–12 and Rose, *Zwischen Empire und Kontinent,* 300–12.

[155] Austin Harrison, *The Pan-Germanic Doctrine: Being a Study of German Political Claims and Aspirations* (London and New York: Harper & Brothers, 1904).

[156] Ibid., vi.

published by the Free Union for Naval Lectures to which Schmoller, von Halle, Schumacher, and Sering had all contributed long essays. It discussed Schmoller's statements on Brazil as a site of possible German colonization as well as von Halle's ideas about connecting the Netherlands and its colonial empire to Germany in some detail.[157] Harrison noted that while in mid 1890s it had been the Kaiser and German government that had pushed for an expansionist program with the German people still rather timid and following, in 1904 it was the reverse: the German government had scaled back its aspirations while the German people – especially those influenced by Pan-German ideas – were disappointed with the meager record of *Weltpolitik* and demanded action.[158] But Harrison could conclude on a confident note in light of the recent developments in Venezuela: "For Anglo-Saxonism, the lesson it teaches is obvious. 'Readiness is all.' Let England, let America, be prepared at all times successfully to meet the Teutonic onrush, if ever it should come. When the 'rash humor' is upon the Germans we can bear with it. Politically Germany has nothing to give us. We can give her all. Her fate lies largely in our destiny."[159]

Harrison was quite perceptive. The movements in the international balance of power in these years were initiated not so much by Germany as by Britain following the experience of the Boer War and Boxer Rebellion. Accommodation, compromises, and alliances were now attractive as Britain had had a taste of the dangers of isolation and vulnerability and as new tensions with Germany emerged that pushed the traditional rivalry with France, Russia and the United States into the background. At the same time, the emergence of two new naval rivals to the United States in Germany and Japan would reinforce an emerging informal entente between the United States and Great Britain.[160] This was not fully recognized by Berlin at the time. Bülow was content to deal with the problems of the day on a case by case basis and lost sight of the larger strategic isolation that was beginning to envelop Germany.[161] It was events not in the Americas but rather in East Asia that would bring about a profound series of geostrategic shifts that would accelerate this process and ultimately contain German *Weltpolitik*.

### The Russo-Japanese War

As tensions between Russia and Japan over Korea mounted in 1903 and early 1904, the Kaiser, Bülow and the German Foreign Office were once more attempting to draw closer to Russia with sights on some kind of a future Russo-German alliance. In the immediate term they were nevertheless expecting to gain from any Russo-Japanese conflict, however it was decided,

---

[157] Ibid., x, xi, 105, 106, 107–8, 110, 124, 239, 240, 258, 260, 344.   [158] Ibid., 7–11.
[159] Ibid., 363; cf. Fiebig-von Hase, *Lateinamerka als Konfliktherd*, 1072–73.
[160] Mehnert, *"Gelbe Gefahr,"* 166–67.   [161] Canis, *Von Bismarck zur Weltpolitik*, 395.

even while the German public's sympathies were mainly with Japan.[162] By that point Russia was near completing the Trans-Siberian Railway – only the stretch around Lake Baikal was missing – which would have connected Port Arthur and Vladivostok with European Russia and dramatically enhanced Russia's military and economic position in Manchuria and Korea.[163] With completion of the railway and closer ties to Russia, Germany would itself be one step closer to the dream of connecting Berlin with northern China by land, just as had been elaborated in Hermann Schumacher's railway memoranda and articles, making such a Russian alliance a natural compliment to Germany's Chinese *Weltpolitik*.[164]

In July 1903 negotiations began between Russia and Japan to settle their differences that would have recognized Russia's claims in Manchuria in return for Russia's recognition of Japan's reciprocal claims in Korea.[165] In the autumn of 1903 Bülow assured the Japanese ambassador that there were no agreements of any kind between Germany and Russia in East Asia or elsewhere and that Germany would observe strict neutrality in the event of war between Japan and Russia. Bülow's thinking at the time was that war in East Asia would reduce the latent danger of war in Europe. In effect it was a subtle encouragement to war.[166]

When the Russo-Japanese negotiations stalled on account of Russian recalcitrance and delaying tactics, Japan launched a surprise attack on the Russian Far East Fleet at Port Arthur on February 8, 1904, and subsequently declared war. Initially Berlin was expecting a Russian victory over Japan, and the Kaiser was particularly outspoken in his sympathy and hopes for the Russians and scorn for the Japanese, reviving once again the specter of the "yellow peril."[167] Bülow did not share Wilhelm's hostility to the Japanese and warned the Kaiser of the potential political harm his one-sided embrace of the Tsar could do Germany, urging the Kaiser to exercise restraint and forge better relations with Japan.[168] In any case, in the ensuing conflict the Japanese had clear advantages in the training, discipline, and morale of their army and navy. And Japan's largely British-built fleet was among the most modern in the world in terms

---

[162] Mehert, "*Gelbe Gefahr*," 114–17; Carol, *Germany and the Great Powers*, 491; Canis, *Der Weg in den Abgrund*, 95–97; Mommsen, *Bürgerstolz und Weltmachtstreben*, 323; Röhl, *Into the Abyss*, 185–89, 263–70.
[163] Canis, *Der Weg in den Abgrund*, 72–73.
[164] See, for example, Schumacher, "Eisenbahnbau und Eisenbahnpläne," 907–8, 915–20.
[165] Canis, *Der Weg in den Abgrund*, 73.
[166] Bülow, *Denkwürdigkeiten*, vol. 1, 629–30; cf. Vogel, *Deutsche Rußlandpolitik*, 154–55.
[167] Röhl, *Into the Abyss*, 270–83, 597; Iikura, "The 'Yellow Peril,'" 88–91; Vogel, *Deutsche Rußlandpolitik*, 161–69.
[168] Bülow, *Denkwürdigkeiten*, vol. 2, 63–65, 87; Röhl, *Into the Abyss*, 271. On Bülow's views on Japan, see also Bülow, *Denkwürdigkeiten*, vol. 1, 436–38; vol. 2, 26–27; Bülow, *Deutsche Politik*, 51–53.

of radio communication, speed, maneuverability, sturdiness, firepower, and armor.[169]

In the opening phases of the conflict, the Japanese set out to destroy the Russian naval forces to gain command of the Yellow Sea and Korean ports in order to land troops for the invasion of Korea, destroying the Russian ships they encountered in Chemulpo (Incheon) and attacking the anchored Russian fleet at Port Arthur, damaging two Russian battleships and a cruiser. Port Arthur was put under distant blockade and the waters outside its harbor were mined, which sank the Russian Far Eastern Fleet's flagship, the *Petropavlosk* killing the commander along with nearly all hands.[170] Meanwhile, the Japanese Imperial Army led a successful land campaign in Manchuria, Korea, and the Liaotung Peninsula, seizing the valuable port of Talien and advancing across the Yalu River into Manchuria as the Japanese navy kept much of the Russian fleet bottled up in Port Arthur. While Russia's Vladivostock squadron was able to successfully raid the Japanese coast and put pressure on Japanese shipping, it, too, was effectively put out of commission following engagement with Japanese armored cruisers in early August 1904. By December Japanese land forces had seized the high ground above Port Arthur and subjected its harbor and fortifications to intense shelling, sinking or disabling every Russian ship in port. It was surrendered to the Japanese on January 2, 1905.[171]

As disaster was unfolding in the Far East, in mid-October 1904 the Tsar dispatched the Baltic Fleet on an eight-month journey to relieve the beleaguered Russian forces in East Asia. While en route through the Dogger Bank near Hull, England on October 21, the Russian convoy mistook harmless English fishing trawlers for Japanese torpedo boats and opened fire on them. The British government reacted with great ferocity, drafting a very sharply worded ultimatum accusing the Russian fleet of behaving like "savages and lunatics."[172] Meanwhile the British press exploded with anger against Germany, which was suspected of having supplied the Russians with this false information. The Royal Navy home squadron was deployed south from Scotland and the squadron in Gibraltar was put on full alert to intercept the Russians. The nightmare of a possible war with Russia, France, and Germany began to make the rounds in London, with the Kaiser suspected as instigator behind the scenes, such was the level of public mistrust between Britain and Germany at the time.[173] Rumors to this effect had already circulated in the

---

[169] Evans and Peattie, *Kaigun*, 84, 92–93, 115–16, 124–26.   [170] Ibid., 95–101.
[171] Ibid., 101–10. See also Pertti Luntinen and Bruce W. Menning, "The Russian Navy at War, 1904–1905," in *Russo-Japanese War*, ed. Steinberg, vol. 1, 229–59.
[172] Coogan, *The End of Neutrality*, 51.
[173] Ibid.; Arthur J. Marder, *From Dreadnought to Scapa Flow: The Royal Navy in the Fisher Era, 1904–1919*, vol. 1 (London and New York: Oxford University Press, 1961), 110–11; Vogel, *Deutsche Rußlandpolitik*, 203; Geppert, *Pressekriege*, 246.

British press in September on account of HAPAG's 1903 contract to supply the Russian fleet with coal in neutral ports.[174] Indeed, in the winter of 1904–5 a full blown war scare erupted between Britain and Germany, with the Kaiser, Bülow, and Tirpitz fearing a British naval attack, lent credibility by the concentration of the Royal Navy in home waters in the summer and autumn of 1904 and the appointment as First Sea Lord of Jackie Fisher in October 1904. The redeployment – which centered on Gibraltar, not Portsmouth – was not to counter a German naval threat but driven by rationalization, cost cutting, and the desire for greater strategic flexibility.[175] And while there was concern about the German navy, it was only in a possible combination with the Russian fleet were the Germans to enter into an alliance with the Tsar, for which there were plenty of rumors in 1904.[176]

Fisher, while prone to using jingoistic language such as repeated threats to "Copenhagen" the German navy, was in fact committed to preserving peace with a powerful British naval deterrent, and bluster had a certain place in that form of deterrence as well as in calming a riled British public.[177] Nevertheless, the British public outcry and Admiralty jingoism left unmistakable impressions of more aggressive British intentions toward Germany than there were in reality, later reinforced when on February 5, 1905, the Civil Lord of the Admiralty Arthur Lee (1868–1947) made threats of a preemptive strike on the German navy.[178]

Adding to the troubles, Tokyo protested HAPAG's coaling operations as a violation of German neutrality, and in December 1904 the British began to limit the cargos of coal HAPAG could load, sparking fears that access to British coaling stations would cease and cripple German overseas trade.[179] Respectable British papers and magazines were demanding an immediate preventive strike against the German navy, while in Germany the Army General Staff was making contingency plans in case of war for a possible occupation of Denmark and preventive strike against France through

---

[174] Röhl, *Into the Abyss*, 283–84. On HAPAG's contract with the Russians, see Cecil, *Albert Ballin*, 73–75.

[175] Nicholas A. Lambert, *Sir John Fisher's Naval Revolution* (Columbia: University of South Carolina Press, 1999), 103–7; Rose, *Zwischen Empire und Kontinent*, 224–27. Cf. Marder, *Anatomy of Sea Power*, 496.

[176] Lambert, *Naval Revolution*, 105–6.

[177] Shawn T. Grimes, *Strategy and War Planning: The British Navy, 1887–1918* (Woodbridge, UK: The Boydell Press, 2012), 58; Marder, *From Dreadnought to Scapa Flow*, vol. 1, 111–13; Offer, *The First World War*, 249–57; Rose, *Zwischen Empire und Kontinent*, 226–27.

[178] See Bülow, *Denkwürdigkeiten*, vol. 2, 65–69; Kelly, *Tirpitz*, 251–53; Röhl, *Into the Abyss*, 285–86; Tirpitz, *Memoirs*, vol. 1, 166–69.

[179] Cecil, *Albert Ballin*, 74–75.

Belgium.[180] While the war scare blew over, elements of the British imperialist press led by *The Times* and *National Review* had worked informally albeit very actively with the Admiralty and the government to shift the British public's anger from Russia toward Germany and its navy with the aim not just of avoiding war with Russia or a Russo-German alliance but to bringing about détente with St. Petersburg as a compliment to the Entente signed with Paris in April 1904.[181] It highlighted just how grave the dangers of strategic isolation were becoming for Germany pursuing a "free hand" policy with a navy large enough irk but too small to deter.

As the Baltic Fleet slowly proceeded toward China, the intervening months before its arrival gave the Japanese navy time to repair and upgrade their ships, as well as plan and train for a decisive engagement with the Baltic Fleet when it arrived in East Asia. At the time Japanese financial resources were extremely strained, and there was little hope of prevailing over the Russians in a protracted land struggle in Manchuria. Thus all bets were placed on launching a bold offensive to destroy the Baltic Fleet in decisive battle, which the Japanese navy planned in the Korea Strait.[182] The Russians fell into this trap. In the ensuing Battle of Tsushima on May 27, 1905, the Japanese Combined Fleet under the command of Admiral Tōgō Heihachirō (1848–1934) launched its attack, putting its battleships and cruisers parallel to the Russian vessels at close range and subjecting the Baltic Fleet to devastating fire with heavy, high-explosive shells, that set fire to the wooden superstructures of many Russian vessels and sowed chaos in the Russian line, forcing the Russians to alter course away from Vladivostock. In that melee the Russian battleship *Oslabaya* was sunk with more than half its crew lost.[183] Toward evening later that day, the Japanese Fleet reengaged the Russian forces, sinking the battleships *Borodino*, *Aleksandr III*, and *Knyaz Suvorov*. Later that night Japanese destroyers and torpedo boats sustained the attack, sinking the battelships *Navarin* and *Sisoi Veliky*. The next day Admiral Tōgō's fleet surrounded and captured the remaining vessels of the Russian Baltic Fleet.[184]

At midday on May 28, 1905, the battle was already over and the war effectively decided. Of the 38 Russian warships and support vessels that entered the Korea Strait, no fewer than 34 had been sunk, scuttled or captured. Some 4,830 Russian sailors had been killed and 5,917 were captured (including two admirals).[185] By contrast, the Japanese navy lost only 110 men killed and three torpedo boats sunk. Other than that, there was only moderate damage to three battleships, and a few destroyers and torpedo boats had been disabled temporarily.[186] It was the most devastating single naval battle in modern history and a staggering Japanese victory that sent shockwaves worldwide.

---

[180] Canis, *Der Weg in den Abgrund*, 108–16; Vogel, *Deutsche Rußlandpolitik*, 201–16.
[181] Geppert, *Pressekriege*, 249–56.   [182] Evans and Peattie, *Kaigun*, 110–14.
[183] Ibid., 115–20.   [184] Ibid., 120–22.   [185] Ibid., 124.   [186] Ibid.

The British naval historian and strategist Julian Corbett would later describe it as "the most decisive naval victory ever recorded" exceeding even Trafalgar.[187] While Japanese casualties in the land campaign were considerable and the strains on Japan's resources severe, by late summer Russia had few options left and was facing massive internal unrest. Chancellor Bülow was understandably alarmed by the prospect of his hoped-for continental ally now also descending into revolution. Pressed as he was by both external pressure and internal unrest, the Tsar sided with the peace party in the Crown Council, conceding defeat and agreeing to Bülow's proposal for President Roosevelt to mediate a peace settlement that was signed in Portsmouth, New Hampshire in September 1905.[188] It should be mentioned here how exceptional the Battle of Tsushima was in the annals of naval warfare: single, decisive naval engagements rarely determined the course of conflicts, but this exception that proved the rule was read by those primed by Mahan's writings or dogmatically committed to ships of the line as a confirmation of the doctrine of "decisive battle" determined by battleships.

The outcome of the conflict in the Far East was not only a tectonic power shift in Asia but an important turning point for Anglo-German relations: it eliminated the prospect of a Russian threat to British interests in China and so shifted Britain's diplomacy back to the European continent, polarizing alliances and ultimately constraining the possibilities of German *Weltpolitik* in ways that few could have imagined back in 1897.[189] It was a disaster not only for the position that Germany had been pursuing in the Far East since 1895, but also for Germany's fleet strategy as part of an alliance calculus. Russia's defeat assured a more accommodating stance in St. Petersburg to London and thus – with the Entente Cordiale already secured with France in 1904 and the added German irritant of the Baghdad Railway – British rapprochement with the Dual Alliance. This led directly to the Anglo-Russian Convention of 1907 that delineated the limits of Russian spheres of influence in Persia, Afghanistan, and Tibet, ending the "Great Game" and effectively putting Anglo-Russian relations on a more friendly track.[190] Henceforth Britain was relieved of significant colonial defense commitments and could focus more squarely on thwarting German alliance strategies, checking its naval ambitions, and totally containing its colonial initiatives.

Russo-German relations also took a serious toll, as it became increasingly clear in St. Petersburg that Berlin had sought to use the conflict in the Far East to strengthen its position vis-à-vis St. Petersburg, exploit Russia's weakness to negotiate a trade treaty favorable to Germany, and to then try to push

---

[187] Hendrix, *Naval Diplomacy*, 144–45.
[188] Canis, *Der Weg in den Abgrund*, 153–54; Bülow, *Denkwürdigkeiten*, vol. 2, 152, 159–62, 169–70.
[189] Clark, *The Sleepwalkers*, 158–59.    [190] Ibid., 87, 140–41, 158.

Russia into an alliance following the Dogger Bank incident. The trade treaty that was signed in July 1904 was subsequently resented by the Russians, and St. Petersburg rejected a German alliance proposal later in the winter of 1904 out of fears that it would undermine the Dual Alliance – French mediation had been critical in preventing the Dogger Bank incident from escalating into an Anglo-Russian war.[191] Germany later tried to use leverage over loans desperately needed by St. Petersburg in 1905 to push Russia into a pro-German position, despite the fact that Germany's capital market was already extremely strained. Indeed, France's much greater liquidity and willingness to lend became powerful glue holding together the Franco-Russian alliance.[192] The net result of these developments was suspicion of German motives on all sides.

Just how isolated Germany became as a result of these tectonic shifts and miscalculations was revealed in the Tangier Crisis that erupted in March 1905. With British, Italian, and Spanish connivance, the French had been emboldened to bring Morocco into their sphere of influence by securing special privileges from the sultan in violation of the 1880 Madrid Convention signed by the European great powers and the United States, which had opened the country to trade and jointly guaranteed the sultan's sovereignty. This was part of a calculated bid by the French foreign minister Théophile Delcassé (1852–1923) to isolate Germany and undermine its alliance with Italy, consciously excluding Germany in its negotiations over the future of Morocco with Spain and Italy. When Bülow sent a reluctant Kaiser to Tangier in late March 1905 to keep the door open in Morocco by affirming the sultan's sovereignty, it was now viewed as a wanton German provocation by Paris and London. It revealed not only the double standards that prevailed in the imperialist horse-trading that was the Anglo-French Entente Cordiale – a French sphere of influence in Morocco was accepted in return for French recognition of British control of Egypt – but the growing reliance of Britain on France for its imperial security.[193]

The Franco-Russian Alliance and the Anglo-French Entente which Holstein and Bülow sought to challenge in Morocco were thus in fact strengthened: in August 1905 the Royal Navy dispatched a flotilla to the Baltic Sea to dissuade a second attempt at a Russo-German alliance sprung on the Tsar by the Kaiser at Björkö in July 1905. In December 1905 Anglo-French military cooperation in the event of a war with Germany was formally discussed for the first time (including dispatching a British expeditionary force to the continent), culminating in general staff talks in January 1906 that over the years that Edward

---

[191] See esp. Vogel, *Deutsche Rußlandpolitik*, 174–231; Lieven, *The End of Tsarist Russia*, 183–85.
[192] Lieven, *The End of Tsarist Russia*, 185–87; Vogel, *Deutsche Rußlandpolitik*, 228–31.
[193] See Charmley, *Splendid Isolation*, 306–23; Clark, *The Sleepwalkers*, 154–58; Geppert, *Pressekriege*, 222–27. Cf. Bülow, *Deutsche Politik*, 95–105.

Grey headed the Foreign Office gradually – and largely secretly – transformed it into an informal military alliance.[194]

Grey, whose commitment to an Anglo-French Entente was deep and predated the Tangier Crisis, held to a rigidly anti-German view of British foreign policy that he shared with his Foreign Office senior colleagues Francis Bertie, Eyre Crowe (1864–1925), Charles Hardinge (1858–1944), and Arthur Nicolson (1849–1928), one that also sought rapprochement with Russia.[195] The Russian leadership, for its part, began to realize that the only power with an interest in prolonging the Russo-Japanese War was Germany, and with Russia's weakened military and financial position, began to fear subordination to Germany. At the subsequent Algeciras Conference in January 1906 to settle the Morocco question, Germany was thus almost completely isolated – only Austria-Hungary stood by, albeit tepidly.[196] Interestingly, the Kaiser's reluctant landing in Tangier and the Algeciras Conference worked to diminish the status of the Kaiser at home, who was now subject to sharp criticism for the first time from the National Liberals and conservatives about the negative impact of his "personal regime" on German foreign policy in Germany's isolation and so-called "encirclement." It also strengthened the radical nationalist voices calling for even larger navy bills so that German diplomacy would be taken more seriously in the future.[197] As we will see in the next chapter, Bülow would draw on these sentiments in the elections of 1906–7 to forge a bloc of conservative and liberal parties.

In January 1907 the half-German and whip smart Eyre Crowe, then a senior clerk in the Western Department in the British Foreign Office specializing on German affairs, circulated an influential secret memorandum to Edward Grey, Herbert Asquith, Richard Haldane and others that in important respects would define policy toward Germany in Edward Grey's Foreign Office thereafter. Written during the Tangier Crisis, Crowe's long memo argued forcefully for the need of the Foreign Office to take a firm line against any future German "blackmail" and to contain German overseas ambitions.[198]

---

[194] Wilson, *The Policy of the Entente*, 35–36, 74–75, 122–34; Mommsen, *Bürgerstolz und Weltmachtstreben*, 332–33.

[195] Wilson, *The Policy of the Entente*, 89–97, 124, 100–20; Clark, *The Sleepwalkers*, 159–67, 200–204. On Grey, see also Margaret MacMillan, *The War that Ended Peace: How Europe Abandoned Peace for the First World War* (London: Profile, 2013), 364–72.

[196] Brechtken, *Scharnierzeit*, 18, 265–67; Canis, *Der Weg in den Abgrund*, 160–61, 166–89; Lieven, *The End of Tsarist Russia*, 186–89; Mommsen, *Bürgerstolz und Weltmachtstreben*, 322–41; Vogel, *Deutsche Rußlandpolitik*, 220–31.

[197] See Daniel, "Einkreisung und Kaiserdämmerung," in Stollberg-Rilinger, *Was heißt Kulturgeschichte*, 315–25; Carroll, *Germany and the Great Powers*, 543–56.

[198] Eyre Crowe, "Memorandum on the Present State of British Relations with France and Germany" (Jan. 1, 1907), in *British Documents on the Origins of the War, 1898–1914*, ed. G. P. Gooch and Harold Temperly, vol. 3 (London: H.M. Stationary Office, 1928), 397–420 (Appendix A).

Combining in equal measure deep admiration for German administrative abilities and the vitality of its culture, science and industry with fear of their implications for Britain's future status, Crowe argued that Germany, as heir to Brandenburg-Prussia, was an expansionist menace to the balance of power that sought "German hegemony, at first in Europe, and eventually the world."[199] The "vague and undefined schemes of Teutonic expansion" were driven by dissatisfaction with Germany's existing colonial empire and presence overseas that now posed a direct threat to the international status quo and thus to British hegemony. With uncanny echoes of the speeches Gustav Schmoller, Max Sering, Ernst von Halle, and Hermann Schumacher gave for the Free Union for Naval Lectures, Crowe argued:

> Emperor, statesmen, journalists, geographers, economists, commercial and shipping houses, and the whole mass of educated and uneducated public opinion continue with one voice to declare: We *must* have real Colonies, where German emigrants can settle and spread the national ideals of the Fatherland, and we *must* have a fleet and coaling stations to keep together the Colonies which we are bound to acquire. To the question, "Why *must?*" the ready answer is: "A healthy and powerful State like Germany, with its 60,000,000 inhabitants, must expand, it cannot stand still, it must have territories to which its overflowing population can emigrate without giving up its nationality." When it is objected that the world is now actually parceled out among independent States, and that territory for colonization cannot be had except by taking it from the rightful possessor, the reply again is: "We cannot enter into such considerations. Necessity has no law. The world belongs to the strong. A vigorous nation cannot allow its growth to be hampered by blind adherence to the *status quo*. We have no designs on other people's possessions, but where States are too feeble to put their territory to the best possible use, it is the manifest destiny of those who can and will do so to take their places."[200]

Crowe then recounted a long history of "typical" German "intriguing," "deception," "dubious dealing," "unprovoked aggressiveness," "violent action," "relentless vindictiveness," "provocative and insulting proceedings," "cynical disregard," and "underhand and disloyal manoevers" toward Britain in the acquisition of colonial territory from Bismarck's acquisition of African colonies to Bülow's bid for the Yangtze region.[201] "Concession after concession" granted by Britain to preserve good relations between the two countries had been abused to advantage and had only fueled a desire for more. "The action of Germany towards this country since 1890," Crowe wrote, "might be likened not inappropriately to that of a professional blackmailer, whose extortions are wrung from his victims by threat of some vague and dreadful consequences in

---

[199] Ibid., 403–4, 414.   [200] Ibid., 405.   [201] Ibid., 408–13.

case of refusal."[202] The only effective policy against such extortion was for Britain to take a resolute stand of refusal toward Germany.

While Crowe's memorandum reflected a degree of German self-loathing and was very much a creature of Edwardian anxiety largely blind to Britain's own insulting and threatening diplomacy toward Germany, it nevertheless contained many perceptive observations about the inherent contradictions and limits of German *Weltpolitik*, notably the diplomatic tensions and international counterbalancing that would invariably result from Germany's wide-ranging ambitions for settler colonies in South America, a German India in Asia Minor, or a fleet to challenge British naval hegemony. Such schemes, Crowe recognized, were achievable only by defiance of practically the entire world. They proved "how little of logical and consistent design and of unrelenting purpose lies behind the impetuous mobility, the bewildering surprises, and the heedless disregard of the susceptibilities of other people that have been so characteristic of recent manifestations of German policy."[203]

Whether German power and influence expanded outwardly by violent means or by peaceful evolution, "the position thereby accruing to Germany would obviously constitute as formidable a menace to the rest of the world...."[204] There was thus no room for an Anglo-German entente. Likewise a policy of concessions, given recent history, was out of the question. Rather, as the German disappointments with Algeciras Conference had shown, close Anglo-French cooperation and "prompt and firm refusal to enter into any one-sided bargains or arrangements" was the only way to induce friendlier Anglo-German relations and thus to contain the German menace.[205] In terms of the German naval program, Crowe recommended that nothing would underscore to the Germans "the practical hopelessness of a never-ending succession of costly naval programmes" than that the British match every new German ship with two.[206] The Crowe memorandum can rightly be seen as an Edwardian version of George F. Kennan's (1904–2005) famous Long Telegram of February 1946 giving a rationale for a policy of containment of the Soviet Union.

There were other interesting and ironic developments that emerged in the aftermath of the Russo-Japanese War and Tangier Crisis. As was discussed at length in Chapter 2, Germany's contributions to Japan's modernization had been significant; in the areas of modern constitutional, commercial, and civil law, state administration, schools and universities, and in military organization and training, Germany's contributions were profoundly important – indeed quite possibly decisive – in creating the legal, administrative, economic, and military capacities that enabled Japan to not only prevent European

---

[202] Ibid., 414, 416.   [203] Ibid., 416–17; cf. Jarausch, *Enigmatic Chancellor*, 163.
[204] Crowe, "Memorandum on the Present State of British Relations," 417.
[205] Ibid., 418–19.   [206] Ibid., 418.

colonization, but to emerge as a modern industrial state, and ultimately in 1905, as a new world power. In offering the legal justification for the annexation of the formerly Russian leaseholds of Port Arthur and Talien on the Liaotung Peninsula, Japanese legal scholars, among them the German-trained Takahashi Sakue (1867–1920), used a German legal precedent, arguing that the leasehold in Kiaochow was equivalent to cession (i.e., in effect identical in status to a colony), thus allowing the Japanese government to disregard China's sovereignty and to extend Japan's colonial claims over these territories.[207] As will be recalled, Japan was forced to relinquish these very territories following the Triple Intervention of 1895, which marked the opening gambit of German *Weltpolitik*. The articles that offered the legal justification for these reinterpretations of international law were published in the *Kokka Gakkai Zasshi,* the very journal Karl Rathgen had initiated at Tokyo University in 1887.[208] In a stunning twenty years Japan had gone from apprentice to master and was now an expanding imperial power with few barriers to regional hegemony East Asia.

## Full Steam to Bankruptcy

The naval implications to Germany of the Russo-Japanese War were profound. By shattering Tsarist Russia as both an Asian and naval power, the war allowed a strategic withdrawal from what had long been a major minefield in Anglo-Russian relations. A British withdrawal from the Americas had already been underway following the two Venezuela crises, given formal expression in the Hay-Pauncefote Treaty of 1901 and the Hay-Herbert Convention of 1903. The 1902 alliance with Japan had started a similar process in East Asia. With the Entente Cordiale of 1904 and now the destruction of much of the Russian Navy in 1905, the two principal naval threats on which the old Two Power Standard had been based were effectively eliminated.

As the strategic situation changed, technological change – notably the increasing range of the torpedo and the viability of submarines – was making battleships much more vulnerable, calling into question their tactical and strategic usefulness in British national defense. In any case, it was clear to naval reformers like Admiral Fisher by 1905 that a rational organization of

---

[207] See Asada Shinji, "Colonizing Kiaochow Bay: From the Perspective of German-Japanese Relations," in *Japan and Germany: Two Latecomers to the World Stage, 1890–1945,* ed. Kudō Akira, Tajima Nobuo, and Erich Pauer, vol. 1 (Folkstone, Kent: Global Oriental, 2009), 91–113, here 105–7.

[208] Ibid., 105–6. See also GStA PK, VI. HA Nl. Schmoller, Nr. 197b, fol. 23, Takimoto Yashio to Gustav Schmoller, Tokyo, June 23, 1905; Gustav Schmoller, "Die künftige englische Handelspolitik, Chamberlain und der Imperialismus," *JbfGVV* 28 (1904): 829–52.

British imperial defenses that made the best use of limited manpower should focus more on the strategic defensive, a "flotilla defense" in the narrow waters of the British coast using submarines and destroyers to deny any would-be attacker the seas, while fast armored cruisers would protect maritime trade. There was really no place in that vision for the battleship.[209] From that perspective, the emerging "Two-Thirds" navy of Imperial Germany – fixated as it was on a rigid and increasingly obsolete numerical ratio of battleships and with no operational range beyond the North and Baltic Seas – posed even less of a threat to Britain, not least since Britain's massive navy now really had only Germany as a potential foe. In September 1906 Admiral Fisher wrote First Lord of the Admiralty Tweedmouth that "our present margin of superiority over Germany (our only possible foe for years) is so great as to render it absurd in the extreme to talk of anything endangering our naval supremacy, *even if we stopped shipbuilding altogether!!!*"[210]

Despite these changes, much of the British Admiralty and many Royal Navy officers (not to mention many parliamentarians and much of the British public) found it very difficult to adjust their thinking to these new strategic and technological realities and continued to insist on global commands and to invoke the time-honored slogans of British maritime supremacy of the Two Power Standard defined by battleships. Within the Admiralty this was driven also by a desire not to appear weak to parliament and the public and to blunt efforts at cost cutting or shifts of resources to the army due to the austerity measures induced by the swollen national debt caused by the Boer War.[211] The Dogger Bank incident had raised anti-German feelings and invasion fears to new heights within the British public and had become a major political factor in any discussion of Royal Navy policy in 1905. Continuing with battleships also accommodated the needs of an emerging British "naval-industrial complex."[212] Not surprisingly, then, Britain continued battleship building and adhering to a revised (and now politically-defined) version of the Two Power Standard. Far more surprising, however, is that Britain would needlessly raise the stakes in 1905 with the decision to build four dreadnoughts, all big-gun, turbine-driven battleships and heavy cruisers.

When intelligence of the planned HMS *Dreadnought* was relayed to Tirpitz for the first time in late February 1905 he was at first deeply shaken and feared that the Reich would likely be far too strapped financially to ever match it, and if it ever did, that it might well precipitate the nightmare of war with Britain.[213] Tirpitz's entire plan had been premised on matching the Royal

---

[209] Lambert, *Naval Revolution*, 107, 116–26.
[210] Fisher quoted in ibid., 142. Emphasis in the original.
[211] Aaron Friedberg, *The Weary Titan: Britain and the Experience of Relative Decline, 1895–1905* (Princeton: Princeton University Press, 1988), 206–7.
[212] See Lambert, *Naval Revolution*, 142–54.    [213] Kelly, *Tirpitz*, 253–54.

Navy to achieve a fixed 2:3 numerical ratio with much smaller ships of the line in which he thought *Germany* would have a qualitative edge, not Britain. Shifting German construction to ships of similar displacement and armament would be extraordinarily costly under already severe Reich financial strain and require expensive enlargement of the Kaiser-Wilhelm Canal connecting the North and Baltic Seas.[214] It seemed an impossible challenge, and yet Tirpitz was neither deterred from his goal of the 2:3 ratio nor from pushing through the necessary qualitative upgrades to match the displacement and armament of the new class of ships. It was in the face of this challenge that the stubborn and dogmatic side of Tirpitz came to the fore – protecting his supreme achievement, the German navy law of 1900 and the bureaucratic empire he had built to sustain it, began to cloud his judgment and would ultimately have negative repercussions for German grand strategy. It was only later that Tirpitz realized the opportunity HMS *Dreadnought* offered Germany by rending the Royal Navy's massive pre-dreadnought fleet obsolete. By leveling the playing field, it practically invited a new arms race.[215]

Under pressure from a noisy Navy League that had been pressing since its general meeting in April 1904 for the navy to build a third double squadron of battleships (i.e., some 19 new ships of the line!), in February 1905 Tirpitz urged the Kaiser to accept an amendment to only build the 6 cruisers that had been struck from the 1900 law and to extend the 3 ship a year building tempo to 1911 (though this was also paired with revised estimates for increasing the displacement of ships to be laid down in the future anticipating vessels approaching dreadnought specification).[216] While overlooked by the Navy League, the amendment bill had thus in fact taken up the *Dreadnought* challenge. However, it was not until late July 1907 that the keel was laid for the roughly 19,000 ton SMS *Nassau*, which while armed with 11-inch guns, was merely an upgrade of existing German ship designs. It had a mixed armament and conventional propulsion, which meant that it was not only slower than *Dreadnought,* but on account of the bulk of its triple-expansion steam engines, inferior in its heavy armament placement. This was no *Dreadnought*. The United States took up the *Dreadnought* challenge at almost exactly the same time, with Congress authorizing the construction of the all-big-gun 22,000 ton USS *Delaware* in 1906, pushed through by none other than Admiral George Dewey, then head of the US Navy's General Board.[217] It was laid down in November 1907. By that point there was consensus in the United States to construct a big-ship navy second in size only to the British.[218]

---

[214] Berghahn, *Der Tirpitz-Plan*, 435–48.   [215] Kelly, *Tirpitz*, 257, 462–63.
[216] Deist, *Flottenpolitik*, 175–77, 184; Kelly, *Tirpitz*, 253–55, 256–57.
[217] George W. Baer, *One Hundred Years of Sea Power: The U.S. Navy, 1890–1990* (Stanford: Stanford University Press, 1993), 24.
[218] Ibid., 40.

**Figure 7.2** "The German Fleet Dragon," *Der wahre Jacob*, June 26, 1906. "The more it eats the more it demands, and in the end it will devour you!"

Tirpitz and the RMA were acutely aware that Reich finances were the biggest constraint on any bolder moves and mobilized the Communications Bureau to shape opinion accordingly. Ernst von Halle published an urgent appeal in support of the March 1905 finance reform proposals in the *Preußische Jahrbücher*, going even further by urging a thoroughgoing financial reform to overcome Germany's fiscal particularism in order to put the Reich's finances on a sound footing of direct taxes.[219] As the financial reforms proposed in 1905 were ultimately stripped of much of their effect by Reichstag opposition and deficits mounted year by year, von Halle would be transferred by the RMA to the Reich Treasury in 1908 to become director of a new "Economic Bureau" to systematically disseminate propaganda for a larger-scale financial reform. The blueprint for that effort was the successful pro-fleet propaganda in the RMA's Communications Bureau in 1897–1900, which included the tried and tested method of

---

[219] Ernst von Halle, "Das Problem der Reichsfinanzreform," *Preußische Jahrbücher* 119, no. 3 (1905): 495–507.

mobilizing professors and other specialists for publicity on behalf of that cause.[220] This will be discussed in Chapter 10.

While Tirpitz and the Communications Bureau went to extraordinary lengths in 1905 to sway the Navy League to support the cruiser amendment as it took draft form and was presented to the Reichstag in the autumn of 1905, Keim and the majority of the Navy League rejected the bill as far too small and continued to agitate for immediate construction of an additional double squadron of battleships. In a December meeting of the Navy League's executive board and then in a meeting of the League's Presidium in January 1906, a leaflet was drafted and then circulated that savaged Germany's inferior fleet as deathtraps and attacked Tirpitz for his deference to the Center Party in producing such a timid draft amendment, urging the Reichstag to take up a much larger navy bill.[221] Simultaneously massive public criticism was being leveled against the Kaiser's "personal regime" and for the failures of *Weltpolitik* in Morocco and elsewhere.[222] As a measure of the success of this popular agitation, it even managed to gain the support of Chancellor Bülow and the Kaiser for a larger bill![223] Tirpitz, invoking fears of a "Copenhagening" of the fleet and threatening his resignation, in the end persuaded the Kaiser and Bülow to accept his draft amendment, which was adopted by the Reichstag Budget Commission unchanged and passed the Reichstag without debate and by a large majority on May 25, 1906. The massive 300-page official memorandum that justified this legislation was written by Ernst von Halle.[224] Meanwhile, however, much of the tax reform package was dismantled by the expected opposition in the Reichstag: the tobacco taxes were rejected unanimously; the beer taxes and stamp duties were reduced drastically by the Center Party and National Liberals; and the inheritance tax was watered down by the conservatives. In the end the net revenue increase of this 1906 reform was only 110 million marks annually.[225] Excessive spending, notably on the navy, would subsequently swell Reich deficits between 1907 and 1909 to an unsustainable 1.35 billion marks.[226]

On May 31, 1906, less than a week after passage of the navy law amendment of 1906, Tirpitz began receiving alarming confidential reports from the German naval attaché in London of major impending upgrades to Britain's heavy cruisers, namely that the new *Invincible* class of cruisers would be equipped with 12 inch guns; an earlier report of this attaché of May 23 had

---

[220] Witt, *Die Finanzpolitik*, 219.
[221] Deist, *Flottenpolitik*, 186–88; Eley, *Reshaping the German Right*, 269.
[222] Mommsen, *Bürgerstoltz und Weltmachtstreben*, 335.
[223] Deist, *Flottenpolitik*, 188; Röhl, *Into the Abyss*, 484.
[224] Kelly, Tirpitz, 260–61; Roth, "Der politische Hintergrund," 69; Reichsmarineamt, *Die Entwicklung der deutschen Seeinteressen im letzten Jahrzehnt* (Berlin: Mittler, 1905).
[225] Hentschel, *Wirtschaft und Wirtschaftspolitik*, 166–67.   [226] Ibid., 167.

already warned that future British dreadnoughts would have 13.5 inch guns and a displacement of 20,000 tons.[227] Tirpitz was so shocked that he asked the attaché to confirm his report, which he did in early July.[228] By September 1906 it was already clear that the modest finance reform of the spring was insufficient to plug holes in the Reich budget due to shortfalls in tax revenue. At the time Bülow was pressing Tirpitz to cut any unessential spending from his budget.[229] The new British developments in heavy cruisers now threatened to topple Tirpitz carefully developed financial calculations. Tirpitz recognized that a new amendment to increase the displacements and armaments of German ships by reducing the service life of vessels and increasing the pace of building to match the Royal Navy's newest initiative was simply out of the question in the 1906-7 Reichstag legislative period so close to a scheduled election and would thus have to wait to be passed by a new Reichstag but no later than 1908-9 or else Germany would fall hopelessly behind.[230] By the early autumn of 1906, however, Bülow was already toying with the idea of having the Kaiser dissolve the Reichstag and call new elections in the hopes of being able to implement a more thoroughgoing Reich finance reform with a more pliable Reichstag majority.[231]

By that point awareness that public finance was Germany's Achilles heel was growing in public. Reflecting on the aftermath of the Russo-Japanese War, Karl Helfferich pointed out that fiscal capacities were important in determining not only the duration of modern warfare but also in the terms of the negotiated peace.[232] Similarly, the Hamburg banker Max Warburg noted that Germany's underdeveloped imperial public finances and rising debts were becoming a strategic liability, as they compromised its capacity to wage modern wars which recent experience had shown were extraordinarily costly.[233] Swelling Reich debts would also worsen a cyclical downturn in 1907 and harm the wider German economy. Despite warnings from experts of a growing shortage of liquidity, the state of Prussia and the Reich issued 550 million marks of new debt in April 1907, all of which could not be

---

[227] Berghahn, *Der Tirpitz-Plan*, 511; Kelly, *Tirpitz*, 269.
[228] Berghahn, *Der Tirpitz-Plan*, 514. [229] Ibid., 527-28.
[230] See Kelly, *Tirpitz*, 270-74. [231] Berghahn, *Der Tirpitz-Plan*, 501-2.
[232] Karl Helfferich, *Das Geld im russisch-japanischen Krieg: Ein finanzpolitischer Beitrag zur Zeitgeschichte* (Berlin: Miller und Sohn, 1906), 238-40. Cf. Miller, "Japan's Other Victory," in Steinberg, *Russo-Japanese War*, vol. 1, 465-83.
[233] Max Warburg, *Finanzielle Kriegsbereitschaft und Börsengesetz: Vortrag auf dem 3. Allg. Deutschen Bankiertag am 5. Sept. 1907* (Hamburg; Ackermann & Wulf, 1907); Warburg, *Aus meinen Aufzeichnungen*, 23. See also Niall Ferguson, "Max Warburg and German Politics: The Limits of Financial Power in Wilhelmine Germany," in *Wilhelminism and Its Legacies: German Modernities, Imperialism and the Meanings of Reform*, ed. Geoff Eley and James Retallack (New York and Oxford: Berghahn Books, 2003), 185-97.

absorbed by the money market and which therefore weakened the liquidity of the bank consortium bringing the debt to market by leaving most of it in their portfolios. Within a few months the price of this debt fell sharply and yields rose, in turn raising German interest rates.[234] With a run on New York banks in October 1907 and a withdrawal of French and British capital that had been drawn to Germany by its higher interest rates, the Reichsbank was left with no other choice but to raise the discount rate repeatedly in October and November 1907 to protect its gold reserves, a situation not helped by Germany's chronic trade deficit. These high discount rates deepened the recession of 1907-8 and came with the negative lasting effect of undermining international confidence in the Reichsbank and German banking system and thus reducing future international capital flows to Germany.[235]

In late 1906 Philip Dumas (1868-1948), British naval attaché in Berlin, reported that the Royal Navy's ships had so overwhelming an advantage in both speed and armament that they could impose a distant blockade of the North Sea and have enough spare ships to undertake a complete destruction of German harbors.[236] Another naval expert assessed the Royal Navy's superiority as so far above the Two Power Standard that the German navy posed "absolutely no danger" – indeed, even the French Navy had a huge advantage over Germany in numbers of battleships, armored cruisers, and torpedo boats in 1906.[237] Yet in these very years the British Naval Defense Department started drawing up new war plans that proposed a wartime naval strategy of economic warfare against Germany in complete repudiation of the Paris Declaration. Indeed, Jackie Fisher made no secret of his contempt for international law and of the "great special anti-German weapon of smashing an enemy's commerce" as early as April 1906.[238] That was some two years before Germany responded to the *Invincible* heavy cruisers by passing a new amendment reducing the service life of its fleet and increasing the pace of construction in March 1908. The move to economic warfare indicated the degree to which the Royal Navy was now beholden to the bluewater strategy of Colomb and Corbett that focused less on decisive battle or the protection of Britain's own shipping lanes and more on command of the sea for the economic strangulation of potential enemies.[239] Indeed, already in November 1906 Corbett was teaching his naval students at Portsmouth that such a defensive strategy could well prove superior to seeking decisive battle.[240] As the strategy evolved it became one of economic warfare, first formally unveiled by Admiral

---

[234] Witt, *Die Finanzpolitik*, 193-94.   [235] Ibid., 194.
[236] Rose, *Zwischen Empire und Kontinent*, 390.
[237] Archibald Hurd quoted in ibid., 391.   [238] Offer, *The First World War*, 233-42, 252.
[239] Hobson, *Imperialism at Sea*, 88-93; Offer, *The First World War*, 221.
[240] Hew Strachan, *The First World War*, vol. 1 (Oxford: Oxford University Press, 2001), 394.

Fisher. It involved not only a crippling blockade but also control of the British merchant fleet and its cargos, cutting off the global flow of money and credit, and control of all telegraph communications. It was accepted as official British wartime strategy in December 1908 by the Committee of Imperial Defence, which was chaired by Prime Minster Asquith and included senior cabinet members and the military chiefs. In any war with Germany, Britain would henceforth adopt a strategy of stopping *all* German trade, financial flows, and global communications – including imports of foodstuffs and raw materials.[241] In short, any future war with Britain would increasingly mean *total war* and the end of German *Weltwirtschaft*.[242]

Oddly, as British grand strategy shifted to the strategic defensive away from decisive battle, *Dreadnought* and the new *Invincible* battle cruisers were weapons of declining strategic and tactical value while stimulating a new arms race that served to undermine one of the very reasons this new class of weapon was introduced in Britain in the first place: economies.[243] Naval expenditure in Britain accelerated significantly after 1908 and would ultimately contribute to a constitutional crisis over the House of Lords veto of Commons spending bills initiated by Lloyd George's (1863–1945) People's Budget in 1909, which was introduced by the need for funds for both old age pensions and large increases in naval spending following a major navy scare.[244]

By this point, growing doubts about Germany's battleship strategy were being aired in public. In the fall of 1907, as a major recession was hitting Germany, the retired Vice-Admiral Karl Galster (1851–1931) published a pamphlet that leveled many criticisms at the basic assumptions of the Tirpitz "Risk Fleet," arguing with remarkable prescience that Germany would be crippled by a distant blockade in the Channel and between Scotland and Norway with or without such a fleet.[245] He argued that priorities had to shift away from building battleships toward torpedo boats and submarines as

---

[241] Offer, *The First World War*, 242–43; in greater detail Lambert, *Planning Armageddon*, 3–5, 102–37.

[242] See Stephen Cobb, *Preparing for Blockade 1885–1914: Naval Contingency for Economic Warfare 1885–1918* (Farnham: Ashgate, 2013), 57–76. Cf. Lambert, *Planning Armageddon*, 102–81.

[243] Eric Grove, "The Battleship *Dreadnought*: Technological, Economic and Strategic Contexts," in *The Dreadnought and the Edwardian Age*, ed. Robert J. Blyth, Andrew Lambert, and Jan Rüger (Farnham, Surrey and Burlington, VT: Ashgate, 2011), 165–81, here 174–75. See also Angus Ross, "Four Lessons that the U.S. Navy Must Learn from the *Dreadnought* Revolution," *Naval War College Review* 63, no. 4 (Autumn 2010): 119–43.

[244] Brooks, *The Age of Upheaval*, 111–23; Sumida, *Naval Supremacy*, Appendix, Table 3.

[245] Karl Paul Hans Galster, *Welche Seekriegs-Rüstung braucht Deutschland?* (Berlin: Boll und Pickardt, 1907). See also Deist, *Flottenpolitik*, 251–52; Hobson, *Militarism at Sea*, 261–62.

cheaper and more effective coastal defenses, as well cruisers, which actually had some prospect of disrupting Britain's maritime trade in war.[246]

There were other problems with Germany's battleship strategy. The exact ratios necessary to serve as an effective naval deterrent to the Royal Navy were based on German naval axioms and in the end were little more than a throw of the dice, as Tirpitz himself later admitted.[247] In any case, the 2:3 ratio that the 1900 navy law foresaw was in reality far too small to serve as a credible deterrent, much less against the qualitatively superior British dreadnoughts. Simple facts of geography made Germany unusually vulnerable to blockade, and the Russo-Japanese War had shown that a fleet kept in port could be contained and denied military action.[248] In truth the larger German navy could never actually pose a credible threat to Britain's command of the seas because Germany lacked its own overseas coaling stations and undersea telegraph cables, restricting it to a wartime operational range of the North and Baltic Seas. The ease with which Britain could deny HAPAG coal in December 1904 made that painfully obvious. As a British close blockade became unlikely, both an offensive and defensive strategy with battleships became fundamentally flawed.

The other assumptions of the "Risk Fleet" were less flawed per se than overturned by events. Anglo-Russian antagonism was not frozen in amber, as was long believed in the Wilhelmstrasse. That rigid Europe-centered strategic perspective overlooked the fact that great powers were dynamic entities that would realign as German, American, and Japanese power grew. British appeasement of the United States after 1895, the Anglo-Japanese Alliance, the Entente Cordiale with France, and the Russo-Japanese War ushered in a diplomatic and strategic revolution that allowed a redeployment of British military assets. The financial breathing room from reduced imperial defensive commitments also allowed for a bold reorganization and modernization of British naval forces, with more of the fleet concentrated in home waters than anticipated by Tirpitz. An effective German naval deterrent under these circumstances would have had to be even larger and deployable to break a distant blockade with the addition of a large submarine fleet whose technology was then just being developed. Thus, as Germany's diplomatic isolation grew, its potential military threat to Britain actually receded.

Finally, the belief that the German battleship navy might make Germany a more attractive alliance partner or offer leverage for extracting colonial concessions proved to be misguided. Leaving aside for a moment the unattractive

---

[246] Epkenhans, *Die wilhelminische Flottenrüstung*, 85; Hobson, *Militarism at Sea*, 262; Ritter, *Staatskunst*, vol. 2, 192.
[247] Hobson, *Militarism at Sea*, 265–67; Kelly, *Tirpitz*, 200–202.
[248] Lambi, *The Navy and German Power Politics*, 249.

defensive liabilities posed by Germany and the growing tensions between its ally Austria-Hungary and Russia over the Balkans, the German navy was still too small to make Germany an attractive ally to either Russia or Britain. It was, however, just large enough to press the neuralgic point of "Naval Supremacy," bound up as it was with British identity, deeply-rooted invasion fear, and popular notions of national security. It was also large enough to stimulate British Foreign Office concern about German "hegemony" on the continent. Memories of the Tangier Crisis and perceptions of German bullying stoked by the dreadnought arms race would thus have the opposite effect, making British diplomacy less accommodating and less flexible, reinforcing preexisting Germanophobia in Edward Grey's Foreign Office, justifying diplomatic and military ties to France and later Russia as a supposed "counterbalance" to an alleged German menace.[249] Indeed, fears were growing in Whitehall in the late summer of 1908 that the larger German fleet might embolden Berlin to risk a war with France thinking that Britain would assess the risk of a naval confrontation with Germany as too high. Given Russia's weakness, German hegemony on the continent would then be the inevitable result.[250]

The long and short of it was that by 1908 Tirpitz's "Risk Fleet" was making Germany less, not more, secure, as it enhanced Germany's diplomatic isolation and – by encouraging an overreliance on Germany's own naval strength – weakened the international commitment to the defense of neutral rights in war. Tirpitz and the RMA would myopically oppose strengthening neutral rights at the Second Hague Conference in 1907 in their dogmatic obsessions with the offensive *potential* of sea power.[251] This led to a willful strategic blindness to the role of powerful neutrals like the United States in enforcing the Paris Declaration and thus a gradual weakening of the common interest in countering Britain's inflated and dangerous bluewater strategic doctrine that, as just discussed, the British CID would begin to formalize in 1908 into a wartime strategy of catastrophic economic warfare against Germany.[252] Of all the great powers, Germany had the most to gain from bolstering international commitment to neutral rights on account of its vulnerable geostrategic position.[253] Germany's refusal at The Hague to also discuss proposals for naval arms limitations made by Britain, the United States, and Spain – on the face of it understandable given Britain's massive naval superiority and the lack of practicable steps in those proposals – raised suspicions about Germany's

[249] Charmley, *Splendid Isolation*, 331–61; Clark, *The Sleepwalkers*, 160–67; Wilson, *The Policy of the Entente*, 100–120.
[250] Canis, *Der Weg in den Abgrund*, 274–75.
[251] Hobson, *Militarism at Sea*, 268–70; Mommsen, *Bürgerstolz und Weltmachtstreben*, 341.
[252] See esp. Lambert, *Planning Armageddon*, 61–101.
[253] Kelly, *Tirpitz*, 276–79; Hobson, *Imperialism at Sea*, 276–84.

commitment to peace, further burdening its diplomacy at a time of increasing international isolation.[254]

As will be discussed in the chapters to follow, Bülow was sensitive to the danger of these developments and aware that any understanding with Britain to overcome Germany's diplomatic isolation required German naval concessions. Bloated German naval spending from the dreadnought arms race would worsen Reich deficits and force a major financial reform in 1908–9 that had similarly thorny constitutional implications as in Britain.[255] On both sides of the North Sea a huge portion of national wealth would be sunk into weapons of dubious tactical and strategic value that, while increasing tensions, did nothing to enhance security or deter conflict and were later not even vindicated by their use in the First World War.[256] As a deterrent to Germany, British dreadnoughts would likewise be a complete failure, as every attempt by the British to negotiate a bilateral reduction in the pace of dreadnought construction with Germany proved a nonstarter before World War I. As we shall see, Germany later shifted resources away from naval construction not because of the acceleration of British dreadnought building after 1909, but because of a military buildup in France and Russia by 1912.[257]

---

[254] Helfferich, *Der Weltkrieg*, vol. 1, 35–36.
[255] Epkenhans, *Die wilhelminische Flottenrüstung*, 465, Tabelle Nr. 14.
[256] Paul Kennedy, "HMS *Dreadnought* and the Tides of History," in *The Dreadnought and the Edwardian Age*, ed. Blyth, Lambert, and Rüger, 213–37, here 223–25.
[257] T. G. Otte, "Grey Ambassador: The *Dreadnought* and British Foreign Policy," in Blyth, Lambert, and Rüger, *The Dreadnought and the Edwardian Age*, 51–78, here 77.

# 8

# Empire in Crisis

## The Colonial Crisis

As the Russo-Japanese War was unfolding in East Asia with its disastrous consequences for Germany, a series of native rebellions began in German East and Southwest Africa that would lead to a growing public perception that Germany's overseas colonies were themselves on a poor footing, losing money, and crisis-prone.[1] In German Southwest Africa a notoriously brutal and ultimately genocidal campaign was fought against the Herero and Nama beginning in January 1904 that by 1907 led to the death of an estimated 60,000 Hereros and 10,000 Nama. In June 1905 the Maji Maji uprising began in German East Africa that would ultimately leave some 75,000 dead. In Southwest Africa alone the Herero and Nama war would tie up 14,000 German troops and cost 600 million marks.[2] These costly wars sparked a heated public debate in 1905–6 about colonial policy that eventually brought German politics to an impasse in late 1906.[3] Quite beyond calling for

---

[1] See esp. Pogge von Strandmann, *Imperilaismus vom grünen Tisch*, 354–98.
[2] See Horst Drechsler, *"Let Us Die Fighting": The Struggle of the Herero and Nama Against German Imperialism (1884–1915)*, trans. Bernd Zöllner (London: Zed Press, 1980); Drechsler, *Aufstände in Südwestafrika: Der Kampf der Herero und Nama 1904 bis 1907 gegen die deutsche Kolonialherrschaft* (Berlin: Dietz Verlag, 1984); Jon M. Bridgman, *The Revolt of the Hereros* (Berkeley, Los Angeles, and London: University of California Press, 1981); Karl-Martin Seeberg, *Der Maji-Maji-Krieg Gegen die deutsche Kolonialherrschaft* (Berlin: Dietrich Riemer Verlag, 1989); Tilman Dedering, "'A Certain Rigorous Treatment of All Parts of the Nation': The Annihilation of the Herero in German South West Africa, 1904," in *Massacre in History*, ed. Mark Levine and Penny Roberts (New York and Oxford: Berghahn Books, 1999), 205–22; Zimmerer and Zeller, eds., *Völkermord in Deutsch-Südwest Afrika*, 45–63; Hull, *Absolute Destruction*, 5–90. Cf. Kuss, *German Colonial Wars*; Benjamin Madley, "Patterns of Frontier Genocide 1803–1910: The Aboriginal Tasmanians, the Yuki of California, and the Herero of Namibia," *Journal of Genocide Research* 6, no. 2 (June 2004): 167–92; Smith, "The Talk of Genocide," 110.
[3] See Mary Evelyn Townsend, *The Rise and Fall of Germany's Colonial Empire 1884–1918* (New York: Howard Fertig, 1966), 225–43; George Dunlap Crothers, *The German Elections of 1907* (New York and London: Columbia University Press, 1941); Beverly Heckart, *From Bassermann to Bebel: The Grand Bloc's Quest for Reform in the Kaiserreich, 1900–1914* (New Haven and London: Yale University Press, 1974); Winfried Becker,

urgent reforms of colonial administration and more enlightened economic development policies, it tarnished Germany's image and questioned the very legitimacy of its colonial endeavor and thus also Germany's status as a world power. The colonial wars and scandals would cost Oscar Stübel his job as director of the Colonial Section of the Foreign Office in November 1905, just as it would his short-lived successor, Ernst zu Hohenlohe-Langenburg (1863–1950) in September 1906.

As the costs of suppressing the native rebellion in Southwest Africa grew in 1905, the young Matthias Erzberger (1875–1921) of the Center Party – who had only been elected to the Reichstag for the first time in 1903 – began to make a name for himself through a campaign against the government's rudderless colonial policy.[4] Erzberger was well informed about colonial affairs through his contacts to Catholic missions. While his criticisms of the expenses and excesses of violence involved in putting down the rebellions were well justified, Erzberger was also an ambitious career politician who harbored deep suspicions toward big business and a personal animus toward Karl Helfferich, who, as discussed in Chapter 7, was himself a staunch advocate of greater involvement of German banks and industrial firms in colonial investments. In March 1905 Erzberger leveled criticisms against the monetary arrangements in German East Africa, which had been given a new currency through negotiation between Hamburg and Berlin banking houses brokered by none other than Helfferich.[5] Another of Erzberger's criticisms centered on a bill granting the Berliner Handelsgesellschaft (a large commercial bank) a guarantee on a loan to build the North Cameroon Railway and payment of the difference between the interest charges and operating income once the railway was in operation. This was a deal that Karl Helfferich had himself also arranged in the Colonial Section between Lenz & Co. (the company building the railway) and the Handeslgesellschaft in late 1904.[6]

In various newspaper articles and then on December 14, 1905, on the floor of the Reichstag, Erzberger attacked the government at length, enumerating the high costs and various failings of Germany's colonial policy and then revealing the details of a supposedly shady deal between Lenz and the railway syndicate that had started but then suspended construction of the North Cameroon Railway on account of cost overruns.[7] This had involved receipt

---

"Kulturkampf als Vorwand: Die Kolonialwahlen von 1907 und das Problem der Parlamentarisierung des Reiches," *Historisches Jahrbuch* 106 (1986): 59–84.

[4] See John S. Lowry, *Big Swords, Jesuits, and Bondelwarts: Wilhelmine Imperialism, Overseas Resistance, and German Political Catholicism, 1897–1906* (Leiden and Boston: Brill, 2015).

[5] Williamson, *Karl Helfferich*, 64–65.   [6] Ibid., 69–71.

[7] *StenBerVR, XI. Legislaturperiode, 12. Sitzung, 1905/06*, vol. 1 (Dec. 14, 1905), 320A-331C; on the North Cameroon Railway and the deal between the Lenz and the syndicate, 326D-330D; cf. Bülow, *Denkwürdigkeiten*, vol. 2, 187.

of a payment and shares by the Cameroon Railway Syndicate in return for allowing Lenz to take a controlling interest in the project, funds that Erzberger claimed were generated by inflated construction costs.[8]

Itching for a fight and himself a highly disputatious *Besserwisser*, Hefferich responded to the specific accusations regarding the Cameroon railway for the government on the floor of the Reichstag.[9] In his response he revealed the difficulties encountered in constructing the railroad (due, among other things, to extremely heavy rainfall) that had increased the construction costs, arguing nevertheless that the costs were not inflated – they had in fact been checked by the Reich Railway Office engineers. He also argued that there were no other options for completing the railroad on account of the risks involved without Reich interest guarantees, but that no mining concessions had been given and that the deal between Lenz and the old syndicate was fair, though ultimately a private matter in which the government had neither an interest nor played a role.[10] Helfferich's rebuttals and Erzberger's counterclaims, which continued into Reichstag sessions on December 15, 1905 and January 18, 1906, revealed the deep hostility between the two men. Most contemporaries agreed that Helfferich had bested Erzberger by effectively rebutting most of these accusations, getting in plenty of digs against his rival in the process. Bülow was so impressed with Helfferich that he secured the Order of the Crown for him from the Kaiser.[11]

Erzberger's attacks, however, did not let up. In January 1906 he claimed that the currency reform Helfferich had worked to implement in East Africa had been a contributing factor in the Maji Maji rebellion.[12] In April criticism extended to Germany's Morocco policy. As the SPD's leader August Bebel was criticizing the government's handling of the Morocco affair on April 5, Bülow collapsed on the floor of the Reichstag from strain and overwork at a time when his entire free-hand foreign policy was coming apart at the seams, highlighted by the Algeciras Act in late March.[13] In late May 1906 the Reichstag refused appropriations to extend the Lüderitz Bay-Kobub railroad to Keetmanhoop in German Southwest Africa. It later also rejected a bill to create an independent Imperial Colonial Office.[14] Throughout the remainder of 1906, especially in September, Erzberger escalated his campaign against the

---

[8] Williamson, *Karl Helfferich*, 72.
[9] *StenBerVR, XI. Legislaturperiode, 12. Sitzung, 1905/06*, vol. 1 (Dec. 14, 1905), 333B-338C.
[10] Ibid.; *StenBerVR, XI. Legislaturperiode, 14. Sitzung, 1905/06*, vol. 1 (Dec. 15, 1905), 399D-403A; *StenBerVR, XI. Legislaturperiode, 23. Sitzung, 1905/1906*, vol. 1 (Jan. 18, 1906), 637D-640C; Williamson, *Karl Helfferich*, 72–73; on the difficulties constructing the railway, 69.
[11] Williamson, *Karl Helfferich*, 75–76.   [12] Ibid., 66.
[13] See Canis, *Der Weg in den Abgrund*, 169–89; cf. Bülow, *Denkwürdigkeiten*, vol. 2, 212–14. See also Lerman, *The Chancellor as Courtier*, 147–48.
[14] Schiefel, *Bernhard Dernburg*, 35.

government's handling of the colonies. By that point Helfferich had left the Colonial Section to work for the Deutsche Bank and take up a position as second director of the Anatolian Railway, in time to avoid the deepening colonial crisis that year.[15] Left to defend German colonial policy in the Reichstag was the inexperienced and hapless Ernst zu Hohenlohe-Langenburg.

By the late summer 1906 Bülow had recovered his strength and started to take the offensive in the colonial crisis by appointing someone with fresh ideas and energy as director of the Colonial Section, ideally an outsider to government not tainted by colonial scandals and with some business experience. While he initially contemplated the brilliant industrialist Walther Rathenau for the post, he ultimately settled on the director of the Darmstädter Bank, Bernhard Dernburg, a left liberal with great financial acumen and much experience working for Siemens and Deutsche Bank in the United States in the 1880s and 1890s. Dernburg was known for his success as a turnaround expert but also for deploying unorthodox methods.[16] Bülow and Dernburg agreed that the keys to prosperous German colonies were trade and industry and colonial reforms along lines long demanded by German businessmen.

Dernburg was named Hohenlohe's successor on September 2, 1906.[17] Not surprisingly, comparisons were made at the time between Dernburg and Joseph Chamberlain, as Chamberlain had also had a background in business before becoming British colonial secretary. Dernburg's appointment was seen as a genuine break with the practice of appointing senior bureaucrats with noble titles to such posts and thus also as an experiment and the beginning of a new era.[18] Indeed, his appointment was described in German and American newspapers as the triumph of "American ideas."[19] Two immediate initiatives Dernburg implemented in office were a reform of the selection of colonial personnel and a survey of the economic status of the colonies, colonial finance, and the profitability of colonial investments.[20]

Despite nasty attacks on his banking background by the Center Party deputy Hermann Roeren (1844–1920) and snide remarks about his Jewish heritage by August Bebel, the leader of the Social Democrats, Dernburg was able to assert himself vigorously and very effectively for his plans for colonial reform and against unsubstantiated accusations leveled at the colonial administration in multiple sessions of the Reichstag in late November and early December 1906, turning the tables on the colonial critics.[21] Dernburg's

---

[15] Williamson, *Helfferich*, 78.
[16] Bülow, *Denkwürdigkeiten*, vol. 2, 266–68; Schiefel, *Bernhard Dernburg*, 37–38, 40–41, 44.
[17] Schiefel, *Bernhard Dernburg*, 38.   [18] Ibid., 40–41, 42–43.   [19] Ibid., 43.
[20] Ibid., 45–46, 47.
[21] Ibid., 52; *StenBerVR, XI. Legislaturperode, 128. Sitzung 1905–06*, vol. 5 (Nov. 28, 1906), 3960D-3969C; *StenBerVR, XI. Legislaturperode, 129. Sitzung 1905/1906*, vol. 5 (Nov. 29, 1906), 3997D-4002D; *StenBerVR, XI. Legislaturperode, 130. Sitzung 1905/06*, vol. 5

blunt style, ability as a speaker, energy, and unwavering confidence turned him into a hero of the colonial cause practically overnight.[22] Ultimately a majority comprised of the Center Party and Social Democrats (along with the Alsatian and Polish parties) rejected the bill for supplemental appropriations of 29 million marks to pay for military operations in Southwest Africa. The rejection gave Bülow an opportunity to ask the Kaiser to dissolve the Reichstag and call fresh elections on December 13, 1906.[23]

The so-called in "Hottentot elections" January and February 1907 would become nothing less than a national referendum on German colonialism and Bülow's *Weltpolitik*. The headquarters for Bülow's campaign was his own chancellory led by Chief of the Reich Chancellery Friedrich Wilhelm von Lobell (1855–1931) and the Foreign Office press secretary Otto Hammann. A special election fund was created from contributions by business magnates of some 587,000 marks that was then funneled to patriotic associations including the Navy League, the Colonial Society, and the Imperial League against Social Democracy. The Navy League received 60,000 marks from this fund and August Keim became an important advisor to Bülow's campaign. The themes emphasized in the campaign thus became much more stridently hostile to both the SPD and Center Party and could draw on the support of radical nationalists in the Pan-German League normally critical of the government.[24] Quite unusual in the campaign was also the very active involvement of Dernburg as a tireless traveling speaker on behalf of the parties supporting the government.[25]

## The "Hottentot Elections"

Throughout the colonial crisis and during the election campaign, Chancellor Bülow and Dernburg could depend on Schmoller and his former students' voluntary and enthusiastic support for the German colonial project. Just as during the debate over the second navy bill in 1899–1900, Schmoller and the

---

(Nov. 30, 1906), 4045A-4048D; *StenBerVR*, XI. *Legislaturperode*, 131. *Sitzung 1905/06*, vol. 5 (Dec. 1, 1906), 4051D-4057D; *StenBerVR*, XI. *Legislaturperode*, 132. *Sitzung 1905/06*, vol. 5 (Dec. 3, 1906), 4084B-4085A, 4096B-4103B, 4116B-4118D; *StenBerVR*, XI. *Legislaturperode*, 133. *Sitzung 1905/06*, vol. 5 (Dec. 4, 1906), 4152C-4154A; *StenBerVR*, XI. *Legislaturperode*, 140. *Sitzung 1905/06*, vol. 5 (Dec. 13, 1906), 4363C-4365A, 4368D-4370A.

[22] See, here, Christian S. Davis, *Colonialism, Antisemitism, and Germans of Jewish Descent in Imperial Germany* (Ann Arbor: University of Michigan Press, 2012), 197–98, 241–42; Schiefel, *Bernhard Dernburg*, 52–53.

[23] See Townsend, *Germany's Colonial Empire*, 225–43; Crothers, *The German Elections of 1907*; Becker, "Kulturkampf als Vorwand," 59–84; Lerman, *The Chancellor As Courtier*, 164–74.

[24] Chickering, *We Men Who Feel Most German*, 258–59; Winzen, *Reichskanzler*, 127–28.

[25] Schiefel, *Bernhard Dernburg*, 56.

other like-minded professors did not participate in the campaign within the political parties or existing colonial and pro-fleet organizations (although like Schmoller, many were members of both of the German Colonial Society and the Navy League). Instead, a new committee of independent academics, artists, writers, and members of the liberal professions was created. The stated aim was to "enlighten" public opinion about the colonies using the tools of *Wissenschaft*. The intention was clearly to prevent being identified with partisan politics and specific interests by donning the aegis of independent scholarship. The close links of Schmoller to Bülow and the new Kolonialdirektor Bernhard Dernburg must have also been an impulse for creating an "independent" pro-colonial organization. As documents reveal, this new body was in fact the brainchild of both Schmoller and the economist Gottfried Zoepfl (1869–1945), then a *Privatdozent* (lecturer) at the University of Berlin.[26] Zoepfl, who was later also active in the pro-fleet propaganda of the RMA's Communications Bureau, had established himself as yet another specialist on *Weltwirtschaft*, having published on trade policy and gained experience as a trade attaché in South America between 1903 and 1906 and as an assistant in the Foreign Office in 1906.[27]

On December 27, 1906 a provisional committee headed by Schmoller published an invitation to a "counter-action" (*Gegenaktion*) planned for January 8, 1907, against those who would seek to restrict Germany to internal politics, play down the value of its colonies, and "suffocate the only just developing sense of responsibility of the German people for its position of world power."[28] The German people, it asserted, "which is just now growing into this position is to be enlightened about the fact that abandonment of its position of world power [*Weltmachtstellung*], and the colonies in particular, is not an option if it does not seek to abandon itself." Despite representing different partisan positions, the signatories of the invitation declared that "a strong and determined majority for the execution of colonial policy is indispensable for the future of the German people."[29] Berlin professors made up the

---

[26] GStA PK, VI. HA Nl. Schmoller, Nr. 13 I, fols. 248–49, Gottfried Zöpfl to Gustav Schmoller, Dec. 29, 1906. His name is spelled Zöpfl, Zoepfl, and sometimes Zoepfel in the manuscript sources.

[27] See, for example, Gottfried Zoepfl, *Fränkische Handelpolitik im Zeitalter der Aufklärung: Ein Beitrag zur deutschen Staats- und Wirtschaftsgeschichte* (Erlangen: A. Deichert'sche Verlagsbuchhandlung Nachf. [G. Böhme], 1894); Zoepfl, *Der Wettbewerb des russischen und amerikanischen Petroleums: Eine Weltwirtschaftliche Studie* (Berlin: Siemenroth & Troschel, 1899). See also Deist, *Flottenpolitik,* 107, 107n 125.

[28] Kolonialpolitisches Aktionskomité, ed., *Schmoller, Dernburg, Delbrück, Schäfer, Sering, Schillings, Brunner, Jastrow, Penck, Kahl über Reichstagsauflösung und Kolonialpolitik: Offizieller stenographischer Bericht über die Versammlung in der Berliner Hochschule für Musik am 8. Januar 1907* (Berlin: Wedekind, 1907), frontispiece.

[29] Ibid.

majority of the forty-two signatories, which included, among others, the painter Anton von Werner (1843–1915) and the composer Richard Strauss (1864–1949).[30] This was to a considerable degree a similar group of people that had formed the Free Union for Naval Lectures in 1899. Several thousand copies of this invitation were sent out, and according to a report later drafted by the organization's business manager Dr. Emil Struve (1864–1915), it was successful beyond expectation.[31]

If there was any doubt about the purpose of the "counter-action," its actual convention on January 8, 1907, in the Royal Academy for Music made it abundantly clear that it existed to agitate and propagandize during the upcoming election.[32] The interest in the meeting was much greater than expected, with the assembly hall having to be closed off because it was overfilled.[33] Schmoller gave a welcoming address and was elected chairman. This was followed by a speech by Kolonialdirektor Bernhard Dernburg, which was greeted with tremendous enthusiasm.[34] Dernburg shared the belief that the colonial crisis was a test of Germany's character. He defined the challenge as putting the colony's soil, its natural resources, plants, animals, and native inhabitants to the benefit of the mother country's economy. The most important of these resources was the native population.[35] The challenge, he noted, was making the "negro" productive and thereby civilized. Some natives would doubtlessly be destroyed by this process just as some wild animals were with the advent of civilization – the greatest of all colonization enterprises, the United States, illustrated that point. By comparison, Dernburg believed that German colonial territories could today be colonized with modern "conservation techniques."[36]

Similar to Schmoller's ruminations at the German Colonial Congress of 1902, Dernburg placed much emphasis on the task of preserving the native populations and making them more productive, but in doing so distinguished between aiding the recovery of the valuable Herero pastoralists and breaking the vagrant and dangerous habits of the "Hottentotten" [Nama].[37] Pandering a bit to his academic audience, he made much of the fact that the "land of poets and thinkers" was endowed with the finest scholars in the *Geisteswissenschaften* and applied sciences, a fact that would greatly aid a new form of rational,

---

[30] Ibid.
[31] GStA PK, VI. HA Nl. Schmoller, Nr. 13 II, fols. 283–84. Geschäftsbericht des Kolonialpolitischen Aktionskomittees, n.d. Struve was Professor of Gesetzeskunde und Handelswissenschaft at the Versuchs- und Lehranstalt für Brauerei in Berlin.
[32] Kolonialpolitisches Aktionskomité, ed., *Schmoller, Dernburg*, 19.
[33] GStA PK, VI. HA Nl. Schmoller, Nr. 13 II, fol. 284, Geschäftsbericht des Kolonialpolitischen Aktionskomittee's, n.d.
[34] Schiefel, *Bernhard Dernburg*, 56–62; Smith, *The German Colonial Empire*, 183–209.
[35] Kolonialpolitisches Aktionskomité, ed., *Schmoller, Dernburg*, 6.   [36] Ibid., 6–8.
[37] Ibid., 14.

Figure 8.1  Bernhard Dernburg ca. 1915.

scientific colonization. He emphasized the important role played in this new form of colonialism by science and technology, hydrology, and electrical technology as well as by geologists, chemists, geographers, botanists, zoologists, and land economists, and not least, by enthnologists, anthroplogists, legal scholars, economists, historians, and statisticians.[38]

Dernburg was particularly animated by the developmental and civilizing possibilities afforded by railways, which he prized as "the most important tool of colonization."[39] These had the capacity to link the production of the colonies to a larger colonial and international network of commerce, and in the process would produce incomes for millions of natives and turn them into consumers. Railways thus acted to habituate the indigenous population to work and elevate them to a higher level of civilization. Drawing on the example of the Uganda Railway, he mentioned that it employed many natives, encouraged agricultural habits, and suppressed raiding.[40] Emphasized along with his optimistic outlook for colonial railways was the relatively light and sustainable overall burden the colonies posed.[41] Pains were also taken to demonstrate how all classes of German society benefited from the colonies,

---

[38] Ibid., 5, 8, 9–10.   [39] Ibid., 8.   [40] Ibid., 9.   [41] Ibid., 11–12.

notably industry and industrial workers.[42] Dernburg's speech was met with enthusiastic interruptions and ended with long applause.

The speeches that followed repeated and reinforced a number of Dernburg's arguments. The Pan-German historian Dietrich Schäfer (1845–1929) brought German colonialism into historical perspective, pointing to the massive growth of the Russian, French, and British Empires since the 1860s, America's recent imperialist expansion, and the utter backwardness of anyone suggesting that Germany was in any position to give up its few colonies in such an aggressive international environment.[43] Max Sering reiterated the notion that railways would create colonial consumers and an industrious class of native small farmers. The colonies also potentially afforded Germany protection from international commodity monopolies.[44] The naturalist and photographer Carl Georg Schillings (1865–1921), drawing on extensive experience in East Africa, advocated thoroughgoing reforms of German colonial administration and training that allowed its officials to gain a detailed knowledge of the languages, character, and political conditions of the indigenous population in order to build trust and better rule them.[45]

The meeting concluded with a vote on a resolution that noted the belated creation of the German Empire and the consequently underdeveloped sense of "world political duty" (*weltpolitische Pflicht*) and the threat posed by a Reichstag majority refusing needed appropriations for Southwest Africa. It proposed the creation of a committee charged with the task of raising awareness for these matters within the electorate, which came to be called the Kolonialpolitisches Aktionskomité (Colonial-Political Action Committee).[46] The target of this agitation, as Schmoller had already outlined in his welcoming address, was the passive electorate, the three million German voters who had not bothered to vote in the last election.[47] As the historian Hans Delbrück made clear, preparations had already been undertaken for the proposed propaganda activities; what was missing were the financial means. The assembled men were thus asked to make contributions on their way out of the meeting.[48] The resolution was accepted unanimously, and a small organizing board was elected to coordinate these activities. This included Max Sering and Gottfried Zoepfl, with Schmoller acting as chairman.[49]

Money contributions to the new Aktionskomité were very generous, and it is notable that the first name on the list of contributors was Karl Rathgen, now at the University of Heidelberg, who would later be appointed to the first chair in political economy at the new German Colonial Institute in Hamburg in 1908, a major initiative of the so-called Dernburg era which will be discussed

---

[42] Ibid., 15.  [43] Ibid., 20–22.  [44] Ibid., 26–27, 31.  [45] Ibid., 33–34.
[46] Ibid., 19.  [47] Ibid., 1.  [48] Ibid., 4, 19.  [49] Ibid., 47.

in the next chapter.[50] Taken together some 2,347 marks in donations were made that evening, with the lion's share from the ranks of professors, artists, and writers living in Berlin.[51] The stenographic report of the January 8 meeting went out to all corners of Germany and was reported on in the major newspapers, which made a point of printing extensive excerpts of Dernburgs's speech.[52]

The Aktionskomité quickly gained a national profile. An indicator of the range of interest generated by this meeting is given by the fact that that Minna Cauer (1841–1922), founder of the Women's Welfare Association Berlin, a bourgeois feminist organization, sent a signed declaration of protest jointly from her organization and the Berlin members of Federation for Women's Suffrage. They took issue with the exclusion of women from the meeting, writing "we condemn the shortsightedness of leading men who want to win the wide masses of the people for questions of world power politics, and go about it by excluding the striving elements of working and the thinking women from striving for the political future of their people. This manner of proceeding directly contradicts the wish recently expressed by Deputy Colonial Director Dernburg that women emigrate to the colonies."[53] There was also much interest from German students. A leader of the Association of German Students wrote the Aktionskomité requesting a "practical *Kolonialpolitiker* with a prominent name but no party figure" to address a "great national, colonial rally" on behalf of the student corporations and associations of the universities in Munich.[54]

## The Colonial-Political Action Committee

Doubtless buoyed by the national resonance of their activities, at the first business meeting of the organizing board of the Aktionskomité under Schmoller three days later it was agreed to have the stenographic report

---

[50] GStA PK, VI. HA Nl. Schmoller, Nr. 13 I, fols. 12–15, Zeichnungen für das Kolonialpolitische Aktionskomitee, n.d. [Jan. 8, 1907].

[51] GStA PK, VI. HA Nl. Schmoller, Nr. 13 II, fol. 284, Geschäftsbericht des Kolonialpolitischen Aktionskomittee's, n.d.

[52] For example, "Die Versammlung des 'Kolonialen Aktionskomités,'" *Berliner Tageblatt*, Jan. 9, 1907.

[53] Quoted in Wildenthal, *German Women for Empire*, 132; cf GStA PK, VI. HA Nl. Schmoller, Nr. 13 I, fol. 197, Statement of protest, Verein Frauenwohl Berlin and the Berlin members of the Deutscher Verband für Frauenstimmrecht; GStA PK, VI. HA Nl. Schmoller, Nr. 13 I, fol. 232, Minna Cauer to Gustav Schmoller, Jan. 10, 1907. On the participation of women's groups in German imperialism, see Birthe Kundrus, "Weiblicher Kulturimperialismus: Die imperialistischen Frauenverbände des Kaiserreichs," in Conrad and Osterhammel, *Das Kaiserreich transnational*, 211–35.

[54] GStA PK, VI. HA Nl. Schmoller, Nr. 13 I, fol. 174, E. Kayser, Verein deutscher Studenten, to Gustav Schmoller, Jan. 15, 1907.

printed as a separate volume and distributed en masse. What is more, an additional pro-colonial publication, a "Colonial-Political Guide" (*Kolonialpolitischer Führer*), was commissioned from a *Privatdozent* at the University of Berlin, Dr. Gustav Roloff (1866–1952), and intended as a short general primer on the basic facts and significance of Germany's colonial possessions. Like the stenographic report, this too was intended for mass circulation.[55] The board also selected a larger number of members from all over Germany to extend the organization beyond Berlin. There were eventually some 138 non-Berlin members, including of course Karl Rathgen but also many other leading economists and statisticians such as Karl Bücher (1847–1930), Johannes Conrad, Heinrich Dietzel (1857–1935), G. F. Knapp, Wilhelm Lexis (1837–1914), Georg von Mayr (1841–1925), Sartorius von Waltershausen, and Georg Schanz (1853–1931).[56] As will be discussed, Hermann Schumacher was at the time in the United States, but there is little doubt he would have been involved had he then been in Germany. Among the more prominent non-economist members of the Aktionskomité were the zoologist Ernst Haeckel (1834–1919) and Nobel Prize-winning physicist Wilhelm Roentgen (1845–1923), and the painters Hans Thoma (1839–1924) and Fritz von Uhde (1848–1911).[57]

A constitutive meeting with these new members was planned for January 19, 1907 in the Prussian Herrenhaus, to be followed by a gala dinner in the Berlin Palast-Hotel, to which Chancellor Bülow and Kolonialdirektor Dernburg were invited as guests of honor.[58] A further organizational meeting was held in Schmoller's home on January 16 to nominate additional board members, among them Wilhelm von Siemens (chairman of the board of Siemens-Schuckertwerke), Gustav von Götzen (1866–1910, governor of German East Africa), and Otto von Hentig (1852–1934, co-founder of the Shantung Railway and Mining companies). This meeting also determined the means of distributing the published stenographic report: along with other agencies, the German Navy League would be entrusted with this task.[59] There is no known evidence of any direct involvement of the RMA's Communications Bureau as a coordinating agency for this election propaganda, as Tirpitz was very much concerned about the anti-Center Party tone of the campaign and wary of burning bridges to an important Reichstag constituency

---

[55] GStA PK, VI. HA Nl. Schmoller, Nr. 13 II, fol. 284, Geschäftsbericht des Kolonialpolitischen Aktionskomittee's, n.d.
[56] GStA PK, VI. HA Nl. Schmoller, Nr. 13 II, fols. 105–13, Verzeichnis der ausserhalb Berlins wohnenden Mitglieder des K.-P-A.K, n.d.
[57] Ibid.
[58] GStA PK, VI. HA Nl. Schmoller, Nr. 13 I, fol. 203, Schmoller to all members of the Kolonialpolitisches Aktionskomitee not present at the January 12 meeting, Jan. 14, 1907.
[59] GStA PK, VI. HA Nl. Schmoller, Nr. 13 II, fol. 6, Minutes of meeting, Wednesday, Jan. 16, 1907.

for fleet appropriations.[60] Still, Ernst von Halle published a stridently pro-colonial propaganda article on colonial history in the *Journal for Colonial Policy, Colonial Law and Colonial Economy* in January 1907 that was distributed in large numbers as an election pamphlet and in which he self-identified as an admiralty councilor and *not* as a professor at the University of Berlin.[61] In any case, there could be no doubt in the minds of most Catholic voters that the Navy Office was anything less than fully behind Bülow, Dernburg, and the Aktionskomité.

Both Bülow and Dernburg accepted invitations to the dinner in writing, suggesting that the initiative came from Schmoller and the Aktionskomité rather than the chancellor's office.[62] In any case, the dinner rapidly became a major political event at which occasion Bülow planned to give an important election speech. The novelty of this arrangement was added to by two factors: members of the press were not invited to the dinner (and were declined invitations when they solicited them) and Bülow refused to have his speech printed and distributed to the press prior to the dinner, fearing *"Zwischenfälle"* (incidents).[63] The dinner was much akin to political dinners then commonly held in Britain and the United States to launch political campaigns, but it was at that time something new in Germany about which the press complained.[64] It is important to add that at the formal constituting meeting of the Aktionskomité that preceded the dinner, the assembled members voted to continue the activities of their new organization beyond the election.[65]

Schmoller's address at the dinner preceding Bülow's election speech reemphasized the aims of the Aktionskomité as enlightening and influencing public opinion and the political parties about the need to preserve the colonies "for the power and honor of Germany" and to facilitate the creation of a Reichstag majority that could work with the chancellor to achieve these goals.[66] Bülow's speech played heavily on the evils of German particularism,

---

[60] Deist, *Flottenpolitik*, 201–2; Kelly, *Tirpitz*, 275.
[61] Ernst von Halle, "Die großen Epochen der neuzeitlichen Kolonialgeschichte," *Zeitschrift für Kolonialpolitik, Kolonialrecht, und Kolonialwirtschaft* 9, no. 1 (Jan. 1907): 19–54. As a pamphlet, see von Halle, *Die großen Epochen der neuzeitlichen Kolonialgeschichte*, Koloniale Abhandlungen, vol. 7 (Berlin: Süssroth, 1907).
[62] GStA PK, VI. HA Nl. Schmoller, Nr. 13 I, fol. 202, Bernhard von Bülow to Gustav Schmoller, Jan. 13, 1907; GStA PK, VI. HA Nl. Schmoller, Nr. 13 I, fol. 187, Dernburg to Schmoller, Jan. 16, 1907.
[63] GStA PK, VI. HA Nl. Schmoller, Nr. 13 I, fols. 180–81, E. Fr. [Ernst Franke] to Gustav Schmoller, Jan. 17, 1907.
[64] *Die Post* (Berlin), Jan. 16, 1907 (Abend-Ausgabe).
[65] GStA PK, VI. HA Nl. Schmoller, Nr. 13 II, fols. 7–8, Minutes of the constituting meeting, Jan. 19, 1907; see also GStA PK, VI. HA Nl. Schmoller, Nr. 13 II, fol. 9, Verzeichnis der Anwesenden, Sitzung des Kolonialpolitischen Aktionskomitees, Jan. 19, 1907.
[66] GStA PK, VI. HA Nl. Schmoller, Nr. 13 I, fols. 163–64, Stenographic report, *Wolff's Telegraphisches Bureau*, 58, no. 301 (Jan. 20, 1907).

confessional divisions, and factional bickering as dangerous remnants of Germany's historical development that manifested itself in endemic petty partisanship and the willingness to sacrifice national welfare for narrow, philistine interests and party doctrines. This was a development that elements of the foreign press hostile to Germany pinned their hopes on, despite the fact that these countries themselves had fought great colonial wars with stoicism and sacrifice. Bülow stated that the claim that the budgetary rights of the Reichstag had been injured was a red herring for what was nothing more than a partisan power struggle of the Center Party in unlikely cahoots with the Social Democrats, normally their sworn enemy. The aim now, he said, was to unite "all national elements from the conservative right to the progressive left, without considerations of religion" for "national duties and obligations."[67] Bülow also took the opportunity to praise Dernburg for restoring the shattered trust in the value of the colonies, which were a touchstone for German vigor and a way of unifying the splintered political tendencies of the Reich. Likewise the organizers of the dinner – scholars, scientists, and artists – were best called on to work against partisanship and to banish the idea that Germany was becoming "again only a nation of thinkers, poets, and dreamers and not also a great, peacefully striving and, in difficult times, unified and courageous nation."[68]

While absent from these activities on account of his duties running the Anatolian Railway in Constantinople, Helfferich published an impassioned plea supportive of Bülow and Dernburg in the pages of the *Kolonialzeitung* a few days after the banquet but before the second ballot.[69] In it, Helfferich argued that the colonial crisis was now nothing less than a "Reich crisis" (*Reichskrisis*) – Germany was at "the crossroads of its *Weltpolitik*" that would determine its fate into the future. Apart from assuring the security of persons and property, Helfferich argued, the single most important measure that had to be taken in the colonies to assure their economic development was the creation an efficient transportation infrastructure.[70] Through shortsightedness and a false sense of economy, Germany had delayed the construction of railways in its African colonies until the second half of the 1890s, and it had only been in the last three years that this had been taken up in earnest and involved German private capital by offering modest interest guarantees.[71]

Signs were now promising. Helfferich pointed out that the Deutsche Bank was now leading a consortium that was building the Daressalam-Morogoro railway in East Africa, and that the consortium had worked with the German East African Company to create the East African Bank. The Disconto-Gesellschaft was involved with the Otavi Company that had

---

[67] Ibid.  [68] Ibid.
[69] Karl Helfferich, "Am Scheideweg der Weltpolitik," *Deutsche Kolonialzeitung*, Jan. 26, 1907, 35–40.
[70] Ibid., 39.  [71] Ibid., 35–37.

built the Swapokmund-Tsumeb railway and was building a line into the copper-rich Otavi region in Southwest Africa. Defending a deal he had himself brokered while working in the Colonial Section, he pointed out that construction and operation of the North Cameroon Railway had been taken up by a consortium led by the Berlin Handelsgesellschaft, which together with the Lenz & Co. had also founded the Colonial Railway Construction and Operation Company, which had taken over operation from the Reich of the Usambara and Lüderitz Bay railroads on terms beneficial to the state. The German West African Bank had been founded by the Dresdner Bank and the West African Corporation. All of that, Helfferich was at pains to point out, had been achieved in the last three years without giving larger land concessions as had been done in the past.

Putting two formerly abusive colonial companies into his sights, Helfferich pointed out that the German East African and the South Cameroon Companies had relinquished many of their territorial privileges and concessions to the Reich in 1902 and 1905, respectively.[72] Helfferich also took some final direct jabs at Matthias Erzberger's claims about the excessive costs and poor performance of the colonies, showing that the value of the German colonies' total trade had nearly doubled between 1901 and 1905 and that many of Erzberger's calculations on the costs of the colonies to the taxpayer and their economic performance were factually erroneous or misleading.[73]

Helfferich concluded his essay by emphasizing the universal civilizing mission that the economic development of the German colonies represented and how that would improve Germany's tarnished image abroad:

> Gaining these territories for civilized humanity will not only vitally strengthen the foundations of our standing in the world, it is at the same time a cultural mission with universal significance. If Germany can devote a part of its surplus energy to this task with seriousness and persistence, it will be able to clear away a good deal of the mistrust with which our every move is followed and interpreted in the entire world. Those who live abroad may have a heightened sensibility for that. ... We appear in the fantasies of other nations as the hungry, roaring lion on the prowl for someone to devour. All upright assurances of our peaceful intentions cannot counter this mistrust that is put into our path everywhere. Here only visible facts will work. When the world sees that we do not leave our colonial possessions aside as worthless, that we have found a wide and rewarding field of activity here for our *"Drang,"* and that we devote ourselves with vigor and confidence to the peaceful conquest and achievement of our colonial empire, then we will appear less hungry and less alarming, and one will not see cravings for occupation wherever we show ourselves.[74]

---

[72] Ibid., 37.   [73] Ibid., 38.   [74] Ibid., 39–40.

Despite Schmoller and the Aktionskomité's attempt to appear "above party," the direct association with Bülow's campaign and the exclusion of the press from the dinner was criticized, as was the general political tendency of these activities. *Die Standarte* dubbed the dinner "the banquet of Baskerville," and complained bitterly about those who would dare exclude the press, noting that it was not Chancellor Bülow – who was deemed far too civilized to do such a thing – but out-of-touch "poets and thinkers" who were to blame.[75]

The perception of partisanship worsened when it was later discovered that two crass political pamphlets had been included in the same shipments of literature sent out for the Aktionskomité to primary school teachers by the Navy League, revealing the extent to which the league was now operating at cross-purposes with the RMA.[76] Again, the Aktionskomité, and Schmoller in particular, found themselves under attack for partisan politicking, interestingly, not only by papers with a Center Party and Social Democratic readership, but also by populist anti-Semites like Theodor Fritsch (1852–1933) who criticized the political activity of the elite "academic guild" that Schmoller represented, undoubtedly irritated by the role of heavy industry and the conspicuous presence of so many Jews in this pro-colonial activity.[77] Declarations had to be published to formally distance the Aktionskomité from these pamphlets and the electoral activities of the Navy League, an association that was vehemently denied by Schmoller and the committee, despite Sering's known direct association with the league and the services of the league in the distribution of the Aktionskomité's published stenographic report of their first meeting.[78] Troubles also began to brew with the German Colonial Society, which viewed the creation of a now permanent Aktionskomité as an unfriendly act and trespass on the turf of its own Colonial-Economic Committee.[79]

Both the unexpected public resonance of their first meeting and the equally unexpected popularity of their publications meant production and distribution

---

[75] "Das Bankett von Baskerville," *Die Standarte* [Berlin], Jan. 24, 1907.

[76] *Die koloniale Lügenfabrik (Erzberger, Stadthagen & Co.)* and *Warum ist der Reichstag am 13. Dezember Aufgelöst* (Berlin: Verlag Paul Köhler, 1907). These were a response to M. Erzberger, *Warum ist der Reichstag aufgelöst worden? Ein Wort an die Wählerschaft* (Berlin: Germania, 1907). See also Diziol, *Der Deutsche Flottenverein*, vol. 1, 69–70.

[77] *Kölnische Volkszeitung*, Feb. 12, 1907; *Vorwärts*, Feb. 14, 1907; "Schmoller und kein Ende," *Hammer. Blätter für deutschen Sinn*, no. 112 (Feb. 1907): 119–20.

[78] GStA PK, VI. HA Nl. Schmoller, Nr. 13 I, fol. 5, Declaration of the Kolonialpolitisches Aktionskomitee to the editors of newspapers, Feb. 11, 1907: Cf. GStA PK, VI. HA Nl. Schmoller, Nr. 13 I, fol. 23, Präsidial-Geschäftsstelle des Flotten-Vereins to Sering. Feb. 4, 1907; GStA PK, VI. HA Nl. Schmoller, Nr. 13 II, fol. 288, Geschäftsbericht des Kolonialpolitischen Aktionskomittee's, n.d.

[79] BArch L, R 8023/511, fol. 4, von Keller, Deutsche Kolonial-Gesellschaft, Abteilung München to the Deutsche Kolonial-Gesellschaft, Jan. 30, 1907.

of pamphlets took on unforeseen dimensions and quickly consumed the relatively generous contributions that had been made before the elections. Gustav Roloff had completed the *Kolonialpolitischer Führer* (Colonial-Political Guide) commissioned by the Aktionskomité just in time for the election, and this and the stenographic report of the first meeting were produced in massive numbers and distributed free of charge throughout the Reich. Some 114,000 alone were sent to German primary school teachers and 300 copies each were sent to no fewer than 250 chambers of commerce, agriculture, and trade.[80] Tens of thousands more were sent to party offices, various voter associations, and newspapers.[81] In all, nearly 700,000 copies of the stenographic report and *Kolonialpolitischer Führer* were distributed at a cost to the committee of over 27,000 marks, and by June 1907, it was running a deficit of 1,627 marks.[82] As a consequence, more contributions had to be solicited from members, and steps were also taken to secure subventions from the Colonial Section of the Foreign Office. Eventually sufficient funds were collected from these various sources to continue the publication activities of the Aktionskomité beyond the election.[83]

## The *Colonial-Political Guide* and *The Railways of Africa*

Given the vast scale of its distribution during the election and after, some words should be said about the content and impact of the *Kolonialpolitischer Führer*. It was written by Gustav Roloff, a lecturer specializing in the history of colonial policy at the University of Berlin.[84] Roloff situated the origin of Germany's colonial empire in an overall expansion of the German economy with the advent of industrialization in the 1850s and the resulting growth of German merchant interests abroad. The economic logic of the colonies as both a potential sources of raw materials and markets thus emerges out of an historical narrative of commercial expansion and *future* needs, in light of the

---

[80] GStA PK, VI. HA Nl. Schmoller, Nr. 13 II, fol. 286, Geschäftsbericht des Kolonialpolitischen Aktionskomittee's, n.d.

[81] GStA PK, VI. HA Nl. Schmoller, Nr. 13 II, fols. 87–88, Kolonialpolitisches Aktionskomité, Bestellung auf 1000 und mehr Exemplare von Berichten und Führern, n.d.

[82] GStA PK, VI. HA Nl. Schmoller, Nr. 13 II, fols. 202, 286–87, Geschäftsbericht des Kolonialpolitischen Aktionskomittee's, n.d.; GStA PK, VI. HA Nl. Schmoller, Nr. 13 II, fol. 2, Schmoller to members of the Kolonialpolitischen Aktionskomité, Mar. 22, 1907; GStA PK, VI. HA Nl. Schmoller, Nr. 13 II, fol. 276, Einnahmen und Ausgaben des Kolonialpolitischen Aktionskomitees bis 15. Juni 1907.

[83] GStA PK, VI. HA Nl. Schmoller, Nr. 13 II, fols. 253–54, Ernst Francke to Gustav Schmoller, Feb. 25, 1907. On the sources of funding for the election campaign, see Dieter Fricke, "Der deutsche Imperialismus und die Reichstagswahlen von 1907," *Zeitschrift für Geschichtswissenschaft*, 9 (1961): 538–76, here 557–66.

[84] For example, Gustav Roloff, *Die Kolonialpolitik Napoleons I.* (Munich and Leipzig: Oldenbourg, 1899).

competitive environment of European imperialism.[85] While taking a very generous view of the economic potential of the colonies – and for that reason taking clear swipes at the Center Party and Social Democrats – this tract is generally free of hyperbole or gratuitous nationalist rhetoric. Much like the arguments presented at the meeting of January 8, it emphasizes the relatively light burden imposed by the colonies and invests much hope in the railways as a precondition for development and civilizing force.[86] Mistreatment of the native population is likewise played down by emphasizing the tremendous overall benefit of European civilization and Germany's relatively good record compared with its rivals.[87] To drive that point home, the *Kolonialpolitischer Führer* included an appendix with brief historical surveys on the difficult colonial experiences of rival colonial powers, emphasizing, for example, the very slow development of the Cape Colony and the colonial scandals and suffering in colonial Virginia, whose white settlers had viciously massacred the native population and coerced vast land concessions.[88]

Finally, the pamphlet deployed the now very familiar menace of the American, British, French, and Russian "giant world empires." It was Germany's mission, Roloff argued, to keep world markets open and defend the independence of smaller states by forging a central European trade bloc that might be joined by other *Kulturstaaten* seeking to escape homogenizing imperial encroachment:

> At the top of a union to which Holland, Belgium, Scandinavia, Austria, perhaps also Italy and a few extra-European states such as Mexico and Chile could belong, Germany would have nothing to fear from the four others [giant empires], and this coalition of territory would have the enormous cultural advantage over the giant empires in that not one nation, not one language dominates, but instead that almost all nations that have created modern *Kultur* would be represented and protected from decline.[89]

Taken together, the speeches and publications of the Aktionskomité saw the novel permutation of interconnected liberal nationalist and liberal imperialist themes. In the first instance, the colonial crisis was presented as a test of Germany's will as a belated and divided nation and colonizer, the success of which hinged on a broad "national" union of pro-colonial parties and interests (liberals and conservatives) against the Reich's colonial detractors. This was itself the core idea of Bülow's political campaign and freely adopted by the liberal and conservative parties, nationalist and imperialist associations, and various interest groups during the election. Indeed, some of the most potent

---

[85] Kolonialpolitisches Aktionskomité, ed., *Kolonialpolitischer Führer* (Berlin: Wedekind, 1907), 3–12.
[86] Ibid., 16–19, 23–24.   [87] Ibid., 25–26.   [88] Ibid., 32–34, 42–43.   [89] Ibid., 31.

imagery of Protestant liberal nationalism, drawing on the notion of *Reichsfeinde* forged during the *Kulturkampf* and years of socialist proscription were shamelessly exploited. The Catholic Center and the SPD were caricatured as sacrificing Germany's national prestige on the altar of humanitarian scruple, budgetary rules, and parliamentary principle, preventing it from properly shouldering its colonial burdens and fulfilling its imperial destiny. Great "national" colonial tasks, it was claimed, were only achievable by broadening the horizon beyond narrow partisan politics. Regrettable though they were, massacres of *Naturvölker* such as the Nama accompanied nearly every great colonial project. They were the price of spreading civilization.

There was likewise much trafficking in a vague but potent term that had entered public consciousness in the 1870s and had since assumed the status of a national trope: reform. Re-christened *Kolonialreform* and loaded with much of the content and expectations of German social reform, it offered "scientific" and technological solutions to the special challenges of the colonies deploying Germany's self image as the most scientifically and technologically advanced European country. It was not surprising that a technology with particularly potent associations with German national unity and progress was employed to make that point: railways. Since Friedrich List, railways had been celebrated as a German unifier, the network that created a national division of labor, facilitated rapid industrialization, and enabled political unification. Similarly, massive hopes were invested in the developmental and civilizing force of expanded African railways. Lastly and more broadly, Germany's imperial mission was conceived as resisting the encroachments of the homogenizing great world empires and preserving the integrity and cultural peculiarity of smaller states and peoples by confederation, an imperialist theme already well developed and disseminated by naval propaganda and very familiar to German readers.

This complex of themes formed a powerful liberal imperialist ideology that was self-consciously modern and could resonate widely. There is no question it helped sway the elections to support Bülow and forge a bloc of liberal and conservative parties. Indeed, the elections of 1907 had the highest voter turnout of any Reichstag election up to that point (84.7 percent) and marked a significant electoral setback for the SPD, the party's support declining nearly by half from 20.4 percent in 1903 to 10.8 percent of the vote in 1907, its first loss of voters since 1887.[90] Significantly, this also represented erosion of support for the SPD in some of the most "red" electoral strongholds of the

---

[90] Nipperdey, *Deutsche Geschichte 1866–1918*, vol. 2, 504–5. In greater depth Jürgen Schmädeke, *Wählerbewegung im Wilhelminischen Deutschland*, vol. 1 (Berlin: Akademie Verlag, 1995), 76–81, 103–26. Jonathan Sperber, *The Kaiser's Voters: Electors and Elections in Imperial Germany* (Cambridge: Cambridge University Press, 1997), 240–54. On the impact of the election on the SPD and the rise of Revisionism, see Carl E. Schorske,

Reich, notably Nuremberg and Leipzig.[91] All of the bloc parties gained Reichstag deputies: while both conservative parties and the National Liberals made modest gains, the two left liberal parties did particularly well, increasing their vote from 9.1 percent in 1903 to 12.4 percent, suggesting that the campaign's themes resonated particularly well for them and boosted voter turnout. Oddly, the Center Party was not much affected by the election, despite its anti-Catholic tone, even managing to increase its vote modestly from 25.2 to 26.4 percent, though it did lose a Reichstag deputy in the second ballot in early February 1907.[92]

Schmoller was elated by these electoral results, writing Bülow that it disproved the utility of repressive measures against the Social Democrats, just as Bülow had long opposed and would hopefully push social democracy into a more moderate position. It also forced the conservatives to take a more friendly line toward the government. He hoped the bloc of conservative, National Liberal and left liberal deputies forged by the election would hold.[93] Bülow wrote back in agreement but without illusions about the difficulties that lay ahead:

> You know what store I place in your deep and prudent judgement! I can largely agree with your view of the new parliamentary situation, its difficulties and possibilities. I see an important gain of the election that it has overcome the widespread sense of hopelessness regarding social democracy and thereby against an inclination to resort to a politics of severe measures and thereby in favor of calmer methods. But we must not be under any illusions about how distant a detachment of the workers' movement from the clutches of social democracy still is. Here the nation, and especially your science, has the most difficult educational task ahead of itself.[94]

The Aktionskomité took this educational task seriously and received assistance for it from the Reich. In late in 1907 it would publish what would be its

---

*German Social Democracy, 1905–1917: The Development of the Great Schism* (Cambridge, MA and London: Harvard University Press, 1955), 59–87.

[91] Short, *Magic Lantern Empire*, 144–45. See in greater detail for Saxony, James Retallack, *Red Saxony: Election Battles and the Spectre of Democracy in Germany, 1860–1918* (Oxford: Oxford University Press, 2017), 393–434.

[92] Nipperdey, *Deutsche Geschichte 1866–1918*, vol. 2, 505, 507. See also in greater detail Schmädeke, *Wählerbewegung*, vol. 1, 192–211, 279–95; Sperber, *The Kaiser's Voters*, 249–52. On the left liberals, Peter Theiner, *Sozialer Liberalismus und deutsche Weltpolitik: Friedrich Naumann im Wilhelminischen Deutschland* (Baden-Baden: Nomos Verlagsgesellschaft, 1983), 169–94.

[93] Gustav Schmoller to Bernhard von Bülow, Feb. 10, 1907, in Bülow, *Denkwürdigkeiten*, vol. 2, 286–87.

[94] GStA PK, VI. HA Nl. Schmoller, Nr. 199a, fol. 70, Bernhard von Bülow to Gustav Schmoller, Feb. 12, 1907.

last publication. This was a shortened and updated version of an extensive official memorandum of 1907 compiled by Gottfied Zoepfl on the railways of Africa entitled *Die Eisenbahnen Afrikas*, for which the Aktionskomité had been given special permission for publication from the Reichstag and the new Colonial Office.[95] This was a detailed survey of the railways of all of the colonial powers in Africa, broken down geographically and featuring many maps. It included a study of the development of the African railways, their construction and management, and the various forms of railway enterprise as well as their profitability, economic impact, and strategic-political significance. In addition to furthering the goals of the government to inspire changes in public sentiment on the colonies and support the government's bills to expand African railways, there are strong indications that Schmoller hoped proceeds from this publication would help finance the Aktionskomité as a permanent pro-colonial body.[96]

A circular announcing *Die Eisenbahnen Afrikas* was sent out to chambers of commerce, large banks and export firms, universities, technological institutes, statistical bureaus, provincial school boards, seminars, associations of the academically trained, and primary school teachers.[97] Schmoller himself believed that this publication had a relevance well beyond railway policy as a valuable contribution to the knowledge of the geography and countries of Africa.[98] Bülow agreed but was also quick to acknowledge its immediate utility to sustaining legislative support for colonial railway bills pending in the Reichstag:

> The contents and kind of portrayal seem to me well suited to serve the goal of spreading and deepening the colonial idea. This generally accessible publication based on official materials showing the urgent necessity of a planned-out colonial railway construction effort will be welcomed with satisfaction by every friend of colonial matters, especially at the current time as important railway questions are being considered.[99]

---

[95] Kolonialpolitisches Aktionskomité, ed., *Die Eisenbahnen Afrikas: Grundlagen und Gesichtspunkte für eine koloniale Eisenbahnpolitik in Afrika: Nach der gleichnamigen amtlichen Denkschrift* (Berlin: Wilhelm Süsserott, 1907); Arthur von Posadowsky-Wehner, ed., *Die Eisenbahnen Afrikas: Grundlagen und Gesichtspunkte für eine koloniale Eisenbahnpolitik in Afrika* (Berlin: Carl Heymanns Verlag, 1907). On Zoepfl's work compiling the memorandum, van Laak, *Imperiale Infrastruktur*, 137–38.

[96] GStA PK, VI. HA Nl. Schmoller, Nr. 13 II, fol. 168, Anlage A. Kolonialpolitisches Aktionskomitee, Jan. 28, 1908.

[97] GStA PK, VI. HA Nl. Schmoller, Nr. 13 II, fol. 163, Struve to Schmoller with enclosures Anlage A (Fol. 168) and B (fols. 164–67), Jan. 30, 1908.

[98] GStA PK, VI. HA Nl. Schmoller, Nr. 13 II, fol. 168, Anlage A. Kolonialpolitisches Aktionskomitee, Jan. 28, 1908.

[99] GStA PK, VI. HA Nl. Schmoller, Nr. 13 II, fol. 181, Bernhard von Bülow to Gustav Schmoller, Dec. 24, 1907.

The wider influence of publications like the *Kolonialpolitischer Führer* and *Die Eisenbahnen Afrikas* was due to their ambiguous status as both election literature with a political tendency and simultaneously as the pronouncements of respected scholars and thus as authoritative material relevant beyond politics. It is known that pro-colonial propaganda literature like this was actively deployed as instructional material in many German *Volksschulen* (primary schools) and *Gymnasien* at the time. These had since 1900 become an arena of intense activity for the German Colonial Society's effort to spread the colonial message among the German youth.[100] An enhanced pro-colonial school curriculum had also been a major topic of discussion at the German Colonial Congress of 1902 and the subject of one of its first resolutions.[101] Similarly, university lecturing in colonial subjects had increased appreciably throughout the states of the Reich, and the examination regimen for future school teachers had been enhanced to test knowledge of Germany's world trade and its colonies.[102]

The generous dissemination of the Aktionskomité's literature through the receptive conduit of school and university instruction was a very effective way of conveying a coherent and compelling liberal imperialist ideology to Germany's youth. This fused economic imperialism with settler colonialism, emphasized the civilizing and unifying role of modern technology, was now global in scope and increasingly racialized in violent colonial encounters in Africa, yet one that also remained anchored in familiar liberal nationalist imagery and ambitions.[103] One irony here was that as the possibilities for an active *Weltpolitik* were narrowing due to Germany's diplomatic and strategic isolation after 1907, a German imperial mindscape was growing, highlighting the incongruity between German aspirations and foreign policy reality. As will be discussed in later chapters, inflated imperial expectations and disappointments would become a potent ingredient in German politics up through the First World War and beyond.[104]

---

[100] Kenneth Holston, "'A Measure of the Nation': Politics, Colonial Enthusiasm and Education in Germany, 1896-1933" (PhD diss., University of Pennsylvania, 1996), 43-138; Jeff Bowersox, *Raising Germans in the Age of Empire: Youth and Colonial Culture, 1871-1914* (Oxford: Oxford University Press, 2013), 54-80.

[101] Deutscher Kolonialkongress, *Verhandlungen 1902*, 828.

[102] Holston, "A Measure of the Nation," 57-58, 86-90.

[103] Short, *Magic Lantern Empire*, 147, 153-59. On the racialization of this nationalism, Sobich, *"Schwarze Bestien, rote Gefahr,"* 19-28, 272-96.

[104] See here Gründer, *Geschichte der deutschen Kolonien*, 213-31; Willeke Sandler, *Empire in the Heimat: Colonialism and Public Culture in the Third Reich* (New York: Oxford University Press, 2018); and Wolfe Schmokel, *Dream of Empire: German Colonialism, 1919-1945* (New Haven: Yale University Press, 1980).

## The Baghdad Railway and the Young Turks – Karl Helfferich in Constantinople

Crisis engulfed not only the German naval project and the colonies but also the Baghdad Railway. As discussed previously, by 1905 it had become the object of intense diplomacy between the great powers as a result of its geostrategic significance and its immense costs, which made international cooperation in its financing unavoidable. The plan to extend the railway from Baghdad to Basra to take advantage of pilgrims on Haj to Mecca and thereby make the railway more profitable embroiled the project in political difficulties with the British, whose sphere of interest included southwestern Mesopotamia and Kuwait.[105] Quite beyond that, the British press and parliament became extraordinarily – indeed irrationally – hostile to the railway when word got out in the spring of 1903 of an agreement on funding construction hammered out between Deutsche Bank and British financiers and sanctioned by the Balfour government, which in fact had made many concessions to the British and would have resulted in joint control over it. The resulting anti-German sentiment secretly whipped up in the press by Chamberlain and his allies in the Co-Efficient Club in the aftermath of the Second Venezuela Crisis was such that Balfour was forced to back Britain out of the deal in April 1903.[106]

The railway's chairman, Arthur von Gwinner, had by 1905 nonetheless managed to successfully internationalize the project's financing without the British, which included the Banque Impérial Ottomane, in which French interests predominated and which the French government had tried – albeit unsuccessfully – to get to withdraw from the project on account of Deutsche Bank retaining a 50 percent controlling stake in the railway. Nevertheless, an agreement was hammered out in 1905 between the two banks to give each other a 25 percent share of any business they secured within the Ottoman Empire, smoothing the way to continued cooperation on the project.[107] By October 1904 a 200 kilometer section of the railway from Konya to Bulgurlu at the base of the Taurus Mountains was completed, but the difficult and extraordinarily costly business of crossing the 3,000 meter high mountains lay ahead and led to a long delay in construction.[108] This diversion of the railway southwest via Konya was due to Russian objections to the railway running on a pre-existing line along the Black Sea between Constantinople and Ankara.[109]

---

[105] Schöllgen, *Imperialismus und Gleichgewicht*, 152–63; Gall, et al., *The Deutsche Bank*, 74.
[106] Geppert, *Pressekriege*, 190–99; Rose, *Zwischen Empire und Kontinent*, 307–8; Schöllgen, *Imperialismus und Gleichgewicht*, 163–76.
[107] Gall, et al., *The Deutsche Bank*, 73–74.
[108] Pohl, *Von Stambuhl bis Bagdad*, 72–75; Barth, *Die deutsche Hochfinanz*, 222–23.
[109] Sean McMeekin, *The Russian Origins of the First World War* (Cambridge, MA and London: Harvard University Press, 2011), 15.

When Helfferich left the Colonial Section to join the Deutsche Bank in late 1905 and in that capacity to then serve as Second Director of the Anatolian Railway in early 1906, this understandably attracted much international attention, with newspapers interpreting it as a sign of greater German political interest in the Baghdad Railway given Helfferich's official connections.[110] That was not far off the mark. Gwinner offered the post to Helfferich on account of both his diplomatic and financial skills, as both the politics and financing of the project were as yet far from settled. In the end Bülow himself persuaded Helfferich to accept the offer rather than take a position offered him in the Reichsbank Direktorium at about the same time.[111] Ironically, it seems that Helfferich had decided to shift his career track out of government because of his disillusionment with politics as a result of the attacks he had been subjected to during the colonial crisis.[112] Some evidence suggests that Bülow, too, had been affected by the rancorous politics over the colonies and sought to shift German overseas initiatives to the Ottoman Empire, which was much less vulnerable than Germany's overseas protectorates and likely to pay political and economic dividends sooner.[113] Given the difficulty of extracting funds for African colonial railway projects from the Reichstag, state subsidized financing of the railway by the Reich, much less direct investment, was out of the question.[114] And anyway, such state-led investment went against the very grain of Bülow's *Weltpolitik*, which was premised instead on large-scale private investments in German spheres of interest to support German industry. As the North Cameroon Railway had shown, Helfferich had demonstrated some skill brokering just such private sector investments that could serve the public interest and thus Bülow's *Weltpolitik*. At the same time, Helfferich's connections to the Foreign Office would come in handy as international diplomacy was necessary not only to untangle the knotty geopolitics of the Baghdad Railway but also to assure its continued financing.

Since the completion of the Konya-Bulgurlu section of the railway in 1904, little progress had been made in securing the financing to continue building the railway. The British prevented directing Ottoman revenue streams from increased customs duties toward the railway, prioritizing instead use of existing Ottoman revenues for debt servicing and administrative reforms in Macedonia.[115] They also sought to internationalize the project to water down German influence by drawing in both France and Russia.[116] For his part,

---

[110] Williamson, *Karl Helfferich*, 78–79. On his appointment and tensions with Marschall von Bieberstein in Constantinople, see Barth, *Die deutsche Hochfinanz*, 231–32.
[111] Williamson, *Karl Helfferich*, 79.   [112] Ibid., 73–76.   [113] Ibid., 80–81.
[114] Ibid., 82.   [115] Ibid., 83–84; Schöllgen, *Imperialismus und Gleichgewicht*, 197–205.
[116] Canis, *Der Weg in den Abgrund*, 221. On the role of the railway in Anglo-German diplomacy between 1904–1908, see esp. Schöllgen, *Imperialismus und Gleichgewicht*, 205–26.

Helfferich approached this challenge pragmatically, aware that any general understanding over the railway with the British was unlikely. Instead he worked with Gwinner and Marschall to expand the bank's economic interests in the Ottoman Empire, such as the irrigation of the Konya Plateau to increase grain and cotton cultivation, the latter – as was discussed in Chapter 7 – a topic that had long interested Helfferich and about which he had published articles while he was working in the Colonial Section. In September 1907 a concession for irrigating some 53,000 hectares in this region was secured by Deutsche Bank and the Anatolian Railway from Sultan Abdul Hamid.[117] The aim was clearly to work toward greater profitability of the railway by increasing the transport of agricultural freight along its route. Subsequently a German company was founded to manage this project, the Gesellschaft für die Bewässerung der Konia Ebene, run jointly by the construction firm Philipp Holzmann & Co. and the Anatolian Railway and headquartered in Frankfurt.[118]

Two years earlier in 1905, the German-Levantine Cotton Company had been founded. Majority owned by Deutsche Bank and the Haidar-Pasha Harbor Company, this firm began purchasing and growing Turkish cotton, subsequently developing model farms and an agricultural school to improve cotton cultivation, as well as a baling operation in Adana to allow cotton exports to Germany.[119] While these and other German investments were bound up with the desire to make the Baghdad Railway profitable, they were driven also by one of the central preoccupations that had long driven German colonialism and continued in the era of *Weltpolitik* to animate scholarship, not least, as was discussed previous chapters, that of von Halle and Helfferich: Germany's dependence on American supplies of cotton. Although often overlooked, Germany's cotton industry was the largest in continental Europe and the third largest in the world by 1900. In terms of value, finished cotton goods far exceeded the coal or the iron and steel industries and were Germany's most significant export product.[120] Unmistakably the contours of an informal empire in Ottoman Anatolia and Mesopotamia were taking form.

In the meantime Gwinner and Helfferich had also successfully consolidated Turkish public debts, which freed up some revenue to offer the guarantees needed to continue construction of the Baghdad Railway.[121] From 1906 on HAPAG began regular service to the Persian Gulf and became more directly

---

[117] Barth, *Die deutsche Hochfinanz*, 234.
[118] Manfred Pohl, *Philipp Holzmann: Geschichte eines Bauunternehmens 1849–1999* (Munich: C. H. Beck, 1999), 109–10. See also BArch K, N 1123 Nl. Helfferich, Bd. 14, Otto Riese, Philipp Holzmann & Co. to Karl Helfferich, Anatolischen Eisenbahn Constantinople, Frankfurt, 15 Juni 1911; BArch K, N 1123 Nl. Helfferich, Bd. 14, Gesellschaft für die Bewässerung der Konia-Ebene to Karl Helfferich, Anatolische Eisenbahn Constantinople, Frankfurt, June 19, 1911.
[119] Pohl, *Von Stambul nach Bagdad*, 111.   [120] Beckert, *Empire of Cotton*, 355.
[121] Helfferich, *Der Weltkrieg*, vol. 1, 132–33; Pohl, *Von Stambul nach Bagdad*, 75–76.

involved in supplying the construction materials of the Baghdad Railway.[122] Not surprisingly, in these very years the British became deeply concerned about the prospect of the Germans ultimately avoiding the British-controlled Suez Canal and developing the shortest route between the North Sea and the Persian Gulf via the Baghdad Railway, which would enhance Germany's competitive position for steamer routes and trade with India and East Asia.[123] Moreover, the Baghdad Railway opened the prospect of closer German economic ties to Persia, which were much welcomed in Teheran at the time, where fears for Persia's independence were being stoked by both Russian ambitions in northern Persia and British troop landings in the Gulf as the country was wracked by revolutionary protests in late 1905–early 1906. In late 1905 the Persian government even proposed that the Germans build a railway between Teheran and Chanikin in western Persia that would be linked to the Baghdad railroad.[124]

Both the British and Russians viewed such proposals with alarm, which worked to bring them together in the 1907 Anglo-Russian Convention, the centerpiece of which was demarcating their respective exclusive spheres of influence in Persia that consciously excluded Germany. Wisely, Bülow opted to defuse the situation in 1907 by focusing for the time being on extending the railway only to Baghdad or Basra.[125] As an informal part of the Anglo-Russian agreement, Foreign Secretary Edward Grey had also promised his Russian counterpart Alexander Izvolsky (1856–1919) British support in opening up the Turkish Straits to Russian warships in the near future, a much-coveted and longstanding Russian aim, one that would offer the Tsarist regime a welcome boost in legitimacy after the debacles of the Russo-Japanese War and Revolution in 1905. Indeed, to the Russians the agreement on Persia was linked directly to the Straits question.[126] While it is most doubtful that the British Foreign Office had any intention of following through on that promise, it did serve to further redirect Russian interest toward the Straits and Balkans in a

---

[122] Ulrich Trumpener, "Germany and the End of the Ottoman Empire," in *The Great Powers and the End of the Ottoman Empire*, ed. Marian Kent, 2nd ed. (London: Frank Cass, 1986), 106–35, here 113.

[123] Eichholtz, *Die Bagdadbahn*, 43.

[124] Schöllgen, *Imperialismus und Gleichgewicht*, 226–27; Canis, *Der Weg in den Abgrund*, 222–24. On German involvement in Persia before 1914, see Jennifer Jenkins, "Experts, Migrants Refugees: Making the German Colony in Iran, 1900–1934," in *German Colonialism in a Global Age*, ed. Naranch and Eley, 147–69, here 149–51.

[125] Canis, *Der Weg in den Abgrund*, 263. On the emergence of the Anglo-Russian Entente in this context, see esp. Schöllgen, *Imperialismus und Gleichgewicht*, 230–33; Charmley, *Splendid Isolation*, 339–45; Rose, *Zwischen Empire und Kontinent*, 429–48 . See also Mommsen, *Bürgerstolz und Weltmachtstreben*, 359; Zara S. Steiner, *Britain and the Origins of the First World War* (New York: St. Martin's Press, 1977), 60.

[126] Charmley, *Splendid Isolation*, 344; Clark, *The Sleepwalkers*, 158; Lieven, *The End of Tsarist Russia*, 194–95, 200, 202.

way that was bound to be dangerous and destabilizing for the Ottoman Empire, Austria-Hungary, and Germany in the longer run. This highlights once again the destabilizing role that British imperial diplomacy played in Europe before 1914.

The biggest problem Helfferich and Gwinner faced in these years was of course the chicken and egg problem of the very expensive construction the railway faced crossing the Taurus and Amanus Mountains to Upper Mesopotamia. The basic problem was the fact that the negotiated railway convention of 1903 only allowed Turkish payment of the critically important operating guarantees once 40 kilometer stretches of railway were actually in operation. Spurred on by Russian provocations in the Balkans during the Sandshak railway crisis in February 1908, the sultan decided in the spring of 1908 that the Baghdad Railway was a strategic priority to counter Russian initiatives and made Ottoman revenues available to extend the railway 340 kilometers past Aleppo to Tel-el-Helif (near Mardin) in Upper Mesopotamia, only some 200 kilometers from Mosul.[127] This gave Helfferich and his co-director, the Swiss-French Edouard Huguenin (1856–1926), an opportunity to devise a plan to resolve the funding conundrum posed by crossing the mountains. Helfferich – supported by future Foreign Secretary Alfred von Kiderlen-Waechter (1852–1912), who was representing Marschall in Constantinople at the time – showed a remarkable degree of independence in taking the lead in negotiating the concession in May 1908 to cross the Taurus and Amanus in what would ultimately be an 840 km extension of the railway from Bulgurlu without any British financial participation. Indeed, he did this against Gwinner's express wishes, who was still holding out for British cooperation.[128]

Helfferich and Huguenin persuaded the sultan to treat the entire 840 km extension as one unit for the purpose of financing, allowing the flotation of a new series of bonds (Series II) to begin construction anywhere along that stretch, which would allow the completion of less expensive stretches on the eastern side of the Taurus to activate the all-important operating guarantees that would generate a surplus of conceded revenue from Series II to finance the expensive construction over the mountains. As an additional surety in securing a later series of bonds (Series III), Helfferich and Huguenin also negotiated claims on revenues from a tax on sheep from the *vilayets* of Konya, Adana, and Aleppo.[129] The project foresaw the connection of the railway to the spur line Mersina-Adana (which had recently been acquired by a German investment group) to the Gulf of Alexandrette, and a connection to Aleppo and thus to the Syrian railway network. In return, the Baghdad Railway committed itself

---

[127] Barth, *Die deutsche Hochfinanz*, 237–38.    [128] Ibid., 238.
[129] Williamson, *Karl Helfferich*, 85–87.

to three advances to the Turkish government of 650,000 Ottoman lira each in 1908.[130] On June 2, 1908, the convention formalizing these arrangements was signed. The Baghdad Railway could proceed. It was a badly-needed boost for Bülow's *Weltpolitik* and a personal triumph for Helfferich, who returned to Berlin in July 1908 to become deputy director of Deutsche Bank's home office.[131]

No sooner had this solution been found than anti-Hamid mutinies began in the Ottoman military followed by demonstrations against the sultan in Constantinople in late June 1908 demanding a restoration of the constitution and elections to parliament. Much was now at stake. The Germans had been strong backers of Hamid, who was a friend of the Kaiser, and they had deep ties to the Ottoman military dating back to the 1880s and now had large-scale commercial interests in Turkey.[132] Britain had, by contrast, long sought to discredit Hamid and to detach Mecca from Ottoman rule in order to rally under the Union Jack the British Empire's 100 million Muslims.[133] By the time of the Young Turk uprising, the Anglo-Russian Convention was already nearly a year old, and both powers were increasingly united in their hostility to the Baghdad Railway project. Nevertheless, the British were as caught by surprise by the events unfolding in the summer of 1908 as the Germans and missed opportunities to take advantage of the circumstances to enhance their position with the new regime in Constantinople.[134] On July 23, 1908, Hamid capitulated. The next day he restored the constitution of 1876 and called for elections to parliament, which reopened in December 1908.

As these events were unfolding, an international oil fever was gripping Mesopotamia. In late May 1908 the British adventurer and oil pioneer William Knox D'Arcy (1849–1917), who had gained possession of a gigantic, nearly 500,000 square mile oil concession in Persia in 1901, struck oil in his drilling operations in Abadan, Persia, just 50 miles southeast of Basra.[135] Unfortunately for the Germans, the Deutsche Bank and the Anatolian Railway had effectively lost their 1904 oil pre-concession in Mesopotamia in 1907 due to delays in completing the geological surveys and attempts to extend the pre-concession from 40 to 60 years, and it was very unlikely under the changed political circumstances that the Young Turks would entertain any renegotiation and renewal of that concession.[136] To add to these complications, later in 1908 the Balkans and Turkish Straits became the flashpoint for an international crisis.

---

[130] Pohl, *Von Stambul bis Bagdad*, 77; Helfferich, *Der Weltkrieg*, vol. 1, 133.
[131] Helfferich, *Der Weltkrieg*, vol. 1, 133; Williamson, *Karl Helfferich*, 87.
[132] Schöllgen, *Imperialismus und Gleichgewicht*, 239–45.
[133] McMeekin, *The Berlin Baghdad Express*, 62–66.   [134] Ibid., 68–69, 77.
[135] Eichholtz, *Die Bagdadbahn*, 26, 35–36.   [136] Ibid., 32; Dokument 6, 83.

Taking advantage of the Young Turk Revolution and following a secret agreement with the Russians initiated by Alexander Izvolsky, Austria precipitously annexed Bosnia and Herzegovina in October 1908, a territory it had legally occupied since 1878 following the Berlin Congress of 1878 but whose seizure under those circumstances was unwise, provocative, and done without informing the Wilhelmstrasse. When Britain refused opening the Straits to Russian warships as Grey had promised in 1907 (as was expected by Izvolsky as part of the deal with Austria) and as Russian Slavophile public opinion turned hostile to the Austrian annexation, Izvolsky backtracked, engineering a crisis that brought Russia and Austria-Hungary to the brink of a war.[137] The Bosnian annexation was denounced sharply by Kaiser Wilhelm as an "irresponsible prank" that ultimately created myriad problems for the Germans in the Balkans and Turkey.[138] As the crisis deepened, it threatened to draw in Germany, France, and even Britain, which under Foreign Secretary Grey und Undersecretary Harding had swung to a strongly pro-Russian (and pro-Serbian) position in the Balkans. This was calculated to preserve the Anglo-Russian Convention – after violating the Madrid Convention over Morocco with France in 1904–5, Whitehall suddenly became committed to upholding the 1878 Berlin Treaty over Bosnia.[139]

The Young Turks who had led the rebellion against the sultan tended to be pro-French and pro-British on account of their liberal politics shaped by years of exile in Paris and London, and due to Hamid's strong ties to Germany, they were initially very hostile to the Germans. To add to the difficulties, a general strike by Turkish railway employees began in early September 1908, putting pressure on both the Anatolian and Baghdad Railways, and the Banque Impérial Ottomane began loosening its ties to the Deutsche Bank in reaction to the changed political situation.[140] In October the Young Turk government took great offense at Austria's annexation of Bosnia-Herzegovina and blamed Germany as Austria's ally – as Helfferich recalled, the Austrian annexation turned the German ambassador to the Porte, Marschall von Bieberstein, from the most to the least influential diplomat in Constantinople practically overnight.[141] Indeed, the Young Turks were so incensed that they considered repudiating the June 1908 convention that had allowed construction of the Baghdad Railway to proceed.[142] From just about every angle, then, in late 1908 the fate of the Baghdad Railway looked as uncertain as ever.

---

[137] Clark, *The Sleepwalkers*, 83–87; Lieven, *The End of Tsarist Russia*, 210–24.
[138] Clark, *Kaiser Wilhelm II*, 187–88.
[139] See Charmley, *Splendid Isolation*, 351–60; Rose, *Zwischen Empire und Kontinent*, 514–57.
[140] Barth, *Die deutsche Hochfinanz*, 241.   [141] Helfferich, *Der Weltkrieg*, vol. 1, 66–68.
[142] McMeekin, *The Berlin Baghdad Express*, 70.

## The Kaiser's Professor – Hermann Schumacher in New York

As crisis was enveloping the German colonial project, alternative arenas of *Weltpolitik* were being explored. One of them was professorial exchanges with the United States. In early February 1906 the president of Columbia University in New York, Nicholas Murray Butler (1862–1947), sent Hermann Schumacher an official letter announcing that he had just been unanimously selected by Columbia's Board of Trustees to serve as the first "Kaiser Wilhelm Professor" in the Faculty of Political Science at Columbia University starting that autumn.[143] Schumacher was astonished by this invitation out of the blue, as he had known nothing at all about this new arrangement. Shortly thereafter he was called to the Prussian Ministry of Culture in Berlin and urged to accept this honor, as the Kaiser had arranged this exchange of professors with Butler and it was hoped this would serve to build intellectual bridges and thus improve relations between Germany and the United States. Diplomacy and trade alone were not up to that task. There was simply no way he could decline such an invitation, he was told.[144]

The original impulses for this exchange had been given as early as 1902 by the Harvard Germanist Kuno Franke (1855–1830) and the German ambassadors to the United States von Holleben and his successor Speck von Sternburg. It had also been endorsed by the International Congress of Arts and Sciences initiated by the German Harvard psychologist Hugo Münsterberg and held in conjunction with the St. Louis World's Exposition in 1904, which a German delegation of forty attended, including Adolf von Harnack (1851–1930, the later founder of the Kaiser-Wilhelm-Gesellschaft), Max Weber, Ferdinand Tönnies (1855–1936), and Ernst Troeltsch (1865–1923).[145] Nicholas Butler – who had studied in Berlin in the mid-1880s – had served on the administrative board of the Congress and had secured the financial means for a US-German professorial exchange with Columbia from the New York-based German American Jewish banker and philanthropist James Speyer (1861–1941). Meanwhile, Friedrich Althoff had brought talks with Harvard's president to successful conclusion in 1904 and secured funding for the German side of the exchange from other German American Jewish and German Jewish philanthropists. Beside Speyer, Jacob Schiff in New York and the Berlin railway industrialist and financier Arthur Koppel (1851–1908) funded the foundation

---

[143] GNN HA, Nl. Schumacher, I, B-15, Nicholas Murray Butler to Hermann Schumacher, New York, Feb. 6, 1906.

[144] GNN HA, Nl. Schumacher, I, B-60, fols. 422–23; Schumacher-Vereinigung, ed., *Hermann Schumacher*, 15–39.

[145] Pommerin, *Der Kaiser und Amerika*, 275–82; Fiebig-von Hase, "Die politische Funktionalisierung der Kultur," 49–50, 54; Karl Heinz Füssl, *Deutsch-amerikanischer Kulturaustausch im 20. Jahrhundert: Bildung – Wissenschaft – Politik* (Frankfurt and New York: Campus Verlag, 2004), 52.

to pay for the exchanges.[146] In August 1905 Butler and the founder and dean of Columbia's Department of Political Science, the German-trained John Burgess, traveled to Germany for an audience with Kaiser Wilhelm to formally inaugurate the exchange with Columbia. The agreement that was signed allowed for professors from universities other than Columbia and Berlin to participate in that exchange.[147]

Foreign policy considerations figured centrally in these exchanges. Trade frictions and naval and colonial competition as well as the Second Venezuela and Tangier Crises and the ongoing refusal of Germany to formally accept the Monroe Doctrine had damaged US-German relations to such an extent that the entry of the United States on the side of Britain against Germany in a future conflict was no longer inconceivable.[148] The professorial exchanges were thus pushed forward by Kaiser Wilhelm as a way to prevent a possible Anglo-American entente, which would have been the death knell of German *Weltpolitik*.[149] Germany's prestige in the arts and sciences, while ebbing in the United States on account of the rapid development of American universities, was still widely acknowledged, and it was hoped the exchanges would reinvigorate Germany's standing in a way that could be leveraged for improved US-German relations and positive international cultural propaganda for Germany.[150] The professor exchanges were thus very much intended as *Weltpolitik* by scholarship.[151]

Gustav Schmoller was involved in these exchange plans from the beginning and had already been approached by Althoff in 1902 to make the case for a professorial exchange with Harvard with his colleagues in Berlin, where the exchange plans faced stiff initial opposition from the faculty.[152] The exchange was ultimately pushed through by Althoff in 1904 on account of its importance to the Kaiser, Chancellor Bülow, and the Foreign Office, underscoring the primarily political motivation and objectives of these exchanges.[153] By early 1905 Schmoller and Farnam were corresponding about suitable American

---

[146] Fiebig-von Hase, "Die politische Funktionalisierung der Kultur," 50, 53, 53n30; Füssl, *Deutsch-amerikanischer Kulturaustausch*, 53.
[147] Fiebig-von Hase, "Die politische Funktionalisierung der Kultur," 51; Füssl, *Deutsch-amerikanischer Kulturaustausch*, 54.
[148] Pommerin, *Der Kaiser und Amerika*, 84; and in greater detail, Mehnert, *"Gelbe Gefahr,"* 119–25.
[149] Fiebig-von Hase, "Die politische Funktionalisierung der Kultur," 45, 57–63.
[150] Ibid., 48–49. See also vom Bruch, *Weltpolitik als Kulturmission*, 31–33; Nagler, "From Culture to *Kultur*," 150. In greater detail, see vom Brocke, "Der deutsch-amerikanische Professorenaustausch," 128–82.
[151] See Bülow, *Deutsche Politik*, 48–49.
[152] Fiebig-von Hase, "Die politische Funktionalisierung der Kultur," 50n18, 51–52.
[153] Ibid., 52–53.

candidates for the exchanges and forwarding their names to Althoff.[154] The Harvard theologian Francis G. Peabody (1847–1936) and the Leipzig chemist Wilhelm Ostwald (1853–1932) were the first professors exchanged between Berlin and Harvard in 1905–6, while John Burgess and Hermann Schumacher were the first professors selected for the exchange with Columbia beginning in 1906–7.[155]

Schumacher ultimately accepted the offer and was eager to observe this country, which since his last visit in 1893 had undergone such tremendous change, epitomized as Schumacher noted, by the imposition of McKinley's protective tariffs in 1890, the founding of the gigantic US Steel Corporation, and the end of the country's "splendid isolation" by its defeat of Spain and seizure of much of its colonial empire.[156] Indeed, his year-long stay in the United States would open Schumacher's eyes as never before to the significance of the United States as a major industrial power, now with an overseas empire, with both coasts soon to be connected by the Panama Canal, and with a new Pacific orientation directed toward Asia facilitated by its presence in Hawaii, Samoa, and the Philippines. He had left an American republic in 1893. He was returning to an empire.

Schumacher took the steamer *Barbarossa* in late August arriving in New York in mid-September 1906. From the start of his stay it was clear that he was very much an honored guest professor, received very warmly by professors John Bates Clark, E. R. A. Seligman, Franklin Henry Giddings (1855–1931), and Munroe Smith (1854–1926) and then accommodated in a bright and spacious room on the seventeenth floor of the new Willard Hotel on 76th Street. Typical of the disarray in the German Foreign Office, no one had bothered to notify the German consulate in New York about the professorial exchange or Schumacher's arrival, so when Schumacher came to call in nostalgic anticipation of seeing the offices again that he remembered so well from his deceased father's time as general consul, he was bitterly disappointed – the consulate could offer no advice about Schumacher's role as an academic ambassador and in general showed a complete lack of interest. He realized then that he was more or less on his own.[157]

Since Schumacher had lived in New York City, Columbia University had blossomed from the shabby college he remembered near where they had once lived on 49th Street into a majestic university in its splendid new facilities

---

[154] GStA PK, VI. HA Nl. Schmoller, Nr. 197a, fols. 87–88, Henry Farnam to Gustav Schmoller, Jan. 5, 1905.
[155] Fiebig-von Hase, "Die politische Funktionalisierung der Kultur," 50–51. The German professors in the Columbia exchange were named "Kaiser-Wilhelm Professors" while the Americans were named "Roosevelt Professors," ibid., 55.
[156] GNN HA, Nl. Schumacher, I, B-60, fol. 424.
[157] GNN HA, Nl. Schumacher, I, B-60, fols. 425–26.

in Morningside Heights, which much impressed Schumacher and, he noted, no German university that he knew of could match. He recalled this as emblematic of the changes that had swept over the country more generally.[158] Schumacher was afforded the honor of giving the inaugural address beginning the 153rd academic year at Columbia on September 26th and started teaching a lecture course and seminar.[159] He was later very impressed with the graduate students in his seminar, which included among others John Maurice Clark (1884–1963) and Richard E. Chaddock (1879–1940) who were later to become influential economists and statisticians,[160] and thought them more mature than their German counterparts. Even the funding and management of the university through an endowment and board of trustees he saw in positive light, as to his mind it brought the university and scholarship into closer connection with the business world than was the case in Germany.[161] Schumacher was also able to rekindle friendships from Schmoller's economics seminar at the University of Berlin, notably to the Wellesley College economist and pacifist Emily Greene Balch, who had impressed him some fifteen years earlier with her keen intelligence. She was then in the midst of writing an important book on Slavic immigration to the United States and would later win the Nobel Peace Prize for her work on behalf of the League of Nations and many other international causes.[162] In general, Schumacher was most impressed by the "great role" that educated women played in American society.[163] Clearly, the Americans were gaining on Germany in higher education. One metric that served to highlight this was the downward trend in American enrollments in German universities between 1880 and 1912. While 1,088 Americans were enrolled in German universities in 1880, these numbers had been falling steadily and by 1912 would decline to 338.[164] Would Germany continue to maintain its preeminence?

Somewhat ominously for US-German relations, the great abolitionist and anti-imperialist German American statesman Carl Schurz – with whom Schumacher's family had maintained very close contact during his father's term as

---

[158] Ibid., fols. 426–27.
[159] GNN HA, NL Schumacher, I, B-15, Columbia University in the City of New York, 1906–1907, The Opening of the 153d Academic Year [brochure]. See also Edwin R.A. Seligman, "Dr. Schumacher and the Kaiser Wilhelm Lectureship," *American Monthly Review of Reviews* XXXIV, no. 5 (Nov. 11, 1906): 548–49.
[160] John M. Clark was later professor at Columbia University and pioneer of the theory of "effective competition," while Robert E. Chaddock was later a professor of statistics at Columbia University and president of the American Statistical Association in 1925.
[161] GNN HA, Nl. Schumacher, I, B-60, fols. 429–32a.
[162] Ibid., fol. 436. Here Schumacher confused Vassar with Wellesley. Emily Greene Balch, *Our Slavic Fellow-Citizens* (New York: Charities Publication Committee, 1910).
[163] GNN HA, Nl. Schumacher, I, B-60, fol. 438.
[164] Nagler, "From Culture to *Kultur*," 143.

general consul in New York – had died in May 1906. Schumacher had been told before embarking on his journey in August that he would likely be asked to speak at a memorial service later that year.[165] This was held in Carnegie Hall on November 21, 1906, and among the speakers beside Hermann Schumacher were former US president Grover Cleveland, the president of Harvard University Charles William Eliot (1834–1926), and president of the Tuskegee Institute Booker T. Washington (1856–1914).[166] While paying tribute to Schurz's German idealism in his speech at the memorial, Schumacher concluded with a plea to better understanding between Germans and Americans in an age rife with the ruthless pursuit of economic and imperial interests:

> For in the midst of the increasing conflicts of economic interests, solutions in harmony with the general welfare can be found and enforced, not by routine politicians, but only by philosophical and wholly sincere men wo are convinced that ultimately great ideas and not petty personal interests must govern the destinies of nations. And that is true of the political conflicts, not only within a nation, but also between nations.[167]

There can be no doubt that he had his American audience foremost in mind with that admonition. There was no small irony in Schumacher – a prominent figure defining German *Weltpolitik* in Asia and enthusiastic propagandist for German naval expansion – addressing an American audience in that manner mourning one of the most outspoken members of the American Anti-Imperialist League and implacable opponent of Theodore Roosevelt and the Spanish-American War.[168]

Over the time he spent in the United States in 1906–7 Schumacher was struck repeatedly by the changes that had been ushered in by the Spanish-American War. While he did not say so at the memorial service, Schumacher observed that Carl Schurz had warned of the dangers of overseas imperialism in the Senate during the January 1899 hearing over the ratification of the Paris Treaty ending the war. At the outbreak of war, the United States had declared it was fighting only to free Cuba from the yoke of Spanish rule. Demands for territorial expansion followed soon thereafter. The United States had since become a world power with a presence in the Caribbean and Philippines

---

[165] GNN HA, Nl. Schumacher, I, B-60, fol. 426.
[166] Ibid., fol. 434; *Address in Memory of Carl Schurz, Carnegie Hall, New York, November 21, 1906* (New York: Committee of the Carl Schurz Memorial, 1906).
[167] "Address of Professor Hermann Schumacher," in *Address in Memory of Carl Schurz*, 33–37, here 36–37.
[168] On Schumacher's account of the tribute to Carl Schurz, GNN HA, Nl. Schumacher, I, B-60, fols. 434–35; On Schurz and the American Anti-Imperialist League, see Kinzer, *The True Flag*, 89–104, 143–46, 153–54, 172–74; Villard, *Memoirs*, vol. 2, 374.

ruling over "foreign races" and requiring larger armed forces, a situation over which in the past Americans had pitied the Europeans.[169]

In 1905 the United States took control of the Dominican Republic's customs, and in October 1906 the US intervened in Cuban politics again by landing marines. It was also busy building the Panama Canal. US Secretary of State Elihu Root had only recently returned from his first "Panamerican journey," which included inspection of the construction work on the canal. Schumacher himself attended the annual banquet of the New York Chamber of Commerce on November 22, 1906, in the Waldorf Astoria, where Root represented President Roosevelt, who was then on his own inspection tour of the canal. It was the largest single gathering Schumacher attended while in the United States and one that left the strongest immediate impression on him.[170] Interestingly, three of the principal subjects the chamber was preoccupied with that year were trade reciprocity with Germany, the protection of private property on the open seas in wartime, and the promotion of South American trade.[171]

In November and December Schumacher gave a number of speeches and public lectures in New York to familiarize Americans with German social and economic conditions. This included talks given to the Union of German Authors in America on Germany's economic interests in East Asia, to Phi Beta Kappa alumni on "Modern Social Problems in Germany," and to the Academy of Political Science on the concentration of German banking.[172] He was also invited to a number of dinners and receptions, among them one hosted by Andrew Carnegie (1835–1919) in honor of Mark Twain (1835–1910) on December 18th, which Woodrow Wilson (1856–1924), then president of Princeton University, also attended. Schumacher's invitation was a result of Carnegie's close friendship with Schurz. Wilson's after dinner speech impressed him while Mark Twain, it turned out, was a better writer than speaker.[173] In any case, there had been some discussions previously between

---

[169] GNN HA, Nl. Schumacher, I, B-6p. fols. 458–58a.
[170] GNN HA, Nl. Schumacher, I, B-60, fols. 440, 451. See George Wilson, *Forty-Ninth Annual Report of the Corporation of the Chamber of Commerce of the State of New York for the Year 1906–07* (New York: Press of the Chamber of Commerce, 1907), 59.
[171] Wilson, *Annual Report*, xiv–xvii.
[172] GNN HA, Nl. Schumacher, I, B-60, fols. 431–32; GNN HA, Nl. Schumacher, I, B-21a, Verband deutscher Schriftsteller in Amerika, Einladung zum Vortrag Hermann Schumachers "Deutschlands wirthschaftliche Interessen in Ostasien," New York, Oct. 27, 1906; Invitation by the Phi Beta Kappa Alumni of New York to Hermann Schumacher's talk "Modern Social Problems in Germany, their Origin and Significance," Dec. 12 [1906]; Invitation of the Academy of Political Science in the City of New York to the talk by Hermann Schumacher "The Concentration in the Banking Business in Germany," Dec. 17 [1906].
[173] GNN HA, Nl. Schumacher, I, B-60, fol. 433; GNN HA, Nl. Schumacher, I, B-21a, Dinner invitation from Andrew Carnegie to Hermann Schumacher in honor of Mr. Samuel L. Clemens, n.d.

Schumacher and the editor of the monthly *The Century*, the poet and reformer Richard Watson Gilder (1844–1909) – who happened to be sitting next to Schumacher at the dinner – about establishing a US-German institute to address the widespread ignorance and misunderstanding about Germany in the United States in the hope that Carnegie would be open to funding it. Nothing came of that, which Schumacher also attributed to the lack of having any consular advice or support.[174]

## The American Empire

Between January and April 1907 Schumacher embarked on journeys to the South, Cuba, and the West. Along the way he made a stop in Washington, DC, where he had been invited to the White House for an evening reception on January 31, 1907.[175] On arriving in Washington the impressions of a provisional capital still under construction in 1893 were banished by the impressive sight of the gigantic, completed new buildings, notably the Library of Congress and Post Office buildings as well as the collection other stately structures, broad avenues, and many open squares in the city. It was, he observed, a city that "anticipated growth."[176] While in 1893 Schumacher had the impression of a stable status quo, since the war with Spain the US had been in the grips of outward expansion much like the growth of American industries had expanded them beyond their state borders into interstate commerce, all putting greater demands on, and thus spurring the growth of, the US federal government.[177] America's overseas imperial expansion, Schumacher noted, had also been accompanied by an extraordinary concentration of political power in Washington, bolstered by anti-trust policy and the conservation movement. Washington was now overshadowing the individual states as the bearer of American national identity, he observed.[178] Washington was, in short, now an imperial capital.

Before arriving in Washington for the reception, Ambassador Speck von Sternburg had written Schumacher that he wanted to introduce him to President Roosevelt.[179] Sternburg, who had known Roosevelt personally since 1889 and was affectionately known by Roosevelt as "Specky," regularly played tennis or went horseback riding with the president and was among Roosevelt's closest confidants.[180] He managed to arrange a meeting with the president the

---

[174] GNN HA, Nl. Schumacher, I, B-60, fols. 433–33a.
[175] GNN HA, Nl. Schumacher, I, B-21a, Invitation to a reception at the White House on January 31, 1907 from Mr. and Mrs. Roosevelt, n.d.
[176] GNN HA, Nl. Schumacher, I, B-6p, fol. 454.   [177] Ibid., fols. 455–56.
[178] GNN HA, Nl. Schumacher, I, B-60, fols. 441–43.
[179] GNN HA, Nl. Schumacher, I, B-6p, fol. 457.
[180] Morris, *Theodore Rex*, 178, 201, 209, 246, 393.

day before the White House reception, but it was, by Schumacher's account, an odd encounter. On meeting, Roosevelt immediately launched into telling Schumacher that he was just reading Hans Delbrück's military history of the Battle of Salamis, the decisive naval engagement between the Greeks and Persians in the narrow Straits of Artemesium between Salamis and Attica, a historical precedent then not infrequently invoked in analyzing the Battle of Tsushima that had decided the recent Russo-Japanese War.[181] Such was the enthusiasm of the president that the introduction became little more than an animated recounting of the battle by Roosevelt. When the president was finished, Sternburg rose and the "audience" was over.[182] Schumacher was unsure of what to make of that encounter, but he entertained the possibility that the president wanted to impress upon him that he was an adherent of the American naval theorist Mahan.[183] At this very time Sternburg was sending the German Foreign Office almost daily reports about the pronounced hostility toward the Japanese and Japanese immigrants of Roosevelt, his government, and the US military leadership, a prelude to an all-out Japanese war scare later that year in which fears of the Japanese navy, threats to the Philippines and Hawaii, and invasion of the US Pacific coast figured prominently.[184]

That Roosevelt's navalism paralleled and in terms of depth even exceeded Kaiser Wilhelm's was well known at the time. He was certainly also much more willing to use the navy in coercive diplomacy than his German counterpart.[185] First as assistant secretary of the US Navy and then as president, he had overseen a breathtaking modernization and expansion of the American battleship navy.[186] By Roosevelt's own reckoning, by March 1905 the US Navy had a fleet of 28 battleships and 12 armored cruisers, putting it on par with the German navy as the second largest battleship force in the world. In terms of material, this force was superior and second only to the British.[187] Indeed, exactly coinciding with Schumacher's January visit to the White House,

---

[181] GNN HA, Nl. Schumacher, I, B-6p, fol. 457; Hans Delbrück, *Geschichte der Kriegskunst im Rahmen der politischen Geschichte,* Erster Theil: Das Alterthum (Berlin: Georg Stilke, 1900), 73–79 (ch. 8).
[182] GNN HA, Nl. Schumacher, I, B-6p, fol. 457.   [183] Ibid.
[184] Mehnert, *"Gelbe Gefahr,"* 125; on the war scare of 1907–8, 87–96, 176–79; on German Foreign Office attempts to exploit US-Japanese tensions to drive a wedge between Washington and London, 125–55.
[185] See Hendrix, *Naval Diplomacy,* 4–12.
[186] See ibid., 12–24; Morris, *The Rise of Theodore Roosevelt,* 137–38, 182, 433–34, 560–61, 581, 592–616; Morris, *Theodore Rex,* 180, 186, 455–56; Dirk Bönker, "Maritime Aufrüstung zwischen Partei- und Weltpolitik: Schlachtflottenbau in Deutschland und den USA um die Jahrhundertwende," in *Zwei Wege in die Moderne,* ed. Fiebig-von Hase and Heideking, 231–59; and in greater detail Bönker, *Militarism in a Global Age.*
[187] Hendrix, *Naval Diplomacy,* 144.

Roosevelt was actively (and ultimately successfully) pushing Congress to approve funds for dreadnought-type battleships.[188] As discussed previously, in December 1902 the US Navy was readied and on the brink of war with Germany and Britain over Venezuela.[189] Following the Venezuela crisis, Roosevelt had dispatched eight US Navy vessels into the Mediterranean for a bit of gunboat diplomacy in Tangiers in May 1904. An American battleships flotilla was dispatched to the Mediterranean again in 1906 for a show of force during the Algeciras Conference. In June 1907 Roosevelt decided to send the "Great White Fleet" of sixteen battleships and various escorts to the Pacific that autumn and then circumnavigate the globe in an act of coercive diplomacy intended to uphold his version of the Monroe Doctrine and intimidate Japan into accepting the US annexation of the Philippines and Hawaii as a result of the war scare of 1907.[190] The contrast to the most provocative example of German gunboat diplomacy after Venezuela – the July 1911 landing of the obsolete German gunboat SMS *Panther* off the coast of Morocco at Agadir to show the flag after the French had dispatched troops to Fez in May in anticipation of annexing Morocco (in flagrant violation of the Franco-German Morocco Treaty of 1909) – is remarkable, especially given the disproportionate outrage and hysteria it would generate in France and Britain.[191]

Roosevelt was initially a strong supporter of the Second Hague Peace Conference of 1907, which preserved the core of the Declaration of Paris affirming neutral rights and immunities by rejecting the doctrine of continuous voyage, establishing an international prize court, excluding food meant for the civilian population as contraband, and by introducing a new "free list" of raw materials essential to national industry that could not be declared contraband in war.[192] This would later be affirmed at the December 1908–February 1909 London Naval Conference and culminated in the Declaration of London of February 26, 1909.[193] Yet as American naval power grew and Britain's strategic pivot toward the United States accelerated, there was a clear erosion of American commitment to these very principles.[194] After the failure to limit naval arms at The Hague in 1907, Roosevelt rejected any arms limitation agreements for the United States in his goal of having the second largest battleship navy in the world after Britain.[195]

---

[188] Ibid., 146–47.    [189] See esp. ibid., 40–53.
[190] Morris, *Theodore Rex*, 323–38, 484–85, 492–95, 509–11; Hendrix, *Naval Diplomacy*, xiii–xvii, 82–103, 155–76; Mehnert, *"Gelbe Gefahr,"* 174–96. On anti-Japanese populism in the US and the war scare of 1907, Mehnert, *"Gelbe Gefahr,"* 87–96, 174–79.
[191] See Canis, *Der Weg in den Abgrund*, 405–29; Clark, *The Sleepwalkers*, 204–14.
[192] See Coogan, *The End of Neutrality*, 90–103.
[193] On the Declaration of London, ibid., 104–47; Offer, *The First World War*, 276.
[194] Coogan, *The End of Neutrality*, 56–69, 102, 114–17, 121–23.
[195] Hendrix, *Naval Diplomacy*, 147.

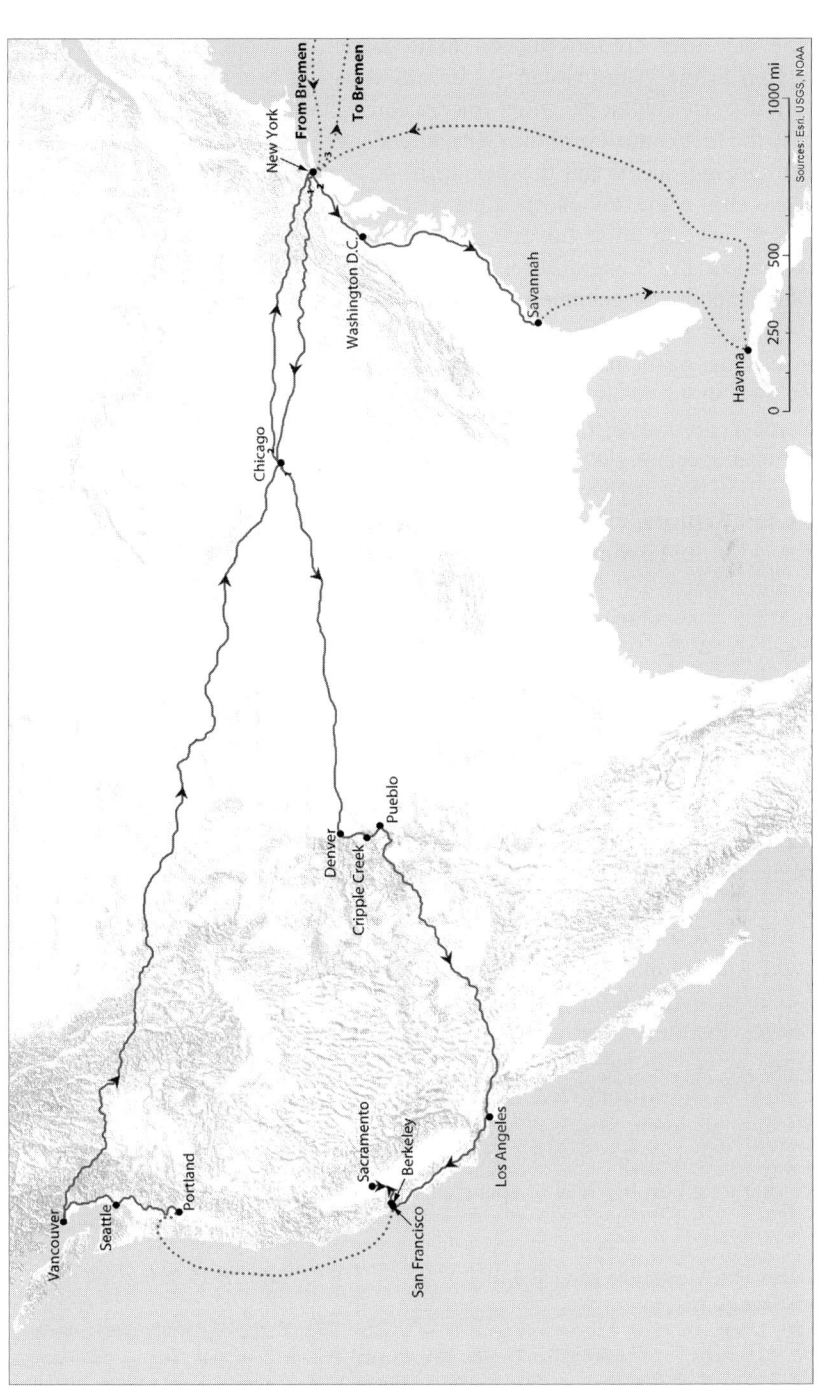

Map 8.1  Hermann Schumacher's journey through the United States and to Cuba, Jan.–April 1907.

The day after his introduction to Roosevelt, Schumacher attended the reception in the White House. As he was engaging in a lively conversation with Roosevelt's oldest daughter, Alice, a commotion erupted in the reception hall as the first councilor of the German embassy paraded across the parquet, spurs clinking, in the full dress uniform of a reserve officer of the cavalry. No one else in the hall except General Leonard Wood (1860–1927) was in uniform, making this spectacle stand out all the more embarrassingly. A woman next to Schumacher whispered to him: "that's what makes us waver in our sympathy for Germany." Schumacher noted that it reinforced his view, gained years earlier witnessing a similar such spectacle at the court of the Korean king, of the misguided German rules that obliged reserve officers to wear their uniforms at all official functions. It was downright destructive to diplomacy, projecting the wrong image of Germany.[196] Indeed, just such superficial spectacles went some way to forging a Germany of the foreign imagination that, as Helfferich later observed, provided the mass psychological basis for Germany's growing diplomatic isolation in the years before the outbreak of the First World War.[197] As mentioned in many examples in the preceding chapters, it was more often the image – not the reality – of German militarism that animated American and especially British opinion. During Germany's *Weltpolitik* images of German power were being built up abroad that were in striking contrast both to Germany's real capacities and its actual foreign policy achievements.

Soon after the reception Schumacher was on his way south to Savannah, the great cotton port, where he planned to meet a friend from Bremen with whom he intended to travel further south. The train journey was unfortunately accompanied by massive delays as the Atlantic Coast Railroad Company was then in bankruptcy proceedings and subject to frequent breakdowns. He regretted that he did not have sufficient time to stay in Georgia long enough to visit W. E. B. Du Bois at Atlanta University, with whom he had been friendly while they were both attending the University of Berlin, or to continue on to Alabama to take up Booker T. Washington's invitation to visit the Tuskegee Institute. Later an automobile accident put an end to a longer journey by car through the South, so Schumacher decided to head directly to Cuba.[198] The Atlanta race riot of the previous September, in which blacks were hunted down, attacked, and lynched indiscriminately in response to sensational newspaper reports alleging black assaults of white women, may have cast a pall on the idea of spending more time in the South.[199]

---

[196] GNN HA, Nl. Schumacher, I, B-6p, fol. 457.  [197] Helfferich, *Der Weltkrieg*, vol. 1, 37.
[198] GNN HA, Nl. Schumacher, I, B-6p, fols. 458a–460.
[199] See Lewis, *W. E. B. Du Bois: Biography of a Race*, 333–37; Lewis, *W. E. B. Du Bois; A Biography*, 224; Ann J. Lane, *The Brownsville Affair: National Crisis and Black Reaction* (Port Washington, NY: Kennikat Press, 1971); Rebecca Burns, *Rage in the*

In Havana Schumacher could still see the wreck of the *Maine* in the harbor, whose explosion had offered the pretext for launching the Spanish-American War. The streets of Havana offered a curious picture of a native population that he observed "one could imagine was easily agitated and hard to govern and the victorious North Americans in uniform and civilian dress walking about with great unselfconsciousness." Still, it did not appear that the two populations were hostile to one another. This, he was told by the German consul in Havana and an English acquaintances of his Bremen travel companion, was to the credit of the US occupation governor Charles Magoon (1861–1920).[200] Rising as a legal clerk in the War Department, Roosevelt had appointed Magoon to serve as governor of the Panama Canal Zone in 1905. He was slated to become vice-governor of the Philippines, but following the contested Cuban presidential election and revolt of 1906 and then the October 1906 landing of US Marines beginning the so-called "Second Occupation" of Cuba, he was installed as governor of Cuba instead. When Schumacher called to visit Magoon in Havana, he was expecting a mere exchange of courtesies and was surprised by what turned into a "long and content-rich conversation" with an unforgettable personality who was willing to entertain Schumacher's many questions willingly and with level-headedness. Schumacher gained the impression from these conversations that the US did not intend to annex Cuba but sought rather to establish order to allow economic activity to flourish. At the end of their conversation, Magoon invited Schumacher to a Sunday picnic on one of the largest tobacco plantations in Cuba.[201]

Schumacher attended Magoon's "Sunday picnic," which turned out to be a large social event. The younger of the Duke brothers, James "Buck" Buchanan Duke (1856–1925), was also in the immediate company of Magoon at the picnic, but Schumacher did not much care for the "ruthless contours" of this multimillionaire or his tobacco trust (American Tobacco Company, later broken up by the Supreme Court). He thought his presence in Cuba was an ill omen for the quality cigar production that Germans had established in Cuba under Spanish rule.[202] The next day, in fact, Schumacher visited the famous German-founded H. Upmann cigar factory, where he had opportunity to observe production and was later ceremonially handed a "Two Dollar Cigar," the pride of the company, and asked to enter his name into a beautiful bound volume that included only a few names of recipients prior to his, among them crowned heads. It was obvious to everyone then, Schumacher noted, that competition with the Duke trust would mean the end, as the best

---

*Gate City: The Story of the 1906 Atlanta Race Riot*, rev. ed. (Athens: University of Georgia Press, 2009).
[200] GNN HA, Nl. Schumacher, I, B-6p, fol. 461.   [201] Ibid., fol. 462.
[202] Ibid., fol. 462–63.

German tobacco plantation had already been brought into the trust, namely the plantation he had visited as a guest of Magoon the day prior![203]

Of even greater interest to Schumacher than Cuban tobacco was the sugar cane industry, which the Germans had conquered through the scientific development of sugar beets and which had turned Germany into the largest sugar producer and sugar exporter in the world. Nevertheless, at the time of Schumacher's visit great changes were underway. First, the United States had annexed the "sugar cane island" Hawaii, and then the Philippines and Puerto Rico shortly after. Now, he observed, the most promising "sugar land" Cuba was being integrated into the US economy. "Large American capital" (*amerikanisches Großkapital*) was now able to purchase raw sugar on the most favorable terms. The largest sugar consumer in the world, it seemed to Schumacher, was beginning a ruthless path toward self-sufficiency in sugar supply. Through new experimental farms, primitive exploitation was giving way to systematic capitalist organization.[204] Schumacher's visit to Cuba under US occupation reinforced fears that the Germans could well see an important export market threatened.

After his journey to Cuba Schumacher had opportunity to travel west in February and March 1907, a part of the country he had not had a chance to see when he visited last in 1893 – the farthest west he got back then was Des Moines. This journey, while it took in some of the natural wonders of the West, was motivated by an interest in the economic development of the West, and given Schumacher's intensive study of the Rhenish-Westphalian mining and steel industry from his home base of Bonn, particularly the development of those sectors. He visited Cripple Creek in Colorado, site of a notoriously violent miners' strike in 1894, but was also interested in and observed the consolidation of mining and smelting that had occurred under Meyer (1828–1905) and then Daniel Guggenheim (1856–1930), which with the Guggenheim's takeover of American Smelting and Refining, had since expanded into Mexico, Bolivia, and Chile. He visited such a smelting works near Denver and was able to speak with a German engineer employed there.[205]

Schumacher also had opportunity to visit an iron works. Previously, Schumacher had seen plenty of iron and steel works in the United States, none of which could stand a comparison with the thorough, systematic organization of their German counterparts in the Rhine-Ruhr. That all changed on visiting the Colorado Fuel and Iron Company in Pueblo, Colorado, the newest and most westerly integrated iron and steel works in the United States at the time. He was, as he recalled, "astounded" by what he saw. The works had a system of internal cost accounting that could not have been more comprehensive,

---

[203] Ibid., fols. 463–64.  [204] Ibid., fol. 464.  [205] Ibid., fols. 466–68.

which was tied up with the fact that the works drew entirely from workers recruited from both coasts comprising some 36 different nationalities, each concentrated into those parts of the works' division of labor for which they were most skilled. If such system and organization was possible in the land of "Buffalo Bill," Schumacher pondered, what might be possible in other parts of American industry?[206]

He also chanced upon an experimental agricultural station for "dry farming" developing new strains of crops from the steppes of Russia and arid regions of Africa, which was at that time working with alfalfa. He was especially impressed by the infectious enthusiasm of the young men working on this experimental farm, who were able to convey directly "the great appeal of the development of a large land" in a way that he had never encountered before. As he recalled, "It was the high point of my visit to Colorado. A conversation of just two hours had opened my eyes – I almost want to say – to a new world."[207] That, he observed, was a foretaste of California, which was next on his itinerary. The areas of irrigated agriculture Schumacher was able to take in in southern California's fertile central valley enabled by the Colorado River, he wrote, produced fruit harvests "the bounty of which the world had not seen before." "Where once there had been dusty desert between the ocean and the snow-covered Sierra Nevada, plantations of oranges, lemons, apricots, grapes... a new image of grand uniformity."[208] One cannot help but be struck by the similarity of Schumacher's impressions with those of Max Sering more than twenty years earlier recounted in Chapter 1.

It was not only California's agriculture that impressed Schumacher. He observed that in 1905 sizable oil fields had been discovered near Los Angeles, which he saw as a significant development as California's industrial development had been hindered thus far by the lack of coal. The new fuel, Schumacher observed, had certain advantages over coal. Likewise, there were ideas afloat to dam the Colorado River to generate electricity.[209] Thus when Schumacher arrived in Los Angeles the city was in a boom atmosphere with the arrival of many entrepreneurs and speculators. The other drivers of this boom mentality were the recent fusion of the Union and Southern Pacific Railroads and the construction of the Panama Canal which promised improved transportation within California and a much shortened connection between the Atlantic and Pacific coasts. Indeed, San Diego was to Schumacher's mind then in the midst of an even greater boom than Los Angeles on account of the promise of the Panama Canal.[210]

By contrast, San Francisco was a shocking picture of devastation and abandonment. Schumacher could smell the smoke from the fires well before

---

[206] Ibid., fols. 468–69.   [207] Ibid., fol. 469.   [208] Ibid., fols. 469–70.
[209] Ibid., fol. 470.   [210] Ibid., fols. 471–72.

the arrival of the train, despite the fact that the earthquake had occurred nearly a year earlier in April 1906. Many of the city's residents were then being accommodated in mining camp-like settlements on the outskirts of the city. Yet the catastrophe had not robbed the city of its lifeblood, which was trade, shipping, and the surrounding agricultural and mining regions.[211] The spirit of the population was likewise alive and much preoccupied by the then raging mayoral race to "clean up government."[212] Indeed, Schumacher noticed that the rebuilding of San Francisco as well as the development of the "backward" West was reinvigorating a basic faith in progress that sustained American society:

> Just as one expected an improvement in the city that would not have been possible without the catastrophe, one expected a "cleansing" [of government] as would not have been possible without political struggle. The American people's proud faith in increasing perfection is strengthened again and again in the development of the backward West. How progress is achieved – whether through the individual, through the city or the state – did not matter. I visited a socialist meeting in New York opened by a finely-dressed bank director with the words: we are all socialists. That was no hollow slogan. So long as striving to make the equality of people a reality had some prospect of attainment, socialism on American soil was harmless; if that striving were to become hopeless, it would become dangerous. In the West progress was still obvious, in the East it was beginning to be lost in the eyes of the masses.[213]

It was while viewing the Golden Gate from Cliff House in San Francisco that Schumacher became fully conscious of the importance of the Pacific to the future of the country and that its political fate was bound up in one way or another with the peoples of Asia. What would it mean, he asked, if hundreds of millions of people in East and South Asia acquired modern production methods and means of war?[214] Clearly, being a "Pacific Power," which the completion of the Panama Canal would reinforce, came with both opportunity and risk.

As noted, at the time of Schumacher's visit the "yellow peril" bogey exercised Theodore Roosevelt and was animating American politics. The changing volume and face of immigration was something that stood out to Schumacher strongly since his last visit in 1893, notably the new immigration from Eastern and Southern Europe, and on the Pacific coast, from China and Japan. Assimilation had proven more difficult with these new immigrants. To the existing "black peril" he noted, a "yellow" one had been added, and with it the rise of nativist calls to remove such "undesirables." Indeed, prohibitions had

---

[211] Ibid., fols. 472–74.   [212] Ibid., fol. 475a.   [213] Ibid., fols. 475a–76.
[214] Ibid., fols. 476–76a.

been passed on immigration from East Asia.[215] In October 1906, San Francisco's school board had ordered Japanese children to attend segregated schools, and shortly after Schumacher's return to the East, in May 1907, racial tensions in San Francisco and other cities boiled over into race riots egged on by the Hearst press.[216] It should be noted here that Roosevelt's coercive diplomacy with the Great White Fleet in 1907 was intended not only to force the Japanese into accepting US annexations in the Pacific, but also to press them to accept restrictions on Japanese emigration to Hawaii and California, which had recently flared tensions between the two countries.[217] Schumacher observed that the new territories seized in the Pacific or annexed from Spain posed an added challenge: they could not be integrated into the existing structure of the United States the way the contiguous territories had been and required a large overseas military presence. But that was not all: "To the regrettable racial divide of whites and negroes, new ones were being added."[218] A closely related problem was the growth of an American proletariat. So long as a frontier existed, it was possible to "Go West" and work toward some prosperity and independence, and there was thus little mass dissatisfaction or a socialist party fueled by it. With the closing of the frontier and restrictions on immigration, that was now changing.[219]

The United States thus presented itself to Schumacher as a complicated, contradictory place: restless, energetic, and hopeful, yet on account of its economic self-sufficiency, dynamism, immigration, and overseas expansionism, a threat to other countries like Germany, just as it was to itself on account of those very forces. Later in his journey and then back in Germany Schumacher would come to see the United States as a great "experimental laboratory for the modern economy," a lab whose experiments also posed explosive dangers.[220]

Schumacher's return journey to New York passed through Sacramento, Portland, Seattle, and Vancouver, and from there he traveled three days and nights by train to Chicago, where he was to give lectures at the University of Chicago in early April 1907.[221] In Chicago he would have a fateful encounter with one of the trustees of the University of Chicago, Charles R. Crane (1858–1939). Crane was a Chicago philanthropist whose family fortune was

---

[215] GNN HA, Nl. Schumacher, I, B-6o, fols. 439–41.
[216] Mehnert, "Gelbe Gefahr," 82–87. See also Hendrix, *Naval Diplomacy*, xiii–xiv.
[217] Mehnert, "Gelbe Gefahr," 174–96. See also Tosh Minohara, "The 'Rat Minister': Komura Jutaro and U.S.-Japan Relations," in *The Russo-Japanese War in Global Perspective: World War Zero*, ed. David Wolff et al., vol. 2 (Leiden and Boston: Brill, 2007), 551–69.
[218] GNN HA, Nl. Schumacher, I, B-6p, fols. 458–58a.
[219] GNN HA, Nl. Schumacher, I, B-6o, fol. 448.
[220] GNN HA, Nl. Schumacher, I, B-6q, fol. 485.
[221] GNN HA, Nl. Schumacher, I, B-6p, fols. 477–78.

made in the plumbing pipe industry and whose work took him to Russia, where he fell in love with the people, culture, and language. He subsequently became an important facilitator of Russian and Slavic studies at the University of Chicago.[222]

Schumacher was slated to visit Crane's pipe factory, but through a lengthy and absorbing conversation in Crane's home sparked by the many Russian landscape paintings in his parlor, the conversation shifted to Russia. Crane impressed upon Schumacher that the large temperate zones of North America and northern Eurasia were the two parts of the earth with the greatest similarity and that the problems they encountered were likewise similar, making experiences gathered in one place valuable in the other. The differences that existed between the two places were not natural but given by the nature of their economic development. For that reason Americans had a right and duty to help the Russians overcome those disparities, and this was in the interest of the United States. For Schumacher, who might have already stumbled upon this idea in his encounter with the "dry farming" experimental station in Colorado, it confirmed that the notion of the United States as a "Pacific Power" was not isolated to California or the West Coast.[223] It turned out that Crane had been hosting Sergei Witte (1849–1915) during the negotiations in Portsmouth, New Hampshire, which ended the Russo-Japanese War. Crane knew many other members of the Tsarist government well, including the outstanding liberal historian and statesman Pavel Milyukov (1859–1943), who had been brought by Crane to lecture at the University of Chicago and likewise been a house guest of Crane. Schumacher described these conversations with Crane as a "concluding high point of my American journeys."[224] The friendship with Crane would be deepened by Crane's later visits to Germany en route to Russia. Crane would eventually serve as ambassador to China and would be part of an American commission led by Elihu Root (Root Commission) and sent to St. Petersburg by Wilson after the United States entered the First World War.[225]

When Schumacher returned to New York and then, after a touching farewell from his students and colleagues at Columbia, embarked on the steamer passage back to Germany, a large stack of books on Russia was waiting for him in his cabin as a gift from Crane.[226] On his return journey Schumacher

---

[222] See, Daniel C. Engerman, "Studying Our Nearest Oriental Neighbor: American Scholars in Late Imperial Russia," in *Americans Experience Russia: Encountering the Enigma, 1917 to the Present*, ed. Choi Chatterjee and Beth Holmgren (New York and Abingdon, Oxon: Routledge, 2013), 12–28, here 22–23.

[223] GNN HA, NL Schumacher, I, B-6p, fols. 479–80. Cf. Kate Brown, "Gridded Lives: Why Kazakhstan and Montana Are Nearly the Same Place," *The American Historical Review* 106, no. 1 (Feb. 2001): 17–48.

[224] GNN HA, Nl. Schumacher, I, B-6p, fol. 480.     [225] Ibid., fols. 483–84.

[226] Ibid., fol. 480a.

had a chance to come to some conclusions about the experiences he had had in the United States as they related to his teaching and scholarship on *Weltwirtschaft*. A German scholarly foundation and reference point, he realized, was inadequate for tackling these international problems. The United States was teeming with economic experiments like no other place on earth, ones that were of great relevance to the rest of the world, he realized. There was no shortage of exceptional energy in its younger and older generations. Indeed, he realized that he had to rethink much of what he thought he knew.[227]

Like Japan, the United States had been successful in its own *Weltpolitik* and had become an expanding, aggressive imperial and naval power with no hindrances to regional hegemony. Britain had not been able to oppose and so appeased that process. But unlike Japan, the United States was astride an entire continent, a land with wide, promising horizons both at home and overseas. Indeed, that abundant land was attractive to Japanese immigrants confined as they were to a cramped, resource-poor archipelago under similar population pressures as Germany and with no land and resource-abundant periphery anywhere in the vicinity. That was already raising tensions with the United States over Japanese immigration and US claims in the Philippines and Hawaii.

To Germany the challenges posed by the United States were different. America's expanded size, resource abundance, and economic dynamism opened the prospect of ever-greater self-sufficiency in sugar and scale economies and other cost advantages in many branches of heavy industry against which German firms might not be able to compete. The ever-present protectionist and nativist forces posed the additional danger of closure of the American market to German exporters. The country was also showing unmistakable signs of self-sufficiency in higher education. Beyond that, Schumacher and many other educated German observers who traveled to the United States in these years, such as Max Weber, saw the United States as the "lap of modernity," forerunner in many features of modernism, not all of them salubrious, ones that they feared could ultimately also engulf their own country.[228]

By contrast, Germany's *Weltpolitik* had clearly stalled by 1908. The enlarged navy had not delivered *Weltgeltung* but rather British animosity and growing diplomatic isolation. No land suitable for settlement had been added since *Weltpolitik* was inaugurated in 1895, and the recent colonial uprisings had shown the German colonies could not absorb German settlers. Under these

---

[227] Ibid., fols. 480a–481.
[228] Wolfgang Mommsen, "Max Weber und die Vereinigten Staaten von Amerika," in *Zwei Wege in die Moderne*, ed. Fiebig-von Hase and Heideking, 91–103; Dirk Kaesler, *Max Weber: Eine Biographie* (Munich: C. H. Beck, 2014), 566–637.

conditions it was undoubtedly a fascinating prospect to project upon Russia, as Crane had done, an American developmental path enabled by American technological transfer, investment, and entrepreneurship. Was there an "America" waiting to be born on the Eurasian continent? Were the vast agricultural lands and natural resources of Russia then not also an outlet for German talent, investment, and technology? This was at the time not as far-fetched a notion as it might seem at first glance. Russian statesmen like Sergei Witte and other members of the pro-German "court" faction in the Tsarist Foreign Ministry, notably Roman Rosen (1847–1921) and Aleksandr Giers (1861–1917), were critical of Russia's misguided and dangerous Slavophile policy in the Balkans pursued by Izvolsky and his successor in the Foreign Ministry Serge Sazonov (1860–1927), advocating instead for a developmental thrust focused on the Black Sea basin, Central Asia, and Siberia. Witte and Rosen in particular were strong advocates of Russian industry and an alliance with Germany, Witte himself seeking to combine German technology, French capital, and Russian resources to forge a continental bloc to counterbalance British and American global dominance.[229] As Domnik Lieven observes, the usual slur that all advocates of an alliance with Germany were reactionaries is false, as both Rosen and Giers were liberal conservatives committed to Russian political and civil rights.[230]

It was no leap from these insights to the geopolitics of Sir Halford MacKinder, who only three years prior in 1904 had given his famous paper "The Geographical Pivot of History" to the Royal Geographical Society, where Eurasia, not command of the seas, was the "pivot" of history.[231] Expanding continental railway networks, the spread of industry eastward into Eurasia, technical progress in the production of raw materials, and the intensification of agriculture all meant that the seas would decline in importance compared to the Eurasian core. Russia was the historical "pivot state" of that core, and a future German-Russian union, Mackinder believed, would offer unparalleled land resources and those for naval expansion ultimately creating an indomitable continental bloc, one that would be able to cut England off from her lines of supply and reduce her to geopolitical insignificance.[232] The Columbian age of sea power was thus coming to an end.

This connected easily with an existing strain of geopolitical thinking in Germany influenced by Friedrich Ratzel – who, as was discussed in Chapter 1, had himself been profoundly shaped by his experiences in the North American West and whose thinking had influenced (and been influenced by) Frederick Jackson Turner and Max Sering – and that would be developed further by his

---

[229] See esp. Lieven, *The End of Tsarist Russia*, 58–59, 70, 109, 133–43.   [230] Ibid., 128.
[231] Halford John Mackinder, "The Geographic Pivot of History," *The Geographical Journal* 23, no. 4 (Apr. 1904): 421–44.
[232] Brechtken, *Scharnierzeit 1895–1907*, 67.

Swedish student Rudolf Kjellén (1864–1922).[233] This argued for a more autarkic Germany in union with the other central European states expanding its influence eastward into Russia, which was viewed by Kjellén and many Swedes and Germans as a growing political menace to central Europe in the immediate prewar years.[234] American self-sufficiency and the Panamerican claims of Roosevelt's version of the Monroe Doctrine seemed, if anything, to reinforce just that perspective. The complete failure of German diplomatic initiatives in 1907–8 to draw the United States into an alliance to jointly assure China's territorial integrity against Japan and the forging of the Triple Entente meant that Germany's leasehold in Shantung was more isolated and vulnerable than ever.[235] The reorientation in German colonial policy under Dernburg away from settler colonialism in Africa after 1908 as well as the growing appeal to Bülow and the Wilhelmstrasse of less vulnerable, contiguous informal empire in Asia Minor and the Near East via the spearhead of the Baghdad Railway reveal that similar such geopolitical ideas were slowly gaining official traction.

---

[233] Friedrich Ratzel, *Politische Geographie* (Munich and Leipzig: Oldenbourg, 1897); David Blackbourn, *The Conquest of Nature: Water, Landscape and the Making of Modern Germany* (New York: Norton, 2007), 294.

[234] Rudolf Kjellén, *Stormakterna: konturer kring samtidens storpolitik,* rev. and enl. ed. (1911; Stockholm: H. Geber, 1913); Kjellén, *Den ryska faran* (Karlskrona: Karlskrona-Tidningen, 1913). During the war Kjellén became an outspoken proponent of German expansionism: Kjellén, *Die Ideen von 1914: Eine weltgeschichtliche Perspektive* (Leipzig: S. Hirzel, 1915).

[235] See Mehnert, *"Gelbe Gefahr,"* 139–55, 197–99; Pommerin, *Der Kaiser und Amerika*, 179–92.

# 9

# Colonial Dreams

### Bernhard Dernburg's Colonial Reforms

In the aftermath of the 1907 Reichstag elections, much hope was invested in the reform of colonial administration promised by Bülow and Bernhard Dernburg. With a major electoral reversal in the SPD and the forging of the Bülow Bloc between the liberal and conservative parties, a new mood predominated in the Reichstag much more accommodating to the government, resulting in the acceptance of the bills that had stalled in late 1906, including the railway bills, supplemental appropriations needed to pay for the war in Southwest Africa, and the bill creating a new Imperial Colonial Office (Reichskolonialamt).[1] It was a welcome shift in what had been nearly three years of colonial scandals and crises.

As discussed previously, Dernburg's colonial economic policy was very driven by the goal of improving indigenous cultivation, connecting the colonies to a German and international division of labor, and making the colonies an attractive destinations for German investment. The most important measure to that end was improving colonial infrastructure. Given the central place that railways were given in the Reichstag election campaign and the hopes invested in them for the colonies, it should not come as too much of a surprise that Dernburg's years as state secretary (1907–10) were marked by something of a railway mania.[2] In early 1907 the "Cocoa Railway" Lome-Agome-Palime was opened. By October of the same year the Daressalam extension of the Pugu-Morogoro line of the German East African Railway was completed. In March 1908 the branch railway Otavi-Grootfontein in German Southwest Africa was finished. Later in June the Seeheim-Kalkfontein stretch of the Lüderitz Railway was begun, with diamonds found on the sixteenth kilometer of the same railway shortly thereafter. The railway project that had helped to precipitate the colonial crisis in December 1906 – the Keepmanshoop extension of the Lüderitz Railway – was completed on June 21, 1908. One year later, the branch railway Seeheim-Kalkfontein, the Mombo-Buiko extension of the

---

[1] Schiefel, *Bernhard Dernburg,* 63–65.
[2] Ibid., 92–96; van Laak, *Imperiale Infrastruktur,* 137–42.

Usambara Railway, and the Bonaberi-Njombe stretch of North Cameroon Railway – which had been the object of such controversy in 1905–6 – were all opened.[3] These investments were facilitated by Dernburg's reform of colonial finance that allowed the protectorates to issue and service their own railway bonds with Reich guarantees, thus decentralizing much of this investment and relying more on private investor capital. Even so, ownership of the railways was retained by the colonial government and colonial railways came under greater state supervision in the Dernburg era.[4]

There can be no doubt that mass distribution of the *Railways of Africa* by the Kolonialpolitisches Aktionskomité in late 1907 helped to smooth the way for relatively easy passage of a major colonial railway bill in the Reichstag in 1908, which paved the way for most of these investments. In all some 125 million marks would be invested in colonial railroads that were expanded by 1,450 kilometers between 1908 and 1911.[5] Dernburg later joked that more colonial railways were built in the four years of his administration than the biggest American railway speculator was able to achieve in those same years.[6]

While Dernburg is certainly owed considerable credit for what was achieved in colonial railways in these years, his railroad program was anticipated by the policy changes Karl Helfferich had helped initiate while working in the Colonial Section of the Foreign Office after 1901 under Dernburg's predecessor, Oscar Stübel, discussed in Chapter 7. This had focused on the economic development of Germany's colonies and their integration into *Weltwirtschaft* through railway infrastructure and the important role that had to be played by private investors in that process. Dernburg himself worked closely with influential figures from the world of German industry and banking, such as Walther Rathenau, Max Warburg, and the director of the Berlin Handelsgesellschaft Carl Fürstenberg (1850–1933) to draw German investment capital to the colonies.[7] Of all the German banking houses, the M.M. Warburg Bank was one of the most active investors in the German colonies in large part due to the patriotic initiative of Max Warburg, who was on friendly terms with Dernburg, and as we shall see, also an important patron of the Hamburg Kolonialinstitut.[8]

When diamonds were found in Southwest Africa in 1908 Dernburg put in place a framework to maximize the effective exploitation of this resource. This involved creating the *Sperrgebiet* (a restricted mining area in the southwestern

---

[3] See Helmut Schroeter and Roel Ramaer, *Die Eisenbahnen in den einst deutschen Schutzgebieten Ostafrika, Kamerun, Togo und die Schantung-Eisenbahn; damals und heute/ German Colonial Railways East Africa, Southwest Africa, Cameroon, Togo and the Shantung Railway; Then and Now* (Krefeld: Röhr-Verlag, 1993).
[4] Schiefel, *Bernhard Dernburg*, 93–94.   [5] Ibid., 94.   [6] Ibid., 96.   [7] Ibid., 91–92.
[8] Warburg, *Aus meinen Aufzeichnugen*, 24; Ferguson, "Max Warburg and German Politics," 188–90.

corner of the colony), the lease of diamond mining rights in it to the Deutsche Diamant-Gesellschaft, and the creation of a diamond board of bankers and colonial officials to monopolize the export of diamonds and fix diamond prices. The advantage of these arrangements was that they allowed for the rapid development of this resource by heavy investment of private capital and by preventing the collapse of international diamond prices, which ultimately benefited both the colony and Reich.[9] This was the face of a colonial *Weltpolitik*, which in truth long predated Dernburg's time in office, witnessing its first experiments in the Venezuelan and Shantung railways and that would find its ultimate expression not so much in the African railways completed under Dernburg than in the Baghdad Railway to be discussed more in the next chapter. However, these and other measures antagonized the white settlers of Southwest Africa and their Pan-German supporters in the Reich, who became persistent critics of Dernburg until his departure from the Colonial Office in 1910.[10] These German overseas railway investments had a darker side, of course. They had burdened colonies with debt and scandal, and as the case of the Boxer Uprising in Shantung makes clear, they had catalyzed colonial unrest. Railways and the debts they had generated had helped to precipitate the Second Venezuela Crisis, and in the case of the Baghdad Railway, had helped to foment tensions with Britain and Russia that encouraged the formation of the Triple Entente in 1907 and Germany's strategic and diplomatic isolation thereafter.

Another prong of Dernburg's colonial reform initiative was to allow greater colonial self-administration and to encourage more self-sufficient colonial finances by unburdening colonial budgets with military expenses and reducing imperial grants to the protectorates.[11] He opposed efforts by Matthias Erzberger to saddle Southwest Africa with the burden of paying for the military intervention that suppressed the Herero and Nama uprising through a colonial wealth tax on the grounds that it would discourage investment. This new approach also involved a greater sensitivity for the customs, languages, and welfare of the indigenous populations, protection of their rights, and a much stronger orientation toward indigenous peasant agriculture away from plantations and forced labor. It also imposed restrictions on German settlers.[12] These were policies reinforced by the impressions Dernburg gained after completing his own inspection tour of East Africa in 1907 and South and Southwest Africa in 1908.[13] To be sure, such policy was driven less by humanitarian than by pragmatic economic and administrative motives. He

---

[9] Schiefel, *Bernhard Dernburg*, 101–4; Smith, *Colonial Empire*, 203–4.
[10] Schiefel, *Bernhard Dernburg*, 104–6, 128–29; Smith, *Colonial Empire*, 207, 209.
[11] Schiefel, *Bernhard Dernburg*, 61, 85–90.    [12] See ibid., 108–20.
[13] Ibid., 60–61, 66–80; R. V. Pierard, "The Dernburg Reform Policy and German East Africa," *Tanzania Notes and Records* 67 (1967): 31–38.

was influenced in that direction by enlightened men of industry, such as Walther Rathenau, and by far-sighted civil servants, particularly Albrecht von Rechenberg (1861–1935), who became governor of German East Africa in 1906). Both Rathenau and von Rechenberg had accompanied Dernburg during his well-publicized travels to Africa.[14]

As will be recalled, many of these policies were anticipated in ideas that Karl Rathgen had first articulated at the Evangelical Social Congress in 1900, emphasizing long-term investments that raised the living standards of the colonial subjects as an end in and of itself. They were also clearly inspired by ideas that Schmoller had expressed at the first German Colonial Congress in 1902, emphasizing indigenous peasant farming and native small enterprise, which were discussed in Chapter 7. The native uprisings in German East and Southwest Africa certainly served to reinforce such a course.[15] Even taking into account Dernburg's initially more conciliatory approach to the Southwest African German settlers, the reforms and restrictions imposed by Dernburg and the Colonial Office after 1907 made it clear that the German colonial empire offered no viable destination for significant numbers of would-be German settlers – these lands were no German equivalent to New Zealand, Australia, Algeria, or South Africa. Once again, this put Dernburg at odds with German settlers' interests and their supporters in the Reich, which led to some backtracking by Dernburg on these policies.[16]

Much as Karl Helfferich had done while working under Stübel, Dernburg also placed great weight on the colonies as a destination for German exports and as a source of key industrial raw materials, albeit with much less success. As Helfferich had pointed out, growing concentration and trustification in the worldwide supply of raw materials such as cotton meant that it was important to have some colonial raw material and export market share as bargaining chips in trade negotiations. The development of colonial railways and other infrastructure would enhance the supply of those raw materials and stimulate colonial demand, Dernburg believed.[17] Under Dernburg, colonial cotton cultivation received a marked new push, and Dernburg himself took a seven-week tour of the United States in 1909 devoted largely to cotton cultivation. His conclusions were practically identical to the findings of von Halle's 1897 study and Helfferich's articles on the *"Baumwollfrage"* published

---

[14] Adolf Zimmermann, *Mit Dernburg nach Ostafrika* (Berlin: C. A. Schwentsche und Sohn, 1908); Hartmut Pogge von Strandmann, ed. *Walther Rathenau, Industrialist, Banker, Intellectual, and Politician: Notes and Diaries 1907–1922*, trans. Caroline Pinder Cracraft (Oxford: Clarendon Press; New York: Oxford University Press, 1985), 27–92. More succinctly, Smith, *Colonial Empire*, 193–202; van Laak, *Imperiale Infrastruktur*, 135–37.

[15] Schiefel, *Bernhard Dernburg*, 69–71, 78–80.

[16] See Bley, *South-West Africa*, 212–19; John Iliffe, *Tanganyika under German Rule 1905–1912* (London: Cambridge University Press, 1969), 82–117.

[17] Schiefel, *Bernhard Dernburg*, 59.

in 1904 discussed in Chapters 1 and 7, respectively: no expansion of cotton cultivation was possible in the United States and a growing portion of the US harvest was being consumed domestically. One policy change that resulted was direct state involvement in experimental cotton stations and cotton cultivation extension services, though one should add here that this led to no sustained increases in colonial cotton output before 1914.[18] African railways had many unintended longer-term consequences that affected this cotton output, especially in German East Africa. There household structure changed dramatically as a consequence of the labor recruitment policies that were part of railway construction, a process that actually undermined peasant agriculture. Thus in East Africa one of the reasons given for railways – to bring peasant crop surpluses into a wider colonial and international division of labor – was ultimately undermined by construction of the railways.[19]

The final major thrust of Dernburg's colonial reforms was developing a competent colonial civil service with a systematic training in a new *Kolonialwissenschaft* (colonial science) equal in status to domestic civil servants. As was discussed in the previous chapter, early on Dernburg had spearheaded personnel reforms in the colonial administration away from *Kolonial-Assessorismus* – the narrowly legally and bureaucratically-trained colonial administrators preoccupied with inflexibly enforcing colonial laws and regulations – toward greater independence of thought and better knowledge of colonial languages, culture, and economic conditions to gain the trust of the colonial subjects and encourage sustained economic development. Greater emphasis was now placed in the training of such officials in practical colonial economics, and more attention would be given to the quality of such officials, their salaries, and possibilities for advancement as well as in fostering internal colonial expertise.[20] A simplification and decentralization of administration and a transition from military to civilian leadership was very much at the heart of these reforms, as was the development of indigenous colonial law that reflected local conditions and customs.[21]

---

[18] Ibid., 97–99. On the new cotton imperialism in German colonial Africa, Beckert, *Empire of Cotton*, 362–75; Thaddeus Sunseri, "The Baumwollfrage: Cotton Colonialism in German East Africa," *Central European History* 34 (2001): 31–51; Zimmerman, *Alabama in Africa*, 112–65.

[19] See Thaddeus Sunseri, "Dispersing the Fields: Railway Labor and Rural Change in Early Colonial Tanzania," *Canadian Journal of African Studies* 32 (1998): 558–83; Bradley D. Naranch, "'Colonized Body,' 'Oriental Machine': Debating Race, Railroads and the Politics of Reconstruction in Germany and East Africa, 1906–10," *Central European History* 33 (2000): 299–338.

[20] Schiefel, *Bernhard Dernburg*, 82–83, 84–85.

[21] See Andreas Eckert and Michael Pesek, "Bürokratische Ordnung und koloniale Praxis: Herrschaft und Verwaltung in Preußen und Afrika," in Conrad and Osterhammel, *Das Kaiserreich transnational*, 87–106; Ulrike Schaper, *Koloniale Verhandlungen:*

There had been growing concern that the education of German officials more generally had not kept up with the times, notably the serious deficits in economics education in evidence in many of them despite the increasing weight of economic forces in German life. This had led to the founding of the Vereinigung für Staatswissenschaftliche Fortbildung (Union for Continuing Education in Political Economy) in Berlin in 1902, the Gesellschaft für wirtschafliche Ausbildung (Society for Economic Education) in Frankfurt in 1904, and other similar initiatives elsewhere in which Sering, Schmoller, Schumacher, and von Halle had actively participated in various capacities.[22] Diplomatic training, as Schumacher would learn, was no exception. He discovered this by chance in 1912 when he gained privileged access to the files of the Foreign Office in Berlin on Germany's China policy. To his surprise, his time-consuming study of these files ultimately yielded remarkably little, as he knew most of the sources from which the reports were drawn and found nothing comparable in quality to the well-informed memos compiled by British diplomats on the Chinese economy.[23] It left an unmistakable impression of incompetence, and though some senior officials in the Foreign Office were well aware of the problem and eager to recruit him to spearhead reforms, Schumacher well knew that powerful traditional forces in the Wilhelmstrasse were firmly aligned against any change and that he, as a lone economics professor, had no hope of prevailing against them.[24]

As we saw in the previous chapter, during the Reichstag election campaign of 1906–7 Dernburg had spoken extensively about a new "scientific colonialism" that he assured the public would make the German colonies more economically productive. That technocratic colonial expertise had to be instilled in would-be colonial administrators in some new way, that is, not in the existing universities – which had obviously failed to prepare them adequately – but in *Handelshochschulen* (business schools) and ideally some new academy devoted specifically to colonial science. But where would that be? And, more importantly, where would the funds for it come from in 1907 given how tight the federal budget was under the dual strain of supplemental appropriations to pay for colonial wars and African railways, on the one hand, and swelling Reich deficits from naval construction, on the other?

---

*Gerichtsbarkeit, Verwaltung und Herrschaft in Kamerun 1884–1916* (Frankfurt: Campus, 2012), 228–302.

[22] vom Bruch, *Wissenschaft, Politik und öffentliche Meinung*, 258–61; GNN HA, Nl. Schumacher, I, B-24, Gesellschaft für wirtschaftliche Ausbildung to Hermann Schumacher, Frankfurt, Jan. 26, 1905; Ernst von Halle, *Die Wirtschaftswissenschaft in der heutigen Beamtenvorbildung: Referat gehalten auf der VI. Ordentlichen Hauptversammlung des Deutschen Volkswirtschaftlichen Verbandes*, Schriften des Deutschen Volkswirtschaftlichen Verbandes, vol. 3, no. 2 (Berlin: Carl Heymanns Verlag, 1909).

[23] GNN HA, Nl. Schumacher, I, B-6v, fols. 609–10.   [24] Ibid., fol. 611.

In many ways Dernburg's very credibility as Colonial Secretary hinged on delivering something tangible on this important front. It would not be in Berlin or anywhere in Prussia that a solution to this problem would present itself, but rather in Hamburg.

## Karl Rathgen and the Hamburg Colonial Institute

The idea of founding an institution of higher learning in Hamburg had been entertained for some years but had repeatedly foundered on the skepticism of Hamburg's merchant elite, who dominated the Bürgerschaft (the Hamburg Assembly) and Senate, and who did not see much practical use in such a costly enterprise. The energetic and ambitious president of the city-state's Upper School Board (Oberschulbehörde) Senator Werner von Melle (1853–1937) had nevertheless been sailing a course in that direction against these headwinds since reforms he spearheaded of Hamburg's system of regular public lectures organized by the General Lecture Agency (Allgemeines Vorlesungswesen) after 1895. This had been reorganized into a regular curriculum with dedicated faculty and an enhanced budget as steps toward the ultimate goal of founding a university.[25] As we saw in the case of Karl Helfferich in Chapter 7, these lecture series drew many talented scholars to Hamburg as guest lecturers, including Gustav Schmoller.[26] By 1906 von Melle had persuaded the Hamburg Senate to approve funding of a permanent professorship of political economy, a position that was deemed a cornerstone for these ambitions in a city defined by international shipping and trade. In the meantime von Melle created a scholarly foundation (Wissenschaftliche Stiftung) to get around the tightfisted Assembly and solicited donations – notably from generous German Jewish businessmen with ties to Hamburg such as Albert Ballin, Alfred Beit (1853–1906), and the Warburg family – that would work toward founding a university. Astonishingly, by the spring of 1907 nearly four million marks had been donated to the foundation, two million alone from Alfred Beit.[27]

The business of hiring a permanent professor of political economy proved more difficult. Once the funds were approved by the Assembly, the intention of the Hamburg Upper School Board was to hire an established professor with a national reputation – ideally someone with expertise in *Weltwirtschaft* and organizational talent. Not surprisingly Hamburg's first-choice candidate was Hermann Schumacher, whom von Melle had gone to the trouble of traveling to meet in Bremen in late summer 1906 just before Schumacher's departure for New York as Kaiser Wilhelm Professor.[28] Melle offered the professorship to him in October, mentioning explicitly that the ultimate goal

---

[25] See Jens Ruppenthal, *Kolonialismus als "Wissenschaft und Technik": Das Hamburgische Kolonialinstitut 1908–1919* (Stuttgart: Franz Steiner Verlag, 2007), 101.
[26] Ibid.   [27] Ibid., 102–7.   [28] Ibid., 108.

was establishing a new university.[29] Schumacher declined, as did those next in line, Alfred Weber and Ludwig Bernhard (1875–1935).[30] It was undoubtedly difficult to persuade established professors to join such an uncertain undertaking.

In mid-April 1907 Dernbug's still vague proposals for a colonial academy and a professorship devoted to colonial science were discussed in the Reichstag Budget Commission. Here a member of the commission familiar with von Melle's efforts to establish a university, Johannes Semler (1858–1914), mentioned that existing institutions and funds were available in Hamburg for such a professorship. Given how tight the Reich budget was at the time, it was not surprising that this news was greeted very positively by the other members of the commission and especially Dernburg. Soon thereafter von Melle was notified of these discussions by Semler. Working closely with the director of Hamburg's Museum of Ethnology, Georg Thilenius (1868–1937), von Melle wasted no time to set the wheels in motion to bring about his plans for a university by way of a colonial institute calculated to appeal to Dernburg and the Colonial Office.[31] Some urgency was given the matter by awareness that plans were afoot to found a Prussian colonial academy involving the Berlin Seminar for Oriental Languages based loosely on a memorandum drafted for the Prussian Ministry of Culture by none other than Ernst von Halle in 1902.[32]

Early in May 1907 Dernburg himself took up contact with von Melle to initiate discussions, and one week later Thilenius was on his way to the new Colonial Office in Berlin to begin the negotiations with Dernburg. Thilenius highlighted the many advantages of establishing a colonial institute in Hamburg that would appeal to Dernburg, notably the synergies possible in training civil servants and businessmen in one institution, the many contacts to colonial merchants and traders in the city, the significance of Hamburg's related museums and institutes (e.g., the Botanical, Ethnological, and Natural History Museums; the observatory; and the Hygienic and Mineralogical-Geological Institutes), the leading role played by the Hamburg Institute for Ships' and Tropical Diseases in Germany, and not least, the direct connections of Hamburg to the rest of the world.[33]

---

[29] GNN HA, Nl. Schumacher, I, C-168, Werner von Melle to Hermann Schumacher, Hamburg, Oct. 26, 1906.
[30] StaHH, 361-6 Hochschulwesen – Dozenten- und Personalakten, I 330, Akte betreffend Übertragung der Professur für Nationalökonomie. Hinterbliebenen-Versorgung, 1907–1921, fols. 3–4, Hamburger Oberschulbehörde, Auszug aus dem Protokolle der ersten Sektion, May 30, 1907.
[31] Ruppenthal, *Kolonialismus*, 110–13.   [32] Ibid., 119–20.
[33] Ibid., 117–19; Deborah J. Neill, "Science and Civilizing Missions: Germans and the Transnational Community of Tropical Medicine," in *German Colonialism in a Global Age*, ed. Naranch and Eley 74–92.

In the meantime the importance of the professorship of political economy had grown considerably, as it could now anchor the proposed institution much more firmly in colonial science.[34] Von Melle wrote Hermann Schumacher with the request to propose someone with suitable expertise on this topic, and Schumacher recommended Karl Rathgen.[35] As Germany's leading authority on the economy of Japan who had subsequently made a reputation for himself in the field of East Asian trade and colonial policy, he was unquestionably an ideal candidate given the new colonial thrust of von Melle and Thilenius's initiative.[36] The challenge was luring him to Hamburg from Heidelberg University, where Rathgen had moved from Marburg in 1900 to replace the incapacitated Max Weber.[37] In the subsequent negotiations, Rathgen was offered significant additional pay by the Wissenschaftliche Stiftung but was obliged in return to commit to holding regular lectures on *Kolonialpolitik* (colonial policy).[38] Rathgen agreed and accepted the offer in early June 1907.[39] Securing this important professorship came not a moment too soon.

In a draft plan for the Hamburg Colonial Institute penned by Thilenius, the new body would come together from an existing core of faculty in Hamburg's Professorenkonvent already teaching for the General Lecture Agency or employed in Hamburg's other institutes and museums. No reorganization or new buildings would thus be needed. Contacts to the Colonial Office would be assured by a commissioner appointed to the Hamburg Upper School Board. All employees of the institute would be paid by the city-state but recognized by the Reich as civil servants. The personnel of a central bureau (proposed by Dernburg) devoted to the centralized collection and

---

[34] Ruppenthal, *Kolonialismus*, 124.
[35] StaHH, 361-6 Hochschulwesen – Dozenten- und Personalakten, I 330, Akte betreffend Übertragung der Professur für Nationalökonomie. Hinterbliebenen-Versorgung, 1907–1921, fols. 3–4, Hamburger Oberschulbehörde Auszug aus dem Protokolle der ersten Sektion, May 30, 1907.
[36] Karl Rathgen, "Entwicklungstendenzen im Außenhandel Chinas und Japans," *JbfGVV* 30 (1906): 1079–94.
[37] See Kaesler, *Max Weber*, 468–75.
[38] StaHH, 361-6 Hochschulwesen – Dozenten- und Personalakten, I 330, Akte betreffend Übertragung der Professur für Nationalökonomie. Hinterbliebenen-Versorgung, 1907–1921, fols. 3–4, Hamburger Oberschulbehörde Auszug aus dem Protokolle der ersten Sektion, May 30, 1907; fol. 5a, Abschrift eines Einschreibens, Hamburg, May 31, 1907. GNN HA, NL Schumacher, I, C-168, Werner von Melle to Hermann Schumacher, Hamburg, June 11, 1907.
[39] StaHH, 361-6 Hochschulwesen – Dozenten- und Personalakten, I 330, Akte betreffend Übertragung der Professur für Nationalökonomie. Hinterbliebenen-Versorgung, 1907–1921, fols. 7–8, Karl Rathgen to Werner von Melle, Heidelberg, June 6, 1907.

disseminating colonial information would be financed by the Reich.[40] This plan much appealed to Dernburg, and from the 5th to 7th of June 1907 Dernburg visited Hamburg accompanied by his deputy Heinrich Schnee (1871–1949, later the last governor of German East Africa) to inspect the city-state's existing educational institutions and continue the discussions. Duly impressed by what he saw and by Hamburg's ability to combine theory and practice (and undoubtedly to absorb most of the costs), all signs pointed to an agreement and a planned opening of the new institute. Due to Dernburg's inspection tour of German East Africa in July 1907, however, final approval of the plan was delayed until January 21, 1908.[41] In the meantime the details of the agreement, the organization of the Colonial Institute, and the content of its curriculum were worked out between Thilenius and Schnee.[42]

The final form of the Kolonialistitut followed Thilenius's proposal quite closely: the Kolonialinstitut was jointly controlled by the Hamburg Senate and Imperial Colonial Office via a new Senate Commission (Senatskommission) headed by von Melle and governed by a Council of Professors (Professorenrat). A Business Advisory Committee (Kauffmännischer Beirat) of three representatives of trade and commerce appointed by Hamburg's Chamber of Commerce was also created to assure that the institution retained its connections with the business world. In addition to the teaching staff and facilities funded or provided by the state of Hamburg, the Colonial Office financed and staffed a Central Office of the Colonial Institute (Zentralstelle des Kolonialinstituts) charged with collecting, archiving, and disseminating comprehensive information on all aspects of colonization. The agreement worked out between the Hamburg Senate and the Colonial Office foresaw that at least twenty colonial officials would be sent to the Kolonialinstitut annually to complete the two-semester course of study before being sent to colonial postings, with the Reich paying a 250 mark lecturing fee per student to the Kolonialinstitut each semester.[43] A subsequent agreement between the Senate and Alfred Tirpitz foresaw a similar fee arrangement for the training of officials of the

---

[40] Ruppenthal, *Kolonialismus*, 120–21.   [41] Ibid., 212–23.
[42] Ibid., 127, 129. See also StaHH, 364-6 Hamburgisches Kolonialinstitut, Nr. 2 Beiakte zur Akte betreffend Errichtung eines Kolonialinstituts in Hamburg, transcription of Prof. Dr. Goerg Thilenius, Museum für Völkerkunde, to Senator von Melle, Hamburg, Nov. 21, 1907; transcription of Geh. Rat Heinrich Schnee, Reichs-Kolonialamt, to Prof. Georg Thilenius, Berlin, Dec. 31, 1907.
[43] StaHH, 364-6 Hamburgisches Kolonialinstitut, Nr. 2 Beiakte zur Akte betreffend Errichtung eines Kolonialinstituts in Hamburg, Antrag betreffend Errichtung eines Kolonialinstituts in Hamburg im Anschluß an die Wissenschaftlichen Anstalten und das Vorlesungswesen, Mitteilung des Senats an die Bürgerschaft, Nr. 70, March 25, 1908, 139–44.

Imperial Navy Office involved in the administration of Kiaochow and the appointment of a Navy Office commissioner to the Senate commission.[44]

The announcement of the founding of the Kolonialinstitut in the spring and then its opening later in 1908 were reported in the German and international press assuring that the project gained a wider public profile.[45] As already suggested, that was undoubtedly very important to Dernburg in cementing the public impression that German colonization was now on a firmer footing and a new systematic, "scientific" path. Soon after the Kolonialinstitut opened its doors to students on October 15, 1908, it held a festive opening ceremony on October 20, 1908, which Dernburg attended and at which he, von Melle, Thilenius, and Vice-Admiral Alfred Breusing (1853–1914, representing Tirpitz) gave short opening remarks and Karl Rathgen gave the festive address.[46] Undoubtedly, the selection of Rathgen to give this speech underscored both his importance as a known quantity on *Weltwirtschaft* and the centrality of his new professorship of *Nationalökonomie* and *Kolonialpolitik* (political economy and colonial policy) to the enterprise.

After congratulating those assembled on the successful founding of the institute in the name of the Reich and his office, Dernburg focused his remarks on the hopes that he had for the institute in breaking down the rigid German social and occupational hierarchies between civil servants, businessmen, planters, and farmers that he hoped would ultimately be transferred to the colonies.[47] Such rigid status hierarchies, he observed, had in the past led to the emigration of many Germans. It was Dernburg's hope that by creating a less rank-stratified society in the colonies, talented and successful German emigrants might be lured to the German colonies and thus be regained for

---

[44] StaHH, 364-6 Hamburgisches Kolonialinstitut, Nr. 11 Vermehrung der Hörerzahl. Allgem., Ausbildung von Offizieren und Beamten der Marine, transcription of a letter by Alfred v. Tirpitz, Staatssekretär des Reichs-Marine-Amtes, to the Senatskommission für die reichs- und auswärtigen Angelegenheiten, Berlin, Aug. 9, 1908; StaHH, 364-6 Hamburgisches Kolonialinstitut, Nr. 11 Vermehrung der Hörerzahl. Allgem., Ausbildung von Offizieren und Beamten der Marine, Alfred v. Tirpitz, Staatssekretär des Reichs-Marine-Amts to Senatskommissar des Hamburgischen Kolonialinstituts Werner von Melle, Berlin, Oct. 9, 1908.

[45] "German Colonial Institute," *The Times,* Apr. 21, 1908; "Vorbereitungen auf den Kolonialdienst," *Hochschul-Nachrichten*, XVIII, no. 213 (July 1908): 289; "Das Reichs-Kolonial-Institut," *Neue Hamburger Zeitung*, Morgen-Ausgabe, Oct. 16, 1908; "Vom Hamburger Kolonialinstitut," *Münchner neueste Nachrichten,* Feb. 24, 1909. See StaHH, 364-6 Hamburgisches Kolonialinstitut, Nr. 222 Pressestimmen und sonstige Äusserungen über das Institut.

[46] Karl Rathgen, *Beamtentum und Kolonialunterricht: Rede, gehalten bei der Eröffnungsfeier des Hamburgischen Kolonialinstituts am 20. Oktober 1908, nebst den weiteren bei der Eröffnungsfeier des Kolonialinstituts gehaltenen Ansprachen* (Hamburg: Leopold Voss, 1908), 7–33.

[47] Ibid., 20–25.

Germany as valuable "*Lehrmeister kolonialer Dinge*" (master teachers in colonial matters).[48] While this reflected Dernburg's past experiences in North America and parallels similar observations made by Sering some twenty-five years earlier (discussed in Chapter 1), it was also undoubtedly shaped by his recent inspection tour of German Southwest Africa, which had also taken him to British South Africa and which, as he hinted strongly in his speech, compared very favorably with the neighboring German colony in that respect.[49] Unquestionably, this was as a liberal critique of the problem of *Kolonial-Assessorismus*, but it was also remarkable how the dream of recovering German settlers who had emigrated from the Reich for the German colonial enterprise continued to figure in the German colonial imagination, even in a man as sober and realistic as Dernburg.

Rathgen's address began by making the point that his comparative analysis of the higher education of colonial officials in Holland, Belgium, France, and England had not led to the discovery of any one viable model for the Hamburg Kolonialinstitut. It also suggested that Germany was not as far behind in this matter as was widely feared.[50] What was clear, he noted, was that in the age of *Weltpolitik* it was no longer possible to leave the governance of colonies to concession companies and poorly prepared, amateur administrators selected by patronage. What was needed now was a professional colonial civil service that could serve as a mediator between the natives and German settlers, planters, and investors whose preparation was grounded in a systematic research of colonial policy problem areas.[51] That is to say, in order to develop a modern *Kolonialunterricht* (colonial education) for this new breed of officials one had to engage in *Kolonialwissenschaft* (colonial science). The realization was dawning, he noted, that a merely practical training for colonial officials would not do; it had to be combined with a formal theoretical education. Maintaining a link between teaching and scholarship was thus indispensable. That had been concluded in France and many of other leading colonial powers, he argued.[52] Initially it was believed that this education would be best imparted directly in an academy situated in the colonies, but experience in British India, Dutch Java, and French Cochinchina had shown that it was unwise to remove impressionable young men from metropolitan intellectual and moral influences and expose them prematurely to an "aboriginal milieu and the prejudices of the white population of the colony."[53]

---

[48] Ibid., 25.
[49] Ibid. See also Ulrike Lindner, *Koloniale Begegnungen: Deutschland und Großbritannien als Imperialmächte in Afrika 1880–1914* (Frankfurt and New York: Campus, 2011), 139–51.
[50] Rathgen, *Beamtentum und Kolonialunterricht*, 38–41.   [51] Ibid., 41–50.
[52] Ibid., 50–52.   [53] Ibid., 52–53.

Rathgen next discussed the education and system of exams of men preparing for the British Indian and Egyptian civil service, which while having shortcomings, he nevertheless saw as a model of sorts, particularly the one-year special subject course that had been developed for those entering the service in Egypt and Sudan, which bore some resemblance to what was being started in Hamburg.[54] Other valuable inspirations came from the Higher Administrative Academy in The Hague, where an elite corps of experienced colonial administrators was being selected to pursue scholarship and give lectures on comparative colonial policy, finances, statistics, and law.[55] Rathgen believed that the tradition of German university scholarship and professional officialdom would work in similar ways in the Kolonialinstitut to unify the necessary scientific training and practical instruction. The aim was not to train colonial technicians; rather, it was to create a uniform colonial officialdom that combined the esprit de corps of the Anglo-Indian Civil Service, the firm loyalty to the state and duty to defend the general interest of German officialdom, and the scientific *Bildung* imparted by German university traditions linking teaching with scholarship.[56] "In institutions of higher learning," Rathgen concluded, "there was no real conflict between scientific and practical instruction. ... And that is why our institute must not simply become a training seminar for some practical expertise."[57]

As is clear from Rathgen's speech, the intellectual links between his vision for *Kolonialwissenschaft* and the older *Staatswissenschaften* remained strong, particularly in its cameralist administrative dimension. The affinities to the "practical imagination" that David Lindenfeld has analyzed within German *Staatswissenschaften* should be noted. Indeed, these ideas for a reformed colonial administrative education showed a striking similarity to a conception of bureaucratic reform that had grown out of German humanism and enlightened absolutism: as administration in the general interest implemented by a competent and impartial bureaucracy, combining formal training in a range of relevant subjects and technologies with deep practical knowledge of their implementation.[58] It may be questioned whether what Rathgen sketched out was wholly in accord with the more practical and immediate aims that Dernburg had for the German colonies or what the businessmen and merchants in Hamburg's Assembly expected from the Kolonialinstitut. In any case, Rathgen's ideas were in broad agreement with von Melle's ultimate goal of founding a university.

The curriculum offered by the Kolonialinstitut for the one-year course of study covered the fields of law, *Staatswissenschaften*, languages, history,

---

[54] Ibid., 54–67.   [55] Ibid., 73.
[56] Ibid., 83–85. Cf. Kolonialpolitisches Aktionskomité, ed., *Schmoller, Dernburg*, 33–34.
[57] Rathgen, *Beamtentum und Kolonialunterricht*, 85.
[58] Lindenfeld, *The Practical Imagination*, 3–4, 11–88.

ethnology, geography, medicine, and the natural sciences from a distinctly colonial perspective. It also included many excursions and exercises to link theory with practice and impart practical skills and knowledge. For example, in the winter semester of 1908–9 (October 15, 1908–March 15, 1909) Rathgen offered courses on "Colonial Policy with Exercises," "The History of Modern Colonial Policy," and "The Colonies in the World Economy including Trade Policy." The course on the colonies in the world economy included guided Saturday excursions every fortnight to view warehouses, processing centers, and industrial sites in and around Hamburg.[59] In the summer semester 1909 (April 15–August 1909) Rathgen offered "Colonial Policy with Exercises" and "The Tasks of Colonial Economic Policy" with the same series of fortnightly excursions offered for the latter.[60] The other subjects offered that first academic year reflected this colonial and practical orientation and included in the field of languages conversational Chinese and Swahili. In law, classes included "Colonial Law," "Native Law," and "Case Law and Administration in German East Africa." In ethnography and geography, "Geography of the German Colonies" and "The Natives of German Colonies" were offered as well as "General Colonial History to 1815" in history. In botany, classes included "Useful Plants of the Colonies, their Cultivation, their Products, and Pests" and "Practical Exercises Identifying and Investigating Plant Products of Trade" and in zoology "The Animal World of our Colonies," "Domestic Animals of the Tropics including Animal Breeding," and "Evaluation and Exploitation of Coastal and Inland Fisheries."[61]

Rathgen's Seminar für Nationalökonomie und Kolonialpolitik (Seminar for Political Economy and Colonial Policy) was the most generously funded of those created in Hamburg to allow for the acquisition of a comprehensive library that included not only standard titles in political economy but specialized literature on the subjects of trade and colonial policy to enable its use for active research.[62] Rathgen was in turn a very energetic scholar who participated in many conferences and gave numerous public lectures beyond Hamburg that were to give the Kolonialinstitut and the new *Kolonialpolitik* a national and international profile. For example, in 1909 he participated in the meetings of the German Colonial Society in Berlin and Dresden, the German Agricultural Society in Berlin, and the congress of the Institut

---

[59] StaHH, 364-6 Hamburgisches Kolonialinstitut, Nr. 28 die Sitzungsberichte des Professorenrats, fols. 8–11, Verzeichnis der Vorlesungen vom 15. Oktober 1908 bis 15. März 1909.
[60] StaHH, 364-6 Hamburgisches Kolonialinstitut, Nr. 28 die Sitzungsberichte des Professorenrats, fols. 10–11, Verzeichnis der Vorlesungen vom 15. April bis 15. August 1909.
[61] Ibid.; StaHH, 364-6 Hamburgisches Kolonialinstitut, Nr. 28 die Sitzungsberichte des Professorenrats, fols. 8–11, Verzeichnis der Vorlesungen vom 15. Oktober 1908 bis 15. März 1909.
[62] Ruppenthal, *Kolonialismus*, 225.

Colonial International in The Hague. That year he also gave a paper at the École de Commerce Solvay in Brussels on African colonial indigenous policy.[63] In 1910 he gave lectures on the political and economic development of Japan to colonial officials in The Hague and was active with his Hamburg colleagues in organizing and participating in the third German Colonial Congress in Berlin.[64]

There can be no doubt that the academic field of *Kolonialpoliitk* made significant strides in Germany by 1910, and not only in the Hamburg Kolonialinstitut. There was already a marked uptick in lecturing on colonial policy in many German universities and business schools by 1909.[65] As exemplified by Rathgen and many of the other economists covered in the preceding chapters, German knowledge of colonial development policy worldwide was notable for both its depth and breadth, based as it was on careful and – more often than not – direct observation of economic development efforts in British and French Africa, the Dutch East Indies, East Asia, Latin America, the Caribbean, and the United States. As was already discussed in Chapter 1, cotton cultivation in the American South especially came to be seen as an important example of productive colonial agriculture with valuable lessons for enhancing the productivity of colonial natives and thus better economic exploitation of the German colonies.[66] There were few people who knew or had written more about that topic in Europe than Ernst von Halle, even if he had no formal association with the Kolonialinstitut or the Colonial Office.

One indicator of the establishment of *Kolonialpolitik* as a new sub-discipline within the German *Staatswissenschaften* around this time was the inclusion of a massive and exhaustive new entry entitled "Colonies and Colonial Policy" in the third, completely revised edition of Johannes Conrad's authoritative

---

[63] Ibid., "Die Neger und die Kultur," *Hamburgerischer Correspondent*, Mar. 16, 1909; "Die Neger und die europäische Kultur," *Fremdenblatt*, Dec. 9, 1908 in StaHH, 361-6 Hochschulwesen – Dozenten- und Personalakten, I 330, Personalakte Prof. Dr. Rathgen, Zeitungsausschnitte zur Personal Akte betreffend Professor Dr. Rathgen.

[64] Ruppenthal, *Kolonialismus*, 225; "Belgiens Bodenpolitik in Kongo," *Vossische Zeitung*, July 30, 1912 in StaHH, 361-6 Hochschulwesen – Dozenten- und Personalakten, I 330, Personalakte Prof. Dr. Rathgen, Zeitungsausschnitte zur Personal Akte betreffend Professor Dr. Rathgen.

[65] Lindenfeld, *The Practical Imagination*, 288, Fig. 13; 292–93.

[66] See Beckert, *Empire of Cotton*, 362–78; Zimmerman, *Alabama in Africa*, 112–72. Cf. Helen Tilley, *Africa as a Living Laboratory: Empire, Development, and the Problem of Scientific Knowledge, 1870-1950* (Chicago and London: The University of Chicago Press, 2011); Dirk van Laak, "Kolonien als 'Laboratorien der Moderne'?" in Conrad and Osterhammel, *Das Kaiserreich transnational*, 257–79; Andrew Zimmerman, "Ruling Africa: Science as Sovereignty in the German Colonial Empire and Its Aftermath," in *German Colonialism in a Global Age*, ed. Naranch and Eley, 93–108.

*Handwörterbuch der Staatswissenschaften*, published in 1910.[67] This entry was written by none other than Gottfried Zoepfl, who was mentioned in the previous chapter as a co-founder of the Kolonialpolitische Aktionskomité.[68] Covering an extraordinary 117 pages of dense text, Zoepfl's entry dealt extensively with colonial policy as a new field within the *Staatswissenschaften*, the nature of colonies, and their historical origins, purposes, and value.[69] Colonial policy itself was unpacked in all of its dimensions – colonial administration, law, politics, corporations, money, finance, communications, trade, and commerce – and each were dealt with in great detail, informed by the past and more recent colonial history of all the European and American colonies worldwide and the perusal of a vast literature in German, Dutch, English, French, and Spanish.[70]

Despite the extraordinary scholarly energy invested during the Dernburg era to keep the German colonies on the political agenda, these efforts were nevertheless always up against a widespread and persistent colonial fatigue (*Kolonialmüdigkeit*) among the German public in these years. Indeed, one cannot help but suspect that the intense scholarly effort directed toward demarcating the new sub-discipline of colonial policy was itself symptomatic of the fact that Germany's colonies had largely disappointed and that *Weltpolitik* had delivered little on the colonial front by the time Dernburg left the Colonial Office in 1910: the only new colonial territory added since 1897 amounted to a small leasehold on the Shantung Peninsula, part of Samoa, and a smattering of tiny islands and atolls in the South Pacific. During his time as colonial secretary, Dernburg did attempt to interest both Bülow and Bethmann Hollweg in acquiring the copper-rich Katanga region of the southern Belgian Congo and a presence somewhere along the Congo River through negotiations with the British, but both initiatives went nowhere, and the latter would influence Foreign Secretary Kiderlen-Waechter's later cack-handed bid to gain the French Congo in the Agadir Crisis in 1911, which will be discussed later in this chapter.[71]

With that in mind, it is perhaps unsurprising that the Kolonialinstitut was actually too large for the relatively modest demand for its courses given Germany's relatively small colonial footprint. In any given semester, most of the matriculated student body was comprised of a modest number of colonial and naval officials (some twenty-two students on average between 1908 and 1914), and the demand for the two-semester course from colonial planters, merchants, and businessmen fell well below expectations.[72] This was a problem exacerbated by the fact that the two-semester course was not accepted for

---

[67] G. Zoepfl, "Kolonien und Kolonialpolitik," *HdS*, 3rd rev. ed., vol. 5, ed. J. Conrad, L. Elster, W. Lexis, and Edg. Loening (Jena: Gustav Fischer, 1910), 921–1038.
[68] Ibid., 1038  [69] Ibid., 921–71.  [70] Ibid., 971–1038.
[71] Schiefel, *Bernhard Dernburg*, 119–27.  [72] Ruppenthal, *Kolonialismus*, 222.

credit toward degrees in any German universities. Rivalries with other institutions with overlapping curricula that competed to train German officials, such as the Berlin Seminar for Oriental Languages, did not help matters.[73] Once again, ambitions far outstripped reality, a now recurring theme in German *Weltpolitik*.

As it turned out, over time the Colonial and Navy Offices developed a rather passive, arms-length relationship with the Kolonialinstitut. It was only infrequently consulted by these offices for its expertise on colonial matters, and the available evidence suggests that the Kolonialinstitut played little if any direct role in shaping German colonial policy after 1908 or that anything like a consensus emerged within the colonial administration over what "scientific" colonial policy entailed before 1914. Some colonial governments were hostile to their officials developing direct contacts with the Kolonialinstitut for fear of internal policy rifts; others were skeptical about the value of the formal training imparted by the Kolonialinstitut versus the practical, local knowledge that they believed could only be imparted by direct on-the-ground experience.[74] All of that said, Dernburg did succeed in improving the formal status and pay of colonial officials and regularizing their career tracks through Reichstag legislation right before his resignation in 1910.[75] What role the Kolonialinstitut might have played in this is unclear.

### Tropical Fever – Hermann Schumacher in Southeast Asia

As colonial fatigue set in and as it became clear that an overseas temperate-zone settler colony was probably off the table for Germany, anxiety about the viability of European settlement in the tropics grew. This was exacerbated by a sharp decline in tropical commodity prices beginning in 1910. In May 1910 the steering committee of Association for Social Policy took up the tropical colonies by launching a large coordinated survey spearheaded by Max Sering that would be published in multiple volumes as "The Settlement of Europeans in the Tropics" in 1912–15.[76] The purpose of the survey was to study "the economic activity and the social life of the whites in the tropical regions ... with special consideration of the question whether continuous settlement had taken place and generations had survived." Further, "the facts, conditions, and successes of European colonization and work in the hot zones

---

[73] Ibid., 173–86, 196–200, 217–24.   [74] Ibid., 151–53, 186–96.
[75] Smith, *Colonial Empire*, 196.
[76] Boese, *Geschichte des Vereins für Sozialpolitik*, 139; Friedrich von Lindequist, *Deutsch-Ostafrika als Siedlungsgebiet für Europäer unter Berücksichtigung Britisch-Ostafrikas und Nyassalands*, in *Die Ansiedlung von Europäern in den Tropen*, ed. Ständiger Ausschuss des Vereins für Socialpoltiik, SdVfS, vol. 147, Erster Teil [part 1] (Leipzig and Munich: Duncker & Humblot, 1912), v.

should be scientifically investigated."[77] Sering was charged with finding experts to cover the German colonies in tropical Africa, the southern states of the United States, and Mexico. Karl Rathgen himself was charged with finding people to cover the west coast of tropical Africa, the East Indies, and Central America, while one of their colleagues and fellow *Aktionskomité* member, Gustav Anton of Jena University, led the survey of the Dutch East Indies.[78] Further studies were commissioned for South America from Gottfried Zoepfl in Berlin and for Uganda and northeastern Africa from Christian Eckert (1874–1952) of the Handelshochschule Cologne, the latter a specialist on shipping who had like Zoepfl been an active member of the *Aktionskomité* in 1906–7.[79]

As was the practice in all of the association's investigations, an elaborate survey questionnaire was developed. It included questions on the health conditions of the white population, requesting statistics on births, deaths, illnesses, the prevalence of infectious diseases, doctors' memoranda on the influence of climate, the impact of work, the differences of the races, the scope for improving the white population, and the origins and class composition of the colonists.[80] Clearly the study was preoccupied with what was then called "the acclimatization question": whether Europeans could survive over multiple generations in the tropics without the feared degenerative effects of the climate and without mixing with the native populations, a question shaped by clear racial biases and eugenic preoccupations current at the time.[81]

While he was not part of this survey, Hermann Schumacher had a unique opportunity to inspect tropical colonies in Southeast Asia in the winter and spring of 1911, a region that on account of its tin, oil, and rubber production had emerged as one of the most important in the world by that point. Schumacher had been asked in October 1910 by his former Bonn tutee, Crown Prince Wilhelm, to accompany him and the princess on a tour of South and East Asia as an expert guide, an idea that appealed to Schumacher given that he had only had limited opportunities to travel into the Chinese interior back in 1897 and was eager to get to know Kiaochow. He also looked forward to

---

[77] von Lindequist, *Deutsch-Ostafrika als Siedlungsgebiet*, v.
[78] GStA PK, VI. HA Nl. Schmoller, Nr. 13 II, fol. 105, Verzeichnis der ausserhalb Berlins wohnenden Mitglieder des K.-P-A.K, n.d.
[79] Ibid., fol. 107; von Lindequist, *Deutsch-Ostafrika als Siedlungsgebiet*, v; Christian Eckert, *Die Seeinteressen Rheinland-Westfalens* (Leipzig: Teubner, 1906).
[80] von Lindequist, *Deutsch-Ostafrika als Siedlungsgebiet*, vi–vii.
[81] Pascal Grosse, *Kolonialismus, Eugenik und bürgerliche Gesellschaft in Deutschland 1850–1918* (Frankfurt and New York: Campus Verlag, 2000); Grosse, "Turning Native? Anthropology, German Colonialism, and the Paradoxes of the 'Acclimatization Question,' 1885–1914," in Penny and Bunzl, *Worldly Provincialism*, 179–97.

traveling back to Europe from Peking via the Trans-Siberian Railway, undoubtedly shaped by his own budding interest in Russia since returning from the United States in 1907.[82] As Schumacher was not equipped for such a journey and could not free himself from his teaching duties until the Christmas break, it was agreed that he would join the Crown Prince in Singapore after the new year, where the journey would continue on to China and Japan aboard the armored cruiser SMS *Gneisenau*, which was part of the German East Asian Squadron.[83]

In late January 1911 Schumacher began his journey by rail to Genoa, and from there he boarded the NDL steamer *Prinzess Alice* for passage to Singapore via Port Said, Suez, Aden, and Colombo.[84] On February 4th in Aden he received disappointing news from Foreign Secretary Kiderlen-Waechter: "Crown Prince returning home this month probably via Bombay."[85] The reason for this sudden turn of events throwing the entire journey into doubt – as he would later discover in Singapore – was an outbreak of *Lungenpest* (pneumonic plague) in northern China.[86] Schumacher was now faced with the dilemma of either continuing on to Singapore or returning to Europe. He decided to "make the best of it" and continue but to decide there whether the journey would continue on to China and Japan or whether he would instead investigate British Malaya and the Dutch East Indies.[87] He was particularly intrigued by Singapore's Malayan hinterlands, where Chinese settlers could be studied in the colonial soil of Southeast Asia. Thus, when the *Gneisenau* arrived in Singapore the decision not to continue on to China and Japan was easier. He would investigate Malaya and the East Indies instead.[88]

Arriving in Singapore, Schumacher was concerned about the tropical diseases he might encounter on his new itinerary but was told that he had nothing to fear from malaria as long as he took quinine. He began his investigation of British Malaya from Singapore along the coast accompanied with the head of a plantation in German East Africa who was there to investigate rubber tree plantings, passing through mangrove forests and visiting many new hevea rubber plantations. Hevea was a crop recently

---

[82] GNN HA, Nl. Schumacher, I, B-22, Hofmarschall Graf Bismarck-Bohlen, Hofmarschall-Amt seiner Kaiserlichen u. Königlichen Hoheit des Kronprinzen des Deutschen Reiches und von Preußen, to Hermann Schumacher, Potsdam, Nov. 1, 1910; GNN HA, Nl. Schumacher, I, B-6qu, fols. 486–87, 513.
[83] GNN HA, Nl. Schumacher, I, B-6qu, fol. 487. GNN HA, Nl. Schumacher, I, B-22, Chef des Marine-Kabinets Müller to Hermann Schumacher, Berlin, Jan. 16, 1911.
[84] GNN HA, Nl. Schumacher, I, B-6qu, fol. 488.
[85] Ibid., fol. 491; GNN HA Nl. Schumacher, I, B-22, Telegram from Kiderlen-Waechter to Hermann Schumacher, Aden, Feb. 4, 1911.
[86] GNN HA, Nl. Schumacher, I, B-6qu, fol. 514.    [87] Ibid., fols. 491–92.
[88] Ibid., fols. 513–14.

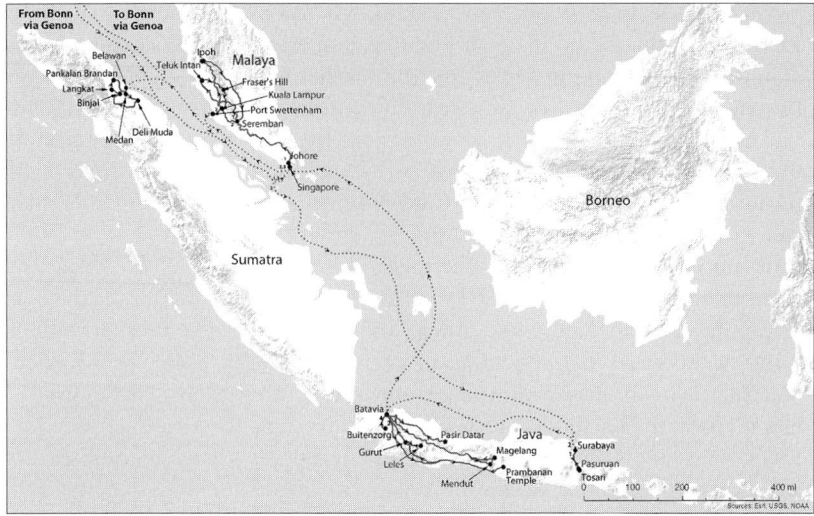

Map 9.1 Hermann Schumacher's journey to Malaya, Java, and Sumatra, Jan.-ca. May 1911.

introduced from Brazil, and its promise as a high-yielding latex plant had led to a boom fueled by speculative investment from London, but expertise about its cultivation in Malaya was still lacking.[89] This rubber boom had been driven by high demand from the American automobile and tire industries, which had raised rubber prices significantly. Among the larger plantations Schumacher visited was one in Perhentian Tinggi (Seremban, Negeri Sembilan). There was much infestation with mosquitos in this region – undoubtedly due to the forest clearings to make way for hevea plantings – and as Schumacher would later discover to his chagrin, malaria.[90]

While in Malaya, Schumacher also traveled to the tin mines of the Kinta Valley and surrounding mountains, in which many Chinese coolies also labored.[91] Malaya was the source of no less than half the world's tin at the time, and speculation on the London tin exchange with its accompanying attempts to corner the market had led to wild price swings that had caused much disruption in Malayan mining. He also noted that the colony had abolished export duties on all tin going to Great Britain in 1904 in an attempt to prevent Standard Oil from shipping the bulk of Malaya's tin to the United States as a cheap return freight in their petroleum ships – the United States had by that point emerged as the world's largest consumer of tin driven by its rapidly-expanding automobile and canned goods industries. This also

---

[89] Ibid., fols. 514–15; GNN HA, Nl. Schumacher, I, B-6r, fols. 516–17.
[90] GNN HA, Nl. Schumacher, I, B-6r, fols. 518–19.    [91] Ibid., fols. 520–22, 527.

protected the English smelters operating in the colony.[92] Schumacher traveled well beyond the Kinta Valley on foot into the jungles of the surrounding mountains and to Fraser's Hill in the borderlands between Selangor and Pahang states in Malaya. His overall impression of tin mining and smelting in Malaya was of pronounced environmental devastation, remarkable primitivism, lack of adequate investment capital, and a colonial government narrowly pursuing the interests of the British motherland with scant interest in raising local levels of education and technology.[93]

Schumacher proceeded from the tin regions back through the jungle to the Malayan capital Kuala Lampur, which was then a city of some 30,000 people still under construction but boasting a fine network of roads, a good water supply, and lovely parks. Here the size and power of the Chinese population in Malaya became especially apparent to Schumacher.[94] He proceeded to conduct much research into materials on plantation farming and tin mining in both Kuala Lampur and Ipoh. Ipoh itself was the seat of the Straits Trading Company at the very center of the Malayan tin industry. A valuable contact to him was the British resident minister in Seremban, who was remarkably well informed about the Malay people, their history, and their customs. Schumacher was nevertheless unnerved by the preferences given by the colonial administration to the Malays over the Chinese, the latter of which to his mind of much greater significance to the colony's development than the former. Reflecting the then widespread European view of the degenerative effects of tropical climates, Schumacher surmised that the tropical zone did not produce "*Herrenvölker*" (master races), and so as in the case of the Chinese it was necessary to import them from the temperate zone to the north.[95] He was unnerved by the tiny European presence in the colony and was doubtful that they could provide adequate protection from the masses of Chinese and Malays.[96]

Due to the swell of European travelers waylaid in Southeast Asia by the plague epidemic in China, Schumacher was unable to get on a ship to Batavia for the next leg of his investigations but was eventually able to secure passage to Surabaya in eastern Java.[97] Java was remarkable to Schumacher not only for its amazing fertility but also its massive population growth, which had resulted in the partitioning of many farms and much deforestation. The Dutch colonial government had in turn sought to counterweigh these pressures by giving preference to small farmers over large plantations in the production of sugar, tea, and cocoa, and in encouraging emigration to Sumatra. It reminded Schumacher much of Cuba.[98] Surabaya, unlike Singapore, was purely an

---

[92] Ibid., fols. 523–26.   [93] Ibid., fols. 520–21, 527–30.   [94] Ibid., fols. 530–31.
[95] Ibid., fols. 532–33.   [96] Ibid., fols. 533a.
[97] GNN HA, Nl. Schumacher, I, B-6s, fols. 534–35.
[98] Ibid., fols. 536, 538–39. Cf. J. N. F. M. à Campo, *Engines of Empire: Steamshipping and State Formation in Colonial Indonesia* (Hilversum: Uitgeverij Verloren, 2002), 251-64.

export hub, notably of sugar. Dutch sugar cultivation had made many strides due to the work of the Dutch botanist Melchoir Treub (1851–1910), director of the botanical gardens in Buitenzorg (Bogor) in western Java, which had improved the quality of cane cultivation and the scale of the sugar mills while also systematically developing the Asian sales market for Javanese sugar. Yet with the presence of large-scale American capital in Cuba (as he had seen in 1907), it was clear to Schumacher that Java was quickly being displaced as the prime site of global sugar production. During his various visits to warehouses in Surabaya he also heard many complaints from German merchants and planters about their mistreatment by the Dutch and English.[99]

After seeking refuge from Surabaya's heat and humidity in Tosari in the Tengger massif for a few days and ascending to the rim of the impressive Bromo volcano, Schumacher continued his journey from Surabaya by ship to Batavia.[100] He then traveled extensively throughout western and central Java, to Magelang and Prambanan in central Java, and to Gurut, Leles, and Bandung in western Java for a closer inspection of Javanese rubber, tea, and tobacco plantations.[101] The main rubber planter in Java was Dr. Willem Rijk Tromp de Haas (1870–1926), and Java was at the time just introducing the Brazilian hevea plant, superior in yield to the native *ficus* species of Java, though at the time there were concerns – given the devastating fungus *Hemilea vastatrix* that had recently decimated Javanese coffee – that hevea would suffer similar problems, and so its adoption was still hesitant and cautious. Schumacher was also able to visit one of the largest tea plantations and tea processing centers on Java in Pasir Datar courtesy of a German agent of the Straits and Sunda Syndicate, a buyer for the Russian market, whose growing demand for tea was being felt in Java and elsewhere in South and Southeast Asia at the time. The expanding webs of global economic connection entangling this part of the world were unmistakable.[102]

Batavia was a much more distinctly European city in terms of plan and architecture than Surabaya, and here the Europeans lived in segregated colonies. While in western Java Schumacher had occasion to observe the rise of Wahhabism among the Arab and even some of the Javanese inhabitants, fed by hajis who had been to Mecca and who had themselves been behind the recent jihad against the Dutch in Sumatra.[103] Of greater concern to the Dutch colonial administration at the time, however, were the Japanese, Schumacher noted. While the Japanese themselves were rare in Java, they were at the time

---

[99] GNN HA, Nl. Schumacher, I, B-6s, fols. 543–44.  [100] Ibid., fols. 546–48, 549–53.
[101] Ibid., fols. 556–64;
[102] Ibid., fols. 565–67; Hermann Schumacher, *Der Reis in der Weltwirtschaft* (Munich and Leipzig: Duncker & Humblot, 1917), iii. On the Sunda Syndicate, à Campo, *Engines of Empire*, 252.
[103] GNN HA, Nl. Schumacher, I, B-6s, fols. 571–73.

awakening in the Javanese an almost vanished national identity: Japanese newsreels and films depicted Japan's victories over the European invaders, while gramophone recordings of Japanese songs were heard celebrating the Japanese age of chivalry. In these developments Schumacher thought he saw an inkling of the mobilization of Asia by the Japanese against European colonizers.[104]

The biggest danger to the Dutch East Indies that Schumacher saw was neither Wahhabism nor the Japanese but rather the indolence and libertinism that had become customary among the Dutch in the colony, which was bound up – as he saw it – with the long practice of intermarriage between the Dutch and natives. That had resulted in the "business of mixed-breeds" (*Mischlingswirtschaft*), that is, the adaptation of the Europeans and their mixed-race progeny to the local lifestyle and work habits of Java, which Schumacher wrote "represented the greatest imaginable contrast to the 'strenuous life.'"[105] Tropical colonialism, it dawned on Schumacher, had not been without negative longer-term consequences for the Dutch motherland, and he now saw a silver lining in the fact that Germany had not possessed such colonies in earlier times and had thus far avoided the apparent degeneracy that it had brought to the Dutch.[106] A number of discussions that Schumacher had with Dutch colonial officials in Batavia revealed that the younger generation of Dutch officials were aware of these dangers and were bringing "a modern spirit and vigor" to the colony.[107]

From Batavia Schumacher took passage on a ship back to Singapore, and from Singapore, on to Sumatra to complete his investigations in the Dutch East Indies. In Sumatra, where the Dutch had only gained sovereignty in 1871, wars with the Sultan of Aceh had been waged over control of the island in 1873–1903, and thus colonization had taken place much later and large plantations predominated.[108] Here Schumacher noted the presence of a significant number of German planters, often ex-officers, who had left Germany to seek their fortunes and who, to his mind, stood in stark contrast to what he saw as the "softened mixed-breed type" that he had observed in Java.[109] His investigations on Sumatra took him through the Sultanates of Deli (Medan) and Langkat and on to Binjai, where he visited a German-owned tobacco plantation and was given a tour by the German director. He was promptly told

---

[104] Ibid., fols. 574–75. Cf. Paul A. Rodell, "Inspiration for Nationalist Aspirations? Southeast Asia and the 1905 Japanese Victory," in Steinberg, *Russo-Japanese War*, vol. 1, 629–54, esp. 633–36. See also Steven G. Marks, "'Bravo, Brave Tiger of the East!': The Russo-Japanese War and the Rise of Nationalism in British Egypt and India," in Steinberg, *Russo-Japanese War*, vol. 1, 609–27.

[105] GNN HA, Nl. Schumacher, I, B-6s, fol. 575.

[106] Ibid., fols. 575–76. The last part of this paraphrased passage was crossed out in the manuscript.

[107] Ibid., fol. 576.    [108] GNN HA, Nl. Schumacher, I, B-6t, fol. 580.    [109] Ibid., fol. 584.

that the plantation was prohibited from employing any additional Germans by the Dutch colonial authorities and that he would himself be leaving in two years. Such visits reinforced Schumacher's impression that the Dutch and English were colluding against the German presence in Southeast Asia and that what Germans had built through successful efforts in places like Sumatra would ultimately be lost.[110]

There was another problem facing such tobacco plantations on Sumatra, and that was that they primarily grew leaves for cigar wrappings, an industry that was then under threat by the massive growth of cigarette consumption driven by large-scale American tobacco cultivation and the mechanization of cigarette production in the hands of American firms. That explained the transition from tobacco to rubber plantings in many parts of Southeast Asia that Schumacher witnessed.[111] The Belgians and English were particularly active in Sumatra investing in these new rubber crops on land that had once been under tobacco, one of which Schumacher was able to inspect at Deli Muda near Medan.[112] Of even greater interest at the time was the development of Sumatran oil, notably in the oil fields of Pankalan Brandan in western Langkat in northern Sumatra and Palembang in southern Sumatra, for which the Royal Dutch Petroleum Company had been founded in 1890, and had fused with the English Shell Transport and Trading Company in 1907. During his time in Sumatra Schumacher was able to tour the Royal Dutch oil fields and refinery at Pankalan Brandan and speak with its management. Oil had grown to such significance that it had become the most valuable export commodity of the Dutch East Indies, even managing to drive Standard Oil out of much of the East Asian oil market reaching all the way to Japan.[113]

Schumacher's view of the viability of European tropical colonization during his journey was much shaped by his visit to the tropical clinic of the Senembah Company, a tobacco plantation in north Sumatra and the conversations he had there with its Dutch-German doctor, the malaria expert Wilhelm Schüffner (1867–1949), who had had some success in improving the health of the company's plantation workers.[114] This visit impressed upon Schumacher the importance of prophylactic and hygienic measures against tropical diseases such as dysentery, worm infestations, and malaria and how the rapid development of tropical medicine and improvements in housing and clothing might allow the adaptation of Europeans to life in the tropics.[115] Yet even these advances left Schumacher doubtful that Europeans would be able preserve their willpower, intellectual energy, and education in the tropics, or that their children would grow to physical and intellectual health in that climate and thus that Europeans would ever be able to settle permanently in the tropics

---

[110] Ibid., fols. 589–90.   [111] Ibid., fol. 591.   [112] Ibid.   [113] Ibid., fols. 592–93.
[114] Ibid., fols. 595–96.   [115] Ibid., fols. 596–98.

without degeneration. He was nevertheless hopeful that rapid improvements in transportation between Europe and the tropics might alleviate the extremes of exploitation that were still all too common in these colonies.[116]

Schumacher's return to Germany from Sumatra that spring went via Singapore, where he spent several days awaiting passage to Genoa and was able to thank many people who had assisted his investigations in Malaya, Java, and Sumatra. One evening in the English club he met the editor of the *Straits Times*, the leading English paper in Southeast Asia, engaging in a long conversation on Anglo-German economic competition that resulted in striking agreement between the two that most points of difference were resolvable. To Schumacher's astonishment, one day before his departure to Genoa the *Straits Times* published a lead article that reported almost exactly the opposite of what the editor had told him in conversation. That morning Schumacher went directly to the editor's office for an explanation and was immediately greeted by him with the words "I had already thought that you would come and feel obliged to give you the following explanation: the article was cabled to me; if I had not soon published it I would no longer be sitting in this room."[117] This stunned Schumacher all the more because earlier the normally sober reporting of the British *North China Daily News* had gone over to a similarly alarmist tone on the Germans, indicating that both papers were no longer reflecting the views prevalent in the colonies but rather opinion in the British metropole.[118]

To Schumacher's mind, German merchants in Southeast Asia either blended in with the English or stood out only for their "petit bourgeois industriousness," posing no menace of any sort. What was more, there was no immigration of Germans to Southeast Asia. As he reflected, Germany was surrounded by neighbors in the heart of the most densely populated continent in the world without a viable formal or informal settler colony elsewhere as a "safety valve" (*Sicherheitsventil*).[119] Britain had the dual advantages of its isolated island geography and abundant settler colonies; France was largely surrounded by coasts and had a nearby settler colonies in North Africa [Algeria and Tunisia]. Was there sufficient appreciation of the special difficulties of Germany's geographic situation in these hostile British attitudes, he asked? These unsettling thoughts deeply troubled Schumacher as he embarked on his homeward journey.[120]

Shortly after leaving port, Schumacher came down with attacks of malarial fever that got steadily worse and then downright deadly over the course of his return passage. Indeed, his condition became so critical that he was given up

---

[116] Ibid., fols. 598–99.  [117] GNN HA, Nl. Schumacher, I, B-6v, fols. 600–601.
[118] Possibly a reference to the *North China Daily News* of May 20, 1911 on German competition of British manufacturers of machinery.
[119] GNN HA, Nl. Schumacher, I, B-6v, fol. 602.  [120] Ibid.

for dead by the ship's doctor and asked to settle his affairs. Somehow he pulled through and gradually regained enough strength by the time he reached Genoa that he was able to complete the rail journey back to Bonn, albeit as a shadow of his former self.[121] That was undoubtedly the *coup de grâce* for the matter of German settlement in the tropics as far as Schumacher was concerned. His experiences in Southeast Asia had clearly also alerted him to the fragile and vulnerable German merchant and planter presence in this important region producing key staples like tea, sugar, and tobacco, the latter two already threatened by American trustification. This was a region whose output of oil, tin, and rubber was of great and growing importance to industry worldwide, but here, too, corners, trusts, and other monopolizing tendencies were to be feared from the British and Dutch.

## Morocco and Espirito Santo

Just a few weeks after Schumacher's return to Germany from Southeast Asia, hopes for gaining a temperate-zone settler colony in Morocco flickered briefly in the German public sparked by the Agadir Crisis in early July 1911.[122] The background was the unilateral violation in the spring of 1911 of a 1909 Franco-German accord on Morocco by a new French government, which among other things ended talks on joint Franco-German management of Moroccan railways and sent French troops to occupy Fez in April 1911 on the pretext of protecting French nationals during a rebellion against Sultan Abdelhafid (1875–1937).[123] Of relevance, too, were the disputed mining concessions that had been acquired from the Moroccan sultan by the German Mannesmann brothers in the Sous region of south-central Morocco following negotiations with the Anglo-French Union des Mines Marocaines in June 1910.[124] After the debacle of the Tangier Crisis and its aftermath, however, the Kaiser himself had no interest at all in Morocco and was eager for it to be put under direct French control, even after the occupation of Fez in late May.

---

[121] Ibid., fols. 604–7.   [122] See Carroll, *Germany and the Great Powers*, 644–49.
[123] See Clark, *The Sleepwalkers*, 194–96; MacMillan, *The War that Ended Peace*, 414–15. Cf. Hammann, *The World Policy of Germany*, 219–21; Helfferich, *Der Weltkrieg*, vol. 1, 77–80.
[124] Hartmut Pogge von Strandmann, "Rathenau, die Gebrüder Mannesmann und die Vorgeschichte der Zweiten Marokkokrise," in *Deutschland in der Weltpolitik des 19. und 20. Jahrhunderts*, ed. Imanuel Geiss and Berndt Jürgen Wendt, Festschrift für Fritz Fischer zum 65. Geburtstag (Düsseldorf: Bertelsmann Universitätsverlag, 1973), 251–70; Pogge von Strandmann, ed., *Walther Rathenau*, 94–95.

He also opposed lodging any German protests and advised Foreign Secretary Kiderlen-Waechter accordingly.[125]

The brash Swabian foreign secretary had other ideas and had meanwhile gained the support of the head of the Pan-German League, Heinrich Claß (1868–1953), for a pro-Morocco publicity campaign and prepared the ground to lodge formal protest.[126] On May 3, Kiderlen-Waechter advised Paris that a French occupation of Fez would be a violation both of the Algeciras Act and Franco-German Morocco Accord of 1909 and would be met with the dispatch of a warship to Agadir to exact compensation. Later in May and June Finance Minister Joseph Caillaux (1863–1944) and the French ambassador Jules Cambon (1845–1935) assured German diplomats and Kiderlen that France would be willing to offer compensation to Germany with territory from French Equatorial Africa.[127] As the French annexation of Morocco seemed immanent and no offers of compensation had been received by Berlin by the end of June, Kiderlen lodged protest by having the Imperial Navy reroute the obsolete gunboat *Panther* – then on its way home for repairs from a Southwest African station – to the Moroccan harbor Agadir and sending a note to the great powers on July 1 assuring them Germany had no intention of seizing Agadir and explaining its position on the Moroccan question.[128]

While the dispatch of the gunboat was officially justified on grounds of protecting Germans and their commercial interests in southern Morocco, Kiderlen was in fact gambling to exploit Pan-German nationalist opinion awakened by the prospect of a settler colony to make claims in Morocco that he intended to exchange in negotiation for the French Congo. This was part of Kiderlen's gambit for "*Mittelafrika*," as discussed in Chapter 4, the idea of linking German Cameroon and East Africa with the Belgian Congo.[129] It was only in seeking to gain such colonial compensation that Kiderlen ultimately persuaded a skeptical Kaiser to support his initiative, even though Wilhelm had no real interest in additional African colonies – *Weltpolitik*, to his mind, was focused on the Near East and East Asia.[130]

As German nationalist politicians and publicists raised hopes for a "German West Morocco" and Rhenish-Westphalian industrialists eyed Morocco's iron

---

[125] Röhl, *Into the Abyss*, 787.
[126] Ibid., 798; Helfferich, *Der Weltkrieg*, vol. 1, 82–83. Cf. Volker Berghahn, *Germany and the Approach of War in 1914* (New York: St. Martin's Press, 1973), 93–98; Klaus Wernecke, *Der Wille zur Weltgeltung: Außenpolitik und Öffentlichkeit im Kaiserreich am Vorabend des Ersten Weltkriegs* (Düsseldorf: Droste Verlag, 1970), 26–31.
[127] Clark, *The Sleepwalkers*, 207. Cf. Hammann, *The World Policy of Germany*, 221; Helfferich, *Der Weltkrieg*, vol. 1, 80.
[128] Hammann, *The World Policy of Germany*, 221–22; Kelly, *Tirpitz*, 323–24.
[129] See Jarausch, *Enigmatic Chancellor*, 120–24; Smith, *Ideological Origins*, 135–40; Smith, *Colonial Empire*, 212–15. Cf. Fischer, *War of Illusions*, 72, 76–88.
[130] Röhl, *Into the Abyss*, 801, 812–13.

ore deposits, behind the scenes Kidlerlen negotiated with the new French premier Joseph Caillaux via the able French ambassador in Berlin, Jules Cambon, but officials in the French foreign ministry led by the rabidly Germanophobe Maurice Herbette (1871–1929) balked, stoking French nationalist opinion with leaks and press releases and pushing the British to stand by France unconditionally or risk a breach of the Anglo-French Entente. Initially inclined to have France give ground because of its obvious provocations in Morocco, Edward Grey, Herbert Asquith, Arthur Nicolson, and Lloyd George now took up a fiery pro-French position that insisted on Britain's inclusion in any Moroccan settlement, mobilizing the Royal Navy and thereby precipitating a European war scare.[131]

For all the jingoistic press noise and risk of war sparked by "the pounce of the *Panther*" in July, a French protectorate was imposed on Morocco later that year by treaty. In the end Germany gained as compensation not the whole of French Congo but rather "Neu-Kamerun," which appeared to many Germans – not inaccurately – as little more than disease-infested swampland to the east and south of German Cameroon. Despite the fact that more generous territorial compensation was prevented by the stubborn unwillingness of the German Colonial Office and pro-colonial groups to cede other German colonies in exchange, the crisis and the apparent German concessions made under joint Anglo-French pressure revealed Germany's diplomatic impotence to the public as never before and resulted in howls of derision against the government's foreign policy and the Kaiser in the nationalist press and Reichstag. Dernburg's successor as Colonial Secretary, Friedrich von Lindequist (1862–1945), who had himself wanted territory in Dahomey to compliment Togo instead of French Congo, resigned in protest of the terms of the treaty in early November 1911. Once again, to the German nationalist press it appeared that Britain had deliberately undermined a German effort to acquire a settler colony for her teeming millions.[132] In France the treaty was

---

[131] See Charmley, *Splendid Isolation*, 365–67; Clark, *The Sleepwalkers*, 204–11; MacMillan, *The War that Ended Peace*, 419–27. On German public opinion at the height of the crisis, Carroll, *Germany and the Great Powers*, 656–90; Wernecke, *Der Wille zur Weltgeltung*, 75–97. Cf. Hammann, *Germany's World Policy*, 222–24; Helfferich, *Der Weltkrieg*, vol. 1, 83–85.

[132] Canis, *Der Weg in den Abgrund*, 433–34, 444–55; Jarausch, *Enigmatic Chancellor*, 124–26; Fischer, *War of Illusions*, 81–94; cf. Helfferich, *Der Weltkrieg*, vol. 1, 85–86. On the German press reaction, Hammann, *The World Policy of Germany*, 222; Carroll, *Germany and the Great Powers*, 691–99; Wernecke, *Der Wille zur Weltgeltung*, 102–30; Geppert, *Pressekriege*, 284–89. On the Pan-German League's reaction, Fischer, *War of Illusions*, 80–83, 88–94; Chickering, *We Men Who Feel Most German*, 265–66. On conservative criticisms, James Retallack, *The German Right 1860-1920* (Toronto, Buffalo, and London: University of Toronto Press, 2006), 389–93. On the diplomatic repercussions, Clark, *The Sleepwalkers*, 212–14; MacMillan, *The War that Ended Peace*, 429–31.

celebrated as a great victory comparable to the seizure of Algeria in 1830, by far the most important French settler colony by that point. With Morocco it now had its "French India."[133]

With hopes for a German presence in Morocco dashed in 1911, German settler ambitions had to resign themselves once again to tropical colonies. Soon thereafter the first of the studies commissioned by the Association for Social Policy on the settlement of Europeans in the tropics was published.[134] Many of these came to some rather sobering conclusions not unlike those of Schumacher following his malarial Southeast Asian sojourn. The last one published was on the single largest German tropical settlement in the world and is, for that reason, worth discussing. This was a survey of the German settlements in the Brazilian state of Espirito Santo compiled by Ernst Wagemann (1884–1956) over a four-month journey to Brazil in 1914.[135] Wagemann had been a colleague of Karl Rathgen as a lecturer in political economy at the Hamburg Kolonialinstitut in 1908–10 before completing his *Habilitation* at the University of Berlin in 1914.[136] Wagemann sought to investigate less the physiological than the economic side of the assimilation and acclimatization questions among the 18,000 German inhabitants in the Brazilian state, who were of great interest to Germans because the third generation of these settlers had been born and were growing into adolescence.[137]

Wagemann found that while the German settlers had preserved their German "*Arbeitskraft*" (work energy) and lived in material conditions superior to the natives, they worked fewer hours than in Germany. Moreover, hygienic conditions were poor and rates of alcoholism very high.[138] Even more worrying was Wagemann's observation that in terms of posture, size, and facial expression, the men appeared to be regressing to "the Brazilian type."[139] The long hours of sleep and intellectual lethargy he witnessed in the colony he attributed to the burdens on the nervous system of the tropical climate.[140]

---

[133] MacMillan, *The War that Ended Peace*, 428–29.
[134] Ständiger Ausschuss des Vereins für Socialpolitik, *Die Ansiedlung von Europäern in den Tropen*, SdVfS, vol. 147, Erster Teil [part 1] (Munich and Leipzig: Duncker & Humblot, 1912); BArch K, N 1210 Nl. Sering, Nr. 108 Protokoll der Sitzung des Ausschusses des Vereins für Sozialpolitik am 24. März 1915.
[135] Ernst Wagemann, *Die deutschen Kolonisten im brasilianischen Staate Espirito Santo*, in *Die Ansiedlung von Europäern in den Tropen*, ed. Ständiger Ausschuss des Vereins für Socialpolitik, SdVfS, vol. 147, Fünfter Teil [part 5] (Munich and Leipzig: Duncker & Humblot, 1915), v.
[136] On Ernst Wagemann, see J. Adam Tooze, *Statistics and the German State: The Making of Modern Economic Knowledge* (Cambridge: Cambridge University Press, 2001).
[137] Wagemann, *Die deutschen Kolonisten*, 4.   [138] Ibid., 79–80, 97–104, 112–13.
[139] Ibid., 114.   [140] Ibid., 115, 139.

Health problems and degeneration were even more pronounced in the hotter lowland regions of German settlement of this Brazilian state.[141]

Still, Wagemann put a brave face on things, concluding that despite such problems "self-reliance, a sense of independence, and self-assurance have increased in the new environment."[142] These German settlers were a "sentry" (*Wachtposten*), he noted, "if not of German political rule, then certainly of German character and German culture!"[143] With this the hopes invested in German farmer settlers that Sering had raised on the Minnesota prairie in 1883 found a final echo in what one can rightly hear as the swan song of German overseas settler colonialism.

### King Leopold's Ghost in Dixie – Karl Rathgen in the American South

As mentioned previously, Karl Rathgen had also been involved in the survey on the settlement of Europeans in the tropics. He gained an opportunity to study conditions in the American South, West Indies, and Central America in the year 1913–14, when he served as Kaiser Wilhelm Professor at Columbia University.[144] This own investigative journey was undertaken between early February and late April 1914 and was very much focused on plantation agriculture, above all on the "negro question," notably the economic and social conditions of the black working population in these regions.[145] This was a topic that meshed closely with his existing research interest in more progressive native policy in colonial Africa. As will be recalled from Chapter 7, Rathgen had been an outspoken advocate for more humane treatment of colonial subjects that focused on their material, intellectual, and moral progress as an end in itself. As early as 1900 he had condemned colonial conquest for the sake of native exploitation as "reprehensible," and this developmental approach to the German colonies had become central to his teaching, research, and public lectures at the Hamburg Kolonialinstitut since its founding.[146] In March 1909 he gave an address to the École de Commerce Solvay in Brussels

---

[141] Ibid., 116.   [142] Ibid., 139.   [143] Ibid., 141.

[144] StaHH, 361-6 Hochschulwesen – Dozenten- und Personalakten, I 330, Personalakte Prof. Dr. Rathgen, Heft 7, Akte betreffend 1.) Entsendung als Kaiser Wilhelm Professor an die Columbia-University in New York 2.) Studienreise nach Mittelamerika, Karl Rathgen to Werner von Melle, Hamburg, Dec. 29, 1912; YUL MA, Farnam Family Papers, Group 203, Series II, Box 182, Folder 1836, Karl Rathgen to Henry Farnam, Hamburg, Feb. 23, 1913.

[145] StaHH, 361-6 Hochschulwesen – Dozenten- und Personalakten, I 330, Personalakte Prof. Dr. Rathgen, Karl Rathgen, Heft 7, Akte betreffend 1.) Entsendung als Kaiser Wilhelm Professor an die Columbia-University in New York 2.) Studienreise nach Mittelamerika, Bericht über eine Studienreise im Süden der Vereinigten Staaten und in West Indien vom 5. Februar bis April 28, 1914, Hamburg, June 1, 1914, fols. 20–21.

[146] Evangelisch-Sozialer Kongress, *Verhandlungen 1900*, 134.

in which he claimed that native policy had become the single most important question faced by European colonizers. And while he was himself still beholden to prevailing notions of white superiority, he insisted in this address that one could not generalize about a "negro race" in Africa; the "negro" of Central Africa was not the "negro" of West or East Africa. As with whites, he argued, blacks had to be treated and educated on an individual basis. Policy toward natives had to shift away from exploiting their labor toward awakening in them economic instincts by the introduction of money and opportunities to acquire landed property, which would help cultivate a modern perspective within the native populations very much on their own.[147]

In the summer of 1912 Rathgen participated as an associate of the prestigious Institut Colonial International in a session held in Brussels devoted to the reform of native land policy in the Belgian Congo, a colony that as the Congo Free State – a corporate territory owned directly by the Belgian king – had been infamous for its land seizures and the horrific abuses of native peoples in the harvesting of rubber under conditions of forced labor.[148] In November 1908, one year before King Loepold's death, the Congo Free States was purchased by Belgium following years of international humanitarian condemnation initiated by the colonial journalist and founder of the Congo Reform Association, Edmund Morel (1873–1924), and the British consul in Congo, Roger Casement (1864–1916).[149] Rathgen's familiarity with the horrendous conditions in the Belgian Congo undoubtedly raised his sensitivity to the abusive practices and racial hatred that prevailed in many other European colonies. He came to the Americas in 1913 haunted by King Leopold's ghost.

Much as Herrmann Schumacher had done before him as the Kaiser Wilhelm Professor, Rathgen spent the autumn in New York teaching at Columbia and giving public lectures in and around New York. Tellingly, this included a lecture at Yale University in late October 1913 on "King Leopold and the Congo" organized and hosted by his old school and university friend Henry Farnam.[150] He would give the same lecture to the New York Germanistic

---

[147] "Die Neger und die Kultur," *Hamburgerischer Correspondent*, March 16, 1909.
[148] K. Rathgen, "Les impôts directs dans les colonies," in *Compte rendu de la session tenue à Bruxelles les 29, 30 et 31 juillet 1912*, ed. Institut colonial international (Brussels: Bbiliothèque Colonial International, 1912), 182–232. See also "Belgiens Bodenpolitik in Kongo," *Vossische Zeitung*, July 30, 1912.
[149] See Adam Hochschild, *King Leopold's Ghost: A Story of Greed, Terror, and Heroism in Colonial Africa* (Boston: Houghton Mifflin, 1998), 177–274.
[150] YUL MA, Farnam Family Papers, Group 203, Series II, Box 182, Folder 1836, Henry Farnam to Karl Rathgen, Oct. 2, 1913, carbon copy; Karl Rathgen to Henry Farnam, New York, Oct. 9, 1913; Henry Farnam to Karl Rathgen, Oct. 13, 1913, carbon copy; Karl Rathgen to Henry Farnam, New York, Oct. 28, 1913.

Society in late January 1914 shortly before embarking on his investigative journey of the US South and Caribbean.[151]

The first destinations on Rathgen's journey in early February were southern agricultural schools and universities to gather information about plantation farming and the "negro question." This took him first to Richmond and then Hampton, Virginia, where he spent three days at the Hampton Institute. After seeing his wife and daughter off in Washington DC for their return to Hamburg via New York, he returned to Virginia, spending several days at the University of Virginia in Charlottesville. He then traveled to North Carolina to the University of North Carolina in Chapel Hill, visiting the tobacco factories in nearby Durham.[152] From there the journey continued on to Atlanta, where he visited the "all colored" Atlanta University. The city's filthiness and outward neglect, but even more so the visibly oppressed condition of the black students attending the university left a very negative impression on Rathgen. From Atlanta he journeyed on to the Tuskegee Institute, where he spent three productive days getting to know the trustees, faculty, and school. He visited the Calhoun Colored School near Montgomery, which had developed a land bank to enable black landownership and had resulted in the creation of 160 independent farm settlements in Lowndes County, Alabama. Alas, the nearby Bell plantation offered a contrasting picture of impoverished and oppressive sharecropping. As he observed in his report to Werner von Melle, "For a German, the impression of the condition of lawlessness and violence that still rules in the center of the Black Belt was particularly strong."[153]

From Montgomery he traveled to the Alabama Polytechnic Institute in Auburn, then to the University of Georgia in Athens, and from there toward the Atlantic coast to Charleston in order to inspect the areas of the new southern cotton industry. It was here that he sought to discover for himself the truth behind the repeated claims made in the German scholarly literature, taken up uncritically from American reports, that on account of the small number of whites residing on some of the Sea Islands off of the coast of South Carolina and Georgia, "the negroes had sunken back to wild barbarism" (*die*

---

[151] "Annual Meeting of the Germanistic Society of America," *Germanistic Society Quarterly* 1, no. 4 (Dec. 1914): 136–62, here 140.

[152] YUL MA, Farnam Family Papers, Group 203, Series II, Box 182, Folder 1837, Karl Rathgen to Henry Farnam, aboard the United Fruit Company's SS Cartago en route between Havana and Colón, March 24, 1914.

[153] StaHH, 361-6 Hochschulwesen – Dozenten- und Personalakten, I 330, Personalakte Prof. Dr. Rathgen, Karl, Heft 7, Bericht über eine Studienreise im Süden der Vereinigten Staaten und in West Indien vom 5. Februar bis 28. April 1914, Hamburg, June 1, 1914, fol. 22.

*Neger in eine wüste Barbarei zurück versunken sein*). It was already striking, Rathgen reported, that the closer he got to these islands the less was known about these supposedly barbarous conditions. Indeed, in Charleston nothing at all was known about them. Rathgen then visited James Island, which had a population of 125 whites and 2,500 blacks. In fact, Rathgen discovered that the conditions of the black population here were indistinguishable from what he had seen on the mainland, indeed if anything they were better: there were three schools, many of the houses had clean white curtains, and agriculture was more intensive than in neighboring regions. He discovered much the same when he visited Saint Helena Island, whose population was 87 percent black. Prosecuted crimes had fallen on the island by one-half between 1880 and 1910. School attendance and illiteracy rates hardly diverged from averages in the rest of the state. As he concluded in a comment tinged with irony, "If one wants to speak of barbarism, unquestionably this does not apply to the negro population."[154]

Rathgen's journey continued from the Sea Islands to the cotton port of Savannah, and from there via St. Augustine to Port Tampa, where he boarded a steamship to Havana. In Cuba he was able to observe the equal rights that blacks enjoyed on the island, which he reported stood in the starkest contrast to what he had seen in the southern states. In Havana and beyond he was able to observe many sugar, tobacco, cotton, and sisal plantations and even met two of his former students from the Kolonialinstitut now working as businessmen on the island. Unfortunately, the continuing journey was hampered by a feared outbreak of bubonic plague in Havana, but he was eventually able to catch passage aboard a United Fruit steamer to Panama in order to visit the Canal Zone, which much interested Rathgen and very much impressed him when he was able to witness its length between Colón and Panama City. From Colón he got on a steamer to Jamaica, spending nine days on the island inspecting plantations – the pronounced racial and social stratification on the island left a strong impression. The plague epidemic diverted his continuing journey until he could board a Norwegian steamer to Honduras. What immediately gained his attention there was "the way North American adventurers and North American capitalist exploitation thrived on the soil of a Central American republic."[155] The United States had landed Marines in Honduras and Nicaragua as recently as 1912, the latest in a series of US military interventions in Central America since the 1890s.[156]

---

[154] Ibid., fols. 25–26.
[155] Ibid.; YUL MA, Farnam Family Papers, Group 203, Series II, Box 182, Folder 1837, Karl Rathgen to Henry Farnam, aboard the United Fruit Company's SS Cartago en route between Havana and Colón, March 24, 1914.
[156] On these so-called Banana Wars, Lester D. Langley, *The Banana Wars: An Inner History of American Empire, 1900–1934* (Lexington, KY: University of Kentucky Press, 1983);

The arrest of American sailors at Tampico, Tamaulipas, on April 9th during the Mexican Revolution and rumors of a German arms shipment to Mexico led President Woodrow Wilson to order the occupation of Veracruz by US Marines on April 21, 1914. The US press exploded in indignation over alleged German arms shipments to President Victoriano Huerta (1850–1916), though it turned out the weapons were in fact supplied by Americans from Remington and Colt and were routed via Hamburg and put aboard a HAPAG steamer to skirt an American arms embargo.[157] Just four days after Wilson's announcement Henry Farnam wrote Rathgen that "This Mexican business is one of the most humiliating things that we have ever drifted into. . . . [M]ost people living at a distance will think that we have acted in a treacherous and high-handed manner in the chase for the almighty dollar, and it will be utterly futile to explain to them that it has all come from a combination of good intentions with an incredibly childish ignorance of the world."[158] It was hard for Germans not to gain the impression that the Caribbean was now an American pond and that the Roosevelt corollary to the Monroe Doctrine sanctioned arbitrary military interventions into the internal affairs of Caribbean and Latin American countries.

Rathgen returned to the United States via Mobile and New Orleans, making the – for Germans anyway – obligatory stops to see the Texas Germans of Austin, New Braunfels, and San Antonio. In New Braunfels, as in so many other cases, what Rathgen witnessed diverged strongly from what had been conveyed in the scholarly literature, perhaps also the somewhat rosy picture conveyed by Ernst von Halle in his book on American cotton discussed in Chapter 1. From Texas the final leg of his investigations took him via northern Louisiana to the Mississippi Delta region and the cotton plantation of Alfred Holt Stone (1870–1955) in Natchez. Holt was later a prominent Mississippi politician and then known as a successful planter and writer who had gained a national profile for his theories of innate black racial inferiority.[159] His

---

Ivan Musicant, *The Banana Wars: A History of United States Military Intervention in Latin America from the Spanish American War to the Invasion of Panama* (New York: Macmillan, 1990).

[157] See Pommerin, *Der Kaiser und Amerika*, 329–34.

[158] YUL MA, Farnam Family Papers, Group 203, Series II, Box 182, Folder 1837, Henry Farnam to Karl Rathgen, April 25, 1914, carbon copy. Cf. Robert E. Quirk, *An Affair of Honor: Woodrow Wilson and the Occupation of Veracruz* (Lexington: University of Kentucky Press for the Mississippi Valley Historical Association, 1962).

[159] Alfred Holt Stone, *Studies in the American Race Problem*, with an Introduction and three papers by Walter F. Wilcox (New York: Doubleday, Page and Co., 1908). On Stone, James G. Hollandsworth, Jr., *Portrait of a Scientific Racist: Alfred Holt Stone* (Baton Rouge: Louisiana State University Press, 2008); Lewis, *W. E. B. Du Bois: Biography of a Race*, 367–69, 372–73, 379; Lewis, *W. E. B. Du Bois: A Biography*, 244–49.

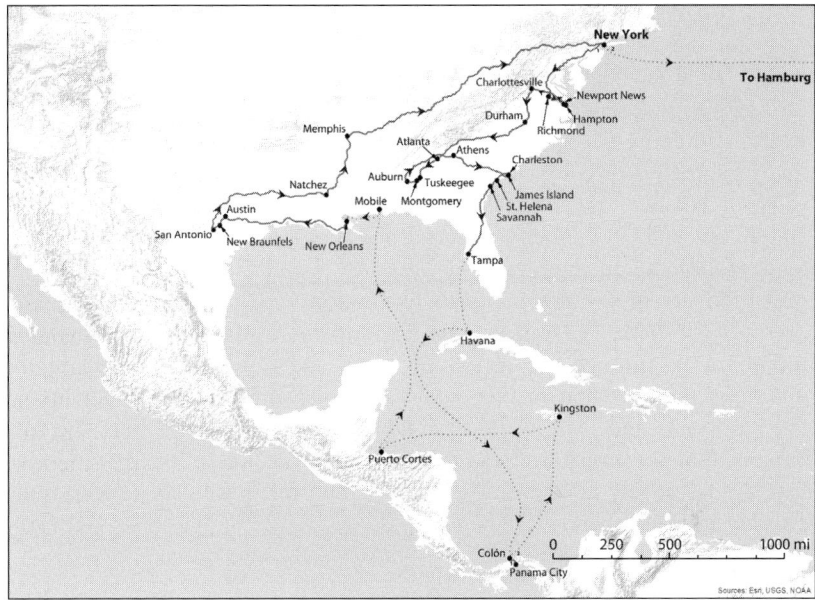

Map 9.2  Karl Rathgen's journey to the American South, Caribbean, Panama, and Honduras, Feb. 5–April 28, 1914.

plantation, Dunleith, on the fertile soil of the Yazoo delta with hundreds of black tenant farmers, was considered a model plantation, and Rathgen gained the impression over the three days he stayed at Dunleith that Stone was a "humane and successful employer," and one known widely, he noted, as an authority on "the negro problem." What insights Stone might have offered Rathgen into this "problem" undoubtedly served to rationalize the lawlessness, violence, injustice, and oppression Rathgen had himself witnessed and criticized repeatedly during his journey through the American South.[160]

Rathgen concluded his journey with a brief stop in Memphis before returning directly to New York City, where he arrived April 28, 1914. Two days later he was on his way back to Hamburg.[161] Right around that time Karl Helfferich was publishing an English translation of a 1913 jubilee essay

---

[160] StaHH, 361-6 Hochschulwesen – Dozenten- und Personalakten, I 330, Personalakte Prof. Dr. Rathgen, Karl Rathgen, Heft 7, Bericht über eine Studienreise im Süden der Vereinigten Staaten und in West Indien vom 5. Februar bis 28. April 1914, Hamburg, June 1, 1914, fol. 24.

[161] YUL MA, Farnam Family Papers, Group 203, Series II, Box 182, Folder 1837, Karl Rathgen to Henry Farnam, New York, April 28, 1914.

on the progress of the German economy since the beginning of Wilhelm II's reign for the New York Germanistic Society.[162] The little book, which was widely read at home and abroad and went through multiple editions, included an assessment of the place of the colonies in Germany's national wealth. While he tried to put a brave face on things by pointing out how many kilometers of colonial railroads had been built and by how much the value of colonial trade had risen, he admitted that the German colonial empire was still "in its incipient stage" and that it would be left to the future for it to become an important consumer of manufactured goods or significant producer of key raw materials like cotton.[163] Even if that were still in prospect, for Rathgen familiarity with conditions in the Belgian Congo and recent travels through the American South and Caribbean had raised the unsettling prospect that in this quest for rubber and cotton, perhaps it was the Europeans and their white descendants in America who were the barbarians, that the entire overseas colonial enterprise was infected with racial hatred, inescapably violent and oppressive, and for those very reasons quite possibly irredeemable.

## Inner Colonization

As was explored in Chapter 1, there had always been a contiguous field of German colonial ambition in the Prussian east. Sering had long viewed the Prussian east through an explicitly American settler colonial lens shaped by his time in North America in 1883. He had been very active promoting German internal colonization efforts since the mid-1880s in the Association for Social Policy and then later as a member of the Agricultural Council (Landwirtschaftsrat) and Prussian Land Economy Collegium.

So what had been achieved on the internal German colonial frontier in the era of *Weltpolitik*? Early in his chancellorship Bülow had considered the question of Prussia's eastern marches one of the most important domestic issues and supported aggressive internal colonization to strengthen "Germandom" in the Polish-speaking parts of eastern Prussia, although not without some reservations.[164] His main objective was purchasing Polish estates with absentee landlords, and in 1902 he saw to a 150 million mark increase in the settlement fund of the Royal Prussian Settlement Commission for the Provinces of West Prussia and Posen created in 1886 and discussed in Chapter 1. By 1907 some 9,000 German farm and some 500 German worker

---

[162] Karl Helfferich, *Germany's Economic Progress and National Wealth 1888–1913* (New York: Germanistic Society, 1914).
[163] Ibid., 82–83.
[164] Bülow, *Denkwürdigkeiten*, vol. 2, 487–90; cf. Bülow, *Deutsche Politik*, 282, 287.

families had been resettled, roughly double the numbers as in all previous years since 1886.[165] By 1911 some 394,000 hectares of land had been purchased by the Prussian state since 1886, of which some 112,000 hectares had been Polish-owned. According to Bülow that land counted some 150,000 German settlers in 450 new villages.[166] Nevertheless, Polish demographic growth swamped these measures, and the population balance in West Prussia and Posen never changed in favor of the Germans.[167] What is more, relations between Germans and Poles deteriorated sharply as a result of these policies, highlighted by the Polish school strike of November 1906 in protest of German-language religious instruction. The reality was that the Settlement Commission was underfunded and Polish landowners and peasants were offended, effectively boycotting its measures and thereby strengthening their Polish identity. Indeed, Bülow was himself impressed by the energy the Poles mobilized to defend themselves.[168] What is more, the Settlement Commission was frequently outbid by private buyers and only ever a small buyer of land in any given year, and of that land purchased, Polish-owned land was only a small fraction.[169] Agricultural conditions had improved and land prices were rising during Bülow's time as chancellor, making it difficult for the Settlement Commission to purchase land from *anyone*, whether Polish or German.[170]

The notorious Prussian Expropriation Act of February 1908 was thus a desperate measure to deal with these realities and placate the agitation of the Eastern Marches Society. It empowered the Prussian government to purchase up to 70,000 hectares of Polish estate land outright. The law immediately generated international approbation. It was also quickly watered down by guidelines exempting vast areas of Polish settlement and was only ever used once in 1912 to purchase four properties totaling some 1,656 hectares. In that purchase the Settlement Commission actually ended up paying *more* for these four properties than it spent for every other property purchased on the free market that year.[171] As it turned out, the law was also fiercely criticized in the Reichstag, which passed a vote of disapproval of the Expropriation Act in January 1913.[172] By most measures, then, the project of official inner

---

[165] Winzen, *Reichskanzler*, 132. For an overview of Bülow's *Polenpolitik,* see Hagen, *Germans, Poles and Jews*, 180–94.
[166] Bülow, *Deutsche Politik*, 284.
[167] Wolfgang Neugebauer, ed., *Handbuch der preussischen Geschichte*, vol. 3 (Berlin and New York: Walter de Gruyter, 2001), 53. Even Bülow admitted this, Bülow, *Deutsche Politik*, 283.
[168] Bülow, *Deutsche Politik*, 281.
[169] Eddie, "The Prussian Settlement Commission," 45, 56–58.   [170] Ibid., 50.
[171] Ibid., 50–51. On the Expropriation Act, see also Bülow, *Deutsche Politik*, 282.
[172] Neugebauer, ed., *Handbuch*, vol. 3, 52.

colonization was a failure.[173] The fact that five times more Germans were settled in the Prussian east (some 120,000) than ever lived in the entire German overseas empire (less than 24,000, mainly in Southwest Africa) should thus not be seen as a metric of the success of these policies but rather stand as testament to how thoroughly German overseas colonies had failed to meet expectations.[174]

Some five years prior in 1908, Max Sering had already come to realize that the work of the Settlement Commission had fallen far short. This was all the more concerning to him since the "giant empires" – the United States, Britain, and Russia – had engaged in grand agricultural colonization projects by that point. He compared German efforts to the more energetic, creative, and far less timid recent inner colonization work in the United States, Canada, Australia, Russia, and even England to prove that the German efforts east of the Elbe had shown little progress, especially in areas beyond West Prussia and Posen, where next to nothing had been done.[175] Sering believed it was because insufficient awareness had been awakened in the German public and insufficient resources had been invested in the effort. Other factors he identified were the expansion of entail, which had restricted the parceling and sale of land; land purchases by urbanites that had driven up land prices; the purchase of additional domain lands by the state, expanding tenant farming; and finally, the practice of keeping heavily-indebted large estates afloat with state subsidized credit.[176]

In 1908 Sering and other like-minded land reformers founded the journal *Archiv für innere Kolonisation*, culminating in 1912 in the founding of the Gesellschaft zur Förderung der inneren Kolonisation (Society for the Promotion of Inner Colonization). Both were clear efforts to raise public awareness and give new life to an issue that had lost traction both with the German public and Prussian government.[177] Other members of the organization included Otto Auhagen (1869–1945), a professor at Berlin's Landwirtschaftliche Hochschule and a specialist on Siberian colonization; Alfred Hugenberg

---

[173] Nelson, "From Manitoba to the Memel," 451; Christopher Clark, *Iron Kingdom: The Rise and Downfall of Prussia, 1600–1947* (Cambridge, MA: Harvard University Press, 2006), 582.

[174] Gründer, *Geschichte der deutschen Kolonien*, 235–45. Cf. Conrad, *Globalisation and the Nation*, 177; Conrad, "Internal Colonialism," in *German Colonialism*, ed. Naranch and Eley, 254; Zimmerman, *Alabama in Africa*, 80–100.

[175] BArch K, N 1210 Nl. Sering, Nr. 19, "Innere Kolonisation," *Frankfurter Oderzeitung*, June 11, 1909; see also Max Sering, *Verhandlungen des Landes-Oekonomie-Kollegiums am 9. Februar 1912 über die Politik der Grundbesitzverteilung in den grossen Reichen* (Berlin: Parey, 1912), 29–30.

[176] Sering, *Verhandlungen des Landes-Oekonomie-Kollegiums*, 30–33.

[177] BArch K, N 1210 Nl. Sering, Nr. 19, Statutes of the Gesellschaft zur Förderung der inneren Kolonisation, n.d. [late 1911 or early 1912]; copy of an invitation to join the Gesellschaft zur Förderung der inneren Kolonisation, Frankfurt an der Oder and Berlin, Jan. 10, 1912, signed by F. von Schwerin and Max Sering.

(1865–1951), a Krupp official and co-founder of the Pan-German League who had served as a leading figure in the Prussian Settlement Commission in Posen; Wolfgang Kapp (1858–1922), the director of the Ostpreußische Generallandschaftsdirektion (an East Prussian public agricultural lending bank); and Friedrich W. L. von Schwerin (1862–1925), the Regierungspräsident of Frankfurt an der Oder and likewise a former senior official in the Prussian Settlement Commission, who was the society's first chairman. Sering served as second chairman.[178]

In early December 1912 an inaugural conference was held by the new society which included many academics and figures from the nationalist press, such as the editors of the *Tägliche Rundschau, Grenzbote*, and *Ostmark* as well as figures from the nationalist societies, notably the Alliance Against Social Democracy and the Eastern Marches Society.[179] Despite certain affinities and involvement of the likes of Hugenberg, the Society for Inner Colonization was not a Pan-German initiative, and its journal's articles remained scholarly in tone and largely devoid of the annexationist aims and jingoistic language of the Pan-German League.[180] Among other things, the journal was not shy about harpooning Pan-German holy cows by, for example, openly admitting the bleak prospects for settler colonialism in Germany's overseas colonies.[181] The *Archiv* was interested in analyzing settler colonization efforts worldwide, featuring articles on the effectiveness of such efforts in places such as England, Sweden, and Russia.[182] Russia in particular was seen as the most parallel inner colonizer to Germany, and thus a great deal of attention was given to Russian eastern migration to the Urals, Siberia, and the Amur region. For that reason there was also great interest in the 1906 agricultural reforms of Premier Petr Stolypin (1862–1911), which had extended private ownership of land to Russian peasants and established an agricultural extension service to improve agricultural techniques and agricultural cooperatives to encourage the growth of an agricultural middle class. Settlement of new lands in the Urals and Siberia had also been encouraged.[183]

---

[178] BArch K, N 1210 Nl. Sering, Nr. 19, Membership list of the Gesellschaft zur Förderung der inneren Kolonisation, n.d. [late 1912]. On Kapp, Heinz Hagenlücke, *Deutsche Vaterlandspartei: Die nationale Rechte am Ende des Kaiserreichs* (Düsseldorf: Droste Verlag, 1997), 116. On Schwerin, Imanuel Geiss, *Der polnische Grenzstreifen 1914–1918: Ein Beitrag zur deutschen Kriegszielpolitik im ersten Weltkrieg* (Lübeck and Hamburg: Matthiesen Verlag, 1960), 80.

[179] Nelson, "The *Archive for Inner Colonization*," in Nelson, *Germans, Poland, and Colonial Expansion*, 69.

[180] Ibid., 76; cf. Smith, *Ideological Origins*, 106–8.

[181] Nelson, "The *Archive for Inner Colonization*," in Nelson, *Germans, Poland, and Colonial Expansion*, 73–74.

[182] Ibid., 71.

[183] Brigitte Löhr, *Die "Zukunft Russlands": Perspektiven russischer Wirtschaftsentwicklung und deutsch-russische Wirtschaftsbeziehungen vor dem Ersten Weltkrieg* (Stuttgart: Franz Steiner, 1985), 137–43.

This interest in the east and Russia was shared by others. Even before his rather sobering experiences in Southeast Asia in 1911, Hermann Schumacher's travels through the American Midwest and West in 1907 had opened his eyes to the economic possibilities offered to Germany by Russia. And well prior to that his view of German opportunities in China had been animated by a Eurasian rail connection made possible by the Trans-Siberian Railway. Astonishingly, even Ernst von Halle had come around to similar views by that point. During the "Hottentot elections" in January 1907 von Halle had been bold enough to openly acknowledge that Germany really had no viable overseas settler colony and that not much could be done about it. But, with an obvious view to the centrifugal forces at work in British Dominions, he saw a silver lining in it: "As much as that [lack of a white settler colony] can be bemoaned from a national standpoint, it's not to be regretted from every angle, as sooner or later they would ripen to independence, and with that, greatly enhance world commercial competition."[184] To his mind the tasks facing Germany were to develop the existing overseas colonies into productive economic units and to restart the colonization project in the Polish east that had been interrupted by the Battle of Tannenberg [Battle of Grunwald, 1410] and the exclusion of Hanseatic merchants from Russia and Scandinavia in the sixteenth and seventeenth centuries.[185] Thus even one of most outspoken former proponents of Mahanian "Sea Power" and German settler colonialism in the Western Hemisphere had shifted his commercial and colonial gaze eastward.

What role might have been played in this reorientation by the new geopolitical theories of MacKinder and Kjellén is unclear, but as was discussed at the end of the previous chapter, the complete failure of German diplomatic initiatives in 1907–8 to draw closer to the United States, the increasingly expansive and aggressive interpretation of the Monroe Doctrine under President Roosevelt, the growing entanglement of Germany with the Ottoman Empire, and the reorientation of German colonial policy away from settler colonialism under Dernburg were all unquestionably reinforcing this "eastern" reorientation. This was also reflected in the activities of Germany's nationalist associations, which showed a distinctly Eurasian continental inclination in the years before the Great War.[186]

---

[184] von Halle, "Die großen Epochen," 53.    [185] Ibid.
[186] Hartmut Pogge von Strandmann, "Nationale Verbände zwischen Weltpolitik und Kontinentalpolitik," in *Marine und Marinepoltik im kaiserlichen Deutschland 1871–1914*, ed. Herbert Schottelius and Wilhelm Deist (Düsseldorf: Droste, 1972), 296–317. See also Mommsen, *Bürgerstolz und Weltmachtsreben*, 524–25.

## Max Sering and Hermann Schumacher in Russia

As discussed in the previous chapter, Hermann Schumacher had a deepening interest in Russia following his observations of experiments in dry farming in the American West and in conversations with Charles Crane in Chicago, who was well connected to senior Russian statesmen such as Serge Witte. His interest was undoubtedly also encouraged by the doubling of trade between Germany and Russia between 1904 and 1911, encouraged by the Russo-German trade treaty of 1904 and recent Russian bumper grain harvests.[187] It was then deepened further in the autumn of 1911 during convalescent leave in the Tirolean Alps to recover from the malaria he contracted in Southeast Asia earlier in the spring. While hiking a mountain pass near Bolzano in early October, he repeatedly chanced upon a large group of Russians roughly his age. After longer conversations with these men, he discovered that they were émigrés, exiled revolutionaries who explained their fate to him in detail and were now living in Vienna. Although he did not know it at the time and could not be certain later, he believed this group included Nikolai Bukharin (1888–1938) and Leon Trotsky (1879–1940). In any case, the discussions with these Russians repeated themselves over several days and became very lively, ranging over social problems, foreign policy, and philosophical questions.[188] Later in his stay he also happened upon Walther Rathenau for the first time in a tavern in Bolzano and struck up an animated conversation with him, once again about Russia. This meeting would not be without consequence, as after the war as German foreign minister Rathenau would invite Schumacher to be part of the German delegation that attended the signing of the Rapallo Treaty with the Soviet Union in 1922.[189]

In 1912, the year following these encounters in the Tirolian Alps, Schumacher was able to visit Russia for the first time. As already mentioned, Schumacher became active in the courses organized by the Vereinigung für Staatswissenschaftliche Fortbildung (Union for Continuing Education in Political Economy) in Berlin intended for civil servants. Notable in this program were the excursions it organized in Germany and abroad. One of these in which both Schumacher and Max Sering participated was to Russia in the spring of 1912 to examine the effects of the agrarian reforms spearheaded by Stolypin and continued by Minister of Agriculture Alexander Krivoshein (1857–1921) after Stolypin's assassination in 1911.[190] These reforms involved

---

[187] Mulligan, *Origins*, 192.     [188] GNN HA, Nl. Schumacher, I, B-6v, fol. 608.
[189] Ibid., fols. 608a–608b. There is a gap in entries from the 1st to the 29th of October 1911 in Walther Rathenau's diary and so no account of this conversation from him, Pogge von Strandmann, ed., *Walther Rathenau*, 135.
[190] GNN HA, Nl. Schumacher, I, B-6v, fol. 628. On Krivoshein, see Lieven, *The End of Tsarist Russia*, 295–96.

the cancellation of redemption payments and dissolution of peasant communes and resulted in large increases in agricultural output and large-scale migration to settle free lands in the Urals and Siberia.[191]

The journey to Russia was organized and directed by Max Sering and Otto Auhagen.[192] It was both a clear admission of the successes the Russians had made in land reforms and internal colonization since the Revolution of 1905 and the growing economic and military strength of Russia. And while a colonial gaze unquestionably informed this German interest, it indicated that German interest in Russia was wider than the Russophobic quarters represented by Theodor Schiemann (1847–1921) or the Pan-German League.[193] In 1912 many avenues of peaceful coexistence to mutual benefit were open to Germany and Russia. As was so often the case in this era, admiration, envy, and fear could coexist.

A group of some 120 German civil servants, agronomists, and economists ultimately participated in this fourteen-day journey to the Russian Empire, which was closely coordinated with Russian officials. The men were booked on a special train that departed Berlin and made a stop first in Warsaw before continuing on to Kiev. In Kiev the group disembarked and was brought to a modern military barracks to observe the exercises of elite Russian troops, a spectacle whose mobility especially impressed the assembled German observers familiar with military matters, Schumacher noted. It was proof to him that the defeat at the hands of the Japanese had accelerated reforms of the Russian military.[194] Clearly, the Russian government was eager to impress upon their German guests Russia's military preparedness. From the barracks the group toured Kiev's famous Monastery of the Caves, which was followed in the evening by a reception by the lord mayor of Kiev, who while conversing with the men in fluent German by day, inexplicably addressed the men in French that evening. Schumacher interpreted this as a clear political message to the visitors of Russia's closeness to France.[195]

---

[191] See David Moon, *The Plough That Broke the Steppes: Agriculture and Environment on Russia's Grasslands, 1700–1914* (Oxford: Oxford University Press, 2013); Wolfgang Faust, *Rußlands Goldener Boden: Der sibirische Regionalismus in der zweiten Hälfte des 19. Jahrhunderts* (Cologne and Vienna: Böhlau Verlag, 1980).

[192] Max Sering, ed., *Russlands Kultur und Volkswirtschaft: Aufsätze und Vorträge im Auftrage der Vereinigung für Staatswissenschaftliche Fortbildung zu Berlin* (Berlin and Leipzig: G. J. Göschen'sche Verlagshandlung, 1913), iii.

[193] James Casteel, "On the Civilizing Mission of the Global Economy: German Observers of the Colonization and Development of Siberia, 1900–1918," in *The Nation State and Beyond: Governing Globalization Processes in the Nineteenth and Early Twentieth Centuries*, ed. Isabella Löhr and Roland Wenzelhuemer (Heidelberg: Springer, 2013), 209–33, here 218.

[194] GNN HA, Nl. Schumacher, I, B-6v, fols. 629–30a.   [195] Ibid., fol. 630a.

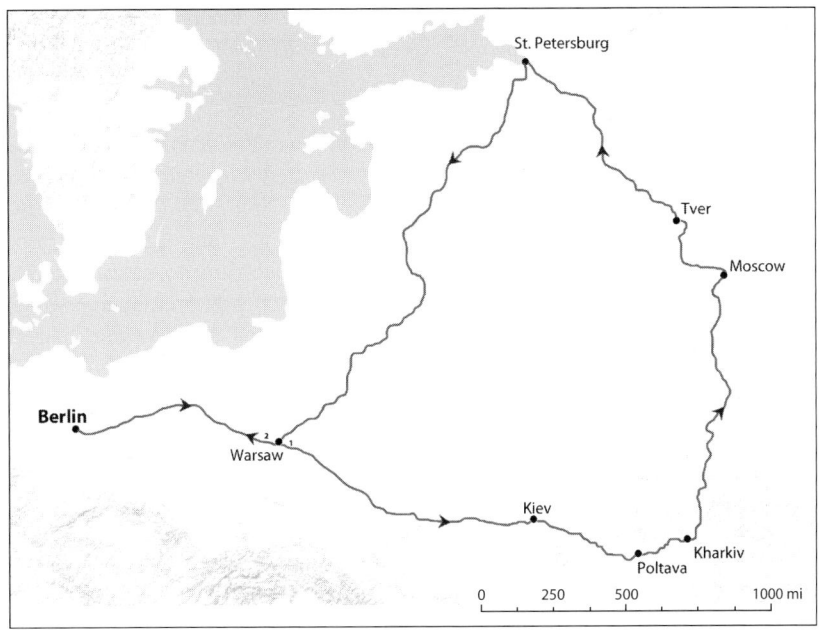

Map 9.3  Hermann Schumacher and Max Sering's journey to the Russian Empire, May–June 1912.

From Kiev the group undertook longer excursions to the surrounding countryside and traveled north of Poltava to inspect some of the new settlements erected in wake of the Russian land reforms. Along the way they passed through many of the "giant villages" (*Riesendörfer*) in the province of Poltava that had been the seat of the agrarian revolution in 1905 and had given the impulse to these reforms. The group was accompanied on its tour by the Danish-Russian agronomist Carl Andreas Koefoed (1855–1948), who had worked to implement the dissolution of the peasant communes (*obshchina*). In the areas of new settlement they toured, the governor of Kharkiv served as guide, accompanied by many other Russian officials.[196] The peasants who greeted them were in their Sunday best and allowed free inspection of their farmsteads everywhere the Germans visited. They offered a remarkable spectacle of clean and tidy domesticity. While aware that a show of sorts was being put on, Schumacher recalled that the overall impression these settlers

---

[196] Ibid., fols. 630a–631. On the peasants in the 1905 Revolution, see Jan Kusber, "Die Bauern und das Jahr 1905: Befunde und Interpretation," in *Das Zarenreich, das Jahr 1905 und seine Wirkungen: Bestandsaufnahmen*, ed. Jan Kusber and Andreas Frings (Berlin: LIT Verlag, 2007), 83–103.

left with the group was unmistakably positive, of a "healthy, hard-working, and sympathetic strain of people" (*gesunden, tüchtigen und sympathischen Volksschlags*).[197] If ever there was evidence of the salubrious effects of inner colonization, here it was.

The next day the journey continued to Moscow. The Kremlin, which had been closed to foreigners since 1905, was unexpectedly opened to the German group. A tour was also organized of the Danilevski Spinning Mill in Moscow, which was unusual to Schumacher's eye on two counts: first of all, it operated with a completely international staff specialized according to national talent (or perhaps cliché, e.g., German bookkeepers, French pattern makers), which much reminded him of the Colorado Fuel and Iron Company that had so impressed him in Pueblo, Colorado, in 1907; secondly, it had an extraordinary collection of Persian patterns and exported nearly all of its cotton cloth to Persia. The cotton itself was grown in Turkestan. Schumacher recalled that while he had visited many cotton mills in his day, he had never seen such a well-organized mill in any other country.[198] The implications were clear: not only were the Russians capable of extraordinary feats of industrial organization, but they could also source critically important raw materials such as cotton domestically. The parallels to the United States were obvious.

The group proceeded from Moscow to the Tver Governorate northeast of Moscow to visit other new peasant settlements, albeit ones that compared unfavorably with what they had seen in the Ukraine. The last leg of the journey took the group to St. Petersburg, which Schumacher observed was now connected to Peking via the Tran-Siberian Railway, but which showed little immediate evidence of that link to the Far East. On the evening before their return to Berlin, the group was fêted by many Russians, including senior members of the government ministries. At this farewell Schumacher was seated next to the deputy minister who had implemented the Krivoshein land reforms. He told Schumacher very candidly that he expected these reforms to fail because they rested on the initiative of a small minority of foreign-educated men facing a backlash from Russian traditionalists – good press from abroad, he hoped, might give their threatened project some badly needed support.[199] Clearly that was also an aim of hosting this German group.

It is important to note here that Chancellor Theobald von Bethmann Hollweg (1856–1921) also traveled to Russia in 1912, albeit in his case over three days in July to St. Petersburg and Moscow. Much like the group of German civil servants and academics, he too gathered mostly positive impressions of the country that disabused him of the prejudices of the German

---

[197] GNN HA, Nl. Schumacher, I, B-6v, fols. 631–32; quotation 632. Cf. Löhr, *Die "Zukunft Russlands,"* 137–43.
[198] GNN HA, Nl. Schumacher, I, B-6v, fols. 632–33.   [199] Ibid., fols. 634–35.

"yellow press" about the country.[200] On reflecting on the journey he observed how much it had refreshed him and how Moscow had fascinated him. Like Sering's group, he was also much taken by the possibilities offered by peaceful engagement with Russia, writing Karl von Eisendecher: "This wealth of natural resources and of inexhaustible human power are factors that especially we, influenced by our effeminate culture, should not fear but also should not underestimate."[201] Bethmann was thereafter committed to defusing tensions with Russia by mutual compromise wherever possible and encouraging the development of bilateral political and economic relations from which both countries were bound to benefit greatly.[202] This is at odds with the mistaken view of Fritz Fischer still widely prevalent in the historiography that Bethmann was possessed only by fear of Russia and that the views of prominent Russophobes dominated German policymaking toward Russia in the years before the First World War, all allegedly pushing Germany toward a preventive war in 1914.[203] To be sure, tensions between Russia and Germany would flare in late 1912 and 1913 during the Balkan wars and a distinctly more uncompromising Russian position toward Vienna and Berlin thereafter that strained these attempts at détente, but they did not derail them or lead to an inevitable war.

Schumacher and Sering returned to Germany with the firm conviction that the German public in general, and German economists in particular (not to mention the Foreign Office and much of the German civil service), knew far too little about Russia. The direct result was the initiative to found the Deutsch-Russische Gesellschaft (German-Russian Society) spearheaded by Max Sering. In late February and early March 1913, a series of talks were held in Berlin and a plan for the new body was drafted at the first formal meeting of the society held March 5.[204] The draft plan justified the founding of the new society on grounds of the widespread ignorance about Russia that the signatories observed in the German public – in spite of the fact that the two countries shared a 200-mile border and that Germany was the largest importer

---

[200] Quoted in Jarausch, *Enigmatic Chancellor*, 119; see also Clark, *The Sleepwalkers*, 326.
[201] Jarausch, *Enigmatic Chancellor*, 119.
[202] Ibid., 457n17; T. G. Otte, "A 'Formidible Factor in European Politics': Views of Russia in 1914," in *The Outbreak of the First World War: Structure, Politics, and Decision-Making*, ed. Jack S. Levy and John A. Vasquez (Cambridge and New York: Cambridge University Press, 2014), 87–111, here 99, 102; Pogge von Strandmann, ed., *Walther Rathenau*, 163.
[203] Fischer, *War of Illusions*, 41–42, 139, 197, 223, 224, 266, 469–70; Lieven, *The End of Tsarist Russia*, 60; Alexander Watson, *Ring of Steel: Germany and Austria-Hungary in World War I* (New York: Basic Books, 2014), 36–37; Troy R. E. Paddock, *Creating the Russian Peril: Education, the Public Sphere, and National Identity in Imperial Germany, 1890–1914* (Rochester, NY: Camden House, 2010), 88–91.
[204] GNN HA, Nl. Schumacher, I, B-28, Wilhelm Crayen to Hermann Schumacher, Berlin, March 8, 1913; Protokoll der 1. Sitzung [der deutsch-russischen Gesellschaft], March 5, 1913.

of Russian goods and Russia imported more goods from Germany than from any other country. By comparison with Britain and France, the signatories observed, very few German scholarly journals devoted themselves to Russia, and there was nothing like the vibrant academic exchanges between those countries and Russia in Germany. The signatories warned of the dangers that such widespread ignorance could hold for Germany.[205] The explicit goal was to "foster understanding about Russia in Germany and to serve the cultural relations of both countries to one another while preserving a thoroughly unpolitical character."[206]

The new organization was to have the qualities of a research institute, and the fields of study under its purview included economics, history, and law, but also ranged very widely to such subjects as ethnography, music, and fine arts. A key point made in the plan was the desire to link scholarship and practice, something that had been a longstanding theme in the work of men like Sering and Schumacher. It thus foresaw initiating travel study, lectures, exhibits, conferences, and the creation of a permanent library and reading room in Berlin. Among the twelve signatories of the plan beside Sering and Schumacher were other members of the group that had visited Russia in the spring of 1912, such as Otto Auhagen, Theodor Schiemann, and Otto Hoetzsch (1876–1946).[207] Interestingly, Hoetzsch had himself spent time traveling in the United States as guest of the New York Germanistic Society in 1907, where undountedly the parallels to Russia must have entered his mind just as they had for Schumacher.[208] Theodor Schiemann, a professor of eastern European history at the University of Berlin, had been active with Schmoller and Sering in the founding of the Kolonialpolitisches Aktionskomité in 1906.[209] Schiemann and Hoetzsch, would subsequently become founders of German *Ostforschung*, with Hoetzsch representing a much more pro-Russian position than Schiemann.[210] Schiemann, who was a Baltic German from Courland and headed Berlin University's Seminar for East European History and Geography, had a much darker view of the Russian Empire shaped by his negative experiences with the Russification policies of Tsar Alexander III. His

---

[205] GNN HA, Nl. Schumacher, I, B-28, Plan der Gründung einer Deutsch-Russischen Gesellschaft, n.d., 1–2.
[206] Ibid., 2.   [207] Ibid., 3.
[208] Fiebig-von Hase, "Die politische Funktionalisierung der Kultur," 68–70, 69n73; Roth, "Der politische Hintergrund," 73.
[209] Kolonialpolitisches Aktionskomité, ed., *Schmoller, Dernburg*, frontispiece.
[210] Klaus Meyer, "Osteuropäische Geschichte," in *Geschichtswissenschaft in Berlin im 19. und 20. Jahrhundert: Persönlichkeiten und Institutionen*, ed. Reimer Hansen (Berlin: de Gruyter, 1992), 553–70; Michael Burleigh, *Germany Turns Eastward: A Study of Ostforschung in the Third Reich* (Cambridge: Cambridge University Press, 1988), 13–18; Fischer, *War of Illusions*, 39–42; Paddock, *Creating the Russian Peril*, 60–64, 66, 69, 70, 72, 73, 83–91, 174–75.

view of Russia was that it was a lawless, corrupt, unruly, and nomadic society with a thin veneer of European culture held together by violent Tsarist absolutism. It was rotten to the core and ripe for collapse.[211]

A conservative Anglophile who was friendly with the Kaiser, Schiemann also wrote an influential foreign policy column for the *Kreuzzeitung*. He was deeply informed about Anglo-Russian relations and the policy of the Entente, as he had since 1909 been translating the top secret communications between the Russian ambassador Alexander von Benckendorff (1849–1917) and the Russian Foreign Ministry forwarded to the Wilhelmstrasse by the Baltic German spy Benno von Siebert (1876–1926) in the Russian embassy in London.[212] Schiemann had also been part of an effort with the radical-liberal editor of *The Economist*, Francis Wrigley Hirst (1873–1953), to improve Anglo-German relations during and after the Agadir Crisis by countering the slanted reporting in the British and German presses. Despite their very different political convictions, what Hirst and Schiemann shared was a deeply critical view of Grey's pro-Russian and anti-German Entente policy.[213] After the failure of the Haldane Mission in March 1912, however, Schiemann began to view prospects for an Anglo-German thaw very pessimistically, convinced that Grey was more committed to Russia than ever and that the Entente was preparing for war.[214] Interestingly, the aims of the German-Russian Society seemed calculated to counter this negative view of Russia within the German public.

As the timing of the founding of the German-Russian Society in 1913 coincided with a tense military standoff between Russia and Austria-Hungary over the status of Albania (the so-called Balkan Winter Crisis of 1912–13), Hoetzsch took up contact with the German Foreign Office on behalf of the society to enquire about any concerns it might have about announcing it in public and was advised that they should hold off on account of these Balkan tensions.[215] The society nevertheless held its first public lecture on March 10, ten days before the Winter Crisis was resolved by negotiation. It is notable that the Hamburg Kolonialinstitut established an independent East European Seminar focused on the history and culture of Russia only a few months later in 1914.[216]

---

[211] Klaus Meyer, *Theodor Schiemann als politischer Publizist* (Frankfurt a. M. and Hamburg: Rütten & Loening, 1956), 88–115.
[212] Ibid., 115–22, 172–76, 245–61; Geppert, *Pressekriege,* 392–93.
[213] Geppert, *Presskriege*, 390–98; Meyer, *Theodor Schiemann*, 176–91.
[214] Geppert, *Presskriege*, 398–99; cf. Pogge von Strandmann, ed., *Walther Rathenau*, 153–54.
[215] GNN HA, Nl. Schumacher, I, B-28, Protokoll der 1. Sitzung [Der deutsch-russischen Gesellschaft], March 5, 1913. Cf. Fischer, *War of Illusions*, 370.
[216] Ruppenthal, *Kolonialismus*, 233, 239.

Pleas from Max Sering in May and June 1913 to gain German Foreign Office support for the society fell on deaf ears, which while undoubtedly a reflection of the ignorant Russophobia that existed within its ranks, was as likely the result of the now familiar pattern of shortsightedness, incompetence, and lack of money that was so evident in the Wilhelmstrasse's handling of similar initiatives in German-Japanese relations discussed in Chapter 7 and that Schumacher had recently confirmed in his perusal of Foreign Office files on China.[217]

## Karl Helfferich and the Balkan Shatterbelt

The delay in announcing the German-Russian Society in public highlights the extent to which Russo-German relations were now hostage to developments in the Balkans. This region was gradually emerging as part of Germany's informal empire before 1914, complimenting its sphere of influence in the Ottoman Empire, and indeed, indispensable to the viability of the Baghdad Railway. In these same years the Balkans and Turkish Straits became the primary sites of Russian diplomatic activity. These Russo-German Balkan entanglements after 1908 were unintentionally encouraged in both instances by British imperial diplomacy that had pushed both countries away from expanding in the periphery back toward the European center. In Germany's case, it was the British containment strategy that had foiled overseas *Weltpolitik* and shifted German energies to the continent, while for Russia it had been the Anglo-Japanese Alliance, the Russo-Japanese War, and the Anglo-Russian Convention of 1907 that had redirected Russian activity back toward Europe from the Far East and Central Asia.[218]

As discussed in the previous chapter, a key turning point in Russo-German relations was Austria-Hungary's provocative and foolish annexation of Bosnia-Herzegovina in October 1908, which Russia and Serbia were forced to accept under German pressure in March 1909. Thereafter Russia had started pursuing a much more aggressive forward policy in the Balkans and Ottoman Empire that represented the triumph of the Moscow-based "country" party in the Russian Foreign Ministry supported by an increasingly anti-German Duma and Russian nationalist press. Under Izvolsky's successor, Serge Sazonov, Grigorii Trubetskoy (1873–1930) as head of the Near Eastern Division, and Nikolai Hartwig (1857–1914) as Russian resident minister to Belgrade, St. Petersburg took a Slovophile Balkan position centered on the territorial expansion of Serbia to bring about a South Slav union. They also

---

[217] Cf. Fischer, *War of Illusions*, 371.
[218] See David McDonald, "Tsushima's Echoes: Asian Defeat and Tsarist Foreign Policy," in Steinberg *Russo Japanese War*, vol. 1, 545–63.

worked toward Russian seizure of the Turkish Straits and Constantinople.[219] This involved the arming of Serbia (generously financed by France) and an offensive policy toward both Austria-Hungary and Ottoman Turkey. The Russian-sponsored Balkan League of Bulgaria, Greece, Montenegro, and Serbia in particular was directed against Austria-Hungary, but Russia soon lost much control over it.[220]

Taking advantage of Italy's war against the Ottoman Empire to gain Libya (set in motion by the precedent of the French seizure of Morocco in 1911), in October 1912 the Balkan League launched a surprise war against the Turks in the Balkans.[221] This led to much territorial expansion of Serbia and an occupation of conquered territory along the Adriatic coast in Turkish Albania, a process accompanied by the destruction of villages and atrocities committed by Serbian troops and paramilitary bands.[222] The Serbs ignored demands by Austria-Hungary to evacuate Albania, and they later defied an international agreement establishing an independent Albania signed in London in July 1913, shielded by Russia and France.[223]

Initially the German Foreign Office took a wholly passive position in the Balkan wars. The Kaiser viewed the struggle of the Serbs, Bulgars, and Greeks as legitimate, creating a useful buffer of states between Austria and Russia that might become a valuable export market for Germany. Indeed, in the years 1909–13 the value of German exports going to Bulgaria, Greece, Romania, and Serbia was growing very robustly. On account of its potential as a breadbasket and its important oil reserves, Romania especially animated German enthusiasts for *"Mitteleuropa"* in these years.[224] The Kaiser himself had no objections at all to Serbia expanding into Albania to the Adriatic and refused to be drawn

---

[219] See Lieven, *The End of Tsarist Russia*, 70–75, 101, 127–30, 172–81, 225, 227, 231–34, 253–55.

[220] Holger Afflerbach, *Der Dreibund: Europäische Großmacht- und Allianzpolitik vor dem Ersten Weltkrieg* (Vienna, Cologne, and Weimar: Bölau Verlag, 2002), 723.

[221] Francesco Caccamo, "Italy, Libya and the Balkans," in *The Wars Before the Great War: Conflict and International Politics before the Outbreak of the First World War*, ed. Dominik Geppert, William Mulligan, and Andreas Rose (Cambridge: Cambridge University Press, 2015), 21–40. Cf. Helfferich, *Der Weltkrieg*, vol. 1, 91–94.

[222] Charmley, *Splendid Isolation*, 372–73, 380–89; Clark, *The Sleepwalkers*, 42–47, 91, 112–13, 251–68; Lieven, *The End of Tsarist Russia*, 246–64; MacMillan, *The War that Ended Peace*, 442–58; Sean McMeekin, *The Russian Origins of the First World War* (Cambridge, MA: Harvard University Press, 2013), 23–27; Uğur Ümit Üngör, "Mass Violence against Civilians during the Balkan Wars," in *The Wars*, ed. Geppert, Mulligan, and Rose, 76–91. Cf. Helfferich, *Der Weltkrieg*, vol. 1, 95–112.

[223] See Clark, *The Sleepwalkers*, 268–301; Lieven, *The End of Tsarist Russia*, 264–79; MacMillan, *The War that Ended Peace*, 458–65.

[224] David Hamlin, *Germany's Empire in the East: Germans and Romania in the Era of Globalization and Total War* (Cambridge: Cambridge University Press, 2017), 27–75.

into a potential military conflict with France and Russia over the matter.[225] That was a view shared by Bethmann Hollweg and Kidereln-Waechter, who were caught by surprise by the war and left to react to events. Their focus was on protecting German economic interests in the Balkans and Ottoman Turkey, working to improve relations with Britain while preserving the Triple Alliance, all of which counseled against any unilateral or Austro-German involvement.[226] In coming to that decision, Bethmann Hollweg was undoubtedly influenced by a desire not to spark a second Bosnian Annexation Crisis, when Berlin had been pressed to back Austria's unwise territorial claim at great cost to Germany's position in Turkey and with lasting damage to Russo-German relations.[227] With hindsight, the inept and weak dual regime in Vienna and Budapest had its hands full and no business annexing any territory at all in 1908, not least since Hungary was at that time causing endless ethnic troubles within the empire through its coercive Magyarization policy.[228]

The German position only shifted as the situation deteriorated sharply in late October–early November 1912 following Austria's mobilization in Bosnia to press the Serbs and Montenegrins, Russia's so-called trial mobilization in Galicia backed by France, and as international opinion swung against Serbia on account of the atrocities in Albania.[229] Rather than backing Austria as its alliance partner directly and risking a war that was now liable to escalate, Bethmann Hollweg and Kiderlen-Waechter announced Germany's intention to seek a negotiated solution involving the great powers in an article in the *Norddeutsche Allgemeine Zeitung* on November 25. They then worked with French premier Raymond Poincaré (1860–1934) and Edward Grey to bring about international mediation in late November and early December 1912 that culminated in an ambassador's conference in London on December 18.[230] Driving home the potential dangers of a wider war, on December 4 – one day after an armistice was signed between Turkey and the Balkan League – Edward Grey had warned the German ambassador in London that a conflict sparked by an Austrian move against Serbia escalating to a Russian attack on Austria

---

[225] Canis, *Der Weg in den Abgrund*, 482; Clark, *Kaiser Wilhelm II*, 190–91; Meyer, *Mitteleuropa*, 82–115; Röhl *Into the Abyss*, 880–86, 889–90.
[226] Afflerbach, *Der Dreibund*, 726–78; Carroll, *Germany and the Great Powers*, 715–24; Clark, *The Sleepwalkers*, 289.
[227] Afflerbach, *Der Dreibund*, 728.
[228] Olaf Leisse, *Der Untergang des Österreichischen Imperiums: Otto Bauer und die Nationalitätenfrage in der Habsburger Monarchie* (Marburg: Tectum Verlag, 2012); Geoffrey Wawro, *A Mad Catastrophe: The Outbreak of World War I and the Collapse of the Habsburg Empire* (New York: Basic Books, 2014), 15–49.
[229] Clark, *The Sleepwalkers*, 266–70; Lieven, *The End of Tsarist Russia*, 240.
[230] Afflerbach, *Der Dreibund*, 736–40; Canis, *Der Weg in den Abgrund*, 487–503; See also Alma Hannig, "Austro-Hungarian foreign policy and the Balkan Wars," in *The Wars*, ed. Geppert, Mulligan, and Rose, 233–48, here 237.

and then a countermove by Germany would draw in France. In that case, Grey said, Britain would likely side with France and Russia.[231] At the ambassador's conference, Russia reluctantly compromised on Serbia's Adriatic claims, and Austria was granted an independent Albania, but the dangerous and financially costly armed standoff between Austria and Russia continued. The German government then gave numerous stern warnings to the Austrians to settle the dispute with the Russians peaceably, steadily keeping up the pressure through January and February 1913.[232]

Karl Helfferich was able to observe the tense situation in Vienna and hear the Austrian government's great displeasure over Germany's lackluster support when he was in Vienna conducting negotiations over the Oriental Railway with the Austrian foreign ministry in late January and early February 1913.[233] Before his departure for Vienna he had met with the new German foreign secretary Gottlieb von Jagow (1863–1935) – Kidrelen-Waechter had died of stroke in late December 1912. Jagow asked Helfferich to "tell the gentlemen at the Ballplatz [also Ballhausplatz, i.e., the Austrian Foreign Ministry] that the Albanian matter worries us here." In Vienna the Austrian section chief for the Balkans tried to impress upon Helfferich the value of an independent Albania as a "dam against a growing South Slav flood." Helfferich doubted the value of such a "dam" and said as much.[234] Later in conversations with the Austrian foreign minister Leopold von Berchthold (1863–1942), Helfferich gained an unmistakable impression of the irrational militancy of Austria's position toward the Serbs due to the perceived threat of Pan-Serbian irredentism to the Habsburg Empire. Berchtold presented the matter as a great showdown between "Teutons and Slavs" and asked Helffeich if Germany really wanted peace at any cost. Taken aback by this statement, Helfferich deflected that every year peace was preserved was a win for Germany on account of its growing population and increasing economic and financial strength.[235]

Berlin ultimately succeeded in pressing Vienna to de-escalate the crisis and negotiate with the Russians in March 1913, playing an important role in ending the armed standoff that could have easily ignited a European and world war.[236] Over the spring and summer of 1913 the German government then worked to bring about closer ties between the Triple Alliance and Serbia, Romania, and Greece, but Berchtold's misguided and self-defeating anti-Serbian policy and designs for an alliance with Bulgaria sabotaged this by stirring up trouble between Bulgaria and Serbia, helping to precipitate the

---

[231] Clark, *The Sleepwalkers*, 328–29, 354–55; cf. Fischer, *War of Illusions*, 154–77.
[232] Canis, *Der Weg in den Abgrund*, 503–8; Fischer, *War of Illusions*, 205–8.
[233] Hefferich, *Der Weltkrieg*, vol. 1, 102–6.    [234] Ibid., 106–7.    [235] Ibid., 108.
[236] See Fischer, *War of Illusions*, 208–9.

Second Balkan War. Once again Germany had to resort to extreme pressure on Austria to prevent a strike on Serbia during these hostilities.[237]

Ultimately, Bulgaria was decisively defeated and lost most of the territory it had gained in the First Balkan War. Germany supported Greek and Romanian territorial claims against Bulgaria in the peace negotiations, but Vienna's stance ultimately offended and alienated Romania. An old and important ally of Germany and Austria-Hungary only growing in significance on account of its grain and oil exports, Romania subsequently drifted toward Serbia and Russia away from the Triple Alliance.[238] Austria's position in the Balkan wars and Treaty of Bucharest was roundly criticized in the German liberal and nationalist press, with voices heard describing the alliance with Austria as a millstone and obstacle to German ambitions.[239] The Albanian matter flared up again in September 1913 over Serbian incursions into northern Albania, but by that point even the Russians were exasperated by the Serbs, so no new escalation was likely. Berlin was by this time also eager to mend fences with Vienna and so approved an Austrian ultimatum to Serbia on October 17 that finally induced Belgrade to withdraw its troops from Albania.[240] Yet very interestingly, not two weeks later the Kaiser advised the Austrian ambassador that his country ought to get back into good graces with the Serbs by offering Belgrade's leadership sizable cash gifts, military exchanges, and a better trade treaty.[241] In early 1914 the agents of the German coal and steel magnate Hugo Stinnes (1870–1924) in Serbia were eager to take advantage of the Austria's loss of credibility to finance Serbian purchases of German machinery.[242]

The conflicting policy visions in the Balkans in Berlin and Vienna in 1912–13 were striking: where the Germans saw opportunities for investment, trade, military cooperation, and potential alliance partners – not least in Serbia – the Austrians thought in terms of building Albanian "dams" and preparing for a violent showdown with the Serbs, waging a kind of proxy war against Serbia via Bulgaria that backfired disastrously. The increasing militarization of both Russian and Austro-Hungarian diplomacy and the willingness of both to unilaterally mobilize armies and take things to the brink over

---

[237] Ibid., 213–18; Canis, *Der Weg in den Abgrund*, 557–79; Afflerbach, *Der Dreibund*, 742–43.
[238] Afflerbach, *Der Dreibund*, 744–46; Hamlin, *Germany's Empire*, 106–14; Hannig, "Austro-Hungarian Foreign Policy," 239–40, 43; Carroll, *Germany and the Great Powers*, 737.
[239] Carroll, *Germany and the Great Powers*, 738–39.
[240] Fischer, *War of Illusions*, 219–20; Clark, *The Sleepwalkers*, 287. Cf. Röhl, *Into the Abyss*, 941–53.
[241] Clark, *The Sleepwalkers*, 290.
[242] Gerald Feldman, "Hugo Stinnes and the Prospect of War Before 1914," in Boemeke, Chickering, and Förster, *Anticipating Total War*, 77–95, here 83.

matters not vital to them – indeed over things as minor as the Serbian possession of an Albanian harbor – was another very dangerous development.[243] To be sure, Serbia's violent provocations and defiance in Albania were maddening, but Albania was not contiguous to Bosnia-Herzegovina, and a Serbian presence on the Adriatic could pose no danger to Austria except as the vaguest naval phantom.[244] Likewise, Slavophile opinion in Russia may have cheered on plucky Serbia and Montenegro, but Russia had only a miniscule trade with these countries and they were hundreds of miles from the vital chokepoints of the Turkish Straits and many hundreds more from the Russian frontier. Such brinksmanship over non-vital interests was symptomatic of weakness and dysfunction in both Vienna and St. Petersburg that now had the potential to trigger a European and indeed world war.

The Balkan wars had a number of other negative consequences for Germany in particular. For one, Russia, France, and Britain viewed Austria-Hungary increasingly as a second-rate power, when not simply as an appendage of Germany, then as a declining entity ripe for dismemberment but propped up and protected by Berlin. Of course Berlin's handling of Vienna in 1912–13 gave them no reason to think otherwise. Disregarding Austro-Hungarian interests in the Balkans became easier, was encouraged by Russia through its Serbian client, and was more or less tolerated in Paris and London, destabilizing the region and Europe more generally.[245] The need to resort to a German-backed ultimatum to get Serbian compliance with an international agreement over Albanian independence brokered by the six great European powers highlights that loss of status and pull.[246]

German pressure on Vienna in 1912–13 also markedly worsened relations with Austria-Hungary, its last remaining reliable alliance partner, raising doubts about whether the Triple Alliance would survive. The only silver lining in this cloud was that the complete failure of Berchtold's anti-Serbian policy seemed to augur for a new course in the Balkans in the Ballhausplatz, promoted by the Archduke Franz Ferdinand (1863–1914), heir to the Austro-Hungarian throne and a committed reformer. He had opposed the unwise annexation of Bosnia-Herzegovina and was a critic of the belligerent stance of the Austrian Chief of the General Staff Blasius von Schemua

---

[243] See Clark, *The Sleepwalkers*, 266–70, 283, 290–92.
[244] Cf. Hannig, "Austro-Hungary and the Balkan Wars," 235.
[245] Günther Kronebitter, "The Perception of the 'Wars before the War' in Austria –Hungary," in The Wars, ed. Geppert, Mulligan, and Rose, 190–203, here 196. See also Charmley, *Splendid Isolation*, 351–61, 369–73, 380–89; Clark, *The Sleepwalkers*, 279–81, 288, 290; Lieven, *The End of Tsarist Russia*, 278–84; Andreas Rose, "From 'Illusion' and 'Angellism' to Détete – British Radicals and the Balkan Wars," in The Wars, ed. Geppert, Mulligan, and Rose, *The Wars*, 320–43, here 335–39; Wawro, *A Mad Catastrophe*, 73–98.
[246] Kronebitter, "The Perception of the 'Wars before the War,'" in The Wars, ed. Geppert, Mulligan, and Rose, 199–200.

(1856–1920) and his successor, the notoriously Serbophobe Franz Conrad von Hötzendorf (1852–1925), who together had helped to militarize Berchthold's misguided Serbian and Russian diplomacy in 1912–13.[247]

Oddly, though Germany had played an important constructive role in restraining Austria in tensions with Russia and in preventing Austrian attacks on Serbia multiple times, German relations with Russia actually deteriorated sharply in late 1913 and early 1914 – indeed, the evidence suggests that Austrian impotence and German restraint in the Balkans in these years may have actually emboldened St. Petersburg.[248] With regard to its continental *Weltpolitik*, the Balkan wars had also much weakened Ottoman Turkey territorially and financially, thus threatening Germany's investments and influence in the Near East, not least the construction of the Baghdad Railway.

To conclude, by 1914 most German colonial initiatives since 1895 had stalled or fallen short. Even compared to Russia, which had suffered multiple imperial setbacks since 1904, German efforts at such things as inner colonization looked feeble and halfhearted. Since 1909 Russia had also much enhanced its continental European position via its Serbian and Montenegrin clients at the expense of Ottoman Turkey (and indirectly Germany), even while gaining zones of influence in northern Persia and the Afghan Hindu-kush as well s bolstering its position in Mongolia and northern Manchuria. Even a relatively weak power such as Italy had gained for itself Libya. It is a remarkable fact that unlike every other great European power, the United States, and Japan, Imperial Germany had not waged wars of conquest or imposed unilateral annexations to expand its colonial territory or spheres of influence – what little that was added between 1895 and 1914 was gained by negotiation (half of Samoa and parts of the so-called sleeping-sickness Congo), purchase (the tiny Caroline, Palau, and Mariana Islands), or gunship diplomacy and lease (Kiaochow). None of it proved suitable for settler colonialism, and all of it except for tiny Samoa represented net financial liabilities to the Reich. Simultaneously, Germany was tied to the Magyar and Balkan follies of an increasingly volatile and dysfunctional Habsburg state, deeply corrosive to better relations with St. Petersburg, Belgrade, or Bucharest. Yet oddly, in the minds of many British, French, Russian, and American officials and their reading publics, it was the Germans who were warlike and expansionist.

For all the election propaganda of 1906–7 and soaring talk that was heard about the German colonies during the Denburg era, von Halle, Rathgen, Sering, Schumacher, and Helfferich knew that there were no broad vistas of overseas development in Germany's existing colonial empire. Germany had no

---

[247] Afflerbach, *Der Dreibund*, 730–33; Clark, *The Sleepwalkers*, 108–9, 116–17; Fischer, *War of Illusions*, 218; Hannig, "Austro-Hungarian Foreign Policy," 240–41, 246; Wawro, *A Mad Catastrophe*, 74–79, 91–98.
[248] See McMeekin, *The Russian Origins*, 24.

colonies producing food grains or key raw materials and commodities like oil, tin, cotton, rubber, tobacco, or sugar on any significant scale, in glaring contrast to what they had seen in North America, the Caribbean, Ottoman Turkey, Russia, and Southeast Asia. They knew no German colonial markets existed worth mentioning that could absorb German manufactured exports and that they were insignificant destinations for investment – they represented only 2 percent of Germany's total overseas invested capital by 1914.[249] No colonies existed that could provide troops or munitions in war either. There were no frontiers to be improved, no viable settler colonies offering social mobility and independence, where many German liberal imperialists had long hoped stakeholders could be created, capacities for self-governance might be developed, and thus a liberal faith in progress could be rekindled. The continuous growth of social democracy was evidence to many that German workers and increasingly even some members of the middle classes – as evidenced by the electoral cooperation between the left liberals and Social Democrats – had given up on that. The Bülow Bloc itself would be short-lived, and in the elections of January 1912 the SPD would poll an unprecedented 4.25 million votes (35 percent of the electorate), nearly 1 million more than in the "Hottentot elections" of 1906–7, making it (with its 110 deputies) by far the largest party in the Reichstag.[250]

As we shall see in the next chapter, this context of stifled colonial ambitions, diplomatic isolation, narrowing horizons, growing European insecurity, and domestic political polarization was behind the frustration of the middle-class public and the rise of radical nationalist critics of German foreign policy between 1908 and 1914. That context is essential for understanding the escalating dreadnought arms race with Great Britain as well the very high stakes of German financial reform in 1908–9 and military spending in 1913–14. It also better explains the great importance invested in the Berlin-Baghdad railroad in the last few years of peace as the only remaining and viable initiative of *Weltpolitik*. Once again, the men who have featured in this book would play important roles in that unfolding drama.

---

[249] Gründer, *Geschichte der deutschen Kolonien*, 235–39.
[250] Schorske, *German Social Democracy*, 228. In greater detail Schmädeke, *Wählerbewegung*, vol. 1, 91–126. Sperber, *The Kaiser's Voters*, 254–64. See also Fischer, *War of Illusions*, 95–111.

# 10

# World Policy Contained

## Fleet Enthusiasm

By 1908 naval propaganda had become part of the background noise of Wilhemine life. While it had been perfected in the RMA into a well-oiled machine that could now dispense with professors, the RMA was losing control to the nationalist associations and above all the Navy League, which as we saw in Chapter 6 was growing into a massive organization with strong local roots. Indeed, if anything by 1908 there was *too much* public enthusiasm for fleet size increases. In the case of the circle of men that is the subject of this book, their own enthusiasm for naval politics had ebbed considerably. That was in part the result of their own maturing careers that had pushed their interests and activities in other directions, which as we saw in the case of Rathgen had moved into tropical colonial policy with his appointment to the Hamburg Kolonialinstitut. Helfferich was much disillusioned with politics after the bruising confrontations over the colonies of the years 1904–6. His work at the Deutsche Bank had deepened his existing interests in money and banking as well as Balkan and Ottoman railway investments. Indeed, as was discussed previously and will be covered in greater depth later in this chapter, Helfferich was deeply involved in the construction of the Baghdad Railway between 1908 and 1914.

For his part, Schumacher had returned from the United States in 1907 and then especially from Southeast Asia in 1911 disillusioned with both overseas colonies and navalism, developing instead a growing interest in contiguous empires such as the United States and Russia. Sering's interests, too, had shifted away from the navy and overseas colonies toward internal colonization in the Prussian east and in Russia, later reinforced both by the rather sobering findings of the study he spearheaded for the Association for Social Policy on tropical colonies and his activity in the Society for the Promotion of Inner Colonization. Even the hardest core navalist of the group, Ernst von Halle, had largely abandoned Mahanism and given up on overseas settler colonies, if not on maritime topics, redirecting his work away from the navy toward research on the shipping industry, the Latin American economy, the reform of economics education in the civil service, and editing his new journal, *Die*

*Weltwitschaft* (The World Economy). Indeed, he himself considered his 1907 book *Die Seemacht in der deutschen Geschichte* (Sea Power in German History) his "final word" (*Schlusswort*) on the topic of the navy.[1] As will be explored later in this chapter, von Halle would in fact leave the RMA's Communications Bureau in 1908 and move to the Reich Treasury to head its new Economic Bureau to spearhead financial reform, which became his prime sphere of political activity before his very untimely death in 1909.

Turning to Schmoller, he published nothing at all on the navy, *Weltpolitik*, or related themes after 1907 except where it touched on financial reform or the 1913 army bill, the former a cause in which he became very active in 1908–9 despite advancing age (he turned 70 in 1908). His own closeness to Bülow would have in any case made him sensitive to the diplomatic dangers of the dreadnought arms race unfolding with Britain. As discussed in Chapter 7, by the fall of 1907 serious doubts had been raised in public about the soundness of Tirpitz's battleship strategy, and by late summer 1908 Bülow felt strongly that concessions in the speed of construction needed to be negotiated in return for a political settlement with Britain to extract Germany from its increasingly isolated diplomatic position.

Be that as it may, in the spring of 1908 the Reichstag easily passed yet another amendment of the navy law that accelerated the dreadnought arms race begun in 1906. It has been noted that the decision to launch German dreadnoughts was taken without much input from the Chancellor, the Foreign Office, or the German Treasury, much less the Admiralty Staff, which speaks to the polycratic and unaccountable nature of German naval decision-making in the Wilhelmine era.[2] What is as remarkable is that it was the Bülow Bloc majority in the Reichstag (especially the National Liberals and left liberals), and not Tirpitz, who in 1907 pushed for a naval amendment that increased the pace of construction. The RMA was in fact planning to wait until the winter of 1909–10 to introduce new legislation and then to only reduce the service life of battleships from twenty-five to twenty years and to stabilize the pace of construction to three ships per year.[3]

The Navy League was pressing for an even more accelerated pace of construction than the parties of the Bülow Bloc. It counted no fewer than 3,006 local branches and 2,924 local agents throughout Germany by 1906 with

---

[1] BPL, Hugo Münsterberg Collection, Ser. 1, Box 7, Folder 1768, Ernst von Halle to Hugo Münsterberg, Grunewald, Oct. 9, 1907; Ernst von Halle, *Die Seemacht in der deutschen Geschichte* (Leipzig: G. J. Göschen'sche Verlagsbuchhandlung, 1907).
[2] Michale Epkenhans, "*Dreadnought*: A 'Golden Opportunity' for Germany's Naval Aspirations?" in The Dreadnought and in Blyth, Lambert, and Rüger, *The Dreadnought and the Edwardian Age*, 79–91, here 85.
[3] See Deist, *Flottenpolik*, 194; Kelly, *Tirpitz*, 279–85.

a total membership that would swell to 324,372 by 1907 and reach 331,910 by 1913, making it by far the largest nationalist pressure group in Germany.[4] Disappointed by the 1906 amendment, in the summer of 1907 the Navy League's pro-fleet agitation had continually pressed for an increase in the pace of construction. When it got wind of Tirpitz's draft amendment with "only" three new ships per year, the league led by August Keim and a large segment of German nationalist public opinion denounced Tirpitz's draft bill as wholly inadequate.[5] Given the importance of Keim and the Navy League to the elections of 1906–7, Bülow and Sering (the latter serving, as will be recalled, in the leadership of the Navy League) supported Keim, and attempts by Tirpitz, the Communications Bureau, and even the Kaiser to force Keim to step down backfired. This led Keim to warn them pointedly in December 1907 that the majority of the Navy League and a large part of German public opinion were behind him and that they could expect a wave of public protest that would damage the Kaiser's image were he forced to step aside.[6]

The Navy League's popular agitation and the bloc parties' initiatives were ultimately so effective that they led the RMA to revise the draft amendment to increase the pace of construction to four ships per year and to seek passage of this legislation far earlier than planned. This pressure also prompted Tirpitz to introduce higher naval estimates to upgrade the armaments and displacements of ships and to shorten the service life of battleships in this new draft amendment.[7] Support for new naval legislation in 1907–8 was not confined to the parties of the bloc or the Navy League. The influential Center Party politician Peter Spahn (1846–1925) spoke in favor of a shortened lifespan and higher estimates as early as August 1907, arguing that Germany needed to follow the lead of the United States, which was building massive 23,000 ton dreadnoughts.[8]

The navy law amendment ultimately passed in the Reichstag on March 27, 1908 with barely any debate and little controversy, such was the consensus in the Bülow Bloc and Center Party over these naval appropriations. Indeed, the amendment was accepted without even a parliamentary resolution on how it would be funded.[9] Along with much higher estimates to build larger and more heavily-armed dreadnought-type battleships, the law increased the pace of new construction to four new ships per year until 1912 and reduced the service life of the fleet from twenty-five to twenty years.[10] It was not until after the passage of this legislation in 1908 that Keim left the leadership of the

---

[4] Eley, *Reshaping the German Right*, 102, 366; cf. Diziol, *Flottenverein*, vol. 1, 103. Diziol's numbers for 1907 are 324,083.
[5] See Deist, *Flottenpolitik*, 210–47.   [6] Ibid., 225–26; Berghahn, *Der Tirpitz-Plan*, 588–91.
[7] Berghahn, *Der Tirpitz-Plan*, 589. See also Deist, *Flottenpolitik*, 211–13.
[8] Kelly, *Tirpitz*, 283–84.   [9] Ibid., 290–91.   [10] Ibid., 288.

Navy League, and even then the populist forces continued to set the tone in this body, particularly through the strength of its local chapters.[11]

As the size and influence of the Navy League and the ease with which such legislation could pass suggests, navalism had made extraordinary inroads into Wilhelmine society by 1908. The Navy League's richly-illustrated magazine *Die Flotte* had a massive monthly circulation reaching 375,000 and was a ubiquitous sight in German hotels, waiting rooms, hospitals, barber shops, passenger ships, and railway dining cars.[12] It ran articles on a wide range of topics related to the navy and all things maritime that appealed to a mass readership of both genders. This went well beyond navy news, naval propaganda, and reports on league affairs to include articles on Germans overseas, the colonies, new maritime technology, shipbuilding, travel, maritime history, and foreign navies as well as naval artwork, poems, and novellas. Other content even devoted itself to water sports and the health benefits and recreational opportunities of the seacoast.[13] The league also organized excursions, lecture series, exhibits, and motion picture screenings.[14] The founding and growth of many German Navy League affiliates abroad in these years indicates, too, that the navy continued to be vested with enormous symbolic weight as a floating agent of a strong and united "Germandom" at home and overseas.[15]

By 1908 German fleet reviews had also become true mass spectacles. The harbor towns closest to such reviews as well as the shipping lines HAPAG and NDL exploited the commercial potential of fleet reviews by organizing tours to see the fleet, while the press ran articles with the leaked information about their location and other details. Such was the enthusiasm that in the summer of 1907 the Kaiser's yacht, on entering a review, was surrounded by a mass of tourist boats bringing sightseers from many ports in Germany whose number exceeded the fleet it came to see.[16] By this time the navy was part of Wilhelmine mass culture, exemplified by the ubiquitous *Matrosenanzug* worn by boys, by postcards, magazines, games, and toys featuring the navy, and by model ship shows and the new medium of film showing ship launches.[17] Indeed, Tirpitz was himself worried about the *excessive* degree of public enthusiasm at ship launches and reviews, as it drew unwelcome attention to the growing fleet during the "danger zone."[18] The German masses participating

---

[11] Eley, *Reshaping the German Right*, 254–79; Chickering, *We Men Who Feel Most German*, 261.

[12] Diziol, *Flottenverein*, vol. 1, 133.   [13] See ibid., 135–44.   [14] Ibid., 144–83.

[15] Stefan Manz, "Nationalism Gone Global: The *Hauptverband Deutscher Flottenvereine in Auslande* 1898–1918," *German History* 30, no. 2 (June 2012): 199–221; Manz, *Constructing a German Diaspora: The "Greater German Empire," 1871–1914* (New York: Routledge, 2014), 98–132.

[16] Rüger, *The Great Naval Game*, 83.   [17] Ibid., 50–82.   [18] Ibid., 69–70.

in Wilhelmine naval culture and in *Flottenpolitik* were active participants in a process over which the RMA, Tirpitz, Bülow, and the Kaiser no longer had full control, if ever they had it.

Why this astonishing investment by the German middle-class public in a battleship navy? As was discussed at length in the earlier chapters, *Weltpolitik* had stalled by 1908. It had been successfully blocked or "countermined" in most overseas engagement since 1895, and often by the British. That was on account of Germany either being too weak or unable to offer anything in return for colonial "favors." Thus the resumé of *Weltpolitik* by 1908 was very thin indeed, amounting to a tiny isolated leasehold in China, a few flyspecks of land in the South Pacific, and an unfinished railroad in Ottoman Turkey. This compared rather poorly with what other younger powers like the Americans and Japanese had attained in those very years, often violently and with British assistance or acquiescence. As *Weltpolitik* failed, Germany's diplomatic isolation grew, and as colonial wars and scandals sullied Germany's reputation as a colonial power in 1904–7, it is only understandable that other measures of *Weltgeltung* (equal world standing), *Weltmachtstellung* (world power position), *Würde* (dignity), and *Ehre* (honor) would grow in importance. Thus Germany's fleet took on much greater symbolic political weight just as HMS *Dreadnought* made its debut. That was a fateful concurrence.

In the eyes of many Germans, dreadnoughts came to be seen as yet another British challenge to one of the few remaining avenues for achieving equal world standing, and thus international dignity and honor, things that had been at the very core of German naval ambitions from the beginning. As the new weapon rendered older British ships obsolete, a favorable ratio with the Royal Navy seemed within reach. Under these circumstances it would have been odd if the Germans *had not* started building dreadnoughts, not least since both the Americans and Japanese were well into their own dreadnought programs by that point. In an era shaped by Social Darwinism and Mahanian doctrines of sea power, and where the naval humiliations of China, Spain, Ottoman Turkey, and Russia were in recent memory, a powerful dreadnought navy was a form of national insurance. As dreadnought navies could be peddled to the public with the appealing peaceful logic of deterrence, navy bills were assured the support of liberals and moderate conservatives, that is, the university-educated and commercial middle classes.

Nevertheless, dreadnoughts in the Anglo-German context were much more than insurance and deterrent weapons. They were powerful national status symbols fulfilling domestic political needs. It is often overlooked that this was as true in Britain as in Germany. In Britain dreadnoughts were loaded with symbolic weight and actively propagated as statements of national efficiency and technological mastery, even as their tactical and strategic value as weapons was increasingly murky. British anxieties about inefficiency, technological obsolescence, and imperial overextension clearly lurked in the background, stoked by the aftermath of the Boer War and economic rivalry with Germany.[19] Public enthusiasm for *Dreadnought* would, moreover, assure parliamentary support for naval estimates during a time of budgetary retrenchment and shifting political priorities. Dreadnoughts were also increasingly loaded in this period with the symbolism of imperial unity, a substitute of sorts for tariff reform and imperial federation.[20] The name *Dreadnought* itself made direct historical associations to no fewer than six English ships of the line dating back to 1573, one of which fought at Trafalgar and was thus calculated to appeal to a British national identity bound up closely with naval supremacy.[21] The noisy politics of the navy law of 1900 and the Bülow tariff of 1902, as well as squabbles over Samoa, the Yangtze Valley, the Venezuelan intervention, and not least Britain's own domestic military politics with its regularly recurring invasion bogey had served to inflate the German threat out of all proportion with Germany's actual naval capacities.[22] With the waning of Britain's relative economic power and growing perceptions of the German threat and as Germany's *Weltpolitik* and diplomacy failed to deliver *Weltgeltung*, dreadnoughts began to play roles as surrogates in both countries after 1908. They became steel and rivet manifestations of the unmet political expectations of the British and German publics.[23]

## Deterrent Illusions

As Jan Rüger has shown, fleet reviews offered an arena for displays of such national status and power expressed through battleships. Such "naval theatre" in Spithead and Kiel served to heighten misunderstanding between Germany and Britain, widening the gap between political rhetoric and strategic rationale, thus actually catalyzing greater antagonism and rivalry between the two countries.[24] As he argues, naval theater "encouraged a culture in which triumphant intransigence and the preparation for war in the name of peace were central features. Rather than communicate the fundamental limitations that confronted both nations and which they had to accept in order to resolve their 'misunderstanding,' the two countries' leading actors either kept quiet or

---

[19] Jan Rüger, "The Symbolic Value of *Dreadnought*," in Lambert, 9–18, here 12. On *Dreadnought's* launch, see also Rüger, *The Great Naval Game*, 67, 78–85, 236–37.
[20] Rüger, *The Great Naval Game*, 175–82.
[21] Andrew Lambert, "The Power of a Name: Tradition, Technology and Transformation," in Blyth, Lambert, and Rüger, *The Dreadnought and the Edwardian Age*, 19–28, here 22–24.
[22] Steiner, *Britain and the Origins*, 48–59. Cf. Kennedy, *Anglo-German Antagonism*, 416, 420.
[23] Rüger, *The Great Naval Game*, 240–44.   [24] Ibid., 247–48.

exploited the naval theatre for their own agendas."[25] Viewed through this lens and set in context, it is hard to see how an abandonment of "Supremacy" or the "Risk Fleet" would have been politically feasible once their assumptions collapsed. Given the massive sunk costs, the tremendous investment in propaganda, the large expenditure of political capital, and the naval-industrial complexes involved in building dreadnought battleships in both Germany and Britain, there were few avenues of escape for men such as Tirpitz and his British counterparts Jackie Fisher, Arthur Wilson, and Winston Churchill. Also, consider public opinion in both countries. Was a German junior partnership with the British Empire acceptable in Berlin? Was greater German parity with Britain politically saleable in London? Thus a mix of rational and irrational motivations began driving German naval policy after 1908 no less than in Britain following the Navy Scare of 1909. The German "Two-Thirds Fleet" and "Risk Fleet" tapped into a mass psychology very similar to the British "Two Power Standard" and "Naval Supremacy" offering deceptively reassuring slogans for deterrence and security to their respective publics, even as the substance became increasingly meaningless, delivering instead more insecurity at higher cost as the perverse dynamic of an arms race took hold.[26] The sheer irrationality of a new weapon originally conceived in a British quest for naval economies contributing to spiraling naval expenditures, national debt, and insecurity deserves to be highlighted. With national identity, honor, and standing at stake, leaders on both sides of the North Sea dug in their heels, denied these realities, and reflexively reiterated their battleship dogmas as this arms race unfolded.

Consider Germany. As the negative diplomatic repercussions of the 1908 navy law amendment began to weigh on Bülow following the encirclement scare of the early summer of 1908, he wrote in his memoirs that he urged the Kaiser to reduce the pace of naval construction in return for negotiating English neutrality in case France were to attack Germany. The Kaiser rejected this proposal violently.[27] He was, Bülow noted, utterly fixated on building ever more battleships at as fast a pace possible.[28] Bülow then asked Tirpitz why it was that the German fleet was so focused on battle with the Royal Navy rather than showing the flag in the Mediterranean or Pacific? Why, he asked (clearly informed by Galster's critiques) were Germany's naval efforts spent solely on building battleships rather than on coastal defenses, torpedo boats, and especially, submarines? Tirpitz answered that the Kaiser feared a "Copenhagening" of the fleet were it to be taken out of home waters. And like a now broken

---

[25] Ibid., 248.  [26] Kelly, *Tirpitz*, 201–2, 262; Röhl, *Into the Abyss*, 821–23.
[27] Bülow, *Denkwürdigkeiten*, vol. 2, 319. Cf. Canis, *Der Weg in den Abgrund*, 271, 281; Alfred von Tirpitz, *Politische Dokumente*, Volume 1: *Der Aufbau der deutschen Weltmacht* (Stuttgart and Berlin: J. G. Cotta'sche Buchhandlung Nachfolger, 1924), 67–68.
[28] Bülow, *Denkwürdigkeiten*, vol. 2, 321.

gramophone record Tirpitz responded with yet another recitation of the "risk theory": battleships would be the decisive factor in an eventual war. In such a war Germany's fleet would leave harbor and force the English into a decisive battle on the open seas, a battle Germany might possibly win. In any case, Germany had good chances and would weaken the Royal Navy so much that German submarines would be able to force England to sue for peace.[29] Bülow evaded the issue, explicitly refusing to pass judgment on the correctness of this strategy.[30] They were now all captives of the "Risk Fleet."

The British leadership stubbornly maintained its own misconceptions. By 1905 the Entente Cordiale, the strategic realignment of the Russo-Japanese War, and technological change had made the Two Power Standard in battleships obsolete. But its hold on elements within the Admiralty and the British public was remarkably stubborn. There was likewise an almost complete inability to recognize that the Germans were becoming nearly as reliant on trade and as vulnerable to its disruption as Britons, and that with a rapidly-growing population but no viable settler colonies, the significance of German trade would only increase over time in assuring continued material prosperity. Thus British attempts to force naval arms limitation agreements on the Germans on the basis of the "Two Power Standard" or "Naval Supremacy" were doomed from the outset. In 1907 and then again in 1908 the Campbell-Bannerman government tried to negotiate a slower pace of German battleship construction from a commanding position of superiority, doing so by invoking the Two Power Standard.[31] Such was the staggering hypocrisy of going to The Hague from that position of superiority to demand naval arms reductions from the Germans that Arthur Balfour took Campbell-Bannerman to task for it on the floor of the Commons in early March 1907.[32] The German response, as just discussed, was to accelerate dreadnought construction in March 1908.

One year later in March of 1909 the Reichstag easily passed the navy budget for the fiscal year with the support of all the bourgeois parties, despite the fact that Admiral Galster's criticisms of German naval policy, deteriorating relations with England, and spiraling construction costs were subjects of lively deliberations in the Reichstag Budget Commission.[33] It was remarkable that not a single Reichstag deputy asked to speak after the report from the

---

[29] Ibid., 320; Ritter, *Staatskunst*, vol. 2, 202. Cf. Berghahn, *Der Tirpitz-Plan*, 602.
[30] Bülow, *Denkwürdigkeiten*, vol. 2, 320. Cf. Bülow, *Deutsche Politik*, 29–31.
[31] Otte, "Grey Ambassador," in Blyth, Lambert and Rüger, *The Dreadnought in the Edwardian Age*, 57–58, 60–61; Offer, *The First World War*, 325.
[32] "Notes and Figures," *The Liberal Magazine* XV, no. 163 (April 1907): 161–99, here 176; Offer, *The First World War*, 325; Charmley, *Splendid Isolation*, 349.
[33] StenBerVR, XII. Legislaturperiode, 233. Sitzung, 1907/09, vol. 9 (March 24, 1909), 7729D–7730D.

commission was delivered to the floor of the Reichstag – the discussion was ended with a "lively bravo" instead.[34] The SPD abstained from the vote, lodging no objections other than some extraneous complaints about the pay, promotion, and working conditions of wharf workers.[35] Bülow believed that this clear signal of public approval of the navy offered German diplomacy a position of strength from which an agreement on naval arms limitations might be negotiated with the British to improve deteriorating relations. He thereupon initiated an extensive and pointed exchange with Tirpitz about it being high time the navy came clean over when Germany would have sufficient naval strength for its defense so that it could reduce the pace of naval construction. Tirpitz evaded the question. He wanted to keep all options open but then promptly undermined Bülow's position with the Kaiser to reject any naval arms limitations.[36]

In early 1909 Britain was gripped by a major naval scare engineered the previous summer to counter cuts to the Cowdor Programme of dreadnought construction implemented by the Liberal government between 1906 and 1908. It was fueled by misinformation, rumors, and cabinet leaks planted deliberately in select newspapers by the Admiralty beginning in the autumn of 1908 that seemed to show Germany secretly accelerating dreadnought construction beyond the 1908 amendment and thus threatening "Supremacy," leading to hysterical calls of "we want eight and we won't wait!" from the British press and Navy League.[37] While no such acceleration of construction was underway in Germany, the scare gripped the British public, unleashing the now very familiar feature of hysterical German invasion stories that ultimately succeeded in pushing the Liberal government to dramatically increase the pace of British dreadnought construction in 1909–10 to eight new ships.[38] No less than in Germany, the British government was now reacting to public opinion, in this instance opinion deliberately manipulated by the Admiralty. The 1909 scare also undermined British public support for the Declaration of London of February 1909 strengthening neutral rights in war, which was already vehemently opposed by First Lord of the Admiralty Reginald McKenna and Admiral Fisher and was ultimately vetoed by the British House

---

[34] Ibid., 7730D.   [35] Ibid., 7731A-C, 7731D–7736D, 7737A-C.
[36] Bülow, *Denkwürdigkeiten*, vol. 2, 427, 465. Cf. Tirpitz, *Politische Dokumente*, vol. 1, 145–52. See also Canis, *Der Weg in den Abgrund*, 325–28; Mommsen, *Bürgerstolz und Weltmachtstreben*, 364.
[37] Geppert, *Pressekriege*, 272–76. Fisher's most important collaborator was James Garvin (1868–1947), chief editor of the *Observer*.
[38] Tirpitz, *Politische Dokumente*, vol. 1, 124–45. See also Nicholas P. Hiley, "The Failure of British Espionage against Germany, 1907–1914," *Historical Journal* 26, no. 4 (1983): 867–89, here 874–79. Cf. Marder, *From Dreadnought to Scapa Flow*, vol. 1, 152–56, 177–78; Matthew Seligmann, "Intelligence Information and the 1909 Naval Scare," *War in History* 17, no. 1 (2010): 37–59.

of Lords.[39] The dreadnought arms race was thus now adding the danger of making it even more likely that in war Britain would target not Germany's fleet but its entire overseas trade in flagrant violation of maritime law and the principles of The Hague and London Conferences.

In the midst of the British navy panic, on June 3, 1909 a conference was held between Bülow, Tirpitz, the German ambassador to London Paul von Metternich, and other senior members of the government, army, and navy on improving Anglo-German relations with sight to a naval agreement.[40] To the surprise of Bülow, Tirpitz now claimed that he had supported a naval agreement on the basis of a 3:4 battleship ratio in new construction in the autumn of 1908, but with the recent acceleration of British dreadnought construction, he no longer did. Germany could not adequately defend itself – the "danger zone" would not be passed until 1915 when fortifications on Heligoland and the widening of the Kaiser-Wilhelm Canal would be completed.[41]

After Bülow's resignation later in the summer of 1909, Bethmann Hollweg actually proposed an Anglo-German battleship ratio of 3:4 as part of a broader political settlement that included a neutrality agreement, but it went nowhere, such was the continuing hold of the need to sustain British battleship "Supremacy" and the importance of the Entente.[42] Yet with the growth of the US Navy, the Two Power Standard was bogus by 1909 and the British government well knew it, though that could not be admitted to the public – the American naval threat was dealt with by willfully denying it existed.[43] That year the British Admiralty quietly decided that a 16:10 battleship ratio with Germany would be sufficient.[44] Japan's growth as a naval power could also be ignored in London, but such was the security anxiety over the expansion of the Japanese Imperial Navy in both Australia and New Zealand following redeployment of the Royal Navy to home waters under Admiral Fisher that both Dominions issued invitations to the US Atlantic Fleet to make stopovers in Auckland and Sydney during its circumnavigation from 1907 to 1909. They did so without bothering to consult the British Colonial or Foreign Offices first. A throng estimated at over half a million welcomed the US Navy to

---

[39] Offer, *The First World War*, 276–80.
[40] Bülow, *Denkwürdigkeiten*, vol. 2, 431–38; Canis, *Der Weg in den Abgrund*, 329–30.
[41] Bülow, *Denkwürdigkeiten*, vol. 2, 433, 434–35, 503–4. Cf. Tirpitz, *Politische Dokumente*, vol. 1, 157–61. See also Canis, *Der Weg in den Abgrund*, 330; Mommsen, *Bürgerstolz und Weltmachtstreben*, 364.
[42] Canis, *Der Weg in den Abgrund*, 343–46; Epkenhans, *Die wilhelminische Flottenrüstung*, 52–64; Jarausch, *Enigmatic Chancellor*, 112–16; Otte, "Grey Ambassador," in Blyth, Lambert and Rüger, *The Dreadnought in the Edwardian Age*, 64–65. Cf. Tirpitz, *Politische Dokumente*, vol. 1, 164–65.
[43] Marder, *From Dreadnought to Scapa Flow*, vol. 1, 182–85; Hendrix, *Naval Diplomacy*, 52–53.
[44] Wilson, *The Policy of the Entente*, 8.

Sydney harbor in August 1908.[45] Australians were voting with their feet about their faith in British "Naval Supremacy."

Having the previous year decided to build eight new dreadnoughts, in the summer of 1910 Prime Minister Asquith signaled a desire for an agreement on naval arms in a speech in the Commons but wasted no time blaming the Germans for previous failures to come to an accord because of their unwillingness to make concessions. Predictably, the British memorandum from Grey forwarded to the Germans assumed the British position of strength would make an impression and demanded concessions on the navy from Germany with nothing concrete in return – a political treaty with Germany, it noted, was out of the question on account of the Entente.[46] In effect this amounted to saying Britain needed to retain a "free hand" to intervene on the side of the Entente in a war started by either France or Russia. In Germany the offer was roundly denounced in National Liberal and conservative circles as just another attempt to assert British "Naval Supremacy."[47] On October 17, 1910, just days after the German government had rejected Asquith's proposal, the Kaiser had an audience with the British Ambassador Sir Edward Goschen (1847–1924) in which he said Germany acknowledged Britain's naval supremacy but could not accept such a degree of supremacy that Britain could attack Germany without incurring the risk of such damage to the Royal Navy that it would no longer be feared by other nations.[48] Just days later at an audience with the Kaiser, Tirpitz reiterated that this "risk" to the Royal Navy was the very "backbone" of His Majesty's naval policy on which Germany's *"Weltmachstellung"* and world peace rested. Were the British capable of building in excess of an acceptable [2:3] risk ratio, "then from an historical standpoint the development of the German fleet would have been a mistake, the fleet politics of Your Majesty an historical fiasco."[49]

By March 1911 the British government appeared willing to concede on account of the unsustainability of British naval spending. In the House of Commons on March 13 Foreign Secretary Grey and McKenna announced accepting a 30:21 margin of superiority over the Germans in battleships, but the Anglo-German negotiations that followed were disrupted by the Agadir Crisis that began to brew one month later and that nearly led to war between the two countries that summer.[50] In reality, this was a short-term concession to supporters of Irish Home Rule, Radicals, and Labour on whom the government was now more reliant following a recent election and unlikely to have

---

[45] Hendrix, *Naval Diplomacy*, 160; Mehnert, "Gelbe Gefahr," 183, 185.
[46] Canis, *Der Weg in den Abgrund*, 367–69.
[47] *Leipziger Tagblatt*, Dec. 5, 1910, quoted in Canis, *Der Weg in den Abgrund*, 370.
[48] Tirpitz, *Politische Dokumente*, vol. 1, 182–84, here 183.     [49] Ibid., 184–85, here 184.
[50] See Ibid., 188–94; Marder, *From Dreadnought to Scapa Flow*, vol. 1, 224–30; Ritter, *Staatskunst*, vol. 2, 211–12; Röhl, *Into the Abyss*, 789–90.

ever been set to paper, as the Liberals were still very much committed to naval superiority, particularly after this crisis.[51] That year Tirpitz himself conceded that even with a favorable 9:14 ratio, Germany's chances in a naval engagement with the Royal Navy were "thoroughly unsatisfactory," but added that this could not be conceded in public.[52] This statement and that of one his closest colleagues in the RMA, Wilhelm Michaelis (1871–1948), suggests that the 2:3 ratio of the 1900 navy law was devised to shield the RMA from Reichstag criticism of "limitless fleet plans," that is, the ratio had always had a political and not a military-strategic logic.[53] As we have seen, much the same could be said about the British Two Power Standard by this point.

The Agadir Crisis precipitated yet another British navy panic, this time whipped up by Grey, Asquith, and Lloyd George and based on the false notion that Germany intended to establish a naval base on the Moroccan Atlantic coast. This was in fact little more than propaganda in a July 1911 Pan-German pamphlet that the German Foreign Office had urged the organization not to publish, albeit unsuccessfully.[54] Regardless, Lloyd George inflated the Morocco issue to such an extent in a speech in Mansion House on July 21 that he turned it into a matter over which Britain might actually wage war to preserve its status as a great power. The British press was carefully managed before the speech to assure full support for the government's position of solidarity with France, including advance circulation of key excerpts of Lloyd George's speech and pressure on skeptical newspaper editors to toe a patriotic line.[55] The resulting navy panic was such that Grey and his faction of Liberal Imperialists launched into secret war planning that succeeded in militarizing the Entente even more: in August 1911 the Committee of Imperial Defence decided that any Franco-German conflict would be met by dispatching a British Expeditionary Force to the European continent, and in September talks were held between the British and French general staffs to coordinate their mobilization and war plans for such an eventuality.[56]

In early 1912 these Anglo-French measures extended to a coordinated strategy to counter German naval expansion, with the Royal Navy moving more warships away from the Mediterranean to the Atlantic and North Sea and France redeploying much of its own navy to the Mediterranean. Churchill recognized the danger of such naval redeployments without firm alliance commitments: if Britain were to back away from supporting France in war, France would have the powerful moral argument that it had left its coasts defenseless on account of its faith in arrangements made with the British

---

[51] Epkenhans, *Die wilhelminische Flottenrüstung*, 68–71; Kelly, *Tirpitz*, 311.
[52] Tirpitz quoted in Kelly, *Tirpitz*, 202.   [53] Ibid., 201; cf. Deist, *Flottenpolitik*, 262.
[54] Chickering, *We Men Who Feel Most German*, 265.
[55] Fischer, *War of Illusions*, 78–79; Geppert, *Pressekriege*, 285.
[56] Wilson, *The Policy of the Entente*, 126–31; Charmley, *Splendid Isolation*, 365–70.

military.[57] As he complained to Asquith in August 1912, "we have all the obligations of an alliance without its advantages and above all its precise definitions."[58] This danger began to dawn on many others in the cabinet and the Liberal Party, forcing Grey to formally disavow that Anglo-French war planning implied any binding obligation to France in a written exchange with the French ambassador Paul Cambon on November 22–23, 1912.[59] As we shall see, the British cabinet were fooling themselves, as it was precisely the moral blackmail of undefended French coasts that would ultimately be decisive in pushing Britain into war less than two years later.[60]

Meanwhile fear spread in Germany that Britain's hostility toward it was implacable, that Germany was now "encircled," that a western European war was a distinct possibility, and that the army had to be strengthened.[61] While both the Kaiser and Bethmann feared antagonizing Britain and imposing further strains on the Reich's budget with additional naval spending, Tirpitz saw an opportunity. He was eager to exploit the shift in public mood to prepare the way for a supplemental navy bill to sustain the pace of battleship construction after 1911, when the four ship annual quota was due to expire and fall to only one or two ships per year.[62] The aimed-for 2:3 battleship ratio was now deployed by Tirpitz explicitly as a propaganda slogan, and a concerted effort was made by the RMA to solicit articles and mobilize the press with it. Details of the not yet published draft bill were even leaked to newspapers.[63]

The Navy League began aggressive agitation reminiscent of August Keim that criticized the government and called on the nation to demand a new navy bill.[64] It was hardly alone. Support for sustained naval spending was widespread riding on a tide of indignation against Britain that was noticeable even in comparatively Anglophile left liberal quarters. In an article in the Viennese *Neue Freie Presse* in late December 1911 that resonated deeply with Schmoller, Lujo Brentano, a leading left liberal supporter of arms control and a lifelong Anglophile, took Britain to task for failing to ratify the Declaration of London

---

[57] Wilson, *The Policy of the Entente*, 143.
[58] Quoted in Charmley, *Splendid Isolation*, 377. See also Wilson, *The Policy of the Entente*, 143–44.
[59] Wilson, *The Policy of the Entente*, 122–23; Clark, *The Sleepwalkers*, 213.
[60] Wilson, *The Policy of the Entente*, 123–24, 143–44; Clark, *The Sleepwalkers*, 213, 543–45.
[61] David G. Herrmann, *The Arming of Europe and the Making of the First World War* (Princeton: Princeton University Press, 1996), 161–72; Fischer, *War of Illusions*, 79, 87–88, 116–21; Ritter, *Staatskunst*, vol. 2, 214–15.
[62] See Berghahn, *Germany and the Approach of War*, 104–12; Fischer, *War of Illusions*, 112–13; Kelly, *Tirpitz*, 325–30. Cf. Tirpitz, *Politische Dokumente*, vol. 1, 197–213.
[63] Tirpitz, *Politische Dokumente*, vol. 1, 213–15; Geppert, *Pressekriege*, 289–94; Ritter, *Staatskunst*, vol. 2, 218–19.
[64] Chickering, *We Men Who Feel Most German*, 266; Geppert, *Pressekriege*, 289–94.

and thus refusing to strengthen neutral rights on the open seas. If the Royal Navy insisted on its resort to "piracy" by refusing to reform the law of the seas, he wrote, the Reich had no choice but "to insist and continue to insist on the main reason for English distrust of Germany: the construction of a fleet in accordance with our interests." Only once England respected the inviolability of private property on the open seas, he argued, would an arms limitation agreement with Germany be possible.[65]

The seeming irreconcilability of the British and German positions was reflected very vividly in the increasingly pained correspondence between William Ashley and Gustav Schmoller following the war scare in the summer and autumn of 1911. As Ashely wrote Schmoller in early January 1912:

> Let me answer you, in the most emphatic language possible, that there is absolutely no desire for war with Germany in the circles in which I move – i.e., among the upper business, professional & academic circles in the Midlands. I am quite certain that there is not the least desire for war anywhere among the working classes. There may, for all I know, be a few foolish people somewhere who play with the idea of war. But I am certain they can only be very few and quite unrepresentative, or I should have come across them. If your view is a common one in Germany, viz. that there is a considerable party in England that wants to force on a war with Germany, it is, indeed, a tragic situation; for there is a common opinion in England which is just the opposite, viz. that there is a considerable party in Germany which wants to force on war with England!
>
> ... The Entente Cordiale with France is certainly pretty generally popular; and any policy of another government is likely to for some time to come to be viewed with dislike which seems to aim at detaching England from France or treating France as if she could not count upon the friendship of England.
>
> ... There is widespread desire for amicable relations with Germany, if they can be attained without abandoning France. And of course you know my own view – that the world is still big enough to allow scope for the necessary and desirable expansion of German energies; and that England ought to welcome such an expansion. The *Weltherrschaft* [world domination] we both have to dread is that of the United States![66]

Later in January, Ashley followed up:

> As I have already told you, I was greatly distressed by your letter; and I have thought myself justified in bringing its substance under the notice of Sir Edward Grey. I have now learnt, on excellent authority, that Sir

---

[65] Lujo Brentano, "Die englische Seeherrschaft und England," *Neue Freie Presse*, Dec. 24, 1911. See also vom Bruch, *Gelehrtenpolitik*, 144–45; 145nn.84–85.
[66] GStA PK, VI. HA Nl. Schmoller, Nr. 204a, fols. 16–18, William Ashley to Gustav Schmoller, Jan. 4, 1912.

Edward Grey's view of influential opinion in Germany is precisely your view of influential opinion in England! All that England desires – so I understand his attitude – is to be able to live on equal terms. But when it is seen that Germany, having created already the largest army in the world, proceeds apparently towards the creation of the largest fleet also, some anxiety is not unnaturally felt by a good many people as to whether it is equal terms or hegemony that Germany desires.[67]

As it turned out, Tirpitz's 1911 draft for the navy law amendment was successfully pared back by the Reich's dire finances, competing demands from the army, and Bethmann's dogged resistance. Moreover, publication of the bill was delayed until after the outcome of Anglo-German talks brokered by the Anglo-German (and Jewish) financier Sir Ernest Cassel (1852–1921) and Albert Ballin in January 1912 and initiated by a visit to Germany by the German-speaking Minister of War Richard Haldane the following month.[68]

On February 9, 1912, just one day after Haldane had arrived in Germany for talks over a set of possible political, colonial, and naval agreements, Churchill gave a speech in Glasgow in which he dismissed the German fleet as a "luxury." This greatly agitated a German public still bitter over their seeming capitulation over Morocco, raising anew suspicions of British aggressive designs and fueling demands not to make any naval compromises.[69] Haldane offered the 16:10 battleship ratio (already quietly adopted by the British Admiralty in 1909) to forestall a rumored German navy law amendment but threatened that Britain would more than match any additional German dreadnoughts by a 2:1 margin, defending the "traditional two-power standard."[70] By this point Britain was "winning" the naval arms race, after all, so why offer anything like a neutrality clause for nothing, the thinking went.[71] Tirpitz and the Kaiser demurred – 16:10 did not equal the 2:3 ratio of the 1900 navy law. Bethmann Hollweg, too, was unwilling to offer Haldane any concessions on the navy short of a full neutrality agreement, but Britain preferred retaining a "free hand." The talks thus went nowhere, and in April

---

[67] GStA PK, VI. HA Nl. Schmoller, Nr. 204c, fols. 7–8, William Ashley to Gustav Schmoller, Jan. 18, 1912.
[68] Kelly, *Tirpitz*, 326–35; Cecil, *Albert Ballin*, 180–98; Warburg, *Aus meinen Aufzeichnungen*, 25–26.
[69] Carroll, *Germany and the Great Powers*, 708–9; Deist, *Flottenpolitik*, 268–97; Herwig, "*Luxury*" Fleet, 77; Kelly, *Tirpitz*, 336.
[70] Kelly, *Tirpitz*, 336–37. Cf. Tirpitz, *Politische Dokumente*, vol. 1, 279–89. See also Marder, *From Dreadnought to Scapa Flow*, vol. 1, 279–80; Otte, "Grey Ambassador," in Blyth, Lambert and Rüger, *The Dreadnought in the Edwardian Age*, 72–74.
[71] Clark, *The Sleepwalkers*, 319. See also Canis, *Der Weg in den Abgrund*, 469–74; Geppert, *Pressekriege*, 398; Rose, "From 'illusion' and 'Angellism,'" in Geppert, Mulligan, and Rose, *The Wars*, 329; Charmley, *Splendid Isolation*, 374–75; Helfferich, *Der Weltkrieg*, vol. 1, 87–91.

1912 a navy law amendment was approved in the Reichstag by a clear majority to add three new ships in 1913 and 1916 and to fund personnel increases making the fleet battle ready year-round with three active squadrons.[72] Churchill's dismissive public characterization of the German fleet in February had been wind in the sails for popular support of the new amendment.[73] Such a policy of strength vis-à-vis Britain to achieve equal status and a neutrality agreement also enjoyed wide support from German bankers, industrialists, and shipbuilders, even among its more enlightened representatives like Walther Rathenau and Arthur von Gwinner.[74]

In 1912 it was acknowledged within the British Committee of Imperial Defence that Germany's economic vulnerability to blockade was about equal to Britain's, but due to the Entente with France and Convention with Russia, a British blockade would be "fatal" to the German economy in war regardless of the German fleet and would force her to sue for peace.[75] At a meeting of the Committee attended by Asquith, Churchill, Haldane, and six other cabinet ministers in early December 1912, Britain's strategy of blockade and the other extreme measures of economic warfare targeting German *Weltwirtschaft* were formalized, including controls of British merchant marine cargos trading with neutral powers, prohibitions on British bills of exchange financing German trade, and stripping the ports of Rotterdam and Antwerp of their neutral status in the event of war. Asquith and his ministers endorsed these measures fully. This bolstered false confidence in Whitehall of Britain's ability to prevail with the Entente were it ever to come to war with Germany, thus making such a future war that much more likely.[76]

On the floor of the Reichstag on December 2, 1912, during the tense military standoff along the Galician border between Russia and Austria-Hungary during the First Balkan War, Bethmann Hollweg calmly reiterated Germany's significant financial interests in Turkey and its alliance commitment to Austria were it to be attacked by a third party.[77] Two days later Edward Grey summoned the Anglophile German ambassador Karl von Lichnowsky (1860–1928) to his office and warned him sternly that a war sparked by an Austrian move against Serbia that led to a Russian invasion of

---

[72] Jarausch, *Enigmatic Chancellor*, 126–30; Kelly, *Tirpitz*, 337–43; Ritter, *Staatskunst*, vol. 2, 229–30; Tirpitz, *Memoirs*, vol. 1, 216–26. Cf. Marder, *From Dreadnought to Scapa Flow*, vol. 1, 280–87; Fischer, *War of Illusions*, 123–31; Röhl, *Into the Abyss*, 844–60.
[73] Carroll, *Germany and the Great Powers*, 700–709; Epkenhans, *Die wilhelminische Flottenrüstung*, 129–30.
[74] Fischer, *War of Illusions*, 134, 139–40; Pogge von Strandmann, ed., *Walther Rathenau*, 153–54.
[75] Offer, *The First World War*, 298; Lambert, *Planning Armageddon*, 162–63.
[76] Lambert, *Planning Armageddon*, 164–81; Clark, *The Sleepwalkers*, 318–25.
[77] StenBerVR, XIII. Legislaturperiode, 75. Sitzung, 1912/14, vol. 4 (Dec. 2, 1912), 2471D–2472D, here 2472B.

Austria and then a countermove by Germany to defend its ally would inevitably draw in France. Were that to happen, Grey said, Britain would likely side with France and Russia. Grey then forwarded the content of his warning to Lichnowsky to the French ambassador Paul Cambon.[78] It is not unreasonable to conclude from this astonishing warning that Britain's grand strategy of blockade and economic warfare, along with the naval redeployments negotiated with France earlier in 1912, had effectively eliminated most of the remaining deterrent value of Germany's battleship navy.

By 1913 Whitehall had come around to realizing that naval arms limitation talks with the Germans were nonstarters that actually harmed bilateral relations.[79] Such talks were by that point in any case largely irrelevant. As a matter of national honor (*nationale Ehrensache*) the German battleship navy was not just impervious to British bullying but actually given a new lease on life by it long after its military rationale had expired.[80] As Albert Hopman (1865–1942) confided to his diary in May 1912, the rivalry with England was the navy's "life elixir."[81] Hopman, then Chief of the RMA's Central Department and Tirpitz's right-hand man, continued his entry by noting that without English rivalry "the German navy loses its raison d'être."[82] When Tirpitz made a favorable reference to the 16:10 battleship ratio offered in 1912 by Haldane and Churchill in the Reichstag's Budget Commission in February 1913, the nationalist press quickly denounced any naval agreement with Britain on that basis.[83]

Despite spiraling costs, dangerously deteriorating relations with Britain, and increasing militarization of the Entente, Reichstag majorities comprised of liberals, conservatives, and the Center Party were found for every navy bill put to a vote before the First World War, with the only consistent criticism of this spending in the SPD, and even that was often remarkably tepid.[84] In the spring of 1914 it was the view of the Reichstag majority that it was Britain, not Germany, that had pushed the naval arms race forward and that had consistently blocked a naval agreement.[85]

---

[78] See Clark, *The Sleepwalkers*, 328–29, 354–55; Lieven, *The End of Tsarist Russia*, 240.

[79] Otte, "Grey Ambassador," in Blyth, Lambert and Rüger, *The Dreadnought in the Edwardian Age*, 75; Richard Langhorne, "The Naval Question in Anglo-German Relations, 1912–14," *The Historical Journal* 14, no. 2 (June 1971): 359–70.

[80] Tirpitz, *Memoirs*, vol. 1, 39–40, 85, 89, 111, 185, 191, 210–11, 230–31, 267; vol. 2, 448, 450; Bülow, *Denkwürdigkeiten*, vol. 2, 322, 429–30; Röhl, *Into the Abyss*, 491–93, 632–40, 789–90, 815–16, 854–60.

[81] Michael Epkenhans, ed., *Das ereignisreiche Leben eines "Wilhelminers": Tagebücher, Briefe und Aufzeichnungen 1901 bis 1920 von Albert Hopman* (Munich: Oldenbourg, 2004), 223.

[82] Ibid.; Kelly, *Tirpitz*, 357, 359–61.   [83] Carroll, *Germany and the Great Powers*, 742.

[84] See Epkenhans, *Die wilhelminische Flottenrüstung*, 83–92, 104–12, 129–30, 138–42, 339–42, 355–58, 413.

[85] Ibid., 356.

As for the Center Party and left liberals, their consistent support of navy bills after 1907 is a striking fact. Bülow confided to Schmoller in January 1913 that he believed the elections of 1906–7 and the forging of the bloc had purged these parties of their opposition in matters naval, military, and colonial:

> If I had not had the courage to dissolve the Reichstag in December 1906, the Center [Party] would scarcely have been healed of it tendency to unseemly horse-trading and brought up to correctness in military, naval, and colonial questions. Without the bloc period the Free-Minded [left liberal Freisinnige Vereinigung] would not have recognized the need to revise their prior negative position in defense and overseas questions.[86]

While Bülow's boasts must be taken with a grain of salt, there was undeniably truth to that claim. The electoral setback of 1907 had had much the same impact on the SPD, where a "national" reformist wing asserted itself ever more on colonial and defense matters.[87] Even if they were no longer active in German fleet politics, Schmoller and his former students had played a key role in helping to forge this consensus within the bourgeois parties by articulating and disseminating a vision for *Weltpolitik* that, while it included the overseas colonies, extended far beyond to East Asia, South America, and the Middle East and that had evolved in the "Hottentot elections" into an increasingly racialized nationalist ideology that fused economic imperialism with settler colonialism.[88] They had, moreover, played a key role in turning the Navy League into a popular mass organization. Public support for the dreadnought arms race was in the end fueled by the striking incongruity that emerged between the soaring hopes and expectations for *Weltpolitik* and a bitterly disappointing reality. The evidence is nevertheless overwhelming that the German battleship navy never developed the capacity to challenge British maritime supremacy and thus never posed a credible military threat to the British Isles or British trade, much less to the British Empire before the outbreak of war in August 1914.[89] By just about any measure, then, the

---

[86] GStA PK, VI. HA Nl. Schmoller, Nr. 205b, fols. 2–4, Bernhard von Bülow to Gustav Schmoller, Jan. 11, 1913; cf. Bülow, *Deutsche Politik*, 132–33.
[87] See Sobich, *"Schwarze Bestien, rote Gefahr,"* 334–46; Schorske, *German Social Democracy*, 146–256. Cf. Gustav Schmoller, "Das Erwachende Verständnis für Aristokratie und Bureaukratie in der radikalen und und sozialistischen Literatur" [1911], in *Zwanzig Jahre*, 91–95.
[88] See Schmokel, *Dream of Empire*; Smith, *Ideological Origins*, 196–258.
[89] Ferguson, *The Pity of War*, 82–87; Kelly, *Tirpitz*, 445–48; Hobson, *Militarism at Sea*, 272–73. Cf. Kennedy, *Anglo-German Antagonism*, 420–31.

dreadnought deterrence strategy was an "historical fiasco" for both countries, not least since it ultimately failed to deter conflict and because dreadnoughts would turn out to play next to no role in determining the outcome of the First World War.[90]

National honor was an expensive business: the German naval budget increased from 347 million marks in 1908 to 480 million marks in 1913.[91] In Britain, gross naval expenditures grew from £ 33.95 million in 1907–8 to £ 48.74 million in 1912–13.[92] In Britain such profligate spending on weapons of dubious military utility but high political value was easily managed, especially after the passage of Lloyd George's People's Budget raised income taxes and death duties, though not without sparking an historic standoff between the Commons and Lords in 1910–11. In Germany, as will be discussed next, that was a different story.

### Financial Reform and the Limits of Professorial Politics

The saga of German financial reform requires stepping back for a moment to focus on the spring of 1908. The big question looming after passage of the March 1908 navy law amendment was how Germany was going to pay for an even faster pace of dreadnought construction while steering clear of national bankruptcy. Already there were ominous signs on the German bond market, which was putting downward pressure on German government debt. As the financial reforms of 1906 had been stripped of much of their effect by the parties of the Reichstag, and as imperial expenditures accelerated with the navy law amendments of 1906 and 1908, Reich deficits became a serious problem that would grow by no less than 38 percent between the start of 1907 and the end of 1909, reaching 1.35 billion marks.[93] Under these circumstances there was no way around a second and more substantial finance reform, and it was clear by the spring of 1908 that the 1909–10 budget needed to begin to reduce that deficit with sizable new annual revenues. As it took form, this new financial reform bill foresaw annual revenue increases of nearly 500 million marks found in a mix of direct and indirect taxes and an increase in per capita matricular contributions from the federal states. It also foresaw a plan for an orderly repayment of imperial debts. The big components included extensions of the 1906 inheritance tax to spouses and children in the form of an estate succession tax and profits from brandy sales by the creation of an imperial brandy sales monopoly. In addition to the familiar (and always unpopular) tax

---

[90] Kennedy, "HMS *Dreadnought*, in Blyth, Lambert, and Rüger, The Dreadnought and the Edwardian Age, 223–25.
[91] Epkenhans, *Die wilhelminische Flottenrüstung*, 465, Tabelle 14.
[92] Lambert, *Naval Revolution*, Appendix 1, 305.
[93] Hentschel, *Wirtschaft und Wirtschaftspolitik*, 167.

increases on beer and tobacco, new taxes on sparkling wine, electricity, natural gas, and advertisements were also proposed.[94]

As the Reich deficits were compounded by the naval arms race, the Reich's financial reform can be seen legitimately as one of the last chapters of peacetime *Weltpolitik*, not least since financial reform intended to give the Reich the tax base to meet the needs of colonial reform and naval construction. As discussed in Chapter 7, Karl Helfferich and Max Warburg had already correctly observed that the Reich's growing debts and fiscal constraints had become strategic liabilities. In light of the failed reform of 1905-6, Bülow was nevertheless well aware that such a substantial reform bill would only have prospects for success in the Reichstag if it were preceded by a major propaganda campaign. Shortly after the appointment of the new state secretary of the Imperial Treasury Reinhold von Sydow (1851–1943) in late February 1908, Bülow confided to him that the model for such a campaign was the successful scholarly propaganda organized by the RMA for the navy law and its amendments, and he recommended that Sydow bring Ernst von Halle into the Treasury to spearhead that effort, a decision the Kaiser himself fully supported.[95] Not surprisingly, the propaganda campaign for financial reform would follow a blueprint now well familiar from the successful campaigns for naval legislation and the Bülow Bloc.

As will be recalled from Chapter 7, von Halle had urged passage of the 1905 reform bill in the pages of *Preußische Jahrbücher* in March 1905 and required little persuasion to now lead this new effort.[96] He was brought to the Treasury in the summer of 1908 to head a new "Economic Bureau" to begin the preparatory work. The treasury secretary secured 100,000 marks for this effort, which was to pay not only for the production of pro-reform scholarship and its publication and distribution, but also for the services of so-called non-official writers.[97] Von Halle wasted no time and had by November 1908 enabled the completion of the first two parts of a four-part memorandum on imperial finance reform just in time for the publication of the proposed taxes of the financial reform bill on November 3, 1908. The first two parts offered a comprehensive view of the finances of all public bodies in Germany as well as a survey of the public finances of France, Great Britain, Japan, Austria-Hungary, Russia, Switzerland, and the United States.[98]

---

[94] Ibid.; Witt, *Die Finanzpolitik*, 243–49, 250, Tabelle XII.
[95] Witt, *Die Finanzpolitik*, 217; Bülow, *Denkwürdigkeiten*, vol. 2, 384–85.
[96] Ernst von Halle, "Das Problem der Reichsfinanzreform," *Preußische Jahrbücher* 119, no. 3 (1905): 495–507.
[97] Witt, *Die Finanzpolitik*, 219.
[98] Reichschatzamt, *Denkschriftenband zur Begründung des Entwurfs eines Gesetzes betreffend Änderungen im Finanzwesen,* Teil 1, Das Finanzwesen der öffentlichen Körperschaften Deutschlands; Teil 2, Die Finanzen von Frankreich, Grossbritannien und Irland, Italien, Japan, Österreich-Ungarn, Russland, der Schweiz, den Vereinigten Staaten von

Von Halle used his deep connections at the University of Berlin and within the German economics profession to solicit articles favoring the financial reform from most of the leading scholars and other specialists in the field, not only his colleagues Gustav Schmoller and Adolph Wagner at the University of Berlin (the latter himself a noted specialist on public finance and proponent of tax fairness), but many other economists elsewhere in Germany, notably Lujo Brentano in Munich, Gustav Cohn (1840–1919) in Göttingen, Johannes Conrad in Halle, Heinrich Dietzel in Bonn, and Gerhart von Schulze-Gaevernitz (1864–1943) in Freiburg.[99] Earlier, in July 1908, Schmoller had received a request directly from the Treasury noting that the Kaiser had asked the chancellor to involve professors in enlightening public opinion about the necessity of financial reform, and the Kaiser had put Schmoller at the top of that list. Would he be willing to oblige?[100] He would and in late September began publishing a series of pro-reform (i.e., pro-inheritance tax) articles timed with the publication and first reading of the finance reform bill. By mid-September von Halle could already report to Schmoller on substantial progress that had been made in getting essays published in newspapers and journals and in organizing public speeches.[101]

By late October and early November the debate over the constitutional questions relating to the fiscal rights of the Reich that always attended tax reform had grown well beyond these issues of federalism. The very institution of Kaiser and its relationship to the government and the Reichstag were now subjects of heated public debate. On Wednesday, October 28, 1908, a little over a week before the publication of the finance reform bill, *The Daily Telegraph* had published a compilation of conversations Kaiser Wilhelm had held with Colonel Edward Stuart-Wortley (1857–1934) while visiting England in November 1907 that became the *Daily Telegraph* Affair.[102] Among other foolish remarks, the Kaiser claimed in the article that Germany's navy was not being prepared against England but for a final showdown in the Far East against the "yellow peril" to determine the future of the Pacific. He also

---

Amerika; Teil 3, Materialien zur Beurteilung der Wohlstandsentwicklung Deutschlands im letzten Menschenalter; Teil 4, Materialien zur Beurteilung der Zusammenhänge zwischen dem öffentlichen Schuldenwesen und dem Kapitalmarkte (Berlin: J. Guttentag Verlagsbuchhandlung, 1908-9).

[99] Witt, *Die Finanzpolitik*, 220.
[100] GStA PK, VI. HA Nl. Schmoller, Nr. 200a, fol. 125, Imperial Treasury Office to Gustav Schmoller, July 6, 1908.
[101] GStA PK, VI. HA Nl. Schmoller, Nr. 200a, fols. 158-59, Ernst von Halle, Imperial Treasury Office, Economic Bureau, to Gustav Schmoller, Sept. 19, 1908.
[102] "The German Emperor and England. Personal Interview. Frank Statement of World Policy. Proofs of Friendship," *The Daily Telegraph*, Oct. 28, 1908, facsimile in Bülow, *Denkwürdigkeiten*, vol. 2, 352-53.

expressed his deep love for Britain and his support during the Boer War, but noted the German public's hostile feelings toward the country.[103]

In Britain the interview confirmed the Germanophobe press' conviction of the implacable hatred of the German people toward their country, while in Germany the Kaiser's expressions of Anglophilia and betrayal of the Boers were taken to task. The backlash in Germany against the Kaiser as a foreign policy liability quickly coalesced to span the entire political spectrum and was unprecedented in its ferocity.[104] Bülow claimed that he objected to the content of the interview and would have advised against publication but had, alas, not read the article, blaming lapses in the Foreign Office. He nevertheless accepted responsibility and tendered his resignation on October 30th, which the Kaiser flatly rejected.[105] Scarcely anyone, not even Bülow, defended the Kaiser when the matter was brought to the floor of the Reichstag on November 4 and debated on November 10 and 11.[106] Rather, Bülow used the crisis to strengthen his hand with the Kaiser, among other things to press him for naval concessions to improve relations with Britain.[107] Understandably the Kaiser felt betrayed by the chancellor and an unbridgeable gulf emerged between them. Whatever his role in causing the crisis, Bülow entered into the campaign for financial reform seriously weakened before the parties of the Reichstag and without the confidence of the emperor.[108] That was an unpromising starting point for financial reform.

As already alluded to, beginning in late September 1908 Schmoller had started publishing his series of articles in the *Tägliche Rundschau* solicited by the Treasury entitled "Historical Perspectives on State Formation and Financial Development" that were later consolidated into a longer essay published in his *Jahrbuch* in early 1909 timed to influence the debate over the financial reform bill in the Reichstag.[109] Schmoller's piece distilled insights from years of research comparing the fiscal history of France, Austria-Hungary, England, Prussia, and the German Empire. These articles, while delving deeply into

---

[103] Ibid; Mehnert, *"Gelbe Gefahr,"* 139–55.
[104] GStA PK, VI. HA Nl. Schmoller, Nr. 200b, fols. 158–61, Henry Farnam to Gustav Schmoller, Dec. 11, 1908; Clark, *Kaiser Wilhelm II*, 176; Geppert, *Pressekriege*, 265–68.
[105] Clark, *Kaiser Wilhelm II*, 172–73; Lerman, *The Chancellor as Courtier*, 222–23; Röhl, *Into the Abyss*, 676–77.
[106] Bülow, *Denkwürdigkeiten*, vol. 2, 365–73; Lerman, *The Chancellor as Courtier*, 223–25; Röhl, *Into the Abyss*, 680–85. Cf. Warburg, *Aus meinen Aufzeichnungen*, 29–32.
[107] Canis, *Der Weg in den Abgrund*, 277–78.
[108] Bülow, *Denkwürdigkeiten*, vol. 2, 353; YUL MA, Farnam Family Papers, Group 203, Box 102, Folder 1832, Gustav Schmoller to Henry Farnam, Berlin, Dec. 21, 1908; Clark, *Kaiser Wilhelm II*, 175–7; Geppert, *Pressekriege*, 262–68; Lerman, *The Chancellor as Courtier*, 221–22. Cf. Röhl, *Into the Abyss*, 663–67, 679–95; Winzen, *Reichskanzler*, 134–46.
[109] Gustav Schmoller, "Historische Betrachtungen über Staatenbildung und Finanzentwicklung," *JbfGVV* 33 (1909): 1–64.

the history of the close relationship between the formation of the modern state and enhanced fiscal capacities, did not flinch from taking Bismarck and Prussian finance ministers to task for leaving the Reich with such a feeble fiscal structure.[110] Even the ablest of that lot, Johannes von Miquel (1828–1901), had focused his prodigious energies on Prussian financial reforms, where much had been achieved, but Schmoller pointed out, he had failed to secure a Reich finance reform in 1893–94.[111] He linked the great epochs of the life of states with the development of financial capacities and warned his readership that in the past the success or failure to adapt those capacities to new demands was closely tied to the rise or decline of those powers, leaving no doubt in the mind of his readers that Germany now stood at just such a crossroads. The extraordinary growth in state obligations from 1860 to the present, he argued, was bound up with the acquisition of colonies and other expansion of territory, as well as the enormous growth in military and naval expenditure driven by international conflicts of interest, for which Germany's fiscal structure was poorly suited.[112] In the past, great financial reforms had nearly always been the result of "shattering state catastrophes" (*erschütternde staatliche Katastrophen*), during wars in which the survival of the state was in question."[113] In Germany today, Schmoller wrote, the biggest hindrance to the reform came from organized interest groups and from the political parties. Recognizing the profound divisions within the Bülow Bloc over direct and indirect taxes, he appealed to "all reasonable people of all parties and classes" to recognize that indirect taxes alone put excessive burdens on the lower classes and that the Reich had to be empowered to levy sizable direct inheritance and estate taxes paid by the well-to-do.[114]

On November 6, three days after the finance reform bill was published, Adolph Wagner along with the legal scholar Wilhelm Penck (who had both been active in the Kolonialpolitisches Aktionskomité in 1906-7) and the Leipzig historian Karl Lamprecht (1856–1915) gave public lectures promoting the bill.[115] Von Halle also succeeded in mobilizing many captains of industry to speak or write on behalf of the reform, which very shrewdly included employers in sectors that would be targeted by the new taxes, such as the tobacco industrialist Julius Lissner (b. 1871), the electrical industrialist Wilhelm von Siemens, and the pioneering advertiser Ernst Growald (1867–1943), among others.[116] The initiative for the actual political agitation was left to

---

[110] Ibid., 55–56.   [111] Ibid., 57.   [112] Ibid., 59.   [113] Ibid., 60.   [114] Ibid., 62–64.
[115] Wilhelm Kahl, Adolph Wagner, and Karl Lamprecht, *Die Nationale Bedeutung der Reichsfinanzreform: Drei Reden, gehalten in Berlin am 6. November 1908* (Berlin and Leipzig: Hillger, 1908).
[116] Julius Lissner, *Zur Klärung tabaksteuerlicher Streitfragen* (Leipzig: A. Deischert'sche Verlagsbuchhandlung, 1908); Wilhelm von Siemens, "Über Elektrizitäts- und Arbeitgebersteuer," *Deutsche Revue* 33, no. 4 (1908): 307–24; Ernst Growald, "Vorschläge zur

the nationalist pressure groups, the Navy League, the Colonial Society, and Pan-German League, which were later coordinated for the campaign under a new umbrella organization, the Vereinigung zur Förderung der Reichsfinanzreform (Union for the Promotion of Imperial Finance Reform).[117] At the time, however, the public's attention was riveted to the *Daily Telegraph* Affair and its implications for the future of the monarchy. There were other distractions. In late September 1908 Franco-German relations deteriorated over a diplomatic dispute related to France's increasingly predominant position in Morocco (the Casablanca Incident), and in October 1908 the Bosnian annexation crisis erupted, bringing Europe to the brink of war. Understandably, with such fare in the newspapers, taxation had a hard time competing for readers.

On the surface at least, the parties of the Bülow Bloc were on board with the chancellor's campaign for the new taxes so long as it was accompanied by assurances from him that all imperial offices would redouble efforts to cut costs. Below the surface and well before the first reading of the various tax proposals beginning on November 19, the German Conservative Party (Deutschkonservative) was wavering in its support for the bill and willing to abandon the bloc for a parliamentary alliance with the Center Party. The German Conservative Party and Agrarian League, meanwhile, agreed to oppose any taxes burdening landownership, rejecting income and wealth taxes as well as any extension of inheritance taxes to spouses and children. The Center Party, too, opposed extensions of the inheritance tax and was itself bent on toppling the bloc and its leaders after the anti-Catholic campaign of the 1906–7 Reichstag elections. All of these groups and parties in turn supported taxes on mobile investment capital, which was bound to be sensitive with the liberal parties.[118] The left liberals, for their part, thought an inheritance tax was an insufficient concession and sought to link it with a demand to reform the Prussian three-class suffrage system, which was practically a declaration of war to the conservatives and bound to explode the bloc.[119]

When the first reading of the bill began, Bülow was aware of the fissures emerging within the bloc and tried to brush over the most divisive matters in a speech that was vague in particulars, emphasizing instead national unity and defense.[120] Bülow was by this point in a much weakened position due to the the *Daily Telegraph* Affair, which had been accompanied by much press criticism of his handling of affairs and calls for his resignation.[121] His speech

---

Reklamesteuer," *Zeitschrift für Sozialwissenschaft* 11, no. 12 (1908): 770–73. On Growald, see David Carlo, *Advertising Empire: Race and Visual Culture in Imperial Germany* (Cambridge, MA and London: Harvard University Press, 2011).

[117] Witt, *Die Finanzpolitik*, 224–25.   [118] Ibid., 231–34.   [119] Ibid., 237–38.
[120] See *StenBerVR, XII. Legislaturperiode, 163. Sitzung, 1907/09*, vol. 7 (Nov. 19, 1908), 5540C-5544D. Cf. Bülow, *Denkwürdigkeiten*, vol. 2, 381–84.
[121] Lerman, *The Chancellor as Courtier*, 223.

was also given in the context of the Bosnian annexation crisis and was thus focused more on the financial and military-strategic liabilities that the Reich's inadequate revenue base imposed upon the country.[122] He reminded the Reichstag deputies that Germany's financial capacities had not changed much since the founding of the Reich in 1871, were still a work in progress, and were now bound up inextricably with keeping Germany secure. As he concluded:

> Gentlemen, the German people are stepping into adulthood, they stand before a great moral task. The task is less conspicuous than a won war; but it is perhaps more useful. Do not forget that world history is ever more becoming a history of economic and financial relations, that more than in the past the power of a state is conditioned by its financial capacity. If we cringe at new taxes, or if we fail to agree on the new taxes, which amounts to the same thing, if we continue the business of borrowing, if the price of our bonds continues to sink, so we endanger our image, so we endanger our security, so we endanger our peace. (Very right!) We endanger our peace because financial preparedness is as important as military [preparedness], to neglect it is just as dangerous and can have just as disastrous consequences as when military preparation has been ignored.[123]

The rather stiff and proper new treasury secretary von Sydow followed Bülow with a four hour-long speech that went into every detail of the reason and means of the taxes to reform Reich finances, but it was a tedious and pedantic effort that had no effect on the Reichstag deputies, with Bülow himself slipping out of the chamber before it was over.[124] The bill was criticized from various angles by German Conservative, Social Democratic, and especially Center Party speakers in the next three Reichstag sessions and only defended by the National Liberals and Free Conservatives.[125] Every proposed tax was criticized in one way or another, with the only taxes with any prospect of passage those on sparkling wine and advertisements together amounting to a trifling 8 million of the 500 million marks needed.[126]

On November 23, a day after the last of the articles Schmoller wrote for the nationalist *Tägliche Rundschau* were published and just as the reform bill was being savaged in the Reichstag, von Halle – no doubt trying to put a brave face on things – wrote Schmoller about the good impression Schmoller's writings on the financial reform bill were making on members of the Reichstag, despite the many setbacks the matter had seen. Reflecting on the impact of the *Daily*

---

[122] Bülow, *Denkwürdigkeiten*, vol. 2, 337–38.
[123] StenBerVR, XII. Legislaturperiode, 163. Sitzung, 1907/09, vol. 7 (Nov. 19, 1908), 5544C.
[124] Ibid., 5544D–5565A; Bülow, *Denkwürdigkeiten*, vol. 2, 385–86.
[125] StenBerVR, XII. Legislaturperiode, 164. Sitzung, 1907/09, vol. 7 (Nov. 20, 1908), 5568C–5598B; 165. Sitzung, 1907/09, vol. 7 (Nov. 21, 1908), 5599D–5611D, 5614D–5631D; 166. Sitzung (Nov. 23, 1908), 5633D–5670D; Witt, *Die Finanzpolitik*, 251–53.
[126] Witt, *Die Finanzpolitik*, 253.

*Telegraph* Affair on these deliberations, he wrote that he thought that the discussion of constitutional issues that had been ongoing for nearly two years but that had recently intensified was quite healthy for the country. Had Kaiser Friedrich been in power longer, he observed, "many of the constitutional issues might have been dealt with; now the dispute takes place 20 years later." Nevertheless, Germany was today more mature and would not be moved by the "*Umsturzgespenst*" (specter of a putsch) so often used by opponents of a healthy development in the past. Financial reform, while more difficult now, was not without hope.[127] In late 1908 and early 1909 in advance of King Edward's visit to Germany in February 1909, Bülow was receiving ominous reports from the Ambassador Metternich in London about how the increased pace of German dreadnought construction since the passage of the 1908 navy law amendment was burdening Anglo-German relations and strengthening the Entente, urging reductions in the naval program for détente with Britain. It was nevertheless important, Metternich wrote, that the proposed finance reform be passed by the Reichstag to show to the world that Germany was not reducing its fleet out of financial necessity.[128]

By January 1909 the finance reform bill was in the Reichstag Tax Commission for further deliberations. The commission included personnel from the Treasury Office, among them Ernst von Halle, who participated in all of its meetings until the end of April 1909.[129] Von Halle was at the same time active in soliciting newspaper articles to try to win over conservatives for the taxes in the reform bill. In Bonn, Hermann Schumacher organized a petition to the Reichstag strongly supporting the financial reform bill signed by numerous prominent citizens, which received national press coverage.[130] In an about-face, Bülow, meanwhile, came out more forcefully in defense of the Kaiser in a speech in the Prussian Chamber of Deputies, acknowledging his own fault in the *Daily Telegraph* Affair more directly in an attempt to unruffle conservative feathers.[131] Be that as it may, the brandy monopoly (supported by the conservatives) was the first casualty of the intra-bloc divisions and defeated by National Liberal, left liberal (as well as Center Party and SPD) opposition. Likewise, the proposed extension of the 1906 inheritance tax to an estate succession tax foundered on the shoals of conservative and – surprisingly – National Liberal opposition in choppy seas produced by plenty of Agrarian League press agitation that painted this proposed tax as an attack on the family.[132] The alternative proposed by the Free Conservatives – a general imperial wealth assessment collected as a property tax at the state level

---

[127] GStA PK, VI. HA Nl. Schmoller, Nr. 200b, fols. 68–69, Ernst von Halle, Reichsschatzamt, to Gustav Schmoller, Nov. 23, 1908.
[128] Bülow, *Denkwürdigkeiten*, vol. 2, 416–19. [129] Witt, *Die Finanzpolitik*, 260.
[130] GNN HA, Nl Schumacher, I, C-237–38, cutting from *Berliner Tageblatt*, Jan. 5, 1909.
[131] Witt, *Die Finanzpolitik*, 262–63, 262n377. [132] Ibid., 265–67.

via various direct taxes in lieu of the estate tax and then forwarded to the Reich as higher matricular contributions – also failed to overcome German Conservative opposition and protest of some federal states in the Federal Council as violating their fiscal sovereignty.[133] Bülow, already weakened from the criticisms leveled at him over mishandling *The Daily Telegraph* interview and with the Kaiser's camarilla intriguing against him, was thus in a very precarious position by March 1909.[134]

The deliberations in the commission over indirect taxes were taken up in the following weeks of March and made little progress. The first hurdle was a proposed tax on cigar bands, which was deemed unfair to tobacco industry workers and relegated to a subcommission. In quick succession thereafter the proposed taxes on electricity, natural gas, and advertisements were stripped from the bill. The Center Party, working closely with the German Conservatives (and supported by Württemberg and Bavaria in the Federal Council), then opposed the proposed tax increases on brandy. Shortly thereafter, on March 24, the German Conservative Party leadership abandoned any further cooperation with the other parties of the bloc, announcing categorical rejection of any estate, inheritance, succession, or wealth taxes on individuals.[135] That was effectively the end of the Bülow Bloc.

That very day Gustav Schmoller, Hans Delbrück, and others, working closely with von Halle in the Economic Bureau of the Treasury, organized the Vereinigung zur Förderung der Reichsfinanzreform (the Union for the Promotion of Imperial Finance Reform), making a public appeal criticizing the narrow partisanship of the interest groups in the Reichstag opposing the Imperial inheritance tax and the slow pace of the Reichstag deliberations.[136] Among those signing on to this appeal were many prominent bankers, industrialists, and professors, including Albert Ballin of HAPAG, Arthur von Gwinner of the Deutsche Bank and Ernst von Mendelssohn-Bartholdy (1846–1909) and Franz von Medelssohn (1865–1935) of the Mendelssohn Bank, as well as Schmoller's colleagues Lujo Brentano, Max Sering, and Adolph Wagner.[137] Shortly thereafter Bülow himself ramped up agitation for the finance reform by appealing directly to the people. For example, he attempted to break rural opposition to the inheritance tax by decreeing that district administrators circulate the articles commissioned by von Halle in the

---

[133] Ibid., 267–70.
[134] Bülow, *Denkwürdigkeiten*, vol. 2, 392, 477–80, 493–95; Lerman, *The Chancellor as Courtier*, 230–32; Witt, *Die Finanzpolitik*, 255, 270–71.
[135] Witt, *Die Finanzpolitik*, 271. See also Hentschel, *Wirtschaft und Wirtschaftspolitik*, 169–72.
[136] See, for example, H. Freiherr von Berlepsch, Hans Delbrück, Ernst Francke, and Gustav Schmoller, "Aufruf," *Frankfurter Zeitung* (Morgenblatt), March 26, 1909.
[137] Witt, *Die Finanzpolitik*, 276, 276n461.

Treasury Office's Economic Bureau in rural newspapers. Meanwhile the Economic Bureau and the rest of the Treasury pulled out all stops in a major propaganda campaign for the inheritance tax, which included an April 20th reception of deputations from Bavaria, Saxony, Württemberg, Baden, and the Agrarian League shortly before deliberations were to begin again in the Reichstag to sow divisions within conservative ranks and give the impression of compromise on the government's tax reform bill.[138]

Alas, the propaganda campaign for the inheritance tax backfired, as the parties participating in the deliberations of the tax commission felt attacked by the accusation of obstructionism. Spearheaded by Center Party deputy Richard Müller (1851–1931) and German Conservative deputy and second chairman of the Agrarian League Gustav Roesicke (1856–1924), Sydow and especially von Halle at the Treasury were bitterly attacked and blamed for the agitation against the work of the Reichstag Tax Commission. One of the criticisms made of the inheritance tax and its supporters in the newspaper of the Agrarian League, the *Deutsche Tageszeitung,* and the conservative *Kreuzzeitung* was that it was inspired by Jews, as the Jewish identity of its supporters and "spiritus rector" Ernst von Halle was by then known.[139] As was discussed in the previous chapters, such accusations were by this point a familiar feature of opposition to Bülow and his *Weltpolitik*, as Jews and those with Jewish backgrounds were prominent among Bülow's supporters and advisors, and in the case of Dernburg, even as members of the government. As was also discussed previously, when Dernburg took office in 1906 he had been subjected to anti-Semitic barbs, and in April and May 1909 Dernburg was again being attacked in colonial newspapers and the *Kreuzzeitung* for judicial reform in the German colonies and for his handling of diamond mining in German Southwest Africa.[140] Although not opposed to colonial judicial reform, it is worth pointing out that even Georg Ledebour (1850–1947) of the SPD was not above anti-Semitic innuendo in his criticisms of Dernburg in March 1909.[141] Tellingly, the German Conservatives supported by the Center Party (and later joined by the Free Conservatives, Anti-Semites, and Poles) sought to shift the tax reforms away from "family" toward "capitalists," proposing taxes on stock dividends and bank and stock market transactions and contemplating a capital gains tax on stocks and real estate.[142] For his part, Roesicke's bitterness was directed particularly viciously against von Halle, who resigned from his position at the Treasury on April 30 citing lack of support from Sydow.

---

[138] Ibid., 276–78.
[139] Peter Pulzer, "Die jüdische Beteiligung an der Politik," in *Juden im Wilhelminischen Deutschland, 1890–1914: Ein Sammelband*, ed. Werner Mosse and Arnold Paucker, 2nd ed. (London and Tübingen: Leo Baeck Institute/Mohr Siebeck, 1998), 143–239, here 227.
[140] Davis, *Colonialism, Antisemitism, and Germans*, 111–12.   [141] Ibid., 226.
[142] Witt, *Die Finanzpolitik*, 279, 286–87.

**Figure 10.1** "Fleet Increases," *Der wahre Jacob*, April 28, 1908. "Germania: (Shows the other Triple Alliance powers the German fleet). The Allies: Marvelous! You paid cash? Germania: Goodness no, all on credit!"

In response to these attacks, Sydow had in the meantime prohibited von Halle's further participation in the meetings of the Reichstag Tax Commission. The anti-Semitic newspaper assaults on von Halle continued well after his departure into May and June 1909.[143] As George Hallgarten later observed, it was a bad omen for Bülow's own fate soon thereafter.[144]

Bülow had on April 28 already threatened the conservatives that he would resign without a finance reform acceptable to the Reichstag majority, that is, a reform also acceptable to the liberals.[145] As Lerman points out, the disarray that was increasingly apparent in the campaign for finance reform was due in no small measure to Bülow's diminished authority and popularity after the *Daily Telegraph* Affair as well as the unclear goals and many errors of judgment and tactics in his negotiations with the Reichstag parties.[146] In the subsequent sessions of the Reichstag Tax Commission, the conservative-

---

[143] Ibid., 260, 280, 280n295; George Hallgarten, *Imperialismus vor 1914: Die soziologischen Grundlagen der Aussenpolitik europäischer Grossmächte vor dem Ersten Weltkrieg*, 2nd rev. and enl. ed., vol. 2 (Munich: C. H. Beck, 1963), 149n1. Cf. *Deutsche Tageszeitung*, May 10, 1909 and *Neue Preußische Zeitung* [*Kreuzzeitung*], June 29, 1909.
[144] Hallgarten, *Imperialismus vor 1914*, vol. 2, 149.    [145] Witt, *Die Finanzpolitik*, 283.
[146] Lerman, *The Chancellor as Courtier*, 236–38.

clerical majority largely succeeded in imposing its tax preferences, with Sydow now backtracking on many taxes he had originally opposed and the left liberals refusing to participate in further deliberations. All that was left of the inheritance tax was a bill for a progressive succession tax that would hit inheriting spouses and children in estates at or exceeding 20,000 marks. It was a watered-down version projected to generate much less revenue, only some 60 million as opposed to 92 million marks in the original bill.[147]

In the opening speech at the second reading of the revised finance reform bill in the Reichstag June 16, Bülow spoke with an unmistakable tone of resignation and disappointment.[148] He criticized the partisan pettiness and doctrinaire stubbornness within the German parties, which he compared unfavorably with British political practice.[149] He also criticized the tactical failings of the left liberals in the deliberations, just as he did the ingratitude and myopia of the conservatives and their stubborn hostility to the wishes of the allied governments to extend Reich revenues with an inheritance tax.[150] The conservatives were digging their own grave by failing to heed the signs of the times, as it opened the path for radicalism, he said.[151] He then put his own political career on the line for the inheritance tax:

> For weeks newspapers have been riled up over whether I will stay or go. That does not depend on the newspapers. That does not depend on the parties. That does not depend on the wishes of my opponents. I will remain as long as His Majesty the Kaiser believes that my participation in foreign and domestic policy is useful to the Reich and as long as according to my own political convictions and my assessment of the situation I believe that I can affect useful results. In the realm of domestic policy I currently see nothing of the same importance for the welfare of the Reich as the speedy completion of financial reform. I fully subordinate my person to this weighty matter. If I gain the conviction that my person stands in the way, that another could arrive at the goal more swiftly, or if a development arises that I cannot support and that I will not support, so it will be possible for me to persuade His Majesty the Kaiser of the opportuneness of my resignation.[152]

On June 24, 1909, a Reichstag majority comprised of the German Conservatives, the Center Party, Poles, Anti-Semites, and Guelphs narrowly defeated the Imperial succession tax bill by a vote of 194 to 186. Among the most closed ranks supporting the failed bill were, interestingly, the left liberals

---

[147] See Witt, *Finanzpolitik*, 281–89; Winzen, *Reichskanzler*, 144–45.
[148] *StenBerVR, XII. Legislaturperiode, 262. Sitzung, 1907/09*, vol. 11 (June 16, 1909), 8585C–8589B.
[149] Ibid., 8586B.    [150] Ibid., 8586D, 8587B–8588A.    [151] Ibid., 8588B-C.
[152] Ibid., 8588D–8589B; cf. Bülow, *Denkwürdigkeitem*, vol. 2, 484–87.

and the SPD and not the Free Conservatives and National Liberals.[153] Two days later Bülow left for Kiel to tender his resignation to the Kaiser, which while accepted in principle at an audience the next day, would not be final until some form of the bill passed.[154] That task was now left to Vice-President of the Ministry of State Bethmann Hollweg and Treasury Secretary Sydow. To the taxes accepted in the second reading of the reform bill (on brandy, beer, tobacco, lighting materials [gas and electricity], and matches) were added increases in import duties on tea and coffee as well as stamp duties on stocks and bonds, checks, receipts, bills of exchange, and real estate transactions. The share to the Reich of the inheritance tax passed in 1906 was also extended to three-quarters of the proceeds. These taxes and tax increases were accepted by the Reichstag after the third reading on July 10, 1909.[155]

Bülow's impending departure as chancellor was bitterly resented by Schmoller. That was a sentiment undoubtedly shared by von Halle, Helfferich, Rathgen, Schumacher, and Sering. In early July 1909 Schmoller wrote Bülow still expressing hope that he would return:

> I cannot refrain from expressing my great pain about your intentions to resign. I am convinced that it is a great misfortune for our fatherland if you go, other than if you intend to return with fresh energy. The ship of state needs a helmsman like you as you have been to the blessing of Prussia and Germany for half a lifetime: outwardly [ a] confident and successful demeanor along with the greatest skill in avoiding a war, and inwardly a moderate conservative government with so many liberal and social reforms as are today essential in avoiding a sudden overthrow, that was the signature of your politics.
>
> That the Center [Party] would fight you was natural; that that liberals did not always operate cleverly is understandable. That the conservatives left you so in the lurch is not excusable by the unreasonableness of its voters. I know of no greater example of crass political ingratitude by a large party. Their political unsoundness of mind may excuse many individual conservatives; from their leaders it is the crudest felony and most narrow-minded shortsightedness.
>
> I understood why you offered the Kaiser your resignation. But I hope he will implore you to stay and give you the powers necessary to break the stubbornness of the conservatives. . . .
>
> Your Sirene Highness, please excuse this effusion of my oppressed patriotic heart. Millions of the best Germans are on your side today, but

---

[153] Witt, *Die Finanzpolitik*, 294–95; Winzen, *Reichskanzler*, 145–46. Cf. Bülow, *Denkwürdigkeiten*, vol. 2, 504–6.
[154] Lerman, *The Chancellor as Courtier*, 242–44. Cf. Bülow, *Denkwürdigkeiten*, vol. 2, 507–16.
[155] Witt, *Die Finanzpolitik*, 297–99.

how few [of them] express it. As I am among the few who may write you, I could not bear to stay wholly silent.[156]

Bülow had no intention to return, nor was there any hope of one being offered by the Kaiser. His resignation was accepted by Wilhelm on July 14, 1909, and on July 17 he and his wife were seen off to Norderney at the Lehrter Bahnhof in Berlin by members of the Reich government, Federal Council, and Prussian Ministry of State.[157] It was the end of an era that had lasted twelve years and had been synonymous with *Weltpolitik*. Less than a year later, Dernburg would tender his resignation, his position in the Reichstag much weakened by the collapse of the bloc and Bülow's departure.[158]

In a very real sense, financial reform – the domestic basis for *Weltpolitik* – had not been undermined by the SPD but by conservative and anti-Semitic intransigence and German particularism.[159] Schmoller had seen Bülow often in the last months of his chancellorship and spent an evening with Bülow, his wife, and Bethmann Hollweg three days before his resignation. In August he wrote Henry Farnam that it had been the large interest groups of industry that had prevented the liberals from accepting direct taxes, while the Agrarian League prevented the conservatives from accepting the inheritance taxes. Bethmann Hollweg would now have to begin the struggle to reform Prussia's suffrage against the Junkers and conservatives. While Bethmann was conservative, Schmoller wrote that he was nevertheless "a modern enlightened person with great high-minded points of view, a very good speaker."[160]

Although Bülow was a political casualty of the failed financial reform, there was one literal casualty: Ernst von Halle. A workaholic if ever there was one, von Halle had been burning the candle at both ends for years, especially in recent months in trying to align public opinion with the finance reform bill. Undoubtedly the strain of his exertions during the campaign in April contributed to a worsening lung infection and to his contracting pleurisy. The degree to which the lack of support from the feckless Sydow and the hateful attacks on his Jewishness to discredit the inheritance tax might have contributed to his illness is not known but can be imagined. In any case, on June 28, 1909, just three days after Bülow tendered his resignation, Ernst von Halle succumbed to

---

[156] BArch K, N 1016 Nl. Bernhard von Bülow, Nr. 119, fols. 1–3, Gustav Schmoller to Bernhard von Bülow, Berlin, July 4, 1909. Partially reprinted in Bülow, *Denkwürdigkeiten*, vol. 3, 349.
[157] Bülow, *Denkwürdigkeiten*, vol. 2, 517–31. Cf. Lerman, *The Chancellor as Courtier*, 243–47.
[158] Schiefel, *Bernhard Dernburg*, 128–29.
[159] On conservative opposition to the government, see Retallack, *The German Right*, 353–63, 374–76.
[160] YUL MA, Farnam Family Papers, Group 203, Series II, Box 182, Folder 1832, Gustav Schmoller to Henry Farnam, Berlin, Aug. 8, 1909.

the disease. He was then only forty-one years old. William Ashely, who had befriended the young von Halle while Ashley was teaching at Harvard in 1893 and von Halle was living in Chicago, was hit hard by the news. On June 30, 1909, he wrote Schmoller that

> I am grieved more than I can say by the news of the death of a dear friend, von Halle. I have not only felt a great respect, from the hour when I first made his acquaintance, for his intellectual powers; I soon became personally greatly attached to him; and for years I have regarded him as one of the most intimate friends of me & mine. My acquaintance with him is one of the few affectionate intimacies which I have formed in adult life; and to me personally the loss is a very severe one. I have written to Frau von Halle: but I feel also impelled to write to you. I don't know how intimate you may have been in recent years; but it was through your introduction that I first came to know him, and he always spoke of you with grateful respect. Will you let me regard you as representing Germany and German science, and allow me to tell you how much I share in the grief which his German friends must feel, and how deeply I deplore the loss to his country? I have again & again warned against the dangers of excessive strain: I have seen him doing the work of two men, with alarm for years. But such was his temperament. I do not know enough of German politics to have an opinion on the events of the last few months; but I feel that *he fell in battle*. It was the death he would have desired.[161]

While Schmoller and von Halle had drifted apart a bit in recent years, they were of course close political allies and shared a strong mutual admiration. There is also no doubt from the intimate and affectionate letter that von Halle's widow Henriette (Henni) von Halle (née Mossner, 1878–1964) wrote Schmoller in response to his condolences that von Halle's death was felt by him as a major loss.[162]

The constitutional issues about imperial direct taxes that had so exercised von Halle since 1905 were left unresolved. One consequence was that as of August 1909 the Imperial Treasury imposed a course of austerity on all Reich offices.[163] The revenue projections of the tax increases that were passed in July proved too optimistic, as on average they brought in only 215 million marks of additional revenue annually by 1913 rather than the 350 million that had been

---

[161] GStA PK, VI. HA Nl. Schmoller, Nr. 201a, fols. 123–24, William Ashley to Gustav Schmoller, June 30, 1909. Emphasis in the original.

[162] GStA PK, VI. HA, Nl. Schmoller, Nr. 201a, fols. 121–22, Henni von Halle to Gustav Schmoller, Hamburg, July 5, 1909. On Henni von Halle, Alexandra Cappel, "'Ihre dankbar ergebene Henni von Halle': Eine 'fröhliche Dilettantin' und ihr Briefwechsel mit Adolf Erman," in *Folia in memoriam Ruth Lindner collecta*, ed. Carina Weiß (Dettelbach: J. H. Röll, 2010), 228–38.

[163] Epkenhans, *Die wilhelminische Flottenrüstung*, 88.

projected.[164] Attempts at reform were made once again in 1912, but conservative intransigence assured failure of a property tax proposed by the Center Party and National Liberals. Only in June 1913, after many rancorous debates in the Federal Councial and Reichstag, did the Reichstag majority including the SPD finally prevail against the conservative parties in passing an Imperial tax on increases in wealth (*Reichsvermögenssteuer*), and even this was insufficient to cover rising German public spending.[165]

The upshot of the failure of German financial reform was that the government of Bethmann Hollweg was forced by financial realities, Germany's growing diplomatic and strategic containment following the Agadir Crisis, and the reorganization and rapid modernization of the Russian army to reduce navy expenditures and shift spending to the army, culminating in the passage in July 1913 of the massive *Wehrvorlage* (army bill).[166] In 1910 the Russian Council of Ministers had agreed to spend an extra 1.413 billion rubles above regular annual military appropriations over a ten year period to build up the Tsarist army and navy. Schmoller obliquely defended the army bill in the Vienna *Neue Freie Presse* in March 1913 on the grounds of this massive Russian rearmament encouraged and financed lavishly by France.[167] This had involved French pressure to speed up the pace of Russian mobilization against Germany in the event of a Franco-German war, culminating in Franco-Russian staff discussions in 1912 in which the Russians promised the French an initial Russian offensive into East Prussia on the fifteenth day of mobilization.[168] That is, the German leadership decided to unilaterally abandon the dreadnought arms race with Britain in 1912 not so much because of the increases in British naval spending after 1909, but rather because of the enhanced military threat posed by Russia and France.[169]

The Reich had to resort once again to massive borrowing to pay for the army bill (1 billion marks and 186 million marks in supplemental defense spending) putting even more pressure on the already illiquid German capital market just as a recession took hold in 1913.[170] By February 1914 spending on the army stopped and shifted to building an air force, where the French had clear superiority.[171] By that point Germany's peacetime army was outnumbered by the French and Russians by some 1.3 million soldiers and its stockpile

---

[164] Hentschel, *Wirtschaft und Wirtschaftspolitik*, 172.
[165] Ibid., 172–73; Fischer, *War of Illusions*, 182–90.
[166] Lieven, *The End of Tsarist Russia*, 226; Herrmann, *The Arming of Europe*, 161–91.
[167] Gustav Schmoller, "Krieg oder Frieden," *Neue Freie Presse*, March 23, 1913, in *Zwanzig Jahre*, 113–20, esp. 118–19, 120.
[168] Lieven, *The End of Tsarist Russia*, 157–58, 265.
[169] Otte, "Grey Ambassador," in Blyth, Lambert and Rüger, *The Dreadnought in the Edwardian Age*, 77. See also Clark, *The Sleepwalkers*, 328–32; Herrmann, *The Arming of Europe*, 130–36, 196–97.
[170] Fischer, *War of Illusions*, 357–59.
[171] Herrmann, *The Arming of Europe*, 138–46, 158–59.

of munitions was sufficient to last only a few months.[172] Nor did things look any better with Berlin's only reliable ally, Austria-Hungary. Due to perpetual problems the monarchy had in raising military revenue from a deadlocked legislature, it had consistently underspent all of the other great European powers save Italy on its military in the ten years before 1914.[173] Its army had, moreover, been deeply compromised to the Russians by the spying of Colonel Alfred Redl (1864–1913) between 1903 and 1913.[174]

In response to the German army bill, France passed the Three Year Law in July 1913 raising the term of French military service to three years and thereby raising France's peacetime military strength to over 700,000 men. One year later, in June 1914, the Russian Duma passed the "Great Program," which was even larger than the German army bill and planned to increase the Russian standing army's strength by an additional 400,000 men by 1917, with two new corps stationed in the west strengthened by additional field guns.[175] Interestingly, French bellicosity toward Germany in these years was such that it even began to worry the Russian ambassador to London Alexander von Benckendorff and other Russian diplomats that France might contemplate a preventive war with Germany while its military was at its peak and before economic and demographic trends weakened France any further vis-à-vis Germany.[176]

From this angle, the German army bill looks much less like Fritz Fischer's "bid for world power" than a desperate attempt to shore up the only credible military deterrent Germany still possessed in a deteriorating continental military balance. Even notorious provocateurs like ex-general Friedrich von Bernhardi (1849–1930), whose *Germany and the Next War* raised eyebrows in 1912 for proposing a preventive war with France and Russia – and who was later cited at length by Fritz Fischer as evidence of Germany's prewar warlike intentions[177] – was at bottom a lament over German pacifism and the unwillingness of the German public to shoulder the fiscal burdens of its military.[178] Certainly despair was growing among Germany's civilian and military leaders that Germany could not win this land arms race with France and Russia in the

---

[172] Niall Ferguson, "Public Finance and National Security: The Domestic Origins of the First World War," *Past and Present* 142 (Feb. 1994): 141–68, here 147; Herrmann, *The Arming of Europe*, 234.
[173] Herrmann, *The Arming of Europe*, 33–34, 68, 97–100, 137, 176–79; for the comparative spending figures in 1904–14, 237, Table B.1; Clark, *The Sleepwalkers*, 217.
[174] Clark, *The Sleepwalkers*, 115–16
[175] See Herrmann, *The Arming of Europe*, 191–98, 205.
[176] Lieven, *The End of Tsarist Russia*, 239–40.
[177] Fischer, *War of Illusions*, 38, 83–84, 171 242–44, 253, 266, 267, 452, 453.
[178] Friedrich von Bernhardi, *Deutschland und der nächste Krieg*, 6th ed. (1912; Stuttgart and Berlin: Cotta, 1913), 9–37, 145–46, 310–37. See also Clark, *The Sleepwalkers*, 236; Ferguson, *The Pity of War*, 15, 136.

long run. Likewise the German public's anxieties were heightened by the sensationally belligerent articles that appeared in *Le Matin* in January 1914 on the vast Russian military preparations on the east European frontier ready to overwhelm Germany, along with the rancorous press war that erupted between the Germany and Russia in the spring of 1914 sparked by a similar article in the *Kölnische Zeitung*.[179] Yet much research has disproven Fritz Fischer's argument that the German civilian and military leadership entertained a "short war" illusion, that a preemptive logic determined German decision-making in the last two years of peace, or that they then rushed into a preemptive war in July 1914.[180] The so-called "war council" of the Kaiser and senior members of the navy and army that convened in secret on December 8, 1912, after the First Balkan War holds almost no significance as a supposed blueprint for preventive war in 1914 as claimed by Fritz Fischer and John Röhl.[181] In reality it was a meeting dealing with the worst case scenarios arising during the deepening Balkan Winter Crisis as were being held in many European capitals at the time. If Germany had wanted a European war, chances of victory were far greater in 1904–5 or 1908–9, but Bülow and the Kaiser had not taken the chance then, and there is no convincing evidence Bethmann Hollweg or the Kaiser were any more inclined to take the country to war in 1911–12 or 1914 when the strategic balance was far worse.[182]

Viewing these developments as somehow leading irresistibly toward a European war is also misleading for other reasons. As was touched on in the previous chapter, the last two years of peace were notable for a genuine attempt to improve Russo-German relations. A similar thrust to détente between Germany and Britain was also initiated by Bethmann Hollweg. It was supported by Lindequist's successor in the Colonial Office Wilhelm

---

[179] Carroll, *Germany and the Great Powers*, 751–68; Clark, *The Sleepwalkers*, 419–18; Gustav Schmoller, "Droht ein russischer Krieg gegen Österreich-Ungarn und Deutschland?" *Neue Freie Presse,* April 12, 1914, in *Zwanzig Jahre,* 121–26, esp. 121, 125–26. Cf. Fischer, *War of Illusions,* 190–99, 373–88.

[180] See Stig Förster, "Dreams and Nightmares: German Military Leadership and the Images of Future Warfare, 1871–1914," in Boemeke, Chickering, and Förster, *Anticipating Total War,* 343–76; Anscar Jansen, *Der Weg in den ersten Weltkrieg: Das deutsche Militär in der Julikrise* (Marburg: Tectum Verlag, 2005), 50–197, 511, 521–22; Jack S. Levy, "The Sources of Preventive Logic in German Decision-Making in 1914," in Levy and Vasquez, *The Outbreak,* 139–66, esp. 158–63.

[181] Fritz Fischer, *War of Illusions,* 161–64; John Röhl, *Into the Abyss,* 908–11.

[182] Sean McMeekin, *July 1914: Countdown to War* (New York: Basic Books, 2013), 386–88; William Mulligan, "Restraints on Preventive War Before 1914," in Levy and Vasquez, *The Outbreak,* 115–38, here 128–33; Pogge von Strandmann, ed., *Walther Rathenau,* 166–68.

Solf and spearheaded by Kiderlen-Waechter's successor, Gottlieb von Jagow in Berlin, and Lichnowsky and Richard von Kühlmann (1873–1948) in the embassy in London.[183] As a rebuttal of Friedrich von Bernhardi under the slogan "German World Policy and No War," this effort sought to accommodate Britain on naval matters and to drop German ambitions in the Balkans and Ottoman Empire in order to focus German expansion on the old goal of "*Mittelafrika*" with the ultimate general aim of avoiding a European war.[184] In London, too, there was an initial willingness to accommodate Germany in colonial matters in order to let off some of the steam of long frustrated *Weltpolitik*.[185] As will be discussed next, the only area where anything like *Weltpolitik* continued successfully was, however, not in Africa but in building the Baghdad Railway, ultimately the only tangible fruit of Anglo-German prewar détente. As we shall see, that was largely a private affair and to the credit of Karl Helfferich and Arthur von Gwinner at the Deutsche Bank.

## The Baghdad Railway and Mesopotamian Oil

As discussed in Chapter 8, the Young Turk regime in Constantinople initially posed a serious challenge to German interests in the Ottoman Empire. Indeed, fears circulated in 1908 that the Baghdad Railway would not be continued with the participation of foreign capital.[186] Nevertheless, for all their Anglophilia the Young Turks were largely abandoned by the British.[187] While the British public welcomed the revolution with enthusiasm, London financiers balked at lending the new regime money.[188] Others sought to gain commercial advantage due to deepening interest in Mesopotamia's oil, which culminated in British proposals for an unguaranteed railway between Baghdad and Basra that pointed to a partitioning of Turkey and a British territorial grab of Lower Mesopotamia.[189] A similar process had already unfolded in Persia, where an initially pro-British Constitutional Revolution was abandoned by the British in 1907 by their support of the Shah and effective partition of the country into exclusive Russian and British spheres formalized under the Anglo-Russian Convention of August 1907. By that point the strategic significance of oil

---

[183] Fischer, *War of Illusions*, 310; Mommsen, *Bürgerstolz und Weltmachtstreben*, 510–11. Cf. Afflerbach, *Der Dreibund*, 737; Charmley, *Splendid Isolation*, 384; Clark, *The Sleepwalkers*, 330.

[184] Anon. [Hans Plehn {1868–1918}], *Deutsche Weltpolitik und kein Krieg!* (Berlin: Puttkammer & Mühlbrecht, 1913), 7–8. See also Carroll, *Germany and the Great Powers*, 744–46; Clark, *The Sleepwalkers*, 334–35; Fischer, *War of Illusions*, 259–71, 310–19; Jarausch, *Enigmatic Chancellor*, 142–43; Kennedy, *Anglo-German Antagonism*, 414–15; Mommsen, *Bürgerstolz und Weltmachtstreben*, 511; Smith, *Ideological Origins*, 138–40.

[185] Steiner, *Britain and the Origins*, 105–9.  [186] Pohl, *Von Stambul bis Bagdad*, 78.

[187] Ibid., 76–78.  [188] Barth, *Die deutsche Hochfinanz*, 240.

[189] Williamson, *Karl Helfferich*, 90–91.

had grown enormously due to the decision by the Royal Navy to fuel their dreadnought battleships with heating and diesel oil. In 1909 the Anglo-Persian Oil Company (APOC) was founded by William D'Arcy with the support of the British government, which by 1910 would employ 2,500 people and in 1912 complete construction of what would become the largest oil refinery in the world in Abadan, Persia, less than 50 miles northeast of the Shat-al-Arab.[190]

Quite consciously, British foreign policy cultivated good relations with France and Russia in 1908 with the explicit aim of jointly dominating the Near East and marginalizing Germany and Austria-Hungary.[191] As Britain's security became ever more rigidly bound up with Russia in the Liberal Foreign Office under Edward Grey and Charles Hardinge, wide latitudes – and in the case of Britain's ambassadors to St. Petersburg, Sir Arthur Nicolson (1906–10) and then Sir George Buchanan (1910–18), encouragements – were given Russia's destabilizing provocations in the Balkans. This not only threatened the Ottoman Empire with disintegration but severely eroded the balance between the Dual and Triple Alliances, enhanced Germany's diplomatic isolation, and thus undermined the very basis of continental European security.[192] In the autumn of 1908, Helfferich himself feared that Ottoman Turkey was about to become a second Egypt.[193] This was a prelude for what would become an all-out "Scramble for Turkey" by 1910–11 that would even draw in American oil and railway interests.[194]

In the immediate term the Germans were left to control the damage and bide their time. In October 1908 Helfferich returned to Constantinople and worked actively to improve the press for the Germans in Turkey by paying the expenses of Paul Weitz (1862–1939), a German correspondent for the *Frankfurter Zeitung* in Constantinople with good contacts to the Young Turks, and subsidizing new Turkish newspapers, accompanied by plenty of baksheesh to Turkish officials. Helfferich and Gwinner themselves took an active role in making good publicity for Germany and the Bagdad railroad and assured that the Deutsche Bank participated in loans to the new regime.[195] On German initiative that autumn, the Deutsche Bank, the Banque Impérial Ottoman, and a group close to the Anglo-German investor Sir Ernest Cassel participated in funding an advance and then loans to help the new regime out of its financial straits. Feelers were also put out to Britain to discuss the many open issues that

---

[190] Eichholtz, *Die Bagdadbahn*, 35–36.   [191] Rose, *Zwischen Empire und Kontinent*, 485.
[192] See ibid., 485–557; Schöllgen, *Imperialismus und Gleichgewicht*, 248–47; Neilsen, *Britain and the Last Tsar*, 294–316; Charmley, *Splendid Isolation*, 354, 358, 359, 363, 373, 382, 386–87. Cf. Bülow, *Denkwürdigkeiten*, vol. 2, 416.
[193] Barth, *Die deutsche Hochfinanz*, 242.   [194] Canis, *Der Weg in den Abgrund*, 354.
[195] Barth, *Die deutsche Hochfinanz*, 243–48, 274; Williamson, *Karl Hefferich*, 89–90.

had stalled construction on the Baghdad Railway in the hopes of some kind of ultimate agreement.[196]

The Germans had an unexpected ally in Ahmed Riza (1859-1930), who while leader of the Young Turk Committee of Union and Progress (CUP) in Paris, was German on his mother's side and pro-German in inclination. Moreover, many other key figures in the CUP were officers in the Ottoman Army, where respect for Germany was deep, and while he was deposed in April 1909, Hamid had in fact gained popularity by his swift restoration of the constitution.[197] Thus by early 1909 the CUP government was on the defensive while the Germans had managed to return to decent standing at the Porte.[198] Their initial hopes for help from Britain dashed, the Young Turks realized that, for better or worse, they were dependent on the Germans more than anyone else to modernize their country and were likely to be able to do so on better terms with them than with any other major European power. For their part, the Germans had more at stake strategically in the preservation of the Ottoman Empire than any other great power and made effective propaganda that they alone among them were pursuing policies that were in Turkey's interests.[199]

Meanwhile, Ernest Cassel had founded the Banque National de Turquie and acquired a significant stake in Turkish investments. Helfferich met with Cassel in Constantinople in the autumn of 1909 to discuss the participation of his bank in the Baghdad Railway. Later that year Cassel came to Berlin and proposed allowing an English company to assume control of the southern stretch of the railway between Baghdad to the Persian Gulf as a way of overcoming British hostility to the project.[200] In October 1909 the Turkish government permitted construction on the Baghdad railroad to continue after a lull of some five years, but proposals for guarantees for streams of revenue to the railway proposed by the bank consortium led by Deutsche Bank were rejected by the new Turkish finance minister Mehemed Djavid Bey (1875-1926).[201] One year later, however, a renewed French initiative (supported by Britain) proposed to challenge the Baghdad Railway with a railroad running from northern Syria through the Euphrates Valley to Baghdad, which as Helfferich recalled, would have been the "deathblow" to the railway.[202] Simultaneously the French sought to exploit Turkey's revenue problems to assert financial controls that aimed at subordinating all Turkish economic

---

[196] Helfferich, *Der Weltkrieg*, vol. 1, 134.
[197] Schöllgen, *Imperialismus und Gleichgewicht*, 242; McMeekin, *The Berlin-Baghdad Express*, 70-71, 72.
[198] McMeekin, *The Berlin-Baghdad Express*, 73.
[199] Schöllgen, *Imperialismus und Gleichgewicht*, 242.
[200] Helfferich, *Der Weltkrieg*, vol. 1, 134-35.    [201] Williamson, *Karl Hefferich*, 91.
[202] Helfferich, *Der Weltkrieg*, vol. 1, 135-36.

policy decisions – including the construction of railroads – in ways preferable to the French and British.[203]

When in the summer of 1910 the Turkish government found itself once again cash strapped and at the mercy of French financiers intent on these drastic restrictions of Turkey's fiscal sovereignty, a consortium of large German, Austrian, and Swiss banks led by Deutsche Bank put together a loan package that Helfferich traveled to Constantinople in November 1910 to negotiate and which ultimately extended 11 million Ottoman lira (204 million marks) to the Turkish government in 1911 and 1912, secured by the customs duties collected in the *vilayet* of Constantinople. This greatly improved German-Turkish relations, though it also put strains on the German credit market, on which the Series II bonds of the Bagdad Railway had been floated only shortly prior and on which the Reich was reliant to finance its own deficits as a result of the watered-down financial reform of 1909.[204]

Soon thereafter Helfferich began negotiations with Djavid Bey on revenue for construction of the 600 kilometer section of the railway between Tel-el-Helif and Baghdad. While Djavid Bey rejected additional revenues, he agreed to a deal much like Helfferich had brokered in 1908, which treated the entire section between Bulgurlu and Baghdad as one unit for financing, allowing Deutsche Bank to use advances on the Series II and not yet issued Series III bonds from the bank consortium to begin construction in Baghdad working northwest.[205] However, no security for later series of bonds (Series IV–VI) to finance construction of the remaining sections of railroad was offered by the Turks, and the projected guaranteed revenues were significantly short of the amounts needed. In the end, political pressure led Helfferich and Gwinner to reluctantly agree to the terms that Djavid Bey offered, as the Ottoman Empire was by that point effectively bankrupt.[206]

In the following year negotiations with the Turks and Russians removed the remaining political obstacles to resuming construction of the railroad. In agreement with the German Foreign Office, Helfferich and Gwinner made arrangements to relinquish partial or full rights to the politically sensitive section of the railway between Baghdad and the Persian Gulf to the Turks in order to give them an opportunity to come to an agreement with the British to complete the railway in this disputed territory by internationalizing it. These supplemental Baghdad railroad accords signed in March 1911 also approved the immediate expansion of the main railway line to Baghdad and gave the railway a concession for a branch line to Alexandrette and the construction

---

[203] Ibid.
[204] Ibid., 136–37; Williamson, *Karl Hefferich*, 92–94; Barth, *Die deutsche Hochfinanz*, 267–72; Pohl, *Von Stambul bis Baghdad*, 78, 80.
[205] Barth, *Die deutsche Hochfinanz*, 259–61.
[206] Williamson, *Karl Helfferich*, 94–95; McMeekin, *The Berlin-Baghdad Express*, 79.

and operation of its strategically important harbor.[207] An agreement with the Russians then signed in August 1911 dropped St. Petersburg's objections to the railway's extension to the Persian Gulf and permitted the construction of a Russian branch line to Tehran in return for Germany's recognition of Russia's sphere of influence in northern Persia and a promise to refrain from any railway construction within it.[208] To avoid sparking Russian ire, the Deutsche Bank was prepared to ignore pleas from both the Ottoman government and the German Foreign Office for more politically and strategically-driven railway investments in Turkey, such as extending the Anatolian Railway from Ankara to Sivas to enhance Ottoman defenses against Russia.[209] And not even the Agadir Crisis in 1911 disrupted the Franco-German banking entente in Turkey – in 1912 the Deutsche Bank estimated that no less than 53 percent of all securities it had underwritten were held abroad, primarily by the French.[210] It was a clear victory for the Germans and a major blow to Britain's persistent opposition to the railway.

By early 1913 the Turkish financial position had worsened considerably on account of the First Balkan War and the resulting loss of European territory from which the state had drawn no less than one-fifth of all Ottoman revenues.[211] Angry over the setbacks in the war and European great power bullying to concede Adrianople to Bulgaria, in late January 1913 a coup d'état led by Ismail Enver Bey (1881–1922) and Mehemed Talaat Bey (1874–1921) brought the Young Turks back into power and a much more explicitly pro-German position at the Porte, which boded well for the Baghdad Railway. That said, Ottoman Turkey's now even more severely strained finances were bound to be a hindrance. In the postwar financial negotiations in Paris in which Gwinner and Helfferich participated on behalf of Deutsche Bank as a major Turkish creditor and which Helfferich chaired, both were aware that any war indemnity would spell the financial ruin of the Ottoman Empire. They thus tried to make the victors liable through their acquisition of Ottoman lands for a share of Turkey's public debt, as the debt was a private organization administered by the great powers whose property could not be seized according to international law. Not surprisingly, this financial maneuver did not convince the Balkan League and Russia. Thus the May 1913 Paris conference failed to produce an agreement, leaving the matter unsettled by the time war broke out in August 1914.[212]

---

[207] Helfferich, *Der Weltkrieg*, vol. 1, 137, 142–43; Williamson, *Karl Helfferich*, 95.
[208] Helfferich, *Der Weltkrieg*, vol. 1, 72–77, 121; Lieven, *The End of Tsarist Russia*, 236.
[209] Barth, *Die deutsche Hochfinanz*, 347–48.   [210] Ibid., 350.   [211] Ibid., 357.
[212] Ibid., 357–59; Williamson, *Karl Helfferich*, 98–100. Cf. Karl Helfferich, "Die türkische Staatsschuld und die Balkanstaaten," *Bank-Archiv: Zeitschrift für Bank- und Börsenwesen* 12, no. 11 (1913): 167–75; Helfferich, *Der Weltkrieg*, vol. 1, 106, 109–10.

Likewise unsettled was the problem of rising construction costs since the original Baghdad Railway concession negotiated between the German and Turkish governments in 1903 and the deteriorating prospects of Turkish railway bonds on the German capital market. Continuing construction required drawing in other banks by showing some prospect of profit on the railway lines. Helfferich thus sought to renegotiate higher interest rates on the railway's existing obligations, operating guarantees for lines that lacked them, and much higher operating guarantees per kilometer. These German-Turkish talks made little progress until they too were overshadowed by war in 1914.[213]

In the meantime, however, the basis for a Franco-German bargain over the Baghdad Railway was emerging. In February 1914, Helfferich, representing the Deutsche Bank, and the General Director of the Banque Impérial Ottoman agreed to demarcate their respective railway interests. Accordingly, northern and eastern Anatolia as well as Syria were recognized as within a French railway sphere, while western Anatolia and the provinces adjacent to the Baghdad Railway were considered German. As part of the deal, Deutsche Bank bought the Banque Ottoman's shares in the Baghdad Railway and the French government agreed to an increase in Turkish customs duties. Likewise, the parties agreed to put Turkish public finances on a broader fiscal basis and to consolidate its public debts with new bonds.[214]

An agreement between Britain and Germany was lubricated by Mesopotamian oil. The Deutsche Bank and its subsidiary the Anatolian Railway had been scrambling unsuccessfully since the drilling success of William D'Arcy in Abadan in 1908 to regain title over their 1904 Mesopotamian oil preconcessions that had been revoked by the Turkish government in 1907. In light of oil-fueled dreadnoughts and the naval arms race with Britain, as well as the growing significance of oil to German industry, Gwinner and Helfferich sought to find ways to regain these claims through the bank's Bagdad Railway concession.[215] At the same time, they pursued a track of reconciliation with the British in order to jointly force the Porte into advantageous oil concessions. In 1909 the bank began negotiations with the British over the thorny matter of the stretch of railway between Basra and the Persian Gulf and a new Mesopotamian oil concession.[216] By then the British Admiralty and Foreign Office were eager for British oil interests, notably Anglo-Persian Oil, Royal Dutch Shell, and Cassel's Banque National de Turquie to secure Mesopotamia's oil for Britain given its strategic importance to the Royal Navy.[217] In Berlin,

---

[213] Williamson, *Karl Helfferich*, 105–6; Barth, *Die deutsche Hochfinanz*, 378–79.
[214] Helfferich, *Der Weltkrieg*, vol. 1, 138–42; Pohl, *Von Stambuhl bis Bagdad*, 89–90; Barth, *Die deutsche Hochfinanz*, 369–75; Schöllgen, *Imperialismus und Gleichgewicht*, 390.
[215] Eichholtz, *Die Bagdadbahn*, 36, 39. See also Dokument 7, Arthur v. Gwinner to Karl Helfferich, Oct. 18, 1910 in ibid., 83.
[216] Ibid., 41, 44, 47.   [217] Ibid., 43.

Bethmann Hollweg and the Reichstag were similarly aware of the economic and strategic significance of oil and eager to find ways to counterbalance the predominant position of Standard Oil through a proposal for an Imperial petroleum monopoly and various schemes for European cooperation.[218]

Meanwhile, the Deutsche Bank and Anatolian Railway were able to use their control over the Baghdad Railway to forge an oil syndicate with these British interests in 1911 in the form of the Turkish Petroleum Company (TPC). Through agreement between Deutsche Bank and this syndicate in 1912, the bank relinquished all claims to Mesopotamian oil to the TPC and agreed that all future negotiations with the Turkish government for valid oil concessions would be sought solely on behalf of the TPC. In return, the Baghdad Railway was allowed to continue its line to Basra and gain access to the British capital market to finance its construction.[219] One year earlier, the Turkish government had agreed to allow the British to control the Basra-Gulf section of the railroad in return for making the mouth of the Shat-al-Arab navigable to large vessels. This arrangement satisfied both the Germans and British, as it gave the Germans their desired outlet to the gulf while allowing the British to retain control of the Persian Gulf coast.[220] In March 1914 a shareholding agreement over the TPC was reached in London, blessed by both the German and British governments, whereby Deutsche Bank and Anglo-Persian Petroleum/Royal Dutch Shell each received 25 percent of the shares of the company, while the D'Arcy Group (APOC) received 50 percent. As a secret addendum to the agreement – about which Helfferich did not even bother to inform the Kaiser – a one-third share of the produced oil was assured the German and British navies each for a period of 30 years.[221] The British and German governments then put joint pressure on the Turks for the oil, which resulted in a proposal for a ninety-nine-year oil concession in the *vilayets* of Mosul and Baghdad along with expansive other rights and tax exemptions to TPC in return for 8 percent of the raw oil produced. Under enormous pressure, Djavid Bey and the Grand Vizier ultimately agreed to it on June 25, 1914.[222] It was a shameless Anglo-German grab for Ottoman oil which foreshadowed the Anglo-French Sykes-Picot Agreement of May 1916 that ultimately partitioned the entire Ottoman Near East and on the basis of which the British Empire would ultimately seize all of Ottoman Mesopotamia.

Ten days earlier, on June 15, 1914, a final agreement between Germany and Great Britain had been signed in London by the German and British foreign ministers after more than a year of very difficult negotiations that formally

---

[218] Barth, *Die deutsche Hochfinanz*, 363–64.   [219] Eichholtz, *Die Bagdadbahn*, 48–50.
[220] Helfferich, *Der Weltkrieg*, vol. 1, 144–50; Williamson, *Karl Helfferich*, 100–1.
[221] Eicholtz, *Die Bagdadbahn*, Dokument 11, 51, 89–90; Barth, *Die deutsche Hochfinanz*, 367.
[222] Eichholtz, *Die Bagdadbahn*, 50–54.

settled all remaining outstanding issues relating to the Baghdad Railway, such as the endpoint of the railway on the Persian Gulf and its control, spur lines of the railway network, navigation of the Tigris and Euphrates, and the construction of harbors in Baghdad and Basra.[223] Under this arrangement the British recognized the Baghdad Railway's transport monopoly and agreed to allow surplus revenue from a planned increase in Turkish customs duties to be directed to complete construction of the railway, while the Germans recognized Britain's sphere of interest in the northern Persian Gulf, agreeing not to extend the railway beyond Basra to Kuwait or challenge Britain's shipping monopoly on the Tigris and Euphrates. Britain also gained the right for a British financial group to take a stake in the railway's capital, as well as in the firms that would build and run the harbor facilities in Baghdad and Basra.[224]

Karl Helfferich was the architect of the German negotiating position via Arthur Zimmermann in the Foreign Office (as by that point the old Ottoman hands Marschall and Kiderlen-Waechter had both died) and worked closely with Richard von Kühlmann in the embassy in London, but he believed that Germany ultimately relinquished more than it gained in these negotiations, effectively buying British cooperation on the railroad at too high a price.[225] It was an admission of the very "junior partnership" that *Weltpolitik* had been devised to strenuously avoid.[226] That said, this agreement, along with previous accords Helfferich had negotiated with the Ottoman government in 1908 and 1911 to finance the railway, the successful internationalization of the railway's financing, the agreement to demarcate railway interests into French and German spheres, and not least, the progress made in actually building the railway by 1914 against enormous diplomatic opposition, financial problems, and engineering challenges was the only example of German *Weltpolitik* in the late Wilhelmine period that succeeded despite steadfast British opposition. Still, when war broke out in 1914 the Baghdad Railway remained unfinished, some 800 kilometers short of the full 1,653 kilometers of track between Konya and Baghdad.[227]

## "World Policy and No War!"

What of the other components of Anglo-German détente? It turned out that the British Colonial Office, Dominions, and Crown Colonies were fiercely

---

[223] Ibid., 59.
[224] Helfferich, *Der Weltkrieg*, vol. 1, 150–54; Pohl, *Von Stambul bis Bagdad*, 90–91; Barth, *Die deutsche Hochfinanz*, 375–85.
[225] Williamson, *Karl Helfferich*, 101–2; Schöllgen, *Imperialismus und Gleichgewicht*, 387, 413, 429.
[226] Schöllgen, *Imperialismus und Gleichgewicht*, 430.
[227] Pohl, *Von Stambul bis Bagdad*, 89.

opposed to making any colonial concessions to Germany – not even an agreement to allow Germany to acquire Walvis Bay and tiny islands off the coast of German Southwest Africa went anywhere.[228] Likewise, attempts to activate British diplomacy to allow Germany to gain a foothold in the Belgian Congo or to demarcate spheres of interest in China stalled.[229] It is true that a secret agreement over a future Anglo-German partition of Portuguese African colonies was concluded in April 1913, but even this hung under a pall, namely the Anglo-Portuguese Windsor Agreement of 1899, which was revealed to the Germans in these negotiations and had in effect secretly reneged on the Anglo-German Angola Treaty of 1898.[230] When Edward Grey insisted that the new Anglo-German Angola Treaty be published together with the old one, Bethmann Hollweg demurred, rightly fearing that it would make him appear a dupe in public and lead to renewed anti-English uproar in the German press and Reichstag.[231]

German bankers and industrialists were also very skeptical about this new Anglola treaty.[232] Still, some very modest success was achieved in areas involving German investment in Portuguese colonial Africa, which the British government was eager to encourage as part of the Angola Treaty. Karl Hellferich, representing a consortium of German banks and overseas trading companies, was able to negotiate a controlling stake with an English investment group in the Portuguese Nyassa Company in Mozambique in 1913–14.[233] Negotiations for German participation in the Benguela-Katanga Railway connecting Portuguese Angola and the copper-rich Katanga province of Belgian Congo were ultimately derailed by the inability to gain a majority stake for German investors on account of energetic French opposition lodged with Whitehall.[234] Other negotiations over investments in railways connecting Portuguese Angolan Port Alexander with German Southwest Africa were not brought to conclusion before the outbreak of war.[235] Thus Bethmann Hollweg's policy of détente with Britain ultimately yielded very little for *Weltpolitik*.

In contrast to German agreements with Britain over the Baghdad Railway and colonial issues, Russia and its Serbian client in the Balkans were following an increasingly belligerent policy toward Germany, Austria-Hungary, and Ottoman Turkey following the Balkan wars that threatened what had been

---

[228] Mommsen, *Bürgerstolz und Weltmachtstreben*, 516–17.   [229] Ibid., 519–23.
[230] Ibid., 517–19.
[231] Ibid., 518–19; Jarausch, *Enigmatic Chancellor*, 142–43; Richard Langhorne, "Anglo-German Negotiations Concerning the Future of the Portuguese Colonies," *The Historical Journal* 16, no. 2 (June 1973): 361–87; Steiner, *Britain and the Origins*, 105–7; Wilson, *The Policy of the Entente*, 10.
[232] Fischer, *War of Illusions*, 314–15.   [233] Helfferich, *Der Weltkrieg*, vol. 1, 119.
[234] Ibid.; Fischer, *War of Illusions*, 315–18.   [235] Helfferich, *Der Weltkrieg*, vol. 1, 119–20.

achieved by pragmatic negotiation and improved trust between London and Berlin. It was fueled by resentment over Turkish reoccupation of Adrianople in the Second Balkan War and the October 1913 submission of Serbia to the Austrian ultimatum over Albania, which had shifted Belgrade's attention northwestward to Bosnia-Herzegovina.[236] While Russian support of Serbian irredentism in Bosnia-Herzegovina played to Slavophile opinion at home and thus served to bolster the Tsar's popular legitimacy, the primary issue driving Russian Balkan policy in the last year of peace was the desire to control the Turkish Straits, a chokepoint through which passed the lion's share of Russian grain exports and that was vital to Ukrainian heavy industry but that had twice been disrupted in the recent Balkan wars at great cost to Russia. Control of the straits was also seen as key to Russian ambitions in the Mediterranean. The Russians were nonetheless well aware that this goal could not be reached by anything short of a European war.[237]

Just how dangerous Russia's preoccupation with the straits was becoming to Germany by 1913–14 was revealed by the Liman von Sanders Crisis that erupted in December 1913, when a German military mission headed by General Otto Liman von Sanders (1855–1929) was dispatched to Constantinople to rebuild the Ottoman military after its crushing defeats in the Balkan wars of 1912–13.[238] While German military missions had been a fixture in Turkey since the late 1880s, the Sanders mission was on a larger scale, and he was to be given command of a Turkish army corps in Constantinople and vast powers to reform the Turkish military. The Russian leadership viewed this German presence with such hostility that foreign minister Sazonov tried to muster a stern joint Entente note to the Porte, and when that failed, to organize an Entente military intervention to occupy land in Asia Minor to pressure Constantinople, also to no avail.[239] In a January 6 memorandum to Tsar Nicholas, Sazonov actually proposed provoking a European war to seize the straits.[240] At a Council of Ministers meeting on January 13, 1914, chaired by premier Vladimir Kokovtsov, the majority of ministers including Sazonov were prepared to go to war with Germany (and Austria-Hungary) over the Liman matter and were assured of full backing from France's foreign minister.[241]

There is something odd about this intense Russian hostility directed against Germany given that an even more immediate threat to the straits and Russian security in the Black Sea was posed by the British naval mission to Turkey headed by Admiral Arthur Limpus (1863–1931), who had arrived in

---

[236] Lieven, *The End of Tsarist Russia*, 277–84.
[237] See McMeekin, *Russian Origins*, 28–30; Lieven, *The End of Tsarist Russia* 73–76, 253–56, 285–87.
[238] Canis, *Der Weg in den Abgrund*, 586–610. Cf. Fischer, *War of Illusions*, 332–54.
[239] Clark, *The Sleepwalkers*, 342–43; Lieven, *The End of Tsarist Russia*, 287–88, 290.
[240] McMeekin, *Russian Origins*, 31.   [241] Ibid., 31–32; Clark, *The Sleepwalkers*, 344.

Constantinople in May 1912 to develop Turkey's navy. This included command of the entire Turkish fleet and the purchase from Armstrong Whitworth and Vickers of two dreadnought-class battleships. In January 1914 the two ships were within weeks of delivery, with the Turks announcing the intention of buying a third such ship already nearly complete, which would render the Russian Black Sea fleet obsolete and give Ottoman Turkey the capacity to not only close the straits but to threaten Russia in the Black Sea basin.[242] Since Russia could not buy such ships abroad because it was prohibited from passing warships through the straits by the Berlin Treaty of 1878, matching the Turks involved massive investments in Russian shipbuilding and construction costs of some 60 percent greater per ton.[243] To make matters worse for the Russians, 2 more Turkish dreadnoughts were then under construction in the United States, while 3 cruisers had been ordered from Italy, 2 submarines from Germany, and 6 minesweepers from France.[244] Indeed, there is evidence that alarm over Ottoman Turkey's immanent naval superiority over Russia and the closing of a window for seizing the straits was the primary catalyst for Russia's willingness to risk a European war in January 1914.[245]

Disturbed by the militancy of the Russian reaction, Berlin backed down by relinquishing command of the Constantinople corps to a Turkish officer on January 16, 1914. Soon thereafter in early February Sazonov chaired an important war planning meeting to assure Russia's army and navy could mobilize to seize Constantinople and the straits on short notice and unilaterally in the event of war.[246] Supported by France, St. Petersburg then pressed London for a more substantial commitment to the Entente, culminating in a proposal for an Anglo-Russian naval convention, an idea pushed by Arthur Nicolson. Edward Grey was himself eager to improve Anglo-Russian relations after the Liman von Sanders Crisis and to preserve the Anglo-Russian Convention, which was under strain over Russian activity in Persia, so he agreed to it in principle in April 1914.[247] Sanctioned by the British cabinet in May, Grey then negotiated the convention in secret in June 1914, but news of it was leaked to the Germans by the Baltic German secretary of the Russian embassy in London.[248] While devoid of much substance, these talks entertained

---

[242] Clark, *The Sleepwalkers*, 342–43; McMeekin, *Russian Origins*, 30–31, 36; Lieven, *The End of Tsarist Russia*, 285–88. See also Chris B. Rooney, "The International Significance of British Naval Missions to the Ottoman Empire, 1908-14," *Middle Eastern Studies* 34, no. 1 (Jan. 1998): 1–29.
[243] Lieven, *The End of Tsarist Russia*, 286.  [244] McMeekin, *Russian Origins*, 36–37.
[245] Ibid., 35–40.  [246] Ibid., 33–36.
[247] Mulligan, *The Origins*, 84–90; McMeekin, *Russian Origins*, 38–39.
[248] See Stephen Schroeder, *Die englisch-russische Marinekonvention: Das Deutsche Reich und die Verhandlungen der Tripleentente am Vorabend des ersten Weltkriegs* (Göttingen: Vandenhoeck & Ruprecht, 2006), 708; Canis, *Der Weg in den Abgrund*, 627–33. See also Charmley, *Splendid Isolation*, 363–95; Ferguson, *The Pity of War*, 60–62; Kennedy,

the possibility of the Royal Navy supporting the landing of a Russian expeditionary force on the German Baltic coast were war to break out with Germany. When queried about these talks by the German ambassador Lichnowsky, Grey evaded and dissembled, suggesting the British were hiding something.[249]

Such duplicity shocked Bethmann Hollweg. It was a major blow to Anglo-German détente that severely undercut the credibility of British peaceful intentions at a time when Russia was on the diplomatic offensive and serious doubts were being raised about the strength of Germany's only remaining reliable ally, Austria-Hungary.[250] It serves to highlight yet again the profoundly destabilizing role Britain was playing in the European power balance by its continued reliance on the Anglo-Russian Convention for its imperial security while at the same time provoking Russia through the Limpus naval mission to Constantinople. Worse, the British Foreign Office under Edward Grey steadfastly refused to clearly define Britain's core European interests or to state openly under what circumstances Great Britain would remain neutral or wage war to defend them. Simply put, British commitments to the Entente in 1914 lacked credibility, as they would have required a formal defensive alliance with France and a conscription army of at least a half million men prepared for an immediate expeditionary operation to the continent, all political non-starters in Britain at the time.[251] Irresponsibly, Grey preferred placating France and Russia through secret diplomacy and non-binding agreements for imperial cover while keeping much of the British cabinet, Parliament, and the public in the dark about the nature of those commitments. In public he professed the fictions that Britain was maintaining the "balance of power" and retaining a "free hand," claiming to let the winds of British public opinion be the ultimate arbiters of war or peace in Europe even as his commitment to the Triple Entente remained as firm as ever.[252]

---

*Anglo-German Antagonism*, 423; Neilson, *Britain and the Last Tsar*, 315–38; Rose, "From 'illusion' to 'Angellism,'" in Geppert, Mulligan, and Rose, *The Wars*, 335–39; Rose, *Zwischen Empire und Kontinent*, 514–57; Wilson, *The Policy of the Entente*, 74–84, 95–99, 115–20.

[249] Canis, *Der Weg in den Abgrund*, 627–33; Clark, *The Sleepwalkers*, 421.
[250] Clark, *The Sleepwalkers*, 422; see also Jarausch, *Enigmatic Chancellor*, 141–43, 151–52; Mulligan, *The Origins*, 88–91.
[251] Lieven, *The End of Tsarist Russia*, 299–301; Wilson, *The Policy of the Entente*, 15–16.
[252] See Wilson, *The Policy of the Entente*, 51–99; Charmley, *Splendid Isolation*, 331–61; Clark, *Sleepwalkers*, 203–4. Cf. Fischer, *War of Illusions*, 156.

# 11

# From World Policy to World War

### The Last Roosevelt Professor

Early in the new year 1914 Gustav Schmoller received a friendly greeting from Madison, Wisconsin. It was from Richard T. Ely, cofounder of the American Economic Association. As mentioned in Chapter 1, Ely had studied in Germany in the late 1870s and had been strongly influenced by that experience and by the example of the Association for Social Policy in creating his association. Ely, who had visited Schmoller in Berlin since his student days, wrote that his wife remembered Schmoller fondly and wished to have a signed picture of him, mentioning that they had pictures of many of the leading German economists in their home. A picture of his already hung in his seminar room at the University of Wisconsin.[1]

As final negotiations over the Baghdad Railway were underway in London in early June 1914, Henry Farnam was very much looking forward to his travel to Europe in July to begin his tenure as the new Roosevelt Professor to Berlin University, attached to the Amerika Institut. This new department had been organized by Hugo Münsterberg for the Prussian Ministry of Culture in 1910 around the sizable library on Americana that Ernst von Halle had accumulated over his lifetime and that his widow had bequeathed to the University of Berlin after his death in 1909. Some five thousand books from von Halle's library were included in the new institute, which was generously supported by Jacob Schiff and James Speyer in New York and Leopold Koppel (1854–1933) in Berlin, the same philanthropic trio that had funded the Kaiser Wilhelm Professorships back in 1904.[2]

Farnam's own appointment as an exchange professor had been reported with much pride in the *Yale News* as soon as it was made official in May 1913.[3] Yale's then president, Arthur T. Hadley, had himself studied political economy

---

[1] GStA PK, VI. HA Nl. Schmoller, Nr. 206a, [no fol. number], Richard T. Ely to Gustav Schmoller, Jan. 2, 1914.
[2] See Roth, "Der Politische Kontext," 69.
[3] "High Honor for Prof. Farnam," *Yale News,* May 14, 1913; cf. "Akademische Nachrichten," *Frankfurter Zeitung* (Abendblatt), Feb. 19, 1914. See YUL MA, Farnam Family Papers, Group 203, Series II, Box 229, Folder 3113.

in Germany in the 1870s and had served as a Roosevelt Professor in Berlin in 1907–8, the year after Hermann Schumacher had been a Kaiser Wilhelm Professor at Columbia. Hadley was quoted in the *Yale News* as saying "Professor Farnam is remarkably well fitted for the position on account of his knowledge of economic legislation, his acquaintance with Germany and the Germans, and his familiarity with the German language."[4] Indeed, since becoming a Yale professor in 1880 Farnam had been a pioneer in both civil service reform and in the promotion of labor legislation in the United States, both of which were much inspired by German precedents. In 1902 he founded and for many years led the Connecticut Civil Service Reform Association and had served as the vice-president of the National Civil Service Reform League in 1900.[5] Together with another of Schmoller's former American students, Adna F. Weber (1870–1968) of the New York Bureau of Labor Statistics, Farnam had founded the American Association for Labor Legislation (AALL) at the annual meeting of the American Economic Association in 1905, with Richard T. Ely serving as the AALL's first president.[6]

In early June 1914 Farnam wrote Schmoller that he and his family would be sailing from New York to Plymouth on July 18 and would spend the first five weeks of their year in Europe in England, planning to arrive in Berlin in the first week of September. He was looking forward to visiting the International Association for Labour Legislation meeting in Berne as well as a conference on social insurance in Paris in September and hoped to see Schmoller before the start of the semester in October.[7] Aboard the NDL steamer *Berlin* on July 23, Farnam wrote that he was looking forward to the annual conference of the Association for Social Policy in Düsseldorf and would enjoy renewing old friendships and making new ones there. He very much looked forward to seeing him in Berlin in October.[8]

While Farnam was on his way to Europe, Schumacher was hosting the American economist John Bates Clark, whom he had gotten to know while serving as Kaiser Wilhelm Professor at Columbia University in 1906–7 – when, as will be recalled from Chapter 9, Schumacher had taught his son, John M. Clark. Schumacher had since deepened his friendship to the elder Clark, and Schumacher's wife Edith had just completed a translation of the

---

[4] High Honor for Prof. Farnam," *Yale News*, May 14, 1913.
[5] *Dictionary of American Biography*, vol. XXI, Supplement 1, 293–95. See also Frank Mann Stewart, *The National Civil Service Reform League: History, Activities and Problems* (Austin: University of Texas, 1902).
[6] Rodgers, *Atlantic Crossings*, 236, 251–54, 261–64, 431–33, 437–39, 481–82.
[7] GStA PK, VI. HA Nl. Schmoller, Nr. 206a, [no fol. no.], Henry Farnam to Gustav Schmoller, June 1, 1914.
[8] GStA PK, VI. HA Nl. Schmoller, Nr. 206b, fol. 1, Henry Farnam to Gustav Schmoller, aboard the steamer *Berlin*, July 23, 1914; cf. Boese, *Geschichte des Vereins für Sozialpolitik*, 143–48.

**Figure 11.1** Henry Walcott Farnam ca. 1910.

Clark's *Essentials of Economic Theory*, which was about to be delivered to its German publisher. On July 30th Clark was with the Schumachers in Bonn and had just returned from a peace conference much moved by its proceedings and then on his way to another in Switzerland. That would be the last time Schumacher would ever see him.[9] Days later the international republic of letters and the integrated world economy of the steamship and railway age would be shattered by war.

## July Crisis

When Austria-Hungary was shaken by the assassination of Archduke Franz Ferdinand and his wife one month earlier, its own foreign policy was overshadowed both by the lamentable status of its military and the restraint it had been forced to show during the two Balkan wars in 1912–13 under German pressure, which had weakened its position in the Balkans and diminished its status as a great power. Because of this weakness and the threat posed to its

---

[9] GNN HA, Nl. Schumacher, I, B-6p, fols. 482–83.

Balkan territories by Serbian irredentism, the Austrian civilian and military leadership quickly came to view the assassination as an existential threat. The jubilation of the Serbian public and press after the murders in Sarajevo, mounting circumstantial evidence of the involvement of agents of the Serbian state in the assassination plot (along with the obfuscations and contradictions of Serbian officials tasked with investigating it), and the post-assassination dissembling and bravado of the Serbian prime minister Nikola Pašić (1845–1926) left little doubt in their minds that Serbia was behind the regicide and needed to be crushed.[10] Thus Emperor Franz Joseph (1846–1916), the Austrian Foreign Ministry, and the military were bent on war with Serbia practically from the onset of the crisis and well before any backing had been given for such a course by Hungary, much less Germany. Even former moderates and those with deep knowledge of the Balkans in the Habsburg government fell in line with this drastic position.[11] Indeed, as discussed in Chapter 10, during the Balkan wars, Austrian diplomacy toward Serbia and Russia had undergone a dangerous militarization that was bound to escalate this newest Balkan crisis.[12]

German policy had never been hostile to Serbia, but the Sarajevo assassination and the apparent involvement in it of agents of the Serbian state brought home to German leaders and the public the fact that Serbian irredentism now posed a direct threat to Austria-Hungary's integrity and thus to an interest vital to Germany as its main alliance partner.[13] Still, the immediate official German response to the assassination was cautious, not belligerent.[14] The presentations of the hawkish Austrian emissary Alexander von Hoyos (1876–1937) and the aging, slippery Austrian ambassador Szögyény-Marich (1841–1916) to the Kaiser, Foreign Office, and chancellor on July 5–6 gave a false picture of consensus in Vienna and Budapest toward a path of swift action against Belgrade, but they were also vague and evasive enough to leave

---

[10] Clark, *The Sleepwalkers*, 42–64, 367–91; Lieven, *The End of Tsarist Russia*, 279–84. Cf. Otte, *July Crisis*, 11–31.
[11] Afflerbach, *Der Dreibund*, 827–33; Clark, *The Sleepwalkers*, 391–403; Otte, *July Crisis*, 39–64; Ritter, *Staatskunst*, vol. 2, 282–97; Watson, *Ring of Steel*, 7–8, 14–28; Wawro, *A Mad Catastrophe*, 106–7. Cf. Annika Mombauer, *Helmuth von Moltke and the Origins of the First World War* (Cambridge: Cambridge University Press, 2001), 151–52.
[12] See Samuel R. Williamson, Jr., *Austria-Hungary and the Origins of the First World War* (New York: Macmillan, 1991), 6–42; Manfred Rauchensteiner, *Der Tod des Doppeladlers: Österreich-Ungarn und der Erste Weltkrieg* (Graz: Verlag Styria, 1993), 68–136; Günther Kronenbitter, *"Krieg im Frieden": Die Führung der k.u.k. Armee und die Großmachtpolitik Österreich-Ungarns 1906–1914* (Munich: Oldenbourg, 2003), 455–86.
[13] Carroll, *Germany and the Great Powers*, 769–75; Clark, *The Sleepwalkers*, 422; Jarausch, *Enigmatic Chancellor*, 153, 156.
[14] See Clark, *The Sleepwalkers*, 399–403.

the impression that steps short of war might be taken.[15] Indeed, Bethmann Hollweg saw German support for Austria at this juncture as part of a broader diplomatic realignment in the Balkans that would isolate Serbia militarily and politically and strengthen the Triple Alliance by adding Bulgaria and Turkey (thereby also securing the Baghdad Railway), as well as developing stronger ties to Romania and Greece.[16]

While the German leadership supported rapid military measures against Serbia, the Kaiser, Bethmann Hollweg, and the Foreign Office were wary of the Serbian matter becoming a European conflict but judged the threat of such a wider war remote if in the climate of international outrage Austria took immediate steps to established a fait accompli. That would force Russia to stand down as it had following the Austrian ultimatum to Serbia in October 1913 after the Second Balkan War. What those measures were the German leadership left Vienna to best determine. An early and unequivocal demonstration of support for Austria, it was believed, would deter the Russians from risking war.[17] Even the more forceful thrust later given this position by the Kaiser, Foreign Secretary Jagow and the German ambassador in Vienna Heinrich von Tschirschky (1858–1916) after the meetings with the Austrians in Berlin stressed swift retributive action to contain the dispute, not provocations that might lead to a wider war.[18] As Kurt Rietzler, Bethmann Hollweg's private secretary, jotted in his diary on July 11 summing up this policy: first establish "a rapid *fait accompli* and then be friendly towards the Entente. Then the shock can be withstood."[19]

That was the German "blank check" to Austria. It is untrue that the German leadership pushed Austria into war or anticipated or made any preparations for wider war as claimed by Fritz Fischer and others.[20] The German military was not involved in these discussions other than to assure the leadership that

---

[15] Ibid., 412–15; see also Otte, *July Crisis*, 64–82. Cf. Fritz Fellner, "Die 'Mission Hoyos,'" in *Vom Dreibund zum Völkerbund: Studien zur Geschichte der internationalen Beziehungen 1882–1919* ed. Heidrun Maschl and Brigitte Mazohl-Wallnig (Vienna: Verlag für Geschichte und Politik, 1994), 112–41.

[16] Jarausch, *Enigmatic Chancellor*, 156–57.

[17] Holger Afflerbach, *Auf Messers Schneide: Wie das Deutsche Reich den Ersten Weltkrieg Verlor* (Munich: C.H. Beck, 2018), 34–35; Clark, *The Sleepwalkers*, 415–19; Otte, *July Crisis*, 82–89.

[18] McMeekin, *July 1914*, 114–16, 119–20; Otte, *July Crisis*, 106, 113–14, 155–56, 159, 168–72.

[19] Quoted in Canis, *Der Weg in den Abgrund*, 659; see also Berghahn, *Germany and the Approach of War*, 190.

[20] Fischer, *Griff nach der Weltmacht*, 56–67; Fischer, *Germany's Aims*, 50–61; Berghahn, *Germany and the Approach of War*, 188; Peter Padfield, *The Great Naval Race: The Anglo-German Naval Rivalry, 1900–1914* (New York: D. McKay Co., 1974), 391; Fritz Fellner, "Austria Hungary," in *Decisions for War 1914*, ed. Keith Wilson (Abingdon, Oxon: Routledge, 1995), 9–25.

they were prepared for all eventualities and to offer their opinion that the likelihood of Russian intervention was low and that no military precautions were warranted. Indeed, no preparations for war of any kind were made to avoid alarming the other powers, underscoring the German hope and expectation of a dispute localized to the Balkans.[21] To be sure, it was ultimately a gamble that risked a European and ultimately a world war, but the ominous risks this policy ran only fully emerge from the hindsight of the unfolding July Crisis and are inflated by our perception that the "blank check" to Austria is among the first in a long chain of events that culminated in the First World War. It is important to stress that neither Bethmann Hollweg nor the Kaiser sought a European war – much less to provoke a world war – when they set out on this policy.[22] As noted in the previous chapter with reference to the 1913 army bill, the German military did not entertain a "short war" illusion, and German decision-making in July 1914 was not aiming to *provoke* a preemptive war.[23]

In calculating the risk of a wider war as remote, the Kaiser, Bethmann Hollweg, and the Foreign Office were banking on Austrian swiftness and a now familiar pattern of Russian bluff on account of insufficient military preparation. They also overestimated the German Army's deterrent effect and assumed that the Tsar and his regime would not support regicide. With hindsight, this put too much stock in Germany's military, the unity and competence of Austria-Hungary's leadership, and the reasonableness of the Tsar and his government not to risk a war they might lose over Serbia, an interest not remotely vital to Russia.[24] In the unlikely event that the Russians were still willing to go to war over it, the thinking went, it would ipso facto establish Russia's belligerent intentions to exploit the crisis to weaken the Triple Alliance, putting it ethically and legally in the wrong and then resulting in a war with Germany before the military balance tilted away from Berlin toward the Dual Alliance. This view clearly underestimated the extent to which the Dual Alliance (and by implication, the Triple Entente) had already

---

[21] Jansen, *Der Weg in den Ersten Weltkrieg*, 198–291, 511–12; Levy, "The Sources of Preventive Logic," in Levy and Vasquez, *The Outbreak*, 158–59, 162–66; Otte, *July Crisis*, 59, 83. Cf. Mombauer, *Helmuth von Moltke*, 189–92.
[22] See Berghahn, *Germany and the Approach of War*, 193; Otte, *July Crisis*, 513.
[23] See Clark, *The Sleepwalkers*, 417; Lieven, *The End of Tsarist Russia*, 337–42; Otte, *July Crisis*, 511–15; Samuel R. Williamson, Jr., "July 1914 Revisited and Revised: The Erosion of the German Paradigm," in Levy and Vasquez, *The Outbreak*, 30–62. Cf. Fischer, *War of Illusions*, 161–458 (chs. 9–21); Mombauer, *Helmuth von Moltke*, 106–81.
[24] See Canis, *Der Weg in den Abgrund*, 658–59; Ronald P. Bobroff, "War Accepted but Unsought: Russia's Growing Militancy in the July Crisis," in Levy and Vasquez, *The Outbreak*, 227–51. Cf. Mark Hewitson, *Germany and the Causes of the First World War* (Oxford and New York: Berg, 2004), 113–89.

embedded a Balkan conflict into its strategic scenarios.[25] This risk calculus thus also assumed that Britain would remain neutral were it ever to come to such a war, itself perhaps a questionable assumption given some of the warnings that had been issued by Edward Grey and Richard Haldane in 1912, but as discussed at the end of the previous chapter, Britain's military commitments to the Entente were vague and ultimately not altogether credible. In any case, the British specialist in the Foreign Office, Wilhelm von Stumm (1869–1935), doubted Britain would get involved and counseled Bethmann Hollweg accordingly.[26] This was reinforced by the fact that ambassador Lichnowsky had informed Edward Grey on July 6 that the German position was that it would be best not to restrain Austria to allow swift action against Serbia and Grey's assurances that an Austrian "action" within certain unspecified bounds would be understood by Whitehall.[27]

The Austro-Serbian isolation strategy must also be seen as an attempt to overcome Bethmann Hollweg and the government's weakness in the face of what appeared to the German public as a timid and ultimately failed *Weltpolitik* – along with perceptions of eroding Reich security – that had been subjects of heavy criticism in the German press and the Reichstag since the Agadir Crisis and had become more acute since the spring of 1914.[28] Germany's passivity and restraint in the two previous Balkan wars and its effort to mediate the Albanian issue with Britain and France had weakened Austria-Hungary and Turkey, emboldened Russia, strengthened and encouraged Serbia, and now with the recent shattering information about the Anglo-Russian naval talks, seemingly tightened the Entente ring around Germany. Isolating and not mediating this latest Balkan conflict and standing by Austria fully was thus clearly informed by these past perceived failures. It was a bid to bolster Germany's position in the Balkans and Near East, to preserve (and keep) its last remaining reliable ally, and thus to improve its continental security. And if it came to a wider war, it would allow Germany to break out of its strategic containment by the Triple Entente to allow for the continuation of peaceful *Weltpolitik*.[29]

The Balkan containment strategy would turn out to be *Weltpolitik*'s final act under conditions of peace, as things went south with it almost from the beginning. Rather than take swift action, the Austrians stalled and dithered,

[25] See Clark, *The Sleepwalkers*, 294–301, 416–23; Jarausch, *Enigmatic Chancellor*, 158–60, 181–84; Lieven, *The End of Tsarist Russia*, 317; Bruce W. Menning, "The Russian Threat Calculation, 1910–1914," in Geppert, Mulligan, and Rose, *The Wars*, 151–75; Otte, *July Crisis*, 89–101, 116–38.
[26] Jarausch, *Enigmatic Chancellor*, 154–55.
[27] Canis, *Der Weg in den Abgrund*, 659; Steiner, *Britain and the Origins*, 220.
[28] See Carroll, *Germany and the Great Powers*, 751–68; Chickering, *We Men Who Feel Most German*, 290; Retallack, *The German Right*, 393–99.
[29] Jarausch, *Enigmatic Chancellor*, 157–59; Hull, *Absolute Destruction*, 199–200.

undermining the German position by failing to capitalize on the international outrage over the assassination and allowing Russia time to coordinate a response with France and Serbia.[30] Much encouragement would be given the Russians to take an uncompromising line by the French ambassador Maurice Paléologue (1859-1944) and President Raymond Poincaré, the latter during a state visit to St. Petersburg with the new French premier René Vivani (1863-1925) on July 20-23. Poincaré, a Lorraine revanchist and strong advocate of a policy of extreme firmness with the Germans since the Adagir Crisis, was aware of Austria's belligerent intentions toward Serbia and Germany's backing of Austria before his arrival in St. Petersburg. He questioned in advance any involvement of Serbia in the assassination, agitated against Austria, affirmed Russia and France's commitment to Serbia, and encouraged a still reluctant foreign minister Sazonov, who was seeking better relations with Germany, to stand tough to the point of war. He then gave the Russians the full political and military backing of France in the event of a Russian escalation over Serbia with Austria on the last day of his visit.[31]

The ultimatum that was eventually produced by Vienna and then delivered 5:00 pm on July 23 – despite prior warnings from St. Petersburg and Paris – was harsh and drafted on the assumption that the Serbs would reject it. It left neither an exit strategy nor much of a window for diplomacy (it expired on the evening of July 25), effectively short-circuiting the great power crisis management that had restrained Russia and Austria and had contained the recent Balkan conflicts, practically assuring an Austrian war with Serbia and thus making one with Russia more likely.[32] Sazonov, Krivoshien, and most of the rest of the Russian Council of Ministers viewed the ultimatum through a peculiarly German lens, as a thinly veiled bid to impose Berlin's will on the Turkish Straits and Near East and establish German hegemony in Europe. Serbia, they argued, was a "vital" Russian interest, part of an historical mission to free the Slavs from foreign rule – giving way on Serbia would, moreover, be the third Russian surrender to an Austro-German ultimatum in five years, usher in the complete collapse of Russian prestige in the Balkans, and spark a massive public backlash at home that might imperil the Tsar.[33] As William

---

[30] See Kronenbitter, "Krieg im Frieden," 487–519; Clark, The Sleepwalkers, 423–30, 451–57; Otte, July Crisis, 101–15; Watson, Ring of Steel, 10–13.
[31] Schmidt, Frankreichs Außenpolitik, 65–104. See also Clark, The Sleepwalkers, 433–50, 471–87. Cf. Otte, July Crisis, 133–38, 198–209.
[32] Canis, Der Weg in den Abgrund, 665; Lieven, The End of Tsarist Russia, 318; Jarausch, Enigmatic Chancellor, 161–62; Otte, July Crisis, 207–8; Schmidt, Frankreichs Außenpolitik, 74–80.
[33] Lieven, The End of Tsarist Russia, 320–26, 331; McMeekin, The Russian Origins, 54–68; McMeekin, July 1914, 182–84, 395–97. Cf. L. C. F. Turner, "The Russian Mobilization in 1914," Journal of Contemporary History 3, no. 1 (Jan. 1968): 65–88, here 75–77.

Mulligan has pointed out, this willingness to risk a European war for great power prestige, as the Russians were plainly willing to do, was a dangerous wild card, a deviation from the prevailing norms of great power decision-making in past European crises foreshadowed to some extent in the Balkan wars.[34] That said, the evidence suggests that the Russians were at this point not interested in starting a European war but eager to demonstrate their resolve in the strongest possible terms in the face of what they perceived – not unreasonably – as a hardening Austro-German position in order to prevent an Austro-Serbian war.[35] It has also been suggested that Russian firmness was intended to demonstrate Russian resolution to the Germans in what were sure to be tough upcoming bilateral trade negotiations.[36]

Throughout most of July 1914 the British government and public were distracted by the matter of Irish Home Rule and the real prospect of a civil war in Ulster. As the Serbian crisis deepened and until as late as the beginning of August, British public opinion and most newspapers with the exception of *The Times* opposed any British intervention, as did most members of the British cabinet.[37] Sir Edward Grey and his closest senior colleagues in the Foreign Office, Undersecretary Arthur Nicolson and Eyre Crowe, however, viewed the July Crisis not as a local Balkan problem but almost single-mindedly as one that pitted the Triple Alliance against the Triple Entente, one in which Britain had obligations to France and Russia. The underlying fear animating this position was the awareness that the 1907 Convention with Russia was in deep trouble and that a failure to show support to St. Petersburg would push Russia into the German camp. While Grey was made well aware of France and Russia's belligerent position by Ambassador Buchanan on July 24 and of the real potential of the crisis to escalate into a European war, he stubbornly held illusions about Germany's ability to rein in Austria, even though he knew that on account of Austria-Hungary's sheer weakness and Germany's isolation and growing fear of Russia that was unlikely. And while Grey asked the French and Russian ambassadors to do what they could to defuse this dangerous situation, Nicolson undermined him, telling Paul Cambon that Grey was excessively apprehensive and paying too much heed to Anglo-German relations. At the same time, Grey's duplicity and evasiveness on Anglo-Russian naval talks in June had greatly undermined the credibility of his peaceful

---

[34] Mulligan, *The Origins*, 216–17.
[35] Lieven, *The End of Tsarist Russia*, 326–31; Bobroff, "War Accepted but Unsought," in Levy and Vasquez, *The Outbreak*, 243–44, 246–49.
[36] Hartmut Pogge von Strandmann, "Germany and the Coming of War," in *The Coming of the First World War*, ed. R. J. W. Evans and Hartmut Pogge von Strandmann (Oxford: Clarendon Press; New York: Oxford University Press, 1988), 87–124, here 104.
[37] See Steiner, *Britain and the Origins*, 215–17; Clark, *The Sleepwalkers*, 488–93.

intentions with Bethmann Hollweg and thus also the effectiveness of any British mediation of the sort that had contained Balkan conflicts in 1912-13.[38]

As early as July 24 Grey told members of the cabinet that Serbia would fight, that Russia would then declare war on Austria, and that this would very likely lead Germany and France into a wider conflict, yet the British Foreign Office did nothing to enlist France to moderate the Russian position or restrain Russia for fear of a further breach in relations with St. Petersburg. Worse, on July 26 Arthur Nicolson issued an uninformed blanket denial of a report from the German ambassador on Russian mobilization efforts near the German frontier and refused to hold back Russia in any way.[39] Meanwhile Bethmann Hollweg and Foreign Secretary Jagow were clinging like limpets to their failing localization strategy, even as Serbia agreed to fulfill most of the terms of the ultimatum and as the signs mounted of further Austrian dithering, a hardening of the Russian position, and accelerating secret Russian mobilization against Austria and Germany.[40] Jagow knew in advance that the ultimatum would be unacceptable to Serbia, yet did nothing to soften it or hold Vienna back, and he passed Edward Grey's suggestion for Austria to soften its position to Vienna without comment.[41] As the first telegrams about the response in St. Petersburg, Paris, and London toward the Austrian ultimatum arrived in Berlin, Bethmann Hollweg judged the situation "not unfavorable"; Sazonov had not bound himself and Paris was appalled by London's lack of commitment.[42] When Serbia agreed to most of the terms of the ultimatum on July 25, Bethmann Hollweg did not rescind the blank check, holding to the belief that a demonstration of German and Austrian firmness would assure containment of the conflict. An Austro-Serbian war was now all but certain.[43]

For their part, the Austrians feigned a willingness to negotiate with the Russians but then first threatened and carried out their own general mobilization. They likewise refused to halt their military operations against Serbia in Belgrade or submit to mediation on the grounds that their mobilization against Serbia was already too advanced and that public opinion and the military would never stand for it. They were by that point receiving conflicting advice from the German chief of the General Staff Helmuth von Moltke

---

[38] See Clark, *The Sleepwalkers*, 322-25, 410-11, 421-23, 491, 495, 546; Jarausch, *Enigmatic Chancellor*, 141-43, 151-52, 157; MacMillan, *The War That Ended Peace*, 555; McMeekin, *July 1914*, 182; Otte, *July Crisis*, 95-96, 142-48, 194-95, 257, 263; Otte, "A 'Formidable Factor,'" in Levy and Vasquez, *The Outbreak*, 89-94; Steiner, *Britain and the Origins*, 229-21.
[39] McMeekin, *July 1914*, 214-16; Charmley, *Splendid Isolation*, 390.
[40] Jarausch, *Enigmatic Chancellor*, 161-67; Steiner, *Britain and the Origins*, 222-23.
[41] Otte, *July Crisis*, 269-72, 293-94, 295, 298.
[42] Quoted in Jarausch, *Enigmatic Chancellor*, 165.
[43] Ibid., 166; Otte, *July Crisis*, 302-11; McMeekin, *July 1914*, 223-40; Pogge von Strandmann, ed. *Walther Rathenau*, 225n60.

(1848–1916), who was demanding an immediate Austrian general mobilization concentrated on Russia. Stuck in their vindictive tunnel vision that was fixated on crushing Serbia, the Austrians stubbornly refused that demand too, threatening the very integrity of the Triple Alliance.[44]

Throughout the July Crisis, Grey remained remarkably opaque on the exact nature of Britain's military commitments to France and Russia that ultimately made a continental European war more likely.[45] The Russian ambassador in Paris, Izvolsky, went so far as to blame Britain for allowing the crisis to escalate into a now looming European war: if Grey had been clearer at the start that Britain would side with France and Russia, he told a British diplomat, Germany and Austria-Hungary would have held back. That view was shared by the French ambassador in London, Paul Cambon, who had feared from the outset that Grey would "wobble and hesitate" and then only join in when it was too late.[46] It was as if Grey had in early July more or less resigned himself to the notion that an Austro-Serbian war legitimated a Russian strike against Austria and largely followed that script to the end of the crisis into world war.[47]

To be sure, Grey abhorred war and tried fecklessly to prevent one, but he was up against very reluctant Liberal cabinet members and a Liberal Party with Anti-Russian feelings, and not least, a very ambivalent British public that prevented him taking a clearer stance for the Triple Entente earlier in the crisis when a world war might still have been averted.[48] That gulf was the outcome of the misguided secretiveness of Britain's Entente diplomacy, itself very much a creature of the difficulty the British political establishment had adjusting to the country's relative economic decline and geostrategic overextension, and most importantly, their inability (or unwillingness) to communicate to the British public and Dominions the steep attending limits and costs that imposed.[49] Dreadnoughts and "naval theatre," as discussed in Chapters 7 and 10, maintained the façade of British world power, but that was no substitute

---

[44] See Canis, *Der Weg in den Abgrund*, 667–68; Jarausch, *Enigmatic Chancellor*, 170, 173, 182–83; MacMillan, *The War That Ended Peace*, 570–71, 576; McMeekin, *July 1914*, 288–90; Otte, *July Crisis*, 431–38; Watson, *Ring of Steel*, 47. Cf. Fischer, *War of Illusions*, 495–96; Berghahn, *Germany and the Approach of War*, 207; Mombauer, *Helmuth von Moltke*, 198–216.

[45] See Wilson, *The Policy of the Entente*, 135–47; Steiner, *Britain and the Origins*, 124, 148, 254, 253; Charmley, *Splendid Isolation*, 390–95.

[46] Quoted in MacMillan, *The War That Ended Peace*, 558; that was apparently also a view shared by Raymond Poincaré, MacMillan, 573.

[47] Clark, *The Sleepwalkers*, 495–98, 501, 502. Cf. Otte, *July Crisis*, 144–48, 194–98, 254–72, 294–302, 316–30, 362–69, 385–94, 449–62.

[48] See Clark, *The Sleepwalkers*, 545; Otte, *July Crisis*, 490–95; Steiner, *Britain and the Origins*, 223–25, 230–31, 233–35, 238.

[49] See Wilson, *The Policy of the Entente*, 4–16, esp. 15–16; Steiner, *Britain and the Origins*, 238, 242–47.

for significant public investments in education and training, infrastructure, a conscription army, effective Indian territorial defenses, and real naval supremacy. The Triple Entente bought Britain some time, retaining great power status and the empire (on which it now increasingly hinged) without the immense burdens of those investments. As the historian Keith Wilson has aptly described this situation, "The battalions were not forthcoming. The talltalk remained."[50] But that came with quasi-alliance liabilities to France and Russia without any clear definition and therefore elastic enough to embroil Britain in a cause as dubious as Serbia's in 1914. These liabilities were dealt with by denying they existed, much as Grey had done throughout the July Crisis, but they pulled Britain into the crisis almost inexorably, albeit too late to avert a world war. As Eyre Crowe was to write to his wife on August 2, "The force of circumstances [was] driving the government where they ought to have gone spontaneously."[51] Once again, the British logic of both imperial and European security converged in a policy of siding with France and Russia and opposing Germany and Austria-Hungary.[52]

The defense of Belgian neutrality, which was used by Grey and Asquith to ultimately push their cabinet to agree to intervention and then as the official British basis for its war ultimatum to Germany, offered no immediate legal justification for Britain to enter into hostilities. It was known and accepted by senior British military and civilian leaders that in any war between Germany and France, the German Army would advance through southern Belgium as a strategic necessity, and it was understood that violating the 1839 treaty guaranteeing Belgian neutrality would thus only offer a British *casus belli* if the signatories to the treaty, which included Germany, agreed collectively to uphold that neutrality.[53] That was the position of the majority of the British cabinet on July 29, which had rejected British military intervention in a previous cabinet meeting July 27, and would "decide not to decide" on August 1 and 2. In the end both Asquith and Grey had to also resort to scare tactics and threats to their own cabinet to get a decision for war – they raised the plainly exaggerated specter of "undefended" French coasts and threatened their resignations and a collapse of the Liberal government, fears and threats that greatly weakened the Radical non-interventionist cause.[54]

---

[50] Wilson, *The Policy of the Entente*, 16.     [51] Quoted in Otte, *July 1914*, 485.
[52] See Clark, *The Sleepwalkers*, 545–47; Otte, *July Crisis*, 521; Steiner, *Britain and the Origins*, 243, 246–47, 255.
[53] Strachan, *The First World War*, vol. 1, 97; Clark, *The Sleepwalkers*, 494; Elie Halévy, *The World Crisis of 1914–1918: An Interpretation Being the Rhodes Memorial Lectures Delivered in 1929* (Oxford: Clarendon Press, 1930), 35.
[54] Clark, *The Sleepwalkers*, 539–47; Otte, *July Crisis*, 489–95; Steiner, *Britain and the Origins*, 224–25, 230–31, 232–36.

There were other factors that ultimately pushed Britain into war with Germany in early August that have usually been ignored. In the last week of July 1914, a calamitous financial crisis erupted that very nearly led to the collapse of the world economy. Indeed, this crisis was of such magnitude that it almost prevented Britain from entering the war at all, so grave were the fears in the British cabinet of potential social disorder on the British Isles. On Friday July 31 the London stock exchange had to suspend trading. The resulting credit crunch forced the Bank of England to suspend gold payments and led the government to resort to extraordinary emergency liquidity measures and extend the annual bank holiday on Monday, August 3 to Wednesday.[55] The decision to issue Berlin a war ultimatum on August 4 following the German invasion of Belgium was thus in the end informed by the belief that Britain's strategy of economic warfare formalized in 1912 would so devastate the German economy that it would preclude heavy British human and material sacrifices and soon end the conflict.[56] That was Britain's "war of illusions."

None of this excuses Germany's risky isolation strategy, its cavalier disregard for the status of Belgium, or Bethmann Hollweg's foolish formalism of insisting on declarations of war to France and Russia (as Russian troops were crossing the East Prussian frontier). Even less excusable was the dogmatic rigidity of German two-front war planning and a German military leadership that could not wait for a Russian attack and fight a defensive war in the Vosges, or the blunder of issuing the Belgians an ultimatum on August 2 rather than advancing unannounced, as was expected by Britain and the other powers.[57] The declarations of war on Russia and France made it appear to the world that Germany was the aggressor and gave Romania and Italy grounds for abandoning their defensive treaty obligations to Germany and Austria.[58] The ultimatum to Belgium invited a response, raising the issue of its neutrality and turning its brave defiance of the Germans into an international cause célèbre.[59] It handed the British leadership an argument for war that it would have had to find – and that Asquith, Grey, and Churchill no doubt would have found – in playing up the plainly more dubious arguments about supposedly "undefended" French coasts, the moral commitments to France, and the need to prevent German "hegemony" in Europe. The Germans were in effect gambling on British neutrality – willfully ignoring the warnings of their

---

[55] Lambert, *Planning Armageddon*, 185–94.
[56] Ibid., 195–201, 204–5; Kennedy, *Anglo-German Antagonism*, 425–26; Steiner, *Britain and the Origins*, 237; Offer, *The First World War*, 308–13; Wilson, *The Policy of the Entente*, 142–47.
[57] Mombauer, *Helmuth von Moltke*, 216–26.   [58] Afflerbach, *Der Dreibund*, 834–48.
[59] Clark, *The Sleepwalkers*, 547–51; MacMillan, *The War That Ended Peace*, 585–87; McMeekin, *July 1914*, 340, 350–52, 355–56, 360–62. See also Jarausch, *Enigmatic Chancellor*, 174–77.

ambassador in London since 1912 of its tenuousness – while at the same time undermining its very basis. That was Germany's real "war of illusions." As Konrad Jarausch sagely observed, the German position in the July Crisis and the unfolding world war was "psychologically and propagandistically defensive. But the means that were adopted ... were offensive."[60] As we shall see, it would be an uphill struggle to disabuse the world of that impression from the very outset of this conflict. While conceding that a non-status quo power like Germany had less of a stake in the international law and norms undergirding the existing order, Isabel Hull has argued convincingly that the German leadership's willingness to flout those laws and norms undermined its position in the international court of public opinion, making it much easier to brand Germany "lawless" and "barbarous" and its methods of war "frightful"[61]

Asquith and Grey deployed the German ultimatum to Belgium to sway still skeptical members of their cabinet and sell this war of choice to the British public.[62] The famous speech Edward Grey gave to a packed House of Commons on August 3 – once the cabinet was behind him and the naval reserves and army had been mobilized – did much to persuade still skeptical parliamentarians and the British public of the need to enter the conflict on the side of the Entente. In it Grey went to the extraordinary step of actually reading aloud the letter he had written the French ambassador Paul Cambon on November 22, 1912, disavowing that coordinated Anglo-French fleet redeployments restricted either party or implied "cooperation in war."[63] But as he argued, most of the French fleet was now in the Mediterranean and its Channel and Atlantic coasts were "absolutely undefended" because of "the feeling of confidence and friendship which has existed between the two countries."[64] In short, Britain had no formal but rather a moral obligation to France, just the thing Churchill had feared could draw Britain into a European war.[65]

In a likely allusion to the then ongoing financial crisis, Grey said Britain would suffer "terribly" in the war "whether we are in it or whether we stand aside." This was not a war for the survival of Britain, Grey admitted candidly, but a war to maintain command of the seas in the Channel and to preserve France, a war for "our respect and good name and reputation before the world," and tellingly, to "escape the most serious and grave economic

---

[60] Jarausch, *Enigmatic Chancellor*, 183.
[61] Isabel Hull, *A Scrap of Paper: Breaking and Making International Law during the Great War* (Ithaca and London: Cornell University Press, 2014), 4, 321–22, 324–25.
[62] See Otte, *July Crisis*, 489–99; Steiner, *Britain and the Origins*, 236–37.
[63] "Great Britain and European Powers. Statement by Sir Edward Grey," *Hansard House of Commons Debates,* 5th Series, vol. LXV (Aug. 3, 1914), cols. 1809–28, here col. 1813.
[64] Ibid., cols. 1815–16. See also Wilson, *The Policy of the Entente*, 144.
[65] Wilson, *The Policy of the Entente*, 143.

consequences."[66] Lurking behind these last words but understood by many in the overflowing chamber that afternoon was the dry rot of Britain's growing industrial obsolescence, its administrative and managerial shortcomings, its entrepreneurial failings, and the loss of overseas markets that had accelerated its relative economic decline vis-à-vis Germany since the late Victorian era. The realization that Britain's status as a great power – because of its tiny army and wholly exposed overseas empire – was now dependent upon France and Russia was plainly also on many minds.[67] Little wonder, then, that doubts arose almost immediately about the government's formal justification for war.[68] The misjudged German assault on the fortress of Liège that commenced Tuesday morning, August 4, simplified things by creating Belgian facts on the ground needed for a British ultimatum to Germany delivered later that afternoon.

From here on out Belgian neutrality and real and imagined German atrocities in Belgium became objects of a shrill – albeit very effective – British propaganda campaign.[69] The Germans gave them plenty of material to work with. Inexperienced but under immense pressure to advance to keep to the Schlieffen Plan's timetables, primed by their commanders to see *franc-tireurs* everywhere, and shocked by the unexpectedly stiff resistance put up by the Belgian military and militia, German troops entering Belgium were prone to overreaction and panic, resulting in large-scale reprisal shootings of civilians and arson, capped by the notorious burning of the city of Louvain.[70] Still, the spontaneity with which the British public embraced an image of German villainy reveals how it had been prepared psychologically for conflict with Germany by decades of invasion stories, navy scares, and anti-German journalism.[71] It is as if the role cast for Germany in Eyre Crowe's 1907 memorandum had been reified.

Helfferich, Rathgen, Schumacher, Sering, and many other German economists, bankers, and businessmen knowledgeable about *Weltwirtschaft* believed

---

[66] "Great Britain and European Powers," cols. 1823, 1825. Cf. Kennedy, *Anglo-German Antagonism*, 428–29.

[67] See Strachan, *The First World War*, vol. 1, 94–95.

[68] Adam Hochschild, *To End All Wars: A Story of Loyalty and Rebellion 1914–1918* (Boston and New York: Houghton Mifflin Harcourt, 2011), 86–87, 90–91, 93–97, 106–8, 111–13, 128–29, 139–40, 187–88, 296–97; Hochschild, *King Leopold's Ghost*, 287–91; Clark, *The Sleepwalkers*, 543; Otte, *July Crisis*, 494; Fritz Stern, *Einstein's German World* (Princeton and Oxford: Princeton University Press, 1999), 202, 204, 209–11.

[69] Lambert, *Planning Armageddon*, 199–210; McMeekin, *July 1914*, 373–75, 379–80; Otte, *July Crisis*, 500–5. On British propaganda, Hochschild, *To End All Wars*, 147–50; Gary S. Messinger, *British Propaganda and the State in the First World War* (Manchester and New York: Manchester University Press), 33–39.

[70] John Horne and Alan Kramer, *German Atrocities, 1914: A History of Denial* (New Haven: Yale University Press, 2001); Hull, *Absolute Destruction*, 208–15; Hull, *Scrap of Paper*, 51–60, 95–140; Larry Zuckerman, *The Rape of Belgium: The Untold Story of World War I* (New York: New York University Press, 2004).

[71] See Steiner, *Britain and the Origins*, 241, 253.

that it was, as Helfferich put it, the "millions of small frictions" accumulated in economic competition worldwide, the eclipse of Britain's *"wirtschaftliche Weltstellung"* (world economic position), and the belief that Germany could be defeated by naval blockade without serious risks to Britain and with confidence in ultimate victory that really drove Whitehall's decision for world war.[72] In 1912 Walther Rathenau had predicted that Britain's "technical-industrial eclipse," fear of continental hegemony, and threat to its colonial empire by the possible loss of naval supremacy might tempt it into a preventive war.[73] That was not that far off. As the only European great power not facing a direct threat to its territorial integrity, it can hardly be denied that such a preventive logic informed by these anxieties drove the British decision for war. Almost prophetically, Rathenau predicted that the longer-term consequence of that war would not be peace but more war until Europe would be eclipsed by the United States.[74] Five years later in July 1917 he made a further prediction in a conversation with General Erich Ludendorff (1865–1937):

> After the war the legend cannot be sustained that Germany was insidiously attacked by four powers. Everyone will see that Austria's ultimatum to Serbia was in fact excessively harsh, that it was an unbelievable stroke of luck that 90 percent of this ultimatum was accepted, undeservedly so, and they will see through the even more incredible deception that this acceptance was followed by the Austrian declaration of war.[75]

## The End of *Weltwirtschaft*

As Britain went to war it quickly became apparent that the dreadnought deterrence strategy had made a hash of British naval wartime operational planning and strategy. The heavy investment in dreadnought battleships for political purposes meant that the Royal Navy did not have enough destroyers to enforce a close blockade of the German coast. The danger of coastal batteries, submarines, mines, and torpedoes as well as the fact that the Royal Navy lacked the North Sea colliers needed to keep the destroyers on regular patrol for such a legal (i.e., enforceable) blockade, ultimately ruled it out.[76]

Patrol submarines had been developed as an alternative means of enforcing a close blockade, but the investment in dreadnoughts meant that these, too, were not available in sufficient numbers at the start of the war. An

---

[72] Helfferich, *Der Weltkrieg*, vol. 1, 44–48.
[73] Walther Rathenau, "England und Wir: Eine Philippika" [1912], in *Gesammelte Schriften*, vol, 1 (Berlin: S. Fischer, 1918), 209–19, here 212.
[74] Ibid., 212–13.
[75] Diary entry July 10, 1917, in *Walther Rathenau*, ed. Pogge von Strandmann, 223.
[76] Strachan, *The First World War*, vol. 1, 393–94.

observational blockade running 300 miles from eastern England to southern Norway deploying cruisers and destroyers was similarly impractical because of insufficient numbers of these vessels, while dreadnoughts could not be used because Britain lacked deepwater shore facilities for such large craft on the English eastern coast and those harbors were vulnerable to submarines. That left an illegal distant blockade of all shipping going in and out of the North Sea as the default strategy, which involved closing off the North Sea between Scotland and western Norway by the British Grand Fleet based in the Orkneys and the English Channel by the Channel Fleet. From the British perspective a distant blockade was all for the better, as visibility in the North Sea was often poor restricting the firing range of the Grand Fleet's dreadnoughts and making them more vulnerable to torpedoes. The investment in dreadnoughts also meant that the Royal Navy lacked minesweepers and escort vessels that would have been necessary for naval operations in the Baltic.[77]

The distant blockade was unambiguously illegal because it was both indiscriminate and legally-technically ineffective: it targeted both neutral and belligerent shipping, was not enforceable on the Baltic coast (violating the 1856 Declaration of Paris), and it expanded the contraband list to foodstuffs (violating the 1909 Declaration of London). As was discussed previously, parallel to the possibility of distant blockade, the Committee of Imperial Defense had developed and ratified with cabinet approval plans for economic warfare in 1912 that aimed at interdicting all trade, communications, and lines of credit to strangle the German economy. While the British Admiralty had supported the 1909 Declaration of London, which had prohibited blockades of neutral ports and given contraband goods a narrow definition, declaring food as conditional contraband (that is, as a good that could only be declared contraband if it was intended for soldiers and would have required a close blockade to implement), Admiralty pressure had led the House of Lords to veto its ratification in 1909.

The dreadnought deterrence strategy had left German naval wartime operational planning and strategy in even greater disarray. The British Grand Fleet did not seek a decisive battle near the Heligoland Bight as German naval planners assumed they would at the outbreak of war. Worse, no viable plans existed for breaking either a close or distant blockade, even though as was discussed in Chapter 7, critics of Tirpitz's "Risk Fleet" in the German navy such as Karl Galster knew that Britain would likely resort to a distant blockade in war. The High Seas Fleet's dreadnoughts were too small in number and under-gunned to challenge the Grand Fleet directly and too valuable to risk in such a gamble. The priority given battleships also meant that Germany had no adequate cruiser fleet to protect shipping or harass and seize enemy ships on

---

[77] Ibid., 388–90, 395–402.

the open seas, even as the spectacularly successful exploits of the German cruiser *Emden* in the Indian Ocean early in the conflict confirmed the effectiveness of such craft. The only available offensive weapon that could be used to break such a blockade and counter economic warfare was the submarine, but Tirpitz's fixation on dreadnought ratios and the political aims of the fleet, as well as his dogged opposition to submarines meant that German submarine construction lagged far behind Britain – only twenty-eight U-boats were available in 1914, whereas Britain had fifty-five.[78] How submarines could be used as a blockade-breaking weapon operating independently of flotilla forces was at the time not yet understood, much less that they could be used as a tool of economic warfare in their own right by sinking merchant ships.

The distant blockade of the North Sea passages and economic warfare were radical weapons, ones that as they were deployed aimed at starving civilians and destroying whole economies in a terrifying new chapter of war that eliminated the distinction between combatants and non-combatants. Thus even if only unintentionally, the failed dreadnought deterrence strategy worked indirectly to escalate the war from the very outset into total war. Indeed, on entering the war on August 4th, the British Admiralty imposed a complete ban on the export of foodstuffs and forage, and within a week the entire German merchant marine had been driven from all waters but the Baltic Sea. All ships carrying foodstuffs, British or neutral, were also prevented from eastbound journeys, even to neutral ports like Rotterdam in clear violation of international law.[79] For their part, the Germans engaged in their own violations of international law by mining parts of the North Sea, which in a curious circularity, was used by Edward Grey to justify non-adherence to the Declaration of London when queried about it by US diplomats – naval mines were actually not covered by the declaration[80]

Worried about the damage to their own economy and their relations with neutrals such as the United States, on August 14, 1914, the British cabinet allowed trade with neutrals to resume and loosened the contraband rules, but a subsequent cabinet subcommittee meeting and an Order in Council of August 20 (and subsequent regulations) affirmed the treatment of foodstuffs headed to Dutch ports as "conditional contraband" subject to Royal Navy seizure in accordance with an interpretation of the "continuous voyage" doctrine that also violated the Declaration of London. Likewise, Britain proceeded to establish a blockade line at the English Channel and outlet of the North Sea between Shetland and Norway that cut off neutral ports.[81] While it

---

[78] See ibid., 405–13, 418; Gary E. Weir, "Tirplitz, Technology and Building U-Boots, 1897–1916," *The International History Review* 6, no. 2 (May 1984): 174–90.
[79] Lambert, *Planning Armageddon*, 211–14, 220–23.
[80] Ibid., 215; Hull, *Scrap of Paper*, 154.
[81] Lambert, *Planning Armageddon*, 225–30, 254–78; Hull, *Scrap of Paper*, 157–61.

would take several months for the Admiralty to work out the details of its distant blockade, Britain went to war with Germany's economy in early August 1914 much as had been planned since 1908 and well before there was any consensus in the cabinet on where a British expeditionary force would be sent.[82]

With nearly all lines of communication severed or severely disrupted, it was not until well into the autumn of 1914 that Henry Farnam managed to regain contact with Germany. Still not having heard anything by November, he wrote Gustav Schmoller another long letter reporting on his misadventure. He wrote that since July he had not heard anything or received any news and hoped that they were faring well. When they had arrived in England in early August, it was impossible to send any letters or telegrams to Germany and to discover if he was even still expected in Berlin. Travel was practically impossible and in any case uncertain. He had cabled President Butler of Columbia, and he had given the advice to return to the United States but to notify officials in Berlin first. Since all other forms of communication were impossible, he had asked the American ambassador to dispatch his letter to Berlin via diplomatic courier but discovered weeks later after his return home that the letter had gone via Washington, and he still did not know if it and several other letters had arrived. The same was true, he wrote, of the letters he had written to Karl Rathgen. But he would not give up trying to make contact with his "old friends" and hoped that he would succeed in getting through.[83]

Farnam reported that as soon as the prospect of a winter in Berlin had disappeared they had decided to return home at the earliest opportunity. In the meantime they had traveled in England, but had been lucky enough, he wrote, to get good cabins on the *Lusitania* on the 12th of September and were back in New York on the 18th. They were all fine, and the lack of their winter things as well as his books and manuscripts was a minor detail against this "*Welttragödie*" (world tragedy).

Everyone was discussing the war, Farnam wrote, and it weighed heavily on the mood of the country. Even those without friends among the belligerents had been made to suffer. Many shops were stocking up because key raw materials like dyestuffs could not be imported anymore, while others could no longer export their goods. The South suffered because it could no longer sell its cotton, Farnam wrote. Many were rendered unemployed and depended on charity, and the schools and charities were having a hard time getting the resources to help them. Still, everywhere there were collections for the Red Cross for the suffering people of Europe. Many women who had not knitted in years, he reported, were knitting for the wounded and giving their output to

---

[82] Lambert, *Planning Armageddon*, 204.
[83] GStA PK, VI. HA Nl. Schmoller, Nr. 206b, fols. 31–32, Henry Farnam to Gustav Schmoller, Yale, New Haven, Nov. 8, 1914.

charitable societies. Even though they received reports about the war from various countries such as Germany, Russia, France, and England, it was hard to get a real impression of what was actually happening, Farnam observed, and even less a sense of the impact of the war on daily life and economic conditions in Europe. "May it all end soon with a lasting peace," he wrote.[84]

On November 30, 1914, Farnam received official word from Nicholas Butler at Columbia that, on receiving news from the Prussian Ministry of Culture earlier that month, the professorial exchanges with the University of Berlin "would be suspended during the present year, or during the war should it unfortunately last longer."[85] By that point American elite opinion had shifted against Germany on account of the German invasion of Belgium, the mistreatment of Belgian civilians, and the looting and arson of Louvain by German troops in August 1914 that resulted in the destruction by fire of the university library.[86] There had been an attempt in the autumn to send a German legal expert to Columbia, Theodor Niemeyer (1857–1939), in order to better present the German legal position in an increasingly heated "war of words" over interpretations of international law with regard to the status of Belgium and German culpability for the outbreak of the war.[87] As Columbia University also had a professorial exchange with France, the French government had in the meantime already put forward its own legal expert in their own exchange for 1914–15, Albert de Geouffre de Lapradelle (1871–1955). With potentially too many legal experts on hand (and undoubtedly much pressure from faculty, students, and trustees), President Butler was put in the awkward position of proposing that the Germans send Niemeyer to Columbia the following academic year. By November the German government had decided that, given the climate of opinion in the United States, it would be hopeless and decided to suspend the Kaiser Wilhelm-Roosevelt professorships altogether.[88]

Similar reasons were given for suspending the exchange with Harvard. There the German American (and, incidentally, Jewish) psychologist Hugo Münsterberg tried to forcefully defend the German position but was derided to such an extent that he felt unable to attend faculty meetings. Later he was pressured to resign by Harvard alumni, denounced as a "Prussianized renegade Jew" by an influential member of Harvard's Board of Overseers, and

---

[84] Ibid.
[85] YUL MA, Farnam Family Papers, Group 203, Series II, Box 229, Folder 3113, Nicholas Murray Butler to Henry Farnam, New York, Nov. 30, 1914.
[86] See Luebke, *Bonds of Loyalty*, 83–86; Michael S. Neiberg, *The Path to War: How the First World War Created Modern America* (New York: Oxford University Press, 2016), 31–32.
[87] Tomás Irish, *The University at War, 1914–25: Britain, France, and the United States* (Basingstoke, Hamps. and New York: Palgrave Macmillan, 2015), 86.
[88] Ibid.

received numerous death threats forcing him to take a one year leave of absence in October 1914. John Burgess, an emeritus professor at Columbia, had also tried to defend the German cause, with much the same result.[89] German cultural capital in the United States – always less than what was imagined in Germany because of shifts in American attitudes toward Germany in the era of *Weltpolitik* – was prone to rapid depreciation in war given how it was waged, and what was left was frittered away by a remarkably inept German Foreign Office and misguided German propaganda efforts.

It was left to Germany's highly capable but overwhelmed ambassador to the United States, Johann Heinrich von Bernstorff (1862–1939), to try to control the damage and make Germany's case to the American public. He was assisted in this thankless task by the ever sharp and energetic Bernhard Dernburg, who on Max Warburg's suggestion to the German Interior Office and under the guise of serving as a representative of the German Red Cross, was charged with raising loans in the United States and the procurement of war-related supplies, accompanying Bernstorff when he returned to New York via a Dutch steamer in August 1914. On their arrival in New York, Bernstorff and Dernburg established a German press office in Manhattan, the German Information Service, which despite the handicap of being cut off from all transatlantic cables to Germany and the frequent obtuse missteps of the Wihlemstrasse on account of its ignorance of the United States, managed to organize an effective propaganda campaign headed and funded by Dernburg in New York.[90]

Dernburg's first propaganda foray included a very sympathetic full-page interview published on page four of the *The New York Times* on September 6, 1914.[91] In it Dernburg expressed puzzlement with the fierce anti-German attitudes he encountered in the United States, deflecting the anger over Belgium by emphasizing the defensive nature of Germany's struggle, his deep ties to the United States, and the debt to the United States owed Germany's colonial endeavors by the example of railroad construction through the wilderness of the West and the flourishing settlements that created. He also

---

[89] Ibid., 69; Margaret Münsterberg, *Hugo Münsterberg: His Life and Work* (New York and London: D. Appleton & Co., 1922), 263–64; Phyllis Keller, *States of Belonging: German-American Intellectuals and the First World War* (Cambridge, MA and London: Harvard University Press, 1979), 7–118, esp. 72–79. See also Bernhard vom Brocke, "'Wissenschaft und Militarismus': Der Aufruf der 93 'an die Kulturwelt!' und der Zusammenbruch der internationalen Gelehrtenrepublik im Ersten Weltkrieg," in *Wilamowitz nach 50 Jahren*, ed. William M. Calder, III, Hellmut Flashar, and Theodor Lindken (Darmstadt: Wissenschaftliche Buschgesellschaft, 1985), 649–716, here 678–79.

[90] See Chad R. Fulwider, *German Propaganda and U.S. Neutrality in World War I* (Columbia: University of Missouri Press, 2016), 55–62; Max Warburg, *Aus meinen Aufzeichnungen*, 35.

[91] "Germany Prepares for Unparalleled Suffering," *The New York Times*, Sept. 6, 1914.

highlighted the wartime *Burgfrieden* (civil truce) announced by the Kaiser between parties and religious creeds on August 4, 1914.[92]

Dernburg cleverly played on the vanities and fears of his American readers by arguing that America's most eminent physicians and surgeons were trained in Germany while the Entente was drawing on the assistance of uncivilized troops from India, the "yellow Japanese," Senegalese, and "Cossack hoards" in its war on Germany. While denouncing Germans as "barbarians" the Entente fought side by side with Russia, whose appalling treatment of the Jews and "revengeful Siberian political convict system has been the scandal of the world for generations." Though Germany had a large and powerful army, for forty-three years Germany had "taken no inch of ground save through peaceful arrangement." The Germans did not covet any territory when it was forced into this war. Asked again about Belgium, Dernburg deflected once again by noting that Germany's treatment of "weaker peoples" had been kindly and helpful, drawing on the example of the German colonies. The investments there had moved them "along that road of racial and social progress." Germany had made major scientific advances against sleeping sickness and venereal disease and spent more than one million dollars per year on medical services in her colonies. Meanwhile, Leopold of Belgium was subjecting the Congo to "wanton cruelty – for personal profit" and "operations which became the scandal of the world." Germany, by contrast, had in its own colonies "made war upon white planters whom we found to have been practically enslaving the blacks." Germany also made major investments in improved farm tools and cultivation, distributed hundreds of tons of cotton seed, established model farms, passed stringent laws protecting natives in land sales to whites, and had built 3,200 miles of railways in Germany's African colonies.[93]

Dernburg argued that it was rich indeed that those countries leveling charges of "inhumanity" against Germany had, unlike Germany, acquired their colonial territory by bayonet and bullet, Britain shelling Alexandria, invading Persia, subjugating the Boers; the French slaughtering the natives of Madagascar and "violently subjugating" Tunis, Morocco, and Indochina; and the Russians invading Turkestan. Germany and the United States were bound together by their common "advanced scientific interests" and an "interlocking higher education system," by the vast German immigration that produced so many great "American patriots of great achievement." The United States, Dernburg argued, was in one sense "the largest German colony in existence" with 3 million Germans and Americans of German descent. He closed his interview with a paean to the great work that the women of

---

[92] Ibid., cols. 1–2.  [93] Ibid., cols. 2–6.

the German Red Cross were doing and appealed to the generosity of the American public to aid this noble humanitarian effort.[94]

Dernburg's work in New York, which extended into the late spring of 1915, included weekly articles that appeared in various other newspapers and magazines, including the *New York Sun*, the *Independent*, and the *North American Review* and was recognized apprehensively by the British for its effectiveness.[95] He was assisted in this work by among others the German American poet and journalist George Sylvester Viereck (1884–1962), editor of the unabashedly pro-German weekly *The Fatherland* founded in August 1914, which managed to gain a circulation of 100,000 by October 1914 with the generous assistance of Dernburg's office.[96] The money for these and other propaganda efforts was deposited by the German government with the Warburg Bank in Hamburg and was then extended to Dernburg by the eminent New York bank house Kuhn, Loeb & Co., headed by the fiercely Germanophile Jacob Schiff, second on Wall Street only to J. P. Morgan.[97] As may be recalled from Chapter 7, before the war the Warburg Bank had sold Kuhn, Loeb & Co.'s American railway securities and Japanese government bonds on the German capital market.[98] As Dernburg and Bernstorff were unable to sell the German treasury bonds that they had brought with them to finance the operations of the embassy and German Information Service, the $ 400,000 extended by Kuhn, Loeb & Co. to Dernburg was essential to these propaganda operations.[99] While selling German treasury bonds on Wall Street was out of the question due to J. P. Morgan's strong Anglophilia and US government bans in September 1914 on lending to belligerents, Schiff personally subscribed to a German war loan via the Warburg Bank. When Woodrow Wilson overturned the ban on American lending in the summer of 1915, Kuhn, Loeb & Co. refused to participate in J. P. Morgan's $ 500 million Anglo-French loan on Schiff's insistence, such was his commitment to Germany.[100]

The contrast between Dernburg's work in New York and perhaps the most prominent early German effort to counter the charges of "barbarism" to influence world opinion – and one in which Schmoller participated directly – could not be more stark. This was the appeal "To the Civilized World!" (*An die Kulturwelt!*), also known as the "Manifesto of Ninety-Three," which Schmoller

---

[94] Ibid., cols. 6–7.   [95] Fulwider, *German Propaganda*, 61–62.
[96] Ibid. 62. On Viereck, see Keller, *States of Belonging*, 121–88, esp. 141–46. See also Luebke, *Bonds of Loyalty*, 91–92, 127–28; Katja Wüstenbecker, *Deutsch-Amerikaner im Ersten Weltkrieg: US-Politik und nationale Identitäten im Mittleren Westen* (Stuttgart: Franz Steiner, 2007), 64–85.
[97] Fulwider, *German Propaganda*, 64.
[98] Chernow, *The Warburgs*, 46–52; Warburg, *Aus meinen Aufzeichnungen*, 19–22; Miller, "Japan's Other Victory," in Steinberg, *Russo-Japanese War*, vol. 1, 471–78.
[99] Fulwider, *German Propaganda*, 63–64.
[100] Chernow, *The Warburgs*, 165–68; see also Neiberg, *The Path to War*, 63–64, 195–99.

himself signed and a copy of which was forwarded to Henry Farnam by Schmoller in the autumn of 1914.[101] In it ninety-three of the most prominent German scientists, scholars, artists, and writers – many of the same men who had been mobilized in the 1906–7 elections – protested the alleged lies being spread about Germany's conduct of the war. They denied that Germany began the war yet justified the violation of Belgian neutrality, denied the mistreatment of Belgian civilians yet justified the reprisal actions in Louvain, denying in turn the violations of international law by German troops. "Militarism" was not the antithesis of German culture, they argued, but rather the guarantor of its survival.[102] Not surprisingly, it immediately elicited a very negative response in the United States as a misuse of academic authority to justify injustice.[103] As Bernhard vom Brocke has argued, "no other manifesto issued during the First World War did more to discredit German scholarship abroad ... than this one."[104] While this faux pas was recognized immediately by enlightened observers in Germany such as the Marburg University professor of law Walther Schücking (1875–1935), the damage was done and affected a massive and sudden shrinkage of Germany's intellectual *Weltstellung*.[105]

The shrinkage of Germany's physical *Weltstellung* was almost as swift. Immediately after the British declaration of war, all of Germany's transatlantic submarine cables were cut by the Royal Navy. On August 12 two companies of the British Gold Coast Regiment seized German Togo's capital Lome, putting Germany's most important overseas wireless station at Kamina out of commission and thus cutting off the rest of the African colonies from Germany.[106] War with Britain's ally Japan followed on August 23, 1914, resulting in the capture of Kiaochow on November 7, 1914, along with its naval base and

---

[101] GStA PK, VI. HA Nl. Schmoller, Nr. 206b, fols. 31–32, Henry Farnam to Gustav Schmoller, Nov. 8, 1914. Here Farnam thanked Schmoller for sending the appeal "To the Civilized World!" On this manifesto, see Schwabe, *Wissenschaft und Kriegsmoral*, 22–23.

[102] vom Brocke, "Wissenschaft und Militarisumus," in Calder, Flashar, and Lindken, *Wilamowitz*, 718; Stern, *Einstein's German World*, 63; Amos Elon, *The Pity of It All: A History of the Jews in Germany, 1743–1933* (New York: Metropolitan Books/Henry Holt, 2002), 325–27.

[103] See GStA PK, VI. HA, Nl. Schmoller, Nr. 92, fols. 29–46, Btr. Kulturbund deutscher Gelehrter und Künstler 1914–1916, open letter of S.H. Church of the Carnegie Institute to Deutsche Vertreter der Wissenschaft und Kunst, Pittsburgh, Nov. 10, 1914, with a copy of a longer letter by Church to Dr. Fritz Schaper, Pittsburgh, Nov. 9, 1914. See also vom Brocke, "Wissenschaft und Militarismus," in Calder, Flashar, and Lindken, *Wilamowitz*, 676–81; Stern, *Einstein's German World*, 210.

[104] vom Brocke, "Wissenschaft und Militarismus," in Calder, Flashar, and Lindken, *Wilamowitz*, 665.

[105] Walther Schücking, "Die deutschen Professoren und der Weltkrieg," *Flugschriften des Bundes "Neues Vaterland,"* no. 5 (1915).

[106] Strachan, *The First World War*, vol. 1, 505–9.

important wireless and undersea cable connections. Kiaochow's German soldiers, sailors, and administrators were transported and interned in Tokushima on Kyushu in Japan for the duration of the war.[107] In the Pacific, a force of New Zealanders had taken German Samoa without a fight in August, and in early September Australian forces took New Guinea and the Bismarck Archipelago, which were surrendered along with the Solomon Islands on September 15. In late September and early October the Japanese seized the Marshall, Mariana, Palau, and Caroline Islands along with the critically important undersea cable and wireless station on Yap.[108] Cameroon, Southwest Africa, and German East Africa held out longer but were almost completely cut off from the outside world and ultimately surrendered to French, South African, and British troops, respectively, between 1915 and 1917.[109]

As for the German surface navy, in early December 1914 the East Asian Cruiser Squadron – by that point cut off from all wireless stations – was completely annihilated after a chase and fierce engagement with the Royal Navy near the Falkland Islands, one that would ultimately prove the most decisive naval battle of the war.[110] This came on the heels of a disastrous skirmish with British battlecruisers around Heligoland in late August 1914. After the sinking of the armored cruiser *Blücher* and the High Seas Fleet's only narrow escape from a trap set by the Royal Navy on the Dogger Bank in January 1915, the Kaiser, the Chief of the High Seas Fleet Ernst Friedrich von Ingenohl (1857–1933), and his successor in February 1915 Hugo von Pohl (1855–1916) realized the grave risks that attended offensive "decisive battle" for which the High Seas Fleet had been built and became reluctant to deploy it. In any case, Bethmann Hollweg and the Kaiser preferred to keep it as a deterrent to British attacks on the German coast and in reserve for eventual peace negotiations.[111]

Despite postwar dissembling over the matter, even Tirpitz acknowledged the suicidal risk involved in launching battleship offensives under these conditions. While it is true that the High Seas Fleet prevented a close blockade, deterred an invasion of the German coast, assured Swedish iron ore imports through a blockade-free Baltic, and made the supply of Russia by its allies more difficult, these benefits were meager given the enormous material, political, and diplomatic costs exacted by the construction of Germany's battleship navy, a weapon that was now relegated to rusting in harbor. With his "risk theory" repudiated and offensive use of the surface navy stifled,

---

[107] Ibid., 455–64; Hayashi Keisuke, *Daiku no sato doitsumura: Bantō horyo shuyōjo* (Itano, Tokushima: Inoue Shōbō, Heisei 5 [1993]), 8–17.
[108] Strachan, *The First World War*, vol. 1, 464–65.   [109] Ibid., 509–643.
[110] Ibid., 466–78.
[111] See ibid., 414–40; Michael Epkenhans, *Tirpitz: Architect of the German High Seas Fleet* (Washington, DC: Potomac Books, 2008), 58–59. Herwig, *"Luxury" Fleet*, 149–58.

Tirpitz would later turn to the submarine, a weapon he had consistently resisted, downplayed, and starved of funds before the war. [112]

## The U-Boat Professors

As the entire German colonial empire was being mopped up or isolated, Germany, too, was increasingly shut off from imports and contact to the rest of the world. As discussed, Britain had been pressured by the United States into rescinding its Order in Council capturing all food on allied or neutral vessels suspected of going to neutral ports or Germany, but in early October 1914 following the entry of German submarines into the English Channel, it was illegally mined by the British between Ostend and Calais up to the mouth of the Thames. In early November the British Admiralty declared the North Sea a "military area" in which they would lay secret minefields. They also banned all foreign fishing vessels from British waters (feared as disguised German minelayers) and moved navigation buoys in these notoriously treacherous waters, measures that were intended to force all ships to rely on British pilots and call at British ports in the Downs and Kirkwall before continuing on their voyage into the North Sea so they could be easily searched for "contraband."[113]

Meanwhile Hermann Schumacher had been summoned in the first weeks of the war by the Prussian Minister of Trade Reinhold von Sydow to attend a meeting of various Prussian and Reich ministry officials in Berlin on the economic aspects of the conflict focused on preventing war profiteering by price controls. To Schumacher's chagrin, the meeting did not have in its remit the more urgent general question of wartime food provisions to which these questions were tied inseparably, nor was there much appreciation of the fact that any price controls needed to consider specific prices as part of a price system. He did, however, gain permission to research the matter and publicize his findings in lectures and articles, which gained the attention of a wider circle of officials.[114] The mayor of Cologne Max Wallraff (1859–1941) subsequently invited Schumacher to inspect the city's war preparations in warehouses only to discover, to his shock, that what had been assembled was only intended for the military – in a state of siege it was expected that the city's civilian

---

[112] Epkenhans, *Tirpitz*, 59–63; Herwig, *"Luxury" Fleet*, 158–61; Jarausch, *Enigmatic Chancellor*, 265; Scheck, *Alfred Tirpitz*, 23–26; Bernd Stegemann, *Die Deutsche Marinepolitik 1916–1918* (Berlin: Duncker & Humblot, 1970), 17–22; Weir, "Tirpitz, Technology," 178–84.

[113] Lambert, *Planning Armageddon*, 297–99. Cf. Alfred von Tirpitz, *Politische Dokumente*, Vol. 2: *Deutsche Ohnmachtspolitik im Weltkriege* (Hamburg and Berlin: Hanseatische Verlagsanstalt, 1926), 281–85.

[114] GNN HA, Nl. Hermann Schumacher, I, B-6u, fols. 641–43.

population would simply flee! Together with the impressions he had gathered in Berlin, this reinforced his view that no thought had been given to the question of feeding the civilian population in wartime by the German leadership.[115] Many other cities in the Rhine-Ruhr recognized the precariousness of the German food supply in the earliest weeks of the war. Already in September, Alfred Hugenberg of Krupp and the coal magnate Hugo Stinnes along with a number of mayors of Ruhr cities pressed the interior secretary Clemens Delbrück (1856-1921) for assistance in founding a corporation two buy up some 2 million tons of wheat to raise prices and thus induce reduced consumption to assure sufficient grain stocks to last until the summer of 1915.[116] At around this time Schumacher was called to advise the Oberpräsident of the Rhine Province Georg von Rheinbaben (1855-1921) about price controls and was able to persuade him that his province could not proceed on its own and needed to coordinate with Westphalia to the north and to subordinate the question of war profits and ad hoc price controls to the more fundamental food question.[117]

In Berlin Sering had been involved in discussions over similar questions within the first week of the war. On August 11 and 13 meetings were organized by Sering, Schmoller, and other economists at the University of Berlin held in the Prussian Ministry of Agriculture to discuss the impact of the war and blockade on Germany's economy. The meeting brought together leading figures from the world of banking and industry as well as senior officials in the Prussian Ministry of Agriculture and Imperial Statistical Office, including Karl Helfferich, Walther Rathenau, the machinery industrialist Ernst von Borsig (1869-1933), and the cotton industrialist Henry James Simon (1851-1932).[118] The meeting made it clear that Germany would soon see serious shortages in fodder grain and oil cake as well as Chile saltpeter and guano phosphates due to the blockade. It recommended inducing an expansion of coke production, as the by-product could be used in the production of synthetic nitrates (the recently-discovered Haber-Bosch process) to cover the shortfalls of imported saltpeter.[119] The biggest shortages would, however, be in imported animal fodder. Massive economies were recommended to reduce waste in the use of potatoes and fodder roots to make up these shortfalls. The

---

[115] Ibid., fols. 643-44.
[116] Gerald D. Feldman, *Army, Industry and Labor in Germany, 1914-1918* (Princeton: Princeton University Press, 1966), 100.
[117] GNN HA, Nl. Hermann Schumacher, I, B-6u, fols. 644-45.
[118] HHStA, Abt. 1088 Teilnachlass Gustav Schmoller, Nr. 14, Max Sering to Gustav Schmoller, Berlin, Aug. 17, 1914 with attached draft confidential summary of deliberations entitled "Die Deutsche Volkswirtschaft Während des Krieges."
[119] Ibid. 1-4.

**Figure 11.2** Max Sering in 1910.

sharing of patents in the mechanical drying of potatoes was recommended in order to induce industry to improve the necessary machinery. Regardless, the conference concluded that the shortage of animal fodder would lead to a serious shortage of milk, meat, and animal fats in the coming winter, shortages that could not be entirely offset by imports from neutral countries such as Denmark, which were themselves also reliant on fodder imports.[120]

The remainder of the discussion was devoted to industry, which was being hit even harder than agriculture by the blockade, especially due to the interruptions of key raw materials like cotton, copper, tin, and rubber. Were the war to last six months, the discussion concluded, many millions of workers in the textile and metallurgical industries would be unemployed.[121] Coinciding with these deliberations, on August 13 Walther Rathenau, encouraged by one of his senior engineers in AEG's metals division, Wichard von Moellendorff (1881–1937), persuaded the Prussian Ministry of War to establish the Kriegsrohstoffabteilung (War Raw Materials Department) to procure, stockpile, and distribute such critically important raw materials. This was done by regulating the right of disposal to firms involved in war-related production

---

[120] Ibid., 4–5.    [121] Ibid., 6–9.

via a system of joint-stock war raw materials corporations supervised by the government and a system of negotiated price ceilings.[122] Many other scientists, businessmen, and bankers – and, notably among them, many prominent German Jews – were involved in official and semi-official capacities in organizing and managing procurement via war corporations/agencies, such as Fritz Haber (1868–1934) in the chemical section of the Prussian Ministry of War, Albert Ballin and Max Warburg in the Zentrale-Einkaufsgesellschaft (Central Procurement Corporation, primarily focused on the purchase of food and animal fodder abroad), and Max Warburg in the Kriegsernährungs- und Übergangswirtschaftsamt (War Nutrition und Transition Economy Agency).[123]

Over the autumn of 1914 Max Sering began to study Germany's grain reserves more closely and grew increasingly concerned, especially as the war bogged down into a stalemate after the Battle of the Marne. His worry was not so much for the immediate term but for the next year, as Germany imported much of its fodder grain such as rye from abroad and reductions in the rye harvest were certain for the year 1915 on account of shortages of nitrates and draft animals shifted for use in the war effort. Assisted by his colleague, the Latvian statistician Karl Ballod (1864–1931) who had participated in the war economy conference in mid-August, Sering compiled a set of statistics on grain stocks and consumption and a memorandum summarizing these observations in the late autumn and winter of 1914–15.[124] The findings were drawn in part from an official survey commissioned by the Reich government from a team of experts (the Eltzbacher Commission) on how war food shortages might be addressed (which had included Ballod) and was then published in December 1914.[125] By that point the Ruhr industrialists and mayors had found a receptive ear for the proposal to establish a War Wheat Corporation in Undersecretary Georg Michaelis of the Prussian Ministry of Finance – who, as will be recalled from Chapter 2, had taught in Japan in the 1880s with Rathgen.

---

[122] Walther Rathenau, "Deutschlands Rohstoffversorgung: Vortrag, gehalten in der 'Deutschen Gesellschaft 1914' am 20. Dezember 1915," in *Gesammelte Schriften*, vol. 5, 25–58; Pogge von Strandmann, ed., *Walther Rathenau*, 186–90; Feldman, *Army, Industry and Labor*, 45–64.

[123] Ferguson, *Paper and Iron*, 99–121; Hans Jaeger, *Unternehmer in der deutschen Politik (1890–1918)* (Bonn: Ludwig Röhrscheid, 1967), 214–19; Margit Szöllösi-Janze, *Fritz Haber 1868–1934: Eine Biographie* (Munich: C. H. Beck, 1998), 256–314; Stern, *Einstein's German World*, 59–196; Warburg, *Aus meinen Aufzeichnungen*, 36–38.

[124] BArch M, N 253 Nl. Tirpitz, Nr. 101, Max Sering and Karl Ballod, Memorandum on the provisioning of Germany with foodstuffs [Jan. 1915], fols. 107–14, here fol. 108.

[125] Paul Eltzbacher, ed., *Die deutsche Volksernährung und der englische Aushungerungsplan* (Braunschweig: F. Vierweg & Sohn, 1914).

This was created on November 17 but was not able to purchase the target volume of wheat and required additional government assistance.[126]

In addition to the expected shortfalls in the grain harvest, Sering observed, the intensity of the war effort on both the home and war front was increasing grain consumption even while the herd of such livestock as pigs remained large. It was thus essential to begin to stock grain for the next year and to prevent the use of bread grains as animal fodder. In line with the findings of the Eltzbacher Commission, he recommended seizure of all bread grain stocks not needed for human consumption and strong restrictions on grain consumption, prohibition of grain exports (even to Austria), and stretching the existing stock of bread grains by combining potato meal and sugar.[127] He also recommended the slaughter of three-quarters of Germany's pig livestock before reaching their slaughter weight and raising prices on edible potatoes by as much as 50 percent to discourage their use as fodder. The situation was even more dire for oats, whose stocks would last four months at the most. Massive rationalization was thus also needed of livestock fed oats, barley, and skim milk as well as a dramatic reduction of human meat consumption from current levels to 80 percent of peacetime consumption starting February 1915, reduced to 48 percent after June 1915.[128] Shortfalls of protein could be compensated with skim milk, whose consumption could be encouraged by reducing railway transport costs. Likewise he recommend reducing beef consumption to 50 percent of peacetime consumption by the summer of 1915.[129]

There was no doubt that lean times were ahead, a diet loaded with carbohydrates and much less protein and fat. These findings and recommendations were later formalized into a printed memorandum submitted to the government in March 1915 signed not only by Sering and Ballod but also by five other of the most prominent contributors to the Eltzbacher Commission report, the professors of physiology Max Rubner (1854–1932) and Nathan Zuntz (1847–1920), and the professors of land economy Otto Lemmermann (1869–1953), Curt Lehmann (1849–1921), and Kurt von Rümker (1859–1940).[130]

Meanwhile, over the first few months of the war the few deployable German submarines had begun to show their potential as independent offensive weapons. The spectacular success of the submarine U-9 in sinking three British armored cruisers in September 1914 with the loss of nearly 1,500 men was a

---

[126] Feldman, *Army, Industry and Labor*, 101; Michaelis, *Für Volk und Staat*, 269–73. See also Gerald D. Feldman, *Hugo Stinnes: Biographie eines Industriellen 1870–1924*, trans. Karl Heinz Siber (Munich: C. H. Beck, 1998), 383.
[127] BArch M, N 253 Nl. Tirpitz, Nr. 101, Max Sering and Karl Ballod, Memorandum on the provisioning of Germany with foodstuffs [Jan. 1915], fols. 108–9.
[128] Ibid., fols. 109–12.   [129] Ibid., fol. 113 r v.
[130] BArch M, N 253 Nl. Tirpitz, Nr. 262, Max Sering et al., "Btr. Die Versorgung der deutschen Bevölkerung mit Nahrungsmitteln," Berlin, March 13, 1915, fols. 92–95.

major blow to the reputation of the Royal Navy and seemed to offer a way to retaliate for Britain's blockade.[131] Just days after the British announcement of its blockade in early November 1914, the chief of the Admiralty Staff Hugo von Pohl sent Bethmann Hollweg a proposal for a submarine blockade, which proposed declaring the waters surrounding the British Isles and Ireland a war zone in which all enemy and neutral ships ran the risk of being torpedoed without warning as a countermeasure to the British North Sea blockade.[132] This was, however, rejected by Bethmann Hollweg because of the very limited number of submarines and thus doubts about the effectiveness of such a blockade as well as the possible negative repercussions on neutrals such as the United States. There was also the problem of international law, as such a blockade involved the suspension of prize rules that obliged submarines to surface, search a ship, and allow crews of merchant ships to escape to lifeboats before seizing or sinking them.[133] The British were less squeamish about such legal rules at sea, commissioning the first of the Royal Navy's Q-ships later that month, merchant ships with hidden deck guns designed to lure German submarines into surfacing so they could be destroyed.[134]

There the matter rested until an interview Alfred Tirpitz had given to an American journalist in late November appeared in German newspapers on December 21. In that interview Tirpitz let loose with blustering comments about Germany's potential ability to impose a submarine blockade to counter the British. After the setback of the Battle of the Marne, the impact of the interview on the German public was electric, as it suggested – quite wrongly – that Germany possessed a sufficiently large U-boat fleet to impose a blockade on Britain, a wonder weapon that could retaliate and force the British to end their blockade and perhaps even secure victory.[135] Oddly, Tirpitz had opposed the November proposal for a submarine blockade on similar grounds as Bethmann Hollweg and continued to advocate a much more limited form of submarine warfare until as late as January 25.[136] Given Tirpitz's known hesitancy on the use of the submarine, these interview comments have been interpreted as a way to test American reaction to the potential unfettered use of the submarine, to distract from the recent naval disasters and inactivity of the German fleet, and to arouse public support for more aggressive forms

[131] See Arno Spindler, *Der Handelskrieg mit U-Booten: Der Krieg zur See 1914–1918*, 5 vols. (Berlin: Mittler & Sohn, 1932–66), vol. 1, 1–10; Kelly, *Tirpitz*, 393; Lambert, *Planning Armageddon*, 283–303; Stegemann, *Marinepolitik*, 22–26.
[132] Spindler, *Der Handelskrieg*, vol. 1, 27; Anlage 1, 196–97.   [133] Ibid., 42–57.
[134] Lawrence Sondhaus, *German Submarine Warfare in World War I: The Onset of Total War at Sea* (Lanham, MD: Rowman & Littlefield, 2017), 74–75.
[135] Spindler, *Der Handelskrieg*, vol. 1, 35–36, 70; Anlage 23, 243–50; also in Tirpitz, *Politische Dokumente*, vol. 2, 623–27.
[136] Herwig, "Luxury" Fleet, 161–62; Kelly, *Tirpitz*, 394–95; Ritter, *Staatskunst*, vol. 3, 146; Spindler, *Der Handelskrieg*, vol. 1, 37–38.

of naval warfare as part of Tirpitz's gambit to become chancellor.[137] In any case, the U-boat genie was now out of the bottle.

As that was unfolding the industrialists, agrarians, and mayors behind the War Wheat Corporation were assisted by Sering in pressing their matter with General von Moltke, which resulted in an appeal directly to Bethmann Hollweg on January 10 for serious government measures to address the growing food shortages.[138] By that point Sering had circulated his findings about dwindling food and fodder grain supplies and his proposals to rationalize food stocks to his colleagues at the University of Berlin, including Gustav Schmoller. Earlier in January both Schmoller and Sering had received an alarming letter and memoranda from William Merton (1848–1916), head of the Frankfurt-based Metallgesellschaft specializing in mining and trading non-ferrous metals, about the acute shortages of phosphates critically important to agriculture and non-ferrous metals similarly critical to munitions production. Merton sought Schmoller's and Sering's help to induce better coordination between government ministries, the army, navy, and war corporations in managing strategic stockpiles of these metals and recommended abandoning proposals for price controls on superphosphate (monocalcium phosphate) to draw in imports from neutrals.[139]

Pressed by the army, interior secretary, and chancellor, in late January and early February the Federal Council approved measures that brought all wheat production under government control, forcing farmers to formally declare their wheat stocks and prohibiting the use of wheat or rye as animal fodder. The War Wheat Corporation was ordered to purchase grain, price ceilings were imposed and an Imperial Allocation Office was created to distribute wheat. Bread rationing was introduced in Berlin in January 1915 and then throughout the Reich in June. As proposed in Sering and Ballod's memoranda and by the Eltzbacher Commission, this resulted in a massive slaughter of pigs in early 1915.[140]

In mid-January news arrived that Karl Helfferich's would be appointed secretary of the Imperial Treasury. When Sering got word of Helfferich's appointment he was much relieved and wrote him an effusive letter of congratulations. It made him "happy and hopeful" to know that a man of his intelligence and ability was taking over this challenging office under such

---

[137] Scheck, *Alfred Tirpitz*, 26; Herwig, *"Luxury" Fleet*, 163; Sondhaus, *German Submarine Warfare*, 23–29.
[138] Feldman, *Army, Industry and Labor*, 101.
[139] GStA PK, VI. HA Nl. Schmoller, Nr. 19, fols. 77–82, Wilhelm Merton to Gustav Schmoller, Jan. 6, 1915, marked *"streng vertraulich!"* with enclosures of memoranda and carbon copies of letters from Merton to Max Sering, Jan. 6, 1914 (fols. 83–84) and Oberregierungspräsident Spahn, Nov. 28, 1914 (fols. 88–91).
[140] Feldman, *Army, Industry and Labor*, 101–2.

Figure 11.3   Karl Helfferich in 1915.

difficult circumstances.[141] As Helfferich had been a vigorous supporter of financial reform in 1912, Sering's hopes and those of many others were clearly pinned on the belief that under the extraordinary circumstances of war the long-needed major reform of Reich finances would finally be ushered in under his auspices. The tax increases of 1912 had failed to stem the flow of red ink – the Reich had a burden of debt exceeding five billion marks on its books when the war started.[142] Max Warburg, who had long warned of this liability in the ability to prosecute war, thought Herfferich's appointment would be "to the greatest blessing of our dear fatherland."[143] Schumacher, too, was very relieved by his appointment, offering his services to Helfferich.[144] As it would turn out

---

[141] BArch K, N 1123 Nl. Helfferich, Bd. 13, Max Sering to Karl Helfferich, Berlin-Grunewald, Jan. 18, 1915.
[142] Williamson, *Karl Helfferich*, 122–23.
[143] BArch K, N 1123 Nl. Helfferich, Bd. 13, Max Warburg to Karl Helfferich, Berlin, Jan. 16, 1915.
[144] BArch K, N 1123 Nl. Helfferich, Bd. 13, Hermann Schumacher to Karl Helfferich, Bonn, Jan. 18, 1915.

and will be discussed later, both as state secretary of the Treasury Office and then as interior secretary in 1916–17, Helfferich would play an important role in Germany's fateful decision to use the new submarine weapon in surprise torpedo attacks against merchant ships. Helfferich at first fully embraced unrestricted submarine warfare only to abandon that standpoint once the risk of war with the United States grew in the late summer of 1915.

As Sering and Ballod's work on dwindling grain stocks was making the rounds, Sering drafted a new memorandum together with his colleague Heinrich Treipel (1868–1946), a noted jurist specializing in international law, justifying a combined retaliatory submarine and airship campaign against Britain's shipping and dock warehouses to break the blockade. This memo was then circulated among his colleagues and sent to Bethmann Hollweg and Admiral Pohl on January 26 with a cover letter signed by Sering, Treipel, and six other illustrious professors of the university that included the classical philologist Ulrich von Wilamowitz- Möllendorff (1848–1931, organizer of the notorious appeal "To the Civilized World!"), the legal scholars Wilhelm Kahl (1849–1932) and Otto von Gierke (1841–1921), the historian Theodor Schiemann, the theologian Adolf von Harnack, and Gustav Schmoller.[145] The cover letter made light of the fact that they, like much of the German public, felt that it was "an economic and military necessity that all available means be applied to annihilate the illegal plan to starve the German people by way of retaliation."[146]

Under separate cover and accompanied by a longer cover letter, that same day Sering sent copies of this memorandum to the chief of the High Seas Fleet Ernst von Ingenohl and RMA secretary Alfred Tirpitz, with the latter also receiving a copy of the memo by Ballod and Sering on the growing food shortages in Germany.[147] In the letter to Tirpitz, Sering wrote that he agreed with Tirpitz's motto "that Germany must not just 'hold out' [*durchhalten*] but move 'forward' [*vorwärts*]," and that the statistics on food stocks had convinced him that "it was high time that we seek to break the blockade by way of retaliation [*Vergeltung*] and to use the same means that it has used violating international law in imposing the blockade to ruthlessly force down England."[148] He noted that in one of the accompanying memoranda he had come to the conclusion – based on reliable British surveys – "that the destruction of supplies in the currently overfilled harbors through airship attacks and the

---

[145] Spindler, *Der Handelskrieg*, vol. 1, Anlage 24, 234–35.   [146] Ibid., Anlage 24, 235.

[147] Ibid., Anlage 24, 234; BArch M, N 253 Nl. Tirpitz, Nr. 101, fols., 104–5, Max Sering to Alfred Tirpitz, Grunewald-Berlin. Jan. 26, 1915. See also Offer, *The First World War*, 354–55.

[148] BArch M, N 253 Nl. Tirpitz, Nr. 101, Max Sering to Alfred Tirpitz, Berlin-Grunewald, Jan. 26, 1915, fol. 105.

throttling of supplies through submarine blockade would force England to yield within a few weeks."[149]

In the accompanying memo on breaking the British blockade, Sering and Treipel then laid out their rationale.[150] First they made light of the fact that a 1905 British blue book indicated that England's own wheat harvest could cover only 22 percent of its wheat consumption and that its imported stocks held in dock warehouses were only sufficient to last three to four weeks or less, being resupplied constantly from overseas. The same source indicated that no less than 45 percent of domestically consumed meat was imported and their frozen stocks in London and Liverpool would last less than one month. Supplies of iron ore and wool would be depleted even more quickly.[151] It quoted the blue book in concluding that if the Royal Navy were to fail to prevent an organized attack on Britain's trade at a time of the year when the stock of wheat and other cereals was low, it would lead to massive price increases and sow such great panic that the country would not be able to continue to prosecute the war.[152] The time was now, Sering and Treipel urged, to begin the submarine blockade and airship campaign to destroy food and raw material stocks in the great harbors, especially London, as the supply of the most important foodstuffs were usually exhausted in January.[153] Import statistics confirmed that supplies of food and fodder grains in warehouses were currently low, that London's harbor was crammed with ships, and that urgent measures were then underway to expand warehouses for wartime stocking: "An air attack on the warehouses, ships, and barges would annihilate monstrous values [of] goods [*ungeheuere Werte vernichten*]. One is even reckoning on that. The last Zeppelin attack on Yarmouth increased insurance rates for goods in London docks against air attacks by 10%."[154] As North American grain shipments would be ending soon, those from the modest Argentinian harvest would be completed in February and March, and those from India would not be arriving until May, interrupting the South American shipments would affect a rapid price rise, as the demise of German merchant shipping

---

[149] Ibid.
[150] BArch M, N 253 Nl. Tirpitz, Nr. 101, Max Sering and Heinrich Treipel, "Denkschrift über die Durchbrechung der Handelssperre gegen Deutschland," n.d. [Jan. 1915], fols. 114–25; duplicated in BArch M, RM 5 Admiralstab der Marine, Max Sering and Heinrich Treipel, "Denkschrift über die Durchbrechung der Handelssperre gegen Deutschland," n.d. [Jan. 1915], fols. 219–23r.
[151] BArch M, N 253 Nl. Tirpitz, Nr. 101, Max Sering and Heinrich Treipel, "Denkschrift über die Durchbrechung der Handelssperre gegen Deutschland," n.d. [Jan. 1915], fols. 115–16.
[152] Ibid., fols. 116–17. This passage was marked by hand for emphasis.
[153] Ibid., fol. 117. These passages were marked by hand for emphasis. [154] Ibid., fol. 120.

and the use of merchant ships for troop transports had raised freight rates by 300–400 percent.[155]

Regarding the blockade, Sering and Treipel argued that there was no doubt that the British embargo of food and fodder violated international law. He noted that during the Russo-Japanese War, Britain and the United States lodged a vehement protest against Russian measures to list rice and other food grains as absolute contraband, forcing the Russians to relent. And while in the current conflict food and fodder had not been declared absolute contraband, they had been treated as such in practice by the Entente powers by applying the theory of continuous voyage and controlling the trade of neutrals, effectively stopping all grain shipments to Germany from across the Atlantic. Thus if the British were to lodge protest to German retaliation against militarily undefended harbors by Zeppelins, they would have no basis to do so.[156] A submarine blockade, by contrast, would be legally unobjectionable. Since the Declaration of London was not ratified by Britain, the only recognized legal criterion for a blockade was its effectiveness. As the Americans were not signatories to the Paris Declaration of 1856 and their official statements indicated that for a blockade to be effective it was sufficient for a squadron of ships to make entry in and out of ports "hazardous," no objections could be expected from the United States. A German submarine blockade, Sering and Treipel wrote, was no more harsh a method than the British mining of the North Sea and their warnings to that effect to neutrals, which was equivalent to an illegal fictive blockade and hindrance to shipping on the open seas.[157] They closed with a chilling passage that enabled sliding down the slippery slope into unrestricted submarine warfare:

> Humanitarian considerations due to the possibly unavoidable harshness involved in destroying blockade breakers must retreat to the thought of the severity and cruelty of victims that England is willing to inflict upon our own people [*Volksgenossen*]. We should not fail to remind the public that six German merchant steamers disappeared without a trace and in all likelihood became victims of English submarines that managed to slip into the Baltic Sea.[158]

If Tirpitz was still skeptical about a submarine blockade, the letter and memoranda from Sering seemed to eliminate any remaining qualms he might have had. On January 27 he had a meeting with Bethmann Hollweg and now expressed complete confidence in a submarine blockade, thinking the danger of antagonizing the United States was slim. And while the chancellor remained worried about precisely that, he was clearly being worn down by public pressure and the exhortations from Sering and the other U-boat professors

---

[155] Ibid., fols. 120–21.   [156] Ibid., fols. 122–23.   [157] Ibid., fol. 124.
[158] Ibid., fol. 125.

that the time to act was now. And indeed, over the next four days he, too, would change his mind. The surface navy's debacle at the Dogger Bank January 24 with the loss of the *Blücher* would be important in bringing around the Kaiser, who thereupon dismissed Ingenohl and appointed Admiral Pohl as his successor, someone who had long been an advocate of submarine warfare.[159]

Pohl, meanwhile, had earlier armed himself with his own expert opinion about the need to begin the submarine blockade forthwith, which he had solicited from an economist at the University of Heidelberg, Hermann Levy (1881–1949), and the director of the Disconto-Gesellschaft, Franz Urbig (1864–1944), among others, though these were rather superficial compared with the memos by Sering, Ballod, and Treipel.[160] In any case, at a meeting in the chancellor's office on February 1 attended by Undersecretary of the Foreign Office Arthur Zimmermann, Chief of the General Staff Erich von Falkenhayn (1861–1922), Secretary of State for the Interior Clemens Delbrück, and Admiral Pohl, Bethmann Hollweg approved a submarine blockade and the declaration of a "war zone" in the waters around Great Britain and Ireland.[161] The decision for what would become unrestricted submarine warfare had been made, one of the weightiest decisions of the war. It was a further escalation into total war erasing the distinction between civilians and combatants. From the beginning it was to prove risky, not least since the British Admiralty ordered the abuse neutral flags to protect British merchant vessels on January 31, 1914, that is, before the German announcement of unrestricted submarine warfare.[162]

On February 4 a public announcement by the Chief of the German Admiralty declared the waters around Great Britain and Ireland including the English Channel a "war zone." As of February 18 every enemy merchant ship found within that zone would be destroyed without warning, and the crews and passengers of targeted vessels could not count on rescue. The announcement stated further that neutral ships, too, ran risk of destruction on the grounds that the British had abused neutral flags. Only the waters north of the Shetland Islands, the eastern North Sea, and a 30 kilometer strip along the Dutch coast were safe.[163] In a subsequent diplomatic note issued February 11 after much protest from neutrals, the Foreign Office justified its actions

---

[159] Spindler, *Der Handelskrieg*, vol. 1, 71, 78–79; Anlage 25, 243–50; Epkenhans, *Tirpitz*, 64–65; Kelly, *Tirpitz*, 395; Sondhaus, *German Submarine Warfare*, 29–30.
[160] Spindler, *Der Handelskrieg*, vol. 1, 69; 225–33, Anlage 19, 20, 21, and 22.
[161] Ibid., 78–84; Jarausch, *Enigmatic Chancellor*, 271–74, 499n14; Röhl, *Into the Abyss*, 1150–51; Watson, *Ring of Steel*, 235–40.
[162] Hull, *Scrap of Paper*, 246; Epkenhans, *Tirpitz*, 64.
[163] Spindler, *Der Handelskrieg*, vol. 1, 87.

against merchant ships on account of the British practice of arming merchant vessels, resisting search, and ramming submarines. It declared further that the German "war zone" would be mined.[164] This was akin to the British announcement that the North Sea was mined, and like that British announcement, clearly intended to scare off neutral vessels from entering British waters.

In Britain the German "war zone" declaration was immediately greeted as an opportunity to tighten the blockade even more. On March 11 the British government responded with a new Order in Council that introduced an unrestricted blockade, stopping all German exports (and thus effectively all German trade) aboard neutral ships and eliminating the distinctions between "conditional" and "absolute" contraband. To prevent re-export to Germany from neutral powers, they also imposed strict import quotas on neutrals calculated to meet the minimum domestic needs of those countries. In December 1915 this was followed up with the Trading with the Enemy Act that "blacklisted" any friendly or neutral firm found trading with Germany or its allies.[165]

The impact of these new British measures was felt by Henry Farnam almost immediately. In January 1915 he had requested that the eight boxes of winter clothing, books, and manuscripts sent to Berlin in advance of his family's arrival be returned to him in New Haven. The boxes were sent to Bremen and then packed aboard the SS *Ogeechee* of the Gans Steamship Company, but on its voyage from Bremen to New York in early April 1915 this neutral American steamer was captured by the Royal Navy and taken to Sharpness, England, where its cargo was confiscated.[166] Interestingly, in January 1915 Farnam was beginning to waver in his sympathies for the German cause, which over the following months would harden into outright aversion. This was fed by the fervent nationalism and arrogant confidence in swift victory conveyed in letters from Gustav Schmoller, as well as the justifications given for violating Belgian neutrality, the apparent German indifference toward the maltreatment of Belgian civilians, the evidence of Germany's role in precipitating the war, and German diplomatic intriguing to pull the United States into the war on the side of the Central Powers. As irksome was the attempt to dismiss the

---

[164] Ibid., 103–4. See also Hull, *Scrap of Paper*, 242–52.
[165] Holger Herwig, *The First World War: Germany and Austria-Hungary, 1914–1918* (London and New York: Arnold, 1997), 287; Watson, *Ring of Steel*, 232; Hull, *Scrap of Paper*, 170–94. In greater detail, Lambert, *Planning Armageddon*, 369–496.
[166] YUL MA, Farnam Family Papers, Group 203, Series II, Box 229, Folder 3113, Sworn Affidavit by Henry W. Farnam before Thomas Hooker, Jr., Notary Public, New Haven, May 3, 1915; *The New York Times Index*, vol. III, no. 2 (April–May–June 1915), 100; William Bayard Hale, *American Rights & British Pretensions on the Seas: The Facts and Documents, Official and Other, Bearing on the Present Attitude of Great Britain toward the Commerce of the United States* (New York: Robert M. McBride & Co, 1915), 172.

negative press about Germany in the United States as "lies."[167] In a very candid letter to his old friend Karl Rathgen in late January 1915, Farnam acknowledged the "wonderful spirit of patriotism" that the Germans had shown and their systematic management of military operations. On the causes of the war, however, many people in the United States were less clear, yet there was wide agreement about certain aspects of the war:

> Indeed the possibility of a conflict between Germany and England had been in the minds of many people, and if one reads what the Germans themselves have been saying with regard to the subject, it seems difficult to accept the theory that the war was forced upon Germany by the jealousy of the English. If the English did want war, they were incredibly stupid in not making better preparations for it.
> 
> It seems to many here as if they had also been decidedly liberal in their treatment of German commerce. In spite of the talk of individuals, the English markets have been open without even a tariff wall to German products, and thousands of German business men have had, and improved, the opportunity to make money in the British Isles and in the British colonies. While almost everyone realizes that some irritation on the part of Germany has naturally been occasioned by the diplomatic setbacks in connection with Africa, this does not justify in their minds the intense hatred of England which has taken possession of the Germans. Nor do most people in this country share the view which I have seen expressed by Germans that the mere existence of the English naval power was a threat to Germany. Other nations, like Norway, have been able to develop a very large commerce in proportion to their own resources, on seas policed by the British navy. This navy has not been used for one hundred years for the purpose of coercing other European nations, and many people feel that it is no menace excepting to a power which sets out to break it down. . . .
> 
> The feature of the war which people find most difficult to justify is the invasion of Belgium. I think that most people here think that the reason originally given by the chancellor that necessity knows no law is the best reason thus far advanced. But we consider that to be a very dangerous doctrine, not only internationally but socially . . . It is an unfortunate fact that many of the explanations sent out by German scholars have distinctly injured the German cause in this country. The claim, e.g., that treaties have been changed or broken by other nations, and that therefore Germany was justified in disregarding the treaty guaranteeing Belgian neutrality, seems to many here to miss the point. Even if there had been no treaty, many people here think that Germany would still have been a

---

[167] YUL MA, Farnam Family Papers, Group 203, Series II, Box 182, Folder 1837; YUL MA, Farnam Family Papers, Group 203, Series II, Box 187, Folder 1883, Henry Farnam to Gustav Schmoller, Sept. 16, 1915 (carbon copy).

trespasser by carrying the war into a country with which she had no quarrel.

A thing which has aroused real resentment among many people here is the apparent effort of German officials to get us into difficulties, both by embroiling us with Japan, and by agitating for the formation of a strong pro-German party in our midst, which would inevitably lead to internal dissentions. This hardly seems honorable or fair. Those of us who know Germany as it used to be, and are fond of its literature, its traditions, and its people, are hoping that the expressions which have produced so painful an impression on the friends of Germany here, are due to the inevitable excitement produced by the war, and that when peace is restored the old Germany will re-assert itself.

I have written you as an old friend with a frankness of which I believe you will appreciate the kindly spirit. I treasure my German memories and my German friends, and it gives me great pain to realize that the actions of the German government and even many utterances of German scholars have deeply offended the moral sense of their friends here. I fear that it will take many years to overcome the feeling of distrust which has been aroused among such people in this country. But I am optimistic enough to look forward to a better time, and in the meantime I hope that the feeling of warm personal regard which I, together with many others, cherish toward our German friends, may be the means of bringing about the resumption of cordial international efforts for social betterment.[168]

Thus the propaganda campaign – the war of words – was won by the Entente within elite and even Germanophile American opinion even before the very ship on which Farnam and his family had returned to the United States in 1914 – the *Lusitania* – was sunk. This swift transformation of American elite opinion in the autumn of 1914 and early 1915 suggests that American perceptions of Germany did not change overnight with the invasion of Belgium or the burning of Louvain but had undergone a gradual but significant shift since the 1880s, later accelerated by the tensions generated between the two countries by trade frictions, American overseas imperialism, and German *Weltpolitik*. Globalization and intensified contact had not only drawn the two nations closer but had also pulled them apart. Very interestingly, the personal ties of friendship maintained since the 1870s were an important conduit for these changed perceptions in Farnam and many other Americans of his class and milieu, but so were the professorial exchanges themselves.[169] Familiarity could and did breed contempt and reinforce one's own national

---

[168] YUL MA, Farnam Family Papers, Group 203, Series II, Box 182, Folder 1838, Henry Farnam to Karl Rathgen, Jan. 27, 1915 (carbon copy).
[169] Nagler, "From Culture to *Kultur*," 146; Fiebig-von Hase, "Die politische Funktionalisierung der Kultur," 47.

identity. That is a conclusion that Hermann Schumacher also came to reflecting on the significance of his early years living overseas.[170]

Despite the enormous public expectations and the inflated image of the submarine generated by wartime propaganda, the 1915 submarine campaign proved to be ineffective.[171] At the start of the war only twenty-seven U-boats were available, of which about a third were diesel models viable for long-distance operations along the British coast. The neglect of German prewar submarine development meant that ramping up wartime production of such vessels would prove very challenging and costly.[172] In the end U-boats failed to induce rapid food price rises or panics in Britain. For example, of over 5,000 merchant ships entering or leaving British harbors in March 1915, only 21 were lost to U-boats. And the 748,000 tons of shipping ultimately lost to this weapon between February and September 1915 was more than made up by 1.3 million tons of new construction in the British Isles and throughout the rest of the empire.[173]

One of the ships lost to U-boats that year was of course the *Lusitania*, whose sinking by a U-20 torpedo May 7, 1915, with the loss of nearly 1,200 lives (128 of them American) caused an international uproar and sharp diplomatic exchanges between the United States and Germany that risked American entry into the conflict.[174] Dernburg tried to defend this German action against an indignant American public. In a speech given at the Hollenden Hotel in Cleveland on May 8, 1915, just one day after the tragedy, Dernburg argued – accurately – that the *Lusitania* was an auxiliary cruiser of the Royal Navy and was carrying tons of metal and munition contraband. While he regretted the loss of life, he blamed the British for not warning American passengers that whey were being used "as a cloak for England's war shipments," that is, as human shields.[175] Needless to say, such honest if very blunt talk was not helpful when American papers were describing the sinking as "premeditated murder" and "savagery carried to its ultimate perfection." Ambassador Bernstorff, who happened to be visiting New York at the time, was besieged

---

[170] GNN HA, Nl. Schumacher, I, B-6x, fol. 723.
[171] See esp. Willi Jasper, *Lusitania: The Cultural History of a Catastrophe*, trans. Stewart Spencer (New Haven: Yale University Press, 2015), 26–50, 92–119.
[172] Herwig, *The First World War*, 287; Herwig, "*Luxury*" *Fleet*, 163–64; Weir, "Tirpitz, Technology," 186–87. Stegemann counts twenty-eight submarines in August 1914, Stegemann, *Marinepolitik*, 26.
[173] Herwig, "*Luxury*" *Fleet*, 165; Ritter, *Staatskunst*, vol. 3, 159; Sondhaus, *German Submarine Warfare*, 50.
[174] Spindler, *Der Handelskrieg*, vol. 2, 86–103, 158–94, 268–87. See also Hull, *Scrap of Paper*, 259–65; Jasper, *Lusitania*, 125–35; Ritter, *Staatskunst*, vol. 3, 159–60; Sondhaus, *German Submarine Warfare*, 41–46.
[175] "Sinking Justified, Says Dr. Dernburg," *The New York Times*, May 9, 1915, 4, col. 1. See also Fulwider, *German Propaganda*, 65–66.

by a mob of angry New Yorkers and reporters and effectively held hostage in his hotel room.[176] Fearing Dernburg might be deported because of the extent of the anti-German backlash, Bernstorff advised him to return to Germany, which he did in mid-June.[177]

By the time of Dernburg's departure, there was growing public suspicion of subversive German activity in the United States. In December 1914 Undersecretary Arthur Zimmermann had foolishly warned the American ambassador that there were 500,000 German reservists resident in the United States prepared to raise arms against the United States were it ever to come to war between the two countries. While a vastly inflated number deployed in diplomatic bluster, this inept threat alarmed the ambassador sufficiently that it was reported to the US secretary of state, raising suspicion about the loyalty of German Americans.[178] By the summer of 1915 American intelligence had uncovered information about a wide range of German subversive activity organized or coordinated by personnel formally attached to the German embassy but receiving their instructions from the German Supreme Army Command (OHL), namely the military attaché Franz von Papen (1879–1969), naval attaché Karl Boy-Ed (1872–1930), trade attaché Heinrich Albert (1874–1960), and the German Army General Staff agent Franz von Rintelen (1878–1949). The headquarters for these activities was the War Intelligence Bureau in New York organized by von Papen and the New York German Consul General's office. They hatched plans to destroy the Welland Canal and railway bridges, tunnels, and war-related factories in Canada by explosives, including one successful attack on a Canadian uniform factory. They successfully planted bombs aboard outgoing Entente munitions transports manufactured by a German chemist in Hoboken, New Jersey. They also organized wildcat strikes of dockworkers, pressed German and Austrian-American workers to abandon their employment in American war-related industries, and disrupted American munitions production by putting in large orders for heavy presses, forging equipment, and explosives through a German shell company, the Bridgeport Projectile Company.[179]

By the end of July 1915 the US government had detailed information about this subversive activity from the arrest of German agents and suspicious persons, as well as documents recovered by the US Secret Service from Heinrich Albert about the extent of German efforts to prevent American weapons and munitions exports to the Entente and the elaborate and

---

[176] Jasper, *Lusitania*, 93–94.
[177] Fulwider, *German Propaganda*, 66; Wüstenbecker, *Deutsch-Amerikaner*, 92.
[178] Jörg Nagler, *Nationale Minoritäten im Krieg: "Feindliche Ausländer" und die amerikanische Heimatfront während des Ersten Weltkriegs* (Hamburg: Hamburger Edition, 2000), 110–11.
[179] Fulwider, *German Propaganda*, 120–33; Nagler, *Nationale Minoritäten*, 113–20.

well-financed work of agents of the German government to influence American public opinion through publications such as *The Fatherland*. Some of the Albert documents were leaked to the press by the Wilson administration and appeared in a series of articles that began to be published by the *New York World* in mid-July 1915. All of this dramatically increased suspicion that German Americans were a fifth column and that it was only a matter of time before targets within the United States would be attacked.[180] Along with outrage over the sinking of the *Lusitania*, these fears and suspicions catalyzed an existing strain of paranoid and violent American nativism that would ultimately explode into the open with dire consequences for the German American community after the US entry into the war in April 1917.

In their diplomatic feud with the Americans in 1915, the German leadership argued that it was forced to resort to its submarine warfare by Britain's illegal blockade and its arming of merchant vessels. A July 23 American diplomatic note then effectively threatened to break off relations if Germany did not condemn the actions of the U-boat crew, assume liability for the damages, and return to cruiser prize rules in submarine warfare. If Germany did those things, it offered to work with the Germans to rescind the most objectionable part of the British blockade. While the German government refused to accept liability for the disaster or repudiate unrestricted submarine warfare, it did promise to safeguard US ships and passengers and later gave instructions to submarines to spare ocean liners and to follow prize rules with non-American ships to allow passengers to scape to safety. Within the German public, however, the sinking of the *Lusitania* was celebrated, and there was enormous public pressure to neither assume responsibility nor restrict submarines so long as the British blockade remained in effect. Even liberal newspapers like the *Berliner Tageblatt* demanded a refusal of apology, arguing that responsibility for the loss of American lives rested solely with the US government.[181] Twenty leading German legal scholars even defended Heinrich Treipel's interpretation of the legality of unrestricted submarine warfare in the pages of the *Zeitschrift für Völkerrecht* (Journal of International Law).[182]

With the risk of the United States entering the war, Helfferich had in the meantime come to change his mind about the "submarine blockade," which he had fully supported earlier in the spring.[183] One important reason was cotton, something he had been studying since his time in the Colonial Section of the Foreign Office and the importance of which he had gained an even greater appreciation of through his various dealings as a banker in Ottoman Turkey

---

[180] Nagler, *Nationale Minoritäten*, 121–25; Neiberg, *The Path to War*, 77–84; Wüstenbecker, *Deutsch-Amerikaner*, 93.
[181] Hull, *Scrap of Paper*, 260–61; Ritter, *Staatskunst*, vol. 3, 160–63, 172–78.
[182] Schwabe, *Wissenschaft und Kriegsmoral*, 98, 235–36n22.
[183] Williamson, *Karl Helfferich*, 158; cf. Helfferich, *Der Weltkrieg*, vol. 2, 300–6.

and the United States. He thought that demonstrating a willingness to work with the US government to restore the Declaration of London could help to mobilize American cotton interests damaged by the blockade. He also knew that a loss of American cotton exports with a US entry into the war would devastate the German textile industry. US entry into the conflict would, moreover, end the Entente's problems financing the war, as it would open the floodgates of US lending and might induce other remaining neutrals to enter the war on the side of the Entente at a critical phase of the war in the Balkans and Russia.[184]

Helfferich took initiative to discuss these concerns with Bethmann Hollweg, and then on August 5th submitted a memorandum advising Bethmann to take up the American offer, reminding the chancellor that the submarine war was no end but merely a means to achieve victory. It was a means to reduce the pressure of the blockade; if there were no results from working with the Americans within a few weeks, he argued, Germany could always return to submarine warfare in its full severity.[185] Tellingly, he admonished the chancellor not to fear the accusation of weakness that might come from the press and public opinion: "when playing for such large stakes, press and public opinion cannot be decisive. Only rational perspectives should be permitted."[186]

Bethmann Hollweg was receptive, as was the Kaiser, but the Chief of the Admiralty Staff Gustav Bachmann (1860–1943), Alfred Tirpitz, and the Foreign Office opposed the initiative. Tirpitz rejected it on the grounds that an apology for the *Lusitania* and a repudiation of a form of warfare formerly affirmed as legal was worse than no answer, as it would put Germany in the wrong and rob its submariners of an effective tool of warfare. To respond as Hefferich advised, he argued, was to give in to American blackmail. Trying to curry favor with opinion in the United States was a hopeless cause in any case, as too much money was at stake in the business of selling the Entente munitions. America had a stake in Germany's demise, he argued, not least since it needed England to hold back Japan.[187]

No sooner had enflamed American opinion died down over the *Lusitania* than the British passenger liner *Arabic* was sunk by the U-24 on August 19, again with the loss of American lives. Though this was apparently done in a defensive action (the submarine commander feared being rammed), a massive

---

[184] Helfferich, *Der Weltkrieg*, vol. 2, 319–21.
[185] Spindler, *Der Handelskrieg*, vol. 1, 190–92. See also Williamson, *Karl Helfferich*, 156–57. Cf. Helfferich, *Der Weltkrieg*, vol. 2, 321–22.
[186] Spindler, *Der Handelskrieg*, vol. 1, 192. Cf. Tirpitz, *Politische Dokumente*, vol. 2, 385–95.
[187] Spindler, *Der Handelskrieg*, vol. 1, 193; Williamson, *Karl Helfferich*, 157–58; Stegemann, *Marinepolitik*, 30–31. Cf. Tirpitz, *Politische Dokumente*, vol. 2, 395–403; BArch M, N 253 Nl. Tirpitz, Nr. 101, fols. 126–30, Report of Hinrich Charles, Secretary of the Chamber of German-American Commerce in New York, Feb. 20, 1915.

outcry ensued once again. The German government responded to the American complaints by forwarding its guidelines on passenger liners issued in the wake of the *Lusitania* disaster, arguing that the sinking had violated these new rules, but the diplomatic feud still threatened to escalate to a US declaration of war. The German government was pressed to accept responsibility for the *Arabic* and pay an indemnity, but the opportunity to cooperate with Woodrow Wilson to rescind the illegal aspects of the British blockade had been sunk with that ship.[188] Tirpitz, for his part, was incensed by these concessions and tendered his resignation as state secretary on August 27, which the Kaiser refused, but he did remove him from his advisory role on the conduct of the naval war on August 30.[189] The "submarine blockade," while never formally repudiated by the German government, was quietly suspended on September 18, 1915 by prohibiting all submarine warfare in the war zone, whether unrestricted or by prize rules.[190] In any case, by that point Royal Navy Q-ships – now often illegally flying neutral flags – had made abiding by prize rules increasingly hazardous, as the men of the U-27 discovered one month earlier when they were sunk by the *Baralong* after surfacing to inspect it.[191]

With constant pressure from Tirpitz, Pohl's successor Henning von Holtzendorff (1853–1919), and other admirals in the navy, as well as strong public support and some softening of the US position regarding use of the submarine against armed merchant ships, submarine warfare was reinstated in late January 1916 against armed merchantmen. This was part of the Verdun offensive that began in February, a desperate gamble by Falkenhayn to secure victory in the west as signs mounted of growing discontent in Germany. Tirpitz once gain pressed for a much more expansive form of submarine warfare, but his repeated insubordination – including a clandestine U-boat propaganda campaign launched by the RMA's Communications Bureau – led to a rift with the Kaiser. On March 15 Tirpitz resigned as secretary of the RMA and was replaced by Admiral Eduard von Capelle (1855–1931).[192]

Tirpitz's resignation fuelled much public backlash and led conservative, National Liberal, and Center Party deputies in the Reichstag to draft a resolution demanding an immediate resumption of unrestricted submarine warfare. However, the near sinking by U-boat of the mistakenly-identified French passenger ship *Sussex* on March 23, 1916 brought relations with the

---

[188] Helfferich, *Der Weltkrieg*, vol. 2, 323–24.
[189] Scheck, *Alfred Tirpitz*, 28; Spindler, *Handelskrieg*, vol. 2, 281. See also Hull, *Scrap of Paper*, 262. Cf. Tirpitz, *Politische Dokumente*, vol. 2, 404–17.
[190] Spindler, *Der Handelskrieg*, vol. 2, 286–87; Stegemann, *Marinepolitik*, 31–32.
[191] Sondhaus, *German Submarine Warfare*, 75.
[192] Kelly, *Tirpitz*, 408, 410–11; Helfferich, *Der Weltkrieg*, vol. 2, 325–49; Herwig, *"Luxury" Fleet*, 165–66; Hull, *Scrap of Paper*, 264–65; Scheck, *Alfred Tirpitz*, 30–31; Williamson, *Karl Helfferich*, 159–60. Cf. Tirpitz, *Politische Dokumente*, vol. 2, 508–22.

United States to a new low. The Americans now declared the submarine an illegitimate weapon incompatible with the rights of neutrals and the protection of non-combatants. Diplomatic relations with Germany would end unless its use cease. The Germans complied on May 4 by reinstating prize rules for all merchant ships, armed or unarmed.[193] As Helfferich recalled, the superficial and tendentious expert memoranda commissioned by the Admiralty to support unrestricted submarine warfare promising English starvation and a quick victory flew in the face of the realities that Britain's economic reserves were largely intact, that there had been excellent harvests worldwide, even in England, and that available shipping volume of British merchant ships had hardly been affected by U-boats.[194]

Even so, the German public's faith in this naval *Wunderwaffe* would grow as the privations imposed by the "hunger blockade" became acute in 1916. To be sure, the blockade was only part of the cause of wartime German hunger. Inconsistent price ceilings and inadequate control over food supplies due to the fragmented nature of German farming were exacerbated by Germany's federal structure and competition between military and civilian authorities, creating thriving black markets that resulted in great inequality of food provision, even under rationing.[195] Hunger was also physiological-psychological, as Germans had become accustomed to diets rich in meats and fats, and the wartime shift toward carbohydrates meant that many people not actually starving felt almost constant hunger.[196] As the preceding discussion has shown, the British blockade greatly enhanced anxiety over food and raw material shortages in the earliest stages of the war. A blockade in 1914 was a very different measure than in the Napoleonic era, when only a tiny fraction of Germany's foodstuffs and raw materials were imported. While in no way excusing unrestricted submarine warfare, the British blockade and the other measures of economic warfare created a climate in which the drastic steps toward unrestricted use of submarines and Zeppelin attacks became acceptable. There can be no doubt that Sering along with Schmoller and their other colleagues at the University of Berlin had played an important role in this process, much in the mold of their *Flottenpolitik* of some 20 years earlier.

As we shall see in the final chapter, the suspension of unrestricted submarine warfare and Tirpitz's dismissal as RMA secretary in 1916 created a growing rift between the government and nationalists committed to *Weltpolitik*. This

---

[193] Afflerbach, *Auf Messers Schneide*, 158–59; Hull, *Scrap of Paper*, 264–65; Ritter, *Staatskunst*, vol. 3, 208–15.
[194] Helfferich, *Der Weltkrieg*, vol. 2, 336; Offer, *The First World War*, 355–62; Scheck, *Alfred Tirpitz*, 31–32.
[195] See Feldman, *Army, Industry and Labor*, 97–116; Offer, *The First World War*, 54–68; Watson, *Ring of Steel*, 231–34, 330–74.
[196] Offer, *The First World War*, 45–53.

group, which included some members of the Center Party and left liberals but had its bastion of strength in the National Liberal and conservative parties, the nationalist *Verbände*, notably the Colonial Society and Navy and Army Leagues, gradually coalesced with the Pan-German League into a *fronde* that accused the government of vacillation and weakness and sought to replace Bethmann Hollweg and the retirement of the Kaiser. The acrimonious debate over German war aims was at the very center of this growing rift, one that pitted those still committed to *Weltpolitik* by other means against those "traitors" to the national cause who sought a peace without annexations or war indemnities. Once again, the men who have featured in this book would play a key role in this process.

# 12

# War Aims, Peace Resolutions, and Defeat

### *Weltpolitik* by Other Means

As the German government was not planning a war in 1914, no official war aims existed when war broke out in August. Bethmann Hollweg's "September Program," on which he was advised by, among others, Karl Helfferich, Arthur von Gwinner, Walther Rathenau, and Wilhelm Solf when quick victory still seemed within reach in early September 1914, was itself little more than a grab bag of goals that had long animated German *Weltpolitik*, in many instances since 1897 and earlier. This included the old idea of a central European customs union ("*Mitteleuropa*," now with an economically subordinated France), a so-called rounding off of Germany's African colonial territory to include Angola, the northern half of Mozambique, French Equatorial Africa, Dahomey, parts of Senegambia, and of course the coveted prize of the Belgian Congo to create "*Mittelafrika*." At the time Bethmann also entertained vague ideas of pushing Russia's borders eastward and creating a new border strip from Russian Polish lands and a set of satellite buffer states in Russian Congress Poland, the Ukraine, and the Baltic, but it was too early in the conflict to settle on any concrete goals in that theater. In addition, there were more specific ideas about possible German annexations of western European territory. In France, Belfort, a coastal strip between Dunkirk and Boulogne, and the iron ore basin of Briey would be ceded as well as Belgian Liège, Verviers, the Province of Luxembourg, the Grand Duchy of Luxembourg, and possibly Antwerp.[1] To be sure these "official" war aims, if they can be called that, were scaled back significantly as the war settled into a stalemate following the Battle of the Marne, but what stands out, even in their later iterations, is their defensiveness: the aim is a semi-autarkic German bloc of states in Europe and Africa, a kind of *Festung* (fortress) *Deutschland* to escape the insecurity of the prewar period.[2] For both domestic political and

---

[1] See Fischer, *Griff nach der Weltmacht*, 107–13; Jaeger, *Unternehmer*, 219–29; Jarausch, *Enigmatic Chancellor*, 195–200; Pogge von Strandmann, ed., *Walther Rathenau*, 184–86; Röhl, *Into the Abyss*, 1135–45; Warburg, *Aus meinen Aufzeichnungen*, 36.

[2] Fischer, *Griff nach der Weltmacht*, 112.

diplomatic reasons, German war aims were not made public and they could not be discussed publicly before the autumn of 1916 due to official censorship imposed by the chancellor in February 1915 prompted by the mass distribution of a Pan-German annexationist memorandum.[3]

How any of the so-called September program would be achieved was unclear and would remain that way throughout the war, but experts were employed by the government to work out the details. One of them was Karl Rathgen. As Farnam was writing his painfully candid letters to his old friend in January 1915, Rathgen was in Brussels on leave from the Hamburg Kolonialinstitut to serve as an expert to the German Colonial Office and the German civil administration of Brussels headed by Maximilian von Sandt (1861–1918).[4] In addition to Rathgen, other economists involved in the brain trust to advise officials on the future of Belgium and its colonies were Hermann Schumacher, Gerhart von Schulze-Gaevernitz, Heinrich Herkner (1863–1932), Edgar Jaffé (1866–1921), and Heinrich Wäntig (1870–1943).[5] Rathgen's work in Brussels seems to have had multiple purposes. Formally he was working with Edmund Brückner (1871–1935, governor of Togo 1911–12), to investigate and manage the administration of the Belgian Congo in wartime in preparation for what was anticipated as an annexation of this territory to complete *"Mittelafrika"* connecting German Cameroon and East Africa, as sketched out in Bethmann Hollweg's September program.[6] As was discussed in Chapter 9, Rathgen was no stranger to Belgium or the topic of the Congo, on which he had in fact lectured both in Brussels and the United States shortly before the war.

By December 1914 Rathgen and these other officials had set up a workplace in the library of the Belgian Colonial Ministry and were going through its files in a systematic manner to gain a clearer picture of what these new colonial responsibilities entailed, made more difficult by the fact that at the outbreak of war the ministry was in the midst of a major reorganization. Making matters worse, all of the Belgian colonial officials had disappeared along with a large number of their files. Rathgen thus doubted that he would be able to find "politically interesting" documents. Nevertheless, he reported to now Lord Mayor of Hamburg Werner von Melle in a long letter that there was a "mass" of valuable information on the economic administration of the Congo and that a division of labor had been worked out between him and the German officials from the Colonial Office to examine the terms of the concession companies operating in the Congo and the economic significance of the colony to

---

[3] Ibid., 192–92; Jarausch, *Enigmatic Chancellor*, 355–56.
[4] Frank Wende, *Die belgische Frage in der deutschen Politik des Ersten Weltkriegs* (Hamburg: Wissenschaftlicher Verlag Eckart Böhme, 1969), 33–39.
[5] Krüger, *Nationalökonomen*, 182–83.
[6] SUB Hamburg, Nl. von Melle, Karl Rathgen to Werner von Melle, Zivilverwaltung Brüssel, Dec. 21, 1914, fols. 13–18, here fols. 13–14.

Figure 12.1   Karl Rathgen ca. 1920.

Belgium, and as Rathgen added in a parenthetical aside, "naturally eventually for Germany." From this letter it is also clear that another side of his stay in Brussels was that he was supervising the collection – or rather, plunder – of colonial information for the Central Office of the Hamburg Kolonialinstitut.[7] No doubt Rathgen was certain that Germany, with its new scientific *Kolonialpolitik* spearheaded by the Kolonialinstitut, would be a much better steward of the Congo's people and resources. While this stay in Brussels in what Rathgen described as "strange times" was not without its interesting sides, he admitted rather understatedly to Melle that "personal relations with former Belgian acquaintances will have their difficulties."[8]

By April 1915 Rathgen had completed a draft of a report to Bethmann Hollweg on the economic significance of the Congo to Belgium, and he was able to extend his stay in Belgium until well into the autumn of 1915 to complete what he called his "political-scientific studies," which included a long official memorandum on these topics.[9] It is hard not to be struck by the

---

[7] Ibid., fols. 14–16.
[8] Ibid., fol. 17. Cf. Warburg, *Aus meinen Aufzeichnungen*, 37; Wende, *Die belgische Frage*, 64–75.
[9] SUB Hamburg, Nl. von Melle, Karl Rathgen to Werner von Melle, Zivilverwaltung Brüssel, April 28, 1915, fols. 19–20; Karl Rathgen to Werner von Melle, Zivilverwaltung Brüssel,

profound irony of Farnam and Rathgen, two lifelong close friends who as recently as October 1913 had seen each other when Rathgen lectured on the Belgian Congo at Yale, now separated by a vast gulf, with Farnam voicing anger about the "rape of Belgium" while Rathgen was actively participating in it, albeit not as a soldier but as a bureaucrat.

As Fritz Fischer revealed in great detail, the issue of war aims was not – and indeed, never could have been – confined to a small circle of senior officials and their advisors but generated a very animated discussion within German society that involved academics, journalists, party leaders, parliamentarians, bankers, and businessmen fueled by longstanding frustrations over Germany's failed prewar *Weltpolitik*.[10] The premium placed on "absolute security" meant that no one imagined returning to the prewar territorial status quo, which made an early negotiated peace practically impossible and eroded the *Burgfrieden* between parties of the left and right and the religious denominations. Often unmoored from the geostrategic realties of the war on account of the limited information available to German civilians about the war's progress, the war aims debate escalated the expectations for an acceptable peace while further inflating the Entente propaganda image of German menace and barbarity and investing the war with even greater moral urgency, making a compromise peace that much more difficult.

On the modest end of the war aims spectrum was Rathgen, who as discussed was definitely on board with annexing the Belgian Congo and consolidating Germany's African possessions with additions of French and Portuguese territory. With respect to European territorial revision, he was far more ambivalent, however. He was close to Friedrich Naumann through their common work in the Evangelical Social Congress and, as victory receded in 1915 and the privations of the blockade came to be felt, he embraced Naumann's highly popular October 1915 proposal for "*Mitteleuropa*" to bring Germany and Austria-Hungary into an explicitly multi-national political, economic, and defensive military union.[11] This was not so much a war aim than a reconceptualization of a longstanding dream of many Reich Germans and Austrians (albeit with a new twist), and in the context of a war in stalemate and the de facto loss of Germany's overseas colonies, a conscious defensive retreat from *Weltwirtschaft* and *Weltpolitik* toward a more autarkic, confederal central Europe and Balkans.[12] It was publicized in Naumann's Working Committee for "*Mitteleuropa*" that involved Rathgen, Herkner, Alfred Weber,

---

Aug. 23, 1915, fols. 23–24; Karl Rathgen to Werner von Melle, Bad Kissingen, Oct. 8, 1915, fols. 25–26.

[10] Fischer, *Griff nach der Weltmacht*, 103–4, 178–216.

[11] Friedrich Naumann, *Mitteleuropa* (Berlin: Georg Reimer, 1915).

[12] Ibid., 199–229. See also Theodor Heuss, *Friedrich Naumann: Der Mann, das Werk, die Zeit*, 2d ed. (Stuttgart and Tübingen: Rainer Wunderlich, 1949), 333–43.

and others and was supported by the German Foreign Office, revealing again how close men like Rathgen and Naumann were to Bethmmann Hollweg, who as will be discussed later in this chapter, was under increasing pressure from an aggressive German war aims movement by 1915 coming from other quarters.[13] That said, at an April 1916 meeting of the Association for Social Policy, most members had doubts about the feasibility of a "central European" customs union, with Hermann Schumacher in particular taking a firm position against it.[14] The main reason for this was his continued commitment to *Weltwirtschaft* and *Weltpolitik*, as will become clearer shortly.

Other left liberals working in Belgium, like Rathgen's colleague Schulze-Gaevernitz's, took a much harder line, insisting on extensive annexations in metropolitan Belgium almost indistinguishable from the Pan-Germans, underscoring the difficulty of making any meaningful distinctions between "liberal imperialism" and the imperialist war aims of the nationalist right during the First World War.[15] The lines were in fact very fluid, as is best illustrated by Hermann Schumacher. Early in the war Schumacher had no formal charge to investigate the practicality of official war aims. Rather, in September 1914 he had participated in a meeting organized by the head of the Essen Chamber of Commerce and attended by the business director of the chamber Wilhelm Hirsch (who had invited Schumacher to be part of the CDI's investigative journey to China in 1897), the coal magnate Hugo Stinnes, the steel industrialist August Thyssen (1842–1926), and a number of other representatives of Rhenish-Westphalian heavy industry. These discussions centered on securing a lasting peace, as expectations were then running high that Germany would soon be victorious. While Schumacher welcomed the group's interest in general economic questions, he was put off by the tenor of the conversation, which had found consensus over the negative view of Russia disseminated by Baltic Germans and the Royal Prussian Settlement Commission, namely a broad eastern annexationist program bent on weakening Russia as much as possible and restricting its access to the Baltic Sea. With an eye to the potential importance of the Trans-Siberian Railway and opportunities for Russo-German economic cooperation, this did not at all sit well with Schumacher.[16]

In any case, more pressing to this group at the time were questions about Rhine River shipping and the competition between the German North Sea ports and those at the mouth of the Rhine and Scheldt at Rotterdam and

---

[13] Heuss, *Friedrich Naumann*, 342; Jarausch, *Enigmatic Chancellor*, 204–17; Krüger, *Nationalökonomen*, 172–73; Theiner, *Sozialer Liberalismus*, 236–58.
[14] Hermann Schumacher, *Meistbegünstigung und Zollunterscheidung* (Munich and Leipzig: Duncker & Humblot, 1916); Jan Vermeiren, *The First World War and German National Identity: The Dual Alliance at War* (Cambridge: Cambridge University Press, 2016), 164.
[15] Krüger, *Nationalökonomen*, 183.
[16] GNN HA, Nl. Schumacher, I, B-6u, fols. 647–47a.

Antwerp, as well as railway rates and canal construction, which were all matters that interested Schumacher much more, and as discussed in earlier chapters, topics on which he had done much research since his time working for the Prussian Ministry of Public Works and journeys in East Asia. Hugo Stinnes, whom he already knew, shared an interest in these and other more general economic questions with Schumacher, thereafter deepened over long conversation with him on a train journey from the Rhineland to Berlin.[17] The result of these deliberations and discussions was that Schumacher was entrusted by Stinnes and the other industrialists to draft a long memorandum on war aims in September and October that was then submitted to Bethmann Hollweg by Stinnes on November 17, 1914.[18] A copy of this memo was also forwarded to Alfred Tirpitz, very likely by Schumacher himself.[19] Fritz Fischer noted that the very center of the unofficial German war aims movement was in western German heavy industry led actively by Stinnes, and he highlighted the significance of Schumacher's memorandum as embodying those war aims and acknowledged its subsequent influence on German war aims policy.[20] It thus deserves a full discussion.

Schumacher's memo began from the premise that the war had to result in a "national gain" to allow a long period of peaceful development and therefore that the war should not be concluded before the complete defeat of Germany's enemies. It was useful to that endeavor and to prevent prolonged peace negotiations, he argued, to articulate a clear and simplified program of expansive demands dictated to a vanquished France and Russia. He also assumed that Britain would not be defeated in the war but that Germany's rivalry with it would be decided at later date. As a foundation for a new "power position" for that longer-term contest and as the most important prize of victory, Germany had first of all to secure a permanent presence along the coast between the Somme River in France and the Dutch frontier adjacent the English coast and the Thames Estuary for direct access to the open ocean. Second, Britain's position in the Mediterranean had to be weakened by taking over France's rights in Morocco and gaining a footing in Tangier or Ceuta across from Gibraltar. Third, Germany needed to gain a footing at the strategic southern entry point to the Red Sea on the Straits of Bab-el-Mandeb across from Aden by cession of French Somaliland. This would also offer the economic

---

[17] Ibid., fols. 648–48a.
[18] Gerald Feldman, "War Aims, State Intervention and Business Leadership in Germany: The Case of Hugo Stinnes," in *Great War, Total War: Combat and Mobilization on the Western Front, 1914–1918*, ed. Roger Chickering and Stig Förster (Washington, DC: German Historical Institute; Cambridge: Cambridge University Press, 2000), 349–67, here 352; Feldman, *Hugo Stinnes*, 386–88. Cf. Fischer, *Griff nach der Weltmacht*, 191.
[19] BArch M, N 253 Nl. Tirpitz, Nr. 101, Hermann Schumacher, Denkschrift über Friedensziele deutscher Politik, Bonn, Sept./Oct. 1914, fols. 59–88.
[20] Fischer, *Griff nach der Weltmacht*, 191, 195–96, 199.

advantage of the railway from Djibouti to Addis Ababa and thus access to Abyssinia. Fourth, Germany was to gain tariff preferences in France and Russia over Britain by the reduction of tariffs on the land frontier with Germany to levels lower than those at their maritime borders. Finally, a war indemnity would need to be extracted from France and Russia of sufficient size to rebuild and expand Germany's battle fleet.[21]

According to Schumacher, Franco-German relations would only become sustainably friendly by a permanent weakening of France's "world political and world economic influence." In addition to the territorial losses along the North Sea and eastern frontier, Mediterranean, and Red Sea and the heavy war indemnity, this would be accomplished by eliminating the foundations of French heavy industry and thus its armaments industry and by dissolving the Dual Alliance with Russia. With respect to Russia, German demands had to be more moderate, with the greater Russian territories remaining intact. Rather, the aim would be to redirect Russian energies eastward and gain frontier lands running from southeastern Silesia via Petrikau (Piotrków), Grodno, Wilna (Vilnius), and Dünaburg (Dvinsk; Duagavpils) up to the Bay of Narva. This meant annexing a strip of land in Russian Poland, the Suwalki, Vilna and Kovno governorates, and the Baltic governorates of Courland, Livonia, and Estonia.[22]

These annexations were justified by Schumacher on the grounds of reducing the distance between East Prussia and Upper Silesia by two hundred kilometers and due to the significant role that "Germandom" had played historically in these regions, notably also the five thousand German settlers along the Vistula. It would also allow Germany to establish a naval base in the eastern Baltic that could threaten the Russian Baltic and St. Petersburg. Above all, Schumacher saw these regions as new fields for extensive German "inner colonization" due to their relatively sparse populations that would forge a "strong Germanic bulwark." This would counterbalance the growth of German industry with an expansion of agricultural lands, increased food self-sufficiency, and increased supply of agricultural laborers.[23]

There can be no doubt that this vision for eastern Europe was shaped by Schumacher's global frame of reference. It is also worth noting here that nowhere in this memorandum was there any discussion of creating border satellite states between Russia and Germany in Finland, Poland, the Ukraine, or Belarusia. Indeed, he explicitly rejected this as potentially harmful to Russo-German relations. Rather, Schumacher envisioned that Germany would return to good graces with Russia and undermine the Dual Alliance by encouraging a crash of the Russian bond market, a default on French loans to Russia, and a

---

[21] BArch M, N 253 Nl. Tirpitz, Nr. 101, Hermann Schumacher, Denkschrift über Friedensziele deutscher Politik, Bonn, Sept./Okt. 1914, fols. 59–61.
[22] Ibid., fols. 63–64.   [23] Ibid., fols. 64–65.

partial national bankruptcy, destroying the basis of the Franco-Russian relationship. Germany would then offer Russia these credits and emerge as Russia's financial savior, gaining for itself in the process a controlling voice in Russian reforms and economic policy as well as valuable economic concessions in return for guaranteeing Russia's credit. This would supposedly strengthen the peace party in St. Petersburg and offer fertile soil for the pursuit of a productive common interest.[24] Unquestionably this vision was shaped by Schumacher's prewar journeys to both the United States and Russia.

Regarding Belgium, Schumacher argued that no thought at all could be given to restoring it to its old form as an independent state. Germany's vital and economic interests demanded retaining control over its coast, Namur, and Liège. In any case, the importance of Antwerp to Germany's *"weltwirtschaftliche Stellung"* (world economic position) demanded its retention under German administration, about which, he added, most of the German public was in agreement. Over time Antwerp might evolve into a status similar to the Hanseatic city-states Hamburg and Bremen. With regard to the rest of Belgium, it was an artificial construct and could be reduced in status to a British-style "self-governing colony."[25] To Schumacher's mind it was important for the Germans to present themselves as liberators to the Germanic Flemings and offer closer ties to Germany as an opportunity, among other things, to gain the protections of German labor legislation, entry into the German Customs Union, Prussian railway administration, and to participate in the world economy in ways that would be impossible for them as Belgians. Germany would thus retain military sovereignty, occupation rights, and diplomatic representation.[26] As for the Walloons with their French language and culture, they were best dealt with by a policy of divide and conquer. Parts of the Walloon territory like Liège could be annexed outright, the rest could be brought under a separate, albeit less autonomous, self-government and gradually dismembered and Germanized by apportioning parts to Flemish administration. Large-scale emigration of Walloons could be encouraged, while the Walloon elite could be dominated by acquisition or expropriation of their industrial assets and by the gradual infiltration of their industrial administration by Germans. Immigration of Italian and Polish workers to Wallonia could likewise be encouraged to water down their influence.[27]

With respect to Germany's colonial empire, Schumacher argued that while Germany should try to regain its colonies, that might not be possible. In any case, what had priority was gaining new, promising colonial territory not scattered all over the globe. A guiding principle was respecting the rights of aboriginals as codified in existing international agreements, such as the 1880 Morocco agreement (Madrid Convention) and the 1885 Congo Act. Ottoman

---

[24] Ibid., fols. 65–66.   [25] Ibid., fol. 69.   [26] Ibid., fols. 67–69.   [27] Ibid., fols. 70–71.

Turkey's rights in Egypt and along the Persian Gulf should be recovered. In line with Germany's claim of being a protector of Islam, all means should be devoted to improving the economic conditions of the native populations to gain the sympathy of these people in Africa, the Near East, India, and China, thereby undermining British rule in these regions. Germany had, moreover, to respect the rights of neutrals by enforcing existing treaties and the policy of the open door as stipulated in the Morocco agreement and Congo Act. Similarly, Schumacher argued that Germany should pursue the policy of the open door in its own colonies, confident that its own capabilities would be vindicated in open competition on a fair playing field. The policy of the open door, he argued, was in Germany's interest, and it should become a champion of this principle and thereby gain the sympathies of neutrals.[28] There can be no doubt that this perspective was much influenced by Schumacher's 1911 journey through British Malaya and the Dutch East Indies, which had reinforced his concern about the exclusion of German investors and planters in this promising region. It is notable too that this is very much a liberal vision of colonial economic policy with its emphasis on respect of existing treaties guaranteeing the open door, advocating open competition, and promoting the economic improvement of native peoples.

Beyond the colonial acquisitions from France in Morocco and Somaliland, Schumacher argued that the aims in Africa should be consolidating territory to make economic development possible. With that in mind he argued that Togo should be enlarged by the addition of neighboring Dahomey, which would encourage cotton cultivation in that colony and give it access to the larger commercial region of the Niger River. Germany should also assume all rights of the Belgian state in the Congo, and on grounds of political, economic and hygienic considerations, gain control of portions of French Equatorial Africa to round off Germany's African possessions. Beyond this formal colonial territory, it was important for Germany to improve its economic position in China and Turkish Asia by taking over Belgium's valuable railway and mining concessions in China and the concessions that France had extracted from Turkey with its last loan to Constantinople.[29]

The remainder of Schumacher's memorandum, which comprised half of this long tract (nearly fifteen of thirty pages), was devoted to purely economic war aims and recommendations. What is striking here is once again the liberal economic vision that runs throughout. Schumacher made light of the fact that the success of German territorial expansion would depend in large measure on changed economic conditions that relied less on the state and much more on private property relations and private law. It was important to gain "unlimited economic rights of disposal" (*unbegrenzte wirtschaftliche Verfügungsgewalt*)

---

[28] Ibid., fols. 71–73.  [29] Ibid., fols. 73–74.

over the annexed territories to make maximal use of agricultural lands, businesses and industrial plant, and transport facilities as freely as possible. That required expropriation of these assets and transfer of them as free property to the German people.[30]

Schumacher claimed that the experience of the Franco-Prussian War and the distortion of the German economy by that war indemnity argued for an investment of any new war indemnity extracted from France and Russia. He proposed using it to fund the army and navy; capitalize funds to care of war invalids, widows, and orphans; expand international telegraph cables and communication services; encourage inner colonization in annexed territories; improve housing; and increase educational and cultural investments.[31] Wherever possible the war indemnity should be paid by the transfer of real assets, such as land, commercial assets (or stock in such), and railways, which the vanquished state would be required to expropriate from its subjects and transfer to Germany within a given timeframe. The advantage of such measures, Schumacher argued, was that Germany would gain "real soil of colonization" immediately "in vital connection with the contiguous motherland, where a growth in economic power represented a growth of national power."[32] Lands to be considered for such action were only those that were of the greatest economic significance, such as the French iron ore basin [of Briey-Longwy] including transfer of all property and stock of industrial assets free and clear; the coal fields of the French departments Nord and Pas-de-Calais as free property or stock in industrial assets; the Russian industrial regions adjacent to Upper Silesia in the same manner; and "areas as wide as possible" in the proposed Polish border strip in the Suwalki, Vilna and Kovno governorates, and the Baltic governorates of Courland, Livonia and Estonia as free property from Russia for German settlers.[33]

A German victory would also allow a major reconfiguration of trade relations. Schumacher argued that the most favored nation trade principle should continue to guide such policy but that it could be adapted to secure advantages for Germany by giving specific trade preferences to the neighboring states along Germany's new borders, albeit with due appreciation and preservation of their economic linkages with their former homeland to preserve their productive capacities. Any preferences would preserve most favored nation legal status by differentiating between maritime and land borders, lowering duties on the latter by 50 percent, which Schumacher argued was justified alone on the grounds of higher land transport costs and the greater significance to Germany of this trade due to its geographical situation as opposed to Great Britain and the United States. This could be legally anchored into any peace treaties. Germany would likewise need to secure the right to treat its

[30] Ibid., fols. 74–75.  [31] Ibid., fols. 75–76.  [32] Ibid., fol. 76.  [33] Ibid., fols. 77–78.

allies and neutrals preferentially. On account of their extreme protectionism, any peace treaty with France and Russia would need to contain clauses that pressed both into new trade treaties by, for example, imposing an immediate reduction of 50–75 percent on current duties on German goods crossing land frontiers. Likewise, agreements on railway transit rates could be included that prohibited discrimination against foreign freight in both countries. These reductions of barriers to trade in France and Russia could then be extended to Germany's allies and neighboring neutrals according to the most favored nation principle, with the proviso that Germany retain the right to offer its allies and European neutrals preferences.[34]

Schumacher proposed that after victory Germany's colonial trade would continue to operate entirely according to the principle of the open door. Tariff preferences between the colony and the metropole were not in Germany's interests, as only a tiny fraction of Germany's colonial trade was with its own colonies and existing treaties such as the Congo Act, the Samoa Treaty, and Morocco Agreement prohibited such preferences. With Germany's highly competitive industry and the economic insignificance of its colonies, Germany would have an even greater interest in the open door after the war. Furthermore, Germany could work to assure that any peace treaty with France prohibited discriminating against German trade with French colonies. It might also be possible, he argued, to negotiate an agreement with Great Britain that prohibited preferences in the Dominion trade and assured the open door in Crown Colonies.[35]

With respect to non-tariff barriers to trade and investment, France and Russia were particularly guilty of imposing discriminatory legislation and regulations that violated the "principle of equal standing" (*Grundsatz der Gleichstellung*).[36] Germany would thus need to assure that any peace treaty with Russia prohibited discrimination against foreigners in domestic travel, acquisition of property, founding of joint-stock companies, taxation and regulation of trade and commerce, and foreign and domestic shipping. Likewise a treaty with France would have to prohibit its discrimination against foreign shipping. It was necessary for Germany to appear to the Russian people in particular as the "champion of its liberties." As he concluded, "the more the war brings about an improvement of the conditions of the broad classes of the Russian population, the less hatred will be left over and the easier it will be to bring about the necessary reconciliation with our great eastern neighbor."[37]

Schumacher's memo is highly significant on a number of counts. Viewed in the context of his prewar writings and experiences, it is entirely in keeping with his understanding of *Weltwirtschaft* and a liberal imperialist *Weltpolitik*.

---

[34] Ibid., fols. 78–85.   [35] Ibid., fols. 85–87.   [36] Ibid., fol. 87.   [37] Ibid., fols. 87–88.

Even the expansive annexationist aims in the west, which include expropriation of important industrial assets in France and Belgium, the control of a French coastal strip, the Flemish coast, and Antwerp, and the reduction of Belgium to the status of a "self-governing colony," with *divide et impera* and emigration (and foreign immigration) used to water down undesired native influences, is right out of the playbook of British liberal imperialism, now extended to European peoples, their lands, and assets. The Flemings, would, after all, enjoy the benefits of German labor legislation, superior Prussian railway administration, access to the German Customs Union, and thus also gain a significance in the world economy that they would never have as part of an "artificial," benighted, independent Belgium. The settler colonialism proposed for the territories in Russia slated for annexation is also entirely compatible with American, British, and French liberal settler colonialism practiced in the American West, Australia, and Algeria, as were the means of domination through finance, which are uncannily reminiscent of Evelyn Baring's (Earl of Cromer, 1841–1917) program for a modern Egypt of 1909.[38] German financial leverage would open up and liberalize the Russian economy and gradually free its people.

There is no talk in the memorandum of "*Mitteleuropa*" or of any defensive tariff walls in Europe or Africa but instead much discussion of the open door, most favored nation status, lowered tariffs, and elimination of other non-tariff barriers to trade and investment, free disposal of lands and assets, and respect of existing treaties that guaranteed openness in the colonies, where native economic improvement and respect of aboriginal rights were underscored. This is an outline for a liberal *Pax Germanica*, one that checks Britain in the Channel and Thames Estuary, the Mediterranean, and the Red Sea, and undermines its position in Egypt and the Persian Gulf by championing Turkish rights, and weakens its position in Africa, India, and China by appealing to Muslim British subjects worldwide. The memorandum stresses the importance of reconciliation with Russia through a magnanimous peace and enhanced German influence over Russian economic policy that would open up Russia to German exports and investments and assure Germany access to the resources, labor, markets, and transportation network of a vast Eurasian domain, one linked to China and East Asia via the Trans-Siberian Railway, ideas that had animated Schumacher since his travels in China, Korea, and Japan in 1897 and reinforced by his travel in the United States in 1907, Southeast Asia in 1911, and Russia in 1912. To borrow from von Clausewitz, this was unquestionably *Weltpolitik* by other means.

The primary political and historical significance of Schumacher's memorandum is that it became the basis of Hugo Stinnes's war aims to which he

---

[38] Earl of Cromer, *Modern Egypt*, 2 vols. (New York: Macmillan, 1908).

would hold consistently until as late as September 1918. Stinnes was unquestionably the leading figure in German heavy industry during the war, whose influence eclipsed even Gustav Krupp's (1870–1950). As already noted, Schumacher's memorandum was presented by Stinnes to Bethmann Hollweg in November 1914, and Stinnes enjoyed direct access to him and his successors, and after August 1916 especially to Field Marshal Paul von Hindenburg (1847–1934) and Erich Ludendorff in the Third Supreme Army Command (OHL).[39] As will be discussed later, Stinnes was so committed to these war aims throughout the war that he became extremely alarmed when the Reichstag majority passed its resolution in July 1917 seeking a peace without annexations, turning him into a staunch supporter of and generous donor to Alfred Tirpitz and Wolfgang Kapp's Fatherland Party in September 1917. Stinnes was, moreover, already a "fanatical" supporter of unrestricted submarine warfare in the summer of 1916 and consistently pressed Ludendorff in that direction in the autumn of 1916.[40]

Schumacher, the Krupp director Hugenberg, Emil Kirdorf (1847–1938), Stinnes, Thyssen, and other scholars and industrialists were able to evade the official ban on war aims discussions by presenting their war aims in eastern and western Europe to the representative commanding general in Westphalia Georg von Gayl (1850–1927) on May 12, 1915, who later forwarded the eighteen accompanying memoranda to Bethmann Hollweg.[41] Moreover, on June 20, 1915 Schumacher along with others in this group were able to give speeches to an invited, semi-public audience in the Berlin Künstlerhaus on German war aims, with Schumacher's speech focusing on war aims in the west, which largely recapitulated the content of his memorandum of September–October 1914 and was later distributed in printed form.[42] Led by the influential Berlin professor of theology Reinhold Seeberg (1859–1935), this group was able to circulate a petition on expansive war aims that managed to secure 1,347 signatures, among them no fewer than 352 from university professors, which included in addition to Schumacher such prominent figures as Wilamowitz-Möllendorff, Otto von Gierke, Friedrich Meinecke (1862–1954), Otto Hintze, Hermann Oncken (1869–1945), Theodor Schiemann, and Heinrich Treipel. After Schumacher revised its final draft, it

---

[39] Feldman, "War Aims," in Chickering and Förster, *Great War, Total War* 350–51; Feldman, *Hugo Stinnes*, 388–92.

[40] Feldman, "War Aims," in Chickering and Förster, *Great War, Total War* 355–57; Feldman, *Hugo Stinnes*, 413–21, 478–80, 489–511. See also Scheck, *Alfred Tirpitz*, 69.

[41] Fischer, *Griff nach der Weltmacht*, 195; Klaus Schwabe, "Ursprung der Verbreitung des Alldeutschen Annexionismus in der deutschen Professorenschaft im Ersten Weltkrieg," *Vierteljahrshefte für Zeitgeschichte* 14, no. 2 (April 1966): 105–58, here 122.

[42] BArch M, RM 3 Reichsmarineamt, Nr. 10311, Hermann Schumacher, "Unsere Kriegsziele, insbesondere im Westen, Vortrag gehalten vor einer eingeladenen Gesellschaft im Künstlerhause in Berlin am 20. Juni 1915."

was submitted to the government on July 8, 1915 and became known as the "Submission of the Intellectuals" (*Intellektuelleneingabe*).[43]

Schumacher's memorandum is also in striking accord with the war aims later developed by Alfred Tirpitz, Henning von Holtzendorff, Albert Hopman, and others in the German navy, notably the Atlantic orientation, the annexation of the French and Flemish coasts along with Antwerp, the permanent weakening of France, the conciliatory peace with Russia without extensive annexations in the east or an independent Poland, and plans for a future reckoning with Great Britain prepared by checking its influence in the Mediterranean and elsewhere.[44] Indeed, at the start of the war the navy had no war aims at all; they were only formally worked out over the course of the autumn of 1914, suggesting strongly that core elements of what Tirpitz and Holtzendorff later elaborated was shaped by Schumacher's memorandum.[45] A version of these naval war aims drawn up by Holtzendorff was later taken up by Hindenburg as part of his own war aims list after he became chief of the German General Staff and head of the OHL in 1916.[46] That is, from at least two different influential angles – Stinnes and the navy – the war aims worked out by Schumacher would come to shape Germany's formal war aims and its conduct of the war.

Generations of historians have had a difficult time coming to grips with Hermann Schumacher's expansive war aims memorandum because they lacked the prewar context of his extensive travel, writings, and involvement in *Weltpolitik*. Thus for Fritz Fischer, Schumacher was merely a shill of Stinnes and Rhenish-Westphalian heavy industry.[47] With his demand for annexations in the west and the reduction of Belgium to the status of a colony, the historian Klaus Schwabe found in Schumacher an extreme outlier among German university professors, one allegedly flattered by the attention of heavy industry and then subtly manipulated by the Pan-Germans Heinrich Claß and Alfred Hugenberg to give voice to an annexationist group of scholars led by Reinhold Seeberg.[48] According to Schwabe, Schumacher was an illiberal "*Schutzzöllner*" (trade protectionist) and part of the "imperialist" group of right-wing industrialists and Pan-Germans, which he then contrasted with a smaller more

---

[43] Schwabe, "Ursprung der Verbreitung," 124–27; Schwabe, *Wissenschaft und Kriegsmoral*, 70. See also vom Brocke, "Wissenschaft und Militarismus," in Calder, Flashar, and Lindken, *Wilamowitz*, 689, 711; Fischer, *Griff nach der Weltmacht*, 199–200; Hagenlücke, *Deutsche Vaterlandspartei*, 67–69; Fritz Ringer, *Decline of the German Mandarins: The German Academic Community* (Middletown, CT: Wesleyan University Press, 1990), 189–90.

[44] Holger Herwig, "Admirals versus Generals: The War Aims of the Imperial German Navy, 1914–1918," *Central European History* 5, no. 3 (Sept. 1972): 208–33, here 212–13, 214–15, 216, 219–20, 222–25, 227–28.

[45] Ibid., 212, 214–15.    [46] Ibid., 216, 220. See also Herwig, *The First World War*, 304–5.

[47] Fischer, *Griff nach der Weltmacht*, 191.

[48] Schwabe, "Ursprung und Verbreitung," 112–13, 114–16, 122–27, 134; Schwabe, *Wissenschaft und Kriegsmoral*, 56, 70.

"liberal" group of scholars represented by Hans Delbrück and Adolf von Harnack who organized a counter declaration eschewing such annexations in the west.[49]

Writing some thirty years later, Gerald Feldman was himself puzzled by Stinnes's "overnight adoption of extreme war aims" as outlined in Schumacher's annexationist memorandum.[50] This is because before the war Stinnes had been a staunch opponent of Pan-German foreign policy ideas. As a major investor in and exporter of British coal, he had instead been a champion of peaceful liberal internationalism and free enterprise as well as a staunch opponent of government control of mining, railways, and other industries.[51] The explanation that Feldman offered for Stinnes's adoption of such war aims centered on his perception of Germany's vulnerability due to its lack of territorial buffers to its major industrial districts in the west, which were within range of French artillery and air raids, as well as the German iron and steel industry's reliance on minette iron ore deposits in eastern France. He also showed that Stinnes believed firmly in the superiority of German management of Belgian industrial assets and treatment of the laboring population and justified expropriation of industrial assets and control of Belgium on those grounds. His support of annexations in both the west and east – albeit more modest in the east to assure an alliance with Russia – were justified as a necessary preparation for a future showdown with the "Anglo-Americans."[52] Feldman also pointed out that Stinnes remained hostile to protectionism and autarky of the sort propagated by Friedrich Naumann's *Mitteleuropa* for closer union with Austria-Hungary and hoped instead for a swift return to free enterprise and global free trade and investment after the war.[53] In the end, however, Feldman remained flummoxed by the supposed irreconcilability of Stinnes's prewar "liberal economic principles" and "the extraordinarily imperialist program he supported during the war."[54]

As Feldman's interpretation began to suggest but did not fully spell out, what linked Stinnes and other liberal industrialists with a global footprint like Carl Duisberg (1861–1935, head of the Bayer chemical works), with Schumacher's memorandum and the Seeberg group was the global vision for a new German political and economic order not susceptible to British blockade, a vision entirely in keeping with prewar *Weltwirtschaft* and *Weltpolitik*, that is, liberal imperialism.[55] Wartime annexation and coercion were couched as means of improvement and progress and as ways of escaping Germany's geostrategic isolation and vulnerability for an even more expansive German

---

[49] Schwabe, *Wissenschaft und Kriegsmoral*, 66, 75, 78–79, 84–87, 90–91.
[50] Feldman, "War Aims," in Chickering and Förster, *Great War, Total War* 350, 352.
[51] Ibid., 350–51, 353.   [52] Ibid., 354–55.   [53] Ibid., 364–65.   [54] Ibid., 365–66.
[55] See Werner Plumpe, *Carl Duisberg 1861–1935: Anatomie eines Industriellen* (Munich: C. H. Beck, 2016), 484–89.

*Weltwirtschaft* and ultimate reckoning with the British Empire. Schwabe's interpretation is thus far off the mark, not least because there is next to no protectionist content in Schumacher's memo, but also because of his unsupported claim that Schumacher and Stinnes sympathized with Pan-German views. Even if that could be shown to be true for Schumacher – for which concrete evidence is lacking – we know enough today about the party-political latitudes that existed within the Pan-German movement and radical nationalism in Imperial Germany to be wary of the reflexive pigeonholing of its adherents as "illiberal" or "conservative," or of lazily equating the Wilhelmine radical right with conservatism.[56]

As the previous chapters have shown, Fischer's presentation of Schumacher as a shill of Rhenish-Westphalian industry is widely off the mark as well. For one, it is based on a very selective and narrow reading of Schumacher's memorandum that reflected Fischer's lack of prewar context to Schumacher's thinking and a misjudgment of the degree of Schumacher's intellectual independence. By obsessing over the annexations in France and Belgium and mischaracterizing them as "Pan-German," both Fischer and Schwabe read the Second World War backward into the First, ignored most of the memorandum and its global vision for a *Pax Germanica*, and implicitly assumed that imperial conquest of western European white people and the expropriation of their lands and resources was different in kind from the conquest of non-whites and the routine appropriation of their lands and resources under western European and North American liberal imperialism before 1914.

As should be clear by now, the opinions of professors involved in the war aims debate also cannot be divided neatly between non-annexationist "liberals" and Pan-German "imperialists."[57] This is supported by the fact that the smaller group of 191 so-called "liberal" professors and senior civil servants (including Lujo Brentano, Bernhard Dernburg, Gustav Schmoller, and Max Weber) who signed the vague counter-petition led by Hans Delbrück and Adolf von Harnack in July 1915 rejecting annexations in Belgium and Poland did so more to support the government because they feared breaking the wartime *Burgfrieden*, not because of any principled aversion to annexation or any commitment to a conciliatory peace.[58] As it turned out, Max Sering, who was on the organizing committee of the Delbrück-Harnack group, was invited by Schumacher to join the organizing committee of the Seeberg group

---

[56] See Chickering, *We Men Who Feel Most German*, 303; Eley, *From Unification to Nazism*, 231–50.
[57] See Schwabe, *Wissenschaft und Kriegsmoral*, 13.
[58] Fischer, *Griff nach der Weltmacht*, 201–2; Schwabe, "Ursprung und Verbreitung," 128–32, 135–37; Schwabe, *Wissenschaft und Kriegsmoral*, 72; Krüger, *Nationalökonomen*, 170–88.

**Figure 12.2** Hermann Schumacher ca. 1910.

one month earlier.[59] While he largely agreed with Schumacher's war aims in Russia, he declined joining the Seeberg group because he thought that the idea of checking England's chain of naval bases hollow, as it was too far removed from wartime reality and because he believed the annexations in the west would create permanently hostile subject populations and would thus not be sustainable. His own view of German war aims was that Belgium should be completely demilitarized and enter into the German Customs Union. He also believed Germany should maintain permanent control of the Belgian coast. Like Schumacher, he believed in extracting very large war indemnities from France and Britain, and in the case of the former, this included the ore basin of Briey. If the war against Russia were to achieve a breakthrough, he hoped to establish a direct link to Constantinople to assure Germany's preeminence in Turkey and to hit at the heart of England's position in the Mediterranean in Egypt, thereby connecting it to Germany's African colonial empire. Like

---

[59] BArch K, N 1210 Nl. Sering, Nr. 116, Invitation from Fürst Hatzfeld, Herzog von Trachtenberg, G. Anschütz, Professor d. Staats- und Völkerrechts, und H. Delbrück, Prof. der Geschichte, Berlin, July 2, 1915. See also Schwabe, "Ursprung und Verbreitung," 130. BArch K, N 1210 Nl. Sering, Nr. 116, Invitation from the preparatory committee of the Verein zur Besprechung der Friedensbedingungen, signed Hermann Schumacher, Berlin, June 9, 1915.

Schumacher, he proposed annexing the French and Belgian Congo, and he also advocated an expansion of the German fleet to establish a basis for true power equality with Britain that would ultimately check its naval hegemony. With regard to the east, again like Schumacher, Sering believed in establishing good relations with Russia over the longer term but believed that ceding Lithuania, Courland, and Polish Russian lands north of the Vistula to Germany would be no hindrance to that aim. In the end Sering had doubts about signing the petition of the Delbrück group because the final draft made it sound as though they were rejecting all annexations.[60] Indeed, he ultimately refused to sign this counter-petition precisely on those grounds.[61]

## "New Germany"

As the war in the east turned in Germany's favor in the summer of 1915 with the conquest of Russian Congress Poland and parts of the Baltic, eyes shifted to more tangible possibilities of an expanded eastern frontier. The official war aims in this theater were influenced most strongly by the Regierungspräsident of Frankfurt an der Oder, Friedrich von Schwerin, who as discussed in Chapters 1 and 9, had worked for the Royal Prussian Settlement Commission and had been a founding member with Max Sering of the Society for the Promotion of Inner Colonization in 1912, serving as its first chairman. Schwerin's views and those of the government were themselves based on memoranda that Max Sering compiled after traveling through the newly conquered Russian territories in September 1915 and the spring of 1916 at the behest of the deputy Prussian minister of war and German Foreign Office.[62]

Sering's first memorandum completed, at the end of September 1915 after his journey to Lithuania and Courland, was shaped strongly by the mental maps he had developed of eastern Europe from his travel in North America and the Russian Empire before the war, and his thoughts were animated by the benefits he had long seen in settler colonialism observed in the American upper Midwest and the Ukraine, as well as his awareness of the problems of tropical

---

[60] BArch K, N 1210 Nl. Sering, Nr. 116, Max Sering to Friedrich von Schwerin, June 18, 1915 (carbon copy); Max Sering to an unnamed "Excellenz" [Foreign Secretary Gottlieb von Jagow], Berlin-Grunewald, July 10, 1915 (carbon copy); Max Sering to an unnamed captain [possibly his son-in-law, Wolfgang von Tirpitz], Berlin-Grunewald, Aug. 6, 1915 (carbon copy); Max Sering to Alfred Weber, Berlin-Grunewald, Aug. 13, 1915 (carbon copy).

[61] Schwabe, *Wissenschaft und Kriegsmoral*, 79.

[62] SBB Krieg 1914/24896, Max Sering, "Bericht über die eroberten Gebiete des Nordostens. Auf Grund einer zweimonatigen Studienreise," n.d. [Sept. 1915]; BArch M, N253 Nl. Tirpitz, Nr. 146, Max Sering, "Die Zukunft Polens," July 29, 1916; cf. Fischer, *Griff nach der Weltmacht*, 126–27, 187–89, 243, 246, 344–46, 349.

colonial settlement from the study he completed for the Association for Social Policy in 1915 discussed in Chapter 9. Long sympathetic to a rapprochement between Russia and Germany, Sering began his memo by arguing that Russo-German relations would be improved in the long run by German territorial acquisitions in Poland and the Baltic because it would create greater demographic and territorial equilibrium between the two empires and bolster Germany's "standing" vis-à-vis the other world powers due to Germany's scattered tropical possessions and her lack of a viable temperate zone settler colony. A "modern world power," he argued, needed both.[63]

Sering argued that the great shift in the world equilibrium of power in the age of railways was the settlement of unpopulated and underpopulated temperate zone regions of the earth, which had created the "giant empires" of Russia, Britain, and the United States. The current war between the British and Russian Empires and the Central Powers would determine whether central european states would continue to coexist with them as equals. That would only be the case with significant territorial changes in eastern Europe, as all temperate zone territories in the rest of the world had been seized. As the conquered Russian territory was contiguous with Germany, Sering assessed its value as equivalent to three to four times the land area in Siberia or the American West.[64] Territorial annexation in the east was thus compared quite explicitly with American westward and Russian eastward expansion and was seen by Sering as offering the basis for a continuation of German *Weltpolitik*.

Invoking the "model" of US westward expansion and gradual assimilation of North American ethnic heterogeneity, Sering argued that the political significance of the territorial acquisitions in the east did not depend upon the complete national or linguistic uniformity of these territories but rather whether the inhabitants could grow into a political and cultural community with the Germans. For various reasons the basis for that was given in what Sering termed the "New Germany" (*Neudeutschland*) emerging in the Baltic. Of these conquered territories, Courland was by far the most valuable, as it was part of a chain of Lutheran states that extended from Holstein to Finland, which in the case of the Russian Baltic governorates of Courland, Livonia, and Estonia, had been much influenced by the Germans, their culture, and language through the Teutonic Order and the Baltic German landed and bourgeois elite that had survived the Russification policies of the Tsars. In Courland these Germans made up some 10 percent of the total population, the remainder of which were Latvian peasants and workers.[65] Likely pondering the rapid assimilation of Germans in the American upper Midwest that he had seen firsthand, Sering believed that through liberal policies tolerating Latvian

---

[63] SBB Krieg 1914/24896, Max Sering, "Bericht über die eroberten Gebiete des Nordostens. Auf Grund einer zweimonatigen Studienreise," n.d. [Sept. 1915], 2–3.
[64] Ibid., 4–5.   [65] Ibid., 5–8.

language elementary school instruction and Latvian associational activity, good administration, and integration of Latvians into German economic life, the adaptable Latvian population would gradually be assimilated and ultimately Germanized. Sering claimed that the Latvian population had been reduced by roughly one half by Russian wartime deportation and resettlement in Siberia, and the remaining population was only growing very slowly while that of German peasants in Courland was growing robustly. He noted, too, that available settler land was in great abundance, both domain lands and empty or indebted Latvian peasant holdings. Thus an energetic German colonization effort supported by the state would be able to purchase hundreds of thousands of hectares of land. German colonists form Russia and Germany could be settled on these lands and would over time facilitate with aid of modern drainage, fertilization, and machinery a two to threefold increase in agricultural productivity.[66]

The Lithuanian governorates of Suwalki, Vilna, and Kovno were, by contrast, more agriculturally backward and much more densely settled with Lithuanian peasants. While the Lithuanians, too, could be Germanized, this would be a more difficult task, as the landed aristocracy was not German as in Courland but Polish or Russian, and the bourgeoisie of the towns and cities was Jewish or Polish or had been Polonized. Given these conditions and the sheer density of settlement, Sering argued that German colonization in the three governorates was currently out of the question.[67] That said, the negative reaction to Russification efforts, Tsarist repression of Catholicism, the corrupt Russian administration, and the growth of a Lithuanian national movement were all auspicious for German control of the governorates. Sering even reported that Lithuanians expected significant economic advantages from integration into the German Customs Union. With a tactful and tolerant administration that respected the local culture and language, quite on their own Lithuanians seeking upward economic mobility and political progress would be drawn to the German language. Rather than autonomy of the sort granted to Alsace-Lorraine, Sering recommended integration of these governorates into Prussia as self-governing provinces, but only after the Polish and Russian landed aristocracy had been removed by forced sale of their estates to the state, with more compensation offered to the Poles in Russian Polish and Belarusian domain lands and forests. That would have the benefit of eventually opening some of these Lithuanian lands to German colonization.[68]

With regard to the conquered Russian Polish territories to the south and east (Congress Poland), Sering recommended a much looser association with Germany on account of both the strong cultural and national identity of the Poles and the extraordinarily high density of its rural population. This would

---

[66] Ibid., 9–16.   [67] Ibid., 16–20.   [68] Ibid., 21–25.

include entry into a German foreign policy, military, and economic compact, including integration into the German Customs Union and transportation network. Sering also considered alleviating Polish population pressures by annexing to Poland contiguous western Belarusian lands.[69]

The overall vision for the "New Germany" in the Baltic sketched out by Sering was of creating an agricultural colonial hinterland that would be able to deliver wood, wheat, flax, animal fodder, milk, poultry, and hardy agricultural laborers from Lithuania, and settler lands for Germans in Courland. Both Lithuania and Courland would gradually be assimilated into "Germandom" as contiguous colonies. As the Lithuanians and Latvians would be exposed to the agricultural, economic, administrative, educational, and cultural advantages offered by Germany, they would adopt the German language and assimilate. With an eye to the yet-to-be conquered governorates of Livonia and Estonia, Sering saw additional such possibilities for settler colonialism and gradual assimilation.[70] In any case, the vision here for the Lithuanians and Latvians is a liberal imperialism tied to the promise of administrative, economic, educational, and civilizational progress enabled by integration and assimilation much like the US conquest of former Mexican territory in the West after the Mexican-American War of 1846–48.

Sering would take up the matter of Poland in greater detail following a second wartime investigative journey through conquered Russian Congress Poland in the spring of 1916. By this point occupied Poland was under a joint Austro-German civil administration and its future status a point of dispute between Vienna and Berlin. Like the German military, Sering was opposed to an integration of Congress Poland into the Habsburg monarchy as was being discussed in the first half of 1915. Sering sought instead a quasi-independent Poland linked to the Reich. In his memorandum, Sering made the case for this as a military buffer state to Russia and a vital interest to Germany. He criticized the proposal to unify Congress Poland and Galicia and its integration into the Habsburg monarchy, which on account of the abysmal performance of its military and dubiousness of a loose "Trialist" Austrian German, Polish, and Magyar administrative structure, would weaken German and Magyar influence and offer no adequate protection to the eastern frontiers of the German Empire. Instead, Sering proposed splitting off Galicia and combining it with Congress Poland into an independent Polish kingdom and installing a scion from a Habsburg branch line as its king. While Sering acknowledged the improbability of the Habsburg court ever agreeing to that, he nevertheless believed that Germany could well live with an independent Polish state linked militarily and economically to the Reich.[71]

---

[69] Ibid., 26.    [70] Ibid., 27–29.

In making this proposal more concrete, Sering argued that Germany would offer Poland protection from Russia and would have an interest in maximizing Poland's economic development as part of the defense of "*Mitteleuropa.*" Poland's entry into trade and transportation agreements with Germany would allow Poland to become an economic intermediary between Russia and Germany, which would be premised on the retention of Poland's commercial links to Russia. Germany's ports in Bremen, Hamburg, and Danzig and the German railway network would finally give Poland access to needed overseas raw materials like cotton, wool, animal skins, raw silk, jute, saltpeter, and phosphates for its textile and shoe industry and its agriculture. German and Polish coal and iron ore mining and iron production in Upper Silesia, Dombrowa, and southern Poland would likewise much benefit from an expanded bilateral trade that had long been systematically hindered by Russian tariffs and other restrictions not in Poland's interests.[72] Bad Russian farm policy and poor administration in Poland had likewise hindered rural investment in land improvement, schools, river navigation, roads, telegraph and telephone networks, and sanitation. These needed investments could only come from Germany but were premised on close economic and military ties between the two countries. Sering believed that they would in a few decades raise Poland's "*allgemeiner Kulturzustand*" (general civilizational standing) to the level of neighboring Prussian Posen.[73]

Sering argued that German industry would have nothing to fear from Polish competition in finished goods, as the lion's share of these were consumed domestically or purchased by Lithuania, Suwalki, Courland, and especially Russia. Thus lower tariffs on Polish industrial exports would have to be negotiated in any peace treaty with Russia. Nevertheless, after having toured through Polish industrial regions and inspecting many cotton and woolen textile factories and observing their workers, Sering was convinced that Poland would be able to assert itself on the world market. He noted that representatives of Polish industry had greater hopes for commercial links with Germany than with Austria-Hungary on account of superior German organization and efficiency. Integration into the Austro-Hungarian Empire would, they argued, have certain benefits in terms of access to important raw materials but would ultimately "paralyze" the Polish economy and hinder Poland's integration into the "world market" (*Weltmarkt*).[74] With respect to the problem of insufficient arable land given Poland's rural overpopulation, Sering repeated his suggestion of annexing to Poland parts of the German-occupied Grodno and Minsk governorates in Belarusia. The Belarusians in these territories, Sering argued, were still an "amorphous mass" without national consciousness and easily

---

[71] BArch M, N 253 Nl. Tirpitz, Nr. 146, Max Sering, "Die Zukunft Polens," July 29, 1916, fols. 114–16.
[72] Ibid., fols. 117–20.   [73] Ibid., fols. 121–22.   [74] Ibid., fols. 124–27.

assimilated into Poland. This would have the added benefit of giving the Poles an incentive to participate in the war to secure these lands to the east.[75]

Sering and the Society for the Promotion of Inner Colonization worked to advance the plans for the east outlined in these two memoranda. This culminated in an article that Sering wrote for a special edition of the monthly *Der Panther* devoted to inner colonization in October 1916.[76] In December, after wartime censorship had been lifted on war aims, the society held its second general meeting devoted to this topic in the rooms of the Prussian Chamber of Deputies attended by a large number of parliamentarians, members of the Prussian Ministry of State, the Oberpräsident of Provincial Saxony, undersecretary of the Prussian Finance Ministry, and the president of the Royal Prussian Settlement Commission.[77] As in the case of Schumacher's war aims memorandum, Fritz Fischer judged Sering's wartime memoranda and writings on the Baltic and Poland as highly influential to official German war aims in the east. As noted, Sering was a close collaborator with Schwerin, the man Fischer considered the "driving force of annexationist and settlement initiatives" during the war and most important advisor to Bethmann Hollweg on annexation of territories in the Russian Empire.[78] Indeed, Bethmann Hollweg and von Jagow's ideas for annexing a Polish border strip and Baltic territories were based on reports and memoranda compiled by Schwerin and Sering, and for the Baltic in particular by the reports that Sering had written.[79]

There was a wide gulf between liberal imperial theory and praxis. For the duration of the war the occupied Baltic (Lithuania, Grodno, Vilna, and Courland) remained a fiefdom of the German Army Oberkommando Ost (Ober Ost), established in September 1915 under Erich Ludendorff. Unlike in Russian Poland, no national appeals went out to the inhabitants of Ober Ost, leaving no doubt that these lands were to be annexed, later confirmed by numerous statements made by Bethmann Hollweg and other senior German leaders throughout the war.[80] Ober Ost subsequently saw much policy

---

[75] Ibid., fols. 127–28.
[76] Max Sering, "Ansiedlungsverhältnisse und Siedlungsmöglichkeiten in den besetzten Gebieten des Ostens," *Der Panther* 4, no. 10 (Oct. 1916): 1265–76; BArch K, N 1210 Nl. Sering, Nr. 28, Gesellschaft zur Förderung der Inneren Kolonisation to Max Sering, Frankfurt a. O., Sept. 5, 1916.
[77] BArch K, N 1210, Nl. Sering, Nr. 28, "Aus der Reichshauptstadt: Die Gesellschaft zur Förderung der inneren Kolonisation." *Deutsche Tageszeitung*, Dec. 15, 1916; Nelson, "The Archive for Inner Colonization," in Nelson, *Germans, Poland, and Colonial Expansion*, 79–85.
[78] Fischer, *Griff nach der Weltmacht*, 126.
[79] Ibid., 127, 187–89, 242–43, 246, 344–49; Geiss, *Der polnische Grenzstreifen*, 81–107.
[80] Abba Strazhas, *Deutsche Ostpolitik im Ersten Weltkrieg: Der Fall Ober Ost 1915-1917* (Wiesbaden: Harrassowitz Verlag, 1993), 108–20.

experimentation with unmistakably colonial features, notably the many measures taken by the military to make over these conquered lands according to a utopian vision of a backward land of opportunity in need of German civilization. This involved establishing uniform and comprehensive administrative and police order with the aid of a massive staff of academically trained specialists. It also involved fully mobilizing the economy, labor, and natural resources of these lands for the war effort with the aim of self-sufficiency. To be sure, there was significant German investment in roads, bridges, railways, telegraphs, factories, and schools in Ober Ost, but such policy was attended by wide-ranging and often arbitrary administrative prohibitions, compulsions, onerous taxes, forced labor, and requisitioning of land, houses, businesses, crops, livestock, and other assets, all a clear prelude to permanent reconfiguration and absorption of Ober Ost into Germany. Central to this colonial project was of course Germanization and German settlement.[81] The common underlying assumption that Ludendorff shared with Sering, Schwerin, and others was that Ober Ost would give Germany the settler frontier that it lacked overseas, one that with comprehensive rational management would help to secure Germany's position as a world power.

Though also subject to severe wartime requisitioning, resource extraction, and forced labor, life was somewhat less oppressive in German-occupied Poland, which had a civilian administration.[82] On November 5, 1916 a Kingdom of Poland was jointly declared by the German and Austro-Hungarian governments with the blessing of the German Army, which was eager to recruit Polish volunteers for the war with Russia. The decision was also undeniably driven by the desire to pull Austria into a German-dominated *"Mitteleuropa"* and show the world (and the center-left majority in the Reichstag) another face of German wartime policy working through newly independent protectorates to burnish its tarnished image from the violation of Belgian neutrality. Thus, in the end annexationist aims, military pragmatism, and liberal imperialist motives of the sort Sering had voiced ultimately informed this decision.[83]

Poland was promised a constitutional monarchy and nominal independence with its own army in that announcement. While a provisional state council was created later that month, the final borders of the new kingdom were an object of disagreement between Berlin and Vienna and yet to be determined. De facto Poland continued to be administered as occupied enemy

---

[81] See ibid., 27–42; Vejas Gabriel Liulevicius, *War Land on the Eastern Front: Culture, National Identity, and German Occupation in World War I* (Cambridge: Cambridge University Press, 2000), 54–81, 94–96. See also Watson, *Ring of Steel*, 398–403.

[82] See Watson, *Ring of Steel*, 407–12.

[83] Jarausch, *Enigmatic Chancellor*, 412–22; Theiner, *Sozialer Liberalismus*, 248–58. Cf. Bülow, *Denkwürdigkeiten*, vol. 3, 246–49.

territory under a German governor. Meanwhile, the proposed annexation of a Polish border strip along the Bobr, Narew, Bug, and Vistula rivers (originally developed by Schwerin in 1915) had to be reduced on account of the new Polish state to a smaller strip of territory following a line from the Narew to Ostrolenka and Mlawa, along with territorial buffers around Thorn, Kalisch, and Upper Silesia. While somewhat reduced, it subsequently evolved under Ludendorff from a defensive buffer into a Germanized agricultural frontier on which Russian Germans were to be settled after the planned forced emigration of Poles and Jews.[84] At its core this, too, was part of the bid for Germany's *Weltmachtstellung* very much analogous to the "New Germany" to be created in Ober Ost.

One year later in 1917 Sering repeated his belief in the importance of an expanded eastern frontier, but now with the added theme of a closer defensive union of the central European nations and new satellite states in western Russia. By this point he had become active with Rathgen, Schulze-Gaevernitz, and Heinrich Herkner in pressing for Naumann's idea of "*Mitteleuropa*" even before the conclusion of peace.[85] In the introduction of an edited book on the future of western Russia with chapters on Finland, the Baltic provinces, Lithuania, Poland, the Ukraine, German colonization in Russia, and the "*Ostjudenfrage*" (eastern Jewish question), Sering argued once again that it was the large-scale settlement of unpopulated and underpopulated temperate zone regions of the world by Europeans made possible by steamships, transcontinental railways, and telegraphs that had created the giant world empires of the United States, the British Empire, and Russia that had tipped the balance of world power over the last two generations. Their railway "imperialism" supplied the rest of the world with food and raw materials, but the idea of autarky animated many of these settler colonies, he claimed, notably the United States, Canada, Australia, and Russia. In the United States this was combined with violent expansionism into Texas, the southern Rockies, the Pacific, Spanish Empire, and the Panama Canal Zone, while the Monroe Doctrine declared US hegemony over Central and South America. Russia had likewise expanded into Central and East Asia, while the British Empire had expanded into Egypt, Indochina, the Transvaaal, and other places.[86]

Sering argued that this only became a danger to the central European states with Britain's entry into the Entente with France and Russia, a deliberate attempt to check German progress as it had with all other economic and naval rivals in the past. And now in alliance with the United States, Britain, France, and Russia were jointly threatening the Central Powers and all other smaller nations, with the ultimate outcome being the extinction of their political

---

[84] Geiss, *Der polnische Grenzstreifen*, 121–44.   [85] Krüger, *Nationalökonomen*, 174.
[86] Max Sering, ed., *Westrußland in seiner Bedeutung für die Entwicklung Mitteleuropas* (Leipzig: B. G. Teubner, 1917), xiv–xvii.

independence and linguistic-cultural plurality. The "union of giant world empires," he wrote, was a "syndicate for the suppression of European nation-states and the smaller and weaker nations more generally."[87] It was clear from the Paris economic conference, he wrote, that England and its allies intended from the beginning to wage a war not just against armies and navies but also against German settlers, merchants, shipping company heads, and industrialists through robbery "in the spirit of brutal mercantilism."[88]

Revealing once again the importance of Sering's North American reference point, he argued that nowhere had he been more impressed with the value of Germans and their culture than in North America, where their talents and energies enjoyed an "unknown independence" under conditions of freedom, but the assimilationist pressures and superficial leveling tendencies of the United States and its oligarchic democracy had worked to destroy that culture and identity.[89] Now, Sering implied, the giant leveling empires were threatening the core of Europe. "*Mitteleuropa*" was the last stand to defend European independence and cultural plurality, a countervailing force to the giant world empires.[90]

Sering argued that the basis for an independent Poland was given, but elsewhere in the occupied east the picture was ethnographically too mixed for independence. Rather, the relative sparsity of the population along with its underdevelopment justified settlement with Germans, namely the estimated two million Russian Germans who had been driven from their farms by the Russians. Seemingly unaware or untroubled by the brutal realities of Ober Ost and Poland under German occupation, Sering argued that closer economic and political links with Germany had undeniable advantages for these people, as they would enjoy a greater degree of autonomy of their culture and language than under Russian rule and the advantages of a more complex division of labor enabled by the elimination of trade barriers. German war aims in the east, Sering argued, sought to free the subject nations from Russia's stifling and uniform imperial yoke and integrate them into a central European economic and defensive union.[91] Even stronger than in his memoranda on the Baltic states and Poland from 1915 and 1916, here Sering justified German annexations and the creation of German-linked satellite states in the Ukraine and elsewhere as offering the liberation of Russian subject peoples, greater cultural and linguistic plurality and autonomy, and economic progress. Once again, the North American reference point for this liberal imperial vision is unmistakable throughout this piece.

Just such a liberal imperialist vision was supported by the center-left Reichstag majority and informed Foreign Secretary Richard von Kühlmann's

---

[87] Ibid., xviii–xix.  [88] Ibid., xx.  [89] Ibid., xxi–xxii.  [90] Ibid., xxiv.
[91] Ibid., xxvi–xxxi.

negotiations with the Bolshevik leadership in Brest beginning on December 22, 1917, following the armistice with the new Soviet government earlier that month. While the resulting treaty is often held up as an example of German wartime rapacity, it reflected a coherent German strategy already begun in Poland, Lithuania, and Courland for a new system of states in eastern Europe built on the principle of popular legitimacy. It was also a peace that the Bolshevik leadership could only refuse with rank hypocrisy, as it offered a modicum of independence to non-Russian subject peoples in Courland, Estonia, Livonia, Lithuania, Poland, and the Ukraine who had suffered much Tsarist political and religious persecution.[92] To be sure, the German negotiations were much shaped by representatives of the OHL who made it plain to the Russian delegation that they were about to lose control over much of western Russia. The Bolsheviks walked out of these negotiations on February 10 and soon thereafter German troops entered Livonia and Estonia, closed in on Petrograd, and advanced to hold Kiev and most of the Ukraine. Thus when the Bolsheviks again sued for peace nine days later a much more overtly imperialist program of domination asserted itself, one that was ultimately dictated to the Bolshevik leadership by the OHL and signed March 3, 1918. The final terms imposed the permanent loss of the Polish, Lithuanian, and Courland governorates, the recognition of an independent Finland and Ukraine, German occupation of Estonia, Livonia, and most of Belarusia, Russian withdrawal from eastern Anatolia, Armenia, and part of Georgia, and the complete demobilization of the Russian army.[93]

While the Treaty of Brest-Litovsk did not involve formal German annexations and was approved by an overwhelming Reichstag majority March 22, it would prove both a diplomatic and military liability. Reconciliation with Russia following such a dictated peace was out of the question, revealing how thoroughly German diplomacy had been militarized. It was also a clear example of the draconian peace terms that France and Britain could expect with a German victory, unmasking previous German peace initiatives and the Reichstag's July 1917 Peace Resolution as hypocrisy. Over twenty German divisions would be tied up in the expansive military occupation of former Russian territory, units that might otherwise have been available as reserve forces for the last-ditch western offensive that began March 21, 1918.[94] More on that to follow.

---

[92] Wilhelm Ribhegge, *Frieden für Europa: Die Politik der deutschen Reichstagsmehrheit 1917/18* (Essen: Reimar Hobbing, 1988), 201–8; Tooze, *Deluge*, 114–15; Watson, *Ring of Steel*, 492–95.

[93] Fischer, *Griff nach der Weltmacht*, 647–62, 708–78; Ribhegge, *Frieden für Europa*, 208–74; Ritter, *Staatskunst*, vol. 4, 109–45; Tooze, *Deluge*, 124–40.

[94] Afflerbach, *Auf Messers Schneide*, 392–97; Ritter, *Staatskunst*, vol. 4, 145–50.

## The Jewish Question

While the war aims debate was a major source of polarization within Germany in 1916–17, other wartime controversies worked to divide Germany and undermine the wartime *Burgfrieden*, perhaps none more openly and viciously than the controversy over the Jewish contributions to the war effort. The debacle of the battle of Verdun, the bloodbath of the Somme, acute manpower problems, strikes and riots in response to growing food shortages, and dissatisfaction with the government of Bethmann Hollweg created a noxious climate in the autumn of 1916 in which scapegoats were sought for a war that showed no sign of ending in victory. The force of anti-Semitic suspicion of wartime shirking in particular began to grow within the army. On October 11, 1916 Minister of War Adolf Wild von Hohenborn (1860–1925) was pressed to order a notorious internal survey of Jewish participation in the war effort.[95] This *Judenzählung* ("Jew count") sought to determine how many Jews fit for military duty were serving in German Army units and whether their service was on the front line or in the rear. A little over one week later, the Center Party leader Matthias Erzberger, who had himself learned of the military's *Judenzählung*, requested that the chancellor conduct a survey of income and religious affiliation of those employed in various war corporations.[96] While it was never granted, this shameless attempt to exploit allegations of "Jewish war profiteering" for political purposes together with revelations of the military's internal survey on the floor of Reichstag shocked the German Jewish community and deeply insulted Jews serving on the front.[97]

Of those appalled by this development and its implications for the war effort was Max Warburg.[98] In early November he wrote the War Ministry and Reich Chancellery demanding an apology. The ministry denied any prejudice and defended the count.[99] It also refused to rescind the count or clear the nimbus of suspicion with the statistical results of the survey, which would have shown that Jews were serving on the front proportionate to their overall population compared to non-Jews: some 100,000 of an overall Jewish population of 550,000 served in the military, over 10,000 alone as volunteers. Indeed, already

---

[95] Werner T. Angress, "The German Army's 'Judenzählung' of 1916: Genesis – Consequences – Significance," *Leo Baeck Institute Year Book* XXIII (1978): 117–35, here 117–25; Tim Grady, *A Deadly Legacy: German Jews and the Great War* (New Haven and London: Yale University Press, 2017), 134–40.

[96] Angress, "The German Army's 'Judenzählung,'" 125; Werner Jochmann, "Die Ausbreitung des Antisemitismus," in *Deutsches Judentum in Krieg und Revolution*, ed. Werner E. Mosse (Tübingen: J. C. B. Mohr, 1971), 409–510, here 424.

[97] Angress, "Judenzählung," 125–27; Jochmann, "Die Ausbreitung," 426–27; Grady, *A Deadly Legacy*, 140–42.

[98] WIA, IV. 69, Max Warburg to Aby Warburg, Oct. 29, 1916.

[99] Grady, *A Deadly Legacy*, 142.

by November 1915 some 710 Jews had been promoted into officer commissions and some 5,000 were awarded the Iron Cross. By war's end some 2,000 would be promoted as officers and 35,000 would receive war decorations of various kinds.[100] Regardless, this confessionalization of the German war effort made anti-Semitic rumor and innuendo respectable and marked an important moment in the history of the Jewish experience in Germany because it called into question, in the most stark manner possible, the basic premises of emancipation, integration, and assimilation, just as it dishonored the extraordinary sacrifices Jews had made in the war and alienated those in the field whose loyalty and willingness to sacrifice was essential if Germany hoped to prevail against numerically and materially superior foes.

In December 1916, in the shadow of the *Judenzählung*, Gustav Schmoller reviewed two books for his *Jahrbuch*. The books were Hans Delbrück's *Regierung und Volkswille* (1914) and Hugo Preuß's (1860–1925) *Das deutsche Volk und die Politik* (1915), both tackling thorny questions about the proper relationship between the German people and their political leadership.[101] In most respects the review was typical of the hundreds Schmoller had penned for his *Jahrbuch*. A monarchist and Prussophile who supported the reform of Prussia's three-class suffrage system but rejected full-scale parliamentarization of the Reich, Schmoller took issue with Hugo Preuß's claim that Germany's political development had been retarded by the perpetuation of authoritarian structures that had hindered the involvement of its citizens in politics.[102] Entirely out of character, however, were his comments about Preuß's activities as "one of the chiefs of Berlin's municipal left-liberals, who, socially supported by Semitic millions, more or less rule our city."[103] He mentioned further that in such circles the political horizon and judgment suffered from the conviction that "in their midst there is such a superiority of intelligence, character and talent that it is unjust and damaging for the state and society that their tightly-knit circle has not fully conquered the universities, the army, and the senior civil service the way they have the city of Berlin and its administration."[104]

While Schmoller conceded a kernel of truth in Preuß's claims and praised his scholarly credentials, he did not agree that Germany's authoritarian system violated the constitutional guarantee of legal equality because some of its citizens still happened to suffer discrimination due to their national origin,

---

[100] Jacob Segall, *Die deutschen Juden als Soldaten im Kriege 1914–1918* (Berlin: Philo-Verlag, 1921), 11, 19, 27–29, 35–38; Wehler, *Gesellschaftsgeschichte*, vol. 4, 128, 131–32.

[101] Gustav Schmoller, "Obrigkeitsstaat und Volksstaat: Ein missverständlicher Gegensatz," *SJ* 40 (1916): 2031–42; reprinted in Gustav Schmoller, *Walter Rathenau und Hugo Preuß: Die Staatsmänner des Neuen Deutschland* (Munich and Leipzig: Duncker & Humblot, 1922), 21–43.

[102] Krüger, *Nationalökonomen*, 205, 207, 211.

[103] Schmoller, *Walter Rathenau und Hugo Preuß*, 24.    [104] Ibid.

religious convictions, political views, or membership in the labor movement.[105] He retorted that "it is not nearly generally correct that we grossly injure the legal equality of our constitution because individual government offices are still not accessible to each unbaptized Jewish applicant, because certain regiments still use their free voting rights to exclude Jews, because not yet all of the many Jewish lecturers in the universities become professors as rapidly as they believe their talent deserves."[106] Adding insult to injury and giving a *völkisch* accent to his anti-Semitic remarks, Schmoller continued his review by writing that

> The great ideal of political and legal equality of rights can only be implemented in such a tempo as the *Volksbewußtsein* [people's consciousness] has adapted itself to the standpoint of the law. Its execution finds hindrances from time to time where a minority of race, of faith etc. seeks rapidly, through free admittance, to make itself the intolerant ruler of the state, the administration in question, the relevant organs, respectively. How rapidly have Jewish lecturers and professors grown in number! How quickly have Jews achieved it that for years in individual clinics only Jewish assistant physicians were employed, how true has the prophesy been shown that in certain faculties the first Jewish full professor would be followed in ten years by five and more. Prejudice against Jews in Prussian political life is close to disappearing and currently it seems to be making room for the opposite in certain places.[107]

The initial reaction to Schmoller's book review of Hugo Preuß was swift. By late December 1916–early January 1917 most of Germany's papers had reported on his review and taken a position on his views. It is astounding that a book review relegated to the back pages of an academic journal could have had such a public impact. This can only be explained by the sensitive climate of opinion produced by the *Judenzählung* and the prominence of the person making these anti-Semitic comments.

One of the first and pithiest papers to comment was the *Berliner Tageblatt*, which noted that in trying to protect the old "*Obrigkeitsstaat*," Schmoller was "in part exaggerating the facts to an extraordinary degree, and in part appealing to base instincts."[108] The *Frankfurter Zeitung* was appalled by what it saw as Schmoller's "tactless anti-Semitism" normally confined to the ultra-conservative and anti-Semitic press.[109] Papers with a specifically Jewish readership did not hide their profound disappointment that a man of Schmoller's stature would stoop to such lows. The *Deutsche Israelitische Zeitung* wrote:

---

[105] Ibid., 23, 24–25.   [106] Ibid., 26.
[107] Ibid., 26–27. Cf. Walther Rathenau, "Staat und Judentum: Eine Polemik" [1911], in *Walther Rathenau: Gesammelte Schriften*, vol. 1 (Berlin: S. Fischer, 1918), 183–207.
[108] "Schmoller gegen den Berliner Freisinn," *BerlinerTageblatt*, Dec. 27, 1916.
[109] "Volksstaat und Gleichberechtigung," *Frankfurter Zeitung*, Jan. 9, 1917 (evening edition).

"One has the impression that it is dear to great Herr Schmoller's heart that the discrimination of Jews could end. That is why he has put himself on the anti-Semitic horse. Not pretty from a man of the reputation of Herr von Schmoller."[110] On the other hand, the anti-Semitic *Die Wahrheit* praised Schmoller's review because it "finally expressed things that others had not dared to say," but it added that Schmoller should have gone further.[111]

Liberal Jewish papers, such as the *Korrespondenz des Centralvereins*, took issue with Schmoller's casual use of statistics in supporting his claims about the number of physician assistants and professors in German universities. In fact, it claimed, only some 1 percent of German professors were Jewish.[112] The editor of the *Deutsche medizinische Wochenschrift* took this even further by refuting, with hard numbers, Schmoller's statements about the supposed Jewish dominance of certain medical clinics. In fact, there was not a single Jewish full professor in any of the German medical faculties, only a few converted Jews.[113] With some bitterness he wrote: "Every true friend of the fatherland must be most painfully moved by the insult that in this area of culture Germany is not on the same level as our western enemies."[114] It seems few were satisfied with what Schmoller had written.

Max Warburg was disturbed to see such a prominent member of Germany's academic establishment legitimating anti-Semitic prejudice and was moved to respond. In a January 1917 letter to Schmoller he wrote:

> Your recent comments about Preuss and Delbrück induce me to send you a manuscript that I have recently completed and which deals with the Jewish question. I also attach a small excerpt from the will of Frederick the Great.
>
> The Jewish question interests me not only as a Jew, but also in the interest of the state. I do not have the impression that you, as far as I understand your comments, do justice to this so important question. I do not seek anything for myself but am simply inspired by the wish to make use of those strengths in Germany which we necessarily need. If we do not do this then the struggle in which we are engaging would in some sense be a mistake. It would interest me much to know of your views of my manuscript, which I ask you to treat with confidentiality.[115]

---

[110] "Professor von Schmoller bei den Antisemiten," *Deutsche Israelitische Zeitung*, Jan. 4, 1917.
[111] "Die Zurückgestellten," *Die Wahrheit*, Jan. 13, 1917.
[112] "Excellenz von Schmollers Universitätsstatistik," *Korrespondenz des Centralvereins deutscher Staatsbürger jüdischen Glaubens*, Jan. 13, 1917.
[113] GStA PK VI. HA Nl. Schmoller, Nr. 1, fols. 328–35, J. Schwalbe to Gustav Schmoller, Jan. 11, 1917.
[114] Ibid.
[115] HHStA Abt. 1088 Teilnachlass Gustav Schmoller, Nr. 11, Max Warburg to Gustav Schmoller, Jan. 6, 1917.

Warburg's manuscript was titled "The Jewish Question in Relation to Overall German Policy." An initial draft of it had been penned in June of 1916, but this was significantly revised with the aid of his brother Aby (1866–1929) in light of the growing anti-Semitism in the late summer and autumn of 1916.[116] Indeed, Warburg had been one of the first prominent German Jews to express his resentment over the *Judenzählung* publicly in November of 1916.[117] In his piece on the "Jewish question," Warburg focused on securing a lasting *Burgfrieden* by working to overcome the ongoing hostility to Jews in Germany. Anti-Semitic prejudices, in particular the exclusion of Jews from reserve officer commissions and the execution of the notorious "Jew count," had given Germany a negative image abroad. Such discrimination also discouraged those whose talents and strengths Germany needed in order to prevail in war. Warburg, making reference to Jewish emigration from Germany, noted that anti-Semitism had cost Germany many able-bodied and talented people in the past, many of whom now enriched states aligned against Germany. It was above all necessary to teach religious tolerance in schools, which had too often become academies for anti-Semitism. Likewise, Germany was one of the few countries where Jews were not promoted to senior positions in government. Humanism and tolerance, he concluded, would greatly improve Germany's position abroad.[118] Thus Warburg identified anti-Semitism as an important hindrance to both Germany's *Weltgeltung* and its war effort.

Schmoller was himself sharply stung by these and other criticisms, so much so that he immediately penned a response and did not wait to publish it in the next number of his *Jahrbuch*. Thus on January 16, 1917 "Die Heutige deutsche Judenfrage" (The Contemporary German Jewish Question) was published in the *Tägliche Rundschau*, a newspaper read widely by those in the liberal professions.[119] In this piece Schmoller was unrepentant about his anti-Semitic remarks, noting that in his review of Preuß and Delbrück he had "added a few completely harmless comments about the fact that mistreated citizens appear here and there in this and that influential position almost as a ruling element."[120] He wrote that he was taken by surprise by the storm of anger in the Jewish and philo-Semitic press and praise in the anti-Semitic press, all of which he chalked up to inadequate discussion of the content of his review. Since he was in no position to respond to the "mountains of mail" he had

---

[116] WIA, IV. 69, Max Warburg to Aby Warburg, June 13, 1916; WIA, FC, Aby Warburg to Max Warburg 25 [Oct. or Nov.?] 1916; WIA, IV. 69, Max Warburg to Aby Warburg, Nov. 25, 1916.

[117] Angress, "Judenzählung," 128–30.

[118] HHStA Abt. 1088 Teilnachlass Gustav Schmoller, Nr. 11, Max Warburg, "Die Judenfrage im Rahmen der deutschen Gesamtpolitik."

[119] Gustav Schmoller, "Die heutige deutsche Judenfrage," *Tägliche Rundschau*, Jan. 16, 1917; also published in *SJ* 41 (1917): 563–67; reprinted in *Zwanzig Jahre*, 177–81.

[120] Schmoller, *Zwanzig Jahre*, 177.

received, he had chosen to write a response articulating his position on the "Jewish question." He began his arguments by making mention of the fact the he himself had lifelong neither been a philo-Semite nor an anti-Semite and that he had "some of my best friends under Jews and half-Jews," possibly a reference to men like Dernburg, von Halle, and Sering but effectively underscoring the racial definition of Jewishness he had introduced in his book review.[121]

Taking an historical perspective, Schmoller discussed the evolution of the relationship between "different races, peoples and religious communities," referring to the fate of the Jews in the Middle Ages as "the fate of racially alien minorities everywhere in cultural history."[122] He then made mention of the dawning realization of the equality of mankind that came with the Enlightenment of the eighteenth century, which was expressed in the political ideas of the nineteenth century, notably legal equality. However, he added that if such ideas were to bear fruit they must be combined with an assimilation as was already occurring in the upper classes of the "racially alien minority."[123] Schmoller then noted that the assimilation of upper-class Jews in Germany had made great progress since 1848–70, marked by growing conversion of Jews to Christian confessions. Nevertheless, assimilation was far from complete. It was hindered by "Jewbaiting by those Germans [*Germanen*] hit by Jewish competition and by the steady immigration of non-assimilated eastern Jewish elements, by the still existing closed-off nature of Jewish circles, especially among middle and lower class Jews."[124] Unlike in France and Britain where the number of Jews was far smaller and where Jewish immigration had been from a Jewish aristocracy of assimilated or semi-assimilated Jews from Italy, Portugal, and Spain, Germany's Jewish immigrants came from the east and resisted assimilation for one or two generations. The agents of assimilation were common schooling and university education, literature, a common world of thought, social intercourse, and most intensively, intermarriage.[125]

Asking himself what could be achieved, he concluded that "an expulsion of all Jews from Germany is impossible, would be a barbarity, would do harm to our culture. All higher culture, the current stock of highest-standing cultures, rest on a mixing of races. . . . We thus have no cause to think that the existence of 615,021 Israelites in a German population of 60 million is problematic. Yes, it would seem that there are convincing reasons to speak of the contrary."[126] Schmoller then said of western German Jewry that it was the most assimilated and "a favorable addition to the Germanic race. It gives us intellectual strength that we more or less lack, or which we lacked in the past; it has very much benefited the German economy."[127] But, he added:

---

[121] Ibid.  [122] Ibid., 178.  [123] Ibid.  [124] Ibid., 178–79.  [125] Ibid., 179.
[126] Ibid.  [127] Ibid.

It carries with it the danger that through its commercial superiority, which it still often exploits through many dubious means, it generates social discord and struggles. The tendency of the Jew, where he is in a position of influence or power, to disadvantage the German [*Germanen*] and Christian is still so frequently at hand that real setbacks in the Jew-friendly attitude of all liberals recur and that ill-feeling among conservative, peasant, small trade, and home industrial circles has not yet disappeared to the extent that it has in western Europe. It is therefore in the interest of the Jews not to dominate certain positions, occupations, and offices excessively and to avoid making such dominance too visible.[128]

Having established what he saw as a way to master the current challenges to full Jewish assimilation, Schmoller returned to some of the issues that had animated his review of Preuß's book, namely Jewish dominance of Berlin's city government and the discrimination of Jews in the officer corps, in effect justifying certain remaining discriminations against Jews in the interest of social harmony.[129] Schmoller concluded his essay by making reference to Lessing's play, *Nathan der Weise*: "If we only had *Nathan-Naturen* among the 600,000 German Jews there would today hardly be a Jewish question; but we also have *Shylock-Naturen*, and the majority of Jews perhaps stand somewhere in between these two extremes."[130] He finished with a call for conciliation between Christians and Jews and expressed his assurance that in a hundred years most of what was the source of complaints on both sides would be overcome. Yet he added: "But the existing beliefs of the masses and the corresponding customs cannot be changed from today to tomorrow."[131]

As Schmoller's essay on the "Jewish question" makes abundantly clear, Schmoller had a basically racial understanding of both "Germanness" and "Jewishness," and while he acknowledged the cultural value of racial mixing, this was only desirable in as much as the "racially alien" element was eventually wholly dissolved into the host race. That is, Schmoller's notion of assimilation had as its final consequence the elimination of Jews as both a people and a religion. It is in this respect particularly revealing that he was willing to discuss Jewish expulsion from Germany, even if he then rejected it as a "barbarity" and as culturally harmful. Instead, Schmoller preferred elimination by way of assimilation. Other aspects of Schmoller's anti-Semitism, notably the social and economic elements, were part of a very familiar repertoire of anti-Semitic prejudices that in effect made Jews responsible for anti-Semitism and thus do not deserve much unpacking or further comment. These prejudices stand as Schmoller's justifications for the remaining discriminations against German Jews, which he believed would give way over time and

---

[128] Ibid., 179–80.  [129] Ibid., 180.  [130] Ibid., 180–81.  [131] Ibid., 181.

through assimilation to full equality. Following Schmoller's strained logic, however, full equality was predicated on the complete disappearance of Jewry. As discussed in Chapter 8, the colonial encounter, *Weltpolitik*, the violent suppression of colonial uprisings, and the bitter politics of the colonial crisis and "Hottentot elections" of 1906-7 – along with the mass dissemination of imperialist propaganda during and after the elections – had worked to racialize German nationhood in its new imperial form. Schmoller had hardly been a passive participant in that process.

The response to Schmoller's provocative essay on the "Jewish question" was, like the reaction to his earlier book review, quite critical, but it also revealed shifts in positions that suggested a convergence of opinion. The liberal Jewish press responded with indignation. For example, the *Deutsche Israelitische Zeitung*, making reference to the concluding sentence of Schmoller's essay where he mentioned the impossibility of overnight changes to public attitudes, wrote: "That today has already lasted 150-200 years. Is that not enough?! It is time that it becomes tomorrow and tomorrow. When one reads the sentence 'an expulsion of the Jews from Germany is impossible' one has to reflect if it is really 1917 or 1519."[132] The *Israelitisches Familienblatt* was even less sparing. It claimed that Schmoller's attempt to elaborate his position was a fudge, combining the trivial with the untrue. It demonstrated the inability to turn anti-Semitism into a science. It is an instinct.[133] A few weeks later the *Jüdische Rundschau* wrote that every few months now the German Jewish community hears of yet another case of a German of high intellectual standing expressing himself as an anti-Semite. This was particularly embarrassing in the case of Schmoller: "There is no other lesson in the case of Schmoller than that within the bounds of an undoubtedly important teacher there can also reside a petty, insignificant politician."[134] In a later issue of the *Deutsche Israelitische Zeitung*, Schmoller's racism was roundly criticized: "Where in Germany are the traceable Germans [*Germanen*]? This is the manner of the Stöckerite terminology."[135]

On the opposite end of the spectrum, anti-Semitic papers and journals criticized Schmoller's argument that the Jews should be assimilated into the German people through intermarriage. In *Der Hammer* the anti-Semitic firebrand Artur Dinter (1876-1948) argued that the German and Jewish races were too alien to each other and should therefore not be mixed, dismissing

---

[132] "Nochmals Herr von Schmoller," *Deutsche Israelitische Zeitung*, Jan. 25, 1917.
[133] "Herr von Schmoller und die Judenfrage," *Israelitisches Familienblatt*, Feb. 1, 1917.
[134] "Der Fall Schmoller," *Jüdische Rundschau*, Feb. 23, 1917.
[135] "Eine gründliche Abfuhr des Geh-Rats Prof. v. Schmoller," *Deutsche Israelitische Zeitung*, March 1, 1917. A reference to the anti-Semitic court preacher and Christian Social Party politician Adolf Stöcker (1835-1909).

**Figure 12.3**   Gustav Schmoller ca. 1915.

Schmoller's "humanitarian-liberal ideas" out of hand.[136] Likewise, Adolf Bartels (1862–1945), drawing heavily on the racist anti-Semitism of Houston Stewart Chamberlain (1855–1927), criticized Schmoller's ideal of eventual Jewish assimilation on the grounds that this was impossible with the Jews, who in fact comprised a state within the state. A mixed race would in any case lead not to higher culture but to cultural degeneration. The Jewish question could only be solved by pure segregation.[137]

As in the case of his review of Hugo Preuß, Schmoller also received much mail in response to his article on the "Jewish question." One such letter was from Willi Major, a young Jewish soldier from Mannheim who was at the time serving on the front in the 8/386th Landwehr regiment. Making reference to discriminations the he knew all too personally, he wrote of the difficulties he

---

[136] GStA PK, VI. HA Nl. Schmoller, Nr. 1, fols. 101–3, Artur Dinter, "Zur Frage der Rassenmischung," *Der Hammer* 16, no. 353 (March 1, 1917).

[137] GStA PK, VI. HA Nl. Schmoller, Nr. 1, fols. 86–88, Adolf Bartels, "Die Heutige deutsche Judenfrage," *Natur und Gesellschaft* IV, no. 6 (March 1917); cf. "Gustav von Schmoller," *Auf Vorposten* 4, no. 9–10 (1917): 220–30.

had had attempting to advance beyond the rank of NCO.[138] It was the same for his four brothers, who were likewise serving in the field. He also wrote of the insults and degradations many of them had suffered, most recently the systematic removal of those Jews who had their normal posts in the rear to the front lines. He wrote that this would undoubtedly result in thousands of young Jewish businessmen emigrating from Germany after the war, just as had occurred in the 60s and 70s of the previous century:

> Germany may be happy to be rid of a part of its Jewish element (or whatever they are), but the new homeland will be even happier to have found new forces [*neue Kräfte*] for commerce in world-wide competition. The multi-billionaires of Wall Street in New York (bankers) are born Germans or of German origin. They have fought against the delivery of munitions [to the Entente powers] and have not participated in purchasing English and French war bonds.
> 
> I thought that I was German and had as my religion the Jewish faith just as one says the Catholic etc. But now we see from the highest posts that they are not playing fair [*von höchsten Stellen auf offene Karte geschielt*]. Does his Excellency know how many billions of war loans the German Jews have signed? How many Jews wounded or dead? How many have been decorated, and how few officers? If we were not Germans, *do we know for what we are bleeding?*[139]

The *Judenzählung* and the resulting debate over the "Jewish question" reflected in Schmoller's writings reveal how the fragile wartime *Burgfrieden* between Christians and Jews was broken in Germany, a country which at the time had one of the most assimilated Jewish populations in the world. It would be a decisive turning point in relations between Jews and non-Jews in Germany with profound lasting aftereffects.[140] The results of the army survey were never publicized, allowing the nimbus of suspicion to remain. In light of their extraordinary patriotism and their important roles in both prewar *Weltpolitik* and the German war effort, it was a shattering experience not just for such Jewish men in the trenches, but also prominent figures like Albert Ballin, Hermann Cohen (1842–1918), Carl Fürstenberg, Fritz Haber, Franz von Mendelssohn, Wilhelm Merton, Walther Rathenau, Henry Simon, and Max Warburg, along with many thousands of ordinary Jewish civilians.[141]

---

[138] GStA PK, VI. HA Nl. Schmoller, Nr. 1, fols. 409–10, Willi Major to Gustav Schmoller, Feb. 23, 1917.

[139] Ibid. Emphasis in the original.

[140] See Till van Rahden, *Jews and Other Germans: Civil Society, Religious Diversity and Urban Politics in Breslau, 1860–1925*, trans. Marcus Brainard (Madison: University of Wisconsin Press, 2008), 231–42; Elon, *The Pity of It All*, 311, 322, 332, 338–40; Grady, *A Deadly Legacy*, 213, 218.

[141] See, for example, Hermann Cohen, "Betrachtungen über Schmoller's Angriff," *Neue Jüdische Monatshefte* 1 (Jan. 25, 1917): 222–30; (Feb. 10, 1917): 256–60; Walther

## The Friends of the Fatherland

Almost simultaneous to the *Judenzählung* and the public controversy it unleashed, the war effort itself took another radical and divisive turn. While unrestricted submarine warfare had been suspended in May 1916, public clamor for it continued unabated and was encouraged and exploited politically by Tirpitz, his ally, the New York-born Prussian civil servant Wolfgang Kapp, and many other like-minded people in and out of the navy. This was part of the *fronde* against Bethmann Hollweg and the Kaiser that also included Crown Prince Wilhelm and ex-chancellor Bülow. As is clear from their correspondence over the summer of 1916, both Schmoller and Tirpitz still looked forward to a *Siegfrieden* and were (falsely) heartened by the outcome of the Battle of Jutland, but they had significant differences of opinion about the future of Belgium, which Schmoller (like Rathgen) wanted to preserve as a unified autonomous state but integrate into the German Customs Union as part of a consolidated "*Mitteleuropa*." Tirpitz, on the other hand, was bent as ever on annexation or otherwise direct control of Belgium, especially the Flemish coast and Antwerp.[142] Bülow, for his part, returned to Germany in May 1915 after failing to keep Italy out of the war as German ambassador to Rome. He then wrote his exculpatory *Deutsche Politik* published in the late summer of 1916, which came out strongly for submarine warfare – and that was reviewed glowingly by Schmoller in his *Jahrbuch* – in part as a gambit to position himself for a return to politics as Bethmann's possible successor, becoming active in anti-Bethmann intrigues.[143] Meanwhile the more radical and uncompromising Tirpitz supported by Kapp and others became less and less shy about attacking Bethmann Hollweg and the Kaiser directly in their campaign to resume unrestricted submarine warfare and have Tirpitz replace Bethmann, with wartime *U-Bootpolitik* gaining an urgent, righteous, and populist tone that gradually wore down those in the civilian government and the military but which also became a threat to the monarchy itself.[144]

---

Rathenau, "Eine Streitschrift vom Glauben" [1917], in *Gesammelte Schriften*, vol. 5, 97–119; Chernow, *The Warburgs*, 171–90; Ferguson, *Paper and Iron*, 141–42; Schulamit Volkov, *Walther Rathenau: Weimar's Fallen Statesman* (New Haven and London: Yale University Press, 2012), 139–45.

[142] BArch M, N 253 Nl. Tirpitz, Nr. 263, fol. 179, Gustav Schmoller to Alfred Tirpitz, June 4, 1916; GStA PK, VI. HA, Nl. Schmoller, Nr. 208b, fols. 14–15, Alfred Tirpitz to Gustav Schmoller, July 13, 1916. Gustav Schmoller, "Die Handels- und Zollannäherung Mitteleuropas," *SJ* 40 (1916): 529–50. Cf. Kelly, *Tirpitz*, 414.

[143] Bülow, *Deutsche Politik*, 39; GStA PK, VI. HA, Nl. Schmoller, Nr. 209, fol. 31, Berhard von Bülow to Gustav Schmoller, Jan. 15, 1917; Gustav Schmoller, "Fürst Bülows Politik," *SJ* 40 (1916): 1609–15; Jarausch, *Enigmatic Chancellor*, 353–62. Cf. Bülow, *Denkwürdigkeiten*, vol. 3, 234–62.

[144] Jarausch, *Enigmatic Chancellor*, 359–60; James Retallack, *Notables of the Right: The Conservative Party and Political Mobilization in Germany, 1876–1918* (Boston: Unwin

When Romania joined the Entente in August 1916 underscoring the failures of the German war effort, Falkenhayn was replaced by Paul von Hindenburg and his deputy Erich Ludendorff as head of the OHL, a duo that was more willing to take risks to achieve expansive war aims and who accumulated power at the expense of Bethmann Hollweg and the Kaiser. The Tirpitz circle and Admiralty Chief Holtzendorff subsequently focused their pressure to resume unrestricted submarine warfare on the OHL. By this point Holtzendorff was armed with new data commissioned from the Magdeburg banker Richard Fuss, the Heidelberg economist Hermann Levy, and the grain merchants Hermann Weil (1868–1927) and Henry P. Newman (1868–1917), among others, predicting a collapse of the British war effort within six months of the resumption of unrestricted submarine warfare. These predictions, as it would turn out, were based on gross underestimations of available British shipping tonnage, the ability of Britain to substitute other grains and grow its own wheat, and the potential of convoys and food rationing as countermeasures. It also miscalculated the scale of the United States' contribution in grain and credit once it was provoked to enter the conflict on the side of the Entente.[145] Max Warburg had warned of many of these very dangers in his own memorandum to Holtzendorff, which urged not provoking the United States with a renewed submarine campaign.[146]

Pressed by Kapp, Tirpitz, Holtzendorff, and Stinnes, by December 1916 Hindenburg and Ludendorff were convinced that submarines would relieve the ground war and demanded reopening unrestricted warfare by February 1, 1917, threatening their resignations if the Kaiser and Bethmann Hollweg did not follow through, a demand repeated in early January with the Kaiser told to dismiss Bethmann Hollweg if he still resisted. The Entente's humiliating rejection of Bethmann Hollweg's December peace proposal and the severe food and fuel shortages the country suffered in January 1917 seemed only to reinforce their case.[147] Reluctantly, on January 9, 1917 Bethmann Hollweg and the Kaiser made the fateful decision to resume unrestricted submarine warfare.[148] As Helfferich himself would later admit, the choice not to resign

---

Hyman, 1988), 219; Kelly, *Tirpitz*, 412; Scheck, *Alfred Tirpitz*, 35–43, 48–61; Stegman, *Die Erben Bismarcks*, 458–76; Stibbe, *German Anglophobia*, 110–64.

[145] See Herwig, *"Luxury" Fleet*, 194–98; Herwig, "Total Rhetoric, Limited War: Germany's U-Boot Campaign, 1917–18," in Chickering and Förster, *Great War, Total War*, 189–206; Offer, *The First World War*, 357–62; Sondhaus, *German Submarine Warfare*, 101–5; Spindler, *Der Handelskrieg*, vol. 3, 361–84; Stegemann, *Marinepolitik*, 51–64.

[146] Warburg, *Aus meinen Aufzeichnungen*, 42–43.

[147] Kelly, *Tirpitz*, 415–17; Feldman, *Hugo Stinnes*, 415–21; Ritter, *Staatskunst*, vol. 3, 368–70; Scheck, *Alfred Tirpitz*, 52, 56–57; Warburg, *Aus meinen Aufzeichnungen*, 45–46; Watson, *Ring of Steel*, 416–48. Cf. Bülow, *Denkwürdigkeiten*, vol. 3, 253.

[148] Erich Ludendorff, ed., *Urkunden der Obersten Heeresleitung über ihre Tätigkeit 1916/18* (Berlin: Mittler und Sohn, 1920), 322–24; Ritter, *Staatskunst*, vol. 3, 370–85.

his office as interior secretary on learning a day later that this "rubicon had been crossed" would turn out to be the most difficult decision of his life.[149] Less than two weeks later on January 22 Woodrow Wilson made his proposal for a "peace without victory" in the US Senate, which Max Warburg urged the German Foreign Office to take seriously as a possible starting point for a negotiated end to the war – he knew that entry into the conflict of the United States provoked by the "*va banque*" game of unrestricted submarine warfare would enhance the "moral, financial, and economic power of Germany's enemies to such a degree that we could not hope for anything from the future."[150] On January 31, the day the German note on the resumption of unrestricted submarine warfare was published, Warburg met with Arthur Zimmermann, Karl Helfferich, and Admiral von Holtzendorff. Although these men had managed to convince themselves that the United States would stay out of the war, the deeply somber and apprehensive mood Warburg observed revealed that they were no longer so sure.[151]

Meanwhile Arthur Zimmermann, who had replaced Jagow as foreign secretary in November 1916, had approved a harebrained scheme devised by the inept head of the East Asia and Latin America desk at the Foreign Office to promise Mexico generous financial assistance and the prospect of reconquering Texas, New Mexico, and Arizona in return for joining the German war effort if the United States could not be kept out of the war as a result of the impending renewed U-boat campaign – California was reserved for the Japanese, with whom the Foreign Office was hoping to sign a separate peace mediated by Mexico.[152] On January 16 this secret and enciphered proposal was forwarded courtesy of the American diplomatic cable to the US State Department, and from there via the German embassy in Washington, DC and legation in Mexico City to President Venustiano Carranza (1859–1920), in the last transmission using an obsolete code. The message was clandestinely intercepted and decrypted by British naval intelligence, which had long been eavesdropping on the American diplomatic communications in London. Both German ciphers were cracked by British cryptanalysts and the content of the "Zimmermann Telegram" was forwarded to American diplomats in London and then to the State Department. The British government obfuscated the

---

[149] Helfferich, *Der Weltkrieg*, vol. 2, 408–12; Warburg, *Aus meinen Aufzeichnungen*, 43–44; Williamson, *Karl Helfferich*, 193–94. Cf. Tirpitz, *Politische Dokumente*, vol. 2, 589–98.
[150] Warburg, *Aus meinen Aufzeichnungen*, 53–54.
[151] Ibid., 54–55; Ferguson, *Paper and Iron*, 138–39; Cecil, *Albert Ballin*, 309–13. Cf. Bülow, *Denkwürdigkeiten*, vol. 3, 263–64.
[152] See Thomas Boghardt, *The Zimmermann Telegram: Intelligence, Diplomacy and America's Entry into World War I* (Annapolis: Naval Institute Press, 2012), 59–79. See also Nieberg, *The Path to War*, 220–21.

source of the telegram and added unconfirmed rumors of Germans allegedly arriving in Mexico in large numbers.[153]

The text of the "Zimmermann Telegram" was ultimately debated in Congress and published in nearly every American newspaper on March 1, 1917. While its impact was both more transient and modest than later claimed by Barbara Tuchman and others, given that US public opinion was already strongly anti-German, it nevertheless smoothed the way for a US declaration of war on Germany on April 6 over its resumption of unrestricted submarine warfare. More than anything else, it revealed once again the astonishing degree of incompetence rife in the Wilhelmstrasse and the militarization of German diplomacy with the ascent of Hindenburg and Ludendorff.[154]

While on account of its extensive finance and supply of the Entente the US was an ally in all but name on the eve of the declaration of war in 1917, once it became a formal belligerent the United States managed to contribute vast additional financial and material resources, and by 1918 the military manpower of the largest industrial and agricultural economy in the world to the Entente, irreversibly tipping the scale against the Central Powers and thus contributing directly to Germany's defeat in November 1918. While early in the new submarine campaign U-boats managed to match or even exceed the needed monthly sunk tonnage projected by the navy, as in 1915–16 even this was only a small fraction of Britain's transatlantic shipping – in the end only 393 of 95,000 vessels convoyed across the Atlantic were lost during the campaign, of which not a single troop transport. No acute food or coal shortages had materialized in Britain by the summer of 1917 as was predicted in Holtzendorff's memorandum. In a twist of irony, nearly one half of the 962,000 US troops that arrived in France by the end of 1918 were transported on German steamers seized by the US government.[155]

The United States' entry into the war in April 1917 coupled with the public anti-Semitism unleashed by the *Judenzählung* was nothing short of catastrophic for the German American community, including its prominent Jewish members given the consistent support they had given the German and Austrian war efforts. The fierce backlash against all things German resulted in the wholesale adoption of the anti-German wartime propaganda so effectively cultivated and exploited by the British. Likewise pro-German

---

[153] Boghardt, *The Zimmermann Telegram*, 90–128.
[154] Ibid., 129–90; cf. Barbara Tuchman, *The Zimmermann Telegram*, 4th ed. (New York: Ballantine Books, 1985), 185, 199; Luebke, *Bonds of Loyalty*, 202–3. See also Bülow, *Denkwürdigkeiten*, vol. 3, 271–72; cf. Friedhelm Koopmann, *Diplomatie und Reichsinteresse: Das Geheimdienstkalkül in der deutschen Amerikapolitik 1914 bis 1917* (Frankfurt a.M.: Peter Lang, 1990), 288–317.
[155] Herwig, "Total Rhetoric," in Chickering and Förster, *Great War, Total War*, 203–4. See also Sondhaus, *German Submarine Warfare*, 144–60; Stegemann, *Marinepolitik*, 103–28.

wartime propaganda and acts of sabotage during the period of American neutrality had managed to spread the notion that German Americans were a fifth column.[156] Thus the entry of the United States into the war was by the summer and autumn of 1917 accompanied by an extraordinary outpouring of hostility against German Americans, such as coerced flag kissing, anthem singing and declarations of loyalty, forced sales of Liberty Bonds, smashing of storefronts and looting of German American shops, smearing of German Americans and their houses, churches, schools, and monuments with yellow paint, verbal and physical assaults, death threats, tar and featherings, public whippings, and many attempted lynchings (one successful in April 1918) – a mood reminiscent of the Atlanta race riots of 1906 and anti-Japanese riots in San Francisco in 1907.[157] German language instruction was banned in the schools of many states, German-language newspapers were restricted or closed down, German American gymnastic and shooting clubs, benevolent and cultural societies, theaters, orchestras, and choirs were restricted, prohibited, dissolved, renamed, or ceased their activities for the duration of the war. German school and library books were burned in public and mobs of super-patriots terrorized German American communities, burning parochial schools and churches. German town, street, park, school, and business names all over the country were Anglicized. Socialist and radical trade union leaders, long suspected of pro-German sentiments or of clandestine bankrolling by Germany, were denounced, attacked by mobs, or arrested. Indeed, so violent and intense was the nativist pressure in the United States by 1918 that many German Americans went to the extraordinary length of changing their surnames. Many ceased speaking German at home and began denying their German heritage and ancestry, creating huge intergenerational rifts within German American families.[158]

On the economic front, German merchant ships, bank assets, credits, investments, real estate, and patents were seized and later confiscated. All told, such British, French, Russian and American wartime action resulted in the seizure of no less than 16.1 of the estimated 20–28 billion marks of German overseas investment.[159] Partnerships were dissolved and Germans working in the United States were registered, their movement restricted and monitored, and in many cases they were interned in special camps. The deep

---

[156] Fulwider, *German Propaganda*, 163–74.
[157] Luebke, *The Bonds of Loyalty*, 3–24, 244–47; Nagler, *Nationale Minoritäten*, 351–52, 355–64; Wüstenbecker, *Deutsch-Amerikaner*, 214–45. See also Jörg Nagler, "Pandora's Box: Propaganda and War Hysteria in the United States During World War I," in Chickering and Förster, *Great War, Total War*, 485–500.
[158] Luebke, *The Bonds of Loyalty*, 241–44, 247–59, 267–93; Nagler, *Nationale Minoritäten*, 365–400; Wüstenbecker, *Deutsch-Amerikaner*, 245–326.
[159] Ferguson, *Paper and Iron*, 102.

business and banking ties, the many intellectual and cultural connections facilitated by German schools and universities, cultural institutions, and philanthropy exemplified by such prominent figures as Hugo Münsterberg, Henry Villard, James Loeb (1867–1933), Jacob Schiff, James Speyer, and Max Warburg's brothers Paul Warburg (1868–1932) and Felix Warburg were broken. As noted, many of these men also happened to be Jewish or have Jewish backgrounds and had worked tirelessly to build bridges between the two countries, and like Schiff, long resisted underwriting Entente loans or financing Entente trade, unlike the virulently anti-German and pro-British J. P. Morgan, whose bank syndicate had organized loans to the Entente of no less than $ 2 billion by 1916.[160] Hugo Münsterberg was himself spared this final indignity by his death from heart failure during a morning lecture at Radcliffe College in mid-December 1916.[161] In short, what personal, cultural, intellectual, business, and banking ties had survived the war until 1917 were now severed, often permanently. This process accelerated the complete assimilation and thus extinction of prewar Christian and Jewish German American culture in the United States. It was the beginning of the end of the Germanosphere in North America that had been built up over the previous three hundred years.

As this was unfolding in the United States, the Kaiser and Bethmann Hollweg were themselves increasingly subject to attack from the nationalist right for their alleged weakness and indecision. On the defensive and reliant on a center-left majority in the Reichstag for passage of semi-annual war loans, both Bethmann and the Kaiser tried to placate this camp, especially as signs of popular discontent grew after the difficult "Turnip Winter" of 1916–17 and the abdication of Nicholas II following revolution in Russia in March 1917. An Easter message of April 7, 1917 from the emperor and chancellor offered the prospect of political reforms such as abolition of the Prussian three-class franchise, direct and secret vote of deputies to the lower house, and a broadening of the social base of members of the upper house of the Prussian Diet, albeit only after the successful conclusion of the war.[162] This did not go nearly far enough for many members of the center-left Reichstag majority reflecting a large and growing segment of the public for whom the war was a distant conflict imposing dire material suffering at home for unclear ends.[163]

As a wave of strikes and unrest began to cripple the country and signs mounted by the early summer that the renewal of unrestricted submarine

---

[160] See Chernow, *The Warburgs*, 157–90; Tooze, *Deluge*, 36–39.
[161] Münsterberg, *Hugo Münsterberg*, 301–2.
[162] "Die 'Osterbotschaft'," in *Deutsche Geschichte*, vol. 8, ed. vom Bruch and Hofmeister, 427–30. See also Jarausch, *Enigmatic Chancellor*, 308–39; Ritter, *Staatskunst*, vol. 3, 536–51. Cf. Bülow, *Denkwürdigkeiten*, vol. 3, 258–61.
[163] Gerd Krumeich, *Die unbewältigte Niederlage: Das Trauma des Ersten Weltkriegs und die Weimarer Republik* (Freiburg: Herder, 2018), 24–71.

warfare had failed, the majority in the Reichstag led by Matthias Erzberger lost confidence in Bethmann Hollweg's leadership, creating an inter-party committee that demanded bolder political reforms and a negotiated peace without annexations or war indemnities. Pleasing neither the Reichstag majority nor nationalist hardliners and the OHL, Bethmann Hollweg was ultimately forced to resign on July 14 and was replaced as chancellor by the undersecretary of the Prussian Finance Ministry, Georg Michaelis.[164] On Erzberger's initiative, the Reichstag ultimately passed a more moderate and nationalistic version of its peace resolution July 19, 1917, one that sought a negotiated peace, albeit one premised on the territorial changes that had occurred during the war.[165] The vague, mealymouthed resolution that even Michaelis could formally accept without committing to anything did not mean a complete abandonment of annexationist war aims per se, but it was viewed by most nationalists in the center-right and far right as a display of German weakness to the Entente and a betrayal of their much more expansive war aims program and thus a de facto abandonment of any future *Weltpolitik*.[166] Indeed, it agitated the anti-Bethmann and anti-Kaiser *fronde* in this camp so much that it became the primary catalyst for organizing the Deutsche Vaterlands-Partei (German Fatherland Party) by Wolfgang Kapp in late August 1917.[167]

The roots of the Fatherland Party go back to the Unabhängiger Auschuß für einen Deutschen Frieden (Independent Committee for a German Peace), which had formed from the committee that had organized the Seeberg petition initiative in 1915 to propagate annexationist war aims and that had culminated in the July 1915 "Submission of the Intellectuals" in which Hermann Schumacher had played a key role. Chaired by Dietrich Schäfer, the Independent Committee had also included Hermann Schumacher, and among many others, Carl Duisberg, Otto Hintze, Emil Kirdorf, Gustav Stresemann (1878–1929), Wilhelm Hirsch, Count Kuno von Westarp (1864–1945), and of course Wolfgang Kapp.[168] The primary field of activity of the Independent Committee in 1916 was getting censorship on the war aims discussion lifted and to press for annexationist war aims and a resumption of unrestricted

---

[164] Jarausch, *Enigmatic Chancellor*, 339–48, 355–77; Ritter, *Staatskunst*, vol. 3, 551–84; Watson, *Ring of Steel*, 455–60. Cf. Helfferich, *Der Weltkrieg*, vol. 3, 93–131; Bülow, *Denkwürdigkeiten*, vol. 3, 264–65, 267–68.

[165] Ribhegge, *Frieden für Europa*, 182–93; Watson, *Ring of Steel*, 460.

[166] "Die Friedensresolution des Deutschen Reichstages," in *Deutsche Geschichte*, vol. 8, ed. vom Bruch and Hofmeister, 450–52; Afflerbach, *Auf Messers Schneide*, 351–64; Helfferich, *Der Weltkrieg*, vol. 3, 139–53; Ritter, *Staatskunst*, vol. 4, 19–26.

[167] Hagenlücke, *Deutsche Vaterlandspartei*, 158–59; Bülow, *Denkwürdigkeiten*, vol. 3, 265, 270–71.

[168] Hagenlücke, *Deutsche Vaterlandspartei*, 73. See also Scheck, *Alfred Tirpitz*, 51; Stegman, *Die Erben Bismarcks*, 465–76; Jarausch, *Enigmatic Chancellor*, 361–62; Plumpe, *Carl Duisberg*, 511–31.

submarine warfare, which it did informally through its network of two thousand representatives throughout the Reich. Under pressure from Ludendorff, official censorship was lifted in November 1916. The Independent Committee then held a large rally in the Prussian Chamber of Deputies in January 1917 in response to the negative reaction of the Entente to Bethmann Hollweg's December 12, 1916 peace proposal.[169] Further, on July 14, 1917 the Independent Committee organized a meeting of its representatives in Berlin and submitted a sharply-worded protest to the emerging peace resolution being debated in the Reichstag, which it argued "would permanently remove the German Empire from the ranks of great powers and lead to an unprecedented economic decline."[170] Later that month Wolfgang Kapp wrote Wilhelm Hirsch that he believed the Independent Committee was the last opportunity to unite all "national forces" into a political initiative that Alfred Tirpitz would be willing to lead.[171]

The ultimate form of that "advance of national forces" against the Peace Resolution was of course the Fatherland Party, formally founded by Kapp in Königsberg on September 2 and which he persuaded Tirpitz to lead as its first chairman. As discussed in Chapter 9, Wolfgang Kapp was a founding member of the Society for the Promotion of Inner Colonization and a new kind of populist nationalist politician who before the war had been no opponent of the reform of Prussia's three-class suffrage. A deep admirer of Bülow's Bloc policies, he first considered Bülow for the Fatherland Party's leadership and had in fact been involved in discussions with the ex-chancellor about this as late as August 1917.[172]

While the organizers and leaders of the Fatherland Party sought a wartime dictatorship and many of them were hostile to Prussian suffrage reform and parliamentarization, that was neither the mobilizing issue of the party nor what it campaigned for in its September 2 appeal that was published in most German newspapers September 9–12, 1917.[173] Instead, securing Germany's postwar *Weltstellung* is front and center.[174] The appeal, which made many heady references to Bismarck and Prussia's unifying legacy for Germany, denounced the Reichstag majority for engaging in divisive disputes over constitutional issues and defeatist peace resolutions to further their party ambitions at the cost of the national unity needed to prevail in war. The party vehemently rejected a *"Hungerfrieden"* (hunger peace), which would, it

---

[169] Hagenlücke, *Deutsche Vaterlandspartei*, 74, 83.   [170] Quoted in ibid., 87.
[171] Ibid., 89.
[172] Ibid., 112–13, 118, 153–55, 403. See also Scheck, *Alfred Tirpitz*, 48, 55, 66–67; Kelly, *Tirpitz*, 419–20.
[173] Stegman, *Die Erben Bismarcks*, 497–519. Cf. Hagenlücke, *Deutsche Vaterlandspartei*, 161.
[174] "Aufruf der Deutschen Vaterlands-Partei," *Norddeutsche Allgemeine Zeitung*, Sept. 12, 1917.

argued, be "a fatal blow to our future development." "The stunting of our *Weltstellung* and unbearable burdens," it claimed, "would destroy our economic position and above all the prospects of our workers. Rather than exporting valuable goods, Germany would once again see its sons emigrate in masses." The party instead offered a "*Siegfrieden*" (a victorious peace, called in the appeal a "Hindenburg Peace") and proposed to work together with all parties of a patriotic bent to achieve that common aim. It declared its complete neutrality in domestic politics and resolved to dissolve itself at the end of the war.[175]

As it turned out, the Fatherland Party was not actually a party that ran candidates but rather an extra-parliamentary nationalist umbrella group uniting all parties and nationalist associations for a final effort to support the government and OHL in securing a victorious peace, focused especially on expansive war aims in the west, particularly Belgium. The primary recurring themes in the public speeches by Tirpitz and other party leaders mirrored Schumacher's war aims memorandum and the war aims of the navy to an uncanny degree: the struggle against England as the key Entente enemy; the need to control Belgium and its coast to secure Germany's *Weltstellung*; the desirability of annexing the French ore basin Briey-Longwy; the need to secure German settler land in the Baltic; and the aim of uniting all Germans regardless of class, confession, and political party in a final push toward an acceptable peace.[176] These goals meshed with the policy of Chancellor Michaelis and now Vice-Chancellor Helfferich, who were inherently hostile to the Peace Resolution and naturally sympathetic to the new party and soon had to answer Reichstag majority questions about suspected official favoritism toward it.[177]

As first chairman of the Fatherland Party, Tirpitz himself had no principled hostility to members of the SPD, much less to the Center Party; he well appreciated the nationalist drift of the reformist wing of the SPD under Gustav Noske (1868–1946) and thought the "traditional caste and class structure outlived."[178] Earlier in the war Tirpitz was already convinced that the war would bring about a change in the German political system and that a government either of the left or right would be acceptable, even contemplating such radical steps as bringing SPD members onto the highest offices of the state.[179] Tirpitz was, moreover, consistently hostile to anti-Semitism and anti-Catholicism, publicly welcoming Jews and Catholics into the Fatherland Party,

---

[175] Ibid.
[176] Hagenlücke, *Deutsche Vaterlandspartei*, 163, 192–215; Scheck, *Alfred Tirpitz*, 68–69; Stibbe, *German Anglophobia*, 184–88.
[177] Hagenlücke, *Deutsche Vaterlandspartei*, 252–61; Scheck, *Alfred Tirpitz*, 72; Helfferich, *Der Weltkrieg*, vol. 3, 182–91; Michaelis, *Für Staat und Volk*, 332–34.
[178] Quoted in Scheck, *Alfred Tirpitz*, 38. [179] Ibid.; Feldman, *Hugo Stinnes*, 507.

something that drove a deep wedge between him and the traditional agrarian reactionaries and *völkisch* nationalists of the Pan-German League in the party.[180] Moreover, his ally and the Fatherland Party's generous financial backer Hugo Stinnes had managed since the spring of 1917 to make some inroads with free trade unionists and some Social Democrats to drop their rejection of annexationist war aims and come to a pragmatic arrangement with heavy industry, a task in which he had been assisted by Hermann Schumacher, who knew the trade union leader August Müller.[181] This was a prelude to the Stinnes-Legien agreement of November 15, 1918, which in return for recognizing trade unions as collective bargaining agents, an eight-hour day, work guarantees for returning veterans, and the creation of co-determining works councils (shop-floor worker organizations) by twenty-one major German employers, seven mainly free (i.e., "yellow" or liberal) and Christian trade unions agreed not to support any socialization (i.e., nationalization) of industry by the new SPD-led government installed after the November 1918 revolution. Indeed, it was Schumacher and Müller who brought Stinnes and the trade union leader Carl Legien (1861–1920) together into these later negotiations, which proved unequivocally that the vast majority of German workers and Social Democrats were at heart pragmatic and reformist, not revolutionary.[182]

The themes of the Fatherland Party's appeal and its speeches clearly resonated with the German public, which by September 1918 counted eight hundred thousand members.[183] While there is some dispute about this number on account of double counting of memberships through affiliated organizations, the range is somewhere between 450,000 and 1,250,000 members organized in 2,536 local chapters, making it one of the largest associations in Imperial Germany rivalling even the combined divided wings of the SPD at the time.[184] Its members were disproportionately Prussian, National Liberal (left liberal in Bremen and Württemberg), university-educated, and bourgeois. Compared to the SPD, its membership was even disproportionately female.[185] The Fatherland Party's supporters welcomed the distinctly uncharismatic, squeaky-voiced Tirpitz in massively overfilled meeting halls as a kind of national savior

---

[180] Kelly, *Tirpitz*, 421; Scheck, *Alfred Tirpitz*, 68, 69–71; Hagenlücke, *Deutsche Vaterlandspartei*, 407.
[181] Feldman, *Hugo Stinnes*, 504–9; GNN HA, Nl. Schumacher, I, B-6w, fols. 672a–672b.
[182] GNN HA, Nl. Schumacher, I, B-6w, fols. 672a–672b; Feldman, *Hugo Stinnes*, 524–30.
[183] Hagenlücke, *Deutsche Vaterlandspartei*, 180.
[184] Ibid., 181, 185; Retallack, *Notables of the Right*, 220; Wehler, *Gesellschaftsgeschichte*, vol. 4, 126–27.
[185] Hagenlücke, *Deutsche Vaterlandspartei*, 180–87, 405–7; Jürgen Kocka, *Facing Total War: German Society 1914–1918* (Cambridge, MA: Harvard University Press, 1984), 98–100.

in the autumn of 1917.[186] They were driven less by a hostility toward the Center Party, left liberals, and SPD, much less by any principled rejection of political reform. Rather, what mobilized them was their rejection of the Reichstag's Peace Resolution and thus its abandonment of *Weltpolitik*. That this was the core issue of the Fatherland Party and the main basis for its surprising popularity has been routinely played down by many historians drawing on Eckart Kehr's model of manipulative *Sammlungspolitik* and Hans-Ulrich Wehler's concept of "social imperialism," who claim instead that the main aim of the party was to block domestic political reform.[187] To be sure, that was *a* motivation of some of its organizers and core supporters – the Fatherland Party was clearly different things to different people, as is clear from its internal divisions that showed the inherent instability and fragmentation within the rightist bloc. Yet the fact remains that the traditional conservative parties were completely marginalized in the party, and preventing domestic political reform – and, indeed, any domestic political topics – were entirely absent from the party's publicity and campaigning. Could large masses of Germans not see through the ruse? Or was it that they were wise to Tirpitz's arch strategy to maintain the authoritarian structures of the Reich to prevent the supposedly radical Social Democrats from gaining political power?

A far more convincing interpretation is that the Fatherland Party's bourgeois supporters were self-motivated because *Weltpolitik* and Germany's "world status" mattered deeply to them, and a victorious peace with annexations and war indemnities was the only way they could conceive that it could be continued and sustained into peacetime. As was discussed in Chapter 10, the extraordinary growth and dynamism of the Navy League by 1914 lends much weight to this argument.

This interpretation hardly denies that continuing the war for such a *Siegfrieden* was a disastrous decision. It is indisputable that the Fatherland Party gave the German war effort a second wind and the needed political cover that enabled the OHL and government to weather the wave of strikes and protests that hit Germany in late January 1918 and to then pull out all stops for Operation Michael, the first phase of the massive Ludendorff Offensive beginning on the western front in March 1918. This was the final gamble that mobilized nearly all available German manpower and materiel for a final victory in the west. The fanatical faith in such a *Siegfrieden* and the nimbus of invincibility surrounding Ludendorff and Hindenburg following victory in

---

[186] Hagenlücke, *Deutsche Vaterlandspartei*, 162–63; Scheck, *Alfred Tirpitz*, 67–68; Kelly, *Tirpitz*, 420–21.
[187] See, for example, Epkenhans, *Tirpitz*, 70–71; Feldman, *Army, Industry and Labor*, 430–31; Hagenlücke, *Deutsche Vaterlandspartei*, 161, 404–5; Scheck, *Alfred Tirpitz*, 48, 67; Stegman, *Die Erben Bismarcks*, 500–502; Wehler, *Gesellschaftsgeschichte*, vol. 4, 127. Cf. Eley, *From Unification to Nazism*, 110–45.

the east actively propagated by the Fatherland Party contributed to a vast overestimation by both the OHL and German public of their remaining military capabilities. It also enabled a willful blindness to the sheer exhaustion of German troops, the inadequacy of transportation, the lack of manpower reserves, and the limited chance of success for an offensive without clear strategic goals.[188]

While the offensive celebrated spectacular early advances and brought German troops within a few days march of Paris, it outstripped its supply lines, stalled, and then ultimately faltered, resulting in casualties of no less than 977,555 men.[189] In August the hungry and demoralized German Army began disintegrating under the blows of Entente counteroffensives, Spanish flu, and growing defeatism, striking and insubordination. But to an increasingly deluded and overstrained Ludendorff, tactical retreats and new defensive lines could not be reconciled with the inflated expectations for a "Hindenburg Peace" that had been whipped up on the German homefront. By September the jig was up. The OHL and civilian leadership had no choice but to seek an armistice on what was hoped – rather naively by that point – would still be Wilsonian terms.[190]

The disappointing turn of those armistice negotiations for which the new civilian leadership could now be blamed and the sudden collapse of an offensive that had been billed by the army as on the cusp of victory as late as August allowed the myth to take hold that the army remained "undefeated in the field" but had been betrayed by Reichstag pacifist socialists, Catholics, and left liberals, by the toleration of striking workers, defeatist scribblers and protesters, and revolutionary Bolsheviks, by war shirkers and profiteers, and of course, by Jews. This joined an already existing wartime narrative of a weak, vacillating, and pandering Bethmann Hollweg and a misled and timidly irresolute Kaiser surrounded by sycophantic advisors who had failed to deploy the battleship navy early in the conflict and had then buckled under American pressure to suspend unrestricted submarine warfare only to resume it when it was too late. The *Judenzählung* and Fatherland Party had prepared fertile ground for this "stab-in-the-back" myth to take root, a myth later cultivated not only by the postwar exculpatory testimony and writings of Ludendorff, Hindenburg, and Tirpitz, but as is often overlooked, by none other than

---

[188] Afflerbach, *Auf Messers Schneide*, 422–43; Ritter, *Staatskunst*, vol. 4, 283–87.
[189] Watson, *Ring of Steel*, 524; cf. Herwig, *The First World War*, 419; Roger Chickering, *Imperial Germany and the Great War, 1914–1918* (Cambridge: Cambridge University Press, 1998), 182.
[190] Afflerbach, *Auf Messers Schneide*, 475–77; Wilhelm Deist, "The Military Collapse of the German Empire: The Reality of the Stab-in-the-Back Myth," trans. E.J. Feuchtwanger, *War in History* 3, no. 2 (1996): 186–207; Ritter, *Staatskunst*, vol. 4, 287–91; Tooze, *Deluge*, 218–31.

Bernhard von Bülow in the third volume of his memoir published in 1931, which lent it additional credibility at a time when Weimar democracy was in an advanced state of decay.[191]

In truth and rather fittingly, the revolution that would topple the Hohenzollern monarchy on November 9, 1918 and spell the end of the empire had its beginnings in a naval mutiny in Kiel starting on October 29, 1918 sparked when the "Risk Fleet" was ordered by Admirals Reinhard Scheer (1863–1928) and Franz von Hipper (1863–1932) to sally forth into the Dover Strait for a last-ditch operation to ambush the Royal Navy. They were acting on their own initiative without orders from Berlin in a bid to affect the armistice negotiations and preserve the navy's honor. To many of the sailors it appeared a suicide mission. Insubordination in Wilhelmshaven and Kiel mushroomed into mutiny and then Worker and Soldiers' Councils that spread all over Germany.[192] The "stab-in-the-back" myth provided convenient cover for such willful insubordination and military striking by German officers, soldiers, and sailors.[193]

What is indisputable is that the German bourgeoisie, its academic elite, and the politicians who had mobilized them for *Weltpolitik* before 1914 were major active agents in the shape of this war and in the contours of Germany's defeat. With the context of the previous chapters, it is possible to see the war aims debate and Fatherland Party as the final iteration of a pattern of Wilhelmine bourgeois political mobilization, albeit not as a diversionary tactic for arch political purposes but as a strategy to forge political consensus for the quest for German world status bound closely to mental maps of the world: in 1897–1900 the mobilizing issue was sea power, in 1906–7 it was colonial reform, in 1908–9 it was financial reform to continue *Weltpolitik*, and in 1916–18 it was a victorious peace. In each instance the bourgeois public was mobilized to pursue *Weltpolitik* as an equal of the other great "world empires." There was no stable alliance with traditional conservatives in any of this mobilization, nor as we have seen, did it always imply loyalty to the crown or government. Indeed, by 1916 the Kaiser himself was a rapidly shrinking and marginalized figure, a force of "inertia and delay" to the radicalizing forces let loose by the war.[194] To be sure, the Fatherland Party's annexationist platform revealed the unreality in which the war aims debate had always been conducted, but the emotional pull of this imperial nationalism cannot be denied. That had everything to do with the way Germany's *Weltmachstellung* was

---

[191] See esp. Bülow, *Denkwürdigkeiten*, vol. 3, 263–64, 281–83, 289.
[192] Herwig, *German Naval Officer Corps*, 247–62; Sondhaus, *German Submarine Warfare*, 209–11.
[193] Richard Bessel, *Germany after the First World War* (Oxford: Clarendon Press; New York: Oxford University Press, 1993), 262–64; Krumeich, *Die unbewältigte Niederlage*, 130–39; Ritter, *Staatskunst*, vol. 4, 461–70.
[194] Clark, *Kaiser Wilhelm II*, 244; Röhl, *Into the Abyss*, 1164–87.

narrated in terms of an all-or-nothing world historical struggle for a national destiny bound to civilizational claims to progress and freedom, one given special urgency by the failure of prewar *Weltpolitik*. This reinforces the conclusion that *Weltpolitik* was less peculiarly illiberal than an intensified – and in war, radicalized and deformed – version of liberal imperialism. The previous chapters have shown how those maps of the world were created *in the world*, how they were disseminated and popularized in Germany, as well as the hold they had on the imagination from peace into total war. These mental maps were never static and were adapted to and shaped by experience. The experience of wartime blockade, hunger and privation, senseless human sacrifice, domestic polarization, defeat, and humiliation altered what it meant to be German in the world to a profound degree, just as the war itself also created a smaller, narrower, de-globalized, and immensely poorer German world. It does not require much imagination to ponder what those experiences might have done to the imperial imaginations in Britain, France, or the United States under similar circumstances.

## Elusive Peace

As Walther Rathenau had predicted in 1912, the war that broke out in 1914 would be the first of a number of unfolding wars that would ultimately lead to the eclipse of Europe by the United States and come to define much of the twentieth century. The "deglobalization" that started in the autumn of 1914 would last nearly forty years, while hot and cold world wars would persist until 1989 throughout which the German question always loomed large.

There was no stable world order around 1900, and the attempt to create one in 1919 was flawed not by vindictiveness or poor design but by the anachronisms and inherent contradictions of liberal imperialism. The problem with the Versailles Treaty was not reparations. While there was controversy over their level, the Germans entered into the peace negotiations accepting them in principle – comprehensive German reparations for damages caused to Allied civilians and their property were in fact part of the Armistice Convention signed on November 11, 1918. The burden of reparation payments was also ultimately much less onerous than John Maynard Keynes (1883–1946) made it out to be in his famous 1919 polemic, *The Economic Consequences of the Peace*.[195] There is today wide agreement that the schedule of payments presented by the Reparations Commission in May 1921 were well within Germany's means to pay, representing at most 8 percent of annual national income. The bulk of the reparations bill (some 82 of the 132 billion gold marks

---

[195] John Maynard Keynes, *The Economic Consequences of the Peace* (1919; New York: Harcourt, Brace and Howe, 1920), 113–225.

owed) was symbolic, that is in purely notional C bonds included to satisfy Allied public opinion. Of the 50 billion gold marks actually owed, Germany ultimately paid only some 20 billion by the time the Lausanne Conference suspended these payments in 1932.[196]

Much more corrosive to the peace were persisting with the naval blockade until July 1919; the acute fuel shortages caused by German coal deliveries to Belgium, France, and Italy; the loss of Germany's entire colonial empire (both overseas and contiguously in West Prussia and Posen); and the confiscation of its merchant marine and largely obsolete but symbolically potent surface navy. These measures – along with the stubborn refusal of the United States to write down debts owed by its Entente allies and the lack of any framework to restore world trade – are key to explaining the ultimate failure of that peace, not reparations.

Continuing with the blockade and extending it to the Baltic and thus tightening it until the ink was dry on the treaty was the only means the Allies had to compel Germany to sign a peace on their terms short of an invasion, but this prolonged severe food and fuel shortages in Germany that resulted in needless civilian suffering and mortality and that worked to discredit the treaty both in Germany and within British and international public opinion.[197] Sensitive as he was to this injustice, Keynes amplified these concerns in his widely-read polemic.[198] By also attacking the personal character and motivations of the drafters of the treaty, questioning the treaty's legality under international law, and exaggerating the burdens of reparations, Keynes' book undermined the treaty's basic legitimacy and emboldened German official foot-dragging and defiance that began immediately after the treaty was signed.[199] The post-Armistice blockade transformed a just war to uphold international law into an unjust one against civilians. As Avner Offer has observed, "the blockade scrambled the moral verdict of the war and planted the seeds of a new *casus belli*."[200]

---

[196] See Étienne Mantoux, *The Carthaginian Peace, or the Economic Consequences of Mr. Keynes* (London and New York: G. Cumberlege, 1946), 133–59; Sally Marks, "The Myths of Reparations," *Central European History* 11, no. 3 (Sept. 1978): 231–55, here 237; Ferguson, *The Pity of War*, 397, 399–432; Leonard Gomes, *German Reparations, 1919-1932: A Historical Survey* (Basingstoke, Hamps.: Palgrave Macmillan, 2010), 71–78; Albrecht Ritschl, *Deutschlands Krise und Konjunktur 1924-1934: Binnenkonjunktur, Auslandsverschuldung und Reparationsproblem zwischen Dawes-Plan und Transfersperre* (Berlin: Akademie Verlag, 2002), 243.

[197] Hull, *Scrap of Paper*, 5–6; Bessel, *Germany after the First World War*, 95–96; Offer, *The First World War*, 383–85, 387–401.

[198] See, for example, Keynes, *Economic Consequences*, 250–51n1.

[199] Ibid., 25–55, 72, 145, 225; Ferguson, *The Pity of War*, 402–19; Gomes, *German Reparations*, 233–38; Tooze, *Deluge*, 295.

[200] Offer, *The First World War*, 401.

If 1919 "was truly a post-colonial moment" as has been claimed by Adam Tooze, it was post-colonial mainly for Germany and only temporarily.[201] It is often overlooked that Anglo-French victory in the Great War had vindicated empire in Britain and France. After the cataclysm of war and the lifeline of troops, food, and resources offered by their colonies, the liberal imperialist mirage of freedom, upward mobility, and prosperity on the lands and backs of others had unmistakable continued attractions. Woodrow Wilson's opposition to colonial empire was lukewarm at best and singularly unpopular with the other victors in Paris. He was ultimately outmaneuvered and placated by Jan Smuts's (1870–1950) proposal for "Mandates," an ingenious liberal imperialist contrivance that placed non-European peoples on a civilizational and racial hierarchy and thus categories of mandates that paid lip service to Wilsonian principles while offering cover for the territorial aims of France, Britain, and the British Dominions, the latter with their own vigorous sub-imperial ambitions in Africa and the Pacific. A Japanese proposal to amend the League of Nations Covenant to recognize the principle of equality among all nations was rejected by the United States and Australia, while the British supported an American amendment to the Covenant that explicitly exempted the Monroe Doctrine.[202]

The League of Nations ultimately sanctioned one the largest Anglo-French colonial grabs in history in the Middle East, Africa, and the Pacific.[203] The colonial unrest that soon erupted in Ireland, Morocco, Egypt, Palestine, Syria, Iraq, India, and Indochina did not substantively alter these imperial ambitions but revealed the distance that always existed between liberal imperial theory and practice. In Ireland the British government sanctioned assassinations, reprisal actions, and mass arrests without trial. Demands for self-government and independence in Egypt were met with martial law, arrests, defiance of election results, and installation of authoritarian puppets. In Iraq members of the constituent assembly were forced under armed British guard to approve a treaty that gave Britain control of their finances and military. Colonial unrest was often suppressed with savage brutality, as in putting down the Yen Bay

---

[201] Tooze, *Deluge*, 283, 285, 287; cf. Marcia Klotz, "The Weimar Republic: A Post-Colonial State in a Still-Colonial World," in *Germany's Colonial Pasts*, ed. Eric Ames, Marcia Klotz, and Laura Wildenthal (Lincoln: University of Nebraska Press, 2005), 135–47.

[202] See Margaret MacMillan, *Paris 1919: Six Months That Changed the World* (New York: Random House, 2001), 98–106; David Reynolds, *The Long Shadow: The Legacy of the Great War in the Twentieth Century* (New York and London: W. W. Norton, 2014), 83–123; Zara Steiner, *The Lights That Failed: European International History 1919–1933* (Oxford: Oxford University Press, 2005), 40–46; Heinrich August Winkler, *The Age of Catastrophe: A History of the West, 1914–1945* (New Haven and London: Yale University Press, 2015), 149–50.

[203] MacMillan, *Paris 1919*, 381–426.

Mutiny in French Indochina or the resort to machine guns in Jallianwala Bagh in Punjab and tanks and airplanes in Syria.[204] Among Egyptian, Indian, Chinese, Vietnamese, Korean, and other disappointed nationalists, the failure of Wilsonian liberal anti-colonialism and the denial of international equality and self-determination to non-whites fueled anticolonial nationalism and pushed many toward Marxist-Leninist revolutionary struggle with profound longer-term repercussions.[205] At the same time, the expanded overseas colonial presence with "Mandates" markedly worsened Britain's strategic overstretch. Getting Britain's own economic house in order with needed public investments in primary schooling, vocational training, technical and scientific education, and infrastructure, or measures to remedy the longstanding problems of technological and managerial backwardness, lack of standardization, limited vertical integration, and loss of market share in British industry gave way to expanded imperial commitments and overseas investments. This only reinforced the long-term track of British relative economic decline and made enforcement of the Paris Peace that much harder.[206]

In the United States, meanwhile, blacks were not rewarded for their wartime service with a repeal of Jim Crow and equal civil rights. Instead race riots shook the country in 1919 resulting in the razing of African American neighborhoods, lynching, and other violence that left 120 dead. A wave of unprecedented strikes, parcel bombs, and a "Red Scare" then swept the country and led to the arrest of six thousand suspected radicals by the FBI and the deportation of hundreds of foreigners. Support for the Ku Klux Klan, which had been revived in 1915, surged to its highest levels ever (some four million members by 1924), reflecting the extreme nativism unleashed by the war. While de facto and de jure second-class citizenship status already existed for blacks, American Indians, Chinese, Japanese, Filipinos, and Hispanics, additional segregation, anti-miscegenation, and eugenic laws were passed and enforcement of existing such laws was tightened in many US states, while at the federal level immigration was curtailed drastically by the 1924 National Origins Act, reducing immigration from Europe to a trickle and prohibiting all immigration from East Asia. Such policies had many parallels in the British Dominions. There Indian and Chinese immigration was restricted, and in South Africa residential segregation, workplace discrimination, and political restrictions were added to long list of black legal disabilities as a prelude to

---

[204] Tooze, *Deluge*, 374–93; Winkler, *Age of Catastrophe*, 150–51, 183–85, 346–56.
[205] Erez Manela, *The Wilsonian Moment: Self-Determination and the International Origins of Anticolonial Nationalism* (Oxford and New York: Oxford University Press, 2007).
[206] Alfred Chandler, *Scale and Scope: The Dynamics of Industrial Capitalism* (Cambridge, MA and London: Belknap Press/Harvard University Press, 1990), 239–336; Charles Kindleberger, *World Economic Primacy: 1500–1990* (New York and Oxford: Oxford University Press, 1996), 137–46.

Apartheid.[207] The hypocrisy of the League of Nations Covenant, French and British liberal imperialism in practice, and the unedifying example of the United States offered poor reference points for liberal internationalism in the 1920s, capped by the debacle that the US Senate failed to ratify the Versailles Treaty and the League of Nations Covenant.

The contradictions of liberal imperialism do not end there. The postwar economic order that Britain, France, and the United States shaped paid lip service to the principles of freedom of commerce, most favored nation, and the open door but was marked by a turn inward toward preferential imperial trade and nationalist protectionism both in Europe and North America. The formation of many new nation states in Europe created new borders, currencies, and tariff walls to protect domestic industry and agriculture where there had once been imperial divisions of labor and relative free trade. As bad, Britain introduced the McKenna duties on luxury goods in 1916 and gradually extended protection to many other products through laws passed in 1919, 1921, and 1932, while the 1931 Abnormal Importations Act empowered the Board of Trade to impose anti-dumping duties of up to 100 percent ad valorem on certain imports. The United States returned to its protectionist past by passing the Fordney-McCumber Act in 1922 which raised ad valorem tariffs to nearly 40 percent on average. In 1930 it followed up with the notorious Smoot-Hawley tariff which raised average tariff rates to 60 percent. Along with the persistence of massive inter-Allied debts and the associated exchange rate volatility, protectionism made a sustained return to prewar free trade based on the gold standard well neigh impossible. It was this context of worldwide protectionism that turned German reparations into such an intractable issue, as German exports were the very lynchpin of meeting those obligations.[208]

Without any honest effort at decolonization, international disarmament, or trade liberalization, the loss of territory and status enshrined by the Versailles Treaty would permanently alienate much of the German public. The war aims

---

[207] See Jeffrey Butler, *Cradock: How Segregation and Apartheid Came to a South African Town*, ed. Richard Elphick and Jeannette Hopkins (Charlottesville and London: University of Virginia Press, 2017); David M. Chalmers, *Hooded Americanism: The History of the Ku Klux Klan* (Durham: Duke University Press, 1987); David Cook-Martin, *Culling the Masses: The Democratic Origins of Racist Immigration Policy in the Americas* (Cambridge, MA: Harvard University Press, 2014); Desmond King, *Making Americans: Immigration, Race, and the Origins of the Diverse Democracy* (Cambridge, MA: Harvard University Press, 2002); Marilyn Lake and Henry Reynolds, *Drawing the Global Colour Line: White Men's Countries and the International Challenge of Racial Equality* (Cambridge: Cambridge University Press, 2008); Peggy Pascoe, *What Comes Naturally: Miscegenation Law and the Making of Race in America* (Oxford: Oxford University Press, 2009); Tooze, *Deluge*, 338–50; Winkler, *The Age of Catastrophe*, 151–56.

[208] Barry Eichengreen, *Golden Fetters: The Gold Standard and the Great Depression* (Oxford and New York: Oxford University Press, 1995), 100–152; Findlay and O'Rourke, *Power and Plenty*, 435–46; Kindleberger, *The World in Depression*, 14–69.

debate, *Judenzählung*, Fatherland Party, and denial and bitterness about Germany's defeat would cast very long shadows here, making many Germans receptive to the "stab-in-the-back" myth and turning a sizable portion of the public into foes of their republic and the postwar world order. With the exception of the Spartakusbund (predecessor of the German Communist Party) and SPD, every major postwar political party – including the Catholic Center – aspired to regain colonies and world power status, most vehemently the German People's Party and German National People's Party (DNVP), the successors of the National Liberal and conservative parties.[209] Karl Helfferich became a leading DNVP Reichstag deputy and notorious for his violent tirades against the republic, the signers of the Armistice (which happened to include his old foe, Matthias Erzberger), and Walther Rathenau, the latter in his capacity first as reconstruction and then foreign minister in 1921–22.[210] This contributed to a poisonous climate that gave license to Wolfgang Kapp's 1920 Putsch and to a wave of right-wing political assassinations that claimed the lives of both Erzberger and Rathenau along with more than 350 others by 1922.[211]

The loss of the German colonies as League of Nations Mandates was decried by German colonial revisionists in the Weimar Republic as a loss of overseas "laboratories" and "schools of the nation," just as they vehemently denied the Allied claims that Germany had mismanaged its colonial stewardships by violence and incompetence and thus had forfeited its civilizational right to govern them.[212] Not surprisingly, the importance of the overseas colonies as a German heritage and legacy was massively inflated after they had been lost. They would remain a neuralgic point throughout the 1920s and 30s, notably through the popular lectures and writings of the most prominent representative of postwar German colonial revisionism, the former Colonial Secretary Heinrich Schnee.[213] And for all its peaceful outward appearance, revision of

---

[209] See Wolfgang Treue, *Deutsche Parteiprogramme seit 1861*, 4th enl. ed. (Göttingen: Musterschmidt-Verlag, 1968), 99–149.

[210] Williamson, *Helfferich*, 291–326, 344–72; Count Harry Kessler, *Walther Rathenau: His Life and Work* (London: Gerald Howe, 1929), 360–74; Volkov, *Walther Rathenau*, 197–205.

[211] Williamson, *Helfferich*, 327–28; Emil Julius Gumbel, *Vier Jahre politischer Mord*, 5th ed. (Berlin-Fichtenau: Verlag der Neuen Gesellschaft, 1922); Martin Sabrow, *Der Rathenaumord: Rekonstruktion einer Verschwörung gegen die Republik von Weimar* (Munich: Oldenbourg, 1994).

[212] van Laak, "Kolonien als 'Laboratorien der Moderne'?" in Conrad and Osterhammel, *Das Kaiserreich transnational* 278. See, for example, Deutscher Kolonialkrieger-Bund, ed., *Unvergessenes Heldentum: Das Kolonisationswerk der deutsche Schutztruppe und Marine* (Berlin: Kolonialwarte, 1924).

[213] Heinrich Schnee, *Braucht Deutschland Kolonien? Ein Vortrag* (Leipzig: Quelle & Meyer, 1921); Schnee, *Nationalismus und Imperialismus* (Berlin: R. Hobbing, 1928); Schnee, *Die*

Germany's eastern frontier and recovery of its former colonies remained *the* two central preoccupations of German foreign policy into the Stresemann era and after.[214]

In the immediate postwar period, however, it was inner colonization that was high on the agenda, lifted on a tide of opinion that Germany had lost the war in large measure because it had not produced enough food to withstand the blockade. Lands in West Prussia, Posen and Memel, the thinking also went, had been ceded to Poland and Lithuania because they had been too thinly settled with Germans. Thus in a remarkable political comeback, President Friedrich Ebert (1871–1925) charged Max Sering with drafting a Reich Settlement Law that was passed in August 1919. It was intended to aid in the demobilization and employment of veterans, apportion lands to German refugees from Poland, boost agricultural output, and forestall future annexation of German lands.[215] German agriculture had been severely damaged by wartime labor, fertilizer, and machinery shortages (grain production in 1919 was a mere 48 percent of 1913 levels). Along with the continuation of the blockade until July 1919, this meant that serious food shortages continued for eight months after the Armistice making the food question an urgent matter and putting an added premium on *Raum* (space).[216]

With the food and space issue given such prominence in the immediate aftermath of the war and the conspicuous absence of decolonization and trade re-liberalization after the Paris peace, it is not altogether surprising that the short-lived contiguous empire of German-occupied Ober Ost would continue to resonate with many Germans in the 1920s, not least since many hundreds of thousands of men had served on the eastern front or as occupation troops. This "mindscape" of colonial settler frontiers fueled postwar colonial fantasies that were reflected in many novels and other writings.[217] One prominent example was Hans Grimm's (1875–1959) long political novel, *Volk ohne Raum* (People without Space, 1926), popular throughout the late 1920s and

---

*deutschen Kolonien vor, in und nach dem Weltkrieg* (Leipzig: Quelle & Meyer, 1935). See also Sandler, *Empire in the Heimat*, 25–51; Schmokel, *Dream of Empire*, 46–75.

[214] See esp. Manfred Berg, *Gustav Stresemann und die Vereinigten Staaten von Amerika: Wirtschaftliche Verflechtung und Revisionspolitik* (Baden-Baden: Nomos Verlagsgesellschaft, 1990), 380–417; Thomas Göthel, *Demokratie und Volkstum: Die Politik gegenüber den nationalen Minderheiten in der Weimarer Republik* (Cologne: Sh-Verlag, 2002).

[215] Nelson, "The *Archive for Inner Colonization*," in Nelson, *Germans, Poland, and Colonial Expansion*, 85–86; Dieter Marc Schneider, *Johannes Schauff (1902–1990): Migration und "Stabilitas" im Zeitalter des Totalitarismen* (Munich: Oldenbourg, 2001), 24–26; FriedaWunderlich, *Farm Labor in Germany, 1810–1945* (Princeton: Princeton University Press, 1961), 148–50, 148n3.

[216] See Bessel, *Germany after the First World War*, 193–219.

[217] Fischer, *Griff nach der Weltmacht*, 817; Liulevicius, *War Land*, 151, 247–72; Liulevicius, *The German Myth of the East*, 130–70.

early 1930s. Grimm had himself been a journalist and then a businessman in South Africa in the years before the First World War, and his novel has considerable autobiographical detail. In it Cornelius Freibott, the longsuffering hero and a returned African settler, gives a speech to the feckless locals of his home town of Jürgenshagen on the Weser, a place whose limited horizons and opportunities he had fled before the war. Freibott fervently believes that Germany's culture of subordination and dependence is a product of centuries of princely tutelage and the failure to expand German territory abroad. He concludes that Germany's current problems spring from the recent loss of colonial territory and the now restricted opportunity for healthy national development:

> It was from the yearning for independence and property and freedom that social turmoil emerged in Germany, the futile yearning of those who achieved enough to deserve property and independence and freedom. Wherever Germans were, as a rule, able to attain property and independence and freedom through their own abilities, such as in our stolen German Southwest Africa, there was no such social turmoil![218]

Grimm's novel tapped into a deep reservoir of popular resentment and aspiration that successive Weimar governments could not ignore and that the National Socialists later cynically exploited.[219] But the popular resonance of the novel suggests more, something that has too often been overlooked: a public familiar and comfortable with the German colonies as a fulfillment of liberal-nationalist freedoms and thus as both a pillar of national identity and the culmination of a national destiny that had been forged into an imperial nationalism through Wilhelmine *Weltpolitik*. The humiliations of a lost war, resentment over the ignominious peace that stripped Germans of their world power trappings, and memories of wartime hunger and privation reshaped this imperialist nationalism in the 1920s and 30s and made it much more receptive to radical ideas and politicians promising a return to the status of *Weltmacht*. Indeed, it was not long before the Weimar-era colonial imagination began to conceive of central and eastern Europe, the Balkans, and even the Soviet Union as objects of German informal empire, an idea that gained practical urgency as world trade collapsed in the early 1930s. It was thus hardly coincidental that as the Nazi regime consolidated power in the mid-1930s – a regime which as we know today was devoid of original ideas – and

---

[218] Hans Grimm, *Volk ohne Raum*, vol. 2 (Munich: Albert Langen, 1931 [1926]), 651.
[219] See Andrew J. Crozier, *Appeasement and Germany's Last Bid for Colonies* (Basingstoke, Hamps.: Macmillan, 1988); Klaus Hildebrand, *Vom Reich zum Weltreich: Hitler, NSDAP und koloniale Frage 1919–1945* (Munich: W. Fink, 1969); Birthe Kundrus, "Colonialism, Imperialism, National Socialism: How Imperial Was the Third Reich?" in Naranch and Eley, *German Colonialism*, 330–46; Schmokel, *Dream of Empire*; Smith, *Ideological Origins*, 224–30.

then charted a course for territorial revisionism and war, *Raumnot* (space needs) and the vision of an autarkic contiguous European empire (*Großraum*) in central and eastern Europe would once again enter the strategic picture.[220]

In the early 1930s the American Secretary of State Cordell Hull (1871 – 1955) recognized that German Nazism and Italian fascism were not just symptoms of radical political nationalism but also the response of "have-not" states driven to autarkic and aggressive imperial alternatives by the restrictive trade policies that had been imposed by the United States, France, and Britain. As he noted, both of these political extremes were "characteristic expressions of great people in revolt against the limitations placed upon their national prosperity by their poverty in natural resources."[221] The work of Adam Tooze, Timothy Snyder, and Carroll Kakel has aided a much fuller appreciation of the fact that the war in the Soviet Union that Nazi Germany began in 1941 was bound up closely with an older liberal imperialist fantasy of Germany in a "superpower" position analogous to the United States, with a vast, resource-rich eastern frontier to deliver American-style material prosperity and food security in the metropole while serving as an outlet for settlers to seek freedom and opportunity in the lands and on the backs of colonial others.[222] That this was ultimately attempted by a criminal regime that unleashed unspeakable horrors on the people of eastern Europe and launched an industrial-scale genocide against European Jewry culminating in the *Shoah* has understandably obscured the long arc of history connecting the American "frontier empire" with German *Weltpolitik* with which this book began.

---

[220] Volker Berghahn, ed., *Quest for Economic Empire: European Strategies of German Big Business in the Twentieth Century* (Providence and Oxford: Berghahn Books, 1996), 13–23, 35–64; Stephen G. Gross, *Export Empire: German Soft Power in Southeastern Europe, 1890– 1945* (Cambridge: Cambridge University Press, 2015), 139–78; Hildebrand, *Vom Reich zum Weltreich*, 143–45; Smith, *Ideological Origins*, 202–3, 211–13; Robert Mark Spaulding, *Osthandel und Ostpolitik: German Foreign Trade Policies in Eastern Europe from Bismarck to Adenauer* (Providence and Oxford: Berghahn Books, 1997) 150–278; Eckart Teichert, *Autarkie und Großraumwirtschaft in Deutschland: Außenwirtschaftspolitische Konzeptionen zwischen Wirtschaftskrise und Zweitem Weltkrieg* (Munich: Oldenbourg, 1984).

[221] Quoted in Arthur Schatz, "The Anglo-American Trade Agreement and Cordell Hull's Search for Peace," *Journal of American History* 57, no. 1 (June 1970): 85–106, here 89.

[222] J. Adam Tooze, *The Wages of Destruction: The Making and Breaking of the Nazi Economy* (New York: Viking, 2007), xxiv–xv, 8–9, 10, 12, 162, 175–76, 467–80; Timothy Snyder, *Bloodlands: Europe Between Hitler and Stalin* (New York: Basic Books, 2010), 15, 19–20, 156–65; Carroll P. Kakel, III, *The American West and the Nazi East: A Comparative and Interpretive Perspective* (Basingstoke, Hamps. and New York: Palgrave Macmillan, 2011).

# EPILOGUE

In March 1946 Hermann Schumacher received a letter from one of his former students, Annelise Schröder-von Halle, who had attended Schumacher's lectures and seminar at the University of Berlin in the 1920s.[1] Schröder had acquired an excellent command of English while living in California in 1925–27 and England in 1930 and was then working as a translator for the American Military Administration in North Baden.[2] As might be guessed, this former student was Ernst von Halle's daughter. She had maintained sporadic contact with the Schumachers over the years, but with the war now over, she was keen to learn of their fate.[3] Schröder-von Halle, her husband, and their two children had themselves survived the war in Salem on Lake Constance but had moved to Heidelberg in July 1945 to be with Anneliese's mother, Henni von Halle, who had herself survived the war in Berlin but had come to Heidelberg to escape the privations and uncertainty of a capital that was being reduced to rubble by bombardment and was later gutted by the last major battle of the war in Europe.[4] The ordeal Schroeder and her family had gone through over the Nazi years can easily be imagined: her mother hailed from a prominent Jewish family in Berlin, and her deceased father, Ernst, was the son of a prominent Jewish attorney and Jewish heiress of a department store fortune in Hamburg. Schröder-von Halle had been a Jew according to the Nuremberg Laws, and her children "*Mischlinge* of the first degree." They were likely only spared deportation and murder by her husband, who had himself managed to survive the war to protect them. Miraculously her mother had survived the Holocaust too. In her letter to Schumacher, Schröder wrote of how very relieved she was that the Nazi years were finally over, that one could now speak openly and expect to be treated decently.[5]

The Schumachers had suffered too, but in other ways. Like von Halle's widow, Hermann Schumacher had survived much of the war in Berlin with his

---

[1] GNN HA, Nl. Hermann Schumacher, I, C-241-43, Annelise Schroeder-von Halle to Hermann Schumacher, Karlsruhe, March 13, 1946.
[2] Ibid.   [3] Ibid.
[4] Ibid.; Cappel, "Ihre dankbar ergebene Henni von Halle," in Weiß, *Folio in memoriam*, 234.
[5] Ibid., 228–29; GNN HA, Nl. Hermann Schumacher, I, C-241-43, Annelise Schroeder-von Halle to Hermann Schumacher, Karlsruhe, March 13, 1946.

wife Edith, née Zitelmann, but their home atop the Fichtelberg in Berlin-Steglitz was destroyed by aerial bombardment and they were forced to flee west as evacuees, settling in Überlingen on Lake Constance.[6] Shortly after the war they moved to Göttingen to be near their daughter Elisabeth (1914–98) and her children. Elisabeth was married to the physicist Werner Heisenberg (1901–76), who had spent time in internment at Farm Hall in England with other leading German nuclear physicists in 1945 before returning to Germany in 1946 and rebuilding his Physics Institute at Göttingen University.[7] Schumacher's oldest son, Hermann Jr. (1910–81) had served in the Wehrmacht in Norway and was held as a POW in the United States. The second oldest son, Ernst Fritz Schumacher (1911–77), later the author of *Small is Beautiful*, had been a Rhodes Scholar in Oxford and was working in London for Unilever before being interned as an enemy alien at the outbreak of the war in 1939. Schumacher's youngest son of barely 18 years, Ernst (1923–41), was killed in action in the Soviet Union in October 1941.[8]

The other men who had formed the circle of scholars around Schumcher had all since died. Ernst von Halle of pleurisy in 1909; Gustav Schmoller while on convalescence at a spa in Bad Harzburg in 1917; Karl Rathgen in 1921; Helfferich violently in a train crash in 1924; and Henry Farnam of post-operative complications in September 1933, living just long enough to watch – no doubt shaking his head – as the Hitler regime consolidated power. Before his own death in 1939 Max Sering had to endure the indignity of being dismissed from his post as professor at the University of Berlin and from the Prussian Academy of Sciences. Officially this was done on account of his consistent opposition to Nazism, but his legal status as a Jewish "*Mischling*" must have also played a role.[9]

Before he died in 1952 Schumacher drafted a memoir which he completed in 1947 but never published. In its foreword he wrote that the tumultuous times he had witnessed over his lifetime sparked a desire to take stock. His brother's life work had been architecture while his own had been *Weltwirtschaft*; much of the former lay in ruins while the latter had largely disintegrated.[10] Yet despite the fact that many cities in western Germany had

---

[6] GNN HA, Nl. Hermann Schumacher, I, B-6x, fols. 713a, 714/718, 733; Werner Heisenberg to Elisabeth Heisenberg, Hechingen, Aug. 21, 1944 and Elisabeth Heisenberg to Werner Heisenberg, Frankfurt, Nov. 14, 1945, in Werner and Elisabeth Heisenberg, *My Dear Li: Correspondence 1937–1946*, ed. Anna Maria Hirsch-Heisenberg, trans. Irene Heisenberg (New Haven and London: Yale University Press, 2016), 220–21, 270.

[7] Heisenberg, *My Dear Li*, 263–72, 282–301.

[8] GNN HA, Nl. Hermann Schumacher, I, B-6x, fols. 709–10, 712b–712d.

[9] HUB, UA, UK Personalia, S 84, Max Sering, Bd. 1 und 2, Max Sering to Rector of the Friedrichs-Wilhelms University of Berlin, Berlin, March 2, 1936 with attached biographical questionnaire.

[10] GNN HA, Nl. Hermann Schumacher, B-6a, Vorwort, Göttingen, Nov. 4, 1949.

been destroyed by bombardment and material shortages were still dire, Schumacher saw that new forms of cooperation between peoples were emerging that he hoped would allow the "confusion of healthy internationalism and healthy nationalism for the well-being of humanity and thereby the German people."[11] The Bretton Woods accord had been signed in the last year of the war, creating the International Monetary Fund and World Bank, and in the year he concluded his memoir, 1947, both the General Agreement on Tariffs and Trade was signed and the Marshall Plan was announced. Before his death Schumacher lived long enough to witness the formation of the German Federal Republic in 1949 and the Schuman Declaration in 1950, which led to the European Coal and Steel Community and the process of European integration initiated by the Treaty of Paris in 1951. These institutions, together with American grants, the security guarantees of the NATO alliance, and the German debt write-downs of the London German External Debt Agreement of 1953, allowed West Germany to slowly reclaim its place in *Weltwirtschaft* in the 1950s and achieve unprecedented levels of economic growth and material prosperity by the early 1960s.

Many have been tempted to chalk up West Germany's remarkable transformation into a stable democracy and peaceful European neighbor to total defeat and occupation and the democratic reforms imposed by the British and Americans, to neoliberal institutions and policy under Konrad Adenauer and Ludwig Erhard, or to the generational change and cultural transformation of the 1960s and 70s. To be sure, these things all contributed to and reinforced West Germany's transformation into a peaceful, stable, open, and democratic society, an effort to which, it must be added here, the historian Fritz Fischer and a younger generation of scholars coming of age then made signal contributions. A useful but tendentious historical narrative was produced in the 1960s and 70s that Germany's World Policy was domestic in origin, a calculated bid by the Kaiser and an alliance of agrarian military and industrial elites to escape domestic crises by outward diversion to prevent democratic reforms, elites who then allegedly planned and started First World War and later brought Hitler to power. Tellingly, this drew on and was influenced by the Weimar-era narrative of Eckart Kehr offering a similar interpretation for his time.[12] While it largely played down or elided the political agency of the middle

---

[11] Ibid.
[12] Kehr, *Battleship Building*; Fischer, *Griff Nach der Weltmacht*; Fischer, *Krieg der Illusionen*; Helmut Böhme, *Deutschlands Weg zur Großmacht: Studien zum Verhältnis von Wirtschaft und Staat während der Reichsgründung 1848–1881* (Cologne: Kiepenheuer und Witsch, 1966); Wehler, *Bismarck und der Imperialismus*; Berghahn, *Der Tirpitz Plan*; Bade, *Friedrich Fabri*; Wolfgang J. Mommsen, "Domestic Factors in German Foreign Policy before 1914," in *Imperial Germany*, ed. James J. Sheehan (New York: New Viewpoints, 1976), 222–68. Cf. Kohut, *Wilhelm II*, 225–34.

and working classes in its narrative and thus much co-responsibility for the twentieth century's German-led disasters, it did help to focus attention on the importance of buttressing West Germany's still fragile democracy when it was under threat from within by ex-Nazis in senior government positions and without by the Neo-Nazi right and the terrorist far left . The durability of the liberal nationalist content of German imperialism, the enthusiastic participation of the middle, and even parts of the working classes in that project, and its continued ressonance well into the 1920s, 30s, and 40s was inconvenient to that narrative, especially since blame could be shifted to a Kaiser and chancellors now long dead, expropriated East Elbian aristocratic landowners, and banking and industrial magnates and their cartels purged or broken up by the occupying allies.[13] This was a story that meshed almost seamlessly with the fable that the German people had been seduced and betrayed by Hitler and the Nazis, a notion lent credibility at the time by the publication and immense popularity of Albert Speer's (1905–1981) deeply deceitful memoir and diaries.[14]

It could be argued that what actually mattered most to the success of West German democracy in the 1960s and 1970s (as opposed to the 1920s and 1930s) was the prosperity enabled by international institutions that liberalized trade within and beyond Europe, the Cold War system of collective security, and the process of decolonization. These things ended the destructive European economic, military, and colonial rivalries of the so-called *Pax Britannica* and interwar period. Democracy was seen to deliver prosperity, stability, and peace for the first time in German history. That, as much as anything else, turned Germans into peaceful democrats. As the centenary of the Versailles Treaty passes and as the world gropes its way through the challenges of the second era of globalization, Germany's past is more relevant than ever as both a caution and way forward.

---

[13] Daniel, "Einkreisung und Kaiserdämmerung," in Stollberg-Rilinger, *Was heißt Kulturgeschichte*, 281–82, 327; cf. Helmut Böhme, "'Primat und Paradigmata': Zur Entwicklung einer bundesdeutschen Zeitgeschichtsforschung am Beispiel des Ersten Weltkriegs," in *Historikerkontroversen*, ed. Hartmut Lehmann (Göttingen: Wallstein, 2000), 87–140.

[14] See Magnus Brechtken, *Albert Speer: Eine deutsche Karriere* (Munich: Siedler, 2017).

# SELECTED BIBLIOGRAPHY

## Manuscript Sources

Boston Public Library (BPL)
    Hugo Münsterberg Collection
Bundesarchiv Koblenz (BArch K)
    N 1001 Nachlass Lujo Brentano
    N 1016 Nachlass Bernhard von Bülow
    N 1123 Nachlass Karl Helfferich
    N 1210 Nachlass Max Sering
Bundesarchiv Lichterfelde (BArch L)
    N 2077 Nachlass Ernst Francke
    R 901/37396 Uebertritt deutscher Gelehrten und Künstler in fremde Dienste, Bd. 11, vom August 1888–Juli 1891
    R 901/39186 Das Unterrichtswesen in Japan, vom Februar 1876 bis Mai 1890
    R 901/39187 Das Unterrichtswesen in Japan, vom Juni 1890 bis September 1900
    R 901/39188 Das Unterrichtswesen in Japan, vom Oktober 1900 bis März 1904
    R 901/39189 Das Unterrichtswesen in Japan, vom 1. April 1904 bis 31. Dezember 1911.
    R 8023/511 R Deutsche Kolonialgesellschaft, Kolonialpolitisches Aktionskomitee
Bundesarchiv Militärarchiv Freiburg (BArch M)
    N 253 Nachlass Alfred von Tirpitz
    RM 2 Kaiserliches Marinekabinett
    RM 3 Reichsmarineamt
    RM 5 Admiralstab der Marine
Geheimes Staatsarchiv preußischer Kulturbesitz, Berlin (GStA PK)
    I. HA Rep. 76 Kultusministerium, V c Sekt. 1, Tit. 11, Teil VII, Nr. 22, Bd. 1 [Die Aus dem Kaiserlichen Japan eingesendeten wissenschaftlichen und Kunstsachen und die Bestimmung darüber vom November 1874 bis März 1902]
    I. HA Rep. 89 Geheimes Zivilkabinett jüngere Periode, Nr. 13369 [Die Asiatischen Staaten/ Japan, Persien, China, Siam, Birma. 1862 bis 1912]
    VI. HA Nachlass Gustav von Schmoller
Germanisches Nationalmuseum Nürnberg, Historisches Archiv (GNN HA)
    Nachlass Hermann Schumacher

Hessisches Hauptstaatsarchiv, Wiesbaden (HHStA)
    Abt. 1088 Teilnachlass Gustav Schmoller
Humboldt-Universität zu Berlin, Universitätsarchiv (HUB UA)
    UK Personalia, S 84, Max Sering
Politisches Archiv der Auswärtigen Amts, Berlin (PA AA)
    P 11799 Personalakte betreffend Dr. jur. Karl Rathgen
    R 62407 Die deutschen Schulen in Japan
    R 63159, Die deutsche Jesuiten-Universität für Japaner in Tokio vom Januar 1913 bis 1925.
Privatnachlass Familie Barthold C. Witte, Bonn-Bad Godesberg (PNFBW)
    Briefe Karl Rathgens an Bernhard Rathgen, Ina von Olshausen, Toni Preller, und Lucie Schmoller, 13. Februar 1882/20. Oktober 1890.
Staatsarchiv der Freien Hansestadt Hamburg (StaHH)
    361-6 Hochschulwesen – Dozenten – und Personalakten I 330, Personalakte Professor Dr. Rathgen
    364-6 Hamburgisches Kolonialinstitut
Staatsbibliothek Berlin (SBB)
    Krieg 1914/24896, Max Sering, Bericht über die eroberten Gebiete des Nordostens. Auf Grund einer zweimonatigen Studienreise, n.d. [1916]
Staats- und Universitätsbibliothek Hamburg Carl von Ossietzky (SUB)
    Nachlass Werner von Melle
Warburg Institute Archives, London (WIA)
    IV Aby Warburg Papers
    Family Correspondence (FC)
Yale University Library, Manuscripts and Archives, New Haven, CT (YUL MA)
    Farnam Family Papers

## Published Primary Sources

### Official Records and Documents

Die Große Politik der Europäischen Kabinette 1871–1914: Sammlung der Diplomatischen Akten des Auswärtigen Amtes
Hansard House of Commons Debates
Stenographische Berichte über die Verhandlungen des Deutschen Reichstages
Stenographische Berichte über die Verhandlungen des Preußischen Hauses der Abgeordneten
Stenographische Berichte über die Verhandlungen des Preußischen Herrenhauses

### Selected Books and Pre-1930 Literature

Ashley, William J. *The Tariff Problem*. London: P. S. King & Son, 1903.
Bartels-Ishikawa, Anna, ed. *Hermann Roesler: Dokumente zu seinem Leben und Werk*. Berlin: Duncker & Humblot, 2007.

Bartels-Ishikawa, Anna, Hansgerd Delbrück, and Itō Yushi, eds. *Die schönste Zeit meines Lebens: Ernst und Felix Delbrücks Briefe aus Japan aus den Jahren 1887 bis 1889*. Dunedin: University of Otago Department of Languages and Cultures, German Section, 2014.

Becker, Bert, ed. *Georg Michaelis: Ein preußischer Jurist im Japan der Meiji-Zeit; Briefe, Tagebuchnotizen, Dokumente, 1885–1889*. Munich: Iudicium, 2001.

Becker, Willy. *Fürst Bülow und England 1897–1909*. Greifswald: L. Bamberg, 1929.

Bernhardi, Friedrich von. *Deutschland und der nächste Krieg*. 6th ed. Stuttgart and Berlin: Cotta, 1913. First published 1912.

Bolles, Albert Sidney. *Industrial History of the United States, from the Earliest Settlements to the Present Time*. Norwich, CT: H. Bill, 1878.

Bueck, H. A. *Der Centralverband deutscher Industrieller 1876–1901*. 3 vols. Berlin: Deutscher Verlag/J. Guttentag, 1902–1905.

Bülow, Bernhard Fürst von. *Deutsche Politik*. Berlin: Reimar Hobbing, 1916.

― *Denkwürdigkeiten*. 4 vols. Edited by Franz von Stockhammern. Berlin: Ullstein, 1930–1931.

Chamberlain, Joseph. "The True Conception of Empire." In *Foreign and Colonial Speeches*, 241–48. London: Routledge, 1897.

― "A Demand for Inquiry." In *Imperial Union and Tariff Reform: Speeches Delivered from May 15 to Nov. 4, 1903*, 1–18. London: Grant Richards, 1903.

Childers, Erskine. *The Riddle of the Sands: A Record of Secret Service Recently Achieved*. With an introduction by Eric J. Grove. Annapolis: Naval Institute Press, 1991. First published 1903.

Cobden, Richard. *The Three Panics: An Historical Episode*. 5th ed. London: Ward & Co, 1862.

Delbrück, Hans. "Stagnation in der inneren und äußeren Politik." *Preußische Jahrbücher* 81 (1895): 383–91.

― *Geschichte der Kriegskunst im Rahmen der politischen Geschichte, Erster Theil: Das Alterthum*. Berlin: Georg Stilke, 1900.

Deutscher Kolonialkongress. *Verhandlungen des Deutschen Kolonialkongresses 1902 zu Berlin am 10. und 11. Oktober 1902*. Berlin: D. Riemer, 1903.

Deutscher Kolonialkrieger-Bund, ed. *Unvergessenes Heldentum: Das Kolonisationswerk der deutschen Schutztruppe und Marine*. Berlin: Kolonialwarte, 1924.

Eckert, Christian. *Die Seeinteressen Rheinland-Westfalens*. Leipzig: Teubner, 1906.

Eltzbacher, Paul, ed. *Die deutsche Volksernährung und der englische Aushungerungsplan*. Braunschweig: F. Vierweg & Sohn, 1914.

Epkenhans, Michael, ed. *Das ereignisreiche Leben eines "Wilhelminers": Tagebücher, Briefe und Aufzeichnungen 1901 bis 1920 von Albert Hopman*. Munich: Oldenbourg, 2004.

Erzberger, Matthias. *Warum ist der Reichstag aufgelöst worden? Ein Wort an die Wählerschaft*. Berlin: Germania, 1907.

Evangelisch-Sozialer Kongress. *Die Verhandlungen des Elften Evangelisch-sozialen Kongresses, abgehalten zu Karlsruhe am 7. und 8. Juni 1900: Nach den stenografischen Protokollen*. Göttingen: Vandenhoeck & Ruprecht, 1900.

Farnam, Henry W. *Die innere französische Gewerbepolitik von Colbert bis Turgot.* Staats- und socialwissenschaftliche Forschungen, vol. 1. Leipzig: Duncker & Humblot, 1878.
*Die amerikanischen Gewerkvereine.* SdVfS, vol. 18. Leipzig: Duncker & Humblot, 1879.
"Deutsch-Amerikanisch Beziehungen in der Volkswirtschaftslehre." In *Die Entwicklung der deutschen Volkswirtschaftslehre im neunzehnten Jahrhundert: Gustav Schmoller zum siebzigsten Wiederkehr seines Geburtstags, 24. Juni 1908*, vol. 1. Edited by S. P. Altmann et al., 1–31. Leipzig: Duncker & Humblot, 1908.
Galster, Karl Paul Hans. *Welche Seekriegs-Rüstung braucht Deutschland?* Berlin: Boll und Pickardt, 1907.
Gooch, G. P., and Harold Temperly, eds. *British Documents on the Origins of the War, 1898–1914.* Vol. 3. London: H. M. Stationary Office, 1928.
Grimm, Hans. *Volk ohne Raum.* Vol. 2. Munich: Albert Langen, 1931. First published 1926.
Gumbel, Emil Julius. *Vier Jahre politischer Mord.* 5th ed. Berlin-Fichtenau: Verlag der Neuen Gesellschaft, 1922.
Hale, William Bayard. *American Rights & British Pretensions on the Seas: The Facts and Documents, Official and Other, Bearing on the Present Attitude of Great Britain toward the Commerce of the United States.* New York: Robert M. McBride & Co, 1915.
Halle, Ernst Levy von. *Die Hamburger Giro-Bank und ihr Ausgang.* Berlin: Puttkammer & Mühlbrecht, 1891.
"Industrielle Unternehmer- und Unternehmungsverbände in den Vereinigten Staaten von Nordamerika." In *Über wirtschaftliche Kartelle in Deutschland und im Auslande: Fünfzehn Schilderungen nebst einer Anzahl Statuten und Beilagen.* Edited by Ständiger Ausschuss des Vereins für Socialpoltik, zweiter Teil [part 2], 93–322. SdVfS, vol. 60. Leipzig: Duncker & Humblot, 1894.
"Münchener Volkswirtschaltliche Studien: Lujo Brentano, Walther Lotz." *Journal of Political Economy* 2, no. 3 (June 1894): 464–68.
"Die Wirtschaftliche Krisis des Jahres 1893 in den Vereinigten Staaten von Nordamerika." *JbfGVV* 18 (1894): 1181–1249.
*Trusts or Industrial Combinations and Coalitions in the United States.* New York and London: Macmillan & Co., 1896.
*Reisebriefe aus Westindien und Venezuela: Skizzen während einer 10 wöchentlichen Tour mit dem Schnelldampfer "Columbia" der Hamburg-Amerika Linie.* Hamburg: A.G. "Neue Börsen-Halle", 1896.
"Das Interesse Deutschlands an der amerikanischen Präsidentenwahl des Jahres 1896." *JbfGVV* 20 (1896): 1353–86.
*Baumwollproduktion und Pflanzungswirtschaft in den Nordamerikanischen Südstaaten.* Vol. 1, *Die Sklavenzeit.* Staats- und socialwissenschaftliche Forschungen, vol. 15, no. 1. Leipzig: Duncker & Humblot, 1897.
"Die Seeinteressen Deutschlands." *JbfGVV* 22 (1898): 221–45.

*Die Blockade der nordamerikanischen Südstaaten*. Berlin: Mittler und Sohn, 1900.

"Die Entwicklung und Bedeutung der deutschen Reederei." In *Handels und Machtpolitik: Reden und Aufsätze im Auftrage der "Freien Vereinigung für Flottenvorträge*." Vol. 2, 2nd ed. Edited by Gustav Schmoller, Max Sering, and Adolph Wagner, 127–74. Stuttgart: J. G. Cotta, 1900.

"Deutschland und die öffentliche Meinung in den Vereinigten Staaten." *Preussische Jahrbücher* 107, no. 2 (1902): 189–212.

*Volks- und Seewirthschaft: Reden und Aufsätze*. Vol. 1. Berlin: Mittler und Sohn, 1902.

"Das Problem der Reichsfinanzreform." *Preußische Jahrbücher* 119, no. 3 (1905): 495–507.

*Baumwollproduktion und Pflanzungswirtschaft in den Nordamerikanischen Südstaaten*. Vol. 2, *Sezessionskrieg und Rekonstruktion: Grundzüge einer Wirtschaftsgeschichte der Baumwollstaaten von 1861–1880*. In Staats- und sozialwissenschaftliche Forschungen, vol. 26, no. 2. Leipzig: Duncker & Humblot, 1906.

"Die großen Epochen der neuzeitlichen Kolonialgeschichte." *Zeitschrift für Kolonialpolitik, Kolonialrecht, und Kolonialwirtschaft* 9, no. 1 (January 1907): 19–54.

*Die Seemacht in der deutschen Geschichte*. Leipzig: G. J. Göschen'sche Verlagsbuchhandlung, 1907.

*Die Wirtschaftswissenschaft in der heutigen Beamtenvorbildung: Referat gehalten auf der VI. Ordentlichen Hauptversammlung des Deutschen Volkswirtschaftlichen Verbandes*, Schriften des Deutschen Volkswirtschaftlichen Verbandes, vol. 3, no. 2. Berlin: Carl Heymanns Verlag, 1909.

Halle, Ernst von, ed. *Amerika: Seine Bedeutung für die Weltwirtschaft und seine wirtschaftliche Beziehungen zu Deutschland insbesondere zu Hamburg*. Hamburg: Verlag der Hamburger Börsenhalle, 1905.

Halle, Ernst von, and Tjard Schwarz, eds. *Die Schiffbauindustrie in Deutschland und im Auslande*. Berlin: Mittler und Sohn, 1902.

Hammann, Otto. *The World Policy of Germany, 1890–1912*. Translated by Maude A. Huttman. New York: Knopf, 1927.

Harrison, Austin. *The Pan-Germanic Doctrine: Being a Study of German Political Claims and Aspirations*. London and New York: Harper & Brothers, 1904.

Heisenberg, Elisabeth. *My Dear Li: Correspondence 1937–1946*. Edited by Anna Maria Hirsch-Heisenberg. Translated by Irene Heisenberg. New Haven, CT and London: Yale University Press, 2016.

Helfferich, Karl. *Die Folgen des deutsch-österreichischen Münzvereins von 1857: Ein Beitrag zur Geld- und Währungs-Theorie*. Strasbourg: Karl J. Trübner, 1894.

*Die Reform des deutschen Geldwesens nach der Gründung des Reiches*. 2 vols. Leipzig: Duncker & Humblot, 1898.

*Handelspolitik: Vorträge, gehalten in Hamburg im Winter 1900/01 im Auftrag der Hamburgischen Oberschulbehörde*. Leipzig: Duncker & Humblot, 1901.

*Zur Reform der kolonialen Verwaltungs-Organisation*. Berlin: Mittler und Sohn, 1905.

*Das Geld im russisch-japanischen Krieg: Ein finanzpolitischer Beitrag zur Zeitgeschichte.* Berlin: Mittler und Sohn, 1906.

"Die türkische Staatsschuld und die Balkanstaaten." *Bank-Archiv: Zeitschrift für Bank- und Börsenwesen* 12, no. 11 (1913): 167–75.

*Germany's Economic Progress and National Wealth 1888–1913.* New York: Germanistic Society, 1914.

*Der Weltkrieg.* 3 vols. Berlin: Ullstein, 1919.

Kahl, Wilhelm, Adolph Wagner, and Karl Lamprecht. *Die nationale Bedeutung der Reichsfinanzreform: Drei Reden, gehalten in Berlin am 6. November 1908.* Berlin and Leipzig: Hillger, 1908.

Kessler, Count Harry. *Walther Rathenau: His Life and Work.* London Gerald Howe, 1929.

Keynes, John Maynard. *The Economic Consequences of the Peace.* New York: Harcourt, Brace and Howe, 1920. First published 1919.

Kjellén, Rudolf. *Stormakterna: konturer kring samtidens storpolitik*, rev. and enl. ed. Stockholm: H. Geber, 1913. First published 1911.

*Den ryska faran.* Karlskrona: Karlskrona-Tidningen, 1913.

*Die Ideen von 1914: Eine weltgeschichtliche Perspektive.* Leipzig: S. Hirzel, 1915.

Koch, Matthias and Sebastian Conrad, eds. *Johannes Justus Rein: Briefe eines deutschen Geographen aus Japan 1873–1875.* Munich: Iudicium, 2006.

Kolonialpolitisches Aktionskomité, ed. *Schmoller, Dernburg, Delbrück, Schäfer, Sering, Schillings, Brunner, Jastrow, Penck, Kahl über Reichstagsauflösung und Kolonialpolitik: Offizieller stenographischer Bericht über die Versammlung in der Berliner Hochschule für Musik am 8. Januar 1907.* Berlin: Wedekind, 1907.

*Kolonialpolitischer Führer.* Berlin: Wedekind, 1907.

*Die Eisenbahnen Afrikas: Grundlagen und Gesichtspunkte für eine koloniale Eisenbahnpolitik in Afrika: Nach der gleichnamigen amtlichen Denkschrift.* Berlin: Wilhelm Süsserott, 1907.

Lindequist, Friedrich von. *Deutsch-Ostafrika als Siedlungsgebiet für Europäer unter Berücksichtigung Britisch-Ostafrikas und Nyassalands.* SdVfS, vol. 147, erster Teil [part 1]. Leipzig and Munich: Duncker & Humblot, 1912.

Ludendorff, Erich, ed. *Urkunden der Obersten Heeresleitung über ihre Tätigkeit 1916/18.* Berlin: Mittler und Sohn, 1920.

Lumm, Karl von. *Karl Helfferich als Währungspolitiker und Gelehrter.* Leipzig: C. L. Hirschfeld, 1926.

Mackinder, Halford John. "The Geographic Pivot of History." *The Geographical Journal* 23, no. 4 (April 1904): 421–44.

Meinecke, Friedrich. *Geschichte des deutsch-englischen Bündnisproblems.* Munich and Vienna: Oldenbourg, 1927.

Michaelis, Georg. *Für Staat und Volk: Eine Lebensgeschichte.* Berlin: Furche Verlag, 1922.

Molodowsky, N. "Germany's Foreign Trade Terms in 1899–1913." *Quarterly Journal of Economics* 41, no. 4 (August 1927): 664–83.

Mosse, Albert, and Lina Mosse. *Fast wie mein eigen Vaterland: Briefe aus Japan, 1886–1889.* Edited by Shirō Ishii, Ernst Lokowandt, and Yūkichi Sakai. Munich: Iudicium, 1995.

Münsterberg, Margaret. *Hugo Münsterberg: His Life and Work.* New York and London: D. Appleton & Co., 1922.

Naumann, Friedrich. *"Asia": Athen, Konstantinopel, Baalbek, Damaskus, Nazaret, Jerusalem, Kairo, Neapel.* 3rd ed. Berlin-Schöneberg: Verlag der "Hilfe," 1900.

——— *Demokratie und Kaisertum: Ein Handbuch für innere Politik.* Berlin-Schöneberg: Buchverlag der "Hilfe," 1905.

——— *Mitteleuropa.* Berlin: Georg Riemer, 1915.

Nauticus. *Altes und neues zur Flottenfrage: Erläuterungen zum Flottengesetz.* Berlin: Mittler und Sohn, 1898.

Peez, Alexander von. *Zur neuesten Handelspolitik: Sieben Abhandlungen.* Vienna: Commissions-Verlag von Georg Szelinski, 1895.

Pogge von Strandmann, Hartmut, ed. *Walther Rathenau, Industrialist, Banker, Intellectual, and Politician: Notes and Diaries 1907–1922.* Translated by Caroline Pinder Cracraft. Oxford: Clarendon Press; New York: Oxford University Press, 1985.

*Die preussische Expedition nach Ost-Asien nach amtlichen Quellen.* Vol. 1. Berlin: Verlag der Königlichen Geheimen Ober-Hofbuchdruckerei [R. v. Decker], 1864.

Rathenau, Walther. *Gesammelte Schriften in fünf Bänden.* 5 vols. Berlin: S. Fischer, 1918.

Rathgen, Karl. *Die Entstehung der Märkte in Deutschland.* Darmstadt: Buchdruckerei von G. Otto, 1881.

——— "Ergebnisse der amtlichen Bevölkerungsstatistik in Japan" (mit einer Karte). *MOAG* 4 (1884–1888), Heft 37: 322–40.

——— *Japans Volkswirtschaft und Staatshaushalt.* Staats- und socialwissenschaftliche Forschungen, vol. 10. Leipzig: Duncker & Humblot, 1891.

——— "Moderne Handelspolitik." *Preußische Jahrbücher* 69 (1892): 84–97.

——— *Englische Auswanderung und Auswanderungspolitik im 19. Jahrhundert.* SdVfS, vol. 72. Leipzig: Duncker & Humblot, 1896.

——— "Über den Plan eines britischen Reichszollvereins." *Preußische Jahrbücher* 86 (1896): 481–523.

——— "Die Kündigung des englischen Handelsvertrags und ihre Gefahr für Deutschlands Zukunft." *JbfGVV* 21 (1897): 1369–86.

——— *Die Japaner und ihre wirtschaftliche Entwicklung.* Leipzig: Teubner, 1905.

——— "Entwicklungstendenzen im Außenhandel Chinas und Japans." *JbfGVV* 30 (1906): 1079–94.

——— "Les impôts directs dans les colonies." In *Compte rendu de la session tenue à Bruxelles les 29, 30 et 31 juillet 1912.* Edited by the Institut colonial international, 182–232. Brussels: Bbiliothèque Colonial International, 1912.

Ratzel, Friedrich. *Die Vereinigten Staaten von Amerika.* Vol. 2, *Politische und Wirtschafts-Geographie.* 2nd ed. Munich: Oldenbourg, 1893.

——— *Politische Geographie.* Munich and Leipzig: Oldenbourg, 1897.

Reichschatzamt. *Denkschriftenband zur Begründung des Entwurfs eines Gesetzes betreffend Änderungen im Finanzwesen.* Teile 1–4. Berlin: J. Guttentag Verlagsbuchhandlung, 1908–9.

Rein, Johannes Justus. "Naturwissenschaftliche Reisestudien in Japan – Nikko," *MOAG* I (1873–1876) Heft 6: 60–61; (Fortsetzung), *MOAG* I (1873–1876) Heft 7: 21–26.

"Naturwissenschaftliche Reisestudien in Japan – Die Kueste von Sendai und Nambu," *MOAG* I (1873–1876), Heft 7: 26–29.

*Japan nach Reisen und Studien im Auftrage der königlich preussischen Regierung dargestellt.* Vol. 1, *Natur und Volk des Mikadoreiches.* Leipzig: Wilhelm Engelmann, 1881.

*Travels and Researches Undertaken at the Cost of the Prussian Government.* New York: A. C. Armstrong and Son, 1884.

*Japan nach Reisen und Studien im Auftrage der königlich preussischen Regierung dargestellt.* Vol. 2, *Land- und Forstwirtschaft, Industrie und Handel.* Leipzig: Wilhelm Engelmann, 1886.

Richthofen, Ferdinand von. *Baron Richthofen's Letters, 1870–72.* Shanghai: North-China Herald Office, 1872.

*China: Ergebnisse eigener Reisen und darauf gegründeter Studien.* 3 vols. Berlin: Dietrich Reimer, 1876–1883.

*Atlas von China: Orographische und geologische Karten, zu des Verfassers Werk: China, Ergebnisse eigener Reisen und darauf gegründeter Studien.* Berlin: Dietrich Reimer, 1885.

Rohrbach, Paul. *Die Bagdadbahn.* Berlin: Wiegandt & Grieben, 1902.

*Deutschland unter den Weltvölkern: Materialien zur auswärtigen Politik.* Berlin-Schöneberg: Buchverlag der "Hilfe," 1903.

Roloff, Gustav. *Die Kolonialpolitik Napoleons I.* Munich and Leipzig: Oldenbourg, 1899.

Royal Commission on the War in South Africa. *Minutes of Evidence Taken Before the Royal Commission on the War in South Africa.* 2 vols. London: Wyman and Sons, 1903.

[Schmoller, Gustav]. *Der französische Handelsvertrag und seine Gegner. Ein Wort der Verständigung von einem Süddeutschen.* Frankfurt a.M.: Sauerländer's Verlag, 1862.

Schmoller, Gustav. "Rede über Strassburgs Blüte und die volkswirtschaftliche Revolution im XIII. Jahrhundert." In *Der Rectoratswechsel an der Universität Strassburg am 31. October 1874.* Strasbourg: Karl J. Trübner, 1874.

*Strassburg zur Zeit der Zunftkämpfe und die Reformen seiner Verfassung und Verwaltung im XV. Jahrhundert: Rede gehalten zur Feier des Stiftungsfestes der Universität Strassburg am 1. Mai 1975.* Strasbourg: Karl. J. Trübner, 1875.

"Korreferat über die Zolltarifvorlage." In *Verhandlungen der sechsten Generalversammlung des Vereins für Socialpolitik über die Zolltarifvorlage am 21. und 22. April 1879.* Edited by Ständiger Ausschuss des Vereins für Socialpoltik, 19–29. SdVfS, vol. 16. Leipzig: Duncker & Humblot, 1879.

"Ueber Zweck und Ziele des Jahrbuchs." *JbfGVV* 5 (1881): 1–18.

"Die amerikanische Konkurrenz und die Lage der mitteleuropäischen, besonders der deutschen Landwirthschaft." *JbfGVV* 6 (1882): 247–84.

"Studien über die wirtschaftliche Politik Friedrichs des Großen und Preußens überhaupt von 1680–1786." *JbfGVV* 8 (1884): 1–61, 345–421, 999–1091; 10 (1886): 1–45, 327–73, 675–727; 11 (1887): 1–58, 789–883.

*Korreferat über innere Kolonisation mit Rücksicht auf die Erhaltung und Vermehrung des mittleren und kleineren ländlichen Grundbesitzes.* SdVfS, vol. 33. Leipzig: Duncker & Humblot, 1886.

"Neuere Literatur über unsere handelspolitische Zukunft." *JbfGVV* 15 (1891): 275–82.

"The Idea of Justice in Political Economy." Translated by Ernst von Halle and Carl M. Schutz. *Annals of the American Academy of Political and Social Science* 4 (March 1894): 1–41.

*The Mercantile System and Its Historical Significance Illustrated Chiefly from Prussian History.* Translated by William J. Ashley. New York: Macmillan, 1896.

*Umrisse und Untersuchungen zur Verfassungs-, Verwaltungs- und Wirtschaftsgeschichte.* Leipzig: Duncker & Humblot, 1898.

"Die wirtschaftliche Zukunft Deutschlands und die Flottenvorlage." In *Zwanzig Jahre Deutscher Politik (1897–1917): Aufsätze und Vorträge von Gustav Schmoller.* Edited by Lucie Schmoller, 1–20. Munich and Leipzig: Duncker & Humblot, 1920. First published 1900.

"Die Wandlungen in der europäischen Handelspolitik des 19. Jahrhunderts: Eine Säkularbetrachtung." *JbfGVV* 24 (1900): 373–82.

"Die Amerikaner." *JbfGVV* 28 (1904): 1477–94.

"Die künftige englische Handelspolitik, Chamberlain und der Imperialismus." *JbfGVV* 28 (1904): 829–52.

"Historische Betrachtungen über Staatenbildung und Finanzentwicklung." *JbfGVV* 33 (1909): 1–64.

"Die Handels- und Zollannäherung Mitteleuropas." *SJ* 40 (1916): 529–50.

"Obrigkeitsstaat und Volksstaat: Ein missverständlicher Gegensatz." *SJ* 40 (1916): 2031–42.

"Die heutige deutsche Judenfrage," *SJ* 41 (1917): 563–67.

*Walter Rathenau und Hugo Preuß: Die Staatsmänner des Neuen Deutschland.* Munich and Leipzig: Duncker & Humblot, 1922.

Schmoller, Gustav, Max Sering, and Adolf Wagner, eds. *Handels- und Machtpolitik: Reden und Aufsätze im Auftrage der "Freien Vereinigung für Flottenvorträge."* 2 vols. 2nd ed. Stuttgart: J. G. Cotta, 1900.

Schmoller, Lucie, ed. *Zwanzig Jahre Deutscher Politik (1897–1917): Aufsätze und Vorträge von Gustav Schmoller.* Munich and Leipzig: Duncker & Humblot, 1920.

Schnee, Heinrich. *Braucht Deutschland Kolonien? Ein Vortrag.* Leipzig: Quelle & Meyer, 1921.

*Nationalismus und Imperialismus.* Berlin: R. Hobbing, 1928.

Schücking, Walther. "Die deutschen Professoren und der Weltkrieg." *Flugschriften des Bundes "Neues Vaterland,"* no. 5 (1915).
Schumacher, Hermann. "Die Organisation des Getreidehandels in den Vereinigten Staaten von Amerika." *JbbfNS* III. Folge, 10 (1895): 361-92, 801-22; 11 (1896): 35-73, 161-236.
———. "Die chinesischen Vertragshäfen, ihre wirtschaftliche Stellung und Bedeutung." *JbbfNS* III. Folge, 16 (1898): 577-97, 721-93; III. Folge, 17 (1899): 55-70; 289-331.
———. "Die Organisation des Fremdhandels in China." *JbfGVV* 23 (1899): 657-91.
———. "Eisenbahnbau und Eisenbahnpläne in China." *Archiv für Eisenbahnwesen* 22 (1899): 901-78, 1194-226; 23 (1900): 1-115.
———. "Deutschlands Interessen in China." In *Handels und Machtpolitik: Reden und Aufsätze im Auftrage der "Freien Vereinigung für Flottenvorträge."* Edited by Gustav Schmoller, Max Sering, and Adolph Wagner, 175-246. Vol. 2, 2nd ed. Stuttgart: J. G. Cotta, 1900.
———. "Die deutschen Schiffahrtsinteressen im Stillen Ozean." In *Weltwirtschaftliche Studien: Vorträge und Aufsätze*, 463-97. Leipzig: Veit & Comp., 1911. First published 1901.
———. "II. Referat." In *Verhandlungen des Vereins für Socialpolitik über die Wohnungsfrage und die Handelspolitik*. Edited by Ständiger Ausschuss des Vereins für Socialpolitik, 153-81. SdVfS, vol. 98. Leipzig: Duncker & Humblot, 1902.
———. "Einleitung." In *Die städtische Handels-Hochschule in Köln, die erste selbständige Handels-Hochschule in Deutschland, eröffnet am 1. Mai 1901*. 3rd ed. Berlin: Julius Springer, 1903.
———. *Weltwirtschaftliche Studien: Vorträge und Aufsätze*. Leipzig: Veit & Comp., 1911.
———. *Meistbegünstigung und Zollunterscheidung*. Munich and Leipzig: Duncker & Humblot, 1916.
———. *Der Reis in der Weltwirtschaft*. Munich and Leipzig: Duncker & Humblot, 1917.
Segall, Jacob. *Die deutschen Juden als Soldaten im Kriege 1914-1918*. Berlin: Philo-Verlag, 1921.
Seligman, Edwin R. A. "Dr. Schumacher and the Kaiser Wilhelm Lectureship." *American Monthly Review of Reviews*, XXXIV, no. 5 (November 11, 1906): 548-49.
Sering, Max. *Geschichte der preussisch-deutschen Eisenzölle von 1818 bis zur Gegenwart*. Staats- und socialwissenschaftliche Forschungen, vol. 4. Leipzig: Duncker & Humblot, 1882.
———. *Die landwirthschaftliche Konkurrenz Nordamerikas in Gegenwart und Zukunft: Landwirthschaft, Kolonisation und Verkehrswesen in den Vereinigten Staaten und Britisch-Nordamerika*. Leipzig: Duncker & Humblot, 1887.
———. *Die innere Kolonisation im östlichen Deutschland*. SdVfS, vol. 56. Leipzig: Duncker & Humblot, 1893.
———. "Die Bodenbesitzverteilung und die Sicherung des Kleingrundbesitzes" [Referat]. In *Verhandlungen des am 20. und 21. März in Berlin abgehaltenen Generalversammlung des Vereins für Socialpolitik über die ländliche*

*Arbeiterfrage und über die Bodenbesitzverteilung und die Sicherung des Kleingrundbesitzes*. Edited by Ständiger Ausschuss des Vereins für Socialpolitik, 135–150. SdVfS, vol. 58. Leipzig: Duncker & Humblot, 1893.

"Die Handelspolitik der Grossstaaten und die Kriegsflotte." In *Handels und Machtpolitik: Reden und Aufsätze im Auftrage der "Freien Vereinigung für Flottenvorträge."* Edited by Gustav Schmoller, Max Sering, and Adolph Wagner, 1–44. Vol. 2, 2nd ed. Stuttgart: J. G. Cotta, 1900.

*Verhandlungen des Landes-Oekonomie-Kollegiums am 9. Februar 1912 über die Politik der Grundbesitzverteilung in den grossen Reichen*. Berlin: Parey, 1912.

Sering, Max, ed. *Russlands Kultur und Volkswirtschaft: Aufsätze und Vorträge im Auftrage der Vereinigung für Staatswissenschaftliche Fortbildung zu Berlin*. Berlin and Leipzig: G. J. Göschen'sche Verlagshandlung, 1913.

*Westrußland in seiner Bedeutung für die Entwicklung Mitteleuropas* Leipzig: B. G. Teubner, 1917.

Small, Albion W. "Some Contributions to the History of Sociology. Section XIX. The Emergence of Sociology in the United States." *American Journal of Sociology*, 30, no. 3. (November 1924): 310–36.

Ständiger Ausschuss des Vereins für Socialpoltik, ed. *Die Ansiedlung von Europäern in den Tropen*, SdVfS, vol. 147 Munich and Leipzig: Duncker & Humblot, 1912–15.

Stieda, Wilhelm. "Zur Erinnerung an Gustav Schmoller und seine Straßburger Zeit." *SJ* 45 (1921): 1155–93.

Studnitz, Arthur von. *Nordamerikanische Arbeiterverhältnisse*. Leipzig: Duncker & Humblot, 1879.

Tirpitz, Alfred von. *My Memoirs*. 2 vols. London: Hurst & Blackett, 1919.

*Politische Dokumente*. Vol. 1, *Der Aufbau der deutschen Weltmacht*. Stuttgart and Berlin: J. G. Cotta'sche Buchhandlung Nachfolger, 1924.

*Politische Dokumente*. Vol. 2, *Deutsche Ohnmachtspolitik im Weltkriege*. Hamburg and Berlin: Hanseatische Verlagsanstalt, 1926.

Treue, Wolfgang. *Deutsche Parteiprogramme seit 1861*. 4th enl. ed. Göttingen: Musterschmidt-Verlag, 1968.

Turner, Frederick Jackson. "The Significance of the Frontier in American History." In *The Frontier in American History*, 1–38. New York: Henry Holt, 1920. First published 1893.

Villard, Henry. *Memoirs of Henry Villard, Journalist and Financier*. 2 vols. Boston and New York: Houghton, Mifflin and Company, 1902.

Wagemann, Ernst. *Die deutschen Kolonisten im brasilianischen Staate Espirito Santo*. In *Die Ansiedlung von Europäern in den Tropen*. Edited by Ständiger Ausschuss des Vereins für Socialpolitik. SdVfS, vol. 147, fünfter Teil [part 5]. Munich and Leipzig: Duncker & Humblot, 1915.

Waltershausen, August Sartorius von. *Die nordamerikanischen Gewerkschaften unter dem Einfluss der fortschreitenden Produktionstechnik*. Berlin: Hermann Bahr, 1886.

*The Worker's Movement in the United States.* Edited by David Montgomery and Marcel van der Linden. Cambridge and New York: Cambridge University Press, 1998. First published 1886.

Warburg, Max. *Finanzielle Kriegsbereitschaft und Börsengesetz: Vortrag auf dem 3. Allg. Deutschen Bankiertag am 5. Sept. 1907.* Hamburg: Ackermann & Wulf, 1907.

*Aus meinen Aufzeichnungen.* New York: Eric M. Warburg, 1952.

Weber, Max. *Die Verhältnisse der Landarbeiter in Deutschland.* Vol. 3, *Die Verhältnisse der Landarbeiter im ostelbischen Deutschland.* SdVfS, vol. 55. Leipzig: Duncker & Humblot, 1892.

*Gesammelte politische Schriften.* Munich: Drei Masken Verlag, 1921.

White, Andrew D. *Autobiography.* Vol. 2. London: Macmillan and Co., 1905.

Whitman, Sidney. *Personal Reminiscences of Prince Bismarck.* New York: D. Appleton & Co., 1903.

Williams, Ernest Edwin. *"Made in Germany."* 5th ed. London: William Heinemann, 1897.

Zimmermann, Adolf. *Mit Dernburg nach Ostafrika.* Berlin: C. A. Schwentsche und Sohn, 1908.

Zoepfl, Gottfried. *Fränkische Handelpolitik im Zeitalter der Aufklärung: Ein Beitrag zur deutschen Staats- und Wirtschaftsgeschichte.* Erlangen: A. Deichert'sche Verlagsbuchhandlung Nachf. [G. Böhme], 1894.

*Der Wettbewerb des russischen und amerikanischen Petroleums: Eine Weltwirtschaftliche Studie.* Berlin: Siemenroth & Troschel, 1899.

"Kolonien und Kolonialpolitik." In *Handwörterbuch der Staatswissenschaften,* 3rd rev. ed., Vol. 5. Edited by J. Conrad, L. Elster, W. Lexis, and Edg. Loening, 921–1038. Jena: Gustav Fischer, 1910.

## Selected Secondary Sources

Afflerbach, Holger. *Der Dreibund: Europäische Großmacht- und Allianzpolitik vor dem Ersten Weltkrieg.* Vienna, Cologne and Weimar: Bölau Verlag, 2002.

*Auf Messers Schneide: Wie das Deutsche Reich den Ersten Weltkrieg Verlor.* Munich: C.H. Beck, 2018.

Ando, Junko. *Die Entstehung der Meiji-Verfassung: Zur Rolle des deutschen Konstitutionalismus im modernen japanischen Staatswesen.* Munich: Iudicium, 2000.

Barth, Boris. *Die deutsche Hochfinanz und die Imperialismen: Banken und Aussenpolitik vor 1914.* Stuttgart: Franz Steiner, 1995.

Beckert, Sven. *Empire of Cotton: A Global History.* New York: Knopf, 2015.

Berghahn, Volker. *Der Tirpitz Plan: Genesis und Verfall einer innenpolitischen Krisenstrategie unter Wilhelm II.* Düsseldorf: Droste Verlag, 1971.

*Germany and the Approach of War in 1914.* New York: St. Martin's Press, 1973.

Bickers, Robert A. *The Scramble for China: Foreign Devils in the Qing Empire, 1832–1914.* London: Allen Lane, 2011.

Blyth, Robert J., Andrew Lambert, and Jan Rüger, eds. *The Dreadnought and the Edwardian Age*. Farnham, Surrey and Burlington, VT: Ashgate, 2011.
Boghardt, Thomas. *The Zimmermann Telegram: Intelligence, Diplomacy and America's Entry into World War I*. Annapolis: Naval Institute Press, 2012.
Böhm, Ekkehard. *Überseehandel und Flottenbau: Hanseatische Kaufmannschaft und deutsche Seerüstung 1879–1914*. Düsseldorf: Bertelsmann Universitätsverlag, 1972.
Bönker, Dirk. *Militarism in a Global Age: Naval Ambitions in Germany and the United States before World War I*. Ithaca: Cornell University Press, 2012.
Brechtken, Magnus. *Scharnierzeit 1895–1907: Persönlichkeitsnetze und internationale Politik in den deutsch-britisch-amerikanischen Beziehungen vor dem Esten Weltkrieg*. Mainz: Philipp von Zabern, 2006.
vom Bruch, Rüdiger. *Wissenschaft, Politik und öffentliche Meinung: Gelehrtenpolitik im Wilhelminischen Deutschland (1890–1914)*. Husum: Matthiesen Verlag, 1980.
*Weltpolitik als Kulturmission: Auswärtige Kulturpolitik und Bildungsbürgertum in Deutschland am Vorabend des Ersten Weltkriegs*. Paderborn: F. Schöningh, 1982.
*Gelehrtenpolitik und akademische Diskurse in Deutschland im 19. und 20. Jahrhundert*. Edited by Björn Hofmeister and Hans-Christoph Liess. Stuttgart: Franz Steiner, 2006.
Canis, Konrad. *Von Bismarck zur Weltpolitik: Deutsche Aussenpolitik 1890 bis 1902*. Berlin: Akademie Verlag, 1997.
*Der Weg in den Abgrund: Deutsche Aussenpolitik 1902–1914*. Paderborn: F. Schöningh, 2011.
Cecil, Lamar. *Albert Ballin: Business and Politics in Imperial Germany, 1888–1918* Princeton: Princeton University Press, 1967.
Charmley, John. *Splendid Isolation? Britain, the Balance of Power and the Origins of the First World War*. London: Hodder & Stoughton, 1999.
Clark, Christopher M. *Kaiser Wilhelm II*. Harlow: Longman, 2000.
*The Sleepwalkers: How Europe Went to War in 1914*. New York: Harper, 2013.
Conrad, Sebastian. *Globalisation and the Nation in Imperial Germany*. Translated by Sorcha O'Hagan. Cambridge: Cambridge University Press, 2010.
Conrad, Sebastian and Jürgen Osterhammel, eds. *Das Kaiserreich transnational: Deutschland in der Welt 1871–1914*. Göttingen: Vandenhoeck & Ruprecht, 2004.
Coogan, John W. *The End of Neutrality: The United States, Britain and Maritime Rights 1899–1915*. Ithaca and London: Cornell University Press, 1981.
Deist, Wilhelm. *Flottenpolitik und Flottenpropaganda: Das Nachrichtenbureau des Reichsmarineamts 1897–1914*. Stuttgart: Deutsche Verlags-Anstalt, 1976.
Diziol, Sebastian. *"Deutsche, werdet Mitglieder des Vaterlandes!": Der Deutsche Flottenverein 1898–1934*. 2 vols. Kiel: Solivagus Praeteritum, 2015.

Eichholtz, Dietrich. *Die Bagdadbahn, Mesopotamien und die deutsche Ölpolitik bis 1918: Aufhaltsamer Übergang ins Erdözeitalter.* Leipzig: Leipziger Universitätsverlag, 2007.

Eley, Geoff. *From Unification to Nazism: Reinterpreting the German Past.* Boston: Allen & Unwin, 1986.

——. *Reshaping the German Right: Radical Nationalism and Political Change after Bismarck.* Ann Arbor: Michigan University Press, 1991. First published 1980, by Yale University Press (New Haven).

Eley, Geoff and James Retallack, eds. *Wilhelminism and Its Legacies: German Modernities, Imperialism and the Meanings of Reform.* New York and Oxford: Berghahn Books, 2003.

Epkenhans, Michael. *Die wilhelminische Flottenrüstung, 1908–1914: Weltmachtstreben, industrieller Fortschritt, soziale Integration.* Munich: Oldenbourg, 1991.

Evans, David C. and Mark R. Peattie, *Kaigun: Strategy, Tactics, and Technology in the Imperial Japanese Navy, 1887–1941.* Annapolis: Naval Institute Press, 1997.

Feldman, Gerald D. *Army, Industry and Labor in Germany, 1914–1918.* Princeton: Princeton University Press, 1966.

——. *Hugo Stinnes: Biographie eines Industriellen 1870–1924.* Translated by Karl Heinz Siber. Munich: C. H. Beck, 1998.

——. "War Aims, State Intervention and Business Leadership in Germany: The Case of Hugo Stinnes." In *Great War, Total War: Combat and Mobilization on the Western Front, 1914–1918.* Edited by Roger Chickering and Stig Förster, 349–67. Washington, DC: German Historical Institute; Cambridge: Cambridge University Press, 2000.

Ferguson, Niall. "Public Finance and National Security: The Domestic Origins of the First World War." *Past and Present* 142 (February 1994): 141–68.

——. *Paper and Iron: Hamburg Business and German Politics in the Era of Inflation, 1897–1927.* Cambridge: Cambridge University Press, 1995.

——. *The Pity of War.* New York: Basic Books, 1999.

Fiebig-von Hase, Ragnhild. *Lateinamerika als Konfliktherd der deutschamerikanischen Beziehungen 1890–1903: Vom Beginn der Panamerikapolitik bis zur Venezuelakrise von 1902/03.* 2 parts. Göttingen: Vandenhoeck & Ruprecht, 1986.

——. "Die politische Funktionalisierung der Kultur: Der sogenannte 'deutsch-amerikanische' Professorenaustausch von 1904–1914." In *Zwei Wege in die Moderne: Aspekte der deutsch-amerikanischen Beziehungen 1900–1918.* Edited by Ragnhild Fiebig-von Hase and Jürgen Heideking, 45–88. Trier: Wissenschaftlicher Verlag Trier, 1998.

Fischer, Fritz. *Griff nach der Weltmacht: Die Kriegszielpolitik des Kaiserlichen Deutschland 1914/18.* 2nd ed. Düssledorf: Droste Verlag, 1962.

——. *War of Illusions: German Policies from 1911 to 1914.* Translated by Marian Jackson. New York: W. W. Norton, 1975.

Fitzpatrick, Matthew P. *Liberal Imperialism in Germany: Expansionism and Nationalism, 1848–1884*. Oxford and New York: Berghahn Books, 2008.

Fulwider, Chad R. *German Propaganda and U.S. Neutrality in World War I*. Columbia: University of Missouri Press, 2016.

Geppert, Dominik. *Pressekriege: Öffentlichkeit und Diplomatie in den deutsch-britischen Beziehungen (1896–1912)*. Munich: Oldenbourg, 2007.

Geppert, Dominik, William Mulligan, and Andreas Rose, eds. *The Wars before the Great War: Conflict and International Politics before the Outbreak of the First World War*. Cambridge: Cambridge University Press, 2015.

Gollwitzer, Heinz. *Die gelbe Gefahr: Geschichte eines Schlagworts: Studien zum imperialistischen Denken*. Göttingen, Vandenhoeck & Ruprecht, 1962.

Grimmer-Solem, Erik. *The Rise of Historical Economics and Social Reform in Germany 1864–1894*. Oxford: Clarendon Press; New York: Oxford University Press, 2003.

——— "Die preußische Bildungspolitik im Spannungsfeld des internationalen Kulturwettbewerbs: der Fall Japan (1869–1914)." In *Kulturstaat und Bürgergesellschaft: Preußen, Deutschland und Europa im 19. und frühen 20. Jahrhundert*. Edited by Bärbel Holtz and Wolfgang Neugebauer, 203–21. Berlin: Akademie Verlag, 2010.

Guettel, Jens-Uwe. *German Expansionism, Imperial Liberalism, and the United States, 1776–1945*. Cambridge and New York: Cambridge University Press, 2012.

Hagenlücke, Heinz. *Deutsche Vaterlandspartei: Die nationale Rechte am Ende des Kaiserreichs*. Düsseldorf: Droste Verlag, 1997.

Hallgarten, George. *Imperialismus vor 1914: Die soziologischen Grundlagen der Aussenpolitik europäischer Grossmächte vor dem Ersten Weltkrieg*. 2nd rev. and enl. ed. Munich: C. H. Beck, 1963.

Hendrix, Henry J. *Theodore Roosevelt's Naval Diplomacy: The U.S. Navy and the Birth of the American Century*. Annapolis: Naval Institute Press, 2009.

Hentschel, Volker. *Wirtschaft und Wirtschaftspolitik im wilhleminischen Deutschland: Organisierter Kapitalismus und Interventionsstaat?* Stuttgart: Klett-Cotta, 1978.

Herold, Heiko. *Reichsgewalt bedeutet Seegewalt: Die Kreuzergeschwader der Kaiserlichen Marine als Instrument der deutschen Kolonial- und Weltpolitik 1885 bis 1901*. Munich: Oldenbourg, 2013.

Herrmann, David G. *The Arming of Europe and the Making of the First World War*. Princeton: Princeton University Press, 1996.

Herwig, Holger H. *The German Naval Officer Corps: A Social and Political History, 1890–1918*. Oxford: Clarendon Press, 1973.

——— *Germany's Vision of Empire in Venezuela 1871–1914*. Princeton: Princeton University Press, 1986.

——— *"Luxury" Fleet: The Imperial German Navy 1888–1918*. London and Atlantic Highlands, NJ: Ashfield, 1987.

——— *The First World War: Germany and Austria-Hungary, 1914–1918*. London and New York: Arnold, 1997.

Hobson, Rolf. *Imperialism at Sea: Naval Strategic Thought, the Ideology of Sea Power, and the Tirpitz Plan, 1875–1914*. Boston and Leiden: Brill, 2002.
Hull, Isabel V. *Absolute Destruction: Military Culture and the Practices of War in Imperial Germany*. Ithaca and London: Cornell University Press, 2005.
― *A Scrap of Paper: Breaking and Making International Law during the Great War*. Ithaca and London: Cornell University Press, 2014.
Jarausch, Konrad H. *Enigmatic Chancellor: Bethmann Hollweg and the Hubris of Imperial Germany*. New Haven: Yale University Press, 1973.
Kehr, Eckart. *Schlachtflottenbau und Partei-Politik 1894–1901: Ein Versuch eines Querschnitts durch die innenpolitischen, sozialen und ideologischen Voraussetzungen des deutschen Imperialismus*. Berlin: Emil Ebering, 1930.
Kelly, Patrick J. *Tirpitz and the Imperial German Navy*. Bloomington and Indianapolis: Indiana University Press, 2011.
Kennedy, Paul M. *The Samoan Tangle: A Study in Anglo-German Relations 1878–1900*. New York: Harper & Row, 1974.
― *The Rise of Anglo-German Antagonism, 1860–1914*. London and Boston: Allen & Unwin, 1980.
Kohut, Thomas A. *Wilhelm II and the Germans: A Study in Leadership*. New York and Oxford: Oxford University Press, 1991.
Kreis, Hannah, and Bertram Schefold. "Die Einführung des Gedankenguts der Deutschen Historischen Schule in Japan: Karl Rathgen und Noburu Kanai—eine weitreichende Lehrer-Schüler-Beziehung und die Gründung des Japanischen Vereins für Sozialpolitik." In *Der Einfluss deutschsprachigen wirtschaftswissenschaftlichen Denkens in Japan*. Edited by Heinz D. Kurz, 29–46. Schriften des Vereins für Socialpolitik, Studien zur Entwicklung der ökonomischen Theorie, 115/XXVII. Berlin: Duncker & Humblot, 2012.
Krumeich, Gerd. *Die unbewältigte Niederlage: Das Trauma des Ersten Weltkriegs und die Weimarer Republik*. Freiburg: Herder, 2018.
Kudō Akira, Tajima Nobuo, and Erich Pauer. *Japan and Germany: Two Latecomers to the World Stage, 1890–1945*. Vol. 1. Folkstone, Kent: Global Oriental, 2009.
Kundrus, Birthe. *Moderne Imperialisten: Das Kaiserreich im Spiegel seiner Kolonien*. Cologne, Weimar and Vienna: Böhlau Verlag, 2003.
Lambert, Nicholas A. *Sir John Fisher's Naval Revolution*. Columbia: University of South Carolina Press, 1999.
― *Planning Armageddon: British Economic Warfare and the First World War*. Cambridge, MA: Harvard University Press, 2012.
Langer, William L. *The Diplomacy of Imperialism 1890–1902*. 2nd ed. New York: Knopf, 1960.
Lerman, Katherine Anne. *The Chancellor as Courtier: Bernhard von Bülow and the Governance of Germany, 1900–1909*. Cambridge: Cambridge University Press, 1990.
Lieven, Dominic. *The End of Tsarist Russia: The March to World War I and Revolution*. New York: Viking, 2015.

Liulevicius, Vejas Gabriel. *War Land on the Eastern Front: Culture, National Identity, and German Occupation in World War I*. Cambridge: Cambridge University Press, 2000.

Löhr, Brigitte. *Die "Zukunft Russlands": Perspektiven russischer Wirtschaftsentwicklung und deutsch-russische Wirtschaftsbeziehungen vor dem Ersten Weltkrieg*. Stuttgart: Franz Steiner, 1985.

MacMillan, Margaret. *Paris 1919: Six Months that Changed the World*. New York: Random House, 2001.

*The War that Ended Peace: How Europe Abandoned Peace for the First World War*. London: Profile, 2013.

Mantoux, Étienne. *The Carthaginian Peace, or the Economic Consequences of Mr. Keynes*. London and New York: G. Cumberlege, 1946.

Manz, Stefan. *Constructing a German Diaspora: The "Greater German Empire," 1871–1914*. New York: Routledge, 2014.

Marder, Arthur J. *The Anatomy of British Sea Power: A History of British Naval Policy in the Pre-Dreadnought Era, 1880–1905*. New York: Knopf, 1940.

*From Dreadnought to Scapa Flow: The Royal Navy in the Fisher Era, 1904–1919*. Vol. 1, *The Road to War, 1904–1914*. London and New York: Oxford University Press, 1961.

Marienfeld, Wolfgang. *Wissenschaft und Schlachtflottenbau in Deutschland 1897–1906. Marine Rundschau*, Beiheft 2 (April 1957). Berin: E. S. Mittler Verlag, 1957.

McMeekin, Sean. *The Russian Origins of the First World War*. Cambridge, MA and London: Harvard University Press, 2011.

*July 1914: Countdown to War*. New York: Basic Books, 2013.

Mehnert, Ute. *Deutschland, Amerika und die "Gelbe Gefahr": Zur Karriere eines Schlagworts in der großen Politik, 1905–1917*. Stuttgart: Franz Steiner, 1995.

Mitchell, Nancy. *The Danger of Dreams: German and American Imperialism in Latin America*. Chapel Hill and London: University of North Carolina Press, 1999.

Mommsen, Wolfgang J. *Bürgerstolz und Weltmachtstreben: Deutschland unter Wilhelm II. 1890 bis 1918*. Berlin: Propyläen, 1995.

Morris, Edmund. *The Rise of Theodore Roosevelt*. New York: Modern Library, 2001. First published 1979.

*Theodore Rex*. New York: Random House, 2001.

Mulligan, William. *The Origins of the First World War*. Cambridge: Cambridge University Press, 2010.

Mühlhahn, Klaus. *Herrschaft und Widerstand in der "Musterkolonie" Kiautschou: Interaktionen zwischen China und Deutschland, 1897–1914*. Munich: Oldenbourg, 2000.

Nagler, Jörg. "From Culture to *Kultur*: Changing American Perceptions of Imperial Germany, 1870–1914." In *Transatlantic Images and Perceptions: Germany and America Since 1776*. Edited by David E. Barclay and Elisabeth

Glaser-Schmidt, 131–54. Washington, DC: German Historical Institute; Cambridge: Cambridge University Press, 1997.

*Nationale Minoritäten im Krieg: "Feindliche Ausländer" und die amerikanische Heimatfront während des Ersten Weltkriegs.* Hamburg: Hamburger Edition, 2000.

Naranch, Bradley, and Geoff Eley, eds. *German Colonialism in a Global Age.* Durham and London: Duke University Press, 2014.

Neitzel, Söhnke. *Weltmacht oder Untergang: Die Weltreichslehre im Zeitalter des Imperialismus.* Paderborn: F. Schöningh, 2000.

Nelson, Robert L. "From Manitoba to the Memel: Max Sering, Inner Colonization and the German East." *Social History* 35, no. 4. (November 2010): 439–57.

Nelson, Robert L., ed. *Germans, Poland, and Colonial Expansion to the East: 1850 Through the Present.* New York: Palgrave Macmillan, 2009.

Nozaki, Toshiro. "Karl Rathgen in Japan (1882–1890)." In *Karl Rathgen (1856–1921) Nationalökonom und Gründungsrektor der Universität Hamburg: Reden, gehalten beim akademischen Festakt zum 150. Geburtstag, 24. Januar 2007*, 19–31. Hamburg: Universität Hamburg, Fakultät Wirtschafts- und Sozialwissenschaften, 2009.

Offer, Avner. *The First World War: An Agrarian Interpretation.* Oxford: Oxford University Press 1989.

Osterhammel, Jürgen. *The Transformation of the World: A Global History of the Nineteenth Century.* Translated by Patrick Camiller. Princeton: Princeton University Press, 2014.

Osterhammel, Jürgen, and Niels P. Petersson, eds. *Geschichte der Globalisierung: Dimensionen, Prozesse, Epochen.* Munich: C. H. Beck, 2003.

Otte, T. G. *The China Question: Great Power Rivalry and British Isolation, 1894–1905.* Oxford: Oxford University Press, 2007.

*July Crisis: The World's Descent into War, Summer 1914.* Cambridge: Cambridge University Press, 2014.

Petersson, Niels P. *Imperialismus und Modernisierung: Siam, China und die europäischen Mächte 1895–1914.* Munich: Oldenbourg, 2000.

Pogge von Strandmann, Hartmut. *Imperialismus vom grünen Tisch: deutsche Kolonialpolitik zwischen wirtschaftlicher Ausbeutung und "zivilisatorischen" Bemühungen.* Berlin: Links, 2009.

Pohl, Manfred. *Von Stambul nach Bagdad: Die Geschichte einer berühmten Eisenbahn.* Munich and Zurich: Piper, 1999.

Pommerin, Rainer. *Der Kaiser und Amerika: Die USA in der Politik der Reichsleitung 1890–1917.* Cologne: Böhlau 1986.

Retallack, James. *Notables of the Right: The Conservative Party and Political Mobilization in Germany, 1876–1918.* Boston: Unwin Hyman, 1988.

*The German Right 1860–1920.* Toronto, Buffalo, and London: University of Toronto Press, 2006.

Ritter, Gerhard. *Staatskunst und Kriegshandwerk: Das Problem des "Militarismus" in Deutschland*, 4 vols. Munich: Oldenbourg, 1954–68.
Rodgers, Daniel T. *Atlantic Crossings: Social Politics in a Progressive Age*. Cambridge, MA: Harvard University Press, 1998.
Röhl, John C. G. *Wilhelm II: The Kaiser's Personal Monarchy*. Translated by Sheila de Bellaigue. Cambridge: Cambridge University Press, 2004.
*Wilhelm II: Into the Abyss of War and Exile, 1900–1941*. Translated by Sheila de Bellaigue and Roy Bridge. Cambridge: Cambridge University Press, 2014.
Rose, Andreas. *Zwischen Empire und Kontinent: Britische Aussenpolitik vor dem Ersten Weltkrieg*. Munich: Oldenbourg, 2011.
Roth, Guenther. "Der politische Kontext von Max Webers Beitrag über die deutsche Wirtschaft in der *Encyclopedia Americana*." *Zeitschrift für Soziologie* 36, no. 1 (February 2007): 65–77.
Rüger, Jan. *The Great Naval Game: Britain and Germany in the Age of Empire*. Cambridge: Cambridge University Press, 2007.
Ruppenthal, Jens. *Kolonialismus als "Wissenschaft und Technik": Das Hamburgische Kolonialinstitut 1908–1919*. Stuttgart: Franz Steiner, 2007.
Scheck, Rafael. *Alfred von Tirpitz and German Right Wing Politics, 1914–1930*. Atlantic Highlands, NJ: Humanities Press, 1998.
Schenck, Paul Christian. *Der deutsche Anteil an der Gestaltung des modernen japanischen Rechts- und Verwaltungswesens: Deutsche Rechtsberater im Japan der Meiji-Zeit*. Stuttgart: Franz Steiner, 1997.
Schiefel, Werner. *Bernhard Dernburg 1865–1937: Kolonialpolitiker und Bankier im Wilhelminischen Deutschland*. Zurich: Atlantis Verlag, 1974.
Schmidt, Stefan. *Frankreichs Außenpolitik in der Julikrise 1914: Ein Beitrag zur Geschichte des Ausbruchs des Ersten Weltkriegs*. Munich: Oldenbourg, 2009.
Schmoller, Gustav. *Auf Messers Schneide: Wie das Deutsche Reich den Ersten Weltkrieg Verlor*. Munich: C.H. Beck, 2018.
Schöllgen, Gregor. *Imperialismus und Gleichgewicht: Deutschland, England und die orientalische Frage*. Munich: Oldenbourg, 1984.
Schwabe, Klaus. *Wissenschaft und Kriegsmoral: Die deutschen Hochschullehrer und die politischen Grundfragen des Ersten Weltkriegs*. Göttingen, Zurich and Frankfurt: Musterschmidt-Verlag, 1969.
Searle, G. R. *The Quest for National Efficiency: A Study in British Politics and Political Thought, 1899–1914*. London and Atlantic Highlands: The Ashfield Press, 1990.
Seligmann, Matthew S. *The Royal Navy and the German Threat, 1901–1914: Admiralty Plans to Protect British Trade in a War against Germany*. New York: Oxford University Press, 2012.
Smith, Woodruff D. *The German Colonial Empire*. Chapel Hill: University of North Carolina Press, 1978.
*The Ideological Origins of Nazi Imperialism*. New York and Oxford: Oxford University Press, 1986.
Sondhaus, Lawrence. *German Submarine Warfare in World War I: The Onset of Total War at Sea*. Lanham, MD: Rowman & Littlefield, 2017.

Spindler, Arno. *Der Handelskrieg mit U-Booten: Der Krieg zur See 1914–1918*, 5 vols. Berlin: Mittler und Sohn, 1932–66.
Stegemann, Bernd. *Die Deutsche Marinepolitik 1916–1918*. Berlin: Duncker & Humblot, 1970.
Stegman, Dirk. *Die Erben Bismarcks: Parteien und Verbände in der Spätphase des wilhelminischen Deutschland, Sammlungspolitik 1897–1918*. Cologne: Kiepenheuer & Witsch, 1970.
Steinberg, Jonathan. *Yesterday's Deterrent: Tirpitz and the Birth of the German Battle Fleet*. New York: Macmillan, 1965.
Steinmetz, Georg. *The Devil's Handwriting: Precoloniality and the German Colonial State in Qingdao, Samoa, and Southwest Africa*. Chicago and London: University of Chicago Press, 2007.
Tooze, J. Adam. *The Deluge: The Great War, America and the Remaking of the Global Order, 1916–1931*. New York: Viking, 2014.
Torp, Cornelius. *The Challenges of Globalization: Economy and Politics in Germany, 1860–1914*. Translated by Alex Skinner. New York: Berghahn Books, 2014.
Vogel, Barbara. *Deutsche Rußlandpolitik: Das Scheitern der deutschen Weltpolitik unter Bülow*. Düsseldorf: Bertelsmann Universitätsverlag, 1973.
Watson, Alexander. *Ring of Steel: Germany and Austria-Hungary in World War I*. New York: Basic Books, 2014.
Wehler, Hans-Ulrich. *Bismarck und der Imperialismus*. 3rd ed. Cologne: Kiepenheuer & Witsch, 1972.
   *Deutsche Gesellschaftsgeschichte*. Vol. 3, *Von der "Deutschen Doppelrevolution" bis zum Beginn des Ersten Weltkrieges 1849–1914*. Munich: C. H. Beck, 1995.
Wildenthal, Lora. *German Women for Empire, 1884–1945*. Durham and London: Duke University Press, 2001.
Williamson, John G. *Karl Helfferich 1872–1924: Economist, Financier, Politician*. Princeton: Princeton University Press, 1971.
Wilson, Keith. *The Policy of the Entente: Essays on the Determinants of British Foreign Policy 1904–1914*. Cambridge: Cambridge University Press, 1985.
Winzen, Peter. *Bülow's Weltmachtkonzept: Untersuchungen zur Frühphase seiner Außenpolitik 1897–1901*. Boppard am Rhein: Harald Boldt Verlag, 1977.
   *Reichskanzler Bernhard Fürst von Bülow: Weltmachtstratege ohne Fortune – Wegbereiter der großen Katastrophe*. Göttingen: Muster-Schmidt Verlag, 2003.
Witt, Peter-Christian. *Die Finanzpolitik des Deutschen Reiches von 1903 bis 1913: Eine Studie zur Innenpolitik des Wilhelminischen Deutschlands*. Lübeck and Hamburg: Matthiesen, 1970.
Wu, Shellen Xiao. *Empires of Coal: Fueling China's Entry Into the Modern World Order, 1860–1920*. Stanford: Stanford University Press, 2015.
Zimmerman, Andrew. *Alabama in Africa: Booker T. Washington, the German Empire, and the Globalization of the New South*. Princeton.: Princeton University Press, 2010.

# INDEX

Abdallahi ibn Muhammad, 139
Abdelhafid, sultan of Morocco, 416
Abdul Hamid II, sultan of the Ottoman Empire, 299
Abyssinia, 547
acclimatization question. *See* tropics
Achenbach, Heinrich, 80–81
Adams, Henry, 32, 316
Adana, 363, 365
Addams, Jane, 70
Addis Ababa, 547
Aden, 87, 139, 245, 546
Adenauer, Konrad, 602
Adrianople, 486, 491
Afghanistan, 120, 176, 324
Africa, German
  *See also* Cameroon, East Africa; Herero and Nama wars; Maji Maji rebellion; Southwest Africa; Togo
Agadir Crisis (1911), 376, 406, 416–17, 437, 456–57, 479, 486, 500
Agrarian League (Bund der Landwirte), 469, 471, 473, 477
agriculture
  barley, 47, 55, 523
  cacao, 152, 155
  coconuts, 218
  coffee, 145, 152, 155, 204, 273, 412
  copra, 218
  cotton, 67, 74–75, 151, 158, 204, 209, 218, 229–30, 293, 296, 363, 378, 394, 405, 423–24, 426, 434, 445, 512, 515, 549
  crisis in Germany, 43, 55, 276
  dairy, 55, 280
  dry farming, 381, 384, 431
  extension services, 395
  horticulture, 47
  Landflucht, 43
  livestock, 43, 55, 72, 229, 523, 564
  maize, 155, 229
  milling, 70, 240
  oil seeds, 55
  peasants, 55–56, 184, 272–73, 275, 427, 429, 433, 559–60
  reforms of, 429
  rice, 88, 105, 529
  rubber, 408–9, 412, 414, 416, 421, 426, 445
  rye, 55, 273, 279, 522, 525
  sugar, 55, 78, 155, 204, 380, 385, 411–12, 416, 423, 445
  tea, 412
  tobacco, 76, 152, 204, 379–80, 412–14, 416, 423, 445
  wheat, 43, 46–47, 49–50, 53, 55, 59, 69, 71, 229, 520, 522, 525, 528, 561, 579
  *See also* colonial science; cotton industry; inner colonization; rubber industry; sugar industry; tobacco industry
Ahmad bin Abd Allah, Muhammad, 139
Alabama, 378
  *See also* Calhoun Colored School; Tuskegee Institute
Alaskan boundary dispute, 315
Albania, 437, 439–42, 491
Albert, Heinrich, 535
Aleppo, 365
Alexander III, tsar of Russia, 436
Alexandrette, Gulf of, 365, 485
Alexandria, 87, 515

## INDEX

Algeciras Conference and Act (1906), 326, 328, 376
Algeria, 13, 252, 267, 394, 415, 419, 552
Algiers, 153, 204
Allgemeine Electricitäts Gesellschaft (AEG), 68
Alsace-Lorraine, 33, 560
  See also Strasbourg
Althoff, Friedrich, 211, 307, 368–70
Alverstone, Richard, 315
American Economic Association, 32, 494–95
American peril, 78, 146, 217
American Tobacco Company, 379
Amoy (Xiamen), 111, 129, 132
Amur River, 251
Anatolia, 487, 567. See also Ottoman Empire
Anatolian Railway, 298–301, 343, 352, 362–63, 366–67, 486–88
Anglo-German Angola Treaty (1898), 253, 490
Anglo-German trade treaty (1865), 143, 203
Anglo-Japanese Alliance (1902), 15, 118, 305, 337, 438
Anglo-Persian Oil Company, 483, 487–88
Anglo-Russian Convention (1907), 195, 364, 366–67, 438, 482, 492–93
Anglo-Russian naval talks (1914), 500, 502
Anglosphere and Anglo-Saxonism, 30, 317–19
Angola, 214, 253, 490, 541
Ankara, 299, 361, 486
anthropology, 13
Anti-Imperialist League, 372
anti-Semitic parties, 354, 473, 475
anti-Semitism, 570, 572, 574–76, 581, 586
Anton, Gustav, 408
Antwerp, 461, 541, 546, 552, 554, 578
  war aims in, 548
Aoki Shūzō, 86–87
*Arabic*, 537
Archiv für innere Kolonisation, 428
Arco-Valley, Emmerich v., 306
Arendt, Otto, 291

Argentina, 63, 315
  trade policy, 145
Arimatsu Hideyoshi, 103
Arizona, 580
Arkansas, 76
Armenia, 567
Armistice (1918), 567, 589–90
arms race
  land forces, 480
  naval, 5, 9, 18, 22–23, 120, 123, 127, 165, 175–76, 247, 287–88, 331, 336, 338–39, 445, 447, 452, 455, 460, 462–63, 465, 479, 487
Armstrong Whitworth & Co. Ltd., 109, 492
army bill (1913), 447, 479–80, 499
Army League (Deutscher Wehrverein), 539
Army, German (Deutsches Heer), 167, 168, 168, 208, 254, 254, 259, 322, 458, 460, 479, 479, 499, 505, 515, 525, 564, 589, 589
  Belgian atrocities, 508
  General Staff, 135, 264, 322, 503, 530, 535, 554
  *Judenzählung* (1916), 24, 568–70, 572, 577–78, 581, 589, 596
  Ludendorff Offensive (1918), 588–89
  Ober Ost, 563–66, 597
  Schlieffen Plan, 508
  Supreme Army Command (OHL), 535, 553
  See also Falkenhayn, Erich v.; Hindenburg, Paul v.; Ludendorff, Erich; Moltke, Helmuth v.
Arnold-Forster, Hugh, 265, 318
Ashley, William James
  Anglo-German relations, views on, 262, 282, 459
  Birmingham University, 262
  Ernst von Halle, relationship with, 65, 76, 261, 478
  Gustav Schmoller, relationship with, 261, 282
  national efficiency, 260
  tariff reform and imperial federation, 282–83

# INDEX

Asquith, Herbert H., 326, 336, 418, 456–58, 461, 505–7
Association for German Scholarship (*doitsugaku kyōkai*), 86, 100
Association for Social Policy (Verein für Socialpolitik), 34–35, 37–38, 41, 57, 62, 64–65, 71, 98, 269, 272, 274, 278, 283, 295, 407, 419, 426, 446, 494–95, 545, 559
Association School (*doisugaku kyōkai gakko*), 98, 100–3, 305–7
Auhagen, Otto, 428, 432, 436
Australia, 235, 239, 267, 394, 428, 455–56, 518, 565, 593
   Chinese immigrants, 239
   subimperialism, 243
   trade policy, 279
Austria-Hungary
   Balkan policy, 338, 367, 438–43, 461
   German trade treaty with, 279
   German trade with, 228, 269, 279
   Germany, relations with, 175, 326, 440, 443, 480
   July Crisis, 496–506, 509
   *Mitteleuropa* and, 173, 226, 356, 544, 555, 564
   Poland, relations with, 561–62
   Russia, relations with, 120, 365, 367, 437, 439, 444, 461, 490–91
   trade policy, 279
Austro-German (Dual) Alliance (1879), 120, 125, 174
automobile industry, 410

Bab-el-Mandeb, 546
Bachmann, Gustav, 537
Baden, 473, 600
Baelz, Erwin, 90
Baghdad Railway, 23, 298, 301–2, 318, 324, 361–63, 365–67, 387, 393, 438, 444, 446, 482, 484, 486–90, 494, 498
Balch, Emily Greene, 60, 62, 371
Balfour, Arthur J., 281, 283, 301, 314, 317–18, 361, 453
Balkan League, 439–40, 486
Balkan wars (1912–13), 120, 435, 439–40, 442–44, 461, 481, 486, 490–91, 496–98, 500, 502

Balkan Winter Crisis (1912–13), 437, 481
Ballin, Albert, 153, 265, 397, 460, 472, 522, 577
Ballod, Karl, 522–23, 525, 527, 530
Baltimore, 234
Bamberger, Ludwig, 296
Bancroft, George, 45
Banque Impérial Ottomane, 301, 361, 367
Banque National de Turquie, 484, 487
*Baralong*, 538
Barbados, 154
Barbarossa, 370
Barbary pirates, 205, 234
Baring, Evelyn (Earl of Cromer), 552
Barnardo, Thomas, 96
Bartels, Adolf, 576
Basra, 300, 302, 361, 364, 366, 482, 487–89
Batavia (Jakarta), 411–13
Battenberg, Louis of, 318
Bavaria, 199, 472–73
Bayer AG, 555
Bebel, August, 140, 342–43
Beckert, Sven, 14
Beijing. *See* Peking
Beit, Alfred, 397
Belarusia (Belarus), 547, 562, 567
Belfort, 541
Belgium, 144, 323, 402, 592
   annexation, plans for, 545, 548, 552, 554–57, 578, 586
   Congo, 125, 172, 406, 417, 421, 426, 490, 515, 541–42, 544, 549, 558
   German atrocities committed in, 508
   German invasion, 2, 505–7, 513–14, 532–33
   German trade treaty with, 279
   Mittteleuropa and, 356
   railway and mining concessions in China, 549
   wartime occupation, 542, 544
Belgrade, 438, 442, 444, 491, 497, 503
Bell, C. F. Moberly, 126
Benckendorff, Alexander K. W. C. v., 437, 480
Benguela-Katanga Railway, 490
Berchthold, Leopold v., 441, 443–44

Berghahn, Volker, 184, 278
Berlin, 495
Berlin, Congress and Treaty of (1878), 367
Berlin, Landwirtschaftliche Hochschule (Higher School of Land Economy), 60, 64, 428
Berlin, University of, 60–62, 65, 85, 92–93, 96, 141–42, 189, 195, 203, 211, 286, 290–91, 316, 345, 350–51, 355, 371, 378, 419, 436, 466, 520, 525, 539, 600
    Amerika Institut, 494
    Institut für Meereskunde (Institute for Oceanography), 211
    professor exchanges, 370, 494, 513
    Seminar for East European History and Geography, 436
    Seminar for Oriental Languages, 84, 292, 306, 398, 407
Berliner Handelsgesellschaft, 341
Bernhard, Ludwig, 398
Bernhardi, Friedrich v., 480, 482
Bernstorff, Johann Heinrich v., 514, 516, 534
Bertie, Francis, 150, 255, 326
Bethmann Hollweg, Theobald v., 406
    Anglo-German détente, 455, 460, 481, 490, 493
    Baghdad Railway, 488
    Balkan policy, 440, 461
    financial reform, 476–77, 479
    July Crisis diplomacy, 481, 498–500, 503, 506
    peace proposal, 585
    resignation, 584
    Russia, views on, 434
    submarine warfare, 524, 527, 529–30, 537, 579
    war aims policy, 17, 541–43, 546, 553, 563
    wartime *fronde* against, 540, 578
    wartime policy, 518, 525, 568, 583, 589
Bidwell, John, 47
*Bildung*, 13, 20, 168, 173, 242, 403
*Bildungsbürgertum* (German university-educated bourgeoisie), 11, 115, 171

bimetallism, 291
Birmingham, 217, 281
Birmingham, University of, 262, 282
Bismarck Archipelago (New Britain), 110, 207
    seizure by Australia in world war, 518
Bismarck, Herbert v., 185–86
Bismarck, Otto v., 56, 106, 118, 171, 174–75, 185–86, 190, 195, 298–99
Björkö Treaty (1905), 325
Blanco, Guzmán, 152
blockade, 121–24, 127, 148, 150, 167, 169, 225, 244, 246, 337, 461–62
    Armistice, 592, 597
    Boer War, 246
    distant, 335–37
    First World War, 509–11, 518, 520, 524, 527, 529, 531, 536, 538–39, 544, 555, 591
    Napoleonic wars, 233
    Russo-Japanese War, 321
    Second Venezuela Crisis, 311–15
    Spanish-American War, 214
    submarine, 524, 527–30, 536, 538
    unrestricted, 531
    US Civil War, 159
*Blücher*, SMS, 518, 530
Blue Riband, 263
Bluewater School, 122, 124, 148, 166, 184
Bluntschli, Johann Caspar, 91, 100
Böckmann, Wilhelm, 155
Boer War (1899–1902), 220–21, 229, 242, 244, 250, 252–53, 256, 259–60, 264, 277, 285, 288, 304, 317, 319
    costs, 259, 330
    mistreatment of Boers, 259
Bogota, 60
Bolzano, 431
Bombay, 300
Bönker, Dirk, 14
Bonn, 380, 416, 466, 471, 496
Bonn, University of, 44, 52, 60, 64, 211, 254, 296, 408

Borsig, Ernst v., 520
Bosnia-Herzegovina, 120, 367, 438, 443, 491
Boston, 38, 65, 72, 76, 157
Boulogne, 541
Boxer Protocol (1901), 256, 303
Boxer Rebellion (1899–1901), 236, 254, 303, 319
Boxers (*yihequan*), 251–53
Boy-Ed, Karl, 535
Brandt, Max v., 80, 84, 106, 111, 115–17, 135
Brazil, 78, 145, 410, 412
    Espirito Santo, German Mennonites in, 419
    German colonization of, 51, 151–52, 226, 284, 312, 319
    German trade and investment, 172
    naval revolts (1893–94), 127
    trade policy, 145
Brechtken, Magnus, 15
Bremen, 29, 60–61, 89, 150, 195, 202, 234–35, 397, 531, 548, 562, 587
Bremen Chamber of Commerce, 60
Bremer Vulkan, 113
Brentano, Lujo, 198, 200, 274
    financial reform, 466
    naval enthusiasm, 458
    naval propaganda, 199
    war aims, 556
Brest-Litovsk, Treaty of (1918), 567
Bretton Woods Conference (1944), 602
Breuer, Möller & Co., 152
Breusing, Alfred, 401
Brewer, William, 45
Bridgeport Projectile Company, 535
Briey-Longwy, German plans to annex, 541, 550, 557, 586
Britain. *See* Great Britain
Brückner, Edmund, 542
Brussels
    École de Commerce Solvay, 405, 420
    wartime occupation, 542–43
Buchanan, George, 483, 502
Bucharest, 185, 444
Bucharest, Treaty of (1913), 442
Bücher, Karl, 350
Buckle, Henry, 83
Bukharin, Nikolai, 431

Bulgaria
    Balkan policy, 439, 441–42, 486
    Germany, relations with, 498
Bulgurlu, 361–62, 365, 485
Bülow Bloc (1907–9), 23, 212, 391, 445, 447–48, 465, 468–69, 472
Bülow, Bernhard Ernst v., 185
Bülow, Bernhard v.
    anti-Bethmann intrigues, 578–79, 585
    background and early career, 185–90
    chancellor, appointment as, 248
    China policy, 196–97, 252–57
    financial reform, 469–70, 475–76
    foreign policy ideas, 190, 192–95
    foreign secretary, appointment as, 185, 193
    Gustav Schmoller, relationship with, 188–90, 279–80, 476–77
    Hammer or Anvil speech, 243–44
    Hottentot elections (1906–7), 344–45, 350–51, 351–52, 358–60
    inner colonization policy, 426–27
    Place in the Sun speech, 195–97
    resignation of chancellorship, 477
    stab-in-the-back myth, 590
    submarine warfare, views on, 578
    tariff bill (1901–2), 278–80
    Wilhelm II, relationship with, 190–91, 466–67
    *See also* Bülow Bloc
Bülow tariff (1902), 23, 212, 269–80, 283, 290, 317, 451
Bund der Industriellen (Federation of Industrialists), 211, 278–79
Bundesrat (Federal Council), 194, 220, 472, 477, 525
*Bundesrath*, 245, 247
Burgess, John W., 32, 369–70, 514
Burma, 120, 225
Butler, Nicholas Murray, 368, 512–13

Caillaux, Joseph, 417–18
Cairo, 87, 290
California
    agriculture, 46–47
    anti-Japanese riots (1907), 383
    Asian immigration, 383
    Berkeley, 47

Chico, 47
Los Angeles, 381
Merced, 47
Monterey, 47
oil industry, 381
Sacramento, 45–47
San Diego, 381
San Francisco, 97, 112, 129, 181, 382
  anti-Japanese riots (1907), 582
Santa Clara, 47
Cambon, Jules, 417–18
Cambon, Paul, 458, 462, 502, 504, 507
Cameroon, 5, 125, 172, 341, 353, 362, 392, 417–18
  colonial abuses in, 293–94, 353
  Mittelafrika and, 542
  seizure by France in world war, 518
Campbell-Bannerman, Henry, 453
Canada, 144, 267, 281–82, 315, 428
  Alaska boundary, 315
  Chinese immigration, 239
  German wartime sabotage in, 535
  immigration to, 143
  imperial federation, 281
  imperial preference, 143–44, 281
  security, 147, 231
  trade, 231, 565
  trade policy, 279
Canadian Pacific Railway, 72, 231
Canis, Konrad, 15
Canton (Guangzhou), 131, 135
Cape Colony. *See* South Africa
Capelle, Eduard v., 538
Caprivi, Leo v., 110, 191
  Anglo-German relations, 175
  New Course, 171, 190
  trade treaties, 145, 201, 269, 276
Caracas. *See* Venezuela
Caribbean. *See* West Indies
Carl Rohde & Co., 109
Carnegie, Andrew, 373
Caroline Islands, 5, 214–15, 218, 444
  seizure by Japan in world war, 518
Carranza, Venustiano, 580
Casement, Roger, 421
Cassel, Ernest, 460, 483–84, 487
Castro, Cipriano, 311, 313–14
Cauer, Minna, 349

Center Party (Deutsche Zentrumspartei), 190
  Bülow tariff, 280
  colonial crisis, 341, 343–44
  Fatherland Party and, 586, 588
  financial reform, 288, 333, 469–73, 475, 479
  Hottentot elections, 344, 350, 352, 354, 356, 358
  Judenzählung, 568
  naval laws, 195, 207, 221, 247, 287–88, 333, 448, 462
  submarine warfare, 538
  wartime polarization, 540
Centralverband deutscher Industrieller (Central Association of German Industrialists), 129, 136, 139, 278, 545
Ceuta, war aims in, 546
Ceylon, 6, 87, 139, 235
Chaddock, Richard E., 371
Chamberlain, Houston Stewart, 576
Chamberlain, Joseph, 343
  Anglo-German alliance proposal, 217
  Anglo-German relations, 142
  Baghdad Railway, 361
  Birmingham University, 262
  First Venezuela Crisis, 146
  great world empires, 159, 161
  Greater Britain, 160–61, 207
  imperial federation, 143, 261, 282
  imperial preference, 142, 144, 281, 283
  imperial vulnerability, 124–25
  Liberal Unionism, 262, 283
  national efficiency, 260–61
  new imperialism, 165, 203, 267
  Samoa, 243
  Spanish-American War, 215
  special relationship with USA, 317
Charmley, John, 22
Chenkiang (Zhenjiang), 134, 238
Chesney, George Tomkyns, 121
Chicago, 38, 43, 45, 65, 67, 69, 71, 230, 383, 431, 478
  Board of Trade, 63, 70
  German immigration, 180
  grain market, 68
  Haymarket Riot (1886), 66

630                                INDEX

Chicago (cont.)
  Hull House, 69
  urban conditions, 67, 69
  World's Columbian Exposition, 57, 63, 65, 69
Chicago, Rock Island, and Pacific Railway, 33
Chicago, University of, 32, 69, 71, 383–84
Chihli province (Zhili), 251
Childers, Erskine, 1, 317
Chile, 61, 151, 356, 380, 520
China, 144
  Chinese Northern Fleet, 109
  Christian missions, 134, 139, 250
  coal deposits and mining, 115, 134, 209, 238
  coaling stations, 135–36, 138, 217
  coastal piracy, 132
  cotton imports, 132
  cotton industry, 132, 240
  geological expeditions, 115
  German arms sales, 113, 252
  German export market, 113, 241
  German knick-knack trade in, 132, 140, 241
  German merchants in, 89, 113, 131–32, 161, 209, 241
  German military mission to, 135
  German sphere of interest in, 238
  German trade commission to (1897), 129–30, 132, 136, 138
  Hanyang Iron Works, 130, 134
  imperial encroachment, 109, 127, 129, 161, 210
  industrial development of, 115, 240
  investments in, 130, 236, 238
  iron industry and mining, 134–35
  Japanese competition in, 210
  Maritime Customs, 135, 241
  military, 128, 135
  mining concessions, 128
  national identity and nationalism, 160, 237, 239
  railway concessions, 116, 128–29, 132, 136
  silk industry, 209
  treaty ports, 79, 132, 134–35, 141, 209, 236, 241
  Weltpolitik and, 22
  See also Boxer Rebellion; Kiaochow; Sino-Japanese War; Tsingtao
China Eastern Railway (Trans-Manchurian Railway), 251
China Northern Railway, 252, 254
China question, 127, 161
Chirol, Valentine, 317
Chita, 136, 252
Churchill, Winston, 31, 317, 452, 457, 460–62, 506–7
Chusan Islands, 129
Clark, Christopher M., 16, 22
Clark, John Bates, 32, 370, 495
Clark, John M., 495
Claß, Heinrich, 417, 554
Cleveland, Grover, 146, 148
Co-Efficient Club, 260, 361
Cohen, Hermann, 577
Cohn, Gustav, 466
Cologne, 152, 211, 262, 269, 408, 519
Colomb, J. C. R., 121, 335
Colombo, 87
colonial administration, 343, 406–7
  reforms of, 341, 348, 391, 395
Colonial Office, Imperial (Reichskolonialamt), 290, 296, 342, 359, 391, 393–94, 398–400, 405–7, 418, 481, 542
colonial policy (*Kolonialpolitik*), 10, 17, 22, 199, 290, 298, 340–41, 343, 345, 355, 387, 399, 401–7, 430, 446
colonial science (*Kolonialwissenschaft*), 395–96, 398–99, 402
Colonial Society, German (Deutsche Kolonialgesellschaft), 110, 151, 344–45, 354, 360, 404, 469, 539
Colorado, 45, 380–81, 384, 434
Colorado Fuel and Iron Company, 380
Colorado River, 381
Columbia, 60, 315
*Columbia* (HAPAG vessel), 153–55
Columbia University, 32, 368, 370–71, 384, 420–21, 495, 512–13
Congo, 231
Congo Act (1885), 548, 551
Congo Free State, 421
  See also Belgium, Congo

Congo River, 406
Congo, French, 5, 406, 417–18
Conklin, Alice, 13
Conrad von Hötzendorf, Franz, 444
Conrad, Johannes, 466
conservatives (Free Conservative Party, German Conservative Party), 15, 23, 190
  Bülow bloc, 326
  colonial crisis, 356
  DNVP and, 596
  Fatherland Party, 588
  financial reform, 333, 469–77, 479
  Hottentot elections, 291, 358
  naval laws, 247, 326, 456, 462
  submarine warfare, 538
  wartime polarization, 539
Consortium for Asian Business, 113
Constanta, 300
Constantinople (Istanbul), 298–300, 302, 352, 361, 365–67, 439, 482–85, 491–93, 549, 557
Copenhagen complex, 195, 333, 452
copper, 72, 81, 229, 232, 270, 353, 406, 490, 521
  wartime shortages, 525
Corbett, Julian, 167, 324, 335
*Cormoran*, SMS, 214
cotton industry, 67, 75–78, 94, 132, 140, 151, 159, 240–41, 270, 281, 363, 422, 424, 434, 520–21, 536, 562
  *Baumwollfrage*, 76, 394
Courland, 436, 559, 563, 567
  war aims in, 547, 550, 558–59, 561–62, 567
Crane, Charles R., 383–84, 386, 431
Crespo, Joaquín, 153–54
Crimean War (1853–56), 120, 123
Crowe, Eyre, 326–28, 502, 505, 508
Cuba, 41, 155, 204, 374, 378, 380, 411, 423
  Mambi Rebellion (1895–98), 157
  Spanish rule, 154, 157
  US interests in, 207, 213, 216, 379–80, 412
  US military intervention, 5, 226, 372, 379
Culebra Island, 312–13

Culture, Prussian Ministry of
  intellectual investment in Japan, 106, 307
Cunard Line, 265
Curaçao, 213, 215
Custance, Reginald, 265
Cyprus, 120, 225
Cyrenaica and Tripolitania (Libya), 5, 439, 444

D'Arcy, William Knox, 366, 483, 487–88
Dahomey (Benin), 418, 541, 549
*Daily Telegraph* Affair, 191, 466, 469, 471
Dakota, 43, 49–50
Dalian. *See* Talien
Danzig, 562
Daye. *See* Huangshi
deglobalization, 591
Dehio, Ludwig, 20
Delagoa Bay, 149–50, 245
Delbrück, Clemens, 520, 530
Delbrück, Ernst, 103
Delbrück, Felix, 103
Delbrück, Hans, 172, 184, 348, 375, 472, 555–56, 558, 569, 571–72
Delcassé, Théophile, 325
Denmark, 154, 213, 322, 521
  trade policy, 279
  *See also* St. Thomas
Dernburg, Bernhard, 514
  colonial crisis, 343
  colonial reforms, 23, 290, 343, 387, 391–95, 406–7, 430
  German wartime propaganda, 514–16, 534–35
  Hamburg Kolonialinstitut, founding of, 396–402
  Hottentot elections, 344, 346–52
  Jewish background, 343, 473
  railways, construction of colonial, 298, 391–92
  state secretary of Colonial Office, 290, 477
Detring, Gustav, 116, 135–36
Deutsch-Asiatische Bank, 113, 253
Deutsche Bank, 296, 343, 362, 366, 446, 472, 482
  African railway investments, 352
  Ottoman cotton investments, 363

Deutsche Bank (cont.)
  Ottoman railway investments, 299, 301, 300, 302, 299, 301, 302, 361, 363, 366, 367, 483–88
  US investments, 68
Deutsche Diamant-Gesellschaft, 393
Deutsche Handels- und Plantagen-Gesellschaft, 218
*Deutschland* (HAPAG vessel), 263
Dewey, George, 215, 312, 314, 331
Diederichs, Otto v., 139
Dietzel, Heinrich, 350, 466
Dingley Act (1897), 143, 145, 200, 229, 270
Dinter, Artur, 575
Disconto-Gesellschaft, 152, 352, 530
Disraeli, Benjamin, 225, 231
Disse, Joseph, 90
Djavid Bey, Mehemed, 484–85, 488
Djibouti, 547
Dogger Bank
  Battle of (1915), 518, 530
  incident (1904), 321, 325, 330
Döhnhoff, Otto v., 107
Dokkyo Daigaku, 307
Dominican Republic, 215, 373
Dortmunder Union, 152
*Dreadnought*, HMS, 330–31, 336, 450–51
dreadnoughts (class of battleships), 23, 330–31, 334, 376, 464, 471, 479, 483, 487, 492
  naval deterrent weapon, as, 337, 339, 452–62, 504
  status symbol, as, 450–52, 462–64
  wartime strategy and, 509–11
  *See also* arms race
Dresdner Bank, 149, 353
Du Bois, W. E. B., 60, 62, 378
Duden, Gottfried, 41
Duisberg, Carl, 555, 584
Duke, James Buchanan, 379
Dumas, Philip, 335
Duncker & Humblot, 37, 203, 291
Dunkirk, 541
Dvinsk, 547

East Africa, 217
East Africa, German, 76, 172, 350, 400, 409, 417
  colonial abuses in, 293, 353
  colonial reforms, 348, 394
  corruption, 341
  currency reform, 295, 342
  Dernburg inspection tour, 393, 400
  Maji Maji rebellion, 340
  Mittelafrika and, 542
  native law and administration, 404
  railways, 352, 391, 395
  siezure of in world war, 518
  wars in, 293
East Elbia, 57, 62, 278, 295
  *See also* Prussia
East Indies, Dutch, 6, 235, 405, 408–9, 411–15, 549 *See also* Java; Sumatra
Eastern Marches Society (Ostmarkenverein), 427, 429
Ebert, Friedrich, 597
Eckert, Christian, 408
Edison General Electric Company, 68
Edward VII, king of the United Kingdom and Ireland and emperor of India (earlier Prince of Wales), 471
Egypt, 78, 87, 120, 123, 127, 139, 225, 290, 325, 483, 565
  British repression in, 593
  civil service, 403
  Earl of Cromer, views on, 552
  German war aims and, 552, 557
  independence movement, 594
  League of Nations, 593
  Ottoman rights in, 549
Eisendecher, Karl v., 45, 435
El Salvador, 145
Eley, Geoff, 286
Elgin Commission, South Africa, 259
Eliot, Charles William, 372
Eltzbacher Commission (1914), 522, 523, 523, 525
Ely, Richard T., 32, 494–95
*Emden*, SMS, 511
England. *See* Great Britain
Entente Cordiale (1904), 127, 183, 283, 324–25, 329, 337, 453
Enver Bey, Ismail, 486
Ernst, Adolf, 154

Erzberger, Matthias
    assassination of, 596
    Bethmann Hollweg's resignation and 584
    colonial crisis, 341–42, 353
    colonial reforms, 393
    Judenzählung, 568
    Reichstag Peace Resolution, 584
Eskisehir, 299
Esquimalt, 231
Essen Chamber of Commerce, 545
Estonia, 559, 561, 567
    war aims in, 547, 550
Ethiopia, 120
Ethnological Museum, 398
eugenics, 408, 594
Eulenburg, Friedrich zu, 79–80, 106, 115
Eulenburg, Philipp zu, 185, 191, 193
European Coal and Steel Community, 602
Evangelical Social Congress, 544
    colonial program, 294, 394
Exchange Survey Commission (Börsen-Enquênte-Kommission), 70
Expropriation Act, Prussian (1908), 427

Fabri, Friedrich, 51
*Falke*, SMS, 315
Falkenhayn, Erich v., 135, 530, 538, 579
Falkland Islands, destruction of German East Asian Cruiser Squadron near, 518
Farnam, Henry, 35
Farnam, Henry Walcott, 33, 44, 263, 477
    American protectionism, views on, 267
    American trade unionism, scholarship on, 37–41
    background and early career, 29, 33, 35–36
    British decline, views on, 260
    frontier thesis, 41–42
    Karl Rathgen, relationship with, 112, 421
    professor exchanges, 369
    Roosevelt Professor, Berlin University (1914–15), 494–95, 512–13, 517
    Spanish-American War, views on, 216
    supporter of Roosevelt, 317
    travel to Japan (1890), 108, 111
    US occupation of Veracruz, views on, 424
    world war, views on, 512–13, 531–33, 542, 544
Fashoda Crisis (1898), 217, 222
Fatherland Party, German (Deutsche Vaterlandspartei), 24, 177, 553, 590
    background and founding of, 584–85
    spring 1918 offensive, support of, 588–89
    stab-in-the-back myth, 589, 596
    war aims program, 585–88
Fenollosa, Henry, 83, 93
Fiebig-von Hase, Ragnhild, 15
Fiji, 218
Finland, 565, 567
First Venezuela Crisis, 146–48
Fischer, Fritz, 21, 24
    Bethmann Hollweg, interpretation of, 435
    Fischer controversy, 15
    interpretation of imperialism, 3–4
    preventive war hypothesis, 480–81, 498
    war aims, 544, 546, 554, 556, 563
    West German historiography, 602
Fisher, John (Jackie), 317–18, 322, 329–30, 335–36, 452, 454–55
Fiske, Bradley, 264
Foochow (Fuzhou), 132
foodstuffs
    armistice shortages of, 592, 597
    blockade of, 510–11, 519, 529
    reliance on imports of, 224, 228, 240, 266, 271, 274, 281, 336, 445
    wartime shortages of, 519, 522, 525, 527, 539, 568, 579, 597
Foreign Office, German (Auswärtiges Amt), 18, 21, 108–9, 115, 118, 151, 153, 169, 185, 192, 214–15, 254, 257, 281, 296, 299, 308, 344–45, 369, 439, 457, 485, 489
    Colonial Section of, 290, 341, 355, 392

Foreign Office, German (Auswärtiges Amt) (cont.)
  incompetence in, 306–7, 370, 396, 438, 467, 514, 580–81
  July Crisis diplomacy, 498–99
  Russophobia in, 435, 437
  wartime diplomacy, 514, 530, 537, 545, 558, 580
  See also Bülow, Bernhard v.; Jagow, Gottlieb v.; Kiderlen-Waechter, Alfred v.; Kühlmann, Richard v.; Marschall v. Bieberstein, Adolf; Zimmermann, Arthur
Formosa, 5, 79, 85, 89, 111, 117, 196, 237
France, 117, 303, 310, 319, 321–22, 325, 338, 362, 367, 417–18, 432, 436, 452, 456–59, 461, 479–80, 483, 492–93, 505, 507, 513, 581, 592
  Army, 339, 479–80
  Balkan policy, 439–40, 462, 500
  colonial administration, 402
  colonialism and imperialism, 9, 123, 127, 139, 161, 169, 204, 231, 244, 367, 415, 418, 469, 593
  German war aims in, 541, 546–47, 549–51, 555–56
  Jews, 573
  July Crisis diplomacy, 501–3
  law, 99
  liberal imperialism, 3, 9, 13–14, 595
  Navy, 122, 176, 178, 183, 237, 247, 304, 457, 462
  public finance, 467
  Three Year Law, 480
  trade policy, 268, 276–77, 279, 599
  war aims in, 554, 557, 567
  See also Agadir Crisis; Fashoda Crisis; Franco-German Morocco Accord; Franco-Russian (Dual) Alliance; Entente Cordiale; Tangier Crisis; Triple Entente
Franco-German Morocco Accord (1909), 417
Franco-Russian (Dual) Alliance (1894), 116–17, 120, 122–23, 127, 174, 192, 217, 325, 479
Franke, Kuno, 368

Frankfurt am Main, 187, 310, 363, 396, 525
Frankfurt an der Oder, 429, 558
Franz, Ferdinand, Austrian archduke, 443, 496
Franz, Joseph, emperor of Austria and king of Hungary, 497
*Frauenlob*, SMS, 79
Frederick the Great, king of Prussia, 571
Free Union for Naval Lectures (Freie Vereinigung für Flottenvorträge), 221, 223, 243, 248, 254, 265, 282, 285, 312, 319, 327, 346
Freiburg, University of, 61, 69, 466
Friedrich, kaiser of Germany, 471
Friedrichsruh, 171, 195
Fritsch, Theodor, 354
Fukuoka, 137
Fukuzawa Yukichi, 82, 107–8
Fürstenberg, Carl, 392, 577
Fuss, Richard, 579
Fuzhou. *See* Foochow

Galicia, 440, 561
Galster, Karl, 336, 510
Gascoyne-Cecil, Robert (Marquess of Salisbury), 30, 124–26, 146, 243, 245–46, 252–56
Gayl, Georg v., 553
Geibel, Carl, 36
*General*, 245
General Agreement on Tariffs and Trade (1947), 602
Genoa, 139, 153, 409, 415–16
genocide, 4, 340, 599
Georgia, 76, 378, 422
  Atlanta, 378, 422, 582
  Savannah, 378, 423
Georgia, University of, 422
Geppert, Dominik, 15
German Agricultural Society (Deutsche Landwirtschafts-Gesellschaft), 404
German Americans, 60, 65, 368, 371, 513, 516
  backlash against in world war, 536, 581–83

Haymarket Riot, 66
 loyalty in world war, 535–36
 rapid assimilation of, 49–51, 151, 566
 socialism of, 41
 Union Civil War service, 30
German Colonial Congress (1902, 1905, 1910), 294, 346, 360, 394, 405
German Confederation (1815–66), 30, 79
German Customs Union, 79, 548, 552, 557, 560–61, 578
German East Africa Company (DOAG), 293
German East Africa Line, 235
German Information Service, New York, 514, 516
German Japan Society (Wa-Doku-Kai), 306
German menace, 2, 186, 328, 338, 544
German National People's Party (DNVP) and, 596
German-Chinese Higher School (Tsingtao), 102, 309
German-Chinese School (Tsingtao), 309
German-Chinese Seminar (Tsingtao), 102, 309
Germanistic Society of New York, 422, 426, 436
German-Levantine Cotton Company, 363
Germanosphere and Germandom (*Deutschtum*), 10, 33, 107–8, 167, 181, 200, 222, 241, 306, 308, 318, 426, 449, 547, 561, 583
German-Russian Society (Deutsch-Russische Gesellschaft), 435–38
Gerstäcker, Friedrich, 41
Gesellschaft für die Bewässerung der Konia Ebene, 363
Gesellschaft für wirtschafliche Ausbildung (Society for Economic Education), 396
giant world empires, 356, 565–66
Gibraltar, 153, 321, 546
Giddings, Henry, 370
Gierke, Otto v., 527, 553
Giers, Aleksandr, 386
Gilder, Richard Watson, 374

Gladstone, William Ewart, 30, 120–21, 225
Glasgow, 460
*Gneisenau*, SMS, 409
Gneist, Rudolf v., 86, 105
Gojong, king of Korea, 137
Gold Coast (Ghana), 517
gold standard, 290, 595
Goschen, Edward, 456
Gotō Shimpei, 98
Göttingen, University of, 35, 466, 601
Götzen, Gustav v., 350
Great Britain, 176
 Admiralty, 121–23, 246–47, 263–65, 288, 314, 317–18, 322–23, 330, 453–55, 460, 487, 510–12, 519, 530
 Army, 139, 245, 259, 264, 317–18, 330, 493, 505, 507–8
 colonial administration, 403, 411
 Colonial Office, 146, 314, 489
 colonialism and imperialism, 4, 119–20, 125, 127, 160–61, 165, 169, 171, 204, 206, 216, 225–26, 231, 244, 367, 415, 552, 593
 Committee of Imperial Defence, 318, 336, 457, 461, 510
 economic warfare, 506, 510–11, 539
 economic warfare, plans for, 335, 338, 461–62
 Foreign Office, 121, 124, 145–46, 150, 181, 186, 252, 254–55, 257, 313, 326, 338, 364, 483, 487, 493, 500, 502–3
 invasion fears, 1, 121, 330, 338
 July Crisis diplomacy, 500, 502–6
 liberal imperialism, 3, 9, 13–14, 170, 177, 552, 595
 Naval Defense Act (1889, 1893), 124, 148
 Naval Supremacy, 121, 330, 338, 451–53, 456, 505, 509
 navy panics, 173, 455, 457
 public opinion, 119, 121, 125–26, 258, 323, 452, 454, 493, 502, 592
 Royal Navy, 122, 147–48, 166, 183, 221, 245–46, 253, 264–66, 288, 313, 321–22, 325, 330, 335, 418, 455, 457, 483, 493, 509–11, 517–18, 524, 534, 538

# INDEX

Great Britain (cont.)
  trade policy, 142–44, 228–29, 280–83
  Two Power Standard, 122, 287, 329–30, 335, 452–53, 455, 457, 460
  *See also* arms race; Anglo-Russian Convention; Anglo-Russian naval talks; Anglosphere and Anglo-Saxonism; Agadir Crisis; blockade; Boer War; dreadnoughts; Fashoda Crisis; First Venezuela Crisis; neutrality and neutral rights; Second Venezuela Crisis; Tangier Crisis; Triple Entente
Great Venezuela Railway (Gran Ferrocaril de Venezuela), 152, 154, 155, 153, 155, 153, 298, 299
Greece, 439, 441, 498
Grey, Edward
  Anglo-German relations, 456, 490, 492
  Balkan war diplomacy, 440
  Declaration of London, non-adherence to, 511
  Entente diplomacy, 326, 364, 367, 418, 437, 457, 459, 483, 492
  Germanophobia, 338
  July Crisis diplomacy, 493, 500, 502–8
Grimm, Hans, 598
Grodno, 547
  war aims in, 562
*Großraum* (greater space), 599
Growald, Ernst, 468
Guam, 5, 215, 230
Guangzhou. *See* Canton
Guangzhouwan (Kwangchow Wan), 5
Guettel, Jens-Uwe, 14
Guggenheim, Daniel, 380
Guggenheim, Meyer, 380
Guiana, British (Guyana), 146
Gutschmidt, Felix v., 112
Gwinner, Arthur v., 301, 361–63, 365, 461, 472, 482–83, 485–87, 541

H. G. & L. F. Blohm, 152
Haas, Willem Rijk Tromp de, 412
Haber-Bosch process, 520
Hadley, Arthur T., 32, 494
Haeckel, Ernst, 350
Hague Peace Conferences (1899, 1907), 220, 338, 376, 453, 455
Haidar-Pasha Harbor Company, 363
Haiti, 154
Haldane, Richard, 260, 262, 326, 437, 460–62, 500
Halifax, 231
Halle, Ernst v., 63
  Americas, writings and views on, 213
  anti-Semitic press attacks on, 473–74
  backgound and early career, 60, 63–65
  Caribbean and Venezuela, travel to (1896), 153–57
  Communications Bureau of Navy Office, work for, 202–7, 210–11, 220, 286, 333
  cotton cultivation and industry, scholarship on, 75–78
  daughter, 600
  Economic Bureau of Treasury Office, work for, 332, 447, 465–66, 468, 470–73
  financial reform bill (1905), writings and support of, 332
  German shipping industry, writings on, 233–36
  Hottentot elections, 351
  industrial trusts in the US, writings on, 71–74
  Nauticus, 202
  Order of the Crown, awarded, 248
  settler colonialism, views on, 430
  United States, writings and views on, 74–75, 150–51, 157–59, 285
Halle, Henriette v., 478, 600
Halle, University of, 35
Hamburg
  Bürgerschaft, 63, 403
  Chamber of Commerce, 127, 400
  General Lecture Agency (Allgemeines Vorlesungswesen), 291, 397
  Klein Flottbeck, 185
  merchants, 217, 397

Senate, 127, 195, 220, 397, 400
shipping, 6, 228, 236
Upper School Board (Oberschulbehörde), 397, 399
Hammann, Otto, 169, 193, 344
Hampton Institute, 422
Handelshochschule (Higher School of Commerce) Cologne, 211
Hangchow (Hangzhou), 132, 134
Hangzhou. *See* Hangchow
Hankou, 111, 118, 134–35
Hanneken, Constantin v., 135
Hannoverischer Maschinenbau A.G., 299
Hanover, 223
*Hans Wagner*, 245
Hanseatic League, 231
HAPAG (Hamburg-Amerikanische Paketfahrt-Aktien-Gesellschaft), 152–53, 235, 255, 262–63, 265, 322, 337, 363, 424, 449, 472
Harbin, 303
*Hardenberg*, SMS, 154
Hardinge, Charles, 326, 367, 483
Harnack, Adolf v., 368, 527, 555–56
Harrison, Austin, 318–19
Hart, Robert, 136
Hartwig, Nikolai, 438
Harvard University, 65, 76, 368–70, 372, 478, 513
Hatzfeldt, Paul v., 149, 214
Havana, 157, 234, 379, 423
Hawaiian Islands, 5, 145, 181, 196, 215, 218, 243, 370, 375–76, 380, 383, 385
Hayakawa Senkichirō, 138
Haydarpasha, 299–300
Hay-Herbert Convention (1903), 315, 329
Hay-Herrán Treaty (1903), 315
Hay-Pauncefote Treaty (1901), 316
Heeringen, August v., 197–99, 202–3, 207–8, 210, 221, 254, 285
Heidelberg, 33, 600
Heidelberg, University of, 96, 348, 399, 530, 579
Heisenberg, Elisabeth, 601
Heisenberg, Werner, 601

Helfferich, Friedrich, 274
Helfferich, Karl
 background and early career, 274, 290–92
 Baghdad Railway, construction of, 298, 301, 362–67, 483–89
 Balkan crises, views on, 441
 colonial crisis, debate over, 341–42
 colonial policy and reform, writings and views on, 295–98, 392, 394
 Colonial Section of Foreign Office, work for, 293
 Communications Bureau of Navy Office, work for, 286
 Deutsche Bank, work for, 343
 DNVP deputy, 596
 fiscal policy, views on, 334, 465
 German colonies, economic assessment of, 425–26
 Hottentot elections, 352–54
 Order of the Crown, awarded, 342
 submarine warfare, views on, 537, 539, 579–80
 trade, views on, 274–76
 treasury secretary, appointment as, 525–27
 vice-chancellor, appointment as, 586
 war aims, 541
 world war, causes of, 508–9
Heligoland Bight, Battle of (1914), 518
Heligoland-Zanzibar Treaty (1890), 171
Hentig, Otto v., 350
Herbette, Maurice, 418
Herero and Nama wars (1904–8), 340, 346, 357, 393
Herkner, Heinrich, 542, 544, 565
*Herzog*, 245–47
Hewins, William A. S., 260–61
Heydt Rescript (1859), 152
Heyking, Edmund v., 135
High Seas Fleet. *See* Navy
Hildebrand, Heinrich, 134
Hildebrand, Klaus, 15
Hillgruber, Andreas, 15
Hindenburg, Paul v., 553–54, 579, 581, 588–89
Hintze, Otto, 62, 553, 584
Hipper, Franz v., 590

Hirsch, Wilhelm, 129, 545, 584–85
Hirst, Francis Wrigley, 437
Historical School of Economics, German, 94
  *See also* Schmoller, Gustav v.
Historikerstreit (1986–89), 15
Hitler, Adolf, 602–3
Ho Amei, 130
Hobson, Rolf, 22, 184
Hoetzsch, Otto, 436
Hoffmann, Theodor Eduard, 84
Hohenborn, Adolf Wild v., 568
Hohenlohe-Langenburg, Ernst zu, 341, 343
Hohenlohe-Schillingsfürst, Chlodwig zu, 148–49, 182, 193, 201, 220
Hokkaido, 79, 137
Holland. *See* Netherlands
Holleben, Theodor v., 32, 106, 108–12, 313–14, 368
Hollmann, Friedrich v., 179, 182
Holst, Hermann v., 69
Holstein, Friedrich August v., 185, 193, 325
Holtzendorff, Henning v., 538, 554, 579–81
Holy Alliance, 120
Honduras, 5, 145, 423
Hong Kong, 89, 115, 117, 130–32, 135, 139, 201, 237, 239–40
Hong Kong and Shanghai Bank, 131
Hopman, Albert, 462, 554
Hottentot elections (1907), 344–52, 354–58
Howaldtwerft, 113
Hoyos, Alexander v., 497
Huangshi (Daye), 134
Hubatsch, Walther, 2
Huerta, Victoriano, 424
Hugenberg, Alfred, 428–29, 520, 553–54
Huguenin, Edouard, 365
Hull, Cordell, 599
Hull, Isabel, 507
Humboldt, Alexander v., 6, 41

Illinois, 43, 46, 52
*Iltis*, SMS, 252
Imperial Navy Office. *See* Navy Office

Imperial University. *See* Tokyo University
Incheon (Chemulpo), 136, 321
India, 13, 78, 120, 228, 552
  Army in world war, 515
  Baghdad Railway and, 300, 302
  British colonial rule, 160–61
  colonial administration, 402–3
  colonial unrest in, 593
  defense of, 121, 123, 505
  Dominion restrictions on immigration from, 594
  German wartime subterfuge, 549
  grain supplies in world war, 528
  Moghul Empire, 160
  Schlagintweit survey, 6
  trade with, 364
Indochina, 88, 139, 515, 565, 593
  Vietnamese nationalists in, 594
Ingenohl, Ernst Friedrich v., 518, 527, 530
inner colonization, 55–57, 426–31, 434, 444, 446, 547, 550, 558, 563, 585, 597
  *See also* Society for the Promotion of Inner Colonization
Inoue Kowashi, 84
Institut Colonial International, 405, 421
International Association for Labour Legislation, 495
International Monetary Fund, 602
International Union for Comparative Jurisprudence and Political Economy, 203, 209
*Invincible*, HMS, 266
Iowa, 43, 52
Iraq, 593
Ireland, 121, 230, 524, 530
  British repression in, 593
  colonial unrest in, 593
  Ulster Crisis (1914), 502
*Irene*, SMS, 214
iron and steel industry, 67, 72, 109, 130, 145, 152, 241, 268, 277, 280, 363, 380, 417, 442, 518, 528, 541, 545, 550, 555, 562
Italy, 5, 9, 444, 492, 592
  German trade treaty with, 279
  German trade with, 228, 269

Italo-Turkish War (1911), 439
Jews, 573
military spending, 480
*Mitteleuropa* and, 173, 356
trade policy, 279
Triple Alliance, 125, 325, 506
world war, 578
Itō Hirobumi, 84, 87
Izvolsky, Alexander, 364, 366–67, 386, 438, 504

Jaffé, Edgar, 542
Jagow, Gottlieb v., 441, 482, 498, 503, 563, 580
J. A. Maffei & Co., 299
Jamaica, 155, 423
James, Edmund J., 32
Jameson Raid (1895), 148, 183
Japan, 6, 9, 15, 19, 29, 32, 176
  administrative reforms, 102–3
  Army, 320
  Boshin War (1868), 80
  Boxer Rebellion, suppression of, 253
  *bunmei-kaika* (civilization and enlightenment movement), 82
  colonialism and imperialism, 81–82, 196, 206, 210, 237, 305, 328–29, 387, 444, 537
  *doitsugaku* (German studies), 83–87
  Dutch East Indies, influence in, 412–13
  Education Ministry, 310
  education reforms, 90–94
  European perceptions of, 6
  factories and factory legislation, 98
  Finance Ministry, 90
  German advisors in, 82, 84, 106, 306
  German Jewish ties to, 310
  German trade with, 110, 137–38, 271
  Germany, education ties to, 19, 309–10
  Germany, relations with, 107–8, 113–18, 181, 192, 302–3, 305–9, 438
  Health and Sanitation, Bureau of, 98
  Home Ministry, 98
  industrialization, 94–95, 137–38, 160, 240, 405
  Jesuits in, 308
  Johannes Justus Rein in, 80–81
  *kokka gakkai* (Association of Political and Social Sciences), 94
  League of Nations Covenant and, 593
  legal and constitutional reforms, 98–101, 103–6
  *meirokusha* (Meiji Six Society), 82–83
  military reforms, 85, 264
  Ministry of Justice, 99, 101, 104
  nation-building, 31
  Navy, 166, 237, 248, 304, 321, 323–24, 455
  *nihon shakai seisaku gakkai* (Japanese Scholars for Social Policy), 97–98
  Police Bureau, Imperial, 103
  Prussian colonial and commerical aims in, 80
  Prussian expedition to (1860–62), 79–80
  *shakai mondai* (social question), 97
  *tennō* (emperor of Japan), 106, 181
  trade policy, 279
  *Weltpolitik* and, 22, 78, 81–82
  *Weltwirtschaft* and, 19
  world war, 517–18
  Zimmermann Telegram and, 580
  *See also* Anglo-Japanese Alliance; Association School; Association for German Scholarship; German Japan Society; Ostasiatische Gesellschaft; Russo-Japanese War; Sino-Japanese War; Tokyo University; yellow peril
Jardine, Matheson & Co., 210
Java, 402, 411–13, 415
  Japanese influences in, 413
  Wahhabism in, 412
Jenisch & Godeffroy, 187
Jenisch, Martin Johann, 187
Jews
  Fatherland Party and, 586
  financial reform bill, role in, 473
  German liberalism and, 9
  Jewish question, 568–78
  *Ostjudenfrage* (eastern Jewish question), 565

Jews (cont.)
  philanthropic activity, 310, 368, 494, 583
  Polish and Russian, 56, 565
  Russia, mistreatment of, 515
  stab-in-the-back myth, 589
  war economy, role in, 522
  *Weltpolitik*, role in, 354, 473
  See also anti-Semitism
Jhering, Rudolf v., 102
Jiaozhou. See Kiaochow
Jinan. See Tsinan
Johann Cesar Godeffroy & Sohn, 217
Judenzählung. See Army
Jutland, Battle of (1916), 578

Kaempfer, Engelbert, 6, 80
Kahl, Wilhelm, 527
*Kaiser*, SMS, 214
*Kaiserin Augusta*, SMS, 214
Kaiser-Wilhelm (Kiel) Canal, 1, 331, 455
Kakel, Caroll P., 599
Kansas, 52
Kapp, Wolfgang, 578–79, 584–85
  Fatherland Party, 553, 584–85
  inner colonization, 429
  Kapp Putsch (1920), 596
Kardorff, Wilhelm v., 201
Kassel, 168, 193
Katō Hiroyuki, 86, 89, 91, 100
Katsura Taro, 85
Kehr, Eckart, 4, 21, 278, 602
  Sammlungspolitik, 588
  social imperialism, 184
Keim, August, 286, 333, 344, 448, 458
Keiō Public School (*keiō gijuku*), 108
Kelly, Patrick J., 22, 177, 185
Kennan, George F., 328
Kessler, Harry, 64
Ketteler, Clemens v., 251–52
Keynes, John Maynard, 591–92
Kharkiv, 433
Kiaochow (Jiaozhou), 5, 102, 129, 136, 138–39, 207, 209, 226, 239, 250, 408
  administration of, 401
  conditions in, 209
  German sphere of influence, 254
  harbor, 238
  landing in and lease of (1897), 139, 140, 141, 192, 196, 329
  naval base, 237, 309
  Navy investments in, 309
  seizure by Japan in world war, 517
  See also Tsingtao (Qingdao)
Kiderlen-Waechter, Alfred v., 365, 406, 409, 489
  Agadir Crisis (1911), 417, 440–41, 482
Kiel, 193, 451, 590
Kiel, University of, 210–11, 272, 292
Kiev, 432–33, 567
Kingston, 157
Kirdorf, Emil, 553, 584
Kitashirakawa Yoshihisa, Japanese prince, 101
Kitchener, Herbert, 139
Kjellén, Rudolf, 387, 430
Klehmet, Reinhold, 213
Kleist, Friedrich v., 153
Knapp, Georg Friedrich, 35–36
Knappe, Wilhelm, 130, 136, 138
Knies, Karl, 96
Knoop, Gustav, 154
Knorr, Eduard, 179
Kobe, 137
Koch, Richard, 290
Koefoed, Carl Andreas, 433
Kokovtsov, Vladimir, 491
Kolonialinstitut, Hamburg (Colonial Institute), 392, 397–407, 437, 542–43
Kolonialpolitisches Aktionskomité (Colonial-Political Action Committee), 348–52, 354–61
Kolonial-Wirtschaftliches Komitee (Colonial Economic Committee), 76
Konya, 299, 361–62, 365, 489
Kopp, Georg v., 195, 308
Koppel, Arthur, 368
Koppel, Leopold, 494
Korea, 5, 109, 111, 117, 135, 137, 231, 252, 305, 319–21
  nationalists, 594
Kovno
  war aims in, 547, 550, 560

Krauss & Co., 299
Kriegsrohstoffabteilung (War Raw Materials Department), 521
Krivoshein, Alexander, 431, 434
Kruger Telegram (1896), 125, 148–50, 169, 171, 180, 183, 317
Kruger, Paul, 148
Krupp, Friedrich Alfred, 129, 152
Krupp, Gustav, 553
Krupp-Gussstahlfabrik, 109–10, 113, 134, 149, 152–53, 168, 221, 252, 299, 429, 520, 553
Kühlmann, Richard v., 482, 566
Kuhn, Loeb & Co., 310, 516
Kundrus, Birthe, 11
Kuwait, 302
Kuwata Kumazō, 97–98
Kyoto, 137

Lambert, Nicholas A., 22
Land Economy Collegium, Prussian funding of Max Sering's North American investigation (1883), 44
Lange, Rudolf, 84, 306
Langkawi, 217
Lapradelle, Albert de Geouffre de, 513
Lascelles, Frank Cavendish, 126
Laughlin, Laurence, 71
Laurenço Marques (Maputo), 245
League of Nations Covenant, 593, 595
*Lebensraum*, 59
Ledebour, Georg, 473
Lee, Arthur, 322
left liberals (Deutsche Freisinnige Partei, Fortschrittspartei, Freisinnige Vereinigung, Freisinnige Volkspartei), 173, 199, 296, 343, 358, 445
  Fatherland Party and, 587
  financial reform, 469, 471, 475
  Hottentot elections, 358
  naval laws, 447, 458, 463
  radical nationalism and, 12
  stab-in-the-back myth, 589
  war aims, 545
  wartime polarization, 540
Lehmann, Curt, 523
Lehmann, Rudolph, 138

Leinung, Gustav, 134
Leipzig, 37, 358
Leipzig, University of, 35–36, 64, 188, 369–70, 468
Leist, Heinrich, 293
Lemmermann, Otto, 523
Lenz & Co., 341
Leopold II, king of the Belgians, 421, 515
Leroy-Beaulieu, Henri, 224
Levy, Hermann, 530, 579
Levy, Heymann Baruch, 63
Lexis, Wilhelm, 350
Li Hongzhang, 109, 116, 135–37, 253
Liaotung (Liaodong) Peninsula, 116, 117, 135, 137, 231, 303, 321, 329
liberal imperialism, 3, 8, 14, 18, 24, 170, 402, 561
  German, defined, 10–12
  National Socialism and, 19
  wartime, 555, 566–67
  world war and, 545, 591
liberalism, 3, 8, 10–11
  bourgeois, 168
  fascism and, 9
  German, defined, 9–10
  nationalism and, 167
  radical nationalism and, 12
Lichnowsky, Karl v., 461, 482, 493, 500
Liebermann, Max, 222
Liebknecht, Karl, 208
Liège, 508, 541, 548
  war aims in, 548
Lieven, Dominik, 386
Liman von Sanders Crisis (1913), 491, 492
Limpus, Arthur, 491, 493
Lindenfeld, David, 403
Lindequist, Friedrich v., 418, 481
Lipke, Gustav, 198
Lissner, Julius, 468
List, Friedrich, 41, 86
Lithuania, 558, 563, 565, 567
  loss of German territory to, 597
  war aims in, 558, 560, 562, 567
Livonia, 559, 561, 567
  war aims in, 547, 550
Lloyd George, David, 336, 418, 457, 464

Lobell, Friedrich Wilhelm v., 344
Lodge, Henry Cabot, 315
Loeb, James, 583
Lohmeyer, Julius, 222
London German External Debt Agreement (1953), 602
London Naval Conference (1908–9), 376
London School of Economics, 260
London, Declaration of (1909), 376, 454, 458, 510–11, 529, 537
Lönholm, Ludwig, 104
Lord Kimberley. *See* Wodehouse, John
Lord Salisbury. *See* Gascoyne-Cecil, Robert (Marquess of Salisbury)
Louisiana, 76
Louvain
  burning of, 508, 513, 517, 533
Ludendorff, Erich, 509, 553, 563–65, 579, 581, 585, 588–89
Lüderitz Railway, 391
Lui Mingchuang, 111
Lüshunkou. *See* Port Arthur
*Lusitania*, 265, 512, 533–34, 536–37
Luxembourg
  war aims in, 541

M. Raspe & Co., 108
M. M. Warburg Bank, 310, 392, 516
Macau, 131
Macdonald, Claude, 136
Macedonia, 362
MacKinder, Halford, 260, 386, 430
Madagascar, 5, 515
Made in Germany (1896), 142, 144
Madrid Convention (1880), 325, 367
Magoon, Charles, 379–80
Mahan, Alfred Thayer, 158, 160, 165–66, 168, 178, 184, 203–4, 324, 375
  sea power ideology, 304, 430
*Maine*, USS, 379
Maji Maji rebellion (1905–7), 340, 342
Malaya, 409, 415, 549
Malet, Edward, 149, 183
Malietoa Laupepa, Samoan king, 218
Malietoa Tanumafili, 218
Manchuria, 5, 116, 127
Manila, 214–15
Manitoba, 49, 51

Mannesmann brothers, 416
Marburg, University of, 142, 399, 517
Marcks, Erich, 62
Mariana Islands, 5, 215, 444
Marienfeld, Wolfgang, 20
Marjoribanks, Edward (Baron Tweedmouth), 330
Marne, First Battle of the (1914), 522, 524, 541
Marschall von Bieberstein, Adolf, 148, 149, 185, 193, 299, 367, 489
Marshall, Alfred, 96
Marshall Islands, 110
  seizure by Japan in world war, 518
Marshall Plan (European Recovery Program, 1947), 602
Maschinenfabrik Esslingen, 299
Mata'afa Iosefo, 218
*Mauretania*, 265
Mauritania, 5
Maxse, Leo, 260, 318
Mayr, Georg v., 350
Mazower, Mark, 8
McKenna duties (1916), 595
McKenna, Reginald, 454, 456
McKinley tariff (1890), 67, 74–75, 145, 229, 370
McKinley, William, 67, 143, 145, 243, 267
McMeekin, Sean, 22
Mecca, 361, 366, 412
Mehnert, Ute, 15
Mehta, Uday, 13
Meinecke, Friedrich, 553
Melchers & Co., 89
Melle, Werner v., 397–401, 403, 422, 542
Mendelssohn-Bartholdy, Ernst v., 472
Mendelssohn & Co., 472
Mendelssohn, Franz v., 472
Menger, Carl, 96
Merton, William, 525, 577
Metallgesellschaft, 525
Metternich zur Gracht, Paul Wolff, 126, 455, 471
Mevissen, Gustav, 211
Mexican-American War (1846–8), 561
Mexico, 5, 41, 356, 380, 580–81
  trade policy, 145

US occupation of Veracruz (1914), 424
Zimmerman Telegram (1917) and, 580
Michaelis, Georg, 101–3, 306, 522, 584, 586
Michaelis, Wilhelm, 457
Mill, John Stuart, 13, 83
Milner, Alfred, 260
Milyukov, Pavel, 384
Min, queen of Korea, 137
Minnesota, 43, 49–50, 59, 151, 420
   Minneapolis, 51, 70
   St. Paul, 49
Minsk
   war aims in, 562
Miquel, Johannes v., 468
Mississippi, 76
   Natchez, 424
Missouri, 52, 76
Mitchell, Nancy, 15
Mitsui Trading Company, 138
*Mittelafrika*, 172, 417, 482, 541–42
*Mitteleuropa*, 62, 173, 439, 541, 544, 552, 555, 562, 564–66, 578
Mitteleuropäischer Wirtschaftsverein (Central European Economic Association), 279
Mocha, 87
Moellendorff, Wichard v., 521
Möllendorff, Paul v., 89, 109, 111, 135, 137
Moltke, Helmuth v., 503, 525
Monroe Doctrine, 75, 146–47, 150–51, 158, 183, 230, 284, 311–14, 387, 565
   League of Nations Covenant and, 593
   Roosevelt corollary, 312, 317, 424, 430
Montana, 49
Montenegro, 439, 443
Montreal, 52
Morefield, Jeanne, 13
Morel, Edmund D., 421
Morgan, J. P., 516, 583
Mori Arinori, 82
Morocco, 5, 252, 325–26, 333, 342, 367, 376, 416–19, 439, 457, 460, 469, 515
   war aims in, 546
   *See also* Agadir Crisis; Tangier Crisis
Moscow, 434
Mosse, Albert, 105
Mosul, 302, 365, 488
Mozambique, 149, 214, 245, 490, 541
Müller, August, 587
Müller, Cesar, 154
Müller, Leopold, 84
Müller, Richard, 473
Mulligan, William, 502
Munich, University of, 64, 274, 466
Münsterberg, Hugo, 65, 368, 494, 513, 583
Murray, David, 83

Nagasaki, 115, 137, 237, 308
Nakamura Masanao, 82
Namier, Louis, 2
Namur
   war aims in, 548
Nanking (Nanjing), 132, 135
Nara, 137
*Nassau*, SMS, 331
Nasse, Erwin, 44
Natal, 225
National Liberals (Nationalliberale Partei), 56, 326, 447
   DNVP and, 596
   Fatherland Party and, 587
   financial reform, 333, 470–71, 476, 479
   Hottentot elections, 358
   naval laws, 447, 456
   submarine warfare, 538
   wartime polarization, 539
National Socialism, 4, 8, 19, 24, 598, 600–1, 603
Naumann, Friedrich, 173, 544, 555, 565
navalism, 22–23, 165, 167–69, 171, 222, 228, 446, 449
   *See also* Mahan, Alfred Thayer; Bluewater School
navy laws (1898, 1900), 23, 185, 203, 213, 237, 247–48, 278, 285, 288, 304, 331, 333, 337, 447–48, 451–52, 457, 460–61, 464–65, 471
Navy League, British, 165, 221, 260, 454

Navy League, German (Deutscher Flottenverein), 12, 221–23, 248, 260, 285–87, 331, 333, 446–49, 458, 463, 469, 588
   Hottentot elections and, 344–45, 350, 354
Navy Office, Imperial (Reichsmarineamt, RMA), 18, 23, 102, 128, 149, 177–78, 180, 182, 197, 202, 211, 221, 285, 287–89, 332, 338, 401, 407, 446–48, 457–58, 465, 527, 538–39
   Communications Bureau (Nachrichtenbureau des Reichsmarineamts), 190, 197, 202–12, 220–21, 223, 286, 332–33, 447
   Hottentot elections and, 351
Navy, Imperial (Kaiserliche Marine), 237
   Admiralty Staff, 265, 447, 524, 537
   East Asian Cruiser Squadron, 110, 113, 180–81, 214, 518
   High Seas Fleet, 2, 277, 510, 518, 527
   naval mutiny (1918), 590
   Navy Cabinet, 179
   *See also* arms race; blockade; dreadnoughts; submarines and submarine warfare
Nebraska, 52
   Omaha, 45
"negro question". *See* United States of America
Nelson, Robert L., 21
the Netherlands, 154, 160, 213, 226, 319
   colonial administration, 412
   *Mitteleuropa* and, 173, 226
   *See also* Dutch East Indies
neutrality and neutral rights, 376
   Boer War, violations of, 245–46
   continuous voyage, 123, 244–45, 376, 511, 529
   erosion of, 454, 531
   Rule of War (1756), 123
   violations of, 510–12, 531
   *See also* Paris, Declaration of (1856)
Nevada, 46, 115
New Guinea, 110, 125, 207, 217, 235
   seizure by Australia in world war, 518
New Haven, 33, 38, 44, 112, 531
new imperialism, 8, 165, 227, 277, 294
New Mexico, 580
New Orleans, 234
New York Chamber of Commerce, 373
New Zealand, 120, 267, 394, 455, 518
   subimperialism, 218
   trade policy, 279
Newchwang (Yingkou), 251
Newman, Henry P., 579
Nicaragua, 5, 146, 213
   US occupation of (1912), 423
Nicholas II, tsar of Russia, 220, 583
Nicolson, Arthur, 326, 418, 483, 492, 502–3
Niebuhr, Barthold, 33
Niebuhr, Cornelia, 33
Niemeyer, Theodor, 513
Nishi Amane, 82–83, 86, 101
Norddeutsche Bank, 152–53
Norddeutscher Lloyd (NDL), 44, 60, 68, 130, 152, 235, 263, 409, 449, 495
North Carolina, 76
North German Confederation (1867–71), 205
Northern Pacific Railroad, 47, 63
North-South Railway (China), 238
Norway, 336, 510–11, 601
   merchant marine, 532
Noske, Gustav, 586
Nyasaland (Malawi), 5
Nyassa Company, 490

*Ogeechee*, 531
Ohio, 52
oil industry
   Anglo-Persian Oil, 483
   California, 381
   Galicia, 302
   Mesopotamia, 302, 366, 487–88
   Persia, 366
   Romania, 302, 439, 442
   Royal Dutch, 414
   Standard Oil, 72, 302, 410, 414
   Sumatra, 414
   Turkish Petroleum, 488
Ōkuma Shigenobu, 84
Oldenberg, Karl, 275

Omdurman, Battle of (1898), 139
Ōmura Jintarō, 306
Oncken, Hermann, 553
Ontario, 52
Oriental Railway, 441
Osaka, 94, 137
Ostasaiatische Gesellschaft (East Asiatic Society, OAG), 80, 82, 107, 110, 138
Osterhammel, Jürgen, 7
Ostpreußische Generallandschaftsdirektion, 429
Ostwald, Wilhelm, 370
Otte, Thomas G., 15, 22
Ottoman Empire, 174
    Anatolia, 125, 298, 300, 363
    German informal empire in, 290, 299–301, 363, 387, 438
    German involvement in military reforms, 366, 491
    Mesopotamia, 300, 302, 361, 363, 365–66, 482, 487–89
    Public Debt Administration, 301
    *See also* Anatolian Railway; Baghdad Railway; Balkan wars; Italo-Turkish War; Liman von Sanders Crisis
Ōyama Iwao, 86

Paasche, Hermann, 142
Palau Islands, 5, 215, 218, 444
    seizure by Japan in world war, 518
Paléologue, Maurice, 501
Palestine
    colonial unrest in, 593
Palmer, William (Earl of Selborne), 247
Panama, 312
    Canal Zone, 5, 316–17, 379, 423, 565
    Colón, 423
    Panama Canal, 272, 316, 370, 373, 379, 381–82, 423, 565
    Panama City, 423
Panamerica, 23, 75, 146, 183, 217, 373, 387
    Panamerican Congress (1889), 145
    Panamericanism, 172, 201, 216, 230
Pan-German League (Alldeutscher Verband), 151, 171, 344, 417, 429, 432, 469, 539, 587

*Panther*, SMS, 313, 315, 376, 417–18
Papen, Franz v., 535
Paraguay, 151
Paris, Declaration of (1856), 123, 246, 510
Paris, Treaty of (1898), 372
Paris, Treaty of (1951), 602
Pašić, Nikola, 497
Patten, Simon N., 32
*Pax Britannica*, 9, 603
*Pax Germanica*, 552, 556
Peabody, Francis G., 370
Peace Resolution (1917), 583–84
Peez, Alexander v., 173
Peking (Beijing), 132, 135–36, 138, 251–53, 409, 434
Pemba, 214
Penck, Wilhelm, 468
Pennsylvania, 39
Pennsylvania Railroad, 40
Penny, Glenn, 14
Persia, 120, 299, 324, 364
    Abadan oil fields, 366, 487
    Abadan oil refinery, 483
    Anglo-Russian agreements on, 364
    Anglo-Russian partition of, 482
    Baghdad Railway connection to, 364
    British oil concessions in, 366
    British sphere of influence in, 302
    German economic ties to, 364
    Russian cotton export market in, 434
    Russian sphere of influence in, 302, 444
Persian Gulf, 300, 302, 364
    HAPAG service to, 363
Pescadores Islands (Penghu), 117
Peters, Carl, 171, 293
Philadelphia, Centennial Exhibition (1876), 280
Philipp Holzmann & Co., 299, 363
Philippine-American War (1899–1902), 216, 251
Philippines, 5, 144, 216, 230, 370
    German ambitions in, 214–15
    Mindanao, 214
    Palwan, 214
    Sulu Archipelago, 214
Philippovich, Eugen v., 61
Pillsbury, Charles, 70

Piotrków, 547
Pitts, Jennifer, 13
Pittsburgh
    Pennsylvania railway riots (1877), 40
Pohl, Hugo v., 518, 524, 527, 530, 538
Pohle, Ludwig, 275
Poincaré, Raymond, 440, 501
Poland, 56, 558, 560–64, 567, 621
    loss of German territory to, 597
    war aims in, 541, 547, 554, 556, 559–66
Polish minority, 56, 426–27
Poltava, 433
population growth, 43, 179, 193, 204, 206, 224–26, 240, 258, 275, 441, 453
Port Arthur (Lüshunkou), 5, 116, 137, 231, 252, 303, 320–21, 329
Portland, 47
Portsmouth, Treaty of (1905), 324
Portsmouth, UK, 322
Portugal
    Jews, 573
    Windsor Treaty, 253
Posen
    as German eastern colonial frontier, 44
Potsdam, 182
Powers, Harry Huntington, 231
Pretoria, 149
Preuß, Hugo, 569–70, 572, 574, 576
Primrose, Archibald (Earl of Rosebery), 260
*Prinzess Alice*, 409
*Prinzess Wilhelm*, SMS, 214
Prussian East Asian expedition (1860–62), 79–80
public finance
    deficits in Imperial (Reich) budget, 288–89, 333–35, 464
    reform of, 464–79
Public Works, Prussian Ministry of, 129, 139–41
Puerto Rico, 5, 154, 216
Puttkamer, Jesko v., 294

Qingdao. *See* Tsingtao
Quebec, 52

Raabe, Wilhelm, 222
Railway Office, Imperial (Reichseisenbahnamt), 342
Ranke, Leopold v., 37
Rathenau, Walther, 343, 392, 431, 461
    assassination of, 596
    British anxieties over Germany, 258–59, 318
    British preventive war, 509
    colonial reform, 394
    *Judenzählung* and, 577
    war aims, 541
    war economy, 520–21
    world war, 591
Rathgen, Bernhard Hederich, 33
Rathgen, Karl
    background and early career, 33, 35–36, 82, 87
    Belgian Congo, scholarship and views on, 420–21
    British imperial preference, views on, 142–44, 160–61
    colonial reform, writings on and support of, 294
    colonial science, development of, 402–5
    East Asia, travel to (1882), 90
    Japanese government, advisor to, 104–5, 107–10
    Kaiser Wilhelm Professor, Columbia University (1913–14), 420
    Korea, China, Formosa, and southern Japan, travel to (1886, 1890), 111
    part of German occupation of Belgium (1914–15), 542–44
    Tokyo University professor, 90–94
    United States South and Caribbean, travel in (1914), 421–26
Ratzel, Friedrich, 41, 58–59, 230, 386
*Raumnot* (space needs), 599
Rechenberg, Albrecht v., 394
Redl, Alfred, 480
Rein, Johannes Justus, 80–81
Reinsurance Treaty (1887), 116, 171, 174
Reuters, 125
Rex, Arthur v., 154

Rheinbaben, Georg v., 520
Rhodes, Cecil, 148
Rhodesia, 5
Richter, Eugen, 173
Richthofen, Ferdinand v., 6, 62, 115, 117, 253
Rietzler, Kurt, 498
Ringer, Fritz, 20
Rintelen, Franz v., 535
Ritter, Gerhard, 2–3, 15, 177
Riza, Ahmed, 484
Roentgen, Wilhelm, 350
Roesicke, Gustav, 473
Roesler, Hermann, 90, 99–100
Röhl, John, 16, 481
Rohrbach, Paul, 172
Roloff, Gustav, 350, 355–56
Romania, 441, 498
   German trade treaty with, 279
   German trade with, 269, 439
   July Crisis, 506
   *Mitteleuropa* and, 439
   world war, 579
Roosevelt, Alice, 378
Roosevelt, Theodore, 374
   Alaska boundary, 315
   Germany, suspicion of in Venezuela, 311–13, 315
   Great White Fleet circumnavigation, 376
   Japanese immigrants, hostility to, 375
   navalism of, 166, 316, 375–76
   Panama Canal, 373
   Roosevelt corollary, 317, 387
   Russo-Japanese War, 324
   Second Venezuela Crisis, 314
   Spanish-American War, 372
   yellow peril, 382–83
Root Commission (1917), 384
Root, Elihu, 315, 384
Roscher, Wilhelm, 86, 188
Rose, Andreas, 15
Rosen, Roman, 386
Rößler, Constantin, 62, 173
Rotterdam, 461
Royal Colonial Institute, 159
Royal Dutch Shell, 487
Royal Navy, 237

rubber industry, 310, 521
Rubner, Max, 523
Rudolph, Carl, 104
Rudorff, Otto, 104
Rüger, Jan, 22, 451
Rümker, Kurt v., 523
Russell, Bertrand, 260
Russia, 116–17, 565
   Army, 479
   Baghdad Railway, opposition to, 364–65
   Balkan policy, 367, 438–39
   colonialism and imperailism, 123, 176, 204, 225, 230, 244
   East Asian policy, 251–52, 303–5
   German perceptions of, 431–38
   Germany, Russia and Eurasian empire, 385–86
   Great Program (1914), 480
   Imperial Navy, 122, 176, 178, 183, 237, 304
   July Crisis diplomacy, 500–2
   *Lombardverbot*, 174
   Ottoman policy and the Entente, 490–93
   Russo-German relations, 324, 438, 440, 481, 501, 547, 559
   Russo-Japanese War (1904–5), 319–25
   Slavophilia, 367, 386, 443, 491
   war aims in, 547–48, 551–52, 558–63, 567
   *See also* Anglo-Russian Convention; Björkö Treaty; Crimean War; Franco-Russian (Dual) Alliance; Reinsurance Treaty; Russo-German trade treaty; Russo-Turkish War; Trans-Siberian Railway; Triple Entente
Russian Germans
   war aims, 565–66
Russo-German trade treaty (1904), 431
Russo-Turkish War (1877–78), 120

Sächsische Maschinenfabrik, 152
Saigon, 88, 96
Salweski, Michael, 184
*Sammlungspolitik*, 192, 207, 588

Samoa, 5, 110, 125–26, 144, 207, 214, 217–22, 230, 232, 242–43, 290, 370, 406, 444, 451
  coaling stations, 218
  seizure by New Zealand in world war, 518
Samsa Bay, 129
Samshui. *See* Sanshui
Samuel Smiles, 83
Sanders, Otto Liman v., 491
Sandshak railway crisis (1908), 365
Sandt, Maximilian v., 542
Sanshui (Samshui), 132
Santo Domingo, 145, 154
Sarajevo, 497
Saskatchewan, 49
Savage Island, 243
Saxony, 129, 473
Sazonov, Serge, 386, 438, 491–92, 501
Scandinavia, 228, 258
  *Mitteleuropa* and, 173, 226, 356
Schäfer, Dietrich, 348, 584
Schantung-Bergbaugesellschaft, 238
Schantung-Eisenbahngesellschaft, 238
Schanz, Georg, 350
Scheer, Reinhard, 590
Scheidtweiler, Peter, 134
Schemua, Blasius v., 443
Schiemann, Theodor, 432, 436–37, 553
Schiff, Jacob, 310, 368, 494, 516, 583
Schillings, Carl Georg, 348
Schlagintweit, brothers (Adolf, Hermann, and Robert), 6
Schleswig, 1
Schlieffen, Alfred v., 508
Schmidt, Stefan, 22
Schmoller, Gustav v.
  background and career, 33–37
  Bülow, relationship with, 188–90, 279–80, 476–77
  colonial reform, views on, 294–95
  financial reform bill, writings on and support of, 466–68, 470, 472, 476–77
  Free Union for Naval Lectures, activity in, 221–23
  German economic future, views on, 223–27
  Historical School of Economics, leader of, 94
  Jewish question, writings on and controversy over, 568–78
  Kolonialpolitisches Aktionskomité, activity in, 345–51
  new imperialism, views on, 267–68
  Schmoller's *Jahrbuch*, 23, 37, 75, 143, 158, 188–89, 197, 203, 209, 269, 467, 569, 572, 578
  submarine warfare, supporter of, 527, 539
  tariff bill (1901–2), views on and support of, 268–69, 276–80
  Tirpitz, relationship with, 198–202
  war aims, 556
  war economy, 520, 525
  wartime propaganda, 516–17, 531
Schmoller, Lucie, 33, 35
Schoenlank, Bruno, 196
Schöllgen, Gregor, 15, 176
Schröder-von Halle, Anneliese, 600
Schücking, Walther, 517
Schuhmann, Leopold, 44
Schulze, Paul, 49
Schulze-Gaevernitz, Gerhart, 466, 542, 545, 565
Schumacher, Edith, 495, 601
Schumacher, Ernst, 601
Schumacher, Ernst Fritz, 601
Schumacher, Fritz, 601
Schumacher, Hermann Albert
  background and early career, 60–63, 210–12
  China question, views and writings on, 141, 236–42, 254
  China, Korea and Japan, travel in (1897), 129–39
  Communications Bureau of the Navy Office, work for, 202, 207–10
  Cuba, travel in (1907), 379–80
  Dutch East Indies and Malaya, travel in (1911), 408–16
  Fatherland Party, 584, 586
  financial reform bill (1908–9), 471
  German-Russian Society, activity in, 435–38

German trade commission to East Asia, secretary of (1897), 129
Kaiser Wilhelm Professor, Columbia University (1906–7), 368, 370–74, 495
postwar experiences, 600–2
Reichstag East Asian exhibit, 140
Russia, travel in (1912), 431–35
Stinnes-Legien agreement (1918), 587
tariff bill (1901–2), views on and support of, 269–72
tutor of Crown Prince Wilhelm, 211
Unites States, travel in (1893), 68–71
United States, travel in (1907), 380–85
war aims, 542, 545–51
war aims, influence and liberal imperialism of, 551–56
war economy, 519–20
world war, causes of, 508
Schumacher, H. A., 60
Schuman Declaration (1950), 602
Schurz, Carl, 60, 67–68, 371, 373
 oppositon to US imperialism, 372
Schwabe, Klaus, 20, 554, 556
Schweinburg, Victor, 221–22
Schweinsberg, Gustav Schenk zu, 135
Schwerin, Friedrich W. L. v., 429, 558, 563–65
Scott-Muravev agreement (1899), 252
Scriba, Julius, 90
Second Venezuela Crisis, 310–16
Seeberg, Reinhold, 553–54
Seehandlung, 301
Seeley, John Robert, 204
Seligman, Edwin R. A., 32, 370
Seminar for Oriental Languages. *See* Berlin, University of
Semler, Johannes, 398
Senden-Bibran, Gustav v., 179, 182
Senegal, 231
Senegambia, 541
Senembah Company, 414
Seoul (Hanjang), 136
Serbia, 367, 438
 Balkan wars, 439–44, 461, 491
 German trade with, 439
 July Crisis, 497–98, 501–5, 509

Pan-Serbian irredentism, 441, 491, 497
Sering, Friedrich Wilhelm, 36
Sering, Max
 background and early career, 36, 44, 61–62, 64–65
 frontier liberal imperialism of, 58–60, 386, 420
 German Navy League, leadership of, 285–86, 354
 German-Russian Society, activity in, 435–38
 inner colonization, 56–57, 428–29
 Kolonialpolitisches Aktionskomité, activity in, 348
 Lithuania and Courland, travel in (1915), 558
 Poland, travel in (1916), 561
 Poland, war aims in, 561–63
 Reich Settlement Law (1919), 597
 Russia, travel in (1912), 431–34
 submarine warfare, supporter of, 527–30, 530, 539
 tariff bill (1901–2), views on and support of, 274
 United States and Canada, travel in (1883), 44–52
 US westward settlement as liberal imperial model, 51–52
 war aims, 556, 558, 564
 war aims as liberal imperialism, 565–66
 war aims in Lithuania and Courland, 558–61
 war economy, 520, 525
 world empires as threats to Germany, 227–33
Settlement Commission, Royal Prussian (Königlich Preußische Ansiedlungskommission), 56, 274, 426–29, 545, 558, 563
Shandong. *See* Shantung
Shanghai, 111, 115, 129, 132, 135, 181, 209, 240, 254, 290
 German troops in during suppression of Boxers, 256
Shanghai-Woosung-Nanking Railway, 129
Shanhaiguan. *See* Shan-hai-kwan
Shan-hai-kwan (Shanhaiguan), 252

Shansi (Shanxi) province, 115
Shantou. *See* Swatow
Shantung Peninsula, 115, 135, 138–39, 209, 238, 250–51, 253–55, 298, 303, 309, 387, 393, 406
Shanxi. *See* Shansi
Shaw, George Bernhard, 260–61
Shaxi (Suzhou, Jiangsu), 135
Shibusawa Eiichi, 137
Shimonoseki, Treaty of (1895), 116, 132, 137
*Shoah*, the, 599
Siam (Thailand), 123, 139
Siebert, Benno v., 437
Siebold, Philipp Franz v., 6, 81
Siemens & Halske, 68, 109, 149, 343
Siemens, Georg v., 296, 300–1
Siemens, Wilhelm v., 222, 350, 468
Siemens-Schuckertwerke, 350
Sierra Nevada, 46–47, 381
Simon, Henry James, 520
Singapore, 79, 409, 411
Sino-French War (1884–85), 109
Sino-Japanese War (1894–95), 116, 127–29, 135, 236, 244, 250, 304
Sinophobia, 81
Sivas, 486
Small, Albion W., 32
Smiles, Samuel, 32
Smith, Munroe, 370
Smith, Woodruff D., 16
Smuts, Jan, 593
Snyder, Timothy, 599
Social Darwinism, 166, 450
Social Democratic Party (Sozialdemokratische Partei Deutschlands, SPD), 13, 140, 596
  as reformist party, 463, 586–87
  elections of 1912, 445
  Fatherland Party and, 586–87
  financial reform, 471, 473, 476–77, 479
  Hottentot elections, 344, 357, 391
  naval laws, 454, 462
social imperialism
  Hans-Ulrich Wehler, 588
social question, 96–97

social reform, 70, 97–98, 173, 188, 191, 222–23, 260–61, 274, 357, 476
socialism, 188, 223
  American, 40, 382
Society for the Promotion of Inner Colonization, 428, 446, 558, 563, 585
Solf, Wilhelm, 172, 482, 541
Solomon Islands, 243
  seizure by Australia in world war, 518
Somaliland
  war aims in, 546, 549
Sombart, Werner, 60
Somme, Battle of the (1916), 568
Soochow (Suzhou), 132
Sophia University (Jōchi Daigaku), 308
South Africa, 120, 126, 281, 394, 402, 598
  Apartheid, 594
  Chinese immigrants, 239
  Drifts Crisis (1895), 149
  Transvaal, 5, 148–50
    German investments in, 149
    railways, 149
South Carolina, 76
  Sea Islands, 422
Southern Pacific Railroad, 381
Southwest Africa, 391
  arid climate of, 267
  coastal islands, 490
  colonial nostalgia, 598
  colonial reform, 394
  Dernburg inspection tour, 393, 402
  diamonds in, 392, 473
  failure as settler colony, 428
  finances, 393
  Herero and Nama wars, 340–41
  Lüderitz Bay-Kobub railroad, 342
  Otavi region, 353
  Port Alexander, railway to, 490
  railways, 391
  seizure by South Africa in world war, 518
  white settlers, 393
Spahn, Peter, 448
Spain
  colonial empire, 207
  colonialism and imperialism, 169

German sympathies for in Spanish-American War, 215
Jews, 573
purchase of Caroline, Palau, and Mariana Islands from, 215
Tangier Crisis, 325
trade policy, 279
See also Spanish-American War
Spanish-American War (1898), 213–17
Spartakusbund (Spartacus League), 596
Speer, Albert, 603
Speyer, James, 368, 494
Spinner, Wilfried, 101, 110
Spring-Rice, Cecil, 214
St. Kitts, 154
St. Louis World's Exposition (1904), 368
St. Lucia, 154
St. Thomas, Danish, 154, 213, 215
*Staatswissenschaften* (political economy), 92, 94, 96, 102–3, 274, 403, 405
Staatswissenschaftliche Gesellschaft, 62
Staatswissenschaftliche Vereinigung, 62
stab-in-the-back myth, 596
Statistical Office, Imperial, 103, 520
Stein, Lorenz v., 86, 99
*Stein*, SMS, 154
Sternburg, Hermann Speck v., 312, 315, 368, 374–75
Stinnes, Hugo, 442, 520, 545–46, 552–55, 579, 587
Stöcker, Adolf, 575
Stolypin, Petr Arkadyevich, 429, 431
Stone, Alfred Holt, 424–25
Stosch, Albrecht v., 180
*Stosch*, SMS, 154
Strachey, John St. Loe, 317–18
Straits and Sunda Syndicate, 412
Straits Trading Company, 411
Strasbourg, 34–35, 87, 223
Strasbourg, University of, 29, 33, 35–36, 44, 60, 274, 290
Strauss, Richard, 346
Stresemann, Gustav, 584, 597
Struve, Emil, 346
Stuart-Wortley, Edward, 466
Stübel, Oskar Wilhelm, 290, 341, 392

Stumm, Carl Ferdinand, 223
Stumm, Wilhelm v., 500
Stürmer, Michael, 15
submarines and submarine warfare, 329, 336, 509
  flotilla defense, 330
  prewar neglect of by Tirpitz, 452, 511
  prize rules and, 524
  success of U-9, 523
  threat to dreadnoughts, 510
  unrestricted, 527–31, 534–40, 580–81
Sudan, 5
Suez Canal, 300, 364
sugar industry, 55, 67, 72, 145, 281, 380
Sumatra, 411–15
Sumner, William G., 32
Suwalki
  war aims in, 547, 550, 560
Suzhou. *See* Soochow
Suzhou, Jiangsu. *See* Shaxi
Swatow (Shantou), 132
Swaziland, 5
Sweden
  trade policy, 279
Switzerland, 258
  German trade treaty with, 279
  German trade with, 269
  *Mitteleuropa* and, 173, 226
Sydow, Reinhold v., 465, 470, 473, 475–77
Sykes-Picot agreement (1916), 488
Syria, 487
  colonial unrest in, 593
Szögyény-Marich, László, 497

Taguchi Ukichi, 82
Takahashi Sakue, 329
Talaat Bey, Mehemed, 486
Talien (Dalian), 5, 231, 321, 329
Tangier
  war aims in, 546
Tangier Crisis (1905–6), 325–26, 328, 338, 416
Taussig, Frank W., 32
Taylor, A. J. P., 2
Taylor, Henry Clay, 311
Technische Hochschule Berlin, 286
Technische Hochschule Karlsruhe, 296
Tennessee, 76

Texas, 580
Texas Germans, 158, 424
Thiel, Hugo, 44
Thilenius, Georg, 398–99, 401
Thoma, Hans, 350
Thyssen, August, 545, 553
Tianjin. *See* Tientsin
Tibet, 176
Tiegel, Ernst, 90
Tientsin (Tianjin), 135
Timor, 214
tin mining and smelting
  Malaya, 410–11
Tirpitz Plan, 185, 278
Tirpitz, Alfred v., 129, 149, 177
  appointment as secretary of Navy Office, 182–83
  background and early career, 177–80
  dreadnought arms race and, 451–64
  dreadnought challenge, 329–39
  East Asian Cruiser Squadron, command of (1896–7), 180–82
  Fatherland Party, 585–88
  Gustav Schmoller, relationship with, 198–202
  naval theories, 183–85, 193–95
  wartime radicalism, 524–25, 538, 578–79
tobacco industry, 67, 379, 422, 468, 472
Tocqueville, Alexis de, 13
Togo, 418, 549
Tōgō Heihachirō, 323
Tokushima, 518
Tokutomi Sohō, 82
Tokyo University, 84, 87, 89–90, 94, 100, 102–4, 108, 138, 329
Tonga, 5, 243
Tönnies, Ferdinand, 368
Tooze, Adam, 8, 593, 599
Torp, Cornelius, 278
total war, 336, 511, 530, 591
Toynbee Hall, 70, 96
Toynbee, Arnold, 261
trade unions, 37–42, 273, 587
Trade, Prussian Ministry of
  investigation of Japan, 80–81
Transandine Railway, 230
Trans-Siberian Railway, 116, 135, 209, 251, 320, 409, 430, 545, 552

Transvaal. *See* South Africa
Transvaal Crisis (1895–6), 1, 169, 182–83, 188
Treasury Office, Imperial (Reichsschatzamt), 471, 473, 527
Treaty of Brest-Litovsk (1918), 566–67
Treipel, Heinrich, 527–30, 536, 553
Treitschke, Heinrich v., 34, 171, 186, 194
Treub, Melchoir, 412
Trinidad, 154, 312–13
Tripartite Convention, Samoan (1899), 243
Triple Alliance (1882), 127, 148, 187, 325, 440–43, 498–99, 502, 504
Triple Entente (1907), 124, 387, 393, 493, 499, 502, 504–5
Troeltsch, Ernst, 368
tropics, 416
  acclimatization question, 408, 414, 419–20
Trotsky, Leon, 431
Trubetskoy, Grigorii, 438
Tsinan (Jinan), 209, 238
Tsingtao (Qingdao), 129
Tsushima, Battle of (1905), 323–24, 375
Tunisia, 415
Turkestan, 230, 434, 515
Turkey. *See* Ottoman Empire
Turkish Petroleum Company, 488
Turner, Frederick Jackson, 57–59, 230, 273
Turner, George, 315
Tuskegee Institute, 151, 372, 378, 422
Tver, 434
Twain, Mark, 373
Tz'u-Hsi, Qing empress dowager, 251

Uhde, Fritz v., 350
Ukraine, 434, 565–67
  war aims in, 541, 547
Unabhängiger Auschuß für einen Deutschen Frieden (Independent Committee for a German Peace), 584
Union des Mines Marocaines, 416
Union of German Authors in America, 373
Union Pacific Railroad, 29, 45, 310

United States of America
  as agricultual challenger, 43–44
  as German liberal imperial model,
    41–42, 51–52
  as industrial challenger, 37–38,
    66–67, 72–75, 78
  Chinese immigrants, 239
  German educational ties to, 30–33
  German immigration, 50, 61, 180, 285
  imperialism, 213–19, 230, 315–16,
    380, 423, 430
  liberal imperialism, 556
  modernity of as threat, 383, 385
  nativism, 317, 536, 581–82, 594
  Navy, 158, 181, 237, 313, 315–16,
    331, 375–76, 455
  "negro question", 31, 383, 420, 422
  professor exchanges with Germany,
    368–69
  trade frictions, 144–46, 158
  trusts, 67–68, 72, 151, 158, 229
  *Weltpolitik* and, 22
  yellow peril, 382
  *See also* Alaska boundary dispute;
    American peril; Anglosphere
    and Anglo-Saxonism; First
    Venezuela Crisis; German-
    Americans; Monroe Doctrine;
    Panamerica; Samoa; Second
    Venezuela Crisis; Spanish
    American War
Upper Volta, 5
Urbig, Franz, 530
Uruguay, 151
Usambara Railway, 392
Utah, 46

Van Dissel, Rhode & Co., 152
Venezuela
  German immigration and
    colonization, 151–52
  German investments in, 152–53
  *Weltpolitik* and, 22
  *See also* First Venezuela Crisis, Great
    Venezuela Railway, Second
    Venezuela Crisis
Verbeck, Guido, 84
Verdun, Battle of (1916), 538, 568
Versailles Treaty (1919), 591, 595

Verviers, 541
Vickers, Sons & Co., 492
Victoria, empress consort of Germany,
  168
Viereck, George Sylvester, 516
Villard, Henry, 47, 63, 68, 583
Vilna, 563
  war aims in, 547, 550, 560
Vilnius, 547
Virginia, 356, 422
Vivani, René, 501
Vladivostok, 136, 252, 320
vom Bruch, Rüdiger, 20

Wadagaki Kenzō, 93
Wagemann, Ernst, 419
Wagner, Adolph, 60–61, 86, 198, 291,
  466, 468, 472
Waldersee, Alfred v., 252–53, 255–57
Wallraff, Max, 519
Waltershausen, August Sartorius v., 42,
  350
Walvis Bay, 214, 490
Wäntig, Heinrich, 542
War Intelligence Bureau, 535
Warburg, Aby, 572
Warburg, Felix, 583
Warburg, Max, 310, 334, 392, 465, 514,
  522, 526
Warburg, Paul, 583
Warsaw, 432
Washburn, W. D., 70
Washington, Booker T., 151, 372, 378
Webb, Beatrice, 260
Webb, Sidney, 260
Weber, Adna F., 495
Weber, Alfred, 62, 398, 544
Weber, Max, 60, 62, 171, 368, 385, 399,
  556
Wehler, Hans-Ulrich, 4, 16, 176, 184, 588
Weihaiwei (Weihai), 5
Weil, Hermann, 579
Weimar Mission, 101–2, 110
Weipert, Heinrich, 104, 138
Weitz, Paul, 483
Wells, H. G., 260
*Weltverkehr* (world commerce), 234
*Weltwirtschaft* (world economy), 234,
  601

Wenckstern, Adolph v., 203
West African Plantation Company Victoria, 293
West Indies, 216
  coaling stations in, 154
West Prussia
  as German eastern colonial frontier, 44
Westarp, Kuno v., 584
Whampoa Dock Co., 131, 240
White, Andrew Dickson, 169
White, Arnold, 149
Whitman, Sidney, 175
Wilamowitz-Möllendorff, Ulrich v., 553
Wildenthal, Laura, 12
Wilhelm I, kaiser of Germany, 81
Wilhelm II, kaiser of Germany, 2, 182, 185, 190, 193, 197, 203, 211
  Agadir Crisis, 416
  background and naval enthusiasm, 128, 150, 166, 168–69
  Balkan wars, 439, 442, 481
  Björkö Treaty, 325
  Boxer Rebellion, 252
  Bülow, relationship with, 191
  *Bundesrath* affair, 245
  character flaws, 16, 175
  confrontational tactics with Reichstag, 182
  *Daily Telegraph* Affair, 466–67, 472
  dreadnought arms race, 452, 456
  financial reform, 466
  July Crisis, 498–99
  Kaiser Wilhelm Professorship, 369
  Kruger Telegram, 148
  naval laws, 220, 246–47
  personal regime, 333
  sensitivity to public opinion, 18, 173–74
  submarine warfare, 538, 578–79
  Tangier Crisis, 326
  Tirpitz, relationship with, 185
  wartime weakness, 579, 583, 589–90
  yellow peril, 137, 239, 320
Wilhelm, crown prince of Germany, 211
  East Asia journey (1911), 409
  radicalism of, 578
  relationship with Schumacher, 408
Williams, Ernest Edwin, 142
Wilson, Herbert Wrigley, 149

Wilson, Keith, 22, 505
Wilson, Woodrow, 373, 384, 424, 516, 538, 580, 593
Windsor Agreement, 490
Winzen, Peter, 186
Wisconsin, University of, 494
Witte, Sergei, 384, 386, 431
Wood, Leonard, 378
Woosung (Wusong), 213
Wuchang (Wuhan), 134
Wuchow (Wuzhou), 132
Wuhan. *See* Wuchang
Württembergische Vereinsbank, 299
Wusong. *See* Woosung
Wuzhou. *See* Wuchow

Xiamen. *See* Amoy
Xujiahui. *See* Zikawei

Yajirō Shinagawa, 86
Yale University, 32–33, 38, 45, 421, 494, 544
Yamagata Aritomo, 85
Yamamoto Gonnohyōe, 166
Yangtze Accord (1900), 255
Yap
  undersea cable and wireless station, 518
yellow peril, 78, 116, 137, 239–40, 320, 466–67
Yingkou. *See* Newchwang
Yokohama, 84, 89, 101, 107, 110–11, 309
Young Turks, 366–67, 482–84, 486

Zander, Kurt, 300–1
Zanzibar, 214
Zappe, Eduard, 89
Zedlitz-Neukirch, Octavio v., 223
Zhang Zhidong, 130, 134
Zhifu. *See* Chih-fu
Zhili. *See* Chihli
Zikawei (Xujiahui), 134
Zimmerman, Andrew, 14
Zimmermann Telegram (1917), 136, 580–81
Zimmermann, Arthur, 18, 136, 291, 489, 530, 535, 580
Zoepfl, Gottried, 345, 348, 359, 406, 408
Zululand, 120
Zuntz, Nathan, 523
Zypen & Charlier, 152